MW00397562

+--+
| **Library of Congress Cataloging-in-Publication Data** |
| Steinhardt, Ralph G.(Ralph Gustav), 1954- |
| International civil litigation: cases and materials on the rise of intermestic law/ by |
| Ralph G. Steinhardt. |
| p. cm. |
| Includes index. |
| ISBN 0-8205-4593-7(hardbound) |
| 1. Civil Procedure (International Law)--Cases. 2. Conflict of Laws--Civil procedure--United |
| States--Cases. I. Title |
| K7615.S74 2002 |
| 340.9—dc21 |
| 2002066101 |
+--+

Editorial Offices
744 Broad Street, Newark, NJ 07102 (973) 820-2000
201 Mission St., San Francisco, CA 94105-1831 (415) 908-3200
701 East Water Street, Charlottesville, VA 22902-7587 (804) 972-7600
www.lexis.com

(Pub.3119)

INTERNATIONAL CIVIL LITIGATION:

CASES AND MATERIALS ON THE RISE OF INTERMESTIC LAW

By

Ralph G. Steinhardt
Arthur Selwyn Miller Research Professor of Law
The George Washington University Law School

To my wife, Donna Scarboro
and our children, Ruth and Tavi

LEVAVI OCULOS

PREFACE

In trying to think and write about the relationship between international law and domestic civil procedure, I've been reminded of G.B. Shaw's famous observation that learning something feels at first like losing something.

On those occasions when it seemed that the something lost as I learned in this case was time or clarity or bearings, I found some solace in Shaw's suggestion that the loss was only "at first" and wasn't some permanent state of being. As the work progressed, I came to hope that the something lost would be the tired ways of thinking about these two traditionally separate disciplines — international law and domestic procedure — with their very different reputations, their axioms and modes of inference, and that these could be replaced by something closer to an understanding of the way law will be practiced and conceived in the twenty-first century. The cases already demonstrate (in ways that law school curricula do not yet reflect) that international law has penetrated other areas of practice — especially litigation — and undermine the received distinction between domestic law and international law. I have tried to demonstrate the breadth of this relationship by drawing cases from a range of fields: human rights and commercial litigation, intellectual property and family law, torts and statutory causes of action, professional responsibility and cyberlaw. In the process, the distinctions that have long given structure to international law (*e.g.*, "public" versus "private" law, state versus non-state actors, treaty versus custom) have proven to obscure more than they illuminate as a practical matter. And the stereotype that international law is practiced by a tiny portion of the profession, working out of "elite" law firms in big cities, has also had to fall away. It may turn out that practicing international law, like speaking prose, is something we do as lawyers whether we know it or not.

There is no single word or phrase that captures this phenomenon, though "transnational law" has its devotees. Whatever the proper phrase is, it has to convey the variety of foreign, domestic, and international sources from which domestic courts derive a rule of decision, as well as the logistical difficulties they face when rules, attorneys, clients, and issues show little if any respect for physical or political borders. Whatever else globalization has meant, the decline of territorial thinking must be near the top of the list. In this book, I have used the neologism "intermestic," combining as it does elements of *inter*national and do*mestic* life. It is admittedly an awkward word that calls too much attention to itself. (Perhaps the word "international" fell equally hard on eighteenth-century ears, when Jeremy Bentham introduced it to the language.) And of course it may prove to have no more staying power than once-fashionable words like "Edsel" or "humours." But it can serve. It certainly captures themes in the cases that do not fall comfortably in either the international or the domestic category, like the contribution domestic law can make to the emergence of international legal standards and vice versa, or the obligation to construe one form of law in light of the other, or the recurring obstacles to the domestic litigation of cases with foreign elements.

Readers will discover too that the cases have been edited lightly (though in virtually every case, some footnotes and citations have been omitted and footnotes have been renumbered). In part, I hope in this way to convey the range of issues that arise in international civil litigation and the pains the judges generally take to resolve them fairly and defensibly. But it is also intended to stress the importance of reading cases as a whole, to encourage the identification of key assumptions in an opinion and the way the implications for doctrine and policy are addressed. This is after all a textbook for law students, a pedagogical tool, and not a desk reference for practitioners understandably eager to resolve a client's issue as quickly and as comprehensively as possible. Readers will also notice that many of the questions that follow the cases invite reflection on both the analytical structure of a doctrine and its defensibility as a matter of policy or rhetoric. That simply reflects my belief that the best students, like the best scholars and the best practitioners, are as fluent in the language of reform and policy-making as they are in the language of black-letter doctrine.

Shaw also apparently said that all professions are conspiracies against the laity. My hope is that this book will in some small way enable all who read it (and the one who wrote it) to remember that a lawyer's first obligation is to do justice.

Washington, D.C.
June 2002

ACKNOWLEDGMENTS

I am pleased here to acknowledge mentors, colleagues, friends, and students, whose suggestions and challenges over the years have improved this book and, in some cases, even made it possible. Many of these people exposed (or prevented) errors even more embarrassing than the ones I fear may remain in the text, and I am grateful to them. Especially helpful were early conversations with Raj Bhala, Joseph Brand, Thomas Buergenthal, Christine Chinkin, Joan Fitzpatrick, Jack Friedenthal, Paul Hoffman, Susan Karamanian, Harold Koh, Harold Maier, Juan Mendez, Tom Morgan, Sean Murphy, Todd Peterson, Steve Saltzburg, Andrew Shacknove, Jon Siegal, Louis Sohn, Andy Spanogle, Herb Somers, Joel Trachtman, and Michael Young. Messrs. Friedenthal and Young, in their capacity as deans of the George Washington University Law School, generously supported this work through summer research grants and frequent words of encouragement. Heather Dean and Adriana Sciortino at Lexis kept a steady hand on the wheel at critical moments. Students too numerous to mention individually have worked from the manuscript in various stages and were unfailingly perceptive in making suggestions for improvements. I have been especially fortunate to work with skilled and dedicated research assistants and advisees: Hdeel Abdelhady, Gabrielle Duvall, Tina Giffin, Jennifer Karmonick, Sif Thorgiersson, Patricia Weinert, and Benjamin Zawacki. My wife, Donna Scarboro, has lived with this project for a long time. Her insights, her judgment, her humor, and her patience make her a co-author in all but name. That each of these people generously saved me from committing certain errors doesn't mean that none remain, and, for those that do, I am solely responsible.

RGS

PERMISSIONS

SUMMARY TABLE OF CONTENTS

———

TABLE OF CONTENTS

———

Page

Page

Page

.

Chapter 1

INTRODUCTION

International Law, International Actors, Domestic Courts

*A strange justice that is bounded by a river! Truth on this side of the
Pyrenees, error on the other.*

— Pascal, PENSÉES § 146[1]

A. ORIENTATION

This book is evidence of a revolution-in-progress. Traditionally, civil litigation in the United States has been considered an exercise in domestic law,
with courts and litigators alike turning to statutes and the common law for
a rule of decision and assuming that the procedures, the parties, and the issues
would remain domestic. First-year law students have studied civil procedure
as a required course, introducing them to the ways of litigation in U.S. courts
on the assumption that litigation stops at the water's edge. By contrast,
international law has been considered a boutique specialization, to be studied
— if at all — only as an upper-level elective. The problem with this conventional approach is that it assumes what experience denies, and practitioners,
students, judges, and teachers must now confront a much more complicated
reality, in which the rules of civil procedure and the rules of international
law routinely intersect, overlap, and sometimes clash.

What happens for example when a child custody case crosses borders and
involves parents from two radically different societies — a case that may turn
ultimately on irreconcilable conceptions of the parent-child relationship in the
two cultures? What happens in borderless corporate transactions when
companies in different countries deal in cyberspace and find themselves in
a domestic court arguing over competing interpretations of their contract? Can
human rights abuses in one country give rise to litigation in another? Is it
legitimate for a domestic court to look beyond a statute or the constitution
and find controlling law in a treaty or in customary international law or even
in the domestic law of some foreign state? What if domestic law and international law are inconsistent with one another? And how will the sheer logistics
of litigation — like serving process, obtaining evidence, enforcing judgments
— be accomplished when borders must be crossed?

Understanding the law that governs these disputes has never been easy.
In fact, the first course taught at the first law school seven hundred years

---

[1] (Francis Kaplan ed. 1982) (1670), *translated in* PETER SAHLINS, BOUNDARIES: THE MAKING
OF FRANCE AND SPAIN IN THE PYRENEES 270 (1989). This introduction is based in part on RALPH
STEINHARDT, "The Internationalization of Domestic Law," THE ALIEN TORT CLAIMS ACT: AN
ANALYTICAL ANTHOLOGY (Anthony D'Amato and Ralph Steinhardt, eds., 1999).

1

ago dealt with the choice-of-law issues that arise whenever a citizen of one city-state sues a citizen of another in a dispute that crosses jurisdictional lines.

But to say that the problems have been predictable and recurring for centuries is not to say that some cohesive body of law has emerged to resolve them. To the contrary, lawyers may well discover that this body of law is more like jazz than it is like arithmetic — that the cases show theme and variation, even improvisation. Some decisions are better reasoned than others, and it is possible to see recurring *forms of argument* at work in the cases. Certainly a major goal of this text is to identify those arguments and the policies behind them in a variety of settings, but there are few mechanical rules that will automatically determine the result in any contested case.

Adding to the traditional complexity of inter-jurisdictional litigation in domestic courts is a rapid, continuing transformation in modern international law. The very distinctions that have long given structure to the discipline of international law have become outmoded in the last half-century and, in some cases, outright dysfunctional. Wolfgang Friedmann famously observed that the essential characteristic of international law in the twentieth century was its transformation "from an essentially negative code of rules of abstention to positive rules of cooperation."[2] In other words, international law, once conceived as a body of law defining states' respective jurisdiction or their reciprocal immunities, could be viewed as a collection of rules of mutual forbearance — rules which tended to preserve more state discretion than they constrained. The transition to "positive rules of cooperation" represented a dramatic expansion in the substantive reach of international standards, as though a law that had primarily been about the "fences" separating states had to be reconceptualized as a matter of "bridges" connecting them.

Even a partial list of contemporary international concerns — gender and race discrimination, the sale of goods, bankruptcy, environmental protection, family law, restrictive business practices, telecommunications, the rights of children — suggests the extent to which the international community has attempted to regulate matters that have historically been within a state's exclusive domestic jurisdiction. You might therefore consider Friedmann's insight as an observation that the scope of exclusive domestic jurisdiction has changed fundamentally and not been allowed to designate some inert, unchanging set of state prerogatives.

We live instead in an era in which international and domestic law converge, so much so that contemporary accounts of the law of nations can proclaim the emergence of "intermestic" law — law that is simultaneously domestic and international.[3] International law has been converted from a separate field of

---

[2] WOLFGANG FRIEDMANN, THE CHANGING STRUCTURE OF INTERNATIONAL LAW 62 (1964). Legal and diplomatic history since 1964, when Friedman first described this transition, have only confirmed the power of his insight.

[3] Though "intermestic" law is an invented word, we should recall that the term "international" law was also consciously introduced into the language — in 1789 by Jeremy Bentham in his INTRODUCTION TO THE PRINCIPLES OF MORALS AND LEGISLATION 296 (Burns and Hart eds. 1970):

> The word *international*, it must be acknowledged, is a new one; though, it is hoped, sufficiently analogous and intelligible. It is calculated to express, in a more significant way, the branch of the law which goes commonly under the name of the *law of nations*: an appellation so uncharacteristic, that, were it not for the force of custom, it would seem rather to refer to internal jurisprudence.

scholarship and practice into an aspect of virtually every field of law, reaching into the regulation of the family, the natural environment, the workplace, and the market. Domestic law has been internationalized and international law has been domesticated to such an extent that practitioners can no longer be certain that their speciality, whatever it is, stops at the water's edge or is in principle immune from the international legal process.

The new international standards moreover take a range of forms, expanding beyond the traditional categories of conventional and customary law, to include uniform legislation, principles, model contracts, and other instances of "soft law." In part, these developments are the culmination of efforts over the last century to harmonize and unify domestic private law around an international standard. But, as shown below, it is also the result of the rise in inter-governmental and non-governmental organizations with broad mandates to solve problems perceived to be communal.

One consequence is that the traditional separation between "public" international law and "private" international law has had to be either abandoned or fundamentally reconceived.[4] One form of that distinction has focused on the class of entities to which each type of law applies: "public international law" is that body of norms regulating relations between co-equal and independent states, and "private international law" governs transborder relations between individuals or business organizations. It is generally assumed that this "entity" test correlates with an "issue" test, such that certain subject areas — like the law of the sea and diplomatic immunity — plainly fall on the public side of the discipline, and other issues — like international business transactions or conflicts of laws — plainly fall on the private side. Though the distinction is *ad hoc*, it does at least account for the dominant ways that practitioners and academics on both sides of the line defined their work in the twentieth century.

The more principled strategy for preserving the distinction might begin with the observation that violations of private international law, unlike public international law, do not engage a state's responsibility as that term is understood in the law of nations. Thus, by tradition, a state can typically violate private international law without triggering an obligation to make reparations and *a fortiori* without justifying another state's resort to arms. It follows that any legal subject which is recognized as lying within a state's exclusive domestic jurisdiction is for that reason a matter of "private international law." In Professor Beckett's words, "Private International Law . . . treats only of matters which are, by the existing law of nations, within a state's exclusive sovereignty to legislate upon as it pleases."[5]

But none of these efforts to police the boundary between public and private international law has been successful in the end, even if the label of private international law is restricted to conflicts of laws. Since the late-nineteenth century, blocs of states have devoted considerable diplomatic "public" energy to the reconciliation of diverse choice-of-law rules in such "private" areas as adoption, marriage, guardianship, capacity of persons, and international civil

---

[4] *See generally* Harold G. Maier, *Extraterritorial Jurisdiction at a Crossroads: An Intersection Between Public and Private International Law*, 76 AMER. J. INT'L L. 280 (1982).

[5] W.E. Beckett, *What is Private International Law?*, 7 BRIT. Y.B. INT'L L. 73, 94 (1926).

procedure. For a variety of reasons, these efforts were not entirely successful, but they did establish a process, and a forum, that eventually enabled states to address more substantive areas of law which needed unification or harmonization, especially commercial and business matters. And to the extent that these conventions involved issues of interpretation, succession, and breach, the public law of treaties inevitably impinged on their private law content.[6]

What may have begun at the end of the nineteenth century as a shared concern with choice-of-law principles has been transformed into a much broader program, addressing business and financial affairs first, and subsequently any behavior with transboundary effects. Indeed, if we consider the variety of regulation in contemporary international law, virtually every law-creating effort can be portrayed as "private" if the criterion is whether it has substantial commercial impact or if it requires substantial compliance through the harmonization of domestic law: human rights, intellectual property, labor law, aviation and space law, economic relations and development — no less than family law and civil procedure — would seem to qualify as "private."

In short, a common dimension of contemporary international relations is the predisposition of states to discover public interests in traditionally private matters, and, as a consequence, the apparatus of "public" international law has been used by states to address a profound range of "private" matters. It follows that there is no pristine or stable distinction between public and private international law based on the type of entity to which each applies or the type of issues that each comprises. States no longer act as though the remedies for breach depend on which type of law has been violated, and practitioners can no longer assume that the patterns of axiom and inference differ depending on which type of law is in play.

The consequence of these related phenomena is that lawyers, regardless of specialization, will increasingly observe the interpenetration of international and domestic standards. In a period of globalization and the proliferation of treaties, the domestic courts in the United States and elsewhere will continue to be confronted with international issues, and intermestic law will continue to evolve.

It is that ongoing revolution-in-progress that this book attempts to lay out. In this Introduction, Part B will review the essential concepts of international law that are relevant to civil litigation in domestic courts. It is not a substitute for the basic course in international law of course, but it may help to orient those who have never completed such a course, or who did but long ago. Part C offers two cases — *Filártiga v. Pena-Irala* and *Marble Ceramic Center*— to illustrate the recurring issues in international civil litigation, around which the rest of the course is organized. The cases are in some ways dramatically different, one a tort case arising out of human rights violations, the other arising out of an international sales contract gone bad. But both reflect in microcosm the fundamental changes in contemporary international law generally. They may be used to illustrate the logistics of transnational litigation (conceiving a cause of action, for example, or serving process or proving the law), but critically they also exemplify the major developments

---

[6] Ralph Steinhardt, *The Privatization of Public International Law*, 25 GEO. WASH. J. INT'L L. & ECON. 523, 531 (1991).

in contemporary international law, including the collapse of the distinctions that have traditionally structured the discipline itself: the progressive narrowing of an exclusive domestic jurisdiction, the declining relevance of the distinction between state and non-state actors, the correlative demise of the public/private distinction, and the attenuation of the distinction between treaty and custom.

B. A SURVIVAL GUIDE TO INTERNATIONAL LAW

The basic premise and its consequences

The basic premise of traditional international law is that the international community consists of numerous, independent, and co-equal states as actors. There is no supranational legislature or police force or court with universal and compulsory powers, and international law consists in the rules governing the legal relationships among states. It is commonly called a "horizontal legal order" because, in contrast to domestic law, there is no authoritative or coercive institution to hand down the law to anyone and enforce it by imprisoning or fining those who violate it. Traditionally, this has meant that a state could not be bound to any international norm to which it had not given its consent, though "consent" could take a variety of forms. It has also meant that the international legal system has been more successful at articulating expectations and incentives than it has been in administering punishments or awarding compensation.

The sources of international law

One particularly important consequence of the "horizontality" of international law is the multiplicity of sources that define a state's legal obligations. Article 38(1) of the Statute of the International Court of Justice articulates the traditional categories of authority in these terms:

> The Court, whose function is to decide in accordance with international law such disputes as are submitted to it, shall apply:
>
> a. international conventions, whether general or particular, establishing rules expressly recognized by the contesting states;
>
> b. international custom, as evidence of a general practice accepted as law;
>
> c. the general principles of law recognized by civilized nations;
>
> d. subject to the provisions of Article 59, judicial decisions and the teachings of the most highly qualified publicists of the various nations, as subsidiary means for the determination of rules of law.

These categories are not hermetically separate from one another, and there is some question whether the list accurately captures the range of relevant authorities in the contemporary world, but the general outlines of these four traditional sources are clear.

In its orthodox conception, international law comprises both contractual and behavioral forms of obligation, corresponding to treaties and customary international law. At first blush, these traditional forms of law seem to derive from two quite separate processes: a dynamic of *ad hoc* consent leading to obligations binding upon the parties to the agreement *versus* a dynamic of habitual usage observed by nations as law and binding upon each of them. As suggested below however, contemporary international law has witnessed — and survived — the proliferation of normative types that do not fit into the either/or world of treaties and custom and which blur any simple-minded distinction between them.

Treaties. Treaties are international agreements that create reciprocal legal obligations among or between the parties, "with corresponding duties of compliance and remedies, including rights of retaliation, in the event of a breach."[7] States have found common ground in an almost bewildering range of areas and declared their mutual self-interest through treaties covering for example: private investment abroad; intellectual and cultural property; the rights of workers and prisoners; international crimes; the environment; arms control and the use of force; borders; gender and race discrimination. Treaties set the conditions for international trade and telecommunications, establish uniform rules for wills and trusts and bankruptcy proceedings, prohibit the testing of nuclear weapons, and even provide for the delivery of mail or the service of process. There is virtually no area of law that remains untouched by treaties.

It is well-established that the word "treaty" need not be used to convey the existence of a binding international agreement. "The terminology used for international agreements is varied. Among the terms used are: treaty, convention, agreement, protocol, covenant, charter, statute, act, declaration, *concordat*, exchange of notes, agreed minute, memorandum of agreement, memorandum of understanding, and *modus vivendi*. Whatever their designation, all agreements have the same legal status, except as their provisions or the circumstances of their conclusion indicate otherwise."[8]

The international law governing treaties is largely contained in the *Vienna Convention on the Law of Treaties* (1969) ("VCLT"),[9] which articulates the fundamental norm that promises must be honored in good faith: "Every treaty in force is binding upon the parties to it and must be performed by them in good faith." This basic idea, *pacta sunt servanda,* brings with it a number of subsidiary principles which also appear in the VCLT. For example, the obligation to respect promises is so powerful that a state's domestic law can be no defense against a charge that it had breached an international treaty. In the words of the VCLT, "[a] party may not invoke the provisions of its internal law as justification for its failure to perform a treaty." And the basic rules of treaty interpretation require that a "treaty shall be interpreted in good faith in accordance with the ordinary meaning to be given to the terms of the treaty in their context and in the light of its object and purpose." Recourse may be had to the legislative history of the treaty, or *travaux preparatoires,* only as a supplementary means of interpretation and only in limited circumstances. States-party may attempt to modify their international obligations

---

[7] BARRY CARTER & PHILLIP TRIMBLE, INTERNATIONAL LAW 109 (2d ed., 1995).

[8] American Law Institute, RESTATEMENT (THIRD) OF THE FOREIGN RELATIONS LAW OF THE UNITED STATES § 301 (comment).

[9] The Vienna Convention on the Law of Treaties is reproduced in the Document Supplement.

under a treaty through *reservations, understandings,* and *declarations,* though in no case may these unilateral modifications violate the object and purpose of the treaty.

Unobjectionable as these contractarian notions are, there are provisions of the VCLT that are controversial precisely because they qualify or undermine the *pure consent theory of international law,* that is, the view that a state's international obligations are strictly a function of its formal and on-going consent. To the extent that the VCLT contemplates international obligation even in the absence of such consent, controversy is inevitable. Article 18 of the VCLT, for example, provides that a state is obliged not to defeat the object and purpose of a treaty it has signed, even if the treaty is not yet in force and even before the state actually ratifies it. Article 38 contemplates the possibility that a treaty can become binding as customary law even on parties that have not signed it, and other provisions recognize the existence of peremptory norms of international law, *jus cogens,* which no treaty may contravene. These norms in effect represent communitarian limits on the power of consent, and they are in principle as applicable to states in treaty relations as they are to private citizens in contractual relations.

Finally with respect to treaties, it is important to note the paradox that a global order increasingly dominated by international treaty law is also increasingly dependent on each state's domestic law, especially "the domestic normative rank treaty provisions enjoy[ed] in the States parties to them."[10] In other words, even as treaties come to address an unprecedented range of subjects, at base their effectiveness is a direct function of how each state gives domestic legal effect to its treaty obligations.

Custom. States recognize the existence of customary international law, arising not out of an explicit agreement to some authoritative text but out of a "general practice accepted as law." The formulation in Article 38(1) suggests two criteria for custom: (i) a general practice among states, meaning that states conform in fact to a standard of behavior or that their conduct follows a consistent, empirical pattern, and (ii) a sense of legal obligation or *opinio juris,* meaning that states behave in these patterned ways not out of ideology or public relations but out of the conviction that the behavior is required by law.

In attempting to give content to this sometimes elusive body of law, international actors (like inter-governmental or non-governmental organizations, arbitrators, tribunals, and advocates) consider evidence in a variety of forms, including diplomatic exchanges, in which states define their legal expectations of one another; treaties in consistent form; the laws, constitutions, and high court decisions in the various countries; the writings of publicists; resolutions and declarations in consistent form in intergovernmental organizations like the UN; decisions of international tribunals and arbitral panels; and compendia or restatements of customary law, like the American Law Institute's RESTATEMENT OF THE FOREIGN RELATIONS LAW OF THE UNITED STATES.

---

[10] Thomas Buergenthal, *Self-Executing and Non-Self-Executing Treaties in National and International Law,* 235 RECUEIL DES COURS 304–400 (1992-IV), at 313.

Although the distinctions between treaty and custom are clear, the relationship between them can be quite complex. Treaties may be used as *evidence* of custom, especially where the treaty enjoys near universal support and the parties understand that the treaty is declaratory of customary law or where the same substantive obligation appears in numerous treaties signed by a variety of states. In this sense, treaties may serve a legislative function for the community at large and not merely a contractual function among the parties. Treaties may in principle also contribute to the demise of custom, as for example in the definition of the territorial sea, the customary breadth of which has moved over time from three miles to six miles to twelve miles in part as the result of international codification. *Jus cogens* also arises at the intersection of treaty law and customary law, consisting in those elite norms of custom from which no derogation by treaty is permitted.

General principles. Article 38(1) also lists "the general principles of law recognized by civilized nations" as a potential source of international law norms. At the core of this category is the recognition that some principles of law seem valid across virtually all human societies or seem basic to the very idea of a legal system generally. International law can arise out of the comparative exercise of finding general principles in the various national (or "municipal") systems of law in the world and applying them at the international plane. For example, virtually all domestic legal systems have some principle like "a party cannot take advantage of its own wrong" or "every violation of a promise or a duty triggers an obligation to make reparation." Although there is nothing explicitly international about these principles, states have reasoned that these principles — in spite of their domestic pedigree — may operate at the international plane. There can in short be a *comparative* element to *international* obligations.

Judicial decisions and writings of publicists. Article 38(1)(d) of the ICJ Statute identifies "as subsidiary means for the determination of rules of law," judicial decisions and the teachings of the most highly qualified publicists of the various nations. Though international law includes no formal notion of precedent or *stare decisis,* the decisions of national courts may nonetheless be relevant in giving content to international law, and the International Court of Justice routinely refers to its own prior decisions on the obvious principle that similar cases should be resolved similarly. The ICJ's determination in one case that a norm had become customary law would be considered virtually conclusive evidence in other settings. Scholarly writing — "the teachings of the most highly qualified publicists of the various nations" — may also exert considerable influence, not because scholars have or claim some authority to make law but because the collection and evaluation of state practice plays a critical *evidentiary* role in determining what the law is.

New sources of authority and the problem of normative variety. Article 38, though long considered the authoritative list of sources of international law, distorts the contemporary practice of international law. The ICJ and other international tribunals, not to mention international lawyers and states in their dealings *inter se*, routinely articulate international obligations on the basis of authorities that are not mentioned in Article 38. Most notable among these are: (i) the resolutions and declarations of intergovernmental organizations, like the United Nations, and their subsidiary agencies, especially when addressing legal issues, adopted by consensus, and consistent with the actual practice of states; (ii) decisions of international courts and arbitral tribunals on issues of general international law; and (iii) the expert submissions of non-governmental organizations on legal issues. The point is not that the work product from these sources is binding *per se*. Rather it is that they offer relevant evidence of what the law in its contemporary forms requires.

The softening of the distinction between treaty and custom and the proliferation of new sources of international law may be seen as part of a larger trend towards the emergence of "soft" forms of law — a range of normativity which complicates the task of defining a state's entitlements and obligations; indeed, the "blurring of the normativity threshold"[11] has been criticized precisely because it seems to expand international law beyond its consensualist base, making it incomprehensible and illegitimate in the process. But this difficulty is hardly new. The difficulty of distinguishing between *lex lata*, the established law, and *lex ferenda*, the emerging law, has long undermined any simple dichotomy between binding law and irrelevant aspiration. Soft law instruments are best conceived as guideposts of greater or lesser persuasive value in discerning the law's trajectory.

Dramatis Personae

States. To qualify as a state, an entity must satisfy certain traditional criteria: territory, population, government, and the capacity to maintain diplomatic relations with other states. These criteria convey the sense that a state must comprise a physically and politically stable community, though history offers ample evidence that these standards are not applied mechanically or apolitically. Some states seem to emerge prematurely and other apparent states are not allowed to emerge at all. There is no centralized process for determining when and if an entity satisfies the statehood criteria, and the judgment that the somewhat formalistic criteria for statehood are satisfied necessarily rests with every other government.

Traditionally, only states could be the subjects of international law, *i.e.*, only states could have rights and obligations cognizable at international law. Only states could enter into treaty relations. Only states' behavior could give rise to customary international law, and to the extent that individuals might bear rights or obligations, it was by virtue of their relationship to, or dependency upon, a state. Statehood connoted independence, the presumptive right to be left alone, to pursue the national interest without interference by other states or the international community at large, and international law was dominated

---

[11] Prosper Weil, *Towards Relative Normativity in International Law?*, 77 AM. J. INT'L L. 413, 415 (1983). Professor Weil continues:

> While prenormative acts do not create rights or obligations on which reliance may be placed before an international court of justice or of arbitration, and failure to live up to them does not give rise to international responsibility, they do create expectations and exert on the conduct of states an influence that in certain cases may be greater than that of rules of treaty or customary law. Conversely the sanction visited upon the breach of a legal obligation is sometimes less real than that imposed for failure to honor a purely moral or political obligation. *Id.*

by norms that preserved independence. As noted by the Permanent Court of International Justice — predecessor to the ICJ — in *The Lotus Case*:[12]

International law governs relations between independent States. The rules of law binding upon States therefore emanate from their own free will as expressed in conventions or by usages generally accepted as expressing principles of law and established in order to regulate the relations between these co-existing independent communities or with a view to the achievement of common aims. Restrictions upon the independence of States cannot therefore be presumed.

The state, having served for centuries as the fulcrum of the international order, is now under sustained attack. As shown below, one counter-force is the regional integration of states and the related rise of intergovernmental organizations, which can in many cases enter into treaty relations themselves, provide a framework for the negotiation and adoption of treaties among states, and contribute to the creation of customary law and general principles. The traditional conception of the state is also under attack (somewhat more literally) from the opposite direction, namely the proliferation of internal separatist movements by indigenous peoples and ethnic minorities, who are themselves the bearers of international rights. In addition, to a limited extent, non-state actors have come to play a quasi-legislative role in the development of international standards: multinational corporations, the International Chamber of Commerce, along with hundreds of other non-governmental organizations, have contributed to the evolution of law in such fields as international trade, transportation, and commercial transactions, even as they have been made subject to it. States, though still at the center of international law, can no longer claim to be the exclusive subjects of international law.

Intergovernmental organizations. Intergovernmental organizations now routinely address substantive issues of law that a prior generation of lawyers would have considered entirely within the domestic realm: environmental protection, communications, human rights, labor standards, commercial law, family law, wills and trusts. Quite apart from the political advantages of such organizations, they provide a ready arena for the negotiation of international instruments and the formal approval of standards, as well as a forum for the authoritative expression of *opinio juris*. They increasingly have a measure of investigative or supervisory authority, and thus contribute to the enforceability of international standards.

There is no suggestion that the United Nations or any other organization operates as an international legislature: under the terms of the U.N. Charter itself, the resolutions of the General Assembly are not binding. But the U.N. and other inter-governmental organizations clearly do provide a forum for the progressive development and codification of international law. Regional groupings of states like the Organization of American States or the Organization of African Unity or the European Union contribute to the creation or articulation of international norms, by developing regional treaties and directives or by attempting to harmonize the domestic laws of their member-states around an international standard. Specialized or functional organizations like the World Bank, the International Telecommunications Union, the

---

[12] *The Lotus Case* (Fr. v. Turkey), 1927 P.C.I.J., Ser. A, No. 10.

International Civil Aviation Organization, or the U.N. Committee on Peaceful Uses of Outer Space similarly contribute to the emergence of international law, through their deliberations and their development of treaties and formal principles.

Intergovernmental organizations have also contributed to the blurring of the received distinction between treaty and custom. The World Trade Organization and the Organization for Security and Cooperation in Europe for example have evolved from legal foundations that were neither strictly conventional nor strictly customary, and their legal work-product must be deliberately distorted to fit into only one of those two analytical boxes.[13] An equally salient example in the contemporary evolution of international commercial law (*lex mercatoria*) is provided by the United Nations Commission on International Trade Law ("UNCITRAL"), which was established to promote "the progressive harmonization and unification of the laws of international trade." UNCITRAL has been largely successful in this effort, operating through multiple types of law, including the promulgation of model laws, the negotiation of conventions, the articulation of standard contracts, and the like. Given the effectiveness of these standards, lawyers who dismiss or minimize this work-product on the ground that it qualifies as neither treaty nor custom (nor any other traditional mode of law) do so at their peril.

Individuals. Prior to the expansion of international human rights law after World War II, individual human beings could be a matter of concern only by virtue of their relationship with a state. The law of *state responsibility* for example "protect[ed] individuals against violations of their rights only when their nationality [was] not that of the offending state,"[14] and turned on the fiction that an injury to an alien was an injury to the state of her nationality. That state could advance a claim for compensation only if it could demonstrate the existence of *real and effective links* to the individual victim.[15] Groups of individuals were also protected by *minority treaties* under the League of Nations on the ground that their collective treatment was a matter of concern to states with ethnic or cultural ties to the protected class. And even the emergence of individual responsibilities and obligations was a function of the relationship between the person and the state. Where conduct like piracy or

---

[13] With respect to GATT/WTO for example, Professor Stephen Zamora has shown that "relatively 'hard' rules, such as interdictions against export subsidies or against the use of quantitative restrictions, are vitiated by a system of enforcement that is 'soft.'" He continues:

> Some international economic "soft law" exists in the form of international instruments that are not intended to be binding, such as codes of conduct, declarations, resolutions, and other non-binding texts. Though not binding on states, the principles set forth in such instruments do influence the economic practices of states; they may also become enforceable rules when adopted by national legislation. One example of this phenomenon can be found in the adoption of UN resolutions on permanent sovereignty over natural resources. These resolutions have influenced national laws, treaties, and judicial case law.

Stephen Zamora, *Economic Relations and Development*, THE UNITED NATIONS AND INTERNATIONAL LAW 232, 258 (Christopher C. Joyner, ed., 1997).

[14] HAROLD MAIER AND THOMAS BUERGENTHAL, PUBLIC INTERNATIONAL LAW 115 (2d ed. 1990).

[15] *Nottebohm Case (Liech. v. Guat.)*, 1955 I.C.J. REP. 4. *Cf. re* the required links between the claimant state and a corporation, *Case concerning the Barcelona Traction, Light and Power Co.* (Belg. v. Spain), 1970 I.C.J. 3.

attacks on diplomats represented a threat to the community of nations, individual responsibility would be imposed.

But the contemporary law of human rights does not depend on the link of nationality or identity group, nor does it indulge the fiction that a government's injury to an alien is an injury to the alien's home state. Rather individuals have rights simply by virtue of being human, including, but not limited to, a right to non-discrimination; due process and other measures of fair treatment in all interactions with the government; freedom of expression, belief, movement, and association; freedom from forced assimilation and *refoulement* (*i.e.* return to a territory where they have a well-founded fear of persecution); freedom from torture and cruel, inhuman, or degrading treatment; economic, social, and cultural rights; the protections of humanitarian law in times of armed conflict.

This body of law is now well-established by treaty and custom, internalized in the domestic laws of states around the world, and enforced episodically through inter-governmental and non-governmental institutions. Article 55 of the U.N. Charter obliges the organization to promote "universal respect for, and observance of, human rights and fundamental freedoms" in order to create the "conditions of stability and well-being which are necessary for peaceful and friendly relations among nations . . . ." The creators of the post-war order thus recognized a direct connection between international peace and security on one hand and the protection of individual human rights, regardless of nationality, on the other. Beginning with the Universal Declaration of Human Rights (1948) and the two human rights covenants,[16] this body of law has expanded dramatically to include treaties governing specific human rights violations (like torture, genocide, and gender and race discrimination) and establishing institutions to enforce these norms (like the International Criminal Court) or to supervise states' compliance with them (like the U.N. Human Rights Committee). Other treaties adopt broad catalogues of rights governing entire regions of the world, notably in Europe and the Americas.

Equally important, international law has come to recognize the possibility of *individual responsibility* for violations of international law. The Nuremberg Tribunal and the contemporary tribunals for war crimes committed in Rwanda and the former Yugoslavia reaffirm that violations of international law are committed by individuals and not by some abstraction called the state. Individual accountability is not limited to human rights and is increasingly common in environmental protection and international criminal law.

Finally, the received distinction between state and non-state actors has come to obscure not only the substance of contemporary international law but its enforcement as well. Private parties — meaning individuals in both human and corporate form — now routinely use the domestic courts to enforce international rules governing investment, trade, civil aviation, pre-trial discovery, banking, commercial transactions, and refugee status.[17] In each

---

[16] *International Covenant on Civil and Political Rights*, adopted Dec. 16, 1966, entered into force Jan. 3, 1976, 999 U.N.T.S. 3; the *International Covenant on Economic, Social, and Cultural Rights*, adopted Dec. 16, 1966, entered into force Mar. 23, 1976, 999 U.N.T.S. 171.

[17] *Chan v. Korean Airlines*, 109 S.Ct. 1676 (1989) (aviation); *Société Nationale Industrielle Aérospatiale v. District Court*, 482 U.S. 522 (1987) (pre-trial discovery); *Cardoza-Fonseca v. Immigration and Naturalization Service*, 480 U.S. 421 (1987) (refugee status); F. Dely, INTERNATIONAL BUSINESS LAW AND LEX MERCATORIA (1992).

of these and similar cases, individuals are the bearers of rights and obligations in ways that would have been anomalous under the traditional conception of international law.

Non-governmental organizations ("NGOs"). In virtually every field of international law, non-governmental organizations have played a profound role in the process by which international norms are created and enforced. In international commercial law for example, the International Chamber of Commerce has articulated the governing rules for documentary credits and trade[18] and the conduct of arbitration.[19] In international environmental law, NGOs are perhaps best known for the direct action they take in bringing environmental concerns to public consciousness, but they have also been involved in the development of legal principles that ultimately command the assent of states, like the Stockholm and Rio Declarations.[20] In international human rights, NGOs like Amnesty International and Article 19 often provide critical triangulation on a government's version of facts and can be effective voices in the adoption of treaties and the use of international standards in domestic proceedings.

Some inter-governmental institutions have formalized the role of NGOs, offering them a consultative status or relying upon them *de facto* for reliable information and analysis. But the variety of these organizations and their internal mandates makes it difficult to generalize about their role in contemporary international law other than to observe their contribution to civil society and the rule of law at the international level.

Dispute resolution

Article 33(1) of the U.N. Charter catalogues a range of methods that are typically used to resolve international disputes:

> The parties to any dispute, the continuance of which is likely to endanger the maintenance of international peace and security, shall, first of all, seek a solution by negotiation, enquiry, mediation, conciliation, arbitration, judicial settlement, resort to regional agencies or arrangements or other peaceful means of their own choice.

Non-judicial methods, like negotiation, mediation or good offices, and conciliation tend to be the least formal means of resolving disputes, preserving maximum flexibility and confidentiality for the parties. Quasi-judicial methods, like arbitration, tend to follow more formal procedures and result in a judgment or award that is typically binding upon the parties. Arbitrations may proceed under treaty, by *ad hoc* agreement (or *compromis)*, or by contract

---

[18] *See, e.g.,* INTERNATIONAL CHAMBER OF COM., Pub. No. 460, INCOTERMS 1990 (1990); INTERNATIONAL CHAMBER OF COM., UNIFORM CUSTOMS AND PRACTICE FOR DOCUMENTARY CREDITS, PUB. NO. 400 (1983).

[19] Elisabeth M. Senger-Weiss, *Enforcing Foreign Arbitral Awards*, 53 DISPUTE RES. J. 70, 72 (Feb. 1998).

[20] REPORT OF THE UNITED NATIONS CONFERENCE ON THE HUMAN ENVIRONMENT, U.N. Doc. A/CONF.48/14/Rev. 1 (1973) ("The Stockholm Declaration"); United Nations Conference on Environment and Development, UNCED Doc. A/CONF.151/5/Rev.1 (1992) ("The Rio Declaration").

between the parties, any one of which may specify the procedures to be followed in the proceeding, including the appointment of the arbitrator(s), the jurisdiction of the panel, the burden of proof, the means of enforcement, *etc.* Though arbitral awards technically bind only the parties to the proceeding, the principles on which the award rests may provide authoritative evidence of what the law is. *See, e.g., The Texaco/Libya Arbitration*,[21] addressing the constraints on a state's power to nationalize the property of aliens, and *The Trail Smelter Case* (United States v. Canada),[22] establishing principles governing the liability of states for transborder pollution.

The judicial methods of dispute settlement include the International Court of Justice, which is the principal judicial organ of the United Nations, and numerous regional and specialized courts, including the European Court of Justice within the European Union, the European Court of Human Rights, the Inter-American Court of Human Rights, the Law of the Sea Tribunal, the war crimes tribunals for the former Yugoslavia and Rwanda, and the International Criminal Court. Although states' record of compliance with international judicial decisions is mixed, the proliferation of international courts suggests the extent to which states are willing to submit to a regime of law, enforced through judicial means. It also suggests that the process by which international norms emerge and are implemented will continue to be profoundly decentralized.

International law as law of the United States

The United States is sometimes described as a *dualistic* system, meaning that the status of an international norm internationally is not necessarily related to its status domestically in the United States. The genetic marker of American dualism is the power of Congress to legislate in derogation of international norms. International law, like other forms of the common law, "bends to the will of Congress."[23] The intention to override international law by statute will not be presumed, and sometimes the courts undertake heroic efforts to interpret legislation so as *not* to violate international standards.[24] But Congress has the constitutional power to adopt legislation that violates international law, and that legislation will be enforced in the courts of the United States. Of course, as previously noted, domestic legislation cannot in principle be a defense to a breach of international law, and an international court may well conclude that the non-conforming legislation is itself a violation of international standards. But within the courts of the United States, the legislation — and not the international law — applies. Dualism in other words means in part that the statute would prevail domestically and the treaty would prevail internationally.

Treaties and executive agreements. From one perspective, dualism assumes a somewhat pathological relationship between international and domestic law,

---

[21] Award of 19 January 1977, 17 INT'L LEGAL MATS. 1 (1978).

[22] 3 U.N. REP. INT'L ARB. AWARDS 1905 (1949).

[23] *The Over the Top*, 5 F.2d 838, 842 (D. Conn. 1925).

[24] *See, e.g., Palestine Liberation Organization v. United States*, 695 F. Supp. 1456 (S.D.N.Y. 1988).

as though one must inevitably trump the other. But it is rare that Congress actually exercises its admitted power to override international law domestically, and the Constitution actually provides for accommodation of international law rather than its repudiation. For example, the place of treaties in the domestic legal system is defined by the Supremacy Clause of the Constitution (Article VI, section 2), which provides that: "This Constitution and the laws of the United States which shall be made in Pursuance thereof; and all treaties made, or which shall be made, under the Authority of the United States, shall be the supreme law of the land; and the judges in every state shall be bound thereby, anything in the constitution or laws of any state to the contrary notwithstanding." At a minimum, this language places treaties on an equal footing with federal statutes, though nothing in the Supremacy Clause itself suggests a limit on the federal treaty power or provides any formula for deciding which prevails if a treaty is in conflict with a statute.

The United States Supreme Court has offered broad guidelines for the resolution of these issues, holding that a treaty in violation of explicit, prohibitory provisions of the Constitution is invalid and that in case of an irreducible conflict between a statute and a treaty the *later-in-time* prevails: a later statute modifies the prior treaty to the extent of the conflict, and a later treaty modifies the prior statute to the extent of the conflict. Inconsistencies between treaty law and state law have generally been resolved in favor of the treaty on the assumption that treaties, as the supreme law of the land, trump contrary state laws, but that assumption is being revisited in light of the Supreme Court's marked expansion in states' rights over the last decade. The question naturally arises whether the resurrection of state power will impose limits on the federal government's treaty power as well.

The courts have also developed the *self-executing treaty doctrine* as a potential limit on the applicability of treaties in U.S. law. By definition, a self-executing treaty becomes law in the United States once it enters into force internationally. It can in other words provide a rule of decision in domestic courts or otherwise be given domestic effect when it enters into force internationally. By contrast, a non-self-executing treaty requires legislation to implement it domestically, and until that legislation is passed, the treaty is not considered domestic law. Unfortunately, as shown in Chapter 4, the courts have not been models of clarity in their conceptualization or application of this doctrine, sometimes declaring a treaty not self-executing when they mean that the plaintiff has no standing to complain or that the treaty does not provide a private right of action or that the treaty is purely aspirational. Sometimes the non-self-executing treaty doctrine appears to be a stand-in for the political question doctrine. To the extent that a treaty uses language of present obligation and does not trench on the constitutional prerogatives of the executive branch or Congress, it is more likely to be deemed self-executing.

In the *interpretation of treaties*, the courts of the United States have frequently declared that they are unqualified to make treaties and have rejected any construction of a treaty that was so detached from the text or the intent of the parties or the *travaux preparatoires* as to create, rather than construe, the agreement in question. "Judicial treaty-making" is the epithet of choice for those interpretations of a treaty which are thought to be excessively creative. The epithet works because it is shorthand for an implied and generalized incapacity that perpetuates the distinction between "making" and "finding" the law. In this view, courts perform their proper function in finding or declaring what the law is, including the obligation of a treaty, and they usurp some political function when their interpretation starts to resemble legislation.

The need to keep interpretation to a minimum has led to the "plain meaning" rule of treaty interpretation, which means that the literal text governs every case, except in the extraordinary case in which "application of the words of the treaty according to their obvious meaning effects a result inconsistent with the intent or expectations of its signatories."[25] In practice, the illegitimacy of "judicial treaty-making" not only favors literal interpretations of treaties, it favors in particular the literalist conclusions of the executive branch. The President, through the Solicitor General and the Legal Advisor to the Department of State, routinely submits briefs and other material to the courts, articulating the executive's position on treaty matters as they may affect a contested case. On a number of specific issues, the president's views are presumptively preferred[26] and frequently decisive, as for example, when the court must identify an authoritative text, or determine the "obvious" meaning of the words in the treaty, or assess the mutual understanding of the parties, or determine the existence of an inconsistency between the obvious meaning and the parties' intentions. The practice of deferring to the executive is thus a powerful corollary to the ideal of "plain meaning" interpretations.

Customary international law. The Supreme Court, in a famously opaque passage in *The Paquete Habana*,[27] declared that:

> [i]nternational law is part of our law, and must be ascertained and administered by the courts of justice of appropriate jurisdiction, as often as questions of right depending upon it are duly presented for their determination. For this purpose, where there is no treaty, and no controlling executive or legislative act or judicial decision, resort must be had to the customs and usages of civilized nations; and as evidence of these, to the works of jurists and commentators, who by years of labor, research and experience, have made themselves peculiarly well acquainted with the subjects of which they treat. Such works are resorted to by judicial tribunals, not for the speculations of their authors concerning what the law ought to be, but for trustworthy evidence of what the law really is.

The origins of the idea that international law is "part of our law" can be traced to the earliest days of the republic.[28] The Court's repeated approval of the

---

[25] *Maximov v. United States*, 373 U.S. 49, 54 (1963); *The Amiable Isabella*, 10 U.S. (6 Wheat.) 1, 72 (1821).

[26] *Sumitomo Shoji America, Inc. v. Avagliano*, 457 U.S. 177, 184–85 (1982) ("Although not conclusive, the meaning attributed to treaty provisions by the Government agencies charged with their negotiation and enforcement is entitled to great weight.")

[27] *The Paquete Habana*, 175 U.S. 677, 708 (1900).

[28] *The Nereide*, 13 U.S. (9 Cranch) 388, 423 (1815) ("the Court is bound by the law of nations which is part of the law of the land.")

Paquete Habana's language has spawned the orthodoxy that customary international law is subsumed in and incorporated by federal common law,[29] that it is enforceable in domestic courts even in the absence of direct legislative authorization,[30] and that, like other forms of federal law, it constrains the actions of the states of the Union.[31] That these principles should find acceptance and expression in the RESTATEMENT (THIRD) OF THE FOREIGN RELATIONS LAW OF THE UNITED STATES — and that the judiciary should in turn invoke the Restatement's language — suggests at a minimum that they are not particularly radical, though it hardly immunizes them from criticism.[32]

The *incorporationist* paradigm is not the only way to conceive the relationship between customary international law and the domestic law of the United States. There is in addition an *interpretativist* approach under which the statutes enacted by Congress "ought never to be construed to violate the law of nations if any other possible construction remains."[33] The idea that international law constrains the interpretation of domestic statutes has been reaffirmed without much reflection or analysis by the federal courts since it was announced in *Murray v. The Schooner Charming Betsy* (1804), and like other canons of statutory construction, is easily dismissed as innocuous or meaningless.

But this perspective masks the potential impact of the *Charming Betsy* principle; indeed, the advocates, courts, and scholars routinely fail to appreciate the consequences of a meaningful requirement that statutes be construed consistently with international law, even though those consequences are far from trivial. It would be significant enough if the norms of customary international law determined only the extraterritorial applicability of domestic statutes. In the era when the law of nations was primarily concerned with jurisdiction and state responsibility, that is precisely what the *Charming Betsy* principle stood for. But the apparent consequences of that principle become even more profound as the international legal system addresses substantive matters of political and economic life traditionally reserved to exclusive domestic jurisdiction. As international law has moved "from an essentially negative code of rules of abstention to rules of cooperation," its

---

[29] *Banco Nacional de Cuba v. Sabbatino*, 376 U.S. 398, 425 (1963).

[30] *First Nat'l City Bank v. Banco para el Comercio Exterior de Cuba*, 462 U.S. 611, 623 (1983).

[31] *See, e.g., Skiriotes v. Florida*, 313 U.S. 69 (1940); Lea Brilmayer, *Federalism, State Authority, and the Preemptive Power of International Law*, [1994] SUP. CT. REV. 295.

[32] Indeed, the historical and doctrinal legitimacy of incorporating the law of nations into domestic law has become a matter of controversy in academic circles, where a spirited minority argues that that axiomatic proposition has been accepted uncritically and with unfortunate consequences. Philip Trimble, *A Revisionist View of Customary International Law*, 33 U.C.L.A. L. REV. 665 (1986); A. M. Weisburd, *State Courts, Federal Courts, and International Cases*, 20 YALE J. INT'L L. 1 (1995); Curtis A. Bradley & Jack L. Goldsmith, *Customary International Law as Federal Common Law: A Critique of the Modern Position*, 110 HARV. L. REV. 815 (1997). For a useful summary of the debate and its resolution, see Harold Koh, *Is International Law Really State Law?*, 111 HARV. L. REV. 1824 (1998). The debate, however, is not new. *See, e.g.,* Edwin D. Dickenson, *Changing Concepts and the Doctrine of Incorporation*, 26 AM. J. INT'L L. 239, 260 (1932); Harold H. Sprout, *Theories as to the Applicability of International Law in the Federal Courts of the United States*, 26 AM.J. INT'L L 280 (1932).

[33] *Murray v. The Schooner Charming Betsy*, 6 U.S. (2 Cranch) 64, 118 (1804).

potential overlap with domestic statutory regimes has become pronounced. There is, in short, an increasingly complex and detailed body of international legal principles that may be relevant to a given statutory problem.

At the same time, domestic jurisprudence has undergone a dramatic transformation of its own, with what Guido Calabresi has called the "statutorification" of United States law.[34] In an historic shift, legislation, rather than the common law, has become the dominant expression of legal norms in the United States. The "orgy of statute making"[35] has provoked and justified a renewed examination of the discipline of statutory construction by courts and commentators. That in turn has spawned new approaches in legal scholarship, as theories of literature, economics, linguistics, and politics assume roles in legal interpretation.

At the intersection of these otherwise unrelated developments lies the *Charming Betsy* principle. At face value, it suggests that the transformation in substantive international law may penetrate domestic law through the presumption that Congress intends to conform its statutes to international standards. It follows that *Charming Betsy* and its progeny offer a potentially potent, though admittedly nondeterminative principle, under which courts, advocates, and scholars faced with issues of statutory construction are obliged to consult international sources.

Doctrines of restraint. Transnational litigation, whether it involves the application of international standards in domestic courts or the application of domestic standards to international parties, can raise prudential concerns. The case may complicate the economic or political relations of the United States with other countries or its status in inter-governmental organizations. A case may implicate the constitutional separation of powers among the judicial, executive, and legislative branches or raise federalism concerns by trenching on the prerogatives of the states of the union. These concerns have led to the development of a variety of doctrines and principles rooted in constitutional law, federal statutes, and the common law, as well as treaties, custom, and international *comity, i.e.* the courtesy or accommodation that states tend to show to one another and expect of one another.

Foreign sovereign immunity, for example, protects foreign states and their agencies or instrumentalities from the jurisdiction of domestic courts and, in the United States, is a matter of federal statutory law. The Foreign Sovereign Immunities Act of 1976[36] empowers the courts to determine issues of sovereign immunity, thereby transferring to the judicial realm a decision that had previously been a matter for the political branches, especially the executive. Substantively, the FSIA establishes a rebuttable presumption that a foreign

---

[34] GUIDO CALABRESI, A COMMON LAW FOR THE AGE OF STATUTES 1 (1982).

[35] GRANT GILMORE, THE AGES OF AMERICAN LAW 95 (1977).

[36] The FSIA provides that "the district courts shall have original jurisdiction [] over any nonjury civil action against a foreign state [] as to any claim for relief in personam with respect to which the foreign state is not entitled to immunity either under sections 1605–1607 of this title or under any applicable international agreement." 28 U.S.C. § 1330. A foreign state includes an agent or instrumentality of a foreign state. 28 U.S.C. § 1603. The FSIA provides the sole and exclusive basis for obtaining jurisdiction over a foreign state in U.S. courts of the United States. *Argentine Republic v. Amerada Hess Shipping Corp.,* 488 U.S. 428, 443 (1989).

state is immune from suit, meaning that the courts lack jurisdiction over claims against that state, unless one of the exceptions enumerated in the statute applies. The exceptions override the presumption of immunity in a variety of settings, including *inter alia* when the state explicitly or implicitly waives its immunity, or commits certain non-commercial torts in the United States, or commits a commercial act with some nexus to the United States. The statute clearly adopts the "restrictive" theory of immunity (as distinct from the older "absolute" theory) under which a state's commercial activities (*jure gestionis*) will not be entitled to sovereign immunity but its public acts (*jure imperii*) will.

The *act of state doctrine* by contrast is judge-made law under which the courts bar themselves from determining the validity of the actions of a foreign government taken within its own territory.[37] In *Banco Nacional de Cuba v. Sabbatino*[38], the Supreme Court ruled that such deference is appropriate, when judicial resolution of the case "may hinder rather than further this country's pursuit of goals both for itself and for the community of nations as a whole in the international sphere."[39] But the rationale and contours of the act of state doctrine have not remained constant, and the courts have repeatedly placed limits on it, invoking the doctrine to protect only official acts, by a government in power, in pursuit of a public purpose,[40] and even then the doctrine is not absolute. It should not apply, for example, when a case involves norms of international law which have been adopted by a clear consensus among states, since, in the words of the Supreme Court, "[t]he courts can then focus on the application of an agreed principle to circumstances of fact rather than on the sensitive task of establishing a principle not inconsistent with the national interest or with international justice."[41] The mere prospect of embarrassment, by itself, is not enough to trigger the doctrine,[42] suggesting that a relatively simple abstention doctrine has been replaced by a more complex formula for determining a rule of decision deserving deference — as in some other choice of law contexts — when it is consistent with the forum's public policy, and not simply because a foreign government is involved.

The *political question doctrine* similarly obliges courts to abstain in a variety of cases, catalogued in *Baker v. Carr*:[43]

---

[37] *Underhill v. Hernandez*, 168 U.S. 250, 252 (1897).

[38] 376 U.S. 398 (1964).

[39] *Id.* at 423.

[40] *See id.* at 428; *Alfred Dunhill of London, Inc. v. Republic of Cuba*, 425 U.S. 682 (1976); *Republic of Philippines v. Marcos*, 806 F.2d 344 (2d Cir. 1986); *Republic of Philippines v. Marcos*, 862 F.2d 1355 (9th Cir. 1988) (en banc), *cert. denied*, 109 S.Ct. 1933 (1989). *Jiminez v. Aristeguieta*, 311 F.2d 547 (5th Cir. 1962).

[41] *Sabbatino*, 376 U.S. at 428. *See also Kalamazoo Spice Extraction Co. v. Provisional Military Gov't of Socialist Ethiopia*, 729 F.2d 422 (6th Cir. 1984) and cases cited therein; RESTATEMENT (THIRD) OF FOREIGN RELATIONS LAW OF THE UNITED STATES, § 443, comment c (1986).

[42] *Kirkpatrick & Co. v. Environmental Tectonics Corp.*, 493 U.S. 400 (1990) ("the act of state doctrine is not some vague doctrine of abstention but a 'principle of decision binding on federal and state courts alike'.")

[43] 369 U.S. 186 (1961).

Prominent on the surface of any case held to involve a political question is found a textually demonstrable constitutional commitment of the issue to a coordinate political department; or a lack of judicially discoverable and manageable standards for resolving it; or the impossibility of deciding without an initial policy determination of a kind clearly for nonjudicial discretion; or the impossibility of a court's undertaking independent resolution without expressing lack of the respect due coordinate branches of government; or an unusual need for unquestioning adherence to a political decision already made; or the potentiality of embarrassment from multifarious pronouncements by various departments on one question.[44]

The Court noted a variety of foreign affairs issues which would raise nonjusticiable political questions,[45] but established also that "it would be error to suppose that every case or controversy which touches foreign relations lies beyond judicial cognizance."[46] The Court's subsequent treatment of the political question doctrine has suggested to courts and commentators alike that it is no longer viable doctrine, but rumors of its death seem exaggerated,[47] especially in cases with foreign affairs implications.[48] The doctrine periodically resurfaces in the domestic litigation of international norms, leading some courts to hold either that the case is nonjusticiable altogether or that the deference owed to the executive in effect "legislates" an answer to the issue.[49]

When other immunities or doctrines of diffidence are asserted, such as head-of-state immunity or diplomatic immunity, judicial deference to executive practice may be pronounced, because in these areas the courts enjoy no statutory prerogative comparable to the Foreign Sovereign Immunities Act. Some courts interpret these doctrines expansively in part because they assume that international law is ultimately just a branch of politics and cannot meaningfully be applied by the domestic judiciary without compromising and embarrassing the political branches in the conduct of foreign relations. Although the embarrassment rationale is a strong theme in the domestic resolution of many issues arising under international law, it is far from determinative in all of them. Especially outside the disputed range of the president's war powers, where nonjusticiable issues of foreign policy are common, the courts have never relinquished the authority to interpret and apply international law, in spite of the potential confusion that their pronouncements might cause.

---

[44] *Id.* at 217.

[45] *See id.* at 213.

[46] *Id.* at 211.

[47] *See Gilligan v. Morgan*, 413 U.S. 1, 11 (1973) ("because this doctrine has been held inapplicable to certain carefully delineated situations, it is no reason for federal courts to assume its demise.")

[48] *See, e.g., Goldwater v. Carter*, 444 U.S. 996 (1979), in which a plurality held the political question doctrine applicable.

[49] *See, e.g.,* the opinion of Judge Bork in *Finzer v. Barry*, 798 F.2d 1450, 1459 (D.C. Cir. 1986), *aff'd in part and rev'd in part sub nom; Boos v. Barry*, 485 U.S. 312 (1988); the concurring opinion of Judge Robb in *Tel-Oren v. Libyan Arab Republic*, 726 F.2d 774, 824–25 (D.C. Cir. 1984), *cert. denied*, 470 U.S. 1003 (1985); *Greenham Women Against Cruise Missiles v. Reagan*, 755 F.2d 34, 37 (2d Cir. 1985); *In re Korean Air Lines Disaster*, 597 F. Supp. 613, 616–17 (D.D.C. 1984).

Over the years, judicial decisions on the merits have overridden the deference urged by the executive branch in such sensitive matters as the protection of diplomats,[50] bilateral aviation relations,[51] asylum determinations,[52] and commercial-strategic relationships with a NATO ally.[53] With respect to justiciability, the separation of powers in foreign affairs plainly does not require a blanket rule of abstention.

These decisions deny that the interpretation of international law is so inherently political as to require deference to the executive's most recent pronouncement on an issue. In a clear display of the courts' common law powers, these decisions distinguish between "the application of law" and the "exercise of judgment" in international affairs, requiring abstention or deference only when the latter is at issue. The fear of embarrassing the executive branch therefore must be broad enough to *favor* the adjudication of those cases in which *not* applying or recognizing international law would be an embarrassing violation of the separation of powers.

C. ILLUSTRATIVE CASES, RECURRING ISSUES

The two cases that follow, *Filártiga* and *Marble Ceramic Center*, might be viewed as merely preliminary decisions at the pre-trial stage in an international case: one determining the jurisdictional reach of an obscure federal statute in a human rights case, the other addressing the effect of a treaty on the parol evidence rule in a commercial case. One is a tort case, the other sounds in contract. One arises primarily under customary international law, the other under treaty law. From one perspective, both decisions are merely procedural, allowing the case to go forward without resolving the underlying dispute on the merits for either party.

But the more complete appreciation of these cases starts with the recognition that they exemplify the fundamental changes in contemporary international law and its role in domestic litigation; indeed, each of the major developments in international law discussed above is reflected at least implicitly in these decisions and their progeny, including, among other things, the progressive narrowing of exclusive domestic jurisdiction, the declining relevance of the distinction between state and non-state actors, the correlative demise of the public/private distinction, and the gradual attenuation of the distinction between treaty and custom.

At a less abstract level, you should also notice certain key issues and their resolution in these cases, because they may recur whenever international law is at issue and whenever international actors are involved in domestic litigation. For example:

1. By what warrant did the domestic courts apply international law? In other words, why was it legitimate for a domestic court to turn to international standards in the first place? How did the courts articulate the status of international law in U.S. law?

---

[50] *Boos,* 485 U.S. 312 (1988).

[51] *Wardair Canada v. Florida Dep't of Revenue,* 477 U.S. 1 (1986).

[52] *INS v. Cardoza-Fonseca,* 480 U.S. 421 (1987).

[53] *Rainbow Navigation Inc. v. Dep't of Navy,* 699 F. Supp. 339 (D.D.C. 1988).

2. To the extent that a treaty or customary norm was relevant, did it provide a rule of decision or perhaps a private right of action? Did it operate of its own force (*e.g.,* by incorporation) or did it simply "tilt" the interpretation of domestic statutes or the common law?

3. How did the parties prove the content of international law, including the requirements of custom or the interpretation of a treaty's text? How were scholarly writings used?

4. The courts will sometimes express reluctance to apply or interpret international law. Were any "doctrines of judicial diffidence" relevant (*e.g.,* the political question doctrine, foreign sovereign immunity, or the act of state doctrine), and if so, how were they resolved?

5. What logistical issues were presented in the case? For example, was personal jurisdiction over the defendant problematic? How was process served? How was discovery (if any) handled?

6. To the extent that the case might have been brought in another country, why was the United States chosen as the forum? Should that choice be respected by the court?

7. Were there any issues of professional responsibility raised by the case?

8. What are the prospects for enforcing the judgment in the United States and elsewhere? If a foreign judgment is involved, what doctrines of transnational *res judicata* are applicable?

DOLLY AND JOEL FILÁRTIGA v. PENA-IRALA
630 F.2d 876 (2d. Cir. 1980)

Upon ratification of the Constitution, the thirteen former colonies were fused into a single nation, one which, in its relations with foreign states, is bound both to observe and construe the accepted norms of international law, formerly known as the law of nations. Under the Articles of Confederation, the several states had interpreted and applied this body of doctrine as a part of their common law, but with the founding of the "more perfect Union" of 1789, the law of nations became preeminently a federal concern.

Implementing the constitutional mandate for national control over foreign relations, the First Congress established original district court jurisdiction over "all causes where an alien sues for a tort only [committed] in violation of the law of nations." Judiciary Act of 1789, . . . codified at 28 U.S.C. § 1350. Construing this rarely-invoked provision, we hold that deliberate torture perpetrated under color of official authority violates universally accepted norms of the international law of human rights, regardless of the nationality of the parties. Thus, whenever an alleged torturer is found and served with process by an alien within our borders, § 1350 provides federal jurisdiction. Accordingly, we reverse the judgment of the district court dismissing the complaint for want of federal jurisdiction.

I

The appellants, plaintiffs below, are citizens of the Republic of Paraguay. Dr. Joel Filártiga, a physician, describes himself as a longstanding opponent of the government of President Alfredo Stroessner, which has held power in Paraguay since 1954. His daughter, Dolly Filártiga, arrived in the United States in 1978 under a visitor's visa, and has since applied for permanent political asylum. The Filártigas brought this action in the Eastern District of New York against Americo Norberto Pena-Irala (Pena), also a citizen of Paraguay, for wrongfully causing the death of Dr. Filártiga's seventeen-year old son, Joelito. Because the district court dismissed the action for want of subject matter jurisdiction, we must accept as true the allegations contained in the Filártigas' complaint and affidavits for purposes of this appeal.

The appellants contend that on March 29, 1976, Joelito Filártiga was kidnapped and tortured to death by Pena, who was then Inspector General of Police in Asunción, Paraguay. Later that day, the police brought Dolly Filártiga to Pena's home where she was confronted with the body of her brother, which evidenced marks of severe torture. As she fled, horrified, from the house, Pena followed after her shouting, "Here you have what you have been looking for so long and what you deserve. Now shut up." The Filártigas claim that Joelito was tortured and killed in retaliation for his father's political activities and beliefs.

Shortly thereafter, Dr. Filártiga commenced a criminal action in the Paraguayan courts against Pena and the police for the murder of his son. As a result, Dr. Filártiga's attorney was arrested and brought to police headquarters where, shackled to a wall, Pena threatened him with death. This attorney, it is alleged, has since been disbarred without just cause.

During the course of the Paraguayan criminal proceeding, which is apparently still pending after four years, another man, Hugo Duarte, confessed to the murder. Duarte, who was a member of the Pena household, claimed that he had discovered his wife and Joelito in flagrante delicto, and that the crime was one of passion. The Filártigas have submitted a photograph of Joelito's corpse showing injuries they believe refute this claim. Dolly Filártiga, moreover, has stated that she will offer evidence of three independent autopsies demonstrating that her brother's death "was the result of professional methods of torture." Despite his confession, Duarte, we are told, has never been convicted or sentenced in connection with the crime.

In July of 1978, Pena . . . entered the United States under a visitor's visa. He was accompanied by Juana Bautista Fernandez Villalba, who had lived with him in Paraguay. The couple remained in the United States beyond the term of their visas, and were living in Brooklyn, New York, when Dolly Filártiga, who was then living in Washington, D. C., learned of their presence. Acting on information provided by Dolly, the Immigration and Naturalization Service arrested Pena and his companion, both of whom were subsequently ordered deported . . . following a hearing. They had then resided in the United States for more than nine months.

Almost immediately, Dolly caused Pena to be served with a summons and civil complaint at the Brooklyn Navy Yard, where he was being held pending deportation. The complaint alleged that Pena had wrongfully caused Joelito's death by torture and sought compensatory and punitive damages of $10,000,000. The Filártigas also sought to enjoin Pena's deportation to ensure his availability for testimony at trial. The cause of action is stated as arising under "wrongful death statutes; the U. N. Charter; the Universal Declaration on Human Rights; the U.N. Declaration Against Torture; the American Declaration of the Rights and Duties of Man; and other pertinent declarations, documents and practices constituting the customary international law of human rights and the law of nations," as well as 28 U.S.C. § 1350, Article II, sec. 2 and the Supremacy Clause of the U. S. Constitution. Jurisdiction is claimed under the general federal question provision, 28 U.S.C. § 1331 and, principally on this appeal, under the Alien Tort Statute, 28 U.S.C. § 1350.

Judge Nickerson stayed the order of deportation, and Pena immediately moved to dismiss the complaint on the grounds that subject matter jurisdiction was absent and for *forum non conveniens*. On the jurisdictional issue, there has been no suggestion that Pena claims diplomatic immunity from suit. The Filártigas submitted the affidavits of a number of distinguished international legal scholars, who stated unanimously that the law of nations prohibits absolutely the use of torture as alleged in the complaint.[4] Pena, in support of his motion to dismiss on the ground of forum non conveniens, submitted the affidavit of his Paraguayan counsel, . . . who averred that Paraguayan law provides a full and adequate civil remedy for the wrong alleged. Dr. Filártiga has not commenced such an action, however, believing that further resort to the courts of his own country would be futile.

Judge Nickerson heard argument on the motion to dismiss . . ., and . . . dismissed the complaint on jurisdictional grounds.[6] The district judge recognized the strength of appellants' argument that official torture violates an emerging norm of customary international law. Nonetheless, he felt constrained by dicta contained in two recent opinions of this Court, *Dreyfus v. von Finck*, 534 F.2d 24 (2d Cir.), *cert. denied*, 429 U.S. 835 (1976); *IIT v. Vencap, Ltd.*, 519 F.2d 1001 (2d Cir. 1975), to construe narrowly "the law of nations," as employed in § 1350, as excluding that law which governs a state's treatment of its own citizens.

The district court continued the stay of deportation for forty-eight hours while appellants applied for further stays. These applications were denied by

---

[4] Richard Falk, the Albert G. Milbank Professor of International Law and Practice at Princeton University, and a former Vice President of the American Society of International Law, avers that, in his judgment, "it is now beyond reasonable doubt that torture of a person held in detention that results in severe harm or death is a violation of the law of nations." Thomas Franck, professor of international law at New York University and Director of the New York University Center for International Studies offers his opinion that torture has now been rejected by virtually all nations, although it was once commonly used to extract confessions. Richard Lillich, the Howard W. Smith Professor of Law at the University of Virginia School of Law, concludes, after a lengthy review of the authorities, that officially perpetrated torture is "a violation of international law (formerly called the law of nations)." Finally, Myres MacDougal, a former Sterling Professor of Law at the Yale Law School, and a past President of the American Society of International Law, states that torture is an offense against the law of nations, and that "it has long been recognized that such offenses vitally affect relations between states."

[6] The court below accordingly did not consider the motion to dismiss on *forum non conveniens* grounds, which is not before us on this appeal.

a panel of this Court . . . and by the Supreme Court two days later. Shortly thereafter, Pena and his companion returned to Paraguay.

II

Appellants rest their principal argument in support of federal jurisdiction upon the Alien Tort Statute, 28 U.S.C. § 1350 , which provides: "The district courts shall have original jurisdiction of any civil action by an alien for a tort only, committed in violation of the law of nations or a treaty of the United States." Since appellants do not contend that their action arises directly under a treaty of the United States,[7] a threshold question on the jurisdictional issue is whether the conduct alleged violates the law of nations. In light of the universal condemnation of torture in numerous international agreements, and the renunciation of torture as an instrument of official policy by virtually all of the nations of the world (in principle if not in practice), we find that an act of torture committed by a state official against one held in detention violates established norms of the international law of human rights, and hence the law of nations.

The Supreme Court has enumerated the appropriate sources of international law. The law of nations "may be ascertained by consulting the works of jurists, writing professedly on public law; or by the general usage and practice of nations; or by judicial decisions recognizing and enforcing that law." *United States v. Smith,* 18 U.S. (5 Wheat.) 153, 160–61 (1820); *Lopes v. Reederei Richard Schroder,* 225 F. Supp. 292, 295 (E.D.Pa. 1963). In *Smith,* a statute proscribing "the crime of piracy [on the high seas] as defined by the law of nations," was held sufficiently determinate in meaning to afford the basis for a death sentence. The Smith Court discovered among the works of Lord Bacon, Grotius, Bochard and other commentators a genuine consensus that rendered the crime "sufficiently and constitutionally defined." *Smith, supra,* at 162.

The Paquete Habana, 175 U.S. 677 (1900), reaffirmed that

> where there is no treaty, and no controlling executive or legislative act or judicial decision, resort must be had to the customs and usages of civilized nations; and, as evidence of these, to the works of jurists and commentators, who by years of labor, research and experience, have made themselves peculiarly well acquainted with the subjects of which they treat. Such works are resorted to by judicial tribunals, not for the speculations of their authors concerning what the law ought to be, but for trustworthy evidence of what the law really is.

Id. at 700. Modern international sources confirm the propriety of this approach.[8]

---

[7] Appellants "associate themselves with" the argument of some of the *amici curiae* that their claim arises directly under a treaty of the United States, . . ., but nonetheless primarily rely upon treaties and other international instruments as evidence of an emerging norm of customary international law, rather then [sic] independent sources of law.

[8] The Statute of the International Court of Justice, Arts. 38 & 59, June 26, 1945, 59 Stat. 1055, 1060 (1945) provides:

Habana is particularly instructive for present purposes, for it held that the traditional prohibition against seizure of an enemy's coastal fishing vessels during wartime, a standard that began as one of comity only, had ripened over the preceding century into "a settled rule of international law" by "the general assent of civilized nations." *Id.* at 694. Thus it is clear that courts must interpret international law not as it was in 1789, but as it has evolved and exists among the nations of the world today. *See Ware v. Hylton,* 3 U.S. (3 Dall.) 199 (1796) (distinguishing between "ancient" and "modern" law of nations).

The requirement that a rule command the "general assent of civilized nations" to become binding upon them all is a stringent one. Were this not so, the courts of one nation might feel free to impose idiosyncratic legal rules upon others, in the name of applying international law. Thus, in *Banco Nacional de Cuba v. Sabbatino,* 376 U.S. 398 (1964), the Court declined to pass on the validity of the Cuban government's expropriation of a foreign-owned corporation's assets, noting the sharply conflicting views on the issue propounded by the capital-exporting, capital-importing, socialist and capitalist nations. *Id.,* at 428–30.

The case at bar presents us with a situation diametrically opposed to the conflicted state of law that confronted the *Sabbatino* Court. Indeed, to paraphrase that Court's statement, *id.* at 428, there are few, if any, issues in international law today on which opinion seems to be so united as the limitations on a state's power to torture persons held in its custody.

The United Nations Charter (a treaty of the United States) makes it clear that in this modern age a state's treatment of its own citizens is a matter of international concern. It provides:

> With a view to the creation of conditions of stability and well-being which are necessary for peaceful and friendly relations among nations . . . the United Nations shall promote . . . universal respect for, and observance of, human rights and fundamental freedoms for all without distinctions as to race, sex, language or religion.

Id., Art. 55. And further:

---

1. The Court, whose function is to decide in accordance with international law such disputes as are submitted to it, shall apply:

(a) international conventions, whether general or particular, establishing rules expressly recognized by the contesting states;

(b) international custom, as evidence of a general practice accepted as law;

(c) the general principles of law recognized by civilized nations;

(d) subject to the provisions of Article 59, judicial decisions and the teachings of the most highly qualified publicists of the various nations, as subsidiary means for the determination of the rules of law.

2. This provision shall not prejudice the power of the Court to decide a case *ex aequo et bono,* if the parties agree thereto.

Art. 59

The decision of the Court has no binding force except between the parties and in respect of that particular case.

All members pledge themselves to take joint and separate action in cooperation with the Organization for the achievement of the purposes set forth in Article 55.

Id., Art. 56.

While this broad mandate has been held not to be wholly self-executing, *Hitai v. Immigration and Naturalization Service,* 343 F.2d 466, 468 (2d Cir. 1965), this observation alone does not end our inquiry.[9] For although there is no universal agreement as to the precise extent of the "human rights and fundamental freedoms" guaranteed to all by the Charter, there is at present no dissent from the view that the guaranties include, at a bare minimum, the right to be free from torture. This prohibition has become part of customary international law, as evidenced and defined by the Universal Declaration of Human Rights, General Assembly Resolution 217 (III)(A) (Dec. 10, 1948) which states, in the plainest of terms, "no one shall be subjected to torture."[10] The General Assembly has declared that the Charter precepts embodied in this Universal Declaration "constitute basic principles of international law." G.A.Res. 2625 (XXV) (Oct. 24, 1970).

Particularly relevant is the Declaration on the Protection of All Persons from Being Subjected to Torture, General Assembly Resolution 3452, 30 U.N. GAOR Supp. (No. 34) 91, U.N.Doc. A/1034 (1975) . . . The Declaration expressly prohibits any state from permitting the dastardly and totally inhuman act of torture. Torture, in turn, is defined as "any act by which severe pain and suffering, whether physical or mental, is intentionally inflicted by or at the instigation of a public official on a person for such purposes as . . . intimidating him or other persons." The Declaration goes on to provide that "[w]here it is proved that an act of torture or other cruel, inhuman or degrading treatment or punishment has been committed by or at the instigation of a public official, the victim shall be afforded redress and compensation, in accordance with national law." This Declaration, like the Declaration of Human Rights before it, was adopted without dissent by the General Assembly. . . .

These U.N. declarations are significant because they specify with great precision the obligations of member nations under the Charter. Since their adoption, "[m]embers can no longer contend that they do not know what human rights they promised in the Charter to promote." . . . . Sohn, "A Short History of United Nations Documents on Human Rights," in The United Nations and Human Rights, 18th Report of the Commission (Commission to Study the Organization of Peace ed. 1968). Moreover, a U.N. Declaration is, according to one authoritative definition, "a formal and solemn instrument, suitable for rare occasions when principles of great and lasting importance

---

[9] We observe that this Court has previously utilized the U.N. Charter and the Charter of the Organization of American States, another non-self-executing agreement, as evidence of binding principles of international law. *See United States v. Toscanino,* 500 F.2d 267 (2d Cir. 1974). In that case, our government's duty under international law to refrain from kidnapping a criminal defendant from within the borders of another nation, where formal extradition procedures existed, infringed the personal rights of the defendant, whose international law claims were thereupon remanded for a hearing in the district court.

[10] Eighteen nations have incorporated the Universal Declaration into their own constitutions. 48 Revue Internationale de Droit Penal Nos. 3 & 4, at 211 (1977).

are being enunciated." 34 U.N. ESCOR, Supp. (No. 8) 15, U.N. Doc. E/cn.4/1/ 610 (1962) (memorandum of Office of Legal Affairs, U.N. Secretariat). Accordingly, it has been observed that the Universal Declaration of Human Rights "no longer fits into the dichotomy of 'binding treaty' against 'non-binding pronouncement,' but is rather an authoritative statement of the international community." E. SCHWELB, HUMAN RIGHTS AND THE INTERNATIONAL COMMUNITY 70 (1964). Thus, a Declaration creates an expectation of adherence, and "insofar as the expectation is gradually justified by State practice, a declaration may by custom become recognized as laying down rules binding upon the States." 34 U.N. ESCOR, *supra*. Indeed, several commentators have concluded that the Universal Declaration has become, in toto, a part of binding, customary international law. . . .

Turning to the act of torture, we have little difficulty discerning its universal renunciation in the modern usage and practice of nations. *Smith, supra,* at 160–61. The international consensus surrounding torture has found expression in numerous international treaties and accords [*citing* the American Convention on Human Rights, Art. 5, ("No one shall be subjected to torture or to cruel, inhuman or degrading punishment or treatment"); the International Covenant on Civil and Political Rights, (identical language); the European Convention for the Protection of Human Rights and Fundamental Freedoms, Art. 3, (semble)]. The substance of these international agreements is reflected in modern municipal, *i.e.*, national law as well. Although torture was once a routine concomitant of criminal interrogations in many nations, during the modern and hopefully more enlightened era it has been universally renounced. According to one survey, torture is prohibited, expressly or implicitly, by the constitutions of over fifty-five nations, including both the United States and Paraguay. Our State Department reports a general recognition of this principle:

> There now exists an international consensus that recognizes basic human rights and obligations owed by all governments to their citizens . . . . There is no doubt that these rights are often violated; but virtually all governments acknowledge their validity.

Department of State, COUNTRY REPORTS ON HUMAN RIGHTS FOR 1979, at 1. We have been directed to no assertion by any contemporary state of a right to torture its own or another nation's citizens. Indeed, United States diplomatic contacts confirm the universal abhorrence with which torture is viewed:

> In exchanges between United States embassies and all foreign states with which the United States maintains relations, it has been the Department of State's general experience that no government has asserted a right to torture its own nationals. Where reports of torture elicit some credence, a state usually responds by denial or, less frequently, by asserting that the conduct was unauthorized or constituted rough treatment short of torture.[15]

---

[15] The fact that the prohibition of torture is often honored in the breach does not diminish its binding effect as a norm of international law. As one commentator has put it, "The best evidence for the existence of international law is that every actual State recognizes that it does exist and that it is itself under an obligation to observe it. States often violate international law, just as individuals often violate municipal law; but no more than individuals do States defend their violations by claiming that they are above the law." J. Brierly, THE OUTLOOK FOR INTERNATIONAL LAW 4–5 (Oxford 1944).

Memorandum of the United States as Amicus Curiae at 16.

Having examined the sources from which customary international law is derived, the usage of nations, judicial opinions and the works of jurists,[16] we conclude that official torture is now prohibited by the law of nations. The prohibition is clear and unambiguous, and admits of no distinction between treatment of aliens and citizens. Accordingly, we must conclude that the dictum in *Dreyfus v. von Finck, supra,*. . . to the effect that "violations of international law do not occur when the aggrieved parties are nationals of the acting state," is clearly out of tune with the current usage and practice of international law. The treaties and accords cited above, as well as the express foreign policy of our own government,[17] all make it clear that international law confers fundamental rights upon all people vis-a-vis their own governments. While the ultimate scope of those rights will be a subject for continuing refinement and elaboration, we hold that the right to be free from torture is now among them. We therefore turn to the question whether the other requirements for jurisdiction are met.

III

Appellee submits that even if the tort alleged is a violation of modern international law, federal jurisdiction may not be exercised consistent with the dictates of Article III of the Constitution. The claim is without merit. Common law courts of general jurisdiction regularly adjudicate transitory tort claims between individuals over whom they exercise personal jurisdiction, wherever the tort occurred. Moreover, as part of an articulated scheme of federal control over external affairs, Congress provided, in the first Judiciary Act, § 9(b), . . . for federal jurisdiction over suits by aliens where principles of international law are in issue. The constitutional basis for the Alien Tort Statute is the law of nations, which has always been part of the federal common law.

It is not extraordinary for a court to adjudicate a tort claim arising outside of its territorial jurisdiction. A state or nation has a legitimate interest in the orderly resolution of disputes among those within its borders, and where the *lex loci delicti commissi* [the law of the place where the wrong was committed] is applied, it is an expression of comity to give effect to the laws of the state where the wrong occurred. Thus, Lord Mansfield in *Mostyn v. Fabrigas, 1 Cowp.* 161 (1774), *quoted in McKenna v. Fisk,* 42 U.S. (1 How.) 241, 248 (1843), said:

---

[16] *See* note 4, *supra: see also Ireland v. United Kingdom*, Judgment of Jan. 18, 1978 (European Court of Human Rights) (holding that Britain's subjection of prisoners to sleep deprivation, hooding, exposure to hissing noise, reduced diet, and standing against a wall for hours was "inhuman and degrading," but not "torture" within meaning of European Convention on Human Rights).

[17] *E.g.*, 22 U.S.C. § 2304(a)(2) ("Except under circumstances specified in this section, no security assistance may be provided to any country the government of which engages in a consistent pattern of gross violations of internationally recognized human rights."); 22 U.S.C. § 2151(a). ("The Congress finds that fundamental political, economic, and technological changes have resulted in the interdependence of nations. The Congress declares that the individual liberties, economic prosperity, and security of the people of the United States are best sustained and enhanced in a community of nations which respect individual civil and economic rights and freedoms.")

If A becomes indebted to B, or commits a tort upon his person or upon his personal property in Paris, an action in either case may be maintained against A in England, if he is there found . . . . As to transitory actions, there is not a colour of doubt but that any action which is transitory may be laid in any county in England, though the matter arises beyond the seas.

Mostyn came into our law as the original basis for state court jurisdiction over out-of-state torts, *McKenna v. Fisk, supra,* (personal injury suits held transitory); *Dennick v. Railroad Co.,* 103 U.S. 11 (1880) (wrongful death action held transitory), and it has not lost its force in suits to recover for a wrongful death occurring upon foreign soil, *Slater v. Mexican National Railroad Co.,* 194 U.S. 120 (1904), as long as the conduct complained of was unlawful where performed. RESTATEMENT (SECOND) OF THE FOREIGN RELATIONS LAW OF THE UNITED STATES § 19 (1965). Here, where *in personam* jurisdiction has been obtained over the defendant, the parties agree that the acts alleged would violate Paraguayan law, and the policies of the forum are consistent with the foreign law, [18] state court jurisdiction would be proper. Indeed, appellees conceded as much at oral argument.

Recalling that *Mostyn* was freshly decided at the time the Constitution was ratified, we proceed to consider whether the First Congress acted constitutionally in vesting jurisdiction over "foreign suits," *Slater, supra,* . . . alleging torts committed in violation of the law of nations. A case properly "aris[es] under the . . . laws of the United States" for Article III purposes if grounded upon statutes enacted by Congress or upon the common law of the United States. *See Illinois v. City of Milwaukee,* 406 U.S. 91, 99–100 (1972); *Ivy Broadcasting Co., Inc. v. American Tel. & Tel. Co.,* 391 F.2d 486, 492 (2d Cir. 1968). The law of nations forms an integral part of the common law, and a review of the history surrounding the adoption of the Constitution demonstrates that it became a part of the common law of the United States upon the adoption of the Constitution. Therefore, the enactment of the Alien Tort Statute was authorized by Article III.

During the eighteenth century, it was taken for granted on both sides of the Atlantic that the law of nations forms a part of the common law. Under the Articles of Confederation, the Pennsylvania Court of Oyer and Terminer at Philadelphia, per McKean, Chief Justice, applied the law of nations to the criminal prosecution of the Chevalier de Longchamps for his assault upon the person of the French Consul-General to the United States, noting that "[t]his law, in its full extent, is a part of the law of this state . . . ." *Respublica v. DeLongchamps,* 1 U.S. (1 Dall.) 113, 119 (1784). Thus, a leading commentator has written:

> It is an ancient and a salutary feature of the Anglo-American legal tradition that the Law of Nations is a part of the law of the land to be ascertained and administered, like any other, in the appropriate case. This doctrine was originally conceived and formulated in England in response to the demands of an expanding commerce and

---

[18] Conduct of the type alleged here would be actionable under 42 U.S.C. § 1983 or, undoubtedly, the Constitution, if performed by a government official.

under the influence of theories widely accepted in the late sixteenth, the seventeenth and the eighteenth centuries. It was brought to America in the colonial years as part of the legal heritage from England. It was well understood by men of legal learning in America in the eighteenth century when the United Colonies broke away from England to unite effectively, a little later, in the United States of America.

Dickenson, *The Law of Nations as Part of the National Law of the United States*, 101 U.Pa.L.Rev. 26, 27 (1952).

Indeed, Dickenson goes on to demonstrate, that one of the principal defects of the Confederation that our Constitution was intended to remedy was the central government's inability to "cause infractions of treaties or of the law of nations, to be punished." 1 Farrand, Records of the Federal Convention 19 (Rev. ed. 1937) (Notes of James Madison). And, in Jefferson's words, the very purpose of the proposed Union was "to make us one nation as to foreign concerns, and keep us distinct in domestic ones." Dickenson, *supra.*

As ratified, the judiciary article contained no express reference to cases arising under the law of nations. Indeed, the only express reference to that body of law is contained in Article I, sec. 8, cl. 10, which grants to the Congress the power to "define and punish . . . offenses against the law of nations." Appellees seize upon this circumstance and advance the proposition that the law of nations forms a part of the laws of the United States only to the extent that Congress has acted to define it. This extravagant claim is amply refuted by the numerous decisions applying rules of international law uncodified in any act of Congress. *E.g., Ware v. Hylton,* 3 U.S. (3 Dall.) 199 (1796); *The Paquete Habana, supra; Sabbatino, supra.* A similar argument was offered to and rejected by the Supreme Court in *United States v. Smith, supra,* and we reject it today. As John Jay wrote in *The Federalist* No. 3, at 22 (1 Bourne ed. 1901), "Under the national government, treaties and articles of treaties, as well as the laws of nations, will always be expounded in one sense and executed in the same manner, whereas adjudications on the same points and questions in the thirteen states will not always accord or be consistent." Federal jurisdiction over cases involving international law is clear.

Thus, it was hardly a radical initiative for Chief Justice Marshall to state in *The Nereide,* 13 U.S. (9 Cranch) 388, 422 (1815), that in the absence of a congressional enactment,[20] United States courts are "bound by the law of nations, which is a part of the law of the land." These words were echoed in *The Paquete Habana, supra:* "international law is part of our law, and must be ascertained and administered by the courts of justice of appropriate jurisdiction, as often as questions of right depending upon it are duly presented for their determination."

The Filártigas urge that 28 U.S.C. § 1350 be treated as an exercise of Congress's power to define offenses against the law of nations. While such

---

[20] The plainest evidence that international law has an existence in the federal courts independent of acts of Congress is the long-standing rule of construction first enunciated by Chief Justice Marshall: "an act of congress ought never to be construed to violate the law of nations, if any other possible construction remains . . . ." *The Charming Betsy,* 6 U.S. (2 Cranch) 64, 67 (1804), quoted in *Lauritzen v. Larsen,* 345 U.S. 571, 578 (1953).

a reading is possible, *see Lincoln Mills v. Textile Workers,* 353 U.S. 448 (1957) (jurisdictional statute authorizes judicial explication of federal common law), we believe it is sufficient here to construe the Alien Tort Statute, not as granting new rights to aliens, but simply as opening the federal courts for adjudication of the rights already recognized by international law. The statute nonetheless does inform our analysis of Article III, for we recognize that questions of jurisdiction "must be considered part of an organic growth, part of an evolutionary process," and that the history of the judiciary article gives meaning to its pithy phrases. *Romero v. International Terminal Operating Co.,* 358 U.S. 354, 360 (1959). The Framers' overarching concern that control over international affairs be vested in the new national government to safeguard the standing of the United States among the nations of the world therefore reinforces the result we reach today.

Although the Alien Tort Statute has rarely been the basis for jurisdiction during its long history,[21] in light of the foregoing discussion, there can be little doubt that this action is properly brought in federal court.[22] This is undeniably an action by an alien, for a tort only, committed in violation of the law of nations. The paucity of suits successfully maintained under the section is readily attributable to the statute's requirement of alleging a *"violation of the law of nations"* (emphasis supplied) at the jurisdictional threshold. Courts have, accordingly, engaged in a more searching preliminary review of the merits than is required, for example, under the more flexible "arising under" formulation. *Compare O'Reilly de Camara v. Brooke,* 209 U.S. 45, 52 (1907) (question of Alien Tort Statute jurisdiction disposed of "on the merits") (Holmes, J.), *with Bell v. Hood,* 327 U.S. 678 (1946) (general federal question jurisdiction not defeated by the possibility that the averments in the complaint may fail to state a cause of action). Thus, the narrowing construction that the Alien Tort Statute has previously received reflects the fact that earlier cases did not involve such well-established, universally recognized norms of international law that are here at issue.

For example, the statute does not confer jurisdiction over an action by a Luxembourgeois international investment trust's suit for fraud, conversion, and corporate waste. *IIT v. Vencap,* 519 F.2d 1001, 1015 (1975). In *IIT,* Judge Friendly astutely noted that the mere fact that every nation's municipal law may prohibit theft does not incorporate "the Eighth Commandment, 'Thou Shalt not steal' . . . [into] the law of nations." It is only where the nations of the world have demonstrated that the wrong is of mutual, and not merely several, concern, by means of express international accords, that a wrong generally recognized becomes an international law violation within the

---

[21] Section 1350 afforded the basis for jurisdiction over a child custody suit between aliens in *Adra v. Clift,* 195 F. Supp. 857 (D.Md. 1961), with a falsified passport supplying the requisite international law violation. In *Bolchos v. Darrel,* 3 Fed. Cas. 810 (D.S.C.1795), the Alien Tort Statute provided an alternative basis of jurisdiction over a suit to determine title to slaves on board an enemy vessel taken on the high seas.

[22] We recognize that our reasoning might also sustain jurisdiction under the general federal question provision, 28 U.S.C. § 1331. We prefer, however, to rest our decision upon the Alien Tort Statute, in light of that provision's close coincidence with the jurisdictional facts presented in this case.

meaning of the statute. Other recent § 1350 cases are similarly distinguishable.[23]

IIT adopted a dictum from *Lopes v. Reederei Richard Schroder,* 225 F. Supp. 292 (E.D.Pa. 1963), to the effect that "a violation of the law of nations arises only when there has been 'a violation by one or more individuals of those standards, rules or customs (a) affecting the relationship between states or between an individual and a foreign state and (b) used by those states for their common good and/or in dealings inter se.'" *IIT, supra,* at 1015, quoting *Lopes, supra,* at 297. We have no quarrel with this formulation so long as it be understood that the courts are not to prejudge the scope of the issues that the nations of the world may deem important to their interrelationships, and thus to their common good. As one commentator has noted:

> the sphere of domestic jurisdiction is not an irreducible sphere of rights which are somehow inherent, natural, or fundamental. It does not create an impenetrable barrier to the development of international law. Matters of domestic jurisdiction are not those which are unregulated by international law, but those which are left by international law for regulation by States. There are, therefore, no matters which are domestic by their "nature." All are susceptible of international legal regulation and may become the subjects of new rules of customary law of treaty obligations.

Preuss, "Article 2, Paragraph 7 of the Charter of the United Nations and Matters of Domestic Jurisdiction," HAGUE RECEUIL (Extract, 149) at 8, *reprinted in* H. Briggs, THE LAW OF NATIONS 24 (1952). Here, the nations have made it their business, both through international accords and unilateral action,[24] to be concerned with domestic human rights violations of this magnitude. The case before us therefore falls within the *Lopes/IIT* rule.

---

[23] *Dreyfus v. von Finck,* 534 F.2d 24 (2d Cir.), *cert. denied,* 429 U.S. 835 (1976), concerned a forced sale of property, and thus sought to invoke international law in an area in which no consensus view existed. *See Sabbatino, supra,* 376 U.S. at 428. Similarly, *Benjamins v. British European Airways,* 572 F.2d 913 (2d Cir. 1978), *cert. denied,* 439 U.S. 1114 (1979), held only that an air disaster, even if caused by "wilful" negligence, does not constitute a law of nations violation. *Id. at 916.* In *Khedivial Line, S. A. E. v. Seafarers' International Union,* 278 F.2d 49 (2d Cir. 1960), we found that the "right" to free access to the ports of a foreign nation was at best a rule of comity, and not a binding rule of international law.

The cases from other circuits are distinguishable in like manner. The court in *Huynh Thi Anh v. Levi,* 586 F.2d 625 (6th Cir. 1978), was unable to discern from the traditional sources of the law of nations "a universal or generally accepted substantive rule or principle" governing child custody, *id. at 629,* and therefore held jurisdiction to be lacking. *Cf. Nguyen Da Yen v. Kissinger,* 528 F.2d 1194, 1201 n.13 (9th Cir. 1975) ("the illegal seizure, removal and detention of an alien against his will in a foreign country would appear to be a tort . . . and it may well be a tort in violation of the 'law of nations'") (§ 1350 question not reached due to inadequate briefing). Finally, the district court in *Lopes v. Reederei Richard Schroder,* 225 F. Supp. 292 (E.D. Pa. 1963) simply found that the doctrine of seaworthiness, upon which the plaintiff relied, was a uniquely American concept, and therefore not a part of the law of nations.

[24] As President Carter stated in his address to the United Nations on March 17, 1977:

> All the signatories of the United Nations Charter have pledged themselves to observe and to respect basic human rights. Thus, no member of the United Nations can claim that mistreatment of the citizens is solely its own business. Equally, no member can avoid its responsibilities to review and to speak when torture or unwarranted deprivation occurs in any part of the world.

Reprinted in 78 *Department of State Bull.* 322 (1977) . . . .

Since federal jurisdiction may properly be exercised over the Filártigas' claim, the action must be remanded for further proceedings. Appellee Pena, however, advances several additional points that lie beyond the scope of our holding on jurisdiction. Both to emphasize the boundaries of our holding, and to clarify some of the issues reserved for the district court on remand, we will address these contentions briefly.

IV

Pena argues that the customary law of nations, as reflected in treaties and declarations that are not self-executing, should not be applied as rules of decision in this case. In doing so, he confuses the question of federal jurisdiction under the Alien Tort Statute, which requires consideration of the law of nations, with the issue of the choice of law to be applied, which will be addressed at a later stage in the proceedings. The two issues are distinct. Our holding on subject matter jurisdiction decides only whether Congress intended to confer judicial power, and whether it is authorized to do so by Article III. The choice of law inquiry is a much broader one, primarily concerned with fairness, *see Home Insurance Co. v. Dick,* 281 U.S. 397 (1930); consequently, it looks to wholly different considerations. *See Lauritzen v. Larsen,* 345 U.S. 571 (1954). Should the district court decide that the *Lauritzen* analysis requires it to apply Paraguayan law, our courts will not have occasion to consider what law would govern a suit under the Alien Tort Statute where the challenged conduct is actionable under the law of the forum and the law of nations, but not the law of the jurisdiction in which the tort occurred.[25]

Pena also argues that "if the conduct complained of is alleged to be the act of the Paraguayan government, the suit is barred by the Act of State doctrine." This argument was not advanced below, and is therefore not before us on this appeal. We note in passing, however, that we doubt whether action by a state official in violation of the Constitution and laws of the Republic of Paraguay, and wholly unratified by that nation's government, could properly be characterized as an act of state. *See Banco Nacionale de Cuba v. Sabbatino, supra; Underhill v. Hernandez,* 168 U.S. 250 (1897). Paraguay's renunciation of torture as a legitimate instrument of state policy, however, does not strip the tort of its character as an international law violation, if it in fact occurred under color of government authority. *See* Declaration on the Protection of All Persons from Being Subjected to Torture, *supra.* . .; *cf. Ex parte Young,* 209 U.S. 123 (1908) (state official subject to suit for constitutional violations despite immunity of state).

---

[25] In taking that broad range of factors into account, the district court may well decide that fairness requires it to apply Paraguayan law to the instant case. *See Slater v. Mexican National Railway Co.,* 194 U.S. 120, (1904). Such a decision would not retroactively oust the federal court of subject matter jurisdiction, even though plaintiff's cause of action would no longer properly be "created" by a law of the United States. *See American Well Works Co. v. Layne & Bowler Co.,* 241 U.S. 257, 260, (1916) (Holmes, J.). Once federal jurisdiction is established by a colorable claim under federal law at a preliminary stage of the proceeding, subsequent dismissal of that claim (here, the claim under the general international proscription of torture) does not deprive the court of jurisdiction previously established. *See Hagans v. Lavine,* 415 U.S. 528, (1974); *Romero v. International Terminal Operating Co.,* 358 U.S. 354 (1959); *Bell v. Hood,* 327 U.S. 678 (1946). *Cf. Huynh Thi Ahn, supra,* 586 F.2d at 633 (choice of municipal law ousts § 1350 jurisdiction when no international norms exist).

Finally, we have already stated that we do not reach the critical question of *forum non conveniens*, since it was not considered below. In closing, however, we note that the foreign relations implications of this and other issues the district court will be required to adjudicate on remand underscores the wisdom of the First Congress in vesting jurisdiction over such claims in the federal district courts through the Alien Tort Statute. Questions of this nature are fraught with implications for the nation as a whole, and therefore should not be left to the potentially varying adjudications of the courts of the fifty states.

In the twentieth century, the international community has come to recognize the common danger posed by the flagrant disregard of basic human rights and particularly the right to be free of torture. Spurred first by the Great War, and then the Second, civilized nations have banded together to prescribe acceptable norms of international behavior. From the ashes of the Second World War arose the United Nations Organization, amid hopes that an era of peace and cooperation had at last begun. Though many of these aspirations have remained elusive goals, that circumstance cannot diminish the true progress that has been made. In the modern age, humanitarian and practical considerations have combined to lead the nations of the world to recognize that respect for fundamental human rights is in their individual and collective interest. Among the rights universally proclaimed by all nations, as we have noted, is the right to be free of physical torture. Indeed, for purposes of civil liability, the torturer has become like the pirate and slave trader before him *hostis humani generis*, an enemy of all mankind. Our holding today, giving effect to a jurisdictional provision enacted by our First Congress, is a small but important step in the fulfillment of the ageless dream to free all people from brutal violence.

Notes and Questions on *Filártiga*

1. *Filártiga and its aftermath.* The denial of a motion to dismiss is of course not a finding of liability, and on remand from the court of appeals, the district court in *Filártiga* avoided a narrow interpretation of the Alien Tort Claims Act:

> The international law prohibiting torture established the standard and referred to the national states the task of enforcing it. By enacting Section 1350, Congress entrusted the task to the federal courts and gave them power to choose and develop federal remedies to effectuate the purposes of the international law incorporated into United States common law. In order to take the international condemnation of torture seriously this court must adopt a remedy appropriate to the ends and reflective of the nature of the condemnation. . . . If the courts of the United States are to adhere to the consensus of the community of humankind, any remedy they fashion must recognize that this case concerns an act so monstrous as to make its perpetrator an outlaw around the globe. . . . [The court went on to award $10,385,364 to the plaintiff in compensatory and punitive damages *inter alia*.]

Filártiga v. Pena-Irala, 577 F. Supp 860, 867–68 (E.D.N.Y. 1984).

Over a hundred cases have been filed under the Alien Tort Claims Act and decided (at least at the pre-trial stage) since 1980, and, though that number may seem small out of context, it is actually surprising that so many cases exist at all, given the high threshold for proving a "tort in violation of the law of nations" and the serendipity of finding both a plaintiff willing to undertake a lawsuit and a defendant within the personal jurisdiction of a U.S. court. There is moreover a qualitative consistency to these decisions that gives them an authority disproportionate to their number: the courts of the United States have generally endorsed the *Filártiga* approach, even as the defendants-of-choice have evolved from the individual who physically commits a violation, to one who orders or tolerates it, to "private" actors — corporations and groups exercising public functions or committing violations that do not require state action. The class of actionable wrongs has similarly evolved beyond torture, genocide, slavery, and the like, to include environmental wrongs, gender violence, and terrorism. As a consequence, a small but coherent body of decisional law has evolved under the ATCA and received the imprimatur of both the executive branch through various *ad hoc* submissions to the courts and the Congress through the enactment of the Torture Victim Protection Act of 1992 ("TVPA").[1] These developments now include the prospect that corporations may be held liable under the Act for their complicity in human rights violations abroad. *See, e.g., Doe v. Unocal,* 963 F. Supp. 880 (C.D. Cal. 1997) (motion to dismiss); *Doe v. Unocal,* 110 F. Supp. 2d 1294 (C. D. Cal. 2000) (summary judgment).

2. *Authority to apply international law.* Under what rationale was it legitimate for a domestic court to apply international law to an event that occurred entirely in a foreign nation?

3. *Proving the content of international law.* Consider the evidence used by the *Filártiga* court to determine that torture was a violation of the law of nations.

A. *Resolutions and declarations of the United Nations.* The Charter of the United Nations does not make the organization an international legislature, and resolutions and declarations are not equivalent to binding legislation. What role do these instruments play in the Second Circuit's opinion?

B. *Treaties in consistent form.* The *Filártiga* court referred to various treaties condemning torture, but was the United States a party to each of these treaties? Does that matter? Of what relevance is the fact that the Torture Convention was at the time of the decision in *draft* form?

C. *Constitutions and laws of the various nations.* What is the Second Circuit's response to the argument that the written laws around the world that prohibit torture are meaningless when states commonly practice torture in violation of their own law? How can the state practice and *opinio juris* requirements of customary international law be satisfied if, at the time of the *Filártiga* decision, torture was practiced to some extent on virtually every continent? Would it matter if some states considered flogging or whipping a form of torture and others did not?

---

[1] Pub.L. No. 102-256, Mar. 12, 1992, 106 Stat. 73, *codified at* 28 U.S.C. § 1350.

D. *Scholarly writings.* Is there reason to think that the writings of scholars and publicists have a greater effect in transnational cases than in domestic cases? What might be the rationale for the difference?

4. *Federal versus state courts.* Under the transitory tort doctrine, as conceived by the Second Circuit, could the Filártigas have sued Pena-Irala in New York state courts? If the framers of Section 1350 were aware of that possibility, why might they have endorsed a federal alternative to litigation in state courts?

5. *Jurisdiction and foreign affairs.* What are the foreign policy implications of this case? Should the court have taken these into account? If a court were sensitive to such concerns, which way should it rule on these facts? Might for example the district court's conclusion that a state's torture of its own citizens is *not* a violation of the law of nations be more embarrassing to the foreign relations of the United States than the appeals court's decision that it *is* a violation of international law? To what evidence should the court turn in determining whether a case is too political or not?

MARBLE CERAMIC CENTER v. CERAMICA NUOVA D'AGOSTINO
144 F.3d 1384 (11th Cir. 1998), *cert. denied,* 526 U.S. 1087 (1999)

This case requires us to determine whether a court must consider parol evidence in a contract dispute governed by the United Nations Convention on Contracts for the International Sale of Goods ("CISG").[1] . . . The plaintiff-appellant, MCC-Marble Ceramic, Inc. ("MCC"), is a Florida corporation engaged in the retail sale of tiles, and the defendant-appellee, Ceramica Nuova d'Agostino S.p.A. ("D'Agostino") is an Italian corporation engaged in the manufacture of ceramic tiles. In October 1990, MCC's president, Juan Carlos Monzon, met representatives of D'Agostino at a trade fair in Bologna, Italy and negotiated an agreement to purchase ceramic tiles from D'Agostino based on samples he examined at the trade fair. Monzon, who spoke no Italian, communicated with Gianni Silingardi, then D'Agostino's commercial director, through a translator, Gianfranco Copelli, who was himself an agent of D'Agostino. The parties apparently arrived at an oral agreement on the crucial terms of price, quality, quantity, delivery, and payment. The parties then recorded these terms on one of D'Agostino's standard, pre-printed order forms and Monzon signed the contract on MCC's behalf. According to MCC, the parties also entered into a requirements contract in February 1991, subject to which D'Agostino agreed to supply MCC with high grade ceramic tile at specific discounts as long as MCC purchased sufficient quantities of tile. MCC completed a number of additional order forms requesting tile deliveries pursuant to that agreement.

MCC brought suit against D'Agostino claiming a breach of the February 1991 requirements contract when D'Agostino failed to satisfy orders in April,

---

[1] United Nations Convention on Contracts for the International Sale of Goods, opened for signature April 11, 1980, S. Treaty Doc. No. 9, 98th Cong., 1st Sess. 22 (1983), 19 I.L.M. 671, reprinted at, 15 U.S.C. app. 52 (1997).

May, and August of 1991. In addition to other defenses, D'Agostino responded that it was under no obligation to fill MCC's orders because MCC had defaulted on payment for previous shipments. In support of its position, D'Agostino relied on the pre-printed terms of the contracts that MCC had executed. The executed forms were printed in Italian and contained terms and conditions on both the front and reverse. According to an English translation of the October 1990 contract, the front of the order form contained the following language directly beneath Monzon's signature:

> [T]he buyer hereby states that he is aware of the sales conditions stated on the reverse and that he expressly approves of them with special reference to those numbered 1-2-3-4-5-6-7-8.

Clause 6(b), printed on the back of the form states:

> [D]efault or delay in payment within the time agreed upon gives D'Agostino the right to . . . suspend or cancel the contract itself and to cancel possible other pending contracts and the buyer does not have the right to indemnification or damages.

D'Agostino also brought a number of counterclaims against MCC, seeking damages for MCC's alleged nonpayment for deliveries of tile that D'Agostino had made between February 28, 1991 and July 4, 1991. MCC responded that the tile it had received was of a lower quality than contracted for, and that, pursuant to the CISG, MCC was entitled to reduce payment in proportion to the defects.[2] D'Agostino, however, noted that clause 4 on the reverse of the contract states, in pertinent part:

> Possible complaints for defects of the merchandise must be made in writing by means of a certified letter within and not later than 10 days after receipt of the merchandise. . . .

Although there is evidence to support MCC's claims that it complained about the quality of the deliveries it received, MCC never submitted any written complaints.

MCC did not dispute these underlying facts before the district court, but argued that the parties never intended the terms and conditions printed on the reverse of the order form to apply to their agreements. As evidence for this assertion, MCC submitted Monzon's affidavit, which claims that MCC had no subjective intent to be bound by those terms and that D'Agostino was aware of this intent. MCC also filed affidavits from Silingardi and Copelli, D'Agostino's representatives at the trade fair, which support Monzon's claim that the parties subjectively intended not to be bound by the terms on the reverse of the order form. The magistrate judge held that the affidavits, even if true, did not raise an issue of material fact regarding the interpretation or applicability of the terms of the written contracts and the district court accepted his recommendation to award summary judgment in D'Agostino's favor. MCC then filed this timely appeal. . . .

Summary judgment is appropriate when the pleadings, depositions, and affidavits reveal that no genuine issue of material fact exists and the moving party is entitled to judgment as a matter of law. *See* Fed.R.Civ.P. 56(c).

---

[2] Article 50 of the CISG permits a buyer to reduce payment for nonconforming goods in proportion to the nonconformity under certain conditions.

The parties to this case agree that the CISG governs their dispute because the United States, where MCC has its place of business, and Italy, where D'Agostino has its place of business, are both States Party to the Convention.[3] *See* CISG, art. 1.[4] Article 8 of the CISG governs the interpretation of international contracts for the sale of goods and forms the basis of MCC's appeal from the district court's grant of summary judgment in D'Agostino's favor.[5] MCC argues that the magistrate judge and the district court improperly ignored evidence that MCC submitted regarding the parties' subjective intent when they memorialized the terms of their agreement on D'Agostino's pre-printed form contract, and that the magistrate judge erred by applying the parol evidence rule in derogation of the CISG.

I. Subjective Intent Under the CISG

Contrary to what is familiar practice in United States courts, the CISG appears to permit a substantial inquiry into the parties' subjective intent, even if the parties did not engage in any objectively ascertainable means of registering this intent.[6] Article 8(1) of the CISG instructs courts to interpret the "statements . . . and other conduct of a party . . . according to his intent" as long as the other party "knew or could not have been unaware" of that intent. The plain language of the Convention, therefore, requires an inquiry into a party's subjective intent as long as the other party to the contract was aware of that intent.

---

[3] The United States Senate ratified the CISG in 1986, and the United States deposited its instrument of ratification at the United Nations Headquarters in New York on December 11, 1986. The Convention entered into force between the United States and the other States Parties, including Italy, on January 1, 1988.

[4] Article 1 of the CISG states in relevant part:

(1) This Convention applies to contracts of sale of goods between parties whose places of business are in different States:

(a) When the States are Contracting States. . . .

[5] Article 8 provides:

(1) For the purposes of this Convention statements made by and other conduct of a party are to be interpreted according to his intent where the other party knew or could not have been unaware what that intent was.

(2) If the preceding paragraph is not applicable, statements made by and conduct of a party are to be interpreted according to the understanding a reasonable person of the same kind as the other party would have had in the same circumstances.

(3) In determining the intent of a party or the understanding a reasonable person would have had, due consideration is to be given to all relevant circumstances of the case including the negotiations, any practices which the parties have established between themselves, usages and any subsequent conduct of the parties.

[6] In the United States, the legislatures, courts, and the legal academy have voiced a preference for relying on objective manifestations of the parties' intentions. For example, Article Two of the Uniform Commercial Code, which most states have enacted in some form or another to govern contracts for the sale of goods, is replete with references to standards of commercial reasonableness. *See, e.g.*, U.C.C. § 2-206 (referring to reasonable means of accepting an offer). . . . Justice Holmes expressed the philosophy behind this focus on the objective in forceful terms: "The law has nothing to do with the actual state of the parties' minds. In contract, as elsewhere, it must go by externals, and judge parties by their conduct." Oliver W. Holmes, The Common Law 242 (Howe ed. 1963) quoted in John O. Honnold, Uniform Law for International Sales under the 1980 United Nations Convention § 107 at 164 (2d ed. 1991) (hereinafter Honnold, Uniform Law).

In this case, MCC has submitted three affidavits that discuss the purported subjective intent of the parties to the initial agreement concluded between MCC and D'Agostino in October 1990. All three affidavits discuss the preliminary negotiations and report that the parties arrived at an oral agreement for D'Agostino to supply quantities of a specific grade of ceramic tile to MCC at an agreed upon price. The affidavits state that the "oral agreement established the essential terms of quality, quantity, description of goods, delivery, price and payment." The affidavits also note that the parties memorialized the terms of their oral agreement on a standard D'Agostino order form, but all three affiants contend that the parties subjectively intended not to be bound by the terms on the reverse of that form despite a provision directly below the signature line that expressly and specifically incorporated those terms.[7]

The terms on the reverse of the contract give D'Agostino the right to suspend or cancel all contracts in the event of a buyer's non-payment and require a buyer to make a written report of all defects within ten days. As the magistrate judge's report and recommendation makes clear, if these terms applied to the agreements between MCC and D'Agostino, summary judgment would be appropriate because MCC failed to make any written complaints about the quality of tile it received and D'Agostino has established MCC's non-payment of a number of invoices . . . .

Article 8(1) of the CISG requires a court to consider . . . evidence of the parties' subjective intent. Contrary to the magistrate judge's report, which the district court endorsed and adopted, article 8(1) does not focus on interpreting the parties' statements alone. Although we agree with the magistrate judge's conclusion that no "interpretation" of the contract's terms could support MCC's position,[8] article 8(1) also requires a court to consider subjective intent while interpreting the conduct of the parties. The CISG's language, therefore, requires courts to consider evidence of a party's subjective intent when signing a contract if the other party to the contract was aware of that intent at the time. This is precisely the type of evidence that MCC has provided through the Silingardi, Copelli, and Monzon affidavits, which discuss not only Monzon's intent as MCC's representative but also discuss the intent of D'Agostino's representatives and their knowledge that Monzon did not intend to agree to the terms on the reverse of the form contract. This acknowledgment that D'Agostino's representatives were aware of Monzon's subjective intent puts

---

[7] MCC makes much of the fact that the written order form is entirely in Italian and that Monzon, who signed the contract on MCC's behalf directly below this provision incorporating the terms on the reverse of the form, neither spoke nor read Italian. This fact is of no assistance to MCC's position. We find it nothing short of astounding that an individual, purportedly experienced in commercial matters, would sign a contract in a foreign language and expect not to be bound simply because he could not comprehend its terms. We find nothing in the CISG that might counsel this type of reckless behavior and nothing that signals any retreat from the proposition that parties who sign contracts will be bound by them regardless of whether they have read them or understood them.

[8] The magistrate judge's report correctly notes that MCC has not sought an interpretation of those terms, but rather to exclude them altogether. We agree that such an approach "would render terms of written contracts virtually meaningless and severely diminish the reliability of commercial contracts."

this case squarely within article 8(1) of the CISG, and therefore requires the court to consider MCC's evidence as it interprets the parties' conduct.[9]

II. Parol Evidence and the CISG

Given our determination that the magistrate judge and the district court should have considered MCC's affidavits regarding the parties' subjective intentions, we must address a question of first impression in this circuit: whether the parol evidence rule, which bars evidence of an earlier oral contract that contradicts or varies the terms of a subsequent or contemporaneous written contract,[10] plays any role in cases involving the CISG. . . .

The CISG itself contains no express statement on the role of parol evidence. It is clear, however, that the drafters of the CISG were comfortable with the concept of permitting parties to rely on oral contracts because they eschewed any statutes of fraud provision and expressly provided for the enforcement of oral contracts. *Compare* CISG, art. 11 (a contract of sale need not be concluded or evidenced in writing) *with* U.C.C. § 2-201 (precluding the enforcement of oral contracts for the sale of goods involving more than $500). Moreover, article 8(3) of the CISG expressly directs courts to give "due consideration . . . to all relevant circumstances of the case including the negotiations . . ." to determine the intent of the parties. Given article 8(1)'s directive to use the intent of the parties to interpret their statements and conduct, article 8(3) is a clear instruction to admit and consider parol evidence regarding the negotiations to the extent they reveal the parties' subjective intent. . . .

Our reading of article 8(3) as a rejection of the parol evidence rule . . . is in accordance with the great weight of academic commentary on the issue. As one scholar has explained:

> [T]he language of Article 8(3) that "due consideration is to be given to all relevant circumstances of the case" seems adequate to override any domestic rule that would bar a tribunal from considering the relevance of other agreements. . . . Article 8(3) relieves tribunals from domestic rules that might bar them from "considering" any evidence between the parties that is relevant. This added flexibility for interpretation is consistent with a growing body of opinion that the "parol

---

[9] Without this crucial acknowledgment, we would interpret the contract and the parties' actions according to article 8(2), which directs courts to rely on objective evidence of the parties' intent. On the facts of this case it seems readily apparent that MCC's affidavits provide no evidence that Monzon's actions would have made his alleged subjective intent not to be bound by the terms of the contract known to "the understanding that a reasonable person . . .would have had in the same circumstances."

[10] The Uniform Commercial Code [§ 2-202] includes a version of the parol evidence rule applicable to contracts for the sale of goods in most states:

> Terms with respect to which the confirmatory memoranda of the parties agree or which are otherwise set forth in a writing intended by the parties as a final expression of their agreement with respect to such terms as are included therein may not be contradicted by evidence of any prior agreement or of a contemporaneous oral agreement but may be explained or supplemented
>
> > (a) by course of dealing or usage of trade . . . or by course of performance . . .; and
> >
> > (b) by evidence of consistent additional terms unless the court finds the writing to have been intended also as a complete and exclusive statement of the terms of the agreement.

evidence rule" has been an embarrassment for the administration of modern transactions.

Honnnold, Uniform Law § 110 at 170–71.[11] [One commentator has disagreed, arguing that] the parol evidence rule often permits the admission of evidence discussed in article 8(3), and that the rule could be an appropriate way to discern what consideration is "due" under article 8(3) to evidence of a parol nature. [David H. Moore, *Note, The Parol Evidence Rule and the United Nations Convention on Contracts for the International Sale of Goods: Justifying Beijing Metals & Minerals Import/Export Corp. v. American Business Center, Inc.*, 1995 BYU L. REV. 1347, 1361–63.] He also argues that the parol evidence rule, by limiting the incentive for perjury and pleading prior understandings in bad faith, promotes good faith and uniformity in the interpretation of contracts and therefore is in harmony with the principles of the CISG, as expressed in article 7.[12]

The answer to both these arguments, however, is the same: although jurisdictions in the United States have found the parol evidence rule helpful to promote good faith and uniformity in contract, as well as an appropriate answer to the question of how much consideration to give parol evidence, a wide number of other States Party to the CISG have rejected the rule in their domestic jurisdictions. One of the primary factors motivating the negotiation and adoption of the CISG was to provide parties to international contracts for the sale of goods with some degree of certainty as to the principles of law that would govern potential disputes and remove the previous doubt regarding which party's legal system might otherwise apply. Courts applying the CISG cannot, therefore, upset the parties' reliance on the Convention by substituting familiar principles of domestic law when the Convention requires a different result. We may only achieve the directives of good faith and uniformity in contracts under the CISG by interpreting and applying the plain language

---

[11] *See also* LOUIS F. DEL DUCA, ET AL., SALES UNDER THE UNIFORM COMMERCIAL CODE AND THE CONVENTION ON INTERNATIONAL SALE OF GOODS, 173–74 (1993); Henry D. Gabriel, *A Primer on the United Nations Convention on the International Sale of Goods: From the Perspective of the Uniform Commercial Code*, 7 IND. INT'L & COMP. L.REV. 279, 281 (1997) ("Subjective intent is given primary consideration. . . . [Article 8] allows open-ended reliance on parol evidence. . . ."); HERBERT BERSTEIN & JOSEPH LOOKOFSKY, UNDERSTANDING THE CISG IN EUROPE 29 (1997) ("[T]he CISG has dispensed with the parol evidence rule which might otherwise operate to exclude extrinsic evidence under the law of certain Common Law countries."); Harry M. Fletchner, *Recent Developments: CISG*, 14 J.L. & COM. 153, 157 (1995) (. . . noting that "[c]ommentators generally agree that article 8(3) rejects the approach to the parol evidence questions taken by U.S. domestic law.") (collecting authority); John E. Murray, Jr., *An Essay on the Formation of Contracts and Related Matters Under the United Nations Convention on Contracts for the International Sale of Goods*, 8 J.L. & COM. 11, 12 (1988) ("We are struck by a new world where there is . . . no parol evidence rule, among other differences."); Peter Winship, *Domesticating International Commercial Law: Revising U.C.C. Article 2 in Light of the United Nations Sales Convention*, 37 LOY. L.REV. 43, 57 (1991).

[12] Article 7 of the CISG provides in pertinent part:

(1) In the interpretation of this Convention, regard is to be had to its international character and to the need to promote uniformity in its application and the observance of good faith in international trade.

(2) Questions concerning matters governed by this Convention which are not expressly settled in it are to be settled in conformity with the general principles on which it is based. . . .

of article 8(3) as written and obeying its directive to consider this type of parol evidence.

This is not to say that parties to an international contract for the sale of goods cannot depend on written contracts or that parol evidence regarding subjective contractual intent need always prevent a party relying on a written agreement from securing summary judgment. To the contrary, most cases will not present a situation (as exists in this case) in which both parties to the contract acknowledge a subjective intent not to be bound by the terms of a pre-printed writing. In most cases, therefore, article 8(2) of the CISG will apply, and objective evidence will provide the basis for the court's decision. Consequently, a party to a contract governed by the CISG will not be able to avoid the terms of a contract and force a jury trial simply by submitting an affidavit which states that he or she did not have the subjective intent to be bound by the contract's terms. . . .

Considering MCC's affidavits in this case, . . . we conclude that the magistrate judge and the district court improperly granted summary judgment in favor of D'Agostino. Although the affidavits are, as D'Agostino observes, relatively conclusory and unsupported by facts that would objectively establish MCC's intent not to be bound by the conditions on the reverse of the form, article 8(1) requires a court to consider evidence of a party's subjective intent when the other party was aware of it, and the Silingardi and Copelli affidavits provide that evidence. This is not to say that the affidavits are conclusive proof of what the parties intended. A reasonable finder of fact, for example, could disregard testimony that purportedly sophisticated international merchants signed a contract without intending to be bound as simply too incredible to believe and hold MCC to the conditions printed on the reverse of the contract. Nevertheless, the affidavits raise an issue of material fact regarding the parties' intent to incorporate the provisions on the reverse of the form contract. If the finder of fact determines that the parties did not intend to rely on those provisions, then the more general provisions of the CISG will govern the outcome of the dispute. . . .

CONCLUSION

MCC asks us to reverse the district court's grant of summary judgment in favor of D'Agostino. The district court's decision rests on pre-printed contractual terms and conditions incorporated on the reverse of a standard order form that MCC's president signed on the company's behalf. Nevertheless, we conclude that the CISG, which governs international contracts for the sale of goods, precludes summary judgment in this case because MCC has raised an issue of material fact concerning the parties' subjective intent to be bound by the terms on the reverse of the pre-printed contract. The CISG also precludes the application of the parol evidence rule, which would otherwise bar the consideration of evidence concerning a prior or contemporaneously negotiated oral agreement. Accordingly, we reverse the district court's grant of summary judgment and remand this case for further proceedings consistent with this opinion.

Notes and Questions on *Marble Ceramic Center*

1. *Application and interpretation of the U.N. Convention on Contracts for the International Sale of Goods (CISG).* You might consider *Marble Ceramic Center* a modest illustration of the extent to which the common law of contracts has been internationalized. But it also offers a cautionary tale of more general application: here after all is a domestic legal doctrine — the parol evidence rule — developed over the years through the common law and typically adopted as state law through Article 2 of the Uniform Commercial Code, being trumped in domestic court by an international agreement developed under the auspices of the United Nations. And *Marble Ceramic Center* is not an isolated example of this phenomenon. *See, e.g., Magellan Int'l Corp.v. Salzgitter Handel GmbH*, 76 F. Supp. 2d. 919 (N.D. Ill. 1999) (addressing the pleading requirements for a breach of contract action under the Convention); *Calzaturificio Claudia v. Olivieri Footwear Ltd.*, 1998 U.S. Dist. LEXIS 4586, No. 96 Civ. 9052 (HB) (THK), (applying the Convention rules eliminating the statute of frauds); *Delchi Carrier SpA v. Rotorex Corp.*, 71 F.3d 1024 (2d Cir. 1995) (calculating the damages available to a buyer under the Convention when the seller delivered nonconforming goods); *Medical Marketing Int'l, Inc. v. Internazionale Medico Scientifica, S.R.L.*, No. CIV.A. 99-0380, 1999 WL 311945 (E.D.La. May 17, 1999) (interpreting the Convention's public laws and regulations provision); *Filanto, S.p.A. v. Chilewich Int'l Corp.*, 789 F. Supp. 1229 (S.D.N.Y. 1992) (interpreting the Convention's provision on the battle-of-forms and noting the Convention's lack of a statute of frauds).

Admittedly, the CISG cannot displace the Uniform Commercial Code altogether in international business transactions, because not all countries are parties to the Convention and because the buyers and sellers involved in any particular contract can opt out of the treaty through a choice-of-law clause. "When two foreign nations are signatories to this Convention, . . . the Convention governs contracts for the sale of goods between parties whose places of business are in these different nations, absent a choice-of-law provision to the contrary." *Calzaturificio Claudia v. Olivieri Footwear Ltd.*, *supra*, at *12 (citing Article 1 of the Convention). Moreover, the inconsistencies between CISG and the UCC are not numerous, and caselaw interpreting the UCC can be useful in interpreting the CISG, when the two contain similar provisions. *Delchi Carrier SpA*, *supra*, 71 F.3d, at 1027. Thus, the CISG and *Marble Ceramic Center* — though significant and characteristic of contemporary trends — no more internationalize all of contract law than modern human rights norms and *Filártiga* internationalize the common law of tort.

But the overlap between these domestic categories of law and international rules — and the impact of that relationship in domestic litigation — should not be minimized. How do *Filártiga* and *Marble Ceramic Center* alter your way of thinking about international law and civil procedure in U.S. courts?

2. *Rationale for the CISG.* In this course, you will encounter many instances of a treaty offering only a partial solution to a transnational problem. To what problem is the CISG a solution, according to the court in *Marble Ceramic Center*? Can the goal of international uniformity be accomplished if the parties to the underlying contract can opt out of the treaty, or is this an instance of the adage that "the perfect is the enemy of the good"? Is it enough in other

words that the convention offers a modest improvement over the *status quo*, even if the problem of inconsistency across borders remains significant?

3. *Authority to apply international law.* By what authority can a federal court displace the state law of contracts through a treaty? Under the Supremacy Clause of the Constitution, "all Treaties made, or which shall be made, under the authority of the United States, shall be the Supreme Law of the Land, and the Judges in every State shall be bound thereby, any Thing in the Constitution or Laws of any State to the Contrary notwithstanding." But does the Supremacy Clause, in combination with CISG, federalize the commercial law of the various states, or is some more substantive congressional authority needed? Does the Treaty Power in the Constitution[1] give the Senate substantive power over that subject matter, or are there other provisions of the Constitution that might? Is it necessary to draw a distinction between the Article I powers of *Congress* and the powers of the *Senate* as specified in the Treaty Power?

4. *The substantive powers of the United Nations.* The CISG was developed under the auspices of the United Nations, confirming that the agenda of the U.N. is not limited to peace, human rights, and economic development. But should it matter in this case that the United Nations is not and was never intended to be an international legislature?

5. *Proving the content of a treaty norm.* To what evidence did the court turn in *Marble Ceramic Center* to determine the content or meaning of the relevant rule? How does this process compare with the *Filártiga* court's approach? What accounts for the difference?

---

[1] Article II, section 2, clause 2, of the Constitution provides: "[The President] shall have Power, by and with the Advice and Consent of the Senate, to make Treaties, provided that two-thirds of the Senators present concur."

Chapter 2

JURISDICTION TO ADJUDICATE

A. THE TRADITIONAL CONSTRAINTS: A FIRST-YEAR ORDEAL REVISITED

In the United States, the power of a court over a person or a corporation is a question of constitutional dimension. In a series of cases beginning with *International Shoe Co. v. State of Washington,* 326 U.S. 310 (1945), the Supreme Court has ruled that a court may exercise jurisdiction over a defendant unless that would be so unfair as to violate the Due Process clause of the U.S. Constitution. Specifically, the defendant must have "certain minimum contacts with [the forum] such that the maintenance of the suit does not offend traditional notions of fair play and substantial justice.'" 326 U.S. at 316 (quoting *Milliken v. Meyer,* 311 U.S. 457, 463 (1940)). The Court has had occasion to apply this standard in a bewildering variety of cases but has done little to reduce the *ad hoc* fact-dependency of these decisions. The one predictable aspect of these cases is the recurrence of fairness arguments grounded in factual details and framed by the minimum contacts test.

The constitutional inquiry has evolved from *International Shoe* into a three-step inquiry: relatedness, purposeful availment, and reasonableness. (i) At the first stage, the court determines whether the plaintiff's claim arises out of or is related to the defendant's conduct within the forum state. Sometimes, a defendant's contacts with a state are so pervasive that a court in that state may exercise personal jurisdiction over it even for claims that are unrelated to those contacts. In other cases, the claim must arise out of, or be related to, the defendant's more limited in-state contacts. (ii) At the second stage, the court will assess the defendant's contacts with the forum state to determine whether they constitute purposeful activity, such that being haled into court there would be foreseeable. In *Hanson v. Denckla*, 357 U.S. 235 (1958), for example, the Court wrote that "there must be some act by which the defendant purposefully avails itself of the privilege of conducting activities within the forum State, thus invoking the benefits and protections of its laws. . . ." (iii) Finally, the Constitution imposes an overall restraint of reasonableness on the exercise of personal jurisdiction. In *World-Wide Volkswagen Corp. v. Woodson*, 444 U.S. 286, 292 (1980), the reasonableness inquiry required the court to consider a range of interests in addition to the burden on the defendant, including:

> the forum State's interest in adjudicating the dispute, the plaintiff's interest in obtaining convenient and effective relief (at least when not protected by the plaintiff's power to choose the forum), the interstate judicial system's interest in obtaining the most efficient resolution of controversies, and the shared interest of the several States in furthering fundamental substantive social policies.

In sum, "[a]n exercise of personal jurisdiction . . . complies with constitutional imperatives only if the defendant's contacts with the forum relate sufficiently to his claim, are minimally adequate to constitute purposeful availment, and render resolution of the dispute in the forum state reasonable." *United States v. Swiss American Bank*, 191 F.3d 30, 36 (1st Cir. 1999).

The right question for our purposes is whether these constitutional principles — articulated in predominantly domestic settings — apply in the same way in international settings. The following cases — *Helicopteros* and *Asahi* — may be familiar to you from the first-year course in civil procedure, but they reappear now because they offer a familiar context for exploring a new set of questions: how does or should the Due Process calculus under the U.S. Constitution change when dealing with foreign actors or foreign conduct? How specifically must a foreign actor "target" a particular state of the union in order to trigger jurisdiction there? Is the required relationship among the defendant, the forum, and the litigation different if the case crosses a border? And how should a doctrine that assumes the existence of physical borders change in a borderless world, like cyberspace?

———

HELICOPTEROS NACIONALES DE COLOMBIA, S. A. v. HALL
466 U.S. 408 (1984)

BLACKMUN, J., delivered the opinion of the Court, in which BURGER, C. J., and WHITE, MARSHALL, POWELL, REHNQUIST, STEVENS, and O'CONNOR, JJ., joined. BRENNAN, J., filed a dissenting opinion.

We granted certiorari in this case to decide whether the Supreme Court of Texas correctly ruled that the contacts of a foreign corporation with the State of Texas were sufficient to allow a Texas state court to assert jurisdiction over the corporation in a cause of action not arising out of or related to the corporation's activities within the State.

I

Petitioner Helicopteros Nacionales de Colombia, S. A. (Helicol), is a Colombian corporation with its principal place of business in the city of Bogota in that country. It is engaged in the business of providing helicopter transportation for oil and construction companies in South America. On January 26, 1976, a helicopter owned by Helicol crashed in Peru. Four United States citizens were among those who lost their lives in the accident. Respondents are the survivors and representatives of the four decedents.

At the time of the crash, respondents' decedents were employed by Consorcio, a Peruvian consortium, and were working on a pipeline in Peru. Consorcio is the alter ego of a joint venture named Williams-Sedco-Horn ([hereinafter Consorcio/]WSH). The venture had its headquarters in Houston, Tex. Consorcio had been formed to enable the venturers to enter into a contract with Petro Peru, the Peruvian state-owned oil company. Consorcio was to construct a pipeline for Petro Peru running from the interior of Peru westward to the

Pacific Ocean. Peruvian law forbade construction of the pipeline by any non-Peruvian entity.

Consorcio/WSH needed helicopters to move personnel, materials, and equipment into and out of the construction area. In 1974, upon request of Consorcio/WSH, the chief executive officer of Helicol, Francisco Restrepo, flew to the United States and conferred in Houston with representatives of the three joint venturers. At that meeting, there was a discussion of prices, availability, working conditions, fuel, supplies, and housing. Restrepo represented that Helicol could have the first helicopter on the job in 15 days. The Consorcio/WSH representatives decided to accept the contract proposed by Restrepo. Helicol began performing before the agreement was formally signed in Peru on November 11, 1974.[1] The contract was written in Spanish on official government stationery and provided that the residence of all the parties would be Lima, Peru. It further stated that controversies arising out of the contract would be submitted to the jurisdiction of Peruvian courts. In addition, it provided that Consorcio/WSH would make payments to Helicol's account with the Bank of America in New York City.

Aside from the negotiation session in Houston between Restrepo and the representatives of Consorcio/WSH, Helicol had other contacts with Texas. During the years 1970-1977, it purchased helicopters (approximately 80% of its fleet), spare parts, and accessories for more than $4 million from Bell Helicopter Company in Fort Worth. In that period, Helicol sent prospective pilots to Fort Worth for training and to ferry the aircraft to South America. It also sent management and maintenance personnel to visit Bell Helicopter in Fort Worth during the same period in order to receive "plant familiarization" and for technical consultation. Helicol received into its New York City and Panama City, Fla., bank accounts over $5 million in payments from Consorcio/WSH drawn upon First City National Bank of Houston.

Beyond the foregoing, there have been no other business contacts between Helicol and the State of Texas. Helicol never has been authorized to do business in Texas and never has had an agent for the service of process within the State. It never has performed helicopter operations in Texas or sold any product that reached Texas, never solicited business in Texas, never signed any contract in Texas, never had any employee based there, and never recruited an employee in Texas. In addition, Helicol never has owned real or personal property in Texas and never has maintained an office or establishment there. Helicol has maintained no records in Texas and has no shareholders in that State. None of the respondents or their decedents were domiciled in Texas,[2] but all of the decedents were hired in Houston by Consorcio/WSH to work on the Petro Peru pipeline project.

Respondents instituted wrongful-death actions in the District Court of Harris County, Tex., against Consorcio/WSH, Bell Helicopter Company, and

---

[1] Respondents acknowledge that the contract was executed in Peru and not in the United States.

[2] Respondents' lack of residential or other contacts with Texas of itself does not defeat otherwise proper jurisdiction. *Keeton v. Hustler Magazine, Inc.,* 465 U.S. 770, 780 (1984); *Calder v. Jones,* 465 U.S. 783, 788 (1984). We mention respondents' lack of contacts merely to show that nothing in the nature of the relationship between respondents and Helicol could possibly enhance Helicol's contacts with Texas. The harm suffered by respondents did not occur in Texas. Nor is it alleged that any negligence on the part of Helicol took place in Texas.

Helicol. Helicol filed special appearances and moved to dismiss the actions for lack of *in personam* jurisdiction over it. The motion was denied. After a consolidated jury trial, judgment was entered against Helicol on a jury verdict of $1,141,200 in favor of respondents.

The Texas Court of Civil Appeals, Houston, First District, reversed the judgment of the District Court, holding that *in personam* jurisdiction over Helicol was lacking. The Supreme Court of Texas, with three justices dissenting, initially affirmed the judgment of the Court of Civil Appeals. Seven months later, however, on motion for rehearing, the court withdrew its prior opinions and, again with three justices dissenting, reversed the judgment of the intermediate court. In ruling that the Texas courts had *in personam* jurisdiction, the Texas Supreme Court first held that the State's long-arm statute reaches as far as the Due Process Clause of the Fourteenth Amendment permits.[3] Thus, the only question remaining for the court to decide was whether it was consistent with the Due Process Clause for Texas courts to assert *in personam* jurisdiction over Helicol.

II

The Due Process Clause of the Fourteenth Amendment operates to limit the power of a State to assert *in personam* jurisdiction over a nonresident defendant. *Pennoyer v. Neff,* 95 U.S. 714 (1878). Due process requirements are satisfied when *in personam* jurisdiction is asserted over a nonresident corporate defendant that has "certain minimum contacts with [the forum] such that the maintenance of the suit does not offend 'traditional notions of fair play and substantial justice.'" *International Shoe Co. v. Washington,* 326 U.S. 310, 316 (1945), quoting *Milliken v. Meyer,* 311 U.S. 457, 463 (1940). When a controversy is related to or "arises out of" a defendant's contacts with the forum, the Court has said that a "relationship among the defendant, the

---

[3] The State's long-arm statute is Tex. Rev. Civ. Stat. Ann., Art. 2031b (Vernon 1964 and Supp. 1982-1983). It reads in relevant part:

> Sec. 3. Any foreign corporation . . . that engages in business in this State, irrespective of any Statute or law respecting designation or maintenance of resident agents, and does not maintain a place of regular business in this State or a designated agent upon whom service may be made upon causes of action arising out of such business done in this State, the act or acts of engaging in such business within this State shall be deemed equivalent to an appointment by such foreign corporation . . . of the Secretary of State of Texas as agent upon whom service of process may be made in any action, suit or proceedings arising out of such business done in this State, wherein such corporation . . . is a party or is to be made a party.

> Sec. 4. For the purpose of this Act, and without including other acts that may constitute doing business, any foreign corporation . . . shall be deemed doing business in this State by entering into contract by mail or otherwise with a resident of Texas to be performed in whole or in part by either party in this State, or the committing of any tort in whole or in part in this State. The act of recruiting Texas residents, directly or through an intermediary located in Texas, for employment inside or outside of Texas shall be deemed doing business in this State.

. . . It is not within our province, of course, to determine whether the Texas Supreme Court correctly interpreted the State's long-arm statute. We therefore accept that court's holding that the limits of the Texas statute are coextensive with those of the Due Process Clause.

forum, and the litigation" is the essential foundation of in *in personam* jurisdiction. *Shaffer v. Heitner,* 433 U.S. 186, 204 (1977).[4]

Even when the cause of action does not arise out of or relate to the foreign corporation's activities in the forum State,[5] due process is not offended by a State's subjecting the corporation to its *in personam* jurisdiction when there are sufficient contacts between the State and the foreign corporation. *Perkins v. Benguet Consolidated Mining Co.,* 342 U.S. 437 (1952) . . . . In *Perkins,* the Court addressed a situation in which state courts had asserted general jurisdiction over a defendant foreign corporation. During the Japanese occupation of the Philippine Islands, the president and general manager of a Philippine mining corporation maintained an office in Ohio from which he conducted activities on behalf of the company. He kept company files and held directors' meetings in the office, carried on correspondence relating to the business, distributed salary checks drawn on two active Ohio bank accounts, engaged an Ohio bank to act as transfer agent, and supervised policies dealing with the rehabilitation of the corporation's properties in the Philippines. In short, the foreign corporation, through its president, "[had] been carrying on in Ohio a continuous and systematic, but limited, part of its general business," and the exercise of general jurisdiction over the Philippine corporation by an Ohio court was "reasonable and just." 342 U.S., at 438, 445.

All parties to the present case concede that respondents' claims against Helicol did not "arise out of," and are not related to, Helicol's activities within Texas.[6] We thus must explore the nature of Helicol's contacts with the State of Texas to determine whether they constitute the kind of continuous and systematic general business contacts the Court found to exist in *Perkins.* We hold that they do not.

It is undisputed that Helicol does not have a place of business in Texas and never has been licensed to do business in the State. Basically, Helicol's

---

[4] It has been said that when a State exercises personal jurisdiction over a defendant in a suit arising out of or related to the defendant's contacts with the forum, the State is exercising "specific jurisdiction" over the defendant.

[5] When a State exercises personal jurisdiction over a defendant in a suit not arising out of or related to the defendant's contacts with the forum, the State has been said to be exercising "general jurisdiction" over the defendant.

[6] Because the parties have not argued any relationship between the cause of action and Helicol's contacts with the State of Texas we, contrary to the dissent's implication, assert no "view" with respect to that issue. The dissent suggests that we have erred in drawing no distinction between controversies that "relate to" a defendant's contacts with a forum and those that "arise out of" such contacts. This criticism is somewhat puzzling, for the dissent goes on to urge that, for purposes of determining the constitutional validity of an assertion of specific jurisdiction, there really should be no distinction between the two.

We do not address the validity or consequences of such a distinction because the issue has not been presented in this case. Respondents have made no argument that their cause of action either arose out of or is related to Helicol's contacts with the State of Texas. Absent any briefing on the issue, we decline to reach the questions (1) whether the terms "arising out of" and "related to" describe different connections between a cause of action and a defendant's contacts with a forum, and (2) what sort of tie between a cause of action and a defendant's contacts with a forum is necessary to a determination that either connection exists. Nor do we reach the question whether, if the two types of relationship differ, a forum's exercise of personal jurisdiction in a situation where the cause of action "relates to," but does not "arise out of," the defendant's contacts with the forum should be analyzed as an assertion of specific jurisdiction.

contacts with Texas consisted of sending its chief executive officer to Houston for a contract-negotiation session; accepting into its New York bank account checks drawn on a Houston bank; purchasing helicopters, equipment, and training services from Bell Helicopter for substantial sums; and sending personnel to Bell's facilities in Fort Worth for training. The one trip to Houston by Helicol's chief executive officer for the purpose of negotiating the transportation-services contract with Consorcio/WSH cannot be described or regarded as a contact of a "continuous and systematic" nature, as *Perkins* described it, and thus cannot support an assertion of *in personam* jurisdiction over Helicol by a Texas court. Similarly, Helicol's acceptance from Consorcio/WSH of checks drawn on a Texas bank is of negligible significance for purposes of determining whether Helicol had sufficient contacts in Texas. There is no indication that Helicol ever requested that the checks be drawn on a Texas bank or that there was any negotiation between Helicol and Consorcio/WSH with respect to the location or identity of the bank on which checks would be drawn. Common sense and everyday experience suggest that, absent unusual circumstances,[7] the bank on which a check is drawn is generally of little consequence to the payee and is a matter left to the discretion of the drawer. Such unilateral activity of another party or a third person is not an appropriate consideration when determining whether a defendant has sufficient contacts with a forum State to justify an assertion of jurisdiction. *See Kulko v. California Superior Court,* ([holding it] arbitrary to subject one parent to suit in any State where other parent chooses to spend time while having custody of child pursuant to separation agreement); *Hanson v. Denckla,* ([declaring that] "The unilateral activity of those who claim some relationship with a nonresident defendant cannot satisfy the requirement of contact with the forum State.")

The Texas Supreme Court focused on the purchases and the related training trips in finding contacts sufficient to support an assertion of jurisdiction. We do not agree with that assessment, for the Court's opinion in *Rosenberg Bros. & Co.* v. *Curtis Brown Co.,* 260 U.S. 516 (1923) (Brandeis, J., for a unanimous tribunal), makes clear that purchases and related trips, standing alone, are not a sufficient basis for a State's assertion of jurisdiction.

The defendant in *Rosenberg* was a small retailer in Tulsa, Okla., who dealt in men's clothing and furnishings. It never had applied for a license to do business in New York, nor had it at any time authorized suit to be brought against it there. It never had an established place of business in New York and never regularly carried on business in that State. Its only connection with New York was that it purchased from New York wholesalers a large portion of the merchandise sold in its Tulsa store. The purchases sometimes were made by correspondence and sometimes through visits to New York by an officer of the defendant. The Court concluded: "Visits on such business, even if occurring at regular intervals, would not warrant the inference that the corporation was present within the jurisdiction of [New York]." *Id.* at 518.

This Court in *International Shoe* acknowledged and did not repudiate its holding in *Rosenberg*. In accordance with *Rosenberg*, we hold that mere

---

[7] For example, if the financial health and continued ability of the bank to honor the draft are questionable, the payee might request that the check be drawn on an account at some other institution.

purchases, even if occurring at regular intervals, are not enough to warrant a State's assertion of *in personam* jurisdiction over a nonresident corporation in a cause of action not related to those purchase transactions.[8] Nor can we conclude that the fact that Helicol sent personnel into Texas for training in connection with the purchase of helicopters and equipment in that State in any way enhanced the nature of Helicol's contacts with Texas. The training was a part of the package of goods and services purchased by Helicol from Bell Helicopter. The brief presence of Helicol employees in Texas for the purpose of attending the training sessions is no more a significant contact than were the trips to New York made by the buyer for the retail store in *Rosenberg*. *See also Kulko v. California Superior Court*, (basing California jurisdiction on 3-day and 1-day stopovers in that State "would make a mockery of" due process limitations on assertion of personal jurisdiction).

III

We hold that Helicol's contacts with the State of Texas were insufficient to satisfy the requirements of the Due Process Clause of the Fourteenth Amendment. Accordingly, we reverse the judgment of the Supreme Court of Texas.

JUSTICE BRENNAN, dissenting.

. . . [T]he undisputed contacts in this case between petitioner Helicol and the State of Texas are sufficiently important, and sufficiently related to the underlying cause of action, to make it fair and reasonable for the State to assert personal jurisdiction over Helicol for the wrongful-death actions filed by the respondents. Given that Helicol has purposefully availed itself of the benefits and obligations of the forum, and given the direct relationship between the underlying cause of action and Helicol's contacts with the forum, maintenance of this suit in the Texas courts "does not offend [the] 'traditional notions of fair play and substantial justice,'" *International Shoe Co. v. Washington* (quoting *Milliken v. Meyer*, 311 U.S. 457, 463 (1940)), that are the touchstone of jurisdictional analysis under the Due Process Clause. . . .

The vast expansion of our national economy during the past several decades has provided the primary rationale for expanding the permissible reach of a State's jurisdiction under the Due Process Clause. By broadening the type and amount of business opportunities available to participants in interstate and foreign commerce, our economy has increased the frequency with which foreign corporations actively pursue commercial transactions throughout the various States. In turn, it has become both necessary and, in my view, desirable to allow the States more leeway in bringing the activities of these nonresident corporations within the scope of their respective jurisdictions. . . .

---

[8] This Court in *International Shoe* cited *Rosenberg* for the proposition that "the commission of some single or occasional acts of the corporate agent in a state sufficient to impose an obligation or liability on the corporation has not been thought to confer upon the state authority to enforce it." 326 U.S., at 318. Arguably, therefore, *Rosenberg* also stands for the proposition that mere purchases are not a sufficient basis for either general or specific jurisdiction. Because the case before us is one in which there has been an assertion of general jurisdiction over a foreign defendant, we need not decide the continuing validity of *Rosenberg* with respect to an assertion of specific jurisdiction, *i.e.*, where the cause of action arises out of or relates to the purchases by the defendant in the forum State.

Moreover, this "trend . . . toward expanding the permissible scope of state jurisdiction over foreign corporations and other nonresidents," [citation omitted], is entirely consistent with the "traditional notions of fair play and substantial justice," *International Shoe,* 326 U.S., at 316, that control our inquiry under the Due Process Clause. As active participants in interstate and foreign commerce take advantage of the economic benefits and opportunities offered by the various States, it is only fair and reasonable to subject them to the obligations that may be imposed by those jurisdictions. And chief among the obligations that a nonresident corporation should expect to fulfill is amenability to suit in any forum that is significantly affected by the corporation's commercial activities.

As a foreign corporation that has actively and purposefully engaged in numerous and frequent commercial transactions in the State of Texas, Helicol clearly falls within the category of nonresident defendants that may be subject to that forum's general jurisdiction. Helicol not only purchased helicopters and other equipment in the State for many years, but also sent pilots and management personnel into Texas to be trained in the use of this equipment and to consult with the seller on technical matters.[9] Moreover, negotiations for the contract under which Helicol provided transportation services to the joint venture that employed the respondents' decedents also took place in the State of Texas. Taken together, these contacts demonstrate that Helicol obtained numerous benefits from its transaction of business in Texas. In turn, it is eminently fair and reasonable to expect Helicol to face the obligations that attach to its participation in such commercial transactions. Accordingly, on the basis of continuous commercial contacts with the forum, I would conclude that the Due Process Clause allows the State of Texas to assert general jurisdiction over petitioner Helicol. . . .

The . . . contacts between petitioner Helicol and the State of Texas . . . are significantly related to the cause of action alleged in the original suit filed by the respondents. Accordingly, in my view, it is both fair and reasonable for the Texas courts to assert specific jurisdiction over Helicol in this case.

By asserting that the present case does not implicate the specific jurisdiction of the Texas courts, the Court necessarily removes its decision from the reality of the actual facts presented for our consideration.[10] Moreover, the Court

---

[9] Although the Court takes note of these contacts, it concludes that they did not "[enhance] the nature of Helicol's contacts with Texas [because the] training was a part of the package of goods and services purchased by Helicol." Presumably, the Court's statement simply recognizes that participation in today's interdependent markets often necessitates the use of complicated purchase contracts that provide for numerous contacts between representatives of the buyer and seller, as well as training for related personnel. Ironically, however, while relying on these modern-day realities to denigrate the significance of Helicol's contacts with the forum, the Court refuses to acknowledge that these same realities require a concomitant expansion in a forum's jurisdictional reach. As a result, when deciding that the balance in this case must be struck against jurisdiction, the Court loses sight of the ultimate inquiry: whether it is fair and reasonable to subject a nonresident corporate defendant to the jurisdiction of a State when that defendant has purposefully availed itself of the benefits and obligations of that particular forum. *Cf. Hanson v. Denckla,* 357 U.S. 235, 253 (1958).

[10] Nor do I agree with the Court that the respondents have conceded that their claims are not related to Helicol's activities within the State of Texas. Although parts of their written and oral arguments before the Court proceed on the assumption that no such relationship exists, other portions suggest just the opposite:

refuses to consider any distinction between contacts that are "related to" the underlying cause of action and contacts that "give rise" to the underlying cause of action. In my view, however, there is a substantial difference between these two standards for asserting specific jurisdiction. Thus, although I agree that the respondents' cause of action did not formally "arise out of" specific activities initiated by Helicol in the State of Texas, I believe that the wrongful-death claim filed by the respondents is significantly related to the undisputed contacts between Helicol and the forum. On that basis, I would conclude that the Due Process Clause allows the Texas courts to assert specific jurisdiction over this particular action.

The wrongful-death actions filed by the respondents were premised on a fatal helicopter crash that occurred in Peru. Helicol was joined as a defendant in the lawsuits because it provided transportation services, including the particular helicopter and pilot involved in the crash, to the joint venture that employed the decedents. Specifically, the respondent Hall claimed in her original complaint that "Helicol is . . . legally responsible for its own negligence through its pilot employee." Viewed in light of these allegations, the contacts between Helicol and the State of Texas are directly and significantly related to the underlying claim filed by the respondents. The negotiations that took place in Texas led to the contract in which Helicol agreed to provide the precise transportation services that were being used at the time of the crash. Moreover, the helicopter involved in the crash was purchased by Helicol in Texas, and the pilot whose negligence was alleged to have caused the crash was actually trained in Texas. This is simply not a case, therefore, in which a state court has asserted jurisdiction over a nonresident defendant on the basis of wholly unrelated contacts with the forum. Rather, the contacts between Helicol and the forum are directly related to the negligence that was alleged in the respondent Hall's original complaint.[11] Because Helicol should have expected to be amenable to suit in the Texas courts for claims directly related to these contacts, it is fair and reasonable to allow the assertion of jurisdiction in this case.

Despite this substantial relationship between the contacts and the cause of action, the Court declines to consider whether the courts of Texas may

---

If it is the concern of the Solicitor General [appearing for the United States as *amicus curiae*] that a holding for Respondents here will cause foreign companies to refrain from purchasing in the United States for fear of exposure to general jurisdiction on unrelated causes of action, such concern is not well founded.

Respondents' cause is not dependent on a ruling that mere purchases in a state, together with incidental training for operating and maintaining the merchandise purchased can constitute the ties, contacts and relations necessary to justify jurisdiction over an unrelated cause of action. However, regular purchases and training coupled with other contacts, ties and relations may form the basis for jurisdiction.

Brief for Respondents 13–14. Thus, while the respondents' position before this Court is admittedly less than clear, I believe it is preferable to address the specific jurisdiction of the Texas courts because Helicol's contacts with Texas are in fact related to the underlying cause of action.

[11] The jury specifically found that "the pilot failed to keep the helicopter under proper control," that "the helicopter was flown into a treetop fog condition, whereby the vision of the pilot was impaired," that "such flying was negligence," and that "such negligence . . .was a proximate cause of the crash." On the basis of these findings, Helicol was ordered to pay over $1 million in damages to the respondents.

assert specific jurisdiction over this suit. Apparently, this simply reflects a narrow interpretation of the question presented for review. It is nonetheless possible that the Court's opinion may be read to imply that the specific jurisdiction of the Texas courts is inapplicable because the cause of action did not formally "arise out of" the contacts between Helicol and the forum. In my view, however, such a rule would place unjustifiable limits on the bases under which Texas may assert its jurisdictional power. . . .

Limiting the specific jurisdiction of a forum to cases in which the cause of action formally arose out of the defendant's contacts with the State would subject constitutional standards under the Due Process Clause to the vagaries of the substantive law or pleading requirements of each State. For example, the complaint filed against Helicol in this case alleged negligence based on pilot error. Even though the pilot was trained in Texas, the Court assumes that the Texas courts may not assert jurisdiction over the suit because the cause of action "did not 'arise out of,' and [is] not related to," that training. If, however, the applicable substantive law required that negligent training of the pilot was a necessary element of a cause of action for pilot error, or if the respondents had simply added an allegation of negligence in the training provided for the Helicol pilot, then presumably the Court would concede that the specific jurisdiction of the Texas courts was applicable.

Our interpretation of the Due Process Clause has never been so dependent upon the applicable substantive law or the State's formal pleading requirements. At least since *International Shoe Co.* v. *Washington,* the principal focus when determining whether a forum may constitutionally assert jurisdiction over a nonresident defendant has been on fairness and reasonableness to the defendant. To this extent, a court's specific jurisdiction should be applicable whenever the cause of action arises out of *or* relates to the contacts between the defendant and the forum. It is eminently fair and reasonable, in my view, to subject a defendant to suit in a forum with which it has significant contacts directly related to the underlying cause of action. Because Helicol's contacts with the State of Texas meet this standard, I would affirm the judgment of the Supreme Court of Texas.

Notes and Questions on *Helicopteros* and the Constitutional Limits on Personal Jurisdiction in Intermestic Cases

1. *Fact-dependency of Helicopteros.* Having read *Helicopteros,* list the factors or affiliations that, either singly or together, might have produced the opposite result. Suppose for example that the plaintiff's cause of action had arisen out of the defendant's in-state purchases. (In what sense exactly did the cause of action in this case *not* arise out of Helicol's contacts in Texas?) Or suppose that Helicol had substantial contacts with the United States but not in Texas (*e.g.,* bank accounts in New York, a corporate office in Miami, a pilot training facility in Los Angeles). Would it be appropriate to aggregate those national contacts for purposes of assessing its exposure to jurisdiction in Texas? If so, on what rationale? Or suppose that Helicol were a Peruvian subsidiary of a

U.S. corporation or owned by exclusively U.S. shareholders. Would that corporate structure strengthen or weaken the case for jurisdiction?

2. *Constitutional significance of sales versus purchases.* Is it defensible to distinguish for jurisdictional purposes between a foreign corporation's *sales* in the forum and its *purchases* there? Is that what the majority in *Helicopteros* did?

3. *Effect of advocacy.* To understand the potential reach of Justice Brennan's dissent (and the malleability of the majority's apparent test), consider how the complaint might have been drafted differently so as to satisfy the test for personal jurisdiction.

4. *Interests of the United States.* How would you articulate the interests of the United States in this case? Were they served or undermined by the result? Assuming that it is not too anthropomorphic to attribute interests to the "United States," should such considerations be relevant in personal jurisdiction cases?

ASAHI METAL INDUSTRY CO., LTD. v. SUPERIOR COURT (CHENG SHIN RUBBER INDUSTRIAL CO., LTD., REAL PARTY IN INTEREST)
480 U.S. 102 (1987)

JUSTICE O'CONNOR announced the judgment of the Court and delivered the unanimous opinion of the Court with respect to Part I, the opinion of the Court with respect to Part II-B, in which THE CHIEF JUSTICE, JUSTICE BRENNAN, JUSTICE WHITE, JUSTICE MARSHALL, JUSTICE BLACKMUN, JUSTICE POWELL, and JUSTICE STEVENS join, and an opinion with respect to Parts II-A and III, in which THE CHIEF JUSTICE, JUSTICE POWELL, and JUSTICE SCALIA join.

This case presents the question whether the mere awareness on the part of a foreign defendant that the components it manufactured, sold, and delivered outside the United States would reach the forum State in the stream of commerce constitutes "minimum contacts" between the defendant and the forum State such that the exercise of jurisdiction "does not offend 'traditional notions of fair play and substantial justice.'" *International Shoe Co. v. Washington,* 326 U.S. 310, 316 (1945), quoting *Milliken v. Meyer,* 311 U.S. 457, 463 (1940).

I

On September 23, 1978, on Interstate Highway 80 in Solano County, California, Gary Zurcher lost control of his Honda motorcycle and collided with a tractor. Zurcher was severely injured, and his passenger and wife, Ruth Ann Moreno, was killed. In September 1979, Zurcher filed a product liability action in the Superior Court of the State of California in and for the County of Solano. Zurcher alleged that the 1978 accident was caused by a sudden loss of air and an explosion in the rear tire of the motorcycle, and alleged that the motorcycle tire, tube, and sealant were defective. Zurcher's complaint named, *inter alia,* Cheng Shin Rubber Industrial Co., Ltd. (Cheng Shin), the Taiwanese manufacturer of the tube. Cheng Shin in turn filed a cross-complaint seeking indemnification from its codefendants and from petitioner, Asahi Metal Industry Co., Ltd. (Asahi), the manufacturer of the tube's valve assembly. Zurcher's claims against Cheng Shin and the other defendants were eventually settled and dismissed, leaving only Cheng Shin's indemnity action against Asahi.

California's long-arm statute authorizes the exercise of jurisdiction "on any basis not inconsistent with the Constitution of this state or of the United States." Cal. Civ. Proc. Code Ann. § 410.10 (West 1973). Asahi moved to quash Cheng Shin's service of summons, arguing the State could not exert jurisdiction over it consistent with the Due Process Clause of the Fourteenth Amendment.

In relation to the motion, the following information was submitted by Asahi and Cheng Shin. Asahi is a Japanese corporation. It manufactures tire valve assemblies in Japan and sells the assemblies to Cheng Shin, and to several other tire manufacturers, for use as components in finished tire tubes. Asahi's sales to Cheng Shin took place in Taiwan. The shipments from Asahi to Cheng Shin were sent from Japan to Taiwan. Cheng Shin bought and incorporated into its tire tubes 150,000 Asahi valve assemblies in 1978; 500,000 in 1979; 500,000 in 1980; 100,000 in 1981; and 100,000 in 1982. Sales to Cheng Shin accounted for 1.24 percent of Asahi's income in 1981 and 0.44 percent in 1982. Cheng Shin alleged that approximately 20 percent of its sales in the United States are in California. Cheng Shin purchases valve assemblies from other suppliers as well, and sells finished tubes throughout the world.

In 1983, an attorney for Cheng Shin conducted an informal examination of the valve stems of the tire tubes sold in one cycle store in Solano County. The attorney declared that of the approximately 115 tire tubes in the store, 97 were purportedly manufactured in Japan or Taiwan, and of those 97, 21 valve stems were marked with the circled letter "A", apparently Asahi's trademark. Of the 21 Asahi valve stems, 12 were incorporated into Cheng Shin tire tubes. The store contained 41 other Cheng Shin tubes that incorporated the valve assemblies of other manufacturers. An affidavit of a manager of Cheng Shin whose duties included the purchasing of component parts stated: "In discussions with Asahi regarding the purchase of valve stem assemblies the fact that my Company sells tubes throughout the world and specifically the United States has been discussed. I am informed and believe that Asahi was fully aware that valve stem assemblies sold to my Company and to others would end up throughout the United States and in California." An affidavit of the president of Asahi, on the other hand, declared that Asahi "has never contemplated that its limited sales of tire valves to Cheng Shin in Taiwan would subject it to lawsuits in California." The record does not include any contract between Cheng Shin and Asahi.

Primarily on the basis of the above information, the Superior Court denied the motion to quash summons, stating: "Asahi obviously does business on an international scale. It is not unreasonable that they defend claims of defect in their product on an international scale."

The Court of Appeal of the State of California issued a peremptory writ of mandate commanding the Superior Court to quash service of summons. The court concluded that "it would be unreasonable to require Asahi to respond in California solely on the basis of ultimately realized foreseeability that the product into which its component was embodied would be sold all over the world including California."

The Supreme Court of the State of California reversed and discharged the writ issued by the Court of Appeal. The court observed: "Asahi has no offices, property or agents in California. It solicits no business in California and has made no direct sales [in California]." Moreover, "Asahi did not design or control the system of distribution that carried its valve assemblies into California." Nevertheless, the court found the exercise of jurisdiction over Asahi to be consistent with the Due Process Clause. It concluded that Asahi knew that some of the valve assemblies sold to Cheng Shin would be incorporated into tire tubes sold in California, and that Asahi benefited indirectly from the sale in California of products incorporating its components. The court considered Asahi's intentional act of placing its components into the stream of commerce — that is, by delivering the components to Cheng Shin in Taiwan — coupled with Asahi's awareness that some of the components would eventually find their way into California, sufficient to form the basis for state court jurisdiction under the Due Process Clause.

We granted certiorari, and now reverse.

II

A

The Due Process Clause of the Fourteenth Amendment limits the power of a state court to exert personal jurisdiction over a nonresident defendant. "[The] constitutional touchstone" of the determination whether an exercise of personal jurisdiction comports with due process "remains whether the defendant purposefully established 'minimum contacts' in the forum State." *Burger King Corp. v. Rudzewicz,* 471 U.S. 462, 474 (1985), quoting *International Shoe Co. v. Washington* . . . . Most recently we have reaffirmed the oft-quoted reasoning of *Hanson v. Denckla,* that minimum contacts must have a basis in "some act by which the defendant purposefully avails itself of the privilege of conducting activities within the forum State, thus invoking the benefits and protections of its laws." *Burger King,* 471 U.S., at 475. "Jurisdiction is proper . . . where the contacts proximately result from actions by the defendant *himself* that create a 'substantial connection' with the forum State." *Ibid.,* quoting *McGee v. International Life Insurance Co.* . . . .

Applying the principle that minimum contacts must be based on an act of the defendant, the Court in *World-Wide Volkswagen Corp.* v. *Woodson,* rejected the assertion that a *consumer's* unilateral act of bringing the defendant's product into the forum State was a sufficient constitutional basis for personal jurisdiction over the defendant. It had been argued in *World-Wide Volkswagen* that because an automobile retailer and its wholesale distributor sold a product mobile by design and purpose, they could foresee being haled into court in the distant States into which their customers might drive. The Court rejected this concept of foreseeability as an insufficient basis for jurisdiction under the Due Process Clause. The Court disclaimed, however, the idea that "foreseeability is wholly irrelevant" to personal jurisdiction, concluding that "[the] forum State does not exceed its powers under the Due Process Clause if it asserts personal jurisdiction over a corporation that delivers its products into the stream of commerce with the expectation that they will be purchased by consumers in the forum State." The Court reasoned:

> When a corporation 'purposefully avails itself of the privilege of conducting activities within the forum State,' it has clear notice that it is subject to suit there, and can act to alleviate the risk of burdensome litigation by procuring insurance, passing the expected costs on to customers, or, if the risks are too great, severing its connection with the State. Hence if the sale of a product of a manufacturer or distributor . . . is not simply an isolated occurrence, but arises from the efforts of the manufacturer or distributor to serve, directly or indirectly, the market for its product in other States, it is not unreasonable to subject it to suit in one of those States if its allegedly defective merchandise has there been the source of injury to its owners or to others. . . .

In *World-Wide Volkswagen* itself, the state court sought to base jurisdiction not on any act of the defendant, but on the foreseeable unilateral actions of the consumer. Since *World-Wide Volkswagen*, lower courts have been confronted with cases in which the defendant acted by placing a product in the stream of commerce, and the stream eventually swept defendant's product into the forum State, but the defendant did nothing else to purposefully avail itself of the market in the forum State. Some courts have understood the Due Process Clause, as interpreted in *World-Wide Volkswagen*, to allow an exercise of personal jurisdiction to be based on no more than the defendant's act of placing the product in the stream of commerce. Other courts have understood the Due Process Clause and the above-quoted language in *World-Wide Volkswagen* to require the action of the defendant to be more purposefully directed at the forum State than the mere act of placing a product in the stream of commerce.

The reasoning of the Supreme Court of California in the present case illustrates the former interpretation of *World-Wide Volkswagen*. The Supreme Court of California held that, because the stream of commerce eventually brought some valves Asahi sold Cheng Shin into California, Asahi's awareness that its valves would be sold in California was sufficient to permit California to exercise jurisdiction over Asahi consistent with the requirements of the Due Process Clause. The Supreme Court of California's position was consistent with those courts that have held that mere foreseeability or awareness was a constitutionally sufficient basis for personal jurisdiction if the defendant's product made its way into the forum State while still in the stream of commerce. . . .

Other courts, however, have understood the Due Process Clause to require something more than that the defendant was aware of its product's entry into the forum State through the stream of commerce in order for the State to exert jurisdiction over the defendant. In the present case, for example, the State

Court of Appeal did not read the Due Process Clause, as interpreted by *World-Wide Volkswagen*, to allow "mere foreseeability that the product will enter the forum state [to] be enough by itself to establish jurisdiction over the distributor and retailer." In *Humble v. Toyota Motor Co.,* 727 F.2d 709 (CA8 1984), an injured car passenger brought suit against Arakawa Auto Body Company, a Japanese corporation that manufactured car seats for Toyota. Arakawa did no business in the United States; it had no office, affiliate, subsidiary, or agent in the United States; it manufactured its component parts outside the United States and delivered them to Toyota Motor Company in Japan. The Court of Appeals, adopting the reasoning of the District Court in that case, noted that although it "does not doubt that Arakawa could have foreseen that its product would find its way into the United States," it would be "manifestly unjust" to require Arakawa to defend itself in the United States. *Id.,* at 710–711 . . . .

We now find this latter position to be consonant with the requirements of due process. The "substantial connection" . . . between the defendant and the forum State necessary for a finding of minimum contacts must come about by *an action of the defendant purposefully directed toward the forum State.* The placement of a product into the stream of commerce, without more, is not an act of the defendant purposefully directed toward the forum State. Additional conduct of the defendant may indicate an intent or purpose to serve the market in the forum State, for example, designing the product for the market in the forum State, advertising in the forum State, establishing channels for providing regular advice to customers in the forum State, or marketing the product through a distributor who has agreed to serve as the sales agent in the forum State. But a defendant's awareness that the stream of commerce may or will sweep the product into the forum State does not convert the mere act of placing the product into the stream into an act purposefully directed toward the forum State.

Assuming, *arguendo*, that respondents have established Asahi's awareness that some of the valves sold to Cheng Shin would be incorporated into tire tubes sold in California, respondents have not demonstrated any action by Asahi to purposefully avail itself of the California market. Asahi does not do business in California. It has no office, agents, employees, or property in California. It does not advertise or otherwise solicit business in California. It did not create, control, or employ the distribution system that brought its valves to California. There is no evidence that Asahi designed its product in anticipation of sales in California. On the basis of these facts, the exertion of personal jurisdiction over Asahi by the Superior Court of California[1] exceeds the limits of due process.

---

[1] We have no occasion here to determine whether Congress could, consistent with the Due Process Clause of the Fifth Amendment, authorize federal court personal jurisdiction over alien defendants based on the aggregate of *national* contacts, rather than on the contacts between the defendant and the State in which the federal court sits. *See Max Daetwyler Corp.* v. *R. Meyer,* 762 F.2d 290, 293–295 (CA3 1985); *DeJames v. Magnificence Carriers, Inc.,* 654 F.2d 280, 283 (CA3 1981) . . . .

B

The strictures of the Due Process Clause forbid a state court from exercising personal jurisdiction over Asahi under circumstances that would offend "traditional notions of fair play and substantial justice." We have previously explained that the determination of the reasonableness of the exercise of jurisdiction in each case will depend on an evaluation of several factors. A court must consider the burden on the defendant, the interests of the forum State, and the plaintiff's interest in obtaining relief. It must also weigh in its determination "the interstate judicial system's interest in obtaining the most efficient resolution of controversies; and the shared interest of the several States in furthering fundamental substantive social policies." *World-Wide Volkswagen,* 444 U.S., at 292 (citations omitted).

A consideration of these factors in the present case clearly reveals the unreasonableness of the assertion of jurisdiction over Asahi, even apart from the question of the placement of goods in the stream of commerce.

Certainly the burden on the defendant in this case is severe. Asahi has been commanded by the Supreme Court of California not only to traverse the distance between Asahi's headquarters in Japan and the Superior Court of California in and for the County of Solano, but also to submit its dispute with Cheng Shin to a foreign nation's judicial system. The unique burdens placed upon one who must defend oneself in a foreign legal system should have significant weight in assessing the reasonableness of stretching the long arm of personal jurisdiction over national borders.

When minimum contacts have been established, often the interests of the plaintiff and the forum in the exercise of jurisdiction will justify even the serious burdens placed on the alien defendant. In the present case, however, the interests of the plaintiff and the forum in California's assertion of jurisdiction over Asahi are slight. All that remains is a claim for indemnification asserted by Cheng Shin, a Taiwanese corporation, against Asahi. The transaction on which the indemnification claim is based took place in Taiwan; Asahi's components were shipped from Japan to Taiwan. Cheng Shin has not demonstrated that it is more convenient for it to litigate its indemnification claim against Asahi in California rather than in Taiwan or Japan.

Because the plaintiff is not a California resident, California's legitimate interests in the dispute have considerably diminished. The Supreme Court of California argued that the State had an interest in "protecting its consumers by ensuring that foreign manufacturers comply with the state's safety standards." The State Supreme Court's definition of California's interest, however, was overly broad. The dispute between Cheng Shin and Asahi is primarily about indemnification rather than safety standards. Moreover, it is not at all clear at this point that California law should govern the question whether a Japanese corporation should indemnify a Taiwanese corporation on the basis of a sale made in Taiwan and a shipment of goods from Japan to Taiwan. . . . The possibility of being haled into a California court as a result of an accident involving Asahi's components undoubtedly creates an additional deterrent to the manufacture of unsafe components; however, similar pressures will be placed on Asahi by the purchasers of its components as long as those who use

Asahi components in their final products, and sell those products in California, are subject to the application of California tort law.

World-Wide Volkswagen also admonished courts to take into consideration the interests of the "several States," in addition to the forum State, in the efficient judicial resolution of the dispute and the advancement of substantive policies. In the present case, this advice calls for a court to consider the procedural and substantive policies of other *nations* whose interests are affected by the assertion of jurisdiction by the California court. The procedural and substantive interests of other nations in a state court's assertion of jurisdiction over an alien defendant will differ from case to case. In every case, however, those interests, as well as the Federal Government's interest in its foreign relations policies, will be best served by a careful inquiry into the reasonableness of the assertion of jurisdiction in the particular case, and an unwillingness to find the serious burdens on an alien defendant outweighed by minimal interests on the part of the plaintiff or the forum State. "Great care and reserve should be exercised when extending our notions of personal jurisdiction into the international field." *United States v. First National City Bank,* 379 U.S. 378, 404 (1965) (Harlan, J., dissenting). *See* Born, *Reflections on Judicial Jurisdiction in International Cases,* to be published in 17 GA. J. INT'L & COMP. L. 1 (1987).

Considering the international context, the heavy burden on the alien defendant, and the slight interests of the plaintiff and the forum State, the exercise of personal jurisdiction by a California court over Asahi in this instance would be unreasonable and unfair.

III

Because the facts of this case do not establish minimum contacts such that the exercise of personal jurisdiction is consistent with fair play and substantial justice, the judgment of the Supreme Court of California is reversed, and the case is remanded for further proceedings not inconsistent with this opinion.

JUSTICE BRENNAN, with whom JUSTICE WHITE, JUSTICE MARSHALL, and JUSTICE BLACKMUN join, concurring in part and concurring in the judgment.

I do not agree with the interpretation in Part II-A of the stream-of-commerce theory, nor with the conclusion that Asahi did not "purposely avail itself of the California market." I do agree, however, with the Court's conclusion in Part II-B that the exercise of personal jurisdiction over Asahi in this case would not comport with "fair play and substantial justice," *International Shoe Co. v. Washington,* 326 U.S. 310, 320 (1945). This is one of those rare cases in which "minimum requirements inherent in the concept of 'fair play and substantial justice'. . . defeat the reasonableness of jurisdiction even [though] the defendant has purposefully engaged in forum activities." *Burger King Corp. v. Rudzewicz,* 471 U.S. 462, 477–478 (1985). I therefore join Parts I and II-B of the Court's opinion, and write separately to explain my disagreement with Part II-A.

Part II-A states that "a defendant's awareness that the stream of commerce may or will sweep the product into the forum State does not convert the mere act of placing the product into the stream into an act purposefully directed toward the forum State." Under this view, a plaintiff would be required to show "[additional] conduct" directed toward the forum before finding the exercise of jurisdiction over the defendant to be consistent with the Due Process Clause. I see no need for such a showing, however. The stream of commerce refers not to unpredictable currents or eddies, but to the regular and anticipated flow of products from manufacture to distribution to retail sale. As long as a participant in this process is aware that the final product is being marketed in the forum State, the possibility of a lawsuit there cannot come as a surprise. Nor will the litigation present a burden for which there is no corresponding benefit. A defendant who has placed goods in the stream of commerce benefits economically from the retail sale of the final product in the forum State, and indirectly benefits from the State's laws that regulate and facilitate commercial activity. These benefits accrue regardless of whether that participant directly conducts business in the forum State, or engages in additional conduct directed toward that State. Accordingly, most courts and commentators have found that jurisdiction premised on the placement of a product into the stream of commerce is consistent with the Due Process Clause, and have not required a showing of additional conduct.

The endorsement in Part II-A of what appears to be the minority view among Federal Courts of Appeals [citations omitted] represents a marked retreat from the analysis in *World-Wide Volkswagen v. Woodson*. In that case, "respondents [sought] to base jurisdiction on one, isolated occurrence and whatever inferences can be drawn therefrom: the fortuitous circumstance that a single Audi automobile, sold in New York to New York residents, happened to suffer an accident while passing through Oklahoma." The Court held that the possibility of an accident in Oklahoma, while to some extent foreseeable in light of the inherent mobility of the automobile, was not enough to establish minimum contacts between the forum State and the retailer or distributor. The Court then carefully explained:

> [This] is not to say, of course, that foreseeability is wholly irrelevant. But the foreseeability that is critical to due process analysis is not the mere likelihood that a product will find its way into the forum State. Rather, it is that the defendant's conduct and connection with the forum State are such that he should reasonably anticipate being haled into Court there.

Id. at 297. The Court reasoned that when a corporation may reasonably anticipate litigation in a particular forum, it cannot claim that such litigation is unjust or unfair, because it "can act to alleviate the risk of burdensome litigation by procuring insurance, passing the expected costs on to consumers, or, if the risks are too great, severing its connection with the State."

To illustrate the point, the Court contrasted the foreseeability of litigation in a State to which a consumer fortuitously transports a defendant's product (insufficient contacts) with the foreseeability of litigation in a State where the defendant's product was regularly *sold* (sufficient contacts). The Court stated:

Hence if the *sale* of a product of a manufacturer or distributor such as Audi or Volkswagen is not simply an isolated occurrence, but arises from the efforts of the manufacturer or distributor to serve, *directly or indirectly*, the market for its product in other States, it is not unreasonable to subject it to suit in one of those States if its allegedly defective merchandise has there been the source of injury to its owner or to others. The forum State does not exceed its powers under the Due Process Clause if it asserts personal jurisdiction over a corporation that delivers its products into the stream of commerce *with the expectation that they will be purchased by consumers* in the forum State.

Id. at 297–298 (emphasis added).

The Court concluded its illustration by referring to *Gray v. American Radiator & Standard Sanitary Corp.,* 22 Ill. 2d 432, 176 N. E. 2d 761 (1961), a well-known stream-of-commerce case in which the Illinois Supreme Court applied the theory to assert jurisdiction over a component-parts manufacturer that sold no components directly in Illinois, but did sell them to a manufacturer who incorporated them into a final product that was sold in Illinois. The Court in *World-Wide Volkswagen* thus took great care to distinguish "between a case involving goods which reach a distant State through a chain of distribution and a case involving goods which reach the same State because a consumer . . . took them there." *Id.* at 306–307 (Brennan, J., dissenting). . . . The California Supreme Court took note of this distinction, and correctly concluded that our holding in *World-Wide Volkswagen* preserved the stream-of-commerce theory.

In this case, the facts found by the California Supreme Court support its finding of minimum contacts. The court found that "[although] Asahi did not design or control the system of distribution that carried its valve assemblies into California, Asahi was aware of the distribution system's operation, and it knew that it would benefit economically from the sale in California of products incorporating its components."[1] Accordingly, I cannot join the determination in Part II-A that Asahi's regular and extensive sales of component parts to a manufacturer it knew was making regular sales of the final product in California is insufficient to establish minimum contacts with California.

JUSTICE STEVENS, with whom JUSTICE WHITE and JUSTICE BLACKMUN join, concurring in part and concurring in the judgment.

The judgment of the Supreme Court of California should be reversed for the reasons stated in Part II-B of the Court's opinion. While I join Parts I and II-B, I do not join Part II-A for two reasons. First, it is not necessary to the Court's decision. . . . Part II-B establishes, after considering the factors set forth in *World-Wide Volkswagen Corp. v. Woodson*, that California's

---

[1] Moreover, the Court found that "at least 18 percent of the tubes sold in a particular California motorcycle supply shop contained Asahi valve assemblies,"and that Asahi had an ongoing business relationship with Cheng Shin involving average annual sales of hundreds of thousands of valve assemblies.

exercise of jurisdiction over Asahi in this case would be "unreasonable and unfair." This finding alone requires reversal; this case fits within the rule that "minimum requirements inherent in the concept of 'fair play and substantial justice' may defeat the reasonableness of jurisdiction even if the defendant has purposefully engaged in forum activities." *Burger King,* 471 U.S. [462], at 477–478 (quoting *International Shoe Co. v. Washington.*) Accordingly, I see no reason in this case for the plurality to articulate "purposeful direction" or any other test as the nexus between an act of a defendant and the forum State that is necessary to establish minimum contacts. Second, even assuming that the test ought to be formulated here, Part II-A misapplies it to the facts of this case. The plurality seems to assume that an unwavering line can be drawn between "mere awareness" that a component will find its way into the forum State and "purposeful availment" of the forum's market. Over the course of its dealings with Cheng Shin, Asahi has arguably engaged in a higher quantum of conduct than "[the] placement of a product into the stream of commerce, without more. . . ." Whether or not this conduct rises to the level of purposeful availment requires a constitutional determination that is affected by the volume, the value, and the hazardous character of the components. In most circumstances, I would be inclined to conclude that a regular course of dealing that results in deliveries of over 100,000 units annually over a period of several years would constitute "purposeful availment" even though the item delivered to the forum State was a standard product marketed throughout the world.

Notes and Questions on *Asahi*

1. *Fact dependency.* What exactly distinguishes the plurality opinion from the concurring opinions in *Asahi*? If you represented a foreign company eager to penetrate the American market but also eager to avoid exposure to lawsuits in all fifty states, what advice would you give on the basis of *Asahi* about structuring its affairs?

2. *Foreseeability and the international stream of commerce.* Will the minimum contacts test be satisfied if a foreign manufacturer places an article in the international stream of commerce, knowing that it will enter the United States? After *Asahi*, what additional factors would be relevant?

In *World-Wide Volkswagen Corp. v. Woodson*, 444 U.S. 286, 292 (1980), plaintiffs purchased an automobile in New York from World-Wide Volkswagen (WWVW), a tri-state distributor in New York, New Jersey and Connecticut. They drove the car to Oklahoma where it was involved in a serious accident. WWVW did not have any place of business in Oklahoma and had never sold a car there, but the plaintiffs sued them in Oklahoma under the state long-arm statute, which conferred jurisdiction up to the limits of the United States Constitution. The Supreme Court ruled that Oklahoma could not exercise jurisdiction over WWVW, rejecting the lower court's view that WWVW should have foreseen that its car would be driven somewhere and therefore might be driven to Oklahoma. To permit suit in these circumstances would be to hold that "[e]very seller of chattels would in effect appoint the chattel his agent for service of process." How these interests might play out in an *international* case was not addressed in *Woodson*, because the foreign manufacturer and exporter of the automobile were no longer in the case when the Supreme Court undertook its review.

But the Court did offer *dicta* on foreseeability which potentially have a profound effect on the vulnerability of foreign defendants to jurisdiction in the United States. Although the Court did not require the actual ability by the defendant to reasonably foresee that he or she might be called into court, foreseeability was not irrelevant. According to the Court, the question is whether

> the defendant's conduct and connection with the forum State are such that he should reasonably anticipate being haled into court there. . . . The Due Process Clause, by ensuring orderly administration of the laws . . . gives a degree of predictability to the legal system that allows potential defendants to structure their primary conduct with some minimum assurance as to where that conduct will and will not render then liable to suit. . . .

> If the sale of a product of a manufacturer or distributor such as Audi or Volkswagen is not simply an isolated occurrence, but arises from the efforts of the manufacturer or distributor to serve, directly or indirectly, the market for its product in other states, it is not unreasonable to subject it to suit in one of those States if its allegedly defective merchandise has there been the source of injury to its owner or to others. The forum State does not exceed its powers under the Due Process Clause if it asserts personal jurisdiction over a corporation that delivers its products into the stream of commerce with the expectation that they will be purchased by consumers in the forum state.

> The mere unilateral activity of those who claim some relationship with a nonresident defendant cannot satisfy the requirement of contact with the forum state. . . .

> [F]inancial benefits accruing to the defendant from a collateral relation to the forum States will not support jurisdiction if they do not stem from a constitutionally cognizable contact with that State. . . .

3. *Proving the defendant's knowledge.* Does the foreseeability standard invite the kind of "dueling affidavits" on display in *Asahi*? Whose knowledge counts in determining whether a corporation "knows" that its products will end up in the United States: Any member of the Board of Directors? The chief executive officer? The president? The director of sales? Is corporate knowledge just a *post hoc* construct of the court?

4. *The relevance of state interests.* The majority in *Asahi* rested part of its analysis on "California's legitimate interest." What's the best argument for doubting the legitimacy of this inquiry by the court?

5. *Impact of international concerns.* Does the international setting of the *Asahi* conflict strengthen or weaken the case for jurisdiction in state court?

6. *Federal versus state law*. Should the jurisdictional calculus change if the cause of action arises under federal or international law instead of state law?

B. SPECIAL PROBLEMS IN THE AFTERMATH OF GLOBALIZATION

[1] The Jurisdictional Consequences of Corporate Structures

Corporate structures can be used to limit liability; indeed, the essence of incorporation is limiting the financial exposure of shareholders to the extent or value of their investment in the corporation, but corporate structures can also be used to limit exposure to jurisdiction. As companies do business around the world through joint ventures, agents, subsidiaries, and branches, the question of when the courts can reach one part of a corporate organization through another part will recur. When is a foreign corporation "present" in a U.S. jurisdiction through its subsidiary or its parent? When is it "doing business" for purposes of state long-arm statutes, such that exercising jurisdiction over it is consistent with *International Shoe* as interpreted?

ROORDA v. VOLKSWAGENWERK, A. G.
481 F. Supp. 868 (D.S.C. 1979)

Ralph Earl Roorda, the plaintiff herein, is a paraplegic, paralyzed from the waist down, and without sight in one eye. He alleges that these injuries were caused by a defective Volkswagen automobile which had been manufactured by defendant, Volkswagenwerk, A.G., (hereinafter referred to as VWAG) in West Germany. The vehicle was sold by VWAG to a dealer in West Germany, who then sold it to a purchaser there. Several transactions later, plaintiff purchased this automobile in Arizona, and while driving it in California in 1970, it overturned, and plaintiff was critically injured. Immediately prior to the institution of this suit, plaintiff changed his domicile from California to South Carolina, and he instituted suit here on November 26, 1976, alleging negligence, breach of warranty, and strict liability in tort. Plaintiff has remained to this date a citizen of South Carolina, residing in Charleston County. Defendant VWAG questions the jurisdiction of this court to hear the merits of this controversy.

The issue confronting this court is whether VWAG was "present" in South Carolina for jurisdictional purposes, when suit was instituted, i.e., whether VWAG's contacts with South Carolina were sufficient to make it amenable to suit in this state and not offend traditional notions of fair play and substantial justice within the meaning of *International Shoe Company v. Washington*, 326 U.S. 310 (1945).

VWAG is a corporation organized and existing under the laws of the Federal Republic of Germany. It manufactures Volkswagen automobiles and parts and accessories for such automobiles. Volkswagen of America (hereinafter referred to as VWOA) is a New Jersey corporation and is the sole "importer" of Volkswagen products in the United States. Neither VWAG nor VWOA is "registered" to do business in South Carolina within the meaning of Sections 15-9-240 and 33-23-10, S.C.Code 1976.

Initially, plaintiff brought suit against VWAG, VWGMBH (a predecessor of VWAG), and VWOA. Plaintiff has agreed that he has no cause of action against the latter two entities and they have been dismissed. Service of process was accomplished on VWAG by service on the Secretary of State of South Carolina pursuant to Section 15-9-240, S.C.Code 1976, and such service was completed by forwarding a copy of the process by registered mail to Toni Schmucker, Chairman of the Board of Management of VWAG, in Wolfsburg, West Germany. Additionally, service of process was made under the same statute on VWOA as agent for defendant, VWAG, and a copy thereof sent by registered mail to VWOA in New Jersey, where VWOA is domiciled.

VWAG does not contest the fact that service was made on it and on VWOA in accordance with the method provided by Section 15-9-240, S.C.Code 1976; VWAG urges, however, that such service is not sufficient to confer jurisdiction upon the court in South Carolina because it transacts no business here. Furthermore, VWAG urges that while its wholly owned subsidiary, VWOA, may be subject to jurisdiction of the South Carolina courts, that fact does not give the courts here jurisdiction over VWAG as plaintiff admittedly has not attempted to pierce the corporate veil of the two corporations so as to make them one and the same and to hold VWAG here under the "alter ego" theory. Plaintiff, on the other hand, contends that the absolute control exercised by VWAG over VWOA mandates a finding that VWOA is the "agent" in South Carolina for VWAG, that VWAG was "present" and "doing business" in South Carolina, and that the service on VWAG directly and on VWOA as its agent in South Carolina has brought VWAG into the jurisdiction of this South Carolina federal court.

This court has received able briefs from counsel, and has heard extensive arguments on the jurisdictional question here involved, and discovery material addressed to this issue has been reviewed. Before deciding the jurisdictional issue raised by the defendant, VWAG, this court must view the entire record to determine the quantity and quality of the contacts which VWAG has had with South Carolina, the forum state. To sustain jurisdiction, plaintiff relies on the relationship between VWAG and VWOA. It is admitted that VWOA, though not "registered" in South Carolina, is present in this state for jurisdictional purposes. A good example of the reason for VWOA's admitted presence in South Carolina is the fact that in the years 1974-76 it had sales here as hereinafter listed:

1974 $ 21,512,926.00

1975 $ 14,710,414.00

1976 $ 8,340,730.00

There are thirteen franchised VW dealerships in South Carolina, said dealers being licensed by VWOA, and VWOA's representatives frequently visit the state transacting business and servicing these dealerships, and, thus, indirectly servicing consumers as well. VWOA's advertising permeates the media in South Carolina; there are other indicia of its admitted "presence" for jurisdictional purposes as well.

Although VWAG contends that it is not "present" in South Carolina for jurisdictional purposes, the record and the reasonable inferences to be drawn therefrom clearly prove the contrary. VWAG is "present" in South Carolina, in this court's opinion, in the intimate and complete control which it exercises over VWOA, so as to make VWOA its South Carolina agent, and, thereby, VWAG may be required to defend this suit in South Carolina without offending the "fair play and substantial justice" rule of *International Shoe, supra*. As sole importer of VW products, VWOA is subject to many direct and indirect controls from VWAG. This corporation is wholly owned by VWAG; its Board of Directors holds practically all of its meetings in Wolfsburg, West Germany, the situs of the corporate headquarters of VWAG; many of the board members of VWOA are on the board of VWAG. Under the agreement between VWAG and VWOA, which agreement is a part of the record herein, VWOA appoints dealerships at locations which must have the approval of VWAG, and VWOA must communicate to all dealers the directives and suggestions made by VWAG. In this manner, VWOA is agent for VWAG to communicate with South Carolina dealers and consumers. Additionally, VWOA must comply with VWAG procedures for ordering and shipping VWAG's products; VWOA must use forms prescribed by VWAG; orders can be rejected only by VWAG and VWOA cannot sue VWAG for delay in delivery; VWAG is not required to observe set installment for delivery of VWOA's orders. Such facts reveal VWAG's complete control over VWOA and control is a fundamental element of agency [citation omitted]. VWAG substantially directs the daily business of VWOA; the very place of business of VWOA must be "located, installed and equipped in a manner reasonably satisfactory" to VWAG; VWOA can only use stationery and business forms printed in accordance with VWAG's specifications; the trademark "VW", and the word "Volkswagen", can only be used from matrices supplied by VWAG; the number of VWOA's office employees and field men for servicing dealers are subject to VWAG's approval, and these VWOA field men have been engaged in systematic contacts with South Carolina in a substantial sense over a period of many years. VWAG has the right to inspect VWOA's records and accounts, including the right to have VWOA's report on market conditions, sales performance, inventories and estimates of requirements. VWOA and VWAG have the same counsel in this case as the affidavits of record reveal. VWOA must submit its yearly and interim financial statements to VWAG. The contract between the parties even provides that delays by VWOA in fulfilling its obligations will compel a penalty payment to VWAG of 1,000 Deutsch Marks per day. Germany is the place of performance of the contract, indicating again VWAG's pervasive role in the relationship between VWOA and VWAG. In fact, VWOA is admittedly the service agent designated by VWAG pursuant to Section 110(e) of the National Traffic and Motor Vehicles Safety Act.

The above discussion convinces this court that there is a sufficient evidentiary basis in this record to support the assertion of jurisdiction over VWAG based on the intimate relationship between VWAG and VWOA and the contacts with this jurisdiction by VWOA. The control VWAG exercises over VWOA is so complete that to find VWOA "present" in South Carolina for jurisdictional purposes (a finding which the defendant does not contest) it is necessary to find that VWAG has the same status. Such a conclusion is mandated for the reasons so ably and logically expressed by Judge Robert W. Hemphill, . . . in *Szantay v. Beech Aircraft Corp.,* 237 F. Supp. 393 (E.D.S.C. 1965). Judge Hemphill reviewed in great detail the relationship found there between the manufacturer, Beech, and its distributor, Hawthorne, and held that such relationship was sufficient to confer jurisdiction over the manufacturer. The court determined that defendant, Beech, a Delaware corporation with its principal place of business in Wichita, Kansas, was present in South Carolina for all purposes because of its relationship with Hawthorne, a South Carolina corporation, despite its assertion that it was not registered in South Carolina, and that it had no agent and did not engage in business activities within this state. To reach this result, Judge Hemphill relied on the contractual relationship, the course of conduct, the control, and the resulting "involvement" between Beech and Hawthorne. *Id.* at 394. Adopting what a later court called "a 'general agency' theory of 'presence,'" Judge Hemphill held that Beech, through its control of Hawthorne, had such substantial contact with South Carolina that finding Beech amenable to service of process in South Carolina did not offend "traditional notions of fair play and substantial justice." Recognizing . . . that "South Carolina has extended its service of process laws to the outer limits allowed by *International Shoe,*" Judge Hemphill disregarded Beech's contentions that it was not registered to do business in South Carolina and that service on Hawthorne, as Beech's agent, did not give the South Carolina court jurisdiction of Beech. Judge Hemphill stated:

> . . . It can only be concluded that South Carolina never intended that a foreign corporation with sufficient "nexus" with the State, which refused or failed to comply with the statutory requirements of the State, could not be sued under the same circumstances where a foreign corporation which did comply with the State law was subject to suit. . . . Further, the Congress has specifically enunciated the policy this Court shall follow, by indicating that a Federal District Court, in diversity cases, shall be available wherever the foreign corporation is doing business. 28 U.S.C. § 1391(c). Plainly, this indication of the Congressional will was designed to remove any possible advantage a foreign corporation might acquire by failing to observe the requirements of State law, as was done here. . . .

Therefore, when a foreign corporation maintains its "presence" in the State jurisdiction, at least up to the time of the institution of suit, without complying with the statutory requirements, it is subject to the same suits and service of process as are domestic corporations and other foreign corporations who have complied with the statutory requirements. This is particularly so when the maintenance of suit will not do violence to the concept of "fundamental fairness" which has evolved through the cases. . . .

The Fourth Circuit Court of Appeals . . . affirmed Judge Hemphill's opinion on the jurisdictional questions. . . .

Many of the terms in the Beech-Hawthorne contract, set forth in *Szantay*, are almost identical to those in the VWOA-VWAG contract. Hawthorne was required to give monthly inventory reports to Beech; Hawthorne could only use signs which Beech provided; when the distributorship agreement terminated, Hawthorne could no longer use the "Beechcraft" name; there was a marked inter-relation of advertising; Beech furnished the forms for Hawthorne to use in accounting; Beech had the right to inspect Hawthorne's facilities, supplies and personnel; Hawthorne was required to use Beech parts unless Beech gave express permission otherwise; Hawthorne used forms furnished by Beech in ordering airplanes; Hawthorne's warranties were closely regulated by Beech; Hawthorne was required to comply with policies, directives, and requirements contained in the Beechcraft Sales Policy Manual; and Hawthorne appointed dealers for the sale of the airplanes at such places as Beech approved.

Many courts in cases involving factual situations almost identical to *Szantay*, in several of which cases Beech was a defendant under similar contracts with local distributors, have followed the reasoning of Judge Hemphill and the approval given his opinion by the Fourth Circuit Court of Appeals [citations omitted]. One of these courts even discussed the "Beech trilogy" and pointed out the unusual control exercised by Beech in its relationship with its distributors:

> . . . Beech's relationship with its distributor was shown by analysis of their intercorporate contracts and memoranda, and by depositions. Its agreement provided that the distributor's staff and service must be *acceptable to Beech*, inventory would be *prescribed by Beech*, parts would be *supplied by Beech*, and facilities would be provided as *deemed necessary by Beech*. Beech provided pricing guidelines, established minimum quotas, supplied all advertising, limited territory, regulated accounting procedures, and controlled warranties, servicing and other aspects of sales. The distributor was pledged to do whatever "Beech may consider essential to the development of [its] territory." *Szantay, supra*, at 399–400. (emphasis in original).

VWAG relies heavily on the case of *Cannon Manufacturing Company v. Cudahy Packing Company*, 267 U.S. 333 (1925), a case in which Cannon, a North Carolina corporation, brought suit in that state against Cudahy, a Maine corporation, with a wholly owned subsidiary corporation that had been incorporated in Alabama, and which subsidiary maintained an office in North Carolina. The Alabama subsidiary was used to market Cudahy's products in North Carolina.[1] Goods sold by the subsidiary were sent directly by the parent to the buyer in North Carolina; however, the subsidiary collected the purchase price. The relationship between the two corporations was noted in detail:

> . . . The Alabama corporation, which has an office in North Carolina, is the instrumentality employed to market Cudahy products within

---

[1] No contention was made that the cause of action involved any activity by the parent in North Carolina.

the State; but it does not do so as defendant's agent. It buys from the defendant and sells to dealers. In fulfillment of such contracts to sell, goods packed by the defendant in Iowa are shipped direct to dealers; and from them the Alabama corporation collects the purchase price. Through ownership of the entire capital stock and otherwise, the defendant dominates the Alabama corporation, immediately and completely; and exerts its control both commercially and financially in substantially the same way, and mainly through the same individuals, as it does over those selling branches or departments of its business not separately incorporated which are established to market the Cudahy products in other States. The existence of the Alabama company as a distinct corporate entity is, however, in all respects observed. Its books are kept separate. All transactions between the two corporations are represented by appropriate entries in their respective books in the same way as if the two were wholly independent corporations. This corporate separation from the general Cudahy business was doubtless adopted solely to secure to the defendant some advantages under the local laws. . . . [267 U.S.] at 335.

The Supreme Court held that regardless of the identity of interest and high degree of control which the parent exercised, the formal separation was sufficiently real to resist jurisdiction of the parent. In this connection, the Supreme Court stated:

The defendant wanted to have business transactions with persons resident in North Carolina, but for reasons satisfactory to itself did not choose to enter the State in its corporate capacity. It might have conducted such business through an independent agency without subjecting itself to the jurisdiction. It preferred to employ a subsidiary corporation. Congress has not provided that a corporation of one State shall be amenable to suit in the federal court for another State in which the plaintiff resides, whenever it employs a subsidiary corporation as the instrumentality for doing business therein. That such use of a subsidiary does not necessarily subject the parent corporation to the jurisdiction was settled by *Conley v. Mathieson Alkali Works,* 190 U.S. 406, 409–411 [and other cases]. In the case at bar, the identity of interest may have been more complete and the exercise of control over the subsidiary more intimate than in the three cases cited, but that fact has, in the absence of an applicable statute, no legal significance. The corporate separation, though perhaps merely formal, was real. It was not pure fiction. There is here no attempt to hold the defendant liable for an act or omission of its subsidiary or to enforce as against the latter a liability of the defendant. . . . [citations omitted].

This court has reviewed literally hundreds of cases in which the *Cudahy* holding, and its present effect on jurisdictional questions, is discussed. It appears to this court that the great majority of the courts which have been involved with a parent-subsidiary issue in which jurisdiction is sought over the parent, have not overruled *Cudahy,* but have found means to avoid the stringent *Cudahy* principle in all instances when the parent completely dominates the activities of the subsidiary, as the facts in the instant case so clearly indicate. While it would be far too burdensome to this court . . . to review in detail the many, many cases which have discussed the present-day effect of *Cudahy*, there are a few cases in which a similar issue as here has been involved that this court feels merit discussion. In *Hitt v. Nissan Motor Co., Ltd.*, 399 F. Supp. 838 (S.D.Fla. 1975), which case concerned a Japanese automobile manufacturer and its American subsidiary, Judge Atkins stated . . .

> *Cannon Manufacturing Co. v. Cudahy Packing Co.* is a watershed case widely cited for the proposition that mere ownership of a subsidiary without more will not subject the foreign parent to the jurisdiction of the state where the subsidiary is doing business. In *Cannon*, the parent corporation dominated its subsidiary through complete stock ownership but formal corporate separateness was carefully maintained in all respects. However, *Cannon* is distinguishable from the case *sub judice* in that *Cannon* involved no question of the constitutional powers of the state or of the federal government but it was merely the Supreme Court's interpretation of what activities constituted "doing business" within a forum and thus involved the concept of "presence" and not the less rigid "minimum contacts" test of *International Shoe.* . . .

In *Freeman v. Gordon & Breach, Science Publishers, Inc.*, 398 F. Supp. 519 (S.D.N.Y. 1975), the court there, reviewing the New York law, which state, like South Carolina, "has extended its service of process laws to the outer limits allowed by *International Shoe*," stated:

> New York courts have held that a parent corporation can be present in the state because of the activities of its subsidiary. However, the activities must amount to more than the mere parent-subsidiary relationship, *Cannon Mfg. Co. v. Cudahy Packing Co.*, 267 U.S. 333, 336 (1925). The parent may be subject to jurisdiction where the subsidiary "performs all the business" which the parent could do "were it here by its own officials." *Frummer v. Hilton Hotels International, Inc.*, 19 N.Y.2d 533, 537, 281 N.Y.S.2d 41, 44, (1967). Additionally, where the subsidiary is "in fact, if not in name" a branch of the parent, the distinctions between the two fall and the parent is amenable to New York's jurisdiction. . . .

While it is true that this court cannot identify any case from the United States Supreme Court which has specifically overruled the principle established in *Cudahy*, it seems apparent to this court, from multitudinous decisions of state and federal courts throughout the United States, that the principle announced twenty years later by the Supreme Court in *International Shoe, supra,* changed the older concept of jurisdiction and substantially eroded the stringent jurisdictional test applied in *Cudahy*.

This court recognizes, when the injury claimed does not arise in the forum state — the situation here involved — that the test for jurisdictional presence of a foreign corporation requires more than the barest minimum contacts. In *Ratliff v. Cooper Laboratories, Inc.*, 444 F.2d 745 (4th Cir. 1971), the court stated:

. . . If "plaintiff's injury does not arise out of something done in the forum state, then other contacts between the corporation and the state must be fairly extensive before the burden of defending a suit there may be imposed upon it without offending 'traditional notions of fair play and substantial justice.'" at p. 748.

This court is of the opinion that the contacts of VWAG in this state, based on its complete control of VWOA, meet the *Ratliff* test. *Ratliff* does not require that the forum state be a major center of the foreign corporation's business, but *Ratliff* dictates only that the forum state be a community into "whose business life the defendant had significantly entered as determined by the quality, substantiality, continuity and systematic nature of its activities." *Ratliff* at 748. VWAG has maintained continuing contact in South Carolina through VWOA's activities in this state, and, certainly, it appears to this court that to require VWAG to defend the instant suit in South Carolina can be done without "offending traditional notions of fair play and substantial justice."[2]

Defendant has asserted, as a bar to jurisdiction here, that plaintiff moved to South Carolina because South Carolina has a six-year statute of limitations for this type of action, and that South Carolina is one of the few states where plaintiff could bring suit because of the time lapse between his injuries (1970) and the institution of suit here (1976). Plaintiff admits this to be a fact; however, a change of domicile for such reason is no bar to jurisdiction if the defendant is factually "present" in this jurisdiction under the principles of *International Shoe, supra,* and *Ratliff, supra.* Citizenship may be changed for the purpose of obtaining federal jurisdiction; however, for there to be a legal change of residence, there must be true intent to reside indefinitely in the new domicile. It is immaterial if a bona fide change to acquire jurisdiction, as is clearly the case here, is made for the purpose of bringing suit in the United States District Court in this state; such bona fide transfer of residence for that purpose is not a new notion. . . .

---

[2] This court notes that the record in this case contains other facts which, while not independently sufficient, do bear generally on the "fair play and substantial justice" theory. For instance, it appears from facts stated in an affidavit, which the court finds to be true, submitted by a former Volkswagen dealer, whose dealership was located in Charleston, South Carolina, from 1955 through 1976, that VWAG representatives visited her place of business to provide her with assistance and advice in the operation of her business, and that VWAG paid the greater part of the cost of bringing Volkswagen dealers to Germany for seminars designed to improve the volume of sales by VWAG to its dealers and by its dealers to the general public. Furthermore, VWAG has recently utilized this court to bring an action for trademark infringement, alleging, among other things, in the complaint in such action (*Volkswagen, A. G. v. Richard F. Hoffman, d/b/a The Bug House,* (D.S.C.), Columbia Division, C/A 78-1891), that VWAG had sold in the United States during the past thirty (30) years over six and one-half million automobiles for a value exceeding Ten Billion Dollars, that during the year 1977 alone over Thirty-Three Million Dollars was spent by VWAG for its dealers in advertising the products and services sold under VWAG's trademark in the United States, and setting forth in said complaint other indicia of control which VWAG exercises over its thirteen dealers in this state. In connection with the aforesaid action, and the insight it affords to the activities of VWAG in South Carolina, it is well to note the established principle that the owner (VWAG) of a trademark must retain some control over the nature and quality of its product and over the activities of its licensees (the Volkswagen dealers in South Carolina) for it to retain its rights in the trademark itself and in order to maintain the secondary meaning of the trademark. *Bramlett v. Arthur Murray, Inc.,* 250 F. Supp. 1011, 1016 (D.S.C. 1966).

South Carolina has a substantial interest in providing a forum for its citizens' suits against foreign corporations which are "present" in this state to the extent that we find the defendant here. Although the plaintiff moved to South Carolina for the sole purpose of instituting this action, he has conclusively proven that his South Carolina citizenship is bona fide, not temporary or illusory, and he is entitled to the same right to use the federal court in this state as any other citizen of South Carolina would possess. This court is not unmindful that the defense of litigation in a foreign jurisdiction is a burdensome inconvenience for any foreign corporation. However, such inconvenience is a part of the price that may properly be demanded of any corporation that extensively engages in international trade. When a foreign parent corporation so pervasively controls the activities of its subsidiary as the control exercised here by VWAG over VWOA, and consideration is given to the tremendous benefits from the business obtained through such relationship, a foreign corporation, like VWAG, should not be heard to complain about the burden of defending litigation in this forum. Therefore, it is

ORDERED, that the motion of the defendant, VWAG, to dismiss the complaint herein for lack of in personam jurisdiction be, and the same hereby is, denied.

BULOVA WATCH CO., INC. v. K. HATTORI & CO., LTD.
508 F. Supp. 1322 (E.D.N.Y 1981)

This motion to dismiss for lack of personal jurisdiction (F.R.Civ.P. 12(b) (2)), presents a classic problem in adjudicating claims against a multinational corporation using subsidiaries to penetrate the American market. Under current doctrine, to be subject to personal jurisdiction by a state, the parent must 1) itself be present because it is doing business in the state (N.Y. CPLR 301); or, 2) under a "long arm" concept, have conducted specific activities out of which the cause of action arose either in the state or outside the state with foreseeable substantial effects in the state (N.Y. CPLR 302); in addition, exercise of judicial power over the person of defendant must not offend our notions of fairness. *See, e.g., International Shoe Co. v. Washington*, 326 U.S. 310 (1945).

Largely for reasons of historical and conceptual development, the doing business concept treats a defendant corporation as if it were present for all purposes in any kind of a suit to the same extent as a real person living and working here would be. The long arm alternative was designed to be used only in limited situations in which an outsider has a transient impact on activities in the state and it applies only to claims arising from that narrow contact.

Multinational activities such as those before us present a factual pattern that sometimes does not quite fit into either of the two tidy conceptual categories reflected in N.Y. CPLR 301 and 302. Here the foreign parent corporation may be considered to be doing business under 301 for limited purposes during the period of penetration of the American market before its subsidiaries have matured to relatively full independence. The implications of this view are that the foreign parent may be deemed to be present for the purpose of expanding into a new market by setting up subsidiaries and dealing with competition, while it may not be doing business for the purposes of day-to-day commercial activity such as dealing in watches, cars, or sealing wax *e.g.,* when a suit is based upon negligent operation of a car operated by an employee of a locally organized subsidiary. Similarly, while not within the strict limits of the 302 long arm provision, the parent's actions might be sufficiently within the CPLR's penumbra so that the combination of 301 and 302 read together covers the particular claims asserted and long arm personal jurisdiction lies. None of this would violate any constitutional requirements.

We do not suggest that the present jurisdictional bases be eliminated, a proposal for the legislature rather than a trial court in any event. Nor do we ignore traditional indicia utilized to measure parent-subsidiary control for jurisdictional purposes. Rather, we note that in this as in so many other areas of the law, stuffing new and complex factual patterns into absolutely rigid legal cubbyholes often results in distortion of the facts. Some give in the categories is desirable lest the law lose touch with the real world.

To any layman it would seem absurd that our courts could not obtain jurisdiction over a billion dollar multinational which is exploiting the critical New York and American markets to keep its home production going at a huge volume and profit. This perception must have a bearing on our evaluation of fairness. The law ignores the common sense of a situation at the peril of becoming irrelevant as an institution.

An apparent growing tendency by the Supreme Court to view jurisdictional bases narrowly in the interest of what it considers to be fairness to defendants is reflected in a few recent cases [citing *Shaffer v. Heitner*, *Rush v. Savchuk*, and *World-Wide Volkswagen Corp. v. Woodson*]. Unreasoned extrapolation of such cases can lead to unfairness to plaintiffs who may be denied a natural forum unless the court carefully analyzes the economic and social realities of the "significant contacts between the litigation and the forum. . . ."

II. FACTS

A. Parties

Plaintiff Bulova Watch Co., Inc. charges K. Hattori & Co., Ltd. and individual defendants Moriya, Segal, Murphy, Waldman and others with unfair competition and disparagement and with engaging in a conspiracy to raid plaintiff's marketing staff in order to appropriate plaintiff's trade secrets.

Bulova is a New York corporation with its principal place of business in Flushing, New York. It manufactures and sells watches and claims to have the largest direct sales marketing system in the watch business.

Hattori is a company incorporated under the laws of Japan with its principal offices in Tokyo. It owns all the stock of Seiko Corporation of America (SCA), a New York corporation. SCA owns all the stock of Seiko Time Corp., Pulsar Time, Inc., and SPD Precision, Inc., all New York corporations. Hattori contracts in Japan for the manufacture of its watches and sells them under the Seiko, Pulsar, and other brand names to its three American sub-subsidiaries. The Japanese parent's annual sales in 1978 were in excess of $1 billion. . . .

A very substantial amount of its total revenue is derived from exports of watches and timepieces, the United States being its largest foreign market. In 1980, over four million Hattori timepieces were sold in this country at prices to the consumer of one hundred twenty-five dollars and higher, far more than half a billion dollars at retail.

Hattori sells products to distributors in over one hundred countries around the world. Wholly-owned subsidiaries of Hattori handle distribution of Hattori's products in about ten of those countries, including the United States. In the rest, or the great majority of the countries in which Hattori's products are sold, sales are made by Hattori or its subsidiaries to independent distributors who conduct their own advertising and other marketing activities and maintain their own repair centers pursuant to agreement or arrangements with Hattori. Hattori has never directly marketed its products in any country except Japan.

From 1967 to 1971, and again from 1975 to July, 1979, Moriya was assigned by Hattori to New York. During the period when the events complained of occurred, he was president and director of SCA and its corporate predecessor, sole director of Pulsar Time and SPD Precision, director of Seiko Time, an officer of two other of Seiko's American distributors, and a director of a third. While in New York, Moriya held the following positions with Hattori: Deputy Manager and Manager, International Marketing Department and Manager, Personnel Department. . . .

B. Allegations

Between July and December of 1978, six members of Bulova's staff, three regional sales managers, and three more senior executive personnel left Bulova to join either a Seiko subsidiary or a Seiko distributor. During December, 1978 four Bulova salesmen joined SPD Precision's Pulsar division which in January, 1979, was separately incorporated as Pulsar Time, Inc. Sometime during 1979 a number of Bulova salesmen were hired by Pulsar Time. What sharply divides plaintiff from defendant is the question of whether these hirings were the result of a conspiracy among defendants to appropriate Bulova's trade secrets and marketing system and to damage Bulova and destroy its business and reputation.

Plaintiff alleges that Hattori and Moriya decided during 1978 to market a new line of watches, Pulsar, a trademark that was acquired by Seiko Time in September, 1978. Plaintiff also alleges that the decision was taken by Hattori and Moriya to organize a clock division of Seiko Time. Seiko watches had been marketed through fifteen Seiko regional distributors, but the Pulsar watches were to be marketed directly to retail outlets. To accomplish this, a direct sales network had to be put quickly into place. It is contended that, as part of the plan, Moriya hired Schwartz, who had been vice-president and director of marketing at Bulova, to head the Pulsar operation.

In the beginning of October, Schwartz and Moriya met to discuss the Pulsar marketing strategy and Schwartz recommended that Moriya hire Cohen as director of sales. Meetings were held between Cohen and Schwartz, and Cohen was offered employment at SPD Precision with the view to directing Pulsar sales. Moriya, Cohen, and Schwartz decided that a sales force of twenty would be required for the first year, 1979, and Cohen was told not to "divulge the name of his new employer" for one month. He recommended the hiring of Waldman, a Bulova regional sales manager. In early December of 1978, Waldman met with Cohen and Schwartz in New York, and the next day Waldman left Bulova to join Pulsar as field sales manager. In order to implement the goal of hiring twenty salesmen by January 1, 1979, the three ex-Bulova employees actively solicited other Bulova employees.

The hirings that ensued apparently resulted in a meeting between Bulova's then head, Flick, and Moriya at the end of the year, following which the solicitation of Bulova salesmen abated. Subsequently, however, additional solicitations are alleged to have been made, and more Bulova salesmen were hired. . . .

Bulova contends that the concerted action of Hattori, Moriya, and the other individual defendants caused serious dislocation and disruption at Bulova's corporate headquarters. The departure of six high level employees is alleged to have damaged sales throughout the country and in New York, and to have contributed substantially to a decrease in sales of some $18 million.

C. Moriya's Crucial Role

Moriya joined Hattori in Japan in 1954 after finishing his schooling. He has never worked for any employer aside from Hattori or its American subsidiaries. As already noted, during the course of his employment with the American subsidiaries, he simultaneously held the Hattori positions of Deputy Manager and Manager of the International Division and Manager of the Personnel Department. Nonetheless, defendants assert that while in the United States "he performed services for the United States subsidiaries and none for Hattori." The court has not been able to see its way to reading the undisputed facts in such an unusual fashion. Common sense, which need not be banished from our reckoning, dictates the conclusion that while in the United States, Moriya loyally performed substantial services for Hattori.

Moriya was no mere liaison officer, and his assignment by Hattori was far from casual. He testified that both his tours were undertaken at the behest of his superiors at Hattori. He was sent first in 1967 when Hattori recognized the potential of America as a market for the sale of its watches, and he was ordered to New York "to take care of marketing." Moriya understood that his assignment was undertaken to further the interests of Hattori and he admitted that he endeavored to carry out this task. Although he was employed by the Hattori subsidiaries, he would not deny that he considered Mr. Unno of Hattori his superior.

While he was in New York as executive vice president of SCA's corporate predecessor, Moriya apparently was instrumental in formulating the marketing strategy that enabled Hattori to establish a formidable position in the American market. . . . It seems plain from Moriya's testimony that he was attempting to advance Hattori's interests and its international marketing aims by formulating plans for the United States in cooperation with Reijiro Hattori and the Hattori Board. Even if we did not need to view the record in a light favorable to plaintiff, there could be no doubt who Moriya's true master was. It is beyond cavil that the establishment of a major presence in the American market is of critical importance to a firm like Hattori. The establishment of such a posture required major marketing planning. Moriya was directly responsible for formulating and implementing that strategy, and at all times his primary allegiance was to Hattori. . . .

III. JURISDICTION OVER K. HATTORI & CO., LTD.

In a diversity action such as this, the question of personal jurisdiction is determined in accordance with the law of the state in which the court sits. Here, New York in personam jurisdictional bases suffice to support federal personal jurisdiction and New York is a convenient forum.

A. Doing Business, N.Y. CPLR 301

1. The Law

CPLR 301 permits the exercise of such jurisdiction over "persons, property, or status as might have been exercised heretofore." It confers personal jurisdiction over unlicensed foreign corporations that are "doing business" in New York.

The definition of "doing business" has been variously stated, but the common denominator is that the corporation is operating within the state "not occasionally or casually, but with a fair measure of permanence and continuity." *Tauza v. Susquehanna Coal Co.,* 220 N.Y. 259, 267, 115 N.E. 915, 917 (1917).

It is no longer a matter of doubt that a foreign corporation can do business in New York through its employees, or through independent agents.

Equally settled is the concept that a corporation may be amenable to New York personal jurisdiction when the systematic activities of a subsidiary in this state may fairly be attributed to the parent. [A] line of cases establishes the rule that a foreign corporation does business in New York if its affiliated company is in effect a "local department separately incorporated,"or it acts as agent by "do[ing] all the business which [the principal] could do were it here by its own officials." *Frummer v. Hilton Hotels International, Inc.,* 19 N.Y.2d at 537.

The parent-subsidiary relationship has not in itself been treated as sufficient to establish personal jurisdiction over the foreign parent. Some additional factor has been needed. Such circumstances include direct and indirect control of the local distributor, treating the subsidiary as an "incorporated division," as an agent or as both. . . .

The two tests that have been utilized in determining the closeness of the economic connection both look to realities rather than to formal relationships. The parent corporations will be found to be present in New York: "First, if the relationship between the foreign parents and local subsidiaries gives rise to a 'valid inference' of an agency relationship;" and second, "if control by the parent of the subsidiary is 'so complete that the subsidiary is, in fact, merely a department of the parent.' "

. . . The factors to be weighed include the significance of the New York business to the defendant's overall activities. While "litigation in a foreign jurisdiction is a burdensome inconvenience for any company, in the appropriate case, where defendant's activities abroad, either directly or through an agent, become as widespread and energetic as the activities in New York conducted by [defendant]," Frummer v. Hilton Hotels International, Inc., [*supra*], such litigation is "part of the price which may be properly demanded of those who extensively engage in international trade."

5. Application of Law to Facts

Moving defendants place great stock in the formal separation of Hattori from its 100% directly-owned subsidiary and its 100% indirectly-owned subsidiaries. They state that the subsidiaries do not receive loans from the parent, that they generally buy from the parent by letter of credit posted with a Japanese bank abroad, that they do their own advertising (although at times they participate in promotions organized by Hattori), and that the parent has no bank account, office or phone listing in New York, is not licensed to do business here, does not assign its "salaried employees" to New York, and is not involved in the personnel policies or the hiring of personnel by its New York subsidiaries.

Plaintiff, on the other hand, points to the complete stock ownership by the parent and additionally draws our attention to the interchange and overlap of directors and officers between parent and subsidiaries, to the fact that intercompany loans are made to other Hattori subsidiaries and are assertedly available, if needed, to the New York subsidiaries, that the financial statements of the New York subsidiaries are consolidated in Hattori's reports filed under the securities and exchange law of Japan, and that unrealized profits and losses arising from sales among the consolidated companies are eliminated in the financial statements. It also relies upon certain advertising materials produced by Hattori and distributed by the public relations firm of the New York subsidiaries that refer to Hattori's "marketing offices in . . . New York" and an "international network of designated distributors . . . supervised by the Tokyo headquarters."

. . . Hattori and its American subsidiaries do maintain some independence — about as much as the egg and vegetables in a western omelette. Just as, from a culinary point of view, we focus on the ultimate omelette and not its ingredients, so, too, from a jurisdictional standpoint, it is the integrated international operation of Hattori affecting activities in New York that is the primary focus of our concern.

Although with time the Hattori subsidiaries might well evolve, along with their parent, into the later stages of multinational development, today Hattori is a highly effective export manufacturer and not a fully developed multinational. It is monocentric more than polycentric. Large and sophisticated as it may be, it is very much the hub of a wheel with many spokes. It is appropriate, therefore, to look to the center of the wheel in Japan when the spokes violate substantive rights in other countries.

Defendant would have the court accept the notion that none of Moriya's work was done for the benefit of Hattori. The metaphoric fiction by which the parent and child corporation are treated as separate is here carried too far. "Metaphors in the law are to be narrowly watched, for starting as devices to liberate thought, they end often by enslaving it" [citing Cardozo]. There are ample grounds to find that plaintiff has made a case that the actions taken by a man adept and experienced in the American market for the specific purpose of expanding significantly Hattori's presence in its major overseas market were undertaken on behalf of Hattori. The fact that Moriya retained prominent titles in Hattori while in New York is significant, although not in itself decisive. So, too, is the fact that at the time of the filing of this complaint, after he had returned to Japan and supposedly severed all his New York connections, Moriya continued as chairman of SCA, chairman of Seiko Time, sole director of SPD Precision and Pulsar, and president of SCA until sometime in November, 1979.

What is decisive is that at the time this complaint was filed, Hattori, through its American subsidiaries, continued to engage in the market penetration and expansion that are its corporate raison d'etre and that are the grounds underlying this action. We have no doubt about the validity of an "inference as to the broad scope of the agency" linking Hattori to the activities of its subsidiaries in New York.

Defendants deny that the subsidiaries meet either the "mere department" or the "agency" test. As to the former, first set forth in *Taca International Airlines, S.A. v. Rolls-Royce of England, Ltd.,* 15 N.Y.2d 97, 256 N.Y.S.2d 129, 204 N.E.2d 329 (1965), defendants seek to distinguish the case by stating that the parent in Taca "controlled" the subsidiary whereas here Hattori does not, and that "important policies" were made by the parent in Taca, but by the subsidiaries here. Suffice it to say that to accept these as distinctions is to beg the jurisdictional question. For what we are deciding is precisely whether or not Hattori controlled its subsidiaries and whether the truly important policies were made, on the one hand, in New York, or, on the other, in Tokyo or in New York on behalf of Tokyo. . . .

The leading "agency" case in New York, *Frummer v. Hilton Hotels International, Inc.,* [supra], involved the question of whether a hotel company was doing business in New York by virtue of its reservation system operated in the state by an affiliated corporation. The test developed there would find jurisdiction if the subsidiary was doing "all the business which the [principal] could do were it here by its own officials." In this case, it is obvious that if the subsidiaries were not in New York and Hattori sought to enter the American market, it would have to do so directly. This market is simply too important to the parent's welfare to use independent and uncontrolled sales agents and distributors as it does in some countries where sales are relatively small. There are undoubtedly special reasons Hattori has chosen to operate in this country by means of incorporated subsidiaries. But these subsidiaries almost by definition are doing for their parent what their parent would otherwise have to do on its own. The question to ask is not whether the American subsidiaries can formally accept orders for their parent, but rather whether, in the truest sense, the subsidiaries' presence substitutes for the presence of the parent. . . .

What the Hattori subsidiaries have done is a far cry from "mere solicitation." To establish marketing and service networks and to formulate and implement distribution systems in the largest export market of a billion dollar company is not "mere solicitation of sales." In any case, once solicitation is found in any substantial degree, "very little more" is necessary to support a conclusion of doing business through the in-state agent. *Aquascutum of London, Inc. v. S.S. American Champion,* 426 F.2d 205, 211 (2d Cir. 1970). There is sufficient evidence at this preliminary stage to support plaintiff's contention that conscious and systematic activities undertaken by Hattori to establish, consolidate and expand a vital market position, satisfy the "very little more" test. . . .

Our holding that the activities of Hattori's subsidiaries allow the court to take jurisdiction of Hattori is buttressed by the fact that the cause of action alleged here is integrally related to the doing of business by Hattori within the state. In *SCM Corporation v. Brother International Corporation,* the court considered whether it had personal jurisdiction of a New York subsidiary of a Japanese parent in a patent infringement case. The court noted the "intimate nature of the relationship" among the affiliated companies, and concluded that these relations justified jurisdiction "especially since the underlying action arises out of and is closely connected with [the] conduct and activity" justifying jurisdiction. It is often said that when a corporation does business in New York, "jurisdiction does not fail because the cause of action sued upon has no relation in its origin to the business here transacted." *Tauza v. Susquehanna Coal Co.,* 220 N.Y. 259, 268, 115 N.E. 915, 917 (1917). Nevertheless, in practice, the cases do reflect judicial weighing of the local agent's participation in the actions surrounding the complaint as a factor strengthening the doing business basis of jurisdiction.

A court might well find substantial unfairness were it to drag a foreign parent into court to defend itself against actions completely unrelated to the subsidiary corporation's purposive activities on behalf of its parent. The holding in this case is simply that while a subsidiary establishes and expands a parent's market position then, so long as that activity is being conducted, and with respect to those activities furthering the parent's ends, the parent is doing business in New York. This is particularly true as to activities directly related to primary steps taken to ensure a place for its subsidiaries, as where action is taken to raid an established competitor's personnel in penetrating the American market.

B. Long Arm Jurisdiction, N.Y. CPLR 302

1. The Law

Plaintiff has also made a sufficient jurisdictional showing to support personal jurisdiction over Hattori under CPLR 302. That provision allows the exercise of jurisdiction over a non-domiciliary where the defendant either commits a tortious act within the state or commits a tortious act outside the state and has substantial contacts with the state. It covers a foreign entity which,

(a) . . . in person or through an agent: (1) transacts any business within the state or contracts anywhere to supply goods or services in the state; or

(2) commits a tortious act within the state . . .; or (3) commits a tortious act without the state causing injury to person or property within the state, . . . if (it) (i) regularly does or solicits business, or engages in any other persistent course of conduct, or derives substantial revenue from goods used or consumed or services rendered, in the state, or (ii) expects or should reasonably expect the act to have consequences in the state and derives substantial revenue from interstate or international commerce.

Jurisdiction is granted only "[as] to a cause of action arising from any of the acts enumerated in th[e] section." N.Y. CPLR 302(a).

2. Application of Law to Facts

Quite aside from our findings with respect to CPLR 301, Hattori transacts business in New York. The cause of action arises out of the actions of the New York subsidiaries in New York on behalf of Hattori.

Defendants contend that plaintiff's claims do not actually relate to the establishment of the Pulsar division, Pulsar Time, Inc., and the Seiko clock sales operation. It seems clear, however, that the gravamen of the complaint is precisely the tortious conduct that is alleged to have occurred just in order that these businesses could be successfully established in New York.

The more important question is whether the actions of the New York subsidiaries can be attributed to Hattori under an agency theory as the statute seems to require. Here, as in the case of CPLR 301, courts look to the realities rather than the formalities of agency to decide whether business has been transacted through an agent.

. . . Planning and establishing significant new product lines and implementing a marketing strategy that entailed the hiring of established salespeople constitute the transaction of business out of which the present complaint arises. As to this business, there is a strong showing that Hattori was informed. When actions of relatively minor significance might subject a foreign party to the jurisdiction of a New York court, it would be anomalous if the systematic and sustained planning for establishing and expanding the New York business of a billion dollar multinational did not. There is jurisdiction under CPLR 302(a)(1).

Similar considerations support finding jurisdiction over Hattori under CPLR 302(a)(2) as well. Plaintiff alleges that Hattori, through Moriya, committed in New York the torts of unfair competition and disparagement and inducing breach of fiduciary duty. While Hattori denies any role in the contested hirings, there is substantial evidence that if there was a tort, substantial tortious acts took place in New York. . . .

WIWA v. ROYAL DUTCH PETROLEUM COMPANY
226 F.3d 88 (2d Cir. 2000), *cert. denied*, 532 U.S. 941 (2001)

. . . Plaintiffs are three Nigerian emigres, and a woman identified only as Jane Doe to protect her safety, who allege that they (or in some cases their deceased next of kin) suffered grave human rights abuses at the hands of the Nigerian authorities. Defendants Royal Dutch Petroleum Company ("Royal Dutch") and Shell Transport and Trading Co., P.L.C. ("Shell Transport") are business corporations, incorporated in the Netherlands and the United Kingdom respectively, that are alleged to have directly or indirectly participated in or directed these abuses. . . . Defendants contend that . . . the court lacked personal jurisdiction over them. We hold that the district court properly exercised jurisdiction over the defendants. . . .

BACKGROUND

A. Allegations of the Complaint

Defendant Royal Dutch is a holding company incorporated and headquartered in the Netherlands. Defendant Shell Transport is a holding company incorporated and headquartered in England. The two defendants jointly control and operate the Royal Dutch/Shell Group, a vast, international, vertically integrated network of affiliated but formally independent oil and gas companies. Among these affiliated companies is Shell Petroleum Development Company of Nigeria, Ltd. ("Shell Nigeria"), a wholly-owned Nigerian subsidiary of the defendants that engages in extensive oil exploration and development activity in the Ogoni region of Nigeria.

The amended complaint ("the complaint") alleges that plaintiffs and their next of kin (hereafter collectively referred to as "Plaintiffs") were imprisoned, tortured, and killed by the Nigerian government in violation of the law of nations at the instigation of the defendants, in reprisal for their political opposition to the defendants' oil exploration activities. According to the complaint, Shell Nigeria coercively appropriated land for oil development without adequate compensation, and caused substantial pollution of the air and water in the homeland of the Ogoni people. A protest movement arose among the Ogoni. Ken Saro-Wiwa was an opposition leader and President of the Movement for the Survival of the Ogoni People (MSOP); John Kpuinen was a leader of the MSOP's youth wing.

Allegedly, Shell Nigeria recruited the Nigerian police and military to attack local villages and suppress the organized opposition to its development activity. Saro-Wiwa and Kpuinen were repeatedly arrested, detained, and tortured by the Nigerian government because of their leadership roles in the protest movement. In 1995, Saro-Wiwa and Kpuinen were hanged, along with other Ogoni leaders, after being convicted of murder by a special military tribunal. Allegedly, they were convicted on fabricated evidence solely to silence political criticism and were not afforded the legal protections required by international law. The complaint further alleges that plaintiff Owens Wiwa (Saro-Wiwa's brother) was illegally detained by Nigerian authorities, that plaintiff Jane Doe was beaten and shot by the Nigerian military in a raid upon her village, and that Saro-Wiwa's family-including Ken Saro-Wiwa's 74-year-old mother-were beaten by Nigerian officials while attending his trial.

According to the complaint, while these abuses were carried out by the Nigerian government and military, they were instigated, orchestrated, planned, and facilitated by Shell Nigeria under the direction of the defendants.

The Royal Dutch/Shell Group allegedly provided money, weapons, and logistical support to the Nigerian military, including the vehicles and ammunition used in the raids on the villages, procured at least some of these attacks, participated in the fabrication of murder charges against Saro-Wiwa and Kpuinen, and bribed witnesses to give false testimony against them.[1]

B. Facts Relating to Jurisdiction in New York

1. Defendants' New York Stock Exchange Listings and Sundry Activities

Neither of the defendants has extensive direct contacts with New York. Both companies list their shares, either directly or indirectly,[2] on the New York Stock Exchange. They conduct activities in New York incident to this listing, including the preparation of filings for the Securities and Exchange Commission (SEC) and the employment of transfer agents and depositories for their shares. Royal Dutch also maintains an Internet site, accessible in New York. They have participated in at least one lawsuit in New York as defendants, without contesting jurisdiction. They have for many years retained New York counsel.

Defendants own subsidiary companies that do business in the United States, including Shell Petroleum Inc. (SPI), a Delaware corporation. SPI in turn owns all the shares of Shell Oil Company (Shell Oil), the well-known oil and gas concern. Shell Oil has extensive operations in New York and is undisputedly subject to the jurisdiction of the New York courts.

2. Defendants' Maintenance of an Investor Relations Office in New York City

The defendants also maintain an Investor Relations Office in New York City, administered by James Grapsi, whose title is "Manager of Investor Relations." The office is nominally a part of Shell Oil. However, all of its functions involve facilitating the relations of the parent holding companies, the defendants Royal Dutch and Shell Transport, with the investment community. The expenses of the office (consisting primarily of rent and salaries) are directly paid in the first instance by Shell Oil, but Shell Oil is reimbursed by the defendants, who therefore bear the full expense of the office. Those expenses average about $45,000 per month, or about $500,000 per year. The Investor Relations Office's duties involve fielding inquiries from investors and potential investors in Royal Dutch and Shell Transport, mailing information about the defendants to thousands of individuals and entities throughout the United States, and organizing meetings between officials of the defendants and investors, potential investors, and financial analysts. Each year the Investor Relations Office organizes about six such sessions and schedules them for various financial centers throughout the United States, including New York. Grapsi manages these functions out of a New York City office located in the Southern District of New York, and characteristically seeks the defendants' approval before scheduling meetings and making other similar decisions.

---

[1] For purposes of this opinion relating to jurisdiction . . ., we assume the truth of the allegations (while implying no views on the truth or falsity of the allegations).

[2] Shares of Royal Dutch are traded directly on the New York Stock Exchange. Shell Transport's shares are traded indirectly in the United States; investors may purchase American Depository Receipts (ADR's) for shares of Shell, rather than shares themselves.

C. Proceedings Below

. . . The amended complaint seeks damages under the ATCA, the Racketeering Influenced and Corrupt Organizations Act (RICO), international law and treaties, Nigerian law, and various state law torts. More specifically, the complaint alleges that the defendants are liable for summary execution; crimes against humanity; torture; cruel, inhuman, and degrading treatment; arbitrary arrest and detention; violations of the rights to life, liberty, security of the person, and peaceful assembly and association; wrongful death; assault and battery; intentional and negligent infliction of emotional distress; and conspiracy. It is not entirely clear whether the liability of the defendants is predicated on their own actions, on a theory of responsibility for the actions of their subsidiary Shell Nigeria, or on a combination of both.

At the time of the filing, two of the four plaintiffs (Blessing Kpuinen and Owens Wiwa) lived in the United States, though not in New York.

The defendants moved to dismiss for lack of personal jurisdiction, *forum non conveniens*, and failure to state a claim. In a Report and Recommendation . . ., Magistrate Judge Henry Pitman recommended that Judge Wood dismiss the case for lack of jurisdiction or, alternatively, for *forum non conveniens*. Explicitly reserving the "difficult" questions of substantive law raised by the defendants' 12(b)(6) motion, Magistrate Judge Pitman found that neither the maintenance of the Investor Relations Office nor the defendants' direct actions in New York, were sufficient to constitute "doing business" in New York, as required to establish general jurisdiction under N.Y. C.P.L.R. § 301. Turning to the *forum non conveniens* issue, he determined that England was an "adequate alternative forum" and that the various factors a court is required to balance in evaluating such a motion favor adjudication of the dispute in England.

Upon plaintiffs' objections to the Magistrate Judge's Report, Judge Wood . . . found that jurisdiction over the defendants was established under § 301 by virtue of their maintenance of the Investor Relations Office in New York, but accepted the Magistrate Judge's recommendation to dismiss for *forum non conveniens*. Plaintiffs moved for reconsideration in light of this court's decision in *Jota v. Texaco, Inc.*, 157 F.3d 153 (2d Cir. 1998). . . . Judge Wood granted their motion, to the extent of conditioning dismissal on the defendants' commitment to consent to service of process in England, comply with all discovery orders, pay any judgment rendered in England, waive a security bond, and waive a statute of limitations defense if an action is begun in England within one year of the conclusion of these proceedings, which conditions defendants accepted. Otherwise the motion was denied.

DISCUSSION

A. Personal Jurisdiction

Under the Federal Rules of Civil Procedure, a court may exercise jurisdiction over any defendant "who could be subjected to the jurisdiction of a court of general jurisdiction in the state in which the district court is located," Fed.R.Civ.P. 4(k)(1)(a), provided of course that such an exercise of jurisdiction comports with the Fifth Amendment's Due Process Clause. The question is therefore whether the defendants may be subjected to the jurisdiction of the courts of the State of New York.

Before the court below, plaintiffs offered multiple theories as to why New York could properly exercise personal jurisdiction over the defendants. While the Magistrate Judge rejected all of these theories, the district court held that, under prevailing law, the activities of the Investor Relations Office on the defendants' behalf in New York were both attributable to the defendants and sufficient to confer jurisdiction. On appeal, defendants make four arguments: (1) these activities are not attributable to the defendants for jurisdictional purposes; (2) these New York activities cannot be considered in the jurisdictional calculus because they are merely "incidental" to a stock market listing and are jurisdictionally inconsequential as a matter of law; (3) the Investor Relations activities are legally insufficient to confer general jurisdiction; and (4) exercising jurisdiction over the defendants would violate the fairness requirement of the Due Process Clause. For the reasons discussed below, we reject each of these contentions and hold that the defendants are subject to personal jurisdiction in the Southern District of New York.[3]

(1) *The Agency Analysis.* Under New York law, a foreign corporation is subject to general personal jurisdiction in New York if it is "doing business" in the state. *See* N.Y. C.P.L.R. § 301 (codifying caselaw that incorporates "doing business" standard); *see also Hoffritz for Cutlery, Inc. v. Amajac, Ltd.,* 763 F.2d 55, 58 (2d Cir. 1985). "[A] corporation is 'doing business' and is therefore 'present' in New York and subject to personal jurisdiction with respect to any cause of action, related or unrelated to the New York contacts, if it does business in New York 'not occasionally or casually, but with a fair measure of permanence and continuity.' " *Id.* (quoting *Tauza v. Susquehanna Coal Co.,* 220 N.Y. 259, 267, 115 N.E. 915 (1917)). In order to establish that this standard is met, a plaintiff must show that a defendant engaged in "continuous, permanent, and substantial activity in New York." *Landoil Resources Corp. v. Alexander & Alexander Servs., Inc.,* 918 F.2d 1039, 1043 (2d Cir. 1990).

The continuous presence and substantial activities that satisfy the requirement of doing business do not necessarily need to be conducted by the foreign corporation itself. In certain circumstances, jurisdiction has been predicated upon activities performed in New York for a foreign corporation by an agent. Under well-established New York law, a court of New York may assert jurisdiction over a foreign corporation when it affiliates itself with a New York representative entity and that New York representative renders services on behalf of the foreign corporation that go beyond mere solicitation and are sufficiently important to the foreign entity that the corporation itself would perform equivalent services if no agent were available. *See, e.g., Frummer v. Hilton Hotels Int'l Inc.,* 19 N.Y.2d 533, 537, 281 N.Y.S.2d 41, 227 N.E.2d 851 (1967) (finding jurisdiction over foreign hotel chain based on the activities of affiliated reservations service); *Gelfand v. Tanner Motor Tours, Ltd.,* 385 F.2d 116, 120–21 (2d Cir. 1967) (applying *Frummer* to find jurisdiction over tour

---

[3] Because we hold that jurisdiction is properly exercised over the defendants on the basis of the activities of the Investor Relations Office, we do not reach any of the other jurisdictional issues raised by the plaintiffs. We express no views on the merits of any of their alternative arguments.

operator based on the activities of affiliated travel agent). To come within the rule, a plaintiff need demonstrate neither a formal agency agreement, nor that the defendant exercised direct control over its putative agent. The agent must be primarily employed by the defendant and not engaged in similar services for other clients.

Both Magistrate Judge Pitman and Judge Wood found that Grapsi and the Investor Relations Office were agents of the defendants for jurisdictional purposes. We agree. While nominally a part of Shell Oil, Grapsi and the Investor Relations Office devoted one hundred percent of their time to the defendants' business. Their sole business function was to perform investor relations services on the defendants' behalf. The defendants fully funded the expenses of the Investor Relations Office (including salary, rent, electricity, mailing costs, etc.), and Grapsi sought the defendants' approval on important decisions.

The defendants nonetheless argue that the relationship does not meet the *Frummer/Gelfand* test. They contend the services of the Investor Relations Office were not sufficiently important that the defendants would have performed them if an agent had been unavailable. We do not find this argument persuasive. While it is true that the Investor Relations Office was not directly involved with the core functions of the defendant's business—the operation of an integrated international oil business, its work was of meaningful importance to the defendants. The defendants are huge publicly-traded companies with a need for access to capital markets. The importance of their need to maintain good relationships with existing investors and potential investors is illustrated by the fact that they pay over half a million dollars per year to maintain the Investors Relations office. In our view, the amount invested by the defendants in the U.S. investor relations activity substantially establishes the importance of that activity to the defendants.

Defendants also contend that, if they were to perform the Investor Relations services themselves, it would not necessarily be in New York. The argument is extremely weak. While of course it is true, especially given technological advances in communication, that such an office could conceivably be located anywhere in the world, the strongest indications are that the defendants selected New York as the locus of the present office because that is the most logical place for it. Insofar as the office concerns itself with investors in the U.S. capital markets, it makes better sense to have the office in the United States, rather than in another country. New York is widely regarded as the capital of U.S. capital markets. It seems most likely that the Investor Relations Office established by Shell Oil for the benefit of its parents and at their insistence was established in New York City because that was the best place for such an office, and that it would most likely be located in New York City regardless of whether operated directly by the defendants, by Shell Oil, or by any other agent.[4] Cf. *Burger King Corp. v. Rudzewicz*, 471 U.S. 462, 475, (1985) (describing as "essential" element in jurisdictional inquiry the question whether "there be some act by which the defendant purposefully

---

[4] Grapsi testified that 100 of the 140 attendees at a December 1996 investor relations meeting for financial writers and members of the international community came from New York and only five came from other locations in the United States.

avails itself of the privilege of conducting activities within the forum State, thus invoking the benefits and protections of its laws"). . . .

The defendants' argument is also difficult to square with the facts of the seminal agency jurisdiction cases, *Frummer* and *Gelfand*. In those cases, the foreign corporations were not absolutely required to choose New York as the locus of their reservations services. *See generally Frummer*, 19 N.Y.2d 533 (involving booking agent that took reservations and performed public relations services for a foreign hotel chain); *Gelfand*, 385 F.2d 116 (involving sales representative that took reservations and performed other services for out-of-state tour operator). They could have located those operations elsewhere, either foregoing the New York market entirely or arranging to service New York customers more circuitously. However, in both those cases, the defendants chose to locate offices in Manhattan to establish easy access to New York's rich market of potential customers, thereby better serving their own interests. The circumstances of the present case support the inference that the defendants made a similar calculation when they chose to locate their Investor Relations Office in New York.

(2) *The Nature of the Activities of the Investor Relations Office.* The defendants contend their Investor Relations Office is an activity that is "incidental" to their listing on the New York Stock Exchange. They cite to a long stream of caselaw reaching back over a century that they argue precludes courts from considering activity "incidental" to stock market listings when evaluating whether a corporation is doing business in the state of New York. We agree that the prevailing caselaw accords foreign corporations substantial latitude to list their securities on New York-based stock exchanges and to take the steps necessary to facilitate those listings (such as making SEC filings and designating a depository for their shares) without thereby subjecting themselves to New York jurisdiction for unrelated occurrences. . . . However, defendants misread the scope of the existing caselaw when they argue that all contacts related to stock exchange listings are stripped of jurisdictional significance.

To begin with, it is not that activities necessary to maintain a stock exchange listing do not count, but rather that, without more, they are insufficient to confer jurisdiction. *See, e.g., Pomeroy v. Hocking Valley Ry. Co.*, 218 N.Y. 530, 536, 113 N.E. 504 (1916) ("The payment, too, of dividends and the transfer of stock while perhaps not sufficient of themselves to constitute the transaction of business . . ., doubtless are of some importance in connection with other facts."). . . Other cases in this line imply a similar result when they suggest that jurisdiction is not available over a corporation whose only contacts with the forum are listings on the New York stock exchanges and ancillary arrangements involving the distribution of their shares.

The Investor Relations Office conducts a broader range of activities on the defendants' behalf than those described in the cited cases as merely "incidental" to the stock exchange listing. These activities, which range from fielding inquiries from investors and potential investors to organizing meetings between defendants' officials and investors, potential investors, and financial analysts, do not properly come within the rule upon which the defendants rely. The defendants' Investor Relations program results not from legal or logistical requirements incumbent upon corporations that list their shares on the New York Stock Exchange, but from the defendants' discretionary determination to invest substantial sums of money in cultivating their relationship with the New York capital markets. It appears the location of the office in New York City has far more to do with the importance of New York as a center of capital markets than with the proximity of the New York Stock Exchange. A company can perfectly well maintain a listing on the New York (or any other) Stock Exchange without maintaining an office nearby to cultivate relations with investors.

In summary, the large body of caselaw the defendants point to at most stands for the proposition that, absent other substantial contacts, a company is not "doing business" in New York merely by taking ancillary steps in support of its listing on a New York exchange. The activities chargeable to the defendants go well beyond this minimum. We conclude that the activities of the Investor Relations Office go beyond the range of activities that have been held insufficient to subject foreign corporations to the jurisdiction of New York courts.

(3) *The Sufficiency of Contacts.* The defendants further contend that the activities of the Investor Relations Office are quantitatively insufficient to confer jurisdiction. . . . We find no merit to this contention. Where, as here, plaintiffs' claim is not related to defendants' contacts with New York, so that jurisdiction is properly characterized as "general," plaintiffs must demonstrate "the defendant's 'continuous and systematic general business contacts.'" *Metropolitan Life Ins. Co. v. Robertson-Ceco Corp.*, 84 F.3d 560, 568 (2d Cir. 1996) (quoting *Helicopteros Nacionales de Colombia, S.A. v. Hall*, 466 U.S. 408, 416 (1984)). Defendants' contacts constitute "a continuous and systematic general business" presence in New York and therefore satisfy the minimum contacts portion of a due process analysis.

Citing to a string of cases holding that solicitation of business plus minimal additional contacts satisfies Section 301, Judge Wood characterized the activities of the Investor Relations Office as satisfying the test of "solicitation plus." The defendants dispute this characterization, arguing that Grapsi did not perform "solicitation" because he did not offer to buy or sell any stock in the corporation. As Judge Wood noted, however, a finding of "solicitation" in the jurisdictional context does not necessarily require "solicitation" in the sense of an offer of contract. Rather, the central question is whether the defendant (or its agent) behaved in such a way so as to encourage others to spend money (or otherwise act) in a manner that would benefit the defendant. *Cf., e.g., Landoil* (trips to New York to service existing accounts constitutes "solicitation"). Judge Wood's characterization of the Investor Relations Office's activities as "solicitation" appears to be a sound interpolation of pre-existing precedent into a new factual context.

However, we need not rely upon such a characterization to support general jurisdiction in this case, because even without relying on the "solicitation plus" formulation, the activities of the Investor Relations Office meet the "doing business" standard. In assessing whether jurisdiction lies against a foreign corporation, both this court and the New York courts have focused on a traditional set of indicia: for example, whether the company has an office in the state, whether it has any bank accounts or other property in the state, whether it has a phone listing in the state, whether it does public relations work there, and whether it has individuals permanently located in the state to promote its interests. The Investor Relations Office, whose activities are attributable to the defendants under the *Frummer* analysis, meets each of these tests. It constitutes a substantial "physical corporate presence" in the State, permanently dedicated to promoting the defendants' interests. *Cf. Landoil*, 918 F.2d at 1045 n. 10 (noting that while periodic business trips to New York to solicit business did not confer jurisdiction, "renting a hotel room . . . on a systematic and regular basis might be the functional equivalent of an office in New York and therefore might be sufficient to establish presence within the state"). We agree with Judge Wood that the continuous presence of the Investor Relations program in New York City is sufficient to confer jurisdiction.

(4) *Fairness.* Finally, the defendants argue that it would violate the fairness requirement of the Due Process Clause for a New York court to exercise jurisdiction over them. Again, we disagree.

Personal jurisdiction may be exercised only when (1) the State's laws authorize service of process upon the defendant, and (2) an assertion of jurisdiction under the circumstances of the case comports with the requirements of due process. The required due process inquiry itself has two parts: whether a defendant has "minimum contacts" with the forum state and whether the assertion of jurisdiction comports with "traditional notions of fair play and substantial justice—that is whether . . . [the exercise of jurisdiction] is reasonable under the circumstances of a particular case." . . .

As noted above, the defendants' contacts go well beyond the minimal. As a general rule, in making the constitutional analysis once a plaintiff has made a "threshold showing" of minimum contacts, the defendant must come forward with a "compelling case that the presence of some other considerations would render jurisdiction unreasonable." *Robertson-Ceco Corp.*, 84 F.3d at 568. The defendants have not made any such compelling showing here.

While it is true that certain factors normally used to assess the reasonableness of subjection to jurisdiction do favor the defendants (they are foreign corporations that face something of a burden if they litigate here, and the events in question did not occur in New York), litigation in New York City would not represent any great inconvenience to the defendants. The defendants control a vast, wealthy, and far-flung business empire which operates in most parts of the globe. They have a physical presence in the forum state, have access to enormous resources, face little or no language barrier, have litigated in this country on previous occasions, have a four-decade long relationship with one of the nation's leading law firms, and are the parent companies of one of America's largest corporations, which has a very significant presence in New York. New York City, furthermore, where the trial would be held, is a major world capital which offers central location, easy access, and extensive facilities of all kinds. We conclude that the inconvenience to the defendants involved in litigating in New York City would not be great and that nothing in the Due Process Clause precludes New York from exercising jurisdiction over the defendants. . . .

Notes and Questions

1. *The evolution of Cannon Manufacturing.* The Supreme Court's formal approach to corporate structures in *Cannon Manufacturing Co. v. Cudahy* exhibits all the virtues and vices of a bright-line rule: so long as the corporate separation "though perhaps merely formal, [is] real . . . [and] not a pure fiction," the parent company will not be subjected to jurisdiction through the in-state activities of its subsidiary. What is the value (and what is the cost) of this formalist approach?

As noted in *Roorda*, the Supreme Court has never directly overruled the *Cannon Manufacturing* approach, but the rule was qualified in *International Shoe*, and later cases have clouded its authority by finding facts which suggest that the corporate separation is fictitious or that the parent has held the subsidiary out as its agent, or that the parent exercises an undue degree of control over the subsidiary. *Compare Pfundstein v. Omnicom Group, Inc.*, 285 N.J. Super., 245, 254, 666 A.2d 1013 (App. Div. 1995) (jurisdiction over a subsidiary corporation that keeps it own books and bank accounts, files income tax returns, is managed by its own board of directors, makes its own employment decisions, and directs its own day-to-day operations, will not be imputed to parent corporation).

On the basis of *Roorda*, *Bulova*, and *Wiwa*, how would you articulate the circumstances in which the *Cannon Manufacturing* rule will not apply? What is the difference between the agency exception and the alter ego exception?

2. *Determinations of liability versus jurisdiction.* The Supreme Court has articulated a generally-applicable principle that a parent corporation may be directly involved in the activities of its subsidiaries without incurring liability so long as that involvement is "consistent with the parent's investor status."

> [I]t is entirely appropriate for directors of a parent corporation to serve as directors of its subsidiary, and that fact alone may not serve to expose the parent corporation to liability for its subsidiary's acts. . . . This recognition that the corporate personalities remain distinct has its corollary in the well established principle of corporate law that directors and officers holding positions with a parent and its subsidiary can and do "change hats" to represent the two corporations separately, despite their common ownership.

United States v. Bestfoods, 524 U.S. 51 (1998). Appropriate parental involvement includes: "monitoring of the subsidiary's performance, supervision of the subsidiary's finance and capital budget decisions, and articulation of general policies and procedures[.]" *Id.*

Should the standards be different if the issue is jurisdiction instead of liability?

3. *Wiwa v. Royal Dutch Shell.* Does *Wiwa* illustrate the jurisdictional doctrines at work in *Roorda* and *Bulova*, or does it articulate a revised approach to personal jurisdiction? Is there anything about the statutory basis for the action in *Wiwa* that supports the Second Circuit's assessment of Royal Dutch Petroleum's in-state actions?

4. *State long-arm jurisdictional standards.* The New York long-arm statute provides that personal jurisdiction over a foreign corporation is proper if that

corporation is "doing business" in the state. Under that standard as interpreted, advertising or soliciting business alone is insufficient to establish jurisdiction, but solicitation combined with a constant presence in New York to promote defendants' interests will. *See, e.g., Landoil Resources Corp. v. Alexander & Alexander Serv.*, 918 F.2d 1039, 1045 (2d Cir. 1990) ("renting a hotel room to solicit business on a systematic and regular basis might be the functional equivalent of an office in New York and therefore might be sufficient to establish presence within the state.") Does this account for the result in *Wiwa*? Should the jurisdiction of the federal courts in transnational cases vary from state-to-state, depending on the peculiarities of the long-arm statute in the state where the federal court sits? *See* Federal Rule of Civil Procedure 4(k)(1)(A) (providing, as noted in *Wiwa*, that a federal district court will have personal jurisdiction if the state in which the court is located could exercise jurisdiction).

[2] Aggregating National Contacts

Personal jurisdiction in international litigation can become especially problematic when a defendant has substantial contacts with the United States as a whole but insufficient minimum contacts with any one state. The federal courts have periodically confronted the issue of when it is appropriate to *aggregate* national contacts for purposes of determining that the exercise of jurisdiction is consistent with "traditional notions of fair play and substantial justice." If aggregation is not allowed, it is possible that no court in the United States will be authorized to exercise personal jurisdiction over a foreign defendant who is fully "present" in the nation but not "in" any one state under *International Shoe*.

Some basic principles of federal law make this problem more difficult than might at first appear. A federal court may not exercise jurisdiction without legislative authorization, and, until 1993, the only general federal permission to exercise long-arm jurisdiction was Rule 4 of the Federal Rules of Civil Procedure, which directed a federal court *inter alia* to borrow the long-arm statute of the state in which it sat. But that led to a significant problem, as noted by the Advisory Committee on the Federal Rules of Civil Procedure,

> when the defendant was a non-resident of the United States having contacts with the United States sufficient to justify the application of United States law . . ., but having insufficient contact with any one state to support jurisdiction under state long-arm legislation, or meet the requirements of the Fourteenth Amendment limitation on state court territorial jurisdiction. In such cases, the defendant was shielded from the enforcement of federal law by the fortuity of a favorable limitation on the power of state courts which was incorporated into federal practice by the former rule [4].

In other words, because there was no general federal long-arm statute, the reach of a federal court was determined by the law of the state in which it sat. There was and could be no "common law rule authorizing service of process." *Omni Capital Int'l v. Rudolf Wolff & Co.*, 484 U.S. 97, 111(1987). In order to establish jurisdiction pursuant to a national contacts theory, a plaintiff was required to identify a federal statute which specifically authorized service of process and established personal jurisdiction over a defendant.

The 1993 Amendments to Rule 4 offered modest guidance in the analysis of cases where the federal interest might be strong but the jurisdictional contacts with any single state were weak. In pertinent part, the amended Rule provides:

4(k) **Territorial Limits of Effective Service.**

(1) Service of a summons . . . is effective to establish jurisdiction over the person of a defendant:

(A) who could be subjected to the jurisdiction of a court of general jurisdiction in the state in which the district court is located, or . . .

(D) when authorized by a statute of the United States.

(2) If the exercise of jurisdiction is consistent with the Constitution and laws of the United States, serving the summons . . . is also effective, with respect to claims arising under federal law, to establish personal jurisdiction over the person of any defendant who is not subject to the jurisdiction of the courts of general jurisdiction of any state.

These provisions effectively authorize federal jurisdiction in three types of circumstances: (i) when the federal court adopts the jurisdictional authority of the courts of the state in which it sits (Rule 4(k)(1)(A)); (ii) when federal legislation grants personal jurisdiction (Rule 4(k)(1)(D)); and (iii) when the Constitution allows the exercise of personal jurisdiction in certain cases arising under federal law (Rule 4(k)(2)). Predictably, it has fallen to the courts to interpret the sparse language of the amended Rule 4 and to define the prerequisites for aggregating contacts, especially under the latter two provisions.[1]

Rule 4(k)(1)(D) of the Federal Rules of Civil Procedure

---

[1] Rule 4(k)(1)(A) means in effect that "[a] state long-arm statute furnishes a mechanism for obtaining personal jurisdiction in federal as well as state courts." *United States v. Swiss American Bank*, 191 F.3d 30, 36 (1st Cir. 1999). Thus for example, "in a diversity case or a case that arises under a federal law which does not provide for service of process on a party outside the state, the issue of personal jurisdiction must be determined according to the law of the forum state. In such cases, the federal district court is constrained by the Fourteenth Amendment's requirements of minimum contacts with the forum state, instead of a national contacts analysis." *Smith v. S&S Dundalk Engineering Works, Ltd.*, 139 F. Supp.2d 610 (D.N.J. 2001) (*citing CFMT, Inc. v. Steag Microtech, Inc.*, 965 F.Supp. 561, 565 (D.Del. 1997) ("In the absence of a federal statute or rule authorizing nationwide or worldwide service of process, a court may not exercise jurisdiction on the basis of a defendant's national aggregated contacts.")). See the discussion of Rule 4(k)(1)(a) in *Wiwa v. Royal Dutch Petroleum, supra.*

GO-VIDEO, INC. v. AKAI ELECTRIC CO., LTD.
885 F.2d 1406 (9th Cir. 1989)

This is an interlocutory appeal from an order of the District Court for the District of Arizona in which we must decide two related questions: first, whether an antitrust plaintiff who serves process pursuant to the provisions of § 12 of the Clayton Act, 15 U.S.C. § 22, may properly establish venue under the Alien Venue Act, 28 U.S.C. § 1391(d); and second, whether it was error for the district court to exercise personal jurisdiction over alien defendants based on an assessment of their contacts with the United States as a whole, rather than their contacts with the forum district. The district court ruled that venue need not be established under the same statute which provides the basis for service of process, that venue lay properly in Arizona under the Alien Venue Act, and that the "national contacts" of the defendants were sufficient for the exercise of personal jurisdiction. We agree and affirm.

I.

The plaintiff in the underlying action, Go-Video, Inc. ("Go-Video"), is a Delaware corporation with its principal place of business in Arizona. Since 1984, Go-Video has apparently been attempting to purchase parts from which it could assemble a "dual deck" video cassette recorder, the "VCR-2," for which it holds a United States patent. In its complaint, Go-Video alleges that a number of foreign manufacturers of consumer electronics, a Japanese electronics trade association (collectively known as the "manufacturing defendants"), various domestic motion picture companies, and a motion picture trade association (the "motion picture defendants") conspired to prevent the marketing of dual deck VCR's in the United States and, pursuant to this allegedly illicit agreement, refused to deal with Go-Video. These actions, Go-Video claims, violated Section 1 of the Sherman Act, 15 U.S.C. § 1.

Go-Video served process on the manufacturing defendants through the long-arm provision of Section 12 of the Clayton Act, 15 U.S.C. § 22, which provides:

> Any suit, action, or proceeding under the antitrust laws against a corporation may be brought not only in the judicial district whereof it is an inhabitant, but also in any district wherein it may be found or transacts business; and all process in such cases may be served in the district of which it is an inhabitant, or wherever it may be found.

As each of the manufacturing defendants was an alien corporation, Go-Video filed suit in the United States District Court for the District of Arizona, alleging venue to be proper under the terms of the Alien Venue Act, codified at 28 U.S.C. § 1391(d): "An alien may be sued in any district."

The appellants here are the remaining manufacturing defendants, four Japanese and one Korean corporation. After being served by Go-Video, some of the manufacturing defendants filed motions to dismiss Go-Video's complaint for lack of personal jurisdiction and improper venue, under Fed.R.Civ.P. 12(b)(2) and (3). All parties eventually filed a "Joint Application for Determination of 'National Contacts' Issue of Law," asking the district court to rule definitively on the personal jurisdiction question. The district court ruled in favor of Go-Video, determining venue to be proper in Arizona and the use of "national contacts" analysis consistent with the approach sanctioned by this court in *Securities Investor Protection Corp. v. Vigman,* 764 F.2d 1309 (9th Cir. 1985) ("*Vigman*").

[The Ninth Circuit ruled that "venue for Go-Video's suit lies properly in the District of Arizona under 28 U.S.C. § 1391(d)."]

[W]e now address the related question whether personal jurisdiction could properly be exercised there. To exercise personal jurisdiction over a non-resident defendant in a federal question case, the district court had to determine that a rule or statute potentially confers jurisdiction over the defendant and then conclude that asserting jurisdiction does not offend the principles of Fifth Amendment due process.

In this case, the district judge looked first to Clayton Act § 12, a statute which . . . authorizes worldwide service of process. Given the scope of permissible service of process, he concluded that § 12 authorizes the exercise of personal jurisdiction over an alien corporation in any judicial district, so long as the corporation had sufficient minimum contacts with the United States at large, thus obviating the normal requirement that Go-Video demonstrate appellants' ties specific to the forum district. After choosing to apply this "national contacts" method of jurisdictional analysis, the judge considered whether Fifth Amendment considerations of fair play and substantial justice militated against the exercise of jurisdiction over the alien corporations. He concluded that such considerations were not offended by exercising jurisdiction over appellants and denied their motions to dismiss for want of personal jurisdiction. Appellants challenge both the proposition that the worldwide service of process provision of section 12 confers jurisdiction over an alien defendant based solely on its national contacts, as well as the district court's conclusion that the constitution is not offended by the exercise of personal jurisdiction based on national contacts analysis. We consider both issues below.[1]

A. National Contacts and Clayton Act § 12

The district court reasoned that, since process, under § 12, could be served anywhere in the country (indeed anywhere in the world) and since venue, under § 1391(d), was proper in any district, personal jurisdiction for an antitrust suit against an alien corporation could be obtained in any judicial district in the United States. Moreover, given the nationwide service provision of the Clayton Act, the court concluded that, in determining whether it could exercise personal jurisdiction over the alien defendants, it was proper to consider their national contacts.[2] In the latter respect particularly, the court

---

[1] Appellants apparently do not question the district court's conclusion that their contacts with the United States met the basic requirement imposed by *International Shoe* and its progeny — that a defendant maintain at least "minimum contacts" with the relevant forum. We thus assume that appellants' contacts are sufficient for the exercise of jurisdiction, as long as the Nation is the appropriate entity against which to assess them.

[2] We note that the Supreme Court has on two occasions explicitly declined to decide the constitutionality of national contacts analysis. *Omni Capital International v. Rudolf Wolff & Co., Ltd.,* 484 U.S. 97 n. 5 (1987); *Asahi Metal Industry v. Superior Court,* 480 U.S. 102 n. * (1987) (plurality opinion).

relied principally on our decision in *Vigman,* in which we held national contacts analysis to be appropriate in a suit in which process had been served on an alien corporation pursuant to § 27 of the Securities Exchange Act.

In *Vigman,* we reasoned that a federal statute which permits the service of process beyond the boundaries of the forum state broadens the authorized scope of personal jurisdiction. Under such a statute, " 'the question becomes whether the party has sufficient contacts with the United States, not any particular state'." Accordingly, we held that "so long as a defendant has minimum contacts with the United States, Section 27 of the [Securities Exchange] Act confers personal jurisdiction over the defendant in any federal district court."

Appellants argue that *Vigman* does not control this case, inasmuch as it concerned a claim under the Securities Exchange Act, not the Clayton Act. There are two logical flaws in this argument. First, we believe that § 27 of the Securities Exchange Act is a peculiarly apt statute from which to analogize to § 12 of the Clayton Act: the two statutes' service of process provisions are nearly identical; indeed, § 27's provision (". . . process may be served in any other district [i.e. districts other than the one in which suit is brought] of which the defendant is an inhabitant or wherever the defendant may be found") was modeled after § 12 (". . . process in such cases may be served in the district of which [the defendant] is an inhabitant, or wherever it may be found"). Second, the reasoning behind the *Vigman* holding is not essentially a function of the particular wording of a statute; rather, it flows from the fact that Congress has authorized service of process nationwide, in fact worldwide. As there is no dispute that § 12 authorizes nationwide service, there is no principled reason not to apply *Vigman's* reasoning in this case.

Vigman hardly stands alone in its adoption of national contacts analysis where Congress has authorized national service [citations omitted]. *See also* Lilly, *Jurisdiction Over Domestic and Alien Defendants*, 69 VA. L. REV. 85, 132 (1983) ("federal statutes conferring 'world-wide service of process' also permit a federal court to base its in personam jurisdiction upon the aggregate contacts [with the United States] of an alien defendant"). In light of *Vigman* and these other decisions, we believe that the district judge was clearly correct in his view and that the worldwide service provision of § 12 justifies its conclusion that personal jurisdiction may be established in any district, given the existence of sufficient national contacts.

B. Constitutional Considerations

Having determined that the district judge correctly concluded that Clayton Act § 12 "potentially confers personal jurisdiction over the [appellants]," we turn to his inquiry into the constitutional aspects of the exercise of personal jurisdiction. Under the due process component of the Fifth Amendment, a court must consider whether the maintenance of the suit (i.e. the exercise of personal jurisdiction over the defendants to the suit) offends traditional notions of fair play and substantial justice. The district judge, without adding much to his § 12 analysis discussed above, concluded that exercising jurisdiction over appellants based on their contacts with the United States was consistent with due process.

Appellants raise two basic objections to this conclusion, arguing first that the Supreme Court has in dictum rejected the theory which supports the constitutionality of national contacts analysis, and second that the burden of defending the suits in Arizona demonstrates, as a practical matter, the unconstitutional results which follow when national contacts analysis is applied. Neither argument has merit.

Appellants' first contention starts with the following passage from *Insurance Corp. of Ireland v. Compagnie des Bauxites de Guinee,* 456 U.S. 694 (1982):

> The requirement that a court have personal jurisdiction flows not from Article III, but from the Due Process Clause. The personal jurisdiction requirement recognizes and protects an individual liberty interest. It represents a restriction on judicial power not as a matter of sovereignty, but as a matter of individual liberty. Thus, the test for personal jurisdiction requires that "the maintenance of the suit . . . not offend 'traditional notions of fair play and substantial justice.' "

Appellants claim that this language rejects the notion that personal jurisdiction should be assessed by reference to the contacts with the Nation when the federal sovereign has provided for the cause of action. Furthermore, appellants contend, the federal cause of action theory is the only one that supports national contacts analysis. Their argument is fallacious, because it both reads too much into the *Bauxites* dictum and incorrectly describes the analytical basis for the national contacts approach.

Two observations are in order concerning the context of the quotation upon which appellants depend so heavily. First, the Supreme Court in *Bauxites* addressed questions only remotely relevant to those relating to the sufficiency of a defendant's contacts with a given forum; the case concerned the appropriateness of declaring certain jurisdictional facts admitted, or jurisdictional objections waived, when a party failed to comply with a district court's discovery orders. The quoted passage serves merely to introduce the discussion of the waivability of certain objections to personal jurisdiction. . . . Clearly, a more complete description of the *Bauxites* quotation demonstrates that, when read in context, appellants' passage has little or no relevance to our case. It simply says nothing about the proposition at issue.

On a less structural and more substantive plane, appellants' argument assumes that national contacts analysis is justified only by a particular notion of federal sovereignty in federal question cases. It is true that some courts have endorsed the national contacts approach based on the (not inarguable) proposition that, since the sovereign in federal question cases is the United States, the relevant contacts inquiry necessarily focuses on the Nation as a whole. Even so, as our decision here demonstrates, national contacts analysis more often finds its basis not in an abstract theory of sovereignty, but in the concrete language of a statute under which Congress has, as it is unquestionably empowered to, authorized nationwide service of process. Indeed, a recent Supreme Court decision implies that a national service provision is a necessary prerequisite for a court even to consider a national contacts approach. *See Omni Capital Int'l v. Rudolf Wolff & Co.,* 484 U.S. 97 (no need to address national contacts argument where no provision of statute authorized nationwide service). . . .

In light of our conclusion that there is no Supreme Court precedent to the contrary, we adhere to our decision in *Vigman* that, when a statute authorizes nationwide service of process, national contacts analysis is appropriate. In such cases, "due process demands [a showing of minimum contacts with the United States] with respect to foreign defendants" before a court can assert personal jurisdiction. See also *Amtrol [Inc. v. Vent-Rite Valve Corp.]*, 646 F. Supp. [1168, D. Mass. 1986,] at 1172 (when service effected under Clayton Act § 12, personal jurisdiction depends on the "familiar 'minimum contacts' analysis[;] however, the relevant forum is not [the state in which suit is brought], but rather the entire United States.")

Appellants' second argument is substantially more simple, and more simply dismissed. They advert to the burden placed on an alien defendant who must litigate in Arizona and conclude that this burden, imposed by virtue of national contacts analysis, is inherently violative of the "fair play and substantial justice" elements of due process. We are not persuaded by appellants' somewhat skeletal argument on this point. As an initial matter, the concerns appellants raise are far more akin to a *forum non conveniens* argument than to a jurisdictional one. Considerations underlying a non-jurisdictional doctrine like *forum non conveniens* must be kept separate from the constitutional and jurisdictional analyses we conduct here. See *Fitzsimmons [v. Barton]*, 589 F.2d [330, 7th Cir. 1979,] at 334 (declining to "import [factors properly suited to *forum non conveniens* analysis] into determination of the constitutionality of exercises of personal jurisdiction"). Second, if there is something peculiarly oppressive about litigating in Arizona, appellants are free to avail themselves of the venue transfer statute, . . . 28 U.S.C. § 1404(a), and seek to have the case transferred to another jurisdiction. As Go-Video observes, appellants have not done so.

CONCLUSION

Go-Video was entitled to serve process under 15 U.S.C. § 22, even while seeking to satisfy venue under 28 U.S.C. § 1391(d). Venue, under § 1391(d), was proper in the District of Arizona. In determining whether it could exercise personal jurisdiction over the appellants, the district court appropriately chose to examine the appellants' national contacts, correctly determined that due process was not offended by this decision, and properly ruled jurisdiction to exist.

Notes and Questions on *Go-Video* and Rule 4(k)(1)(D)

1. *Aggregation in the Supreme Court.* On two occasions, the Supreme Court has had the opportunity to address the constitutionality of aggregating national contacts for the purpose of establishing personal jurisdiction and has ducked the question both times. *Omni Capital Int'l v. Rudolf Wolff & Co.*, 484 U.S. 97, 102 (1987); *Asahi Metal Indus. Co. v. Superior Court*, 480 U.S. 102, 113 (1987). If there are no federalism concerns when the defendant is a foreign corporation from a foreign country, and if it is no more burdensome to defend

in one state than in any other, how might national aggregation offend the Due Process Clause?

2. *Broad statutory authorizations of process.* In addition to the Clayton Act as applied in *Go-Video*, numerous federal statutes permit world-wide or nation-wide service of process by any federal district court to any place that the foreign defendant "may be found" or "transacts business." Notably included are the Racketeer Influenced and Corrupt Organizations Act, 18 U.S.C. § 1965; the Federal Interpleader Act, 28 U.S.C. § 2361; the federal securities laws, 15 U.S.C. §§ 77v and 78aa; the Telemarketing and Consumer Fraud and Abuse Prevention Act, 15 U.S.C. § 6101; and the Federal Bankruptcy Code § 101 (23) (A) 1-4 and the Federal Rules of Bankruptcy Procedure, Rule 7004(d). What concerns might a court have about interpreting these acts in the same way as the *Go-Video* court?

3. *Triggering the Go-Video rule.* Under *Go-Video*, must the statute explicitly authorize the aggregation of national contacts, or would it be enough for the statute to authorize service so long as it was "consistent with the Due Process Clause"?

4. *Fifth versus Fourteenth Amendment due process standards.* The jurisdiction of the federal courts is determined by the Due Process Clause in the Fifth Amendment rather than the Fourteenth Amendment, which applies to the state courts. Is there reason to think that the requirements of these two provisions are not identical, and that the consequences in personal jurisdiction cases might be profound? Consider Justice White's observation in *World-Wide Volkswagen, supra*, that the Fourteenth Amendment is not simply concerned with fairness but also with the protection of "co-equal sovereigns in a federal system." By contrast, "when a *federal court* is hearing and deciding a *federal question* case there are no problems of 'co-equal sovereigns.' That is a Fourteenth Amendment concern which is not present in actions founded on federal substantive law." *Handley v. Indiana & Michigan Elec. Co.*, 732 F.2d 1265, 1271 (6th Cir. 1984) (emphasis supplied). *See also United Rope Distrib., Inc. v. Seatriumph Marine Corp.*, 930 F.2d 532 (7th Cir. 1991) ("When a national court applies national law, the due process clause requires only that the defendant possess sufficient contacts with the United States.")

5. *Aggregation and venue.* Should the venue provision of the act constrain the aggregation of national contacts? In *GTE Media Serv., Inc. v. Bellsouth Corp.*, 199 F.3d 1343 (D.C. Cir. 2000), the Court of Appeals for the District of Columbia held that the "invocation of the nationwide service clause rests on satisfying the venue provision" of the statute, *id.* at 1350, meaning that the defendant must be an inhabitant of, be found in, or transact business in the judicial district where the suit is brought. Under *GTE Media*,

> a plaintiff who wishes to use Section 12 for service of process must also establish venue under that provision. A plaintiff relying on the general alien statute to establish venue would then have to rely on the long-arm statute of the forum state to obtain service of process. See Fed. R. Civ. P. 4(k)(1)(A). The end result is that a foreign corporation may only be sued where it has some sort of local contacts, either contacts with the judicial district in which the suit is brought sufficient to satisfy the venue provision of Section 12 or contacts with

the forum state sufficient to allow for service of process under the relevant state long-arm statute.

William S. Dodge, *Antitrust and the Draft Hague Judgments Convention*, 32 LAW & POL. INT'L BUS. 363 (2001), at n. 21. Not all courts agree with the analysis of the court in *GTE Media. See, e.g., In re Magnetic Audiotape Antitrust Litigation*, 171 F. Supp. 2d 179, 2001 WL 434866 (S.D.N.Y. 2001)

6. *Aggregation under various categories of subject matter jurisdiction.* Suppose the federal court's subject matter jurisdiction were founded on diversity of citizenship or the Alien Tort Claims Act. Would the argument for aggregation of contacts be stronger or weaker than in federal question cases?

———

Rule 4(k)(2)

PYRENEE, LTD. v. WOCOM COMMODITIES LTD.
984 F. Supp. 1148 (E.D. Ill. 1997)

This suit represents the second attempt to litigate against the defendants in the United States to recover for an alleged commodity fraud scheme that occurred principally in Hong Kong. . . .

Pyrenee brings this lawsuit alleging violations of the Commodity Exchange Act ("CEA") in connection with trades that Wocom Commodities or Wocom Limited placed (or, in some cases, feigned placing) on the Chicago Mercantile Exchange ("CME"). Instead of executing the trades as Pyrenee requested, Wocom allegedly "bucketed" some, that is, conducted the trades privately in its Hong Kong office, and "stole the ticks" on others, that is, placed the trades but misrepresented their price and kept the difference. The legality of these rather complicated schemes is not at issue here. As an initial matter, we must confront the jurisdictional issues that Wocom raises in its motion. Reduced to its essentials, the motion contends that this Court lacks subject matter jurisdiction and personal jurisdiction over Pyrenee's claims; should these grounds fail, Wocom urges us to dismiss the suit on *forum non conveniens* or statute of limitations grounds. Although we find . . . personal jurisdiction, we ultimately dismiss this suit for its resolution in Hong Kong, a more convenient forum under the circumstances.

RELEVANT FACTS

A. The Parties' National Affiliations

The Wocom entities [Wocom Commodities and Wocom Limited] are Hong Kong corporations that do business in Hong Kong[, . . .] trading in spot bullion, foreign currency, foreign exchange, and United States commodities and futures. . . . Neither [defendant] has ever had offices in the United States or solicited customers from the United States. Nor have they registered as members of any United States exchange. As non-members, [they] must rely on a United States-based registered futures commission merchant to place their customers' trades on American exchanges.

Pyrenee was organized under the laws of Liberia and is registered there as an "Offshore Company." Offshore companies are not permitted to trade in Liberia, which serves as a tax haven for businesses that operate elsewhere. Pyrenee alleges that it does business in the United States as Pyrenee Real Estate Holding Co., a California business enterprise based in San Francisco and Menlo Park, CA. . . . Pyrenee's President, Michael Mak, is a Hong Kong citizen and resident. From 1980 to 1985, he lived in California, directing the operations of Pyrenee Real Estate Holding Co.

B. Trading in Pyrenee's Account

In May 1985, Mak returned to Hong Kong and opened a trading account with Wocom in Pyrenee's name. Mak signed a "General Agreement for Customer Accounts" ("the Agreement"), which provided that Wocom would act as Pyrenee's broker in executing trades for, among other things, foreign currency futures on various exchanges. Wocom acknowledged that any commodity trades in the United States would be subject to the Commodity Futures Trading Commission Act of 1974 and "any applicable Federal or State laws or regulations having the force of law." In the event of a legal dispute, the Agreement granted Pyrenee the right to proceed in any court of competent jurisdiction.

From May 1985 to June 1996, Mak conducted trading in the Pyrenee account from Hong Kong, spending much of his time in Wocom's offices for this purpose and for the purpose of placing trades in a personal account he maintained with Wocom. In July 1996, Mak went back to the United States for six months. Mak remained in California until December 1996, all the while directing trading in Pyrenee's Wocom account. Mak testifies that he frequently discussed Pyrenee's account with Wocom representatives on the phone during this time, but his affidavit does not specify who initiated the calls. Wocom claims it had no idea that Mak had returned to the United States, or for that matter, that Pyrenee maintained offices in California as a real estate holding company. Wocom's Director and General Manager testifies that all daily confirmations of Pyrenee's trades were sent to Mak's Hong Kong address. Mak states that the trade confirmations were forwarded to him in California, and contends that he made it clear to Wocom officials that California was his operational base in the latter half of 1996. According to Mak, Wocom acknowledged his change in residence by complying with requests to "notify" him (but it is unclear by what means) in California when various commodities reached threshold prices.

It was during the period of Mak's California residence — July to December 1986 — that Wocom allegedly began mishandling the Pyrenee account. Pyrenee claims that Wocom engaged in two distinct types of commodity fraud: "bucketing" and "stealing the ticks." Bucketing has been described as

> a method of doing business wherein orders of customers for the purchase or sale of commodities for future delivery, instead of being executed by bona fide purchases and sales with other traders, are simply matched and offset in the soliciting firm's own office and the firm itself takes the opposite side of the customer's orders.

Purdy v. CFTC, 968 F.2d 510, 520 (5th Cir. 1992). In accordance with this scheme, Wocom allegedly ignored Mak's requests to place foreign currency trades for Pyrenee on the CME and conducted the trades in its own offices instead, putting itself on the opposite side and reaping the profits. Secondly, Wocom allegedly "stole the ticks" from trades that it actually placed for Pyrenee on the CME. In other words, Wocom placed Pyrenee's trades as requested, but then "confirmed the orders at a less favorable price than executed at the exchange and kept the difference." Pyrenee allegedly did not discover this fraudulent activity until August 1994. . . .

D. Actions in the United States

. . . Mak . . . filed suit in the United States alleging that Wocom had bucketed trades in his personal futures account. That suit, which was filed one year before this litigation, was dismissed . . . for lack of subject matter jurisdiction. The Seventh Circuit affirmed the district court's ruling . . . [W]hile Mak's appeal was pending, Pyrenee brought this action in connection with its corporate account, alleging in Count I that Wocom bucketed Pyrenee's commodity futures trades and including in Count II a claim that was not formally asserted in Mak's action — tick stealing from Pyrenee's futures trades. Pyrenee claims that Wocom's bucketing and tick stealing both violate section 4b of the CEA.[1] We now turn to the issue of whether we have jurisdiction over these claims and, if so, whether we should nevertheless dismiss the action on *forum non conveniens* grounds.

ANALYSIS

* * *

II. Personal Jurisdiction

A. Legal Standards Governing Personal Jurisdiction

As is the case with subject matter jurisdiction, the plaintiff bears the burden of establishing personal jurisdiction. The court must assume the plaintiff's jurisdictional allegations are true unless controverted by the defendant's affidavits. Should the affidavits conflict, the court must resolve the discrepancy in favor of the plaintiff. The plaintiff's burden is to provide evidence that establishes a prima facie case for personal jurisdiction. In federal question cases, the prima facie case requirements are twofold: (1) haling the defendant into court must comport with Fifth Amendment Due Process; and (2) the defendant must be amenable to service of process.

These two prongs collapse into one, however, when the federal claim is brought against a foreign defendant who lacks "sufficient contacts to satisfy the due process concerns of the long-arm statute of any particular state." *World Tanker Carriers Corp. v. M/V Ya Mawlaya*, 99 F.3d 717, 720 (5th Cir. 1996). In such cases, the service of process provisions in Federal Rule of Civil Procedure 4(k)(2) apply. Rule 4(k)(2) conditions both personal jurisdiction and amenability to process on fulfilling federal constitutional dictates:

> If the exercise of jurisdiction is consistent with the Constitution and laws of the United States, serving a summons or filing a waiver of service is also effective, with respect to claims arising under federal

---

[1] This section prohibits any member of a contract market or its agent from defrauding any person in connection with the making of a futures contract on any contract market.

law, to establish personal jurisdiction over the person of any defendant who is not subject to the jurisdiction of the courts of general jurisdiction of any state.

Therefore, in Rule 4(k)(2) cases, the court makes only one inquiry: does the foreign defendant have sufficient contacts with the United States as a whole in order to satisfy Fifth Amendment Due Process requirements? This is . . . dubbed the "minimum contacts test" — the same constitutional analysis that the Seventh Circuit performs in all federal question cases. *See Martinez de Ortiz,* 910 F.2d at 382 (where claim raises a federal question, due process commands sufficient contacts only with the United States as a whole); *United Rope Distribs., Inc. v. Seatriumph Marine Corp.,* 930 F.2d 532, 534 (7th Cir. 1991) ("When a national court applies national law, the due process clause requires only that the defendant possess sufficient contacts with the United States."). Since Pyrenee does not contend that Wocom's contacts with this forum satisfy the Illinois long-arm statute, and relies exclusively on Rule 4(k)(2) to establish personal jurisdiction, we limit our analysis to determining whether Wocom maintains sufficient contacts with the United States for personal jurisdiction to lie under Rule 4(k)(2).

B. The Minimum Contacts Test Is Met

The minimum contacts test ensures that exercising federal jurisdiction in a particular case comports with "traditional notions of fair play and substantial justice." Minimum contacts exist if the defendant "should reasonably anticipate being haled into court" in the relevant forum because the defendant "has purposefully availed itself of the privilege of conducting activities" there. District courts in our Circuit have remarked how easily this due process requirement is satisfied, and indeed, we find that to be the case here.

By engaging in United States commodity trading through a United States agent and by acknowledging that its trading is subject to the laws of the United States, Wocom has purposefully availed itself of the privileges associated with conducting activity in this country. Wocom admits that brokering trades on United States exchanges in accordance with American laws is a regular part of its business. In addition, Wocom's General Agreement for Customer Accounts provides that "all commodity transactions for execution on Contract Markets in the United States are subject to the provisions of the Commodity Futures Trading Commission Act of 1974 and the rules and regulations promulgated thereunder . . . ." Along the same lines, the Agreement anticipates foreign jurisdiction arising from trading disputes. These concessions to United States regulation are compounded by the fact that Wocom's United States trades on the CME were significant steps in completing the fraud alleged in this case. Under these circumstances, we find that Pyrenee has met its burden of establishing a prima facie case for personal jurisdiction under Rule 4(k)(2) and its minimum contacts requirement.

Up until this point, we have devoted our resources to determining whether Pyrenee has satisfied the formal requisites for jurisdiction. We find that it has. We nevertheless decline to exercise our powers of jurisdiction because Wocom has met its burden of proving that Hong Kong is the more convenient forum for this dispute. [The court dismissed the case on *forum non conveniens* grounds. *See* Chapter 3 *infra.*]

Notes and Questions on *Pyrenee Ltd.* and Rule 4(k)(2)

1. *The burden of proof under Rule 4(k)(2).* "The fabric [of Rule 4(k)(2)] contains three strands: (1) the plaintiff's claim must be one arising under federal law; (2) the putative defendant must be beyond the jurisdictional reach of any state court of general jurisdiction [the so-called "negation requirement"]; and (3) the federal courts' exercise of personal jurisdiction over the defendant must not offend the Constitution or other federal law." *United States v. Swiss American Bank*, 191 F.3d 30, 38 (1st Cir. 1999).

But who should bear the burden of proving that each of these three criteria — especially the negation requirement — is satisfied?

> "[A] plaintiff ordinarily must shoulder the burden of proving personal jurisdiction over the defendant. Some district courts, relying on this shibboleth, have assigned outright to plaintiffs the burden of proving the Rule 4(k)(2) negation requirement. This paradigm in effect requires a plaintiff to prove a negative fifty times over — an epistemological quandary which is compounded by the fact that the defendant typically controls much of the information needed to determine the existence and/or magnitude of its contacts with any given jurisdiction. There is a corresponding problem with assigning the burden of proof on the Rule 4(k)(2) negation requirement to defendants: doing so threatens to place a defendant in a "Catch-22" situation, forcing it to choose between conceding its potential amenability to suit in federal court (by denying that any state court has jurisdiction over it) or conceding its potential amenability to suit in some identified state court.
>
> Faced with such dilemmas, courts historically have tailored special burden-of-proof regimes for specific classes of cases in order to strike an equitable balance. We believe that Rule 4(k)(2) is fertile territory for such an innovation. The architects of the rule—and Congress, by adopting it — clearly intended to . . . ensure that persons whose contacts with this country exceeded the constitutional minimum could not easily evade civil liability in the American justice system. At the same time, however, the drafters also wrote the rule to preserve the established modalities for obtaining personal jurisdiction previously available under Rule 4(k)(1)(A) as the primary avenue to service on foreign defendants. The desire to achieve this secondary purpose led the authors of the rule to restrict its reach to those defendants with sufficient nationwide contacts to subject them to federal jurisdiction, but whose contacts were too exiguous to permit any state court to exercise personal jurisdiction over them. Viewed in this light, the application of traditional burden-of-proof principles to Rule 4(k)(2) cases not only would be inequitable, but also would shield foreign defendants

who were constitutionally within the reach of federal courts from the exercise of personal jurisdiction, and, thus, thwart the core purpose that underlies the rule.

In our view, this core purpose can be achieved much more salubriously by crafting a special burden-shifting framework. To accomplish the desired end without placing the judicial thumb too heavily on the scale, we will not assign the burden of proof on the negation issue to either party in a monolithic fashion. We prefer instead to draw upon the burden-shifting arrangement devised by the Court to cope with somewhat analogous problems of proof in the discrimination context. . . .

We hold that a plaintiff who seeks to invoke Rule 4(k)(2) must make a prima facie case for the applicability of the rule. This includes a tripartite showing (1) that the claim asserted arises under federal law, (2) that personal jurisdiction is not available under any situation-specific federal statute, and (3) that the putative defendant's contacts with the nation as a whole suffice to satisfy the applicable constitutional requirements. The plaintiff, moreover, must certify that, based on the information that is readily available to the plaintiff and his counsel, the defendant is not subject to suit in the courts of general jurisdiction of any state. If the plaintiff makes out his prima facie case, the burden shifts to the defendant to produce evidence which, if credited, would show either that one or more specific states exist in which it would be subject to suit or that its contacts with the United States are constitutionally insufficient. . . . Should the defendant default on its burden of production, the trier may infer that personal jurisdiction over the defendant is not available in any state court of general jurisdiction. If, however, the defendant satisfies its second-stage burden of production, then the aforementioned inference drops from the case.

What happens next depends on how the defendant satisfies its burden. If the defendant produces evidence indicating that it is subject to jurisdiction in a particular state, the plaintiff has three choices: he may move for a transfer to a district within that state, or he may discontinue his action (preliminary, perhaps, to the initiation of a suit in the courts of the identified state), or he may contest the defendant's proffer. If the plaintiff elects the last-mentioned course, the defendant will be deemed to have waived any claim that it is subject to personal jurisdiction in the courts of general jurisdiction of any state other than the state or states which it has identified, and the plaintiff, to fulfill the negation requirement, must prove that the defendant is not subject to suit in the identified forum(s).

Of course, the defendant may satisfy its burden of production by maintaining that it cannot constitutionally be subjected to jurisdiction in any state court. In that event, the defendant will be deemed to have conceded the negation issue, and the plaintiff, to succeed in his Rule 4(k)(2) initiative, need only prove that his claim arises under federal law and that the defendant has contacts with the United States as a whole sufficient to permit a federal court constitutionally to exercise personal jurisdiction over it.

We think that this schematic fairly balances the equities and comports with congressional intent, particularly since we envision the defendant's burden as a burden of production only. The plaintiff at all times retains the devoir of persuasion on the ultimate issue. And while the burden-shifting framework puts defendants in an admittedly uncomfortable litigating position, that is to some degree the object of Rule 4(k)(2)."

Id. at 40.

2. *Rule 4(k)(2) and state substantive law.* Suppose that a plaintiff's claims arise under California unfair competition law, but the lawsuit is filed in federal district court in Los Angeles under the diversity statute. Could Rule 4(k)(2) — as interpreted in *Pyrenee Ltd.* — be used to establish personal jurisdiction on the basis of the defendant's aggregate contacts with the United States?

According to the Advisory Committee Notes, Rule 4(k)(2) does not establish personal jurisdiction "if the only claims are those arising under state law or the law of another country, even though there might be diversity or alienage subject matter jurisdiction as to such claims." Why not, and why might the rule have been drafted that way?

3. *The meaning of "federal law" for purposes of Rule 4(k)(2).* Rule 4(k)(2) applies only "with respect to claims arising under federal law." Suppose the plaintiff's claim arises under a treaty of the United States or customary international law. Is that sufficiently "federal" to trigger the rule?

Chapter 3

DETERMINING THE PROPER FORUM

Transnational litigation routinely requires the courts to decide whether they *should* hear cases that are admittedly within their power. The court may well have personal jurisdiction over a foreign defendant and subject matter jurisdiction over the case, for example, but the plaintiff's choice of forum is nonetheless unfair to the defendant or imprudent from the court's institutional perspective. The difficulties of gathering evidence abroad, not to mention the prospect of harassing a defendant through distant litigation, may lead a court in its discretion to dismiss a case precisely because the chosen forum is seriously inconvenient or inappropriate. Even when the parties attempt by contract to pre-select a forum for the resolution of disputes, the court may nonetheless invoke its discretionary power to dismiss the case.

The purpose of this chapter is to explore the possibility that this discretion has a structure to it, even if the idea of convenience — standing alone — can be an amorphous concept.

Forum non conveniens is the common law doctrine under which a court may decline to exercise judicial jurisdiction, when some significantly more convenient alternative forum exists. In the United States, the touchstone for all litigation under the *forum non conveniens* doctrine is *Gulf Oil Corp. v. Gilbert*, 330 U.S. 501 (1947), and its companion case, *Koster v. Lumbermens Mut. Cas. Co.*, 330 U.S. 518 (1947). In those decisions, the Supreme Court endorsed a presumption in favor of the plaintiff's choice of forum, directing that that choice be disturbed only rarely and in compelling circumstances.

Specifically, the court is to engage in a two-step process. *First*, it must determine if an adequate alternative forum exists, and much litigation turns on the adequacy of the apparent alternative: what if the applicable law in the alternative forum is less favorable to the plaintiff in the alternative forum? What if the statute of limitations has run there? What if the court is unsure about the quality of justice meted out in an alternative forum that is available? What if the unavailability of a foreign forum is the plaintiff's own fault? *Second*, assuming that an adequate alternative forum exists, the court must balance a constellation of factors involving the private interests of the parties and any public interests that may be at stake, all for the purpose of determining whether trial in the chosen forum would "establish . . . oppressiveness and vexation to a defendant . . . out of all proportion to plaintiff's convenience," or whether the "chosen forum [is] inappropriate because of considerations affecting the court's own administrative and legal problems." *Koster*, *supra*, at 524.

To guide the lower courts' discretion, the Supreme Court has provided a list of "private interest factors" affecting the convenience of the litigants, and a list of "public interest factors" affecting the convenience of the forum:

The factors pertaining to the private interests of the litigants included the "[1] relative ease of access to sources of proof; [2] availability of compulsory process for attendance of unwilling, and the cost of obtaining attendance of willing, witnesses; [3] possibility of view of premises, if view would be appropriate to the action; and [4] all other practical problems that make trial of a case easy, expeditious and inexpensive." *Gilbert*, 330 U.S., at 508. The public factors bearing on the question included [1] the administrative difficulties flowing from court congestion; [2] the "local interest in having localized controversies decided at home;" [3] the interest in having the trial of a diversity case in a forum that is at home with the law that must govern the action; [4] the avoidance of unnecessary problems in conflict of laws, or in the application of foreign law; and [5] the unfairness of burdening citizens in an unrelated forum with jury duty. *Id.*, at 509.

Piper Aircraft Co. v. Reyno, 454 U.S. 235 (1982). The defendant bears the burden of establishing that an adequate alternative forum exists and that the pertinent factors "tilt[] strongly in favor of trial in the foreign forum." *R. Maganlal & Co.v. M.G. Chemical Co. Inc.*, 942 F.2d 164, 167 (2d Cir. 1991), again with the understanding that "the plaintiff's choice of forum should rarely be disturbed." *Gilbert*, 330 U.S. at 508.

Neither *Gilbert* nor *Koster* was an international case. Both tested the reach of the *forum non conveniens* doctrine in cases involving different states of the Union, and the question now is whether the public and private factors announced in these cases need to be modified in transnational cases or replaced altogether with a different set of criteria. After all, globalization — whether in the form of e-commerce, international intellectual property, or human rights law — puts paradoxical pressure on the *forum non conveniens* doctrine. From one perspective, the rise of transnational litigation will raise the prospect of court proceedings in a distant forum under unfamiliar rules, suggesting that foreign defendants will increasingly argue that the exercise of jurisdiction would be imprudent even if it is constitutional. On the other hand, the very forces that give rise to transnational litigation may reduce the inconvenience of foreign litigation, especially with the digitization of information, nearly instantaneous communication, the internationalization of virtually every economy on earth, and the harmonization of law across borders. How exactly should a doctrine with its roots in the eighteenth century change to reflect these contemporary realities?

A. THE INCONVENIENT FORUM DOCTRINE IN A SHRINKING WORLD

In the United States, the presence of corporate defendants, combined with generous standards of personal jurisdiction, substantial damage awards, and the rules governing attorneys fees, make a U.S. forum especially attractive to foreign plaintiffs. "As a moth is drawn to the light, so is a litigant drawn to the United States. If he can only get his case into their courts, he stands to win a fortune." *Smith Kline & French Labs. v. Bloch*, [1983] 2 All. E.R. 72, 74. Should the U.S. courts take the nationality of the parties into account in applying the doctrine of *forum non conveniens*? If not, what presumptions and standards should apply in U.S. courts in those common circumstances when one party is based in the United States and the other is not?

PIPER AIRCRAFT CO. v. REYNO
454 U.S. 235 (1982)

These cases arise out of an air crash that took place in Scotland. Respondent, acting as representative of the estates of several Scottish citizens killed in the accident, brought wrongful-death actions against petitioners that were ultimately transferred to the United States District Court for the Middle District of Pennsylvania. Petitioners moved to dismiss on the ground of *forum non conveniens*. After noting that an alternative forum existed in Scotland, the District Court granted their motions. The United States Court of Appeals for the Third Circuit reversed. The Court of Appeals based its decision, at least in part, on the ground that dismissal is automatically barred where the law of the alternative forum is less favorable to the plaintiff than the law of the forum chosen by the plaintiff. Because we conclude that the possibility of an unfavorable change in law should not, by itself, bar dismissal, and because we conclude that the District Court did not otherwise abuse its discretion, we reverse.

I

In July 1976, a small commercial aircraft crashed in the Scottish highlands during the course of a charter flight from Blackpool to Perth. The pilot and five passengers were killed instantly. The decedents were all Scottish subjects and residents, as are their heirs and next of kin. There were no eyewitnesses to the accident. At the time of the crash, the plane was subject to Scottish air traffic control. The aircraft, a twin-engine Piper Aztec, was manufactured in Pennsylvania by petitioner Piper Aircraft Co. (Piper). The propellers were manufactured in Ohio by petitioner Hartzell Propeller, Inc. (Hartzell). At the time of the crash, the aircraft was registered in Great Britain and was owned and maintained by Air Navigation and Trading Co., Ltd. (Air Navigation). It was operated by McDonald Aviation, Ltd. (McDonald), a Scottish air taxi service. Both Air Navigation and McDonald were organized in the United Kingdom. The wreckage of the plane is now in a hangar in Farnsborough, England.

The British Department of Trade investigated the accident shortly after it occurred. A preliminary report found that the plane crashed after developing a spin, and suggested that mechanical failure in the plane or the propeller was responsible. At Hartzell's request, this report was reviewed by a three-member Review Board, which held a 9-day adversary hearing attended by all interested parties. The Review Board found no evidence of defective equipment and indicated that pilot error may have contributed to the accident. The pilot, who had obtained his commercial pilot's license only three months earlier, was flying over high ground at an altitude considerably lower than the minimum height required by his company's operations manual. . . .

[A] California probate court appointed respondent Gaynell Reyno administratrix of the estates of the five passengers. . . . Several days after her appointment, Reyno commenced separate wrongful-death actions against Piper and Hartzell in the Superior Court of California, claiming negligence and strict liability. . . . Reyno candidly admits that the action against Piper and Hartzell was filed in the United States because its laws regarding liability, capacity to sue, and damages are more favorable to her position than are those of Scotland. Scottish law does not recognize strict liability in tort. Moreover, it permits wrongful-death actions only when brought by a decedent's relatives. The relatives may sue only for "loss of support and society." . . .

. . . [A]fter the suit had been transferred [to a federal district court in Pennsylvania pursuant to 28 U.S.C. § 1404(a)], both Hartzell and Piper moved to dismiss the action on the ground of *forum non conveniens*. The District Court granted these motions . . . rel[ying] on the balancing test set forth by this Court in *Gulf Oil Corp. v. Gilbert*, and its companion case, *Koster v. Lumbermens Mut. Cas. Co.* . . . . [When] the District Court analyzed the facts of [this] case[,] it began by observing that an alternative forum existed in Scotland; Piper and Hartzell had agreed to submit to the jurisdiction of the Scottish courts and to waive any statute of limitations defense that might be available. It then stated that plaintiff's choice of forum was entitled to little weight. The court recognized that a plaintiff's choice ordinarily deserves substantial deference. It noted, however, that Reyno "is a representative of foreign citizens and residents seeking a forum in the United States because of the more liberal rules concerning products liability law," and that "the courts have been less solicitous when the plaintiff is not an American citizen or resident, and particularly when the foreign citizens seek to benefit from the more liberal tort rules provided for the protection of citizens and residents of the United States."

The District Court next examined several factors relating to the private interests of the litigants, and determined that these factors strongly pointed towards Scotland as the appropriate forum. Although evidence concerning the design, manufacture, and testing of the plane and propeller is located in the United States, the connections with Scotland are otherwise "overwhelming." The real parties in interest are citizens of Scotland, as were all the decedents. Witnesses who could testify regarding the maintenance of the aircraft, the training of the pilot, and the investigation of the accident — all essential to the defense — are in Great Britain. Moreover, all witnesses to damages are located in Scotland. Trial would be aided by familiarity with Scottish topography, and by easy access to the wreckage.

The District Court reasoned that because crucial witnesses and evidence were beyond the reach of compulsory process, and because the defendants would not be able to implead potential Scottish third-party defendants, it would be "unfair to make Piper and Hartzell proceed to trial in this forum." The survivors had brought separate actions in Scotland against the pilot, McDonald, and Air Navigation. "[I]t would be fairer to all parties and less costly if the entire case was presented to one jury with available testimony from all relevant witnesses." Although the court recognized that if trial were held in the United States, Piper and Hartzell could file indemnity or contribution actions against the Scottish defendants, it believed that there was a significant risk of inconsistent verdicts.[1]

The District Court concluded that the relevant public interests also pointed strongly towards dismissal. The court determined that Pennsylvania law would apply to Piper and Scottish law to Hartzell if the case were tried in the Middle District of Pennsylvania.[2] As a result, "trial in this forum would be hopelessly complex and confusing for a jury." In addition, the court noted that it was unfamiliar with Scottish law and thus would have to rely upon experts from that country. The court also found that the trial would be enormously costly and time-consuming; that it would be unfair to burden citizens with jury duty when the Middle District of Pennsylvania has little connection with the controversy; and that Scotland has a substantial interest in the outcome of the litigation.

In opposing the motions to dismiss, respondent contended that dismissal would be unfair because Scottish law was less favorable. The District Court explicitly rejected this claim. It reasoned that the possibility that dismissal might lead to an unfavorable change in the law did not deserve significant weight; any deficiency in the foreign law was a "matter to be dealt with in the foreign forum."

On appeal, the United States Court of Appeals for the Third Circuit reversed and remanded for trial. The decision to reverse appears to be based on two alternative grounds. First, the Court held that the District Court abused its discretion in conducting the *Gilbert* analysis. Second, the Court held that dismissal is never appropriate where the law of the alternative forum is less favorable to the plaintiff. . . . In this opinion, we begin by considering whether the Court of Appeals properly held that the possibility of an unfavorable change in law automatically bars dismissal. Since we conclude that the Court of Appeals erred, we then consider its review of the District Court's *Gilbert* analysis to determine whether dismissal was otherwise appropriate. . . .

II

The Court of Appeals erred in holding that plaintiffs may defeat a motion to dismiss on the ground of *forum non conveniens* merely by showing that the substantive law that would be applied in the alternative forum is less

---

[1] The District Court explained that inconsistent verdicts might result if petitioners were held liable on the basis of strict liability here, and then required to prove negligence in an indemnity action in Scotland. Moreover, even if the same standard of liability applied, there was a danger that different juries would find different facts and produce inconsistent results.

[2] Under *Klaxon v. Stentor Electric Mfg. Co.*, 313 U.S. 487 (1941), a court ordinarily must apply the choice-of-law rules of the State in which it sits. However, where a case is transferred pursuant to 28 U.S.C. § 1404(a), it must apply the choice-of-law rules of the State from which the case was transferred. *Van Dusen v. Barrack*, 376 U.S. 612 (1946). Relying on these two cases, the District Court concluded that California choice-of-law rules would apply to Piper, and Pennsylvania choice-of-law rules would apply to Hartzell. It further concluded that California applied a "governmental interests" analysis in resolving choice-of-law problems, and that Pennsylvania employed a "significant contacts" analysis. The court used the "governmental interests" analysis to determine that Pennsylvania liability rules would apply to Piper, and the "significant contacts" analysis to determine that Scottish liability rules would apply to Hartzell.

favorable to the plaintiffs than that of the present forum. The possibility of a change in substantive law should ordinarily not be given conclusive or even substantial weight in the *forum non conveniens* inquiry.

We expressly rejected the position adopted by the Court of Appeals in our decision in *Canada Malting Co. v. Paterson Steamships, Ltd.*, 285 U.S. 413 (1932). That case arose out of a collision between two vessels in American waters. The Canadian owners of cargo lost in the accident sued the Canadian owners of one of the vessels in federal district court. The cargo owners chose an American court in large part because the relevant American liability rules were more favorable than the Canadian rules. The district court dismissed on grounds of *forum non conveniens*. The plaintiffs argued that dismissal was inappropriate because Canadian laws were less favorable to them. This Court nonetheless affirmed:

> We have no occasion to enquire by what law the rights of the parties are governed, as we are of the opinion that, under any view of that question, it lay within the discretion of the District Court to decline to assume jurisdiction over the controversy. . . . '[T]he court will not take cognizance of the case if justice would be as well done by remitting the parties to their home forum.

The Court further stated that "[t]here was no basis for the contention that the District Court abused its discretion."

It is true that *Canada Malting* was decided before *Gilbert*, and that the doctrine of *forum non conveniens* was not fully crystallized until our decision in that case. However, *Gilbert* in no way affects the validity of *Canada Malting*. Indeed, by holding that the central focus of the *forum non conveniens* inquiry is convenience, *Gilbert* implicitly recognized that dismissal may not be barred solely because of the possibility of an unfavorable change in law. Under *Gilbert*, dismissal will ordinarily be appropriate where trial in the plaintiff's chosen forum imposes a heavy burden on the defendant or the court, and where the plaintiff is unable to offer any specific reasons of convenience supporting his choice.[3] If substantial weight were given to the possibility of an unfavorable change in law, however, dismissal might be barred even where trial in the chosen forum was plainly inconvenient.

The Court of Appeals' decision is inconsistent with this Court's earlier *forum non conveniens* decisions in another respect. Those decisions have repeatedly emphasized the need to retain flexibility. In *Gilbert*, the Court refused to identify specific circumstances "which will justify or require either grant or denial of remedy." Similarly, in *Koster*, the Court rejected the contention that where a trial would involve inquiry into the internal affairs of a foreign corporation, dismissal was always appropriate. "That is one, but only one, factor which may show convenience." And in *Williams v. Green Bay & Western R. Co.*, 326 U.S. 549, 557 (1946), we stated that we would not lay down a rigid rule to govern discretion, and that "[e]ach case turns on its facts." If central

---

[3] In other words, *Gilbert* held that dismissal may be warranted where a plaintiff chooses a particular forum, not because it is convenient, but solely in order to harass the defendant or take advantage of favorable law. This is precisely the situation in which the Court of Appeals' rule would bar dismissal.

emphasis were placed on any one factor, the *forum non conveniens* doctrine would lose much of the very flexibility that makes it so valuable.

In fact, if conclusive or substantial weight were given to the possibility of a change in law, the *forum non conveniens* doctrine would become virtually useless. Jurisdiction and venue requirements are often easily satisfied. As a result, many plaintiffs are able to choose from among several forums. Ordinarily, these plaintiffs will select that forum whose choice-of-law rules are most advantageous. Thus, if the possibility of an unfavorable change in substantive law is given substantial weight in the *forum non conveniens* inquiry, dismissal would rarely be proper. . . .

The Court of Appeals' approach is not only inconsistent with the purpose of the *forum non conveniens* doctrine, but also poses substantial practical problems. If the possibility of a change in law were given substantial weight, deciding motions to dismiss on the ground of *forum non conveniens* would become quite difficult. Choice-of-law analysis would become extremely important, and the courts would frequently be required to interpret the law of foreign jurisdictions. First, the trial court would have to determine what law would apply if the case were tried in the chosen forum, and what law would apply if the case were tried in the alternative forum. It would then have to compare the rights, remedies, and procedures available under the law that would be applied in each forum. Dismissal would be appropriate only if the court concluded that the law applied by the alternative forum is as favorable to the plaintiff as that of the chosen forum. The doctrine of *forum non conveniens*, however, is designed in part to help courts avoid conducting complex exercises in comparative law. As we stated in *Gilbert*, the public interest factors point towards dismissal where the court would be required to "untangle problems in conflict of laws, and in law foreign to itself."

Upholding the decision of the Court of Appeals would result in other practical problems. At least where the foreign plaintiff named an American manufacturer as defendant, a court could not dismiss the case on grounds of *forum non conveniens* where dismissal might lead to an unfavorable change in law. The American courts, which are already extremely attractive to foreign plaintiffs,[4] would become even more attractive. The flow of litigation into the United States would increase and further congest already crowded courts.[5]

. . .

---

[4] First, all but 6 of the 50 American States — Delaware, Massachusetts, Michigan, North Carolina, Virginia, and Wyoming — offer strict liability. Rules roughly equivalent to American strict liability are effective in France, Belgium, and Luxembourg. West Germany and Japan have a strict liability statute for pharmaceuticals. However, strict liability remains primarily an American innovation. Second, the tort plaintiff may choose, at least potentially, from among 50 jurisdictions if he decides to file suit in the United States. Each of these jurisdictions applies its own set of malleable choice-of-law rules. Third, jury trials are almost always available in the United States, while they are never provided in civil law jurisdictions. Even in the United Kingdom, most civil actions are not tried before a jury. Fourth, unlike most foreign jurisdictions, American courts allow contingent attorney's fees, and do not tax losing parties with their opponents' attorney's fees. Fifth, discovery is more extensive in American than in foreign courts.

[5] In holding that the possibility of a change in law unfavorable to the plaintiff should not be given substantial weight, we also necessarily hold that the possibility of a change in law favorable to defendant should not be considered. Respondent suggests that Piper and Hartzell filed the motion to dismiss, not simply because trial in the United States would be inconvenient, but also

We do not hold that the possibility of an unfavorable change in law should never be a relevant consideration in a *forum non conveniens* inquiry. Of course, if the remedy provided by the alternative forum is so clearly inadequate or unsatisfactory that it is no remedy at all, the unfavorable change in law may be given substantial weight; the district court may conclude that dismissal would not be in the interests of justice.[6] In these cases, however, the remedies that would be provided by the Scottish courts do not fall within this category. Although the relatives of the decedents may not be able to rely on a strict liability theory, and although their potential damages award may be smaller, there is no danger that they will be deprived of any remedy or treated unfairly.

III

The court of appeals also erred in rejecting the district court's *Gilbert* analysis. The court of appeals stated that more weight should have been given to the plaintiff's choice of forum, and criticized the district court's analysis of the private and public interests. However, the district court's decision regarding the deference due plaintiff's choice of forum was appropriate. Furthermore, we do not believe that the district court abused its discretion in weighing the private and public interests.

The district court acknowledged that there is ordinarily a strong presumption in favor of the plaintiff's choice of forum, which may be overcome only when the private and public interest factors clearly point towards trial in the alternative forum. It held, however, that the presumption applies with less force when the plaintiff or real parties in interest are foreign.

The district court's distinction between resident or citizen plaintiffs and foreign plaintiffs is fully justified. In *Koster*, the Court indicated that a plaintiff's choice of forum is entitled to greater deference when the plaintiff has chosen the home forum.[7] When the home forum has been chosen, it is

---

because they believe the laws of Scotland are more favorable. She argues that this should be taken into account in the analysis of the private interests. We recognize, of course, that Piper and Hartzell may be engaged in reverse forum-shopping. However, this possibility ordinarily should not enter into a trial court's analysis of the private interests. If the defendant is able to overcome the presumption in favor of plaintiff by showing that trial in the chosen forum would be unnecessarily burdensome, dismissal is appropriate— regardless of the fact that defendant may also be motivated by a desire to obtain a more favorable forum.

[6] At the outset of any *forum non conveniens* inquiry, the court must determine whether there exists an alternative forum. Ordinarily, this requirement will be satisfied when the defendant is "amenable to process" in the other jurisdiction. *Gilbert*, 330 U.S., at 506–507. In rare circumstances, however, where the remedy offered by the other forum is clearly unsatisfactory, the other forum may not be an adequate alternative, and the initial requirement may not be satisfied. Thus, for example, dismissal would not be appropriate where the alternative forum does not permit litigation of the subject matter of the dispute. Cf. *Phoenix Canada Oil Co. Ltd. v. Texaco, Inc.*, 78 F.R.D. 445 (Del. 1978) (court refuses to dismiss, where alternative forum is Ecuador, it is unclear whether Ecuadorean tribunal will hear the case, and there is no generally codified Ecuadorean legal remedy for the unjust enrichment and tort claims asserted).

[7] In *Koster*, we stated that "[i]n any balancing of conveniences, a real showing of convenience by a plaintiff who has sued in his home forum will normally outweigh the inconvenience the defendant may have shown." . . . As the district court correctly noted in its opinion, the lower federal courts have routinely given less weight to a foreign plaintiff's choice of forum. . . . A citizen's forum choice should not be given dispositive weight, however. Citizens or residents deserve somewhat more deference than foreign plaintiffs, but dismissal should not be automati-

reasonable to assume that this choice is convenient. When the plaintiff is foreign, however, this assumption is much less reasonable. Because the central purpose of any *forum non conveniens* inquiry is to ensure that the trial is convenient, a foreign plaintiff's choice deserves less deference.

The *forum non conveniens* determination is committed to the sound discretion of the trial court. It may be reversed only when there has been a clear abuse of discretion; where the court has considered all relevant public and private interest factors, and where its balancing of these factors is reasonable, its decision deserves substantial deference. Here, the court of appeals expressly acknowledged that the standard of review was one of abuse of discretion. In examining the district court's analysis of the public and private interests, however, the court of appeals seems to have lost sight of this rule, and substituted its own judgment for that of the district court.

In analyzing the private interest factors, the district court stated that the connections with Scotland are "overwhelming." This characterization may be somewhat exaggerated. Particularly with respect to the question of relative ease of access to sources of proof, the private interests point in both directions. As respondent emphasizes, records concerning the design, manufacture, and testing of the propeller and plane are located in the United States. She would have greater access to sources of proof relevant to her strict liability and negligence theories if trial were held here.[8] However, the district court did not act unreasonably in concluding that fewer evidentiary problems would be posed if the trial were held in Scotland. A large proportion of the relevant evidence is located in Great Britain.

The court of appeals found that the problems of proof could not be given any weight because Piper and Hartzell failed to describe with specificity the evidence they would not be able to obtain if trial were held in the United States. It suggested that defendants seeking *forum non conveniens* dismissal must submit affidavits identifying the witnesses they would call and the testimony these witnesses would provide if the trial were held in the alternative forum. Such detail is not necessary. Piper and Hartzell have moved for dismissal precisely because many crucial witnesses are located beyond the reach of compulsory process, and thus are difficult to identify or interview. Requiring extensive investigation would defeat the purpose of their motion. Of course, defendants must provide enough information to enable the district court to balance the parties' interests. Our examination of the record convinces us that sufficient information was provided here. Both Piper and Hartzell submitted affidavits describing the evidentiary problems they would face if the trial were held in the United States.[9]

---

cally barred when a plaintiff has filed suit in his home forum. As always, if the balance of conveniences suggests that trial in the chosen forum would be unnecessarily burdensome for the defendant or the court, dismissal is proper. . . .

[8] In the future, where similar problems are presented, district courts might dismiss subject to the condition that defendant corporations agree to provide the records relevant to the plaintiff's claims.

[9] . . . The affidavit provided to the district court by Piper states that it would call the following witnesses: the relatives of the decedents; the owners and employees of McDonald; the persons responsible for the training and licensing of the pilot; the persons responsible for servicing and maintaining the aircraft; and two or three of its own employees involved in the design and manufacture of the aircraft.

The district court correctly concluded that the problems posed by the inability to implead potential third-party defendants clearly supported holding the trial in Scotland. Joinder of the pilot's estate, Air Navigation, and McDonald is crucial to the presentation of petitioners' defense. If Piper and Hartzell can show that the accident was caused not by a design defect, but rather by the negligence of the pilot, the plane's owners, or the charter company, they will be relieved of all liability. It is true, of course, that if Hartzell and Piper were found liable after a trial in the United States, they could institute an action for indemnity or contribution against these parties in Scotland. It would be far more convenient, however, to resolve all claims in one trial. The court of appeals rejected this argument. Forcing petitioners to rely on actions for indemnity or contributions would be "burdensome" but not "unfair." Finding that trial in the plaintiff's chosen forum would be burdensome, however, is sufficient to support dismissal on grounds of *forum non conveniens*.

The district court's review of the factors relating to the public interest was also reasonable. On the basis of its choice-of-law analysis, it concluded that if the case were tried in the Middle District of Pennsylvania, Pennsylvania law would apply to Piper and Scottish law to Hartzell. It stated that a trial involving two sets of laws would be confusing to the jury. It also noted its own lack of familiarity with Scottish law. Consideration of these problems was clearly appropriate under *Gilbert*; in that case we explicitly held that the need to apply foreign law pointed towards dismissal.[10] The court of appeals found that the district court's choice-of-law analysis was incorrect, and that American law would apply to both Hartzell and Piper. Thus, lack of familiarity with foreign law would not be a problem. Even if the court of appeals' conclusion is correct, however, all other public interest factors favored trial in Scotland.

Scotland has a very strong interest in this litigation. The accident occurred in its airspace. All of the decedents were Scottish. Apart from Piper and Hartzell, all potential plaintiffs and defendants are either Scottish or English. As we stated in *Gilbert*, there is "a local interest in having localized controversies decided at home." Respondent argues that American citizens have an interest in ensuring that American manufacturers are deterred from producing defective products, and that additional deterrence might be obtained if Piper and Hartzell were tried in the United States, where they could be sued on the basis of both negligence and strict liability. However, the incremental deterrence that would be gained if this trial were held in an American court is likely to be insignificant. The American interest in this accident is simply not sufficient to justify the enormous commitment of judicial time and resources that would inevitably be required if the case were to be tried here.

IV

The court of appeals erred in holding that the possibility of an unfavorable change in law bars dismissal on the ground of *forum non conveniens*. It also erred in rejecting the district court's *Gilbert* analysis. The district court properly decided that the presumption in favor of the respondent's forum

---

[10] Many *forum non conveniens* decisions have held that the need to apply foreign law favors dismissal. Of course, this factor alone is not sufficient to warrant dismissal when a balancing of all relevant factors shows that the plaintiff's chosen forum is appropriate.

choice applied with less than maximum force because the real parties in interest are foreign. It did not act unreasonably in deciding that the private interests pointed towards trial in Scotland. Nor did it act unreasonably in deciding that the public interests favored trial in Scotland. Thus, the judgment of the court of appeals is reversed.

[Concurring and dissenting opinions omitted.]

Notes and Questions on *Piper*

1. *Discretionary standard for forum non conveniens dismissal*. *Piper*, like *Gilbert*, reinforces the trial court's discretion to dismiss a case on *forum non conveniens* grounds (1) when there is an adequate alternative forum and (2) when "trial in the chosen forum would 'establish . . . oppressiveness and vexation to a defendant . . . out of all proportion to plaintiff's convenience,' or when the 'chosen forum [is] inappropriate because of considerations affecting the court's own administrative and legal problems."

A. *Adequacy of the alternative forum*. Under *Piper*, an alternative forum is adequate if (i) the defendants are subject to service of process there; and (ii) the forum permits "litigation of the subject matter of the dispute." That the law of the foreign forum differs from American law "should ordinarily not be given conclusive or even substantial weight" in assessing the adequacy of the forum. Addressing the relationship between choice-of-law and the *forum non conveniens* doctrine, the *Piper* court said that an "unfavorable change of law may be given substantial weight" if the "remedy provided by the alternative forum is *so clearly inadequate or unsatisfactory that it is no remedy at all*." This is clearly intended to be — and has been interpreted to be — a difficult standard to satisfy. In one famous application of the *Piper* standards, *In re Union Carbide Gas Plant Disaster at Bhopal, India, in December 1984*, 634 F. Supp. 842 (S.D.N.Y. 1986), *aff'd as modified*, 809 F.2d 195 (2d Cir.), *cert. denied*, 484 U.S. 871 (1987), for example, numerous actions had been filed against Union Carbide, a U.S. corporation, for death, injuries, and damages sustained as result of a gas leak at a chemical plant at Bhopal, India. The district court granted the motion to dismiss on grounds of *forum non conveniens*, ruling that the Indian legal system was better able to determine the cause of the accident and to fix liability, not least because the overwhelming majority of witnesses, evidence, and claimants were in India. The Indian government's substantial interest in the accident and the outcome of the litigation compelled a conditional dismissal in favor of an Indian forum. On appeal, the Second Circuit sustained the dismissal and ruled that the defendant had been properly required to agree to submit to the jurisdiction of Indian courts and to waive the statute of limitations. The strategic advantages sought by the foreign plaintiffs in U.S. courts — especially the standards governing liability, standing, measure of damages, discovery, and the enforceability of judgments — were insufficient to keep the action in the United States. Even substantial differences in procedure do not satisfy the *Piper* "no-remedy-at-all" standard. *See, e.g., Lueck v. Sundstrand Corp.*, 236 F.3d 1137 (9th Cir. 2001).

B. *Balancing the public and private interest.* Once the adequacy of the alternative forum is established, the court must articulate and weigh the public and private interests identified in *Gilbert*, to determine which forum "will be most convenient and will best serve the ends of justice." *Peregrine Myanmar Ltd. v. Segal*, 89 F.3d 41, 46 (2d Cir. 1996). There has been some variation in the formulation of these factors but they generally include, on the "public" side, (1) having local disputes settled locally; (2) avoiding problems of applying foreign law; and (3) avoiding burdening jurors with cases that have no impact on their community. On the "private" side, the factors include (1) ease of access to evidence; (2) the cost for witnesses to attend trial; (3) the availability of compulsory process; and (4) other factors that might shorten trial or make it less expensive. On those rare occasions when a lower court's dismissal is overturned on appeal as an abuse of discretion, the failure either to address these factors or to show that they cut strongly in favor of the defendant is frequently decisive. *See, e.g, Reid-Walen v. Hansen*, 933 F.2d 1390 (8th Cir. 1991).

2. *The selective presumption in favor of the plaintiff's choice of forum. Piper* establishes "a strong presumption in favor of the plaintiff's choice of forum." As a consequence, dismissal is usually inappropriate unless "the balance of convenience tilts strongly in favor of trial in the foreign forum." *R. Maganlal & Co. v. M.G. Chem. Co.*, 942 F.2d 164, 167 (2d Cir. 1991). The presumption clearly weakens if the plaintiff is a foreign national, as *Piper* itself demonstrates.

A. In principle, why should the plaintiff's choice of forum get substantial deference given the prospect of forum-shopping and the court's prerogative to determine its own jurisdiction? Would a plaintiff class that includes U.S. and foreign plaintiffs be entitled to the same deference as a U.S.-citizen plaintiff suing alone? And, if forum-shopping is so bad, what should the *Piper* court have made of the fact that the defendants were also forum-shopping in their motion to dismiss?

B. Consider the following provision of the Treaty of Friendship, Commerce, and Navigation (FCN) between the United States and Costa Rica:

> The citizens of the high contracting parties shall reciprocally receive and enjoy full and perfect protection for their persons and property, and shall have free and open access to the courts of justice in the said countries respectively, for the prosecution and defense of their just rights; and they shall be at liberty to employ, in all cases, the advocates, attorneys, or agents of whatever description, whom they may think proper, and *they shall enjoy in this respect the same rights and privileges therein as native citizens.*

10 Stat. 916 (emphasis supplied). Similar provisions appear routinely in the scores of FCN treaties (and bilateral investment treaties) to which the United States is a party. Is a *Piper*-like convenience test that takes nationality into account consistent with the obligation not to discriminate on the basis of nationality, as expressed in these conventions?

3. *Authority and rationale.* The *forum non conveniens* doctrine is controversial, both in its application on particular facts and in principle. Dissenting in *Gulf Oil v. Gilbert*, for example, Justice Black expressed concern about the court's "abdication" of its responsibility: "the courts of the United States are bound to proceed to judgment . . . in every case to which their jurisdiction extends. They cannot abdicate their authority or duty in any case in favor of another jurisdiction." 330 U.S. at 515. Where do courts get the authority to decline jurisdiction they have been given by the legislature? Whose inconvenience counts?

4. *Legislative policy and forum non conveniens.* What would be the consequences if a jurisdiction explicitly rejected the doctrine of *forum non conveniens*? *See Dow Chemical Co. v. Castro Alfaro*, 786 S.W.2d 674 (Tex. 1990) (Justice Hecht, dissenting from the ruling that Texas would not recognize the *forum non conveniens* doctrine, asked: "Why . . . should Texas be the only state in the country [sic], perhaps the only jurisdiction on earth, possibly the only one in history, to offer to try personal injury cases from around the world? Do Texas taxpayers want to pay extra for judges and clerks and courthouses and personnel to handle foreign litigation?. . . As the courthouse for the world, will Texas entice employers to move here, or people to do business here, or even anyone to visit?") Is this hyperbole?

If you were a member of a state legislature, would you attempt to codify or constrain the *forum non conveniens* doctrine? Consider Section 1.05 of the Uniform Interstate and International Procedure Act provides:

> When the court finds that in the interest of substantial justice the action should be heard in another forum, the court may stay or dismiss the action in whole or in part on any conditions that may be just.

Is Section 1.05 an improvement over the *forum non conveniens* doctrine as it has emerged from the *Gilbert-Koster-Piper* line of cases?

5. *The relationship between forum non conveniens and transfer.* In *Piper*, the court of appeals had based its decision in part on an analogy between dismissals on grounds of *forum non conveniens* and transfers between federal courts pursuant to 28 U.S.C. § 1404(a). The analogy was critical because the Supreme Court had earlier ruled that a § 1404(a) transfer should not result in a change in the applicable law. *Van Dusen v. Barrack*, 376 U.S. 612 (1964). In reversing the court of appeals, the Supreme Court in *Piper* rejected the analogy and distinguished § 1404(a) from *forum non conveniens* dismissals:

> Congress enacted § 1404(a) to permit change of venue between federal courts. Although the statute was drafted in accordance with the doctrine of *forum non conveniens*, it was intended to be a revision rather than a codification of the common law. District courts were given more discretion to transfer under § 1404(a) than they had to dismiss on grounds of *forum non conveniens*. The reasoning employed in *Van Dusen v. Barrack* is simply inapplicable to dismissals on grounds of *forum non conveniens*. That case did not discuss the common-law doctrine. Rather, it focused on "the construction and application" of § 1404(a). Emphasizing the remedial purpose of the statute, *Barrack* concluded that Congress could not have intended a transfer to be accompanied by a change in law. The statute was designed as a "federal

housekeeping measure," allowing easy change of venue within a unified federal system. The Court feared that if a change in venue were accompanied by a change in law, forum-shopping parties would take unfair advantage of the relaxed standards for transfer. The rule was necessary to ensure the just and efficient operation of the statute.

On the other hand, even if *Piper* rejects any direct analogy between transfer and *forum non conveniens,* it is at least arguable that similar logistical concerns should be addressed similarly. Consider Judge Newman's observation that "[i]t will often be quicker and less expensive to transfer a witness or a document than to transfer a lawsuit." *Calavo Growers of California v. Generali Belgium,* 632 F.2d 963, 969 (2d Cir. 1980).

6. *Forum non conveniens "within" diversity.* The Supreme Court has never resolved the question whether, under *Erie R. Co. v. Tompkins,* 304 U.S. 64 (1938), state or federal law of *forum non conveniens* should apply in a diversity case. *Cf. American Dredging Co. v. Miller,* 510 U.S. 443 (1994) ("the doctrine is one of procedure rather than substance"). Generally, no resolution has been necessary because the standards are generally similar if not identical; indeed, in *Piper* itself, the lower courts decided that Pennsylvania and California standards for *forum non conveniens* dismissals were virtually identical to federal law. But how should courts approach the hard case, where the choice of one state's law might determine the outcome of the *forum non conveniens* calculus?

7. *Forum non conveniens "without" diversity.* Should *forum non conveniens* be more acceptable when jurisdiction is based on the diversity of the parties (28 U.S.C. § 1332) than when jurisdiction is based on the existence of a federal question (28 U.S.C. § 1331)? As you read the following case, consider whether the Alien Tort Claims Act (28 U.S.C. § 1350) is closer to a diversity case or a federal question case.

WIWA v. ROYAL DUTCH PETROLEUM CO.
226 F.3d 88 (2d Cir. 2000), *cert. denied,* 532 U.S. 941 (2001)

This case concerns the application of *forum non conveniens* doctrine to suits under the Alien Tort Claims Act (ATCA), involving claimed abuses of the international law of human rights. Plaintiffs are three Nigerian emigres, and a woman identified only as Jane Doe to protect her safety, who allege that they (or in some cases their deceased next of kin) suffered grave human rights abuses at the hands of the Nigerian authorities. Defendants Royal Dutch Petroleum Company ("Royal Dutch") and Shell Transport and Trading Co., P.L.C. ("Shell Transport") are business corporations, incorporated in the Netherlands and the United Kingdom respectively, that are alleged to have directly or indirectly participated in or directed these abuses. The district court dismissed the action for *forum non conveniens* after determining that England is an adequate alternative forum and that a balancing of public interest and private interest factors make the British forum preferable. Plaintiffs appeal, arguing, *inter alia*, that the district court erred in not affording sufficient weight to the plaintiffs' choice of forum and to the interests of the United States in providing a forum for the adjudication of claims of abuse of international human rights. . . . We hold that the district court properly exercised jurisdiction over the defendants. As to the dismissal for *forum non conveniens*, we reverse.

[*See* Ch. 2, *supra* at p.84, for the factual background of this case.]

DISCUSSION

A. Personal Jurisdiction [The Court of Appeals ruled that personal jurisdiction was proper. *See* Chapter 2, *supra*.]

B. *Forum Non Conveniens*

Plaintiffs appeal from the decision of the district court to dismiss for *forum non conveniens*. The grant or denial of a motion to dismiss for *forum non conveniens* is generally committed to the district court's discretion. The deference accorded to a district court's discretion, however, presupposes that the court used the correct standards prescribed by the governing rule of law. We believe that, as a matter of law, in balancing the competing interests, the district court did not accord proper significance to a choice of forum by lawful U.S. resident plaintiffs or to the policy interest implicit in our federal statutory law in providing a forum for adjudication of claims of violations of the law of nations. . . .

[W]e assume *arguendo* that there are no rules of British law that would prevent a British court from reaching the merits. We believe the order of dismissal must nonetheless be reversed as the defendants have not established as *Gilbert* requires that the pertinent factors tilt sufficiently strongly in favor of trial in the foreign forum. In our view, the district court failed to give weight to three significant considerations that favor retaining jurisdiction for trial: (1) a United States resident plaintiff's choice of forum, (2) the interests of the United States in furnishing a forum to litigate claims of violations of the international standards of the law of human rights, and (3) the factors that led the district court to dismiss in favor of a British forum were not particularly compelling. For the reasons developed below, we believe that they are outweighed by the considerations favoring exercise of the court's jurisdiction.

(1) *Deference to the Choice of a United States Forum by a Lawful United States Resident Plaintiff.* By definition, the doctrine of *forum non conveniens* contemplates the dismissal of lawsuits brought by plaintiffs in their favored forum in favor of adjudication in a foreign court. Nonetheless, a plaintiff's choice of forum is entitled to substantial deference and should only be disturbed if the factors favoring the alternative forum are compelling. . . .

While any plaintiff's selection of a forum is entitled to deference, that deference increases as the plaintiff's ties to the forum increase. *See, e.g., Murray v. British Broad. Corp.,* 81 F.3d 287, 290 (2d Cir. 1996) (holding that a domestic plaintiff's choice of forum is entitled to more deference than a foreign plaintiff's); *see also Piper* (noting that the choice of a forum by its citizens and residents is entitled to greater deference than a stranger's choice); *Koster* ("[A] real showing of convenience by a plaintiff who has sued in his home forum will normally outweigh the inconvenience the defendant may have shown."). In a decision handed down since oral argument in this case, we overturned a *forum non conveniens* dismissal in a case brought by a United States citizen involving events occurring outside the United States where the defendant was unable to " 'establish such oppressiveness and vexation . . . as to be out of all proportion to plaintiff's convenience' " and where there were no compelling public interest considerations favoring litigation in the alterative foreign forum. *Guidi* [*v. Inter-Continental Hotels Corp.*, 224 F.3d 142 (2d Cir. 2000),] at 145–46 (quoting *Koster*).

These cases do not reflect a rigid rule of decision protecting U.S. citizen or resident plaintiffs from dismissal for *forum non conveniens*. Rather, they illustrate the manner in which a court must take into account the hardship dismissal would cause to a resident plaintiff when evaluating the *Gilbert* factors; in the words of this court, the cited cases represent a "consistent, pragmatic application" of the *Gilbert* factors to actions in which a plaintiff has particular ties to the forum state. The *Gilbert* test requires a balancing of factors, and a plaintiff's lawful U.S. residence can be a meaningful factor supporting the plaintiff's choice of a U.S. forum. . . .

That is the case not because of chauvinism or bias in favor of U.S. residents. It is rather because the greater the plaintiff's ties to the plaintiff's chosen forum, the more likely it is that the plaintiff would be inconvenienced by a requirement to bring the claim in a foreign jurisdiction. Also, while our courts are of course required to offer equal justice to all litigants, a neutral rule that compares the convenience of the parties should properly consider each party's residence as a factor that bears on the inconvenience that party might suffer if required to sue in a foreign nation.

During the last two decades, our caselaw and that of the Supreme Court has clearly and unambiguously established that courts should offer greater deference to the selection of a U.S. forum by U.S. resident plaintiffs when evaluating a motion to dismiss for *forum non conveniens*. [W]e [have previously] rejected the proposition that courts must accord "a talismanic significance to the citizenship or residence of the parties," and held that "citizenship [and] residence no longer are absolutely determinative factors," in the *forum non conveniens* analysis. [W]e [are required to] apply the *Gilbert* factors in evaluating a *forum non conveniens* motion, even when the plaintiff is a U.S. citizen or resident; *Murray* and *Piper* point to the important role the plaintiff's residence and citizenship potentially play in the *Gilbert* analysis; and *Guidi* illustrates that a plaintiff's U.S. citizenship and residence is entitled to consideration in favor of retaining jurisdiction, such that the *Gilbert* factors will favor dismissal (in the absence of strong public interest factors favoring dismissal) only if the defendant can establish " 'such oppressiveness and vexation . . . as to be out of all proportion to plaintiff's convenience.' " *Guidi*, 224 F.3d at 146 (quoting *Koster*).[1]

---

[1] We read *Guidi* as allowing for the possibility that, under certain circumstances, the public interest factors favoring dismissal might (by themselves or in combination with inconvenience to the defendant not quite rising to the level of "oppressiveness and vexation") be strong enough to justify dismissal, notwithstanding the absence of "oppressiveness and vexation." See *Guidi*, (stating the *forum non conveniens* dismissal against a U.S. citizen seeking to invoke a U.S. forum may be appropriate if defendant presents a "clear showing of facts which . . . make trial in the

In this case, the district court weighed against the plaintiffs that none of them were residents of the Southern District of New York but did not count in favor of their choice of a U.S. forum that two of them were residents of the United States. This was error. . . . The benefit for a U.S. resident plaintiff of suing in a U.S. forum·is not limited to suits in the very district where the plaintiff resides, especially considering that the defendant may not be amenable to suit in the plaintiff's district of residence. *See, e.g., Guidi* (the "home forum" of an American citizen for *forum non conveniens* purposes is any "United States court"). . . . In deciding whether to dismiss a case brought by a lawful U.S. resident plaintiff for *forum non conveniens*, the district should consider whether, in view of the plaintiff's U.S. residence, such a dismissal would cause plaintiff significant hardship.

In all of our cases in which we have deemed a plaintiff "foreign" and accorded that plaintiff's choice of forum less deference, the plaintiffs involved were foreign corporations or foreign-national individuals residing abroad. We have never accorded less deference to a foreign plaintiff's choice of a United States forum where that plaintiff was a U.S. resident.

In short, the district court applied an incorrect standard of law when it failed to credit the fact that two of the plaintiffs were United States residents as a consideration favoring plaintiff's choice of a U.S. forum.

(2) *The Application of Forum Non Conveniens Doctrine to ATCA Cases*. The plaintiffs also argue that the ATCA, as supplemented by the Torture Victim Prevention [sic] Act (TVPA), reflects a United States policy interest in providing a forum for the adjudication of international human rights abuses, and that this policy interest should have a role in the balancing of the *Gilbert* factors.

The Alien Tort Claims Act was adopted in 1789 as part of the original Judiciary Act. In its original form, it made no assertion about legal rights; it simply asserted that "[t]he district courts shall have original jurisdiction of any civil action by an alien for a tort only, committed in violation of the law of nations or a treaty of the United States." For almost two centuries, the statute lay relatively dormant, supporting jurisdiction in only a handful of cases. *See, e.g., Filártiga v. Pena-Irala*, 630 F.2d 876, 887 & n. 21 (2d Cir. 1980) (identifying only two previous cases that had relied upon the ATCA for jurisdiction). As the result of increasing international concern with human rights issues, however, litigants have recently begun to seek redress more frequently under the ATCA.

These suits produced several important decisions interpreting the meaning and scope of the 1789 Act. For example, in *Filártiga v. Pena-Irala*, this court held that deliberate torture perpetrated under the color of official authority violates universally accepted norms of international human rights law, and that such a violation of international law constitutes a violation of the domestic law of the United States, giving rise to a claim under the ATCA whenever the perpetrator is properly served within the borders of the United

---

chosen forum inappropriate because of considerations affecting the court's own administrative and legal problems" (quoting *Koster*). Furthermore, *Guidi*'s focus on the balancing of defendant's inconvenience against plaintiff's implicitly recognizes that, depending on the particular circumstances, the degree of inconvenience that dismissal would impose on a U.S. resident will vary.

States. More recently, we held in *Kadic v. Karadzic* that the ATCA reaches the conduct of private parties provided that their conduct is undertaken under the color of state authority or violates a norm of international law that is recognized as extending to the conduct of private parties.

In passing the Torture Victim Prevention [sic] Act in 1991, Congress expressly ratified our holding in *Filártiga* that the United States courts have jurisdiction over suits by aliens alleging torture under color of law of a foreign nation, and carried it significantly further. While the 1789 Act expressed itself in terms of a grant of jurisdiction to the district courts, the 1991 Act (a) makes clear that it creates liability under U.S. law where under "color of law, of any foreign nation" an individual is subject to torture or "extra judicial killing," and (b) extends its remedy not only to aliens but to any "individual," thus covering citizens of the United States as well. The TVPA thus recognizes explicitly what was perhaps implicit in the Act of 1789 — that the law of nations is incorporated into the law of the United States and that a violation of the international law of human rights is (at least with regard to torture) *ipso facto* a violation of U.S. domestic law.

Whatever may have been the case prior to passage of the TVPA, we believe plaintiffs make a strong argument in contending that the present law, in addition to merely permitting U.S. district courts to entertain suits alleging violation of the law of nations, expresses a policy favoring receptivity by our courts to such suits. Two changes of statutory wording seem to indicate such an intention. First is the change from addressing the courts' "jurisdiction" to addressing substantive rights; second is the change from the ATCA's description of the claim as one for "tort . . . committed in violation of the law of nations . . ." to the new Act's assertion of the substantive right to damages under U.S. law. This evolution of statutory language seems to represent a more direct recognition that the interests of the United States are involved in the eradication of torture committed under color of law in foreign nations.

In *Jota v. Texaco, Inc.*, 157 F.3d 153, 159 (2d Cir. 1998), we recognized the plaintiff's argument that "to dismiss . . . [a claim pursuant to the ATCA under *forum non conveniens*] would frustrate Congress's intent to provide a federal forum for aliens suing domestic entities for violation of the law of nations." We expressed "no view" on the question but directed the district court to consider the issue on remand. In this case, the issue is again advanced (in slightly different form, as *Jota* did not involve torture and the defendants in this case are not domestic entities). Dismissal on grounds of *forum non conveniens* can represent a huge setback in a plaintiff's efforts to seek reparations for acts of torture. Although a *forum non conveniens* dismissal by definition presupposes the existence of another forum where the suit may be brought, dismissal nonetheless requires the plaintiff to start over in the courts of another nation, which will generally at least require the plaintiff to obtain new counsel, as well as perhaps a new residence.

One of the difficulties that confront victims of torture under color of a nation's law is the enormous difficulty of bringing suits to vindicate such abuses. Most likely, the victims cannot sue in the place where the torture occurred. Indeed, in many instances, the victim would be endangered merely by returning to that place. It is not easy to bring such suits in the courts of another nation. Courts are often inhospitable. Such suits are generally time consuming, burdensome, and difficult to administer. In addition, because they assert outrageous conduct on the part of another nation, such suits may embarrass the government of the nation in whose courts they are brought. Finally, because characteristically neither the plaintiffs nor the defendants are ostensibly either protected or governed by the domestic law of the forum nation, courts often regard such suits as "not our business."

The new formulations of the Torture Victim Protection Act convey the message that torture committed under color of law of a foreign nation in violation of international law is "our business," as such conduct not only violates the standards of international law but also as a consequence violates our domestic law. In the legislative history of the TVPA, Congress noted that universal condemnation of human rights abuses "provide[s] scant comfort" to the numerous victims of gross violations if they are without a forum to remedy the wrong. This passage supports plaintiffs' contention that in passing the Torture Victim Prevention [sic] Act, Congress has expressed a policy of U.S. law favoring the adjudication of such suits in U.S. courts. If in cases of torture in violation of international law our courts exercise their jurisdiction conferred by the 1789 Act only for as long as it takes to dismiss the case for *forum non conveniens*, we will have done little to enforce the standards of the law of nations.

This is not to suggest that the TVPA has nullified, or even significantly diminished, the doctrine of *forum non conveniens*. The statute has, however, communicated a policy that such suits should not be facilely dismissed on the assumption that the ostensibly foreign controversy is not our business. The TVPA in our view expresses a policy favoring our courts' exercise of the jurisdiction conferred by the ATCA in cases of torture, unless the defendant has fully met the burden of showing that the *Gilbert* factors "tilt[] strongly in favor of trial in the foreign forum."

(3) *The Forum Non Conveniens Analysis in this Case.* We turn to the analysis of the *forum non conveniens* factors in their application to this case. We believe the rule of law applied by the district court was faulty, as noted above, in the following respects: (a) The district court counted against retention of jurisdiction that the plaintiffs were not residents of the Southern District of New York while failing to count in favor of retention that two of the plaintiffs were residents of the United States, and (b) the court failed to count in favor of retention the interest of the United States, as expressed in the TVPA, in providing a forum for the adjudication of claims of torture in violation of the standards of international law. Furthermore, the Magistrate Judge, whose findings were adopted by the district court, gave no consideration to the very substantial expense and inconvenience (perhaps fatal to the suit) that would be imposed on the impecunious plaintiffs by dismissal in favor of a British forum, and the inconvenience to the defendants that ultimately justified the dismissal seems to us to have been minimal. . . .

The issue of *forum non conveniens* is not settled by adding to the mix the considerations favoring retention arising from the U.S. residence of two of the plaintiffs and the policy expressed in the TVPA favoring adjudication of claims of torture in violation of international law. If the defendants advanced substantial interests supporting dismissal in favor of a British forum, we would either remand to the district court for reconsideration or, if the defendants interests were sufficiently substantial, sustain the dismissal notwithstanding our identification of interests in favor of retention that the district court did not consider. In our view, however, the defendants have offered only minimal considerations in support of an English forum. This is not a case like *Piper* where there is an obviously better suited foreign forum for the adjudication of the dispute. Nor does it involve substantial physical evidence that is difficult or expensive to transport. For any nonparty witnesses, the inconvenience of a trial in New York is not significantly more pronounced than the inconvenience of a trial in England.

In arguing that England is a more appropriate forum, defendants rely upon arguments such as the inconvenience of shipping documents from England to the United States and the additional cost for a Nigerian witness of flying to New York rather than London. These considerations are indeed a legitimate part of the *forum non conveniens* analysis, but (a) the defendants have not demonstrated that these costs are excessively burdensome, especially in view of the defendants' vast resources, and (b) the additional cost and inconvenience to the defendants of litigating in New York is fully counterbalanced by the cost and inconvenience to the plaintiffs of requiring them to reinstitute the litigation in England — especially given the plaintiffs' minimal resources in comparison to the vast resources of the defendants. These considerations cannot justify overriding the plaintiffs' choice of forum.

Defendants argue that England has a public interest in adjudicating this action. In particular, they argue that (1) Shell Transport is a British corporation whose liability for the actions of its subsidiary is likely to be governed by British law; and (2) Nigeria was, at the time of the actions in question, a member of the Commonwealth of Nations. Although these factors do bear consideration, they are not overriding. To the same extent that England may have an interest in adjudicating matters affecting a British corporation, the United States courts have an interest in adjudicating matters affecting its residents. Also, while one defendant is a British corporation whose actions are governed by British law, the second defendant is not British, but Dutch. The fact that Nigeria was at the time a member of the voluntary consortium of nations constituting the Commonwealth is of no particular significance.

[CONCLUSION]

In order to be granted dismissal based on *forum non conveniens*, the defendants bear the burden of establishing that the *Gilbert* factors "tilt[] strongly in favor of trial in the foreign forum." We believe they have failed as a matter of law to meet this burden. The factors weighing against dismissal include (1) the substantial deference courts are required to give to the plaintiff's choice of forum, (2) the enormous burden, expense, and difficulty the plaintiffs would suffer if required to begin the litigation anew in England,[2] (3) the policy

---

[2] As the Magistrate Judge noted in his report, the plaintiffs lack meaningful financial resources and will be substantially burdened by the expense of bringing this litigation in England. Nonetheless, he concluded that the plaintiffs' lack of resources is a "neutral factor" because the plaintiffs have not established that it will be less expensive to try the case in New York than

favoring our court's retention of such suits brought by plaintiffs who are residents of the United States, and (4) the policy expressed in the TVPA favoring adjudication of claims of violations of international prohibitions on torture. These factors are more than sufficient to overcome the defendants' weak claim for dismissal based on *forum non conveniens*.[3] We therefore remand to the district court for further proceedings. Because the district court dismissed for *forum non conveniens*, it never considered the defendants' motion to dismiss under Federal Rule of Civil Procedure 12(b)(6) for failure to state a claim.[4] We remand for consideration of that motion.

Notes and Questions on *Wiwa*

1. *The adequacy of the foreign forum in light of foreign law.* In their appellate argument, the plaintiffs argued that the United Kingdom was not an adequate alternative forum because certain doctrines of British law would bar a British court from reaching the subject matter of the dispute — specifically double actionability, transmissibility, and the act of state doctrine. In the court's words, "[a]s the parties' experts describe the British law, the doctrine of double accountability [sic] states that, with limited exceptions, torts committed in other countries are actionable in England only if they would be actionable under both English law and the law of the country in which the act was committed. . . . The doctrine of transmissibility holds that the question whether a decedent's claims transfer to his survivors is determined by the law of the decedent's nation. The act of state doctrine bars, on comity grounds, the consideration of certain claims arising out of the official actions of foreign governments."

A. Why isn't this line of argument completely foreclosed by *Piper*?

B. If the court were inclined to grant a *forum non conveniens* dismissal in *Wiwa* (or any other case), what conditions might it endorse as part of the

---

in England. The record, however, contains substantial evidence that trial in New York will be less expensive and burdensome for the plaintiffs. The plaintiffs have already obtained excellent pro bono counsel to litigate this matter in the courts of the United States; there is no guarantee that they will be able to obtain equivalent representation in England without incurring substantial expenses. Two of the plaintiffs lived in the United States when the action was brought. The cost and difficulties of relocating themselves to England for the duration of the litigation is likely to be onerous. Finally, the plaintiffs and their attorneys have already made substantial investments of time, money, and energy in pursuing this litigation in the U.S. courts. Requiring the plaintiffs to replicate them in the British courts would substantially increase their burden. For these reasons, we believe that the Magistrate Judge should have given greater consideration to the burden on the impecunious plaintiffs, rather than focusing his consideration of the convenience factors almost entirely on the convenience of the defendants.

[3] The other considerations favoring retention of jurisdiction sufficiently outweigh the defendants' claim for dismissal that we would reach the same result without consideration of the policy interest we have found to be expressed by the TVPA.

[4] Defendants also urged below that the Netherlands was an adequate alternative forum and more convenient than the United States. Although the district court did not rule on the defendants' request for dismissal in favor of a Dutch forum, we need not remand for consideration of this question, because dismissal in favor of trial in the Netherlands would share the disadvantages that have led us to reject the dismissal in favor of trial in England.

dismissal? Or phrasing the question somewhat more adversarially, what undertakings might the court extract from the defendant in exchange for the dismissal?

2. *Forum non conveniens and statutes.* Understanding that *forum non conveniens,* like all common law doctrines, "bends to the will of Congress," what are the criteria for determining whether a federal or state statute actually does that? Are you convinced that the Alien Tort Claims Act or the Torture Victim Protection Act meets those criteria? What is the significance of the court's observation in a footnote that "we would reach the same result without consideration of the policy interest we have found to be expressed by the TVPA?"

In some cases, the courts will find a statutory override of the *forum non conveniens* doctrine grounded not in the federal interests behind the law as in *Wiwa,* but in the language of the statute itself, especially if there is an exclusive venue provision requiring venue in the United States. *See, e.g.,* the Jones Act, 46 U.S.C. App. § 688(a) or the Federal Employers' Liability Act, 45 U.S.C. § 56. Thus, if the court's choice-of-law analysis determines that one of these statutes applies, a *forum non conveniens* dismissal would be inappropriate. "Where no such law is implicated, the choice of law determination is given much less deference on [sic] a *forum non conveniens* inquiry." *Lueck v. Sundstrand Corp.,* 236 F.3d 1137, 1148 (9th Cir. 2001).

3. *Differentiating between international law and foreign law for purposes of forum non conveniens. Piper* suggested that the difficulty of discerning and applying foreign law could be one factor in favor of a *forum non conveniens* dismissal. *Wiwa* suggests that discerning and applying international law need not cut the same way. What should happen when *multiple* foreign laws are potentially involved? Should an abundance of adequate alternative forums cut *against* dismissal, as the following case suggests?

BOOSEY & HAWKES MUSIC PUBLISHERS., LTD. v. WALT DISNEY CO.
145 F.3d 481 (2d Cir. 1998)

Boosey & Hawkes Music Publishers Ltd., an English corporation and the assignee of Igor Stravinsky's copyrights for "The Rite of Spring," brought this action alleging that the Walt Disney Company's foreign distribution in video cassette and laser disc format of the film *Fantasia,* featuring Stravinsky's work, infringed Boosey's rights. In 1939, Stravinsky licensed Disney's distribution of "The Rite of Spring" in the motion picture. Boosey, which acquired Stravinsky's copyright in 1947, contends that the license does not authorize distribution in video format.

The district court granted partial summary judgment to Boosey, declaring that Disney's video format release was not authorized by the license agreement. Disney appeals from that ruling. The court granted partial summary judgment to Disney, dismissing Boosey's claims for breach of contract and violation of the Lanham Act; the court also dismissed Boosey's foreign copyright claims under the doctrine of *forum non conveniens*. Boosey appeals from these rulings. We hold that summary judgment was properly granted to Disney with respect to Boosey's Lanham Act claims, but that material issues of fact barred the other grants of summary judgment. We . . . reverse the order dismissing for *forum non conveniens*. . . .

During 1938, Disney sought Stravinsky's authorization to use "The Rite of Spring" . . . throughout the world in a motion picture. Because under United States law the work was in the public domain, Disney needed no authorization to record or distribute it in this country, but permission was required for distribution in countries where Stravinsky enjoyed copyright protection. In January 1939, the parties executed an agreement giving Disney rights to use the work in a motion picture in consideration of a fee to Stravinsky of $6000. Disney released *Fantasia*, starring Mickey Mouse, in 1940. The film contains no dialogue. It matches a pantomime of animated beasts and fantastic creatures to passages of great classical music, creating what critics celebrated as a "partnership between fine music and animated film." The soundtrack uses compositions of Bach, Beethoven, Dukas, Schubert, Tchaikovsky, and Stravinsky, all performed by the Philadelphia Orchestra under the direction of Leopold Stokowski. . . . For more than five decades, Disney exhibited "The Rite of Spring" in *Fantasia* under the 1939 license. In 1991, Disney first released *Fantasia* in video format. The video has been sold in foreign countries, as well as in the United States. To date, the *Fantasia* video release has generated more than $360 million in gross revenue for Disney.

Boosey brought this action in February 1993. The complaint sought (1) a declaration that the 1939 Agreement did not include a grant of rights to Disney to use the Stravinsky work in video format; (2) damages for copyright infringement in at least 18 foreign countries; [and additional causes of action.] . . . [T]he district court invoked *forum non conveniens* to dismiss all of Boosey's claims of copyright infringement because they involved the application of foreign law. . . . [Taken as a whole,] the decision below . . . declared Disney an infringer, but granted Boosey no relief, leaving it to sue in the various countries under whose copyright laws it claims infringement. This appeal followed. . . .

Foreign Copyright Claims

Invoking the doctrine of *forum non conveniens*, the district court dismissed Boosey's second cause of action, which sought damages for copyright infringement deriving from Disney's sales of videocassettes of *Fantasia* in at least eighteen foreign countries. The court below concluded that these claims should be tried "in each of the nations whose copyright laws are invoked." Boosey appeals, seeking remand to the district court for trial.

District courts enjoy broad discretion to decide whether to dismiss an action under the doctrine of *forum non conveniens*. Nevertheless, this discretion is subject to "meaningful appellate review." *R. Maganlal & Co. v. M.G. Chem. Co., Inc.*, 942 F.2d 164, 167 (2d Cir. 1991). A dismissal for *forum non conveniens* will be upset on appeal where a defendant has failed to demonstrate that "an adequate alternative forum exists" and that "the balance of convenience tilts strongly in favor of trial in the foreign forum." . . . The district court first must determine whether there exists an alternative forum with jurisdiction to hear the case. If so, the court then weighs the factors set out in *Gilbert* . . . to decide which "forum . . . will be most convenient and will best serve the ends of justice."

The district court failed to consider whether there were alternative fora capable of adjudicating Boosey's copyright claims. It made no determination whether Disney was subject to jurisdiction in the various countries where the court anticipated that trial would occur and did not condition dismissal on Disney's consent to jurisdiction in those nations.[1] Furthermore, consideration of the *Gilbert* factors makes plain that *forum non conveniens* is inappropriate here. The district court must carefully weigh the private and public interests set forth in *Gilbert* and may grant the *forum non conveniens* motion only if these considerations strongly support dismissal. Relevant private interests of the litigants include access to proof, availability of witnesses, and "all other practical problems that make trial of a case easy, expeditious and inexpensive." *Gilbert*, 330 U.S. at 508.

The private interests of the litigants favor conducting the litigation in New York where the plaintiff brought suit. Disney does not allege that a New York forum is inconvenient. The necessary evidence and witnesses are available and ready for presentation. A trial here promises to begin and end sooner than elsewhere, and would allow the parties to sort out their rights and obligations in a single proceeding. This is not a circumstance where the plaintiff's choice of forum is motivated by harassment. Indeed, it seems rather more likely that Disney's motion seeks to split the suit into 18 parts in 18 nations, complicate the suit, delay it, and render it more expensive.

In dismissing the cases, the court relied on the "public interests" identified in *Gilbert*. It reasoned that the trial would require extensive application of foreign copyright and antitrust jurisprudence, bodies of law involving strong national interests best litigated "in their respective countries. "The court concluded as well that these necessary inquiries into foreign law would place an undue burden on our judicial system."

While reluctance to apply foreign law is a valid factor favoring dismissal under *Gilbert*, standing alone it does not justify dismissal. *See Piper Aircraft Co. v. Reyno*, 454 U.S. 235, 260 n.29 (1968) ("The need to apply foreign law . . . alone is not sufficient to warrant dismissal."). District courts must weigh this factor along with the other relevant considerations. Numerous countervailing considerations suggest that New York venue is proper: defendant is a U.S. corporation, the 1939 agreement was substantially negotiated and signed in New York, and the agreement is governed by New York law. The plaintiff has chosen New York and the trial is ready to proceed here. Everything before us suggests that trial would be more "easy, expeditious and inexpensive" in the district court than dispersed to 18 foreign nations. We

---

[1] We need not decide, therefore, whether *forum non conveniens* dismissal requires the dismissing court to ascertain a single alternative court with jurisdiction over the claims, because, at a minimum, our jurisprudence requires a pre-dismissal determination that the claims be justiciable somewhere.

therefore vacate the dismissal of the foreign copyright claims and remand for trial.

Note on the *Fantasia* Case and Multiterritorial Copyright Cases

In the current state of international law, battling a multinational infringer of a copyright can require a nation-by-nation offensive. Multiple international agreements address copyrights and other forms of intellectual property, including the Berne Convention, the Agreement on Trade Related Aspects of Intellectual Property Rights, and the World Intellectual Property Organization Copyright Treaty. Regional agreements — like the North American Free Trade Agreement and the European Community Trademark — also exist. Taken together, these agreements establish a relatively uniform if minimal system for the registration and protection of copyrights. But they do little to address the piecemeal, territorial nature of copyright enforcement, and on remand in *Boosey & Hawkes*, the district court expressed its dependence on expert testimony in ascertaining and applying foreign copyright law, *Boosey & Hawkes Music Publishers, Ltd. v. Walt Disney Co.*, 2000 U.S. Dist. LEXIS 1643 (S.D.N.Y. Feb. 17, 2000), pursuant to F.R.C.P. Rule 44.1. As Professor Nimmer has explained:

> Even if the United State Copyright Act is clearly inoperative with respect to acts occurring outside of its jurisdiction, it does not necessarily follow that American courts are without [subject matter] jurisdiction in such a case. If the plaintiff has a valid cause of action under the copyright laws of a foreign country, and if personal jurisdiction of the defendant can be obtained in an American court, it is arguable that an action may be brought in such court for infringement of a foreign copyright law. This would be on a theory that copyright infringement constitutes a transitory cause of action, and hence, may be adjudicated in the courts of a sovereign other than the one in which the cause of action arose.

3 NIMMER ON COPYRIGHT § 17.03. The logistical difficulty that this creates may be preferable to allowing multiple lawsuits in various countries around the world, but *Fantasia*-like consolidation of foreign copyright infringement claims in U.S. courts is not a universal approach. *Compare Creative Technology Ltd. v. Aztech System Pte., Ltd.*, 61 F.3d 696 (9th Cir. 1995); *Stewart v. Adidas A.G.*, 1997 WL 218431 (S.D.N.Y.). *See generally* Jane C. Ginsburg, *Extraterritoriality and Multi-territoriality in Copyright Infringement*, 37 VA. J. INT'L L. 587 (1997); Curtis A. Bradley, *Territorial Intellectual Property Rights in an Age of Globalism*, 37 VA. J. INT'L L. 505 (1997). Perhaps *forum non conveniens* is an especially inappropriate and unwieldy doctrine for the enforcement of intellectual property rights, but until there is international agreement about the extent of artists' and creators' rights — let alone a centralized procedure for registration and enforcement — the *Gilbert-Piper* doctrine will recur, with all of its territorialism and its indeterminacy.

B. FORUM-SELECTION CLAUSES

[1] Reversing the Presumption against Forum-Selection Clauses

THE BREMEN v. ZAPATA OFF-SHORE CO.
407 U.S. 1 (1972)

MR. CHIEF JUSTICE BURGER delivered the opinion of the Court. We granted certiorari to review a judgment of the United States court of appeals for the Fifth Circuit declining to enforce a forum-selection clause governing disputes arising under an international towage contract between petitioners and respondent. The circuits have differed in their approach to such clauses. For the reasons stated hereafter, we vacate the judgment of the court of appeals.

In November 1967, respondent Zapata, a Houston-based American corporation, contracted with petitioner Unterweser, a German corporation, to tow Zapata's ocean-going, self-elevating drilling rig *Chaparral* from Louisiana to a point off Ravenna, Italy, in the Adriatic Sea, where Zapata had agreed to drill certain wells. . . . The contract submitted by Unterweser contained the following provision, which is at issue in this case: "Any dispute arising must be treated before the London Court of Justice." In addition, the contract contained two clauses purporting to exculpate Unterweser from liability for damages to the towed barge.[1]

After reviewing the contract and making several changes, but without any alteration in the forum-selection or exculpatory clauses, a Zapata vice president executed the contract and forwarded it to Unterweser in Germany, where Unterweser accepted the changes, and the contract became effective. . . . Unterweser's deep sea tug Bremen departed Venice, Louisiana, with the *Chaparral* in tow bound for Italy. . . . [W]hile the flotilla was in international waters in the middle of the Gulf of Mexico, a severe storm arose. The sharp roll of the *Chaparral* in Gulf waters caused its elevator legs, which had been raised for the voyage, to break off and fall into the sea, seriously damaging the *Chaparral*. In this emergency situation, Zapata instructed the Bremen to tow its damaged rig to Tampa, Florida, the nearest port of refuge.

. . . Zapata, ignoring its contract promise to litigate "any dispute arising" in the English courts, commenced a suit in admiralty in the United States district court at Tampa, seeking $3,500,000 damages against Unterweser *in personam* and the *Bremen in rem*, alleging negligent towage and breach of contract. Unterweser responded by invoking the forum clause of the towage

---

[1] The General Towage Conditions of the contract included the following:

1. . . .[Unterweser and its] masters and crews are not responsible for defaults and/or errors in the navigation of the tow.

2. . . . b) Damages suffered by the towed object are in any case for account of its Owners.

In addition, the contract provided that any insurance of the *Chaparral* was to be "for account of" Zapata. Unterweser's initial telegraphic bid had also offered to "arrange insurance covering towage risk for rig if desired." As Zapata had chosen to be self-insured on all its rigs, the loss in this case was not compensated by insurance.

contract, and moved to dismiss for lack of jurisdiction or on *forum non conveniens* grounds, or in the alternative to stay the action pending submission of the dispute to the "London Court of Justice." Shortly thereafter . . . before the district court had ruled on its motion to stay or dismiss the United States action, Unterweser commenced an action against Zapata seeking damages for breach of the towage contract in the High Court of Justice in London, as the contract provided. Zapata appeared in that court to contest jurisdiction, but its challenge was rejected, the English courts holding that the contractual forum provision conferred jurisdiction. . . .

[T]he district court denied Unterweser's . . . motion to dismiss or stay Zapata's initial action. In denying the motion, that court . . . reiterat[ed] the traditional view of many American courts that "agreements in advance of controversy whose object is to oust the jurisdiction of the courts are contrary to public policy and will not be enforced." Apparently concluding that it was bound by [precedent], the district court gave the forum-selection clause little, if any, weight. Instead, the court treated the motion to dismiss under normal *forum non conveniens* doctrine applicable in the absence of such a clause . . . . Under that doctrine "unless the balance is strongly in favor of the defendant, the plaintiff's choice of forum should rarely be disturbed." The district court concluded: "The balance of conveniences here is not strongly in favor of [Unterweser] and [Zapata's] choice of forum should not be disturbed." . . .

[The Court of Appeals affirmed the district court's judgment.] It noted that (1) the flotilla never "escaped the Fifth Circuit's mare nostrum, and the casualty occurred in close proximity to the district court"; (2) a considerable number of potential witnesses, including Zapata crewmen, resided in the Gulf Coast area; (3) preparation for the voyage and inspection and repair work had been performed in the Gulf area; (4) the testimony of the *Bremen* crew was available by way of deposition; (5) England had no interest in or contact with the controversy other than the forum-selection clause. The court of appeals majority further noted that Zapata was a United States citizen and "the discretion of the district court to remand the case to a foreign forum was consequently limited" — especially since it appeared likely that the English courts would enforce the exculpatory clauses. In the court of appeals' view, enforcement of such clauses would be contrary to public policy in American courts under *Bisso v. Inland Waterways Corp.*, 349 U.S. 85 (1955), and *Dixilyn Drilling Corp. v. Crescent Towing & Salvage Co.*, 372 U.S. 697 (1963). Therefore, "the district court was entitled to consider that remanding Zapata to a foreign forum, with no practical contact with the controversy, could raise a bar to recovery by a United States citizen which its own convenient courts would not countenance."[2]

We hold . . . that far too little weight and effect were given to the forum clause in resolving this controversy. For at least two decades, we have witnessed an expansion of overseas commercial activities by business enterprises based in the United States. The barrier of distance that once tended

---

[2] The court of appeals also indicated in passing that even if it took the view that choice-of-forum clauses were enforceable, unless "unreasonable" it was "doubtful" that enforcement would be proper here because the exculpatory clauses would deny Zapata relief to which it was "entitled" and because England was "seriously inconvenient" for trial of the action.

to confine a business concern to a modest territory no longer does so. Here we see an American company with special expertise contracting with a foreign company to tow a complex machine thousands of miles across seas and oceans. The expansion of American business and industry will hardly be encouraged if, notwithstanding solemn contracts, we insist on a parochial concept that all disputes must be resolved under our laws and in our courts. Absent a contract forum, the considerations relied on by the court of appeals would be persuasive reasons for holding an American forum convenient in the traditional sense, but in an era of expanding world trade and commerce, the absolute aspects of the doctrine [as applied in the lower courts] have little place and would be a heavy hand indeed on the future development of international commercial dealings by Americans. We cannot have trade and commerce in world markets and international waters exclusively on our terms, governed by our laws, and resolved in our courts.

Forum-selection clauses have historically not been favored by American courts. Many courts, federal and state, have declined to enforce such clauses on the ground that they were "contrary to public policy," or that their effect was to "oust the jurisdiction" of the court. Although this view apparently still has considerable acceptance, other courts are tending to adopt a more hospitable attitude toward forum-selection clauses. This view, advanced in the well-reasoned dissenting opinion in the instant case, is that such clauses are *prima facie* valid and should be enforced unless enforcement is shown by the resisting party to be "unreasonable" under the circumstances. We believe this is the correct doctrine to be followed by federal district courts sitting in admiralty. It is merely the other side of the proposition recognized by this Court in *National Equipment Rental, Ltd. v. Szukhent,* 375 U.S. 311 (1964), holding that in federal courts, a party may validly consent to be sued in a jurisdiction where he cannot be found for service of process through contractual designation of an "agent" for receipt of process in that jurisdiction. In so holding, the Court stated: "It is settled . . . that parties to a contract may agree in advance to submit to the jurisdiction of a given court, to permit notice to be served by the opposing party, or even to waive notice altogether."

This approach is substantially that followed in other common-law countries including England. It is the view advanced by noted scholars and that adopted by the RESTATEMENT OF THE CONFLICT OF LAWS. It accords with ancient concepts of freedom of contract and reflects an appreciation of the expanding horizons of American contractors who seek business in all parts of the world. Not surprisingly, foreign businessmen prefer, as do we, to have disputes resolved in their own courts, but if that choice is not available, then in a neutral forum with expertise in the subject matter. Plainly, the courts of England meet the standards of neutrality and long experience in admiralty litigation. The choice of that forum was made in an arm's-length negotiation by experienced and sophisticated businessmen, and absent some compelling and countervailing reason, it should be honored by the parties and enforced by the courts.

The argument that such clauses are improper because they tend to "oust" a court of jurisdiction is hardly more than a vestigial legal fiction. It appears to rest at core on historical judicial resistance to any attempt to reduce the power and business of a particular court and has little place in an era when all courts are overloaded and when businesses once essentially local now operate in world markets. It reflects something of a provincial attitude regarding the fairness of other tribunals. No one seriously contends in this case that the forum-selection clause "ousted" the district court of jurisdiction over Zapata's action. The threshold question is whether that court should have exercised its jurisdiction to do more than give effect to the legitimate expectations of the parties, manifested in their freely negotiated agreement, by specifically enforcing the forum clause.

There are compelling reasons why a freely negotiated private international agreement, unaffected by fraud, undue influence, or overweening bargaining power,[3] such as that involved here, should be given full effect. In this case, for example, we are concerned with a far from routine transaction between companies of two different nations contemplating the tow of an extremely costly piece of equipment from Louisiana across the Gulf of Mexico and the Atlantic Ocean, through the Mediterranean Sea to its final destination in the Adriatic Sea. In the course of its voyage, it was to traverse the waters of many jurisdictions. The *Chaparral* could have been damaged at any point along the route, and there were countless possible ports of refuge. That the accident occurred in the Gulf of Mexico and the barge was towed to Tampa in an emergency were mere fortuities. It cannot be doubted for a moment that the parties sought to provide for a neutral forum for the resolution of any disputes arising during the tow. Manifestly, much uncertainty and possibly great inconvenience to both parties could arise if a suit could be maintained in any jurisdiction in which an accident might occur or if jurisdiction were left to any place where the *Bremen* or Unterweser might happen to be found.[4] The

---

[3] The record here refutes any notion of overweening bargaining power. Judge Wisdom, dissenting, in the court of appeals noted:

> Zapata has neither presented evidence of nor alleged fraud or undue bargaining power in the agreement. Unterweser was only one of several companies bidding on the project. No evidence contradicts its Managing Director's affidavit that it specified English courts 'in an effort to meet Zapata Off-Shore Company half way.' Zapata's Vice President has declared by affidavit that no specific negotiations concerning the forum clause took place. But this was not simply a form contract with boilerplate language that Zapata had no power to alter. The towing of an oil rig across the Atlantic was a new business. Zapata did make alterations to the contract submitted by Unterweser. The forum clause could hardly be ignored. It is the final sentence of the agreement, immediately preceding the date and the parties' signatures. . . .

[4] At the very least, the clause was an effort to eliminate all uncertainty as to the nature, location, and outlook of the forum in which these companies of differing nationalities might find themselves. Moreover, while the contract here did not specifically provide that the substantive law of England should be applied, it is the general rule in English courts that the parties are assumed, absent contrary indication, to have designated the forum with the view that it should apply its own law. It is therefore reasonable to conclude that the forum clause was also an effort to obtain certainty as to the applicable substantive law.

The record contains an affidavit of a Managing Director of Unterweser stating that Unterweser considered the choice-of-forum provision to be of "overriding importance" to the transaction. He stated that Unterweser towage contracts ordinarily provide for exclusive German jurisdiction and application of German law, but that "in this instance, in an effort to meet [Zapata] half way, [Unterweser] proposed the London Court of Justice. Had this provision not been accepted by [Zapata], [Unterweser] would not have entered into the towage contract . . . ." He also stated that the parties intended, by designating the London forum, that English law would be applied.

elimination of all such uncertainties by agreeing in advance on a forum acceptable to both parties is an indispensable element in international trade, commerce, and contracting. There is strong evidence that the forum clause was a vital part of the agreement,[5] and it would be unrealistic to think that the parties did not conduct their negotiations, including fixing the monetary terms, with the consequences of the forum clause figuring prominently in their calculations. . . .

Thus, in the light of present-day commercial realities and expanding international trade, we conclude that the forum clause should control, absent a strong showing that it should be set aside. Although their opinions are not altogether explicit, it seems reasonably clear that the district court and the court of appeals placed the burden on Unterweser to show that London would be a more convenient forum than Tampa, although the contract expressly resolved that issue. The correct approach would have been to enforce the forum clause specifically unless Zapata could clearly show that enforcement would be unreasonable and unjust, or that the clause was invalid for such reasons as fraud or overreaching. Accordingly, the case must be remanded for reconsideration.

We note, however, that there is nothing in the record presently before us that would support a refusal to enforce the forum clause. The court of appeals suggested that enforcement would be contrary to the public policy of the forum under *Bisso v. Inland Waterways Corp.*, 349 U.S. 85 (1955), because of the prospect that the English courts would enforce the clauses of the towage contract purporting to exculpate Unterweser from liability for damages to the *Chaparral*. A contractual choice-of-forum clause should be held unenforceable if enforcement would contravene a strong public policy of the forum in which suit is brought, whether declared by statute or by judicial decision. It is clear, however, that whatever the proper scope of the policy expressed in *Bisso*, it does not reach this case. *Bisso* rested on considerations with respect to the towage business strictly in American waters, and those considerations are not controlling in an international commercial agreement. Speaking for the dissenting judges in the court of appeals, Judge Wisdom pointed out:

> We should be careful not to over-emphasize the strength of the [*Bisso*] policy. . . . Two concerns underlie the rejection of exculpatory agreements: that they may be produced by overweening bargaining power; and that they do not sufficiently discourage negligence. . . . Here the conduct in question is that of a foreign party occurring in international waters outside our jurisdiction. The evidence disputes any notion of overreaching in the contractual agreement. And for all we know, the uncertainties and dangers in the new field of transoceanic towage of

---

A responsive affidavit by Hoyt Taylor, a vice president of Zapata, denied that there were any discussions between Zapata and Unterweser concerning the forum clause or the question of the applicable law.

[5] Zapata has denied specifically discussing the forum clause with Unterweser, but, as Judge Wisdom pointed out, Zapata made numerous changes in the contract without altering the forum clause, which could hardly have escaped its attention. Zapata is clearly not unsophisticated in such matters. The contract of its wholly owned subsidiary with an Italian corporation covering the contemplated drilling operations in the Adriatic Sea provided that all disputes were to be settled by arbitration in London under English law, and contained broad exculpatory clauses.

oil rigs were so great that the tower was unwilling to take financial responsibility for the risks, and the parties thus allocated responsibility for the voyage to the tow. It is equally possible that the contract price took this factor into account. I conclude that we should not invalidate the forum-selection clause here unless we are firmly convinced that we would thereby significantly encourage negligent conduct within the boundaries of the United States.

Courts have also suggested that a forum clause, even though it is freely bargained for and contravenes no important public policy of the forum, may nevertheless be "unreasonable" and unenforceable if the chosen forum is *seriously* inconvenient for the trial of the action. Of course, where it can be said with reasonable assurance that at the time they entered the contract, the parties to a freely negotiated private international commercial agreement contemplated the claimed inconvenience, it is difficult to see why any such claim of inconvenience should be heard to render the forum clause unenforceable. We are not here dealing with an agreement between two Americans to resolve their essentially local disputes in a remote alien forum. In such a case, the serious inconvenience of the contractual forum to one or both of the parties might carry greater weight in determining the reasonableness of the forum clause. The remoteness of the forum might suggest that the agreement was an adhesive one, or that the parties did not have the particular controversy in mind when they made their agreement; yet even there the party claiming should bear a heavy burden of proof.[6] Similarly, selection of a remote forum to apply differing foreign law to an essentially American controversy might contravene an important public policy of the forum. For example, so long as *Bisso* governs American courts with respect to the towage business in American waters, it would quite arguably be improper to permit an American tower to avoid that policy by providing a foreign forum for resolution of his disputes with an American towee.

This case, however, involves a freely negotiated international commercial transaction between a German and an American corporation for towage of a vessel from the Gulf of Mexico to the Adriatic Sea. As noted, selection of a London forum was clearly a reasonable effort to bring vital certainty to this international transaction and to provide a neutral forum experienced and capable in the resolution of admiralty litigation. Whatever "inconvenience" Zapata would suffer by being forced to litigate in the contractual forum as it agreed to do was clearly foreseeable at the time of contracting. In such circumstances, it should be incumbent on the party seeking to escape his contract to show that trial in the contractual forum will be so gravely difficult and inconvenient that he will for all practical purposes be deprived of his day in court. Absent that, there is no basis for concluding that it would be unfair, unjust, or unreasonable to hold that party to his bargain.

---

[6] *See, e.g.,* Model Choice of Forum Act § 3 (3), comment: "On rare occasions, the state of the forum may be a substantially more convenient place for the trial of a particular controversy than the chosen state. If so, the present clause would permit the action to proceed. This result will presumably be in accord with the desires of the parties. It can be assumed that they did not have the particular controversy in mind when they made the choice-of-forum agreement since they would not consciously have agreed to have the action brought in an inconvenient place."

In the course of its ruling on Unterweser's second motion to stay the proceedings in Tampa, the district court did make a conclusory finding that the balance of convenience was "strongly" in favor of litigation in Tampa. However, as previously noted, in making that finding the court erroneously placed the burden of proof on Unterweser to show that the balance of convenience was strongly in its favor.[7] Moreover, the finding falls far short of a conclusion that Zapata would be effectively deprived of its day in court should it be forced to litigate in London. Indeed, it cannot even be assumed that it would be placed to the expense of transporting its witnesses to London. It is not unusual for important issues in international admiralty cases to be dealt with by deposition. Both the district court and the court of appeals majority appeared satisfied that Unterweser could receive a fair hearing in Tampa by using deposition testimony of its witnesses from distant places, and there is no reason to conclude that Zapata could not use deposition testimony to equal advantage if forced to litigate in London as it bound itself to do. Nevertheless, to allow Zapata opportunity to carry its heavy burden of showing not only that the balance of convenience is strongly in favor of trial in Tampa (that is, that it will be far more inconvenient for Zapata to litigate in London than it will be for Unterweser to litigate in Tampa), but also that a London trial will be so manifestly and gravely inconvenient to Zapata that it will be effectively deprived of a meaningful day in court, we remand for further proceedings. . . .

Notes and Questions on *The Bremen*

1. *Rationale for the Bremen rule*. What is the rationale for the traditional common law rule limiting party autonomy in the selection of the forum? In the Supreme Court's view, what circumstances have changed to justify the modification of that traditional rule?

2. *Bremen and forum-selection clauses*. What are *The Bremen's* limits on the parties' ability to specify the forum in advance? Would the result be the same for example if the forum-selection clause had not been negotiated but had simply been included in a form contract between the same parties? Or suppose the selected forum had not been England, with its maritime history, but some

---

[7] Applying the proper burden of proof, Justice Karminski in the High Court of Justice at London made the following findings, which appear to have substantial support in the record:

[Zapata] pointed out that in this case the balance of convenience so far as witnesses were concerned pointed in the direction of having the case heard and tried in the United States district court at Tampa in Florida because the probability is that most, but not necessarily all, of the witnesses will be American. The answer, as it seems to me, is that a substantial minority at least of witnesses are likely to be German. The tug was a German vessel and was, as far as I know, manned by a German crew . . . . Where they all are now or are likely to be when this matter is litigated I do not know, because the experience of the Admiralty Court here strongly points out that maritime witnesses in the course of their duties move about freely. The homes of the German crew presumably are in Germany. There is probably a balance of numbers in favour of the Americans, but not, as I am inclined to think, a very heavy balance.

It should also be noted that if the exculpatory clause is enforced in the English courts, many of Zapata's witnesses on the questions of negligence and damage may be completely unnecessary.

other forum whose only connection to the contract was that it was mutually inconvenient for the parties. Same result?

3. *Bremen and statutes*. From one perspective, the Supreme Court in *The Bremen* was simply modifying a rule of common law admiralty it had adopted in *Bisso v. Inland Waterways Corp.*, and the Court acknowledged that its decision was for "federal district courts sitting in admiralty." 407 U.S. at 10. It is one thing for the Court to alter a common law rule and quite another to sustain a forum-selection clause that is in violation of, or inconsistent with, a statute, as *dicta* in *The Bremen* suggest: "[a] contractual choice-of-forum clause should be held unenforceable if enforcement would contravene a strong public policy of the forum in which suit is brought, whether declared by statute or by judicial decision." But it was not until the 1990's that the Supreme Court actually faced the argument that the underlying policy of a federal statute prohibited the selection of a foreign court. *See Carnival Lines Inc. v. Shute*, 499 U.S. 585 (1991) and *Vimar Seguros y Reaseguros, S.A. v. M/V Sky Reefer*, 515 U.S. 528 (1995), *infra*, p. 151.

4. *Forum-selection clauses and arbitration*. In *Mitsubishi Motors Corp. v. Soler Chrysler-Plymouth, Inc.*, 473 U.S. 614 (1985), *infra* p. 151, the Court extended *The Bremen* to foreign arbitration clauses, reasoning that agreements to arbitrate are simply specialized types of forum-selection clauses. Reinforcing *The Bremen*'s attack on provincialism, the Court noted that, if international arbitral institutions "are to take a central place in the international legal order, national courts will need to 'shake off the old judicial hostility to arbitration,' and also their customary and understandable unwillingness to cede jurisdiction of a claim arising under domestic law to a foreign or transnational tribunal." On what grounds might you resist the assumption that foreign arbitral tribunals and foreign courts should be treated equivalently?

5. *Limits on the Bremen rule*. *Bremen*'s endorsement of forum-selection clauses did not mean that such clauses were (or are) invariably enforced. *See, e.g., Copperweld Steel Co. v. Demag-Mannesmann-Bohler*, 578 F.2d 953 (3d Cir. 1978). If the clause were "manifestly unreasonable," the trial court would have the discretion to disregard it. In *Copperweld*,

the district court gave the following reasons for its decision not to enforce the forum-selection clause: (1) that the facility which was the subject of the action was located in Warren, Ohio, and was likely to become the object of an intensive inspection during the trial; (2) that the facility was fabricated by Birdsboro Corporation, a Pennsylvania contractor, in this country; (3) that all of the records concerning operation of the plant were in this country; (4) that all of Copperweld's personnel who operated the plant were in this country; (5) that all of Copperweld's personnel who negotiated the contract were in this country; (6) that certain of Demag's personnel involved in the sale were in this country and that Demag was doing business in the United States and maintained offices in Pittsburgh, Pennsylvania; (7) that practically all of the activities undertaken in connection with the contract took place in the English language; (8) that almost all of the witnesses were English speaking; and (9) that conducting the litigation in Germany would have required translation with inherent inaccuracies. Furthermore, all of the plant's customers were in this country and if their testimony were necessary, the district court envisioned difficulties in compelling their attendance in a German forum.

Id. The court of appeals found no abuse of discretion in the decision of the district court to retain jurisdiction.

CARNIVAL CRUISE LINES, INC. v. SHUTE
499 U.S. 585 (1991)

JUSTICE BLACKMUN delivered the opinion of the Court. In this admiralty case, we primarily consider whether the United States court of appeals for the Ninth Circuit correctly refused to enforce a forum-selection clause contained in tickets issued by petitioner Carnival Cruise Lines, Inc., to respondents Eulala and Russell Shute.

I

The Shutes, through an Arlington, Wash., travel agent, purchased passage for a 7-day cruise on petitioner's ship, the *Tropicale*. Respondents paid the fare to the agent who forwarded the payment to petitioner's headquarters in Miami, Fla. Petitioner then prepared the tickets and sent them to respondents in the State of Washington. The face of each ticket, at its left-hand lower corner, contained this admonition:

SUBJECT TO CONDITIONS OF CONTRACT ON LAST PAGES **IMPORTANT**! PLEASE READ CONTRACT — ON LAST PAGES 1, 2, 3

The following appeared on "contract page 1" of each ticket:

TERMS AND CONDITIONS OF PASSAGE CONTRACT TICKET . . . .

3. (a) The acceptance of this ticket by the person or persons named hereon as passengers shall be deemed to be an acceptance and agreement by each of them of all of the terms and conditions of this Passage Contract Ticket. . . .

8. It is agreed by and between the passenger and the Carrier that all disputes and matters whatsoever arising under, in connection with or incident to this Contract shall be litigated, if at all, in and before a Court located in the State of Florida, U. S. A., to the exclusion of the Courts of any other state or country.

The last quoted paragraph is the forum-selection clause at issue.

II

Respondents boarded the *Tropicale* in Los Angeles, Cal. The ship sailed to Puerto Vallarta, Mexico, and then returned to Los Angeles. While the ship was in international waters off the Mexican coast, respondent Eulala Shute was injured when she slipped on a deck mat during a guided tour of the ship's galley. Respondents filed suit against petitioner in the United States district court for the Western District of Washington, claiming that Mrs. Shute's injuries had been caused by the negligence of Carnival Cruise Lines and its employees.

Petitioner moved for summary judgment, contending that the forum clause in respondents' tickets required the Shutes to bring their suit against petitioner in a court in the State of Florida. Petitioner contended, alternatively, that the district court lacked personal jurisdiction over petitioner because petitioner's contacts with the State of Washington were insubstantial. The district court granted the motion . . . . The court of appeals reversed. . . .

Turning to the forum-selection clause, the court of appeals acknowledged that a court concerned with the enforceability of such a clause must begin its analysis with *The Bremen v. Zapata Off-Shore Co.*, where this Court held that forum-selection clauses, although not "historically . . . favored," are "prima facie valid." The appellate court concluded that the forum clause should not be enforced because it "was not freely bargained for." As an "independent justification" for refusing to enforce the clause, the court of appeals noted that there was evidence in the record to indicate that "the Shutes are physically and financially incapable of pursuing this litigation in Florida" and that the enforcement of the clause would operate to deprive them of their day in court and thereby contravene this Court's holding in *The Bremen*.

III

We begin by noting the boundaries of our inquiry. First, this is a case in admiralty, and federal law governs the enforceability of the forum-selection clause we scrutinize. Second, we do not address the question whether respondents had sufficient notice of the forum clause before entering the contract for passage. Respondents essentially have conceded that they had notice of the forum-selection provision. Brief for Respondents 26 ("The respondents do not contest the incorporation of the provisions nor [sic] that the forum-selection clause was reasonably communicated to the respondents, as much as three pages of fine print can be communicated"). Additionally, the court of appeals evaluated the enforceability of the forum clause under the assumption, although "doubtful," that respondents could be deemed to have had knowledge of the clause.

Within this context, respondents urge that the forum clause should not be enforced because, contrary to this Court's teachings in *The Bremen*, the clause was not the product of negotiation, and enforcement effectively would deprive respondents of their day in court. Additionally, respondents contend that the clause violates the Limitation of Vessel Owner's Liability Act, 46 U. S. C. App. § 183c. We consider these arguments in turn.

IV

A

Both petitioner and respondents argue vigorously that the Court's opinion in *The Bremen* governs this case, and each side purports to find ample support for its position in that opinion's broad-ranging language. This seeming paradox derives in large part from key factual differences between this case and *The Bremen*, differences that preclude an automatic and simple application of *The Bremen's* general principles to the facts here.

[The Court then discussed its general holding in *The Bremen*, that] "a freely negotiated private international agreement, unaffected by fraud, undue influence, or overweening bargaining power, such as that involved here, should be given full effect." The Court further generalized that "in the light of present-day commercial realities and expanding international trade we conclude that the forum clause should control absent a strong showing that it should be set aside." The Court did not define precisely the circumstances that would make it unreasonable for a court to enforce a forum clause. Instead, the Court discussed a number of factors that made it reasonable to enforce the clause at issue in *The Bremen* and that, presumably, would be pertinent in any determination whether to enforce a similar clause.

In this respect, the Court noted that there was "strong evidence that the forum clause was a vital part of the agreement, and [that] it would be unrealistic to think that the parties did not conduct their negotiations, including fixing the monetary terms, with the consequences of the forum clause figuring prominently in their calculations." Further, the Court observed that it was not "dealing with an agreement between two Americans to resolve their essentially local disputes in a remote alien forum," and that in such a case, "the serious inconvenience of the contractual forum to one or both of the parties might carry greater weight in determining the reasonableness of the forum clause." The Court stated that even where the forum clause establishes a remote forum for resolution of conflicts, "the party claiming [unfairness] should bear a heavy burden of proof."

In applying *The Bremen*, the court of appeals in the present litigation took note of the foregoing "reasonableness" factors and rather automatically decided that the forum-selection clause was unenforceable because, unlike the parties in *The Bremen*, respondents are not business persons and did not negotiate the terms of the clause with petitioner. Alternatively, the court of appeals ruled that the clause should not be enforced because enforcement effectively would deprive respondents of an opportunity to litigate their claim against petitioner.

The Bremen concerned a "far from routine transaction between companies of two different nations contemplating the tow of an extremely costly piece of equipment from Louisiana across the Gulf of Mexico and the Atlantic Ocean, through the Mediterranean Sea to its final destination in the Adriatic Sea." These facts suggest that, even apart from the evidence of negotiation regarding the forum clause, it was entirely reasonable for the Court in *The Bremen* to have expected [the parties] to have negotiated with care in selecting a forum for the resolution of disputes arising from their special towing contract. In contrast, respondents' passage contract was purely routine and doubtless nearly identical to every commercial passage contract issued by petitioner and most other cruise lines. In this context, it would be entirely unreasonable for us to assume that respondents — or any other cruise passenger — would negotiate with petitioner the terms of a forum-selection clause in an ordinary commercial cruise ticket. Common sense dictates that a ticket of this kind will be a form contract the terms of which are not subject to negotiation, and that an individual purchasing the ticket will not have bargaining parity with the cruise line. But by ignoring the crucial differences in the business contexts in which the respective contracts were executed, the court of appeals' analysis seems to us to have distorted somewhat this Court's holding in *The Bremen*.

In evaluating the reasonableness of the forum clause at issue in this case, we must refine the analysis of *The Bremen* to account for the realities of form passage contracts. As an initial matter, we do not adopt the court of appeals' determination that a nonnegotiated forum-selection clause in a form ticket contract is never enforceable simply because it is not the subject of bargaining. Including a reasonable forum clause in a form contract of this kind well may be permissible for several reasons: First, a cruise line has a special interest in limiting the fora in which it potentially could be subject to suit. Because a cruise ship typically carries passengers from many locales, it is not unlikely that a mishap on a cruise could subject the cruise line to litigation in several different fora. Additionally, a clause establishing *ex ante* the forum for dispute resolution has the salutary effect of dispelling any confusion about where suits arising from the contract must be brought and defended, sparing litigants the time and expense of pretrial motions to determine the correct forum and conserving judicial resources that otherwise would be devoted to deciding those motions. Finally, it stands to reason that passengers who purchase tickets containing a forum clause like that at issue in this case benefit in the form of reduced fares reflecting the savings that the cruise line enjoys by limiting the fora in which it may be sued.

We also do not accept the court of appeals' "independent justification" for its conclusion that *The Bremen* dictates that the clause should not be enforced because "there is evidence in the record to indicate that the Shutes are physically and financially incapable of pursuing this litigation in Florida." We do not defer to the court of appeals' findings of fact. . . . [T]he district court made no finding regarding the physical and financial impediments to the Shutes' pursuing their case in Florida. The court of appeals' conclusory reference to the record provides no basis for this Court to validate the finding of inconvenience. Furthermore, the court of appeals did not place in proper context this Court's statement in *The Bremen* that "the serious inconvenience of the contractual forum to one or both of the parties might carry greater weight in determining the reasonableness of the forum clause." The Court made this statement in evaluating a hypothetical "agreement between two Americans to resolve their essentially local disputes in a remote alien forum." In the present case, Florida is not a "remote alien forum," nor — given the fact that Mrs. Shute's accident occurred off the coast of Mexico — is this dispute an essentially local one inherently more suited to resolution in the State of Washington than in Florida. In light of these distinctions, and because respondents do not claim lack of notice of the forum clause, we conclude that they have not satisfied the "heavy burden of proof," required to set aside the clause on grounds of inconvenience.

It bears emphasis that forum-selection clauses contained in form passage contracts are subject to judicial scrutiny for fundamental fairness. In this case, there is no indication that petitioner set Florida as the forum in which disputes were to be resolved as a means of discouraging cruise passengers from pursuing legitimate claims. Any suggestion of such a bad-faith motive is belied by two facts: Petitioner has its principal place of business in Florida, and many of its cruises depart from and return to Florida ports. Similarly, there is no evidence that petitioner obtained respondents' accession to the forum clause by fraud or overreaching. Finally, respondents have conceded that they were given notice of the forum provision and, therefore, presumably retained the option of rejecting the contract with impunity. In the case before us, therefore, we conclude that the court of appeals erred in refusing to enforce the forum-selection clause.

B

Respondents also contend that the forum-selection clause at issue violates [The Limitation of Vessel Owners' Liability Act,] 46 U. S. C. App. § 183c. That statute, enacted in 1936, provides:

> It shall be unlawful for the . . . owner of any vessel transporting passengers between ports of the United States or between any such port and a foreign port to insert in any rule, regulation, contract, or agreement any provision or limitation (1) purporting, in the event of loss of life or bodily injury arising from the negligence or fault of such owner or his servants, to relieve such owner . . . from liability, or from liability beyond any stipulated amount, for such loss or injury, or (2) purporting in such event to lessen, weaken, or avoid the right of any claimant to a trial by court of competent jurisdiction on the question of liability for such loss or injury, or the measure of damages therefor. All such provisions or limitations contained in any such rule, regulation, contract, or agreement are hereby declared to be against public policy and shall be null and void and of no effect.

By its plain language, the forum-selection clause before us does not take away respondents' right to "a trial by [a] court of competent jurisdiction" and thereby contravene the explicit proscription of § 183c. Instead, the clause states specifically that actions arising out of the passage contract shall be brought "if at all," in a court "located in the State of Florida," which, plainly, is a "court of competent jurisdiction" within the meaning of the statute.

Respondents appear to acknowledge this by asserting that, although the forum clause does not directly prevent the determination of claims against the cruise line, it causes plaintiffs unreasonable hardship in asserting their rights and therefore violates Congress' intended goal in enacting § 183c. Significantly, however, respondents cite no authority for their contention that Congress' intent in enacting § 183c was to avoid having a plaintiff travel to a distant forum in order to litigate. The legislative history of § 183c suggests instead that this provision was enacted in response to passenger-ticket conditions purporting to limit the shipowner's liability for negligence or to remove the issue of liability from the scrutiny of any court by means of a clause providing that "the question of liability and the measure of damages shall be determined by arbitration." There was no prohibition of a forum-selection clause. Because the clause before us allows for judicial resolution of claims against petitioner and does not purport to limit petitioner's liability for negligence, it does not violate § 183c.

The judgment of the court of appeals is reversed.

JUSTICE STEVENS, with whom JUSTICE MARSHALL joins, dissenting.

The Court prefaces its legal analysis with a factual statement that implies that a purchaser of a Carnival Cruise Lines passenger ticket is fully and fairly notified about the existence of the choice of forum clause in the fine print on the back of the ticket. Even if this implication were accurate, I would disagree with the Court's analysis. But, given the Court's preface, I begin my dissent by noting that only the most meticulous passenger is likely to become aware of the forum-selection provision [in paragraph 8] . . . .

Of course, many passengers, like the respondents in this case, will not have an opportunity to read paragraph 8 until they have actually purchased their tickets. By this point, the passengers will already have accepted the condition set forth in paragraph 16(a), which provides that "the Carrier shall not be liable to make any refund to passengers in respect of . . . tickets wholly or partly not used by a passenger." Not knowing whether or not that provision is legally enforceable, I assume that the average passenger would accept the risk of having to file suit in Florida in the event of an injury, rather than canceling — without a refund — a planned vacation at the last minute. The fact that the cruise line can reduce its litigation costs, and therefore its liability insurance premiums, by forcing this choice on its passengers does not, in my opinion, suffice to render the provision reasonable.

Even if passengers received prominent notice of the forum-selection clause before they committed the cost of the cruise, I would remain persuaded that the clause was unenforceable under traditional principles of federal admiralty law and is "null and void" under the terms of Limitation of Vessel Owners' Liability Act, 46 U. S. C. App. § 183c, which was enacted in 1936 to invalidate expressly stipulations limiting shipowners' liability for negligence.

Exculpatory clauses in passenger tickets have been around for a long time. These clauses are typically the product of disparate bargaining power between the carrier and the passenger, and they undermine the strong public interest in deterring negligent conduct. For these reasons, courts long before the turn of the century consistently held such clauses unenforceable under federal admiralty law. Thus, in a case involving a ticket provision purporting to limit the shipowner's liability for the negligent handling of baggage, this Court wrote:

> It is settled in the courts of the United States that exemptions limiting carriers from responsibility for the negligence of themselves or their servants are both unjust and unreasonable, and will be deemed as wanting in the element of voluntary assent; and, besides, that such conditions are in conflict with public policy. This doctrine was announced so long ago, and has been so frequently reiterated, that it is elementary. . . .

Clauses limiting a carrier's liability or weakening the passenger's right to recover for the negligence of the carrier's employees come in a variety of forms. Complete exemptions from liability for negligence or limitations on the amount of the potential damage recovery, requirements that notice of claims be filed within an unreasonably short period of time, provisions mandating a choice of law that is favorable to the defendant in negligence cases, and forum-selection clauses are all similarly designed to put a thumb on the carrier's side of the scale of justice.

Forum-selection clauses in passenger tickets involve the intersection of two strands of traditional contract law that qualify the general rule that courts will enforce the terms of a contract as written. Pursuant to the first strand, courts traditionally have reviewed with heightened scrutiny the terms of contracts of adhesion, form contracts offered on a take-or-leave basis by a party with stronger bargaining power to a party with weaker power. Some commentators have questioned whether contracts of adhesion can justifiably be enforced at all under traditional contract theory because the adhering party generally enters into them without manifesting knowing and voluntary consent to all their terms.

The common law, recognizing that standardized form contracts account for a significant portion of all commercial agreements, has taken a less extreme position and instead subjects terms in contracts of adhesion to scrutiny for reasonableness. Judge J. Skelly Wright set out the state of the law succinctly in *Williams v. Walker-Thomas Furniture Co.*, 350 F.2d 445, 449–450 (1965) (footnotes omitted):

> Ordinarily, one who signs an agreement without full knowledge of its terms might be held to assume the risk that he has entered a one-sided bargain. But when a party of little bargaining power, and hence little real choice, signs a commercially unreasonable contract with little or no knowledge of its terms, it is hardly likely that his consent, or even an objective manifestation of his consent, was ever given to all of the terms. In such a case the usual rule that the terms of the agreement are not to be questioned should be abandoned and the court should consider whether the terms of the contract are so unfair that enforcement should be withheld.

The second doctrinal principle implicated by forum-selection clauses is the traditional rule that "contractual provisions, which seek to limit the place or court in which an action may . . . be brought, are invalid as contrary to public policy." Although adherence to this general rule has declined in recent years, particularly following our decision in *The Bremen*, the prevailing rule is still that forum-selection clauses are not enforceable if they were not freely bargained for, create additional expense for one party, or deny one party a remedy. A forum-selection clause in a standardized passenger ticket would clearly have been unenforceable under the common law before our decision in *The Bremen*, and, in my opinion, remains unenforceable under the prevailing rule today.

The Bremen, which the Court effectively treats as controlling this case, had nothing to say about stipulations printed on the back of passenger tickets. That case involved the enforceability of a forum-selection clause in a freely negotiated international agreement between two large corporations providing for the towage of a vessel from the Gulf of Mexico to the Adriatic Sea. The Court recognized that such towage agreements had generally been held unenforceable in American courts, but held that the doctrine of those cases did not extend to commercial arrangements between parties with equal bargaining power.

The federal statute that should control the disposition of the case before us today was enacted in 1936 when the general rule denying enforcement of forum-selection clauses was indisputably widely accepted. The principal subject of the statute concerned the limitation of shipowner liability, but as . . . the House Report explains, the section that is relevant to this case was added as a direct response to shipowners' ticketing practices. . . .

The stipulation in the ticket that Carnival Cruise sold to respondents certainly lessens or weakens their ability to recover for the slip and fall incident that occurred off the west coast of Mexico during the cruise that originated and terminated in Los Angeles, California. It is safe to assume that the witnesses — whether other passengers or members of the crew — can be assembled with less expense and inconvenience at a west coast forum than in a Florida court several thousand miles from the scene of the accident.

A liberal reading of the 1936 statute is supported by both its remedial purpose and by the legislative history's general condemnation of "all such practices." Although the statute does not specifically mention forum-selection clauses, its language is broad enough to encompass them. The absence of a specific reference is adequately explained by the fact that such clauses were already unenforceable under common law and would not often have been used by carriers, which were relying on stipulations that purported to exonerate them from liability entirely. . . .

The Courts of Appeals, construing an analogous provision of the Carriage of Goods by Sea Act, have unanimously held invalid as limitations on liability forum-selection clauses requiring suit in foreign jurisdictions. Commentators have also endorsed this view. The forum-selection clause here does not mandate suit in a foreign jurisdiction, and therefore arguably might have less of an impact on a plaintiff's ability to recover. However, the plaintiffs in this case are not large corporations but individuals, and the added burden on them of conducting a trial at the opposite end of the country is likely proportional to the additional cost to a large corporation of conducting a trial overseas.[1]

Under these circumstances, the general prohibition against stipulations purporting "to lessen, weaken, or avoid" the passenger's right to a trial certainly should be construed to apply to the manifestly unreasonable stipulation in these passengers' tickets. Even without the benefit of the statute, I would continue to apply the general rule that prevailed prior to our decision in *The Bremen* to forum-selection clauses in passenger tickets. I respectfully dissent.

Notes and Questions on *Carnival Lines*

1. *Bremen and Carnival Cruise Lines.* How if at all does the majority opinion in *Carnival Lines* alter *The Bremen*'s analysis of forum-selection clauses? Has

---

[1] The Court does not make clear whether the result in this case would also apply if the clause required Carnival passengers to sue in Panama, the country in which Carnival is incorporated.

the traditional prohibition on private forum arrangements been completely reversed, or can you articulate some recognizable limits?

2. *Standards for resisting enforcement.* What must parties resisting the enforcement of a forum-selection clause show in order to demonstrate that they "would effectively be deprived of their days in court?"

3. *Determining the respective burdens.* Why exactly is an increase in the Shutes' transaction costs of litigation not a lessening of Carnival Lines' liability within the meaning of the Limitation of Vessel Owners' Liability Act?

4. *Adhesion contracts.* Is the result in *Carnival Lines* an indication that (i) forum-selection clauses will be enforced even if they appear in an adhesion contract, or (ii) the contract in this case is not an adhesion contract in the first place?

5. *Classification of motion.* Procedurally, how should the courts classify a motion to dismiss on the basis of a foreign forum-selection clause? The courts have variously portrayed them as motions to dismiss for failure to state a claim under Rule 12(b)(6), F.R.C.P., *e.g., Silva v. Encyclopedia Britannica, Inc.*, 239 F.3d 385 (1st Cir. 2001); or as motions to dismiss for improper venue under Rule 12(b)(3), *e.g., Lipcon v. Underwriters at Lloyd's, London*, 148 F.3d 1285 (11th Cir. 1998); or as motions for lack of subject matter jurisdiction under Rule 12(b)(1), *e.g., AVC Netherland B.V. v. Atrium Inv. Partnership*, 740 F.2d 148, 153 (2d Cir. 1984). What important differences might the classification make?

---

[2] Forum-Selection Clauses and Statutes: *Mitsubishi Motors, Sky Reefer*, and their Aftermath

The courts of the United States have increasingly confronted the implications of the dictum in *The Bremen* that "[a] contractual choice-of-forum clause should be held unenforceable if enforcement would contravene a strong public policy of the forum in which suit is brought, whether declared by statute or by judicial decision." The majority in *Carnival Lines* concluded that nothing in the Limitation of Vessel Owners' Liability Act bars the enforcement of the forum-selection clause, because the clause would not inevitably "lessen, weaken, or avoid the right of any claimant to a trial by [a] court of competent jurisdiction on the question of liability for . . . loss or injury, or the measure of damages therefor." On its face, the selected court — Florida — was entirely competent to hear and resolve the Shute's claim. The sheer logistical difficulty that the Shutes might face in bringing a transcontinental case was not enough in the majority's view to trigger the statutory prohibition. To the contrary, the clause was enforced over the dissent's argument that the cost and inconvenience of traveling thousands of miles and maintaining a lawsuit in Florida "lessens or weakens [the plaintiffs'] ability to recover."

The dictum in *The Bremen* and the result in *Carnival Lines* raise the problem of reconciling the international community's interest in the cosmopolitan resolution of disputes with the nation's interest in enforcing its regulatory statutes. What little remains of the ancient predisposition against forum-selection clauses is the courts' unwillingness to allow private parties to circumvent the legitimate regulatory reach of the nation's law. Outright statutory prohibitions of forum-selection clauses are virtually non-existent, and therefore courts have had to determine whether and when the policies behind a statute are incompatible with — and therefore trump — a contractual choice of forum outside the United States. What must a statute do or say to reverse the presumption of enforceability?

In *Mitsubishi Motors Corp. v. Soler Chrysler-Plymouth*, 473 U.S. 614 (1985), the chosen forum was an arbitral tribunal in Japan applying Japanese law, and the party resisting enforcement of the clause claimed that enforcing the clause would compromise certain rights under U.S. antitrust law. The Court enforced the clause on the assumption that the lower court would retain jurisdiction over the case even as it went forward through arbitration and that the court "will have the opportunity at the award-enforcement stage to ensure that the legitimate interest in the enforcement of the . . . laws has been addressed." 473 U.S., at 638. The Court also noted an outer limit in principle on the enforceability of foreign arbitration clauses: if "the choice-of-forum and choice-of-law clauses operated in tandem as a prospective waiver of a party's right to pursue statutory remedies . . ., we would have little hesitation in condemning the agreement as against public policy."

Similarly, in *Vimar Seguros y Reaseguros, S.A. v. M/V Sky Reefer*, 515 U.S. 528 (1995), the Supreme Court ruled that a foreign arbitration clause in a maritime bill of lading does not lessen liability in violation of Section 3(8) of the Carriage of Goods by Sea Act, 46 U.S.C. App. § 1300 *et seq.*, ("COGSA"), which provides in part:

> Any clause, covenant, or agreement in a contract of carriage relieving the carrier or the ship from liability for loss or damage to or in connection with the goods, arising from negligence, fault, or failure in the duties and obligations provided in this section, or lessening such liability otherwise than as provided in this chapter, shall be null and void and of no effect.

46 U.S.C. App. § 1303(8). The Court focused on the specific forms of liability "provided in this section," noting that the standards of conduct laid out in COGSA were designed to stop carriers from capping damages, imposing unreasonable limitations periods for the filing of claims, and attempting to exempt themselves from liability altogether.

> Thus, § 3, entitled "Responsibilities and liabilities of carrier and ship," requires that the carrier "exercise due diligence to . . . [m]ake the ship seaworthy" and "[p]roperly man, equip, and supply the ship" before and at the beginning of the voyage, § 3(1), "properly and carefully load, handle, stow, carry, keep, care for, and discharge the goods carried," § 3(2), and issue a bill of lading with specified contents, § 3(3). 46 U.S.C. App. §§ 1303(1), (2), and (3). Section 3(6) allows the cargo owner to provide notice of loss or damage within three days and to bring suit within one year. These are the substantive obligations and particular procedures that § 3(8) prohibits a carrier from altering to its advantage in a bill of lading. Nothing in this section, however, suggests that the statute prevents the parties from

agreeing to enforce these obligations in a particular forum. By its terms, it establishes certain duties and obligations, separate and apart from the mechanisms for their enforcement.

As in *Mitsubishi*, the lower court retained jurisdiction over the case, allowing the Supreme Court to observe again that U.S. courts "will have the opportunity at the award-enforcement stage to ensure that the legitimate interest in the enforcement of the . . . laws has been addressed. . . . Were there no subsequent opportunity for review and we were persuaded that 'the choice-of-forum and choice-of-law clauses operated in tandem as a prospective waiver of a party's right to pursue statutory remedies . . ., we would have little hesitation in condemning the agreement as against public policy.' "

According to the Supreme Court then, nothing in the Limitation of Vessel Owners' Liability Act (*Carnival Lines*), the antitrust laws (*Mitsubishi*), or COGSA (*Sky Reefer*) is enough to reverse the presumption that foreign forum-selection clauses are enforceable, at least so long as (i) U.S. courts retain jurisdiction over the case at the enforcement stage and (ii) the choice-of-forum and choice-of-law clauses do not amount to a waiver of the right to pursue statutory remedies. As the following cases suggest, however, the law governing forum-selection clauses that overlap regulatory statutes may not have reached some final stage of development.

RICHARDS v. LLOYD'S OF LONDON
135 F.3d 1289 (9th Cir.) (*en banc*), *cert. denied*, 525 U.S. 943 (1998)

The primary question this case presents is whether the antiwaiver provisions of the Securities Act of 1933 and the Securities Exchange Act of 1934 void choice-of-law and choice-of-forum clauses in an international transaction. The district court found that they do not. The appeal has been argued twice. Upon reconsideration *en banc*, . . . we affirm the district court.

[Over six hundred U.S. investors in insurance syndicates managed by Lloyd's of London ("Names") sued Lloyd's], claim[ing] that Lloyd's actively sought the investment of United States residents to fill an urgent need to build up capital. According to the Names, Lloyd's concealed information regarding the possible consequences of the risks undertaken and deliberately and disproportionately exposed the Names to massive liabilities for which sufficient underwriting capital or reinsurance was unavailable. This appeal does not address the merits of the underlying claims. It addresses only the Names' contention that their disputes with Lloyd's should be litigated in the United States despite contract clauses binding the parties to proceed in England under English law. [The specific clauses in question appeared in a contract called a General Undertaking and provided:

2.1 The rights and obligations of the parties arising out of or relating to the Member's membership of, and/or underwriting of insurance business at, Lloyd's and any other matter referred to in this Undertaking shall be governed by and construed in accordance with the laws of England.

2.2 Each party hereto irrevocably agrees that the courts of England shall have exclusive jurisdiction to settle any dispute and/or controversy of whatsoever nature arising out of or relating to the Member's membership of, and/or underwriting of insurance business at, Lloyd's. . . .]

. . . The Names make three arguments for repudiating the choice clauses. They contend (1) that the antiwaiver provisions of the federal securities laws void such clauses, (2) that the choice clauses are invalid because they offend the strong public policy of preserving an investor's remedies under federal and state securities law and RICO [The Racketeer Influenced and Corrupt Organizations Act] and (3) that the choice clauses were obtained by fraud. We will address each of these in turn.

I

We analyze the validity of the choice clause under *The Bremen v. Zapata Off-Shore Co.*, 407 U.S. 1 (1972), where the Supreme Court stated that courts should enforce choice-of-law and choice-of-forum clauses in cases of "freely negotiated private international agreement[s]." *Bremen*, 407 U.S. at 12–13.[1]

A

The Names dispute the application of *Bremen* to this case. They contend that *Bremen* does not apply to cases where Congress has spoken directly to the immediate issue — as they claim the antiwaiver provisions do here. The Securities Act of 1933 (the " '33 Act") provides that:

> Any condition, stipulation, or provision binding any person acquiring any security to waive compliance with any provision of this subchapter or of the rules and regulations of the Commission shall be void.

15 U.S.C. § 77n. The 1934 Securities Exchange Act (the " '34 Act") contains a substantially similar provision. 15 U.S.C. § 78cc(a). The Names seize on these provisions and claim that they void the choice clauses in their agreement with Lloyd's.

Certainly the antiwaiver provisions are worded broadly enough to reach this case. They cover "any condition, stipulation, or provision binding any person acquiring any security to waive compliance with any provision of this subchapter. . . ." Indeed, this language is broad enough to reach any offer or sale of anything that could be alleged to be a security, no matter where the transaction occurs.

Nevertheless, this attempt to distinguish *Bremen* fails. In *Bremen* itself, the Supreme Court contemplated that a forum-selection clause may conflict with relevant statutes. *Bremen*, 407 U.S. at 15 ("A contractual choice-of-forum clause should be held unenforceable if enforcement would contravene a strong public policy of the forum in which suit is brought, whether declared *by statute* or by judicial decision.") (emphasis added).

Moreover, in *Scherk v. Alberto-Culver Co.*, 417 U.S. 506 (1974), the Supreme Court explicitly relied on *Bremen* in a case involving a securities transaction.

---

[1] While the contract in *Bremen* did not contain a choice of law clause, the Supreme Court explicitly recognized that the forum-selection clause also acted as a choice-of-law clause.

Echoing the language of *Bremen*, the Court found that "[a] contractual provision specifying in advance the forum in which disputes shall be litigated and the law to be applied is . . . an almost indispensable precondition to achievement of the orderliness and predictability essential to any international business transaction." *Id.* at 516. *See Bremen*, 407 U.S. at 13–14 ("[A]greeing in advance on a forum acceptable to both parties is an indispensable element in international trade, commerce, and contracting."). This passage should leave little doubt as to the applicability of *Bremen* to the case at hand.

Indeed, were we to find that *Bremen* did not apply, the reach of United States securities laws would be unbounded. The Names simply prove too much when they assert that "*Bremen*'s judicially-created policy analysis under federal common law is not controlling when Congress has expressed its will in a statute." This assertion, if true, expands the reach of federal securities law to any and all such transactions, no matter how remote from the United States. We agree with the Fifth Circuit that "we must tread cautiously before expanding the operation of U.S. securities law in the international arena." *Haynsworth v. The Corporation*, 121 F.3d 956, 966 (5th Cir. 1997).

B

[The court had no difficulty concluding that the Names' contract was international and therefore comes within the doctrine announced in *The Bremen*.] The Names signed a contract with English entities to participate in an English insurance market and flew to England to consummate the transaction. That the Names received solicitations in the United States does not somehow erase these facts. Moreover, Lloyd's insistence that individuals travel to England to become a Name does not strike us as mere ritual. Lloyd's likely requires this precisely so that those who choose to be the Names understand that English law governs the transaction. Entering into the Lloyd's market in the manner described is plainly an international transaction.

II

We now apply *Bremen* to this case. *Bremen* emphasized that "in the light of present-day commercial realities and expanding international trade we conclude that the forum clause should control absent a strong showing that it should be set aside." The Court reasoned that "[t]he elimination of all [] uncertainties [regarding the forum] by agreeing in advance . . . is an indispensable element in international trade, commerce, and contracting." Thus, "absent some compelling and countervailing reason [a forum selection clause] should be honored by the parties and enforced by the courts." The party seeking to avoid the forum-selection clause bears "a heavy burden of proof."

The Supreme Court has identified three grounds for repudiating a forum-selection clause: first, if the inclusion of the clause in the agreement was the product of fraud or overreaching; second, if the party wishing to repudiate the clause would effectively be deprived of his day in court were the clause enforced; and third, "if enforcement would contravene a strong public policy of the forum in which suit is brought." The Names contend that the first and third grounds apply in this case.

<h1 style="text-align:center">A</h1>

The Names' strongest argument for escaping their agreement to litigate their claims in England is that the choice clauses contravene a strong public policy embodied in federal and state securities law and RICO. *See Bonny v. Society of Lloyd's,* 3 F.3d 156, 160–61 (7th Cir. 1993) (expressing "serious concerns" that the choice clauses offend public policy but ultimately ruling in Lloyd's favor), *cert. denied,* 510 U.S. 1113 (1994).

We follow our six sister circuits that have ruled to enforce the choice clauses. *See Haynsworth,* 121 F.3d 956; *Allen v. Lloyd's of London,* 94 F.3d 923 (4th Cir. 1996); *Shell v. R.W. Sturge, Ltd.,* 55 F.3d 1227 (6th Cir. 1995); *Bonny,* 3 F.3d 156; *Roby,* 996 F.2d 1353; and *Riley v. Kingsley Underwriting Agencies, Ltd.,* 969 F.2d 953 (10th Cir.), *cert. denied,* 506 U.S. 1021 (1992). We do so because we apply *Scherk* and because English law provides the Names with sufficient protection.

In *Scherk,* the Supreme Court was confronted with a contract that specified that all disputes would be resolved in arbitration before the International Chamber of Commerce in Paris, France. The arbitrator was to apply the law of the state of Illinois. The Court enforced the forum-selection clause despite then hostile precedent.

The Court's treatment of [*Wilko v. Swan,* 346 U.S. 427 (1953), *overruled by Rodriguez de Quijas v. Shearson / American Express, Inc.,* 490 U.S. 477, 485 (1989)] leaves little doubt that the choice clauses in this case are enforceable. In *Wilko,* the Supreme Court ruled that "the right to select the judicial forum is the kind of 'provision' that cannot be waived under § 14 of the Securities Act." In *Scherk,* the Court had before it a case where both the district court and the Seventh Circuit found a forum-selection clause invalid on the strength of *Wilko.*

In distinguishing *Wilko,* the Supreme Court stated that there were "significant and, we find, crucial differences between the agreement involved in *Wilko* and the one signed by the parties here." *Scherk,* 417 U.S. at 515, 94 S.Ct. at 2455. The first and primary difference that the Court relied upon was that "Alberto-Culver's contract . . . was a truly international agreement." The Court reasoned that such a contract needs, as "an almost indispensable precondition," a "provision specifying in advance the forum in which disputes shall be litigated and the law to be applied." Moreover, the Supreme Court has explained that, in the context of an international agreement, there is "no basis for a judgment that only United States laws and United States courts should determine this controversy in the face of a solemn agreement between the parties that such controversies be resolved elsewhere." [*Scherk,*] at 517 n. 11. To require that " 'American standards of fairness' must . . . govern the controversy demeans the standards of justice elsewhere in the world, and unnecessarily exalts the primacy of United States law over the laws of other countries."

These passages from *Scherk,* we think, resolve the question whether public policy reasons allow the Names to escape their "solemn agreement" to adjudicate their claims in England under English law. *Scherk* involved a securities transaction. The Court rejected *Wilko*'s holding that the antiwaiver provision of the '34 Act prohibited choice clauses. It also recognized that enforcing the forum-selection clause would, in some cases, have the same effect as choosing foreign law to apply. Yet the Court did not hesitate to enforce the forum-selection clauses. It believed that to rule otherwise would "reflect a 'parochial concept that all disputes must be resolved under our laws and in our courts.'" As the Supreme Court has explained, "'[w]e cannot have trade and commerce in world markets and international waters exclusively on our terms, governed by our laws, and resolved in our courts.'" (quoting *Bremen*).

Relying on *Mitsubishi Motors Corp. v. Soler Chrysler-Plymouth, Inc.*, 473 U.S. 614 (1985), the Names argue that federal and state securities laws are of "fundamental importance to American democratic capitalism." They claim that enforcement of the choice clauses will deprive them of important remedies provided by our securities laws. The Supreme Court disapproved of such an outcome, the Names contend, when it stated that "in the event the choice-of-forum and choice-of-law clauses operated in tandem as a prospective waiver of a party's right to pursue statutory remedies for antitrust violations, we would have little hesitation in condemning the agreement as against public policy." *Id.* at 637 n. 19.

Without question this case would be easier to decide if this footnote in *Mitsubishi* had not been inserted. Nevertheless, we do not believe dictum in a footnote regarding antitrust law outweighs the extended discussion and holding in *Scherk* on the validity of clauses specifying the forum and applicable law. The Supreme Court repeatedly recognized in *Scherk* that parties to an international securities transaction may choose law other than that of the United States, yet it never suggested that this affected the validity of a forum-selection clause.[2]

B

Of course, were English law so deficient that the Names would be deprived of any reasonable recourse, we would have to subject the choice clauses to another level of scrutiny. *See Carnival Cruise Lines, Inc. v. Shute*, 499 U.S. 585, 595 (1991) ("It bears emphasis that forum-selection clauses contained in form passage contracts are subject to judicial scrutiny for fundamental fairness."). In this case, however, there is no such danger. *See Haynsworth*, 121 F.3d at 969 ("English law provides a variety of protections for fraud and misrepresentations in securities transactions."). *Cf. British Midland Airways Ltd. v. International Travel, Inc.*, 497 F.2d 869, 871 (9th Cir. 1974) (This court is "hardly in a position to call the Queen's Bench a kangaroo court.").

---

[2] The Names also point to *Vimar Seguros y Reaseguros, S.A. v. M/V Sky Reefer*, 515 U.S. 528 (1995), as support for their position. In *Vimar*, the Supreme Court expressed concern that a forum-selection clause combined with a choice-of-law clause would deprive a party of remedies under the Carriage of Goods by Sea Act ("COGSA"). The Court's reasoning in *Vimar*, however, does not extend to the instant case as *Vimar* involved COGSA, a statute designed to address international transactions. *Id.* at 537 ("COGSA is the culmination of a multilateral effort to establish uniform ocean bills of lading to govern the rights and liabilities of carriers and shippers inter se in international trade.") (internal quotations and citation omitted).

We disagree with the dramatic assertion that "[t]he available English remedies are not adequate substitutes for the firm shields and finely honed swords provided by American securities law." *Richards v. Lloyd's of London*, 107 F.3d 1422, 1430 (9th Cir. 1997). The Names have recourse against both the Member and Managing Agents[3] for fraud, breach of fiduciary duty, or negligent misrepresentation. Indeed, English courts have already awarded substantial judgments to some of the other Names.[4]

While it is true that the Lloyd's Act [of 1982, passed by Parliament,] immunizes Lloyd's from many actions possible under our securities laws, Lloyd's is not immune from the consequences of actions committed in bad faith, including fraud. The Names contend that entities using the Lloyd's trade name willfully and fraudulently concealed massive . . . liabilities in order to induce them to join syndicates. If so, we have been cited to no authority that Lloyd's partial immunity would bar recovery.

C

The addition of RICO claims does not alter our conclusion. This court has already held that the loss of RICO claims does not suffice to bar dismissal for *forum non conveniens*. *Lockman Found. v. Evangelical Alliance Mission*, 930 F.2d 764, 768–69 (9th Cir. 1991). We agree with our sister circuit that has considered this issue and extend the logic of *Lockman* to this case.

D

The Names also argue that the choice clauses were the product of fraud. They claim that at the time of signing the General Undertaking, Lloyd's knew that the Names were effectively sacrificing valid claims under U.S. law by signing the choice clauses and concealed this fact from the Names. Had the Names known this fact, they contend, they never would have agreed to the choice clauses. The Names never allege, however, that Lloyd's misled them as to the legal effect of the choice clauses. Nor do they allege that Lloyd's fraudulently inserted the clauses without their knowledge. Accordingly, we view the allegations made by the Names as going only to the contract as a whole, with no allegations as to the inclusion of the choice clauses themselves.

Absent such allegations, these claims of fraud fail. The Supreme Court has noted that simply alleging that one was duped into signing the contract is not enough. *Scherk*, 417 U.S. at 519 n. 14 (The fraud exception in *Bremen* "does not mean that any time a dispute arising out of a transaction is based upon an allegation of fraud . . . the clause is unenforceable."). For a party to escape a forum-selection clause on the grounds of fraud, it must show that "the inclusion of that clause in the contract was the product of fraud or coercion." *Id*. . . .

[W]e decide that the district court correctly ruled to enforce the choice clauses. . . .

---

[3] [Editor's note: Agents controlled each insurance syndicate and were responsible for its financial status. They were not employees of Lloyd's.]

[4] The Names complain that the Member and Managing Agents are insolvent. If so, this is truly unfortunate. It does not, however, affect our analysis of the adequacy of English law.

THOMAS, Circuit Judge, with whom Judge PREGERSON and Judge HAW-KINS join, dissenting.

The majority espouses a reasonable foreign policy, but one which emanates from the wrong branch of government. Congress has already explicitly resolved the question at hand. In the Securities Act of 1933 and the Securities Exchange Act of 1934 (the "Acts"), Congress expressly provided that investors cannot contractually agree to disregard United States securities law. Thus, in applying the "reasonableness" policy-weighing approach of *M/S Bremen v. Zapata Off-Shore Co.*, 407 U.S. 1 (1972), the majority displaces Congress' specific statutory directive. Furthermore, even assuming that the *Bremen* analysis applies here, the circumstances surrounding this dispute compel the conclusion that enforcement of the choice clauses would be unreasonable. Accordingly, I respectfully dissent.

I.

Unlike the conflict the *Bremen* Court envisioned between statutes and forum-selection clauses, the Acts do not merely declare "a strong public policy" against the waiver of compliance with United States securities laws. Rather, the Acts explicitly and unconditionally prohibit such a waiver. The language of the Securities Act of 1933 is clear and unambiguous:

> Any condition, stipulation, or provision binding any person acquiring any security to waive compliance with any provision of this subchapter or of the rules and regulations of the Commission shall be void.

15 U.S.C. § 77n. The Securities Exchange Act of 1934 contains a similar restriction. *See* 15 U.S.C. § 78cc(a). . . .

With adoption of those sections, Congress announced a *per se* rule that American laws cannot be ignored in this context. Courts should not employ amorphous public policy to emasculate plain statutory language. . . . The majority's fears notwithstanding, it is unnecessary to displace Congress' reasoned judgment in order to contract the "boundless" reach of United States securities laws. First, because plaintiffs alleging securities fraud will at some point have to establish that the disputed transactions involved "securities," as defined under United States law, plaintiffs cannot gain unfettered access to the protection of the securities laws simply by alleging that they have purchased securities. Second, the plaintiffs here do not seek to invoke the Acts' substantive remedies in the context of transactions that enjoy only an incidental nexus with the United States. Lloyd's recruited the plaintiffs, residents of the United States, in the United States, often using United States brokerage firms and recruiters, and availed itself of the United States mails to disseminate information about becoming a Name. In short, Lloyd's purpose-fully devoted considerable time and resources to recruiting American investors through specifically American media. . . .

The majority argues that the Supreme Court's reliance on *Bremen* in *Scherk v. Alberto-Culver Co.*, 417 U.S. 506 (1974), should control here. However, the majority overlooks the crucial differences between the instant dispute and the facts underlying *Scherk*. *Scherk* involved a contract that contained an agreement to arbitrate any disputes arising out of the contract in Paris, France.

This contract specified that "[t]he laws of the State of Illinois, U.S.A. shall apply to and govern this agreement, its interpretation and performance." *Scherk*, 417 U.S. at 508. In contrast, the choice clauses here not only select the forum — the courts of England — but mandate that English law shall govern any controversy. Thus, the reasoning and conclusions of *Scherk* should not extend to this case. To the extent that the *Scherk* Court approved a hypothetical choice-of-law clause that prescribed the application of foreign law, such approval was dicta and cannot bind the parties here.

Furthermore, the Lloyd's underwriting agreements had substantial connections with the United States, in contrast with the sparse contacts between the United States and the contract in *Scherk*. In *Scherk*, an American company made an initial contact with Scherk, a German citizen, in Germany, pursued negotiations with *Scherk* in both Europe and the United States, and finally executed a contract in Vienna, Austria, providing for the transfer of the ownership of Scherk's enterprises. The closing of this transaction occurred in Geneva, Switzerland. In comparison, the sole component of Lloyd's campaign to recruit American Names that took place in England was the committee meeting that new Names attended in London. Otherwise, every aspect of the solicitation occurred in the United States. To characterize this extensive and multifaceted recruitment campaign as the mere receipt of "solicitations," as does the majority, is to understate the impact of Lloyd's activities in the United States. The *Scherk* majority itself recognized that a contract with "insignificant or attenuated" contacts with foreign countries might well prompt a refusal to enforce a forum-selection clause, let alone a clause choosing foreign law. . . .

II.

In addition to violating the Acts' express antiwaiver provisions, the choice clauses are unenforceable because they are " 'unreasonable' under the circumstances." *Bremen*, 407 U.S. at 10. Initially, the Supreme Court has twice stated that the type of clauses at issue here are invalid when they prospectively disable parties from pursuing statutory remedies. *See Mitsubishi Motors Corp. v. Soler Chrysler-Plymouth, Inc.*, 473 U.S. 614, 637 n. 19 (1985), quoted in *Vimar Seguros y Reaseguros, S.A. v. M/V Sky Reefer*, 515 U.S. 528, 540 (1995). Indeed, in *Vimar*, the Court went so far as to declare that "[t]he relevant question" was "whether the substantive law to be applied [would] reduce the carrier's obligations to the cargo owner below what [the Carriage of Goods by Sea Act] requires." *Vimar*, 515 U.S. at 539. In other words, the Court implicitly rejected the argument that a forum-selection clause must be enforced even if some of the claims that could have been brought in the forum of the lawsuit must be forfeited.

As applied here, the logic of *Mitsubishi* and *Vimar* militates against enforcing the choice clauses. Not only do the choice clauses preclude the plaintiffs from seeking the substantive remedies the Acts offer, but the protections they provide under English law are markedly inferior to the Acts'. . . . Nor is there any English remedy against Lloyd's for negligent misrepresentation as provided by section 12(2) of the Securities Act of 1933, because the 1982 Lloyd's Act expressly immunizes Lloyd's from any claim for "negligence or other tort" unless bad faith was involved.[1] . . . Thus, the choice clauses should not be enforced, because they afford a level of protection far lower than the remedies the Acts provide.

The stark differences between American and English securities laws in turn reveal additional public policy reasons for invalidating the choice clauses. Enforcing the choice clauses gravely disadvantages American businesses, because foreign businesses, like Lloyd's, can recruit investors without expending the time and money involved in fulfilling the requirements of the Acts—a burden that American businesses cannot legally evade. Invalidating the choice clauses therefore eliminates any artificial advantage that Lloyd's may have enjoyed in competing in the American insurance market. In addition, the Acts furnish a necessary regulatory check upon an otherwise virtually autonomous organization. As the British government itself concedes, Lloyd's is a self-governing body charged with regulatory functions. Hence, a refusal to enforce the choice clauses would not reflect a lack of deference to English law and courts, but would simply arise from the realization that externally imposed restraints may sometimes be appropriate to control the behavior of a self-regulating organization. . . .

III.

Increasing access to international capital markets is a laudable goal, but one need not trample on United States securities laws to achieve it. Indeed, securitization of insurance risk is increasing, with some public offerings involving Lloyd's exposures. However, these insurance risk-backed securitized investments are marketed in conformance with securities law, with full disclosure to the investor. Indeed, the facts alleged in this case make a powerful argument for vigorous application of American securities laws. A company, whether foreign or domestic, should not be able to mislead American investors with impunity into assuming unlimited liability for known losses with no possibility of financial gain. When Congress voided waiver clauses, it meant what it said. The antiwaiver provisions of the Acts, whether as clear statutory directives or as embodiments of public policy, render the choice clauses unenforceable. The district court's dismissal of the plaintiffs' claims under the Acts should be reversed. Hence, I respectfully dissent.

Notes and Questions on *Lloyd's of London*

1. *Strategies for attacking the result in Lloyd's of London*. Assume that you represent Richards and the other American Names in this case. If the U.S. Supreme Court granted *certiorari* on the question of whether the Ninth Circuit

---

[1] While the plaintiffs may sue Members' and Managing Agents, who are not exempt from the 1982 Lloyd's Act, the Members' and Managing Agents are insolvent. The majority regards this insolvency, if true, as "truly unfortunate," but deems it irrelevant to the "analysis of the adequacy of English law." However, it is equally reasonable to find English law all the more inadequate to address the plaintiffs' grievances, because the insolvency of one class of potential defendants so materially damages the plaintiffs' chances for recovery.

had misapplied *The Bremen*, *Carnival Lines*, and their progeny, what arguments would you make?

2. *Statutory prohibitions*. If the antiwaiver provisions of the securities laws are insufficient to block the enforcement of a forum-selection clause, what statutory formulation — short of an outright prohibition on forum-selection clauses — would work? If the exclusive venue provisions of the Jones Act and the Federal Employees Liability Act are sufficient to block the common law *forum non conveniens* doctrine, are they also sufficient to override forum-selection clauses? *See, e.g.,* the Jones Act, 46 U.S.C. App. § 688(a) or the Federal Employers' Liability Act, 45 U.S.C. § 56.

3. *Aftermath*. In a wide variety of cases, Lloyd's of London has successfully invoked the forum-selection clauses in its General Undertakings with the American Names. As shown in Chapter 7, *infra*, Lloyd's has also successfully invoked transnational *res judicata* doctrines to enforce in U.S. courts the judgments it has won abroad. *See, e.g., Society of Lloyd's v. Ashenden*, 233 F.3d 473 (7th Cir. 2000).

---

[3] Attempts at Harmonization and Simplification

If a client were looking for a short, comprehensive restatement of the law governing forum-selection clauses, what would you say? Would it look like either of the following?

MODEL CHOICE OF FORUM ACT (selected provisions)
17 AM. J. COMP. L. 292 (1969)

§ 1. *Definitions*. As used in this Act, "state" means any foreign nation, and any state, district, commonwealth, territory or insular possession of the United States.

§ 2. *Action in this State by Agreement*.

(a) If the parties have agreed in writing that an action on a controversy may be brought in this state and the agreement provides the only basis for the exercise of jurisdiction, a court of this state will entertain the action if

    (1) the court has power under the law of this state to entertain the action;

    (2) this state is a reasonably convenient place for the trial of the action;

    (3) the agreement as to the place of the action was not obtained by misrepresentation, duress, the abuse of economic power, or other unconscionable means; and

(4) the defendant, if within the state, was served as required by law of this state in the case of persons within the state, or, if without the state, was served either personally or by registered [or certified] mail directed to his last known address.

. . . .

§ 3. *Action in Another Place by Agreement.* If the parties have agreed in writing that an action shall on a controversy be brought only in another state and it is brought in a court of this state, the court will dismiss or stay the action, as appropriate, unless

(1) the court is required by statute to entertain the action;

(2) the plaintiff cannot secure effective relief in the other state, for reasons other than delay in bringing the action;

(3) the other state would be a substantially less convenient place for the trial of the action than this state;

(4) the agreement as to the place of the action was obtained by misrepresentation, duress, the abuse of economic power, or other unconscionable means; or

(5) it would for some other reason be unfair or unreasonable to enforce the agreement.

§ 4. *Uniformity of Interpretation.* This Act shall be so construed as to effectuate its general purpose to make uniform the law of those states which enact it. . . .

CONFLICT OF JURISDICTION MODEL ACT (selected provisions)

§ 1. *Declaration of Public Policy.* It is an important public policy of this State to encourage the early determination of the adjudicating forum for transnational civil disputes, to discourage vexatious litigation and to enforce only those foreign judgments which were not obtained in connection with vexatious litigation, parallel proceedings, or litigation in inconvenient forums.

§ 2. *Discretion to Enforce Judgments.* [The CJMA prohibits recognition of a foreign judgment in parallel proceedings unless a local court has first designated the foreign court a proper "adjudicating forum." The factors for selecting the proper forum are laid out in Section 3.]

§ 3. *Factors in Selection of Adjudicating Forum.* A determination of the adjudicating forum shall be made in consideration of the following factors:

a. the interests of justice among the parties and of worldwide justice;

b. the public policies of the countries having jurisdiction of the dispute, including the interest of the affected courts in having proceedings take place in their respective forums;

c. the place of occurrence, and of any effects, of the transaction or occurrence, and of any effects, of the transaction or occurrence out of which the dispute arose;

d. the nationality of the parties;

e. substantive law likely to be applicable and the relative familiarity of the affected courts with that law;

f. the availability of a remedy and the forum most likely to render the most complete relief;

g. the impact of the litigation on the judicial systems of the courts involved, and the likelihood of prompt adjudication in the court selected;

h. location of witnesses and availability of compulsory process;

i. location of documents and other evidence and ease or difficulty associated with obtaining, reviewing, or transporting such evidence;

j. place of first filing and connection of such place to the dispute;

k. the ability of the designated forum to obtain jurisdiction over the person and property that are the subject of the proceeding;

l. whether designation of an adjudicating forum is a superior method to parallel proceedings in adjudicating the dispute;

m. the nature and extent of litigation that has proceeded over the dispute and whether a designation of an adjudicating forum will unduly delay or prejudice the adjudication of the rights of the original parties; and

n. a realigned plaintiff's choice of forum should rarely be disturbed.

. . .

————————

Why do you suppose the CJMA has been adopted in only one state since 1989, when it was proposed by the American Bar Association Section on International Law and Practice?

————————

Chapter 4

FINDING THE APPLICABLE LAW: CHOICE OF LAW AND THE JURISDICTION TO PRESCRIBE

At some point in every transnational case (and sometimes at several points), the court is required to choose which law from which jurisdiction should apply to resolve the dispute. It is not uncommon for the laws of different jurisdictions to control different issues within a single case, especially if the case is brought in one nation, on the basis of a cause of action that arose in another, involving parties from a third. The court is obliged to make a defensible choice of law for each issue that arises — everything from standing and the elements of the claim, to the burden of proof, the measure of damages, and evidentiary privileges. In this chapter, the problem of choosing law in a transnational case brought in the courts of the United States is divided into five separate topics:

1. What constitutional constraints are there on the court's choice of law?

2. What are the various approaches to choice of law among the states of the Union (and when are these approaches binding on the federal courts sitting in those states)?

3. To what extent does international law and comity limit a court's choice of law?

4. When will a court recognize the parties' autonomy in choosing the law to govern the dispute between them?

5. In what circumstances is it appropriate for the court to apply international law, rather than the law of any particular jurisdiction, and what unique difficulties arise when international law provides the rule of decision?

A. CONSTRAINTS OF DOMESTIC LAW

[1] Constitutional Limitations on State Choice-of-Law Rules

In contrast to issues of personal jurisdiction, where analysis under the Due Process Clause has been fundamental, the constitutional dimension of choice-of-law decisions has been surprisingly modest. That is especially true of the Due Process Clause, the Equal Protection Clause, the Privileges and Immunities Clause, and the Full Faith and Credit Clause, which — even taken together — do little to limit the constitutional space left for states and state courts to devise their own choice-of-law rules. The case of *Allstate Insurance v. Hague*, excerpted below, illustrates the breadth of that state power. On the other hand, transnational cases will frequently implicate the federal interest in foreign affairs, and so the constitutional provisions limiting state legislative powers may operate as a limit on the discretion of states to choose their own law. The case of *Crosby v. National Foreign Trade Council*, also excerpted below, illustrates those potential limits.

---

[a] Horizontal Choice of Law: Due Process and the Full Faith and Credit Clause

ALLSTATE INSURANCE CO. v. HAGUE
449 U.S. 302 (1981)

JUSTICE BRENNAN announced the judgment of the Court and delivered an opinion, in which JUSTICE WHITE, JUSTICE MARSHALL, and JUSTICE BLACKMUN joined.

This Court granted certiorari to determine whether the Due Process Clause of the Fourteenth Amendment[1] or the Full Faith and Credit Clause of Art. IV, § 1,[2] of the United States Constitution bars the Minnesota Supreme Court's choice of substantive Minnesota law to govern the effect of a provision in an insurance policy issued to respondent's decedent.

I

Respondent's late husband, Ralph Hague, died of injuries suffered when a motorcycle on which he was a passenger was struck from behind by an automobile. The accident occurred in Pierce County, Wis., which is immediately across the Minnesota border from Red Wing, Minn. The operators of both vehicles were Wisconsin residents, as was the decedent, who, at the time of the accident, resided with respondent in Hager City, Wis., which is one and one-half miles from Red Wing. Mr. Hague had been employed in Red Wing for the 15 years immediately preceding his death and had commuted daily from Wisconsin to his place of employment.

Neither the operator of the motorcycle nor the operator of the automobile carried valid insurance. However, the decedent held a policy issued by petitioner Allstate Insurance Co. covering three automobiles owned by him and containing an uninsured motorist clause insuring him against loss incurred from accidents with uninsured motorists. The uninsured motorist coverage was limited to $15,000 for each automobile.[3]

---

[1] The Due Process Clause of the Fourteenth Amendment provides that no State "shall . . . deprive any person of life, liberty, or property, without due process of law. . . ."

[2] The Full Faith and Credit Clause, Art. IV, § 1, provides: "Full Faith and Credit shall be given in each State to the public Acts, Records, and judicial Proceedings of every other State. And the Congress may by general Laws prescribe the Manner in which such Acts, Records, and Proceedings shall be proved, and the Effect thereof."

[3] Ralph Hague paid a separate premium for each automobile including an additional separate premium for each uninsured motorist coverage.

After the accident, but prior to the initiation of this lawsuit, respondent moved to Red Wing. Subsequently, she married a Minnesota resident and established residence with her new husband in Savage, Minn. At approximately the same time, a Minnesota Registrar of Probate appointed respondent personal representative of her deceased husband's estate. Following her appointment, she brought this action in Minnesota District Court seeking a declaration under Minnesota law that the $15,000 uninsured motorist coverage on each of her late husband's three automobiles could be "stacked" to provide total coverage of $45,000. Petitioner defended on the ground that whether the three uninsured motorist coverages could be stacked should be determined by Wisconsin law, since the insurance policy was delivered in Wisconsin, the accident occurred in Wisconsin, and all persons involved were Wisconsin residents at the time of the accident.

The Minnesota District Court disagreed. Interpreting Wisconsin law to disallow stacking, the court concluded that Minnesota's choice-of-law rules required the application of Minnesota law permitting stacking. The court refused to apply Wisconsin law as "inimical to the public policy of Minnesota" and granted summary judgment for respondent.

The Minnesota Supreme Court, sitting en banc, affirmed the District Court. The court, also interpreting Wisconsin law to prohibit stacking, applied Minnesota law after analyzing the relevant Minnesota contacts and interests within the analytical framework developed by Professor Leflar. *See* Leflar, *Choice-Influencing Considerations in Conflicts Law*, 41 N. Y. U. L. REV. 267 *(1966)*. The state court, therefore, examined the conflict-of-laws issue in terms of (1) predictability of result, (2) maintenance of interstate order, (3) simplification of the judicial task, (4) advancement of the forum's governmental interests, and (5) application of the better rule of law. Although stating that the Minnesota contacts might not be, "in themselves, sufficient to mandate application of [Minnesota] law," under the first four factors, the court concluded that the fifth factor — application of the better rule of law — favored selection of Minnesota law. The court emphasized that a majority of States allow stacking and that legal decisions allowing stacking "are fairly recent and well considered in light of current uses of automobiles." In addition, the court found the Minnesota rule superior to Wisconsin's "because it requires the cost of accidents with uninsured motorists to be spread more broadly through insurance premiums than does the Wisconsin rule." Finally, after rehearing en banc, the court buttressed its initial opinion by indicating "that contracts of insurance on motor vehicles are in a class by themselves" since an insurance company "knows the automobile is a movable item which will be driven from state to state." From this premise the court concluded that application of Minnesota law was "not so arbitrary and unreasonable as to violate due process."

II

It is not for this Court to say whether the choice-of-law analysis suggested by Professor Leflar is to be preferred or whether we would make the same choice-of-law decision if sitting as the Minnesota Supreme Court. Our sole function is to determine whether the Minnesota Supreme Court's choice of its own substantive law in this case exceeded federal constitutional limitations. Implicit in this inquiry is the recognition, long accepted by this Court, that a set of facts giving rise to a lawsuit, or a particular issue within a lawsuit, may justify, in constitutional terms, application of the law of more than one jurisdiction. *See generally Clay v. Sun Insurance Office, Ltd.,* 377 U.S. 179, 181–182 (1964) (hereinafter cited as Clay II). As a result, the forum State may have to select one law from among the laws of several jurisdictions having some contact with the controversy.

In deciding constitutional choice-of-law questions, whether under the Due Process Clause or the Full Faith and Credit Clause,[4] this Court has traditionally examined the contacts of the State, whose law was applied, with the parties and with the occurrence or transaction giving rise to the litigation. *See Clay II, supra,* at 183. In order to ensure that the choice of law is neither arbitrary nor fundamentally unfair, see *Alaska Packers Assn. v. Industrial Accident Comm'n,* 294 U.S. 532, 542 (1935), the Court has invalidated the choice of law of a State which has had no significant contact or significant aggregation of contacts, creating state interests, with the parties and the occurrence or transaction.[5]

Two instructive examples of such invalidation are *Home Ins. Co. v. Dick,* 281 U.S. 397 (1930), and *John Hancock Mutual Life Ins. Co. v. Yates,* 299 U.S. 178 (1936). In both cases, the selection of forum law rested exclusively on the presence of one nonsignificant forum contact . . . .

Dick and *Yates* stand for the proposition that if a State has only an insignificant contact with the parties and the occurrence or transaction, application of its law is unconstitutional. *Dick* concluded that nominal residence — standing alone — was inadequate; *Yates* held that a postoccurrence change of residence to the forum State — standing alone — was insufficient to justify application of forum law. Although instructive as extreme examples of selection of forum law, neither *Dick* nor *Yates* governs this case. For in contrast to those decisions, here the Minnesota contacts with the parties and the occurrence are obviously significant. Thus, this case is like *Alaska Packers, Cardillo v. Liberty Mutual Ins. Co.,* 330 U.S. 469 (1947), and *Clay II* — cases where this Court sustained choice-of-law decisions based on the contacts of the State, whose law was applied, with the parties and occurrence.

---

[4] This Court has taken a similar approach in deciding choice-of-law cases under both the Due Process Clause and the Full Faith and Credit Clause. In each instance, the Court has examined the relevant contacts and resulting interests of the State whose law was applied. *See, e.g., Nevada v. Hall,* 440 U.S. 410, 424 (1979). Although at one time, the Court required a more exacting standard under the Full Faith and Credit Clause than under the Due Process Clause for evaluating the constitutionality of choice-of-law decisions, *see Alaska Packers Assn. v. Industrial Accident Comm'n,* 294 U.S. 532, 549–550 (1935) (interest of State whose law was applied was no less than interest of State whose law was rejected), the Court has since abandoned the weighing-of-interests requirement. *Carroll v. Lanza,* 349 U.S. 408 (1955). . . .

[5] Prior to the advent of interest analysis in the state courts as the "dominant mode of analysis in modern choice of law theory," Silberman, *Shaffer v. Heitner: The End of an Era,* 53 N. Y. U. L. REV. 33, 80, n. 259 (1978), the prevailing choice-of-law methodology focused on the jurisdiction where a particular event occurred. *See, e.g.,* RESTATEMENT OF CONFLICT OF LAWS (1934). For example, in cases characterized as contract cases, the law of the place of contracting controlled the determination of such issues as capacity, fraud, consideration, duty, performance, and the like. *Id.,* § 332. In the tort context, the law of the place of the wrong usually governed traditional choice-of-law analysis. RESTATEMENT, *supra,* § 378. . . .

In *Alaska Packers*, the Court upheld California's application of its Workmen's Compensation Act, where the most significant contact of the worker with California was his execution of an employment contract in California. The worker, a nonresident alien from Mexico, was hired in California for seasonal work in a salmon canning factory in Alaska. As part of the employment contract, the employer, who was doing business in California, agreed to transport the worker to Alaska and to return him to California when the work was completed. Even though the employee contracted to be bound by the Alaska Workmen's Compensation Law and was injured in Alaska, he sought an award under the California Workmen's Compensation Act. The Court held that the choice of California law was not "so arbitrary or unreasonable as to amount to a denial of due process," because "[without] a remedy in California, [he] would be remediless," and because of California's interest that the worker not become a public charge.[6]

In *Cardillo v. Liberty Mutual Ins. Co., supra,* a District of Columbia resident, employed by a District of Columbia employer and assigned by the employer for the three years prior to his death to work in Virginia, was killed in an automobile crash in Virginia in the course of his daily commute home from work. The Court found the District's contacts with the parties and the occurrence sufficient to satisfy constitutional requirements, based on the employee's residence in the District, his commute between home and the Virginia workplace, and his status as an employee of a company "engaged in electrical construction work in the District of Columbia and surrounding areas."

Similarly, *Clay II* upheld the constitutionality of the application of forum law. There, a policy of insurance had been issued in Illinois to an Illinois resident. Subsequently, the insured moved to Florida and suffered a property loss in Florida. Relying explicitly on the nationwide coverage of the policy and the presence of the insurance company in Florida and implicitly on the plaintiff's Florida residence and the occurrence of the property loss in Florida, the Court sustained the Florida court's choice of Florida law.

The lesson from *Dick* and *Yates*, which found insufficient forum contacts to apply forum law, and from *Alaska Packers*, *Cardillo*, and *Clay II*, which found adequate contacts to sustain the choice of forum law,[7] is that for a

---

[6] The Court found no violation of the Full Faith and Credit Clause, since California's interest was considered to be no less than Alaska's, even though the injury occurred in Alaska while the employee was performing his contract obligations there. . . .

[7] The Court has upheld choice-of-law decisions challenged on constitutional grounds in numerous other decisions. *See Nevada v. Hall, supra* (upholding California's application of California law to automobile accident in California between two California residents and a Nevada official driving car owned by State of Nevada while engaged in official business in California); *Carroll v. Lanza,* 349 U.S. 408 (1955) (upholding Arkansas' choice of Arkansas law where Missouri employee executed employment contract with Missouri employer and was injured on job in Arkansas but was removed immediately to a Missouri hospital); *Watson v. Employers Liability Assurance Corp.,* 348 U.S. 66 (1954) (allowing application of Louisiana direct action statute by Louisiana resident against insurer even though policy was written and delivered in another State, where plaintiff was injured in Louisiana); *Pacific Employers Ins. Co. v. Industrial Accident Comm'n,* 306 U.S. 493 (1939) (holding Full Faith and Credit Clause not violated where California applied own Workmen's Compensation Act in case of injury suffered by Massachusetts employee temporarily in California in course of employment). Thus, *Nevada v. Hall* and *Watson v. Employers*

State's substantive law to be selected in a constitutionally permissible manner, that State must have a significant contact or significant aggregation of contacts, creating state interests, such that choice of its law is neither arbitrary nor fundamentally unfair. Application of this principle to the facts of this case persuades us that the Minnesota Supreme Court's choice of its own law did not offend the Federal Constitution.

III

Minnesota has three contacts with the parties and the occurrence giving rise to the litigation. In the aggregate, these contacts permit selection by the Minnesota Supreme Court of Minnesota law allowing the stacking of Mr. Hague's uninsured motorist coverages.

First, and for our purposes a very important contact, Mr. Hague was a member of Minnesota's work force, having been employed by a Red Wing, Minn., enterprise for the 15 years preceding his death. While employment status may implicate a state interest less substantial than does resident status, that interest is nevertheless important. The State of employment has police power responsibilities towards the nonresident employee that are analogous, if somewhat less profound, than towards residents. Thus, such employees use state services and amenities and may call upon state facilities in appropriate circumstances.

In addition, Mr. Hague commuted to work in Minnesota, a contact which was important in *Cardillo v. Liberty Mutual Ins. Co.,* and was presumably covered by his uninsured motorist coverage during the commute. The State's interest in its commuting nonresident employees reflects a state concern for the safety and well-being of its work force and the concomitant effect on Minnesota employers.

That Mr. Hague was not killed while commuting to work or while in Minnesota does not dictate a different result. To hold that the Minnesota Supreme Court's choice of Minnesota law violated the Constitution for that reason would require too narrow a view of Minnesota's relationship with the parties and the occurrence giving rise to the litigation. An automobile accident need not occur within a particular jurisdiction for that jurisdiction to be connected to the occurrence. Similarly, the occurrence of a crash fatal to a Minnesota employee in another State is a Minnesota contact. If Mr. Hague had only been injured and missed work for a few weeks, the effect on the Minnesota employer would have been palpable and Minnesota's interest in having its employee made whole would be evident. Mr. Hague's death affects Minnesota's interest still more acutely, even though Mr. Hague will not return to the Minnesota work force. Minnesota's work force is surely affected by the level of protection the State extends to it, either directly or indirectly. Vindication of the rights of the estate of a Minnesota employee, therefore, is an important state concern.

Liability Assurance Corp. upheld application of forum law where the relevant contacts consisted of plaintiff's residence and the place of the injury. *Pacific Employers Ins. Co. v. Industrial Accident Comm'n* and *Carroll v. Lanza* relied on the place of the injury arising from the respective employee's temporary presence in the forum State in connection with his employment.

Mr. Hague's residence in Wisconsin does not — as Allstate seems to argue — constitutionally mandate application of Wisconsin law to the exclusion of forum law. If, in the instant case, the accident had occurred in Minnesota between Mr. Hague and an uninsured Minnesota motorist, if the insurance contract had been executed in Minnesota covering a Minnesota registered company automobile which Mr. Hague was permitted to drive, and if a Wisconsin court sought to apply Wisconsin law, certainly Mr. Hague's residence in Wisconsin, his commute between Wisconsin and Minnesota, and the insurer's presence in Wisconsin should be adequate to apply Wisconsin's law.[8] Employment status is not a sufficiently less important status than residence, when combined with Mr. Hague's daily commute across state lines and the other Minnesota contacts present, to prohibit the choice-of-law result in this case on constitutional grounds.

Second, Allstate was at all times present and doing business in Minnesota.[9] By virtue of its presence, Allstate can hardly claim unfamiliarity with the laws of the host jurisdiction and surprise that the state courts might apply forum law to litigation in which the company is involved. "Particularly since the company was licensed to do business in [the forum], it must have known it

---

[8] Of course Allstate could not be certain that Wisconsin law would necessarily govern any accident which occurred in Wisconsin, whether brought in the Wisconsin courts or elsewhere. Such an expectation would give controlling significance to the wooden *lex loci delicti* doctrine. While the place of the accident is a factor to be considered in choice-of-law analysis, to apply blindly the traditional, but now largely abandoned, doctrine, would fail to distinguish between the relative importance of various legal issues involved in a lawsuit as well as the relationship of other jurisdictions to the parties and the occurrence or transaction. If, for example, Mr. Hague had been a Wisconsin resident and employee who was injured in Wisconsin and was then taken by ambulance to a hospital in Red Wing, Minn., where he languished for several weeks before dying, Minnesota's interest in ensuring that its medical creditors were paid would be obvious. Moreover, under such circumstances, the accident itself might be reasonably characterized as a bistate occurrence beginning in Wisconsin and ending in Minnesota. Thus, reliance by the insurer that Wisconsin law would necessarily govern any accident that occurred in Wisconsin, or that the law of another jurisdiction would necessarily govern any accident that did not occur in Wisconsin, would be unwarranted. . . .

If the law of a jurisdiction other than Wisconsin did govern, there was a substantial likelihood, with respect to uninsured motorist coverage, that stacking would be allowed. Stacking was the rule in most States at the time the policy was issued. Indeed, the Wisconsin Supreme Court, in [a separate case] identified 29 States, including Minnesota, whose law it interpreted to allow stacking, and only 9 States whose law it interpreted to prohibit stacking. Clearly then, Allstate could not have expected that an antistacking rule would govern any particular accident in which the insured might be involved and thus cannot claim unfair surprise from the Minnesota Supreme Court's choice of forum law.

[9] The Court has recognized that examination of a State's contacts may result in divergent conclusions for jurisdiction and choice-of-law purposes. See *Kulko v. California Superior Court,* 436 U.S. 84, 98 (1978) (no jurisdiction in California but California law "arguably might" apply); *Shaffer v. Heitner,* 433 U.S., at 215 (no jurisdiction in Delaware, although Delaware interest "may support the application of Delaware law"); *cf. Hanson v. Denckla,* 357 U.S. 235, 254, and n. 27 (1958) (no jurisdiction in Florida; the "issue is personal jurisdiction, not choice of law," an issue which the Court found no need to decide). Nevertheless, "both inquiries 'are often closely related and to a substantial degree depend upon similar considerations.'" *Shaffer,* 433 U.S., at 224–225 (Brennan, J., concurring in part and dissenting in part). Here, of course, jurisdiction in the Minnesota courts is unquestioned, a factor not without significance in assessing the constitutionality of Minnesota's choice of its own substantive law. *Cf. id.,* at 225 ("the decision that it is fair to bind a defendant by a State's laws and rules should prove to be highly relevant to the fairness of permitting that same State to accept jurisdiction for adjudicating the controversy").

might be sued there, and that [the forum] courts would feel bound by [forum] law."[10] Moreover, Allstate's presence in Minnesota gave Minnesota an interest in regulating the company's insurance obligations insofar as they affected both a Minnesota resident and court-appointed representative — respondent — and a longstanding member of Minnesota's work force — Mr. Hague.

Third, respondent became a Minnesota resident prior to institution of this litigation. The stipulated facts reveal that she first settled in Red Wing, Minn., the town in which her late husband had worked. She subsequently moved to Savage, Minn., after marrying a Minnesota resident who operated an automobile service station in Bloomington, Minn. Her move to Savage occurred "almost concurrently" with the initiation of the instant case. There is no suggestion that Mrs. Hague moved to Minnesota in anticipation of this litigation or for the purpose of finding a legal climate especially hospitable to her claim.[11] The stipulated facts, sparse as they are, negate any such inference.

While *John Hancock Mutual Life Ins. Co. v. Yates,* 299 U.S. 178 (1936), held that a postoccurrence change of residence to the forum State was insufficient in and of itself to confer power on the forum State to choose its law, that case did not hold that such a change of residence was irrelevant. Here, of course, respondent's *bona fide* residence in Minnesota was not the sole contact Minnesota had with this litigation. And in connection with her residence in Minnesota, respondent was appointed personal representative of Mr. Hague's estate by the Registrar of Probate for the County of Goodhue, Minn. Respondent's residence and subsequent appointment in Minnesota as personal representative of her late husband's estate constitute a Minnesota contact which gives Minnesota an interest in respondent's recovery, an interest which the court below identified as full compensation for "resident accident victims" to keep them "off welfare rolls" and able "to meet financial obligations."

In sum, Minnesota had a significant aggregation[12] of contacts with the parties and the occurrence, creating state interests, such that application of its law was neither arbitrary nor fundamentally unfair. Accordingly, the choice of Minnesota law by the Minnesota Supreme Court did not violate the Due Process Clause or the Full Faith and Credit Clause.

AFFIRMED.

JUSTICE STEWART took no part in the consideration or decision of this case. [JUSTICE STEVENS' concurrence, in which he distinguishes the

---

[10] There is no element of unfair surprise or frustration of legitimate expectations as a result of Minnesota's choice of its law. Because Allstate was doing business in Minnesota and was undoubtedly aware that Mr. Hague was a Minnesota employee, it had to have anticipated that Minnesota law might apply to an accident in which Mr. Hague was involved. . . . Indeed, Allstate specifically anticipated that Mr. Hague might suffer an accident either in Minnesota or elsewhere in the United States, outside of Wisconsin, since the policy it issued offered continental coverage. At the same time, Allstate did not seek to control construction of the contract since the policy contained no choice-of-law clause dictating application of Wisconsin law.

[11] The dissent suggests that considering respondent's postoccurrence change of residence as one of the Minnesota contacts will encourage forum shopping. This overlooks the fact that her change of residence was bona fide and not motivated by litigation considerations.

[12] We express no view whether the first two contacts, either together or separately, would have sufficed to sustain the choice of Minnesota law made by the Minnesota Supreme Court.

requirements of the Full Faith and Credit Clause from the requirements of the Due Process Clause, is omitted.]

JUSTICE POWELL, with whom THE CHIEF JUSTICE and JUSTICE REHN-QUIST join, dissenting.

My disagreement with the plurality is narrow. I accept with few reservations Part II of the plurality opinion, which sets forth the basic principles that guide us in reviewing state choice-of-law decisions under the Constitution. The Court should invalidate a forum State's decision to apply its own law only when there are no significant contacts between the State and the litigation. This modest check on state power is mandated by the Due Process Clause of the Fourteenth Amendment and the Full Faith and Credit Clause of Art. IV, § 1. I do not believe, however, that the plurality adequately analyzes the policies such review must serve. In consequence, it has found significant what appear to me to be trivial contacts between the forum State and the litigation.

I

At least since *Carroll v. Lanza, supra,* the Court has recognized that both the Due Process and the Full Faith and Credit Clauses are satisfied if the forum has such significant contacts with the litigation that it has a legitimate state interest in applying its own law. The significance of asserted contacts must be evaluated in light of the constitutional policies that oversight by this Court should serve. Two enduring policies emerge from our cases.

First, the contacts between the forum State and the litigation should not be so "slight and casual" that it would be fundamentally unfair to a litigant for the forum to apply its own State's law. *Clay v. Sun Ins. Office, Ltd., supra.* The touchstone here is the reasonable expectation of the parties. . . .

Second, the forum State must have a legitimate interest in the outcome of the litigation before it. *Pacific Ins. Co. v. Industrial Accident Comm'n,* 306 U.S. 493 (1939). The Full Faith and Credit Clause addresses the accommodation of sovereign power among the various States. Under limited circumstances, it requires one State to give effect to the statutory law of another State. To be sure, a forum State need not give effect to another State's law if that law is in "violation of its own legitimate public policy" [citing *Nevada v. Hall, supra*]. Nonetheless, for a forum State to further its legitimate public policy by applying its own law to a controversy, there must be some connection between the facts giving rise to the litigation and the scope of the State's lawmaking jurisdiction.

. . . The State has a legitimate interest in applying a rule of decision to the litigation only if the facts to which the rule will be applied have created effects within the State, toward which the State's public policy is directed. To assess the sufficiency of asserted contacts between the forum and the litigation, the court must determine if the contacts form a reasonable link between the litigation and a state policy. In short, examination of contacts addresses whether "the state has an interest in the application of its policy in this instance." Currie, *The Constitution and the Choice of Law: Governmental Interests and the Judicial Function*, in B. Currie, SELECTED ESSAYS ON

THE CONFLICT OF LAWS 188, 189 (1963) (Currie). If it does, the Constitution is satisfied. . . .

In summary, the significance of the contacts between a forum State and the litigation must be assessed in light of these two important constitutional policies. A contact, or a pattern of contacts, satisfies the Constitution when it protects the litigants from being unfairly surprised if the forum State applies its own law, and when the application of the forum's law reasonably can be understood to further a legitimate public policy of the forum State.

II

Recognition of the complexity of the constitutional inquiry requires that this Court apply these principles with restraint. Applying these principles to the facts of this case, I do not believe, however, that Minnesota had sufficient contacts with the "persons and events" in this litigation to apply its rule permitting stacking. I would agree that no reasonable expectations of the parties were frustrated. The risk insured by petitioner was not geographically limited. The close proximity of Hager City, Wis., to Minnesota, and the fact that Hague commuted daily to Red Wing, Minn., for many years should have led the insurer to realize that there was a reasonable probability that the risk would materialize in Minnesota. Under our precedents, it is plain that Minnesota could have applied its own law to an accident occurring within its borders. The fact that the accident did not, in fact, occur in Minnesota is not controlling because the expectations of the litigants before the cause of action accrues provide the pertinent perspective.

The more doubtful question in this case is whether application of Minnesota's substantive law reasonably furthers a legitimate state interest. The plurality attempts to give substance to the tenuous contacts between Minnesota and this litigation. Upon examination, however, these contacts are either trivial or irrelevant to the furthering of any public policy of Minnesota.

First, the postaccident residence of the plaintiff-beneficiary is constitutionally irrelevant to the choice-of-law question. *John Hancock Mut. Life Ins. Co. v. Yates, supra.* The plurality today insists that *Yates* only held that a postoccurrence move to the forum State could not "in and of itself" confer power on the forum to apply its own law, but did not establish that such a change of residence was irrelevant. What the *Yates* Court held, however, was that "there was no occurrence, nothing done, to which the law of Georgia could apply." Any possible ambiguity in the Court's view of the significance of a postoccurrence change of residence is dispelled by *Home Ins. Co. v. Dick, supra,* cited by the *Yates* Court, where it was held squarely that Dick's postaccident move to the forum State was "without significance."

This rule is sound. If a plaintiff could choose the substantive rules to be applied to an action by moving to a hospitable forum, the invitation to forum shopping would be irresistible. Moreover, it would permit the defendant's reasonable expectations at the time the cause of action accrues to be frustrated, because it would permit the choice-of-law question to turn on a postaccrual circumstance. Finally, postaccrual residence has nothing to do with facts to which the forum State proposes to apply its rule; it is unrelated to the substantive legal issues presented by the litigation.

Second, the plurality finds it significant that the insurer does business in the forum State. The State does have a legitimate interest in regulating the practices of such an insurer. But this argument proves too much. The insurer here does business in all 50 States. The forum State has no interest in regulating that conduct of the insurer unrelated to property, persons, or contracts executed within the forum State. The plurality recognizes this flaw and attempts to bolster the significance of the local presence of the insurer by combining it with the other factors deemed significant: the presence of the plaintiff and the fact that the deceased worked in the forum State. This merely restates the basic question in the case.

Third, the plurality emphasizes particularly that the insured worked in the forum State.[13] The fact that the insured was a nonresident employee in the forum State provides a significant contact for the furtherance of some local policies. The insured's place of employment is not, however, significant in this case. Neither the nature of the insurance policy, the events related to the accident, nor the immediate question of stacking coverage is in any way affected or implicated by the insured's employment status. The plurality's opinion is understandably vague in explaining how trebling the benefits to be paid to the estate of a nonresident employee furthers any substantial state interest relating to employment. Minnesota does not wish its workers to die in automobile accidents, but permitting stacking will not further this interest. The substantive issue here is solely one of compensation, and whether the compensation provided by this policy is increased or not will have no relation to the State's employment policies or police power.

Neither taken separately nor in the aggregate do the contacts asserted by the plurality today indicate that Minnesota's application of its substantive rule in this case will further any legitimate state interest. The plurality focuses only on physical contacts *vel non*, and in doing so pays scant attention to the more fundamental reasons why our precedents require reasonable policy-related contacts in choice-of-law cases. Therefore, I dissent.

Notes and Questions on *Allstate*

1. *Understanding the Allstate test.* Consider each of the major contacts cited by the plurality in *Allstate Insurance v. Hague* in justification for applying the Minnesota law: (i) the plaintiff's husband had been employed in Minnesota

---

[13] The plurality exacts double service from this fact, by finding a separate contact in that the insured commuted daily to his job. This is merely a repetition of the facts that the insured lived in Wisconsin and worked in Minnesota. The State does have an interest in the safety of motorists who use its roads. This interest is not limited to employees, but extends to all nonresident motorists on its highways. This safety interest, however, cannot encompass, either in logic or in any practical sense, the determination whether a nonresident's estate can stack benefit coverage in a policy written in another State regarding an accident that occurred on another State's roads.

Cardillo v. Liberty Mutual Ins. Co., supra, hardly establishes commutation as an independent contact; the case merely approved the application of a forum State's law to an industrial accident occurring in a neighboring State when the employer and the employee both resided in the forum State.

for fifteen years before his death; (ii) Allstate did business in Minnesota; and (iii) the plaintiff had moved to Minnesota prior to filing the suit. How would you articulate the connection between these contacts — individually or collectively — with the issue before the court?

2. *Allstate tested in Phillips Petroleum v. Shutts.* The precedents cited in *Allstate* suggest that the operative test for determining the constitutionality of a state's choice-of-law rules has two elements. First, the court will presumptively allow the forum to apply its own law provided that such a decision is fundamentally fair, meaning that no party is *unfairly surprised* by the application of that state's law. Especially where the parties have gotten the benefit of the forum state's law, it has generally been thought fair to impose the burdens of that law as a *quid pro quo. See, e.g., Home Ins. Co. v. Dick, supra. Clay II, supra.* Second, a state's law can only be applied if that state has an interest in the case other than as the forum chosen by the plaintiff, meaning that the policies and principles behind its laws are implicated on the facts of the case.

The impact of this latter criterion is illustrated by *Phillips Petroleum Co. v. Shutts*, 472 U.S. 797 (1985), in which the Supreme Court applied *Allstate* to invalidate an application of state law by that state's courts. In that case, a nationwide class action was brought against Phillips Petroleum in Kansas state court on behalf of royalty holders in all fifty states and some foreign countries, who had been deprived of interest on certain royalty payments that Phillips Petroleum had delayed. Although "over 99% of the gas leases and some 97% of the plaintiffs in the case had no apparent connection to the state of Kansas except for this lawsuit," 472 U.S., at 815, the Kansas Supreme Court allowed the application of Kansas law to every claim in the class. Phillips Petroleum sought review in the Supreme Court on the ground that the application of Kansas law in such circumstances violated the Due Process Clause and the Full Faith and Credit Clause.

The Court reiterated its observation in *Allstate* that "a particular set of facts giving rise to litigation could justify, constitutionally, the application of more than one jurisdiction's laws." (It also noted that there were significant differences between the law of Kansas and the laws of other states — notably Oklahoma, Louisiana, and Texas — making it impossible to pretend that the choice of law made no substantive difference in the case.) But the essence of the Court's analysis was its application of the *Allstate* standard:

> For a State's substantive law to be selected in a constitutionally permissible manner, that State must have a significant contact or significant aggregation of contacts, creating state interests, such that choice of its law is neither arbitrary nor fundamentally unfair.

None of the contacts asserted by the Kansas Supreme Court in justification of its decision to apply Kansas law across the class action satisfied this test — including the facts that Phillips Petroleum owned property and conducted substantial business in the state, that Kansas courts were familiar with this type of lawsuit, or that hundreds (from among the thousands) of the plaintiffs were Kansas residents. The Supreme Court continued:

> We also give little credence to the idea that Kansas law should apply to all claims because the plaintiffs, by failing to opt out [of the class

action], evinced their desire to be bound by Kansas law. Even if one could say that the plaintiffs "consented" to the application of Kansas law by not opting out, plaintiff's desire for forum law is rarely, if ever controlling. In most cases the plaintiff shows his obvious wish for forum law by filing there. "If a plaintiff could choose the substantive rules to be applied to an action . . . the invitation to forum shopping would be irresistible." *Allstate*, 449 U.S., at 337 (opinion of Powell, J.). Even if a plaintiff evidences his desire for forum law by moving to the forum, we have generally accorded such a move little or no significance. In *Allstate*, the plaintiff's move to the forum was only relevant because it was unrelated and prior to the litigation. Thus the plaintiffs' desire for Kansas law, manifested by their participation in this Kansas lawsuit, bears little relevance.

472 U.S., at 820.

The Court summarized its approach to fairness in this setting as giving important weight to the expectation of the parties:

> There is no indication that when the leases involving land and royalty owners outside of Kansas were executed, the parties had any idea that Kansas law would control. Neither the Due Process Clause nor the Full Faith and Credit Clause requires Kansas "to substitute for its own [laws], applicable to persons and events within it, the conflicting statute of another state," *Pacific Employees Ins. Co. v. Industrial Accident Comm'n*, 306 U.S. 493, 502 (1939), but Kansas "may not abrogate the rights of parties beyond its borders having no relation to anything done or to be done within them," *Home Ins. Co. v. Dick*, [281 U.S. 391], at 410. *Id.*

How exactly are Kansas' contacts with the issues and the parties in *Phillips Petroleum* constitutionally insufficient when compared with Minnesota's contacts with the issues and the parties in *Allstate*?

3. *Applying Allstate to an international case. Allstate* was an exclusively domestic case, involving courts and parties from two states of the Union. But suppose that the facts were "internationalized," and specifically that each of the contacts with Wisconsin were turned into contacts with Canada — meaning that the decedent lived in Canada, took out insurance policies, and was killed there. Would that strengthen or weaken the argument that the application of Minnesota law violates due process? Would it matter if the decedent and his wife were Canadian citizens throughout the litigation?

---

[b] Vertical Choice of Law: Federalism, Preemption, and the Foreign Affairs Power

The result in *Allstate* suggests that the Due Process and Full Faith and Credit Clauses of the Constitution pose only minimal constraints on the decision of a state's courts to apply that state's law to multistate or horizontal disputes. But transnational cases may also implicate the vertical relationship between the states and the national government in ways that were irrelevant in *Allstate*; indeed, as shown in the following cases, the legislative discretion of the states in such cases may well be limited by the Supremacy Clause[1] and the Foreign Commerce Clause[2] of the Constitution, not to mention the foreign affairs powers of the national government — a power not mentioned explicitly in the Constitution but derived from its structure and the nature of federalism.[3]

In *Zchernig v. Miller*, 389 U.S. 429 (1968), the plaintiff challenged an Oregon probate law that allowed a foreign citizen to inherit from a decedent's estate only if U.S. citizens could inherit from a decedent's estate in the foreign citizen's country. The Court held that Oregon's statute, as applied, was an unconstitutional "intrusion by the State into the field of foreign affairs which the Constitution entrusts to the President and the Congress." Expressing concern that the law as applied invited state courts to approve or disapprove the policies of foreign nations, the Court concluded that "the type of probate law that Oregon enforces affects international relations in a persistent and subtle way. . . . [I]nternational controversies of the gravest moment, sometimes even leading to war, may arise from real or imagined wrongs to another's subjects inflicted, or permitted, by a government." *Id.* at 441. The *Zchernig* power — specifically the authority of the courts to invalidate state laws that intrude too fundamentally on the foreign affairs powers of the United States government — has been routinely acknowledged but rarely invoked.

In *Crosby v. National Foreign Trade Council*, 530 U.S. 363 (2000), excerpted below, the Supreme Court invalidated a Massachusetts statute restricting the authority of state agencies to purchase goods or services from companies doing business with Burma. Under the Supremacy Clause, federal statutes may explicitly declare that they preempt state law, but even without an express provision to that effect, state law must yield to a congressional enactment in at least two circumstances. First, when Congress intends federal law to "occupy the field," state law in that area is preempted under the doctrine of "field preemption." And even when Congress has not occupied the field, state law is still preempted to the extent of any conflict with a federal statute. " 'Conflict preemption' is found where under the circumstances of a particular case, the challenged state law stands as an obstacle to the accomplishment

---

[1] Article VI, cl. 2 provides:

> This Constitution, and the Laws of the United States which shall be made in Pursuance thereof; and all Treaties made, or which shall be made, under the Authority of the United States, shall be the supreme law of the Land; and the Judges in every State shall be bound thereby, any Thing in the Constitution or Laws of any State to the Contrary notwithstanding.

[2] Article I, sec. 8, cl. 3 provides in part:

> The Congress shall have power . . . [t]o regulate Commerce with foreign Nations. . . .

[3] Compare Article I, § 10:

> No State shall . . . enter into any Treaty, Alliance, or Confederation [or] grant letters of Marque or Reprisal . . . [or] without the Consent of the Congress, lay any Imposts or Duties on Imports or Exports, except what may be absolutely necessary for executing [its] inspection Laws . . . . No State shall, without the Consent of Congress . . . enter into any Agreement or Compact with another State, or with a foreign power, or engage in War, unless actually invaded, or in such imminent Danger as will not admit of delay.

and execution of the full purposes and objectives of Congress." *Kroll v. Finery*, 242 F.3d 1359, 1364 (Fed. Cir. 2001). When Congress exercises its power under the Foreign Commerce Clause, pre-emption is possible though not inevitable, as *Gerling Global Reinsurance Corp v. Low*, summarized *infra*, makes clear.

Of course, the recent resurrection of federalism by the Supreme Court might have suggested that the ability of a state to apply its own law in international cases would enjoy a kind of renaissance, meaning that even this traditional constitutional limitation could become as flimsy as other constitutional provisions. *Compare, e.g., United States v. Lopez*, 514 U.S. 549 (1995) (invalidating federal Gun-Free School Zones Act on the ground that it exceeded Congress' authority over interstate commerce); *Alden v. Maine*, 527 U.S. 706 (1999) (invalidating overtime provisions of federal Fair Labor Standards Act, as applied to state workers, on the ground that Congress had no power to subject the state to suit in state courts without the state's consent); *Brzonkala v. Morrison*, 529 U.S. 598 (2000) (invalidating civil remedy provision of the federal Violence Against Women Act, on the ground that the provision was not a regulation of activity that substantially affects interstate commerce). The Supreme Court's decision in *Crosby* suggests that, when the state law interferes too much in the conduct of foreign relations, or undermines the president's singular powers in foreign relations, it will be invalidated despite the recent trend towards state power. *Gerling Global Insurance*, *infra*, offers some initial evidence that the lower courts may resist the broadest implications of *Crosby* and will continue to give states a wide berth of discretion, even when their actions have international consequences.

CROSBY v. NATIONAL FOREIGN TRADE COUNCIL
530 U.S. 363 (2000)

Justice SOUTER delivered the opinion of the Court.

The issue is whether the Burma law of the Commonwealth of Massachusetts, restricting the authority of its agencies to purchase goods or services from companies doing business with Burma,[1] is invalid under the Supremacy Clause of the National Constitution owing to its threat of frustrating federal statutory objectives. We hold that it is.

I

In June 1996, Massachusetts adopted "An Act Regulating State Contracts with Companies Doing Business with or in Burma (Myanmar)." The statute generally bars state entities from buying goods or services from any person (defined to include a business organization) identified on a "restricted purchase list" of those doing business with Burma. Although the statute has no

---

[1] The Court of Appeals noted that the ruling military government of "Burma changed [the country's] name to Myanmar in 1989," but the court then said it would use the name Burma since both parties and *amici curiae*, the state law, and the federal law all do so. We follow suit, noting that our use of this term, like the First Circuit's, is not intended to express any political view.

general provision for waiver or termination of its ban, it does exempt from boycott any entities present in Burma solely to report the news, or to provide international telecommunication goods or services, or medical supplies. . . . There are three exceptions to the ban: (1) if the procurement is essential, and without the restricted bid, there would be no bids or insufficient competition; (2) if the procurement is of medical supplies; and (3) if the procurement efforts elicit no "comparable low bid or offer" by a person not doing business with Burma, meaning an offer that is no more than 10 percent greater than the restricted bid. To enforce the ban, the Act requires petitioner Secretary of Administration and Finance to maintain a "restricted purchase list" of all firms "doing business with Burma."

In September 1996, three months after the Massachusetts law was enacted, Congress passed a statute imposing a set of mandatory and conditional sanctions on Burma. *See* Foreign Operations, Export Financing, and Related Programs Appropriations Act, 1997, § 570, 110 Stat. 3009-166 to 3009-167 (enacted by the Omnibus Consolidated Appropriations Act, 1997, § 101(c), 110 Stat. 3009-121 to 3009-172). The federal Act has five basic parts, three substantive and two procedural.

First, it imposes three sanctions directly on Burma. It bans all aid to the Burmese Government except for humanitarian assistance, counternarcotics efforts, and promotion of human rights and democracy. The statute instructs United States representatives to international financial institutions to vote against loans or other assistance to or for Burma, and it provides that no entry visa shall be issued to any Burmese government official unless required by treaty or to staff the Burmese mission to the United Nations. These restrictions are to remain in effect "[u]ntil such time as the President determines and certifies to Congress that Burma has made measurable and substantial progress in improving human rights practices and implementing democratic government."

Second, the federal Act authorizes the President to impose further sanctions subject to certain conditions. He may prohibit "United States persons" from "new investment" in Burma, and shall do so if he determines and certifies to Congress that the Burmese Government has physically harmed, rearrested, or exiled Daw Aung San Suu Kyi (the opposition leader selected to receive the Nobel Peace Prize), or has committed "large-scale repression of or violence against the Democratic opposition." "New investment" is defined as entry into a contract that would favor the "economical development of resources located in Burma," or would provide ownership interests in or benefits from such development, but the term specifically excludes (and thus excludes from any Presidential prohibition) "entry into, performance of, or financing of a contract to sell or purchase goods, services, or technology."

Third, the statute directs the President to work to develop "a comprehensive, multilateral strategy to bring democracy to and improve human rights practices and the quality of life in Burma." He is instructed to cooperate with members of the Association of Southeast Asian Nations (ASEAN) and with other countries having major trade and investment interests in Burma to devise such an approach, and to pursue the additional objective of fostering dialogue between the ruling State Law and Order Restoration Council (SLORC) and democratic opposition groups.

As for the procedural provisions of the federal statute, the fourth section requires the President to report periodically to certain congressional committee chairmen on the progress toward democratization and better living conditions in Burma as well as on the development of the required strategy. And the fifth part of the federal Act authorizes the President "to waive, temporarily or permanently, any sanction [under the federal Act] . . . if he determines and certifies to Congress that the application of such sanction would be contrary to the national security interests of the United States."

On May 20, 1997, the President issued the Burma Executive Order, Exec. Order No. 13047. He certified . . . that the Government of Burma had "committed large-scale repression of the democratic opposition in Burma" and found that the Burmese Government's actions and policies constituted "an unusual and extraordinary threat to the national security and foreign policy of the United States," a threat characterized as a national emergency. The President then prohibited new investment in Burma "by United States persons," any approval or facilitation by a United States person of such new investment by foreign persons, and any transaction meant to evade or avoid the ban. The order generally incorporated the exceptions and exemptions addressed in the statute. Finally, the President delegated to the Secretary of State the tasks of working with ASEAN and other countries to develop a strategy for democracy, human rights, and the quality of life in Burma, and of making the required congressional reports.

II

Respondent National Foreign Trade Council . . . is a nonprofit corporation representing companies engaged in foreign commerce; 34 of its members were on the Massachusetts restricted purchase list in 1998. Three withdrew from Burma after the passage of the state Act, and one member had its bid for a procurement contract increased by 10 percent under the provision of the state law allowing acceptance of a low bid from a listed bidder only if the next-to-lowest bid is more than 10 percent higher.

In April 1998, the Council filed suit in the United States District Court for the District of Massachusetts, seeking declaratory and injunctive relief against the petitioner state officials charged with administering and enforcing the state Act . . . . The Council argued that the state law unconstitutionally infringed on the federal foreign affairs power, violated the Foreign Commerce Clause, and was preempted by the federal Act. After detailed stipulations, briefing, and argument, the District Court permanently enjoined enforcement of the state Act, holding that it "unconstitutionally impinge[d] on the federal government's exclusive authority to regulate foreign affairs." *National Foreign Trade Council v. Baker*, 26 F. Supp. 2d 287, 291 (D. Mass. 1998).

The United States Court of Appeals for the First Circuit affirmed on three independent grounds. [*National Foreign Trade Council v. Natsios*, 181 F.3d 38 (1st Cir. 1999)], at 45. It found the state Act unconstitutionally interfered with the foreign affairs power of the National Government[;] violated the dormant Foreign Commerce Clause, U.S. Const. Art. I, § 8, cl. 3; and was preempted by the congressional Burma Act. The State's petition for certiorari challenged the decision on all three grounds and asserted interests said to be shared by other state and local governments with similar measures. . . . We granted certiorari . . ., and now affirm.

III

A fundamental principle of the Constitution is that Congress has the power to preempt state law. Art. VI, cl. 2; *Gibbons v. Ogden*, 9 Wheat. 1, 211 (1824). Even without an express provision for preemption, we have found that state law must yield to a congressional Act in at least two circumstances. When Congress intends federal law to "occupy the field," state law in that area is preempted. And even if Congress has not occupied the field, state law is naturally preempted to the extent of any conflict with a federal statute. We will find preemption where it is impossible for a private party to comply with both state and federal law, and where "under the circumstances of [a] particular case, [the challenged state law] stands as an obstacle to the accomplishment and execution of the full purposes and objectives of Congress." What is a sufficient obstacle is a matter of judgment, to be informed by examining the federal statute as a whole and identifying its purpose and intended effects:

> For when the question is whether a Federal act overrides a state law, the entire scheme of the statute must of course be considered and that which needs must be implied is of no less force than that which is expressed. If the purpose of the act cannot otherwise be accomplished—if its operation within its chosen field else must be frustrated and its provisions be refused their natural effect—the state law must yield to the regulation of Congress within the sphere of its delegated power.

Savage [*v. Jones*, 225 U.S. 501, 533 (1912).]

Applying this standard, we see the state Burma law as an obstacle to the accomplishment of Congress's full objectives under the federal Act. We find that the state law undermines the intended purpose and "natural effect" of at least three provisions of the federal Act, that is, its delegation of effective discretion to the President to control economic sanctions against Burma, its limitation of sanctions solely to United States persons and new investment, and its directive to the President to proceed diplomatically in developing a comprehensive, multilateral strategy towards Burma. . . .

A

First, Congress clearly intended the federal act to provide the President with flexible and effective authority over economic sanctions against Burma. Although Congress immediately put in place a set of initial sanctions (prohibiting bilateral aid, support for international financial assistance, and entry by Burmese officials into the United States), it authorized the President to terminate any and all of those measures upon determining and certifying that there had been progress in human rights and democracy in Burma. It invested the President with the further power to ban new investment by United States persons, dependent only on specific Presidential findings of repression in Burma. And, most significantly, Congress empowered the President "to waive, temporarily or permanently, any sanction [under the federal act] . . . if he determines and certifies to Congress that the application of such sanction would be contrary to the national security interests of the United States."

This express investiture of the President with statutory authority to act for the United States in imposing sanctions with respect to the government of Burma, augmented by the flexibility to respond to change by suspending sanctions in the interest of national security, recalls Justice Jackson's observation in *Youngstown Sheet & Tube Co. v. Sawyer*, 343 U.S. 579, 635 (1952): "When the President acts pursuant to an express or implied authorization of Congress, his authority is at its maximum, for it includes all that he possesses in his own right plus all that Congress can delegate." . . . [T]he President's power in the area of foreign relations is least restricted by Congress. . . . Within the sphere defined by Congress, then, the statute has placed the President in a position with as much discretion to exercise economic leverage against Burma, with an eye toward national security, as our law will admit. And it is just this plenitude of Executive authority that we think controls the issue of preemption here. The President has been given this authority not merely to make a political statement but to achieve a political result, and the fullness of his authority shows the importance in the congressional mind of reaching that result. It is simply implausible that Congress would have gone to such lengths to empower the President if it had been willing to compromise his effectiveness by deference to every provision of state statute or local ordinance that might, if enforced, blunt the consequences of discretionary Presidential action.

And that is just what the Massachusetts Burma law would do in imposing a different, state system of economic pressure against the Burmese political regime. . . . [T]he state statute penalizes some private action that the federal Act (as administered by the President) may allow, and pulls levers of influence that the federal Act does not reach. But the point here is that the state sanctions are immediate, . . . and perpetual, there being no termination provision. . . . This unyielding application undermines the President's intended statutory authority by making it impossible for him to restrain fully the coercive power of the national economy when he may choose to take the discretionary action open to him, whether he believes that the national interest requires sanctions to be lifted, or believes that the promise of lifting sanctions would move the Burmese regime in the democratic direction. Quite simply, if the Massachusetts law is enforceable the President has less to offer and less economic and diplomatic leverage as a consequence. In *Dames & Moore v. Regan*, 453 U.S. 654 (1981), we used the metaphor of the bargaining chip to describe the President's control of funds valuable to a hostile country; here, the state Act reduces the value of the chips created by the federal statute. It thus stands as an obstacle to the accomplishment and execution of the full purposes and objectives of Congress.

B

Congress manifestly intended to limit economic pressure against the Burmese Government to a specific range. The federal Act confines its reach to United States persons, imposes limited immediate sanctions, places only a conditional ban on a carefully defined area of "new investment," and pointedly exempts contracts to sell or purchase goods, services, or technology. . . .

The State has set a different course, and its statute conflicts with federal law at a number of points by penalizing individuals and conduct that Congress has explicitly exempted or excluded from sanctions. While the state Act differs from the federal in relying entirely on indirect economic leverage through third parties with Burmese connections, it otherwise stands in clear contrast to the congressional scheme in the scope of subject matter addressed. It restricts all contracts between the State and companies doing business in Burma, except when purchasing medical supplies and other essentials (or when short of comparable bids). It is specific in targeting contracts to provide financial services, and general goods and services, to the Government of Burma, and thus prohibits contracts between the State and United States persons for goods, services, or technology, even though those transactions are explicitly exempted from the ambit of new investment prohibition when the President exercises his discretionary authority to impose sanctions under the federal Act.

As with the subject of business meant to be affected, so with the class of companies doing it: the state Act's generality stands at odds with the federal discreteness. The Massachusetts law directly and indirectly imposes costs on all companies that do any business in Burma, save for those reporting news or providing international telecommunications goods or services, or medical supplies. It sanctions companies promoting the importation of natural resources controlled by the government of Burma, or having any operations or affiliates in Burma. The state Act thus penalizes companies with pre-existing affiliates or investments, all of which lie beyond the reach of the federal act's restrictions on "new investment" in Burmese economic development. The state Act, moreover, imposes restrictions on foreign companies as well as domestic, whereas the federal Act limits its reach to United States persons.

The conflicts are not rendered irrelevant by the State's argument that there is no real conflict between the statutes because they share the same goals and because some companies may comply with both sets of restrictions. The fact of a common end hardly neutralizes conflicting means, and the fact that some companies may be able to comply with both sets of sanctions does not mean that the state Act is not at odds with achievement of the federal decision about the right degree of pressure to employ. "[C]onflict is imminent" when "two separate remedies are brought to bear on the same activity," *Wisconsin Dept. of Industry v. Gould, Inc.*, 475 U.S. 282, 286 (1986). Sanctions are drawn not only to bar what they prohibit but to allow what they permit, and the inconsistency of sanctions here undermines the congressional calibration of force.

C

Finally, the state Act is at odds with the President's intended authority to speak for the United States among the world's nations in developing a "comprehensive, multilateral strategy to bring democracy to and improve human rights practices and the quality of life in Burma." Congress called for Presidential cooperation with members of ASEAN and other countries in

developing such a strategy, *ibid.*, directed the President to encourage a dialogue between the government of Burma and the democratic opposition, *ibid.*,
and required him to report to the Congress on the progress of his diplomatic
efforts. As with Congress's explicit delegation to the President of power over
economic sanctions, Congress's express command to the President to take the
initiative for the United States among the international community invested
him with the maximum authority of the National Government, *cf. Youngstown
Sheet & Tube Co.*, 343 U.S., at 635, in harmony with the President's own
constitutional powers, U.S. Const., Art. II, § 2, cl. 2 ("[The President] shall
have Power, by and with the Advice and Consent of the Senate, to make
Treaties" and "shall appoint Ambassadors, other public Ministers and Consuls"); § 3 ("[The President] shall receive Ambassadors and other public
Ministers"). This clear mandate and invocation of exclusively national power
belies any suggestion that Congress intended the President's effective voice
to be obscured by state or local action.

Again, the state Act undermines the President's capacity in this instance
for effective diplomacy. It is not merely that the differences between the state
and federal Acts in scope and type of sanctions threaten to complicate
discussions; they compromise the very capacity of the President to speak for
the Nation with one voice in dealing with other governments. We need not
get into any general consideration of limits of state action affecting foreign
affairs to realize that the President's maximum power to persuade rests on
his capacity to bargain for the benefits of access to the entire national economy
without exception for enclaves fenced off willy-nilly by inconsistent political
tactics. When such exceptions do qualify his capacity to present a coherent
position on behalf of the national economy, he is weakened, of course, not only
in dealing with the Burmese regime, but in working together with other
nations in hopes of reaching common policy and "comprehensive" strategy.

While the threat to the President's power to speak and bargain effectively
with other nations seems clear enough, the record is replete with evidence
to answer any skeptics. First, in response to the passage of the state Act, a
number of this country's allies and trading partners filed formal protests with
the National Government ([*e.g.*] . . . Japan, the European Union (EU), and
ASEAN). . . .

Second, the EU and Japan have gone a step further in lodging formal
complaints against the United States in the World Trade Organization (WTO),
claiming that the state Act violates certain provisions of the Agreement on
Government Procurement, and the consequence has been to embroil the
National Government for some time now in international dispute proceedings
under the auspices of the WTO. In their brief before this Court, EU officials
point to the WTO dispute as threatening relations with the United States,
and note that the state Act has become the topic of "intensive discussions"
with officials of the United States at the highest levels, those discussions
including exchanges at the twice yearly EU-U.S. Summit.

Third, the Executive has consistently represented that the state Act has
complicated its dealings with foreign sovereigns and proven an impediment
to accomplishing objectives assigned it by Congress. Assistant Secretary of
State Larson, for example, has directly addressed the mandate of the federal

Burma law in saying that the imposition of unilateral state sanctions under the state Act "complicates efforts to build coalitions with our allies" to promote democracy and human rights in Burma. "[T]he EU's opposition to the Massachusetts law has meant that U.S. government high level discussions with EU officials often have focused not on what to do about Burma, but on what to do about the Massachusetts Burma law." This point has been consistently echoed in the State Department. . . .

This evidence in combination is more than sufficient to show that the state Act stands as an obstacle in addressing the congressional obligation to devise a comprehensive, multilateral strategy. . . .

IV

The State's remaining argument is unavailing. It contends that the failure of Congress to preempt the state Act demonstrates implicit permission. The State points out that Congress has repeatedly declined to enact express preemption provisions aimed at state and local sanctions, and it calls our attention to the large number of such measures passed against South Africa in the 1980s, which various authorities cited have thought were not preempted. The State stresses that Congress was aware of the state Act in 1996, but did not preempt it explicitly when it adopted its own Burma statute. The State would have us conclude that Congress's continuing failure to enact express preemption implies approval, particularly in light of occasional instances of express preemption of state sanctions in the past.

The argument is unconvincing on more than one level. A failure to provide for preemption expressly may reflect nothing more than the settled character of implied preemption doctrine that courts will dependably apply, and in any event, the existence of conflict cognizable under the Supremacy Clause does not depend on express congressional recognition that federal and state law may conflict. The State's inference of congressional intent is unwarranted here, therefore, simply because the silence of Congress is ambiguous. Since we never ruled on whether state and local sanctions against South Africa in the 1980s were preempted or otherwise invalid, arguable parallels between the two sets of federal and state Acts do not tell us much about the validity of the latter.

V

Because the state Act's provisions conflict with Congress's specific delegation to the President of flexible discretion, with limitation of sanctions to a limited scope of actions and actors, and with direction to develop a comprehensive, multilateral strategy under the federal Act, it is preempted, and its application is unconstitutional, under the Supremacy Clause. The judgment of the Court of Appeals for the First Circuit is affirmed.

Note on *Gerling Global Reinsurance Corp. v. Low*
240 F.3d 739 (9th Cir. 2001), *cert. dismissed sub nom., American Inc., Ass'n v. Low,* __ U.S. __ (2002)

In 1999, the state of California adopted the Holocaust Victim Insurance Relief Act, which required all insurers doing business in California that had sold Holocaust-era insurance policies to persons in Europe to file certain information about those policies with the state Commissioner of Insurance.[1] The reporting requirement also applied to insurance companies that do business in California and are "related" to a company that sold Holocaust-era policies, even if the relationship arose after the policies were issued. The law also required the Commissioner to store the information in a public "Holocaust Era Insurance Registry" and to "suspend the certificate of authority to conduct insurance business in the state of any insurer that fails to comply" with the reporting requirements.

Three insurance companies and one trade organization of insurance companies who did business in California sued the Commissioner, seeking declaratory and injunctive relief, claiming that the HVIRA violated the Commerce Clause, the Due Process Clause, and the foreign affairs power, among other objections. The district court issued a preliminary injunction, ruling that "plaintiffs have established a probability of success under the foreign affairs doctrine and the Commerce Clause" and holding that the companies had established the likelihood of irreparable injury.

On appeal, the Ninth Circuit reversed and remanded.

The Commerce Clause. The court of appeals first noted that Congress had carved out a zone of discretion for states in the regulation of the insurance industry. The McCarran-Ferguson Act, 15 U.S.C. §§ 1011–1014 (1945) (McCarran Act) provides in part that

> Congress hereby declares that the continued regulation and taxation by the several States of the business of insurance is in the public interest, and that silence on the part of the Congress shall not be construed to impose any barrier to the regulation or taxation of such business by the several States.

Id. at § 1011. Section 1012(a) provides that the "business of insurance . . . shall be subject to the laws of the several States which relate to the regulation or taxation of such business." The district court had ruled that the McCarran Act did not apply to this case because the HVIRA amounted to an impermissible extraterritorial regulation. Specifically, citing the legislative history of the HVIRA, the district court had ruled that the statute encourages the resolution

---

[1] The information that the insurance companies must provide is: (1) the number of insurance policies; (2) the holder, beneficiary, and current status of each policy; and (3) the city of origin, domicile, or address for each policyholder listed in each policy. In addition, the insurer must certify that: (1) the proceeds of the policies were paid; or (2) the beneficiaries or heirs could not be located after diligent search, and the proceeds were distributed to Holocaust survivors or charities; or (3) a court of law has certified a plan for distributing the proceeds; or (4) the proceeds have not been distributed. The implementing regulations state that, if "the insurer states that it has no actual policies to report because the records are no longer in the possession of the insurer or its related company(ies), it shall provide a complete explanation of that statement." Any insurer who knowingly files false information is subject to a penalty of up to $5,000.

of claims concerning Holocaust-era policies "through an international process" and thereby attempts to "regulate the decision making authority of European insurance companies to pay or not to pay claims on European policies."

The court of appeals rejected this analysis. Unlike other state laws which had been struck down, the HVIRA did not seek "to regulate directly the conduct of an insurer in another jurisdiction. . . . [but sought] only to obtain information about conduct in another jurisdiction, without affecting directly any of that conduct. . . ." The court continued:

> HVIRA, by its terms, does not regulate 'the decision making authority of European insurance companies to pay or not to pay claims on European policies' in any way. HVIRA requires California companies only to provide information about Holocaust-era insurance policies that they (or any of their affiliates) issued. It is true that, by enacting HVIRA, California's legislature intended to help California residents recover on unpaid policies that were entered into in foreign countries by giving them access to information. It also is likely that California's legislature simply intended to protect its residents from insurance companies that have not paid valid insurance claims. In any event, however, the legislature's stated purpose in enacting a statute is not dispositive of a dormant Commerce Clause challenge. The Commerce Clause seeks to prevent extraterritorial economic "effects," not pur-poses. *See Healy v. Beer Institute*, 491 U.S. 324, 336 (1989) ("The critical inquiry is whether the practical effect of the regulation is to control conduct beyond the boundaries of the State." Extraterritorial regulation "is invalid regardless" of the intent of the enacting legisla-ture.) . . . HVIRA, on its face, does not regulate foreign insurance policies, or control the substantive conduct of a foreign insurer, or otherwise affect 'the business of insurance' in any other country.

> In conclusion, Congress has expressly delegated to the states the power to regulate insurance, free from the constraints of the dormant Commerce Clause. . . . HVIRA is a California insurance regulation of California insurance companies that affects foreign commerce only indirectly. Consequently, the McCarran Act applies and the dormant Commerce Clause does not. . . .

The "One-Voice" Orthodoxy. Plaintiffs also challenged the HVIRA on the ground that it interfered with the constitutionally-grounded exclusive powers of the federal government in all matters touching on foreign relations, including international commerce. The court of appeals, interpreting *Barclays Bank PLC v. Franchise Tax Board*, 512 U.S. 298 (1994) and *Wardair Canada, Inc. v. Florida Department of Revenue*, 477 U.S. 1 (1986) concluded that,

> before we can hold that an otherwise constitutional state statute that affects foreign commerce is unconstitutional because it prevents the federal government from speaking with "one voice," we must examine whether the federal government has chosen to permit the states to act.

The court noted that Congress had passed the U.S. Holocaust Assets Commission Act of 1998 (Holocaust Act), Pub.L. 105-186, 112 Stat. 611, as amended Pub.L. 106-155, § 2, 113 Stat. 1740 (1999) (codified at 22 U.S.C. § 1621 note),

> in order "to establish a commission to examine issues pertaining to the disposition of Holocaust-era assets in the United States . . . and to make recommendations to the President on further action, and for other purposes." The Holocaust Act instructs the Commission to "conduct a thorough study and develop a historical record of" certain assets, "if such assets came into the possession or control of the Federal Government." . . . Congress was aware that domestic [state] governmental entities were conducting research into the activities of Holocaust-era insurers. . . . On the basis of the text, context, and history of the Holocaust Act, we conclude that Congress was aware of the states' involvement in this area and, at least implicitly, encouraged laws like HVIRA.

The court also rejected the argument that the HVIRA impermissibly interfered with certain policy initiatives of the executive branch to obtain compensation for Holocaust victims, ruling that the state law and the executive initiatives actually reinforced one another and concluding that Congress, not the executive branch, had constitutional authority to "regulate Commerce with foreign Nations."

The Foreign Affairs Power. The lower court had ruled that the HVIRA had more than an "incidental effect on foreign countries" and had the potential to "disrupt and embarrass" the federal government in its foreign relations. But the court of appeals disagreed as a matter of law, noting that "[t]he federal government's foreign affairs power is not mentioned expressly in the text of the Constitution but, rather, is derived from the structure of the Constitution and the nature of federalism. The power is rarely invoked by the courts; the Supreme Court has not applied it in more than 30 years, since *Zschernig v. Miller*, 389 U.S. 429 (1968). . . ." The court of appeals did not consider the *Crosby* court's invalidation of the Massachusetts Burma law to be controlling because "the Supreme Court affirmed the First Circuit's ruling that the Burma Law was preempted by federal law under the Supremacy Clause, but the Court did not rule on the foreign affairs question." The court of appeals continued:

> We are not persuaded that *Zschernig* applies to HVIRA. In *Zschernig*, the Oregon probate statute violated the foreign affairs power because, as applied, it allowed Oregon judges to insult foreign nations. In *Clark* [*v. Allen*, 331 U.S. 503 (1947),], the Court held that a similar California statute, on its face, did not violate the Constitution. HVIRA regulates insurance companies that do business in California and are, or are related to, companies that issued Holocaust-era insurance policies. No Plaintiff is a foreign government, nor is any Plaintiff owned in whole or in part by a foreign government; they are, simply, businesses. Unlike the statute considered in [*Crosby*], HVIRA does not refer to any particular country. . . . [W]e hesitate to apply *Zschernig* to a facial challenge to state statutes involving "foreign affairs" (a) but that mainly involve foreign commerce and (b) that are not directed at a particular country. HVIRA, on its face, involves commerce alone, and

it is not, on its face, directed at any particular foreign country. For those reasons, we conclude that *Zschernig* does not govern.

The Due Process Claim. Certain plaintiffs argued that the HVIRA violates the "legislative prong" of the Due Process Clause, which "limits the power of a forum state to apply its substantive law to factual and legal situations with which it has little or no contact." One argued that the HVIRA "violates the most basic notions of fundamental fairness" because it takes "away the licenses of California insurers for failure to perform tasks that are literally impossible, making the reporting requirement "arbitrary and irrational." *Cf. Gerling Global Reinsurance Corp. v. Nelson*, 123 F. Supp. 2d 1298, 1303–04 (N.D. Fla. 2000), in which the court ruled that a Florida Holocaust-era insurance statute violates the legislative prong of the Due Process Clause, noting, under Eleventh Circuit precedent, that there must be "some minimal contact between a State and the regulated subject before it can, consistently with the requirements of due process, exercise legislative jurisdiction." In the California case, however, the court of appeals observed that the lower court had did not reached the due process issue and that it had not been fully developed in the record or briefed. It therefore left the preliminary injunction in place "in order to give the district court an opportunity to consider whether Plaintiffs are likely to succeed on the merits. . . ." The court of appeals affirmed on the ground the statute violated the Due Process Clause as applied to the German companies. 267 F. 3d 1228 (11th Cir. 2001).

Notes and Questions on *Crosby*, *Gerling*, and the Transnational Consequences of the Federalist Renaissance

1. *The power of characterization.* Would it alter the result to characterize *Crosby*, not as a foreign relations case, but as a state-procurement case or a state-spending case? Could that bring it within the revival of federalist powers as in *Lopez*, *Brzonkala*, and *Alden*, *supra*?

The Court had previously rejected the argument that a state's "statutory scheme . . . escapes preemption because it is an exercise of the State's spending power rather than its regulatory power." *Wisconsin Dept. of Industry v. Gould, Inc.*, 475 U.S. 282, 287 (1986). According to the *Crosby* court:

> In *Gould*, we found that a Wisconsin statute debarring repeat violators of the National Labor Relations Act from contracting with the State was preempted because the state statute's additional enforcement mechanism conflicted with the federal Act. The fact that the State "ha[d] chosen to use its spending power rather than its police power" did not reduce the potential for conflict with the federal statute.

2. *Crosby and the measure of federal pre-emption.* One interpretation of *Crosby* is that it lowers the standard for finding federal pre-emption of state law when foreign relations are involved. Prior to *Crosby*, when Congress intended to preempt state action that might affect foreign affairs, it frequently said so explicitly. *See, e.g.*, Export Administration Act of 1979, 50 U.S.C. app.

§ 2407(c) (specifying that federal Anti-Arab boycott provisions "preempt any law, rule or regulation"). And, after state and municipal laws proliferated in the 1980's condemning racist policies in South Africa, Congress adopted the Comprehensive Anti-Apartheid Act of 1986 (CAAA) without explicitly prohibiting those laws, leading some authorities to conclude that local divestment or selective purchasing laws were not preempted. *See, e.g., Board of Trustees v. Mayor and City Council of Baltimore*, 317 Md. 72, 79–98 (1989) (holding that local divestment ordinance was not preempted by CAAA), *cert. denied subnom., Lubman v. Mayor and City Council of Baltimore*, 493 U.S. 1093 (1990); Constitutionality of South African Divestment Statutes Enacted by State and Local Governments, 10 OP. OFF. LEGAL COUNSEL 49, 64–66 (state and local divestment and selective purchasing laws not preempted by pre-CAAA federal law); H.R. Res. Nos. 99-548, 99-549 (1986) (denying preemptive intent of CAAA); 132 CONG. REC. 23119-23129 (1986) (House debate on resolutions); *id.*, at 23292 (Sen. Kennedy, quoting testimony of Laurence H. Tribe). In the *Crosby* litigation itself, various members of Congress appeared *amicus curiae* to argue that, when Congress revoked its federal sanctions in response to the democratic transition in South Africa, it declined to preempt the state and local measures, merely "urg[ing]" both state and local governments and private boycott participants to rescind their sanctions. The *Crosby* court's response was that Congress's silence is inescapably ambiguous:

> A failure to provide for pre-emption expressly may reflect nothing more than the settled character of implied preemption doctrine that courts will dependably apply, and in any event, the existence of conflict cognizable under the Supremacy Clause does not depend on express congressional recognition that federal and state law may conflict. The State's inference of congressional intent is unwarranted here, therefore, simply because the silence of Congress is ambiguous. Since we never ruled on whether state and local sanctions against South Africa in the 1980s were preempted or otherwise invalid, arguable parallels between the two sets of federal and state Acts do not tell us much about the validity of the latter.

Is the refusal to infer constitutional power from Congressional silence consistent with *Dames & Moore v. Regan*, 453 U.S. 654 (1981)? In *Dames & Moore*, the Court had to determine the legality of executive branch settlements of U.S. claims against foreign governments — a practice the Court traced through U.S. history. The Court found significance in the fact that "Congress has consistently failed to object to this longstanding practice of claim settlement by executive agreement, even when it has had an opportunity to do so." *Id.* at 682. Will Congressional silence only be given weight if its effect is to augment executive power? Is that wrong?

3. *Due process as a limitation on the choice of law.* Notice that the issue on remand in *Gerling* in some ways echoes the due process arguments in *Allstate*. At oral argument in *Gerling* on appeal, counsel for the state acknowledged that the HVIRA might require the suspension of the license of a California insurer who was unable to produce the information required by the statute, even if the failure to comply was compelled by European privacy laws or the company's lack of control over the information. Counsel argued specifically

that a company's failure to comply should be evaluated "as part of a due process analysis, and that's where we think that issue properly lies." Why under the Due Process Clause might you expect a more searching review of California's Holocaust insurance laws in *Gerling* than of Minnesota's choice-of-law rules in *Allstate*?

4. *Gerling and Crosby reconciled?* Notice that the *Gerling* court, in determining whether the state law was preempted by federal law, declared that "the Holocaust Act, HVIRA, and the executive branch initiatives share the same policy objective, although they seek to achieve that policy objective by varying techniques." Is this line of argument foreclosed by *Crosby*?

[2] The Received State Systems

Virtually unconstrained by constitutional limitations, the various states have embraced a range of approaches to the choice of law. Some states have adopted "jurisdiction-selecting rules" which apply the law of a state without regard to the content of the law or the policies served by the law or the interests that the state might have in the litigation. These states might, for example, choose a strictly territorial approach to the choice of law, and select the jurisdiction with the requisite territorial link to the case: in tort, states might apply the *lex loci delicti* ("the law of the place of the wrong"), typically meaning the law of the place where the accident occurred, even if some other state had other, less fortuitous connections to the parties or their behavior. Similarly, in contract cases, the law of the place where the contract was made might control. In determining the validity of a marriage, a state fixed on the territorial approaches would consider the law of the place where the marriage was celebrated. These territorialist or "vested rights" rules were gathered in the early part of the twentieth century into the Restatement (First) of Conflict of Laws, closely associated with the work of Professor Joseph Beale.

The rigidity of this approach lead almost immediately to the creation of escape devices — reasons to ignore the jurisdiction-selecting results of the First Restatement. A forum court, for example, might articulate broad notions of local public policy that would allow it to ignore the contrary rules of the *lex loci*, or recharacterize a case from tort to contract (or an issue from substance to procedure) so as to manipulate the selection of a different jurisdiction's rules. As a consequence, the principal virtue of the First Restatement approach — predictability and an imperviousness to forum-shopping — could not be served. Equally important, the rigidity of the First Restatement ran counter to the prevailing legal philosophy of the day, Legal Realism, which radically undermined the view of law as some objective or mechanical exercise. Law was instead to be considered functional, serving social purposes or interests first.

A Second Restatement of Conflicts, under the direction of its reporter, Professor Willis Reese, abandoned the hard-and-fast rules of the First Restatement, establishing that the law of the state with "the most significant relationship" to a case (or to an issue within the case) would prevail. Under this approach, the territorial rule became a rebuttable presumption that could be overcome by demonstrating that some other state had a more significant relationship or contact with the case or the issue (in which case that state's law would control). So for example, in tort, the court might start with the presumption that the law of the place where the injury occurred should control, but then consider other contacts that the parties might have with other states (residence, place of business, *etc.*). As suggested in *Pancotto,* excerpted below, the Second Restatement, with its combination of presumptions and escape devices, has become a popular approach.

A third alternative open to states in selecting a process to resolve choice-of-law disputes is known as "interest analysis," and is closely associated with the work of Professor Brainerd Currie. He suggested that courts should be guided by the state interests and policies implicit in all substantive rules, and his approach therefore stands in stark contrast to "jurisdiction-selecting rules." It focuses exclusively on the content of the laws in conflict and selects a law only if the policies behind it are advanced by its application in the case. Many courts have combined the interest analysis with the "most significant relationship" test of the Second Restatement to establish a flexible but structured alternative to territorialism. Predictability has not been served, but the approach is defended as offering something closer to justice.

International litigation in domestic courts must operate within this complicated patchwork of doctrines and techniques. As you consider the following case, try to imagine an approach to such issues that would offer predictability and serve justice simultaneously.

PANCOTTO v. SOCIEDADE de SAFARIS de MOZAMBIQUE, S.A.R.L.
422 F. Supp. 405 (N.D. Ill. 1976)

The plaintiff, Rosemary Pancotto, has brought this diversity action to recover damages for a personal injury she sustained in 1973 while on a hunting safari in Mozambique. Pending for decision is the motion of defendant, Sociedade de Safaris de Mozambique (Safrique), to apply the law of Mozambique to the substantive issues in the action, and for a determination of the relevant Mozambique law. Defendant has complied with the notice provisions of Fed. R.Civ.P. 44.1. Under the rule of *Klaxon v. Stentor Electric Mfg. Co.,* 313 U.S. 487 (1941), a federal court sitting in diversity applies the conflicts law of the state in which it sits. Thus, our task regarding the first part of defendant's motion is to determine and apply the Illinois choice-of-law rule.

Illinois modified its choice of law rules for tort cases in *Ingersoll v. Klein,* 46 Ill.2d 42 (1970). "In our opinion, the local law of the State where the injury occurred should determine the rights and liabilities of the parties, unless Illinois has a more significant relationship with the occurrence and the parties, in which case, the law of Illinois should apply."

The first step in the choice-of-law analysis is to isolate the substantive legal issues and determine whether the various states' tort rules conflict. If a potential conflict is discovered, the next step is to examine the contacts with the states, evaluating the importance of each contact in relation to the legal issues of the case. Finally, under the Illinois choice of law rule, the law of the state or country of the place of injury is followed, unless Illinois is more significantly interested in the resolution of a particular legal issue.

I. The Defendant's Liability

Defendant's motion identifies the two substantive legal issues to be addressed by this choice of law analysis, each of which will be considered in turn: (1) the defendant's liability; and (2) the appropriate measure of damages. A cursory look at the defendant's materials outlining Mozambique law indicates that the standard of care there was different from Illinois'.[1] Briefly, the Mozambique standard of care upon which defendant relies was the "diligence with which a law abiding male head of a family would act." Portuguese Civil Code, Art. 487(2). Although this standard of care bears an analytical similarity to Illinois' reasonable man standard, it may be more or less demanding of an alleged wrongdoer. This putative difference could lead to a different result if Mozambique rather than Illinois law is applied.[2] Consequently, we are faced with a true conflict of laws and must evaluate the parties' contacts with the two states to determine which law should control.

Ingersoll refers us to what is now RESTATEMENT (SECOND) OF CONFLICTS OF LAWS § 145 (1971),[3] for a listing of the contacts to be evaluated in

---

[1] At the time of plaintiff's injury in 1973, Mozambique was a territory of Portugal and applied the Portuguese Civil Code. *See* Affidavit of Marcel Molins. We take judicial notice that Mozambique in 1975 became an independent nation, with its own law. However, to the extent that Mozambique law is controlling, it is the law as it existed at the time of the alleged wrong.

[2] Furthermore, Article 503(1) of the Portuguese Civil Code, which we discuss, *infra,* appears to impose liability without fault on those in control of a vehicle used for travel on land. Certainly such a "no-fault" substantive rule could lead to a result different from that presently available under Illinois law.

[3] Section 145 provides:

(1) The rights and liabilities of the parties with respect to an issue in tort are determined by the local law of the state which, with respect to that issue, has the most significant relationship to the occurrence and the parties under the principles stated in Section 6 [see below].

(2) Contacts to be taken into account in applying the principles of Section 6 to determine the law applicable to an issue include:

(a) the place where the injury occurred,

(b) the place where the conduct causing the injury occurred,

(c) the domicil, residence, nationality, place of incorporation and place of business of the parties, and

(d) the place where the relationship, if any, between the parties is centered.

These contacts are to be evaluated according to their relative importance with respect to the particular issue.

Section 6 provides:

(1) A court, subject to constitutional restrictions, will follow a statutory directive of its own state on choice of law.

(2) When there is no such directive, the factors relevant to the choice of the applicable rule of law include:

determining which jurisdiction is most significantly concerned with the liability of the alleged tortfeasor. The first of these is the place where the injury occurred. The parties do not dispute that plaintiff sustained her injuries in Mozambique. Mrs. Pancotto accompanied her husband and sons on a hunting safari directed by defendant. She was taking pictures of other members of the hunting party when a swamp buggy driven by a Safrique employee ran into her.

The place of injury has an interest in applying its own tort principles to discourage harmful behavior within its borders. This interest in controlling the tortfeasor's conduct is strongest when the alleged tort is intentional. If the harmful contact is unintentional, however, the interest of the place of injury is attenuated. Realistically, the negligent tortfeasor is not affected by a state's civil liability laws because he does not premeditate before he acts. Nonetheless, to the extent that such conduct is shaped by legal standards, Mozambique was, at the time of the alleged wrong, interested in the choice of the standard of care to be imposed upon the defendant.

The second contact listed in the Restatement is the place of the conduct which caused injury, which is again clearly Mozambique. The interest of the jurisdiction where the conduct occurred is similar if not identical to that of the place of injury. Again, however, Mozambique's valid interest in controlling harmful conduct assumes less importance when the alleged tortfeasor was not governed by conscious reference to a behavioral standard.

The Restatement's third contact is the domicile or place of business of the parties. This consideration refers us to both Illinois law and that of Mozambique. The plaintiff's domicile, Illinois, is interested in compensating both the victim and her creditors. Mozambique, on the other hand, as the defendant's domicile and principal place of business, is concerned that defendant's conduct conforms to its standards, and may also have an interest in insulating a domiciliary from liability.

The Restatement's final contact point is the place where the parties' relationship is centered. The relationship here has an international flavor. The safari was arranged in large part by intercontinental telephone calls and cables. In addition, certain employees of the defendant visited the plaintiff's husband in Illinois approximately three times prior to the safari, although the parties dispute the business as opposed to personal significance of the visits. Regardless of the nature of the Illinois contacts, they obviously were preparatory to an extended, well-planned interaction in Mozambique. Plaintiff's ultimate presence in that country was hardly fortuitous. In short, although the relationship had international aspects, it can fairly be characterized as centering in Mozambique.

(a) the needs of the interstate and international systems,

(b) the relevant policies of the forum,

(c) the relevant policies of other interested states and the relative interests of those states in the determination of the particular issue,

(d) the protection of justified expectations,

(e) the basic policies underlying the particular field of law,

(f) certainty, predictability and uniformity of result, and

(g) ease in the determination and application of the law to be applied.

These contacts and the state interests evoked by them indicate that both Illinois and Mozambique are interested in the resolution of the liability issue. Both jurisdictions' interests are significant. The numerous Mozambique contacts highlight that government's interest in controlling the conduct of those who take action within its borders, and the interest in affording the protection of its laws to its domiciliaries. Illinois, on the other hand, has a strong interest in seeing that its residents are adequately compensated for tortious injuries. The Illinois interest, although based upon a single contact, cannot for that reason be automatically dismissed as less significant. A contact assumes significance only in view of the legal issue to which it relates. Our evaluation of the contacts indicates that both Illinois and Mozambique are validly interested in the resolution of the issue of defendant's liability, and we hesitate to characterize either jurisdiction's interest as more significant.

In general, the Illinois courts have chosen their own law rather than the law of the place of injury only if the majority of the significant contacts were in Illinois, and the tort's occurrence in the foreign state was fortuitous. *See, e.g., Ingersoll, supra.* Given that both states here may assert significant although distinct interests in the outcome of the liability issue, the Illinois choice of law rule directs the application of the law of the place of injury, Mozambique.

We now turn to a determination of the Mozambique law governing liability for the acts of misconduct alleged in the complaint.

Rule 44.1 [of the Federal Rules of Civil Procedure] gives district courts wide discretion in the materials to which they may resort to determine the content of foreign law. The defendant has provided copies of the relevant sections of the Portuguese Civil Code, both in that language and in translation. In addition, defendant offers the affidavit of Mr. Marcel Molins, an expert witness conversant with the law of Portugal, who comments upon the law pertinent to the issues of liability and damages. Regarding liability, these combined resources indicate that Portuguese law sets out two standards for liability, either of which might apply to the facts alleged in the complaint. The first standard seems to be a rough equivalent, allowing for cultural differences, of the common law reasonable man standard. Under this standard, "[fault] is judged, in the absence of another legal criterion, by the diligence with which a law-abiding male head of a family would act in the face of the circumstances of each case." Art. 487(2). The injured person carries the burden of proving that the opposing party was at fault as measured by this standard, unless there is a legal presumption of fault. Art. 487.

A second standard may be available, however, under the facts alleged here. As in the United States, in Mozambique liability was sometimes imposed without regard to fault. Under the Portuguese Civil Code this concept is called objective liability, and appears to be theoretically equivalent to our concept of strict liability in tort. Under the Portuguese Code, the operation of a land vehicle is considered inherently hazardous. Thus, Art. 503(1) provides that "[one] who has effective control of a vehicle for travel on land and uses it for his own purposes or by means of an agent, is chargeable for the damage originating in the risks inherent in the vehicle, even though it is not in movement." A Safrique employee was operating the swamp buggy at the time of

Mrs. Pancotto's injury. Mr. Molins admits that the available Mozambique case law does little to clarify the meaning and application of the term "for his own purposes." But, on the record as presently constituted, a fact finder could find that the vehicle was "for travel on land", was under the control of Safrique, and was used "by means of an agent" in which event it would appear that defendant would be liable for risks inherent in the vehicle, *i.e.*, striking a pedestrian.

Without further testimony on the matter, we are not prepared to decide at this time which standard of liability would be applied by a Mozambique court. We also need edification on the question whether the common law reasonable man standard and the Mozambique "male head of a family" standard are equivalents or whether the latter imposes a greater or lesser standard of care than does the former. Therefore, in preparation for trial, the parties are directed to submit supplemental materials addressing these issues.

II. The Measure of Damages

A brief look at Mozambique's and Illinois' laws on recoverable damages reveals an acute conflict. Illinois permits recovery for medical expenses due to the injury, and, *inter alia*, compensation for the injury itself, for disfigurement, and for pain and suffering. In contrast, Art. 508 of the Portuguese Civil Code limits liability for travel accidents to 600 contos, or approximately $6,600 in United States dollars. This limit is not inflexible, however. A Mozambique court may apparently, in its discretion, award damages to the full extent of the plaintiff's out-of-pocket loss, although the typical recovery is less generous. And, under Mozambique law, the plaintiff recovers nothing for pain and suffering, disfigurement, or loss of enjoyment of life as she might under Illinois law.

The defendant argues that the Illinois choice of law rule dictates the application of Mozambique law to this issue also. And, in fact, the analysis of the two jurisdictions' interests in the measure of damages leads to such a result. As the place of conduct, injury, defendant's domicile, and the place where the parties' relationship centered, Mozambique has a strong interest in the resolution of this issue. As plaintiff's domicile and the place where the consequences of the injury are felt, Illinois is concerned that plaintiff receives compensation. Plaintiff, however, contends that the application of Mozambique's damage limitation would be so grossly repugnant to Illinois' public and constitutional policy of providing a remedy for all injuries that an Illinois court would refuse to follow Mozambique law, even if the *Ingersoll* rule would normally dictate its application.

With no Illinois cases in point, the parties discuss certain cases in which the New York courts have faced similar contentions. Of these, *Rosenthal v. Warren,* 475 F.2d 438 (2d Cir. 1973), is the closest factually to the case here. As a federal court sitting in New York, the *Rosenthal* court was concerned with the proper application of New York's choice-of-law rule, which differs from the Illinois rule.[4] Despite this difference in orientation, *Rosenthal* points

---

[4] New York employs the "interest analysis" approach to conflicts of law, and applies the law of the jurisdiction which because of its relationship to the parties or the occurrence has the greatest concern with the specific issues raised in the case. *Rosenthal v. Warren,* 475 F.2d 438 (2d Cir. 1973). Applying this rule, the New York courts have attached heavy weight to their state's vital

out the important factors to consider in determining whether the forum state's public policy should overrule the law of a foreign jurisdiction.

The plaintiff's decedent in *Rosenthal* was domiciled in New York. Accompanied by the plaintiff, his wife and later his executrix, the decedent traveled to Boston for medical treatment by a physician domiciled in Massachusetts. The decedent died while recuperating in a Massachusetts hospital after surgery performed by the physician. The decedent's wife subsequently sued the physician and the hospital in a New York state court.

The defendants argued that the Massachusetts wrongful death statute, with its $50,000 limit on damages, should apply. The court rejected Massachusetts' statute in favor of New York's full compensation policy. Before doing so, the court confronted and thoroughly analyzed the factors militating against the forum's application of its own public policy. First, the court considered whether the defendants had patterned their conduct upon the Massachusetts statute. A doctor does not, however, ordinarily think of wrongful death limitations before performing surgery; consequently the doctor could not claim he acted in reliance upon a Massachusetts behavioral standard. Second, the court considered whether the defendants would be unfairly surprised by the application of New York law. Neither the doctor nor the hospital had a strictly local clientele or practice. Consequently, it could not be said that they justifiably expected to be affected only by Massachusetts law. Third, the court considered whether defendants had purchased insurance in reliance upon the Massachusetts limitation. The defendants' policies, however, made no distinction between recoveries for personal injuries and recoveries for wrongful death. As a result, the defendants could not convincingly argue that they relied upon the Massachusetts limit. Finally, the court evaluated the policy behind the Massachusetts limitation to determine whether application of the New York law would frustrate an important Massachusetts interest. Finding that the few remaining wrongful death limitations are vestiges of the mistaken view that a common law action for wrongful death did not exist, the court declined to apply an archaic and unjust policy, particularly in view of its own policy to assure just and fair compensation for the victims of tortious conduct.

In short, *Rosenthal* indicates that the defendant's reliance, and principles of fundamental fairness and governmental policy, should be balanced in determining whether the forum's measure of damages, grounded upon a strong public policy, may be applied against a foreign defendant.

Applying these principles to the factual context here yields some similar conclusions. The tort alleged in the complaint is unintentional, rendering any argument of behavioral reliance untenable. And, as in *Rosenthal*, the defendant here anticipated and welcomed, if not solicited, business contacts with persons outside the jurisdiction. The last two *Rosenthal* considerations, however, are not so easily dismissed. Defendant's counsel has submitted an affidavit attesting that defendant told him it carries no insurance. The competency of this affidavit is questionable as counsel has no personal

---

concern that injured domiciliaries are compensated for their loss. *E.g., Miller v. Miller,* 22 N.Y.2d 12 (1969). In contrast, Illinois follows the approach of the Second Restatement, and applies the law of the place of injury unless Illinois has a more significant interest in the outcome of a specific issue.

knowledge of this fact. He has assured us, however, that competent evidence will be forthcoming before trial. If we place aside the question of the competency of the affidavit, the lack of insurance suggests that defendant relied upon Mozambique's damage limitation. Moreover, although a New York court can confidently characterize wrongful death limitations as an archaic minority rule, we have no knowledge of the status of damage limitations for personal injury actions in the world community of nations.

Despite these countervailing considerations, our educated prediction is that the Illinois courts would refuse to enforce the Portuguese limitation as unreasonable and contrary to Illinois public policy. Illinois' public policy is found in its Constitution, laws, judicial decisions, and also in its customs, morals, and notions of justice. *Marchlik v. Coronet Ins. Co.,* 40 Ill.2d 327 (1968). There is perhaps no more compelling Illinois public policy than one expressed in the state's Constitution, which provides that every person should find a certain remedy in the law for injuries to his person. Ill. Const. Art. I, § 12. On occasion, the Illinois courts have accepted reasonable limits on recoveries for personal injuries, as for example in the Dram Shop Act and the Wrongful Death Act. Ill.Rev.Stat. ch. 43, § 135; ch. 70, §§ 1, 2 (1973). But as the Illinois Supreme Court noted in its recent decision invalidating Illinois' medical malpractice law, these statutes created actions unknown at common law. Thus, the courts were not disturbed when the newly created right was accompanied by a limited remedy. But if the right existed at common law, damage limitations without a *quid pro quo* have been disfavored. Moreover, the damage limitations incorporated into Illinois legislation have been more consistent with potential out-of-pocket loss. The Dram Shop Act limits damages to $20,000, Ill.Rev.Stat. ch. 43, § 135; the recently voided malpractice act carried a $500,000 limit.

Of course, we are not dealing here with a law of Illinois, but one from a foreign country. Recently liberated from foreign rule, the economic and social conditions in Mozambique are quite different from those in Illinois. Recognizing such international disparities, the court in *Ciprari v. Servicos Aereos Cruzeiro,* 245 F. Supp. 819 (S.D.N.Y. 1965), applied the Brazilian Code, which limited damages to an amount less than $100. The court, however, emphasized the unique justifications for the limitation, which applied only to accidents involving Brazil's national airline. In particular, the court cited Brazil's public policy of protecting the financial integrity of an infant national industry, and the overtones of national security in Brazil's special interest in the national airline. On the contrary, no exceptional national concern is asserted here. Instead, the damage limitation is general, applying to all injuries sustained in travel accidents. The parties have cited no public policy to be advanced by the law and we hesitate to speculate on the question.

In the absence of an articulated national policy, the final inquiry is whether the application of the Illinois law would unfairly prejudice the defendant. Although the defendant is a Mozambique corporation, its trade is international in scope. Safrique allows travel agencies to use its name in advertisements for sporting magazines with national circulation. If Safrique induces residents of other countries to visit Mozambique and profits from the excursions, it is hardly unfair to require Safrique to compensate its clients for tortious injuries inflicted by Safrique employees. Concomitantly, Safrique cannot claim that its clients' residencies take it by surprise. Indeed, Safrique deliberately engages in a business which thrives on international tourism.

A final aspect of the question of prejudice involves counsel's allegation that defendant carries no liability insurance. Safrique's failure to obtain insurance, however, is not alleged to have been motivated by the Mozambique damage limitation. Without supplemental affidavits, this neglect is as easily attributed to oversight as to a calculated business decision that it might cost more in premiums than to directly compensate a victim to the statutory limit.

In conclusion, although the Illinois choice of law rule indicates the application of Mozambique's law to the substantive issues in this action, we feel the Illinois courts would refuse to enforce the Mozambique policy of providing a remedy for personal injuries. Foreign substantive law is not unenforceable simply because it differs from our own law, but because the differences are against public policy. The refusal to enforce a foreign law should not be lightly made. But when no justification is offered for a policy which contravenes a sound public policy of the forum, and the defendant is not unfairly surprised, we believe that the Illinois courts would decline to apply the foreign limitation.

Defendant's motion to apply the substantive law of Mozambique is granted as to the issue of liability and denied as to the issue of damages. In advance of trial, the parties are directed to submit supplemental memoranda describing the appropriate Mozambique standard of care to be applied to the facts to be proved at trial, and commenting upon the equivalence of the Portuguese "male head of a family" standard of care to the common law reasonable man standard.

Notes and Questions on *Pancotto* and the Knock-kneed Army of State Techniques

1. *Problem.* In order to clarify how the various state approaches might work in a domestic setting, suppose you represent a railroad worker, who lives in Mississippi and works for a railroad company incorporated in Mississippi, with its principal place of business in that state. One day, one of her co-workers makes a mistake in coupling the cars together. Your client is working on the train, and just after it crosses the border into Alabama, the cars part, and your client is severely injured. She's treated briefly in an Alabama hospital, but she comes back to her home state for long-term rehabilitation, and she eventually sues her employer in a Mississippi court for negligence. Suppose further that Alabama has a fellow servant rule (under which the company is not liable for the negligence of a fellow worker) and that Mississippi has no such rule. Your client's case turns on which state's law applies. On the question of whether the Alabama fellow-servant rule applies, (i) what is the test and what is the likely result under the First Restatement approach? (ii) Under the Second Restatement? (iii) Under interest analysis?

2. *The received systems in a transnational setting.* Is one of these approaches preferable in international litigation, or are the pros and cons of each approach roughly the same in that setting?

3. *Dépeçage.* Notice that Mozambique law governs certain issues in *Pancotto* but not all of them. This splitting process — in which different issues in a single case may be resolved by reference to the laws of different jurisdictions — is known as *dépeçage.* Can you articulate the standards for distinguishing between those issues to which Mozambique law properly applies from those to which it does not?

B.   INTERNATIONAL LEGAL CONSTRAINTS ON THE CHOICE OF LAW

[1]   International Jurisdictional Standards and the Reach of Domestic Law

Domestic courts are routinely asked to consider which of two (or more) nations' laws applies to a particular transaction, person, event, or thing. The traditional assumption was that a nation's law was strictly territorial, meaning that every nation had plenary authority to apply its law within its own territory, to the exclusion of all others, and, absent some special arrangement or understanding, the applicability of its law stopped at its borders. As noted by Joseph Story in his influential *Commentaries on the Conflict of Laws* (1841), "no state or nation can, by its laws, directly affect, or bind property out of its own territory, or bind persons not resident therein . . . for it would be wholly incompatible with the equality and exclusiveness of the sovereignty of all nations, that any one nation should be at liberty to regulate either persons or things not resident within its own territory."

But in an increasingly international order, states claimed (and recognized) other sovereign interests — non-territorial connections — that could justify the application of their own law in a given case. States were in fact considerably better at identifying which interests would suffice for this purpose than they were at resolving the disputes that arose between them whenever two or more states had different but adequate connections to a case. Over time, the international community has come to recognize five broad categories of such interests, subsumed under the heading *jurisdiction to prescribe*: territoriality, nationality of the actor, nationality of the victim ("passive personality"), the protective principle, and universality. One rough approximation of the international understanding of jurisdiction appears in §§ 402 *et seq.* of the RESTATEMENT (THIRD) OF FOREIGN RELATIONS LAW OF THE UNITED STATES (1987):

> § 402. Subject to § 403, a state has jurisdiction to prescribe law with respect to:
>
> (1) (a) conduct that, wholly or in substantial part, takes place within its territory;
>
>   (b) the status of persons, or interests in things, present within its territory;

(c) conduct outside its territory that has or is intended to have substantial effect within its territory;

(2) the activities, interests, status, or relations of its nationals outside as well as within its territory; and

(3) certain conduct outside its territory by persons not its nationals that is directed against the security of the state or against a limited class of other state interests.

§ **403**. (1) Even when one of the bases for jurisdiction under § 402 is present, a state may not exercise jurisdiction to prescribe law with respect to a person or activity having connections with another state when the exercise of such jurisdiction is unreasonable.

(2) Whether exercise of jurisdiction over a person or activity is unreasonable is determined by evaluating all relevant factors, including, where appropriate:

(a) the link of the activity to the territory of the regulating state, *i.e.*, the extent to which the activity takes place within the territory, or has substantial, direct, and foreseeable effect upon or in the territory;

(b) the connections, such as nationality, residence, or economic activity, between the regulating state and the person principally responsible for the activity to be regulated, or between that state and those whom the regulation is designed to protect;

(c) the character of the activity to be regulated, the importance of the regulation to the regulating state, the extent to which other states regulate such activities, and the degree to which the desirability of such regulation is generally accepted;

(d) the existence of justified expectations that might be protected or hurt by the regulation;

(e) the importance of the regulation to the international political, legal, or economic system;

(f) the extent to which the regulation is consistent with the traditions of the international system;

(g) the extent to which another state may have an interest in regulating the activity; and

(h) the likelihood of conflict with regulation by another state.

(3) When it would not be unreasonable for each of two states to exercise jurisdiction over a person or activity, but the prescriptions by the two states are in conflict, each state has an obligation to evaluate its own as well as the other state's interest in exercising jurisdiction, in light of all the relevant factors, Subsection 2; a state should defer to the other state if that state's interest is clearly greater.

§ **404**. A state has jurisdiction to define and prescribe punishment for certain offenses recognized by the community of nations as of universal concern, such as piracy, slave trade, attacks on or hijacking of aircraft, genocide, war crimes, and perhaps certain acts of terrorism, even where none of the bases of jurisdiction indicated in § 402 is present.

As shown in the cases below, the operation of jurisdictional principles is far more complicated and contentious than these *Restatement* formulations suggest. But one shouldn't let the important disagreements at the margins of these categories hide the standard cases at the core of each one:

Territoriality. The commentary that accompanies Section 402(1) declares that the "territorial principle is by far the most common basis for the exercise of jurisdiction to prescribe, and it has generally been free from controversy." That assessment is somewhat optimistic, but it is true that the full range of a state's law is routinely assumed to apply to conduct that occurs or property that is within its boundaries (subparagraphs 1(a) and (b)). This is frequently referred to as *subjective territoriality*. But the *Restatement* also follows the practice of states in allowing the application of a state's law to "conduct outside its territory that has or is intended to have substantial effect within its territory" (subparagraph 1(c)). This effects-based jurisdiction is referred to as *objective territoriality* and has generated serious international conflict, especially in the extraterritorial application of U.S. regulatory statutes, as shown below.

Nationality. The *Restatement* provides that states also have jurisdiction to prescribe as to "the activities, interests, status, or relations of its nationals outside as well as within its territory," meaning that international law permits states to apply their laws to their citizens (Section 402(2)). The fact that U.S. citizens — wherever they may be — are subject *inter alia* to U.S. laws regarding tax, selective service, and trading with the enemy, offers the standard illustration of nationality-based jurisdiction to prescribe.

Passive personality. Many countries, though not historically the United States, have attempted to legislate *protections* for their citizens anywhere in the world, and not just *obligations*. In these cases, jurisdiction to prescribe is based on the citizenship of a victim instead of an actor. For example, some states will allow extraterritorial libel actions against foreign defendants on the ground that one of their own citizens was the target of the libel. The United States has traditionally resisted the passive personality principle on the ground that it subjected U.S. citizens to a range of laws of which they could have no notice. But at least in criminal proceedings, the United States has cautiously followed this principle where the victim was chosen precisely because of his or her U.S. citizenship, as for example in criminal prosecutions for terrorist acts.

Protective principle. States generally assert the right to apply their laws against conduct that is directed against the security or essential governmental functions of that state. Typically for example, a state may criminalize espionage, passport fraud, and counterfeiting of its currency, regardless of the citizenship of the perpetrator or the physical location of the offensive conduct. Though invoked primarily in criminal instead of civil cases, the protective principle might apply in transnational civil cases in which the underlying criminal statute provided a private right of action.

Universality. A handful of international wrongs are sufficiently threatening to the international community as a whole that each individual state has an interest in combatting it through the application of its own law. Genocide, piracy, war crimes, and slave-trading are generally considered the exemplars of wrongs within each state's universal criminal jurisdiction. Though universality tends to underlie primarily *criminal* prosecutions for such conduct, civil actions based on universality are neither uncommon nor unjustified, as *Filártiga* and its progeny demonstrate (p. 22, *supra*). (You may also notice that universality in Section 404 is the only basis for prescriptive that is *not* explicitly subject to the reasonableness factors in Section 403.)

The modern law of prescriptive jurisdiction, with its move away from strictly territorial rules, can be traced to the 1927 judgment of the Permanent Court of International Justice in the *Lotus* case. In that case, France had challenged Turkey's right to prosecute a French officer whose negligence at sea caused an accident in which several Turkish sailors died. Though the case arose in the criminal setting, the PCIJ adopted language with broad implications. It rejected the French suggestion that international law presumptively barred the extraterritorial application of a nation's laws and declared:

> Far from laying down a general prohibition to the effect that states may not extend the application of their laws and the jurisdiction of their courts to persons, property, and acts outside their territory, [international law] leaves them in this respect a wide measure of discretion which is only limited in certain cases by prohibitive rules; as regards other cases every state remains free to adopt the principles which it regards as best and most suitable. . . . The territoriality of criminal law, therefore is not an absolute principle of international law and by no means coincides with territorial sovereignty. . . . [T]he courts of many countries, even of countries which have given their criminal legislation a strictly territorial character, interpret criminal law in the sense that offenses, the authors of which at the moment of commission are in the territory of another state, are nevertheless to be regarded as having been committed in the national territory, if one of the constituent elements of the offense, and more especially its effects, have taken place there.

P.C.I.J., Ser. A, No. 10, at 19, 23 (1927). Although the contemporary significance of the *Lotus* decision is disputed, the core of the judgment — namely its rejection of purely territorial approaches to prescriptive jurisdiction — has been followed by states. Especially in matters of commercial regulation and antitrust law, states frequently have simultaneous but conflicting interests, and it routinely — though not invariably — falls to the courts to resolve them. The purpose of this section is to expose the matrix of doctrine and technique that the U.S. courts use in such cases.

One final introductory observation is necessary. To say that a state is justified in *prescribing* its law is not to say that it can for that reason alone *enforce* its law. The enforcement function or *jurisdiction to enforce* is strictly territorial, and no state may exercise sovereign powers — like arrest or investigation or prosecution — in the territory of another without consent. A state may well have international authority to prescribe law as to a particular person or transaction but be powerless to enforce it without cooperation from another state. The decision that a certain law applies is only the first step in enforcing it.

UNITED STATES v. ALUMINUM CO. OF AMERICA
148 F.2d 416 (2d Cir. 1945)

This appeal comes to us by virtue of a certificate of the Supreme Court [because that Court could not muster a quorum of six qualified justices in the case. The government had filed a complaint against Aluminum Company of America (Alcoa) and Aluminum, Limited (Limited), alleging that they had violated the antitrust laws of the United States by "monopolizing interstate and foreign commerce, particularly in the manufacture and sale of 'virgin' aluminum ingot." Limited, a Canadian corporation, had been established for the purpose of acquiring Alcoa's properties outside the United States and was controlled by Alcoa's shareholders at the time of the suit. Among other allegations, the government charged that Alcoa and Limited had entered into an international cartel with various European aluminum companies (the Alliance). Among the issues in the appeal was whether the defendants' conduct violated Section 1 of the Sherman Antitrust Act.] . . .

Whether 'Limited' itself violated that section depends upon the character of the 'Alliance.' It was a Swiss corporation, created in pursuance of an agreement entered into on July 3, 1931, the signatories to which were a French corporation, two German, one Swiss, a British, and 'Limited.' The original agreement, or 'cartel,' provided for the formation of a corporation in Switzerland which should issue shares, to be taken up by the signatories. This corporation was, from time to time, to fix a quota of production for each share, and each shareholder was to be limited to the quantity measured by the number of shares it held, but was free to sell at any price it chose. The corporation fixed a price every year at which it would take off any shareholder's hands any part of its quota which it did not sell. No shareholder was to 'buy, borrow, fabricate or sell' aluminum produced by anyone not a shareholder except with the consent of the board of governors, but that must not be 'unreasonably withheld.' . . . [U]ntil 1936, when the new arrangement was made, imports into the United States were not included in the quotas. . . .

The agreement of 1936 abandoned the system of unconditional quotas, and substituted a system of royalties. Each shareholder was to have a fixed free quota for every share it held, but as its production exceeded the sum of its quotas, it was to pay a royalty, graduated progressively in proportion to the excess; and these royalties the 'Alliance' divided among the shareholders in proportion to their shares. . . . Although this agreement, like its predecessor, was silent as to imports into the United States, when that question arose during its preparation, as it did, all the shareholders agreed that such imports should be included in the quotas. . . .

Did either the agreement of 1931 or that of 1936 violate § 1 of the Act? The answer does not depend upon whether we shall recognize as a source of liability a liability imposed by another state. On the contrary, we are concerned only with whether Congress chose to attach liability to the conduct outside the United States of persons not in allegiance to it. That being so, the only question open is whether Congress intended to impose the liability, and whether our own Constitution permitted it to do so: as a court of the United States, we cannot look beyond our own law. Nevertheless, it is quite true that we are not to read general words, such as those in this Act, without regard to the limitations customarily observed by nations upon the exercise of their powers; limitations which generally correspond to those fixed by the 'Conflict of Laws.' We should not impute to Congress an intent to punish all whom its courts can catch, for conduct which has no consequences within the United States. *American Banana Co. v. United Fruit Co.*, 213 U.S. 347, 357 [(1909)]. On the other hand, it is settled law — as 'Limited' itself agrees — that any state may impose liabilities, even upon persons not within its allegiance, for conduct outside its borders that has consequences within its borders which the state reprehends; and these liabilities other states will ordinarily recognize. It may be argued that this Act extends further.

Two situations are possible. There may be agreements made beyond our borders not intended to affect imports, which do affect them, or which affect exports. Almost any limitation of the supply of goods in Europe, for example, or in South America, may have repercussions in the United States if there is trade between the two. Yet when one considers the international complications likely to arise from an effort in this country to treat such agreements as unlawful, it is safe to assume that Congress certainly did not intend the Act to cover them. Such agreements may on the other hand intend to include imports into the United States, and yet it may appear that they had no effect upon them. That situation might be thought to fall within the doctrine that intent may be a substitute for performance in the case of a contract made within the United States; or it might be thought to fall within the doctrine that a statute should not be interpreted to cover acts abroad which have no consequence here.

We shall not choose between these alternatives; but for argument, we shall assume that the Act does not cover agreements, even though intended to affect imports or exports, unless its performance is shown actually to have had some effect upon them. Where both conditions are satisfied, the situation certainly falls within such decisions as *United States v. Pacific & Arctic R. & Navigation Co.*, 228 U.S. 87; *Thomsen v. Cayser*, 243 U.S. 66; and *United States v. Sisal Sales Corporation*, 274 U.S. 268. . . . It is true that in those cases, the persons held liable had sent agents into the United States to perform part of the agreement; but an agent is merely an animate means of executing his principal's purposes, and, for the purposes of this case, he does not differ from an inanimate means . . . .

Both agreements would clearly have been unlawful, had they been made within the United States; and it follows from what we have just said that both were unlawful, though made abroad, if they were intended to affect imports and did affect them. . . . [The court then found that "the intent [of the 1936 agreement] was to set up a quota system for imports" and that proving such an intent shifted the burden of proof to "Limited," creating in effect a presumption that the agreement had had the requisite effects in the United States.] For these reasons we think that the agreement of 1936 violated Section 1 of the Act.

Notes and Questions on *Alcoa* and the Two-Pronged Test

1. What is the test for jurisdiction according to Judge Hand? Does that standard apply only in cases based on objective territoriality or does it apply to every application of U.S. law outside of the United States?

2. One of the most over-interpreted, cryptic sentences in the work of Learned Hand is his pronouncement in *Alcoa*, "as a court of the United States, we cannot look beyond our own law." In context, is this a directive *not* to consider international law? What does it mean?

BOURESLAN and THE EQUAL EMPLOYMENT OPPORTUNITY COMMISSION v. ARABIAN AMERICAN OIL CO.
499 U.S. 244 (1991)

REHNQUIST, C.J., delivered the opinion of the Court, in which WHITE, O'CONNOR, KENNEDY, and SOUTER, joined.

These cases present the issue whether Title VII applies extraterritorially to regulate the employment practices of United States employers who employ United States citizens abroad. The United States Court of Appeals for the Fifth Circuit held that it does not, and we agree with that conclusion.

Petitioner Boureslan is a naturalized United States citizen who was born in Lebanon. The respondents are two Delaware corporations, Arabian American Oil Company (Aramco), and its subsidiary, Aramco Service Company (ASC). Aramco's principal place of business is Dhahran, Saudi Arabia, and it is licensed to do business in Texas. ASC's principal place of business is Houston, Texas.

In 1979, Boureslan was hired by ASC as a cost engineer in Houston. A year later he was transferred, at his request, to work for Aramco in Saudi Arabia. Boureslan remained with Aramco in Saudi Arabia until he was discharged in 1984. After filing a charge of discrimination with the Equal Employment Opportunity Commission (EEOC or Commission), he instituted this suit in the United States District Court for the Southern District of Texas against Aramco and ASC. He sought relief under both state law and Title VII of the

Civil Rights Act of 1964, 42 U. S. C. §§ 2000e–2000e-17, on the ground that
he was harassed and ultimately discharged by respondents on account of his
race, religion, and national origin.

Respondents filed a motion for summary judgment on the ground that the
District Court lacked subject-matter jurisdiction over Boureslan's claim
because the protections of Title VII do not extend to United States citizens
employed abroad by American employers. The District Court agreed and
dismissed Boureslan's Title VII claim; it also dismissed his state-law claims
for lack of pendent jurisdiction and entered final judgment in favor of
respondents. [The Fifth Circuit affirmed.] . . .

Both parties concede, as they must, that Congress has the authority to
enforce its laws beyond the territorial boundaries of the United States. *Cf.*
Foley Bros., Inc. v. Filardo, 336 U.S. 281, 284–285 (1949). Whether Congress
has in fact exercised that authority in this case is a matter of statutory
construction. It is our task to determine whether Congress intended the
protections of Title VII to apply to United States citizens employed by
American employers outside of the United States. It is a longstanding
principle of American law "that legislation of Congress, unless a contrary
intent appears, is meant to apply only within the territorial jurisdiction of
the United States." *Foley Bros.,* 336 U.S., at 285. This "canon of construction
. . . is a valid approach whereby unexpressed congressional intent may be
ascertained." *Ibid.* It serves to protect against unintended clashes between
our laws and those of other nations which could result in international discord.

In applying this rule of construction, we look to see whether "language in
the [relevant Act] gives any indication of a congressional purpose to extend
its coverage beyond places over which the United States has sovereignty or
has some measure of legislative control." *Foley Bros., supra,* at 285. We
assume that Congress legislates against the backdrop of the presumption
against extraterritoriality. Therefore, unless there is "the affirmative intention of the Congress clearly expressed," we must presume it "is primarily
concerned with domestic conditions." *Foley Bros., supra,* at 285. Boureslan and
the EEOC contend that the language of Title VII evinces a clearly expressed
intent on behalf of Congress to legislate extraterritorially. They rely principally on two provisions of the statute. First, petitioners argue that the
statute's definitions of the jurisdictional terms "employer" and "commerce" are
sufficiently broad to include United States firms that employ American
citizens overseas. Second, they maintain that the statute's "alien exemption"
clause, 42 U. S. C. § 2000e-1, necessarily implies that Congress intended to
protect American citizens from employment discrimination abroad. . . . We
conclude that petitioners' evidence, while not totally lacking in probative
value, falls short of demonstrating the affirmative congressional intent
required to extend the protections of Title VII beyond our territorial borders.

Title VII prohibits various discriminatory employment practices based on
an individual's race, color, religion, sex, or national origin. *See* §§ 2000e-2,
2000e-3. An employer is subject to Title VII if it has employed 15 or more
employees for a specified period and is "engaged in an industry affecting
commerce." An industry affecting commerce is "any activity, business, or
industry in commerce or in which a labor dispute would hinder or obstruct

commerce or the free flow of commerce and includes any activity or industry 'affecting commerce' within the meaning of the Labor-Management Reporting and Disclosure Act of 1959 [(LMRDA)] [29 U. S. C. 401 *et seq.*].'' § 2000e(h). "Commerce," in turn, is defined as "trade, traffic, commerce, transportation, transmission, or communication among the several States; or between a State and any place outside thereof; or within the District of Columbia, or a possession of the United States; or between points in the same State but through a point outside thereof." § 2000e(g).

Petitioners argue that by its plain language, Title VII's "broad jurisdictional language" reveals Congress's intent to extend the statute's protections to employment discrimination anywhere in the world by a United States employer who affects trade "between a State and any place outside thereof." More precisely, they assert that since Title VII defines "States" to include States, the District of Columbia, and specified territories, the clause "between a State and any place outside thereof" must be referring to areas beyond the territorial limit of the United States.

Respondents offer several alternative explanations for the statute's expansive language. They contend that the "or between a State and any place outside thereof" clause "provides the jurisdictional nexus required to regulate commerce that is not wholly within a single state, presumably as it affects both interstate and foreign commerce", but not to "regulate conduct exclusively within a foreign country." They also argue that since the definitions of the terms "employer," "commerce," and "industry affecting commerce" make no mention of "commerce with foreign nations," Congress cannot be said to have intended that the statute apply overseas. . . .

We need not choose between these competing interpretations as we would be required to do in the absence of the presumption against extraterritorial application discussed above. Each is plausible, but no more persuasive than that. The language relied upon by petitioners — and it is they who must make the affirmative showing — is ambiguous, and does not speak directly to the question presented here. The intent of Congress as to the extraterritorial application of this statute must be deduced by inference from boilerplate language which can be found in any number of congressional Acts, none of which have ever been held to apply overseas. *See, e.g.,* Consumer Product Safety Act, 15 U. S. C. § 2052 (a)(12); Federal Food, Drug, and Cosmetic Act, 21 U. S. C. § 321(b); Transportation Safety Act of 1974, 49 U. S. C. App. § 1802(1); Labor-Management Reporting and Disclosure Act of 1959, 29 U. S. C. § 401 *et seq.*; Americans with Disabilities Act of 1990, 42 U. S. C. § 1201 *et seq.*

Petitioners' reliance on Title VII's jurisdictional provisions also finds no support in our case law; we have repeatedly held that even statutes that contain broad language in their definitions of "commerce" that expressly refer to "foreign commerce" do not apply abroad. For example, in *New York Central R. Co. v. Chisholm,* 268 U.S. 29 (1925), we addressed the extraterritorial application of the Federal Employers' Liability Act (FELA), 45 U. S. C. § 51 *et seq.* FELA provides that common carriers by railroad while engaging in "interstate or foreign commerce" or commerce between "any of the States or territories and any foreign nation or nations" shall be liable in damages to its employees who suffer injuries resulting from their employment. § 51. Despite this broad jurisdictional language, we found that the Act "contains no words which definitely disclose an intention to give it extraterritorial effect," *Chisholm, supra,* at 31, and therefore there was no jurisdiction under FELA for a damages action by a United States citizen employed on a United States railroad who suffered fatal injuries at a point 30 miles north of the United States border into Canada.

Similarly, in *McCulloch v. Sociedad Nacional de Marineros de Honduras,* 372 U.S. 10 (1963), we addressed whether Congress intended the National Labor Relations Act (NLRA), 29 U.S.C. §§ 151–168, to apply overseas. Even though the NLRA contained broad language that referred by its terms to foreign commerce, § 152(6), this Court refused to find a congressional intent to apply the statute abroad because there was not "any specific language" in the Act reflecting congressional intent to do so.

The EEOC places great weight on an assertedly similar "broad jurisdictional grant in the Lanham Act" that this Court held applied extraterritorially in *Steele v. Bulova Watch Co.,* 344 U.S. 280, 286 (1952). In *Steele,* we addressed whether the Lanham Act, designed to prevent deceptive and misleading use of trademarks, applied to acts of a United States citizen consummated in Mexico. The Act defined commerce as "all commerce which may lawfully be regulated by Congress." The stated intent of the statute was "to regulate commerce within the control of Congress by making actionable the deceptive and misleading use of marks in such commerce." While recognizing that "the legislation of Congress will not extend beyond the boundaries of the United States unless a contrary legislative intent appears," the Court concluded that in light of the fact that the allegedly unlawful conduct had some effects within the United States, coupled with the Act's "broad jurisdictional grant" and its "sweeping reach into 'all commerce which may lawfully be regulated by Congress,'" the statute was properly interpreted as applying abroad.

The EEOC's attempt to analogize these cases to *Steele* is unpersuasive. The Lanham Act by its terms applies to "all commerce which may lawfully be regulated by Congress." The Constitution gives Congress the power "to regulate Commerce with foreign Nations, and among the several States, and with the Indian Tribes." U.S. Const., Art. I, § 8, cl. 3. Since the Act expressly stated that it applied to the extent of Congress' power over commerce, the Court in *Steele* concluded that Congress intended that the statute apply abroad. By contrast, Title VII's more limited, boilerplate "commerce" language does not support such an expansive construction of congressional intent. Moreover, unlike the language in the Lanham Act, Title VII's definition of "commerce" was derived expressly from the LMRDA, a statute that this Court had held, prior to the enactment of Title VII, did not apply abroad. *McCulloch, supra,* at 15.

Thus, petitioner's argument based on the jurisdictional language of Title VII fails both as a matter of statutory language and of our previous case law. Many Acts of Congress are based on the authority of that body to regulate commerce among the several States, and the parts of these Acts setting forth the basis for legislative jurisdiction will obviously refer to such commerce in one way or another. If we were to permit possible, or even plausible, interpretations of language such as that involved here to override the presumption against extraterritorial application, there would be little left of the presumption.

Petitioners argue that Title VII's "alien exemption provision," 42 U. S. C. § 2000e-1, "clearly manifests an intention" by Congress to protect United States citizens with respect to their employment outside of the United States. The alien-exemption provision says that the statute "shall not apply to an employer with respect to the employment of aliens outside any State." Petitioners contend that from this language a negative inference should be drawn that Congress intended Title VII to cover United States citizens working abroad for United States employers. There is "no other plausible explanation [that] the alien exemption exists," they argue, because "if Congress believed that the statute did not apply extraterritorially, it would have had no reason to include an exemption for a certain category of individuals employed outside the United States." Since "the statute's jurisdictional provisions cannot possibly be read to confer coverage only upon aliens employed outside the United States," petitioners conclude that "Congress could not rationally have enacted an exemption for the employment of aliens abroad if it intended to foreclose all potential extraterritorial applications of the statute."

Respondents resist petitioners' interpretation of the alien-exemption provision and assert two alternative raisons d'etre for that language. First, they contend that since aliens are included in the statute's definition of employee, and the definition of commerce includes possessions as well as "States," the purpose of the exemption is to provide that employers of aliens in the possessions of the United States are not covered by the statute. Thus, the "outside any State" clause means outside any State, but within the control of the United States. . . .

Second, respondents assert that by negative implication, the exemption "confirms the coverage of aliens in the United States." They contend that this interpretation is consistent with our conclusion in *Espinoza v. Farah Mfg. Co.,* 414 U.S. 86 (1973), that aliens within the United States are protected from discrimination both because Title VII uses the term "individual" rather than "citizen," and because of the alien-exemption provision.

If petitioners are correct that the alien-exemption clause means that the statute applies to employers overseas, we see no way of distinguishing in its application between United States employers and foreign employers. Thus, a French employer of a United States citizen in France would be subject to Title VII — a result at which even petitioners balk. The EEOC assures us that in its view the term "employer" means only "American employer," but there is no such distinction in this statute and no indication that the EEOC in the normal course of its administration had produced a reasoned basis for such a distinction. Without clearer evidence of congressional intent to do so than is contained in the alien-exemption clause, we are unwilling to ascribe to that body a policy which would raise difficult issues of international law by imposing this country's employment-discrimination regime upon foreign corporations operating in foreign commerce.

This conclusion is fortified by the other elements in the statute suggesting a purely domestic focus. The statute as a whole indicates a concern that it not unduly interfere with the sovereignty and laws of the States. *See, e.g.*, 42 U. S. C. § 2000h-4 (stating that the Act should not be construed to exclude the operation of state law or invalidate any state law unless inconsistent with the purposes of the Act). . . . While Title VII consistently speaks in terms of "States" and state proceedings, it fails even to mention foreign nations or foreign proceedings.

Similarly, Congress failed to provide any mechanisms for overseas enforcement of Title VII. For instance, the statute's venue provisions, § 2000e-5(f)(3), are ill-suited for extraterritorial application as they provide for venue only in a judicial district in the State where certain matters related to the employer occurred or were located. And the limited investigative authority provided for the EEOC, permitting the Commission only to issue subpoenas for witnesses and documents from "any place in the United States or any Territory or possession thereof," 29 U. S. C. § 161, incorporated by reference into 42 U. S. C. § 2000e-9, suggests that Congress did not intend for the statute to apply abroad.

It is also reasonable to conclude that had Congress intended Title VII to apply overseas, it would have addressed the subject of conflicts with foreign laws and procedures. In amending the Age Discrimination in Employment Act of 1967 (ADEA), 29 U. S. C. § 621 *et seq.*, to apply abroad, Congress specifically addressed potential conflicts with foreign law by providing that it is not unlawful for an employer to take any action prohibited by the ADEA "where such practices involve an employee in a workplace in a foreign country, and compliance with [the ADEA] would cause such employer . . . to violate the laws of the country in which such workplace is located." § 623(f)(1). Title VII, by contrast, fails to address conflicts with the laws of other nations. . . .

Our conclusion today is buttressed by the fact that "when it desires to do so, Congress knows how to place the high seas within the jurisdictional reach of a statute." *Argentine Republic v. Amerada Hess Shipping Corp.*, 488 U.S. 428, 440 (1989). Congress' awareness of the need to make a clear statement that a statute applies overseas is amply demonstrated by the numerous occasions on which it has expressly legislated the extraterritorial application of a statute. *See, e.g.*, The Export Administration Act of 1979, 50 U. S. App. § 2415(2) (defining "United States person" to include "any domestic concern (including any permanent domestic establishment of any foreign concern) and any foreign subsidiary or affiliate (including any permanent foreign establishment) of any domestic concern which is controlled in fact by such domestic concern"); Coast Guard Act, 14 U. S. C. § 89(a) (Coast Guard searches and seizures upon the high seas); 18 U. S. C. § 7 (Criminal Code extends to high seas); 19 U. S. C. § 1701 (Customs enforcement on the high seas); Comprehensive Anti-Apartheid Act of 1986, 22 U. S. C. § 5001(5)(A) (definition of "national of the United States" as "a natural person who is a citizen of the United States . . ."); the Logan Act, 18 U. S. C. § 953 (applying Act to "any citizen . . . wherever he may be . . ."). Indeed, after several courts held that the ADEA did not apply overseas, Congress amended § 11(f) to provide: "The term 'employee' includes any individual who is a citizen of the United States employed by an employer in a workplace in a foreign country." 29 U. S. C. § 630(f). . . . Congress also amended § 4(g)(1), which states: "If an employer controls a corporation whose place of incorporation is in a foreign country, any practice by such corporation prohibited under this section shall be presumed to be such practice by such employer." § 623(h)(1). The expressed purpose of these changes was to "make provisions of the Act apply to citizens of the United States employed in foreign countries by U.S. corporations or their subsidiaries." S. Rep. No. 98-467, p. 2 (1984).

Congress, should it wish to do so, may similarly amend Title VII and in doing so will be able to calibrate its provisions in a way that we cannot. Petitioners have failed to present sufficient affirmative evidence that Congress intended Title VII to apply abroad.

[The concurring opinion of Justice Scalia is omitted.]

Justice MARSHALL, with whom Justices BLACKMUN and STEVENS join, dissenting.

Like any issue of statutory construction, the question whether Title VII protects United States citizens from discrimination by United States employers abroad turns solely on congressional intent. As the majority recognizes, our inquiry into congressional intent in this setting is informed by the traditional "canon of construction which teaches that legislation of Congress, unless a contrary intent appears, is meant to apply only within the territorial jurisdiction of the United States." *Foley Bros., Inc. v. Filardo,* 336 U.S. 281, 285 (1949). But contrary to what one would conclude from the majority's analysis, this canon is not a "clear statement" rule, the application of which relieves a court of the duty to give effect to all available indicia of the legislative will. Rather, as our case law applying the presumption against extraterritoriality well illustrates, a court may properly rely on this presumption only after exhausting all of the traditional tools "whereby unexpressed congressional intent may be ascertained." *Ibid.* When these tools are brought to bear on the issue in this case, the conclusion is inescapable that Congress did intend Title VII to protect United States citizens from discrimination by United States employers operating overseas. Consequently, I dissent.

I

Because it supplies the driving force of the majority's analysis, I start with "the canon . . . that legislation of Congress, unless a contrary intent appears, is meant to apply only within the territorial jurisdiction of the United States." The majority recasts this principle as "the need to make a clear statement that a statute applies overseas." . . . In my view, the majority grossly distorts the effect of this rule of construction upon conventional techniques of statutory interpretation.

Our most extensive discussion of the presumption against extraterritoriality can be found in *Foley Brothers, supra.* The issue in that case was whether the Eight Hour Law — a statute regulating the length of the workday of employees hired to perform contractual work for the United States — applied to construction projects in foreign nations. After noting "the assumption that Congress is primarily concerned with domestic conditions," the Court concluded that there was "nothing in the Act itself, as amended, nor in the legislative history, which would lead to the belief that Congress entertained any intention other than the normal one in this case." The Court put particular emphasis on "the scheme of the Act," including Congress' failure to draw a "distinction . . . therein between laborers who are aliens and those who are citizens of the United States." "The absence of any [such] distinction," the Court explained, "indicates . . . that the statute was intended to apply only to those places where the labor conditions of both citizen and alien employees are a probable concern of Congress." The Court also engaged in extended analyses of the legislative history of the statute, and of pertinent administrative interpretations.

The range of factors that the Court considered in *Foley Brothers* demonstrates that the presumption against extraterritoriality is not a "clear-statement" rule. Clear-statement rules operate less to reveal actual congressional intent than to shield important values from an insufficiently strong legislative intent to displace them. When they apply, such rules foreclose inquiry into extrinsic guides to interpretation, and even compel courts to select less plausible candidates from within the range of permissible constructions. The Court's analysis in *Foley Brothers* was by no means so narrowly constrained. Indeed, the Court considered the entire range of conventional sources "whereby unexpressed congressional intent may be ascertained," including legislative history, statutory structure, and administrative interpretations. Subsequent applications of the presumption against extraterritoriality confirm that we have not imposed the drastic clear-statement burden upon Congress before giving effect to its intention that a particular enactment apply beyond the national boundaries. *See, e.g., Steele v. Bulova Watch Co.,* 344 U.S. 280, 286–287 (1952) (relying on "broad jurisdictional grant" to find intention that Lanham Act applies abroad).

The majority also overstates the strength of the presumption by drawing on language from cases involving a wholly independent rule of construction: "that 'an act of congress ought never to be construed to violate the law of nations if any other possible construction remains. . . .'" *McCulloch v. Sociedad Nacional, supra,* at 21, (quoting *The Charming Betsy,* 2 Cranch 64, 118 (1804) (Marshall, C. J.)); *see Benz v. Compania Naviera Hidalgo, S. A.,* 353 U.S. 138, 146–147 (1957). At issue in *Benz* was whether the Labor Management Relations Act of 1947 "applied to a controversy involving damages resulting from the picketing of a foreign ship operated entirely by foreign seamen under foreign articles while the vessel is temporarily in an American port." Construing the statute to apply under such circumstances would have displaced labor regulations that were founded on the law of another nation and that were applicable solely to foreign nationals. In language quoted in the majority's opinion, the Court stated that there must be present "the affirmative intention of the Congress clearly expressed" before it would infer that Congress intended courts to enter "such a delicate field of international relations." *Benz, supra,* at 147. Similarly, in *McCulloch*, the Court focused on the absence of "'the affirmative intention of the Congress clearly expressed,'" in declining to apply the National Labor Relations Act to foreign-flag vessels with foreign crews. Extraterritorial application in *McCulloch* would have violated not only "the well-established rule of international law that the law of the flag state ordinarily governs the internal affairs of a ship," but also regulations issued by the State Department.

Far from equating *Benz* and *McCulloch's* clear-statement rule with *Foley's* presumption against extraterritoriality, the Court has until now recognized that *Benz* and *McCulloch* are reserved for settings in which the extraterritorial application of a statute would "implicate sensitive issues of the authority of the Executive over relations with foreign nations." *NLRB v. Catholic Bishop of Chicago,* 440 U.S. 490, 500 (1979); *see Weinberger v. Rossi,* 456 U.S. 25, 32 (1982) (*McCulloch* rule designed to avoid constructions that raise "foreign policy implications"). The strictness of the *McCulloch* and *Benz* presumption permits the Court to avoid, if possible, the separation-of-powers and international-comity questions associated with construing a statute to displace the domestic law of another nation. Nothing nearly so dramatic is at stake when Congress merely seeks to regulate the conduct of United States nationals abroad.

Because petitioners advance a construction of Title VII that would extend its extraterritorial reach only to United States nationals, it is the weak presumption of *Foley Brothers,* not the strict clear-statement rule of *Benz* and *McCulloch,* that should govern our inquiry here. Under *Foley Brothers,* a court is not free to invoke the presumption against extraterritoriality until it has exhausted all available indicia of Congress' intent on this subject. Once these indicia are consulted and given effect in this case, I believe there can be no question that Congress intended Title VII to protect United States citizens from discrimination by United States employers abroad.

II

Title VII states:

> It shall be an unlawful employment practice for an employer . . . to fail or refuse to hire or to discharge any individual, or otherwise to discriminate against any individual with respect to his compensation, terms, conditions, or privileges of employment, because of such individual's race, color, religion, sex, or national origin. 42 U. S. C. § 2000e-2(a)(1).

Under the statute, "the term 'employer' means a person engaged in an industry affecting commerce who has fifteen or more employees," § 2000e(b); "the term 'commerce' means trade, traffic, commerce, transportation, transmission, or communication among the several States; or between a State and any place outside thereof. . . ." § 2000e(g).

These terms are broad enough to encompass discrimination by United States employers abroad. Nothing in the text of the statute indicates that the protection of an "individual" from employment discrimination depends on the location of that individual's workplace; nor does anything in the statute indicate that employers whose businesses affect commerce between "a State and any other place outside thereof" are exempted when their discriminatory conduct occurs beyond the Nation's borders. While conceding that it is "plausible" to infer from the breadth of the statute's central prohibition that Congress intended Title VII to apply extraterritorially, the majority goes to considerable lengths to show that this language is not sufficient to overcome the majority's clear-statement conception of the presumption against extraterritoriality. However, petitioners claim no more — and need claim no more, given additional textual evidence of Congress' intent — than that this language is consistent with a legislative expectation that Title VII apply extraterritorially, a proposition that the majority does not dispute.

Confirmation that Congress did in fact expect Title VII's central prohibition to have an extraterritorial reach is supplied by the so-called "alien exemption" provision. The alien-exemption provision states that Title VII "shall not apply to an employer with respect to the employment of aliens outside any State." 42 U. S. C. § 2000e-1. Absent an intention that Title VII apply "outside any State," Congress would have had no reason to craft this extraterritorial exemption. And because only discrimination against aliens is exempted, employers remain accountable for discrimination against United States citizens abroad.

. . . The history of the alien-exemption provision confirms the inference that Congress expected Title VII to have extraterritorial application. As I have explained, the Court in *Foley Brothers* declined to construe the Eight Hour Law to apply extraterritorially in large part because of "the absence of any distinction between citizen and alien labor" under the Law. . . .

Finally, the majority overstates the importance of Congress' failure expressly to disclaim extraterritorial application of Title VII to foreign employers. As I have discussed, our cases recognize that application of United States law to United States nationals abroad ordinarily raises considerably less serious questions of international comity than does the application of United States law to foreign nationals abroad. It is the latter situation that typically presents the foreign-policy and conflicts-of-law concerns that underlie the clear-statement rule of *McCulloch* and *Benz*. Because two different rules of construction apply depending on the national identity of the regulated parties, the same statute might be construed to apply extraterritorially to United States nationals but not to foreign nationals. *Compare Steele v. Bulova Watch Co., supra,* at 285–287 (applying Lanham Act to United States national for conduct abroad) *with Vanity Fair Mills, Inc. v. T. Eaton Co.,* 234 F.2d 633, 642–643 (CA2) (declining to apply Lanham Act to foreign national for conduct abroad), *cert. denied,* 352 U.S. 871 (1956). . . .

The extraterritorial application of Title VII is supported not only by its language and legislative history but also by pertinent administrative interpretations. Since 1975, the EEOC has been on record as construing Title VII to apply to United States companies employing United States citizens abroad . . . .

In the hands of the majority, the presumption against extraterritoriality is transformed from a "valid approach whereby unexpressed congressional intent may be ascertained," *Foley Bros.,* 336 U.S., at 285, into a barrier to any genuine inquiry into the sources that reveal Congress' actual intentions. Because the language, history, and administrative interpretations of the statute all support application of Title VII to United States companies employing United States citizens abroad, I dissent.

Notes and Questions on *Boureslan*

1. Are *Alcoa* and *Boureslan* inconsistent with one another? If so, how might they be distinguished? Did the majority in *Boureslan* apply international law in determining the jurisdictional reach of Title VII?

2. *The legislative aftermath of Boureslan.* Many courts have followed the principles articulated in *Boureslan* and declined to give extraterritorial effect to U.S. legislation when there is no clear evidence that Congress intended the legislation to apply abroad. *See, e.g., Gushi Brothers Co. v. Bank of Guam,* 28 F.3d 1535 (9th Cir. 1994) (Bank Holding Company Act); *Subafilms Ltd. v. MGM-Pathe Communications Co.,* 24 F.3d 1088 (9th Cir.), *cert. denied,* 513 U.S. 1001 (1994) (copyright laws); *Van Blaricom v. Burlington Northern Railroad Co.,* 17 F.3d 1224 (9th Cir. 1994) (certain regulatory powers of the ICC under the Interstate Commerce Act). But the specific result in *Boureslan* was overturned by Congress in the Civil Rights Act of 1991, 105 Stat. 1077. The 1991 amendment, *inter alia* addressing the term "employee," provided: "With respect to employment in a foreign country, such term includes an individual who is a citizen of the United States." This narrow amendment does not of course translate into a general obligation to apply Title VII extraterritorially. *Reyes-Gaona v. North Carolina Growers Assoc., Inc.,* 250 F.3d 861 (4th Cir. 2001) (ADEA does not apply to a foreign national who unsuccessfully applies in foreign country for employment in the United States). Is the new amendment in violation of international law as articulated in §§ 402–404 of the RESTATEMENT (THIRD) OF FOREIGN RELATIONS LAW?

3. *Extraterritoriality in other regulatory settings.* When Congress has deliberately criminalized certain international acts — like drug trafficking and terrorism — the courts have had little difficulty overcoming the presumption against extraterritorial application of the laws. But in civil cases that arise in regulatory fields, the courts have developed a variety of criteria that avoid the under-inclusiveness of strictly territorial application and the aggression inherent in regulating foreign conduct. For example, U.S. laws regulating securities fraud apply to transactions "between any foreign country and any State" — the very jurisdictional phrase at issue in *Boureslan. See* Securities Act, 15 U.S.C. § 77b(7); Securities Exchange Act, 15 U.S.C. § 78c(a)(17). But in a series of cases predating *Boureslan* — and apparently surviving it — the lower courts have adopted alternative tests for applying the securities laws transnationally, and those tests are reminiscent of the *Alcoa* standards. *See, e.g., Itoba Ltd. v. Lep Group PLC,* 54 F.3d 118 (2d Cir. 1995) (combining "pertinent principles of both the conduct and effects tests," without addressing or citing *Boureslan*). Some decisions focus primarily on one or the other of *Alcoa's* two prongs, *i.e.* whether the fraudulent conduct wherever it occurs has "substantial effects" in the United States, *see, e.g., Consolidated Gold Fields PLC v. Minorco, S.A.,* 871 F.2d 252 (2d Cir. 1989), or whether the defendant's conduct occurred in the United States, was more than "merely preparatory," and satisfied all the elements necessary to establish a violation of the securities laws, and that conduct was "a substantial or significant contributing cause of the decision to purchase stock." *In re Gaming Lottery Securities Litigation,* 58 F. Supp.2d 62, 73 (S.D.N.Y. 1999). *See generally In re Baan Securities Litigation,* 103 F. Supp. 2d 1 (D.D.C. 2000).

[2] The Role of Comity

HARTFORD FIRE INSURANCE CO. v. CALIFORNIA
509 U.S. 764 (1993)

SOUTER, J., announced the opinion of the Court, in which REHNQUIST, C. J., and WHITE, BLACKMUN, and STEVENS, JJ., joined.

The Sherman Act makes every contract, combination, or conspiracy in unreasonable restraint of interstate or foreign commerce illegal. These consolidated cases present questions about the application of that Act to the insurance industry . . . abroad. The plaintiffs (respondents here) allege that both domestic and foreign defendants (petitioners here) violated the Sherman Act by engaging in various conspiracies to affect the American insurance market. A . . . group of foreign defendants argues that the principle of international comity requires the District Court to refrain from exercising jurisdiction over certain claims against it. We hold that . . . the principle of international comity does not preclude District Court jurisdiction over the foreign conduct alleged.

I

The two petitions before us stem from consolidated litigation comprising the complaints of 19 States and many private plaintiffs alleging that the defendants, members of the insurance industry, conspired in violation of § 1 of the Sherman Act to restrict the terms of coverage of commercial general liability (CGL) insurance available in the United States. . . . According to the complaints, the object of the conspiracies was to force certain primary insurers (insurers who sell insurance directly to consumers) to change the terms of their standard CGL insurance policies to conform with the policies the defendant insurers wanted to sell. . . .

[Plaintiffs alleged a conspiracy among a group of London reinsurers and brokers to limit the types of insurance offered in the United States market, in violation of the Sherman Act.] The District Court . . . dismissed the three claims that named only certain London-based defendants, invoking international comity and applying the Ninth Circuit's decision in *Timberlane Lumber Co. v. Bank of America, N. T. & S. A.*, 549 F.2d 597 (1976). . . . The Court of Appeals reversed. [A]s to the three claims brought solely against foreign defendants, the court applied its *Timberlane* analysis, but concluded that the principle of international comity was no bar to exercising Sherman Act jurisdiction. . . .

III

. . .

At the outset, we note that the District Court undoubtedly had jurisdiction of these Sherman Act claims, as the London reinsurers apparently concede. *See* Tr. of Oral Arg. 37 ("Our position is not that the Sherman Act does not apply in the sense that a minimal basis for the exercise of jurisdiction doesn't exist here. Our position is that there are certain circumstances, and that this is one of them, in which the interests of another State are sufficient that the exercise of that jurisdiction should be restrained"). Although the proposition was perhaps not always free from doubt, *see American Banana Co. v. United Fruit Co.,* 213 U.S. 347 (1909), it is well established by now that the Sherman Act applies to foreign conduct that was meant to produce and did in fact produce some substantial effect in the United States.[1] Such is the conduct alleged here: that the London reinsurers engaged in unlawful conspiracies to affect the market for insurance in the United States and that their conduct in fact produced substantial effect.[2]

According to the London reinsurers, the District Court should have declined to exercise such jurisdiction under the principle of international comity.[3] The Court of Appeals agreed that courts should look to that principle in deciding whether to exercise jurisdiction under the Sherman Act. This availed the London reinsurers nothing, however. To be sure, the Court of Appeals believed that "application of [American] antitrust laws to the London reinsurance market 'would lead to significant conflict with English law and policy,' " and that "[s]uch a conflict, unless out-weighed by other factors, would by itself be reason to decline exercise of jurisdiction." But other factors, in the court's view, including the London reinsurers' express purpose to affect United States commerce and the substantial nature of the effect produced, out-weighed the supposed conflict and required the exercise of jurisdiction in this litigation.

When it enacted the FTAIA, Congress expressed no view on the question whether a court with Sherman Act jurisdiction should ever decline to exercise such jurisdiction on grounds of international comity. *See* H. R. Rep. No. 97-686, p. 13 (1982) ("If a court determines that the requirements for subject

---

[1] Justice Scalia believes that what is at issue in this litigation is prescriptive, as opposed to subject-matter, jurisdiction. The parties do not question prescriptive jurisdiction, however, and for good reason: it is well established that Congress has exercised such jurisdiction under the Sherman Act. *See* G. Born & D. Westin, *International Civil Litigation in United States Courts* 542, n. 5 (2d ed. 1992) (Sherman Act is a "prime example of the simultaneous exercise of prescriptive jurisdiction and grant of subject matter jurisdiction").

[2] Under § 402 of the Foreign Trade Antitrust Improvements Act of 1982 (FTAIA), 15 U.S. C. § 6a, the Sherman Act does not apply to conduct involving foreign trade or commerce, other than import trade or import commerce, unless "such conduct has a direct, substantial, and reasonably foreseeable effect" on domestic or import commerce. § 6a(1)(A). The FTAIA was intended to exempt from the Sherman Act export transactions that did not injure the United States economy, *see* H. R. Rep. No. 97-686, pp. 2–3, 9–10 (1982), and it is unclear how it might apply to the conduct alleged here. Also unclear is whether the Act's "direct, substantial, and reasonably foreseeable effect" standard amends existing law or merely codifies it. We need not address these questions here. Assuming that the FTAIA's standard affects this litigation, and assuming further that that standard differs from the prior law, the conduct alleged plainly meets its requirements.

[3] Justice Scalia contends that comity concerns figure into the prior analysis whether jurisdiction exists under the Sherman Act. This contention is inconsistent with the general understanding that the Sherman Act covers foreign conduct producing a substantial intended effect in the United States, and that concerns of comity come into play, if at all, only after a court has determined that the acts complained of are subject to Sherman Act jurisdiction. *See United States v. Aluminum Co. of America,* 148 F.2d 416, 444 (CA2 1945) ("It follows from what we have . . . said that [the agreements at issue] were unlawful [under the Sherman Act], though made abroad, if they were intended to affect imports and did affect them"); *Mannington Mills, Inc. v. Congoleum Corp.,* 595 F.2d 1287, 1294 (CA3 1979) (once court determines that jurisdiction exists under the Sherman Act, question remains whether comity precludes its exercise). *But cf. Timberlane Lumber Co. v. Bank of America, N. T. & S. A.,* 549 F.2d 597, 613 (CA9 1976). In any event, the parties conceded jurisdiction at oral argument, and we see no need to address this contention here.

matter jurisdiction are met, [the FTAIA] would have no effect on the court['s] ability to employ notions of comity . . . or otherwise to take account of the international character of the transaction") (citing *Timberlane*). We need not decide that question here, however, for even assuming that in a proper case, a court may decline to exercise Sherman Act jurisdiction over foreign conduct (or, as Justice Scalia would put it, may conclude by the employment of comity analysis in the first instance that there is no jurisdiction), international comity would not counsel against exercising jurisdiction in the circumstances alleged here. The only substantial question in this litigation is whether "there is in fact a true conflict between domestic and foreign law." *Societe Nationale Industrielle Aerospatiale v. United States Dist. Court for Southern Dist. of Iowa*, 482 U.S. 522, 555 (1987) (Blackmun J., concurring in part and dissenting in part). The London reinsurers contend that applying the Act to their conduct would conflict significantly with British law, and the British Government, appearing before us as amicus curiae, concurs. They assert that Parliament has established a comprehensive regulatory regime over the London reinsurance market and that the conduct alleged here was perfectly consistent with British law and policy. But this is not to state a conflict. "The fact that conduct is lawful in the state in which it took place will not, of itself, bar application of the United States antitrust laws," even where the foreign state has a strong policy to permit or encourage such conduct. RESTATEMENT (THIRD) FOREIGN RELATIONS LAW § 415, Comment j. No conflict exists, for these purposes, "where a person subject to regulation by two states can comply with the laws of both." RESTATEMENT (THIRD) FOREIGN RELATIONS LAW § 403, Comment e.[4] Since the London reinsurers do not argue that British law requires them to act in some fashion prohibited by the law of the United States, or claim that their compliance with the laws of both countries is otherwise impossible, we see no conflict with British law. *See* RESTATEMENT (THIRD) FOREIGN RELATIONS LAW § 403, Comment e, § 415, Comment j. We have no need in this litigation to address other considerations that might inform a decision to refrain from the exercise of jurisdiction on grounds of international comity. . . .

JUSTICE SCALIA delivered . . . a dissenting opinion with respect to Part II. . . .

Petitioners, various British corporations and other British subjects, argue that certain of the claims against them constitute an inappropriate extraterritorial application of the Sherman Act. It is important to distinguish two distinct questions raised by this petition: whether the District Court had jurisdiction, and whether the Sherman Act reaches the extraterritorial conduct alleged here. On the first question, I believe that the District Court had subject-matter jurisdiction over the Sherman Act claims against all the defendants (personal jurisdiction is not contested). Respondents asserted nonfrivolous claims under the Sherman Act, and 28 U.S.C. § 1331 vests district courts with subject-matter jurisdiction over cases "arising under" federal statutes. As precedents such as *Lauritzen v. Larsen*, 345 U.S. 571 (1953) make clear, that is sufficient

---

[4] Justice Scalia says that we put the cart before the horse in citing this authority, for he argues it may be apposite only after a determination that jurisdiction over the foreign acts is reasonable. But whatever the order of cart and horse, conflict in this sense is the only substantial issue before the Court.

to establish the District Court's jurisdiction over these claims. *Lauritzen* involved a Jones Act claim brought by a foreign sailor against a foreign shipowner. The shipowner contested the District Court's jurisdiction, apparently on the grounds that the Jones Act did not govern the dispute between the foreign parties to the action. Though ultimately agreeing with the shipowner that the Jones Act did not apply, the Court held that the District Court had jurisdiction.

> As frequently happens, a contention that there is some barrier to granting plaintiff's claim is cast in terms of an exception to jurisdiction of subject matter. A cause of action under our law was asserted here, and the court had power to determine whether it was or was not well founded in law and in fact." 345 U.S. at 575.

The second question — the extraterritorial reach of the Sherman Act — has nothing to do with the jurisdiction of the courts. It is a question of substantive law turning on whether, in enacting the Sherman Act, Congress asserted regulatory power over the challenged conduct. *See EEOC v. Arabian American Oil Co.,* 499 U.S. 244, 248 (1991) (Aramco) ("It is our task to determine whether Congress intended the protections of Title VII to apply to United States citizens employed by American employers outside of the United States"). If a plaintiff fails to prevail on this issue, the court does not dismiss the claim for want of subject-matter jurisdiction — want of power to adjudicate; rather, it decides the claim, ruling on the merits that the plaintiff has failed to state a cause of action under the relevant statute. *See American Banana Co. v. United Fruit Co.,* 213 U.S. 347, 359 (1909) (holding that complaint based upon foreign conduct "alleges no case under the [Sherman Act]").

There is, however, a type of "jurisdiction" relevant to determining the extraterritorial reach of a statute; it is known as "legislative jurisdiction," *Aramco, supra*, at 253; RESTATEMENT (FIRST) CONFLICT OF LAWS § 60 (1934), or "jurisdiction to prescribe," 1 RESTATEMENT (THIRD) OF FOREIGN RELATIONS LAW OF THE UNITED STATES 235 (1987) (hereinafter Restatement (Third)). This refers to "the authority of a state to make its law applicable to persons or activities," and is quite a separate matter from "jurisdiction to adjudicate," *see id.* at 231. There is no doubt, of course, that Congress possesses legislative jurisdiction over the acts alleged in this complaint: Congress has broad power under Article I, § 8, cl. 3, "to regulate Commerce with foreign Nations," and this Court has repeatedly upheld its power to make laws applicable to persons or activities beyond our territorial boundaries where United States interests are affected. But the question in this litigation is whether, and to what extent, Congress has exercised that undoubted legislative jurisdiction in enacting the Sherman Act.

Two canons of statutory construction are relevant in this inquiry. The first is the "longstanding principle of American law 'that legislation of Congress, unless a contrary intent appears, is meant to apply only within the territorial jurisdiction of the United States.'" *Aramco, supra*, at 248 (quoting *Foley Bros., Inc. v. Filardo,* 336 U.S. 281, 285 (1949)). Applying that canon in *Aramco*, we held that the version of Title VII of the Civil Rights Act of 1964 then in force did not extend outside the territory of the United States, even though the statute contained broad provisions extending its prohibitions to, for example, "'any activity, business, or industry in commerce'" (quoting 42 U.S.C. § 2000e(h)). We held such "boilerplate language" to be an insufficient indication to override the presumption against extraterritoriality. The Sherman Act contains similar "boilerplate language," and if the question were not governed by precedent, it would be worth considering whether that presumption controls the outcome here. We have, however, found the presumption to be overcome with respect to our antitrust laws; it is now well established that the Sherman Act applies extraterritorially.

But if the presumption against extraterritoriality has been overcome or is otherwise inapplicable, a second canon of statutory construction becomes relevant: "An act of congress ought never to be construed to violate the law of nations if any other possible construction remains." *Murray v. Schooner Charming Betsy*, 6 U.S. 64, 2 Cranch 64, 118 (1804) (Marshall, C.J.). This canon is "wholly independent" of the presumption against extraterritoriality. *Aramco*, at 264 (Marshall, J., dissenting). It is relevant to determining the substantive reach of a statute because "the law of nations," or customary international law, includes limitations on a nation's exercise of its jurisdiction to prescribe. *See* RESTATEMENT (THIRD) §§ 401-416. Though it clearly has constitutional authority to do so, Congress is generally presumed not to have exceeded those customary international-law limits on jurisdiction to prescribe.

Consistent with that presumption, this and other courts have frequently recognized that, even where the presumption against extraterritoriality does not apply, statutes should not be interpreted to regulate foreign persons or conduct if that regulation would conflict with principles of international law. For example, in *Romero v. International Terminal Operating Co.*, 358 U.S. 354 (1959), the plaintiff, a Spanish sailor who had been injured while working aboard a Spanish-flag and Spanish-owned vessel, filed a Jones Act claim against his Spanish employer. The presumption against extraterritorial application of federal statutes was inapplicable to the case, as the actionable tort had occurred in American waters. The Court nonetheless stated that, "in the absence of a contrary congressional direction," it would apply "principles of choice of law that are consonant with the needs of a general federal maritime law and with due recognition of our self-regarding respect for the relevant interests of foreign nations in the regulation of maritime commerce as part of the legitimate concern of the international community." "The controlling considerations" in this choice-of-law analysis were "the interacting interests of the United States and of foreign countries."

Romero referred to, and followed, the choice-of-law analysis set forth in *Lauritzen v. Larsen*, 345 U.S. 571 (1953). As previously mentioned, *Lauritzen* also involved a Jones Act claim brought by a foreign sailor against a foreign employer. The *Lauritzen* Court recognized the basic problem: "If [the Jones Act were] read literally, Congress has conferred an American right of action which requires nothing more than that plaintiff be 'any seaman who shall suffer personal injury in the course of his employment.'" The solution it adopted was to construe the statute "to apply only to areas and transactions in which American law would be considered operative under prevalent doctrines of international law." To support application of international law to limit the facial breadth of the statute, the Court relied upon — of course

— Chief Justice Marshall's statement in *Schooner Charming Betsy*. It then set forth "several factors which, alone or in combination, are generally conceded to influence choice of law to govern a tort claim." *See also McCulloch v. Sociedad Nacional de Marineros de Honduras*, 372 U.S. 10, 21–22 (1963) (applying *Schooner Charming Betsy* principle to restrict application of National Labor Relations Act to foreign-flag vessels).

Lauritzen, *Romero*, and *McCulloch* were maritime cases, but we have recognized the principle that the scope of generally worded statutes must be construed in light of international law in other areas as well. More specifically, the principle was expressed in *United States v. Aluminum Co. of America*, the decision that established the extraterritorial reach of the Sherman Act. In his opinion for the court, Judge Learned Hand cautioned "we are not to read general words, such as those in [the Sherman] Act, without regard to the limitations customarily observed by nations upon the exercise of their powers; limitations which generally correspond to those fixed by the 'Conflict of Laws.'"

More recent lower court precedent has also tempered the extraterritorial application of the Sherman Act with considerations of "international comity." . . . The "comity" they refer to is not the comity of courts, whereby judges decline to exercise jurisdiction over matters more appropriately adjudged elsewhere, but rather what might be termed "prescriptive comity": the respect sovereign nations afford each other by limiting the reach of their laws. That comity is exercised by legislatures when they enact laws, and courts assume it has been exercised when they come to interpreting the scope of laws their legislatures have enacted. It is a traditional component of choice-of-law theory. *See* J. STORY, COMMENTARIES ON THE CONFLICT OF LAWS § 38 (1834) (distinguishing between the "comity of the courts" and the "comity of nations," and defining the latter as "the true foundation and extent of the obligation of the laws of one nation within the territories of another"). Comity in this sense includes the choice-of-law principles that, "in the absence of contrary congressional direction," are assumed to be incorporated into our substantive laws having extraterritorial reach. Considering comity in this way is just part of determining whether the Sherman Act prohibits the conduct at issue.[1]

In sum, the practice of using international law to limit the extraterritorial reach of statutes is firmly established in our jurisprudence. In proceeding to apply that practice to the present cases, I shall rely on the Restatement (Third) for the relevant principles of international law. Its standards appear fairly supported in the decisions of this Court construing international choice-of-law principles (*Lauritzen*, *Romero*, and *McCulloch*) and in the decisions of other federal courts, especially *Timberlane*. Whether the Restatement precisely reflects international law in every detail matters little here, as I believe this

---

[1] Some antitrust courts, including the Court of Appeals in the present cases, have mistaken the comity at issue for the "comity of courts," which has led them to characterize the question presented as one of "abstention," that is, whether they should "exercise or decline jurisdiction." *Mannington Mills, Inc. v. Congoleum Corp.*, 595 F.2d 1287, 1294, 1296 (CA3 1979); *see also In re Insurance Antitrust Litigation*, 938 F.2d 919, 932 (CA9 1991). As I shall discuss, that seems to be the error the Court has fallen into today. Because courts are generally reluctant to refuse the exercise of conferred jurisdiction, confusion on this seemingly theoretical point can have the very practical consequence of greatly expanding the extraterritorial reach of the Sherman Act.

litigation would be resolved the same way under virtually any conceivable test that takes account of foreign regulatory interests.

Under the Restatement, a nation having some "basis" for jurisdiction to prescribe law should nonetheless refrain from exercising that jurisdiction "with respect to a person or activity having connections with another state when the exercise of such jurisdiction is unreasonable." RESTATEMENT (THIRD) § 403(1). The "reasonableness" inquiry turns on a number of factors including, but not limited to: "the extent to which the activity takes place within the territory [of the regulating state]," § 403(2)(a); "the connections, such as nationality, residence, or economic activity, between the regulating state and the person principally responsible for the activity to be regulated," § 403(2)(b); "the character of the activity to be regulated, the importance of regulation to the regulating state, the extent to which other states regulate such activities, and the degree to which the desirability of such regulation is generally accepted," § 403(2)(c); "the extent to which another state may have an interest in regulating the activity," § 403(2)(g); and "the likelihood of conflict with regulation by another state," § 403(2)(h). Rarely would these factors point more clearly against application of United States law. The activity relevant to the counts at issue here took place primarily in the United Kingdom, and the defendants in these counts are British corporations and British subjects having their principal place of business or residence outside the United States. Great Britain has established a comprehensive regulatory scheme governing the London reinsurance markets, and clearly has a heavy "interest in regulating the activity," § 403(2)(g). Finally, § 2(b) of the McCarran-Ferguson Act allows state regulatory statutes to override the Sherman Act in the insurance field, . . . suggesting that "the importance of regulation to the [United States]," is slight. Considering these factors, I think it unimaginable that an assertion of legislative jurisdiction by the United States would be considered reasonable, and therefore it is inappropriate to assume, in the absence of statutory indication to the contrary, that Congress has made such an assertion.

It is evident from what I have said that the Court's comity analysis, which proceeds as though the issue is whether the courts should "decline to exercise . . . jurisdiction," rather than whether the Sherman Act covers this conduct, is simply misdirected. I do not at all agree, moreover, with the Court's conclusion that the issue of the substantive scope of the Sherman Act is not in the cases. To be sure, the parties did not make a clear distinction between adjudicative jurisdiction and the scope of the statute. Parties often do not, as we have observed (and have declined to punish with procedural default) before. It is not realistic, and also not helpful, to pretend that the only really relevant issue in this litigation is not before us. In any event, if one errone-ously chooses, as the Court does, to make adjudicative jurisdiction (or, more precisely, abstention) the vehicle for taking account of the needs of prescriptive comity, the Court still gets it wrong. It concludes that no "true conflict" counseling nonapplication of United States law (or rather, as it thinks, United States judicial jurisdiction) exists unless compliance with United States law would constitute a violation of another country's law. That breathtakingly broad proposition, which contradicts the many cases discussed earlier, will bring the Sherman Act and other laws into sharp and unnecessary conflict with the legitimate interests of other countries — particularly our closest trading partners.

In the sense in which the term "conflict" was used in *Lauritzen* and is generally understood in the field of conflicts of laws, there is clearly a conflict in this litigation. The petitioners here, like the defendant in *Lauritzen*, were not compelled by any foreign law to take their allegedly wrongful actions, but that no more precludes a conflict-of-laws analysis here than it did there. Where applicable foreign and domestic law provide different substantive rules of decision to govern the parties' dispute, a conflict-of-laws analysis is necessary.

Literally, the only support that the Court adduces for its position is § 403 of the Restatement (Third) — or more precisely Comment e to that provision, which states:

> Subsection (3) [which says that a State should defer to another state if that State's interest is clearly greater] applies only when one state requires what another prohibits, or where compliance with the regulations of two states exercising jurisdiction consistently with this section is otherwise impossible. It does not apply where a person subject to regulation by two states can comply with the laws of both . . . .

The Court has completely misinterpreted this provision. Subsection (3) of § 403 (requiring one State to defer to another in the limited circumstances just described) comes into play only after subsection (1) of § 403 has been complied with — i.e., after it has been determined that the exercise of jurisdiction by both of the two States is not "unreasonable." That prior question is answered by applying the factors (*inter alia*) set forth in subsection (2) of § 403, that is, precisely the factors that I have discussed in text and that the Court rejects.

Notes and Questions on *Hartford Insurance*, Comity, and the Balancing Test

1. *Reconciling the principal cases.* Is the approach in *Hartford Insurance* consistent with *Alcoa* and *Boureslan*? Should *Boureslan* have compelled the opposite result in *Hartford Insurance*? Does Justice Souter's failure to deal with the *Boureslan* principle suggest that the presumption against extraterritoriality has been weakened generally or only in the context of the antitrust laws? *See* William Dodge, *Understanding the Presumption Against Extraterritoriality*, 16 BERKELEY J. INT'L L. 85 (1998).

2. *The meaning of comity.* In his opinion for the majority in *Hartford Insurance*, Justice Souter argues that comity need only be extended if there were a true conflict between U.S. and British law and that there is no such conflict because the defendants "do not argue that British law requires them to act in some fashion prohibited by the law of the United States, or claim that their compliance with the laws of both countries is otherwise impossible." Are you convinced that comity — the accommodation shown by one sovereign to

another — should apply in only these narrow circumstances? Is a true conflict, as Justice Souter understands it, perhaps the one circumstance in which comity should *not* be shown?

3. *The balancing test and its discontents.* As noted in Justice Scalia's dissent, several lower courts have restricted the extraterritorial application of the antitrust laws, sometimes invoking notions of international comity, and sometimes offering multifactor analyses of the respective interests of both the parties and the states involved in the case. The cases cited by Justice Scalia include *Timberlane Lumber Co. v. Bank of America, N. T. & S. A.,* 549 F.2d 597, 608–615 (9th Cir. 1976); *Mannington Mills, Inc. v. Congoleum Corp.,* 595 F.2d 1287, 1294–1298 (3rd Cir. 1979); *Montreal Trading Ltd. v. Amax Inc.,* 661 F.2d 864, 869–871 (10th Cir. 1981); *Laker Airways Limited v. Sabena, Belgian World Airlines,* 731 F.2d 909, 938 and n. 109 (D.C. Cir. 1984).

But these cases are not necessarily consistent with one another in their approaches to determining the extraterritorial reach of the antitrust laws. In *Timberlane,* for example, the court modified the *Alcoa* test, by adding a balancing test to the jurisdictional inquiry. Specifically, even if a court were convinced that the alleged restraint affected or was intended to affect the foreign commerce of the United States, and was of such a type and magnitude as to be cognizable as a violation of the Sherman Act, the court would still be obliged to answer "the additional question which is unique to the international setting of whether the interests of, and links to, the United States — including the magnitude of the effect on American foreign commerce — are sufficiently strong, vis-à-vis those of other nations, to justify an assertion of extraterritorial authority." In answering that question,

> The elements to be weighed include the degree of conflict with foreign law or policy, the nationality or allegiance of the parties and the locations or principal places of business or corporations, the extent to which enforcement of either state can be expected to achieve compliance, the relative significance of the effects on the United States as compared with those elsewhere, the extent to which there is explicit purpose to harm or affect American commerce, the foreseeability of such effect, and the relative importance to the violation charged of conduct within the United States as compared with conduct abroad.

The resemblance between these elements and Section 403 of the RESTATEMENT is clear and intentional.

But not all courts have agreed that interest-balancing could or would produce defensible results. In *Laker Airways Ltd. v. Sabena,* 731 F.2d 909, 948–52 (D.C. Cir. 1984), for example, the court doubted both the legitimacy and the practicality of the *Timberlane* test:

> Even as the political branches of the respective countries have set in motion the legislative policies which have collided in this litigation, they have deprived courts of the ability meaningfully to resolve the problem. The American and English courts are obligated to attempt to reconcile two contradictory laws, each supported by recognized prescriptive jurisdiction, one of which is specifically designed to cancel out the other.

The suggestion has been made that this court should engage in some form of interest balancing, permitting only a "reasonable" assertion of prescriptive jurisdiction to be implemented. However, this approach is unsuitable when courts are forced to choose between a domestic law which is designed to protect domestic interests, and a foreign law which is calculated to thwart the implementation of the domestic law in order to protect foreign interests allegedly threatened by the objectives of the domestic law. Interest balancing in this context is hobbled by two primary problems: (1) there are substantial limitations on the court's ability to conduct a neutral balancing of the competing interests, and (2) the adoption of interest balancing is unlikely to achieve its goal of promoting international comity.

. . . Most proposals for interest balancing consist of a long list of national contacts to be evaluated and weighed against those of the foreign country. These interests may be relevant to the desirability of allocating jurisdiction to a particular national forum. However, their usefulness breaks down when a court is faced with the task of selecting one forum's prescriptive jurisdiction over that of another.

Many of the contacts to be balanced are already evaluated when assessing the existence of a sufficient basis for exercising prescriptive jurisdiction. Other factors, such as "the extent to which another state may have an interest in regulating the activity," and "the likelihood of conflict with regulation by other states" are essentially neutral in deciding between competing assertions of jurisdiction. Pursuing these inquiries only leads to the obvious conclusion that jurisdiction could be exercised or that there is a conflict, but does not suggest the best avenue of conflict resolution. These types of factors are not useful in resolving the controversy.

Those contacts which do purport to provide a basis for distinguishing between competing bases of jurisdiction, and which are thus crucial to the balancing process, generally incorporate purely political factors which the court is neither qualified to evaluate comparatively nor capable of properly balancing. One such proposed consideration is "the degree to which the desirability of such regulation [of restrictive practices] is generally accepted." We doubt whether the legitimacy of an exercise of jurisdiction should be measured by the substantive content of the prescribed law. Moreover, although more and more states are following the United States in regulating restrictive practices, and even exercising jurisdiction based on effects within territory, the differing English and American assessment of the desirability of anti-trust law is at the core of the conflict. An English or American court cannot refuse to enforce a law its political branches have already determined is desirable and necessary.

The court is also handicapped in any evaluation of "the existence of justified expectations that might be protected or hurt by the regulation in question." In this litigation, whether the reliance of Laker and its creditors on United States antitrust laws is justified depends upon whether one accepts the desirability of United States anti-trust law.

Whether the defendants could justifiably have relied on the inapplicability of United States law to their conduct alleged to have caused substantial effects in the United States is based on the same impermissible inquiry. The desirability of applying ambiguous legislation to a particular transaction may imply the presence or absence of legislative intent. However, once a decision is made that the political branches intended to rely on a legitimate base of prescriptive jurisdiction to regulate activities affecting foreign commerce within the domestic forum, the desirability of the law is no longer an issue for the courts.

The "importance of regulation to the regulating state" is another factor on which the court cannot rely to choose between two competing, mutually inconsistent legislative policies. We are in no position to adjudicate the relative importance of antitrust regulation or nonregulation to the United States and the United Kingdom. It is the crucial importance of these policies which has created the conflict. A proclamation by judicial fiat that one interest is less "important" than the other will not erase a real conflict.

Given the inherent limitations of the Judiciary, which must weigh these issues in the limited context of adversarial litigation, we seriously doubt whether we could adequately chart the competing problems and priorities that inevitably define the scope of any nation's interest in a legislated remedy. This court is ill-equipped to "balance the vital national interests of the United States and the [United Kingdom] to determine which interests predominate." When one state exercises its jurisdiction and another, in protection of its own interests, attempts to quash the first exercise of jurisdiction", it is simply impossible to judicially 'balance' these totally contradictory and mutually negating actions." [citing *In re Uranium Antitrust Litigation*, 480 F.Supp. 1138, 1148 (N.D.Ill. 1978).]

Besides the difficulty of properly weighing the crucial elements of any interest balancing formula, one other defect in the balancing process prompts our reluctance to adopt this analysis in the context of preservation of jurisdiction. Procedurally, this kind of balancing would be difficult, since it would ordinarily involve drawn-out discovery and requests for submissions by political branches. There was no time for this process in the present case. Either jurisdiction was protected or it was lost. It is unlikely that the employment of a hasty and poorly informed balancing process would have materially aided the district court's evaluation of the exigencies and equities of Laker's request for relief.

. . . We might be more willing to tackle the problems associated with the balancing of competing, mutually inconsistent national interests if we could be assured that our efforts would strengthen the bonds of international comity. However, the usefulness and wisdom of interest balancing to assess the most "reasonable" exercise of prescriptive jurisdiction has not been affirmatively demonstrated. This approach has not gained more than a temporary foothold in domestic law. . . . Additionally, there is no evidence that interest balancing represents a rule of international law. Thus, there is no mandatory rule requiring its adoption here, since Congress cannot be said to have implicitly legislated subject to these international constraints.

If promotion of international comity is measured by the number of times United States jurisdiction has been declined under the "reasonableness" interest-balancing approach, then it has been a failure. Implementation of this analysis has not resulted in a significant number of conflict resolutions favoring a foreign jurisdiction. A pragmatic assessment of those decisions adopting an interest-balancing approach indicates none where United States jurisdiction was declined when there was more than a *de minimis* United States interest. Most cases in which use of the process was advocated arose before a direct conflict occurred when the balancing could be employed without impairing the court's jurisdiction to determine jurisdiction. When push comes to shove, the domestic forum is rarely unseated.

Despite the real obligation of courts to apply international law and foster comity, domestic courts do not sit as internationally constituted tribunals. Domestic courts are created by national constitutions and statutes to enforce primarily national laws. The courts of most developed countries follow international law only to the extent it is not overridden by national law. Thus, courts inherently find it difficult neutrally to balance competing foreign interests. When there is any doubt, national interests will tend to be favored over foreign interests. This partially explains why there have been few times when courts have found foreign interests to prevail.

If you are persuaded by the *Laker* critique of interest-balancing, what alternative approach would you propose?

C. PARTY AUTONOMY

In principle, the choice-of-law in transnational cases can be affected by the private contractual choices of the parties, and not just by the public standards of constitutional, international, and state law. The courts have crafted a rebuttable presumption in favor of freedom of contract (or party autonomy) in selecting the applicable law. *See* RESTATEMENT (SECOND) OF CONFLICT OF LAWS §§ 187, 188 (1971).[1] This works especially well when the parties use

---

[1] Section 187 provides:

(1) The law of the state chosen by the parties to govern their contractual rights and duties will be applied if the particular issue is one which the parties could have resolved by an explicit provision in their agreement directed to that issue.

(2) The law of the state chosen by the parties to govern their contractual rights and duties will be applied, even if the particular issue is one which the parties could not have resolved by an explicit provision in their agreement directed to that issue, unless either

(a) the chosen state has no substantial relationship to the parties or the transaction and there is no other reasonable basis for the parties' choice, or

the reference to some jurisdiction's law to fill in the silent gaps of their contract. Of course, the doctrines under which any contract can be invalidated apply to choice-of-law clauses as well, with the result that the presumption in favor of party autonomy can be overcome if the contract or the clause were procured through fraud or overreaching — as shown below.

But there are two critical complications: first, suppose the parties used the choice-of-law mechanism to circumvent the legitimate regulatory interest of governments. Could they select the law of some exotic jurisdiction knowing that the contemplated transaction would be illegal under the law everywhere else, including their home states? And if that is clearly not to be allowed, how should the courts distinguish between "mandatory" laws, which are *not* subject to private choice-of-law arrangements, and "secondary" laws, which are? Second, is there something unique about *international* cases (especially the need to promote international commerce), which compels the courts to respect party autonomy more than they would in an entirely domestic case?

The cases in this section invite you to consider the presumption in favor of party autonomy — and its complications — in two very different settings: a transnational tort case involving an aggressive deck chair (*Milanovich*) and a sophisticated transnational contract potentially involving paramount principles of federal policy (the *Triad* litigation). In each case, the analysis is framed by the Supreme Court's decision in *The Bremen v. Zapata Off-Shore Co.,* 407 U.S. 1 (1972). As summarized by the court in *Mitsubishi Motors Corp. v. Soler Chrysler-Plymouth, Inc.,* 473 U.S. 614 (1985),

> In *The Bremen,* an American oil company, seeking to evade a contractual choice of an English forum and, by implication, English law, filed a suit in admiralty in a United States District Court against the German corporation which had contracted to tow its rig to a location in the Adriatic Sea. Notwithstanding the possibility that the English

---

> (b) application of the law of the chosen state would be contrary to a fundamental policy of a state which has a materially greater interest than the chosen state in the determination of the particular issue and which, under the rule of § 188, would be the state of the applicable law in the absence of an effective choice of law by the parties. . . .

Section 188 provides:

> (1) The rights and duties of the parties with respect to an issue in contract are determined by the local law of the state which, with respect to that issue, has the most significant relationship to the transaction and the parties under the principles stated in Section 6. [For the text of Section 6, see footnote 3 of the *Pancotto* case, *supra.*]

> (2) In the absence of an effective choice of law by the parties (*see* § 187), the contacts to be taken into account in applying the principles of § 6 to determine the law applicable to an issue include:

> (a) the place of contracting,

> (b) the place of negotiation of the contract,

> (c) the place of performance,

> (d) the location of the subject matter of the contract, and

> (e) the domicil, residence, nationality, place of incorporation and place of business of the parties.

These contacts are to be evaluated according to their relative importance with respect to the particular issue. . . .

court would enforce provisions in the towage contract exculpating the German party which an American court would refuse to enforce, this Court gave effect to the choice-of-forum clause. It observed:

> The expansion of American business and industry will hardly be encouraged if, notwithstanding solemn contracts, we insist on a parochial concept that all disputes must be resolved under our laws and in our courts. . . . We cannot have trade and commerce in world markets and international waters exclusively on our terms, governed by our laws, and resolved in our courts. 407 U.S., at 9.

> Recognizing that "agreeing in advance on a forum acceptable to both parties is an indispensable element in international trade, commerce, and contracting," the decision in *The Bremen* clearly eschewed a provincial solicitude for the jurisdiction of domestic forums.

The Bremen is considered in depth in Chapter 3, *supra*, which deals with the problem of determining the appropriate forum. It makes an appearance here, because the courts do not always distinguish between the parties' choice of forum and their choice of law, and both may be challenged under *The Bremen* if the underlying agreement was *inter alia* "[affected] by fraud, undue influence, or overweening bargaining power," or if "enforcement would be unreasonable and unjust."

GREGORY MILANOVICH v. COSTA CROCIERE, S.p.A.
954 F.2d 763 (D.C. Cir. 1992)

Appellants Gregory Milanovich and Marjorie Koch-Milanovich appeal the grant of summary judgment to appellees Costa Crociere, S.p.A., an Italian cruise line corporation, and Costa Cruises, Inc., a New York corporation serving as Costa Crociere's general sales agent. For reasons given below, we vacate the judgment and remand for further proceedings on appellants' claim.

I. Background

Appellants Gregory Milanovich and Marjorie Koch-Milanovich, a husband and wife residing in the District of Columbia, booked passage for a one-week Caribbean cruise on an Italian flag vessel owned by appellee Costa Crociere, S.p.A. The cruise disembarked from San Juan, Puerto Rico, [and] . . . while the ship was in international waters, the deck chair upon which Mr. Milanovich was sitting collapsed, allegedly causing him serious injury. . . . [T]he Milanoviches [subsequently] made a written demand for damages on appellee Costa Cruises, Inc.

Three months later, . . . appellants filed a personal injury action in the United States District Court for the District of Columbia. The suit was filed one year and fifty-three days after the date of the accident. The cruise company promptly moved for summary judgment claiming that the suit was time-barred by a provision of the passage ticket establishing a one-year time limit for bringing personal injury actions. Appellants opposed summary judgment arguing that another provision of the ticket invoked Italian law as the "ruling law of the contract," and that under Italian law, the one-year limitation was unenforceable.[1] They submitted uncontroverted expert testimony that under Articles 1341 and 1342 of the Italian Civil Code, provisions expressly referenced in the passage ticket,[2] liability limiting provisions in certain kinds of "adhesion" contracts, of which a passenger ticket is one, are unenforceable against the nondrafting party unless that party gives specific written assent to such provisions. Without such written approval, they contended, the one-year limitation period in this case was unenforceable.[3]

The district court disagreed. The court reasoned that federal maritime law governed this contract, and that under federal maritime choice-of-law rules, the governing law of the contract is determined by a "center of gravity" analysis, not by the contractual intent of the parties alone. Because of the preponderance of U.S. contacts — appellants are U.S. citizens, the cruise was advertised in the U.S., the tickets were purchased and delivered in the U.S., and the ship left from and returned to a U.S. port — the court held that U.S. law, not Italian law, provided the rule of decision regarding the validity of the one-year limitation clause. Applying U.S. law, the court found that this provision had been effectively incorporated into the contract and was legally enforceable.[4]

---

[1] Appellants' passage ticket came in a 13-page booklet, measuring 8 1/2 by 3 1/2 inches, setting out the terms and conditions of carriage. The following notice was printed on the front of the booklet in red letters against a white background:

IMPORTANT NOTICE

Each passenger should carefully examine this ticket, particularly the conditions on pages 2-10.

A similar notice appeared in the upper left hand corner of the actual ticket: "By accepting or using this ticket the passenger agrees to the terms and conditions appearing on pages 2-10 of Passage Ticket Booklet."

Article 30, printed in small type on page 9 of the ticket, provided that "no action or proceeding against the Company for . . . injury . . . to the passenger shall be instituted, unless . . . the action or suit . . . is commenced within one year from the date when the . . . injury occurred." Art. 35, printed on the next page of the ticket and entitled "RULING LAW OF THIS CONTRACT," provided that "this passage ticket is subject to the Italian law."

[2] The following passage, translated from the Italian, appeared on page 10 of the ticket immediately following Article 35's invocation of Italian law:

THE HOLDER OF THIS PASSAGE TICKET, DO [sic] HEREBY DECLARE TO THE EFFECTS AND UNDER PROVISIONS OF ART. 1341 AND 1342 OF THE ITALIAN CIVIL CODE IN FORCE, THAT HE IS AWARE AND ADHERES TO ALL CONDITIONS AND CLAUSES SET FORTH IN THIS PASSAGE TICKET CONTRACT AND THAT HE SPECIFICALLY APPROVES CLAUSES . . . 30 . . . AND 35.

[3] Appellants also argued that even if enforceable, under Italian law, the one-year limitation period was tolled by their demand letter. Because we find that the limitation period is not enforceable, we do not reach this question.

[4] The court reasoned that under U.S. law, liability limiting provisions in passenger cruise tickets are incorporated into the contract between the passenger and the cruise line if "the contents of the ticket 'reasonably communicated' the presence of the limitation term to the passenger against whom it might be invoked." Surveying the relevant case law, the court noted that

the general characteristics of those tickets held to be sufficiently communicative have included a boldface or otherwise distinguishable warning to the passenger to read the fine print; placement of this warning on the cover of the ticket booklet; repetition of

In a supplemental memorandum and order, the district court considered, and rejected, appellants' argument that the district court had failed to appreciate the significance of the Supreme Court's decision in *The Bremen v. Zapata Off-Shore Co.,* 407 U.S. 1 (1972), in which the Court enforced a contractual choice-of-forum clause in a maritime towage contract.[5] The district court reasoned that

> it is doubtful if the Supreme Court anticipated an extension of the rule of *The Bremen* so far from the [commercial] circumstances of that case as to allow a passenger ticket for a pleasure cruise to dictate, as a matter of contract alone, the terms and conditions upon which a shipowner would be liable to its passengers for personal injury . . . . The proposition may be tested by asking whether, were the situation reversed and the limitations clause less favorable to the Milanoviches under Italian law than under the applicable provision of U.S. maritime law, would it nevertheless be enforced under the rule of *The Bremen* in the circumstances of this case.

Implicitly answering that question in the negative, the district court reiterated that American law, not Italian law, governed this contract and that appellants' suit was time-barred. On appeal, the Milanoviches challenge the district court's refusal to enforce the choice-of-law provision contained in their passage ticket.[6]

II. Analysis

The Milanoviches' cruise ticket is a maritime contract and thus the substantive law to be applied in this case is the general federal maritime law, including maritime choice-of-law rules [citations omitted]. The question we ultimately face is whether a provision of that contract limiting the time for suit was validly incorporated and is legally enforceable. The resolution of those questions depends, however, on the body of contract law with which we examine the contract.

The contract contains a provision purporting to adopt Italian law as the law of the contract, but to follow that direction and use Italian contract law to

---

the warning elsewhere; contrast between the warning and the background on which it is printed; and opportunity afforded the passenger to study the provisions of the ticket by which he is to be bound.

Measured against these criteria, the court concluded that "the tickets given the plaintiffs here reasonably communicated that [they] contained information of which it was in their interest to be aware."

[5] In *The Bremen,* 407 U.S. 1 (1972), the American and German parties to the contract stipulated that the English High Court of Justice would be the exclusive forum for any disputes relating to the contract. The Supreme Court recognized that the English court would apply English law and, in so doing, enforce provisions of the contract that an American court would not.

[6] Because we agree with appellants that the district court erred in refusing to enforce the contractual choice-of-law provision, we do not reach appellants' alternative arguments that (1) the reference to Articles 1341 and 1342 of the Italian Civil Code in the ticket incorporated the requirement of those provisions that the limitation period be specifically approved and therefore the one-year limitation was invalid strictly as a matter of American contract law, and (2) the passage ticket did not "reasonably communicate" to appellants the presence of the one-year limitation clause.

decide whether the provision telling us to use Italian law is valid would obviously be "putting the barge before the tug." What law should govern whether a choice-of-law provision is a valid part of a maritime contract is a difficult question, but one we need not decide because both parties here have assumed that American contract law principles control. If the choice-of-law provision is enforceable, we will use the law that it selects to evaluate the enforceability of the remainder of the contract terms.

Under American law, contractual choice-of-law provisions are usually honored. RESTATEMENT (SECOND) OF CONFLICT OF LAWS § 187 (1971). This principle applies even when the choice-of-law clause is contained in a contract of adhesion, although courts typically scrutinize such contracts to prevent substantial injustice to the adherent. Thus, in *Siegelman v. Cunard White Star,* 221 F.2d 189 (2d Cir. 1955), the court enforced a choice-of-law provision in a cruise ship passage ticket where "there [did] not appear to be an attempt . . . to evade American policy" and "there [was] no suggestion that English law [the stipulated law of the contract] is oppressive to passengers." *See also Jansson v. Swedish American Line,* 185 F.2d 212, 218 (1st Cir. 1950) (noting that "when the parties contract with the law of some particular jurisdiction in view, the law of that jurisdiction will be applicable in determining the interpretation and validity of the contract").

The district court here, however, ignored the choice-of-law clause, reasoning that *The Bremen*, in which the Supreme Court enforced a similar clause,[7] was distinguishable because it involved commercial parties of equal bargaining strength. Appellees, in turn, argue that the district court properly disregarded the choice-of-law clause — a clause that they drafted and included in this adhesion contract — because a contractual choice-of-law clause is only one factor to be considered in a court's choice-of-law analysis. We find neither argument persuasive.

First, while there are indeed statements by some district courts that a choice-of-law clause is only one factor in determining the applicable law, they appear to express mainly the courts' understandable reluctance to automatically enforce the terms of these adhesion contracts against the passenger. *See Caruso v. Italian Line,* 184 F. Supp. 862, 863 (S.D.N.Y. 1960) ("although a recital of the law governing the contract may be determinative in a proper case, it is here but one consideration in determining choice of law because its consensual nature is clearly fictitious"); *Mulvihill v. Furness, Withy & Co.,* 136 F. Supp. 201, 206 (S.D.N.Y. 1955) (applying U.S. law where interpretation of limitation clause "involves important considerations of internal public policy"). While these concerns warrant heightened judicial scrutiny of choice-of-law provisions in passage tickets, they do not sanction their utter disregard, especially where there are no countervailing polices of the forum implicated and where it is the nondrafting party that seeks enforcement of the choice-of-law provision.

Second, the district court's conclusion that the reasoning of *The Bremen* is limited to the commercial context has been undermined by the Supreme

---

[7] As noted above, *The Bremen* involved a choice-of-forum clause, but the Supreme Court recognized that enforcing the provision would have the effect of subjecting the contract to foreign law. *See supra* note 5.

Court's recent decision in *Carnival Cruise Lines, Inc. v. Shute,* 111 S. Ct. 1522 (1991), in which the Court extended the logic of *The Bremen* to contracts governing pleasure cruises. In *Carnival Cruise,* an injured cruise ship passenger filed suit in his home state despite a stipulation in the passage ticket requiring all suits to be filed in Florida. The Court recognized that the choice-of-forum clause was not the subject of bargaining, but nonetheless considered whether it was "reasonable" and therefore enforceable under American law. The Court noted that "forum-selection clauses contained in form passage contracts are subject to judicial scrutiny for fundamental fairness," but concluded that this particular choice-of-forum clause was reasonable and that the plaintiff had failed to satisfy the "heavy burden of proof" required to set aside the clause on grounds of inconvenience (quoting *The Bremen,* 407 U.S. at 17).

Under *The Bremen* and *Carnival Cruise,* then, courts should honor a contractual choice-of-law provision in a passenger ticket unless the party challenging the enforcement of the provision can establish that "enforcement would be unreasonable and unjust," "the clause was invalid for such reasons as fraud or overreaching," or "enforcement would contravene a strong public policy of the forum in which suit is brought."[8]

Appellees do not argue that enforcement of the choice-of-law provision would be unreasonable or unjust, or that they have been the victim of fraud, bad faith, or overreaching; after all, appellees drafted the choice-of-law provision and included it in the form passage contract. Instead, appellees argue that a particular policy of the forum would be contravened by enforcement of the contractual choice-of-law clause. Under 42 U.S.C. § 183b(a), they say, it is unlawful

> for the . . . owner of any sea-going vessel . . . transporting passengers . . . from or between ports of the United States and foreign ports to provide . . . a shorter period for . . . the institution of suits on [claims for loss of life or bodily injury] than one year.

Appellees argue that this provision implicitly sanctions a maximum limitation period of one year and was enacted "to provide uniformity of treatment and predictability of outcome for American passengers" regardless of the nationality of the carrier. Enforcing a choice-of-law clause that will permit suit beyond one year from the date of the accident, appellees argue, would contravene this public policy.

The plain language of 42 U.S.C. § 183b, however, reveals that the provision seeks only to prevent time limitations of less than one year. Enforcing the choice-of-law clause here obviously does not contravene that policy. To the extent there is an affirmative forum policy regarding time bars to suit, it is embodied in 46 U.S.C. § 763(a), which provides for a three-year statute of

---

[8] Of course, a preliminary question exists as to whether the choice-of-law clause was validly incorporated into the passage ticket. Under American maritime law, the terms and conditions in a passage ticket are deemed to be incorporated as long as they are "reasonably communicated" to the passenger. Appellees forcefully argue that the one-year limitation clause was "reasonably communicated" to appellants. They thus necessarily concede that the choice-of-law clause, printed in identical type on the very next page of the ticket, was also "reasonably communicated" to appellants and was therefore validly incorporated into the passage ticket.

limitations for maritime torts. Enforcing the choice-of-law clause here would clearly not undermine that policy.

III. Conclusion

The Milanvoches' passage ticket designates Italian law as the ruling law of the contract. Appellees, the parties opposing enforcement of that provision, have not demonstrated that the choice-of-law clause is unjust or unreasonable or that its enforcement would violate American public policy. We therefore see no reason to deny enforcement of this express provision of the Milanoviches' passage ticket. Under Italian law, as it was explained by appellants' expert without contradiction by appellees, the contract's one-year limitation on suit is invalid, and thus appellants' action was timely filed. The summary judgment of the district court is vacated and the case is remanded for further proceedings to adjudicate appellants' personal injury claim.

Notes and Questions on *Milanovich*

1. *The limits of party autonomy.* The contractual provisions at issue in the case were not in any meaningful sense negotiated, and yet they were enforced. What is the rationale for respecting party autonomy in the choice of law in such circumstances? Compare *Carnival Cruise Lines v. Shute, supra,* p. 142.

2. Were there any substantial public policies that might have compelled the opposite result in *Milanovich*?

3. In what sense is the analysis in *Milanovich* compelled more by equities than law?

TRIAD FINANCIAL ESTABLISHMENT v. TUMPANE COMPANY
611 F. Supp. 157 (N.D.N.Y. 1985)

Plaintiff, Triad Financial Establishment ("Triad") brings this breach of contract action against defendant, The Tumpane Company ("Tumco"), seeking more than $3.5 million in commissions allegedly owed to Triad under the contracts between the parties. Presently before the court are cross-motions for summary judgment. . . .

Plaintiff Triad is a Liechtenstein entity controlled by Adnan Khashoggi, a well-known Saudi Arabian businessman. Triad describes itself as a "marketing and consulting organization" that "assists its clients in locating, identifying, and participating in international business ventures, particularly in Saudi Arabia." Defendant Tumco is a New York corporation with its principal place of business in Vancouver, Washington. Tumco is primarily engaged in providing support services such as housing, transportation, food services, and health facilities for large military projects.

In 1971, the United States agreed to equip and modernize the Royal Saudi Air Force of the Kingdom of Saudi Arabia through a long range, multibillion dollar program called "Peace Hawk" ("Peace Hawk" or "program"). In accordance with the terms of the Foreign Military Sales Contract, the Northrop Corporation ("Northrop") was designated the prime contractor for the entire program. Defendant Tumco was interested in being named as the sole-source subcontractor for support services on the Peace Hawk program. On December 1, 1971, Triad and Tumco entered into two agreements wherein Tumco appointed Triad as its marketing agent to assist Tumco in obtaining the Peace Hawk support services subcontract from Northrop.

Triad contends that it has performed all of its obligations under the agreement and is entitled to commissions in excess of $3.5 million. Tumco contends that it does not owe Triad any commissions and has counterclaimed for the return of $1.7 million already paid to Triad under the agreements. . . .

The Conflict of Law Issues

. . . [T]he Marketing Agreement between the parties contains a forum-selection clause designating New York as the jurisdiction that would govern the interpretation of the contracts. New York courts will normally honor the parties' choice of forum provided the forum selected has a substantial relationship to the parties or the transaction and the application of the forum's law would not be contrary to a fundamental policy of a state with a materially greater interest than the forum state.[1] Thus, New York courts do not consider themselves bound by a forum-selection clause if its application would override the policies of a state with a materially greater interest in the controversy.

Tumco contends that Saudi Arabia has a far greater interest in this litigation than New York does and, consequently, Saudi law should apply notwithstanding the forum selection clause. Triad contends that Saudi Arabia has no interest in this controversy and accordingly, this court should honor the parties' choice of forum. In determining what law should apply, this court must weigh the relative interests of the states involved to determine which state has the greatest interest at stake in this litigation. The court must also consider which forum has the most significant relationship with the parties and transaction.

Plaintiff Triad is a Liechtenstein entity. Defendant Tumco is incorporated in New York with its main office in Vancouver, Washington. At the height of the Peace Hawk program, Tumco had only two employees in New York compared with 3750 in Saudi Arabia, 500 in Montana, 250 in California, 200 in Spain, and 100 in Washington. None of the relevant agreements were negotiated, executed, or performed in New York. It appears that New York's only significant contact with this litigation is via the forum-selection clause contained in the Marketing Agreement.

In contrast, Saudi Arabia has a significant connection to this litigation and a compelling interest in the application of the law. Although Triad is a

---

[1] The parties agree that New York's policy with regard to this issue is based on the RESTATEMENT (SECOND) OF CONFLICT OF LAWS § 187 . . . . Tumco contends that this case falls squarely within § 187(2)(b).

Liechtenstein entity, it has characterized itself as a "Saudi sales agent." Its reputation as an effective marketing agent is based almost entirely on Mr. Khashoggi's purported influence in Saudi Arabia. In addition, the Northrop-Tumco contracts, which are predicates to the Triad-Tumco contracts, were negotiated primarily in Saudi Arabia and call for performance entirely in Saudi Arabia. Moreover, Saudi Arabia has a compelling interest in having its law applied to this controversy. The Kingdom of Saudi Arabia prohibits the payment of agent's fees on contracts for arms and related services. The Saudi prohibition was formally expressed in Decree No. 1275 which was issued on September 17, 1975. The Decree prohibits the payment of any agent's fees in connection with the sale of armaments or related equipment:

> 1. No firm holding a contract with the Saudi Government for the supply of arms or equipment required by the Saudi Government may pay any sum as a commission to any intermediary, sales agent, representative, or broker. This prohibition shall apply regardless of the nationality of the firm or the nationality of the intermediary, sales agent, representative, or broker. It shall apply also whether the contract was concluded directly between the Saudi Government and the firm or through a third-party state. No recognition is accorded to any commission agreement previously concluded by any of such firm with any party, and such agreement shall have no validity vis-a-vis the Saudi Government.

> 2. If among the foreign firms mentioned in paragraph 1 above there are any that are obligated by commission agreements that they have made, they are to stop payment of the commissions due after having been warned by this decision. . . .

The Saudis enacted Decree No. 1275 in an attempt to root out corruption and bribery in military contracts. To allow a forum-selection clause to circumvent this strong Saudi policy would render Decree No. 1275 meaningless. In contrast, New York has no policy at stake in this litigation. New York has little or no interest in upholding Triad's claim for fees. In view of the significant connection to Saudi Arabia, the fundamental Saudi policy against agent's fees in military contracts, and the negligible relation between this case and New York, the court finds that Saudi Arabian law should apply.

NORTHROP CORPORATION v. TRIAD INTERNATIONAL MARKETING S.A.
811 F.2d 1265 (9th Cir. 1987)

In October 1970, Northrop and Triad entered into a "Marketing Agreement," under which Triad became Northrop's exclusive marketing representative to solicit contracts for aircraft and related maintenance, training, and support services for the Saudi Air Force, in return for commissions on sales. Northrop made substantial sales to Saudi Arabia and paid Triad a substantial part of the commissions due under the Marketing Agreement.

On September 17, 1975, the Council of Ministers of Saudi Arabia issued Decree No. 1275, prohibiting the payment of commissions in connection with armaments contracts.[1] Northrop ceased paying commissions to Triad. Triad protested, and demanded payment of the commissions remaining due under the Agreement. The dispute was submitted to arbitration. The arbitrators sustained Triad's claim in part, denied it in part, and entered an award in Triad's favor.

Triad filed an action to confirm the arbitrators' award, and Northrop filed suit to vacate it. The district court vacated the award in some respects. Triad appealed . . . We reverse. . . .

I

The arbitrators noted that the essence of Northrop's defense was that Saudi Arabia's Decree No. 1275 applied to the Marketing Agreement, and made illegal any commission payment to Triad under the Agreement. "This contention," the arbitrators said, "necessitates a consideration of the meaning and effect of paragraph 13 of the Marketing Agreement."

Paragraph 13 of the Marketing Agreement provided: "[T]he validity and construction of this Agreement shall be governed by the laws of the State of California." It further provided: "Any controversy or claim between the parties hereto arising out of or in connection with this Agreement . . . shall be settled by arbitration," and "[t]he award of a majority of the arbitrators . . . shall be final and binding upon the parties."

The arbitrators noted that Northrop had proposed inclusion of paragraph 13 in the Marketing Agreement to make it

> unnecessary for Northrop to make an in-depth study of the law of countries such as Saudi Arabia, Iran, etc., to know what its rights and obligations would be. Instead of having varying and even inconsistent results under the same contractual provisions as a result of applying different laws, depending on where the marketing was to occur, this clause resulted in uniformity of interpretation and application of the contract. Northrop was familiar with the law of California and knew what to expect from it.

Accordingly, the arbitrators interpreted paragraph 13 as requiring that the local law of California determine the effect of Saudi Arabia Decree No. 1275

---

[1] That Decree provides in relevant part:

First: No company under contract with the Saudi Arabian government for the supply of arms or related equipment shall pay any amount as commission to any middleman, sales agent, representative, or broker irrespective of their nationality, and whether the contract was concluded directly between the Saudi Arabian government and the company or through another state. Any commission arrangement already concluded by any of these companies with any other party shall be considered void and not binding for the Saudi Arabian government;

Second: If any of the foreign companies described in Article I (one) were found to have been under obligation for the payment of commission, payment of such commission shall be suspended after notifying the concerned companies of this decision. Relevant commissions shall be deducted from the total amount of the contract for the account of the Saudi Arabian government.

on Northrop's obligation to pay commissions to Triad, pursuant to the Marketing Agreement. Northrop does not disagree with this determination.

Northrop argued [that] the Marketing Agreement was invalid under California Civil Code § 1511. This statute provides "performance of an obligation . . . is excused . . . [w]hen such performance . . . is prevented . . . by the operation of law. . . ." Cal.Civ.Code § 1511(1). Northrop reasoned [that] Saudi Decree No. 1275 rendered the Marketing Agreement unlawful under California Civil Code § 1511 because the Decree "prevented" payment of commissions to Triad and thus "excused" Northrop's performance of its obligations under the Agreement. . . .

The arbitrators concluded [that, . . .] despite the issuance of Decree No. 1275, Northrop could still pay Triad the commissions the Marketing Agreement called for, and Triad could still give advice, translate documents, make local arrangements, and perform the other services the Agreement required. Moreover, as Triad points out, before Decree No. 1275 issued, Triad had successfully solicited the sales contracts Northrop sought and thus had already completed performance of its principal obligation under the Marketing Agreement.

Northrop argued that to honor its obligation to Triad, Northrop would be required to violate Decree No. 1275. The arbitrators adopted Judge Hamley's statement for this court in a similar case and responded: "It may be that Boeing has gotten itself into some trouble with the government of Kuwait by setting up and terminating a selling agency in a manner allegedly violative of Kuwait law. But as between Boeing and Alghanim, we think the contract provision must govern." *Alghanim v. Boeing Co.*, 477 F.2d 143, 150 (9th Cir. 1973).

II

. . . The question the arbitrators decided . . . was . . . the proper interpretation of the requirement of paragraph 13 of the Marketing Agreement that claims arising in connection with the Agreement be settled by arbitration and that California law be applied in resolving them. More specifically, the question was whether paragraph 13 required the arbitrators to apply California Civil Code § 1511 to determine the effect of Saudi Arabia Decree No. 1275 on the obligations of the parties under the Agreement, and, if so, what that determination should be. This issue arose from the very terms of the Marketing Agreement. Its resolution was an inescapable part of the arbitrators' task of interpreting and applying the Agreement and resolving the dispute between these parties. Courts are bound to enforce an award based upon the arbitrators' resolution of such an issue "even in the face of 'erroneous findings of fact or misinterpretations of law.'" *French v. Merrill Lynch, Pierce, Fenner & Smith*, 784 F.2d 902, 906 (9th Cir. 1986) (quoting *American Postal Workers*, 682 F.2d at 1285) (footnote omitted).

This case is not unlike *George Day Construction Co. v. United Brotherhood of Carpenters*, 722 F.2d 1471 (9th Cir. 1984). A clause in the contract in *George Day Construction* provided that the terms of the contract were intended to be consistent with federal and state law. The arbitrators interpreted this contract provision as authorizing the arbitrators to look to external law to resolve the parties' dispute. In reviewing the award, the court held that both the arbitrators' interpretation of this provision and their resolution of the legal questions the dispute raised as to the parties' contractual obligations were entitled to deferential review.

Similarly, in this case it was within the arbitrators' authority to interpret paragraph 13 as requiring that all disputes under the Agreement be determined by the arbitrators in accordance with California law. This interpretation required the arbitrators to decide questions of California law relevant to the parties' dispute as to their obligations under the Agreement. "In such circumstances, the arbitrator may and indeed must do so to fulfill his function under the agreement, and a court should not review the merits of his performance in any more depth than it reviews the merits of his interpretation of other contractual provisions." Kaden, *Judges and Arbitrators: Observations on the Scope of Judicial Review*, 80 COLUM. L. REV. 267, 286 (1980).

The arbitrators' conclusions on legal issues are entitled to deference here. The legal issues were fully briefed and argued to the arbitrators; the arbitrators carefully considered and decided them in a lengthy written opinion. To now subject these decisions to *de novo* review would destroy the finality for which the parties contracted and render the exhaustive arbitration process merely a prelude to the judicial litigation which the parties sought to avoid.

III

In stating the rule of deferential review afforded arbitration awards, the Supreme Court also noted a limitation: "the interpretations of the law by the arbitrators in contrast to manifest disregard are not subject, in the federal courts, to judicial review for error in interpretation." *Wilko v. Swan*, 346 U.S. 427, 436–37 (1953). Although the "manifest disregard of law" standard is not easily defined, it is clear it has not been met in this case.

By the very terms of the rule of deferential review, mere error in interpretation of California law would not be enough to justify refusal to enforce the arbitrators' decision. Moreover, it is far from evident that the arbitrators misread California law at all. No California case clearly contrary to the arbitrators' interpretation has been called to our attention. It was not unreasonable for the arbitrators to distinguish the cases upon which Northrop relied on the ground stated by the arbitrators. . . .

The district court examined the language and history of Saudi Arabia Decree No. 1275 in some detail and concluded that it prohibited the payment of the commissions involved in this case. But as we have said, the question was whether payment was prohibited under California law, not Saudi law, and the answer to that question turned not upon whether Decree No. 1275 stated a rule of Saudi law under which the payment would be illegal, but rather upon whether the existence of such a rule in Saudi law excused performance under California Civil Code § 1511.

Northrop also argues that if the Saudi Decree did not excuse performance of the Marketing Agreement under California Civil Code § 1511, the choice-of-law clause in the Agreement should be set aside and the Saudi Decree should be applied directly to invalidate the Marketing Agreement under the principle announced in RESTATEMENT (SECOND) OF CONFLICTS § 187(2)(b) (1971). However, choice-of-law and choice-of-forum provisions in international commercial contracts are "an almost indispensable precondition to achievement of the orderliness and predictability essential to any international business transaction," and should be enforced absent strong reasons to set them aside. *Scherk v. Alberto-Culver Co.*, 417 U.S. 506, 516–20 (1974); *The Bremen v. Zapata Off-Shore Co.*, 407 U.S. 1 (1972). We agree with the arbitrators that the general principle of conflicts Northrop cites is not sufficient standing alone to overcome the strong policy consideration announced in *Scherk* and *Bremen*. . . .

Notes and Questions on the *Triad* Litigation

1. What accounts for the difference in the results in *Tumpane* and *Northrop*?

2. How would you articulate the post-*Triad* test for when party autonomy in the choice of law will be respected? In approaching this question, consider the following observations of the Fourth Circuit Court of Appeals in *Barnes Group, Inc. v. C&C Products, Inc.*, 716 F.2d 1023, 1029 (4th Cir. 1983):

> While contemporary doctrine recognizes a sphere of party autonomy within which contractual choice-of-law provisions will be given effect,[1] it also limits the extent to which deft draftsmanship will be allowed to bypass legislative judgments as to basic enforceability or validity [citations omitted]. This is implicit in the RESTATEMENT (SECOND) OF CONFLICTS § 187(2)(b), which provides that a contractual choice-of-law clause will not be given effect on matters such as "capacity, formalities and substantial validity,"[2] *id.* comment d, when "application of the law of the chosen state would be contrary to a fundamental policy of a state which has a materially greater interest than the chosen state in the determination of the particular issue and which . . . would be the state of the applicable law in the absence of an effective choice of law by the parties."[3]

What authorities would you consult to determine the content of a state's "fundamental policy"?

---

[1] Parties are not "legislating" when they choose governing law, "because the forum has adopted a choice-of-law rule which provides that the law chosen by the parties shall be applied." Reese, *Contracts and the Restatement of Conflict of Laws, Second*, 9 INT'L & COMP.L.Q. 531, 534 (1960).

[2] In contrast, parties enjoy full autonomy to choose controlling law with regard to matters within their contractual capacity. *See* RESTATEMENT (SECOND) OF CONFLICTS § 187(1) (1971).

[3] The Restatement also specifies two other circumstances . . . in which a contractual choice of law will not be given effect in matters concerning capacity and substantive validity: where the state whose law is chosen has no substantial relationship to the contract; and where the choice-of-law clause is the result of misrepresentation, duress, undue influence, or mistake. *See* RESTATEMENT (SECOND) OF CONFLICTS § 187(2)(a) & comment b.

D. CHOOSING INTERNATIONAL LAW

[1] Treaties as the Rule-of-Decision: The Self-Executing Treaty Doctrine

Under the Supremacy Clause of the Constitution, "all treaties made, or which shall be made, under the authority of the United States" are part of the supreme law of the land, on a par with "[t]his Constitution, and the Laws of the United States which shall be made in Pursuance thereof." U.S. CONST., art. VI. But not all treaties are created equal, and the Supreme Court held early in the Republic that only a "self-executing treaty" would create domestic law under the Supremacy Clause, with the understanding that its international status was a very different question. In other words, the United States might be bound internationally by a treaty, but it would become enforceable in the courts of the United States only if it were self-executing. By definition, a non-self-executing treaty becomes domestic law only if and when it has been implemented by federal statute.

The distinction has been easier to define than to apply for nearly two centuries. According to Chief Justice Marshall in *Foster v. Neilson*, 27 U.S. (2 Pet.) 253, 314 (1829), *overruled on other grounds*, *United States v. Percheman*, 32 U.S. (7 Pet.) 51 (1833):

> Our constitution declares a treaty to be the law of the land. It is, consequently, to be regarded in courts of justice as equivalent to an act of the legislature, whenever it operates of itself, without the aid of any legislative provision. But when the terms of the stipulation import a contract — when either of the parties engages to perform a particular act, the treaty addresses itself to the political, not the judicial department; and the legislature must execute the contract, before it can become a rule for the court.

See also The Head Money Cases, 112 U.S. 580, 598–99 (1884):

> A treaty, then, is the law of the land as an act of Congress is, whenever its provisions prescribe a rule by which the rights of the private citizen or subject may be determined. And when such rights are of a nature to be enforced in a court of justice, that court resorts to the treaty for a rule of decision for the case before it as it would to a statute.

The cases and materials in this section invite you to consider the criteria that courts use to distinguish self-executing treaties from non-self-executing treaties, and the various (sometimes inconsistent) uses to which the doctrine is put.

As a first cut, consider the test used in the Ninth Circuit Court of Appeals for determining whether a treaty is self-executing or not. *See Islamic Republic of Iran v. Boeing Co.,* 771 F.2d 1279, 1283 (9th Cir. 1985):

> (1) "the purposes of the treaty and the objectives of its creators," (2) "the existence of domestic procedures and institutions appropriate for direct implementation," (3) "the availability and feasibility of alternative enforcement methods," and (4) "the immediate and long-range social consequences of self-or non-self-execution."

Id. (quoting *People of Saipan v. United States Dep't of Interior*, 502 F.2d 90, 97 (9th Cir. 1974).) "The first factor [] is critical to determine whether an executive agreement [or treaty] is self-executing, while the other factors are most relevant to determine the extent to which the agreement is self-executing." *Id*. If the treaty parties' intent is clear from the treaty's language, courts will not inquire into the remaining factors. *Id*. Thus, if the parties intend the treaty to become domestic law without legislative implementation, enforceable in domestic courts through the initiative of non-state actors, the courts are likely to declare the treaty self-executing. Intent can be inferred from the *travaux* or legislative history of the treaty, though the actual language in the treaty is routinely considered the best indicator of the parties' intent: did they use language of present action (as distinct from some requirement of future action as in *Foster v. Neilson, supra*)? Did they use the language of obligation rather than aspiration? And the Senate in giving its advice and consent to a treaty can attach a "non-self-executing" reservation, understanding, or declaration, which effectively directs the courts to await Congressional implementation before enforcing it domestically.

The open-endedness of these criteria and their complicated interrelationships are compounded by a cruel reality: the courts do not consistently mean any one thing when they declare a treaty to be not self-executing. A treaty will sometimes be held to be self-executing when the courts conclude that it *trenches on some Constitutional prerogative* of the Congress. The Constitution, for example, grants Congress certain powers over patents, the alienation of federal land, and federal appropriations. A treaty purporting to address these subjects would likely be deemed non-self-executing and require some form of congressional implementation before it could be enforced in U.S. courts. A court may also use the rhetoric of self-execution when it means that plaintiffs have *no standing to invoke the treaty*, *i.e.*, the plaintiffs are not within the class intended to be protected by the agreement. Alternatively, and with increasing frequency, to call a treaty non-self-executing is to say that the treaty *does not create a private right of action*: whatever enforcement mechanisms are contemplated by the parties to a treaty, a lawsuit in a domestic court filed by private individuals is not among them. In other cases, "non-self-executing" is a synonym for *"aspirational" or "hortatory,"* and the failure of the treaty-parties to use the language of current obligation will imply that the treaty requires legislative implementation. Courts suspicious that the political question doctrine is only to be invoked narrowly may nonetheless decide that a treaty provides no *"judicially manageable standards"* or *trenches on some executive prerogative in foreign affairs*, and the self-executing treaty doctrine will provide a useful dispositive hook. "What Professor Henkin said about the political-question doctrine is an even more apt description of the doctrine of self-executing treaties: the doctrine 'is an unnecessary, deceptive packaging of several established doctrines that has misled lawyers and courts to find in it things that were never put there and make it far more than the sum of its parts.'" Carlos Vazquez, *Treaty-Based Rights and Remedies of Individuals*, 92 COLUM. L. R. 1082 (1992) (citing Louis Henkin, *Is There A 'Political Question' Doctrine?*, 85 YALE L.J. 597, 622 (1976)).

RESTATEMENT (THIRD) FOREIGN RELATIONS LAW OF THE UNITED STATES

§ 111. International Law and Agreements as Law of the United States

(1) International law and international agreements of the United States are law of the United States and supreme over the law of the several States.

(2) Cases arising under international law or international agreements of the United States are within the Judicial Power of the United States and, subject to Constitutional and statutory limitations and requirements of justiciability, are within the jurisdiction of the federal courts.

(3) Courts in the United States are bound to give effect to international law and to international agreements of the United States, except that a "non-self-executing" agreement will not be given effect as law in the absence of necessary implementation.

(4) An international agreement of the United States is "non-self-executing"

(A) if the agreement manifests an intention that it shall not become effective as domestic law without the enactment of implementing legislation;

(B) if the Senate in giving consent to a treaty, or Congress by resolution, requires implementing legislation; or

(C) if implementing legislation is constitutionally required.

ASAKURA v. CITY OF SEATTLE
265 U.S. 332 (1924)

MR. JUSTICE BUTLER delivered the opinion of the Court. Plaintiff in error is a subject of the Emperor of Japan, and, since 1904, has resided in Seattle, Washington. Since July, 1915, he has been engaged in business there as a pawnbroker. The city passed an ordinance, which took effect July 2, 1921, regulating the business of pawnbroker and repealing former ordinances on the same subject. It makes it unlawful for any person to engage in the business unless he shall have a license, and the ordinance provides "that no such license shall be granted unless the applicant be a citizen of the United States." Violations of the ordinance are punishable by fine or imprisonment or both. Plaintiff in error brought this suit in the Superior Court of King County, Washington, against the city, its Comptroller, and its Chief of Police to restrain them from enforcing the ordinance against him. He attacked the ordinance on the ground that it violates the treaty between the United States and the Empire of Japan, proclaimed April 5, 1911, 37 Stat. 1504. . . . It was shown that he had about $5,000 invested in his business, which would be broken up and destroyed by the enforcement of the ordinance. The Superior Court granted the relief prayed. On appeal, the Supreme Court of the State held the ordinance valid and reversed the decree. . . .

Does the ordinance violate the treaty? Plaintiff in error invokes and relies upon the following provisions:

> The citizens or subjects of each of the High Contracting Parties shall have liberty to enter, travel and reside in the territories of the other to carry on trade, wholesale and retail, to own or lease and occupy houses, manufactories, warehouses and shops, to employ agents of their choice, to lease land for residential and commercial purposes, and generally to do anything incident to or necessary for trade upon the same terms as native citizens or subjects, submitting themselves to the laws and regulations there established. . . . The citizens or subjects of each . . . shall receive, in the territories of the other, the most constant protection and security for their persons and property,
> . . . .

A treaty made under the authority of the United States "shall be the supreme law of the land; and the judges in every State shall be bound thereby, any thing in the constitution or laws of any State to the contrary notwithstanding." Constitution, Art. VI, § 2.

The treaty-making power of the United States is not limited by any express provision of the Constitution, and, though it does not extend "so far as to authorize what the Constitution forbids," it does extend to all proper subjects of negotiation between our government and other nations. The treaty was made to strengthen friendly relations between the two nations. As to the things covered by it, the provision quoted establishes the rule of equality between Japanese subjects while in this country and native citizens. Treaties for the protection of citizens of one country residing in the territory of another are numerous, and make for good understanding between nations. The treaty is binding within the State of Washington. The rule of equality established by it cannot be rendered nugatory in any part of the United States by municipal ordinances or state laws. It stands on the same footing of supremacy as do the provisions of the Constitution and laws of the United States. It operates of itself without the aid of any legislation, state or national; and it will be applied and given authoritative effect by the courts.

The purpose of the ordinance complained of is to regulate, not to prohibit, the business of pawnbroker. But it makes it impossible for aliens to carry on the business. It need not be considered whether the State, if it sees fit, may forbid and destroy the business generally. Such a law would apply equally to aliens and citizens, and no question of conflict with the treaty would arise. The grievance here alleged is that plaintiff in error, in violation of the treaty, is denied equal opportunity. . . . Decree reversed.

HAITIAN REFUGEE CENTER, INC. v. GRACEY
600 F. Supp. 1396 (D.D.C. 1985)

The complaint in this case raises several challenges to the interdiction by United States officials of visaless aliens on the high seas. This program of interdiction was ordered by the President in 1981. The plaintiffs herein are the Haitian Refugee Center ("HRC"), a nonprofit membership corporation located in Miami, Florida, and two of its members. The defendants are the Commandant of the U.S. Coast Guard, and the Commissioner of the Immigration and Naturalization Service ("INS"). The Court currently has before it a motion to dismiss, and cross-motions for summary judgment. Upon consideration of the motions, the supporting memoranda, oral argument, and the entire record herein, the court has decided to grant the defendants' motion to dismiss for failure to state a claim upon which relief can be granted.

FACTS

On September 29, 1981, President Reagan authorized the interdiction of certain vessels containing undocumented aliens on the high seas. The President had found that the illegal migration of many undocumented aliens into the United States was "a serious national problem detrimental to the interests of the United States", and that international cooperation to intercept vessels trafficking in such migrants was a necessary and proper means of ensuring the effective enforcement of United States immigration laws. By Executive Order No. 12324, also dated September 29, 1981, President Reagan ordered the Secretary of State to enter into cooperative arrangements with appropriate foreign governments for the purpose of preventing illegal migration to the United States by sea. He ordered the Secretary of Transportation to issue instructions to the Coast Guard in order to enforce the suspension of undocumented aliens and the interdiction of any "defined" vessel carrying such aliens. Among the defined vessels were the vessels of foreign nations with which the United States has arrangements authorizing it to stop and board such vessels.

Executive Order 12324 also ordered the Secretary of Transportation to direct the Coast Guard "to return the vessel and its passengers to the country from which it came, when there is reason to believe that an offense is being committed against the United States immigration laws, or appropriate laws of a foreign country with which we have an arrangement to assist." The Order provided, however, "that no person who is a refugee will be returned without his consent." The Coast Guard actions were to be taken only outside United States territorial waters. Indeed, plaintiffs admit that the instant suit challenges only actions taken beyond the territorial boundaries of the United States. The President also ordered the Attorney General, in consultation with the Secretaries of State and Transportation, to take appropriate steps "to ensure the fair enforcement of our laws relating to immigration . . . and the strict observance of our international obligations concerning those who genuinely flee persecution in their homeland."

On September 23, 1981, the United States and Haiti entered into a cooperative arrangement for the purpose of preventing illegal migration of undocumented Haitians to the United States by sea. The arrangement permits United States authorities to board Haitian flag vessels on the high seas, to inquire regarding the condition and destination of the vessels, and the status of those on board. If a violation of United States or appropriate Haitian law is discovered, the vessel and passengers may be returned to Haiti. The arrangement provided that "it is understood that under these arrangements the United States Government does not intend to return to Haiti any Haitian migrants whom the United States authorities determine to qualify for refugee status." The Government of Haiti also agreed that Haitians returned to their country who are not traffickers will not be subject to prosecution for illegal departure. Lastly, the United States agreed to the presence of a representative of the Navy of Haiti as liaison aboard any United States vessel engaged in the implementation of the cooperative arrangement. . . .

UNITED STATES OBLIGATIONS TOWARD REFUGEES ON THE HIGH SEAS

The United States is a party to the 1967 Protocol Relating to the Status of Refugees, which incorporates Articles 2 to 34 of the 1951 Convention Relating to the Status of Refugees. 19 U.S.T. 6223; T.I.A.S. No. 2545. The Protocol defines a "refugee" as any person who, "owing to well-founded fear of being persecuted for reasons of race, religion, nationality, membership of a particular social group or political opinion is outside the country of his nationality and is unable or, owing to such fear, is unwilling to avail himself of the protection of that country."

Article 33 of the Convention, incorporated into the Protocol, provides as follows:

> No Contracting State shall expel or return ("refouler") a refugee in any manner whatsoever to the frontiers of territories where his life or freedom would be threatened on account of his race, religion, nationality, membership in a particular social group or political opinion.

The Protocol does not specify the procedures for determining refugee status. Those procedures are apparently left to each contracting nation. Although Congress has directed the Attorney General to establish procedures for use when an alien arrives in the United States or seeks admission to the United States from a foreign country, neither Congress nor the Attorney General has established any procedures for use on the high seas.

THE COMPLAINT

In the present complaint, the plaintiffs attack the United States program of high seas interdiction of Haitians, which is carried out pursuant to the cooperative arrangement with Haiti. Alleging that "the human rights situation in Haiti [is] . . . very grave," and that "hundreds of thousands of Haitians have fled . . . to escape . . . political persecution," the plaintiffs bring several causes of action against the interdiction program.

In Count I, the plaintiffs contend that the actions of defendants under the interdiction program violate the rights of Haitians under the Refugee Act of 1980 and the Immigration and Nationality Act. In Count II, plaintiffs contend that defendants have deprived Haitian refugees on interdicted vessels of their liberty and rights afforded them by the Refugee Act and the Immigration and Nationality Act, in violation of the Fifth Amendment of the Constitution. In Count III, plaintiffs allege that the interdiction program fails to satisfy the "nonrefoulment obligation" imposed by the United Nations Protocol and Universal Declaration of Human Rights by creating a substantial risk that political refugees will be forcibly returned to face persecution. Plaintiffs also contend that the program violates the provision against racial and other discrimination in Article 3 of the United Nations Convention. Count IV charges a violation of the extradition statute, and the Extradition Treaty between the United States and Haiti.

After addressing the preliminary issue of standing, the Court addresses each of these counts below. None of them states a claim upon which relief can be granted. . . .

Count III — The United Nations Protocol and the Universal Declaration of Human Rights Do Not Provide Rights Upon Which Plaintiffs May Rely.

In Count III, the plaintiffs invoke the 1967 United Nations Protocol Relating to the Status of Refugees and the Universal Declaration of Human Rights. Because neither document affords any rights to the interdicted Haitians, Count III cannot form the basis for any relief.

The plaintiffs claim that the program of interdiction violates the non-refoulement obligations of the United Nations Protocol. However, it has long been established that for a treaty to provide rights enforceable in a United States Court, the treaty must be one which is self-executing. *See Foster v. Neilson,* 27 U.S. (2 Pet.) 253, 314 (1829). "Unless a treaty is self-executing, it must be implemented by legislation before it gives rise to a private cause of action." *Mannington Mills, Inc. v. Congoleum Corp.,* 595 F.2d 1287, 1298 (3d Cir. 1979).

The United Nations Protocol is not self-executing. *Bertrand v. Sava,* 684 F.2d 204, 218–19 (2d Cir. 1982). In *Bertrand,* the Second Circuit held that "the Protocol's provisions were not themselves a source of rights under our law unless and until Congress implemented them by appropriate legislation." This conclusion is compelled by the terms of the treaty itself, which provided that the signatories were to communicate to the United Nations the "laws and regulations which they adopt to ensure the application of the Present Protocol." 19 U.S.T. 6226. Treaties with "such provisions are uniformly declared executory." *United States v. Postal,* 589 F.2d 862, 876–77 (5th Cir.), *cert. denied,* 444 U.S. 832 (1979).

Congress has implemented the Protocol, at least in part, through the Refugee Act of 1980. However, that statute does not provide any rights to aliens outside of the United States. 8 U.S.C. § 1158. Thus, the plaintiffs can find no relief in the United Nations Protocol.

The plaintiffs also assert in Count III that the interdiction program violates Haitians' rights under the Universal Declaration of Human Rights, which was adopted by the General Assembly of the United Nations in 1948. G.A. Res. 217, 3 U.N. GAOR, U.N. Doc. 1/777 (1948). This declaration is merely a nonbinding resolution, not a treaty. "It is not and does not purport to be a statement of law or of legal obligation." *In re Alien Children Education Litigation,* 501 F. Supp. 544, 593 (S.D. Tex. 1980) (quoting 5 Whiteman, Digest of International Law 243 (1965), in turn quoting Mrs. Franklin D. Roosevelt, then-U.S. representative in the General Assembly). It is plain, therefore, that this declaration provides no right of action for the plaintiffs. . . .

CONCLUSION

Although the plaintiffs have standing to bring this suit, none of the four Counts contained in the instant complaint states a cause of action upon which this Court may grant relief. Because the interdiction program herein attacked occurs outside the jurisdiction of the United States, neither the statutes nor the treaty upon which plaintiffs rely can provide any relief. Because the interdicted Haitians never reach the shores of the United States, they are entitled to no protections contained within the Fifth Amendment of the Constitution. The plaintiffs also can find no relief in the United Nations Protocol Relating to the Status of Refugees and the Universal Declaration of Human Rights.

It is clear that the President instituted the interdiction program pursuant to ample constitutional and statutory authority. *See generally Knauff v. Shaughnessy,* 338 U.S. 537, 542–43 (1950). This program is carried out pursuant to an agreement with Haiti, and is therefore intricately interwoven with matters of foreign relations. Because such programs "are so exclusively entrusted to the political branches of government", this Court's review is correspondingly narrow. *Harisiades v. Shaughnessy,* 342 U.S. 580 (1952). Therefore, the result which the Court today reaches should not surprise the plaintiffs. Although the actions of the plaintiffs, and their representatives, are commendable, and stem from the highest form of humanitarian concern, the Court cannot allow its sympathy for the plight of the Haitians to blind it from the law. The Court simply can find no basis for relief. . . .

PEOPLE OF SAIPAN v. UNITED STATES DEPARTMENT OF INTERIOR
502 F.2d 90 (9th Cir. 1974)

Plaintiffs, citizens of the Trust Territory of the Pacific Islands (known also as Micronesia), sued in the district court to challenge the execution by the High Commissioner of the Trust Territory of a lease permitting Continental Airlines to construct and operate a hotel on public land adjacent to Micro Beach, Saipan. Plaintiffs appeal a judgment of dismissal. The district court held that . . . the Trusteeship Agreement does not vest plaintiffs with individual legal rights which they can assert in a federal court. We affirm the judgment, but, for the reasons set out below, we do so without prejudice to the right of the plaintiffs to refile in the district court should the High Court of the Trust Territory deny that it has jurisdiction to review the legality of the actions of the High Commissioner.

. . . In brief, Continental applied in 1970 to the Trust Territory government for permission to build a hotel on public land adjacent to Micro Beach, Saipan, an important historical, cultural, and recreational site for the people of the islands. Pursuant to the requirements of the Trust Territory Code, Continental's application was submitted to the Mariana Islands District Land Advisory

Board for its consideration. In spite of the Board's unanimous recommendation that the area be reserved for public park purposes, the District Administrator of the Marianas District recommended approval of a lease. The High Commissioner himself executed the lease on behalf of the Trust Territory government. An officer appointed by the President of the United States with the advice and consent of the Senate, the High Commissioner is the highest official in the executive branch of the Trust Territory government.

Following its execution in 1972, the lease was opposed by virtually every official body elected by the people of Saipan. Indeed, the record in this case shows that the High Commissioner's decision was officially supported only by the United States Department of the Interior, the Trust Territory Attorney General (a United States citizen), and the District Administrator of the Marianas District (appointed by the High Commissioner, serving directly under him, and subject to removal by him). Later in 1972, an action against some of the parties here was commenced before the High Court of the Trust Territory to enjoin construction of the hotel. The High Court, while denying defendants' motions to dismiss on certain nonfederal causes of action, held that [the National Environmental Policy Act] (NEPA) did not apply to actions of the Trust Territory government, as plaintiffs had contended. Soon afterward, the plaintiffs filed this action in the United States District Court for the District of Hawaii, and the High Court thereupon stayed proceedings before it pending the outcome of this action. . . .

Plaintiffs . . . asserted below and assert here that the action of the governmental defendants in leasing public land to an American corporation against the expressed opposition of the elected representatives of the people of Saipan and without compliance with NEPA is a violation of their duties under the Trusteeship Agreement. The district court rejected this argument, holding that the Trusteeship Agreement[1] did not vest the citizens of the Trust Territory with rights which they can assert in a district court.

We cannot accept the full implications of this holding. We do not dispute the district court's conclusion that compliance with NEPA was not required by the Trusteeship Agreement. We do, however, disagree with the holding insofar as it can be read to say that the Trusteeship Agreement does not create for the islanders substantive rights that are judicially enforceable.

The district court relied for its conclusion on language in *Pauling v. McElroy*, 164 F. Supp. 390, 393 (D.D.C. 1958), *aff'd on other grounds*, 278 F.2d 252 [(D.C. Cir.)], *cert denied*, 364 U.S. 835 (1960). *Pauling* concerned an attempt to enjoin United States officials from proceeding with nuclear tests in the Marshall Islands, an area within the trusteeship. The controversy there, unlike the one here, involved the Trusteeship Agreement's grant of broad discretion to use the area for military purposes. We do not find *Pauling* to

---

[1] [Editor's note: Article 6 of the Trusteeship Agreement, 61 Stat. at 3302–3303, provided in pertinent part that the United States as administering authority shall:

1. foster the development of such political institutions as are suited to the trust territory and shall promote the development of the inhabitants of the trust territory toward self-government or independence . . .; 2. promote the economic advancement and self-sufficiency of the inhabitants . . .; 3. promote the social advancement of the inhabitants . . .; and 4. promote the educational advancement of the inhabitants . . . .]

support the defendants' contention here that the plaintiffs cannot invoke the provisions of the Trusteeship Agreement to challenge the High Commissioner's power to lease local public land for commercial exploitation by private developers.

The right of Rhodesian and American citizens to maintain an action in the courts of the United States seeking enforcement of the United Nations embargo against Rhodesia was recently recognized in *Diggs v. Shultz*, 470 F.2d 461 ([D.C. Cir.] 1972), *cert. denied*, 411 U.S. 931 (1973). On the merits, the court denied specific relief because of Congressional action which was held to have abrogated the United Nations Security Council Resolution, but the right to seek enforcement in federal court was firmly established. That decision, if correct, suggests that the islanders here can enforce their treaty rights, if need be in federal court.

Article 73 of the United Nations Charter (1945), which discusses non-self-governing territories generally, provides:

> Members of the United Nations which have or assume responsibilities for the administration of territories whose peoples have not yet attained a full measure of self-government recognize the principle that the interests of the inhabitants of these territories are paramount, and accept as sacred trust the obligation to promote to the utmost, within the system of international peace and security established by the present Charter, the well-being of the inhabitants of these territories, and, to this end:
>
> > a. To ensure, with due respect for the culture of the peoples concerned, their political, economic, social, and educational advancement, their just treatment, and their protections against abuses
> >
> > . . . .

See also United Nations Charter art. 76, describing the basic objectives of the trusteeship system. Although the plaintiffs have argued that these articles of the United Nations Charter, standing alone, create affirmative and judicially enforceable obligations, we assume without deciding that they do not.

However, pursuant to Article 79 of the Charter,[2] the general principles governing the administration of trust territories were covered in more detail in a specific trusteeship agreement for the Trust Territory of the Pacific Islands. Specifically, Article 6 of the Trusteeship Agreement requires the United States to "promote the economic advancement and self-sufficiency of the inhabitants, and to this end . . . regulate the use of natural resources" and to "protect the inhabitants against the loss of their lands and resources . . . ."

Defendants contend, though, that provisions of the Trusteeship Agreement, including Article 6, can be enforced only before the Security Council of the United Nations.[3] We disagree, concluding that the Trusteeship Agreement

---

[2] "The terms of trusteeship for each territory to be placed under the trusteeship system, including any alteration or amendment, shall be agreed upon by the states directly concerned, including the mandatory power in the case of territories held under mandate by a Member of the United Nations, and shall be approved as provided for in Articles 83 and 85." United Nations Charter art. 79.

[3] Unlike the other ten trusteeships set up after World War II, pursuant to agreements between

can be a source of rights enforceable by an individual litigant in a domestic court of law.

The extent to which an international agreement establishes affirmative and judicially enforceable obligations without implementing legislation must be determined in each case by reference to many contextual factors: the purposes of the treaty and the objectives of its creators, the existence of domestic procedures and institutions appropriate for direct implementation, the availability and feasibility of alternative enforcement methods, and the immediate and long-range social consequences of self-or non-self-execution. . . .

The preponderance of features in this Trusteeship Agreement suggests the intention to establish direct, affirmative, and judicially enforceable rights. The issue involves the local economy and environment, not security; the concern with natural resources and the concern with political development are explicit in the agreement and are general international concerns as well; the enforcement of these rights requires little legal or administrative innovation in the domestic fora; and the alternative forum, the Security Council, would present to the plaintiffs obstacles so great as to make their rights virtually unenforceable.

Moreover, the Trusteeship Agreement constitutes the plaintiffs' basic constitutional document . . . . For all these reasons, we believe that the rights asserted by the plaintiffs are judicially enforceable. However, we see no reason why they could not and should not have been enforced in the High Court of the Trust Territory. The district court found that:

> . . . The lease approval was a "local" decision of the High Commissioner acting within the scope of his duties as chief executive of the Trust Territory Government. The officials of the Interior Department did not negotiate, counsel, advise or participate in the decision. Nor was the lease ever sent to the Department for approval or concurrence in any form. . . .

Surely, the judicial branch of the Trust Territory government has the authority to determine whether or not the action of its chief executive complies with a provision in its own constitutional document. . . .

Admittedly, the substantive rights guaranteed through the Trusteeship Agreement are not precisely defined. However, we do not believe that the agreement is too vague for judicial enforcement. Its language is no more general than such terms as "due process of law," "seaworthiness," "equal protection of the law," "good faith," or "restraint of trade," which courts interpret every day. Moreover, the High Court can look for guidance to its own recently enacted environmental quality and protection act, T.T.Pub.L. No. 4C-78 of Apr. 14, 1972, codified at 63 T.T.C. §§ 501–509, to the relevant principles of international law and resource use which have achieved a substantial degree of codification and consensus . . . and to the general direction, although not

---

the United Nations and various nations, the Trust Territory was designated as a 'strategic' trust. Trusteeship Agreement art. 1, 61 Stat. 3301. This designation results in the United States being responsible to the Security Council for the administration of the Trust Territory — where the United States possesses veto power (United Nations Charter art. 27, 59 Stat. 1041) — rather than to the General Assembly. United Nations Charter art. 83(1).

necessarily the specific provisions, of NEPA. These sources should provide a sufficiently definite standard against which to test the High Commissioner's approval of a 50-year lease of unique public lands to an American corporation, allegedly in disregard of the protests of the islands' elected officials and without a showing of consideration of cultural and environmental factors. . . .

We hold, then, that the plaintiffs must initially pursue their remedies in the local court. If our assumption that the High Court has the power to review the decision of the High Commissioner proves to be invalid, then the federal district court must assume jurisdiction of this case. We refuse to leave the plaintiffs without a forum which can hear their claim that the High Commissioner has violated the duties assumed by the United States in the Trusteeship Agreement. . . .

TRASK, Circuit Judge (concurring). I join in the decision of the majority but follow a different course to the common conclusion. First of all, it appears clear to me that the Charter of the United Nations is not self-executing and does not in and of itself create rights which are justiciable between individual litigants. . . . I agree with the federal appellees and with the court in *Pauling v. McElroy*, *supra*, that the Trusteeship Agreement is not self-executing.[1]

Notes and Questions on the Self-Executing Treaty Doctrine

1. The cases addressing the self-executing treaty doctrine often arise in a criminal setting, with defendants invoking treaties as an objection to the criminal jurisdiction of the United States. *See, e.g., United States v. Postal*, 589 F.2d 862 (5th Cir. 1979). But the relevance of the doctrine in international civil litigation is no less clear. The non-discrimination provisions in Friendship, Commerce, and Navigation treaties like the one at issue in *Asakura* are routinely held to be self-executing. On the other hand, the phrase "self-executing treaty doctrine" appears nowhere in the *Asakura* opinion. How can you tell that the case says anything relevant about the doctrine?

2. *Applying the self-executing treaty doctrine*. What arguments would you make to the effect that the *Gracey* court erred in holding that the Refugee Convention is not self-executing?

---

[1] The language of the Agreement, and in particular that of Article 6, the specific provision at issue in this suit, evinces a series of general commitments undertaken by the United States in furtherance of particular social objectives. That these phrases may become workable through judicial construction, as the majority opines, does not detract from the probability that, had the drafters of the instrument intended the document to have the effect of a statute, more precise language delimiting the rights of Micronesians would have been employed.

Yet, a series of actions all ultimately founded upon congressional authority have so executed the Agreement that its provisions may now properly be regarded as judicially enforceable. Thus, the Agreement was approved by the President pursuant to a joint resolution of Congress, and implemented by Executive orders promulgated pursuant to congressional authority, 48 U.S.C. § 1681. Finally, the Trust Territory Government, created by the Department of the Interior, has declared the Agreement "to be in full force and to have the effect of law in the Trust Territory." 1 T.T.C. § 101(1). . . .

A. In this connection, compare Article 33, quoted in the opinion, with the following provision of the treaty:

Art. 34. The Contracting States shall as far as possible facilitate the assimilation and naturalization of refugees. They shall in particular make every effort to expedite naturalization proceedings and to reduce as far as possible the charges and costs of such proceedings.

Notice that it is possible in principle for some provisions of a treaty to be self-executing even if other provisions of the same treaty are not.

B. Compare also Article X(1) of the Interim Convention on Conservation of North Pacific Fur Seals (1957):

Each party agrees to enact and enforce such legislation as may be necessary to guarantee the observance of this convention and to make effective its provisions with appropriate penalties for violation thereof.

3. *Misquotation of the treaty.* In *Gracey*, Judge Richey misquoted the Refugee Protocol, stating that the Court's "conclusion is compelled by the terms of the treaty itself, which provided that the signatories were to communicate to the United Nations the 'laws and regulations which they adopt [sic] to ensure the application of the present Protocol.'" In fact, the article cited refers to the "laws and regulations which they *may* adopt. . . ." Is the omission reversible error?

4. *Executive agreements and the self-executing treaty doctrine.* Executive agreements, though they do not become treaties through the operation of the Treaty Power of the Constitution, are nonetheless considered "treaties" for purposes of the Supremacy Clause, meaning that executive agreements — when they become relevant in domestic proceedings — will be subject to the self-executing treaty doctrine. In *Islamic Republic of Iran v. Boeing*, 771 F.2d 1279 (9th Cir. 1985), Iran initiated an action against Boeing for damages resulting from an airplane crash. Boeing, having provided operations support for aircraft in Iran, counterclaimed for damages arising out of the Iranian revolution in 1979. The court's jurisdiction depended on whether certain executive agreements entered into by the president diverted the counterclaims to the Iran-U.S. Claims Tribunal and out of the federal district courts. Applying the four-part test described in the introductory note, the court ruled that the executive agreements were not self-executing and therefore did not divest it of jurisdiction.

5. *The effect of Executive submissions and Senate declarations.* Article 3 of the Torture Convention provides in part that:

No State Party shall expel, return ('refouler') or extradite a person to another State where there are substantial grounds for believing that he would be in danger of being subjected to torture.

In his Letter of Submittal to the President, the Secretary of State included a "Declaration Regarding the Non-Self-Executing Nature of the Convention," which reads in part: "The United States declares that the provisions of Articles 1 through 16 of the Convention are not self-executing." The Senate adopted and incorporated this statement in its Resolution of Advice and Consent to the Ratification of the Convention, 136 Cong. Rec. S17486 (Oct. 27, 1990).

Thus, despite the language of present action in Article 3, and despite the fact that the determination of whether a treaty is self-executing or not is a judicial function, the understanding of the political branches can readily prevent a treaty from becoming self-executing. *See Extradition of Cheung*, 968 F. Supp. 791, 803 n. 17 (D. Conn. 1997).

6. *Self-executing treaties and the latter-in-time rule*. A self-executing treaty is juridically equal to a statute, meaning, in case of a conflict between them, that the latter-in-time prevails to the extent of the conflict. Congress may also legislate in violation of treaty obligations, and it well-established in those circumstances that the latter-in-time prevails. *See, e.g., The Chinese Exclusion Cases*, 130 U.S. 581, 599–602 (1889); *South African Airways v. Dole*, 817 F.2d 119, 125–26 (D.C. Cir.), *cert denied*, 484 U.S. 896 (1987). But these admitted powers are exercised rarely: outright repudiation of treaties by legislation is extraordinary, both because Congress is unwilling to be perceived as violating international standards and because the courts are reluctant to find a conflict that triggers these supremacy doctrines in the first place. From this perspective, the more characteristic judicial concern is the interpretive guideline captured in Justice Marshall's classic statement in *The Charming Betsy, supra*: statutes enacted by Congress "ought never to be construed to violate the law of nations if any other possible construction remains." 6 U.S. (2 Cranch) 64, 118 (1804). That means that the latter-in-time rule is respectable black-letter doctrine but also that implicit overrides are disfavored: Congress must explicitly override the pre-existing international standard. *See, e.g., United States v. Palestine Liberation Org.*, 695 F. Supp. 1456 (S.D.N.Y. 1988).

7. *Constitutional prerogatives and the self-executing treaty doctrine*. As noted above, Section 111(4)(c) of the Restatement (Third) suggests that there is a constitutional dimension to self-execution, the clear implication being that there are some treaties which, as a matter of U.S. constitutional law, require implementation through Congressional action, or which, if enforced by individuals in domestic courts, might invade the constitutional prerogatives of the executive branch. Aside from the examples suggested in the introductory note, what constitutional provisions would you consider particularly relevant in this regard?

8. *Subsequent disposition of the issue in Gracey*. The specific issue before the district court in *Gracey* — whether Article 33 of the Refugee Convention is self-executing or not — arose again in 1992, when Haitian refugees challenged an Executive Order by President Bush requiring all Haitian "boat people" to be forcibly returned to Haiti. Two circuit courts of appeals reached inconsistent conclusions on the self-execution issue. *Compare Haitian Refugee Center, Inc. v. Baker*, 953 F.2d 1498 (11th Cir.) (per curiam), *cert. denied*, 112 S.Ct. 1245 (1992), *with Haitian Centers Council, Inc. v. McNary*, 969 F.2d 1326, 1350 (2d Cir. 1992), *cert. granted*, 113 S.Ct. 1326 (1992). In 1993, the U.S. Supreme Court decided that nothing in Article 33 of the Refugee Convention limited the discretion of the President to interdict Haitians on the high seas and return them to Haiti. The analysis turned on a textual interpretation of Article 33 only, and the self-execution issue was not addressed.

9. *Non-self-executing treaties as guides to interpretation of statutes*. The courts have uniformly held that there is no private cause of action under the

International Covenant on Civil and Political Rights, in part because the Senate declared key provisions of the Covenant non-self-executing. 138 Cong. Rec. S4783, at S4784 (Daily ed. Apr. 2, 1992). *Jama v. Immigration and Naturalization Service*, 22 F. Supp. 2d 353 (D.N.J. 1998); *Hawkins v. Comparet-Cassani*, 33 F. Supp.2d 1244, 1257 (C.D. Cal. 1999); *Ralk v. Lincoln County*, 81 F. Supp. 2d 1372, 1380 (S.D. Ga. 2000). Suppose a party invoked the covenant not as a rule of decision, but as a guide in the interpretation of the statute governing habeas corpus or the Eighth Amendment prohibition on cruel and unusual punishments. Same result?

[2] The *Charming Betsy* Principle: Interpreting Domestic Statutes in Light of International Law

In *Murray v. The Schooner Charming Betsy*, 6 U.S. (2 Cranch) 64, 118 (1804), Justice John Marshall offered an interpretive guideline for accommodating international law and domestic legislation: the statutes enacted by Congress, he said, "ought never to be construed to violate the law of nations if any other possible construction remains." *See also* RESTATEMENT (THIRD) OF THE FOREIGN RELATIONS LAW OF THE UNITED STATES, § 114 ("Where fairly possible, a United States statute is to be construed so as not to conflict with international law or with an international agreement of the United States.") The *Charming Betsy* principle has been reaffirmed without much reflection or analysis by the federal courts since it was announced, and, like other canons of construction, is sometimes dismissed as innocuous or meaningless. But domestic courts continue to invoke the principle as a kind of default drive: if Congress means to legislate in violation of international law, and says so explicitly, the violation may persist at the international plane, but the statute will prevail in U.S. courts. The logic of *Charming Betsy* requires the courts to attempt reasonable saving constructions of a statute before assuming that Congress has actually exercised its authority to legislate in derogation of international standards.

As noted in Chapter 1, the *Charming Betsy* principle stands at the intersection of two unrelated but significant developments in contemporary law. The first is the truism that the international community now routinely attempts to regulate matters that have historically been the subject of exclusively domestic legislation, including restrictive business practices, gender and race discrimination, family law, labor rights, and environmental protection. In this process, the potential overlap between international legal principles and domestic statutory regimes has become pronounced. The second is the historic shift by which legislation, rather than the common law, has become the dominant modality or expression of legal norms in the United States. As a consequence of this progressively statutory aspect of U.S. law, lawyers have developed a continuing concern with the messy discipline of statutory construction.

The Charming Betsy and its progeny offer a potentially potent though admittedly nondeterminative principle, under which advocates and courts faced with issues of statutory construction should do three things. *First*, they must assess the meaning and the status of any pertinent international norms, using the traditional evidentiary standards laid out by the Supreme Court for determining custom or the meaning of a treaty, *see The Paquete Habana*, 175 U.S. 677, 708 (1900). In the era when the law of nations was primarily concerned with jurisdiction and state responsibility, the *Charming Betsy* had a corresponding jurisdictional cast. *See, e.g., Lauritzen v. Larsen*, 345 U.S. 571 (1953). As the international legal system comes to address more substantive matters of political and economic life, the *Charming Betsy* principle takes on a potentially more substantive cast as well. *Second*, if the international norm is relevant and nothing in the statute repudiates it, or if an inconsistency between the norm and the statute can be resolved fairly through reasoned interpretation, the court should adopt the interpretation that preserves maximum scope for both. *Third*, if the conflict between the international norm and the statute is unavoidable and irreducible, then the court must resort to the supremacy axioms — like the power of Congress to legislate in violation of international law, or the latter-in-time rule, or justiciability doctrines — to resolve the conflict.

In *Maria v. McElroy*, 68 F. Supp. 2d 206 (E.D.N.Y. 1999), for example, the court ruled that the Antiterrorism and Effective Death Penalty Act of 1996 and the Illegal Immigration Reform and Immigrant Responsibility Act of 1996 could apply retroactively to find that an alien with strong family connections in the United States is nonetheless deportable, but the court also found that the alien would be entitled to a hearing on whether deportation should be stayed for humanitarian reasons:

> The retroactive deprivation of [the alien's] statutory right to humanitarian relief from deportation would arguably be contrary to both the International Covenant on Civil and Political Rights and customary international human rights law." Specifically, "retroactive application of the [statute] threatens precisely the type of arbitrary family break-up that the ICCPR guards against. . . . [It would also] be a violation of customary international human rights law, to which the United States is bound as a member of the community of nations — violations that Congress, it can be assumed, would want to avoid; this is a factor that must be given weight in statutory construction. . . . The congressional scheme [of the statute] can be fully vindicated without retroactively eliminating the right to a humanitarian hearing.

In other words, Congress had not explicitly overruled international standards, nor had it legislated in a way that necessarily pre-empted international argumentation, and as a result the international standards in the ICCPR shed light on the proper interpretation of the statute. That the ICCPR has generally been deemed non-self-executing in U.S. courts suggests that treaties as expression of customary law can play an interpretive role even when they do not provide a rule of decision.

Chapter 5

INTERNATIONAL JUDICIAL ASSISTANCE: SERVICE OF PROCESS AND THE PRODUCTION OF EVIDENCE

A. SERVICE OF PROCESS

Under international law, no state may exercise its sovereignty in the territory of another without consent. Extraterritorial arrests and extraterritorial seizures of evidence by government officials are plainly illegal in the absence of the territorial state's consent, but considerably less dramatic exercises of power may also violate this basic standard. Consider for example the service of judicial documents like subpoenas and complaints. Litigation in the United States routinely begins when one party serves documents directly on the other, but in many nations, service is a public function which, if undertaken by private parties, can violate local law. Serving the defendant in person or by mail can be equally unlawful.

In order to avoid conflict, states have adopted various means of cooperation or *international judicial assistance* in the serving of documents. Notable among these are the Hague Convention on the Service Abroad of Judicial and Extrajudicial Documents in Civil or Commercial Matters ("Hague Convention") and the Inter-American Convention on Letters Rogatory, both of which are in the Document Supplement. In the absence of a treaty framework for service, counsel may revert to the mechanism of the letter rogatory, in which counsel asks the forum court to seek assistance from the foreign court, a request that is transmitted through diplomatic channels, honored (or not) through the foreign judiciary, and returned through diplomatic channels. Neither the treaty regimes nor the letters rogatory are entirely seamless, as shown below.

Quite apart from international standards and procedures, the U.S. Constitution defines the minimal requirements of service, especially of the complaint in a case brought in the United States against a foreign national. Under the Due Process Clause, "foreign nationals are assured of either personal service, which typically will require service abroad and trigger the Convention, or substituted service that provides 'notice reasonably calculated, under all the circumstances, to apprise interested parties of the pendency of the action and afford them an opportunity to present their objections.'" *Volkswagernwerk AG v. Schlunk, infra, quoting Mullane v. Central Hanover Bank & Trust Co.,* 339 U.S. 306, 314 (1950). As shown below, federal and state laws may also constrain the lawful means of service.

The service of documents may seem an especially dull, "merely" logistical exercise. But the law of service offers a virtual clinic in the relationship among various sources of law in transnational cases. At some point, the service issue is likely to turn on the interpretation of treaties, customary international law, and federal statutes and rules. Developing the ability to work with each type of law — and reconcile them when necessary — is an essential skill for the transnational advocate. And from a purely practical perspective, illegal or ineffective service is a standard and powerful defense to the enforcement or recognition of a judgment, and counsel, eager to enforce a judgment at the end of a proceeding, should be careful at the beginning to lay the right groundwork.

FEDERAL STATUTORY PROVISIONS

28 U.S.C. § 1696. Service in foreign and international litigation

(a) The district court of the district in which a person resides or is found may order service upon him of any documents issued in connection with a proceeding in a foreign or international tribunal. The order may be made pursuant to a letter rogatory issued, or request made, by a foreign or international tribunal upon application of any interested person and shall direct the manner of service. Service pursuant to this subsection does not, of itself, require the recognition or enforcement in the United States of a judgment, decree, or order rendered by a foreign or international tribunal.

(b) This section does not preclude service of such document without an order of court.

28 U.S.C. § 1781. Transmittal of letter rogatory or request

(a) The Department of State has power, directly, or through suitable channels —

(1) to receive a letter rogatory issued, or request made, by a foreign or international tribunal, to transmit it to the tribunal, officer, or agency in the United States to whom it is addressed, and to receive and return it after execution; and

(2) to receive a letter rogatory issued, or request made, by a tribunal in the United States, to transmit it to the foreign or international tribunal, officer, or agency to whom it is addressed, and to receive and return it after execution.

(b) This section does not preclude —

(1) the transmittal of a letter rogatory or request directly from a foreign or international tribunal to the tribunal, officer, or agency in the United States to whom it is addressed and its return in the same manner; or

(2) the transmittal of a letter rogatory or request directly from a tribunal in the United States to the foreign or international tribunal,

officer, or agency to whom it is addressed and its return in the same manner.

FEDERAL RULES OF CIVIL PROCEDURE
RULE 4(f)

Rule 4. Summons

* * *

(f) Service Upon Individuals in a Foreign Country. Unless otherwise provided by federal law, service upon an individual from whom a waiver has not been obtained and filed, other than an infant or an incompetent person, may be effected in a place not within any judicial district of the United States:

(1) by any internationally agreed means reasonably calculated to give notice, such as those means authorized by the Hague Convention on the Service Abroad of Judicial and Extrajudicial Documents; or

(2) if there is no internationally agreed means of service or the applicable international agreement allows other means of service, provided that service is reasonably calculated to give notice:

(A) in the manner prescribed by the law of the foreign country for service in that country in an action in any of its courts of general jurisdiction; or

(B) as directed by the foreign authority in response to a letter rogatory or letter of request; or

(C) unless prohibited by the law of the foreign country, by

(i) delivery to the individual personally of a copy of the summons and the complaint; or

(ii) any form of mail requiring a signed receipt, to be addressed and dispatched by the clerk of the court to the party to be served; or

(3) by other means not prohibited by international agreement as may be directed by the court.

CONVENTION ON THE SERVICE ABROAD OF JUDICIAL AND EXTRAJUDICIAL DOCUMENTS IN CIVIL OR COMMERCIAL MATTERS (1964) (selected provisions)
Done At The Hague March 18, 1970 and entered into force for the United States October 7, 1972[1]

The States signatory to the present Convention,

Desiring to create appropriate means to ensure that judicial and extrajudicial documents to be served abroad shall be brought to the notice of the addressee in sufficient time,

Desiring to improve the organization of mutual judicial assistance for that purpose by simplifying and expediting the procedure,

Have resolved to conclude a Convention to this effect and have agreed upon the following provisions:

ARTICLE 1

The present Convention shall apply in all cases, in civil or commercial matters, where there is occasion to transmit a judicial or extrajudicial document for service abroad. This Convention shall not apply where the address of the person to be served with the document is not known.

ARTICLE 2

Each contracting State shall designate a Central Authority which will undertake to receive requests for service coming from other contracting States and to proceed in conformity with the provisions of articles 3 to 6. Each State shall organise the Central Authority in conformity with its own law.

ARTICLE 3

The authority or judicial officer competent under the law of the State in which the documents originate shall forward to the Central Authority of the State addressed a request conforming to the model annexed to the present Convention, without any requirement of legalisation or other equivalent formality. The document to be served or a copy thereof shall be annexed to the request. The request and the document shall both be furnished in duplicate.

---

[1] As of this writing, the following states are parties to the Hague Service Convention: Antigua and Barbuda, Barbados, Belgium, Belize, Botswana, Canada, China, Cyprus, Czech Republic, Denmark, Djibuti, Egypt, Fiji, Finland, France, Germany, Greece, Ireland, Israel, Italy, Japan, Kiribati, Latvia, Luxembourg, Malawi, Netherlands, Nevis, Norway, Pakistan, Poland, Portugal, St. Christopher, St. Lucia, St. Vincent & the Grenadines, Seychelles, Slovak Republic, Solomon Islands, Spain, Sweden, Switzerland, Turkey, Tuvalu, the United Kingdom, the United Sates, and Venezuela. Many of these states have adopted reservations, understandings, and declarations that limit the types of service considered lawful. A representative sample of these reservations appears in the Document Supplement.

ARTICLE 4

If the Central Authority considers that the request does not comply with the provisions of the present Convention, it shall promptly inform the applicant and specify its objections to the request.

ARTICLE 5

The Central Authority of the State addressed shall itself serve the document or shall arrange to have it served by an appropriate agency, either—

(a) by a method prescribed by its internal law for the service of documents in domestic actions upon persons who are within its territory, or

(b) by a particular method requested by the applicant, unless such a method is incompatible with the law of the State addressed.

Subject to sub-paragraph (b) of the first paragraph of this article, the document may always be served by delivery to an addressee who accepts it voluntarily. If the document is to be served under the first paragraph above, the Central Authority may require the document to be written in, or translated into, the official language or one of the official languages of the State addressed.

That part of the request, in the form attached to the present Convention, which contains a summary of the document to be served, shall be served with the document.

ARTICLE 8

Each contracting State shall be free to effect service of judicial documents upon persons abroad, without application of any compulsion, directly through its diplomatic or consular agents. Any State may declare that it is opposed to such service within its territory, unless the document is to be served upon a national of the State in which the documents originate.

ARTICLE 9

Each contracting State shall be free, in addition, to use consular channels to forward documents, for the purpose of service, to those authorities of another contracting State which are designated by the latter for this purpose. Each contracting State may, if exceptional circumstances so require, use diplomatic channels for the same purpose.

ARTICLE 10

Provided the State of destination does not object, the present Convention shall not interfere with—

(a) the freedom to send judicial documents, by postal channels, directly to persons abroad,

(b) the freedom of judicial officers, officials or other competent persons of the State of origin to effect service of judicial documents directly through the judicial officers, officials or other competent persons of the State of destination,

(c) the freedom of any person interested in a judicial proceeding to effect service of judicial documents directly through the judicial officers, officials or other competent persons of the State of destination.

ARTICLE 11

The present Convention shall not prevent two or more contracting States from agreeing to permit, for the purpose of service of judicial documents, channels of transmission other than those provided for in the preceding articles and, in particular, direct communication between their respective authorities.

. . .

ARTICLE 13

Where a request for service complies with the terms of the present Convention, the State addressed may refuse to comply therewith only if it deems that compliance would infringe its sovereignty or security. It may not refuse to comply solely on the ground that, under its internal law, it claims exclusive jurisdiction over the subject-matter of the action or that its internal law would not permit the action upon which the application is based. The Central Authority shall, in case of refusal, promptly inform the applicant and state the reasons for the refusal.

ARTICLE 14

Difficulties which may arise in connection with the transmission of judicial documents for service shall be settled through diplomatic channels.

ARTICLE 15

Where a writ of summons or an equivalent document had to be transmitted abroad for the purpose of service, under the provisions of the present Convention, and the defendant has not appeared, judgment shall not be given until it is established that—

(a) the document was served by a method prescribed by the internal law of the State addressed for the service of documents in domestic actions upon persons who are within its territory, or

(b) the document was actually delivered to the defendant or to his residence by another method provided for by this Convention,

and that in either of these cases the service or the delivery was effected in sufficient time to enable the defendant to defend.

Each contracting State shall be free to declare that the judge, notwithstanding the provisions of the first paragraph of this article, may give judgment even if no certificate of service or delivery has been received, if all the following conditions are fulfilled—

(a) the document was transmitted by one of the methods provided for in this Convention,

(b) a period of time of not less than six months, considered adequate by the judge in the particular case, has elapsed since the date of the transmission of the document,

(c) no certificate of any kind has been received, even though every reasonable effort has been made to obtain it through the competent authorities of the State addressed.

Notwithstanding the provisions of the preceding paragraphs the judge may order, in case of urgency, any provisional or protective measures.

ARTICLE 16

When a writ of summons or an equivalent document had to be transmitted abroad for the purpose of service, under the provisions of the present Convention, and a judgment has been entered against a defendant who has not appeared, the judge shall have the power to relieve the defendant from the effects of the expiration of the time for appeal from the judgment if the following conditions are fulfilled—

(a) the defendant, without any fault on his part, did not have knowledge of the document in sufficient time to defend, or knowledge of the judgment in sufficient time to appeal, and

(b) the defendant has disclosed a prima facie defence to the action on the merits.

An application for relief may be filed only within a reasonable time after the defendant has knowledge of the judgment.

. . .

ARTICLE 19

To the extent that the internal law of a contracting State permits methods of transmission, other than those provided for in the preceding articles, of documents coming from abroad, for service within its territory, the present Convention shall not affect such provisions.

ARTICLE 21

Each contracting State shall, at the time of the deposit of its instrument of ratification or accession, or at a later date, inform the Ministry of Foreign Affairs of the Netherlands of the following—

(a) the designation of authorities, pursuant to articles 2 and 18,

(b) the designation of the authority competent to complete the certificate pursuant to article 6,

(c) the designation of the authority competent to receive documents transmitted by consular channels, pursuant to article 9.

Each contracting State shall similarly inform the Ministry, where appropriate, of—

(a) opposition to the use of methods of transmission pursuant to articles 8 and 10,

(b) declarations pursuant to the second paragraph of article 15 and the third paragraph of article 16,

(c) all modifications of the above designations, oppositions and declarations.

---

[1]   To What Problem is the Hague Convention a Solution?

VOLKSWAGENWERK AG v. SCHLUNK
486 U.S. 694 (1988)

JUSTICE O'CONNOR delivered the opinion of the Court.

This case involves an attempt to serve process on a foreign corporation by serving its domestic subsidiary which, under state law, is the foreign corporation's involuntary agent for service of process. We must decide whether such service is compatible with the Convention on Service Abroad of Judicial and Extrajudicial Documents in Civil and Commercial Matters, Nov. 15, 1965 (Hague Service Convention), [1969] 20 U.S.T. 361, T. I. A. S. No. 6638.

I

The parents of respondent Herwig Schlunk were killed in an automobile accident in 1983. Schlunk filed a wrongful death action on their behalf in the Circuit Court of Cook County, Illinois. Schlunk alleged that Volkswagen of America, Inc. (VWoA), had designed and sold the automobile that his parents were driving, and that defects in the automobile caused or contributed to their deaths. Schlunk also alleged that the driver of the other automobile involved in the collision was negligent; Schlunk has since obtained a default judgment against that person, who is no longer a party to this lawsuit. Schlunk successfully served his complaint on VWoA, and VWoA filed an answer denying that it had designed or assembled the automobile in question. Schlunk then amended the complaint to add as a defendant Volkswagen Aktiengesellschaft (VWAG), which is the petitioner here. VWAG, a corporation established under the laws of the Federal Republic of Germany, has its place of business in that country. VWoA is a wholly owned subsidiary of VWAG. Schlunk attempted to serve his amended complaint on VWAG by serving VWoA as VWAG's agent.

VWAG filed a special and limited appearance for the purpose of quashing service. VWAG asserted that it could be served only in accordance with the Hague Service Convention, and that Schlunk had not complied with the Convention's requirements. The Circuit Court denied VWAG's motion. It first observed that VWoA is registered to do business in Illinois and has a registered agent for receipt of process in Illinois. The court then reasoned that VWoA and VWAG are so closely related that VWoA is VWAG's agent for service of process as a matter of law, notwithstanding VWAG's failure or refusal to appoint VWoA formally as an agent. The court relied on the facts that VWoA is a wholly owned subsidiary of VWAG, that a majority of the members of the board of directors of VWoA are members of the board of VWAG, and that VWoA is by contract the exclusive importer and distributor of VWAG products sold in the United States. The court concluded that, because service was accomplished within the United States, the Hague Service Convention did not apply.

The Circuit Court certified two questions to the Appellate Court of Illinois. For reasons similar to those given by the Circuit Court, the Appellate Court determined that VWoA is VWAG's agent for service of process under Illinois law, and that the service of process in this case did not violate the Hague Service Convention. After the Supreme Court of Illinois denied VWAG leave to appeal, VWAG petitioned this Court for a writ of certiorari to review the Appellate Court's interpretation of the Hague Service Convention. We granted certiorari to address this issue, which has given rise to disagreement among the lower courts.

II

The Hague Service Convention is a multilateral treaty that was formulated in 1964 by the Tenth Session of the Hague Conference of Private International Law. The Convention revised parts of the Hague Conventions on Civil Procedure of 1905 and 1954. The revision was intended to provide a simpler way to serve process abroad, to assure that defendants sued in foreign jurisdictions would receive actual and timely notice of suit, and to facilitate proof of service abroad. Representatives of all 23 countries that were members of the Conference approved the Convention without reservation. Thirty-two countries, including the United States and the Federal Republic of Germany, have ratified or acceded to the Convention.

The primary innovation of the Convention is that it requires each state to establish a central authority to receive requests for service of documents from other countries. Once a central authority receives a request in the proper form, it must serve the documents by a method prescribed by the internal law of the receiving state or by a method designated by the requester and compatible with that law. Art. 5. The central authority must then provide a certificate of service that conforms to a specified model. Art. 6. A state also may consent to methods of service within its boundaries other than a request to its central authority. Arts. 8–11, 19. The remaining provisions of the Convention that are relevant here limit the circumstances in which a default judgment may be entered against a defendant who had to be served abroad and did not appear, and provide some means for relief from such a judgment. Arts. 15, 16.

Article 1 defines the scope of the Convention, which is the subject of controversy in this case. It says: "The present Convention shall apply in all cases, in civil or commercial matters, where there is occasion to transmit a judicial or extrajudicial document for service abroad." . . . This language is mandatory, as we acknowledged last term in *Societe Nationale Industrielle Aerospatiale v. United States District Court*, 482 U.S. 522, 534, n. 15 (1987). By virtue of the Supremacy Clause, U.S. Const., Art. VI, the Convention pre-empts inconsistent methods of service prescribed by state law in all cases to which it applies. Schlunk does not purport to have served his complaint on VWAG in accordance with the Convention. Therefore, if service of process in this case falls within Article 1 of the Convention, the trial court should have granted VWAG's motion to quash. When interpreting a treaty, we "begin 'with the text of the treaty and the context in which the written words are used.'" *Societe Nationale, supra,* at 534 (quoting *Air France v. Saks,* 470 U.S. 392, 397 (1985)). Other general rules of construction may be brought to bear on difficult or ambiguous passages. "Treaties are construed more liberally than private agreements, and to ascertain their meaning we may look beyond the written words to the history of the treaty, the negotiations, and the practical construction adopted by the parties." *Air France v. Saks, supra,* at 396. The Convention does not specify the circumstances in which there is "occasion to transmit" a complaint "for service abroad." But at least the term "service of process" has a well-established technical meaning. Service of process refers to a formal delivery of documents that is legally sufficient to charge the defendant with notice of a pending action. The legal sufficiency of a formal delivery of documents must be measured against some standard. The Convention does not prescribe a standard, so we almost necessarily must refer to the internal law of the forum state.

If the internal law of the forum state defines the applicable method of serving process as requiring the transmittal of documents abroad, then the Hague Service Convention applies. The negotiating history supports our view that Article 1 refers to service of process in the technical sense. The committee that prepared the preliminary draft deliberately used a form of the term "notification" (formal notice), instead of the more neutral term "remise" (delivery), when it drafted Article 1. Then, in the course of the debates, the negotiators made the language even more exact. The preliminary draft of Article 1 said that the present Convention shall apply in all cases in which there are grounds to transmit or to give formal notice of a judicial or extrajudicial document in a civil or commercial matter to a person staying abroad. . . .

To be more precise, the delegates decided to add a form of the juridical term "signification" (service), which has a narrower meaning than "notification" in some countries, such as France, and the identical meaning in others, such as the United States. The delegates also criticized the language of the preliminary draft because it suggested that the Convention could apply to transmissions abroad that do not culminate in service. The final text of Article 1 eliminates this possibility and applies only to documents transmitted for service abroad. The final report (Rapport Explicatif) confirms that the Convention does not use more general terms, such as delivery or transmission, to define its scope because it applies only when there is both transmission of a document from the requesting state to the receiving state, and service upon the person for whom it is intended.

The negotiating history of the Convention also indicates that whether there is service abroad must be determined by reference to the law of the forum state. The preliminary draft said that the Convention would apply "where there are grounds" to transmit a judicial document to a person staying abroad. The committee that prepared the preliminary draft realized that this implied that the forum's internal law would govern whether service implicated the Convention. The reporter expressed regret about this solution because it would decrease the obligatory force of the Convention. Nevertheless, the delegates did not change the meaning of Article 1 in this respect. . . .

VWAG protests that it is inconsistent with the purpose of the Convention to interpret it as applying only when the internal law of the forum requires service abroad. One of the two stated objectives of the Convention is "to create appropriate means to ensure that judicial and extrajudicial documents to be served abroad shall be brought to the notice of the addressee in sufficient time." The Convention cannot assure adequate notice, VWAG argues, if the forum's internal law determines whether it applies. VWAG warns that countries could circumvent the Convention by defining methods of service of process that do not require transmission of documents abroad. Indeed, VWAG contends that one such method of service already exists and that it troubled the Conference: *notification au parquet.*

Notification au parquet permits service of process on a foreign defendant by the deposit of documents with a designated local official. Although the official generally is supposed to transmit the documents abroad to the defendant, the statute of limitations begins to run from the time that the official receives the documents, and there allegedly is no sanction for failure to transmit them. At the time of the 10th Conference, France, the Netherlands, Greece, Belgium, and Italy utilized some type of *notification au parquet.*

There is no question but that the Conference wanted to eliminate *notification au parquet.* It included in the Convention two provisions that address the problem. Article 15 says that a judgment may not be entered unless a foreign defendant received adequate and timely notice of the lawsuit. Article 16 provides means whereby a defendant who did not receive such notice may seek relief from a judgment that has become final. Like Article 1, however, Articles 15 and 16 apply only when documents must be transmitted abroad for the purpose of service. VWAG argues that, if this determination is made according to the internal law of the forum state, the Convention will fail to eliminate variants of *notification au parquet* that do not expressly require transmittal of documents to foreign defendants. Yet such methods of service of process are the least likely to provide a defendant with actual notice.

The parties make conflicting representations about whether foreign laws authorizing *notification au parquet* command the transmittal of documents for service abroad within the meaning of the Convention. The final report is itself somewhat equivocal. It says that, although the strict language of Article

1 might raise a question as to whether the Convention regulates *notification au parquet*, the understanding of the drafting Commission, based on the debates, is that the Convention would apply. Although this statement might affect our decision as to whether the Convention applies to *notification au parquet*, an issue we do not resolve today, there is no comparable evidence in the negotiating history that the Convention was meant to apply to substituted service on a subsidiary like VWoA, which clearly does not require service abroad under the forum's internal law. Hence, neither the language of the Convention nor the negotiating history contradicts our interpretation of the Convention, according to which the internal law of the forum is presumed to determine whether there is occasion for service abroad. Nor are we persuaded that the general purposes of the Convention require a different conclusion. One important objective of the Convention is to provide means to facilitate service of process abroad. Thus, the first stated purpose of the Convention is "to create" appropriate means for service abroad, and the second stated purpose is "to improve the organization of mutual judicial assistance for that purpose by simplifying and expediting the procedure." By requiring each state to establish a central authority to assist in the service of process, the Convention implements this enabling function. Nothing in our decision today interferes with this requirement.

VWAG correctly maintains that the Convention also aims to ensure that there will be adequate notice in cases in which there is occasion to serve process abroad. Thus, compliance with the Convention is mandatory in all cases to which it applies, and Articles 15 and 16 provide an indirect sanction against those who ignore it. Our interpretation of the Convention does not necessarily advance this particular objective, inasmuch as it makes recourse to the Convention's means of service dependent on the forum's internal law. But we do not think that this country, or any other country, will draft its internal laws deliberately so as to circumvent the Convention in cases in which it would be appropriate to transmit judicial documents for service abroad. For example, there has been no question in this country of excepting foreign nationals from the protection of our Due Process Clause. Under that Clause, foreign nationals are assured of either personal service, which typically will require service abroad and trigger the Convention, or substituted service that provides "notice reasonably calculated, under all the circumstances, to apprise interested parties of the pendency of the action and afford them an opportunity to present their objections." *Mullane v. Central Hanover Bank & Trust Co.,* 339 U.S. 306, 314 (1950).[1]

---

[1] The concurrence believes that our interpretation does not adequately guarantee timely notice, which it denominates the "primary" purpose of the Convention, albeit without authority. The concurrence instead proposes to impute a substantive standard to the words, "service abroad." Evidently, a method of service would not be deemed to be "service abroad" within the meaning of Article 1 unless it provides notice to the recipient "in due time." This due process notion cannot be squared with the plain meaning of the words, "service abroad." The contours of the concurrence's substantive standard are not defined, and we note that it would create some uncertainty even on the facts of this case. If the substantive standard tracks the Due Process Clause of the Fourteenth Amendment, it is not self-evident that substituted service on a subsidiary is sufficient with respect to the parent. In the only cases in which it has considered the question, this Court held that the activities of a subsidiary are not necessarily enough to render a parent subject to a court's jurisdiction, for service of process or otherwise. *Cannon Mfg. Co. v. Cudahy*

Furthermore, nothing that we say today prevents compliance with the Convention even when the internal law of the forum does not so require. The Convention provides simple and certain means by which to serve process on a foreign national. Those who eschew its procedures risk discovering that the forum's internal law required transmittal of documents for service abroad, and that the Convention therefore provided the exclusive means of valid service. In addition, parties that comply with the Convention ultimately may find it easier to enforce their judgments abroad. For these reasons, we anticipate that parties may resort to the Convention voluntarily, even in cases that fall outside the scope of its mandatory application.

III

In this case, the Illinois long-arm statute authorized Schlunk to serve VWAG by substituted service on VWoA, without sending documents to Germany. *See* Ill. Rev. Stat., ch. 110, P2-209(a)(1) (1985). VWAG has not petitioned for review of the Illinois Appellate Court's holding that service was proper as a matter of Illinois law. VWAG contends, however, that service on VWAG was not complete until VWoA transmitted the complaint to VWAG in Germany. According to VWAG, this transmission constituted service abroad under the Hague Service Convention.

VWAG explains that, as a practical matter, VWoA was certain to transmit the complaint to Germany to notify VWAG of the litigation. Indeed, as a legal matter, the Due Process Clause requires every method of service to provide "notice reasonably calculated, under all the circumstances, to apprise interested parties of the pendency of the action and afford them an opportunity to present their objections." *Mullane v. Central Hanover Bank & Trust Co., supra.* VWAG argues that, because of this notice requirement, every case involving service on a foreign national will present an "occasion to transmit a judicial . . . document for service abroad" within the meaning of Article 1. VWAG emphasizes that in this case, the Appellate Court upheld service only after determining that "the relationship between VWAG and VWoA is so close that it is certain that VWAG 'was fully apprised of the pendency of the action' by delivery of the summons to VWoA."

We reject this argument. Where service on a domestic agent is valid and complete under both state law and the Due Process Clause, our inquiry ends and the Convention has no further implications. Whatever internal, private communications take place between the agent and a foreign principal are beyond the concerns of this case. The only transmittal to which the Convention applies is a transmittal abroad that is required as a necessary part of service. And, contrary to VWAG's assertion, the Due Process Clause does not require an official transmittal of documents abroad every time there is service on a foreign national. Applying this analysis, we conclude that this case does not present an occasion to transmit a judicial document for service abroad within the meaning of Article 1. Therefore the Hague Service Convention does not

---

Packing Co., 267 U.S. 333, 336–337 (1925). Although the particular relationship between VWAG and VWoA might have made substituted service valid in this case, a question that we do not decide, the factbound character of the necessary inquiry makes us doubt whether the standard suggested by the concurrence would in fact be "remarkably easy" to apply.

apply, and service was proper. The judgment of the Appellate Court is affirmed.

JUSTICE BRENNAN, with whom JUSTICE MARSHALL and JUSTICE BLACKMUN join, concurring in the judgment.

We acknowledged last Term, and the Court reiterates today, that the terms of the Convention on Service Abroad of Judicial and Extrajudicial Documents in Civil or Commercial Matters, are "mandatory," not "optional" with respect to any transmission that Article 1 covers. *Societe Nationale Industrielle Aerospatiale v. United States District Court,* 482 U.S. 522, 534 (1987). Even so, the Court holds, and I agree, that a litigant may, consistent with the Convention, serve process on a foreign corporation by serving its wholly owned domestic subsidiary, because such process is not "service abroad" within the meaning of Article 1. The Court reaches that conclusion, however, by depriving the Convention of any mandatory effect, for in the Court's view the "forum's internal law" defines conclusively whether a particular process is "service abroad," which is covered by the Convention, or domestic service, which is not. I do not join the Court's opinion because I find it implausible that the Convention's framers intended to leave each contracting nation, and each of the 50 States within our Nation, free to decide for itself under what circumstances, if any, the Convention would control. Rather, in my view, the words "service abroad," read in light of the negotiating history, embody a substantive standard that limits a forum's latitude to deem service complete domestically.

The first of two objectives enumerated in the Convention's preamble is "to create appropriate means to ensure that judicial . . . documents to be served abroad shall be brought to the notice of the addressee in sufficient time . . . ." Until the Convention was implemented, the contracting nations followed widely divergent practices for serving judicial documents across international borders, some of which did not ensure any notice, much less timely notice, and therefore often produced unfair default judgments. Particularly controversial was a procedure, common among civil-law countries, called *"notification au parquet,"* which permitted delivery of process to a local official who was then ordinarily supposed to transmit the document abroad through diplomatic or other channels. Typically, service was deemed complete upon delivery of the document to the official whether or not the official succeeded in transmitting it to the defendant and whether or not the defendant otherwise received notice of the pending lawsuit.[1]

---

[1] The head of the United States delegation to the Convention described *notification au parquet* as follows:

> This is a system which permits the entry of judgments *in personam* by default against a nonresident defendant without requiring adequate notice. There is also no real right to move to open the default judgment or to appeal, because the time to move to open judgment or to appeal will generally have expired before the defendant finds out about the judgment. Under this system of service, the process-server simply delivers a copy of the writ to a public official's office. The time for answer begins to run immediately. Some effort is supposed to be made through the Foreign Office and through diplomatic channels to give the defendant notice, but failure to do this has no effect on the validity of the service. . . . There are no . . . limitations and protections [comparable to due process or personal jurisdiction] under the *notification au parquet* system. Here jurisdiction lies merely if the plaintiff is a local national; nothing more is needed." S. Exec. Rep. No. 6, at 11–12 (statement by Philip W. Amram). . . .

The United States delegation to the Convention objected to *notification au parquet* as inconsistent with "the requirements of 'due process of law' under the Federal Constitution." The head of the delegation has derided its " 'injustice, extravagance, [and] absurdity . . . .' " In its classic formulation, he observed, *notification au parquet* " 'totally sacrificed all rights of the defense in favor of the plaintiff.' " The Convention's official reporter noted similar " 'spirited criticisms of the system' . . . which we wish to see eliminated."

In response to this and other concerns, the Convention prescribes the exclusive means for service of process emanating from one contracting nation and culminating in another. As the Court observes, the Convention applies only when the document is to be "transmit[ted] . . . for service abroad"; it covers not every transmission of judicial documents abroad, but only those transmissions abroad that constitute formal "service." It is common ground that the Convention governs when the procedure prescribed by the internal law of the forum nation or state provides that service is not complete until the document is transmitted abroad. That is not to say, however, as does the Court, that the forum nation may designate any type of service "domestic" and thereby avoid application of the Convention.

Admittedly, as the Court points out, the Convention's language does not prescribe a precise standard to distinguish between "domestic" service and "service abroad." But the Court's solution leaves contracting nations free to ignore its terms entirely, converting its command into exhortation. Under the Court's analysis, for example, a forum nation could prescribe direct mail service to any foreigner and deem service effective upon deposit in the mailbox, or could arbitrarily designate a domestic agent for any foreign defendant and deem service complete upon receipt domestically by the agent even though there is little likelihood that service would ever reach the defendant. In fact, so far as I can tell, the Court's interpretation permits any contracting nation to revive *notification au parquet* so long as the nation's internal law deems service complete domestically, even though, as the Court concedes, "such methods of service are the least likely to provide a defendant with actual notice," and even though "there is no question but that the Conference wanted to eliminate *notification au parquet*." . . .

My difference with the Court does not affect the outcome of this case, and, given that any process emanating from our courts must comply with due process, it may have little practical consequence in future cases that come before us. Our Constitution does not, however, bind other nations haling our citizens into their courts. Our citizens rely instead primarily on the forum nation's compliance with the Convention, which the Senate believed would "provide increased protection (due process) for American Citizens who are involved in litigation abroad." And while other nations are not bound by the Court's pronouncement that the Convention lacks obligatory force, after today's decision their courts will surely sympathize little with any United States national pleading that a judgment violates the Convention because (notwithstanding any local characterization) service was "abroad."

It is perhaps heartening to "think that [no] countr[y] will draft its internal laws deliberately so as to circumvent the Convention in cases in which it would be appropriate to transmit judicial documents for service abroad," although from the defendant's perspective "circumvention" (which, according to the Court, entails no more than exercising a prerogative not to be bound) is equally painful whether deliberate or not. The fact remains, however, that had we been content to rely on foreign notions of fair play and substantial justice, we would have found it unnecessary, in the first place, to participate in a Convention "to ensure that judicial . . . documents to be served abroad [would] be brought to the notice of the addressee in sufficient time," 20 U.S.T., at 362.

Notes and Questions on *Schlunk*

1. *Relationship of treaty to local law.* "United States courts have consistently and properly held that litigants wishing to serve process in countries that are parties to the Service Convention must follow the procedures provided by that Convention unless the nation involved permits more liberal procedures." Brief for the United States as *Amicus Curiae, Volkswagenwerk, A.G. v. Falzon*, 465 U.S. 1014 (1984). It is widely understood that the Convention procedures, when they apply, are exclusive and mandatory. Is it wrong or paradoxical for the *Schlunk* court to look to local law to determine the applicability of the Hague Service Convention?

2. *Treaty compliance and the enforceability of a subsequent judgment.* Appearing *amicus curiae* in *Schlunk*, the Federal Republic of Germany informed the court that it interpreted the Hague Service Convention as the exclusive means of serving process on defendants in Germany. Serving an involuntary agent outside the Convention framework would not qualify as lawful service if recognition and enforcement of the judgment were later sought in a German court. In its *amicus* brief, the government of the United States made a similar point: "we expect that respondent's failure to employ the Convention's procedures may raise serious obstacles to obtaining foreign assistance in enforcing any judgment that he might ultimately receive." As a consequence, the expedient allowed in *Schlunk* may be self-defeating. Counsel has a powerful practical incentive to comply voluntarily with the Convention.

3. *Minimal state standards governing service.* Suppose a state law named the state Attorney General as the mandatory agent for the receipt of process for all foreign corporations doing business in that state. Assume that that officer is required only to make "best efforts" to assure that the foreign corporation receives actual notice. Invoking the law, plaintiff serves the state official but makes no effort to serve the defendant corporation directly. Would service be sustained under *Schlunk* on the ground that the Convention was again not applicable? *Compare Curcuruto v. Cheshire*, 864 F. Supp. 1410 (S.D. Ga. 1994), *with Melia v. Les Grands Chais de France*, 135 F.R.D. 28 (D.R.I. 1991). *See also Paradigm Entertainment, Inc. v. Video System Co., Ltd.*, 2000 WL 251731 at *7 (N.D.Tex. 2000) (holding that substitute service pursuant to Texas state law is not inconsistent with Article 10(a) of the Hague Convention). What are the likely long-term international consequences if such expedients are deemed "domestic service" to which the Convention is inapplicable after *Schlunk*?

4. *Service outside the treaty.* Suppose no treaty applied to define the means of service in a case (*e.g.* service is to be attempted in a country that is not

a party to the Hague Convention or any similar regional agreement). Under Rule 4(f), what alternatives are available, and what standards would have to be satisfied before service would be considered effective? Is the court authorized to make something up and call it service? *See Tinicum Properties v. Garnett*, 1992 U.S. Dist. LEXIS 6564 (E.D. Pa. 1992), *infra*.

5. *Waiver.* Under F.R.C.P. Rule 4(d), a party may waive service of summons. What is the best argument for *not* extending the waiver option to service under the Hague Convention? Could a party thereby waive something that is not hers to waive?

6. *Remedies for violation of the treaty.* What should the proper range of remedies be for attempting service in violation of the convention? *See Rhodes v. J.P. Sauer,, infra*, and *Teknekron Management, Inc. v. Quante Ternmeldet-echnik*, 115 F.R.D. 175 (D. Nev. 1987). What law should apply to resolve this issue?

---

[2]   Problems in the Aftermath of the Hague Convention

[a]   Did the Hague Convention survive being *Schlunk*ed?

HEREDIA v. TRANSPORT S.A.S., Inc. and PRESENZA
101 F. Supp. 2d 158 (S.D.N.Y. 2000)

Plaintiff is a resident of Bronx County, New York. Defendants are both citizens of Quebec, Canada. [P]laintiff and defendant Presenza were involved in an automobile accident . . . in Bronx County, New York. At the time of the accident, Presenza was driving a truck registered to defendant Transport. . . . [P]ursuant to New York [law governing the] procedures for service of non-resident motorists, plaintiff delivered the summons and complaint to an authorized agent in the office of New York's Secretary of State (the "Secretary of State"). The following day, the Secretary of State sent notice of service and a copy of the summons and complaint by registered mail to Presenza in Quebec, Canada. Presenza signed the return receipt, indicating that he had received the notice of service and a copy of the summons and complaint. The summons, complaint, and notice of service were written only in English, while the return receipt was written in both English and French. . . .

A. Applicability of the Hague Convention

[I]t is undisputed that plaintiff served a copy of the summons and complaint upon the Secretary of State, and that the Secretary of State subsequently acted on behalf of plaintiff by sending notice of the service and a copy of the summons and complaint to the defendant by registered mail with return receipt requested. Accordingly, plaintiff complied with the service requirements of section 253 [of the state vehicle and traffic law] which provides as follows:

> Service of such summons shall be made by mailing a copy thereof to the Secretary of State . . . and such service shall be sufficient service upon such non-resident provided that notice of such service and a copy of the summons and complaint are forthwith sent by or on behalf of the plaintiff to the defendant by certified mail or registered mail with return receipt requested.

Although plaintiff followed the procedure established by section 253, proper service of the summons must also comply with the Convention on Service Abroad of Judicial and Extrajudicial Documents in Civil and Commercial Matters, Nov. 15, 1965, 20 U.S.T. 361 ("Hague Convention" or "Convention"). Article 1 of the Hague Convention states that "[t]he present Convention shall apply in all cases, in civil or commercial matters, where there is occasion to transmit a judicial or extrajudicial document for service abroad." In *Volkswagenwerk v. Schlunk*, 486 U.S. 694 (1988), the Supreme Court analyzed the applicability of the Hague Convention and found that "[i]f the internal law of the forum state defines the applicable method of serving process as requiring the transmittal of documents abroad, then the Hague Service Convention applies." Section 253 requires that the Secretary of State mail copies of the summons and complaint to non-resident defendants. Thus, New York law requires the transmittal of documents abroad and the Hague Convention applies. Accordingly, plaintiff's service must meet the requirements of the Hague Convention in addition to the procedures established by section 253.

As a preliminary matter, it should be noted that service of process by registered mail is one of several methods of service permitted by the Hague Convention. Article 10 of the Convention states: "Provided the State of destination does not object, the present Convention shall not interfere with . . . the freedom to send judicial documents, by postal channels, directly to persons abroad." This freedom to send judicial documents includes service of process. *Ackermann v. Levine*, 788 F.2d 830, 838–39 (2d Cir. 1986) ("The service of process by registered mail did not violate the Hague Convention. Plaintiffs declined to follow the service route allowed under Article 5 of the Convention, which permits service via a 'Central Authority' of the country in which service is to be made. Instead, plaintiffs chose to follow the equally acceptable route allowed under Articles 8 and 10"). Canada does not object to service by postal channels. Thus, service by registered mail in Quebec is adequate service under the Convention.

B. Translation Requirement

In their opposition to plaintiff's motion to remand, defendants contend that service was improper under the Hague Convention because the summons and complaint were not translated from English into French, Presenza's native language and the official language of Quebec province. However, it is well-settled that the translation requirement is triggered only when it is the Central Authority that serves the document, an alternative method of service that is set forth in Article 5 of the Convention. ("If the document is to be served [by the Central Authority], the Central Authority may require the document to be written in, or translated into, the official language . . . of the State addressed."). Canada does require translation of documents into French for recipients of service under Article 5. There is, however, no similar requirement by Canada or by the Convention for translation when service is effected by direct mail under Article 10. Thus, where service is made by registered mail under Article 10, the served documents need not be translated. *See Taft [v. Moreau]*, 177 F.R.D. [201 (D.Vt. 1997] at 203 ("Documents served upon Quebec residents or citizens under Article 10(a) need not be translated into French in order to comply with the Hague Convention."); *Lemme v. Wine of Japan Import*, 631 F.Supp. 456, 464 (E.D.N.Y. 1986) ("In the first place, the translation 'requirement' is triggered only when it is the Central Authority that serves the document. . . . Where the method used is direct postal service under section 10(a), the document need not be translated."); *Weight v. Kawasaki Heavy Indus.*, 597 F.Supp. 1082, 1086 (E.D.Va. 1984) ("A Japanese translation is required only when the service of process is transmitted through the 'Central Authority' pursuant to Article 5 of the Convention. . . . However, Article 10(a) of the Convention contains no such requirement for direct postal service.").

Defendants seek to distinguish *Lemme* and *Weight* by noting that service here was made in Canada, not Japan. However, under the Convention, service in Japan and Canada are identical. Neither country requires translation for Article 10 service. . . .

Plaintiff's service of process comport[ed] with the procedures set forth in section 253 [and] the requirements of the Hague Convention. . . .

---

[b] "Sending" versus "Serving"

SUZUKI MOTOR CO., LTD. v. SUPERIOR COURT and
PEGGY ARMANTA (real party in interest)
200 Cal. App. 3d 1476 (Cal. Court of Appeal 1988)

Suzuki is a Japanese corporation which is named as a defendant in an action now pending in the superior court entitled *Peggy Armenta v. Bellflower Suzuki*. Peggy Armenta, the plaintiff in that action and the real party in interest in this proceeding, allegedly sustained personal injuries while operating a 1984 Suzuki four-wheel, all-terrain vehicle. Ms. Armenta filed a complaint for products liability and negligence against a number of defendants, including Suzuki. Plaintiff purported to effect service of process upon Suzuki by sending the summons, together with copies of the complaint, certificate of assignment, and amendment to the complaint, via registered mail to Suzuki's office in Hamamatsu, Japan. These documents, which actually were received by Suzuki, were not translated into Japanese.

Suzuki moved to quash service of process, asserting that service was improper under the provisions of the California Code of Civil Procedure, as well as the provisions of the Hague Convention. In support of its motion to quash, Suzuki filed the declaration of Hidetoshi Asakura, a partner with the law firm of Graham & James, licensed to practice law in Japan and California.

In his declaration, Mr. Asakura expounded on the acceptable methods of service of process in Japan and concluded that plaintiff here had failed to conform to these methods, and thereby had also failed to conform to the requirements of the Hague Convention for service of process in the Convention's signatory states. Plaintiff did not contest the information contained in Mr. Asakura's declaration, but relied instead on the First District's decision in *Shoei Kako, Co. v. Superior Court,* 33 Cal. App.3d 808 [109 Cal.Rptr. 402] (1973).

The superior court refused to grant the motion to quash service, and rightly so, in light of the [doctrine] . . . that a lower court which refuses to follow a binding precedent of a higher court is acting in excess of jurisdiction, and because there has been no holding contrary to that of *Shoei Kako* in this or any other appellate district. We, however, are not bound by the holding in *Shoei Kako,* particularly because it was based in part on a unique factual record before that court, a record which differs substantially from that now before us. Therefore, as explained below, we hold that the service of process described above was not effective . . . .

Discussion

In 1969, the United States signed the Convention on the Service Abroad of Judicial and Extrajudicial Documents in Civil or Commercial Matters (the Hague Convention or the Convention). Japan became a signatory to the Convention in 1970. The Convention provides several acceptable methods for service of process abroad. These methods are: (1) service through the receiving country's designated "Central Authority" for service of foreign process (art. 5); (2) delivery by the Central Authority to an addressee who accepts service "voluntarily" so long as the method used is not incompatible with the law of the receiving state (art. 5); (3) service through diplomatic or consular agents of the sending state (art. 8); (4) service through the judicial officers, officials or other competent persons of the receiving state (art. 10, subdivisions (b) and (c)); and (5) service as permitted by the internal law of the receiving state for documents coming from abroad (art. 19).

Real party in interest urges that there is yet another method of service of process which meets the requirements of the Convention, to wit, service by registered mail as allowed by California Code of Civil Procedure sections 413.10[1] and 415.30[2] and article 10, subdivision (a) of the Convention, which

---

[1] Code of Civil Procedure section 413.10 reads as follows: "Except as otherwise provided by statute, a summons shall be served on a person: . . . (c) Outside the United States, as provided in this chapter or as directed by the court in which the action is pending, or, if the court before or after service finds that the service is reasonably calculated to give actual notice, as prescribed by the law of the place where the person is served or as directed by the foreign authority in response to a letter rogatory. These rules are subject to the provisions of the Convention on the 'Service Abroad of Judicial and Extrajudicial Documents' in Civil or Commercial Matters (Hague Service Convention)."

[2] Code of Civil Procedure section 415.30 reads, in pertinent part: "(a) A summons may be served by mail as provided in this section. A copy of the summons and of the complaint shall be mailed (by first-class mail or airmail, postage prepaid) to the person to be served, together with two copies of the notice and acknowledgment provided for in subdivision (b) and a return envelope, postage prepaid, addressed to the sender . . . .(c) Service of a summons pursuant to this section is deemed complete on the date a written acknowledgment of receipt of summons is executed, if such acknowledgment thereafter is returned to the sender."

provides that "Provided the State of destination does not object, the present Convention shall not interfere with — (a) the freedom to send judicial documents, by postal channels, directly to persons abroad, . . ." According to real party in interest and the court in *Shoei Kako*, this section of the Convention allows service of process by mail.

The *Shoei Kako* court analyzed the issue of the interpretation of the section, concluding that the Convention permitted signatories to exclude the methods of service outlined in articles 8 and 10 by filing objections to them. Japan objected to article 10, subdivisions (b) and (c), which provide for service via the judicial officers, officials, or other competent persons of the receiving state. Japan, however, did not object to article 10, subdivision (a). Downplaying the fact that article 10, subdivision (a) specifically refers to the sending of judicial documents rather than the service of such documents, the *Shoei Kako* court interpreted article 10, subdivision (a), like article 10, subdivisions (b) and (c), as also referring to the service of process by mail. According to that court, "The reference to 'the freedom to send judicial documents by postal channels, directly to persons abroad' would be superfluous unless it was related to the sending of such documents for the purpose of service. The mails are open to all." Therefore, it concluded that Japan's failure to object specifically to subdivision (a) meant such service was acceptable.

The *Shoei Kako* court also relied on article 15 of the Convention to hold that service by registered mail was proper. Article 15 provides, in relevant part, "Where a writ of summons or an equivalent document had to be transmitted abroad for the purpose of service, under the provisions of the present Convention, and the defendant has not appeared, judgment shall not be given until it is established that — (a) the document was served by a method prescribed by the internal law of the State addressed for the service of documents in domestic actions upon persons who are within its territory, or (b) the document was actually delivered to the defendant or to his residence by another method provided for by this Convention, and that in either of these cases the service or the delivery was effected in sufficient time to enable the defendant to defend . . . ." According to the *Shoei Kako* court, the record before it indicated that Japan's internal law allowed service by mail with evidence of delivery as an effective mode of service of process, and the record also indicated that the defendant in the case before it had actually received the summons and complaint by "a method provided for by [the] Convention," i.e., service by registered mail, the *Shoei Kako* court having determined that service by registered mail was a method allowed under article 10, subdivision (a).

Here, the record before us indicates that Japan does not have an internal legal system which allows service of process by registered mail. As indicated by the declaration of Mr. Asakura, and confirmed by a law review article . . ., Japan, unlike California, does not allow either attorneys or lay people to serve process by mail. To effectuate service of process through the mail, the court clerk stamps the outside of the envelope containing the required documents with a notice of special service (*tokubetsu sootatsu*) and the mail carrier acts as a special officer of the court by recording proof of delivery on a special proof of service form and returning this proof of service to the court. Significantly, real party in interest did not controvert these facts when she opposed Suzuki's motion to quash.

Given the fact that Japan itself does not recognize a form of service sufficiently equivalent to America's registered mail system, it is extremely unlikely that Japan's failure to object to article 10, subdivision (a) was intended to authorize the use of registered mail as an effective mode of service of process, particularly in light of the fact that Japan specifically objected to the much more formal modes of service by Japanese officials which were available in article 10, subdivisions (b) and (c). Instead, it seems much more likely that Japan interpreted article 10, subdivision (a) as allowing only the transmission of judicial documents, rather than the service of process. This interpretation is all the more reasonable given the fact that the Convention persistently refers to "service" as opposed to "send," e.g., "forward documents, for the purpose of service" (art. 9); "transmission of judicial documents *for service*" (art. 14, italics added); and "transmitted abroad *for the purpose of service*" (arts. 15 and 16, italics added), in contrast to "the freedom to send judicial documents, by postal channels, directly to persons abroad, . . ." (art. 10, subd. (a)).

It is a well-recognized canon of statutory interpretation that words in a statute or similar enactment are to be given their common and ordinary meaning and that every word and phrase used is presumed to have a meaning and to perform a useful function. To interpret the phrase "to send" as used in article 10, subdivision (a) of the Convention to mean "to serve" would fly in the face of both these rules; the common and ordinary meaning of "to send" is "to cause to be conveyed by an intermediary to a destination" or "to dispatch, as by mail or telegraph" . . . not "to serve," and the fact the Convention's drafters used both the phrase "to send" and the phrase "service of process" indicates they intended each phrase to have a different meaning and function.

Real party in interest relies on various cases which do not interpret "to send" as we do, including the . . . case of *Ackermann v. Levine,* 788 F.2d 830 (2d Cir. 1986), which cites *Shoei Kako* with approval, and which, as did the court in *Shoei Kako*, interprets "to send" as meaning "to serve." In *Ackermann*, German plaintiffs served a summons and complaint on a New York defendant by registered mail. The Second Circuit held that service of process by registered mail was effective under article 10, subdivision (a) of the Hague Convention, because (1) the use of the word "send" in that subdivision was intended to mean "service" and (2) the United States had not objected to the use of "postal channels" under article 10, subdivision (a) as it could have chosen to do.[3] The *Ackermann* court also noted with approval several other cases which had held that Japan, too, had not objected to mail "service" under article 10, subdivision (a).

The result in *Ackermann*, as in the cases to which the *Ackermann* court referred with approval, turns on the interpretation of the word "send" as meaning "serve." As noted above, this interpretation simply does not make sense. The *Ackermann* court relied on a treatise which concluded that the use

---

[3] It is also worth noting, as a further distinguishing feature of *Ackermann*, that the United States, which was the "receiving" country in *Ackermann*, did not object to any subdivision of article 10, whereas Japan, the "receiving" country here, did object to subdivisions (b) and (c). This differentiation between the subdivisions by Japan indicates to us, as set out more specifically in this opinion, that Japan did not believe "to send," as that phrase is used in subdivision (a), meant "to serve."

of the word "send" rather than the otherwise consistently used "service" " 'must be attributable to careless drafting.' " However, whether the phrase "to send" was used because of careless drafting or not, it appears that Japan understood it to mean "to send," not "to serve," as it is implausible that a country which does not use basic postal channels for service of process by its own nationals on their fellows, and which objected to the more rigorous methods of service set out in article 10, subdivisions (b) and (c), would have failed to object to subdivision (a) if it had understood that section to relate to service of process.

Ackermann has been cited with approval by a recent opinion from the Central District of California, *Newport Components v. NEC Home Electronics,* 671 F.Supp. 1525 (C.D.Cal. 1987). . . . In *Newport Components,* the district court was faced with the same issue raised here. Noting that there was a split among the courts as to the meaning of article 10, subdivision (a), the *Newport Components* court cast its lot with the *Ackermann* line of cases, without any independent discussion of the import of subdivision (a)'s use of the verb "to send," and after finding the following reasoning from *Shoei Kako* particularly persuasive: "If it be assumed that the purpose of the convention is to establish one method to avoid the difficulties and controversy attendant to the use of other methods . . ., it does not necessarily follow that other methods may not be used if effective proof of delivery can be made."

We, however, do not find this reasoning persuasive. If the signatories' intent was to establish a particular method of service to avoid the controversy attendant on the use of other methods, and if signatories were allowed, as they were, to object to particular modes of service, then it makes no sense to allow private litigants to by-pass the agreed-upon methods and to use other methods, even methods to which some signatories objected, even if effective proof of delivery using such alternate and objected-to methods can be made. . . .

In sum, we do not find the *Ackermann* line of cases persuasive, and therefore take the position taken by other commentators and courts that service of process by registered mail is not one of the methods authorized by the Convention for service of process on Japanese defendants. . . . This holding compels the corollary holding, based on the fact that a California court may not exercise jurisdiction in violation of an international treaty, that Suzuki is entitled to have its motion to quash service of process granted.

BANKSTON v. TOYOTA MOTOR CORP.
889 F.2d 172 (8th Cir. 1989)

Appellants Charles Bankston, Sr. and Regina Dixon filed suit in the United States District Court for the Western District of Arkansas against Toyota Motor Corporation, a Japanese corporation, seeking damages resulting from an accident involving a Toyota truck. The appellants first attempted service of process upon Toyota by serving an affiliated United States corporation in Torrance, California, as Toyota's purported agent. Toyota filed a motion to dismiss for improper service of process. The district court denied Toyota's motion but granted the appellants 45 days in which to serve Toyota in accordance with the Hague Convention.

The appellants next attempted to serve process upon Toyota by sending a summons and complaint by registered mail, return receipt requested, to Tokyo, Japan. The documents were in English and did not include a translation into Japanese. The receipt of service was signed and returned to appellants. Toyota renewed its motion to dismiss, arguing that the appellants' proposed method of service still did not comply with the Hague Convention.

The district court concluded that Article 10(a) of the Hague Convention does not permit service of process upon a Japanese corporation by registered mail [but] . . . gave the appellants an additional sixty days in which to effect service in compliance with the Hague Convention [and] . . . certified the issue for interlocutory appeal to this court. . . .

The crucial article for this discussion is Article 10, under which appellants herein purportedly attempted to serve process upon Toyota by registered mail. Article 10 provides in relevant part:

Provided the State of destination does not object, the present Convention shall not interfere with —

(a) the freedom to send judicial documents, by postal channels, directly to persons abroad,

(b) the freedom of judicial officers, officials or other competent persons of the State of origin to effect service of judicial documents directly through the judicial officers, officials or other competent persons of the State of destination,

(c) the freedom of any person interested in a judicial proceeding to effect service of judicial documents directly through the judicial officers, officials or other competent persons of the State of destination.

Japan has objected to subparagraphs (b) and (c), but not to subparagraph (a). The issue before this court is whether subparagraph (a) permits service on a Japanese defendant by direct mail. In recent years, two distinct lines of Article 10(a) interpretation have arisen. Some courts have ruled that Article 10(a) permits service of process by mail directly to the defendant without the necessity of resorting to the central authority, and without the necessity of translating the documents into the official language of the nation where the documents are to be served.

In general, these courts reason that since the purported purpose of the Hague Convention is to facilitate service abroad, the reference to " 'the freedom to send judicial documents by postal channels, directly to persons abroad' would be superfluous unless it was related to the sending of such documents for the purpose of service." *Ackermann v. Levine,* 788 F.2d 830, 839 (2d Cir. 1986) . . . . These courts have further found that the use of the "send" rather than "service" in Article 10 (a) "must be attributed to careless drafting."

The second line of interpretation, advocated by Toyota, is that the word "send" in Article 10(a) is not the equivalent of "service of process." The word "service" is specifically used in other sections of the Convention, including subsections (b) and (c) of Article 10. If the drafters of the Convention had meant for subparagraph (a) to provide an additional manner of service of judicial documents, they would have used the word "service." Subscribers to this interpretation maintain that Article 10(a) merely provides a method for sending subsequent documents after service of process has been obtained by means of the central authority.

We find this second line of authority to be more persuasive. It is a "familiar canon of statutory construction that the starting point for interpreting a statute is the language of the statute itself. Absent a clearly expressed legislative intention to the contrary, that language must ordinarily be regarded as conclusive." *Consumer Prod. Safety Comm'n v. GTE Sylvania, Inc.,* 447 U.S. 102, 108 (1980). In addition, where a legislative body "includes particular language in one section of a statute but omits it in another section of the same Act, it is generally presumed that [the legislative body] acts intentionally and purposely in the disparate inclusion or exclusion." *Russello v. United States,* 464 U.S. 16, 23 (1983). In *Suzuki Motor Co. v. Superior Court,* the court found that because service of process by registered mail was not permitted under Japanese law, it was "extremely unlikely" that Japan's failure to object to Article 10(a) was intended to authorize the use of registered mail as an effective mode of service of process, particularly in light of the fact that Japan had specifically objected to the much more formal modes of service by Japanese officials which were available in Article 10(b) and (c).

We conclude that sending a copy of a summons and complaint by registered mail to a defendant in a foreign country is not a method of service of process permitted by the Hague Convention. We affirm the judgment of the district court and remand this case with directions that appellants be given a reasonable time from the date of this Order in which to effectuate service of process over appellee Toyota Motor Corporation in compliance with the terms of the Hague Convention.

GIBSON, Circuit Judge, concurring. I concur in the court's opinion today in every respect. The court correctly interprets the Hague Convention. I write separately only to express nagging concerns I have about the practical effect of our opinion. Automobiles are subject to a plethora of regulations requiring particular equipment and detailed warnings. Should an automobile manufactured in Japan carry a disclosure that, if litigation ensues from its purchase and use, service of process on the Japanese manufacturer can only be obtained under the Hague Convention? Should the purchaser also be informed that this special service of process will cost $800 to $900, as we are told, and must include a translation of the suit papers in Japanese? These decisions we must leave to others. I write only to express my discomfort with the practical effect of Toyota's insistence on strict compliance with the letter of the Hague Convention.

STATEMENT OF JAPANESE DELEGATION BEFORE THE HAGUE CONFERENCE ON PRIVATE INTERNATIONAL LAW
28 I.L.M. 1558 (1989)

Japanese position on Article 10(a) of the Hague Convention on the Service Abroad of Judicial and Extrajudicial Documents in Civil or Commercial Matters:

> Japan has not declared that it objects to the sending of judicial documents, by postal channels, directly to persons abroad. In this connection, Japan has made it clear that no objection to the use of postal channels for sending judicial documents to persons in Japan does not necessarily imply that the sending by such a method is considered valid service in Japan; it merely indicates that Japan does not consider it as infringement of its sovereign power.

UNITED STATES DEPARTMENT OF STATE OPINION REGARDING THE *BANKSTON* CASE AND SERVICE BY MAIL TO JAPAN UNDER THE HAGUE SERVICE CONVENTION
30 I.L.M. 260 (1991)

In the decision of the United States Court of Appeals for the Eighth Circuit, *Bankston v. Toyota Motor Company*, No. 89-1249, November 13, 1989, the Court concluded that service of summons and complaint by registered mail to a defendant in a foreign country is not a method of service permitted by the Hague Convention. The United States Department of State has recently stated that it believes the decision to be incorrect. This view is contained in a March 14 letter from the United States Department of State Deputy Legal Adviser, Alan J. Kreczko, to the Administrative Office of United States Courts and the National Center for State Courts, excerpts of which are reproduced below:

> I am writing with reference to the interpretation of United States treaty obligations in the recent *Bankston* decision. As you are aware, while courts in the United States have final authority to interpret international treaties for the purposes of their application as law in the United States, they give great weight to treaty interpretations made by the Executive Branch. RESTATEMENT (THIRD) OF FOREIGN RELATIONS LAW OF THE UNITED STATES, section 326(2) (1986).

> "The United States Government did not have an opportunity to express its views on the issues before the 8th Circuit Court in *Bankston*. . . . The Circuit Court in *Bankston*, examining Toyota's motion to dismiss for improper service on the defendant in Japan by registered mail rather than under procedures set out in the Hague Service Convention (to which both the United States and Japan are parties), concluded that service of summons and complaint by

registered mail to a defendant in a foreign country (Japan) is not a method of service of process permitted by the Hague Convention.

"We understand from appellant's/plaintiff's counsel that the time period for filing a petition for a rehearing in *Bankston* has elapsed. We understand further that neither the plaintiff nor the Court of Appeals was aware of a statement made by the delegate of Japan in April, 1989 at a meeting of representatives of countries that have joined the Hague Service Convention that appears to be relevant to the basic question addressed in the *Bankston* case. The Japanese statement in question was the result of efforts by the Departments of State and Justice to encourage the Government of Japan to clarify its position with regard to the service of process in Japan by mail from another country party to the Hague Service Convention. . . .

"We consider that the Japanese statement represents the official view of the Japanese Government that Japan does not consider service of process by mail in Japan to violate Japanese judicial sovereignty and that Japan does not claim that such service would be inconsistent with the obligations of any other country party to the Hague Service Convention vis-a-vis Japan. The Japanese statement suggests, however, that it is possible, and even likely, that service in Japan by mail, which may be considered valid service by courts in the United States, would not be considered valid service in Japan for the purposes of Japanese law. Thus, a judgment by a court in the United States based on service on the defendant in Japan by mail, while capable of recognition and enforcement throughout the United States, may well not be capable of recognition and enforcement in Japan by the courts of that country.

"We therefore believe that the decision of the Court of Appeals in *Bankston* is incorrect to the extent that it suggests that the Hague Convention does not permit as a method of service of process the sending of a copy of a summons and complaint by registered mail to a defendant in a foreign country. . . ."

Notes and Questions

1. *The diplomacy of service.* How do you interpret the Japanese statement? What do you suppose the Legal Adviser's Office was trying to accomplish with its letter? If you were a judge in a case like *Bankston* or *Suzuki*, how much weight would you give to the letter and on what rationale? Is the Legal Adviser's position on the Japanese statement a matter of wishful interpretation?

2. *"Sending" vs. "Serving".* The issue raised in *Suzuki* and *Bankston* has remarkable staying power, and the courts continue to adopt irreconcilable interpretations of Article 10 of the Hague Service Convention. From one perspective, the dispute is about the reach and meaning of Article 10(a). But it is also about the proper approach to the interpretation of treaties generally.

Consider the following excerpt from *Lafarge Corp. v. M/C/ Macedonia Hellas*, 2000 WL 687708, *10 (E.D.La. 2000):

> The circuits are split as to whether Article 10(a) permits service of process via mail on a non-resident, foreign defendant. The conflict turns on whether Article 10(a)'s use of the term "send," encompasses "service." Courts holding that Article 10(a) is meant to apply to service of process conclude that use of the word "send" instead of "service" can be attributed to careless drafting.[1] Further, these courts reason that a determination that the term "send" does not include "service" is not in accord with the broad purpose of the Hague Convention as a whole. . . .

> In contrast, other courts hold that service of process under the Hague Convention is controlled strictly by Article 5. *See, e.g., Bankston v. Toyota Motor Corp.*, 889 F.2d 172 (8th Cir. 1989). Such courts argue that use of the term "service" appears in subparagraphs (b) and (c) of Article 10. These courts reason that if the drafters meant the term "send" to include "service," they would have used the term "service" in Article 10(a). Under this line of authority, service of process must be effected under Article 5 of the Hague Convention. In other words, service by mail is deemed insufficient or defective. . . .

> The Fifth Circuit has yet to rule on this issue. District courts within the Fifth Circuit continue to disagree. *Compare Bayoil Supply & Trading of Bahamas v. Jorgen Jahre Shipping AS*, 54 F. Supp. 2d 691 (S.D. Tex. 1999) (concluding the Hague Convention, pursuant to Article 10(a), permits service of process by direct or registered mail); *Ortega Dominguez v. Pyrgia Shipping Corp.*, 1998 WL 204798 (E.D. La. Apr. 24, 1998) (same); *Hutchins v. Beneteau (USA) Ltd.*, 1990 WL 17533 (E.D. La. Feb. 15, 1990) (same); *Smith v. Dainichi Kinzoku Kogyo Co.*, 680 F. Supp. 847 (W.D. Tex. 1988) (same); *Friede & Goldman, Ltd. v. Gotaverken Arendal Consultants, AB*, 2000 WL 288375 (E.D. La.), *with Greene v. LeDorze*, 1998 WL 158632 (N.D. Tex. Mar. 24, 1998) (concluding Article 10(a) does not permit service of process by direct or registered mail); *Postal v. Princess Cruises, Inc.*, 163 F.R.D. 497 (N.D. Tex. 1995) (same); *Pennebaker v. Kawasaki Motors Corp.*, 155 F.R.D. 153 (S.D. Miss. 1994) (same); *Hunter Douglas Metals, Inc. v. New Bay Fin. Shipping Co.*, 1988 WL 115234 (E.D. La. Oct. 28, 1988) (same); *Pochop v. Toyota Motor Co.*, 111 F.R.D. 464 (S.D. Miss. 1986) (same).

> Other courts reason that where the receiving country ratified the Hague Convention without express prohibition of service by mail, service by mail pursuant to Article 10(a) is proper.[2] This line of reasoning is

---

[1] *See Ackermann v. Levine*, 788 F.2d 830 (2d Cir. 1986); *see also Koehler v. Dodwell*, 152 F.3d 304 (4th Cir. 1998) (stating that the liberal service options provided in the treaty include service by mail); *Coblentz GMC/Freightliner, Inc. v. General Motors Corp.*, 724 F. Supp. 1364 (M.D. Ala. 1989), *aff'd*, 932 F.2d 977 (11th Cir. 1991).

[2] *See, e.g., Ackermann*, 788 F.2d 830; *G.A. Modefine, S.A. v. Burlington Coat Factory Warehouse Corp.*, 164 F.R.D. 24 (S.D.N.Y. 1995); *Curcuruto v. Chelshire*, 864 F. Supp. 1410 (S.D.Ga. 1994); *Melia v. Les Grandes Chais de France*, 135 F.R.D. 28 (D.R.I. 1991); *Hammond v. Honda Motor*

based on Article 21, which provides an opt out procedure for signatories to the Hague Convention, stating: "[e]ach contracting State shall, at the time of the deposit of its instrument of ratification or accession, or at a later date, inform the Ministry of Foreign Affairs of the Netherlands of the following . . . opposition to the use of methods of transmission pursuant to articles 8 and 10. . . ." *Id.* In this case, there is no evidence that Greece has objected to service of process via mail, and thus service by mail is not an invalid method of transmission under the treaty. . . . [E]ven though the internal law of Greece does not allow service by direct mail, and Greek law imposes additional requirements for service to be effective, Article 10(a) of the Hague Convention provides the rule of decision in this case because Greece has not specifically objected to this provision. See Hague Convention, attachment of notification of States which are parties, Greece (approving Convention and objecting only to Article 15).

. . . The court finds that this conclusion is warranted by both the broad spirit and overall purpose of the Convention—to create appropriate means of serving abroad judicial and extrajudicial documents. It is undisputed that a copy of the summons and complaint reached [the defendant] in Greece. The court finds that to allow the distinction between "send" and "service" to prohibit service of process directly by mail would elevate form over substance.

3. How would you proceed if you needed to accomplish service of process in Japan and were constrained by time and cost? Given the results in *Suzuki Motor* and *Bankston*, what do you make of the *Heredia* court's observation that, "under the Convention, service in Japan and Canada are identical?"

---

[c] Varieties of Substituted Service

DAVIES v. JOBS & ADVERTS ONLINE, GmbH
94 F. Supp. 2d 719 (E.D. Va. 2000)

In this breach of contract action against a German corporation, plaintiff has twice elected not to effect service of process via the Hague Convention, choosing instead to serve, in the first instance, the Clerk of the Virginia State Corporation Commission, and in the second instance, defendant's lawyer and registered agent for its wholly-owned subsidiary. For the reasons that follow, service in both instances is insufficient.

In January 1998, plaintiff entered into a written employment contract with defendant, a German corporation, in Virginia. In essence, defendant agreed

---

Co., 128 F.R.D. 638 (D.S.C. 1989); *Montgomery, Zukerman, Davis, Inc. v. Diepenbrock*, 698 F.Supp. 1453 (S.D.Ind. 1988); *Turick v. Yamaha Motor Corp., U.S.A.*, 121 F.R.D. 32 (S.D.N.Y. 1988); *Newport Components, Inc. v. NEC Home Electronics (U.S.A.), Inc.*, 671 F.Supp. 1525 (C.D.Cal. 1987); *Lemme v. Wine of Japan Import, Inc.*, 631 F.Supp. 456 (E.D.N.Y. 1986); *Zisman v. Sieger*, 106 F.R.D. 194 (N.D.Ill. 1985); *Weight v. Kawasaki Heavy Indus., Ltd.*, 597 F.Supp. 1082 (E.D.Va. 1984).

to employ plaintiff as the president of its wholly-owned U.S. subsidiary, Jobs & Adverts USA, Inc. ("J & A USA"). . . . By its terms, the contract could be canceled by either party on three months notice, or by defendant, at any time, for cause. After plaintiff had served as J & A USA's president for several months and failed to generate any revenue, defendant invoked the three months notice provision and terminated plaintiff's contract . . . . Following this, defendant claims that an audit of J & A USA's books revealed that plaintiff had breached her fiduciary duty to J & A USA by, inter alia, compensating herself in excess of her annual salary, and by paying family members significant sums allegedly in compensation for services performed, without revealing their relationship to her. In addition, plaintiff failed to return all company records after her termination, as required by the contract. In light of these discoveries, defendant reclassified plaintiff's termination as "for cause," and accordingly declined to pay plaintiff the three months severance pay required under the contract for termination without cause. . . .

[P]laintiff filed the instant suit against defendant, J & A USA's German parent. To effect service of process, plaintiff served the Clerk of the State Corporation Commission in Richmond, Virginia.[1] The Clerk of the State Corporation Commission, as part of effecting service pursuant to Virginia Code § 12.1–19.1, sent a copy of the complaint to defendant in Germany.[2] On these facts, defendant moved to dismiss on the ground that, Rule 4(f), Fed.R.Civ.P., which governs service of process on individuals and corporations in foreign countries, required plaintiff to follow the provisions of the Hague Convention in serving the complaint upon defendant. The . . . defendant's motion was granted insofar as it sought a determination that service of process via the Clerk of the State Corporation Commission was defective. Rather than dismissing the action, the Court granted plaintiff sixty days in which to cure the deficient service by serving process on defendant in accordance with the Hague Convention.

Thereafter, plaintiff served Kelm, defendant's outside counsel, with a copy of the complaint, asserting that (i) he is defendant's agent, and therefore is an appropriate person to receive service of process for defendant and (ii) J & A USA is defendant's agent and, as Kelm is J & A USA's registered agent, service on him constitutes proper service on defendant. Defendant seeks dismissal once again on grounds of insufficiency of process and insufficiency of service of process, pursuant to Rules 12(b)(4) and (b)(5), Fed.R.Civ.P.

Plaintiff has made two attempts to serve defendant, and both must be examined for their sufficiency. The first issue to be resolved is whether plaintiff's attempt at serving defendant through the Clerk of the State Corporation Commission was indeed insufficient. This question can confidently be answered in the affirmative, as this attempt at service triggered the

---

[1] Virginia Code § 13.1-758 authorizes service of process on foreign corporations that transact business in Virginia without first obtaining a certificate of authority by serving the Clerk of the State Corporation Commission. Assuming for the purposes of this motion that defendant transacted business in Virginia, it did so without a certificate of authority.

[2] Section 12.1-19.1 provides that whenever the Clerk of the Commission is deemed by statute to be the agent for service of process for a foreign corporation transacting business in Virginia, the party seeking service shall leave two copies of the process at the Clerk's office, and the Clerk then will mail the process to the defendant at the address supplied by the party seeking service.

provisions of the Hague Convention, and it is undisputed that plaintiff did not comply with those provisions. Virginia Code § 12.1–19.1 mandates that whenever the Clerk of the Commission is deemed to be the agent for service of process for a foreign corporation doing business in Virginia, the Clerk must mail the process to the defendant at the address supplied by the party seeking service. In this case, the address supplied by plaintiff was defendant's address in Germany; thus, the Clerk of the Corporation Commission, as required, mailed the process to defendant in Germany. This mailing triggered the application of the Hague Convention because all service abroad is governed by the Hague Convention. *See Randolph v. Hendry*, 50 F. Supp.2d 572, 575 (S.D.W.Va. 1999) (noting that Article 1 of the Hague Convention provides that its terms apply "in all cases . . . where there is occasion to transmit a judicial or extrajudicial document for service abroad").[3] Indeed, "substituted service on a foreign corporation under Virginia law necessarily involves the transmission of documents abroad within the contemplation of the Hague Convention." *Fleming v. Yamaha Motor Corp., USA*, 774 F. Supp. 992, 994–95 (E.D.Va. 1991). Thus, it is insufficient to serve a foreign defendant, as plaintiff here sought to do, via the Clerk of the State Corporation Commission, without complying with the dictates of the Hague Convention.

The second issue presented by the motion at bar is whether plaintiff properly effected service on defendant through her service on Kelm, defendant's outside counsel and J & A USA's registered agent.[4] In asserting that service of process on Kelm was sufficient to effect service on defendant, plaintiff relies on Virginia Code § 13.1-758, which states, in pertinent part, that "[s]uits, actions and proceedings may be begun against a foreign corporation that transacts business in this Commonwealth without a certificate of authority by serving process on any director, officer or agent of the corporation . . . ."[5] It is undisputed that Kelm was not designated as defendant's agent for receipt of service of process, but this is not dispositive, as an agent's authority to

---

[3] Rule 4(f), Fed.R.Civ.P., states that service upon an individual or corporation outside the United States may be effected "by any internationally agreed means reasonably calculated to give notice, such as those authorized by the Hague Convention on the Service Abroad of Judicial and Extrajudicial Documents." Generally, the Hague Convention, to which Germany is a signatory, requires that a plaintiff serve the complaint and accompanying documents on a designated "central authority" in the defendant's country and translate the complaint and accompanying documents into the defendant's language. To accomplish this, a litigant should obtain a Request for Service Form, currently Form USM-94, from the United States Marshal's Service. The completed request form and the documents to be served, along with the accompanying translations must then be mailed to the appropriate central authority with a designation of the method of service to be used. The address of any signatory country's central authority can be obtained from the State Department. . . .

The Hague Convention also allows for the direct transmission of judicial documents to persons abroad, provided that the state of destination does not object to service by mail. Germany, however, has expressly objected to service by mail, and requires that service be effected on the central authority. . . .

[4] Were Kelm or J & A USA suitable entities to receive service of process for defendant, the Hague Convention would not apply, as it is applicable only where papers must be sent abroad to effect service.

[5] Also applicable is Virginia Code § 8.01-301, which states that process may be served on a foreign corporation transacting business in Virginia without authorization "by personal service on any agent of [the] foreign corporation . . . ."

accept service may be implied in fact. Accordingly, plaintiff relies on Kelm's role as defendant's counsel as establishing the requisite agency relationship. This reliance is misplaced, however, as numerous federal courts have held that "[t]he mere relationship between a defendant and his attorney does not, in itself, convey authority to accept service" [citations omitted]. Rather, the party seeking to establish the agency relationship must show "that the attorney exercised authority beyond the attorney-client relationship, including the power to accept service" [citations omitted]. Indeed, even where an attorney has broad power to represent a client, "these powers of representation alone do not create a specific authority to receive service" [citations omitted]. Plaintiff here has presented no evidence to establish that defendant either explicitly or implicitly authorized Kelm to accept service of process in this action, or that Kelm ever represented to anyone that he had such authority. Without such evidence, Kelm cannot be defendant's agent for the purposes of receiving service of process merely by virtue of the fact that he is defendant's attorney. Indeed, were that the rule, a foreign party would never hire a lawyer to challenge the sufficiency of service of process because otherwise the party seeking service could simply serve the lawyer. Such a result would be contrary to both law and common sense. Thus, service on Kelm was insufficient to effect service on defendant.

Nor was service on Kelm, as the registered agent of J & A USA, defendant's wholly-owned subsidiary, sufficient to effect service on defendant. It is clear, under Virginia law, that service of process on a foreign defendant's wholly-owned subsidiary is not sufficient to effect service on the foreign parent so long as the parent and the subsidiary maintain separate corporate identities.[6] Plaintiff has presented no evidence to indicate that J & A USA is not a separate and distinct entity from defendant, its parent. To the contrary, the evidence shows that J & A USA has maintained separate and independent offices, financial records, ledgers, bank accounts, and filed separate tax returns. Moreover, J & A USA has filed the requisite corporate records, including Articles of Incorporation and a 1999 annual report, with the Virginia State Corporation Commission. These facts preclude a finding, on this record, that J & A USA has failed to maintain a corporate identity separate from defendant, its parent corporation, and consequently service on J & A USA cannot be substituted for service of process on defendant.

In conclusion, on this record, it is clear that both of plaintiff's attempts to serve process on defendant have been insufficient.

---

[6] Other jurisdictions have different rules. For example, in *Volkswagenwerk Aktiengesellschaft v. Schlunk*, the Supreme Court held that the Hague Convention did not apply to service of process in that case because service was complete when plaintiff served Volkswagen's domestic subsidiary pursuant to an Illinois statute which provided that service on a domestic subsidiary was equivalent to service on the parent corporation. Virginia, however, has no such statute allowing for substituted service on a foreign corporation's domestic subsidiary.

[d]   The Proper Remedy for Violating the Convention

RHODES v. J.P. SAUER & SOHN, INC., SIG ARMS, INC.
98 F. Supp. 2d 746 (W.D. La. 2000)

Plaintiffs Charles A. Rhodes, Jr. and Judy Valentine Rhodes filed a petition for damages under the Louisiana Products Liability Act, [alleging] that Charles Rhodes was injured when a gun manufactured by the defendants malfunctioned and discharged. The defendants timely removed to this court based on diversity of citizenship jurisdiction. . . . Sauer filed this motion, claiming that it had not been served properly. Sauer is organized under the laws of the Federal Republic of Germany, and has its principal place of business in Eckernford, Germany. Plaintiffs attempted to serve a copy of their petition for damages on Sauer via Federal Express, without German translations. Sauer contends that this method of service failed to comport with the requirements of Rule 4(f)(1) of the Federal Rules of Civil Procedure. Sauer therefore asks that we dismiss the plaintiffs' suit against it based on improper service of process.

Pursuant to Rule 12(b)(5), upon motion of the defendant, this court may dismiss an action for insufficiency of process. In order to achieve proper service for purposes of Rules 12(b)(5), a party must follow the requirements of Rule 4 of the Federal Rules of Civil Procedure. Rule 4(f) of the Federal Rules of Civil Procedure governs service on individuals in a foreign country. Service on a corporation of a foreign country that has not waived proper service may be effected "by any internationally agreed means reasonably calculated to give notice, such as those means authorized by the Hague Convention on the Service Abroad if Judicial and Extrajudicial Documents." Fed.R.Civ.P. 4(f)(1). . . . If the Hague Convention is applicable, its provisions preempt inconsistent methods of service prescribed by state law.

Pursuant to Article 21 of the Hague Convention, each signatory nation may retain or reject certain general provisions and enact specific requirements for valid service within that country. Articles 2 and 3 of the Hague Convention require signatory countries to designate a Central Authority to receive requests for service, and require that a request for service of judicial documents and the documents to be served be forwarded to the Central Authority. Although Article 10 of the Hague Convention contemplates service by mail, Germany has specifically rejected the validity of this mode of service. Article 5 allows the signatory State to require that the document to be served be translated into the official language of the State. Germany is one of the countries that has such a requirement.

Sauer contends that the service attempted here did not comport with the requirements of the Hague Convention in that the plaintiffs failed to (1) use and serve the necessary forms promulgated by the Hague Convention; (2) properly transmit the papers to the appropriate Central Authority; (3) translate the citation and petition into German; and (4) obtain service of the papers by the Central Authority. Plaintiffs concede that they did not translate the summons into German . . . . Further, in their opposition to Sauer's motion to dismiss, they do not refute Sauer's assertion that they failed to transmit properly their complaint to the appropriate Central Authority in Germany or obtain service through the designated Central Authority.

Foreign defendants are permitted to "insist on service pursuant to the Hague Convention." *Sheets v. Yamaha*, 891 F.2d 533, 536 (5th Cir. 1990). Since the plaintiffs did not comply with the service and translation requirements of the Hague Convention as adopted by the Federal Republic of Germany, they failed to effectuate valid service on Sauer under Rule 4(f)(1). The plaintiffs argue, however, that this court has jurisdiction over Sauer because they properly served Sig Arms, Inc. ("Sig"), Sauer's domestic subsidiary, and Louisiana law allows service of process on a foreign corporation by serving its domestic subsidiary.

The plaintiffs cite *Schlunk* for the proposition that a plaintiff may serve a corporation in a foreign country by serving its domestic subsidiary. . . . The plaintiffs have failed to note a key distinction between their case and the circumstances presented in *Schlunk*. The plaintiff in Schlunk did not attempt to transmit documents abroad, but instead served VwoA as the agent of VWAG. Where the plaintiff actually attempts to send the pleadings to a corporation in a foreign nation, however, the plaintiff does become responsible for serving process under the mandates of the Hague Convention. In *Sheets*, the plaintiff brought suit against Yamaha Motor Corporation, U.S.A. (Yamaha U.S.A.) and Yamaha Motor Company, Ltd. (Yamaha Japan). Plaintiff attempted to serve process on Yamaha Japan pursuant to the Louisiana long-arm statute. Yamaha Japan then attempted to quash service for failure to comply with the Hague Convention. In determining that the plaintiff had not made proper service on Yamaha Japan, the court pointed out that, even if the Louisiana long-arm statute permits service on a foreign corporation by serving its domestic subsidiary, the plaintiff had never served Yamaha U.S.A. as agent for its parent, Yamaha Japan. Instead, the plaintiff had attempted to mail a copy of the pleadings directly to Yamaha Japan. The court noted that the plaintiff's transmittal of documents to Japan had triggered the application of Hague Convention procedures.

Sheets is instructive here. In this case, there is no indication that the plaintiffs served Sig as the agent of Sauer.[1] In fact, regardless of whether Sig

---

[1] Further, we reject plaintiffs' argument that Sig is the domestic subsidiary of Sauer. In *Green v. Champion*, 577 So.2d 249, 257–58 (La. Ct. App. 1st Cir. 1991), the court laid forth non-dispositive factors that indicate whether two companies are really just one single business enterprise. They include: common stock ownership; common directors or officers; unified administrative control; common financing; inadequate capitalization; corporation paying the salaries and other expenses or losses of another corporation; receiving no business other than that given to it by its affiliated corporations; corporation using the property of another corporation as its own; noncompliance with corporate formalities; common employees; services rendered by the employees of one corporation on behalf of another corporation; common offices; centralized accounting; undocumented transfers of funds between corporations; unclear allocation of profits and losses between corporations; and excessive fragmentation of a single enterprise into separate corporations. The affidavit of Hermann Kleutzer, Executive Vice President of Sig Arms, Inc, makes clear that Sig and Sauer do not own corporate stock in each other. Sig and Sauer do not share expenses, profits, losses, office facilities, bookkeeping, equipment, or other property. These considerations lead us to the conclusion that Sig and Sauer are separate corporate entities. Service on Sig thus would not effectuate proper service on Sauer, regardless of whether the Rhodes had served Sig as the agent for Sauer.

is the domestic subsidiary of Sauer, it is evident that the plaintiffs attempted to serve pleadings on Sauer by mailing the documents directly to Sauer in Germany. This transmittal of documents invokes the Hague Convention and requires strict compliance with its mandates. Accordingly, having found that plaintiffs failed to serve Sauer in accordance with the Hague Convention and having found that service of process on Sig was not valid service on Sauer, the court concludes that plaintiffs have not properly served Sauer in this case.

B. Motion to Dismiss Pursuant to Rule 12(b)(5)

Sauer asks this court to dismiss plaintiffs' case against them for improper service of process. The "general rule" is that " 'when a court finds that service is insufficient but curable, it generally should quash the service and give the plaintiff an opportunity to re-serve the defendant.' " *Gregory v. United States Bankruptcy Court*, 942 F.2d 1498, 1500 (10th Cir. 1991). At the same time, dismissal without opportunity to cure is appropriate where proper service would be futile. Proper service would be futile, for instance, where this court would not have personal jurisdiction over the defendant.

The Louisiana long-arm statute permits the exercise of jurisdiction over a nonresident defendant as far as is permitted by due process. Our inquiry, therefore, is whether the exercise of personal jurisdiction over a nonresident defendant comports with federal constitutional requirements. The Supreme Court has held that due process is satisfied when the defendant (1) has purposefully availed himself of the benefits and protections of the forum state by establishing "minimum contacts" with the forum state such that he could anticipate being haled into that state's courts and (2) the exercise of jurisdiction does not offend traditional notions of fair play and substantial justice.

In their petition for damages, plaintiffs assert that Sauer is authorized and is currently conducting business in Louisiana. This is sufficient to establish minimum contacts with Louisiana. We conclude that, should service be executed properly, this court would have personal jurisdiction over Sauer. Given that there is no indication that service on Sauer would be futile, the court determines that dismissal of plaintiffs' case against Sauer is inappropriate.

---

[e]   Service in Countries that Are Not Parties to the Hague Convention

TINICUM PROPERTIES ASSOCIATES v. GARNETT
1992 U.S. Dist. LEXIS 6564 (E.D. Pa. 1992)

The plaintiff has moved pursuant to Federal Rule Civil Procedure 4(i)(1)(E)[1] for an order specifying a special service of process upon the

---

[1] [Editor's Note: For the current version of the applicable rule, *see* p. [261], *supra*. Although the *Tinicum* court's analysis was bounded by a now-superceded rule, its approach to service in countries that are not parties to the Hague Convention remains illustrative.]

defendant. The defendant does not reside in the United States. Currently, the defendant resides in Saudi Arabia. Plaintiff instituted this action as a result of defendant's indebtedness under a personal guarantee of a lease agreement, entered into in the Commonwealth of Pennsylvania. Saudi Arabia is not a signatory of the Hague Convention on Service of Process. The plaintiff has tried to serve the defendant by mailing a copy of the complaint and summons to the plaintiff's address in Saudi Arabia. No acknowledgment of service was received. The plaintiff served a copy on an attorney who had represented the defendant in non-related litigation. That attorney refused service as he was not authorized by the defendant to accept on the defendant's behalf. The plaintiff attempted without success to have the United States Embassy and the defendant's employer assist in service.

Federal Rule of Civil Procedure 4(i) allows alternate provisions for service of process in a foreign country.

The rule states as follows:

> (1) Manner. When the federal or state law referred to in subdivision (e) of this rule authorizes service upon a party not an inhabitant of or found within the state in which the district court is held, and service is to be effected upon the party in a foreign country, it is also sufficient if service of the summons and complaint is made: (A) in the manner prescribed by the law of the foreign country for service in that country in an action in any of its courts of general jurisdiction; or (B) as directed by the foreign authority in response to a letter rogatory, when service in either case is reasonably calculated to give actual notice; or (c) upon an individual, by delivery to the individual personally . . .; or (D) by any form of mail, requiring a signed receipt, to be addressed and dispatched by the clerk of the court to the party to be served; or (E) as directed by order of the court.

Pennsylvania law permits the exercise of personal jurisdiction over a defendant who entered into a contract in Pennsylvania.

The plaintiff is given five service options under Rule 4(i)(1). The plaintiff has chosen to use 4(i)(1)(E), which allows the Court to fashion an alternative form of service. Because Saudi Arabia is not a signatory to the Hague Convention, mail service under Rule 4(i)(1)(D) would be appropriate. However, service under 4(i)(1)(D) requires the clerk of the court to mail the summons and complaint which is something the plaintiff, for whatever reason, has chosen not to request. *Lampe v. Xouth, Inc.*, 952 F.2d 697, 702 (3d Cir. 1991) (clerk of court must mail summons and complaint under 4(i)(1)(D)). The service options in 4(i)(1)(A) & (B) require the plaintiff to use the service methods of Saudi Arabia or request a letter rogatory issue. Neither option has been chosen. Rule 4(i)(1)(C) permits personal service upon the individual. According to correspondence received from the plaintiff, the plaintiff has, to date, been unable to contact a Saudi Arabian attorney or process server willing to serve the defendant. The plaintiff has, therefore, requested the Court to fashion a method of service which will comply with due process and the federal rules.

The Court is permitted under Rule 4(i)(1)(E) to tailor the method of service to the necessities of the case, but due process requires that the Court fashion a method reasonably calculated to give actual notice and afford an adequate opportunity to be heard. *Avianca, Inc. v. Corriea*, 705 F.Supp. 666, 684 (D.D.C. 1989). The *Avianca* court noted that several courts have permitted service by registered mail where the defendant has been able to evade conventional service methods. *See International Controls Corp. v. Vesco*, 593 F.2d 166, 175 (2d Cir. 1979) (allowed service by regular mail where bodyguard at residence prevented personal service); *Levin v. Ruby Trading Corp.*, 248 F. Supp. 537, 541 (S.D.N.Y. 1965) (service by mail to defendant and two of his attorneys sufficient); *New England Merchants Nat'l Bank v. Iran*, 508 F. Supp. 49, 52 (S.D.N.Y. 1980) (substituted service by telex permitted). The provisions of Rule 4(i)(1)(D) authorizing service by mail from the clerk does not prohibit any other form of mail service.

The Court also notes that the defendant was aware that an action was to be filed by his letter to plaintiff's attorney. Although that letter predates the attempted service on the defendant, it demonstrates that he has at least some knowledge of the pendency of this action. The Court orders service to be made pursuant to Fed.R.Civ.P. 4(i)(1)(E) in the following manner:

1. A copy of the Summons and Complaint shall be sent by regular mail and certified mail, return receipt requested, to the defendant at the following addresses:
(a) Mr. William Garnett
c/o RAYMES, Raytheon Middle East Service
11 Chestnut Street
Andover, MA 01810
(b) Mr. William Garnett
Raytheon Middle East Services
Kaheel Al-Azdey Street
Jeddah, 21431, Saudi Arabia
(c) Mr. William Garnett
915 Lovering Avenue
Wilmington, DE 19086

2. Although the Court makes no finding that Raymond Radulski, Esq., is currently the defendant's attorney or is authorized in any way to receive service, the Court will also require a copy of the Summons and Complaint to be delivered by regular and certified mail to Raymond Radulski, Esq., solely for the purpose of providing another means of actual notice to the defendant. Therefore, a copy of the Summons and Complaint will be delivered by regular and certified mail to Raymond Radulski, Esq., 712 West Street, Wilmington, DE 19801.

3. A copy of this Memorandum and Order shall accompany each mailing.

The Court finds that these provisions will insure that the defendant receives notice. The mailings are to be addressed to current and recent past address of the defendant.

B. OBTAINING EVIDENCE ARBOAD

A distinguishing (and often resented) characteristic of civil litigation in the United States is that the litigants themselves are supposed to have nearly unlimited access to all information that might be relevant in the case. Rule 26(b) of the Federal Rules of Civil Procedure gives the parties to a civil action broad authority to "obtain discovery regarding any matter, not privileged, which is relevant to the subject matter involved in the pending action." The sheer scope of this authority is confirmed by the fact that "[t]he information sought need not be admissible at the trial if the information sought appears reasonably calculated to lead to the discovery of admissible evidence." *Id.* Without prior judicial approval, the litigants may seek this information out through a variety of techniques, the most common being: depositions upon oral examination, Rules 28, 30, and 32; requests for production of documents, Rules 34 and 35; written interrogatories to parties, Rule 33; and requests for admissions Rule 36. Non-parties may also be compelled to produce evidence, and if they are unwilling to cooperate, the court may issue a subpoena requiring the non-party witness to testify at oral deposition and to produce documents. The state rules of civil procedure tend to be similar to these federal provisions.

The parties' discovery powers in U.S. litigation, combined with the power of the court under Rule 37 to impose sanctions for non-compliance, offer a fertile breeding ground for international conflict, especially with those legal systems in which pre-trial discovery and the gathering of evidence is an exclusively judicial function. The expansive "pretrial procedure presently permitted by many American courts is so completely alien to the procedure in most other jurisdictions that an attitude of suspicion and hostility is created, which sometimes causes discovery which would be considered proper, even narrow, in this country to be regarded as a fishing expedition elsewhere."[1] In response to what they perceive as unilateral, extraterritorial, invasive, and privatized discovery — all in violation of their sovereign prerogative — some countries have adopted *blocking statutes* or *non-disclosure statutes*, which specifically prohibit compliance with U.S. discovery orders for the production of evidence located within the foreign state's territory. As shown in the first case excerpted below, secrecy laws governing key industries like banking or transportation or energy can have a similar effect.

In high-profile litigation, especially in antitrust and securities regulation cases where massive transnational discovery is routine, discovery requests and orders can provoke formal protests. A famous and characteristic example arose out of a case in which U.S. courts ordered discovery of sensitive information located in Canada (and elsewhere) pertaining to the monopolization of the market for uranium. According to a diplomatic note submitted by the Secretary of State for External Affairs of Canada to the Ambassador of the United States:

> A situation in which courts of the United States imposed sanctions
> for failure to produce documents or information located in Canada
> where such production would violate Canadian laws and regulations

---

[1] Carter, *Existing Rules and Procedures*, 13 INT'L LAW. 5 (1979).

> would be a matter of serious concern to the Government of Canada
> because it would subordinate to the procedures of U.S. courts the
> authority of the Government of Canada to prohibit the disclosure of
> certain information in Canada relating to the production and market-
> ing of Canadian uranium. Such a failure on the part of courts in the
> United States to recognize the authority of the Canadian government
> to prohibit such disclosure would be contrary to generally accepted
> principles of international law and would have an adverse impact on
> relations between the U.S.A. and Canada. . . . The Government of
> Canada wishes to state its serious objection to the imposition of any
> sanction by the judicial branch of the United States Government for
> failing to produce documents or to disclose information located in Can-
> ada where such production or disclosure would require a person or
> corporation in Canada to perform an act or omission in Canada which
> is prohibited by the Uranium Information Security Regulations or any
> other law of Canada.

17 CANAD. Y.B. INT'L L. 334 (1979). The court's resolution of the discovery
dispute, *In re Uranium Antitrust Litigation*, has become a standard touchstone
in similar cases and is excerpted below.

In an effort to prevent or manage these potential conflicts, many countries
— including the United States and most Western European nations — have
become parties to the Hague Convention on the Taking of Evidence Abroad
in Civil or Commercial Matters ("Hague Evidence Convention"), which, like
the Hague Service Convention, obliges parties to designate a "Central Authority" to provide *judicial assistance* in the completion of official acts. Specifically,
the Central Authority will process *letters of request* that it receives from other
parties to the Convention by transmitting them to the appropriate local court
or agency for action, and the evidence produced is then returned to the
requesting court. The Hague Evidence Convention builds on a long-standing
practice in which *letters rogatory* were used to request some particular act
of judicial assistance in the territory of another state. When the Hague
Evidence Convention is inapplicable, courts with transnational cases may
attempt to apply the discovery provisions of the Federal Rules of Civil
Procedure as though the case did not cross borders, or they may revert to the
somewhat *ad hoc* technique of issuing letters rogatory. Each of these alternatives is explored in this chapter.

At this initial stage, we need only appreciate that domestic courts with
transnational discovery disputes face the unenviable task of reconciling what
may appear to be irreconcilable interests, none of which is trivial: respect for
foreign law and international treaties; awareness of the diplomatic prerogatives of the executive branch; and adherence to the law of the United States,
with its preference for party-directed discovery, not to mention the court's
interest in having its own orders respected to the letter.

Not surprisingly, when the rules must accommodate interests this various
and antagonistic, the result in a case can turn on fine gradations of fact. As
you read through the following provisions of the Restatement, and the cases
on which they are based, consider which facts seem to make a difference in
the result. Consider in particular the type of evidence sought and its importance to the litigation, the precise requirements of the foreign law and the

form, civil or penal, that its sanctions take, the discovery technique at issue (*e.g.*, depositions versus production of documents), the type of sanction to be imposed in the United States for non-compliance, the balance of hardships to the parties, and whether the entity resisting discovery is a party (or is related to or controlled by a party) or not.

---

[1] The Risk of Controversy

RESTATEMENT (THIRD) FOREIGN RELATIONS LAW OF THE UNITED STATES

§ 442. Requests for Disclosure: Law of the United States

(1) (a) A court or agency in the United States, when authorized by statute or rule of court, may order a person subject to its jurisdiction to produce documents, objects, or other information relevant to an action or investigation, even if the information or the person in possession of the information is outside the United States.

(b) Failure to comply with an order to produce information may subject the person to whom the order is directed to sanctions, including finding of contempt, dismissal of a claim or defense, or default judgment, or may lead to a determination that the facts to which the order was addressed are as asserted by the opposing party.

(c) In deciding whether to issue an order directing production of information located abroad, and in framing such an order, a court or agency in the United States should take into account the importance to the investigation or litigation of the documents or other information requested; the degree of specificity of the request; whether the information originated in the United States; the availability of alternative means of securing the information; and the extent to which noncompliance with the request would undermine important interests of the United States, or compliance with the request would undermine important interests of the state where the information is located.

(2) If disclosure of information located outside the United States is prohibited by a law, regulation, or order of a court or other authority of the state in which the information or prospective witness is located, or of the state of which a prospective witness is a national,

(a) a court or agency in the United States may require the person to whom the order is directed to make a good faith effort to secure permission from the foreign authorities to make the information available;

(b) a court or agency should not ordinarily impose sanctions of contempt, dismissal, or default on a party that has failed to comply with the order for production, except in cases of deliberate concealment or removal of information or of failure to make a good faith effort in accordance with paragraph (a);

(c) a court or agency may, in appropriate cases, make findings of fact adverse to a party that has failed to comply with the order for production, even if that party has made a good faith effort to secure permission from the foreign authorities to make the information available and that effort has been unsuccessful.

§ 473. Obtaining Evidence in Foreign State

(1) Under international law, a state may determine the conditions for taking evidence in its territory in aid of litigation in another state, but the state of the forum may determine its admissibility, probative value, and effect. . . .

(2) Under the Hague Evidence Convention,

(a) each contracting state is required to designate a Central Authority to which letters of request for assistance in obtaining evidence for use in civil or commercial litigation may be addressed by courts of other contracting states, and the Central Authority must direct that any letter of request meeting the requirements of the Convention be executed expeditiously, in accordance with the procedures, including measures of compulsion, for obtaining evidence for use in the requested state's courts;

(b) a contracting state may determine the conditions for taking evidence in its territory, without compulsion, by diplomatic or consular officers, or by commissioners designated by a court in another contracting state, for use in civil or commercial litigation pending in that state.

(3) A person required or requested to give evidence for use in a foreign state, whether pursuant to the Hague Evidence Convention or through other arrangements for judicial assistance, may refuse to do so insofar as he has a privilege or a duty of nondisclosure under either the law of the state of origin of the request or of the state in which the evidence is sought.

§ 474 Obtaining Evidence in or for use in Foreign State: Law of the United States

(1) United States district court may execute a letter rogatory issued by a foreign tribunal by ordering a person residing or found in the district to give testimony or to produce a document or other thing for use in a proceeding in the foreign tribunal.

(2) A United States district court, in order to obtain evidence for use in a proceeding before it, may

(a) issue a commission to a United States consul, or to any other person not related to the parties or their attorneys, to take testimony in a foreign state;

(b) issue a letter rogatory requesting a court or other appropriate authority in a foreign state to direct the taking of evidence in that state; or

(c) issue a subpoena ordering a national or resident of the United States in a foreign state to give evidence as directed by the court,

provided the procedure is not inconsistent with the law of the state where the evidence is to be taken.

These provisions of the Restatement (Third) encapsulate statutory, decisional, and international law, as the following materials demonstrate.

SELECTED PROVISIONS FROM U.S. CODE, TITLE 28

§ 1781. Transmittal of letter rogatory or request

(a) The Department of State has power, directly, or through suitable channels—

(1) to receive a letter rogatory issued, or request made, by a foreign or international tribunal, to transmit it to the tribunal, officer, or agency in the United States to whom it is addressed, and to receive and return it after execution; and

(2) to receive a letter rogatory issued, or request made, by a tribunal in the United States, to transmit it to the foreign or international tribunal, officer, or agency to whom it is addressed, and to receive and return it after execution.

(b) This section does not preclude—

(1) the transmittal of a letter rogatory or request directly from a foreign or international tribunal to the tribunal, officer, or agency in the United States to whom it is addressed and its return in the same manner; or

(2) the transmittal of a letter rogatory or request directly from a tribunal in the United States to the foreign or international tribunal, officer, or agency to whom it is addressed and its return in the same manner.

§ 1782. Assistance to foreign and international tribunals and to litigants before such tribunals

(a) The district court of the district in which a person resides or is found may order him to give his testimony or statement or to produce a document or other thing for use in a proceeding in a foreign or international tribunal, including criminal investigations conducted before formal accusation. The order may be made pursuant to a letter rogatory issued, or request made, by a foreign or international tribunal or upon the application of any interested person and may direct that the testimony or statement be given, or the document or other thing be produced, before a person appointed by the court. By virtue of his appointment, the person appointed has power to administer any necessary oath and take the testimony or statement. The order may prescribe the practice and procedure, which may be in whole or part the practice and procedure of the foreign country or the international tribunal, for taking the testimony or statement or producing the document or other thing. To the extent that the order does not prescribe otherwise, the testimony or statement shall be taken, and the document or other thing produced, in accordance with the Federal Rules of Civil Procedure.

A person may not be compelled to give his testimony or statement or to produce a document or other thing in violation of any legally applicable privilege.

(b) This chapter does not preclude a person within the United States from voluntarily giving his testimony or statement, or producing a document or other thing, for use in a proceeding in a foreign or international tribunal before any person and in any manner acceptable to him.

§ 1783. Subpoena of person in foreign country

(a) A court of the United States may order the issuance of a subpoena requiring the appearance as a witness before it, or before a person or body designated by it, of a national or resident of the United States who is in a foreign country, or requiring the production of a specified document or other thing by him, if the court finds that particular testimony or the production of the document or other thing by him is necessary in the interest of justice, and, in other than a criminal action or proceeding, if the court finds, in addition, that it is not possible to obtain his testimony in admissible form without his personal appearance or to obtain the production of the document or other thing in any other manner.

(b) The subpoena shall designate the time and place for the appearance or for the production of the document or other thing. Service of the subpoena and any order to show cause, rule, judgment, or decree authorized by this section or by section 1784 of this title shall be effected in accordance with the provisions of the Federal Rules of Civil Procedure relating to service of process on a person in a foreign country. The person serving the subpoena shall tender to the person to whom the subpoena is addressed his estimated necessary travel and attendance expenses, the amount of which shall be determined by the court and stated in the order directing the issuance of the subpoena.

§ 1784. Contempt

(a) The court of the United States which has issued a subpoena served in a foreign country may order the person who has failed to appear or who has failed to produce a document or other thing as directed therein to show cause before it at a designated time why he should not be punished for contempt.

(b) The court, in the order to show cause, may direct that any of the person's property within the United States be levied upon or seized, in the manner provided by law or court rules governing levy or seizure under execution, and held to satisfy any judgment that may be rendered against him pursuant to subsection (d) of this section if adequate security, in such amount as the court may direct in the order, be given for any damage that he might suffer should he not be found in contempt. Security under this subsection may not be required of the United States.

(c) A copy of the order to show cause shall be served on the person in accordance with section 1783(b) of this title.

(d) On the return day of the order to show cause or any later day to which the hearing may be continued, proof shall be taken. If the person is found in contempt, the court, notwithstanding any limitation upon its power generally to punish for contempt, may fine him not more than $100,000 and direct that the fine and costs of the proceedings be satisfied by a sale of the property levied upon or seized, conducted upon the notice required and in the manner provided for sales upon execution.

SOCIETE INTERNATIONALE S. A. v. ROGERS
357 U.S. 197 (1958)

MR. JUSTICE HARLAN delivered the opinion of the Court.

[Section 5 (b) of the Trading with the Enemy Act, 50 U.S.C.A. App. § 5(b), authorizes the United States during a period of war or national emergency to seize "any property or interest of any foreign country or national." Section 9(b) of the Act authorizes recovery of seized assets by "any person not an enemy or ally of enemy" to the extent of such person's interest in the assets. This litigation began in 1948 when Societe Internationale, a Swiss holding company also known as Interhandel, sought to recover assets which had been seized by the Alien Property Custodian during World War II, because they had been found to be "owned by or held for the benefit of" I. G. Farbenindustrie, a German firm and an enemy national within the meaning of the Act. These assets, valued at more than $100,000,000, consisted of cash in American banks and approximately 90% of the capital stock of General Aniline & Film Corporation, a Delaware corporation ("GAF"). Interhandel argued that it had owned the GAF stock and cash at the time of vesting and hence, as the national of a neutral power, was entitled to recovery.

The Government disputed Interhandel's claim of ownership and asserted that it was in any event an "enemy" since it was intimately connected with I. G. Farben and hence was affected with "enemy taint" despite its "neutral" incorporation. More particularly, the Government alleged that from the time of its incorporation in 1928, petitioner had conspired with I. G. Farben, H. Sturzenegger & Cie, a Swiss banking firm, and others "to conceal, camouflage and cloak the ownership, control and domination by I. G. Farben of properties and interests located in countries, including the United States, other than

Germany, in order to avoid seizure and confiscation in the event of war between such countries and Germany."

Because the ownership of Interhandel was so central an issue, the government moved under Rule 34 of the Federal Rules of Civil Procedure for an order requiring petitioner to make available for inspection and copying a large number of the banking records of Sturzenegger & Cie. Rule 34, in conjunction with Rule 26(b), provides that upon a motion "showing good cause therefore," a court may order a party to produce for inspection nonprivileged documents relevant to the subject matter of pending litigation "which are in his possession, custody, or control." In support of its motion the Government alleged that the records sought were relevant to showing the true ownership of the GAF stock and that they were within petitioner's control because petitioner and Sturzenegger were substantially identical. The district court found that Sturzenegger's papers were in Interhandel's control within the meaning of Rule 34 and granted the government's motion.

Thereafter the Swiss Federal Attorney in effect confiscated the Sturzenegger records, leaving them in Sturzenegger's hands but stopping their production in the U.S. The Federal Attorney had exercised his authority pursuant to certain provisions of Swiss law:

> Article 273, Swiss Penal Code: Economic intelligence service in the interest of foreign countries: Whoever elicits a manufacturing or business secret in order to make it accessible to a foreign official, agency or to a foreign organization or private enterprise or to agents of the same, [and] whoever makes accessible a manufacturing or business secret to a foreign official agency, or to a foreign organization or private enterprise or to agents of the same, shall be punished by imprisonment and in serious cases by penitentiary. In addition to that penalty, a fine may be imposed.

> Article 47, Swiss Banking Law of 1934: Any person who wilfully . . . (b) in his capacity as organ, officer or employee of a bank, as auditor or assistant auditor, as member of the Banking Commission, officer or employee of its secretarial office, violates his duty to observe silence or the professional secrecy, or whoever induces or attempts to induce a person to commit such an offense, shall be fined not more than twenty thousand francs, and/or shall be imprisoned for not longer than six months. If the offender acted negligently, the penalty is a fine of not more than ten thousand francs.

There followed protracted maneuvers involving repeated motions for relief by Interhandel, repeated extensions of the deadline for compliance, the procurement of waivers from many of Sturzenegger's clients, and the production of nearly 200,000 documents. Some documents, notably the bank's books of account, were never produced, but Interhandel ultimately offered a plan — approved by the Swiss government — under which a neutral expert would examine the files and identify documents he deemed relevant, which

Interhandel could then seek to produce. The district court rejected the plan and, on motion by the government, dismissed Interhandel's recovery action.[1]

Interhandel had resisted the court's production order on the ground that disclosure of the bank records would violate Swiss penal laws and therefore might lead to criminal sanctions, including fine and imprisonment. The district court found that Interhandel had acted in good faith in trying to comply with the discovery order, but still dismissed its recovery action for noncompliance. The Court of Appeals affirmed, but observed: "That [petitioner] and its counsel patiently and diligently sought to achieve compliance . . . is not to be doubted." The Supreme Court granted certioriari.

In its opinion, the Supreme Court first sustained the propriety of the original production order under Rule 34 on the ground that the documents in question were still in petitioner's "control," even with the Swiss government's prohibition order. The Court then considered the propriety of dismissing Interhandel's recovery action for noncompliance with the discovery order. The Court declared: "Whatever its reasons, petitioner did not comply with the production order. Such reasons, and the willfulness or good faith of petitioner, can hardly affect the fact of noncompliance and are relevant only to the path which the District Court might follow in dealing with petitioner's failure to comply," it concluded that Interhandel's noncompliance constituted a refusal to obey within the meaning of Rule 37, even though Interhandel had not wilfully refused but had been prevented by intervening state authority from doing so. It then considered whether the sanction of dismissal, though within the terms of Rule 37, was excessive.]

We must discard at the outset the strongly urged contention of the Government that dismissal of this action was justified because petitioner conspired with I. G. Farben, Sturzenegger & Cie, and others to transfer ownership of General Aniline to it prior to 1941 so that seizure would be avoided and advantage taken of Swiss secrecy laws. In other words, the Government suggests that petitioner stands in the position of one who deliberately courted legal impediments to production of the Sturzenegger records, and who thus cannot now be heard to assert its good faith after this expectation was realized. Certainly these contentions, if supported by the facts, would have a vital bearing on justification for dismissal of the action, but they are not open to the Government here. The findings below reach no such conclusions; indeed, it is not even apparent from them whether this particular charge was ever passed upon below. Although we do not mean to preclude the Government from seeking to establish such facts before the District Court upon remand, or any other facts relevant to justification for dismissal of the complaint, we

---

[1] Rule 37 described the consequences of a refusal to make discovery. Subsection (b), which is entitled "Failure to Comply With Order," provides in pertinent part:

> Rule 37(b)(2). Failure to Comply with Order. . . . If any party . . . refuses to obey . . . an order made under Rule 34 to produce any document or other thing for inspection . . ., the court may make such orders in regard to the refusal as are just, and among others the following: (iii) An order striking out pleadings or parts thereof . . ., or dismissing the action or proceeding or any part thereof . . . .

Rule 41 (b) is concerned with involuntary dismissals and reads in part: "For failure of the plaintiff to prosecute or to comply with these rules or any order of court, a defendant may move for dismissal of an action or of any claim against him."

must dispose of this case on the basis of the findings of good faith . . . adopted by the District Court, and approved by the Court of Appeals. The provisions of Rule 37 which are here involved must be read in light of the provisions of the Fifth Amendment that no person shall be deprived of property without due process of law, and more particularly against the opinions of this Court in *Hovey v. Elliott,* 167 U.S. 409, and *Hammond Packing Co. v. Arkansas,* 212 U.S. 322. These decisions establish that there are constitutional limitations upon the power of courts, even in aid of their own valid processes, to dismiss an action without affording a party the opportunity for a hearing on the merits of his cause. . . .

These two decisions leave open the question whether Fifth Amendment due process is violated by the striking of a complaint because of a plaintiff's inability, despite good-faith efforts, to comply with a pretrial production order. . . . Certainly substantial constitutional questions are provoked by such action. Their gravity is accented in the present case where petitioner, though cast in the role of plaintiff, cannot be deemed to be in the customary role of a party invoking the aid of a court to vindicate rights asserted against another. Rather, petitioner's position is more analogous to that of a defendant, for it belatedly challenges the Government's action by now protesting against a seizure and seeking the recovery of assets which were summarily possessed by the Alien Property Custodian without the opportunity for protest by any party claiming that seizure was unjustified under the Trading with the Enemy Act. Past decisions of this Court emphasize that this summary power to seize property which is believed to be enemy-owned is rescued from constitutional invalidity under the Due Process and Just Compensation Clauses of the Fifth Amendment only by those provisions of the Act which afford a nonenemy claimant a later judicial hearing as to the propriety of the seizure.

The findings below, and what has been shown as to petitioner's extensive efforts at compliance, compel the conclusion on this record that petitioner's failure to satisfy fully the requirements of this production order was due to inability fostered neither by its own conduct nor by circumstances within its control. It is hardly debatable that fear of criminal prosecution constitutes a weighty excuse for nonproduction, and this excuse is not weakened because the laws preventing compliance are those of a foreign sovereign. Of course, this situation should be distinguished from one where a party claims that compliance with a court's order will reveal facts which may provide the basis for criminal prosecution of that party under the penal laws of a foreign sovereign thereby shown to have been violated. Here the findings below establish that the very fact of compliance by disclosure of banking records will itself constitute the initial violation of Swiss laws. In our view, petitioner stands in the position of an American plaintiff subject to criminal sanctions in Switzerland because production of documents in Switzerland pursuant to the order of a United States court might violate Swiss laws. Petitioner has sought no privileges because of its foreign citizenship which are not accorded domestic litigants in United States courts. It does not claim that Swiss laws protecting banking records should here be enforced. It explicitly recognizes that it is subject to procedural rules of United States courts in this litigation and has made full efforts to follow these rules. It asserts no immunity from them. It asserts only its inability to comply because of foreign law.

In view of the findings in this case, the position in which petitioner stands in this litigation, and the serious constitutional questions we have noted, we think that Rule 37 should not be construed to authorize dismissal of this complaint because of petitioner's noncompliance with a pretrial production order when it has been established that failure to comply has been due to inability, and not to willfulness, bad faith, or any fault of petitioner.

This is not to say that petitioner will profit through its inability to tender the records called for. In seeking recovery of the General Aniline stock and other assets, petitioner recognizes that it carries the ultimate burden of proof of showing itself not to be an "enemy" within the meaning of the Trading with the Enemy Act. The Government already has disputed its right to recovery by relying on information obtained through seized records of I. G. Farben, documents obtained through petitioner, and depositions taken of persons affiliated with petitioner. It may be that in a trial on the merits, petitioner's inability to produce specific information will prove a serious handicap in dispelling doubt the Government might be able to inject into the case. It may be that in the absence of complete disclosure by petitioner, the District Court would be justified in drawing inferences unfavorable to petitioner as to particular events. So much indeed petitioner concedes. But these problems go to the adequacy of petitioner's proof and should not on this record preclude petitioner from being able to contest on the merits.

On remand, the District Court possesses wide discretion to proceed in whatever manner it deems most effective. It may desire to afford the Government additional opportunity to challenge petitioner's good faith. It may wish to explore plans looking towards fuller compliance. Or it may decide to commence at once trial on the merits. We decide only that on this record dismissal of the complaint with prejudice was not justified.

The judgment of the Court of Appeals is reversed and the case is remanded to the District Court for further proceedings in conformity with this opinion.

***

Notes and Questions on *Rogers*

1. *The Rogers approach.* The two-step analysis pursued by the court in *Rogers* has been followed — and refined or modified — by a variety of courts since 1958. The court was careful to distinguish between the propriety of the production order and the propriety of the sanction for non-compliance. Can you think of other settings where necessity or compulsion ("just following orders") was no defense but could be considered in mitigation of punishment?

2. *Options on remand.* What sanctions short of dismissal remain open to the court on remand in this case?

3. *Rogers and statutes.* To what extent was the result in the case determined by the policies behind the Trading with the Enemy Act? Can you identify other federal statutes likely to be at issue in civil litigation which might be (a) more and (b) less compelling than the TWEA?

4. *Civil vs. criminal contexts.* Would it have made any difference if the foreign law imposed civil sanctions instead of criminal or penal sanctions? Should it?

In the Matter of Grand Jury Subpoena Duces Tecum
addressed to First National City Bank

UNITED STATES v. FIRST NATIONAL CITY BANK (*"CITIBANK"*)
396 F.2d 897 (2d Cir. 1968)

The issue presented on this appeal is of considerable importance to American banks with branches or offices in foreign jurisdictions. We are called upon to decide whether a domestic bank may refuse to comply with a valid Grand Jury subpoena *duces tecum* requiring the production of documents in the possession of a foreign branch of the bank on the ground that compliance would subject it to civil liability under the law of the foreign state. . . .

On March 7, 1968, First National City Bank of New York [Citibank] was served with a subpoena *duces tecum* in connection with a federal Grand Jury investigation of certain alleged violations of the antitrust laws by several of its customers.[1] The subpoena required the production of documents located in the bank's offices in New York City and Frankfurt, Germany, relating to any transaction . . . for the benefit of its customers C.F. Boehringer & Soehme, G.m.b.H., a German corporation, and Boehringer Mannheim Corporation, a New York corporation [referred to jointly as "Boehringer"].[2] Citibank complied with the subpoena insofar as it called for the production of material located in New York, but failed to produce or divulge any documents reposited in Frankfurt. Indeed, the bank even refused to inquire or determine whether any relevant papers were overseas. Instead, William T. Loveland, Citibank's vice-president responsible for the decision to defy the subpoena, appeared before the Grand Jury and asserted that the bank's action was justified because compliance would subject Citibank to civil liability and economic loss in Germany.

On May 8, 1968, Judge Pollack conducted an initial hearing at which the sole witness was Dr. Martin Domke, an expert in German law. He testified on behalf of Citibank that under the "bank secrecy law" of Germany, a bank — including a foreign bank (such as Citibank) licensed to do business in Germany — cannot divulge information relating to the affairs of its customers even in response to the process of a court of the United States. To do so, he claimed, would amount to a breach of the bank's "self evident" contractual obligation which flows from the business relationship between bank and customer. Domke made it clear that bank secrecy was not part of the statutory law of Germany; rather, it was in the nature of a privilege that could be waived by the customer but not the bank. He insisted that a violation of bank secrecy

---

[1] Citibank is organized under the laws of the United States and has its principal place of business in the Southern District of New York.

[2] Citibank does not contend that records located in its Frankfurt branch are not within the possession, custody, and control of the head office.

could subject the bank to liability in contract or tort but not to criminal sanctions or their equivalent. But, he made it plain, that it was a simple matter for a bank customer to obtain an *ex parte* restraining order enjoining a bank from disclosing privileged material and that a violation of such an injunction would be punished under a general provision of the criminal law governing violations of court orders.[3] As a result of this testimony, the district judge appropriately decided to adjourn this hearing in order to afford an opportunity to Citibank to ascertain whether its customers would obtain such an injunction and which would have the effect of subjecting the bank to criminal penalties if it complied with the subpoena. This did not prove fruitful however, for the very next day, the court was advised by Citibank's counsel that Boehringer did not intend to take advantage of the readily available injunctive procedures under German law. Instead, the judge was told that Boehringer had informed Citibank that it would have to "suffer the consequences" if it obeyed the subpoena. It was suggested that Boehringer would sue the bank for breach of contract and would also use its influence within German industrial circles to cause Citibank to suffer business losses.[4]

In any event, Citibank remained adamant in its refusal to produce the documents located in Frankfurt and on May 21, 1968, a second hearing was held, this time on the government's order to show cause why the bank and Loveland should not be held in civil contempt. Domke testified once again as did a government expert, Dr. Magdalena Schoch. Both witnesses discussed with great particularity the precise nature of German bank secrecy[5] and Citibank's prospective liability under German law if it were sued for disclosing privileged information. Domke made the point that compulsion by an American court would not be accepted as an excuse for violating bank secrecy and that in a civil suit under German law, the court would determine "in its free discretion" the amount of damages, if any. Schoch insisted, however, that Citibank would have a number of valid defenses in the event Boehringer ever sued.[6] Moreover, Schoch's testimony made clear that in a criminal proceeding

---

[3] Section 890 of the German Code of Civil Procedure provides that:

> If the defendant violates his duty to omit an act or to suffer the commission of an act, the Court of first instance, on application of the plaintiff, must punish him, the defendant, for each violation with a fine or with jail up to six months. . . .

Although this section is found in the Code of Civil Procedure the penalties it prescribes are considered criminal sanctions.

[4] Dr. Domke testified that if he were representing Boehringer in Germany, he would advise his client not to seek an injunction enforceable under Section 890, *see* note 3, *supra*, until the court in the United States had decided whether to enforce the subpoena.

[5] In addition, an official of the German Consulate General in New York, introduced a statement from the Bundesbank — the central bank of Germany roughly equivalent to the Federal Reserve Bank — defining the German policy of bank secrecy. This statement was in broad terms, not addressed to the specific facts of the instant litigation, and did not add to or contradict the testimony of either expert witness in any significant way.

[6] Dr. Schoch testified that if Citibank were sued by Boehringer, the bank could plead compulsion by an American court as a complete defense to the action. She indicated that performance of the bank's contract with Boehringer would be excused under German doctrines of impossibility of performance and of requiring only the "good faith" performance of contracts taking into consideration ordinary usage. Similar defenses were said to apply if Citibank were sued in tort. Moreover, Dr. Schoch indicated that Section 25 of Citibank's written contract with Boehringer — which provides that "The bank is not liable for any losses caused by disturbances of its

in Germany bank secrecy does not provide a basis for refusing to obey a court order to provide evidence. [7]

In a reasoned opinion, Judge Pollack concluded that Citibank had failed to present a legally sufficient reason for its failure to comply with the subpoena. He determined that it was manifest that Citibank would not be subject to criminal sanctions or their equivalent under German law, that it had not acted in good faith, [8] and that there was only a "remote and speculative" possibility that it would not have a valid defense if it were sued for civil damages. Accordingly, he adjudged the bank and Loveland to be in civil contempt and fined the bank $2,000 per day for its failure to act; he sentenced Loveland to 60 days' imprisonment. [9] For the reasons stated below, we conclude that Judge Pollack's order was justified and affirm.

The basic legal question confronting us is not a total stranger to this Court. With the growing interdependence of world trade and the increased mobility of persons and companies, the need arises not infrequently, whether related to civil or criminal proceedings, for the production of evidence located in foreign jurisdictions. It is no longer open to doubt that a federal court has the power to require the production of documents located in foreign countries if the court has *in personam* jurisdiction of the person in possession or control of the material. *See, e.g., First National City Bank of New York v. I.R.S.*, 271 F.2d 616 (2d Cir. 1959), *cert. denied*, 361 U.S. 948 (1960). Thus, the task before us, as Citibank concedes, is not one of defining power but of developing rules governing the proper exercise of power. The difficulty arises, of course, when the country in which the documents are located has its own rules and policies dealing with the production and disclosure of business information — a circumstance not uncommon. This problem is particularly acute where the documents are sought by an arm of a foreign government. The complexities of the world being what they are, it is not surprising to discover nations having diametrically opposed positions with respect to the disclosure of a wide range of information. It is not too difficult, therefore, to empathize with the party

---

operations or by domestic or foreign acts of authorities at home or abroad" — would provide another defense to a civil suit since the process of an American court would be considered the act of a "foreign authority." . . . She testified further that Boehringer would have to prove actual damages resulting from the disclosure but could not recover for "loss of face or mental upset." (And, we note that, in any event, any disclosure by Citibank would be made to the Grand Jury whose proceedings are kept secret.) Finally, Schoch gave her opinion that Citibank would have an action for damages against Boehringer under German law if Boehringer made good its threat to cause Citibank to lose business.

[7] The subpoena *duces tecum*, requiring the actual production of documents or other matter, is a procedural device unknown to German law. Instead, a party or witness is apparently required to testify with respect to relevant information; he need not, however, produce actual records.

[8] Judge Pollack based his finding of lack of good faith on the fact that Citibank, as noted above, had failed to even make a simple inquiry into the nature or extent of the records available at the Frankfurt branch. In addition, the expert testimony was clear that the bank secrecy doctrine applied only to material entrusted to a bank within the framework of any confidential relationship of bank and customer but not to records that were the bank's own work product. Citibank failed to produce any documents reflecting its own work product that were within the terms of the subpoena or to indicate that none existed.

[9] By the terms of the District Court's order, Citibank and Loveland were cited for *civil* contempt, both penalties to cease upon compliance with the subpoena. Also, the punishment could not extend beyond the expiration of the life of the Grand Jury.

or witness subject to the jurisdiction of two sovereigns and confronted with conflicting commands. . . .

In any event, under the principles of international law, "A state having jurisdiction to prescribe or enforce a rule of law is not precluded from exercising its jurisdiction *solely* because such exercise requires a person to engage in conduct subjecting him to liability under the law of another state having jurisdiction with respect to that conduct." RESTATEMENT (SECOND), FOREIGN RELATIONS LAW OF THE UNITED STATES, § 39 (1) (1965). It is not asking too much however, to expect that each nation should make an effort to minimize the potential conflict flowing from their joint concern with the prescribed behavior. *Id.* at § 39 (2).

Where, as here, the burden of resolution ultimately falls upon the federal courts, the difficulties are manifold because the courts must take care not to impinge upon the prerogatives and responsibilities of the political branches of the government in the extremely sensitive and delicate area of foreign affairs. Mechanical or overbroad rules of thumb are of little value; what is required is a careful balancing of the interests involved and a precise understanding of the facts and circumstances of the particular case.

With these principles in mind, we turn to the specific issues presented by this appeal. Citibank concedes, as it must, that compliance with the subpoena does not require the violation of the criminal law of a foreign power, as in *Societe Internationale v. Rogers,* 357 U.S. 197 (1958) (discovery under the Federal Rules of Civil Procedure); or risk the imposition of sanctions that are the substantial equivalent of criminal penalties, as in *Application of Chase Manhattan Bank,* 297 F.2d 611, 613 (2d Cir. 1962); or even conflict with the public policy of a foreign state as expressed in legislation. . . . Instead, all that remains, as we see it, is a possible prospective civil liability flowing from an implied contractual obligation between Citibank and its customers that, we are informed, is considered implicit in the bank's license to do business in Germany.

But, the government urges vigorously, that to be excused from compliance with an order of a federal court, a witness, such as Citibank, must show that following compliance it will suffer criminal liability in the foreign country. We would be reluctant to hold, however, that the mere absence of criminal sanctions abroad necessarily mandates obedience to a subpoena. Such a rule would show scant respect for international comity; and, if this principle is valid, a court of one country should make an effort to minimize possible conflict between its orders and the law of a foreign state affected by its decision. The vital national interests of a foreign nation, especially in matters relating to economic affairs, can be expressed in ways other than through the criminal law. For example, it could not be questioned that, insofar as a court of the United States is concerned, a statement or directive by the Bundesbank (the central bank of Germany) or some other organ of government, expresses the public policy of Germany and should be given appropriate weight. Equally important is the fact that a sharp dichotomy between criminal and civil penalties is an imprecise means of measuring the hardship for requiring compliance with a subpoena.

In *Application of Chase Manhattan Bank, supra,* this Court affirmed the modification of a subpoena because strict obedience would have resulted in a violation of Panamanian law punishable by a fine of not more than 100 Balboas (equivalent to $100); we held that a violation was the equivalent of a misdemeanor under our criminal law. It would be a gross fiction to contend that if the Bundesbank were to revoke the license of Citibank for a violation of bank secrecy the impact would be less catastrophic than having to pay an insignificant fine because the revocation is theoretically not "equivalent to a misdemeanor" or criminal sanction. We are not required to decide whether penalties must be under the "criminal law" to provide a legally sufficient reason for noncompliance with a subpoena; but, it would seem unreal to let all hang on whether the label "criminal" were attached to the sanction and to disregard all other factors. In any event, even were we to assume *arguendo* that in appropriate circumstances civil penalties or liabilities would suffice, we hold that Citibank has failed to provide an adequate justification for its disobedience of the subpoena.

In evaluating Citibank's contention that compliance should be excused because of the alleged conflict between the order of the court below and German law, we are aided materially by the rationale of the recent RESTATE-MENT (SECOND), FOREIGN RELATIONS LAW OF THE UNITED STATES, § 40 (1965):

> Where two states have jurisdiction to prescribe and enforce rules of law and the rules they may prescribe require inconsistent conduct upon the part of a person, each state is required by international law to consider, in good faith, moderating the exercise of its enforcement jurisdiction, in the light of such factors as
>
> (a) vital national interests of each of the states,
>
> (b) the extent and the nature of the hardship that inconsistent enforcement actions would impose upon the person,
>
> (c) the extent to which the required conduct is to take place in the territory of the other state,
>
> (d) the nationality of the person, and
>
> (e) the extent to which enforcement by action of either state can reasonably be expected to achieve compliance with the rule prescribed by that state.

In the instant case, the obvious, albeit troublesome, requirement for us is to balance the national interests of the United States and Germany and to give appropriate weight to the hardship, if any, Citibank will suffer.

The important interest of the United States in the enforcement of the subpoena warrants little discussion. The federal Grand Jury before which Citibank was summoned is conducting a criminal investigation of alleged violations of the antitrust laws. These laws have long been considered cornerstones of this nation's economic policies, have been vigorously enforced and the subject of frequent interpretation by our Supreme Court. We would have great reluctance, therefore, to countenance any device that would place relevant information beyond the reach of this duly impaneled Grand Jury or impede or delay its proceedings. Judge Learned Hand put the issue in perspective many years ago: "The suppression of truth is a grievous necessity at best, more especially where as here the inquiry concerns the public interest; it can be justified at all only where the opposing private interest is supreme." *McMann v. S.E.C.,* 87 F.2d 377, 378, (2d Cir. 1937), *cert. denied, McMann v. Engle,* 301 U.S. 684 (1937).

We examine the importance of bank secrecy within the framework of German public policy with full recognition that it is often a subtle and difficult undertaking to determine the nature and scope of the law of a foreign jurisdiction. There is little merit, however, in Citibank's suggestion that the mere existence of a bank secrecy doctrine requires us to accept on its face the bank's assertion that compliance with the subpoena would violate an important public policy of Germany. While we certainly do not intend to deprecate the importance of bank secrecy in the German scheme of things, neither can we blind ourselves to the doctrine's severe limitations as disclosed by the expert testimony. We have already made the assumption that the absence of criminal sanctions is not the whole answer to or finally determinative of the problem. But, it is surely of considerable significance that Germany considers bank secrecy simply a privilege that can be waived by the customer and is content to leave the matter of enforcement to the vagaries of private litigation. Indeed, bank secrecy is not even required by statute. *See* Restatement, *supra,* § 40, comment (c): "A state will be less likely to refrain from exercising its jurisdiction when the consequence of obedience to its order will be a civil liability abroad."

Moreover, Section 300 of the Criminal Code of Germany provides that:

> Anybody who without authority discloses the secrets of another, shall be punished by imprisonment for a term not to exceed six months or by a fine, if the secret was intrusted or became known to him in his capacity as a (1) Physician, dentist, pharmacist [and similar professions]; (2) Attorneys, patent attorney, notary public, defense counsel, auditor, Certified Public Accountant, or tax consultant.

It is not of little significance that a German court has noted, "The fact that bank secrecy has not been included in the penal protection of Section 300 of the Criminal Code must lead to the conclusion that the legislature did not value the public interest in bank secrecy as highly as it did the duty of secrecy of doctors and attorneys." District Court of Frankfurt (1953). Further, Section 53 of the German Code of Criminal Procedure grants the right of refusal to testify to a number of persons, ranging from clergymen and mid-wives to publishers and printers; again reference to bankers is conspicuously absent.[10] It would be anomalous if Citibank, deprived of any right to assert bank secrecy in a criminal investigation conducted in Germany, could — in the absence of statutes imposing greater limitations upon foreign governments — benefit from German bank secrecy in a criminal investigation in the United States.[11]

---

[10] The omission of bankers cannot be considered accidental. Bankers are apparently privileged to refuse testimony in a civil proceeding. *See* Article 383 of the German Code of Civil Procedure.

[11] While it may be true that the subpoena *duces tecum* is unknown to German law, *see* note 7, *supra,* the important point is that bank secrecy is no bar to as much disclosure as German law ever requires in a criminal proceeding; it should have no greater impact in a criminal proceeding in this country.

In addition, it is noteworthy that neither the Department of State nor the German Government has expressed any view on this case or indicated that, under the circumstances present here, enforcement of the subpoena would violate German public policy or embarrass German-American relations.[12] The Supreme Court commented on this aspect in other litigation involving Citibank: "[If] the litigation might in time be embarrassing to United States diplomacy, the District Court remains open to the Executive Branch, which, it must be remembered, is the moving party in the present proceeding." *United States v. First National City Bank,* 379 U.S. 378 (1965). We are fully aware that when foreign governments, including Germany, have considered their vital national interests threatened, they have not hesitated to make known their objections to the enforcement of a subpoena to the issuing court. *See, e.g., In re Grand Jury Investigation of the Shipping Industry,* 186 F. Supp. 298, 318 (D.D.C. 1960). So far as appears, both the United States and German governments have voiced no opposition to Citibank's production of the subpoenaed records.

We turn now to the nature and extent of the alleged hardships to which Citibank would be subjected if it complied with the subpoena. It advances two grounds on which it will suffer injury. First, it states that it will be subjected to economic reprisals by Boehringer and will lose foreign business that will harm it and the economic interests of the United States. It paints a dismal picture of foreign companies boycotting American banks for fear that their business records will be subject to the scrutiny of our courts. A partial answer is that the protection of the foreign economic interests of the United States must be left to the appropriate departments of our government, especially since the government is the moving litigant in these proceedings. . . . Second, Citibank complains that it will be subjected to civil liability in a suit by Boehringer. . . . We have already rejected the contention that Citibank's alleged loss of business abroad is a sound justification for disobedience of the subpoena. In any event, Judge Pollack concluded that risk of civil damages was slight and speculative, and we agree. The chance that Boehringer will suffer compensable damages is quite remote and Citibank appears to have a number of valid defenses if it is sued, both under the terms of the contract and principles of German civil law. . . .

Finally, additional factors support our conclusion that the district judge was correct in citing Citibank and Loveland for civil contempt. As noted above, Citibank has failed to produce or segregate documents or records which reflect the bank's own work product. And, the expert testimony indicated that disclosure of such material would not violate any policy of bank secrecy. Moreover, one of the companies being investigated by the Grand Jury — Boehringer Mannheim Corporation — is incorporated in New York. Whatever one may think of requiring disclosure of records of a German corporation reposited in a bank in Germany, surely an American corporation cannot insulate itself from a federal Grand Jury investigation by entering into a contract with an American bank abroad requiring bank secrecy. If indeed Citibank might suffer civil liability under German law in such circumstances, it must confront the

---

[12] The Consulate General of Germany did, however, introduce a document describing the nature of bank secrecy. *See* note 5, *supra.*

choice mentioned in *First National City Bank v. I.R.S., supra,* — the need to "surrender to one sovereign or the other the privileges received therefrom" or, alternatively, a willingness to accept the consequences.

Notes and Questions on *Citibank*

1. *Effects of control.* How might the result in this case be different if the documents in question were in the control of a joint venture partner or a corporate parent instead of Citibank's branch office in Germany?

2. *Relationship between the Second and Third Restatements.* Consider again the list of factors that the court was to balance under § 40 of the 1965 RESTATEMENT (SECOND) OF FOREIGN RELATIONS LAW (1965):

   (a) vital national interests of each of the states,

   (b) the extent and the nature of the hardship that inconsistent enforcement actions would impose upon the person,

   (c) the extent to which the required conduct is to take place in the territory of the other state,

   (d) the nationality of the person, and

   (e) the extent to which enforcement by action of either state can reasonably be expected to achieve compliance with the rule prescribed by that state.

What changes were made to this list by § 442(1)(c) of the Restatement (Third), *supra,* and why do you suppose those changes were thought to be necessary?

3. *Balancing and the judicial function.* Is it legitimate for a U.S. court to engage in any exercise in which political interests are "balanced" against one another? Consider the concurring opinion of Judge Easterbrook in *Reinsurance Company of America, Inc. v. Administratia Asigurarilor de Stat,* 902 F.2d 1275 (7th Cir. 1990):

> . . . I would be most reluctant to accept an approach that calls on the district judge to throw a heap of factors on a table and then slice and dice to taste. Although it is easy to identify many relevant considerations as the ALI's [American Law Institute's] Restatement [(Third) of Foreign Relations Law] does, a court's job is to reach judgments on the basis of rules of law, rather than to use a different recipe for each meal.

4. *Civil vs. criminal contexts redux.* Reading *Citibank* and *Rogers* together, what difference does it make that the foreign secrecy law takes civil instead of criminal form? Does (or should) it matter whether the U.S. proceeding in which the evidence is sought is civil or criminal? Does (or should) it matter whether the U.S. government is a party to the suit regardless of the civil or criminal nature of the case?

5. Is it accurate or misleading to say that *Rogers* and *Citibank* do little more than adopt a comity test?

IN RE URANIUM ANTITRUST LITIGATION
480 F. Supp. 1138 (N.D. Ill. 1979)

[Westinghouse had entered into long-term, fixed-price contracts with various electric utility companies for the sale of uranium. When the price of uranium escalated on the world market in the 1970s, Westinghouse repudiated its contracts and filed an antitrust action against numerous uranium producers, alleging a conspiracy to monopolize the market. Westinghouse sought discovery of documents relating to questions of jurisdiction and liability, thought to be in the possession of foreign producers or located outside the United States. Most of the defendants refused to comply with the discovery requests, and Westinghouse sought an order from the court compelling production. The court ordered that "all parties should either comply with outstanding discovery demands for 'foreign documents' or file . . . objections to the production of such documents, including . . . objections to demands for any such documents whose production was said to be forbidden by foreign law. The term 'foreign documents' was defined to include all documents whose disclosure was in any way affected by foreign law." Several of the defendants invoked foreign laws barring disclosure as grounds for noncompliance with the plaintiffs' discovery requests.

According to the court's memorandum opinion, "five sets of foreign laws are involved. Three of those are regulations or statutes of Canada, Australia, and South Africa which were enacted or modified . . . for the express purpose of frustrating the jurisdiction of the United States courts over the activities of the alleged international uranium cartel. Those laws generally prohibit the production of any document relating to uranium marketing activities from 1972 through 1975 and also prohibit communications that would result in the disclosure of the contents of such documents. The fourth statute is the Ontario Business Records Protection Act, which was enacted in Canada in 1947. That Act forbids the production of any business records requested by a foreign tribunal if a provincial court issues an order to that effect. Because no such order has been sought or issued to date, this Act has little or no applicability here. The final statutes are Articles 162 and 273 of the Swiss Penal Code, which prohibit the disclosure of a "business or manufacturing secret." Because a violation can be avoided if a person with a secrecy interest in some matter consents to its disclosure, and because [the affected defendants] expect to secure all necessary consents within a short span of time, the Swiss statutes also have limited applicability here. All of these statutes impose criminal penalties for their violation, including fines and imprisonment."]

The parties have offered differing views on the proper standards to be applied in deciding whether to issue a production order for documents located in a country which prohibits their removal or disclosure. Plaintiffs argue that Rule 37 requires a bifurcated two-step procedure for compelling production and imposing sanctions. They contend that the question of whether a discovery order should issue is solely a matter of American law; foreign nondisclosure laws are only relevant in deciding whether sanctions should be imposed for non-compliance. Defendants argue that we should instead use a balancing test to consider all circumstances, including foreign law, before entering an order compelling discovery. We take a middle course between these opposing positions, finding that a number of factors must be considered before issuing a production order, but that the inquiry is not as comprehensive as defendants suggest.

At the outset, we should identify the type of jurisdiction exercised by a court in issuing an order to produce foreign documents. In the field of foreign relations law, two types of jurisdiction have been defined. Prescriptive jurisdiction refers to the capacity of a state under international law to make a rule of law. It is exemplified by the enactment of the Federal Rules of Civil Procedure, *e.g.*, Rule 37. Enforcement jurisdiction, on the other hand, refers to the capacity of a state under international law to enforce a rule of law. When a court enters an order compelling production of documents under Rule 37, it exercises its enforcement jurisdiction. RESTATEMENT (SECOND) OFFOREIGN RELATIONS LAW OF THE UNITED STATES, § 6 (1965). The jurisdiction of American courts is unquestioned when they order their own nationals to produce documents located within this country. But jurisdiction is less certain when American courts order a defendant to produce documents located abroad, especially when the country in which the documents are situated prohibits their disclosure.

As a general rule, a court has the power to order a person subject to its jurisdiction to perform an act in another state. RESTATEMENT (SECOND) OF CONFLICT OF LAWS, § 53 (1971). There are two preconditions for the exercise of this power. First, the court must have personal jurisdiction over the person. Second, the person must have control over the documents. The location of the documents is irrelevant.

On the issue of control, there are certain corollary principles which apply to multinational corporations. The test for determining whether an American court can order an American parent corporation to produce the documents of its foreign subsidiary was stated in *In re Investigation of World Arrangements*, 13 F.R.D. 280, 285 (D.D.C. 1952):

> [I]f a corporation has power, either directly or indirectly, through another corporation or series of corporations, to elect a majority of the directors of another corporation, such corporation may be deemed a parent corporation and in control of the corporation whose directors it has the power to elect to office.

Thus, for example, if the parent owns more than 50% of the foreign subsidiary's stock, it possesses the necessary control.

The test is less clear in situations where an order is directed to the American subsidiary of a foreign corporation to produce documents from its head office located abroad. One court has held that a subpoena duces tecum was enforceable if it was served on the subsidiary's offices in the United States, even though the corporation's board of directors had passed a resolution prohibiting the removal of the requested records from Canada and even though all the board members were residents of Canada. *In re Grand Jury Subpoenas Duces Tecum, supra,* 72 F. Supp. at 1020. The court's reasoning as to how the American officers had control over the withheld documents seems to rest on the theory that it was sufficient that the documents were in the possession of the corporation and that a subpoena had been served on some of its officers. More helpful guidance can be drawn from *Societe Internationale v. McGranery,* 111 F. Supp. 435, 440–42 (D.D.C. 1953), in which the court held that plaintiff, a Swiss corporation, had control over the papers of its Swiss-based bank, H. Sturzenegger & Cie.[1] The court attached significance to the fact that Sturzenegger was a director and officer of plaintiff and was "perhaps" a dominant personality in plaintiff's affairs. After an extensive examination of the corporate affiliations of the two partners, the court concluded that "[t]hrough the interlocked web of corporate organization, management and finance there runs the thread of a fundamental identity of individuals in the pattern of control." 111 F. Supp. at 442. Thus, the issue of control is more a question of fact than of law, and it rests on a determination of whether the defendant has practical and actual managerial control over, or shares such control with, its affiliate, regardless of the formalities of corporate organization.

Once personal jurisdiction over the person and control over the documents by the person are present, a United States court has power to order production of the documents. The existence of a conflicting foreign law which prohibits the disclosure of the requested documents does not prevent the exercise of this power. This proposition has been accepted by both the American Law Institute (RESTATEMENT (SECOND) OFFOREIGN RELATIONS LAW OF THE UNITED STATES, § 39), and by the Supreme Court, *Societe Internationale v. Rogers, supra.* However, American courts should not ignore the fact that such a law exists. When two states, both having jurisdiction, prescribe inconsistent conduct, American courts have developed certain rules of self-restraint governing the appropriate exercise of their power. . . .

[The court summarized its lengthy discussion of *Societe Internationale* by concluding as follows:] [W]e possess the power to enter an order against defendants under Rule 37(a) compelling them to produce documents located abroad if the particular defendant is within the personal jurisdiction of this court and has control over the requested documents. *Societe* teaches that the decision whether to exercise that power is a discretionary one which is informed by three main factors: 1) the importance of the policies underlying the United States statute which forms the basis for the plaintiffs' claims; 2) the importance of the requested documents in illuminating key elements of the claims; and 3) the degree of flexibility in the foreign nation's application of its nondisclosure laws. Relying on the Court's additional suggestion that each case must depend upon its particular facts, several defendants urge that we consider several other factors that we have not yet discussed. However, in the circumstances of this case, we find that these other factors are of limited or no utility.

Several defendants cite the RESTATEMENT (SECOND) OFFOREIGN RELATIONS LAW OF THE UNITED STATES, § 40(a) or rely on broad notions of "international comity" for the proposition that we should balance the vital national interests of the United States and the foreign countries to determine which interests predominate. Aside from the fact that the judiciary has little expertise, or perhaps even authority, to evaluate the economic and social policies of a foreign country, such a balancing test is inherently unworkable in this case.

---

[1] The court's holding on the control issue was accepted both by the Court of Appeals and by the Supreme Court, *Societe Internationale v. Rogers,* 357 U.S. 197, 204 (1958).

The competing interests here display an irreconcilable conflict on precisely the same plane of national policy. Westinghouse seeks to enforce this nation's antitrust laws against an alleged international marketing arrangement among uranium producers, and to that end has sought documents located in foreign countries where those producers conduct their business. In specific response to this and other related litigation in the American courts, three foreign governments have enacted nondisclosure legislation which is aimed at nullifying the impact of American antitrust legislation by prohibiting access to those same documents. It is simply impossible to judicially "balance" these totally contradictory and mutually negating actions. . . .

Many defendants ask us to consider communications from foreign governments to the U.S. State Department which have protested the issuance of production orders by American courts in similar circumstances. We believe those communications are relevant to the decision whether to issue a production order only insofar as they indicate the degree of accommodation or adjustment which the foreign government may be willing to make in its nondisclosure laws. We reserve any further consideration of these communications to the hearing on sanctions, if that becomes necessary.

Finally we have on this question . . . been benefitted with statements *amici curiae* from the Governments of Canada, Australia, South Africa, and Switzerland. By far the most extensive of these is the Canadian statement which urges that we defer to the critical importance which Canada attaches to its national policies and regulations. But as we have earlier observed, a balancing test is inherently unworkable in this case, and were it not we would be hard pressed not to accede to the strong national policy of this country to enforce vigorously its anti-trust laws. . . .

The remaining question is whether we should exercise our discretionary power to issue those orders, after weighing the three factors described earlier in this memorandum. We conclude that we should.

The first consideration is the strength of the Congressional policies underlying the statute which forms the basis for plaintiffs' action. Plaintiffs' complaint challenges activities by the defendants which, if true, would constitute massive violations of this nation's antitrust laws. "These laws have long been considered cornerstones of this nation's economic policies, have been vigorously enforced and the subject of frequent interpretation by our Supreme Court." *United States v. First National City Bank,* 396 F.2d 897, 903 (2d Cir. 1968). "They are as important to the preservation of economic freedom and our free-enterprise system as the Bill of Rights is to the protection of our fundamental personal freedoms." *United States v. Topco Associates, Inc.,* 405 U.S. 596, 610 (1972). More specifically, Congressional concern with the very practices at issue here, and with the antitrust implications of those practices, is evidenced by extensive subcommittee investigations into the alleged international uranium cartel. Governmental concern with this issue achieved choate form when the Justice Department convened a grand jury which eventually charged Gulf with criminal antitrust violations arising out of the same transactions identified by Westinghouse. The existence of this public enforcement action does not supplant plaintiffs' private civil action. Indeed, Congress specifically intended to encourage civil antitrust actions by allowing private litigants to gain certain estoppel advantages from government anti-trust actions. From these indicators, it is clear that the policies supporting an inquiry into corporate activities and structure are at least as weighty, and probably stronger, with the antitrust statutes here than they were with the Trading with the Enemy Act in *Societe Internationale*.

The second consideration is whether the requested documents are crucial to the determination of a key issue in the litigation. Plaintiffs' showing on this factor is simply overwhelming. All of the discovery requests now at issue are directly relevant to a number of fundamental issues in the complaint, answers, affirmative defenses, and counterclaims in this litigation. Plaintiffs seek vital information relating to, among other things, the time period when the alleged conspiracy of uranium producers was carrying out its activities, defendants' alleged efforts to conceal their conspiracy, the impact of that alleged conspiracy on United States interstate and foreign commerce, the defendants' defenses of sovereign compulsion, and information on uranium sales and market conditions. Plaintiffs have submitted voluminous exhibits which give a sketchy picture strongly supporting their allegations in these areas but also suggesting that there are larger gaps in defendants' document production. . . .

The third consideration involves an appraisal of the chances for flexibility in a country's application of its nondisclosure laws. The degree of leniency in the application of the nondisclosure laws varies from country to country. South Africa has taken the most flexible position. It has allowed Westinghouse to inspect [one defendant's] uranium-related documents in that country, and is currently considering a request from [another defendant] to allow a similar inspection of its documents. Australia has rejected all past requests for a waiver of its regulations, but interprets its laws as authorizing the Attorney General to grant such waivers. The Attorney General is presently considering requests for waivers from [three defendants]. Canada has taken a completely inflexible position. It has consistently rejected all requests for waivers, stating that its government officials have no authority to grant them. It has opposed Westinghouse's unsuccessful efforts to secure letters rogatory from a Canadian court for production of uranium-related documents. It has rejected all requests to modify or amend the regulations and has refused to give any assurances of non-prosecution for any violations. Canada has also sent numerous diplomatic notes to the U.S. State Department in which it has expressed a firm position that any disclosure of documents covered by its regulations would be inimical to its national interests. Canada's position has not been relaxed by its *amicus* submission.

On balance, we have concluded the issuance of Rule 37(a) orders is required. The entry of such orders may lead to a further narrowing of the defendants' foreign law objections. That process has already been evidenced by the increased disclosures which have occurred since Westinghouse filed the present motions. Even if some defendants subsequently conclude, as they now suggest, that they have already done everything within their powers to comply with such an order, we do not think an order at this time would be a futile gesture. The order will serve to declare Westinghouse's right to the discovery it seeks, thereby framing the competing interests of the United States and the foreign governments on a plane where the potential moderation of the exercise of their conflicting enforcement jurisdictions can be meaningfully considered. We do not seek to force any defendant to violate foreign law. But we do seek to make each defendant feel the full measure of each sovereign's conflicting commands, so that, in the words of Chief Judge Kaufman of the Second Circuit, it now "must confront . . . the need to "surrender to one sovereign or the other the privileges received therefrom' or, alternatively a willingness to accept the consequences." *United States v. First National City Bank,* 396 F.2d 897, 905 (2d Cir. 1968).

Notes and Questions on *Uranium Antitrust Litigation*

1. *Jurisdictional discovery*. States have consistently upheld their own authority to compel discovery from persons or entities within their personal jurisdiction, and even to compel limited discovery of jurisdictional facts to determine whether the "target" of a discovery order is within the personal jurisdiction of the court or not. *Insurance Corp. of Ireland, Ltd. v. Compagnie des Bauxites de Guinee*, 456 U.S. 694 (1982). In order to prevent abuse of jurisdictional discovery, some courts have required the party seeking discovery to demonstrate "a reasonable probability that ultimately it will succeed in establishing the facts necessary for the exercise of jurisdiction." *In re Marc Rich & Co. v. United States*, 707 F.2d 663, 670 (2d Cir.), *cert. denied*, 463 U.S. 1215 (1983). Is that the right test?

2. *Burden of proof*. After the decision in *Uranium Antitrust Litigation*, what must a party resisting discovery on the basis of foreign law prove in order to get protection?

3. *"Control"*. Rule 34 of the Federal Rules of Civil Procedure allows discovery of documents in the "possession, custody, or control" of other parties. When a U.S. parent company effectively controls a foreign subsidiary, the courts have generally required the parent to produce the subsidiary's documents. What should the test of control be? Should it be the same as that for alter ego jurisdiction, *supra*, Chapter 2, or should a lesser showing of interconnectedness suffice for purposes of civil discovery? Under what conditions, if any, might a court rule that a U.S. subsidiary of a foreign parent "controls" the parent's documents or some relevant subset of them?

4. Are jurisdictional conflicts over transnational discovery one of those areas of the law where a clear rule is *less* preferable than a vague one?

---

[2]   Managing the Risk: The Hague Evidence Convention and its Discontents

CONVENTION ON THE TAKING OF EVIDENCE ABROAD IN CIVIL OR COMMERCIAL MATTERS (selected provisions)
Done at The Hague on March 18, 1970, and entered into force for the United States October 7, 1972

The States signatory to the present Convention,

Desiring to facilitate the transmission and execution of Letters of Request and to further the accommodation of the different methods which they use for this purpose,

Desiring to improve mutual judicial co-operation in civil or commercial matters,

Have resolved to conclude a Convention to this effect and have agreed upon the following provisions—

CHAPTER I—LETTERS OF REQUEST

ARTICLE 1

In civil or commercial matters a judicial authority of a Contracting State may, in accordance with the provisions of the law of that State, request the competent authority of another Contracting State, by means of a Letter of Request, to obtain evidence, or to perform some other judicial act. A Letter shall not be used to obtain evidence which is not intended for use in judicial proceedings, commenced or contemplated. The expression 'other judicial act' does not cover the service of judicial documents or the issuance of any process by which judgments or orders are executed or enforced, or orders for provisional or protective measures.

ARTICLE 2

A Contracting State shall designate a Central Authority which will undertake to receive Letters of Request coming from a judicial authority of another Contracting State and to transmit them to the authority competent to execute them. Each State shall organize the Central Authority in accordance with its own law. Letters shall be sent to the Central Authority of the State of execution without being transmitted through any other authority of that State.

ARTICLE 3

A Letter of Request shall specify—

(a) the authority requesting its execution and the authority requested to execute it, if known to the requesting authority;

(b) the names and addresses of the parties to the proceedings and their representatives, if any;

(c) the nature of the proceedings for which the evidence is required, giving all necessary information in regard thereto;

(d) the evidence to be obtained or other judicial act to be performed.

Where appropriate, the Letter shall specify, inter alia—

(e) the names and addresses of the persons to be examined;

(f) the questions to be put to the persons to be examined or a statement of the subject-matter about which they are to be examined;

(g) the documents or other property, real or personal, to be inspected;

(h) any requirement that the evidence is to be given on oath or affirmation, and any special form to be used;

(i) any special method or procedure to be followed under Article 9.

A Letter may also mention any information necessary for the application of Article 11. No legalization or other like formality may be required.

ARTICLE 4

A Letter of Request shall be in the language of the authority requested to execute it or be accompanied by a translation into that language. Nevertheless, a Contracting State shall accept a Letter in either English or French, or a translation into one of these languages, unless it has made the reservation authorized by Article 33. . . . Any translation accompanying a Letter shall be certified as correct, either by a diplomatic officer or consular agent or by a sworn translator or by any other person so authorized in either State.

ARTICLE 5

If the Central Authority considers that the request does not comply with the provisions of the present Convention, it shall promptly inform the authority of the State of origin which transmitted the Letter of Request, specifying the objections to the Letter.

ARTICLE 7

The requesting authority shall, if it so desires, be informed of the time when, and the place where, the proceedings will take place, in order that the parties concerned, and their representatives, if any, may be present. This information shall be sent directly to the parties or their representatives when the authority of the State of origin so requests.

ARTICLE 9

The judicial authority which executes a Letter of Request shall apply its own law as to the methods and procedures to be followed. However, it will follow a request of the requesting authority that a special method or procedure be followed, unless this is incompatible with the internal law of the State of execution or is impossible of performance by reason of its internal practice and procedure or by reason of practical difficulties. A Letter of Request shall be executed expeditiously.

ARTICLE 10

In executing a Letter of Request the requested authority shall apply the appropriate measures of compulsion in the instances and to the same extent as are provided by its internal law for the execution of orders issued by the authorities of its own country or of requests made by parties in internal proceedings.

ARTICLE 11

In the execution of a Letter of Request the person concerned may refuse to give evidence in so far as he has a privilege or duty to refuse to give the evidence—

(a) under the law of the State of execution; or

(b) under the law of the State of origin, and the privilege or duty has been specified in the Letter, or, at the instance of the requested authority, has been otherwise confirmed to that authority by the requesting authority.

A Contracting State may declare that, in addition, it will respect privileges and duties existing under the law of States other than the State of origin and the State of execution, to the extent specified in that declaration.

ARTICLE 12

The execution of a Letter of Request may be refused only to the extent that—

(a) in the State of execution the execution of the Letter does not fall within the functions of the judiciary; or

(b) the State addressed considers that its sovereignty or security would be prejudiced thereby.

Execution may not be refused solely on the ground that under its internal law the State of execution claims exclusive jurisdiction over the subject-matter of the action or that its internal law would not admit a right of action on it.

CHAPTER II—TAKING OF EVIDENCE BY DIPLOMATIC OFFICERS, CONSULAR AGENTS AND COMMISSIONERS

ARTICLE 15

In a civil or commercial matter, a diplomatic officer or consular agent of a Contracting State may, in the territory of another Contracting State and within the area where he exercises his functions, take the evidence without compulsion of nationals of a State which he represents in aid of proceedings commenced in the courts of a State which he represents. A Contracting State may declare that evidence may be taken by a diplomatic officer or consular agent only if permission to that effect is given upon application made by him or on his behalf to the appropriate authority designated by the declaring State.

ARTICLE 16

A diplomatic officer or consular agent of a Contracting State may, in the territory of another Contracting State and within the area where he exercises his functions, also take the evidence, without compulsion, of nationals of the State in which he exercises his functions or of a third State, in aid of proceedings commenced in the courts of a State which he represents, if—

(a) a competent authority designated by the State in which he exercises his functions has given its permission either generally or in the particular case, and

(b) he complies with the conditions which the competent authority has specified in the permission.

. . . .

CHAPTER III—GENERAL CLAUSES

ARTICLE 23

A Contracting State may at the time of signature, ratification or accession, declare that it will not execute Letters of Request issued for the purpose of obtaining pre-trial discovery of documents as known in Common Law countries.

ARTICLE 27

The provisions of the present Convention shall not prevent a Contracting State from—

(a) declaring that Letters of Request may be transmitted to its judicial authorities through channels other than those provided for in Article 2;

(b) permitting, by internal law or practice, any act provided for in this Convention to be performed upon less restrictive conditions;

(c) permitting, by internal law or practice, methods of taking evidence other than those provided for in this Convention.

SOCIETE NATIONALE INDUSTRIELLE AEROSPATIALE v. U.S. DISTRICT COURT
482 U.S. 522 (1987)

JUSTICE STEVENS delivered the opinion of the Court.

The United States, the Republic of France, and 15 other Nations have acceded to the Hague Convention on the Taking of Evidence Abroad in Civil or Commercial Matters. . . ., sometimes referred to as the "Hague Convention" or the "Evidence Convention," [which] prescribes certain procedures by which a judicial authority in one contracting state may request evidence located in another contracting state. The question presented in this case concerns the extent to which a federal district court must employ the procedures set forth in the Convention when litigants seek answers to interrogatories, the production of documents, and admissions from a French adversary over whom the court has personal jurisdiction.

I

The two petitioners are corporations owned by the Republic of France.[1] They are engaged in the business of designing, manufacturing, and marketing aircraft. One of their planes, the "Rallye," was allegedly advertised in American aviation publications as "the World's safest and most economical STOL ["short takeoff and landing"] plane." On August 19, 1980, a Rallye crashed in Iowa, injuring the pilot and a passenger. Dennis Jones, John George, and Rosa George brought separate suits based upon this accident in the United States District Court for the Southern District of Iowa, alleging that petitioners had manufactured and sold a defective plane and that they were guilty of negligence and breach of warranty. Petitioners answered the complaints, apparently without questioning the jurisdiction of the District Court. . . .

Initial discovery was conducted by both sides pursuant to the Federal Rules of Civil Procedure without objection.[2] When plaintiffs served a second request for the production of documents pursuant to Rule 34, a set of interrogatories

---

[1] Petitioner Societe Nationale Industrielle Aerospatiale is wholly owned by the Government of France. Petitioner Societe de Construction d'Avions de Tourisme is a wholly owned subsidiary of Societe Nationale Industrielle Aerospatiale.

[2] Plaintiffs made certain requests for the production of documents pursuant to Rule 34(b) and for admissions pursuant to Rule 36. Apparently, the petitioners responded to those requests without objection, at least insofar as they called for material or information that was located in the United States. In turn, petitioners deposed witnesses and parties pursuant to Rule 26, and served interrogatories pursuant to Rule 33 and a request for the production of documents pursuant to Rule 34. Plaintiffs complied with those requests.

pursuant to Rule 33, and requests for admission pursuant to Rule 36, however, petitioners filed a motion for a protective order. The motion alleged that because petitioners are "French corporations, and the discovery sought can only be found in a foreign state, namely France," the Hague Convention dictated the exclusive procedures that must be followed for pretrial discovery. In addition, the motion stated that under French penal law, the petitioners could not respond to discovery requests that did not comply with the Convention.[3]

The Magistrate denied the motion insofar as it related to answering interrogatories, producing documents, and making admissions.[4] After reviewing the relevant cases, the Magistrate explained:

> To permit the Hague Evidence Convention to override the Federal Rules of Civil Procedure would frustrate the courts' interests, which particularly arise in products liability cases, in protecting United States citizens from harmful products and in compensating them for injuries arising from use of such products.

The Magistrate made two responses to petitioners' argument that they could not comply with the discovery requests without violating French penal law. Noting that the law was originally " 'inspired to impede enforcement of United States antitrust laws,' " and that it did not appear to have been strictly enforced in France, he first questioned whether it would be construed to apply to the pretrial discovery requests at issue.[5] Second, he balanced the interests in the "protection of United States citizens from harmful foreign products and compensation for injuries caused by such products" against France's interest in protecting its citizens "from intrusive foreign discovery procedures." The Magistrate concluded that the former interests were stronger, particularly because compliance with the requested discovery will "not have to take place in France" and will not be greatly intrusive or abusive.

[On review,] the Court of Appeals for the Eighth Circuit . . . held that "when the district court has jurisdiction over a foreign litigant the Hague Convention does not apply to the production of evidence in that litigant's possession, even

---

[3] Article 1A of the French "blocking statute," French Penal Code Law No. 80-538, provides [in translation by the Court]:

> Subject to treaties or international agreements and applicable laws and regulations, it is prohibited for any party to request, seek or disclose, in writing, orally or otherwise, economic, commercial, industrial, financial or technical documents or information leading to the constitution of evidence with a view to foreign judicial or administrative proceedings or in connection therewith.

Article 2 provides:

> The parties mentioned in [Article 1A] shall forthwith inform the competent minister if they receive any request concerning such disclosures.

[4] The Magistrate stated, however, that if oral depositions were to be taken in France, he would require compliance with the Hague Evidence Convention.

[5] He relied on a passage in [a law review article] stating that "the legislative history [of the Law] shows only that the Law was adopted to protect French interests from abusive foreign discovery procedures and excessive assertions of extraterritorial jurisdiction. Nowhere is there an indication that the Law was to impede litigation preparations by French companies, either for their own defense or to institute lawsuits abroad to protect their interests, and arguably such applications were unintended."

though the documents and information sought may physically be located within the territory of a foreign signatory to the Convention." The Court of Appeals disagreed with petitioners' argument that this construction would render the entire Hague Convention "meaningless," noting that it would still serve the purpose of providing an improved procedure for obtaining evidence from nonparties. The court also rejected petitioners' contention that considerations of international comity required plaintiffs to resort to Hague Convention procedures as an initial matter ("first use"), and correspondingly to invoke the federal discovery rules only if the treaty procedures turned out to be futile. The Court of Appeals believed that the potential overruling of foreign tribunals' denial of discovery would do more to defeat than to promote international comity. Finally, the Court of Appeals concluded that objections based on the French penal statute should be considered in two stages: first, whether the discovery order was proper even though compliance may require petitioners to violate French law; and second, what sanctions, if any, should be imposed if petitioners are unable to comply. The Court of Appeals held that the Magistrate properly answered the first question and that it was premature to address the second.[6] . . . We granted certiorari.

II

In the District Court and the Court of Appeals, petitioners contended that the Hague Evidence Convention "provides the exclusive and mandatory procedures for obtaining documents and information located within the territory of a foreign signatory."[7] We are satisfied that the Court of Appeals correctly rejected this extreme position. We believe it is foreclosed by the plain language of the Convention. Before discussing the text of the Convention, however, we briefly review its history.

The Hague Conference on Private International Law, an association of sovereign states, has been conducting periodic sessions since 1893. The United States participated in those sessions as an observer in 1956 and 1960, and as a member beginning in 1964 pursuant to congressional authorization. In that year, Congress amended the Judicial Code to grant foreign litigants, without any requirement of reciprocity, special assistance in obtaining evidence in the United States. In 1965, the Hague Conference adopted a Convention on the Service Abroad of Judicial and Extrajudicial Documents in Civil or Commercial Matters (Service Convention), to which the Senate gave

---

[6] "The record before this court does not indicate whether the Petitioners have notified the appropriate French Minister of the requested discovery in accordance with Article 2 of the French Blocking Statute, or whether the Petitioners have attempted to secure a waiver of prosecution from the French government. Because the Petitioners are corporations owned by the Republic of France, they stand in a most advantageous position to receive such a waiver. However, these issues will only be relevant should the Petitioners fail to comply with the magistrate's discovery order, and we need not presently address them." 782 F.2d, at 127.

[7] The Republic of France likewise takes the following position in [its brief in] this case:

THE HAGUE CONVENTION IS THE EXCLUSIVE MEANS OF DISCOVERY IN TRANSNATIONAL LITIGATION AMONG THE CONVENTION'S SIGNATORIES UNLESS THE SOVEREIGN ON WHOSE TERRITORY DISCOVERY IS TO OCCUR CHOOSES OTHERWISE.

its advice and consent in 1967. The favorable response to the Service Convention, coupled with the longstanding interest of American lawyers in improving procedures for obtaining evidence abroad, motivated the United States to take the initiative in proposing that an evidence convention be adopted. The Conference organized a special commission to prepare the draft convention, and the draft was approved without a dissenting vote on October 26, 1968. It was signed on behalf of the United States in 1970 and ratified by a unanimous vote of the Senate in 1972. The Convention's purpose was to establish a system for obtaining evidence located abroad that would be "tolerable" to the state executing the request and would produce evidence "utilizable" in the requesting state.

. . . The Convention was fairly summarized in the Secretary of State's letter of submittal to the President:

> The willingness of the Conference to proceed promptly with work on the evidence convention is perhaps attributable in large measure to the difficulties encountered by courts and lawyers in obtaining evidence abroad from countries with markedly different legal systems. Some countries have insisted on the exclusive use of the complicated, dilatory and expensive system of letters rogatory or letters of request. Other countries have refused adequate judicial assistance because of the absence of a treaty or convention regulating the matter. The substantial increase in litigation with foreign aspects arising, in part, from the unparalleled expansion of international trade and travel in recent decades had intensified the need for an effective international agreement to set up a model system to bridge differences between the common law and civil law approaches to the taking of evidence abroad.
>
> Civil law countries tend to concentrate on commissions rogatoires, while common law countries take testimony on notice, by stipulation and through commissions to consuls or commissioners. Letters of request for judicial assistance from courts abroad in securing needed evidence have been the exception, rather than the rule. The civil law technique results normally in a resume of the evidence, prepared by the executing judge and signed by the witness, while the common law technique results normally in a verbatim transcript of the witness's testimony certified by the reporter.
>
> Failure by either the requesting state or the state of execution fully to take into account the differences of approach to the taking of evidence abroad under the two systems and the absence of agreed standards applicable to letters of request have frequently caused difficulties for courts and litigants. To minimize such difficulties in the future, the enclosed convention, which consists of a preamble and forty-two articles, is designed to:
>
> 1. Make the employment of letters of request a principal means of obtaining evidence abroad;
>
> 2. Improve the means of securing evidence abroad by increasing the powers of consuls and by introducing in the civil law world, on a limited basis, the concept of the commissioner;

3. Provide means for securing evidence in the form needed by the court where the action is pending; and

4. Preserve all more favorable and less restrictive practices arising from internal law, internal rules of procedure and bilateral or multilateral conventions.

What the convention does is to provide a set of minimum standards with which contracting states agree to comply. Further, through articles 27, 28 and 32, it provides a flexible framework within which any future liberalizing changes in policy and tradition in any country with respect to international judicial cooperation may be translated into effective change in international procedures. At the same time it recognizes and preserves procedures of every country which now or hereafter may provide international cooperation in the taking of evidence on more liberal and less restrictive bases, whether this is effected by supplementary agreements or by municipal law and practice.

III

In arguing their entitlement to a protective order, petitioners correctly assert that both the discovery rules set forth in the Federal Rules of Civil Procedure and the Hague Convention are the law of the United States. This observation, however, does not dispose of the question before us; we must analyze the interaction between these two bodies of federal law. Initially, we note that at least four different interpretations of the relationship between the federal discovery rules and the Hague Convention are possible. Two of these interpretations assume that the Hague Convention by its terms dictates the extent to which it supplants normal discovery rules. First, the Hague Convention might be read as requiring its use to the exclusion of any other discovery procedures whenever evidence located abroad is sought for use in an American court. Second, the Hague Convention might be interpreted to require first, but not exclusive, use of its procedures. Two other interpretations assume that international comity, rather than the obligations created by the treaty, should guide judicial resort to the Hague Convention. Third, then, the Convention might be viewed as establishing a supplemental set of discovery procedures, strictly optional under treaty law, to which concerns of comity nevertheless require first resort by American courts in all cases. Fourth, the treaty may be viewed as an undertaking among sovereigns to facilitate discovery to which an American court should resort when it deems that course of action appropriate, after considering the situations of the parties before it as well as the interests of the concerned foreign state. In interpreting an international treaty, we are mindful that it is "in the nature of a contract between nations," *Trans World Airlines, Inc. v. Franklin Mint Corp.*, 466 U.S. 243, 253 (1984), to which "general rules of construction apply." We therefore begin "with the text of the treaty and the context in which the written words are used." *Air France v. Saks,* 470 U.S. 392, 397 (1985). The treaty's history, " 'the negotiations, and the practical construction adopted by the parties' " may also be relevant. *Id.* at 396 (quoting *Choctaw Nation of Indians v. United States,* 318 U.S. 423, 431–432 (1943)). We reject the first two of the possible interpretations as inconsistent with the language and negotiating history of the Hague Convention. The preamble of the Convention specifies its purpose "to facilitate the transmission and execution of Letters of Request" and to "improve mutual judicial cooperation in civil or commercial matters." The preamble does not speak in mandatory terms which would purport to describe the procedures for all permissible transnational discovery and exclude all other existing practices.[8] The text of the Evidence Convention itself does not modify the law of any contracting state, require any contracting state to use the Convention procedures, either in requesting evidence or in responding to such requests, or compel any contracting state to change its own evidence-gathering procedures.

The Convention contains three chapters. Chapter I, entitled "Letters of Requests," and chapter II, entitled "Taking of Evidence by Diplomatic Officers, Consular Agents and Commissioners," both use permissive rather than mandatory language. Thus, Article 1 provides that a judicial authority in one contracting state "may" forward a letter of request to the competent authority in another contracting state for the purpose of obtaining evidence. Similarly, Articles 15, 16, and 17 provide that diplomatic officers, consular agents, and commissioners "may . . . without compulsion," take evidence under certain conditions. The absence of any command that a contracting state must use Convention procedures when they are not needed is conspicuous.

Two of the Articles in chapter III, entitled "General Clauses," buttress our conclusion that the Convention was intended as a permissive supplement, not a pre-emptive replacement, for other means of obtaining evidence located abroad. Article 23 expressly authorizes a contracting state to declare that it will not execute any letter of request in aid of pretrial discovery of documents in a common-law country. Surely, if the Convention had been intended to replace completely the broad discovery powers that the common-law courts in the United States previously exercised over foreign litigants subject to their jurisdiction, it would have been most anomalous for the common-law contracting parties to agree to Article 23, which enables a contracting party to revoke its consent to the treaty's procedures for pretrial discovery.[9] In the absence of explicit textual support, we are unable to accept the hypothesis that the common-law contracting states abjured recourse to all pre-existing discovery procedures at the same time that they accepted the possibility that a contracting party could unilaterally abrogate even the Convention's procedures.[10]

---

[8] The Hague Conference on Private International Law's omission of mandatory language in the preamble is particularly significant in light of the same body's use of mandatory language in the preamble to the Hague Service Convention. Article 1 of the Service Convention provides: "The present Convention shall apply in all cases, in civil or commercial matters, where there is occasion to transmit a judicial or extrajudicial document for service abroad." As noted, *supra*, the Service Convention was drafted before the Evidence Convention, and its language provided a model exclusivity provision that the drafters of the Evidence Convention could easily have followed had they been so inclined. Given this background, the drafters' election to use permissive language instead is strong evidence of their intent.

[9] Thirteen of the seventeen signatory states have made declarations under Article 23 of the Convention that restrict pretrial discovery of documents.

[10] "The great object of an international agreement is to define the common ground between sovereign nations. Given the gulfs of language, culture, and values that separate nations, it is essential in international agreements for the parties to make explicit their common ground on the most rudimentary of matters." *Trans World Airlines, Inc. v. Franklin Mint Corp.*, 466 U.S.

Moreover, Article 27 plainly states that the Convention does not prevent a contracting state from using more liberal methods of rendering evidence than those authorized by the Convention. Thus, the text of the Evidence Convention, as well as the history of its proposal and ratification by the United States, unambiguously supports the conclusion that it was intended to establish optional procedures that would facilitate the taking of evidence abroad. . . . We conclude accordingly that the Hague Convention did not deprive the District Court of the jurisdiction it otherwise possessed to order a foreign national party before it to produce evidence physically located within a signatory nation.[11]

IV

While the Hague Convention does not divest the District Court of jurisdiction to order discovery under the Federal Rules of Civil Procedure, the optional character of the Convention procedures sheds light on one aspect of the Court of Appeals' opinion that we consider erroneous. That court concluded that the

---

243, 262 (1984) (STEVENS, J., dissenting). The utter absence in the Hague Convention of an exclusivity provision has an obvious explanation: The contracting states did not agree that its procedures were to be exclusive. The words of the treaty delineate the extent of their agreement; without prejudice to their existing rights and practices, they bound themselves to comply with any request for judicial assistance that did comply with the treaty's procedures. The separate opinion reasons that the Convention procedures are not optional because unless other signatory states "had expected the Convention to provide the normal channels for discovery, [they] would have had no incentive to agree to its terms." We find the treaty language that the parties have agreed upon and ratified a surer indication of their intentions than the separate opinion's hypothesis about the expectations of the parties. Both comity and concern for the separation of powers counsel the utmost restraint in attributing motives to sovereign states which have bargained as equals. Indeed, JUSTICE BLACKMUN notes that "the Convention represents a political determination — one that, consistent with the principle of separation of powers, courts should not attempt to second guess." Moreover, it is important to remember that the evidence-gathering procedures implemented by the Convention would still provide benefits to the signatory states even if the United States were not a party.

[11] The opposite conclusion of exclusivity would create three unacceptable asymmetries. First, within any lawsuit between a national of the United States and a national of another contracting party, the foreign party could obtain discovery under the Federal Rules of Civil Procedure, while the domestic party would be required to resort first to the procedures of the Hague Convention. This imbalance would run counter to the fundamental maxim of discovery that "mutual knowledge of all the relevant facts gathered by both parties is essential to proper litigation." *Hickman v. Taylor*, 329 U.S. 495, 507 (1947).

Second, a rule of exclusivity would enable a company which is a citizen of another contracting state to compete with a domestic company on uneven terms, since the foreign company would be subject to less extensive discovery procedures in the event that both companies were sued in an American court. Petitioners made a voluntary decision to market their products in the United States. They are entitled to compete on equal terms with other companies operating in this market. But since the District Court unquestionably has personal jurisdiction over petitioners, they are subject to the same legal constraints, including the burdens associated with American judicial procedures, as their American competitors. A general rule according foreign nationals a preferred position in pretrial proceedings in our courts would conflict with the principle of equal opportunity that governs the market they elected to enter.

Third, since a rule of first use of the Hague Convention would apply to cases in which a foreign party is a national of a contracting state, but not to cases in which a foreign party is a national of any other foreign state, the rule would confer an unwarranted advantage on some domestic litigants over others similarly situated.

Convention simply "does not apply" to discovery sought from a foreign litigant that is subject to the jurisdiction of an American court. Plaintiffs argue that this conclusion is supported by two considerations. First, the Federal Rules of Civil Procedure provide ample means for obtaining discovery from parties who are subject to the court's jurisdiction, while before the Convention was ratified it was often extremely difficult, if not impossible, to obtain evidence from nonparty witnesses abroad. Plaintiffs contend that it is appropriate to construe the Convention as applying only in the area in which improvement was badly needed. Second, when a litigant is subject to the jurisdiction of the district court, arguably the evidence it is required to produce is not "abroad" within the meaning of the Convention, even though it is in fact located in a foreign country at the time of the discovery request and even though it will have to be gathered or otherwise prepared abroad. Nevertheless, the text of the Convention draws no distinction between evidence obtained from third parties and that obtained from the litigants themselves; nor does it purport to draw any sharp line between evidence that is "abroad" and evidence that is within the control of a party subject to the jurisdiction of the requesting court. Thus, it appears clear to us that the optional Convention procedures are available whenever they will facilitate the gathering of evidence by the means authorized in the Convention. Although these procedures are not mandatory, the Hague Convention does "apply" to the production of evidence in a litigant's possession in the sense that it is one method of seeking evidence that a court may elect to employ.

V

Petitioners contend that even if the Hague Convention's procedures are not mandatory, this Court should adopt a rule requiring that American litigants first resort to those procedures before initiating any discovery pursuant to the normal methods of the Federal Rules of Civil Procedure. The Court of Appeals rejected this argument because it was convinced that an American court's order ultimately requiring discovery that a foreign court had refused under Convention procedures would constitute "the greatest insult" to the sovereignty of that tribunal. We disagree with the Court of Appeals' view. It is well known that the scope of American discovery is often significantly broader than is permitted in other jurisdictions, and we are satisfied that foreign tribunals will recognize that the final decision on the evidence to be used in litigation conducted in American courts must be made by those courts. We therefore do not believe that an American court should refuse to make use of Convention procedures because of a concern that it may ultimately find it necessary to order the production of evidence that a foreign tribunal permitted a party to withhold. Nevertheless, we cannot accept petitioners' invitation to announce a new rule of law that would require first resort to Convention procedures whenever discovery is sought from a foreign litigant. Assuming, without deciding, that we have the lawmaking power to do so, we are convinced that such a general rule would be unwise. In many situations the Letter of Request procedure authorized by the Convention would be unduly time consuming and expensive, as well as less certain to produce needed evidence than direct use of the Federal Rules.[12] A rule of first resort in all cases would therefore be inconsistent with the overriding interest in the "just, speedy, and inexpensive determination" of litigation in our courts. *See* Fed. Rule Civ. Proc. 1.

Petitioners argue that a rule of first resort is necessary to accord respect to the sovereignty of states in which evidence is located. It is true that the process of obtaining evidence in a civil-law jurisdiction is normally conducted by a judicial officer rather than by private attorneys. Petitioners contend that if performed on French soil, for example, by an unauthorized person, such evidence-gathering might violate the "judicial sovereignty" of the host nation. Because it is only through the Convention that civil-law nations have given their consent to evidence-gathering activities within their borders, petitioners argue, we have a duty to employ those procedures whenever they are available. We find that argument unpersuasive. If such a duty were to be inferred from the adoption of the Convention itself, we believe it would have been described in the text of that document. Moreover, the concept of international comity[13] requires in this context a more particularized analysis of the respective interests of the foreign nation and the requesting nation than petitioners' proposed general rule would generate.[14] We therefore decline to hold as a blanket matter that comity requires resort to Hague Evidence Convention procedures without prior scrutiny in each case of the particular facts, sovereign interests, and likelihood that resort to those procedures will prove effective.[15] The American Law Institute has summarized this interplay

---

[12] We observe, however, that in other instances a litigant's first use of the Hague Convention procedures can be expected to yield more evidence abroad more promptly than use of the normal procedures governing pretrial civil discovery. In those instances, the calculations of the litigant will naturally lead to a first-use strategy.

[13] Comity refers to the spirit of cooperation in which a domestic tribunal approaches the resolution of cases touching the laws and interests of other sovereign states. This Court referred to the doctrine of comity among nations in *Emory v. Grenough*, 3 Dall. 369, 370 (1797) (dismissing appeal from judgment for failure to plead diversity of citizenship, but setting forth an extract from a treatise by Ulrich Huber (1636–1694), a Dutch jurist):

'By the courtesy of nations, whatever laws are carried into execution, within the limits of any government, are considered as having the same effect every where, so far as they do not occasion a prejudice to the rights of the other governments, or their citizens. . . . .

See also Hilton v. Guyot, 159 U.S. 113, 163–164 (1895):

"Comity," in the legal sense, is neither a matter of absolute obligation, on the one hand, nor of mere courtesy and good will, upon the other. But it is the recognition which one nation allows within its territory to the legislative, executive or judicial acts of another nation, having due regard both to international duty and convenience, and to the rights of its own citizens or of other persons who are under the protection of its laws.

[14] The nature of the concerns that guide a comity analysis is suggested by the Restatement of Foreign Relations Law of the United States (Revised) § 437(1)(c) (Tent. Draft No. 7, 1986) (approved May 14, 1986) (Restatement) [now at § 442, *supra*]. While we recognize that § [442] of the Restatement may not represent a consensus of international views on the scope of the district court's power to order foreign discovery in the face of objections by foreign states, these factors are relevant to any comity analysis . . . .

[15] The French "blocking statute," *supra*, does not alter our conclusion. It is well settled that such statutes do not deprive an American court of the power to order a party subject to its jurisdiction to produce evidence even though the act of production may violate that statute. *See Societe Internationale Pour Participations Industrielles et Commerciales*; *S. A. v. Rogers*, 357 U.S. 197, 204–206 (1958). Nor can the enactment of such a statute by a foreign nation require American courts to engraft a rule of first resort onto the Hague Convention, or otherwise to provide the

of blocking statutes and discovery orders: "When a state has jurisdiction to prescribe and its courts have jurisdiction to adjudicate, adjudication should (subject to generally applicable rules of evidence) take place on the basis of the best information available. . . . [Blocking] statutes that frustrate this goal need not be given the same deference by courts of the United States as substantive rules of law at variance with the law of the United States." *See* RESTATEMENT § 437 [442], Reporter's Note 5, pp. 41, 42. "On the other hand, the degree of friction created by discovery requests . . . and the differing perceptions of the acceptability of American-style discovery under national and international law, suggest some efforts to moderate the application abroad of U.S. procedural techniques, consistent with the overall principle of reasonableness in the exercise of jurisdiction."

Some discovery procedures are much more "intrusive" than others. In this case, for example, an interrogatory asking petitioners to identify the pilots who flew flight tests in the Rallye before it was certified for flight by the Federal Aviation Administration, or a request to admit that petitioners authorized certain advertising in a particular magazine, is certainly less intrusive than a request to produce all of the "design specifications, line drawings and engineering plans and all engineering change orders and plans and all drawings concerning the leading edge slats for the Rallye type aircraft manufactured by the Defendants." Even if a court might be persuaded that a particular document request was too burdensome or too "intrusive" to be granted in full, with or without an appropriate protective order, it might well refuse to insist upon the use of Convention procedures before requiring responses to simple interrogatories or requests for admissions. The exact line between reasonableness and unreasonableness in each case must be drawn by the trial court, based on its knowledge of the case and of the claims and interests of the parties and the governments whose statutes and policies they invoke.

American courts, in supervising pretrial proceedings, should exercise special vigilance to protect foreign litigants from the danger that unnecessary, or unduly burdensome, discovery may place them in a disadvantageous position. Judicial supervision of discovery should always seek to minimize its costs and inconvenience and to prevent improper uses of discovery requests. When it is necessary to seek evidence abroad, however, the district court must supervise pretrial proceedings particularly closely to prevent discovery abuses.

---

nationals of such a country with a preferred status in our courts. It is clear that American courts are not required to adhere blindly to the directives of such a statute. Indeed, the language of the statute, if taken literally, would appear to represent an extraordinary exercise of legislative jurisdiction by the Republic of France over a United States district judge, forbidding him or her to order any discovery from a party of French nationality, even simple requests for admissions or interrogatories that the party could respond to on the basis of personal knowledge. It would be particularly incongruous to recognize such a preference for corporations that are wholly owned by the enacting nation. Extraterritorial assertions of jurisdiction are not one-sided. While the District Court's discovery orders arguably have some impact in France, the French blocking statute asserts similar authority over acts to take place in this country. The lesson of comity is that neither the discovery order nor the blocking statute can have the same omnipresent effect that it would have in a world of only one sovereign. The blocking statute thus is relevant to the court's particularized comity analysis only to the extent that its terms and its enforcement identify the nature of the sovereign interests in nondisclosure of specific kinds of material.

For example, the additional cost of transportation of documents or witnesses to or from foreign locations may increase the danger that discovery may be sought for the improper purpose of motivating settlement, rather than finding relevant and probative evidence. Objections to "abusive" discovery that foreign litigants advance should therefore receive the most careful consideration. In addition, we have long recognized the demands of comity in suits involving foreign states, either as parties or as sovereigns with a coordinate interest in the litigation. *See Hilton v. Guyot*, 159 U.S. 113 (1895). American courts should therefore take care to demonstrate due respect for any special problem confronted by the foreign litigant on account of its nationality or the location of its operations, and for any sovereign interest expressed by a foreign state. We do not articulate specific rules to guide this delicate task of adjudication.[16]

VI

In the case before us, the Magistrate and the Court of Appeals correctly refused to grant the broad protective order that petitioners requested. The Court of Appeals erred, however, in stating that the Evidence Convention does not apply to the pending discovery demands. This holding may be read as indicating that the Convention procedures are not even an option that is open to the District Court. It must be recalled, however, that the Convention's specification of duties in executing states creates corresponding rights in requesting states; holding that the Convention does not apply in this situation would deprive domestic litigants of access to evidence through treaty procedures to which the contracting states have assented. Moreover, such a rule would deny the foreign litigant a full and fair opportunity to demonstrate appropriate reasons for employing Convention procedures in the first instance, for some aspects of the discovery process. Accordingly, the judgment of the Court of Appeals is vacated, and the case is remanded for further proceedings consistent with this opinion.

JUSTICE BLACKMUN, with whom JUSTICE BRENNAN, JUSTICE MARSHALL, and JUSTICE O'CONNOR join, concurring in part and dissenting in part.

Some might well regard the Court's decision in this case as an affront to the nations that have joined the United States in ratifying the Hague Convention. . . . The Court ignores the importance of the Convention by relegating it to an "optional" status, without acknowledging the significant achievement in accommodating divergent interests that the Convention represents. Experience to date indicates that there is a large risk that the

---

[16] Under the Hague Convention, a letter of request must specify "the evidence to be obtained or other judicial act to be performed," Art. 3, and must be in the language of the executing authority or be accompanied by a translation into that language. Art. 4. Although the discovery request must be specific, the party seeking discovery may find it difficult or impossible to determine in advance what evidence is within the control of the party urging resort to the Convention and which parts of that evidence may qualify for international judicial assistance under the Convention. This information, however, is presumably within the control of the producing party from which discovery is sought. The district court may therefore require, in appropriate situations, that this party bear the burden of providing translations and detailed descriptions of relevant documents that are needed to assure prompt and complete production pursuant to the terms of the Convention.

case-by-case comity analysis now to be permitted by the Court will be performed inadequately and that the somewhat unfamiliar procedures of the Convention will be invoked infrequently. I fear the Court's decision means that courts will resort unnecessarily to issuing discovery orders under the Federal Rules of Civil Procedure in a raw exercise of their jurisdictional power to the detriment of the United States' national and international interests. The Court's view of this country's international obligations is particularly unfortunate in a world in which regular commercial and legal channels loom ever more crucial.

I do agree with the Court's repudiation of the positions at both extremes of the spectrum with regard to the use of the Convention. Its rejection of the view that the Convention is not "applicable" at all to this case is surely correct: the Convention clearly applies to litigants as well as to third parties, and to requests for evidence located abroad, no matter where that evidence is actually "produced." The Court also correctly rejects the far opposite position that the Convention provides the exclusive means for discovery involving signatory countries. I dissent, however, because I cannot endorse the Court's case-by-case inquiry for determining whether to use Convention procedures and its failure to provide lower courts with any meaningful guidance for carrying out that inquiry. In my view, the Convention provides effective discovery proce-dures that largely eliminate the conflicts between United States and foreign law on evidence gathering. I therefore would apply a general presumption that, in most cases, courts should resort first to the Convention procedures. An individualized analysis of the circumstances of a particular case is appropriate only when it appears that it would be futile to employ the Conven-tion or when its procedures prove to be unhelpful.

I

Even though the Convention does not expressly require discovery of materi-als in foreign countries to proceed exclusively according to its procedures, it cannot be viewed as merely advisory. The Convention was drafted at the request and with the enthusiastic participation of the United States, which sought to broaden the techniques available for the taking of evidence abroad. The differences between discovery practices in the United States and those in other countries are significant, and "no aspect of the extension of the Ameri-can legal system beyond the territorial frontier of the United States has given rise to so much friction as the request for documents associated with investiga-tion and litigation in the United States." RESTATEMENT OFFOREIGN RELATIONS LAW OF THE UNITED STATES (Revised) § 437 [442], Reporters' Note 1, p. 35 (Tent. Draft No. 7, Apr. 10, 1986). Of particular import is the fact that discovery conducted by the parties, as is common in the United States, is alien to the legal systems of civil-law nations, which typically regard evidence gathering as a judicial function. . . .

It is not at all satisfactory to view the Convention as nothing more than an optional supplement to the Federal Rules of Civil Procedure, useful as a means to "facilitate discovery" when a court "deems that course of action appropriate." Unless they had expected the Convention to provide the normal channels for discovery, other parties to the Convention would have had no incentive to agree to its terms. The civil-law nations committed themselves to employ more effective procedures for gathering evidence within their borders, even to the extent of requiring some common-law practices alien to their systems. . . .

II

By viewing the Convention as merely optional and leaving the decision whether to apply it to the court in each individual case, the majority ignores the policies established by the political branches when they negotiated and ratified the treaty. The result will be a duplicative analysis for which courts are not well designed. The discovery process usually concerns discrete interests that a court is well equipped to accommodate — the interests of the parties before the court coupled with the interest of the judicial system in resolving the conflict on the basis of the best available information. When a lawsuit requires discovery of materials located in a foreign nation, however, foreign legal systems and foreign interests are implicated as well. The presence of these interests creates a tension between the broad discretion our courts normally exercise in managing pretrial discovery and the discretion usually allotted to the Executive in foreign matters.

It is the Executive that normally decides when a course of action is important enough to risk affronting a foreign nation or placing a strain on foreign commerce. It is the Executive, as well, that is best equipped to determine how to accommodate foreign interests along with our own.[1] Unlike the courts, "diplomatic and executive channels are, by definition, designed to exchange, negotiate, and reconcile the problems which accompany the realization of national interests within the sphere of international association." *Laker Airways, Ltd. v. Sabena; Belgian World Airlines,* 731 F.2d 909, 955 (1984). The Convention embodies the result of the best efforts of the Executive Branch, in negotiating the treaty, and the Legislative Branch, in ratifying it, to balance competing national interests. As such, the Convention represents a political determination — one that, consistent with the principle of separation of powers, courts should not attempt to second-guess.

Not only is the question of foreign discovery more appropriately considered by the Executive and Congress, but in addition, courts are generally ill equipped to assume the role of balancing the interests of foreign nations with that of our own. Although transnational litigation is increasing, relatively few judges are experienced in the area and the procedures of foreign legal systems are often poorly understood. As this Court recently stated, it has "little competence in determining precisely when foreign nations will be offended by particular acts." *Container Corp. v. Franchise Tax Bd.,* 463 U.S. 159, 194 (1983). A pro-forum bias is likely to creep into the supposedly neutral balancing process[2] and courts not surprisingly often will turn to the more

---

[1] Our Government's interests themselves are far more complicated than can be represented by the limited parties before a court. The United States is increasingly concerned, for example, with protecting sensitive technology for both economic and military reasons. It may not serve the country's long-term interest to establish precedents that could allow foreign courts to compel production of the records of American corporations.

[2] One of the ways that a pro-forum bias has manifested itself is in United States courts' preoccu-

familiar procedures established by their local rules. In addition, it simply is not reasonable to expect the Federal Government or the foreign state in which the discovery will take place to participate in every individual case in order to articulate the broader international and foreign interests that are relevant to the decision whether to use the Convention. Indeed, the opportunities for such participation are limited. . . .

III

The principle of comity leads to more definite rules than the ad hoc approach endorsed by the majority. The Court asserts that the concept of comity requires an individualized analysis of the interests present in each particular case before a court decides whether to apply the Convention. There is, however, nothing inherent in the comity principle that requires case-by-case analysis. The Court frequently has relied upon a comity analysis when it has adopted general rules to cover recurring situations in areas such as choice of forum, maritime law, and sovereign immunity, and the Court offers no reasons for abandoning that approach here.

Comity is not just a vague political concern favoring international cooperation when it is in our interest to do so. Rather it is a principle under which judicial decisions reflect the systematic value of reciprocal tolerance and goodwill. *See* Maier, *Extraterritorial Jurisdiction at a Crossroads: An Intersection Between Public and International Law*, 76 AM. J. INT'L L. 280, 281–285 (1982); J. Story, Commentaries on the Conflict of Laws §§ 35, 38 (8th ed. 1883).[3] As in the choice-of-law analysis, which from the very beginning has been linked to international comity, the threshold question in a comity analysis is whether there is in fact a true conflict between domestic and foreign law. When there is a conflict, a court should seek a reasonable accommodation that reconciles the central concerns of both sets of laws. In doing

---

pation with their own power to issue discovery orders. All too often courts have regarded the Convention as some kind of threat to their jurisdiction and have rejected use of the treaty procedures. It is well established that a court has the power to impose discovery under the Federal Rules of Civil Procedure when it has personal jurisdiction over the foreign party. *See Societe Internationale v. Rogers*, 357 U.S. 197, 204–206 (1958). But once it is determined that the Convention does not provide the exclusive means for foreign discovery, jurisdictional power is not the issue. The relevant question, instead, becomes whether a court should forgo exercise of the full extent of its power to order discovery. The Convention, which is valid United States law, provides an answer to that question by establishing a strong policy in favor of self-restraint for the purpose of furthering United States interests and minimizing international disputes.

There is also a tendency on the part of courts, perhaps unrecognized, to view a dispute from a local perspective. "Domestic courts do not sit as internationally constituted tribunals. . . . The courts of most developed countries follow international law only to the extent it is not overridden by national law. Thus courts inherently find it difficult neutrally to balance competing foreign interests. When there is any doubt, national interests will tend to be favored over foreign interests." *Laker Airways, Ltd. v. Sabena, Belgian World Airlines*, 731 F.2d 909, 951 (1984) (footnotes omitted); *see also In re Uranium Antitrust Litigation*, 480 F.Supp. 1138, 1148 (N.D. Ill. 1979).

[3] Justice Story used the phrase "comity of nations" to "express the true foundation and extent of the obligation of the laws of one nation within the territories of another." § 38. "The true foundation on which the administration of international law must rest is, that the rules which are to govern are those which arise from mutual interest and utility, from a sense of the inconveniences which would result from a contrary doctrine, and from a sort of moral necessity to do justice, in order that justice may be done to us in return." § 35.

so, it should perform a tripartite analysis that considers the foreign interests, the interests of the United States, and the mutual interests of all nations in a smoothly functioning international legal regime.[4] . . .

[In the usual case, the courts should require first use of the Convention.] There are, however, some situations in which there is legitimate concern that certain documents cannot be made available under Convention procedures. Thirteen nations have made official declarations pursuant to Article 23 of the Convention, which permits a contracting state to limit its obligation to produce documents in response to a letter of request. These reservations may pose problems that would require a comity analysis in an individual case, but they are not so all-encompassing as the majority implies — they certainly do not mean that a "contracting party could unilaterally abrogate . . . the Convention's procedures." First, the reservations can apply only to *letters of request for documents*. Thus, an Article 23 reservation affects neither the most commonly used informal Convention procedures for taking of evidence by a consul or a commissioner nor formal requests for depositions or interrogatories. Second, although Article 23 refers broadly to "pre-trial discovery," the intended meaning of the term appears to have been much narrower than the normal United States usage. The contracting parties for the most part have modified the declarations made pursuant to Article 23 to limit their reach. Indeed, the emerging view of this exception to discovery is that it applies only to "requests that lack sufficient specificity or that have not been reviewed for relevancy by the requesting court." Thus, in practice, a reservation is not the significant obstacle to discovery under the Convention that the broad wording of Article 23 would suggest. . . .

The second major United States interest is in fair and equal treatment of litigants. The Court cites several fairness concerns in support of its conclusion that the Convention is not exclusive and apparently fears that a broad endorsement of the use of the Convention would lead to the same "unacceptable asymmetries." Courts can protect against the first two concerns noted by the majority — that a foreign party to a lawsuit would have a discovery advantage over a domestic litigant because it could obtain the advantages of the Federal Rules of Civil Procedure, and that a foreign company would have an economic competitive advantage because it would be subject to less extensive discovery — by exercising their discretionary powers to control discovery in order to ensure fairness to both parties. A court may "make any order which justice requires" to limit discovery, including an order permitting discovery only on specified terms and conditions, by a particular discovery method, or with limitation in scope to certain matters. *See* Fed. Rule Civ. Proc. 26(c). If, for instance, resort to the Convention procedures would put one party at a disadvantage, any possible unfairness could be prevented by postponing that party's obligation to respond to discovery requests until completion of the

---

[4] Choice-of-law decisions similarly reflect the needs of the system as a whole as well as the concerns of the forums with an interest in the controversy. "Probably the most important function of choice-of-law rules is to make the interstate and international systems work well. Choice-of-law rules, among other things, should seek to further harmonious relations between states and to facilitate commercial intercourse between them. In formulating rules of choice of law, a state should have regard for the needs and policies of other states and of the community of states." RESTATEMENT (SECOND) OF CONFLICT OF LAWS § 6, Comment d, p. 13 (1971).

foreign discovery. Moreover, the Court's arguments focus on the nationality of the parties, while it is actually the locus of the evidence that is relevant to use of the Convention: a foreign litigant trying to secure evidence from a foreign branch of an American litigant might also be required to resort to the Convention.

The Court's third fairness concern is illusory. It fears that a domestic litigant suing a national of a state that is not a party to the Convention would have an advantage over a litigant suing a national of a contracting state. This statement completely ignores the very purpose of the Convention. The negotiations were proposed by the United States in order to facilitate discovery, not to hamper litigants. Dissimilar treatment of litigants similarly situated does occur, but in the manner opposite to that perceived by the Court. Those who sue nationals of noncontracting states are disadvantaged by the unavailability of the Convention procedures. This is an unavoidable inequality inherent in the benefits conferred by any treaty that is less than universally ratified.

In most instances, use of the Convention will serve to advance United States interests, particularly when those interests are viewed in a context larger than the immediate interest of the litigants' discovery. The approach I propose is not a rigid per se rule that would require first use of the Convention without regard to strong indications that no evidence would be forthcoming. All too often, however, courts have simply assumed that resort to the Convention would be unproductive and have embarked on speculation about foreign procedures and interpretations. When resort to the Convention would be futile, a court has no choice but to resort to a traditional comity analysis. But even then, an attempt to use the Convention will often be the best way to discover if it will be successful, particularly in the present state of general inexperience with the implementation of its procedures by the various contracting states. An attempt to use the Convention will open a dialogue with the authorities in the foreign state and in that way a United States court can obtain an authoritative answer as to the limits on what it can achieve with a discovery request in a particular contracting state. . . .

Use of the Convention would help develop methods for transnational litigation by placing officials in a position to communicate directly about conflicts that arise during discovery, thus enabling them to promote a reduction in those conflicts. In a broader framework, courts that use the Convention will avoid foreign perceptions of unfairness that result when United States courts show insensitivity to the interests safeguarded by foreign legal regimes. Because of the position of the United States, economically, politically, and militarily, many countries may be reluctant to oppose discovery orders of United States courts. Foreign acquiescence to orders that ignore the Convention, however, is likely to carry a price tag of accumulating resentment, with the predictable long-term political cost that cooperation will be withheld in other matters. Use of the Convention is a simple step to take toward avoiding that unnecessary and undesirable consequence.

IV

I can only hope that courts faced with discovery requests for materials in foreign countries will avoid the parochial views that too often have characterized the decisions to date. Many of the considerations that lead me to the conclusion that there should be a general presumption favoring use of the Convention should also carry force when courts analyze particular cases. The majority fails to offer guidance in this endeavor, and thus it has missed its opportunity to provide predictable and effective procedures for international litigants in United States courts. It now falls to the lower courts to recognize the needs of the international commercial system and the accommodation of those needs already endorsed by the political branches and embodied in the Convention.

Notes and Questions on *Aerospatiale*

1. *Analyzing Aerospatiale.* How would you articulate the difference between the majority opinion and the opinion of Justice Blackmun? In what ways might the majority opinion balkanize the lower courts' approaches to subsequent discovery disputes?

2. *Public treaty/private incentive.* What is the incentive for a private litigant to pursue discovery through the Hague Evidence Convention voluntarily?

3. *Pre-trial documents under the convention.* The vast majority of parties to the Hague Evidence Convention, other than the United States, have adopted declarations under Article 23, to the effect that they "will not execute Letters of Request issued for the purpose of obtaining pretrial discovery of documents as known in common law countries." Given the importance of pre-trial discovery of documents to litigants in the United States, what is the value of the convention for them? *See* RESTATEMENT (THIRD) OF FOREIGN RELATIONS LAW, § 473, cmt. h, noting that Article 23 "applies only to letters of request for discovery of documents, and does not preclude examination before trial of witnesses pursuant to a letter of request" as for example through interrogatories, request of admissions, and depositions.

4. *Comparing Aerospatiale and Schlunk.* From one perspective, *Aerospatiale* is to the Hague Evidence Convention as *Schlunk* is to the Hague Service Convention, *supra*. But how are the two treaties handled differently in the two cases, and what accounts for the difference?

---

[3]   The Aftermath of *Aerospatiale*

[a]   The Methodology of Balancing: Will Foreign Interests *Ever* Prevail over U.S. Interests in a U.S. Court?

RICHMARK CORP. v. TIMBER FALLING CONSULTANTS
959 F.2d 1468 (9th Cir. 1992)

This case presents a number of difficult questions regarding a sensitive area of law and foreign relations. Timber Falling Consultants, Inc. (TFC) won a default judgment for fraud and breach of contract against Beijing Ever Bright Industrial Co. (Beijing), a corporation organized under the laws of the People's Republic of China (PRC) and an arm of the PRC government. As part of an effort to execute that judgment, TFC sought discovery of Beijing's assets worldwide. Beijing resisted those discovery efforts, and refused to comply when ordered to do so by the district court. The district court imposed discovery sanctions, held Beijing in contempt, and ordered contempt fines of $10,000 a day. Beijing contends that PRC secrecy laws prevent it from complying with the discovery order and that it would be subject to prosecution in the PRC were it to comply. It appeals the discovery order, the discovery sanction, the contempt order, and the district court's refusal to vacate the contempt order.

While we acknowledge the importance of the interests the State Secrecy statute is designed to protect, we conclude in the circumstances of this case that the PRC's laws limiting disclosure cannot excuse Beijing's failure to comply with the district court's orders. For this reason, we affirm the discovery and contempt orders. . . .

FACTUAL AND PROCEDURAL BACKGROUND

Beijing contracted to purchase lumber from Richmark Corp. Richmark in turn retained TFC to procure the timber. After the contract fell through, Richmark sued TFC. TFC counterclaimed against Richmark and cross-claimed against all other parties involved, including Beijing, alleging fraud and breach of contract. Beijing failed to appear, apparently because of the interruption in United States-PRC relations which followed the Tienanmen square incident. All other claims on both sides were dismissed by the district court, but TFC was awarded a $2.2 million default judgment against Beijing. . . .

Beijing appealed this judgment to the Ninth Circuit. Beijing did not post a supersedeas bond or letter of credit, however, so TFC was free to begin efforts to collect the judgment while the appeal was pending. In an attempt to do so, TFC served Beijing with a number of discovery requests and interrogatories which sought to identify Beijing's assets worldwide. Beijing did not respond to those requests, and instead moved for a stay of discovery pending resolution of its . . . motion for relief from the judgment [which the district court denied.]. TFC in turn filed a motion to compel discovery [which the district court granted.] . . .

[Beijing petitioned the court of appeals for a stay of discovery and then] for the first time requested advice from its government on how to respond to TFC's discovery requests. Specifically, Beijing sought guidance as to whether PRC "State Secrecy Laws" prohibited it from disclosing the requested information concerning its assets. This request was passed by the State Secrecy Bureau to another arm of the State Council, the Ever Bright Group, which was in charge of overseeing Beijing's operations. . . . The Ever Bright Group sent written notification to Beijing that almost all of its financial information was classified a state secret and could not be disclosed.

Meanwhile, following the denial of the stay petition by the Ninth Circuit, TFC moved for contempt and discovery sanctions against Beijing. In its answer, Beijing for the first time raised the issue of the State Secrecy Laws. The district court denied the request for sanctions, but it rejected Beijing's contention that PRC law prevented it from complying as "untimely and without merit," and again ordered Beijing to respond to TFC's discovery requests. Beijing moved the district court for a protective order against discovery, on the same grounds. The district court denied this motion. . . .

Beijing still refused to comply with the discovery orders, [and] . . . the district court held Beijing in contempt of its [prior] orders. It awarded TFC its attorney's fees and costs incurred in seeking discovery as a discovery sanction, and imposed contempt fines of $10,000 a day, payable to TFC, until Beijing complied with the discovery orders. However, the district court indicated that it would vacate the contempt order if Beijing complied with the discovery orders within 60 days.

Beijing provided the limited amount of information the Ever Bright Group allowed it to disclose,[1] and moved the district court to vacate the contempt sanctions [which the district court denied]. Beijing appeals on a variety of grounds from the discovery order, the contempt order, and the denial of its motion to vacate. . . .

DISCUSSION

. . . Beijing contends that the state secrecy laws prohibit it from disclosing the information the district court ordered it to provide, that it would be subject to criminal prosecution if it did disclose such information, and that this prohibition necessitates the reversal of the discovery order and the contempt sanctions against it. The district court explicitly accepted Beijing's contention that the PRC's State Secrets Act barred disclosure of the information in question. We do so as well.[2]

That does not end the inquiry, however. The PRC's admitted interest in secrecy must be balanced against the interests of the United States and the plaintiffs in obtaining the information. In *Societe Internationale Pour Participations Industrielles et Commerciales v. Rogers,* 357 U.S. 197 (1958) (*Societe Internationale*), the Supreme Court confronted a similar issue. In that case, the petitioner, a Swiss company, objected to discovery requests on the grounds that producing Swiss bank records would violate Swiss law. The Swiss Federal Attorney had issued an order prohibiting their disclosure. The district court expressly concluded that the Swiss company acted in good faith in seeking to comply, and the company did disclose over 190,000 documents during discovery. The Supreme Court held that the company had failed to comply with the order, but concluded that the sanction of dismissal of its complaint

---

[1] Specifically, Beijing disclosed the nature of its business, the names and addresses of its offices, and the value and location of its furniture, equipment, and machinery. It refused to disclose the value and location of its cash, real property, bank accounts, stock and bond holdings, other financial portfolios, notes, inventories, accounts receivable, or any other information concerning its assets.

[2] For this reason, the "act of state" doctrine does not apply. That doctrine comes into play only where a United States court declares invalid the official act of a foreign sovereign. In this case, we expressly accept as valid the Ever Bright Group's letter interpreting the State Secrets Act. We have neither the power nor the expertise to determine for ourselves what PRC law is.

was inappropriate. It reached this conclusion because "petitioner's failure to satisfy fully the requirements of this production order was due to inability fostered neither by its own conduct nor by circumstances within its control. It is hardly debatable that fear of criminal prosecution constitutes a weighty excuse for nonproduction . . . ."

Cases since *Societe Internationale*, however, have emphasized that a foreign-law prohibition will not always excuse compliance with a discovery order. In *Societe Nationale Industrielle Aerospatiale v. United States District Court*, 482 U.S. 522 (1987) (*Aerospatiale*), the Supreme Court stated that "it is well settled that such [foreign 'blocking'] statutes do not deprive an American court of the power to order a party subject to its jurisdiction to produce evidence even though the act of production may violate that statute."[3]

Instead, *Aerospatiale* endorsed the balancing test contained in the RESTATE-MENT (THIRD) OF FOREIGN RELATIONS LAW § 442(1)(c). Under that test, factors that are relevant in deciding whether or not foreign statutes excuse noncompliance with discovery orders include:

> the importance to the investigation or litigation of the documents or other information requested; the degree of specificity of the request; whether the information originated in the United States; the availability of alternative means of securing the information; and the extent to which noncompliance with the request would undermine important interests of the United States, or compliance with the request would undermine important interests of the state where the information is located.

As the Court noted, this list of factors is not exhaustive. Other factors that we have considered relevant are " 'the extent and the nature of the hardship that inconsistent enforcement would impose upon the person, . . . [and] the extent to which enforcement by action of either state can reasonably be expected to achieve compliance with the rule prescribed by that state.' " [*United States v. Vetco*, 691 F.2d 1281, 1288 (9th Cir.) (quoting the RESTATE-MENT (SECOND) OFFOREIGN RELATIONS LAW § 40)[, *cert. denied*, 454 U.S. 1098 (1981)).] We consider each factor in turn.

Importance of the Documents. Where the outcome of litigation "does not stand or fall on the present discovery order," or where the evidence sought is cumulative of existing evidence, courts have generally been unwilling to override foreign secrecy laws. Where the evidence is directly relevant, however, we have found this factor to weigh in favor of disclosure. In this case, the information sought is not only relevant to the execution of the judgment, it is crucial. Without information as to Beijing's assets, TFC cannot hope to enforce the judgment. The execution proceedings, and in some sense the underlying judgment itself, will be rendered meaningless. The importance of the documents to the litigation weighs in favor of compelling disclosure.

Specificity of the Request. A second consideration in evaluating a discovery request is how burdensome it will be to respond to that request. Generalized searches for information, the disclosure of which is prohibited under foreign

---

[3] The Court went on to note that "it would be particularly incongruous to recognize such a preference for corporations that are wholly owned by the enacting nation." *Id.* at 545 n.29.

law, are discouraged. In this case, Beijing has not objected to the burdensome nature of the discovery request, apart from the fact of its illegality. While TFC sought a great deal of information, all of it was directed at identifying Beijing's current assets in order to execute the judgment. Further, TFC's request was reasonably limited in time: it sought only recent financial documents. Beijing has not made this factor an issue, and it does not favor nondisclosure here.

Location of Information and Parties. The fact that all the information to be disclosed (and the people who will be deposed or who will produce the documents) are located in a foreign country weighs against disclosure, since those people and documents are subject to the law of that country in the ordinary course of business. In this case, Beijing has no United States office. All of its employees, and all of the documents TFC has requested, are located in the PRC. This factor weighs against requiring disclosure.

Alternate Means of Obtaining Information. If the information sought can easily be obtained elsewhere, there is little or no reason to require a party to violate foreign law. In this circuit, the alternative means must be "substantially equivalent" to the requested discovery. Beijing has not suggested any such alternatives . . . .

One possible alternative would be to seek information from Beijing's nominal parent corporation, China Ever Bright Holdings Co., which is incorporated in Hong Kong. However, as Beijing itself takes pains to note, China Ever Bright is a separate entity from Beijing, and financial information about China Ever Bright is not relevant to Beijing's financial position. A second alternative would be to subpoena information from sources in the United States who have dealt with Beijing and might have financial information. TFC in fact has attempted to do this, issuing subpoenas to the Bank of China, Mesta Engineering Corp., Shougang Mechanical Equipment of Pennsylvania, and Solid Beam Industrial Co. TFC was not successful in obtaining information from these sources. Indeed, it failed in part because Beijing and its affiliates actively opposed those subpoenas. Further, Beijing concedes that any information received from these sources would not include the core financial information requested by TFC. Finally, TFC has requested depositions of various Beijing officials, which obviously cannot be provided by anyone other than Beijing.

TFC appears to have done everything in its power to collect information which will enable it to enforce the judgment. To date, it has been unsuccessful. The absence of other sources for the information TFC seeks is a factor which weighs strongly in favor of compelling disclosure.

Balance of National Interests. This is the most important factor. We must assess the interests of each nation in requiring or prohibiting disclosure, and determine whether disclosure would "affect important substantive policies or interests" of either the United States or the PRC. RESTATEMENT (THIRD) OF FOREIGN RELATIONS LAW § 442 comment c.[4] In assessing the strength of the

---

[4] Initially, Beijing contends that the court is not empowered to look beyond the Chinese government's assertion of its interest in preventing disclosure to determine the strength of that interest. Beijing is in error. As we have recognized, in balancing sovereign interests the court is "necessarily interested in the depth and nature of [the foreign sovereign's] interest." *Timberlane Lumber Co. v. Bank of America,* 549 F.2d 597, 607 (9th Cir. 1976). Indeed, Beijing itself appears to concede in its brief that the court must balance the competing national interests at stake.

PRC's interests, we will consider "expressions of interest by the foreign state," "the significance of disclosure in the regulation . . . of the activity in question," and "indications of the foreign state's concern for confidentiality prior to the controversy."

In this case, the PRC's State Secrecy Bureau has directly expressed an interest in the outcome of this case. In its response to Beijing's request for guidance, the Bureau wrote: "This Bureau hereby orders your Company not to disclose or provide the information and documents requested by the United States District Court for the District of Oregon except Items 1, 2, 3(f), 9 and 10. Your Company shall bear any or all legal consequences should you not comply with this order."

However, the State Secrecy Bureau did not express interest in the confidentiality of this information prior to the litigation in question. Indeed, Beijing routinely disclosed information regarding its assets, inventory, bank accounts, and corporate structure to the general public, for example through a trade brochure, and to companies with whom it did business. The State Secrecy Bureau did not object to the voluntary disclosure of any of this information. It is only now, when disclosure will have adverse consequences for Beijing, that the PRC has asserted its interest in confidentiality.

Further, neither Beijing nor the PRC has identified any way in which disclosure of the information requested here will significantly affect the PRC's interests in confidentiality. Those interests, as set forth by the State Secrecy Laws themselves, are in "matters involving national security and interest." *Collection of the Laws of the People's Republic of China* 1363, Art. 2 (1989). This is defined to include information which "concerns the national economy and social development" or disclosure of which may "diminish the country's economic, technological and scientific strength." *Id.* at Art. 8, Art. 4(7). There is no indication that Beijing, much less the economy of the PRC as a whole, will be adversely affected at all by disclosure of this information. The only likely "adverse" effect on the PRC economy will be that TFC may be able to collect its judgment, something the PRC has no legitimate state interest in preventing.

The PRC, then, has asserted an interest (albeit one whose strength is unknown) in the confidentiality of the information in question. This interest must be weighed against the United States' interests in vindicating the rights of American plaintiffs and in enforcing the judgments of its courts. The former interest has been described as "substantial," and the latter as "vital," To be sure, these interests are not so strong that they would compel disclosure in all cases. In this case, however, because Beijing and the PRC have been unable to identify any way in which the PRC's interests will be hurt by disclosure, the interests of the United States must prevail. The balancing of national interests is therefore a factor which weighs in favor of disclosure.

Hardship to Beijing. The effect that a discovery order is likely to have on the foreign company is another factor to be considered. If Beijing is likely to face criminal prosecution in the PRC for complying with the United States court order, that fact constitutes a "weighty excuse" for nonproduction. In this case, Beijing has in fact been ordered by the Chinese government to withhold the information, and has been told that it will bear the "legal consequences" of disclosing the information.[5] Beijing therefore seems to be placed in a difficult position, between the Scylla of contempt sanctions and the Charybdis of possible criminal prosecution.

However, if the hardship is self-imposed, or if Beijing could have avoided it, the fact that it finds itself in an undesirable position will not work against disclosure of the requested information. In this case, the discovery dispute arose only because Beijing refused to post a supersedeas bond or letter of credit to stay execution of the judgment pending appeal, as required by [the Federal Rules of Civil Procedure.] Beijing even now could post a supersedeas bond pending the outcome of its petition for certiorari, or it could pay the judgment. Either of these courses of action would keep it from having to violate either the district court's orders or the PRC's laws. . . . Because Beijing could — and still can — avoid the hardship disclosure would place on it, that hardship is not a factor weighing against disclosure.

Likelihood of Compliance. If a discovery order is likely to be unenforceable, and therefore to have no practical effect, that factor counsels against requiring compliance with the order. In this case, it may be impossible to force Beijing to comply. The imposition of sanctions in the amount of $10,000 a day, sanctions which have already grown larger than the underlying judgment, has failed to move Beijing. It is perhaps unrealistic to expect that a PRC court will enforce an order requiring Beijing to violate PRC law. Compliance therefore seems unlikely, a factor counseling against compelling discovery.

Nonetheless, the discovery and contempt orders may be of some significance. While Beijing apparently has no assets in the United States, it has in the past done substantial business in this country. Should it wish to do business here in the future, it would have to pay the judgment or risk having its assets seized and its business interrupted. In addition, a clear statement that foreign corporations which avail themselves of business opportunities in the United States must abide by United States laws might have a substantial effect on the way Beijing and other corporations do business in the United States in the future. . . .

In short, full compliance by Beijing with the order of the district court is unlikely. The order may nonetheless produce partial compliance, and might be effective in other ways as well. While the likelihood of noncompliance does weigh against compelling disclosure, we think the weight of this factor is lessened by these mitigating circumstances.

Conclusion. Taking all of the aforementioned factors into consideration, the balance tips significantly (although not overwhelmingly) in TFC's favor. The United States has a strong interest in enforcing its judgments which out-weighs the PRC's interest in confidentiality in this case. The information sought is vital to the litigation and cannot be obtained elsewhere. Finally, Beijing can avoid any hardship it may face by following normal litigation procedure and posting a supersedeas bond. If it does so, both the district court and TFC have indicated a willingness to forego contempt sanctions. The only factors weighing against compelling disclosure are that Beijing has the

---

[5] Beijing has not, however, provided any indication of what those consequences are likely to be.

information in the PRC and may choose not to disclose it in spite of the court's order. Were these factors alone sufficient, a foreign corporation could avoid its discovery obligations in almost every instance. We therefore conclude that the order compelling discovery should be upheld in spite of the PRC secrecy statute.

In reaching this conclusion, we are not unmindful of the difficulties foreign corporations face in doing business in the United States, nor of the rather delicate nature of relations between sovereign states. We sincerely hope that today's decision will not adversely affect the cordial business relationship between the United States and the PRC. However, international business requires the accommodation of different legal climates. Just as United States companies doing business in the PRC must expect to abide by PRC law, when Beijing availed itself of business opportunities in this country, it undertook an obligation to comply with the lawful orders of United States courts. We do not minimize the difficult situation in which Beijing has been placed. Here, however, where the PRC has not demonstrated a strong interest in keeping the requested information confidential, and where Beijing has options open to it which violate neither United States nor PRC law, Beijing cannot escape compliance with the district court's discovery orders. . . .

Beijing next contends that, even if the discovery order was valid, the contempt sanction should be vacated because Beijing has attempted in good faith to comply with the court's orders. It is true that contempt is inappropriate where a party has taken "all the reasonable steps" it can take to comply. The RESTATEMENT (THIRD) OF FOREIGN RELATIONS LAW § 442(2)(b) provides that "a court or agency should not ordinarily impose sanctions of contempt . . . on a party that has failed to comply with the order for production, except in cases of deliberate concealment or removal of information or of failure to make a good faith effort" to secure permission from the foreign government to disclose the information.

In *Vetco*, we required a foreign corporation asserting a blocking statute as a defense to make an affirmative showing of its good faith in seeking permission to disclose the information. 691 F.2d at 1287 ("This case is not controlled by *Societe Internationale*. We have no finding that appellants have made good faith efforts to comply with the summonses. . ."; *see also* RESTATEMENT (THIRD) OF FOREIGN RELATIONS LAW § 442 comment h ("Parties to litigation . . . may be required to show that they have made serious efforts before appropriate authorities of states with blocking statutes to secure release or waiver from a prohibition against disclosure.")

Beijing has made no such affirmative showing here. The district court did not find that Beijing acted in good faith in attempting to obtain a waiver. Nor is good faith evident from the record. Beijing fought disclosure for several months before raising the foreign law problem, even after the district court issued an order. . . compelling disclosure. Beijing's effort to seek a waiver consisted of a letter to the Ministry of Justice . . . in which it noted the "broad scope" of the discovery order, pointed out to the Ministry the legal provision it felt barred disclosure, and asked whether it was permitted to disclose the information under the State Secrets Act. While Beijing did ask whether there was "a procedure through which Beijing Ever Bright may seek the permission of the government to disclose the information it is not presently permitted to disclose," it did not in fact seek such permission, but rather requested only "guidance" on the legal question. In spite of this, Beijing asserted that the State Secrets Act prevented it from complying . . . two months before the Ministry even responded to this request. Beijing does not appear to have made a good faith effort to clarify PRC law or to seek a waiver of the secrecy statutes before refusing to comply with the district court order. For these reasons, the district court acted within its discretion in sanctioning Beijing for its noncompliance. . . .

REINSURANCE COMPANY OF AMERICA, INC. v. ADMINISTRATIA ASIGURARILOR de STAT
(Administration of State Insurance)
902 F.2d 1275 (7th Cir. 1990)

[Reinsurance Company of America (RCA), an Illinois corporation engaged in the reinsurance business, won a summary judgment against Administratia Asigurarilor de Stat (ADAS), an insurance corporation wholly owned by the Romanian government, for breach of contract and was awarded damages in the amount of $337, 597.00. In an effort to enforce its judgment, RCA served various post-judgment interrogatories, with which ADAS only partially complied. It objected to some of RCA's inquiries on the ground that compliance would violate Romanian law prohibiting disclosure of state secrets. RCA then filed a motion to compel ADAS to respond. The district court denied the motion to compel, indicating that the balance of the interests weighed in favor of Romania's laws protecting national secrecy. RCA appeals.]

RCA contends . . . that the district court abused its discretion by denying its request for post-judgment interrogatories. RCA, in an effort to collect its damage award, filed a series of these interrogatories with the district court. . . . ADAS refused to respond to three of these inquiries. Each of the interrogatories in controversy asked ADAS to provide information regarding insurance contracts with firms in the United States, Canada, and the United Kingdom.[1] In explaining this refusal to furnish a response, ADAS claimed

---

[1] Specifically, ADAS objected to interrogatories 2, 6, and 9. These interrogatories provided:

2. For each and every person, partnership or corporation maintaining a residence or which is domiciled in the United States, which is insured or reinsured by ADAS and which has exposures in the United States, Canada and/or the United Kingdom, identify the following:

    (a) The name and address of the insured or reinsured;

    (b) The policy treaty or facultative certificates which provide the coverage; and

    (c) The policy limit for each coverage in U.S. dollars.

6. State whether ADAS has in force any reinsurance agreements with any ceding companies located in the United States, Canada and/or the United Kingdom, pursuant to which funds held by such ceding companies earn interest which is ultimately payable to ADAS, and if so, identify for each:

    (a) The name of the ceding company;

    (b) The business address of the ceding company;

that Romanian law forbade disclosure of the requested information.[2] Judge Grady denied RCA's motion to compel responses to the three disputed interrogatories. Because we agree with this decision, we affirm.

When the laws of the United States and those of a foreign country are in conflict, as they are here, this circuit, along with several others, has employed a balancing test derived from Section 40, RESTATEMENT (SECOND) OF FOREIGN RELATIONS LAW (1965) ("Section 40"). Section 40 provides:

> Where two states have jurisdiction to prescribe and enforce rules of law and the rules they may prescribe require inconsistent conduct upon the part of a person, each state is required by international law to consider, in good faith, moderating the exercise of its enforcement jurisdiction in light of such factors as
>
> (a) vital national interests of each of the states,
>
> (b) the extent and the nature of the hardship that inconsistent enforcement actions would impose upon the person,
>
> (c) the extent to which the required conduct is to take place in the territory of the other state,
>
> (d) the nationality of the person, and
>
> (e) the extent to which enforcement by action of either state can reasonably be expected to achieve compliance with the rule prescribed by that state.

> (c) The date on which each agreement was entered into; and
>
> (d) The termination date, if any, for each agreement.

9. State whether ADAS has accepted reinsurance submissions from brokers or agents located in the United Kingdom who ADAS knows or believes receives business offerings from reinsurance brokers located in the United States and/or Canada, and if so, state:

> (a) Whether the United Kingdom brokers or agents issue cover-notes or other formal evidence of coverage on behalf of ADAS;
>
> (b) Whether the United Kingdom brokers or agents collect premiums which are ultimately due to ADAS, and if so;
>
> (c) Identify the brokers, agents or companies located in the United States and Canada who remit such premiums, and provide their business addresses.

[2] ADAS particularly raises two points of Romanian law defining "state secrets" and "service secrets." A rough translation of the relevant law, as quoted by the district court, provides:

> Art. 2. It is considered State secret according to the stipulations of the Penal Code, any information data and documents which evidently show this character as well as those declared and qualified as such by a Council of Ministers decision. The transmission or divulging of information data and documents which constitute State secrets, loss, detained outside Service duties, distruction [sic] alteration or taking away of documents with such character negligence which led to one of these facts or which enabled other persons to take possession of information data or documents which might endanger the economic, technical-scientific military or political interests of the State as well as other infringement of the norms regarding the protection of the State secret, constitute unusually grave facts and are punished by penal law.
>
> Art. 4. The information, data and documents which according to the present law do not constitute State secrets but are not destined to publicity are Service secrets and cannot be divulged.
>
> Art. 251. The divulgement of the State secret, if this does not constitute infringement of art. 169, and also the divulgement of data or information which, although it does not constitute State secrets are not destined to publicity, if the act is of the nature to affect public interest, are punished by imprisonment from 6 months to 5 years.

Applying this test, Judge Grady determined that because Romanian law considered the requested information a "service secret" and punished disclosure with criminal sanctions, and the law was apparently vigorously enforced, the balance favored ADAS's refusal to respond to the interrogatories over RCA's right to such responses. As the following discussion of the Section 40 factors demonstrates, Judge Grady's conclusion is correct.

Initially, we must balance the "vital national interests" of both the United States and Romania. We approach this task with some misgivings. As Judge Marshall of the Northern District of Illinois noted, "the judiciary has little expertise, or perhaps even authority to evaluate the economic and social policies of a foreign country." *In re Uranium Antitrust Litigation,* 480 F. Supp. 1138, 1148 (N.D.Ill. 1979). Moreover, when allegedly considering only "vital national interests," we are left with the rather ridiculous assignment of determining which competing national interest is the more vital.

Whatever the semantic difficulties of our test, the courts of the United States undoubtedly have a vital interest in providing a forum for the final resolution of disputes and for enforcing these judgments. This rather general interest, however, is not as compelling as those interests implicated in other Section 40 cases cited by RCA. For instance, in *Graco, Inc v. Kremlin, Inc.,* 101 F.R.D. 503 (N.D.Ill. 1984), the court held that the United States had a compelling interest in ensuring that its patent laws were not undermined by a French blocking statute. Similarly, vital interests are involved when a commercial dispute implicates the integrity of American antitrust laws, *see, e.g., In re Uranium Antitrust Litigation,* 480 F. Supp. at 1149. When the United States itself is a party in the litigation, the national interest involved may become compelling. Thus, enforcement of the tax laws and security laws have been considered compelling national interests.

In the case at hand, though, we are presented with a private dispute between two reinsurance corporations. The disputed materials are the subject of a post-judgment interrogatory request and not vital to the case-in-chief. While there is unquestionably a vital national interest in protecting the finality of judgments and meaningfully enforcing these decisions, this interest alone does not rise to the level of those found in these earlier cases.

Against this, we must weigh on the opposing side of the balance the Romanian interest in protecting its state and so-called "service" secrets. Given the scope of its protective laws and the strict penalties it imposes for any violation, Romania places a high price on this secrecy. Unlike a blocking statute, Romania's law appears to be directed at domestic affairs rather than merely protecting Romanian corporations from foreign discovery requests. *Cf. Compagnie Francaise D'Assurance v. Phillips Petroleum Co.,* 105 F.R.D. 16, 30 (S.D.N.Y. 1984) (French blocking statute "never expected nor intended to be enforced against French subjects but was intended rather to provide them with tactical weapons and bargaining chips in foreign courts."); *Graco,* 101 F.R.D. at 508 ("The Blocking Statute obviously is a manifestation of French displeasure with American pre-trial discovery procedures."). Given this choice between the relative interests of Romania in its national secrecy and the American interest in enforcing its judicial decisions, we have determined that

Romania's, at least on the facts before us, appears to be the more immediate and compelling.[3]

The remaining factors are far less problematic. In evaluating the extent and nature of the hardship imposed upon ADAS by inconsistent enforcement actions, Section 40(b), our sole reference is the affidavit provided by Mr. Dumitriu, a Romanian attorney. Mr. Dumitriu states that the officers of ADAS would face criminal sanctions for revealing "service" secrets as classified by the Romanian government. Moreover, Dumitriu's affidavit states that the law protecting state and "service" secrets is vigorously enforced, thus, satisfying the factor under Section 40(e). RCA contends that Section 40(c), the extent to which the required conduct is to take place in the territory of the foreign state, was mismeasured by the district court. We disagree. All the information which plaintiff sought through these interrogatories is located within Romania. The offices of ADAS are located within Romania as well. Any responses to RCA's interrogatories would have to be prepared in Romania using this information. Obviously, ADAS could deliver this material to a site in the United States and prepare some of the responses there, as plaintiff contends. Yet, this does not affect the very real threat faced by officials at ADAS who would have to remove this information from Romania. Finally, it is undisputed that Section 40(d), the consideration of the nationality of the person in question, weighs in favor of ADAS. This is a Romanian corporation whose offices are located only within that country. Those persons forced to comply with this discovery order would be Romanian citizens subject to the criminal sanctions of the law protecting state secrets. Thus, considering all five factors provided under Section 40 — the competing national interests involved, the hardship to ADAS of compliance, the place of compliance, the nationality of ADAS and the likelihood of enforcement of the criminal sanctions — we conclude that on balance the district court correctly denied RCA's motion to compel responses to the interrogatories.

Complicating our determination, however, is the recent publication of the RESTATEMENT (THIRD) OF FOREIGN RELATIONS LAW OF THE UNITED STATES . . . and now we must review our precedent in light of this new standard. Section 442 of the Third Restatement considers the specific problem of conflicting jurisdiction over discovery. The new section provides:

> Requests for Disclosure: Law of the United States
>
> (1)(a) A court or agency in the United States, when authorized by statute or rule of court, may order a person subject to its jurisdiction to produce documents, objects, or other information relevant to an action or investigation, even if the information or the person in possession of the information is outside the United States.

---

[3] We pause to note that between the argument of this case and this decision, there has been a profound and much celebrated change in the political structure of Romania. The high priority which national secrecy enjoyed under the old regime is presumably no longer in vogue. Neither plaintiff nor defendant, however, has brought supplemental information to this court regarding this matter. Thus, we must decide this case on the facts before us. Should the parties believe that new facts have materially altered the foundation of our judgment, they are free to resubmit their claims. We note, however, that relevant changes in the law must be presented to the court rather than illusory changes in the political climate which provide little basis for re-evaluating this decision.

(b) Failure to comply with an order to produce information may subject a person to whom the order is directed to sanctions, including finding of contempt, dismissal of a claim of defense, or default judgment, or may lead to a determination that the facts to which the order was addressed are as asserted by the opposing party.

(c) In deciding whether to issue an order directing production of information located abroad, and in framing such an order, a court or agency of the United States should take into account the importance to the investigation or litigation of the documents or other information requested; the degree of specificity of the request; whether the information originated in the United States; the availability of alternative means of securing the information; and the extent to which noncompliance with the request would undermine important interests of the state where the information is located.

Thus, the new Section 442 follows the path announced by this court in *First National Bank of Chicago* that "the fact that foreign law may subject a person to criminal sanctions in the foreign country if he produces certain information does not automatically bar a domestic court from compelling production." 699 F.2d at 345. The new Section 442 provides a modified balancing test substantially similar to that of *First National Bank of Chicago* and Section 40. Although there are certain differences in emphasis, the factors to be considered remain largely synonymous and do not alter our determination that the district court's judgment was reasonable and correct.

Section 442, however, does make one significant change to the old standard by introducing an element of good faith to be included at the court's discretion. The new language provides in part:

(2) If disclosure of information located outside the United States is prohibited by law, regulation, or order of a court or other authority of the state in which the information is located, . . .

(a) a court or agency of the United States may require the person to whom the order is directed to make a good faith effort to secure permission from the foreign authorities to make the information available[.]

Thus, at its discretion, the district court may require a good faith effort from the parties to seek a waiver of any blocking provisions. For example, the Eleventh Circuit held that a bank must comply with a grand jury subpoena and produce records located in the Bahamas despite alleged conflict with a Bahamian bank secrecy rule. *United States v. Bank of Nova Scotia I,* 691 F.2d 1384 (11th Cir. 1982). The court held that, because the bank had not made a good faith effort to obtain the approval of the Bahamian authorities, and because there was no realistic threat of enforcement of the rule, the bank could not refuse to comply with the subpoena. Similarly, in *United States v. First National Bank of Chicago*, this court remanded a case to the Northern District of Illinois in order to determine whether First Chicago must make a good faith effort to receive permission from the Greek authorities to produce bank information located in Greece but unavailable due to the bank secrecy provisions of Greek law.

Here, the district court did not discuss the question of a good faith effort by ADAS to seek a waiver of Romania's secrecy laws. Given our holding in *First National Bank of Chicago*, we could remand this case for additional consideration of this issue. However, such a step is unnecessary. Our earlier case is easily distinguishable from the one at hand. In *First National Bank of Chicago*, the Greek law at issue appeared to provide a limited exception for furnishing certain information. Thus, it was unclear whether compliance would have resulted in criminal sanctions. Moreover, a treaty existed between the United States and Greece for the purposes of diplomatically resolving such banking disputes. Given this welter of uncertainty, there appeared at least the possibility of obtaining permission from the Greek authorities if First Chicago made a good faith effort.

By contrast, here, the law is apparently strictly applied. There are no exceptions to Romania's secrecy law. There exists no treaty between these governments to diplomatically resolve such problems. Unlike both *First National Bank of Chicago* and *Nova Scotia*, there would be little purpose to requiring a good faith effort to comply with the discovery request. Therefore, the district court's decision not to impose a requirement of a good faith effort upon ADAS was reasonable. The denial of RCA's motion to compel responses was consistent with our prior holdings as well as the new standard under RESTATEMENT (THIRD) § 442 and not an abuse of discretion. . . . [T]he court properly considered the relevant factors under Section 40 and determined that the interests of the Romanian government outweighed those of the United States and that the potential hardship to ADAS tipped the balance against asserting jurisdiction. Thus, RCA's motion to compel responses to certain post-judgment interrogatories was properly denied. Moreover, upon reviewing the facts before us, we find that the district court was within its discretion in not requiring ADAS to make a good faith effort to seek a waiver of the applicable Romanian law. Therefore, for the foregoing reasons, the decision of the district court is affirmed.

EASTERBROOK, Circuit Judge, concurring.

Events have overtaken this case. Romania adopted a strict code of secrecy out of fear that sunlight would jeopardize the regime. Under Romanian law, anything that is not a "State secret" is a "Service secret" — in other words, everything is a secret. The regime fell nonetheless, and not because of loose lips. Revolution in Romania means that yesterday's secrecy laws are of little moment. What the Securitate kept under covers, its successors broadcast.

We have not heard from Romania's lawyer, perhaps because he has no idea who speaks for his client. I therefore join the court's opinion, which observes that the plaintiff may return to the district court for a fresh decision under contemporary law. The court applies a balancing approach that the parties agree is apt. Given this agreement, we have no occasion to decide whether to follow the RESTATEMENT (THIRD) OF FOREIGN RELATIONS § 442 (1987), to the extent we may create a federal common law of privileges.

If we were free of the parties' agreement, I would be most reluctant to accept an approach that calls on the district judge to throw a heap of factors on a table and then slice and dice to taste. Although it is easy to identify many relevant considerations, as the ALI's RESTATEMENT does, a court's job is to reach judgments on the basis of rules of law rather than to use a different recipe for each meal.

Two sources of law dominate here. The first is Fed.R.Evid. 501, which says that when state law supplies the rule of decision (as Illinois law does in this case), it also supplies the law with respect to privileges. Fed.R.Civ.P. 69, which governs this enforcement action, also directs the court to follow state law. Does (would?) Illinois follow the RESTATEMENT OF FOREIGN RELATIONS in deciding whether documents held abroad are privileged? The parties do not discuss the question.

The other rules come from the Foreign Sovereign Immunities Act, 28 U.S.C. §§ 1602-11. Defendant in this case ("AAS"), an arm of the Romanian government, is open to suit under § 1605(a)(2) because the claim is based on its commercial activity within the United States. With a default judgment in hand, plaintiff seeks to discover AAS's assets. AAS invokes Romania's secrecy laws, which forbid it to disclose any information in its hands, even information about assets located outside Romania. Their effect is that no judgment against Romania may be collected. I doubt that general interest-balancing principles of the sort discussed in the RESTATEMENT may countermand the decision of Congress that courts of the United States may impose liability. The FSIA provides that a prevailing party may execute against the foreign government's assets except to the extent the statute creates exceptions, see §§ 1609-11. This catalog of what is, and is not, available to satisfy a judgment eclipses any attempt by the foreign defendant to create its preferred list by using its domestic secrecy law. If we allow foreign states to exempt themselves after the fashion of (the old) Romania, we might as well forget about the FSIA.

Even the RESTATEMENT is no longer as favorable to foreign defendants as it once was. The catalog of relevant interests in § 442(1)(c) of the THIRD RESTATEMENT is not to be used generally to assess demands for information. It is designed to inform the discretionary decision whether to impose one of the sanctions mentioned in Fed.R.Civ.P. 37 and § 442(1)(b), such as contempt of court or a default judgment. As a rule, parties are entitled to seek information and, without regard to balancing national interests, the foreign party must make a good faith effort to secure its release, § 442(2)(a) and (b). If release is not forthcoming, then

> a court or agency may, in appropriate cases, make findings of fact adverse to a party that has failed to comply with the order for production, even if that party has made a good faith effort to secure permission from the foreign authorities to make the information available and that effort has been unsuccessful.

§ 442(2)(c). In other words, the party seeking the information obtains its equivalent despite foreign secrecy rules. The balancing approach of § 442(1)(c) in conjunction with the adverse inference under § 442(2)(c) means that the party caught between inconsistent obligations to two nations with equal sovereign authority is not subject to extra penalty, such as imprisonment or fines exceeding the stakes of the case. A party may lose no more than the case — and then only if the law favors the adverse party once the facts have been deemed admitted under § 442(2)(c). Such an approach is a careful accommodation of the legitimate interests of the parties and the nations alike, all without authorizing unconfined "balancing" of the "importance" of the nations' policies.

If I thought we had to do such balancing, I would be at sea. If I knew how to balance incommensurables, I would be hard pressed to agree with courts saying (as the district judge did) that a suit by the government is "more important" than private litigation. In a capitalist economy enforcement of contracts is a subject of the first magnitude. The gravity of the nation's interest is no less when it decides to enforce vital rules through private initiative. A court would need to know the "importance" of the substantive rule, which is not well correlated with the enforcement mechanism. (The antitrust laws are "more important" than the littering laws, although the former are largely enforced by private suits and the latter by public prosecutions.)

Section 442(2)(c) breaks down in a case such as this one in which the judgment has been rendered and the prevailing party seeks to discover assets. This problem, which the RESTATEMENT does not discuss, is closer in principle to the rule of § 442(2)(c) than to that of § 442(1). Ascertaining assets under Rule 69 is not a "sanction" for misconduct. A prevailing party is entitled to relief; so much has been determined by the judgment. At this point resort to secrecy laws does nothing but nullify the rendering nation's substantive law. Because the FSIA does not contemplate such a step, foreign secrecy laws are not sufficient to block disclosures under Rule 69.

Notes and Questions on the Balancing Test in *Richmark* and *RCA*

1. *Interpreting the principal cases*. Are *Richmark* and *RCA* irreconcilable, distinguishable, or neither? Is the "good faith" of a party easier to determine than the depth of a foreign government's "interest" in its own law?

2. *Government corporations*. Reading *Richmark* and *RCA* together, on what principle should U.S. courts be more deferential (or less) in compelling discovery from corporations that are owned by foreign governments?

3. *"Present ability" and "control"*. In *Richmark* and similar cases, why couldn't Beijing — or parties similarly situated — argue that it has no "present ability" to comply with the discovery order because to do so would violate PRC law? Alternatively, why could they not argue that the documents were not in their "control" within the meaning of Rule 34 of the Federal Rules of Civil Procedure?

---

[b] The Exclusivity of the Hague Evidence Convention

IN RE PERRIER BOTTLED WATER LITIGATION
138 F.R.D. 348 (D. Conn. 1991)

. . . [T]hese suits were initiated following the public announcement that quantities of benzene, a possible carcinogen, had been identified in Perrier Water. Plaintiffs have asserted claims for violations of the Racketeer Influenced and Corrupt Organizations Act (RICO), 18 U.S.C. §§ 1961 *et seq.*, and for breach of warranty under sections 2-313 and 2-314 of the Uniform Commercial Code ("U.C.C."), in addition to others. After various complaints were lodged in several districts across the country, the Judicial Panel on Multidistrict Litigation ordered many of these cases to be transferred to and consolidated for pretrial purposes in this District. Defendants in these actions include, inter alia, Perrier Group of America, Inc. ("Perrier Group"), Great Waters of France, Inc. ("Great Waters"), and Source Perrier, S.A. ("Source Perrier"), a French corporation.

Claiming that defendants have failed to answer interrogatories or respond to requests for production adequately, or, in some cases, at all, plaintiffs have filed a motion to compel. Defendants oppose this motion. Furthermore, defendant Source Perrier has filed a motion for a protective order directing that any discovery requested of it proceed pursuant to the provisions of the Hague [Evidence] Convention. Plaintiffs oppose this request, and argue for the application of the discovery procedures set forth in the Federal Rules of Civil Procedure. . . .

Defendant Source Perrier seeks a Court Order requiring plaintiffs to utilize the procedures established by the Hague Evidence Convention in seeking discovery of information and material in Source Perrier's possession or control. Unlike the United States, where the Federal Rules provide private parties with broad powers to conduct their own pre-trial discovery, civil-law countries, such as France, of which Source Perrier is a resident, view the evidence gathering process as an exercise of judicial sovereignty to be entrusted entirely to the courts. Several civil-law countries have publicly expressed their disfavor of foreign citizens gathering evidence within their territory without sending requests through the judicial branches of their governments.[1] . . . In an attempt to establish procedures for obtaining evidence located abroad that a state executing a request would find "tolerable", and which the state from which a request came would find "utilizable", *Societe,* 482 U.S. at 530 (1987), seventeen nations, including the United States, joined the Hague Evidence Convention.

---

[1] [According to the French government,] "the French conception of sovereignty and 'ordre public' implies that, on French territory, the collection of evidence may not be undertaken by an agency other than a [French] court or magistrate appointed by that court." France has even enacted a penal law proscribing private parties from gathering evidence for litigation abroad. Article 1A of the French "blocking statute" provides: "subject to treaties or international agreements and applicable laws and regulations, it is prohibited for any party to request, seek or disclose, in writing, orally or otherwise, economic, commercial, industrial, financial or technical documents or information leading to the constitution of evidence with a view to foreign judicial or administrative proceedings or in connection therewith." *Societe Nat. Indus. Aero. v. United States District Court,* 482 U.S. 522, 526 (1987).

The Convention establishes three procedures through which parties to a litigation in one country may obtain evidence located in another country. The first is a "letter of request" from the trial court to the appropriate authority in the foreign country, requesting a foreign court "to obtain evidence, or to perform a requested act." Convention, Arts. 1–14. Under the second procedure, a diplomatic officer or consular agent of the requesting country gathers the evidence in the foreign country for use in the litigation. *Id.* at Arts. 15, 16. Lawyers may only use this second procedure if "a competent authority designated by the state in which he exercises his functions has given its permission either generally or in the particular case, and he complies with the conditions which the competent authority has specified in the permission." *Id.* at Art. 16(a), (b). The third procedure permits a court of the foreign state where the parties seek the evidence to appoint a commissioner to gather such evidence. *Id.* at Arts. 17–22. The trial court may make such an appointment with the consent of the appropriate foreign authorities.

In *Societe*, the Supreme Court analyzed the interaction of the discovery procedures set forth in the Federal Rules and the Convention, noting that both are the law of the United States. After review of the language of the Convention, and its history, the Court rejected the notion that the Convention requires the use of its procedures to the exclusion of the Federal Rules procedures whenever evidence located abroad is sought for use in an American court. The Court further rejected the suggestion that American courts should adopt a rule of "first resort" to the procedures of the Convention.

Ultimately, the Court concluded that the Convention established optional procedures to facilitate the taking of evidence abroad. In making a determination whether to require use of the Convention procedures, or to permit discovery pursuant to the Federal Rules, the Supreme Court instructed that courts must consider the particular facts of each case, the sovereign interests at issue, and the likelihood that resort to Convention procedures will prove effective. Leaving the determination to be made on a case-by-case basis by the trial court, the Supreme Court advised that American courts "should exercise special vigilance to protect foreign litigants from the danger that unnecessary, or unduly burdensome, discovery may place them in a disadvantageous position."

For the most part, lower court decisions since *Societe* have followed the analytical framework just described, though they have not generally concluded that the procedures set forth by the Convention should be utilized. *See, e.g., Haynes v. Kleinwefers,* 119 F.R.D. 335 (E.D.N.Y. 1988); and *Benton Graphics v. Uddeholm Corp.,* 118 F.R.D. 386 (D.N.J. 1987). One Court which found use of the Convention procedures appropriate, however, was the Northern District of New York, in *Hudson v. Hermann Pfauter GmbH & Co.,* 117 F.R.D. 33 (N.D.N.Y. 1987). In that case, Judge Munson found that, on the facts of that particular case, under either the approach taken by Justice Blackmun in his concurring and dissenting opinion in *Societe*, which Judge Munson preferred,[2]

---

[2] Justice Blackmun wrote that he would require a general presumption that courts should first resort to the Convention procedures. To reach this conclusion, he performed a tripartite analysis which included examination of foreign nations' interests, the interests of the United States, and the mutual interests of all nations in a smoothly functioning international legal regime. Justice Blackmun eschewed the notion that this analysis should be done on a case-by-case basis.

or under the *Societe* majority's analysis, the Convention's procedures should be utilized in the first instance by those litigants.

Although this Court concurs with the sentiments expressed in Judge Munson's dicta concerning his preference for Justice Blackmun's approach, the majority opinion in *Societe* was unambiguous as to how lower courts are to analyze whether to require use of the Convention procedures. Thus, whether these plaintiffs must utilize the Convention procedures to obtain the discovery they seek is a function of a three-pronged inquiry, including (1) examination of the particular facts of the case, particularly with regard to the nature of the discovery requested; (2) the sovereign interests in issue; and (3) the likelihood that the Convention procedures will prove effective. *See id.*; *Benton,* 118 F.R.D. at 390. The Court concurs with the *Benton* Court that a party who seeks the application of Convention procedures rather than the Federal Rules bears the burden of persuading the trial court.

On the first prong of this examination, . . . the Court views plaintiffs' . . . interrogatories as . . . excessive. Although plaintiffs have submitted a replacement set of interrogatories to be answered by Source Perrier that are far fewer in number, the Court concurs in defendants' assessment that certain of these interrogatories could also be characterized as abusive. For example, the first interrogatory requests Source Perrier to identify each person who investigated the manufacture of Perrier water. Plaintiffs instruct that "investigate" means

> to observe, study closely, inquire into systematically, examine, scrutinize, inquire into officially or unofficially, routinely, sporadically, or on a one time basis . . . .

Plaintiffs further instruct that "manufacture of Perrier" refers

> to all endeavors, physical and mental, related to the operations that result in the finished bottled product Perrier Water . . . .

Especially when the size of Source Perrier is considered, it is obvious that plaintiffs' request seeks an extraordinary volume of information, much of it irrelevant to the cases at hand. Similarly, interrogatory #10 requests Source Perrier to identify, among other things, all persons responsible for administering document retention policies concerning the manufacture of Perrier Water. The term "document", as described in the instructions, means virtually any piece of paper or print-out containing data. Requiring Source Perrier to identify any person who possesses documents relating to the manufacture of Perrier Water is a request for information that goes far beyond what might be relevant in this lawsuit, or what is reasonably calculated to lead to relevant material.

Plaintiffs' memorandum also makes clear that its document requests have not been replaced, but are equally applicable to Source Perrier. Certain of these requests call for an incredible quantity of information. For example, request #5 of the first set calls for all advertising copy and all documents referring to advertising campaigns for Perrier in the United States.

In sum, plaintiffs' discovery requests are not narrowly tailored inquiries designed solely to target discreet and material information. Rather, although many of the requests seek discoverable information, they call for extremely broad responses from Source Perrier, much of which is likely to be immaterial, and intrusive.

Turning to the second prong of the analysis, the sovereign interests in issue, plaintiffs suggest that since Source Perrier is a privately-owned corporation, the French government has no particular interest in the outcome of the litigation. Plaintiffs, however, have missed the point of the Hague Evidence Convention. In this context, a foreign state's sovereign interests are implicated, if at all, in seeking discovery from citizens of the foreign state, within the boundaries of that state, without the permission of that state. Justice Blackmun explained that

> the act of taking evidence in a common-law country from a willing witness, without compulsion and without a breach of the peace, in aid of a foreign proceeding, is a purely private matter, in which the host country has no interest and in which its judicial authorities have normally no wish to participate. To the contrary, the same act in a civil-law country may be a public matter, and may constitute the performance of a public judicial act by an unauthorized foreign person. It may violate the 'judicial sovereignty' of the host country, unless its authorities participate or give their consent.

Societe, 482 U.S. at 557–58 (Blackmun, J., concurring in part). Accordingly, the appropriate inquiry on this issue is the "host" country's amenability to the manner of discovery sought to be utilized by the plaintiffs.

Although not all civil-law countries have expressed their disfavor of private litigants' use of the Federal Rules' procedures within its borders, of those which have, France has been among the most emphatic. Indeed, as defendants point out, and as the Court has earlier described in part, France has even amended its civil and penal codes to incorporate the Hague Evidence Convention, and proscribe foreign litigants' use of alternative, unauthorized procedures. The simple fact that, in joining the Convention, France has consented to its procedures is an expression of France's sovereign interests and weighs heavily in favor of the use of those procedures.

Finally, turning to the third prong of the *Societe* majority's test — whether Convention procedures will be effective —, plaintiffs raise the spectre that the process of using Convention devices might prove "amazingly cumbersome and enervating", and include time delays resulting from translation requirements, and appeals within the French judicial system stemming from potential refusals to execute letters of request. Nevertheless, the Court shares Judge Munson's belief that the major obstacle to the effective use of the Convention procedures, if one there be, is litigants' lack of familiarity with them. Although, in theory, learning-curve costs might make Convention procedures more costly in terms of efficiency, such inconveniences alone pale beside the importance of respecting France's sovereign interests, and the Court's concern for fairness to foreign litigants.

In any event, and notwithstanding plaintiffs' unsupported speculation, there is no reason, on the record before the Court, to believe that Convention procedures will be ineffective in producing the discovery to which plaintiffs are entitled. As noted above, France has amended its civil code specifically to permit use of Convention procedures by foreign litigants. *Compare Hudson,* 117 F.R.D. at 39 (even where West Germany declared it would not permit performance of certain Convention procedures, plaintiffs made insufficient showing that remaining procedures would be unavailing). Indeed, Justice Blackmun responded to apprehensions similar to those expressed by plaintiffs, explaining that "experience with the Convention suggests [that] contracting parties have honored their obligations to execute letters of request expeditiously and to use compulsion if necessary." Finally, even if Convention procedures should prove unsuccessful in producing the discovery to which plaintiffs are entitled, the Court retains the authority to order Source Perrier to produce the requested material under the provisions of the Federal Rules.

In sum, all three prongs of the test set forth in *Societe* suggest utilization of Convention procedures. Accordingly, defendants' motion for a protective order is granted such that the Court hereby orders plaintiffs to employ the procedures set forth in the Hague Evidence Convention in pursuing any discovery from Source Perrier, or of materials or information otherwise located in France. Should these procedures prove unavailing, and upon request, the Court shall consider modification of this Order. . . .

IN RE BENTON GRAPHICS v. UDDEHOLM CORP.
118 F.R.D. 386 (D.N.J. 1987)

This litigation involves allegations of fraud and breach of contract against several defendants, including two Swedish Companies, Uddeholms, A.B. and Uddeholm Strip Steel, A.B. The plaintiff, Benton Graphics, Inc., originally brought the instant motion on for an order compelling responses to interrogatories and the production of documents. The defendants opposed this motion claiming that the principles of comity required that discovery must first be sought under the applicable Hague Convention procedures. Because the United States Supreme Court was then considering the interplay of the Federal Rules of Civil Procedure and the Hague Convention in *Aerospatiale,* I stayed my decision until that case was decided. . . .

In *Aerospatiale,* the Supreme Court rejected the position that a party would first be required to utilize Hague Convention procedures whenever discovery is sought of a foreign litigant. However, the Court also rejected the position that the Convention is never applicable when discovery is sought abroad. Rather, the court adopted an intermediate case-by-case approach. The Court found that "the text of the Evidence Convention as well as the history of the proposal and ratification by the United States unambiguously supports the conclusion that it was intended to establish optional procedures that would facilitate the taking of evidence abroad." According to the Court, these optional procedures did not deprive a district court of the jurisdiction it otherwise possessed to order a party to produce evidence located in a signatory country. However, the Court did find that "the Hague Convention does 'apply' to the production of evidence in a litigant's possession in the sense that it is one method of seeking evidence that a court may elect to employ". Nonetheless, the court declined to find that comity requires resort to Hague Evidence Convention procedures "without prior scrutiny in each case of the particular facts, sovereign interests, and likelihood that resort to those procedures will prove effective."

While stating that resort to convention procedures was only optional, the Court observed that "some discovery procedures are much more intrusive than others". Therefore, district courts must take special care to ensure that foreign litigants are not subject to unnecessary or unduly burdensome discovery. Due respect must be accorded special problems encountered by a foreign litigant because of its nationality, location, or any sovereign interest expressed by a foreign state.

However, while emphasizing that careful consideration must be given to a foreign litigant's claim of abusive discovery, the Court held that, "even if a court might be persuaded that a particular document request was too burdensome or too 'intrusive' to be granted in full, with or without an appropriate protective order, it might well refuse to insist upon the use of Convention procedures before requiring responses to simple interrogatories or requests for admissions. The exact line between reasonableness and unreasonableness in each case must be drawn by the trial court, based on its knowledge of the case and of the claims and interests of the parties and the governments whose statutes and policies they invoke."

In sum, the Hague Convention is an optional procedure that may be utilized by a district court after considering 1) the particular facts of the case, 2) the sovereign interests involved, and 3) the likelihood that resort to the Convention would be an effective discovery device. Whether a particular document request is too burdensome is left to the sound discretion of the trial court in light of the facts of the case, and the respective interests of the parties and foreign governments involved.

In the instant motion, a major dispute is whether either party carries the burden in determining whether the Federal Rules or Convention procedures should be followed. The plaintiff claims that the Supreme Court's analysis in *Aerospatiale* strongly suggests that the party seeking to supplant the Federal Rules with the Convention must demonstrate its reasons. Plaintiff relies on the Court's rejection of the position that the Hague Convention never applies to foreign litigants over which the court has jurisdiction because "such a rule would deny the foreign litigant a full and fair opportunity to demonstrate appropriate reasons for employing the Convention procedures in the first instance." Thus, the plaintiff argues that parties seeking to invoke the Convention are required "to demonstrate appropriate reasons for employing the Convention" in lieu of the federal rules.

On the other hand, the defendants contend that the burden rests with the party who seeks to avoid using Convention procedures. Specifically, defendants argue that a party seeking discovery outside the Convention should be required to show by clear and convincing evidence that the Convention's procedures would be inefficient or unnecessarily burdensome. Anything less, according to the defendants, would derogate from the United States' obligations under the Convention and violate the judicial sovereignty of Sweden.

Essentially, the defendants would like to adopt the position of the four justices who filed an opinion dissenting in part and concurring in part.

While the majority opinion is not crystal clear on the issue of who bears the burden of establishing which discovery procedure to utilize, I agree with the plaintiff that the party seeking to utilize Convention procedures must demonstrate appropriate reasons. *But see Hudson v. Hermann Pfauter GmbH & Co.,* 117 F.R.D. 33 (N.D.N.Y. 1987).[1] This is consistent with the policy expressed by the Court in *Aerospatiale* that foreign competitors voluntarily marketing their product in the United States should be subject to the same judicial burdens as their domestic counterparts. If foreign litigants seek resort to the Convention, fairness requires that they have the burden of proof. Therefore, foreign litigants attempting to supplant the federal rules with Convention procedures must demonstrate why the particular facts and sovereign interests support using the Convention. They must also demonstrate that resort to these procedures will prove effective.

To undertake a review of whether the Convention should apply to this case, it is appropriate to start with a review of the facts of the case beginning with the parties. Plaintiff, Benton Graphics, Inc., is a New Jersey corporation in the business of manufacturing and distributing doctor blades for use in the gravure printing industry. Defendant, Uddeholm Strip Steel, A.B. is a Swedish Corporation which manufactures and distributes steel products, including carbon steel for use in manufacturing doctor blades. Until 1981, Uddeholm Strip Steel was a division of defendant Uddeholm, A.B. and not separately incorporated. Defendant Uddeholm Corporation, U.S.A. imports and distributes in the United States steel and steel products manufactured by Uddeholm Strip Steel, A.B. Defendant Thomas Knudsen is the former vice-president of Uddeholm Corporation, U.S.A.

Between 1979 and 1985, Benton Graphics entered into a series of contracts with defendants to purchase doctor blades. Prior to 1980, defendants manufactured and sold doctor blades under the designation UHB-20R steel. After 1980, defendants manufactured and sold to Benton a different grade carbon steel under the designation UHB-18-CR. Benton claims that defendant Knudsen represented on numerous occasions that the steel delivered to Benton since 1980 was UHB-20R. In February 1986, Benton brought this action against defendants alleging breach of contract, breach of warranty, fraud, and RICO

---

[1] In *Hudson*, the court found that the burden should be placed on the party opposing the use of Convention procedures to demonstrate that those procedures would be ineffective. In reaching this decision the district court relied upon Justice Blackmun's concurring and dissenting opinion in *Aerospatiale*. Justice Blackmun held that a court "should perform a tripartite analysis that considers the foreign interests, the interests of the United States, and the mutual interests of all nations in a smoothly functioning international legal regime", when determining whether the Convention should be utilized in the first instance. In agreeing with Justice Blackmun, the court, in *Hudson* also noted that international policy considerations transcend the interests of the individual litigants. I disagree with the *Hudson* court's analysis because it relies too heavily on the concurring and dissenting opinion of Justice Blackmun in *Aerospatiale*. While Justice Blackmun's opinion certainly is thoughtful and well reasoned, it is not the opinion of the majority of the members on the Supreme Court. In *Aerospatiale*, the majority did not elevate theoretical policy concerns over the effect Convention procedures would have upon particular litigants. Rather, the Court specifically directed district courts to analyze the interests of the parties and the intrusiveness of the discovery sought.

violations based on the theory that defendants conspired to misrepresent the grade of steel sold to Benton between 1980 and 1985. Benton claims that there is a material difference between UHB 20R and UHB 18CR steel and that defendants intentionally withheld this information from Benton. Defendants deny these allegations.

In the instant motion, defendants have made no attempt to relate the "particular facts" of this case to the discovery sought. Defendants only argue that the interrogatories and requests for documents are overbroad and burdensome. I note that the defendants have not identified the specific interrogatories or document requests that are overbroad or burdensome. They have not alleged that the discovery is unduly expensive or that the discovery is being sought for the "improper purpose of motivating settlement rather than finding relevant and probative evidence" [citing *Aerospatiale*]. Moreover, defendants have failed to allege any special problems because of their nationality or the location of their operations.

Because defendants have largely failed to specifically identify their objections, it is impossible for me to determine which, if any, requests are overbroad and burdensome. However, having reviewed the interrogatories, I believe that a number of the requests are not "simple" and may require streamlining if we are to proceed under the federal rules. For example, a number of questions seek information held by "any employee of Uddeholm Strip Steel"; these appear too encompassing. I believe these questions can be limited to a defined group of individuals from Uddeholm who were involved in the manufacture of and the decision to sell UHR-18-CR grade steel in place of UHB-20R steel products. It is this that is important and not whether any employee had certain knowledge which may never have been communicated to any of the persons in control until the commencement of this litigation. Furthermore, these questions, as phrased, include even clerical employees. Identification of such persons, while being of little or no moment, would, however, involve substantial investigation by the foreign litigants. This type of expansive discovery without concomitant relevance is not what the Court envisioned when it handed down the *Aerospatiale* decision:

> Some discovery procedures are much more "intrusive" than others. In this case, for example, an interrogatory asking petitioners to identify the pilots who flew flight tests in the Rallye before it was certified for flight by the Federal Aviation Administration, or a request to admit that petitioners authorized certain advertising in a particular magazine, is certainly less intrusive than a request to produce all of the "design specifications, line drawings and engineering plans and all engineering change orders and plans and all drawings concerning the leading edge slats for the Rallye type aircraft manufactured by the Defendants."

Aerospatiale, 482 U.S. at 545.

Thus, the parties shall have 10 days to confer in an effort to limit and resolve the scope of the discovery requests to ensure that they are reasonable and not overly burdensome, keeping in mind that discovery requests that are too "intrusive" may be limited by this court. After making such good faith effort to reach accommodation, I will permit the defendants to address any specific objections to interrogatories or document requests within ten days thereafter.[2] Defendants are cautioned that they must explain why specific discovery sought is overbroad or burdensome. Plaintiff will be entitled to respond to any potential objections within ten days after defendants' objections are filed with this court.

Notwithstanding defendants' blanket objections to all discovery, I do not find that the "particular facts" of this case require resort to Convention procedures. The discovery sought in this case largely relates to the composition, qualities, and testing of defendants' steel. Several of the defendants and all relevant tests are located in Sweden. This is conceded by defendants. It is essential that plaintiff and its experts have access to the tests if this litigation is to proceed in any semblence of a timely fashion. The foreign defendants have identified no special problem with responding to the requested discovery because of their nationality. Since discovery of these tests and other relevant information can be accomplished efficiently under the federal rules the "particular facts" of this case do not necessitate resort to the Convention.

The second factor which must be analyzed before ordering use of the Convention is the sovereign interest involved. Defendants argue that "critical sovereign interests of Sweden" support utilizing Convention procedures. They have submitted the duly authenticated Declaration of Wanja Tornberg, Assistant Under-Secretary of the Swedish Ministry for Foreign Affairs, (the "Tornberg Declaration"). According to Tornberg, use of the Hague Convention serves a number of important Swedish interests including:

(a) It serves as an essential link and an effective mechanism for cooperation between different legal systems.

(b) It minimizes conflicts between the legal requirements of different states.

(c) It satisfies the urging of the United States for Sweden and other civil law nations to provide a means for complying with requests for pretrial discovery of documentary evidence in a manner which is consistent with the laws of Sweden.

(d) It discourages "fishing expedition" methods of obtaining unspecified evidence, which are regarded as unacceptable in Sweden and in other civil law nations.

(e) It effectively balances the divergent interests promoted by the United States' and Sweden's conflicting rules on who bears the costs associated with compliance. The rule in Sweden, as in most civil law countries, is that the losing party reimburses the winner for litigation expenses. Unlike the general rule in the United States, the Swedish rule forces plaintiffs to evaluate carefully the merits of a case before bringing it.

(f) It enables Swedish courts to limit discovery in sensitive and protected areas under Swedish law such as trade secrets and national security.

These "critical sovereign interests" are merely general reasons why Sweden prefers civil law discovery procedures to the more liberal discovery permitted

---

[2] Whether a particular document request or interrogatory is overbroad or burdensome is left to the discretion of the trial court. A decision that a discovery request is overbroad and burdensome does not necessitate the use of Convention procedures for other valid interrogatories or document requests.

under the federal rules. Defendants cite no reasons how the specific discovery sought by Benton implicates any specific sovereign interest of Sweden. Defendant claims that the Swedish government may have the right to protect some of the information requested. However, defendant does not explain which discovery is objectionable nor why it might have to be protected. No allegations are made that trade secrets are involved or that Benton is engaged in a "fishing expedition". In short, because defendant has not explained, and I do not see why Benton's discovery requests in their entirety or any particular request, violate any special sovereign interests of Sweden, resort to the Hague Convention is not required.

Lastly, I must consider whether Convention procedures in this case will prove effective. Here, I find that they will not. The Tornberg declaration states that the defendants' letter of request should be processed by the Swedish authorities in approximately two months. That is an approximation based upon past history; there are certainly no guarantees. This case has already endured numerous delays and discovery should proceed apace. Another delay while the Swedish authorities determine what discovery will be permitted and the further litigation undoubtedly spawned by their decision may bring actual discovery to a standstill. Therefore, in light of the lengthy history of discovery in this case and the potential for additional delays, I do not find that Convention procedures will prove effective.

In conclusion, plaintiff's motion compelling responses to interrogatories and the production of documents in accordance with the Federal Rules of Civil Procedure is granted.

Notes and Questions

1. *Reconciling the principal cases.* What are the differences in approach between *Perrier* and *Benton*, and what accounts for those differences?

2. *Hudson v. Pfauter*, 117 F.R.D. 33 (N.D.N.Y. 1987), was the first post-*Aerospatiale* decision to address the exclusivity of the Hague Evidence Convention. Under the tripartite analysis in Justice Blackmun's separate opinion, the *Hudson* court ruled that the party opposing the use of the Convention bore the burden of proof, a burden that had not been met on the facts of that case. The court found that Convention procedures were less intrusive than those under the Federal Rules of Civil Procedure and therefore less offensive to the foreign sovereign. The interests of the United States, though formidable, could be served satisfactorily through Convention procedures. In the event that those procedures were unproductive, the Federal Rules offer a fallback procedure. The court also found that the first resort to the Convention would promote international cooperation and the development of an ordered international system. As noted by the court in *Benton*, the *Hudson* approach has its detractors and cannot be considered the prevailing analysis among the federal district courts.

3. *Jurisdictional discovery versus discovery on the merits.* In *Vitamins Antitrust Litigation*, 120 F. Supp. 2d 45 (D.D.C. 2000), *infra,* the court had to decide whether to "require first resort to Hague procedures for jurisdictional

discovery or whether the three-prong test established . . . in *Aerospatiale* governs even in cases where personal jurisdiction has not yet been conclusively established." Because *Aerospatiale* assumed that the foreign defendants were within the personal jurisdiction of the court and therefore never addressed the applicability of the Convention to the preliminary issue of personal jurisdiction, the court felt free to exercise the discretion given to trial courts by the *Aerospatiale* majority and reasoned that "the only reason to depart . . . from the three-part balancing test would be if . . . the foreign nations' sovereign interests are more threatened by potential application of the Federal Rules at the jurisdictional discovery stage that they would be with merits discovery." Because the discovery requests were narrowly tailored and because personal jurisdiction was not fanciful or speculative, the court concluded that the likelihood of offense to foreign nations was no greater at the preliminary stage than on the merits as in *Aerospatiale*.

The court asserted that "this conclusion is supported by the large majority of the lower court decisions that have considered this issue." *See Rich v. KIS California, Inc.*, 121 F.R.D. 254, 260 (M.D.N.C. 1988) (holding that jurisdictional discovery need not be taken under Hague because *Aerospatiale* "did not carve out any exception for disputes involving personal jurisdiction" and "[s]ufficient protection is given by the Supreme Court's admonishment to district courts to be particularly sensitive to claims of abuse of discovery made by foreign litigants"); *Fishel v. BASF Group*, 175 F.R.D. 525, 529 (S.D. Iowa 1997) (concluding that the reasoning and holding of *Aerospatiale* provide that the Hague procedures are optional and do not divest federal district courts of authority to order discovery under the Federal Rules); *In re Bedford Computer Corp.*, 114 B.R. 2, 5–6 (Bankr.D.N.H. 1990) (citing *Rich* and allowing discovery strictly related to jurisdictional issues to proceed under the Federal Rules). In fact, there are only two cases that support defendants' position and both are far from convincing. *See Jenco v. Martech Int'l, Inc.*, No. 86-4229, 1988 WL 54733 (E.D. La. May 19, 1988) (holding, with almost no meaningful analysis, that certain jurisdictional discovery requests must be made under Hague because "[w]hile judicial economy may dictate that the Federal Rules of Civil Procedure should be used, the interests of protecting a foreign litigant in light of the jurisdictional problems are paramount"); *Knight v. Ford Motor Co.*, 260 N.J. Super. 110, 615 A.2d 297, 301 n. 11 (L.Div. 1992) (noting, in dicta, that "[i]f jurisdiction does not exist over a foreign party . . ., the Convention may provide the only recourse for obtaining evidence.")

4. *Federalism, Aerospatiale, and the state courts.* Because state law must yield when it is inconsistent with the provisions of a treaty, *United States v. Pink*, 315 U.S. 203(1942), some litigants have argued that the Hague Convention pre-empts or trumps the discovery laws of each state. But the broadest form of that argument has not succeeded. *See, e.g., Scarminach v. Goldwell GmbH*, 140 Misc.2d 103, 531 N.Y.S.2d 188 (Sup Ct. Monroe Co. 1998) ("The preemption argument . . . would require that the Convention procedures provide the exclusive, rather than an optional, method to obtain evidence abroad, a conclusion expressly rejected by the Supreme Court [in *Aerospatiale*]"); *Bank of Tokyo-Mitsubishi, Ltd. v. Kvaerner*, 175 Misc. 2d 408, 671 NYS 2d 902 (Sup. Ct. N.Y. Co. 1998) ("Resort to the Hague Convention, which would effectively shield the documents from production, should not be required where the court

has jurisdiction over a party and that party has control over its subsidiaries whose documents are sought pursuant to the usual [state law] procedures"). This is true even if a foreign sovereign state objects to the taking of evidence outside the treaty framework. *In re Asbestos Litigation,* 623 A.2d 546 (Sup. Ct. Del. 1992):

> The fact that a foreign government might regard discovery outside the Hague Convention procedures as an affront is not . . . dispositive; the Court can envision circumstances under which the sovereign interests of a foreign country might be disregarded because of competing interests. For example, if a foreign country forbids discovery of a type which is permitted in the U.S., or if there is reason to expect less than full cooperation from that country, use of Hague Convention procedures might be inappropriate. The sovereign interests of foreign governments are important but not overriding considerations.

But some state courts have determined that the Hague Convention does displace state law in certain narrow circumstances. The Convention may for example provide the only means of obtaining discovery from a foreign entity that is neither a party to the litigation nor affiliated in any legal sense with the parties before the court. *See, e.g., In Matter of Agusta,* 171 A.D.2d 595, 567 N.Y.S.2d 664 (1st Dept. 1991); *Intercontinental Credit Corporation v. Roth,* 154 Misc.2d 639, 595 N.Y.S.2d 602 (Sup Ct. N.Y. Co. 1991) ("[W]hen discovery is sought from a nonparty in a foreign jurisdiction, application of the Hague Convention . . . which encompasses principles of international comity, is virtually compulsory").

The Supremacy Clause at a minimum means that the federal court's interpretation of a treaty binds the state courts. But is the authority of the federal court diminished when comity rather than law is the basis for the federal court's decision? Would it be a violation of the Supremacy Clause for a state court to give the Hague Convention *greater* scope than the Supreme Court did in *Aerospatiale?*

---

[c] The Doctrine and the Logistics of Obtaining Evidence Outside the Convention Framework

IN RE VITAMINS ANTITRUST LITIGATION
120 F. Supp. 2d 45 (D.D.C. 2000)

[In this sprawling case involving transnational price-fixing, a special master was appointed to frame the discovery process, a task made especially complex by the fact that the defendants came from a variety of countries, some of which were signatories to the Hague Evidence Convention and some of which were not. Defendants UCB S.A., and Eisai Co., Ltd. ("ECL"), in particular, were Belgian and Japanese companies respectively, and neither Belgium nor Japan were parties to the convention. In pre-trial proceedings, the court had to determine which process should be followed to discover facts going to the court's personal jurisdiction over the defendants as distinct from facts going to the merits of the case. A special master recommended that the position of these "non-signatory defendants be analyzed under the [tripartite] *Aerospatiale* [balancing] test." But the court rejected the special master's recommendation.]

Since *Aerospatiale* is concerned exclusively with the question of whether to apply the Federal Rules or the Hague Convention to discovery being sought from a signatory country, the Supreme Court's holding in that case is clearly limited to countries that have adopted the Hague Convention procedures for the taking of evidence. *See McKesson Corp. v. Islamic Republic of Iran*, 185 F.R.D. 70 (D.D.C. 1999) (holding that *Aerospatiale* is "of limited assistance to this case since Iran is not a party to the Hague Evidence Convention"); *see also Japan Halon Co., Ltd. v. Great Lakes Chemical Corp.*, 155 F.R.D. 626, 627 (N.D.Ind. 1993) ("The court also agrees with defendants that because Japan is not a signatory to the Hague Convention on Evidence, any analysis of case law on that point is rendered moot"). Since Japan and Belgium chose not to adopt the Hague evidence procedures, any analysis of the *Aerospatiale* factors would seem wholly irrelevant to these nations.

Unfortunately, after finding that *Aerospatiale* is inapplicable to defendants ECL and UCB S.A., the Court is left with little guidance as to what analysis it should employ in order to determine whether to proceed under the Federal Rules or the laws of these non-signatory countries for jurisdictional discovery in this case. When asked by these defendants at the hearing what test should be applied to their situation, their response was simply: the general principles of comity and territorial preferences as expressed in international treaties and laws. In the absence of any other prescribed analysis, the Court will defer to these two defendants and analyze their situation under principles of comity, affording special attention to the international territorial preference which favors discovery procedures governed by the law of the territory where discovery is sought in the absence of any conflict between the Federal Rules and the laws of that territory. Therefore, the Court will first consider whether there is in fact any conflict between the evidence laws of Japan and Belgium and the United States; and second, in the event that there is a conflict, the Court will analyze the principles of comity in order to determine whether these principles require use of the nonsignatories' laws in this case. . . .

The record shows that Japan did not join the Hague Convention apparently out of fear of American-type discovery procedures; that under Japanese law "the scope of witness examination and document discovery is narrowly tailored to the allegations"; and that when the one-hundred-year-old Code of Civil Procedure Law was revised in 1996, [according to one expert submission,] "the Japanese legislature refused to adopt the American-type discovery system (particularly, the out-of-court deposition and document-request procedure) as excessively intrusive and therefore undesirable in the non-litigious Japanese society." Although limited pretrial discovery of witnesses and documents is allowed under the laws of Japan, document requests must identify specifically the documents sought, and various documentary and testimonial privileges would prevent the taking of much evidence even if the specificity requirements were met. . . . Therefore, the Court finds that there are indeed inherent conflicts between the Japanese discovery procedures and the Federal Rules.

Apparently recognizing the conflicts between the Japanese system and the Federal Rules, ECL asserts that its offer to voluntarily, upon proper service, make one deponent available to testify in Tokyo "provided that the plaintiffs narrow the topics to be covered" and to produce documents "provided that the plaintiffs narrow the scope of their request" will permit plaintiffs to obtain "reasonable discovery" under the laws of Japan. The Court agrees with the Special Master's finding that plaintiffs will not likely be able to obtain the necessary pretrial testimony and documentary evidence found to be proper by the Special Master and through adoption by this Court under the Laws of Japan. First, the Court is not satisfied with ECL's quite reserved and contingent offer for voluntary discovery; the Court has now decided that plaintiffs' revised requests, the very ones ECL says must be further revised, are narrowly tailored and should be answered. Second, the Court is convinced, considering Japan's antipathy to even the Hague procedures, that plaintiffs' discovery requests would not be sufficiently specific to meet the requirements of the Japanese Civil Code.[1] Therefore, despite the Court's respect for the principles of comity and Japan's sovereign interests in protecting its citizens from unduly burdensome discovery, this Court cannot find that these concerns outweigh the need for prompt and efficient resolution of the jurisdictional questions in this case. Accordingly, the Court will adopt the Special Master's recommendation that jurisdictional discovery against ECL proceed under the Federal Rules. . . .

UCB S.A. argues that it is in a unique position among these foreign defendants in that it did not plead guilty or enter into a leniency agreement and plaintiffs submitted no affidavit respecting discovery under Belgian law. With regard to the first contention, the Court recognizes that UCB S.A. did not plead guilty or enter into any agreement in this case; therefore, plaintiffs' case against UCB S.A. is arguably more speculative than against the other defendants. Nevertheless, plaintiffs' allegations against UCB S.A., as against all other defendants in this case, are quite detailed and are far from blind fishing expeditions. Therefore, the Court finds no evidence that plaintiffs' discovery requests against UCB S.A. are unjustified or unduly burdensome to this defendant. Second, with respect to plaintiffs' failure to submit contrary evidence, the Court agrees with UCB S.A. that their expert's testimony is unrebutted but it disagrees with the defendant's assertion that the evidence provided by this expert necessarily requires a ruling in favor of applying Belgian discovery procedures in this case.

UCB S.A.'s own expert stated that Belgium generally disfavors pretrial discovery in civil litigation. In fact, Belgian scholars cited by [UCB's expert] say that pretrial discovery in Belgium is "tantamount to a private house search of the opposing party" and these scholars note that "if Belgium were to ratify the Hague Evidence Convention it would make a reservation under article 23 of the Convention in order to avoid inquisitorial acts which are not

---

[1] In fact, ECL has not cited to this Court a single case holding that Japanese discovery procedures should supplant the Federal Rules. Plaintiffs cite *Japan Halon Co.*, 155 F.R.D. at 627, where the court found that following Japanese procedures in pursuing discovery would be futile. Although that case is not directly analogous because the Japanese company in *Japan Halon Co.* invoked the jurisdiction of that court, the court's findings and conclusions regarding the ineffectiveness of Japanese discovery procedures is [sic] relevant to the issue here.

meant to gather specific evidentiary materials pertaining to a pending procedure, or consist in fact of 'fishing expeditions.' " [UCB's expert] does say that "a foreign litigant is able to obtain specified documents and deposition testimony" and that under Belgium law, Belgian courts are required to execute letters rogatory properly issued "so long as the discovery sought by such letters rogatory is specific and narrow and does not breach fundamental rules of Belgium." However, there is no indication that plaintiffs' requests would meet this criteria.

After considering the entire record in this case, the Court disagrees with UCB S.A. that Belgian law affords "a reasonable and effective method of obtaining jurisdictional discovery" in this case. The Court finds that the Letters of Request procedure available under Belgian law is unlikely to secure for plaintiffs the jurisdictional discovery approved by this Court. Document and deposition discovery would most likely be thwarted by the stringent requirements for specificity. Therefore, despite the strong interest in comity and the respect that this Court has for Belgium's sovereign interests,[2] the Court will adopt the Special Master's recommendation that jurisdictional discovery involving UCB S.A. proceed under the Federal Rules because it finds that Belgium's procedures significantly conflict with the Federal Rules and that these procedures would not result in prompt and effective jurisdictional discovery in this case.

Notes and Questions

1. *Arguments on appeal.* Are you persuaded by the court's analysis in *Vitamins Litigation*? What are the defendants' best arguments on appeal? What difference did it make that the discovery sought was jurisdictional?

2. *Advantages of treaty participation.* In light of the cases collected in this chapter, is the legal position of signatories to the Hague Convention any better in U.S. courts than that of non-signatories?

3. *Letters rogatory.* The conclusion that the Hague Convention is inapplicable does not necessarily imply that the case will proceed as though it were an entirely domestic case. The parties and the court might revert to the traditional practice of seeking judicial assistance from the foreign state through letters rogatory, as outlined in the following guidance from the U.S. State Department.

------

[2] The Court notes that Belgium's sovereign interests are particularly strong since this defendant has not pled guilty or entered into any agreement and therefore has admitted no involvement in this price-fixing conspiracy. For this reason, the Court was particularly concerned with UCB S.A.'s situation and afforded them individual consideration; however, after reviewing the entire record in this case, the Court finds that Belgium's sovereign interests will not be unduly offended by this jurisdictional discovery and that the unlikelihood of effective discovery under Belgian procedures and the need for a rapid and effective resolution of the jurisdictional questions in this case necessitate a finding in favor of the Federal Rules in this case.

UNITED STATES DEPARTMENT OF STATE
PREPARATION OF LETTERS ROGATORY (selections)
http://travel.state.gov/letters_rogatory.html

WHAT IS A LETTER ROGATORY:

A letter rogatory is a formal request from a court in one country to "the appropriate judicial authorities" in another country requesting compulsion of testimony or documentary or other evidence or effect service of process. Although statutory authority generally refers to the instrument as a "letter rogatory", the terms "letter rogatory" and "letter of request" (which is used specifically in the Hague Evidence Convention) have come to be virtually synonymous in actual practice. In some countries which do not permit the taking of depositions of willing witnesses, letters rogatory are the only method of obtaining evidence or serve process. Letters rogatory can be used in civil and criminal matters, and have been used in administrative matters. The execution of a request for judicial assistance by the foreign court is based on comity between nations, absent a specific treaty obligation such as the Hague Evidence Convention or Mutual Legal Assistance in Criminal Matters (MLAT) treaties. Consular Conventions generally include language which authorizes transmission of letters rogatory through diplomatic channels. This does not obligate the foreign country to execute the request, but simply provides a formal avenue by which the requests may be made. If there is no Consular Convention in force between the United States and the foreign country, letters rogatory are received by foreign authorities on the basis of comity. Letters rogatory are a time consuming, cumbersome process and should not be utilized unless there are no other options available.

HOW IS A LETTER ROGATORY EXECUTED:

The foreign court will execute a letter rogatory in accordance with the laws and regulations of the foreign country. In obtaining evidence, for example, in most cases an American attorney will not be permitted to participate in such a proceeding. Occasionally a local, foreign attorney may be permitted to attend such a proceeding and even to put forth additional questions to the witness. Not all foreign countries utilize the services of court reporters or routinely provide verbatim transcripts. Sometimes the presiding judge will dictate his recollection of the witness's responses.

AUTHORITY FOR ISSUANCE OF A LETTER ROGATORY:

The power of federal courts to issue letters rogatory derives from 28 U.S.C. 1781 and from the court's "inherent" authority.

COMPULSION OF EVIDENCE:

When a witness is not willing to testify or produce documents or other evidence voluntarily, the assistance of foreign authorities generally must be sought. The customary method of compelling evidence is by letter rogatory. See Rule 28(b), Fed. R. Civ. P.

. . .

SAMPLE LETTERS ROGATORY:

There is annexed a basic sample letter rogatory. (Caveat: Do not draft the letter rogatory as a request from the President of the United States, but rather as a request from the requesting court.)

GUIDELINES ON DRAFTING LETTERS ROGATORY:

Letters rogatory should be written in simple, non-technical English and should not include unnecessary information which may confuse court in the receiving foreign state. Avoid use of the term "discovery". Similarly, to avoid the appearance of a "fishing expedition" which may result in refusal of the foreign country to execute the request, try not to use phrases such as "any and all documents". Requests for documents should be as specific as possible. If particular procedures to be followed by the foreign court are preferable, include the specifics in the letter rogatory (for example, verbatim transcript, place witness under oath, permission for American or foreign counsel to attend or participate in proceedings if possible, etc.)

The letter rogatory should be addressed "To Appropriate Judicial Authority of (Insert name of Country)." The essential elements of a letter rogatory are:

(a) a request for international judicial assistance is being made in the interests of justice;

(b) a brief synopsis of the case, including identification of the parties and the nature of the claim and relief sought to enable the foreign court to understand the issues involved;

(c) type of case [civil, criminal, administrative];

(d) the nature of the assistance required [compel testimony or production of evidence; service of process];

(e) name, address, and other identifiers, such as corporate title, of the person abroad to be served or from whom evidence is to be compelled, documents to be served;

(f) list of questions to be asked, where applicable, generally in the form of written interrogatories;

(g) list of documents or other evidence to be produced;

(h) the requesting court should include a statement expressing a willingness to provide similar assistance to judicial authorities of the receiving state [28 U.S.C. 1782];

(i) the requesting court should include a statement expressing a willingness to reimburse the judicial authorities of the receiving state for costs incurred in executing the requesting court's letter rogatory.

AUTHENTICATION REQUIREMENTS:

Letters rogatory must be issued under the seal of the court and the signature of the judge. . . . For most countries, the seal of the court and signature of the judge is sufficient. . . . Some countries require further authentication of letters rogatory. Do not waste time and money on these additional steps unless your local foreign counsel, this office, or some other authoritative source advises that it is necessary. If there is no specific flyer for the country in question, consult the geographic division of the Office of American Citizens Services and Crisis Management.

TRIPLE CERTIFICATION, CHAIN AUTHENTICATION, AND AUTHENTICATION BY THE FOREIGN EMBASSY IN THE UNITED STATES:

As noted above, these additional authentication steps are not required by most countries. Some countries require Triple Certification of the letter rogatory which means that the judge signs the documents; the clerk certifies that the judge is the judge; the judge certifies that the clerk is the clerk. This is also known as an exemplification certificate. In addition to the triple certification or exemplification process, some foreign countries require that the letter rogatory be authenticated by the embassy or consulate of the foreign country in the United States. This is accomplished by "chain authentication" summarized below. . . .

TRANSLATION REQUIREMENTS:

The letters rogatory and any accompanying documents must be translated into the official language of the foreign country. The translator should execute an affidavit as to the validity of the translation before a notary.

NUMBER OF COPIES REQUIRED:

Forward to the Department of State for transmittal to the foreign authorities: the original English version bearing the seal of the court and signature of the judge [or a certified copy]; a photocopy of the English; the original translation and a photocopy of the translation. The original documents will be served upon the designated recipient or deposited with the foreign court in connection with a request for evidence, and the copies returned to the court in the U.S. as proof of execution. For requests involving multiple witnesses in diverse locations, either prepare a separate letter rogatory for each witness, or provide a certified copy of the single letter rogatory (plus translation and duplicate copy noted above) for each witness. The foreign country may assign the matter to different courts. The U.S. embassy will endeavor to ensure that evidence obtained will be transmitted to the court in the U.S. as it is received from the Foreign Ministry rather than held by the Foreign Ministry until all the evidence has been obtained. The same procedures apply to requests involving service of process upon multiple persons.

TRANSMITTAL OF THE REQUEST:

Letters rogatory generally may be transmitted to foreign judicial authorities through the "diplomatic channel". The "diplomatic channel" is a circuitous route by which the documents are sent to the foreign court. Unless the foreign country accepts transmittal directly from court-to-court or through local foreign counsel, you will be confronted with the difficulties of at least some portion of the diplomatic channel described below. If your local counsel in the foreign country advise that letters rogatory may be transmitted directly by your foreign counsel to the foreign court, you may elect to avoid the time consuming diplomatic channel. If the Department of State information about a particular country reflects that use of the diplomatic channel is required, you may wish to seek clarification of contrary guidance from other sources.

. . .

WHAT IS THE DIPLOMATIC CHANNEL?

The documents proceed along the following lines:
1. Drafted by American attorney . . .
2. Issued Under Seal of American court and Signature of Judge . . .
3. Returned by Issuing Court to American Attorney . . .
4. Sent by Attorney to U.S. State Department or U.S. Embassy Abroad . . .
5. Received by U.S. Embassy . . .
6. Sent to Ministry of Foreign Affairs under cover of a diplomatic note . . .
7. Sent to foreign Ministry of Justice . . .
8. Sent to by Ministry of Justice Foreign Court of Competent Jurisdiction . . .
9. Executed by Foreign Court subject to Court's Calender . . .
10. Returned to Ministry of Foreign Affairs . . .
11. Returned to U.S. Embassy . . .
12. Returned to U.S. Department of State . . .
13. Returned to Requesting Court.
14. Requesting Attorney Receives Evidence from Requesting American Court.

COSTS:

Effective February 1, 1998, there is a $455.00 consular fee for services related to execution of a letter rogatory. Foreign authorities may also charge fees, therefore, counsel are requested to submit a certified bank check in the amount of $500.00 payable to the U.S. Embassy (insert name of capital of the foreign country, for example, "U.S. Embassy Tokyo") as a deposit against which the U.S. consular fee, and any foreign fees may be deducted. . . .

RETAINING LOCAL FOREIGN COUNSEL:

28 U.S.C. 1781(b)(2) permits American courts to transmit letters rogatory directly to the executing authority in the foreign country. Although many countries require that letters rogatory be transmitted to the foreign government through the "diplomatic channel" by the U.S. embassy, local counsel can be helpful in subsequent inquiries. Where the foreign government does not object to direct transmission, for example through a local foreign attorney, this can save time. While retention of the services of a foreign attorney to aid in the progress of a letter rogatory is not generally required (although some countries, such as the Bahamas mandate such assistance), requesting counsel in the U.S. may find it useful to retain local counsel to provide guidance on preparation of the request and to expedite the process.

REFUSAL TO HONOR AMERICAN LETTERS ROGATORY:

Foreign countries have declined to honor American letters rogatory where a foreign domestic blocking statute prohibits release of the evidence requested.

. . .

TIME REQUIRED TO EXECUTE A LETTER ROGATORY:

Generally letters rogatory worldwide, including those sent to the United States, take from six months to a year to execute.

RETURN OF EXECUTED LETTER ROGATORY:

When a letter rogatory is executed by the foreign authorities, it is returned to the requesting court in the United States by this office via certified mail. Requesting counsel is also notified. At the request of the court, the executed letter rogatory and proof of service/evidence can be returned directly to requesting counsel. If transmittal by commercial express delivery service is preferred, please include your account number in the covering letter.

. . .

EXAMPLE — LETTER ROGATORY: SAMPLE REQUEST FOR INTERNATIONAL JUDICIAL ASSISTANCE

NAME OF COURT IN SENDING STATE
REQUESTING JUDICIAL ASSISTANCE

NAME OF PLAINTIFF	
V.	DOCKET NUMBER
NAME OF DEFENDANT	

REQUEST FOR INTERNATIONAL JUDICIAL ASSISTANCE
(LETTER ROGATORY)

[NAME OF THE REQUESTING COURT] PRESENTS ITS COMPLIMENTS TO THE APPROPRIATE JUDICIAL AUTHORITY OF (NAME OF RECEIVING STATE), AND REQUESTS INTERNATIONAL JUDICIAL ASSISTANCE TO [OBTAIN EVIDENCE/EFFECT SERVICE OF PROCESS] TO BE USED IN A [CIVIL, CRIMINAL, ADMINISTRATIVE] PROCEEDING BEFORE THIS COURT IN THE ABOVE CAPTIONED MATTER. A [TRIAL/HEARING] ON THIS MATTER IS SCHEDULED AT PRESENT FOR [DATE] IN [CITY, STATE, COUNTRY].

THIS COURT REQUESTS THE ASSISTANCE DESCRIBED HEREIN AS NECESSARY IN THE INTERESTS OF JUSTICE. THE ASSISTANCE REQUESTED IS THAT THE APPROPRIATE JUDICIAL AUTHORITY OF [NAME OF RECEIVING STATE] [COMPEL THE APPEARANCE OF THE BELOW NAMED INDIVIDUALS TO GIVE EVIDENCE/PRODUCE DOCUMENTS] [EFFECT SERVICE OF PROCESS UPON THE BELOW NAMED INDIVIDUALS].

[NAMES OF WITNESSES/PERSONS TO BE SERVED]
[NATIONALITY OF WITNESSES/PERSONS TO BE SERVED]
[ADDRESSED OF WITNESSES/PERSONS TO BE SERVED]
[DESCRIPTION OF DOCUMENTS OR OTHER EVIDENCE TO BE PRODUCED]

FACTS

[THE FACTS OF THE CASE PENDING BEFORE THE REQUESTING COURT SHOULD BE STATED BRIEFLY HERE, INCLUDING A LIST OF THOSE LAWS OF THE SENDING STATE WHICH GOVERN THE MATTER PENDING BEFORE THE COURT IN THE RECEIVING STATE.]

QUESTIONS

[IF THE REQUEST IS FOR EVIDENCE, THE QUESTIONS FOR THE WITNESSES SHOULD BE LISTED HERE].

[LIST ANY SPECIAL RIGHTS OF WITNESSES PURSUANT TO THE LAWS OF THE REQUESTING STATE HERE].

[LIST ANY SPECIAL METHODS OR PROCEDURES TO BE FOLLOWED].

[INCLUDE REQUEST FOR NOTIFICATION OF TIME AND PLACE FOR EXAMINATION OF WITNESSES/DOCUMENTS BEFORE THE COURT IN THE RECEIVING STATE HERE].

<u>RECIPROCITY:</u>

THE REQUESTING COURT SHOULD INCLUDE A STATEMENT EXPRESSING A WILLINGNESS TO PROVIDE SIMILAR ASSISTANCE TO JUDICIAL AUTHORITIES OF THE RECEIVING STATE.

<u>REIMBURSEMENT FOR COSTS:</u>

THE REQUESTING COURT SHOULD INCLUDE A STATEMENT EXPRESSING A WILLINGNESS TO REIMBURSE THE JUDICIAL AUTHORITIES OF THE RECEIVING STATE FOR COSTS INCURRED IN EXECUTING THE REQUESTING COURT'S LETTER ROGATORY.

SIGNATURE OF REQUESTING JUDGE
TYPED NAME OF REQUESTING JUDGE
NAME OF REQUESTING COURT
CITY, STATE, COUNTRY

DATE
[SEAL OF COURT]

C. U.S. DISCOVERY IN AID OF FOREIGN LITIGATION: 28 U.S.C. § 1782

IN THE MATTER OF THE APPLICATION OF TIME, INC.
1999 U.S. Dist. LEXIS 15858 (E.D. La. Oct. 6, 1999),
affirmed without opinion, 209 F.3d 719 (5th Cir. 2000)

Time, Inc. ("Time") has moved, pursuant to 28 U.S.C. § 1782, for the issuance of subpoenas to James R. Moffett and Freeport McMoRan Copper & Gold Inc. ("Freeport") to obtain deposition testimony and documents for use in pending court proceedings in Indonesia, to which Moffett and Freeport are not parties. Moffett and Freeport (hereinafter sometimes referred to collectively as "Freeport") filed a timely opposition memorandum. . . .

In May 1999, Time published an article in the Asian edition of its "Time" magazine that was highly critical of former Indonesian president General Suharto. The article asserted that "during his thirty-two year reign, General Suharto, his children, and his close friends amassed a vast fortune through rampant corruption, hidden ownership, nepotism, and abuse of power." General Suharto responded to the article by filing a civil suit for defamation against Time Asia and six of its editors and reporters in the Central Jakarta District Court of Indonesia. General Suharto alleges in his complaint that the article defamed him by falsely reporting that (1) he amassed a fortune for himself, family members, and close friends through an entity known as "Suharto Inc.," which he says does not exist; (2) he shifted billions of dollars from a Swiss bank account to an Austrian bank account, when General Suharto says that he never possessed money in either country; (3) the "Suharto companies" very likely never paid more than 10% of their real tax obligations, which General Suharto denies and alleges that no such company exists; (4) and by publishing a picture of General Suharto hugging a picture of a house that General Suharto says he does not own, which painted a false portrait of him as a greedy man. He seeks retractions, an apology, and $27 billion in damages.

Freeport operates in Indonesia the largest copper and gold mine in the world. Moffett is Freeport's chief executive officer. In the instant application pursuant to 28 U.S.C. § 1782, Time seeks deposition testimony and documents from Freeport and Moffett concerning a broad expanse of topics, primarily concerned with the financial dealings of General Suharto, his family members, and close friends in connection with the Indonesian mine. Time asserts this information will be relevant and useful in its defense of the defamation action.

ANALYSIS

A. Section 1782 Contains No Blanket Discoverability Requirement

Congress has enacted legislation to enable discovery to proceed in the United States in connection with foreign judicial proceedings. The applicable statute provides:

> The district court of the district in which a person resides or is found may order him to give his testimony . . . or to produce a document or other thing for use in a proceeding in a foreign or international tribunal. . . . The order may be made pursuant to a . . . request made, by a foreign or international tribunal or upon the application of any interested person. . . . The order may prescribe the practice and procedure, which may be in whole or part the practice and procedure of the foreign country or the international tribunal, for taking the testimony or statement or producing the document or other thing. To the extent that the order does not prescribe otherwise, the testimony or statement shall be taken, and the document or other thing produced, in accordance with the Federal Rules of Civil Procedure.

28 U.S.C. § 1782(a). Thus, the application need show only that it is made (1) "by a foreign or international tribunal" or "any interested person," (2) "for use in a proceeding in a foreign or international tribunal," and (3) that the person or entity from whom the discovery is sought is a resident of or can be found in the district where the application is filed. *In re Bayer AG*, 146 F.3d 188, 193 (3d Cir. 1998).

The three prima facie requirements of the statute are met in the instant case. Moffett and Freeport are admittedly residents of or found in New Orleans. Time has provided a declaration stating that its Hong Kong office was served with the Indonesian lawsuit and it has hired an Indonesian attorney. Time's New Orleans counsel has stated that its Indonesian attorney has appeared in the Indonesian court on Time's behalf and that the case is proceeding, although Time intends to file or has filed a motion to dismiss on jurisdictional and substantive grounds. This Court has no knowledge what the outcome of that motion may be or when it may be decided. On the current record, Time has established that it is an interested person and that the discovery is sought for use on the merits in the Indonesian civil proceeding. Therefore, the Court has discretion to order the discovery.

Freeport argues, however, that the statute imposes a fourth requirement that the laws of the foreign jurisdiction must permit the discovery. Time concedes that the Indonesian court has no discovery procedures. The Fifth Circuit has squarely stated that "[t]here is no discoverability requirement in the text of § 1782." *In re Letter Rogatory from the First Court of First Instance in Civil Matters, Caracas*, 42 F.3d 308, 310 (5th Cir. 1995). Nonetheless, there is disagreement in the federal courts whether the statute requires discoverability. The issue in *Letter Rogatory* was whether the Court should impose such a requirement when the information was being requested by a foreign tribunal. The Court held it would not inquire into discoverability because the requesting "foreign court is, presumably, the arbiter of what is discoverable under its procedural rules."

The Fifth Circuit in *Letter Rogatory* distinguished private litigants who request discovery under Section 1782. In such cases, the Court said,

> courts in the United States have routinely undertaken a discoverability determination when the request for information comes from a private litigant. The reason for this is to avoid assisting a foreign litigant who desires to circumvent the forum nation's discovery rules by diverting a discovery request to an American court. The case law in this area is very clear.

However, the Fifth Circuit's statement about private litigants was dictum because the only issue in *Letter Rogatory* was whether to require discoverability when the Court was presented with a letter rogatory from a foreign court. Moreover, the case law on this issue is no longer, if it ever was, as clear as the Fifth Circuit stated in January 1995.

In the absence of Fifth Circuit authority on point, I find the reasoning of the Third Circuit in *Bayer AG*, 146 F.3d at 193–96, and the Second Circuit in *Euromepa S.A. v. R. Esmerian, Inc.*, 51 F.3d 1095, 1099–1100 (2d Cir. 1995), persuasive. As these and other cases have noted, concern about possible offense to a foreign nation whose procedures do not include pretrial discovery can be addressed as a factor that informs the Court's discretion, rather than as a blanket prohibition against such discovery. . . . The well-reasoned position of much of the case law, as explained by the Third Circuit, is that a blanket restrictive requirement is contrary to the language and purpose of Section 1782. I agree.

First, the language of the statute is clear, and it includes no discoverability requirement. Imposing such a requirement would be inconsistent with both the letter and spirit of the statute. If Congress had intended to impose such a restrictive element, at a time when it was enacting liberalizing amendments to the statute, it could have done so easily and explicitly. *Bayer AG*, 146 F.3d at 192–93. It is not this Court's function to rewrite statutes.

Second, the legislative history and purpose of Section 1782 do not support a blanket discoverability requirement.

> The legislative history is . . . devoid of any indication that Congress intended to limit the scope of § 1782 to those situations in which the discovery sought would be discoverable under the laws of the foreign jurisdiction. . . . Congress's overarching goals were to provide efficient means of assistance to foreign courts and litigants and encourage other nations to return the favor by providing similar assistance to United States courts. Neither of these congressional purposes requires courts to impose a discoverability requirement as a bright-line rule.

Id. at 193.

Third, the policy concerns expressed by some courts as the basis for inventing a discoverability requirement in Section 1782 are not persuasive. For example, the First Circuit in [*In re Application of Asta Medica, S.A.*, 981 F.2d 1, 7 (1st Cir. 1992)] was concerned that a foreign party could invoke Section 1782 and obtain broad, American-style discovery that would not be available for that party's American adversary. "In essence, that is simply another way of imposing a reciprocity requirement, a requirement we [the Third Circuit][have previously] rejected . . . . Any patent unfairness can be dealt with by the district court crafting an appropriate discovery order." *Bayer AG*, 146 F.3d at 194. Moreover, that situation does not exist here, when it is the American litigant seeking discovery from American nonparties.

An additional concern is that granting a Section 1782 application when the requested discovery would not be available in the foreign jurisdiction

> would lead some nations to conclude that United States courts view their laws and procedures with contempt, thereby frustrating Congress's desire to stimulate foreign tribunals to provide reciprocal assistance to litigants before our own courts. We agree that . . . we ought to avoid a construction of the statute that would lead other nations to conclude that we do not respect their laws and procedures. . . . It does not follow that the inability to obtain discovery means that the foreign court objects to the inquiry. In many of such situations it may signify merely the unavailability of an applicable procedure.

Bayer AG, 146 F.3d at 194.

The question whether a foreign tribunal would take offense at the discovery can be handled by the district court in the exercise of its discretion. It may "consider any materials, typically statutes or case law from the foreign jurisdiction, that may be presented by the parties" on this issue. "Inasmuch as relevant evidence is presumptively discoverable under § 1782, the burden of demonstrating offense to the foreign jurisdiction, or any other facts warranting the denial of a particular application, should rest with the party opposing the application. . . ." Freeport has offered nothing but a conclusory statement that the Indonesian court would "likely" be offended by Time's application for discovery. It is difficult to see how an Indonesian court would be offended by discovery requests from one American company to another and to an American citizen, both nonparties to the litigation who are not subject to the Indonesian court's jurisdiction, particularly when it appears that the Indonesian court has "wide discretion in deciding what evidence to admit at trial," and conversely to reject proffered evidence.

"[T]here is no reason to assume that because a country has not adopted a particular discovery procedure, it would take offense at its use." *Id.* at 194 (quoting Hans Smit, *Recent Developments in International Litigation*, 35 S. TEX. L. REV. 215, 236 (1994) (hereinafter "Recent Developments") ("although a foreign court might not compel production of the evidence in the manner employed by an American court, it might very well, and ordinarily would, readily accept and rely on the evidence obtained with the help of the American court,")). Time's Indonesian lawyer has asserted without contradiction that the Indonesian judges have absolute discretion to decide what evidence to admit. Freeport has not provided any evidence to this Court that information discovered through American processes will be inadmissible in Indonesia for that reason.

The Third Circuit recognized [in *Bayer AG*] that there are some instances in which permitting discovery of certain evidence may cause offense to the courts of the foreign jurisdiction. "Some countries may regard information held by spouses or children to be privileged; others may have different limits. The comity concerns we expressed against 'use of U.S. discovery procedures to evade the limitations placed on domestic pre-trial disclosure by foreign tribunals,' are applicable only when the substance of the discovery is objectionable." *Id.* at 195. Again, Freeport has provided no evidence that the substance of the discovery is *per se* objectionable to an Indonesian court.

Finally, "[t]his case raises the question of the degree to which federal district courts, in deciding whether to order discovery under 28 U.S.C. § 1782(a) in aid of a foreign litigation, should delve into the mysteries of foreign law." *Euromepa*, 51 F.3d at 1096. The Second Circuit's answer, with which I agree, is that "an extensive examination of foreign law regarding the existence and extent of discovery in the forum country is [not] desirable." For, as a chief architect of section 1782's current version . . . stated:

> [The statute's] drafters . . . did not want to have a request for cooperation turn into an unduly expensive and time-consuming fight about foreign law. That would be quite contrary to what they sought to be achieved. They also realized that, although civil law countries do not have discovery rules similar to those of common law countries, they often do have quite different procedures for discovering information that could not properly be evaluated without a rather broad understanding of the subtleties of the applicable foreign system. It would, they judged, be wholly inappropriate for an American district court to try to obtain this understanding for the purpose of honoring a simple request for assistance.

Id. (quoting Smit, *Recent Developments* at 235). In *Euromepa*, the district court, which had imposed a discoverability requirement, found itself embroiled in a battle-by-affidavit of international legal experts, [which] resulted in the district court's admittedly "superficial" ruling on French law. We think that it is unwise — as well as in tension with the aims of section 1782 — for district judges to try to glean the accepted practices and attitudes of other nations from what are likely to be conflicting and, perhaps, biased interpretations of foreign law. . . . [W]e do not read the statute to condone speculative forays into legal territories unfamiliar to federal judges. Such a costly, time-consuming, and inherently unreliable method of deciding section 1782 requests cannot possibly promote the "twin aims"[1] of the statute.

Id. at 1099–1100.

Nothing in the history or purpose of Section 1[7]82 indicates that such battles over the interpretation of foreign law are necessary or desirable before implementing the liberal employment of discovery granted by the statute. Rather, the discoverability of the information sought and whether allowing the discovery would offend the foreign tribunal are factors for the Court to consider in exercising its discretion.

In connection with this inquiry, the Second Circuit requires the district court to consider only "authoritative proof that a foreign tribunal would reject evidence obtained with the aid of section 1782." *Euromepa*, 51 F.3d at 1100. The burden is not, as Freeport suggests, on Time to show discoverability. Rather, it is Freeport's burden to show that the foreign tribunal would refuse the evidence. According to the uncontradicted declaration of Time's Indonesian lawyer, the Indonesian court has unlimited discretion to decide what evidence to admit. Freeport's expert Indonesian attorney states that the usual procedure is for the Indonesian court to receive written exhibits and to hear testimony of witnesses, and that the courts generally consider it the responsibility of a party to produce its own evidence. This declaration does not establish that evidence discovered via Section 1782 would be inadmissible in the Indonesian civil proceeding.

Accordingly, the Court finds that Section 1782 does not impose a blanket discoverability requirement and that Time's application is not objectionable on that basis. Therefore, the Court will examine the discovery requests themselves. . . .

B. Relevance and Breadth of the Discovery

The reference to the Federal Rules of Civil Procedure in Section 1782 suggests that under ordinary circumstances, the standards for discovery under those rules should also apply when discovery is sought under the statute. Consistent with the statute's modest prima facie elements and Congress's goal of providing equitable and efficacious discovery procedures, district courts should treat relevant discovery materials sought pursuant to § 1782 as discoverable unless the party opposing the application can demonstrate facts sufficient to justify the denial of the application. [The court determined that the requested discovery was "grotesquely overbroad" F.R.C.P. 26(b), under

---

[1] The statute has the "twin aims of providing efficient means of assistance to participants in international litigation in our federal courts and encouraging foreign countries by example to provide similar means of assistance to our courts." *Id.* at 1097.

which, as summarized in the opinion, "the Court shall limit the discovery if it determines that the discovery sought is unreasonably cumulative or duplicative, or is obtainable from some other source that is more convenient, less burdensome, or less expensive; or the burden or expense of the proposed discovery outweighs its likely benefit."]

Notes and Questions on Section 1782 and *Application of Time, Inc.*

1. *Fairness and Section 1782*. The courts that have grafted a foreign discoverability requirement onto Section 1782 have expressed concern that the law otherwise allows one party to a foreign lawsuit to obtain American-style discovery against another party, specifically to circumvent the limitations on discovery under foreign law — as a substitute for foreign procedures rather than as an aid or supplement to them as Congress intended. *See, e.g., In re Application of Asta Medica, SA*, 981 F.2d 1 (1st Cir. 1992). Should Congress redraft the statute to foreclose this possibility, or can U.S. courts be trusted to do so through protective orders? If the latter, what criteria should the U.S. court use in determining whether, in Judge Jacobs' words, "the discovery sought here aids the proceedings abroad or . . . distorts the adversarial symmetry existing there"? *See In the Matter of the Application of Euromepa v. Esmerian, Inc.*, 51 F.3d 1095 (2d Cir. 1995) (Jacobs, J., dissenting).

2. *The applicable standard*. The court in *Application of Time, Inc.*, wished to avoid an extensive examination of foreign law, fearing that it might lead to an inconclusive "battle-by-affidavit" among expert witnesses. What alternative standard does it suggest for determining how and whether to proceed under Section 1782? Does the requirement of "authoritative proof that a foreign tribunal would reject evidence obtained with the aid of Section 1782" constrain the courts' discretion too much? And would anything less than a foreign court's injunction forbidding U.S. discovery qualify as "authoritative proof" if expert witness affidavits are excluded? Is there reason to doubt that such an injunction would be respected by a U.S. court? Would a requirement that the petitioner first exhaust local discovery options be effective or preferable?

3. *Alternative approaches*. Consider the expedient proposed by the Second Circuit Court of Appeals in *In re Male v. Hungarian Airlines*, 964 F.2d 97, 102 (2d Cir.), *cert. denied*, 506 U.S. 861 (1992), under which the court could require a petitioner under § 1782

> to prepare a discovery plan, make a showing that the discovery is "not obtainable from [some] other source that is more convenient, less burdensome, or less expensive," such as the [foreign] court, and then require [the petitioner] to take the discovery plan before the [foreign] court for a determination as to which requests are relevant before coming to the United States district court for actual discovery.

Would such a plan necessarily prevent the U.S. courts from becoming "global 'Special Masters for Discovery'"? *See id.* at 103 (Feinberg, J., dissenting).

4. *"Interested person."* The liberal standard for "interested person" under Section 1782 allows a party to a foreign lawsuit — and not necessarily a foreign governmental official or a foreign court — to enlist the assistance of a U.S. court directly in the process of discovery. Should Congress redraft the statute to correct this departure from the orthodox framework for judicial assistance, under which one court assists another court in its judicial functions?

Chapter 6

DOCTRINES OF RESTRAINT AND DIFFIDENCE

In this chapter, we explore the concrete consequences of an abstraction, namely "the perfect equality and absolute independence of sovereigns," *The Schooner Exchange*, 11 U.S. (7 Cranch) 116, 136 (1812). Sovereignty has its privileges especially in a court-room, including the expectation that every foreign state will be immune from the jurisdiction of all other states' courts, or the presumption that one government's official actions will not be judged in the domestic courts of other nations, or the obligation to respect the inviolability of diplomats, heads-of-state, and diplomatic missions. The courts of the United States have developed an extensive body of law that both preserves and qualifies each of these privileges, drawing on statutes, the Constitution, treaties, custom, and the common law. But the law evolves: as the line blurs between states and private actors — especially as states leave their traditional perch as market regulators and become market participants — these privileges change, and the courts are required to recalibrate the balance between their respect for sovereignty and their obligation to resolve the disputes brought before them. What emerges from that tension are doctrines of restraint and diffidence, under which the courts are — or rule themselves to be — powerless over certain parties and certain issues. In this chapter, we focus on these doctrines:

> *foreign sovereign immunity*, that is, the immunity from jurisdiction that foreign states (and their agencies and instrumentalities) have in federal and state courts in the United States. This body of law is now codified in the Foreign Sovereign Immunities Act of 1976 (excerpted below and reproduced in its entirety in the Documents Supplement);

> *the act of state doctrine*, a judicially-created doctrine under which the domestic courts presume the validity of a foreign government's official acts within its own territory;

> *the political question doctrine*, under which certain issues are non-justiciable, that is, inappropriate for judicial resolution, especially to the extent that they implicate the executive branch's authority over foreign affairs;

> *diplomatic and consular immunity*, under which certain representatives of a foreign state receive a functional immunity from criminal process, and to some extent from civil process as well; and

> *head-of-state immunity*, under which sitting heads-of-state enjoy as close to an absolute immunity as U.S. law allows.

As you consider each of these doctrines, notice the interplay between the "hard" sources of law, like statutes and treaties, and "soft" sources, like the courts' discretion to characterize acts in a particular way or the in-court power of *ad hoc* submissions from the political branches of the U.S. government.

A. FOREIGN SOVEREIGN IMMUNITY

[1] History and Structure of the Foreign Sovereign Immunity Doctrine

In *Siderman de Blake v. Argentina*, 965 F.2d 699 (9th Cir. 1992), *cert. denied*, 507 U.S. 1017 (1993), the court offered a brief history of foreign sovereign immunity in the United States. The full text of the opinion appears below, but the court's treatment of the underlying concepts offers a useful orientation to the topic:

> Until 1952, foreign states and their agencies and instrumentalities enjoyed virtually absolute immunity from suit in the courts of the United States. Chief Justice John Marshall authored the seminal opinion that considered and recognized the immunity of a foreign state from suit in a United States court. In *The Schooner Exchange v. M'Faddon*, 11 U.S. (7 Cranch) 116 (1812), the Court upheld a French plea of immunity against an American citizen's assertion of title to an armed national vessel of France that had entered the territorial waters of the United States. In his opinion for the Court, Chief Justice Marshall first emphasized the "exclusive and absolute" nature of a nation's territorial jurisdiction, any exception to which could arise only from the consent or waiver of that nation. He then explained:
>
> > The world being composed of distinct sovereignties, possessing equal rights and equal independence, . . . all sovereigns have consented to a relaxation in practice, in cases under certain peculiar circumstances, of that absolute and complete jurisdiction within their respective territories which sovereignty confers.
>
> Thus, Chief Justice Marshall announced that the common practice of nations forms the foundation for the doctrine of foreign sovereign immunity, while a given state's agreement to grant immunity in a particular case is a matter of grace, comity, and respect for the equality and independence of other sovereigns. Although *The Schooner Exchange* did not announce a rule of absolute sovereign immunity, in the following 140 years absolute immunity became the norm, principally because the courts practiced consistent deference to the Executive Branch, which "ordinarily requested immunity in all actions against friendly foreign sovereigns."
>
> In 1952, however, the Acting Legal Adviser of the State Department, Jack Tate, sent a letter to the Acting Attorney General announcing that the State Department was adopting the "restrictive" principle of foreign sovereign immunity. Under the restrictive principle, as defined in the Tate Letter, "the immunity of the sovereign is recognized with

regard to sovereign or public acts (*jure imperii*) of a state, but not with respect to private acts (*jure gestionis*)." 26 Dep't of State Bull. 984 (1952), reprinted in *Alfred Dunhill of London, Inc. v. Republic of Cuba*, 425 U.S. 682 (1976). With the issuance of the Tate Letter, the United States joined the emerging international consensus that private acts of a sovereign — commercial activities being the primary example — were not entitled to immunity. While the Tate Letter altered the Executive Branch's view of foreign sovereign immunity, it did not provide the courts with concrete legislative standards for determining whether to assert jurisdiction over actions against foreign states. Thus, the courts continued to defer to the Executive Branch. When the State Department issued a suggestion of immunity in a particular case, the court followed it; when the State Department remained silent, the court relied on prior suggestions for precedential assistance in determining immunity.

With the enactment of the [Foreign Sovereign Immunities Act (FSIA)] in 1976, Congress replaced the regime of deference to Executive suggestion with a comprehensive legislative framework "governing claims of immunity in every civil action against a foreign state or its political subdivisions, agencies, or instrumentalities." *Id.* at 488; H.R. Rep. No. 1487, 94th Cong., 2d Sess. 7, reprinted in 1976 U.S. Code Cong. & Admin. News 6604, 6606 ("A principal purpose of this bill is to transfer the determination of sovereign immunity from the executive branch to the judicial branch . . . .") In essence, the FSIA codified the restrictive theory of sovereign immunity, which had become widely accepted in international law. Structurally, the FSIA sets forth the general rule that foreign states are immune from the jurisdiction of both federal and state courts in the United States, subject to certain exceptions. 28 U.S.C. §§ 1330(a) & 1604. A federal court lacks subject matter jurisdiction over a claim against a foreign state unless the claim falls within an exception to immunity under the FSIA. *See* 28 U.S.C. § 1330(a); *see also Argentine Republic v. Amerada Hess Shipping Corp.,* 488 U.S. 428, 439 (1989) (FSIA is "sole basis for obtaining jurisdiction over a foreign state in federal court").

As a threshold matter, therefore, a court adjudicating a claim against a foreign state must determine whether the FSIA provides subject matter jurisdiction over the claim. The existence of subject matter jurisdiction under the FSIA is a question of law subject to *de novo* review. . . .

FOREIGN SOVEREIGN IMMUNITIES ACT OF 1976 (selected provisions)

§ 1330. Actions against foreign states

(a) The district courts shall have original jurisdiction without regard to amount in controversy of any nonjury civil action against a foreign state as defined in section 1603(a) of this title as to any claim for relief in personam with respect to which the foreign state is not entitled to immunity either under sections 1605–1607 of this title or under any applicable international agreement.

(b) Personal jurisdiction over a foreign state shall exist as to every claim for relief over which the district courts have jurisdiction under subsection (a) where service has been made under section 1608 of this title.

(c) For purposes of subsection (b), an appearance by a foreign state does not confer personal jurisdiction with respect to any claim for relief not arising out of any transaction or occurrence enumerated in sections 1605–1607 of this title.

§ 1602. Findings and declaration of purpose

The Congress finds that the determination by United States courts of the claims of foreign states to immunity from the jurisdiction of such courts would serve the interests of justice and would protect the rights of both foreign states and litigants in United States courts. Under international law, states are not immune from the jurisdiction of foreign courts insofar as their commercial activities are concerned, and their commercial property may be levied upon for the satisfaction of judgments rendered against them in connection with their commercial activities. Claims of foreign states to immunity should henceforth be decided by courts of the United States and of the States in conformity with the principles set forth in this chapter.

§ 1603. Definitions

For purposes of this chapter -

(a) A "foreign state", except as used in section 1608 of this title, includes a political subdivision of a foreign state or an agency or instrumentality of a foreign state as defined in subsection (b).

(b) An "agency or instrumentality of a foreign state" means any entity -

   (1) which is a separate legal person, corporate or otherwise, and

   (2) which is an organ of a foreign state or political subdivision thereof, or a majority of whose shares or other ownership interest is owned by a foreign state or political subdivision thereof, and

   (3) which is neither a citizen of a State of the United States as defined in section 1332 and (d) of this title, nor created under the laws of any third country.

(c) The "United States" includes all territory and waters, continental or insular, subject to the jurisdiction of the United States.

(d) A "commercial activity" means either a regular course of commercial conduct or a particular commercial transaction or act. The commercial character of an activity shall be determined by reference to the nature of the course of conduct or particular transaction or act, rather than by reference to its purpose.

(e) A "commercial activity carried on in the United States by a foreign state" means commercial activity carried on by such state and having substantial contact with the United States.

§ 1604. Immunity of a foreign state from jurisdiction

Subject to existing international agreements to which the United States is a party at the time of enactment of this Act a foreign state shall be immune from the jurisdiction of the courts of the United States and of the States except as provided in sections 1605 to 1607 of this chapter.

§ 1605. General exceptions to the jurisdictional immunity of a foreign state

(a) A foreign state shall not be immune from the jurisdiction of courts of the United States or of the States in any case -

(1) in which the foreign state has waived its immunity either explicitly or by implication, notwithstanding any withdrawal of the waiver which the foreign state may purport to effect except in accordance with the terms of the waiver;

(2) in which the action is based upon a commercial activity carried on in the United States by the foreign state; or upon an act performed in the United States in connection with a commercial activity of the foreign state elsewhere; or upon an act outside the territory of the United States in connection with a commercial activity of the foreign state elsewhere and that act causes a direct effect in the United States;

(3) in which rights in property taken in violation of international law are in issue and that property or any property exchanged for such property is present in the United States in connection with a commercial activity carried on in the United States by the foreign state; or that property or any property exchanged for such property is owned or operated by an agency or instrumentality of the foreign state and that agency or instrumentality is engaged in a commercial activity in the United States;

(4) in which rights in property in the United States acquired by succession or gift or rights in immovable property situated in the United States are in issue;

(5) not otherwise encompassed in paragraph (2) above, in which money damages are sought against a foreign state for personal injury or death, or damage to or loss of property, occurring in the United States and caused by the tortious act or omission of that foreign state or of any official or employee of that foreign state while acting within the scope of his office or employment; except this paragraph shall not apply to -

(A) any claim based upon the exercise or performance or the failure to exercise or perform a discretionary function regardless of whether the discretion be abused, or

(B) any claim arising out of malicious prosecution, abuse of process, libel, slander, misrepresentation, deceit, or interference with contract rights;

(6) in which the action is brought, either to enforce an agreement made by the foreign state with or for the benefit of a private party to submit to arbitration all or any differences which have arisen or which may arise between the parties with respect to a defined legal relationship, whether contractual or not, concerning a subject matter capable of settlement by arbitration under the laws of the United States, or to confirm an award made pursuant to such an agreement to arbitrate, if

(A) the arbitration takes place or is intended to take place in the United States,

(B) the agreement or award is or may be governed by a treaty or other international agreement in force for the United States calling for the recognition and enforcement of arbitral awards,

(C) the underlying claim, save for the agreement to arbitrate, could have been brought in a United States court under this section or section 1607, or

(D) paragraph (1) of this subsection is otherwise applicable; or

(7) not otherwise covered by paragraph (2), in which money damages are sought against a foreign state for personal injury or death that was caused by an act of torture, extrajudicial killing, aircraft sabotage, hostage taking, or the provision of material support or resources (as defined in section 2339A of title 18) for such an act if such act or provision of material support is engaged in by an official, employee, or agent of such foreign state while acting within the scope of his or her office, employment, or agency, except that the court shall decline to hear a claim under this paragraph -

(A) if the foreign state was not designated as a state sponsor of terrorism under section 6(j) of the Export Administration Act of 1979 (50 U.S.C. App. 2405(j)) or section 620A of the Foreign Assistance Act of 1961 (22 U.S.C. 2371) at the time the act occurred, unless later so designated as a result of such act; and

(B) even if the foreign state is or was so designated, if -

(i) the act occurred in the foreign state against which the claim has been brought and the claimant has not afforded the foreign state a reasonable opportunity to arbitrate the claim in accordance with accepted international rules of arbitration; or

(ii) neither the claimant nor the victim was a national of the United States (as that term is defined in section 101(a)(22) of the Immigration and Nationality Act) when the act upon which the claim is based occurred.

. . .

(f) No action shall be maintained under subsection (a)(7) unless the action is commenced not later than 10 years after the date on which the cause of action arose. All principles of equitable tolling, including the period during which the foreign state was immune from suit, shall apply in calculating this limitation period.

. . .

§ 1608. Service; time to answer; default

(a) Service in the courts of the United States and of the States shall be made upon a foreign state or political subdivision of a foreign state:

(1) by delivery of a copy of the summons and complaint in accordance with any special arrangement for service between the plaintiff and the foreign state or political subdivision; or

(2) if no special arrangement exists, by delivery of a copy of the summons and complaint in accordance with an applicable international convention on service of judicial documents; or

(3) if service cannot be made under paragraphs (1) or (2), by sending a copy of the summons and complaint and a notice of suit, together with a translation of each into the official language of the foreign state, by any form of mail requiring a signed receipt, to be addressed and dispatched by the clerk of the court to the head of the ministry of foreign affairs of the foreign state concerned, or

(4) if service cannot be made within 30 days under paragraph (3), by sending two copies of the summons and complaint and a notice of suit, together with a translation of each into the official language of the foreign state, by any form of mail requiring a signed receipt, to be addressed and dispatched by the clerk of the court to the Secretary of State in Washington, District of Columbia, to the attention of the Director of Special Consular Services — and the Secretary shall transmit one copy of the papers through diplomatic channels to the foreign state and shall send to the clerk of the court a certified copy of the diplomatic note indicating when the papers were transmitted.

As used in this subsection, a "notice of suit" shall mean a notice addressed to a foreign state and in a form prescribed by the Secretary of State by regulation.

(b) Service in the courts of the United States and of the States shall be made upon an agency or instrumentality of a foreign state:

(1) by delivery of a copy of the summons and complaint in accordance with any special arrangement for service between the plaintiff and the agency or instrumentality; or

(2) if no special arrangement exists, by delivery of a copy of the summons and complaint either to an officer, a managing or general agent, or to any other agent authorized by appointment or by law to receive service of process in the United States; or in accordance with an applicable international convention on service of judicial documents; or

(3) if service cannot be made under paragraphs (1) or (2), and if reasonably calculated to give actual notice, by delivery of a copy of the summons and complaint, together with a translation of each into the official language of the foreign state—

(A) as directed by an authority of the foreign state or political subdivision in response to a letter rogatory or request or

(B) by any form of mail requiring a signed receipt, to be addressed and dispatched by the clerk of the court to the agency or instrumentality to be served, or

(C) as directed by order of the court consistent with the law of the place where service is to be made.

(c) Service shall be deemed to have been made—

(1) in the case of service under subsection (a)(4), as of the date of transmittal indicated in the certified copy of the diplomatic note; and

(2) in any other case under this section, as of the date of receipt indicated in the certification, signed and returned postal receipt, or other proof of service applicable to the method of service employed.

(d) In any action brought in a court of the United States or of a State, a foreign state, a political subdivision thereof, or an agency or instrumentality of a foreign state shall serve an answer or other responsive pleading to the complaint within sixty days after service has been made under this section.

(e) No judgment by default shall be entered by a court of the United States or of a State against a foreign state, a political subdivision thereof, or an agency or instrumentality of a foreign state, unless the claimant establishes his claim or right to relief by evidence satisfactory to the court. A copy of any such default judgment shall be sent to the foreign state or political subdivision in the manner prescribed for service in this section.

---

[2] The Statute in Operation

ARGENTINE REPUBLIC v. AMERADA HESS SHIPPING CORP.
488 U.S. 428 (1989)

CHIEF JUSTICE REHNQUIST delivered the opinion of the Court. Two Liberian corporations sued the Argentine Republic in a United States District Court to recover damages for a tort allegedly committed by its armed forces on the high seas in violation of international law. We hold that the District Court correctly dismissed the action, because the Foreign Sovereign Immunities Act of 1976 (FSIA), 28 U. S. C. § 1330 *et seq.*, does not authorize jurisdiction over a foreign state in this situation.

Respondents alleged the following facts in their complaints. Respondent United Carriers, Inc., a Liberian corporation, chartered one of its oil tankers, the *Hercules*, to respondent Amerada Hess Shipping Corporation, also a Liberian corporation. The contract was executed in New York City. Amerada Hess used the *Hercules* to transport crude oil from the southern terminus of the Trans-Alaska Pipeline in Valdez, Alaska, around Cape Horn in South America, to the Hess refinery in the United States Virgin Islands. On May 25, 1982, the *Hercules* began a return voyage, without cargo but fully fueled, from the Virgin Islands to Alaska. At that time, Great Britain and petitioner Argentine Republic were at war over an archipelago of some 200 islands —

the Falkland Islands to the British, and the Islas Malvinas to the Argentin-eans — in the South Atlantic off the Argentine coast. On June 3, United States officials informed the two belligerents of the location of United States vessels and Liberian tankers owned by United States interests then traversing the South Atlantic, including the *Hercules*, to avoid any attacks on neutral shipping.

By June 8, 1982, after a stop in Brazil, the *Hercules* was in international waters about 600 nautical miles from Argentina and 500 miles from the Falk-lands; she was outside the "war zones" designated by Britain and Argentina. At 12:15 Greenwich mean time, the ship's master made a routine report by radio to Argentine officials, providing the ship's name, international call sign, registry, position, course, speed, and voyage description. About 45 minutes later, an Argentine military aircraft began to circle the *Hercules*. The ship's master repeated his earlier message by radio to Argentine officials, who acknowledged receiving it. Six minutes later, without provocation, another Argentine military plane began to bomb the *Hercules*; the master immediately hoisted a white flag. A second bombing soon followed, and a third attack came about two hours later, when an Argentine jet struck the ship with an air-to-surface rocket. Disabled but not destroyed, the *Hercules* reversed course and sailed to Rio de Janeiro, the nearest safe port. At Rio de Janeiro, respondent United Carriers determined that the ship had suffered extensive deck and hull damage, and that an undetonated bomb remained lodged in her No. 2 tank. After an investigation by the Brazilian Navy, United Carriers decided that it would be too hazardous to remove the undetonated bomb, and on July 20, 1982, the *Hercules* was scuttled 250 miles off the Brazilian coast.

Following unsuccessful attempts to obtain relief in Argentina, respondents commenced this action in the United States District Court for the Southern District of New York for the damage that they sustained from the attack. United Carriers sought $10 million in damages for the loss of the ship; Amerada Hess sought $1.9 million in damages for the fuel that went down with the ship. Respondents alleged that petitioner's attack on the neutral *Hercules* violated international law. They invoked the District Court's jurisdic-tion under the Alien Tort Statute, 28 U. S. C. § 1350, which provides that "[t]he district courts shall have original jurisdiction of any civil action by an alien for a tort only, committed in violation of the law of nations or a treaty of the United States." Amerada Hess also brought suit under the general admiralty and maritime jurisdiction, and "the principle of universal jurisdic-tion, recognized in customary international law." The District Court dismissed both complaints for lack of subject-matter jurisdiction, ruling that respon-dents' suits were barred by the FSIA.

A divided panel of the United States Court of Appeals for the Second Circuit reversed. The Court of Appeals held that the District Court had jurisdiction under the Alien Tort Statute, because respondents' consolidated action was brought by Liberian corporations, it sounded in tort ("the bombing of a ship without justification"), and it asserted a violation of international law ("attacking a neutral ship in international waters, without proper cause for suspicion or investigation"). Viewing the Alien Tort Statute as "no more than a jurisdictional grant based on international law," the Court of Appeals said that "who is within" the scope of that grant is governed by "evolving standards of international law," . . . citing *Filártiga v. Pena-Irala*, 630 F.2d 876, 880 (CA2 1980). The Court of Appeals reasoned that Congress' enactment of the FSIA was not meant to eliminate "existing remedies in United States courts for violations of international law" by foreign states under the Alien Tort Statute. The dissenting judge took the view that the FSIA precluded respondents' action. We granted certiorari, and now reverse.

We start from the settled proposition that the subject-matter jurisdiction of the lower federal courts is determined by Congress "in the exact degrees and character which to Congress may seem proper for the public good." *Cary v. Curtis,* 3 How. 236, 245 (1845); *see Insurance Corp. of Ireland v. Compagnie des Bauxites de Guinee*, 456 U.S. 694, 701 (1982) (jurisdiction of lower federal courts is "limited to those subjects encompassed within the statutory grant of jurisdiction"). In the FSIA, Congress added a new chapter . . . to Title 28 of the United States Code, 28 U. S. C. § 1602–1611, which is entitled "Jurisdictional Immunities of Foreign States."[1] Section 1604 provides that "[s]ubject to existing international agreements to which the United States [was] a party at the time of the enactment of this Act[,] a foreign state shall be immune from the jurisdiction of the courts of the United States and of the States except as provided in sections 1605 to 1607 of this chapter." The FSIA also added § 1330(a) to Title 28; it provides that "[t]he district courts shall have original jurisdiction without regard to amount in controversy of any nonjury civil action against a foreign state . . . as to any claim for relief in personam with respect to which the foreign state is not entitled to immunity under sections 1605–1607 of this title or under any applicable international agreement." § 1330(a).[2]

We think that the text and structure of the FSIA demonstrate Congress' intention that the FSIA be the sole basis for obtaining jurisdiction over a foreign state in our courts. Sections 1604 and 1330(a) work in tandem: § 1604 bars federal and state courts from exercising jurisdiction when a foreign state is entitled to immunity, and § 1330(a) confers jurisdiction on district courts to hear suits brought by United States citizens and by aliens when a foreign state is not entitled to immunity. As we said in *Verlinden*, the FSIA "must be applied by the district courts in every action against a foreign sovereign, since subject-matter jurisdiction in any such action depends on the existence of one of the specified exceptions to foreign sovereign immunity."[3]

---

[1] From the Nation's founding until 1952, foreign states were "generally granted . . .complete immunity from suit" in United States courts, and the Judicial Branch deferred to the decisions of the Executive Branch on such questions. *Verlinden B. V. v. Central Bank of Nigeria*, 461 U.S. 480, 486 (1983). In 1952, the State Department adopted the view that foreign states could be sued in United States courts for their commercial acts, but not for their public acts. "For the most part," the FSIA "codifies" this so-called "restrictive" theory of foreign sovereign immunity.

[2] Respondents did not invoke the District Court's jurisdiction under 28 U. S. C. § 1330(a). They did, however, serve their complaints upon petitioner's Ministry of Foreign Affairs in conformity with the service of process provisions of the FSIA, 28 U. S. C. § 1608(a), and the regulations promulgated thereunder by the Department of State.

[3] Subsection (b) of § 1330 provides that "[p]ersonal jurisdiction over a foreign state shall exist as to every claim for relief over which the district courts have [subject-matter] jurisdiction under subsection (a) where service has been made under [28 U. S. C. § 1608]." Thus, personal jurisdiction, like subject-matter jurisdiction, exists only when one of the exceptions to foreign

The Court of Appeals acknowledged that the FSIA's language and legislative history support the "general rule" that the Act governs the immunity of foreign states in federal court. The Court of Appeals, however, thought that the FSIA's "focus on commercial concerns" and Congress' failure to "repeal" the Alien Tort Statute indicated Congress' intention that federal courts continue to exercise jurisdiction over foreign states in suits alleging violations of international law outside the confines of the FSIA. The Court of Appeals also believed that to construe the FSIA to bar the instant suit would "fly in the face" of Congress' intention [expressed in the legislative history of the statute] that the FSIA be interpreted pursuant to " 'standards recognized under international law.'

Taking the last of these points first, Congress had violations of international law by foreign states in mind when it enacted the FSIA. For example, the FSIA specifically denies foreign states immunity in suits "in which rights in property taken in violation of international law are in issue." 28 U. S. C. § 1605 (a)(3). Congress also rested the FSIA in part on its power under Art. I, § 8, cl. 10, of the Constitution "[t]o define and punish Piracies and Felonies committed on the high Seas, and Offenses against the Law of Nations." From Congress' decision to deny immunity to foreign states in the class of cases just mentioned, we draw the plain implication that immunity is granted in those cases involving alleged violations of international law that do not come within one of the FSIA's exceptions.

As to the other point made by the Court of Appeals, Congress' failure to enact a *pro tanto* repealer of the Alien Tort Statute when it passed the FSIA in 1976 may be explained at least in part by the lack of certainty as to whether the Alien Tort Statute conferred jurisdiction in suits against foreign states. Enacted by the First Congress in 1789, the Alien Tort Statute provides that "[t]he district courts shall have original jurisdiction of any civil action by an alien for a tort only, committed in violation of the law of nations or a treaty of the United States." The Court of Appeals did not cite any decision in which a United States court exercised jurisdiction over a foreign state under the Alien Tort Statute, and only one such case has come to our attention — one which was decided after the enactment of the FSIA.[4]

In this Court, respondents argue that cases were brought under the Alien Tort Statute against foreign states for the unlawful taking of a prize during wartime. The Alien Tort Statute makes no mention of prize jurisdiction, and § 1333(2) now grants federal district courts exclusive jurisdiction over "all proceedings for the condemnation of property taken as a prize." In *The*

---

sovereign immunity in §§ 1605–1607 applies. Congress' intention to enact a comprehensive statutory scheme is also supported by the inclusion in the FSIA of provisions for venue, 28 U. S. C. § 1391(f), removal, § 1441(d), and attachment and execution, §§ 1609–1611. Our conclusion here is supported by the FSIA's legislative history. *See, e.g.*, H. R. Rep. No. 94-1487, p. 12 (1976) (H. R. Rep.); S. Rep. No. 94-1310, pp. 11–12 (1976) (S. Rep.) (FSIA "sets forth the sole and exclusive standards to be used in resolving questions of sovereign immunity raised by sovereign states before Federal and State courts in the United States," and "prescribes . . .the jurisdiction of U.S. district courts in cases involving foreign states").

[4] *See Von Dardel v. Union of Soviet Socialist Republics*, 623 F. Supp. 246 (DC 1985) (alternative holding). The Court of Appeals did cite its earlier decision in *Filártiga v. Pena-Irala*, 630 F.2d 876 (1980), which involved a suit under the Alien Tort Statute by a Paraguayan national against a Paraguayan police official for torture; the Paraguayan Government was not joined as a defendant.

Santissima Trinidad, 7 Wheat. 283, 353–354 (1822), we held that foreign states were not immune from the jurisdiction of United States courts in prize proceedings. That case, however, was not brought under the Alien Tort Statute but rather as a libel in admiralty. Thus there is a distinctly hypothetical cast to the Court of Appeals' reliance on Congress' failure to repeal the Alien Tort Statute, and respondents' arguments in this Court based on the principle of statutory construction that repeals by implication are disfavored.

We think that Congress' failure in the FSIA to enact an express *pro tanto* repealer of the Alien Tort Statute speaks only faintly, if at all, to the issue involved in this case. In light of the comprehensiveness of the statutory scheme in the FSIA, we doubt that even the most meticulous draftsman would have concluded that Congress also needed to amend *pro tanto* the Alien Tort Statute and presumably such other grants of subject-matter jurisdiction in Title 28 as § 1331 (federal question), § 1333 (admiralty),§ 1335 (inter-pleader), § 1337 (commerce and antitrust), and § 1338 (patents, copyrights, and trademarks). Congress provided in the FSIA that "[c]laims of foreign states to immunity should henceforth be decided by courts of the United States in conformity with the principles set forth in this chapter," and very likely it thought that should be sufficient. § 1602 (emphasis added); *see also* H. R. Rep., at 12; S. Rep., at 11 (FSIA "intended to preempt any other State and Federal law (excluding applicable international agreements) for according immunity to foreign sovereigns").

For similar reasons we are not persuaded by respondents' arguments based upon the rule of statutory construction under which repeals by implication are disfavored. This case does not involve two statutes that readily could be seen as supplementing one another, nor is it a case where a more general statute is claimed to have repealed by implication an earlier statute dealing with a narrower subject. We think that Congress' decision to deal comprehensively with the subject of foreign sovereign immunity in the FSIA, and the express provision in § 1604 that "a foreign state shall be immune from the jurisdiction of the courts of the United States and of the States except as provided in §§ 1605–1607," preclude a construction of the Alien Tort Statute that permits the instant suit. The Alien Tort Statute by its terms does not distinguish among classes of defendants, and it of course has the same effect after the passage of the FSIA as before with respect to defendants other than foreign states. . . .

Having determined that the FSIA provides the sole basis for obtaining jurisdiction over a foreign state in federal court, we turn to whether any of the exceptions enumerated in the Act apply here. These exceptions include cases involving the waiver of immunity, § 1605(a)(1), commercial activities occurring in the United States or causing a direct effect in this country, § 1605(a)(2), property expropriated in violation of international law, § 1605(a)(3), inherited, gift, or immovable property located in the United States, § 1605(a)(4), noncommercial torts occurring in the United States, § 1605(a)(5), and maritime liens, § 1605(b).[5] We agree with the District Court that none of

---

[5] [Editor's note: Following this decision, the Congress adopted additional exceptions, none of which alters the analysis or the result in this case.]

the FSIA's exceptions applies on these facts.[6]

Respondents assert that the FSIA exception for noncommercial torts, § 1605(a)(5), is most in point. This provision denies immunity in a case

> in which money damages are sought against a foreign state for personal injury or death, or damage to or loss of property, occurring in the United States and caused by the tortious act or omission of that foreign state or of any official or employee of that foreign state while acting within the scope of his office or employment.

28 U. S. C. § 1605(a)(5). Section 1605(a)(5) is limited by its terms, however, to those cases in which the damage to or loss of property occurs in the United States. Congress' primary purpose in enacting § 1605(a)(5) was to eliminate a foreign state's immunity for traffic accidents and other torts committed in the United States, for which liability is imposed under domestic tort law. In this case, the injury to respondents' ship occurred on the high seas some 5,000 miles off the nearest shores of the United States. Despite these telling facts, respondents nonetheless claim that the tortious attack on the *Hercules* occurred "in the United States." They point out that the FSIA defines "United States" as including all "territory and waters, continental and insular, subject to the jurisdiction of the United States," § 1603(c), and that their injury occurred on the high seas, which is within the admiralty jurisdiction of the United States. They reason, therefore, that "by statutory definition" petitioner's attack occurred in the United States.

We find this logic unpersuasive. We construe the modifying phrase "continental and insular" to restrict the definition of United States to the continental United States and those islands that are part of the United States or its possessions; any other reading would render this phrase nugatory. Likewise, the term "waters" in § 1603(c) cannot reasonably be read to cover all waters over which United States courts might exercise jurisdiction. When it desires to do so, Congress knows how to place the high seas within the jurisdictional reach of a statute.[7] We thus apply "[t]he canon of construction which teaches that legislation of Congress, unless contrary intent appears, is meant to apply only within the territorial jurisdiction of the United States." *Foley Brothers v. Filardo,* 336 U.S. 281, 285 (1949); *see also Weinberger v. Rossi,* 456 U.S. 25, 32 (1982). Because respondents' injury unquestionably occurred well outside the 3-mile limit then in effect for the territorial waters of the United States, the exception for noncommercial torts cannot apply.[8]

---

[6] The Court of Appeals majority did not pass on whether any of the exceptions to the FSIA applies here. It did note, however, that respondents' arguments regarding § 1605(a)(5) were consistent with its disposition of the case. The dissent found none of the FSIA's exceptions applicable on these facts.

[7] *See, e.g.,* 14 U. S. C. § 89(a) (empowering Coast Guard to search and seize vessels "upon the high seas and waters over which the United States has jurisdiction" for "prevention, detection, and suppression of violations of laws of the United States"); 18 U. S. C. § 7 ("special maritime and territorial jurisdiction of the United States" in Federal Criminal Code extends to United States vessels on "[t]he high seas, any other waters within the admiralty and maritime jurisdiction of the United States, and out of the jurisdiction of any particular State"); 19 U. S. C. § 1701 (permitting President to declare portions of "high seas" as customs-enforcement areas).

[8] The United States has historically adhered to a territorial sea of 3 nautical miles, *see United States v. California,* 332 U.S. 19, 32–34 (1947), although international conventions permit a

The result in this case is not altered by the fact that petitioner's alleged tort may have had effects in the United States. Respondents state, for example, that the *Hercules* was transporting oil intended for use in this country and that the loss of the ship disrupted contractual payments due in New York. Under the commercial activity exception to the FSIA, § 1605(a)(2), a foreign state may be liable for its commercial activities "outside the territory of the United States" having a "direct effect" inside the United States.[9] But the noncommercial tort exception, § 1605(a)(5), upon which respondents rely, makes no mention of "territory outside the United States" or of "direct effects" in the United States. Congress' decision to use explicit language in § 1605(a)(2), and not to do so in § 1605(a)(5), indicates that the exception in § 1605(a)(5) covers only torts occurring within the territorial jurisdiction of the United States. Respondents do not claim that § 1605(a)(2) covers these facts.

We also disagree with respondents' claim that certain international agreements entered into by petitioner and by the United States create an exception to the FSIA here. As noted, the FSIA was adopted "[s]ubject to international agreements to which the United States [was] a party at the time of [its] enactment." § 1604. This exception applies when international agreements "expressly conflic[t]" with the immunity provisions of the FSIA, hardly the circumstances in this case. Respondents point to the Geneva Convention on the High Seas, [1962] 13 U. S. T. 2312, and the Pan American Maritime Neutrality Convention, 47 Stat. 1989, 1990-1991. These conventions, however, only set forth substantive rules of conduct and state that compensation shall be paid for certain wrongs.[10] They do not create private rights of action for foreign corporations to recover compensation from foreign states in United States courts.

Nor do we see how a foreign state can waive its immunity under § 1605(a)(1) by signing an international agreement that contains no mention of a waiver of immunity to suit in United States courts or even the availability of a cause of action in the United States. We find similarly unpersuasive the argument of respondents and Amicus Curiae Republic of Liberia that the Treaty of Friendship, Commerce and Navigation [between the United States and

---

territorial sea of up to 12 miles. *See* 2 RESTATEMENT (THIRD) OF FOREIGN RELATIONS LAW OF THE UNITED STATES § 511 (1987). On December 28, 1988, the President announced that the United States would henceforth recognize a territorial sea of 12 nautical miles. *See* Presidential Proclamation No. 5928, 3 CFR 547 (1988).

[9] Section 1605(a)(2) provides, in pertinent part, that foreign states shall not be immune from the jurisdiction of United States courts in cases "in which the action is based . . . upon an act outside the territory of the United States in connection with a commercial activity of the foreign state elsewhere and that act causes a direct effect in the United States."

[10] Article 22(1), (3), of the Geneva Convention on the High Seas, for example, states that a warship may only board a merchant ship if it has a "reasonable ground for suspecting" the merchant ship is involved in piracy, the slave trade, or traveling under false colors. If an inspection fails to support the suspicion, the merchant ship "shall be compensated for any loss or damage that may have been sustained." Article 23 contains comparable provisions for the stopping of merchant ships by aircraft. Similarly, Article 1 of the Pan American Maritime Neutrality Convention, permits a warship to stop a merchant ship on the high seas to determine its cargo, and whether it has committed "any violation of blockade," but the warship may only use force if the merchant ship "fails to observe the instructions given it." Article 27 provides: "A bel[l]igerent shall indemnify the damage caused by its violation of the foregoing provisions. It shall likewise be responsible for the acts of persons who may belong to its armed forces."

Liberia] carves out an exception to the FSIA. Article I of this Treaty provides, in pertinent part, that the nationals of the United States and Liberia "shall enjoy freedom of access to the courts of justice of the other on conforming to the local laws." The FSIA is clearly one of the "local laws" to which respondents must "conform" before bringing suit in United States courts.

We hold that the FSIA provides the sole basis for obtaining jurisdiction over a foreign state in the courts of this country, and that none of the enumerated exceptions to the Act apply to the facts of this case. The judgment of the Court of Appeals is therefore reversed.

JUSTICE BLACKMUN, with whom JUSTICE MARSHALL joins, concurring in part. I join the Court's opinion insofar as it holds that the FSIA provides the sole basis for obtaining jurisdiction over a foreign state in federal court. I, however, do not join the latter part of the Court's opinion to the effect that none of the FSIA's exceptions to foreign sovereign immunity apply in this case. As the majority notes, the Court of Appeals did not decide this question, and, indeed, specifically reserved it. Moreover, the question was not among those presented to this Court in the petition for certiorari, did not receive full briefing, and is not necessary to the disposition of the case. Accordingly, I believe it inappropriate to decide here, in the first instance, whether any exceptions to the FSIA apply in this case. . . .

Notes and Questions on *Amerada Hess*

1. *Immunity for violations of international law.* If international law by definition limits what a sovereign can lawfully do, doesn't it follow that it can be no act of sovereignty to violate international norms? And if that's true, doesn't it follow that violations of international norms cannot be protected by the FSIA? Consider the following observation made by the Second Circuit Court of Appeals in *Amerada Hess*: "If sovereign acts were immunized from scrutiny under international law, the exception would nearly swallow the rule. For example the emerging international law prohibition of genocide . . . would make little sense, even in theory, if sovereign states were not covered by the prohibition." 830 F.2d at 426.

A. Was the Second Circuit wrong in this analysis? Even if it was right, is there good reason for *not* following its premise to the conclusion that no violation of international law can qualify for sovereign immunity in U.S. courts?

B. Is there any sense in which it might be said that the decision of the Second Circuit Court of Appeals, though trying to enforce principles of international law, was itself in violation of international law?

C. Assuming that the Second Circuit's decision was inconsistent with the statute as enacted by Congress, what exactly was Congress trying to accomplish in the FSIA? More specifically, what was the essential trade-off made by Congress in the legislation, and at what cost?

2. *When is a state a state?* The FSIA leaves the key term "foreign state" undefined. Although the statute clarifies that immunity can attach to the state

itself, its political subdivisions, and its agencies and instrumentalities, 28 U.S.C. § 1603(a), how should a court determine whether a potential defendant qualifies as a foreign state in the first place?

Section 201 of the RESTATEMENT (THIRD) OF FOREIGN RELATIONS LAW provides that "a 'state' is an entity which has a defined territory and permanent population, under the control of its own government, and which engages in, or has the capacity to engage in, formal relations with other such entities." Notice that there is no requirement that an entity be recognized by the U.S. government in order to be a state, suggesting that an unrecognized state might still be entitled to immunity under the FSIA so long as the other criteria for statehood were satisfied. But the courts have generally followed the practice of the executive branch in determining whether an entity should be treated as a state. *See, e.g., Kadic v. Karadzic,* 70 F.3d 232 (2d Cir. 1995); *Klinghoffer v. S.N.C. Achille Lauro,* 937 F.2d 44 (2d Cir. 1991). Can this practice be squared with the statute's transfer of authority over immunity decisions from the State Department to the courts? Is there an alternative approach?

3. *Immunity for individuals.* Should individual officials of foreign governments also be entitled to immunity under the FSIA? Suppose for example the pilot of the plane that bombed the *Hercules* could be found in the United States. Would he be entitled to claim sovereign immunity on the same terms as the state of Argentina? Is there a textual basis in § 1603(b) of the statute itself for concluding that he would *not*? Are there reasons other than the text for concluding that he *must*?

The FSIA has been interpreted to protect individuals acting in an official capacity for a foreign government, even when they are officers of a corporation considered to be an agency or instrumentality of a foreign sovereign. *See, e.g., El-Fadl v. Central Bank of Jordan,* 75 F.3d 668 (D.C.Cir. 1996). But immunity is not available when the individual officer acts beyond her authority. *See, e.g., Trajano v. Marcos (In re Estate of Ferdinand E. Marcos Human Rights Litig.),* 978 F.2d 493, 497 (9th Cir. 1992), *cert. denied,* 508 U.S. 972 (1993). The clear implication is that a government official can fall within the definition of an "agency or instrumentality of a foreign state" and will be entitled to foreign sovereign immunity on the same terms as states unless she acts outside the scope of her authority.

The rationale for this result is clear enough. In *Chuidian v. Philippine Nat'l Bank,* 912 F.2d 1095, 1103–06 (9th Cir. 1990), the court concluded that there was little practical difference between a suit against a state and a suit against an individual acting in her official capacity, and, if plaintiffs could circumvent the FSIA by naming individual officials instead of the state, the statute — with all of its safeguards and standards — would be meaningless. Plaintiffs could avoid the FSIA altogether through a strategic selection of defendants and artful pleading. The court concluded that the FSIA serves purposes that are too important to be manipulated in that way.

The difficult litigated question is therefore how to determine the scope of a foreign official's authority. In *Trajano, supra,* the Ninth Circuit defined "beyond the scope of the official's authority" to include anything the sovereign has not empowered the official to do. And "[w]here the officer's powers are limited by statute, his actions beyond those limitations are considered individual and not sovereign actions. The officer is not doing the business which the sovereign has empowered him to do." *In re Estate of Ferdinand Marcos, Human Rights Litigation*, 25 F.3d 1467, 1470 (9th Cir. 1994). Under these standards, some examples of *ultra vires* or unauthorized acts are fairly easy to define. *See, e.g., Chuidian,* 912 F.2d at 1106 ("An obvious example would be if a dispute occurs pertaining to the sale of an employee's personal house, his government employment provides him no shield to liability.")

But suppose the defendant is not acting in an obviously personal capacity (as with the selling of her own house), but abuses the governmental authority she has admittedly been granted. Should immunity attach? Would the abuse of her authority be determined under the law (or practice) of the foreign state? *See Phaneuf v. Republic of Indonesia,* 106 F.3d 302 (9th Cir. 1997). Or should a domestic court turn to the more familiar "color of law" jurisprudence from U.S. decisions? And how — if at all — is international law relevant to the issue?

On occasion, the courts have been asked to consider the argument that international law should limit what a sovereign may lawfully authorize an official to do, and that a foreign law offering blanket authorization for anything its officers do is not entitled to recognition through the FSIA. For example, in the human rights litigation against Ferdinand Marcos, the former president of the Philippines, the plaintiffs alleged among other things that Marcos violated international law as well as the constitution and laws of the Philippines in that he "under color of law, ordered, orchestrated, directed, sanctioned and tolerated the continuous and systematic violation of human rights of plaintiffs and the class through the military, para-military and intelligence forces he controlled." The Ninth Circuit declined to extend sovereign immunity to him:

> Although sometimes criticized as a ruler and at times invested with extraordinary powers, Ferdinand Marcos does not appear to have had the authority of an absolute autocrat. He was not the state, but the head of the state, bound by the laws that applied to him. Our courts have had no difficulty in distinguishing the legal acts of a deposed ruler from his acts for personal profit that lack a basis in law. As in the case of the deposed Venezuelan ruler, Marcos Perez Jimenez, the latter acts are as adjudicable and redressable as would be a dictator's act of rape.

Republic of the Philippines v. Marcos, 862 F.2d 1355, 1361 (9th Cir. 1988) (citing *Jimenez v. Aristeguieta,* 311 F.2d 547 (5th Cir. 1962), *cert. denied,* 373 U.S. 914 (1963). Does that imply that individual officials can never qualify for sovereign immunity if their actions violate international standards? Does it imply greater immunity for absolute autocrats than for officials whose authority is defined and limited by law? Is there a problem with either of these results?

4. *Personal jurisdiction under the FSIA.* How do the courts get personal jurisdiction over foreign governments? The FSIA itself provides that "[p]ersonal jurisdiction over a foreign state shall exist as to every claim for relief over which the district courts have [subject-matter] jurisdiction under subsection (a) where service has been made under [28 U. S. C. § 1608]." 28

U.S.C. § 1330(b). Under the statute, in other words, subject matter jurisdiction plus proper service equals personal jurisdiction. But if foreign states are considered "persons" for purposes of the Due Process Clause, they should also be entitled as a matter of constitutional law to the minimum contacts test of *International Shoe, Asahi*, and their progeny.

In *Republic of Argentina v. Weltover*, 504 U.S. 607 (1992), *infra*, the Supreme Court decided simply to "assum[e], without deciding, that a foreign state is a 'person' for purposes of the Due Process Clause," and minimum contacts were assumed to exist where the "direct effects" prong of the commercial activity exception had been satisfied. *See also El-Hadad v. Embassy of the United Arab Emirates*, 69 F. Supp.2d 69, 77 n. 7 (D.D.C. 1999) ("because the D.C. Circuit has not yet resolved whether the due process clause applies to foreign states, the Court considers the [foreign state] a 'person' and conducts the constitutional due process analysis" in commercial activity exception case); *Creighton Ltd. v. Government of the State of Qatar*, 181 F.3d 118 (D.C. Cir. 1999) (continuing the assumption that foreign states are persons for purposes of the Due Process Clause). As noted in *Flatow v. Islamic Republic of Iran*, 999 F. Supp. 1, 19–20 (D.D.C. 1998),

> Most courts have simply assumed that foreign states were entitled to Constitutional Due Process protections, just as courts have assumed that foreign corporations are entitled to Constitutional Due Process protections, at least with respect to the assertion of personal jurisdiction. Once these trends were initiated, on the basis of an assumption, courts have been reluctant to reexamine this issue . . . . The merger of subject matter and personal jurisdictional inquiries under the FSIA has contributed to the confusion in the jurisprudence of personal jurisdiction over foreign states. The majority of cases brought under the FSIA involve commercial activity, which requires an evaluation of the activity's effects in the United States. "Direct effects" language closely resembles that of Constitutional Due Process "minimum contacts." Tandem consideration of these overlapping yet fundamentally discrete analyses as a matter of practice in several Circuits has exacerbated the situation.

A. Does this assumption make sense given the focus or purpose of the Due Process Clause? *Cf. World Wide Minerals Ltd. v. Kazakhstan*, 116 F. Supp. 2d 98 (D.D.C. 2000):

> In *Flatow*, this court stated that the traditional minimum contacts test was subsumed in the exceptions to FSIA. This ruling drew on the Supreme Court's suggestion [in *Weltover*] that a foreign state might not be a "person" for due process considerations. Since *Flatow*, this circuit has raised the issue but not decided it. Consistent with the decision in *Flatow*, we find that no minimum contacts analysis is required concerning defendants the Republic of Kazakhstan, the State Committee of the Republic of Kazakhstan on the Management of State Property, and the National Atomic Company Kazatomprom. The jurisdictional analysis instead depends on the presence or absence of one of the exceptions to FSIA.

B. Should the analysis change if jurisdiction is based on some provision of the FSIA *other than* the commercial activity exception?

5. *Service of process under the FSIA.* Section § 1608(a) and (b), *supra*, outline the methods for serving process upon foreign entities. The courts have generally ruled that Congress intended to require strict compliance with section 1608(a) as to service upon foreign states and their political subdivisions. But substantial compliance — meaning actual notice of the suit and the consequences thereof — can be sufficient to satisfy the requirements of section 1608(b) as to service upon an agency or instrumentality of a foreign state. *See, e.g., Magness v. Russian Federation*, 247 F.3d 609 (5th Cir. Tex. 2001). As shown below in connection with the execution of judgments under the FSIA, this is not the only issue under the FSIA that turns on the distinction between the state and its agencies or instrumentalities, though both are entitled to the rebuttable presumption of immunity under 28 U.S.C. § 1604. Why would Congress draw this distinction for some purposes (*e.g.*, service of process and execution of judgments) but not for other purposes (*e.g.*, the presumption of immunity)?

6. *Shifting burdens.* Notice the distribution of the burden of production, persuasion, and proof under the FSIA. The party claiming immunity "bears the burden of establishing its immunity, including the burden of proof that no exception applies." *Phaneuf v. Republic of Indonesia*, 106 F.3d 302 (9th Cir. 1997); *see also Princz v. Federal Republic of Germany*, 26 F.3d 1166, 1171 (D.C. Cir. 1994) ("It is the burden of the foreign sovereign in each case to establish its immunity by demonstrating that none of the exceptions is applicable.") In practice, the defendant must first present a *prima facie* case that it is a sovereign state. Then "the burden of production shifts to the plaintiff to offer evidence that an exception applies." *Id.* If the plaintiffs' allegations bring the claim within a FSIA exception, the burden then reverts to the party claiming immunity to prove by a preponderance of the evidence that the exception does not apply. In other words, once a party offers evidence that an FSIA exception to immunity applies, the party claiming the immunity bears the burden of proving that the exception is inapplicable. *Aquamar S.A. v. Del Monte Fresh Produce N.A., Inc.*, 179 F.3d 1279, 1290 (11th Cir. 1999).

7. *Amerada Hess and the Alien Tort Claims Act.* What if anything, does the Supreme Court's decision in *Amerada Hess* do to the holding in *Filártiga*, *supra*?

THE PROBLEM OF ATTRIBUTION: THE *BANCEC* LITIGATION

Sections 1603(a) and (b) of the FSIA make it clear that agencies and instrumentalities of foreign states, including certain state-owned corporations, are entitled to the presumption of immunity. It may be overcome of course if one of the exceptions applies, but as an initial matter, they qualify for sovereign immunity. In practice though, there is the problem of attributing actions to a particular agency or instrumentality and proceeding against the right defendant. The complexity of the modern state makes it particularly difficult for courts to attribute a plaintiff's injury to a particular part of the foreign bureaucratic machine. In the *Bancec* litigation, *infra*, the Supreme Court was obliged to determine when it would respect and when it would disregard the formalities that separate a national government from its agencies or its agencies from one another.

FIRST NATIONAL CITY BANK v. BANCO PARA EL COMERCIO EXTERIOR de CUBA
462 U.S. 611 (1983)

Justice O'CONNOR delivered the opinion of the Court. In 1960, the Government of the Republic of Cuba established respondent Banco Para El Comercio Exterior de Cuba (Bancec) to serve as "[a]n official autonomous credit institution for foreign trade . . . with full juridical capacity . . . of its own. . . ." Law No. 793, Art. 1 (1960). In September 1960, Bancec sought to collect on a letter of credit issued by petitioner First National City Bank (now Citibank) in its favor in support of a contract for delivery of Cuban sugar to a buyer in the United States. Within days after Citibank received the request for collection, all of its assets in Cuba were seized and nationalized by the Cuban Government. When Bancec brought suit on the letter of credit in United States District Court, Citibank counterclaimed, asserting a right to set off the value of its seized Cuban assets. The question before us is whether Citibank may obtain such a setoff, notwithstanding the fact that Bancec was established as a separate juridical entity. Applying principles of equity common to international law and federal common law, we conclude that Citibank may apply a setoff.

I

. . . Bancec was established by Law No. 793, of April 25, 1960, as the legal successor to the Banco Cubano del Comercio Exterior (Cuban Foreign Trade Bank), a trading bank established by the Cuban Government in 1954 and jointly owned by the Government and private banks. . . . Bancec's stated purpose was "to contribute to, and collaborate with, the international trade policy of the Government and the application of the measures concerning foreign trade adopted by the 'Banco Nacional de Cuba,'" Cuba's central bank (Banco Nacional). Bancec was empowered to act as the Cuban Government's exclusive agent in foreign trade. The Government supplied all of its capital and owned all of its stock. The General Treasury of the Republic received all of Bancec's profits, after deduction of amounts for capital reserves. A Governing Board consisting of delegates from Cuban governmental ministries governed and managed Bancec. Its president was Ernesto Che Guevara, who also was Minister of State and president of Banco Nacional. A General Manager appointed by the Governing Board was charged with directing Bancec's day-to-day operations in a manner consistent with its enabling statute.

In contracts signed on August 12, 1960, Bancec agreed to purchase a quantity of sugar from El Institutio Nacional de Reforma Agraria (INRA), an instrumentality of the Cuban Government which owned and operated Cuba's nationalized sugar industry, and to sell it to the Cuban Canadian Sugar Company. The latter sale agreement was supported by an irrevocable letter of credit in favor of Bancec issued by Citibank on August 18, 1960, which Bancec assigned to Banco Nacional for collection. Meanwhile, in July 1960, the Cuban Government enacted Law No. 851, which provided for the nationalization of the Cuban properties of United States citizens. By Resolution No. 2 of September 17, 1960, the Government ordered that all of the Cuban property of three United States banks, including Citibank, be nationalized through forced expropriation. The "Bank Nationalization Law," Law No. 891, of October 13, 1960, declared that the banking function could be carried on only by instrumentalities created by the State, and ordered Banco Nacional to effect the nationalization.

On or about September 15, 1960, before the banks were nationalized, Bancec's draft was presented to Citibank for payment by Banco Nacional. The amount sought was $193,280.30 for sugar delivered at Pascagoula, Mississippi. On September 20, 1960, after its branches were nationalized, Citibank credited the requested amount to Banco Nacional's account and applied the balance in Banco Nacional's account as a setoff against the value of its Cuban branches.

On February 1, 1961, Bancec brought this diversity action to recover on the letter of credit in the United States District Court for the Southern District of New York. On February 23, 1961, by Law No. 930, Bancec was dissolved and its capital was split between Banco Nacional and "the foreign trade enterprises or houses of the Ministry of Foreign Trade," which was established by Law No. 934 the same day. All of Bancec's rights, claims, and assets "peculiar to the banking business" were vested in Banco Nacional, which also succeeded to its banking obligations. All of Bancec's "trading functions" were to be assumed by "the foreign trade enterprises or houses of the Ministry of Foreign Trade." By Resolution No. 1, dated March 1, 1961, the Ministry of Foreign Trade created Empresa Cubana de Exportaciones (Empresa), which was empowered to conduct all commercial export transactions formerly conducted by Bancec "remaining subrogated in the rights and obligations of said bank [Bancec] as regards the commercial export activities."

On March 8, 1961, after Bancec had been dissolved, Citibank filed its answer, which sought a setoff for the value of its seized branches, not an affirmative recovery of damages.[1] . . . [T]he District Court granted judgment in favor of Citibank. The court rejected Bancec's contention that its separate juridical status shielded it from liability for the acts of the Cuban Government[:]

> Under all of the relevant circumstances shown in this record, . . . it is clear that Bancec lacked an independent existence, and was a mere arm of the Cuban Government, performing a purely governmental function. The control of Bancec was exclusively in the hands of the

[1] Citibank's answer alleged that the suit was "brought by and for the benefit of the Republic of Cuba by and through its agent and wholly-owned instrumentality, . . . which is in fact and in law and in form and function an integral part of and indistinguishable from the Republic of Cuba."

Government, and Bancec was established solely to further Governmental purposes. Moreover, Bancec was totally dependent on the Government for financing and required to remit all of its profits to the Government. . . .

Bancec is not a mere private corporation, the stock of which is owned by the Cuban Government, but an agency of the Cuban Government in the conduct of the sort of matters which even in a country characterized by private capitalism, tend to be supervised and managed by Government. Where the equities are so strong in favor of the counterclaiming defendants, as they are in this case, the Court should recognize the practicalities of the transactions. . . . The Court concludes that Bancec is an alter ego of the Cuban Government.

Without determining the exact value of Citibank's assets seized by Cuba, the court held that "the value of the confiscated branches . . . substantially exceeds the sums already recovered, and therefore the set-off pleaded here may be granted in full in favor of Citibank." It therefore entered judgment dismissing the complaint. . . .

The United States Court of Appeals for the Second Circuit reversed. While expressing agreement with the District Court's "descriptions of Bancec's functions and its status as a wholly-owned instrumentality of the Cuban government," the court concluded that "Bancec was not an alter ego of the Cuban government for the purpose of [Citibank's] counterclaims." It stated that, as a general matter, courts would respect the independent identity of a governmental instrumentality created as "a separate and distinct juridical entity under the laws of the state that owns it" — except "when the subject matter of the counterclaim assertible against the state is state conduct in which the instrumentality had a key role." . . .

II

A. As an initial matter, Bancec contends that the Foreign Sovereign Immunities Act of 1976 immunizes an instrumentality owned by a foreign government from suit on a counterclaim based on actions taken by that government. Bancec correctly concedes that, under 28 U.S.C. § 1607(c), an instrumentality of a foreign state bringing suit in a United States court is not entitled to immunity "with respect to any counterclaim — . . . to the extent that the counterclaim does not seek relief exceeding in amount or differing in kind from that sought by the [instrumentality.]" It contends, however, that as a substantive matter, the FSIA prohibits holding a foreign instrumentality owned and controlled by a foreign government responsible for actions taken by that government.

We disagree. The language and history of the FSIA clearly establish that the Act was not intended to affect the substantive law determining the liability of a foreign state or instrumentality, or the attribution of liability among instrumentalities of a foreign state. Section 1606 of the FSIA provides in relevant part that "[a]s to any claim for relief with respect to which a foreign state is not entitled to immunity . . ., the foreign state shall be liable in the same manner and to the same extent as a private individual under like circumstances. . . ." The House Report on the FSIA states: "The bill is not

intended to affect the substantive law of liability. Nor is it intended to affect
. . . the attribution of responsibility between or among entities of a foreign
state; for example, whether the proper entity of a foreign state has been sued,
or whether an entity sued is liable in whole or in part for the claimed wrong."
H.R. REP. No. 94-1487, p. 12 (1976), U.S.C.C.A.N. 1976, pp. 6604, 6610. . . .

B. We must next decide which body of law determines the effect to be given
to Bancec's separate juridical status. Bancec contends that internationally
recognized conflict-of-law principles require the application of the law of the
state that establishes a government instrumentality — here Cuba — to
determine whether the instrumentality may be held liable for actions taken
by the sovereign.

We cannot agree. As a general matter, the law of the state of incorporation
normally determines issues relating to the internal affairs of a corporation.
Application of that body of law achieves the need for certainty and predictability of result while generally protecting the justified expectations of parties
with interests in the corporation. Different conflicts principles apply, however,
where the rights of third parties external to the corporation are at issue. To
give conclusive effect to the law of the chartering state in determining whether
the separate juridical status of its instrumentality should be respected would
permit the state to violate with impunity the rights of third parties under
international law while effectively insulating itself from liability in foreign
courts. We decline to permit such a result.[2]

Bancec contends in the alternative that international law must determine
the resolution of the question presented. Citibank, on the other hand, suggests
that federal common law governs. The expropriation claim against which
Bancec seeks to interpose its separate juridical status arises under international law, which, as we have frequently reiterated, "is part of our law . . . ."
The Paquete Habana, 175 U.S. 677, 700 (1900). As we set forth below, the
principles governing this case are common to both international law and federal common law, which in these circumstances is necessarily informed both
by international law principles and by articulated congressional policies.

---

[2] Pointing out that 28 U.S.C. § 1606 contains language identical to the Federal Tort Claims
Act (FTCA), 28 U.S.C. § 2674 (1976 ed.), Bancec also contends alternatively that the FSIA, like
the FTCA, requires application of the law of the forum state — here New York — including its
conflicts principles. We disagree. Section 1606 provides that "[a]s to any claim for relief with
respect to which a foreign state is not entitled to immunity . . ., the foreign state shall be liable
in the same manner and to the same extent as a private individual in like circumstances." Thus,
where state law provides a rule of liability governing private individuals, the FSIA requires the
application of that rule to foreign states in like circumstances. The statute is silent, however,
concerning the rule governing the attribution of liability among entities of a foreign state. In *Banco
Nacional de Cuba v. Sabbatino,* 376 U.S. 398 (1964), this Court declined to apply the State of
New York's act of state doctrine in a diversity action between a United States national and an
instrumentality of a foreign state, concluding that matters bearing on the nation's foreign relations
"should not be left to divergent and perhaps parochial state interpretations." When it enacted
the FSIA, Congress expressly acknowledged "the importance of developing a uniform body of law"
concerning the amenability of a foreign sovereign to suit in United States courts. H.R.Rep. No.
94-1487, p. 32. In our view, these same considerations preclude the application of New York law
here.

III

A. Before examining the controlling principles, a preliminary observation is appropriate. The parties and amici have repeatedly referred to the phrases that have tended to dominate discussion about the independent status of separately constituted juridical entities, debating whether "to pierce the corporate veil," and whether Bancec is an "alter ego" or a "mere instrumentality" of the Cuban Government. In *Berkey v. Third Avenue R. Co.*, 244 N. Y. 84, 155 N. E. 58 (1926), Justice (then Judge) Cardozo warned in circumstances similar to those presented here against permitting worn epithets to substitute for rigorous analysis. "The whole problem of the relation between parent and subsidiary corporations is one that is still enveloped in the mists of metaphor. Metaphors in law are to be narrowly watched, for starting as devices to liberate thought, they end often by enslaving it." With this in mind, we examine briefly the nature of government instrumentalities.

Increasingly during this century, governments throughout the world have established separately constituted legal entities to perform a variety of tasks. The organization and control of these entities vary considerably, but many possess a number of common features. A typical government instrumentality, if one can be said to exist, is created by an enabling statute that prescribes the powers and duties of the instrumentality, and specifies that it is to be managed by a board selected by the government in a manner consistent with the enabling law. The instrumentality is typically established as a separate juridical entity, with the powers to hold and sell property and to sue and be sued. Except for appropriations to provide capital or to cover losses, the instrumentality is primarily responsible for its own finances. The instrumentality is run as a distinct economic enterprise; often it is not subject to the same budgetary and personnel requirements with which government agencies must comply.

These distinctive features permit government instrumentalities to manage their operations on an enterprise basis while granting them a greater degree of flexibility and independence from close political control than is generally enjoyed by government agencies. These same features frequently prompt governments in developing countries to establish separate juridical entities as the vehicles through which to obtain the financial resources needed to make large-scale national investments. . . .

Separate legal personality has been described as "an almost indispensable aspect of the public corporation." Provisions in the corporate charter stating that the instrumentality may sue and be sued have been construed to waive the sovereign immunity accorded to many governmental activities, thereby enabling third parties to deal with the instrumentality knowing that they may seek relief in the courts. Similarly, the instrumentality's assets and liabilities must be treated as distinct from those of its sovereign in order to facilitate credit transactions with third parties. Thus what the Court stated with respect to private corporations in *Anderson v. Abbott*, 321 U.S. 349 (1944), is true also for governmental corporations: "Limited liability is the rule, not the exception; and on that assumption large undertakings are rested, vast enterprises are launched, and huge sums of capital attracted."

Freely ignoring the separate status of government instrumentalities would result in substantial uncertainty over whether an instrumentality's assets would be diverted to satisfy a claim against the sovereign, and might thereby cause third parties to hesitate before extending credit to a government instrumentality without the government's guarantee. As a result, the efforts of sovereign nations to structure their governmental activities in a manner deemed necessary to promote economic development and efficient administration would surely be frustrated. Due respect for the actions taken by foreign sovereigns and for principles of comity between nations, *see Hilton v. Guyot*, 159 U.S. 113, 163–164 (1895), leads us to conclude — as the courts of Great Britain have concluded in other circumstances — that government instrumentalities established as juridical entities distinct and independent from their sovereign should normally be treated as such.

We find support for this conclusion in the legislative history of the FSIA. During its deliberations, Congress clearly expressed its intention that duly created instrumentalities of a foreign state are to be accorded a presumption of independent status. In its discussion of FSIA § 1610(b), the provision dealing with the circumstances under which a judgment creditor may execute upon the assets of an instrumentality of a foreign government, the House Report states:

> Section 1610(b) will not permit execution against the property of one agency or instrumentality to satisfy a judgment against another, unrelated agency or instrumentality. There are compelling reasons for this. If U.S. law did not respect the separate juridical identities of different agencies or instrumentalities, it might encourage foreign jurisdictions to disregard the juridical divisions between different U.S. corporations or between a U.S. corporation and its independent subsidiary. However, a court might find that property held by one agency is really the property of another.

H. R. REP. No. 94-1487, pp. 29–30 (1976). Thus, the presumption that a foreign government's determination that its instrumentality is to be accorded separate legal status is buttressed by this congressional determination. We next examine whether this presumption may be overcome in certain circumstances.

B. In discussing the legal status of private corporations, courts in the United States[3] and abroad,[4] have recognized that an incorporated entity . . . is not

---

[3] *See* 1 W. Fletcher, CYCLOPEDIA OF THE LAW OF PRIVATE CORPORATIONS § 41 (Rev. Perm. Ed. 1983): "[A] corporation will be looked upon as a legal entity as a general rule, and until sufficient reason to the contrary appears; but, when the notion of legal entity is used to defeat public convenience, justify wrong, protect fraud, or defend crime, the law will regard the corporation as an association of persons."

[4] In *Case Concerning The Barcelona Traction, Light & Power Co.*, 1970 I.C.J. 3, the International Court of Justice acknowledged that, as a matter of international law, the separate status of an incorporated entity may be disregarded in certain exceptional circumstances:

> Here, . . . as elsewhere, the law, confronted with economic realities, has had to provide protective measures and remedies in the interests of those within the corporate entity as well as of those outside who have dealings with it: the law has recognized that the independent existence of the legal entity cannot be treated as an absolute. It is in this context that the process of 'lifting the corporate veil' or 'disregarding the legal entity' has been found justified and equitable in certain circumstances or for certain purposes.

to be regarded as legally separate from its owners in all circumstances. Thus, where a corporate entity is so extensively controlled by its owner that a relationship of principal and agent is created, we have held that one may be held liable for the actions of the other. In addition, our cases have long recognized "the broader equitable principle that the doctrine of corporate entity, recognized generally and for most purposes, will not be regarded when to do so would work fraud or injustice." *Taylor v. Standard Gas Co.*, 306 U.S. 307, 322 (1939). In particular, the Court has consistently refused to give effect to the corporate form where it is interposed to defeat legislative policies. And in *Bangor Punta Operations, Inc. v. Bangor & Aroostook R. Co.*, 417 U.S. 703 (1974), we concluded:

> Although a corporation and its shareholders are deemed separate entities for most purposes, the corporate form may be disregarded in the interests of justice where it is used to defeat an overriding public policy. . . . [Where] equity would preclude the shareholders from maintaining an action in their own right, the corporation would also be precluded. . . . [The] principal beneficiary of any recovery and itself estopped from complaining of petitioners' alleged wrongs, cannot avoid the command of equity through the guise of proceeding in the name of . . . corporations which it owns and controls.

C. We conclude today that similar equitable principles must be applied here. In *National City Bank v. Republic of China*, 348 U.S. 356 (1955), the Court ruled that when a foreign sovereign asserts a claim in a United States court, "the consideration of fair dealing" bars the state from asserting a defense of sovereign immunity to defeat a setoff or counterclaim. *See* 28 U. S. C. § 1607(c). As a general matter, therefore, the Cuban Government could not bring suit in a United States court without also subjecting itself to its adversary's counterclaim. Here there is apparently no dispute that, . . . "the devolution of [Bancec's] claim, however viewed, brings it into the hands of the Ministry [of Foreign Trade], or Banco Nacional," each a party that may be held liable for the expropriation of Citibank's assets. Bancec was dissolved even before Citibank filed its answer in this case, apparently in order to effect "the consolidation and operation of the economic and social conquests of the Revolution," particularly the nationalization of the banks ordered by Law No. 891. Thus, the Cuban Government and Banco Nacional, not any third parties that may have relied on Bancec's separate juridical identity, would be the only beneficiaries of any recovery. In our view, this situation is similar to that in the *Republic of China* case. "We have a foreign government invoking our law but resisting a claim against it which fairly would curtail its recovery. It wants our law, like any other litigant, but it wants our law free from the claims of justice."

The wealth of practice already accumulated on the subject in municipal law indicates that the veil is lifted, for instance, to prevent the misuse of the privileges of legal personality, as in certain cases of fraud or malfeasance, to protect third persons such as a creditor or purchaser, or to prevent the evasion of legal requirements or of obligations. . . . In accordance with the principle expounded above, the process of lifting the veil, being an exceptional one admitted by municipal law in respect of an institution of its own making, is equally admissible to play a similar role in international law. . . .

Giving effect to Bancec's separate juridical status in these circumstances, even though it has long been dissolved, would permit the real beneficiary of such an action, the Government of the Republic of Cuba, to obtain relief in our courts that it could not obtain in its own right without waiving its sovereign immunity and answering for the seizure of Citibank's assets — a seizure previously held by the Court of Appeals to have violated international law. We decline to adhere blindly to the corporate form where doing so would cause such an injustice.

Respondent contends, however, that the transfer of Bancec's assets from the Ministry of Foreign Trade or Banco Nacional to Empresa and Cubazucar effectively insulates it from Citibank's counterclaim. We disagree. Having dissolved Bancec and transferred its assets to entities that may be held liable on Citibank's counterclaim, Cuba cannot escape liability for acts in violation of international law simply by retransferring the assets to separate juridical entities. To hold otherwise would permit governments to avoid the requirements of international law simply by creating juridical entities whenever the need arises. We therefore hold that Citibank may set off the value of its assets seized by the Cuban Government against the amount sought by Bancec.

IV

Our decision today announces no mechanical formula for determining the circumstances under which the normally separate juridical status of a government instrumentality is to be disregarded.[5] Instead, it is the product of the application of internationally recognized equitable principles to avoid the injustice that would result from permitting a foreign state to reap the benefits of our courts while avoiding the obligations of international law.

Notes and Questions on *Bancec*

1. *Rationale versus result.* The Court in *Bancec* found domestic and international authority for the presumption against breaching the corporate independence of government instrumentalities. But it also stressed a pragmatic rationale for the presumption:

> [f]reely ignoring the separate status of government instrumentalities would result in substantial uncertainty over whether an instrumentality's assets would be diverted to satisfy a claim against the sovereign, and might thereby cause third parties to hesitate before extending credit to a government instrumentality. As a result, the efforts of sovereign nations to structure their governmental activities in a

---

[5] The District Court adopted, and both Citibank and the Solicitor General urge upon the Court, a standard in which the determination whether or not to give effect to the separate juridical status of a government instrumentality turns in part on whether the instrumentality in question performed a "governmental function." We decline to adopt such a standard in this case, as our decision is based on other grounds. We do observe that the concept of a "usual" or a "proper" governmental function changes over time and varies from nation to nation.

manner deemed necessary to promote economic development and efficient administration would surely be frustrated.

What is the best argument that the principle in *Bancec* was not actually applied in the case? Is there something about the peculiar posture of the case (involving Citibank's set-off claim) that accounts for the Court's approach?

2. *Rebutting the Bancec presumption.* The presumption of independence, though overcome by the unusual facts of *Bancec*, is not easily trumped:

> The Court [in *Bancec*] recognized . . . that consistent with the law of private corporations, principles of equity may require the presumption of separateness to be overcome in certain circumstances, such as "where a corporate entity is so extensively controlled by its owner that a relationship of principal and agent is created," or if giving effect to separate legal entities "would work fraud or injustice" or would "defeat legislative policies." The central fact relied upon by the Supreme Court in holding that a setoff was fair was that the entities that may be held liable for the expropriation of Citibank's assets are the only beneficiaries of any recovery on the original suit. Bancec's rights had been transferred either to Banco Nacional de Cuba ("Banco Nacional"), which had a major role in the nationalization of Citibank's assets, or to Cuba, which had dissolved Bancec shortly after bringing its action. Giving posthumous effect to Bancec's separate juridical status would thus allow Cuba, the real beneficiary of the action, "to obtain relief in our courts that it could not obtain in its own right without waiving its sovereign immunity and answering for the seizure of Citibank's assets." The Court also rejected Bancec's contention that the counterclaim could not be asserted because the Bancec claim had been transferred to another Cuban government agency that had no role in the expropriation. The Court ruled that the transfer was a device to gain a litigation advantage and therefore was an abuse of the corporate form. Accordingly, barring Citibank's counterclaim would work an injustice.

Pravin Banker Associates, Ltd. v. Banco Popular del Peru, 9 F. Supp.2d 300 (S.D.N.Y 1998) (holding that the corporate independence of a foreign state-owned enterprise would not be disregarded in order to allow execution against the enterprise of a judgment entered against the foreign nation). Clearly, overcoming the presumption of independence is not some routine operation. But what standards — other than the notoriously vague admonition to avoid injustice — does the Supreme Court articulate? And what is the relationship between these principles under the FSIA and the principles governing a state court's personal jurisdiction over a foreign parent through the in-state activities of its subsidiary or agent? *See* Chapter 2, *supra*.

3. *Consequences of corporate independence.* Under the terms of the FSIA, what difference can it make (and at which points in the litigation) whether the corporate form is disregarded by the court or not?

4. *Choice of law.* The *Bancec* court relied in part on federal statutes, the decisions of British courts, and the decision of the International Court of Justice in *The Barcelona Traction Case.* How much weight did the court give

to Cuban law, and on what basis? Is it appropriate for a domestic court to give weight to the laws of a foreign state whose legal, political, and economic system is fundamentally different from that of the United States?

Does the Court's choice-of-law analysis imply that a forum state's law should determine whether an individual tortfeasor is an employee of the foreign sovereign for purposes of the non-commercial tort exception to the FSIA? For an affirmative answer, see *Randolph v. Budget Rent-A-Car*, 97 F.3d 319, 325 (9th Cir. 1996). *Compare First Fidelity Bank, N.A. v. Antigua & Barbuda-Permanent Mission*, 877 F.2d 189, 194–96 & n. 3 (2d Cir. 1989) (assuming without deciding that state law determines whether ambassador's borrowing of money constituted Antigua's commercial activity, as well as to waiver inquiry).

----

[3] Litigating the Exceptions to Foreign Sovereign Immunity

[a] The Commercial Activity Exception

§ 1605. General exceptions to the jurisdictional immunity of a foreign state.

(a) A foreign state shall not be immune from the jurisdiction of courts of the United States or of the States in any case -

(2) in which the action is based upon a commercial activity carried on in the United States by the foreign state; or upon an act performed in the United States in connection with a commercial activity of the foreign state elsewhere; or upon an act outside the territory of the United States in connection with a commercial activity of the foreign state elsewhere and that act causes a direct effect in the United States; . . .

[1] The Supreme Court Speaks

REPUBLIC OF ARGENTINA v. WELTOVER, INC.
504 U.S. 607 (1992)

JUSTICE SCALIA delivered the opinion of the Court. This case requires us to decide whether the Republic of Argentina's default on certain bonds issued as part of a plan to stabilize its currency was an act taken "in connection with a commercial activity" that had a "direct effect in the United States" so as to subject Argentina to suit in an American court under the Foreign Sovereign Immunities Act of 1976.

I

Since Argentina's currency is not one of the mediums of exchange accepted on the international market, Argentine businesses engaging in foreign transactions must pay in United States dollars or some other internationally accepted currency. In the recent past, it was difficult for Argentine borrowers to obtain such funds, principally because of the instability of the Argentine currency. To address these problems, petitioners, the Republic of Argentina and its central bank, Banco Central (collectively Argentina), in 1981 instituted a foreign exchange insurance contract program (FEIC), under which Argentina effectively agreed to assume the risk of currency depreciation in cross-border transactions involving Argentine borrowers. This was accomplished by Argentina's agreeing to sell to domestic borrowers, in exchange for a contractually predetermined amount of local currency, the necessary United States dollars to repay their foreign debts when they matured, irrespective of intervening devaluations.

Unfortunately, Argentina did not possess sufficient reserves of United States dollars to cover the FEIC contracts as they became due in 1982. The Argentine Government thereupon adopted certain emergency measures, including refinancing of the FEIC-backed debts by issuing to the creditors government bonds. These bonds, called "Bonods," provide for payment of interest and principal in United States dollars; payment may be made through transfer on the London, Frankfurt, Zurich, or New York market, at the election of the creditor. Under this refinancing program, the foreign creditor had the option of either accepting the Bonods in satisfaction of the initial debt, thereby substituting the Argentine Government for the private debtor, or maintaining the debtor/creditor relationship with the private borrower and accepting the Argentine Government as guarantor.

When the Bonods began to mature in May 1986, Argentina concluded that it lacked sufficient foreign exchange to retire them. Pursuant to a Presidential Decree, Argentina unilaterally extended the time for payment and offered bondholders substitute instruments as a means of rescheduling the debts. Respondents, two Panamanian corporations and a Swiss bank who hold, collectively, $1.3 million of Bonods, refused to accept the rescheduling and insisted on full payment, specifying New York as the place where payment should be made. Argentina did not pay, and respondents then brought this breach-of-contract action in the United States District Court for the Southern District of New York, relying on the Foreign Sovereign Immunities Act of 1976 as the basis for jurisdiction. Petitioners moved to dismiss for lack of subject-matter jurisdiction, lack of personal jurisdiction, and *forum non conveniens*. The District Court denied these motions, and the Court of Appeals affirmed. We granted Argentina's petition for certiorari, which challenged the Court of Appeals' determination that, under the Act, Argentina was not immune from the jurisdiction of the federal courts in this case.

II

The Foreign Sovereign Immunities Act of 1976 (FSIA), establishes a comprehensive framework for determining whether a court in this country, state or federal, may exercise jurisdiction over a foreign state. Under the Act, a "foreign state shall be immune from the jurisdiction of the courts of the United States and of the States" unless one of several statutorily defined exceptions applies. The FSIA thus provides the "sole basis" for obtaining jurisdiction over a foreign sovereign in the United States. *See Argentine Republic v. Amerada Hess Shipping Corp.*, 488 U.S. 428 (1989). The most significant of the FSIA's exceptions — and the one at issue in this case — is the "commercial" exception of § 1605(a)(2), which provides that a foreign state is not immune from suit in any case

> in which the action is based upon a commercial activity carried on in the United States by the foreign state; or upon an act performed in the United States in connection with a commercial activity of the foreign state elsewhere; or upon an act outside the territory of the United States in connection with a commercial activity of the foreign state elsewhere and that act causes a direct effect in the United States."

§ 1605(a)(2).

In the proceedings below, respondents relied only on the third clause of § 1605(a)(2) to establish jurisdiction, and our analysis is therefore limited to considering whether this lawsuit is (1) "based . . . upon an act outside the territory of the United States"; (2) that was taken "in connection with a commercial activity" of Argentina outside this country; and (3) that "caused a direct effect in the United States."[1] The complaint in this case alleges only one cause of action on behalf of each of the respondents, *viz.*, a breach-of-contract claim based on Argentina's attempt to refinance the Bonods rather than to pay them according to their terms. The fact that the cause of action is in compliance with the first of the three requirements — that it is "based upon an act outside the territory of the United States" (presumably Argentina's unilateral extension) — is uncontested. The dispute pertains to whether the unilateral refinancing of the Bonods was taken "in connection with a commercial activity" of Argentina, and whether it had a "direct effect in the United States." We address these issues in turn.

A

Respondents and their amicus, the United States, contend that Argentina's issuance of, and continued liability under, the Bonods constitute a "commercial activity" and that the extension of the payment schedules was taken "in connection with" that activity. The latter point is obvious enough, and Argentina does not contest it; the key question is whether the activity is "commercial" under the FSIA. The FSIA defines "commercial activity" to mean:

> Either a regular course of commercial conduct or a particular commercial transaction or act. The commercial character of an activity shall be determined by reference to the nature of the course of conduct or particular transaction or act, rather than by reference to its purpose.

28 U. S. C. § 1603(d).

This definition, however, leaves the critical term "commercial" largely undefined: The first sentence simply establishes that the commercial nature of an

---

[1] It is undisputed that both the Republic of Argentina and Banco Central are "foreign states" within the meaning of the FSIA. *See* 28 U. S. C. §§ 1603(a), (b) ("Foreign state" includes certain "agenc[ies] or instrumentalit[ies] of a foreign state").

activity does not depend upon whether it is a single act or a regular course of conduct; and the second sentence merely specifies what element of the conduct determines commerciality (i.e., nature rather than purpose), but still without saying what "commercial" means. Fortunately, however, the FSIA was not written on a clean slate. . . . [T]he Act (and the commercial exception in particular) largely codifies the so-called "restrictive" theory of foreign sovereign immunity first endorsed by the State Department in 1952. The meaning of "commercial" is the meaning generally attached to that term under the restrictive theory at the time the statute was enacted.

This Court did not have occasion to discuss the scope or validity of the restrictive theory of sovereign immunity until our 1976 decision in *Alfred Dunhill of London, Inc. v. Republic of Cuba*, 425 U.S. 682. [In that case,] there was little disagreement over the general scope of the [commercial act] exception. The plurality noted that, after the State Department endorsed the restrictive theory of foreign sovereign immunity in 1952, the lower courts consistently held that foreign sovereigns were not immune from the jurisdiction of American courts in cases "arising out of purely commercial transactions". The plurality further recognized that the distinction between state sovereign acts, on the one hand, and state commercial and private acts, on the other, was not entirely novel to American law. The plurality stated that the restrictive theory of foreign sovereign immunity would not bar a suit based upon a foreign state's participation in the marketplace in the manner of a private citizen or corporation. A foreign state engaging in "commercial" activities "do[es] not exercise powers peculiar to sovereigns"; rather, it "exercise[s] only those powers that can also be exercised by private citizens." The dissenters did not disagree with this general description.

Given that the FSIA was enacted less than six months after our decision in *Alfred Dunhill* announced, we think the plurality's contemporaneous description of the then-prevailing restrictive theory of sovereign immunity is of significant assistance in construing the scope of the Act. In accord with that description, we conclude that when a foreign government acts, not as regulator of a market, but in the manner of a private player within it, the foreign sovereign's actions are "commercial" within the meaning of the FSIA. Moreover, because the Act provides that the commercial character of an act is to be determined by reference to its "nature" rather than its "purpose," the question is not whether the foreign government is acting with a profit motive or instead with the aim of fulfilling uniquely sovereign objectives. Rather, the issue is whether the particular actions that the foreign state performs (whatever the motive behind them) are the type of actions by which a private party engages in "trade and traffic or commerce."

Thus, a foreign government's issuance of regulations limiting foreign currency exchange is a sovereign activity, because such authoritative control of commerce cannot be exercised by a private party; whereas a contract to buy army boots or even bullets is a "commercial" activity, because private companies can similarly use sales contracts to acquire goods. The commercial character of the Bonods is confirmed by the fact that they are in almost all respects garden-variety debt instruments: They may be held by private parties; they are negotiable and may be traded on the international market (except in Argentina); and they promise a future stream of cash income. We recognize that, prior to the enactment of the FSIA, there was authority suggesting that the issuance of public debt instruments did not constitute a commercial activity. There is, however, nothing distinctive about the state's assumption of debt (other than perhaps its purpose) that would cause it always to be classified as *jure imperii* . . . . Because the FSIA has now clearly established that the "nature" governs, we perceive no basis for concluding that the issuance of debt should be treated as categorically different from other activities of foreign states.

Argentina contends that, although the FSIA bars consideration of "purpose," a court must nonetheless fully consider the context of a transaction in order to determine whether it is "commercial." Accordingly, Argentina claims that the Court of Appeals erred by defining the relevant conduct in what Argentina considers an overly generalized, acontextual manner and by essentially adopting a *per se* rule that all "issuance of debt instruments" is "commercial." . . . We have no occasion to consider such a *per se* rule, because it seems to us that even in full context, there is nothing about the issuance of these Bonods (except perhaps its purpose) that is not analogous to a private commercial transaction.

Argentina points to the fact that the transactions in which the Bonods were issued did not have the ordinary commercial consequence of raising capital or financing acquisitions. Assuming for the sake of argument that this is not an example of judging the commerciality of a transaction by its purpose, the ready answer is that private parties regularly issue bonds, not just to raise capital or to finance purchases, but also to refinance debt. That is what Argentina did here: by virtue of the earlier FEIC contracts, Argentina was already obligated to supply the United States dollars needed to retire the FEIC-insured debts; the Bonods simply allowed Argentina to restructure its existing obligations. Argentina further asserts (without proof or even elaboration) that it "received consideration [for the Bonods] in no way commensurate with [their] value." Assuming that to be true, it makes no difference. Engaging in a commercial act does not require the receipt of fair value, or even compliance with the common-law requirements of consideration.

Argentina argues that the Bonods differ from ordinary debt instruments in that they "were created by the Argentine Government to fulfill its obligations under a foreign exchange program designed to address a domestic credit crisis, and as a component of a program designed to control that nation's critical shortage of foreign exchange." In this regard, Argentina relies heavily on *De Sanchez v. Banco Central de Nicaragua*, 770 F.2d 1385 (1985), in which the Fifth Circuit took the view that "often, the essence of an act is defined by its purpose"; that unless "we can inquire into the purposes of such acts, we cannot determine their nature"; and that, in light of its purpose to control its reserves of foreign currency, Nicaragua's refusal to honor a check it had issued to cover a private bank debt was a sovereign act entitled to immunity. Indeed, Argentina asserts that the line between "nature" and "purpose" rests upon a "formalistic distinction [that] simply is neither useful nor warranted."

We think this line of argument is squarely foreclosed by the language of the FSIA. However difficult it may be in some cases to separate "purpose" (i.e., the reason why the foreign state engages in the activity) from "nature" (i.e., the outward form of the conduct that the foreign state performs or agrees to perform), the statute unmistakably commands that to be done, 28 U. S. C. § 1603(d). We agree with the Court of Appeals that it is irrelevant why Argentina participated in the bond market in the manner of a private actor; it matters only that it did so. We conclude that Argentina's issuance of the Bonods was a "commercial activity" under the FSIA.

B

The remaining question is whether Argentina's unilateral rescheduling of the Bonods had a "direct effect" in the United States, 28 U. S. C. § 1605(a)(2). In addressing this issue, the Court of Appeals rejected the suggestion in the legislative history of the FSIA that an effect is not "direct" unless it is both "substantial" and "foreseeable." That suggestion is found in the House Report, which states that conduct covered by the third clause of § 1605(a)(2) would be subject to the jurisdiction of American courts "consistent with principles set forth in section 18, Restatement of the Law, Second, Foreign Relations Law of the United States (1965)." Section 18 states that American laws are not given extraterritorial application except with respect to conduct that has, as a "direct and foreseeable result," a "substantial" effect within the United States. Since this obviously deals with jurisdiction to legislate rather than jurisdiction to adjudicate, this passage of the House Report has been charitably described as "a bit of a non sequitur," *Texas Trading & Milling Corp. v. Federal Republic of Nigeria*, 647 F.2d 300, 311 (CA2 1981), *cert. denied*, 454 U.S. 1148 (1982).

Of course the generally applicable principle *de minimis non curat lex* ensures that jurisdiction may not be predicated on purely trivial effects in the United States. But we reject the suggestion that § 1605(a)(2) contains any unexpressed requirement of "substantiality" or "foreseeability." As the Court of Appeals recognized, an effect is "direct" if it follows "as an immediate consequence of the defendant's . . . activity."

The Court of Appeals concluded that the rescheduling of the maturity dates obviously had a "direct effect" on respondents. It further concluded that that effect was sufficiently "in the United States" for purposes of the FSIA, in part because "Congress would have wanted an American court to entertain this action" in order to preserve New York City's status as "a preeminent commercial center." The question, however, is not what Congress "would have wanted" but what Congress enacted in the FSIA. Although we are happy to endorse the Second Circuit's recognition of "New York's status as a world financial leader," the effect of Argentina's rescheduling in diminishing that status (assuming it is not too speculative to be considered an effect at all) is too remote and attenuated to satisfy the "direct effect" requirement of the FSIA.

We nonetheless have little difficulty concluding that Argentina's unilateral rescheduling of the maturity dates on the Bonods had a "direct effect" in the United States. Respondents had designated their accounts in New York as the place of payment, and Argentina made some interest payments into those accounts before announcing that it was rescheduling the payments. Because

New York was thus the place of performance for Argentina's ultimate contractual obligations, the rescheduling of those obligations necessarily had a "direct effect" in the United States: Money that was supposed to have been delivered to a New York bank for deposit was not forthcoming. We reject Argentina's suggestion that the "direct effect" requirement cannot be satisfied where the plaintiffs are all foreign corporations with no other connections to the United States. We expressly stated in *Verlinden* that the FSIA permits "a foreign plaintiff to sue a foreign sovereign in the courts of the United States, provided the substantive requirements of the Act are satisfied."

Finally, Argentina argues that a finding of jurisdiction in this case would violate the Due Process Clause of the Fifth Amendment, and that, in order to avoid this difficulty, we must construe the "direct effect" requirement as embodying the "minimum contacts" test of *International Shoe Co. v. Washington*, 326 U.S. 310, 316 (1945). Assuming, without deciding, that a foreign state is a "person" for purposes of the Due Process Clause, we find that Argentina possessed "minimum contacts" that would satisfy the constitutional test. By issuing negotiable debt instruments denominated in United States dollars and payable in New York and by appointing a financial agent in that city, Argentina " 'purposefully availed itself of the privilege of conducting activities within the [United States].'

We conclude that Argentina's issuance of the Bonods was a "commercial activity" under the FSIA; that its rescheduling of the maturity dates on those instruments was taken in connection with that commercial activity and had a "direct effect" in the United States; and that the District Court therefore properly asserted jurisdiction, under the FSIA, over the breach-of-contract claim based on that rescheduling. Accordingly, the judgment of the Court of Appeals is affirmed.

SAUDI ARABIA v. NELSON
507 U.S. 349 (1993)

JUSTICE SOUTER delivered the opinion of the Court. The Foreign Sovereign Immunities Act of 1976 entitles foreign states to immunity from the jurisdiction of courts in the United States, subject to certain enumerated exceptions. § 1605. One is that a foreign state shall not be immune in any case "in which the action is based upon a commercial activity carried on in the United States by the foreign state." § 1605(a)(2). We hold that respondents' action alleging personal injury resulting from unlawful detention and torture by the Saudi Government is not "based upon a commercial activity" within the meaning of the Act, which consequently confers no jurisdiction over respondents' suit.

I

Because this case comes to us on a motion to dismiss the complaint, we assume that we have truthful factual allegations before us, though many of those allegations are subject to dispute. Petitioner Kingdom of Saudi Arabia owns and operates petitioner King Faisal Specialist Hospital in Riyadh, as well as petitioner Royspec Purchasing Services, the hospital's corporate purchasing agent in the United States. The Hospital Corporation of America, Ltd. (HCA), an independent corporation existing under the laws of the Cayman Islands, recruits Americans for employment at the hospital under an agreement signed with Saudi Arabia in 1973.

In its recruitment effort, HCA placed an advertisement in a trade periodical seeking applications for a position as a monitoring systems engineer at the hospital. The advertisement drew the attention of respondent Scott Nelson in September 1983, while Nelson was in the United States. After interviewing for the position in Saudi Arabia, Nelson returned to the United States, where he signed an employment contract with the hospital, satisfied personnel processing requirements, and attended an orientation session that HCA conducted for hospital employees. In the course of that program, HCA identified Royspec as the point of contact in the United States for family members who might wish to reach Nelson in an emergency.

In December 1983, Nelson went to Saudi Arabia and began work at the hospital, monitoring all "facilities, equipment, utilities and maintenance systems to insure the safety of patients, hospital staff, and others." He did his job without significant incident until March 1984, when he discovered safety defects in the hospital's oxygen and nitrous oxide lines that posed fire hazards and otherwise endangered patients' lives. Over a period of several months, Nelson repeatedly advised hospital officials of the safety defects and reported the defects to a Saudi Government commission as well. Hospital officials instructed Nelson to ignore the problems.

The hospital's response to Nelson's reports changed, however, on September 27, 1984, when certain hospital employees summoned him to the hospital's security office where agents of the Saudi Government arrested him.[1] The agents transported Nelson to a jail cell, in which they "shackled, tortured and beat" him, and kept him four days without food. Although Nelson did not understand Arabic, government agents forced him to sign a statement written in that language, the content of which he did not know; a hospital employee who was supposed to act as Nelson's interpreter advised him to sign "anything" the agents gave him to avoid further beatings. Two days later, government agents transferred Nelson to the Al Sijan Prison "to await trial on unknown charges."

At the prison, Nelson was confined in an overcrowded cell area infested with rats, where he had to fight other prisoners for food and from which he was taken only once a week for fresh air and exercise. Although police interrogators repeatedly questioned him in Arabic, Nelson did not learn the nature of the charges, if any, against him. For several days, the Saudi Government failed to advise Nelson's family of his whereabouts, though a Saudi official

---

[1] Petitioners assert that the Saudi Government arrested Nelson because he had falsely represented to the hospital that he had received a degree from the Massachusetts Institute of Technology and had provided the hospital with a forged diploma to verify his claim. The Nelsons concede these misrepresentations, but dispute that they occasioned Scott Nelson's arrest.

eventually told Nelson's wife, respondent Vivian Nelson, that he could arrange for her husband's release if she provided sexual favors.

Although officials from the United States Embassy visited Nelson twice during his detention, they concluded that his allegations of Saudi mistreatment were "not credible" and made no protest to Saudi authorities. It was only at the personal request of a United States Senator that the Saudi Government released Nelson, 39 days after his arrest, on November 5, 1984. Seven days later, after failing to convince him to return to work at the hospital, the Saudi Government allowed Nelson to leave the country.

In 1988, Nelson and his wife filed this action against petitioners in the United States District Court for the Southern District of Florida seeking damages for personal injury. The Nelsons' complaint sets out 16 causes of action, which fall into three categories: [(i) various intentional torts, including battery, unlawful detainment, wrongful arrest and imprisonment, false imprisonment, inhuman torture, disruption of normal family life, and infliction of mental anguish; (ii) negligent failure to warn Nelson of otherwise undisclosed dangers of his employment, namely, that if he attempted to report safety hazards, the hospital would likely retaliate against him and the Saudi Government might detain and physically abuse him without legal cause; and (iii) derivative injury to Vivian Nelson from petitioners' actions.] Presumably because the employment contract provided that Saudi courts would have exclusive jurisdiction over claims for breach of contract, the Nelsons raised no such matters.

The District Court dismissed for lack of subject-matter jurisdiction under the Foreign Sovereign Immunities Act of 1976. It rejected the Nelsons' argument that jurisdiction existed, under the first clause of § 1605(a)(2), because the action was one "based upon a commercial activity" that petitioners had "carried on in the United States." Although HCA's recruitment of Nelson in the United States might properly be attributed to Saudi Arabia and the hospital, the District Court reasoned, it did not amount to commercial activity "carried on in the United States" for purposes of the Act. The court explained that there was no sufficient "nexus" between Nelson's recruitment and the injuries alleged. "Although [the Nelsons] argue that but for [Scott Nelson's] recruitment in the United States, he would not have taken the job, been arrested, and suffered the personal injuries," the court said, "this 'connection' [is] far too tenuous to support jurisdiction" under the Act. Likewise, the court concluded that Royspec's commercial activity in the United States, purchasing supplies and equipment for the hospital, had no nexus with the personal injuries alleged in the complaint; Royspec had simply provided a way for Nelson's family to reach him in an emergency.

The Court of Appeals reversed. It concluded that Nelson's recruitment and hiring were commercial activities of Saudi Arabia and the hospital, carried on in the United States for purposes of the Act, and that the Nelsons' action was "based upon" these activities within the meaning of the statute. There was, the court reasoned, a sufficient nexus between those commercial activities and the wrongful acts that had allegedly injured the Nelsons: "the detention and torture of Nelson are so intertwined with his employment at the Hospital," the court explained, "that they are 'based upon' his recruitment and hiring" in the United States. The court also found jurisdiction to hear the claims against Royspec. After the Court of Appeals denied petitioners' suggestion for rehearing en banc, we granted certiorari. We now reverse.

II

The Foreign Sovereign Immunities Act "provides the sole basis for obtaining jurisdiction over a foreign state in the courts of this country" [quoting *Amerada Hess, supra*]. Under the Act, a foreign state is presumptively immune from the jurisdiction of United States courts; unless a specified exception applies, a federal court lacks subject-matter jurisdiction over a claim against a foreign state.

Only one such exception is said to apply here. The first clause of § 1605(a)(2) of the Act provides that a foreign state shall not be immune from the jurisdiction of United States courts in any case "in which the action is based upon a commercial activity carried on in the United States by the foreign state." The Act defines such activity as "commercial activity carried on by such state and having substantial contact with the United States," § 1603(e), and provides that a commercial activity may be "either a regular course of commercial conduct or a particular commercial transaction or act," the "commercial character of [which] shall be determined by reference to" its "nature," rather than its "purpose," § 1603(d).

There is no dispute here that Saudi Arabia, the hospital, and Royspec all qualify as "foreign state[s]" within the meaning of the Act. For there to be jurisdiction in this case, therefore, the Nelsons' action must be "based upon" some "commercial activity" by petitioners that had "substantial contact" with the United States within the meaning of the Act. Because we conclude that the suit is not based upon any commercial activity by petitioners, we need not reach the issue of substantial contact with the United States.

We begin our analysis by identifying the particular conduct on which the Nelsons' action is "based" for purposes of the Act. Although the Act contains no definition of the phrase "based upon," and the relatively sparse legislative history offers no assistance, guidance is hardly necessary. In denoting conduct that forms the "basis," or "foundation," for a claim, . . . the phrase is read most naturally to mean those elements of a claim that, if proven, would entitle a plaintiff to relief under his theory of the case. *See Callejo v. Bancomer, S. A.*, 764 F.2d 1101, 1109 (CA5 1985) (focus should be on the "gravamen of the complaint"); *accord, Santos v. Compagnie Nationale Air France*, 934 F.2d 890, 893 (CA7 1991) ("An action is based upon the elements that prove the claim, no more and no less"). What the natural meaning of the phrase "based upon" suggests, the context confirms. . . . Section 1605(a)(2) contains two clauses following the one at issue here. The second allows for jurisdiction where a suit "is based . . . upon an act performed in the United States in connection with a commercial activity of the foreign state elsewhere," and the third speaks in like terms, allowing for jurisdiction where an action "is based . . . upon an act outside the territory of the United States in connection with a commercial activity of the foreign state elsewhere and that act causes a direct effect in the United States." Distinctions among descriptions juxtaposed against each other are naturally understood to be significant, and Congress manifestly understood there to be a difference between a suit "based upon" commercial activity and one "based upon" acts performed "in connection with" such activity. The only reasonable reading of the former term calls for something more than a mere connection with, or relation to, commercial activity.[2]

In this case, the Nelsons have alleged that petitioners recruited Scott Nelson for work at the hospital, signed an employment contract with him, and subsequently employed him. While these activities led to the conduct that eventually injured the Nelsons, they are not the basis for the Nelsons' suit. Even taking each of the Nelsons' allegations about Scott Nelson's recruitment and employment as true, those facts alone entitle the Nelsons to nothing under their theory of the case. The Nelsons have not, after all, alleged breach of contract, but personal injuries caused by petitioners' intentional wrongs and by petitioners' negligent failure to warn Scott Nelson that they might commit those wrongs. Those torts, and not the arguably commercial activities that preceded their commission, form the basis for the Nelsons' suit.

Petitioners' tortious conduct itself fails to qualify as "commercial activity" within the meaning of the Act, although the Act is too "obtuse" to be of much help in reaching that conclusion. [citation omitted.] We have seen already that the Act defines "commercial activity" as "either a regular course of commercial conduct or a particular commercial transaction or act," and provides that "the commercial character of an activity shall be determined by reference to the nature of the course of conduct or particular transaction or act, rather than by reference to its purpose." If this is a definition, it is one distinguished only by its diffidence; as we observed in our most recent case on the subject, it "leaves the critical term 'commercial' largely undefined." *Republic of Argentina v. Weltover, Inc.*, 504 U.S. 607 (1992). We do not, however, have the option to throw up our hands. The term has to be given some interpretation, and congressional diffidence necessarily results in judicial responsibility to determine what a "commercial activity" is for purposes of the Act.

We took up the task . . . in *Weltover*, which involved Argentina's unilateral refinancing of bonds it had issued under a plan to stabilize its currency. . . . We explained in *Weltover*, that a state engages in commercial activity under the restrictive theory where it exercises " 'only those powers that can also be exercised by private citizens,' " as distinct from those " 'powers peculiar to sovereigns.' " Put differently, a foreign state engages in commercial activity for purposes of the restrictive theory only where it acts "in the manner of a private player within" the market. *See* RESTATEMENT (THIRD) OF FOREIGN RELATIONS LAW OF THE UNITED STATES § 451 (1987) ("Under international law, a state or state instrumentality is immune from the jurisdiction of the courts of another state, except with respect to claims arising out of activities of the kind that may be carried on by private persons").

We emphasized in *Weltover* that whether a state acts "in the manner of" a private party is a question of behavior, not motivation:

---

[2] We do not mean to suggest that the first clause of § 1605(a)(2) necessarily requires that each and every element of a claim be commercial activity by a foreign state, and we do not address the case where a claim consists of both commercial and sovereign elements. We do conclude, however, that where a claim rests entirely upon activities sovereign in character, as here, jurisdiction will not exist under that clause regardless of any connection the sovereign acts may have with commercial activity.

Because the Act provides that the commercial character of an act is to be determined by reference to its "nature" rather than its "purpose," the question is not whether the foreign government is acting with a profit motive or instead with the aim of fulfilling uniquely sovereign objectives. Rather, the issue is whether the particular actions that the foreign state performs (whatever the motive behind them) are the type of actions by which a private party engages in "trade and traffic or commerce."

We did not ignore the difficulty of distinguishing " 'purpose' (i.e., the reason why the foreign state engages in the activity) from 'nature' (i.e., the outward form of the conduct that the foreign state performs or agrees to perform)," but recognized that the Act "unmistakably commands" us to observe the distinction. Because Argentina had merely dealt in the bond market in the manner of a private player, we held, its refinancing of the bonds qualified as a commercial activity for purposes of the Act despite the apparent governmental motivation. Unlike Argentina's activities that we considered in *Weltover*, the intentional conduct alleged here (the Saudi Government's wrongful arrest, imprisonment, and torture of Nelson) could not qualify as commercial under the restrictive theory. The conduct boils down to abuse of the power of its police by the Saudi Government, and however monstrous such abuse undoubtedly may be, a foreign state's exercise of the power of its police has long been understood for purposes of the restrictive theory as peculiarly sovereign in nature. . . .[3] Exercise of the powers of police and penal officers is not the sort of action by which private parties can engage in commerce. "Such acts as legislation, or the expulsion of an alien, or a denial of justice, cannot be performed by an individual acting in his own name. They can be performed only by the state acting as such." Lauterpacht, *The Problem of Jurisdictional Immunities of Foreign States*, 28 Brit. Y. B. Int'l L. 220, 225 (1952).

The Nelsons and their amici urge us to give significance to their assertion that the Saudi Government subjected Nelson to the abuse alleged as retaliation for his persistence in reporting hospital safety violations, and argue that the character of the mistreatment was consequently commercial. One amicus, indeed, goes so far as to suggest that the Saudi Government "often uses detention and torture to resolve commercial disputes." But this argument does not alter the fact that the powers allegedly abused were those of police and penal officers. In any event, the argument is off the point, for it goes to purpose, the very fact the Act renders irrelevant to the question of an activity's commercial character. Whatever may have been the Saudi Government's motivation for its allegedly abusive treatment of Nelson, it remains the case that the Nelsons' action is based upon a sovereign activity immune from the subject-matter jurisdiction of United States courts under the Act.

---

[3] The State Department's practice prior to the passage of the Act supports this understanding. Prior to the Act's passage, the State Department would determine in the first instance whether a foreign state was entitled to immunity and make an appropriate recommendation to the courts. . . . [T]he Department recognized immunity with respect to claims involving the exercise of the power of the police or military of a foreign state. JUSTICE WHITE points to an episode in which the State Department declined to recognize immunity with respect to a claim by Jamaican nationals, working in the United States, against the British West Indies Central Labour Organization, a foreign governmental agency. In our view that episode bears little relation to this case, for the Jamaican nationals did not allege mistreatment by the police of a foreign state.

In addition to the intentionally tortious conduct, the Nelsons claim a separate basis for recovery in petitioners' failure to warn Scott Nelson of the hidden dangers associated with his employment. The Nelsons allege that, at the time petitioners recruited Scott Nelson and thereafter, they failed to warn him of the possibility of severe retaliatory action if he attempted to disclose any safety hazards he might discover on the job. In other words, petitioners bore a duty to warn of their own propensity for tortious conduct. But this is merely a semantic ploy. For aught we can see, a plaintiff could recast virtually any claim of intentional tort committed by sovereign act as a claim of failure to warn, simply by charging the defendant with an obligation to announce its own tortious propensity before indulging it. To give jurisdictional significance to this feint of language would effectively thwart the Act's manifest purpose to codify the restrictive theory of foreign sovereign immunity.

III

The Nelsons' action is not "based upon a commercial activity" within the meaning of the first clause of § 1605(a)(2) of the Act, and the judgment of the Court of Appeals is accordingly reversed.

JUSTICE WHITE, with whom JUSTICE BLACKMUN joins, concurring in the judgment. According to respondents' complaint, Scott Nelson's employer retaliated against him for reporting safety problems by "summon[ing him] . . . to the hospital's security office from which he was transported to a jail cell." Once there, he allegedly was "shackled, tortured and beaten by persons acting at the direction, instigation, provocation, instruction or request of" petitioners — Saudi Arabia, King Faisal Specialist Hospital, and Royspec. The majority concludes that petitioners enjoy sovereign immunity because respondents' action is not "based upon a commercial activity." I disagree. I nonetheless concur in the judgment because in my view the commercial conduct upon which respondents base their complaint was not "carried on in the United States."

I

A

As the majority notes, the first step in the analysis is to identify the conduct on which the action is based. Respondents have pointed to two distinct possibilities. The first, seemingly pressed at trial and on appeal, consists of the recruiting and hiring activity in the United States. Although this conduct would undoubtedly qualify as "commercial," I agree with the majority that it is "not the basis for the Nelsons' suit," for it is unrelated to the elements of respondents' complaint.

In a partial change of course, respondents suggest to this Court both in their brief and at oral argument that we focus on the hospital's commercial activity in Saudi Arabia, its employment practices and disciplinary procedures. Under this view, the Court would then work its way back to the recruiting and hiring activity in order to establish that the commercial conduct in fact had "substantial contact" with the United States. The majority never reaches this second stage, finding instead that petitioners' conduct is not commercial because it "is not the sort of action by which private parties can engage in commerce." If by that the majority means that it is not the manner in which private parties ought to engage in commerce, I wholeheartedly agree. That, however, is not the relevant inquiry. Rather, the question we must ask is whether it is the manner in which private parties at times do engage in commerce.

B

To run and operate a hospital, even a public hospital, is to engage in a commercial enterprise. The majority never concedes this point, but it does not deny it either, and to my mind the matter is self-evident. By the same token, warning an employee when he blows the whistle and taking retaliatory action, such as harassment, involuntary transfer, discharge, or other tortious behavior, although not prototypical commercial acts, are certainly well within the bounds of commercial activity. The House and Senate Reports accompanying the legislation virtually compel this conclusion, explaining as they do that "a foreign government's . . . employment or engagement of laborers, clerical staff or marketing agents . . . would be among those included within" the definition of commercial activity. H. R. Rep. No. 94-1487, p. 16 (1976) (House Report); S. Rep. No. 94-1310, p. 16 (1976) (Senate Report). Nelson alleges that petitioners harmed him in the course of engaging in their commercial enterprise, as a direct result of their commercial acts. His claim, in other words, is "based upon commercial activity." Indeed, I am somewhat at a loss as to what exactly the majority believes petitioners have done that a private employer could not. As countless cases attest, retaliation for whistle-blowing is not a practice foreign to the marketplace. . . . On occasion, private employers also have been known to retaliate by enlisting the help of police officers to falsely arrest employees. More generally, private parties have been held liable for conspiring with public authorities to effectuate an arrest, and for using private security personnel for the same purposes.

Therefore, had the hospital retaliated against Nelson by hiring thugs to do the job, I assume the majority — no longer able to describe this conduct as "a foreign state's exercise of the power of its police," — would consent to calling it "commercial." For, in such circumstances, the state-run hospital would be operating as any private participant in the marketplace and respondents' action would be based on the operation by Saudi Arabia's agents of a commercial business. . . .

At the heart of the majority's conclusion, in other words, is the fact that the hospital in this case chose to call in government security forces. I find this fixation on the intervention of police officers, and the ensuing characterization of the conduct as "peculiarly sovereign in nature," to be misguided. To begin, it fails to capture respondents' complaint in full. Far from being directed solely at the activities of the Saudi police, it alleges that agents of the hospital summoned Nelson to its security office because he reported safety concerns and that the hospital played a part in the subsequent beating and imprisonment. Without more, that type of behavior hardly qualifies as sovereign. Thus, even assuming for the sake of argument that the role of the official police somehow affected the nature of petitioners' conduct, the claim cannot be said to "rest entirely upon activities sovereign in character." At the very least it "consists of both commercial and sovereign elements," thereby presenting the specific question the majority chooses to elude. The majority's single-minded focus on the exercise of police power, while certainly simplifying the case, thus hardly does it justice. . . .

Nevertheless, I reach the same conclusion as the majority because petitioners' commercial activity was not "carried on in the United States." The Act defines such conduct as "commercial activity . . . having substantial contact with the United States." Respondents point to the hospital's recruitment efforts in the United States, including advertising in the American media, and the signing of the employment contract in Miami. . . . [W]hile these may very well qualify as commercial activity in the United States, they do not constitute the commercial activity upon which respondents' action is based. Conversely, petitioners' commercial conduct in Saudi Arabia, though constituting the basis of the Nelsons' suit, lacks a sufficient nexus to the United States. Neither the hospital's employment practices, nor its disciplinary procedures, has any apparent connection to this country. On that basis, I agree that the Act does not grant the Nelsons access to our courts.

JUSTICE KENNEDY, . . . concurring in part and dissenting in part.

I join all of the Court's opinion except the last paragraph of Part II, where, with almost no explanation, the Court rules that, like the intentional tort claim, the claims based on negligent failure to warn are outside the subject-matter jurisdiction of the federal courts. These claims stand on a much different footing from the intentional tort claims for purposes of the Foreign Sovereign Immunities Act (FSIA). In my view, they ought to be remanded to the District Court for further consideration.

I agree with the Court's holding that the Nelsons' claims of intentional wrongdoing by the hospital and the Kingdom of Saudi Arabia are based on sovereign, not commercial, activity, and so fall outside the commercial activity exception to the grant of foreign sovereign immunity contained in 28 U.S.C. § 1604. The intentional tort counts of the Nelsons' complaint recite the alleged unlawful arrest, imprisonment, and torture of Mr. Nelson by the Saudi police acting in their official capacities. These are not the sort of activities by which a private party conducts its business affairs; if we classified them as commercial, the commercial activity exception would in large measure swallow the rule of foreign sovereign immunity Congress enacted in the FSIA.

By the same token, however, the Nelsons' claims alleging that the hospital, the Kingdom, and Royspec were negligent in failing during their recruitment of Nelson to warn him of foreseeable dangers are based upon commercial activity having substantial contact with the United States. As such, they are within the commercial activity exception and the jurisdiction of the federal courts. Unlike the intentional tort counts of the complaint, the failure to warn counts do not complain of a police beating in Saudi Arabia; rather, they complain of a negligent omission made during the recruiting of a hospital employee in the United States. To obtain relief, the Nelsons would be obliged to prove that the hospital's recruiting agent did not tell Nelson about the foreseeable hazards of his prospective employment in Saudi Arabia. Under the Court's test, this omission is what the negligence counts are "based upon."

Omission of important information during employee recruiting is commercial activity as we have described it. It seems plain that recruiting employees is an activity undertaken by private hospitals in the normal course of business. Locating and hiring employees implicates no power unique to the sovereign. In explaining the terms and conditions of employment, including the risks and rewards of a particular job, a governmental entity acts in "the manner of a private player within" the commercial marketplace. Under the FSIA, as a result, it must satisfy the same general duties of care that apply to private actors under state law. If a private company with operations in Saudi Arabia would be obliged in the course of its recruiting activities subject to state law to tell a prospective employee about the risk of arbitrary arrest and torture by Saudi authorities, then so would King Faisal Specialist Hospital.

The recruiting activity alleged in the failure to warn counts of the complaint also satisfies the final requirement for invoking the commercial activity exception: that the claims be based upon commercial activity "having substantial contact with the United States." 28 U.S.C. § 1603(e). Nelson's recruitment was performed by Hospital Corporation of America, Ltd. (HCA), a wholly owned subsidiary of a United States corporation, which, for a period of at least 16 years beginning in 1973, acted as the Kingdom of Saudi Arabia's exclusive agent for recruiting employees for the hospital. HCA in the regular course of its business seeks employees for the hospital in the American labor market. HCA advertised in an American magazine, seeking applicants for the position Nelson later filled. Nelson saw the ad in the United States and contacted HCA in Tennessee. After an interview in Saudi Arabia, Nelson returned to Florida, where he signed an employment contract and underwent personnel processing and application procedures. Before leaving to take his job at the hospital, Nelson attended an orientation session conducted by HCA in Tennessee for new employees. These activities have more than substantial contact with the United States; most of them were "carried on in the United States." 28 U.S.C. § 1605(a)(2). In alleging that the petitioners neglected during these activities to tell him what they were bound to under state law, Nelson meets all of the statutory requirements for invoking federal jurisdiction under the commercial activity exception.

Having met the jurisdictional prerequisites of the FSIA, the Nelsons' failure to warn claims should survive petitioners' motion under Federal Rule of Civil Procedure 12(b)(1) to dismiss for want of subject-matter jurisdiction. . . .

JUSTICE STEVENS, dissenting. Under the Foreign Sovereign Immunities Act of 1976 (FSIA), a foreign state is subject to the jurisdiction of American courts if two conditions are met: The action must be "based upon a commercial activity" and that activity must have a "substantial contact with the United States." These two conditions should be separately analyzed because they serve two different purposes. The former excludes commercial activity from the scope of the foreign sovereign's immunity from suit; the second identifies the contacts with the United States that support the assertion of jurisdiction over the defendant.

In this case, as JUSTICE WHITE has demonstrated, petitioner Kingdom of Saudi Arabia's operation of the hospital and its employment practices and disciplinary procedures are "commercial activities" within the meaning of the statute, and respondent Scott Nelson's claim that he was punished for acts performed in the course of his employment was unquestionably "based upon" those activities. Thus, the first statutory condition is satisfied; petitioner is not entitled to immunity from the claims asserted by respondent.

Unlike JUSTICE WHITE, however, I am also convinced that petitioner's commercial activities — whether defined as the regular course of conduct of operating a hospital or, more specifically, as the commercial transaction of engaging respondent "as an employee with specific responsibilities in that enterprise," — have sufficient contact with the United States to justify the exercise of federal jurisdiction. Petitioner Royspec maintains an office in Maryland and purchases hospital supplies and equipment in this country. For nearly two decades the hospital's American agent has maintained an office in the United States and regularly engaged in the recruitment of personnel in this country. Respondent himself was recruited in the United States and entered into his employment contract with the hospital in the United States. Before traveling to Saudi Arabia to assume his position at the hospital, respondent attended an orientation program in Tennessee. The position for which respondent was recruited and ultimately hired was that of a monitoring systems manager, a troubleshooter, and, taking respondent's allegations as true, it was precisely respondent's performance of those responsibilities that led to the hospital's retaliatory actions against him.

Whether the first clause of § 1605(a)(2) broadly authorizes "general" jurisdiction over foreign entities that engage in substantial commercial activity in this country, or, more narrowly, authorizes only "specific" jurisdiction over particular commercial claims that have a substantial contact with the United States, petitioners' contacts with the United States in this case are, in my view, plainly sufficient to subject petitioners to suit in this country on a claim arising out of their nonimmune commercial activity relating to respondent. If the same activities had been performed by a private business, I have no doubt jurisdiction would be upheld. And that, of course, should be a touchstone of our inquiry; for as JUSTICE WHITE explains, when a foreign nation sheds its uniquely sovereign status and seeks out the benefits of the private marketplace, it must, like any private party, bear the burdens and responsibilities imposed by that marketplace. I would therefore affirm the judgment of the Court of Appeals.[1]

Notes and Questions on *Weltover* and *Nelson*

1. *Characterization.* Reading *Weltover* and *Nelson* together, how would you articulate the test for commercial activity? Is it solely a matter of unbounded characterization by the judge?

2. *Causality.* Is there a sense in which the primary distinction between the majority and dissenting opinions in *Nelson* reflects a difference in the test of

---

[1] My affirmance would extend to respondents' failure to warn claims. I am therefore in agreement with Justice Kennedy's analysis of that aspect of the case.

causality, with one side using a "but for" test and the other relying on a narrower notion of proximate cause?

3. *Formalism.* Altering the facts slightly in these two cases can illustrate just how formalistic the Court's approach to the commercial activity exception is. Suppose for example that Argentina had accomplished the rescheduling of the debt, not through bonds, but through outright regulation — say in the form of central bank rules on the repayment of foreign debt. The Court itself suggests that the result under the commercial activity exception would be very different, declaring that "a foreign government's issuance of regulations limiting foreign currency exchange is a sovereign activity, because such authoritative control of commerce cannot be exercised by a private party." Similarly, in *Nelson*, if the hospital had hired thugs for security — even off-duty police officers — and they had done precisely the same thing to the Nelsons, the result under the commercial activity exception might well have been different. The precise form that the government's action takes determines whether it qualifies as commercial activity or not. As the following cases suggest, this puts a premium on the courts' power to characterize a government's action.

[2] The Lower Courts At Work: The Power of Characterization

MOL, INC. v. BANGLADESH
736 F.2d 1326 (9th Cir.), *cert. denied*, 469 U.S. 1037 (1984)

MOL, Inc. sues Bangladesh for termination of a licensing agreement for the export of rhesus monkeys from Bangladesh. Because the granting and revocation of a license to export a natural resource are sovereign acts, we have no jurisdiction over this claim.

In 1977, a division of the Bangladesh Ministry of Agriculture granted MOL, Inc., an Oregon corporation, a ten-year license to capture and export rhesus monkeys. The licensing agreement specified quantities and prices and required MOL to build in Bangladesh in 1978 a breeding farm for rhesus monkeys. By its terms, the agreement was granted "on the grounds and sole condition that the primates exported by [MOL] from Bangladesh shall be used exclusively for the purposes of medical and other scientific research by highly skilled and competent personnel for the general benefit of all peoples of the world." To enable Bangladesh to monitor uses of the monkeys, it required MOL to keep available records on each monkey and arrange for duplicate records in Bangladesh. The agreement provided for arbitration of disputes, each party selecting one arbitrator. Bangladesh reserved the right to terminate the agreement "without notice if [MOL] has failed to fulfill its obligations under this Agreement."

In November 1977, India banned the export of its rhesus monkeys. As India had been the major exporter of these animals, which are valuable for research because of their anatomical and behavioral similarity to humans, Bangladesh became an important supplier. Although world monkey prices rose while MOL's payments to Bangladesh remained fixed, Bangladesh complied with the licensing agreement through the spring of 1978. Bangladesh threatened to cancel the agreement in May 1978 because MOL had not built the breeding farm or exported agreed quantities. MOL denied any departure from the agreement. In September 1978, it delivered some Bangladesh monkeys to the United States armed services for radiobiological research.

Bangladesh announced on January 3, 1979, that it was terminating the agreement because MOL had not constructed the breeding farm in 1978 and had breached the requirement that the monkeys be used only for humanitarian purposes. It claimed that MOL sold the monkeys to the armed services for "neutron bomb radiation experiments." When MOL sought arbitration, Bangladesh refused, asserting its right to terminate for breach by MOL. Apparently MOL asked the State Department to intervene. Despite these efforts and MOL's reassurances that monkeys would not be used for radiation experiments, Bangladesh did not reinstate the licensing agreement.

In 1982, MOL sued Bangladesh for $15 million. Bangladesh did not appear, and MOL moved for default. Amicus curiae, Attorneys for Animal Rights, moved to dismiss for lack of jurisdiction under the FSIA. The district court denied the default judgment and dismissed the action, holding it barred . . . by the FSIA. . . .

MOL argues that Bangladesh does not enjoy sovereign immunity because its acts fall under the commercial activity exception of the FSIA. That Act denies immunity in any case in which the action is based "upon an act outside the territory of the United States in connection with a commercial activity of the foreign state elsewhere and that act causes a direct effect in the United States." The exception turns on whether the act is commercial:

> A "commercial activity" means either a regular course of commercial conduct or a particular commercial transaction or act. The commercial character of an activity shall be determined by reference to the nature of the course of conduct or particular transaction or act, rather than by reference to its purpose . . . .

A crucial step in determining whether the basis of this suit was a commercial activity is defining the "act complained of here." The court must then decide whether that act is commercial or sovereign. MOL asserts that the activity here relates to Bangladesh's contracting to sell monkeys. It admits that licensing the exploitation of natural resources is a sovereign activity. It argues, however, that this suit arises not from license revocation but from termination of a contract. In essence, Bangladesh lost its sovereign status when it contracted and then terminated pursuant to contract terms. The argument seems persuasive because, in breaking the agreement, Bangladesh itself spoke in commercial terms, basing its termination on MOL's alleged breaches. The true nature of the action, however, does not depend on terminology.

Bangladesh was terminating an agreement that only a sovereign could have made. This was not just a contract for trade of monkeys. It concerned Bangladesh's right to regulate imports and exports, a sovereign prerogative.

It concerned Bangladesh's right to regulate its natural resources, also a uniquely sovereign function. A private party could not have made such an agreement. MOL complains that this conclusion relies on the purpose of the agreement, in contradiction of the FSIA. But consideration of the special elements of export license and natural resource looks only to the nature of the agreement and does not require examination of the government's motives. In short, the licensing agreement was a sovereign act, not just a commercial transaction. Its revocation was sovereign by nature, not commercial. Bangladesh has sovereign immunity from this suit.

TEXAS TRADING & MILLING CORP. v. FEDERAL REPUBLIC OF NIGERIA
647 F.2d 300 (2d Cir. 1981)

These four appeals grow out of one of the most enormous commercial disputes in history, and present questions which strike to the very heart of the modern international economic order. An African nation, developing at breakneck speed by virtue of huge exports of high-grade oil, contracted to buy huge quantities of Portland cement, a commodity crucial to the construction of its infrastructure. It overbought, and the country's docks and harbors became clogged with ships waiting to unload. Imports of other goods ground to a halt. More vessels carrying cement arrived daily; still others were steaming toward the port. Unable to accept delivery of the cement it had bought, the nation repudiated its contracts. In response to suits brought by disgruntled suppliers, it now seeks to invoke an ancient maxim of sovereign immunity *par in parem imperium non habet* ["an equal has no dominion over an equal"] to insulate itself from liability. But Latin phrases speak with a hoary simplicity inappropriate to the modern financial world. For the ruling principles here, we must look instead to a . . . vaguely-worded statute, the Foreign Sovereign Immunities Act of 1976 ("FSIA" or "Act"), a law described by its draftsmen as providing only "very modest guidance" on issues of preeminent importance. For answers to those most difficult questions, the authors of the law "decided to put [their] faith in the U.S. courts." Guided by reason, precedent, and equity, we have attempted to give form and substance to the legislative intent. Accordingly, we find that the defense of sovereign immunity is not available in any of these four cases. . . .

The facts of the four appeals are remarkably parallel, and can be stated in somewhat consolidated form. Early in 1975, the Federal Military Government of the Federal Republic of Nigeria ("Nigeria") embarked on an ambitious program to purchase immense amounts of cement. We have already had occasion in another case to call the program "incredible," but the statistics speak for themselves. Nigeria executed 109 contracts, with 68 suppliers. It purchased, in all, over sixteen million metric tons of cement. The price was close to one billion dollars. Four of the 109 contracts were made with American companies that were plaintiffs below in the cases now before us [including Texas Trading & Milling Corp. ("Texas Trading")] . . . .

In short, performance under the contracts was to proceed as follows. Nigeria was to establish letters of credit. The suppliers were to ship cement. Each time a supplier had loaded a ship and insured its cargo to Lagos/Apapa, the supplier could take documents so proving to the bank named in the contract and, "at sight," be paid for the amount of cement it shipped. The ship might sink on the way to Nigeria, or it might never leave the Spanish port at all, but on presentation of proper documents showing a loaded ship and an insured cargo, the supplier had a right to be paid. Demurrage was to operate in the same manner: if a ship was detained in Nigerian waters, the supplier would receive certain documents. It could present the documents to the bank, and receive payment.

After receiving notice that the letters of credit had been established, the suppliers set out to secure subcontracts to procure the cement, and shipping contracts to transport it. They, through their subcontractors, began to bag the cement and load it on ships, as suppliers across the globe were doing the same. Hundreds of ships arrived in Lagos/Apapa in the summer of 1975, and most were carrying cement. Nigeria's port facilities could accept only one to five million tons of cement per year; at any rate, they could not begin to unload the over sixteen million tons Nigeria had slated for delivery in eighteen short months. Based on prior experience, Nigeria had made the contracts expecting only twenty percent of the suppliers to be able to perform. By July, when the harbor held over 400 ships waiting to unload, 260 of them carrying cement, Nigeria realized it had misjudged the market considerably.

With demurrage piling up at astronomical rates, and suppliers, hiring, loading, and dispatching more ships daily, Nigeria decided to act. On August 9, 1975, Nigeria caused its Ports Authority to issue Government Notice No. 1434, a regulation which stated that, effective August 18, all ships destined for Lagos/Apapa would be required to convey to the Ports Authority, two months before sailing, certain information concerning their time of arrival in the port. The regulation also stated vaguely that the Ports Authority would "co-ordinate all sailing," and that it would "refus[e] service" to vessels which did not comply with the regulation. Then, on August 18, Nigeria cabled its suppliers and asked them to stop sending cement, and to cease loading or even chartering ships. In late September, Nigeria took the crucial step: Central Bank instructed Morgan [Guaranty Trust Company] not to pay under the letters of credit unless the supplier submitted in addition to the documents required by the letter of credit as written a statement from Central Bank that payment ought to be made. Morgan notified each supplier of Nigeria's instructions, and Morgan commenced refusing to make payment under the letters of credit as written. Almost three months later, on December 19, 1975, Nigeria promulgated Decree No. 40, a law prohibiting entry into a Nigerian port to any ship which had not secured two months' prior approval, and imposing criminal penalties for unauthorized entry.

Nigeria's unilateral alteration of the letters of credit took place on a scale previously unknown to international commerce. Officers of Morgan explained the potential consequences of Nigeria's action to representatives of Central Bank; Central Bank was adamant that Morgan not pay. After a meeting with Central Bank personnel, one Morgan officer stated that Central Bank's

Deputy Governor "responded that the [Nigerian] Government was willing to go to court if we did pay." Within weeks of Nigeria's instructions to Morgan not to pay without the additional documentation, Morgan warned Central Bank in a telex: "We believe that there is an increasing possibility that litigation against you may be instituted in New York."

Nigeria's next step was to invite its suppliers to cancel the contracts. As part of the program, Nigeria convened a meeting at Morgan's offices in New York, to discuss Nigeria's position with members of the American financial community. Over forty suppliers eventually did settle. Nigeria asked Morgan to effect several of the settlement payments; some were for settling with suppliers not located in the United States.

Cement suppliers who did not settle sued in courts all over the world. . . . The complaints alleged that Central Bank's September instructions to Morgan, changing the terms of payment under the letters of credit, constituted anticipatory breaches of both the cement contracts (requiring Nigeria to establish "irrevocable" letters of credit with certain terms of payment) and the letters of credit (requiring Central Bank to authorize payment when certain documents were presented to Morgan). Defendants do not seriously dispute that their actions constitute such anticipatory breaches; their defenses go more to the propriety of jurisdiction under the FSIA. . . .

In structure, the FSIA is a marvel of compression. Within the bounds of a few tersely-worded sections, it purports to provide answers to three crucial questions in a suit against a foreign state: the availability of sovereign immunity as a defense, the presence of subject matter jurisdiction over the claim, and the propriety of personal jurisdiction over the defendant. Through a series of intricately coordinated provisions, the FSIA seems at first glance to make the answer to one of the questions, subject matter jurisdiction, dispositive of all three. This economy of decision has come, however, at the price of considerable confusion in the district courts. In fact, Congress intended the sovereign immunity and subject matter jurisdiction decisions to remain slightly distinct, and it drafted the Act accordingly. Moreover, Congress has only an incomplete power to tie personal jurisdiction to subject matter jurisdiction; its prerogatives are constrained by the due process clause. These cases present an opportunity to untie the FSIA's Gordian knot, and to vindicate the Congressional purposes behind the Act.

Before undertaking the threshold "commercial activity" analysis, our first task is to identify what particular conduct in this case is relevant. Subsection 1603(d) states that "commercial activity" might consist of either "a regular course of commercial conduct" or "a particular commercial transaction or act." The words "regular course of conduct" seem to authorize courts to cast the net wide, and to identify a broad series of acts as the relevant set of activities. Here, the relevant "course of conduct" is undoubtedly Nigeria's massive cement purchase program. Alternatively, each of its contracts or letters of credit with these four plaintiffs would qualify as "a particular transaction."

The determination of whether particular behavior is "commercial" is perhaps the most important decision a court faces in an FSIA suit. This problem is significant because the primary purpose of the Act is to "restrict" the immunity of a foreign state to suits involving a foreign state's public acts. If the activity is not "commercial," it satisfies none of the three clauses of § 1605(a)(2), and the foreign state is (at least under that subsection) immune from suit. Unfortunately, the definition of "commercial" is the one issue on which the Act provides almost no guidance at all. Subsection 1603(d) advances the inquiry somewhat, for it provides: "The commercial character of an activity shall be determined by reference to the nature of the course of conduct or particular transaction or act, rather than by reference to its purpose." No provision of the Act, however, defines "commercial." Congress deliberately left the meaning open and, as noted above, "put [its] faith in the U.S. courts to work out progressively, on a case-by-case basis the distinction between commercial and governmental." We are referred to no less than three separate sources of authority to resolve this fundamental definitional question.

The first source is statements contained in the legislative history itself. Perhaps the clearest of them was made by then Chief of the Foreign Litigation Section of the Civil Division, Department of Justice: "If a government enters into a contract to purchase goods and services, that is considered a commercial activity. It avails itself of the ordinary contract machinery. It bargains and negotiates. It accepts an offer. It enters into a written contract and the contract is to be performed." The House Report seems to conclude that a contract or series of contracts for the purchase of goods would be *per se* a "commercial activity," and the illustrations cited by experts who testified on the bill — contracts, for example, for the sale of army boots or grain — support such a rule. Or, put another way, if the activity is one in which a private person could engage, it is not entitled to immunity.

The second source for interpreting the phrase "commercial activity" is the "very large body of case law which exist[ed]" in American law upon passage of the Act in 1976. Testifying on an earlier version of the bill, then Legal Adviser of the Department of State, stated:

> [T]he restrictive theory of sovereign immunity from jurisdiction, which has been followed by the Department of State and the courts since it was articulated in the familiar letter of Acting Legal Adviser Jack B. Tate of May 29, 1952, would be incorporated into statutory law. This theory limits immunity to public acts, leaving so-called private acts subject to suit. The proposed legislation would make it clear that immunity cannot be claimed with respect to acts or transactions that are commercial in nature, regardless of their underlying purpose. . . .

Finally, current standards of international law concerning sovereign immunity add content to the "commercial activity" phrase of the FSIA. Section 1602 of the Act, entitled "Findings and declaration of purpose," contains a cryptic reference to international law, but fails wholly to adopt it. The legislative history states that the Act "incorporates standards recognized under international law," and the drafters seem to have intended rather generally to bring American sovereign immunity practice into line with that of other nations. At this point, there can be little doubt that international law follows the restrictive theory of sovereign immunity.

Under each of these three standards, Nigeria's cement contracts and letters of credit qualify as "commercial activity." Lord Denning, writing in *Trendtex Trading Corp. v. Central Bank of Nigeria*, (1977) 2 W.L.R. 356, 369, 1 All E.R.

881, with his usual erudition and clarity, stated: "If a government department goes into the market places of the world and buys boots or cement as a commercial transaction that government department should be subject to all the rules of the marketplace." Nigeria's activity here is in the nature of a private contract for the purchase of goods. Its purpose to build roads, army barracks, whatever is irrelevant. Accordingly, courts in other nations have uniformly held Nigeria's 1975 cement purchase program and appurtenant letters of credit to be "commercial activity," and have denied the defense of sovereign immunity. We find defendants' activity here to constitute "commercial activity," and we move on to the next step of analysis.

We need look no further than the third clause of § 1605(a)(2) to find statutory subject matter jurisdiction here. That clause provides: "A foreign state shall not be immune in any case in which the action is based upon an act outside the territory of the United States in connection with a commercial activity of the foreign state elsewhere and that act causes a direct effect in the United States." The focus of our analysis is to determine whether "the act cause[d] a direct effect in the United States" within the meaning of the FSIA. . . .[1] The "direct effect" clause has been the subject of considerable commentary, but remains somewhat abstruse. The House Report, for example, states only that the direct effect clause "would subject [commercial] conduct [abroad] to the exercise of jurisdiction by the United States consistent with principles set forth in section 18, Restatement of the Law, Second, Foreign Relations Law of the United States (1965)." The reference is a bit of a *non sequitur,* since § 18 concerns the extent to which substantive American law may be applied to conduct overseas, not the proper extraterritorial jurisdictional reach of American courts *n'importe quelle* substantive law. . . .[2] We are left with the words, "direct effect in the United States," and with Congress's broad mandate in passing the FSIA: "Under section 1605(a)(2), no act of a foreign state, tortious or not, which is connected with the commercial

---

[1] We need not belabor the point that the specific act or acts upon which these suits are based the anticipatory repudiation of the cement contracts and letters of credit took place at least in part "outside the territory of the United States." It was from Nigeria that Central Bank sent the instructions amending the letters of credit; it was in Nigeria that Nigeria instructed Central Bank to do so. Congress in writing the FSIA did not intend to incorporate into modern law every ancient sophistry concerning "where" an act or omission occurs. Conduct crucial to modern commerce — telephone calls, telexes, electronic transfers of intangible debits and credits — can take place in several jurisdictions. Outmoded rules placing such activity "in" one jurisdiction or another are not helpful here.

Moreover, should defendants establish that the "act" or "commercial activity" the action is "based upon" took place not "outside the territory of the United States" but inside it, then the first or second clauses of § 1605(a)(2) might become relevant. We need not decide the question. Given Congress's broad approach in the language of § 1605(a)(2), it is not at all improbable that a suit could be brought under more than one clause. . . . Moving to the second phrase of the clause, we have little doubt that the acts these actions are "based upon" were "in connection" with defendants' commercial activity. Breach of an agreement is necessarily performed "in connection with" that agreement, or with a series of similar agreements.

[2] As a result, certain limitations built into the text of § 18, such as the requirement that the "direct effect" be "substantial" or "foreseeable," are not necessarily apposite to the direct effect clause of § 1605(a)(2). To the extent the substantiality and foreseeability requirements of the legislative reach cases are designed to minimize unnecessary conflict between United States and foreign substantive law, 28 U.S.C. § 1606 renders the requirements irrelevant, since it implies that federal substantive law will not always govern in FSIA cases.

activities of a foreign state would give rise to immunity if the act takes place in the United States or has a direct effect within the United States."

Fortunately, a certain amount of case law interprets both components of the problematic phrase: "direct" and "in the United States." For a paradigm of "direct," we look to the vivid examples of *Harris v. VAO Intourist, Moscow*, 481 F. Supp. 1056 (E.D.N.Y. 1979), and *Upton v. Empire of Iran*, 459 F. Supp. 264 (D.D.C. 1978), *aff'd mem.*, 607 F.2d 494 (D.C.Cir. 1979). In *Harris*, a man lost his life in a hotel fire; in *Upton*, a man was injured when the roof of a building collapsed on him. Both men undoubtedly suffered "direct" effects.

Applying the term to a corporation is not so simple. Unlike a natural person, a corporate entity is intangible; it cannot be burned or crushed. It can only suffer financial loss. Accordingly, the relevant inquiry under the direct effect clause when plaintiff is a corporation is whether the corporation has suffered a "direct" financial loss. To discover whether breach of a contract causes this type of loss, we look to *Carey v. National Oil Corp.*, 592 F.2d 673, 676–77 (2d Cir. 1979) (*per curiam*). In *Carey*, we decided that a direct effect can arise not only from a tort, *e. g., Harris* and *Upton*, *supra*, but from cancellation of a contract for the sale of oil as well. Here, under either theory of recovery, breach of the cement contracts or breach of the letters of credit, the effect of the suppliers was "direct." They were beneficiaries of the contracts that were breached.

Finally, the most difficult aspect of the direct effect clause concerns its phrase, "in the United States." State law abounds with decisions locating "effects" for personal jurisdiction purposes. But those cases are not precisely on point, for they are concerned more with federalism, and less with international relations, than was Congress in passing the FSIA. Reliance on state cases is not necessary here because the financial loss in these cases occurred "in the United States" for two much simpler reasons. First, the cement suppliers were to present documents and collect money in the United States, and the breaches precluded their doing so. Second, each of the plaintiffs is an American corporation. Whether a failure to pay a foreign corporation in the United States or to pay an American corporation overseas creates an effect "in the United States" under § 1605(a)(2) is not before us. Both factors are present here, and the subsection is clearly satisfied.

The foregoing analysis demonstrates that neither "direct" nor "in the United States" is a term susceptible of easy definition. A corporation is no more than a series of conduits, filtering profit or loss through each stage from the company's customers to its shareholders, who may themselves be fictional entities as well. Harm to any component is somewhat "indirect," and locating the site of the injury, especially when the harm consists in an omission, is an enterprise fraught with artifice. Courts construing either term should be mindful more of Congress's concern with providing "access to the courts" to those aggrieved by the commercial acts of a foreign sovereign, than with cases defining "direct" or locating effects under state statutes passed for dissimilar purposes. Before the FSIA, plaintiffs enjoyed a broad right to bring suits against foreign states, subject only to State Department intervention and the presence of attachable assets. Congress, in the FSIA, certainly did not intend significantly to constrict jurisdiction; it intended to regularize it. The question is, was the effect sufficiently "direct" and sufficiently "in the United States" that Congress would have wanted an American court to hear the case? No rigid parsing of § 1605(a)(2) should lose sight of that purpose. We have no doubt that Congress intended to bring suits like these into American courts, and we hold that statutory subject matter jurisdiction here exists. [The court's analysis of the constitutional limits on the exercise of personal jurisdiction is deleted.]

Our rulings today vindicate more than Congressional intent. They affirm the right of all participants in the marketplace of the world to be treated as equals, and to ascribe to principles of trade which found their birth in the law merchant, centuries ago. Corporations can enter contracts without fear that the defense of sovereign immunity will be inequitably interposed, and foreign states can bargain without paying a premium required by a trader in anticipation of a judgment-proof client. Commerce is fostered, and all interests are advanced. . . .

Notes and Questions on *MOL* and *Texas Trading*

1. *MOL and Texas Trading reconciled.* How is the effective termination of the contract in *MOL* sovereign in a way that is distinguishable from the termination of any other contract that a state might conclude with a private party? Should the arguments that prevailed in *MOL* also have worked in *Texas Trading*? Would your reaction to the result in *MOL* change if it could be demonstrated that private persons could not have engaged in the sale of these particular monkeys because of a treaty banning trade in endangered species?

2. *MOL and Weltover.* Does the result in *MOL* survive the Supreme Court's decision in *Weltover*? To what extent does the result in *MOL* turn on "purpose" arguments, which are foreclosed by § 1603(d)?

3. *OPEC and the commercial activity exception.* Should the market division and price-fixing undertaken by the Organization of Petroleum Exporting Countries ("OPEC") subject its member states to the jurisdiction of the U.S. courts under § 1605(a)(2)? *See Int'l Ass'n of Machinists and Aerospace Workers v. OPEC*, 649 F.2d 1354 (9th Cir. 1981), *cert. denied*, 454 U.S. 1163 (1982), *subsequently disapproved on procedural grounds in Siderman de Blake v. Republic of Argentina*, 965 F.2d 699, 707 (9th Cir. 1992), *cert. denied*, 507 U.S. 1017 (1993), *infra*.

4. *Direct effects test.* According to the court in *Texas Trading*, "*Harris* and *Upton* involved Americans injured overseas, but since the injured parties there were natural persons, not corporations, it is easy to locate the 'effect' outside the United States. Whether an American corporation injured overseas incurs a direct effect in the United States remains an open question." We know from subsequent decisions that "mere financial loss" in the United States is not a sufficient jurisdictional effect for purposes of 1605(a)(2). What should constitute a direct effect when a U.S. corporation is injured abroad? What are the best arguments — pro and con — for a *per se* finding of sufficient effects in these circumstances?

5. *Sovereign immunity and geopolitics.* The Tate Letter was condemned by Soviet scholars of international law as a legalistic effort by the United States to counteract the growing market power of state trading companies from communist countries. For decades, debate over the sovereign immunity doctrine was a theater for East-West conflict. With the end of the Cold War, the foreign critique of the FSIA has assumed a North-South dimension, as though the sovereign immunity doctrine were being deployed specifically to constrain the economic choices of the less developed countries, especially those without oil reserves. On the basis of the cases you have read, do you see any truth to that observation? Could the defendants' imputed "good faith" in *MOL* and imputed "bad faith" in *Texas Trading* account for the difference?

6. *The commercial activity exception and human rights violations.* Human rights violations can take commercial form and may be actionable under Section 1605(a)(2). For example, in *Siderman de Blake v. Republic of Argentina,* 965 F.2d 699 (9th Cir. 1992), *cert. denied,* 507 U.S. 1017 (1993), the victims of abuse sued the government of Argentina, alleging that their commercial properties (a resort hotel and related companies) had been seized by the government as part of a campaign of repression and discrimination. Because the government had continued to operate the properties after seizure, the court had

> no doubt that the Siderman's claims are based on commercial activity being conducted by Argentina. The activities that form the basis of the claims — Argentina's continuing management of INOSA [the family business], its operation of the Hotel Gran Corona, and its receipt of profits from the company's operations — are clearly activities "of a kind in which a private party might engage."

The court also determined that there was an adequate nexus between these activities and the United States, noting *inter alia*:

> [the] evidence that Argentina advertises the Hotel Gran Corona in the United States and solicits American guests through its U.S. agent, Aerolinas Argentinas, the national airline of Argentina. [The plaintiffs] have alleged further that numerous Americans have stayed at the Hotel, which accepts all the major American credit cards, including Mastercard, Visa, and American Express. On the present record, we believe that these allegations are sufficient to demonstrate that the commercial activities Argentina is conducting through INOSA have "substantial contact with the United States."

One court — *Doe v. Unocal Corp.,* 963 F. Supp. 880 (C.D.Cal. 1997) — concluded that the Ninth Circuit's approach in *Siderman* should not survive the Supreme Court's subsequent decision in *Nelson.* On the other hand, can you think of an argument — grounded in factual distinctions between the two cases — that would allow *Siderman* to remain good law even after *Nelson*?

7. *A jurisprudential perspective.* It may be naive to expect doctrinal coherence in the decisions interpreting the commercial activity exception. Modern schools of jurisprudence across the political spectrum suggest that we no longer have some pristine or simple notion of the proper functions of government and that the distinction between public and private is constantly shifting. The FSIA offers precious little guidance for distinguishing commercial from non-commercial activity, and what guidelines exist are perhaps

better conceived as markers for argument in an adversarial setting than as markers for decision in a judicial setting. Of course, with the proliferation of decisions under § 1605(a)(2), advocates now have a substantial body of decisional law they can use by reference and by analogy, even if the principles distinguishing the results may be difficult to articulate. If anything, the open-endedness of the commercial activity exception — far from making advocacy impossible — makes it essential.

---

[b] The Waiver Exception

§ 1605. General exceptions to the jurisdictional immunity of a foreign state.

(a) A foreign state shall not be immune from the jurisdiction of courts of the United States or of the States in any case —

(1) in which the foreign state has waived its immunity either explicitly or by implication, notwithstanding any withdrawal of the waiver which the foreign state may purport to effect except in accordance with the terms of the waiver; . . .

FOREMOST-McKESSON, INC. v. ISLAMIC REPUBLIC OF IRAN
905 F.2d 438 (D.C. Cir. 1990)

[Foremost, a U.S. company, and its subsidiaries held a powerful minority interest in the Pak Dairy in Iran from 1959 to 1979, providing the dairy's top management and controlling its board of directors. Following the revolution that brought the Ayatollah Khomeini to power, Foremost's interest in the dairy was divested by various co-defendants, including by allegation the Iranian government. In January 1982, Foremost sued to recover damages for the value of its interest, allegedly in excess of $7 million. The gravamen of the complaint was that the defendants had used their "majority position to lock [Foremost] out of the management of the dairy and to deny [Foremost] its share of company earnings." In its "Answer to Complaint," Iran did not respond to the factual allegations in the complaint, nor did it raise any affirmative defenses. It did however interpose the Algiers Accords of 19 January 1981, and Executive Order 12294, 46 FED. REG. 14111 (1981), which created the Iran-U.S. Claims Tribunal at The Hague and effectively transferred commercial disputes from U.S. courts to the new tribunal for binding arbitration. Executive Order 12294 "suspended" all "claims which may be presented to the Tribunal" and provided that such claims "shall have no legal effect in any action now pending in any court of the United States."

The case came before the Iran-U.S. Claims Tribunal, which ruled partially in Foremost's favor, awarding in excess of $1.4 million — an amount that was paid out of a security account established at The Hague pursuant to other provisions of the Algiers Accords.

In April 1988, Foremost sought to recover the balance of its claimed losses, "revived" its original lawsuit,[1] and moved for summary judgment against Iran on the issue of liability, the District Court allowed Iran to amend its 1982 Answer and to file a motion to dismiss, both of which raised the issue of foreign sovereign immunity for the first time. Plaintiffs argued *inter alia* that Iran had waived its foreign sovereign immunity by failing to raise the immunity defense in its 1982 Answer and by signing a Treaty of Amity with the United States.]

Foremost argues that by filing the 1982 Answer without asserting the defense of sovereign immunity, Iran permanently waived its immunity "by implication," pursuant to 28 U.S.C. § 1605(a)(l). We cannot agree. Section l605(a)(l) provides that a foreign sovereign is not "immune from the jurisdiction of courts of the United States . . . in any case . . . in which the foreign state has waived its immunity either explicitly or by implication." Foremost is correct in asserting that, in most instances, a state's failure to assert sovereign immunity in a responsive pleading will constitute a waiver of the defense. But the situation here is different because, in 1982, Iran did not respond substantively to any of the averments in the complaint or pose any defenses to the claims; instead, Iran merely argued that the action should proceed in another forum, which it then did. Iran's actions in these circumstances did not constitute an implied waiver.

It is true that the House Report accompanying FSIA provides that "[a]n implicit waiver would . . . include a situation where a foreign state has filed a responsive pleading in an action without raising the defense of sovereign immunity." H. Rep. No. 1487, 94th Cong., 2d Sess. 18 (1976), U.S. CODE CONG. & ADMIN. NEWS 1976, pp. 6604, 6616. We agree with the Seventh Circuit, however, that the example of an implied waiver given in the legislative history — filing a responsive pleading without raising an immunity defense — demonstrates that Congress anticipated, at a minimum, that waiver would not be found absent a conscious decision to take part in the litigation and a failure to raise sovereign immunity despite the opportunity to do so. *Frolova v. Union of Soviet Socialist Republics*, 761 F.2d 370, 378 (7th Cir. 1985). Iran's 1982 Answer does not exhibit such a conscious decision or opportunity.

The 1982 Answer does not admit or deny any of the averments upon which Foremost relied; nor does it state any defenses to the claims Foremost asserted. Indeed, Iran explicitly stated in the 1982 Answer that "the action commenced by the filing of plaintiffs' complaint has no legal effect other than to toll the applicable statute of limitations" and that "no response to plaintiffs' complaint is required." As though to dispel any doubt, Iran further stated that "[t]he foregoing is without prejudice to any of defendant's rights against the United States or plaintiffs, either in this forum or before the Arbitral Tribunal." While such statements would not, in most contexts, excuse the failure to assert a defense in a responsive pleading, the circumstances of this

---

[1] The Supreme Court explained in *Dames & Moore v. Regan,* 453 U.S. 654, 684–85 (1981), that "those claims not within the jurisdiction of the Claims Tribunal will 'revive' and become judicially enforceable in United States courts."

case are unusual because of the Executive Order. Iran contended, and Foremost conceded below, that Executive Order No. 12294 did not even contemplate the filing of a responsive pleading in cases, like this one, that were referred to the Claims Tribunal under the Algiers Accords. We need not reach the issue whether the 1982 Answer is a responsive pleading for purposes of the Federal Rules of Civil Procedure. In the unusual circumstances of this case, it is clear that Iran did not make a "conscious decision to take part in the litigation" before the District Court.

Application of the implied waiver provision in the instant case would be inconsistent with the substantial precedent construing the implied waiver provision narrowly. The legislative history of FSIA gives three examples of circumstances in which courts have found implied waivers: (1) a foreign state has agreed to arbitration in another country; (2) a foreign state has agreed that the law of a particular country governs a contract; or (3) a foreign state has filed a responsive pleading in an action without raising the defense of sovereign immunity. In reviewing the case law bearing on the breadth of the implicit waiver provision, the Seventh Circuit noted that "[c]ases involving arbitration clauses illustrate that provisions allegedly waiving sovereign immunity are narrowly construed" and that the narrow construction of the implicit waiver clause is also evident in "the line of cases holding that a contract's waiver of immunity does not apply to third parties not privy to the contract." *Frolova*, 761 F.2d at 377. . . . The *Frolova* court further noted that, with regard to contract provisions, "courts rarely find that a nation has waived its sovereign immunity, particularly with respect to suits brought by third parties, without strong evidence that this is what the foreign state intended."

In rejecting the plaintiffs contention that the foreign sovereign had implicitly waived its immunity by not defending the action, the Seventh Circuit further noted that

> [t]he case law evidences a reticence to find a waiver from the nature of a foreign state's participation in litigation. For example, in *Castro v. Saudi Arabia*, 510 F. Supp. [309, 311–12 (W.D. Tex. 1980)], the court held that the defendant's failure to timely answer the complaint did not waive sovereign immunity. And in *Canadian Overseas Ores Ltd. v. Compania de Acero del Pacifico S.A.*, 727 F.2d 274, 277–78 (2d Cir. 1984), the court ruled that the district court did not err in finding that sovereign immunity was not waived, although the defendant never filed a responsive pleading but instead filed several motions which did not assert sovereign immunity, and a Rule 12(b)(1) motion to dismiss based on sovereign immunity was not filed until over two and one-half years after the complaint was filed.

Id., at 378.[2]

Finally, the mechanistic application of the implied waiver urged by Foremost would be inconsistent with the notions of "grace and comity" that

---

[2] In *Practical Concepts, Inc. v. Republic of Bolivia*, [811 F.2d 1543 (D.C. Cir. 1987),] this court concluded that, even though Bolivia's telegram acknowledging receipt of process might be an "appearance" under Federal Rule of Civil Procedure 55(b)(2), it was not an "appearance" for purposes of FSIA so as to bar Bolivia's assertion of sovereign immunity for the first time in its objection to a default judgment.

underlie the statutory scheme. In effecting these underlying policy concerns, this court noted in *Practical Concepts* that "[i]ntolerant adherence to default judgments against foreign states could adversely affect this nation's relations with other nations and 'undermine the State Department's continuing efforts to encourage. . . foreign sovereigns generally[] to resolve disputes within the United States' legal framework.'" 811 F.2d at 1551 n. 19 (quoting Brief for the United States as Amicus Curiae). In this regard, the District Court "speculate[d] that an intolerant elevation of form over substance in this case, by deeming Iran's original 'answer' to have waived the defense of sovereign immunity, will almost certainly undermine the confidence of foreign states in the fairness of our legal system." We agree.

On the record before us, we conclude that the District Court properly permitted Iran to amend the 1982 Answer to include the defense of sovereign immunity. . . .

Foremost [also] claims that, under the Treaty of Amity, Iran waived its sovereign immunity as to suits arising out of commercial activity in which it is involved. Thus, according to Foremost, there is no jurisdictional issue to be addressed under FSIA. We cannot agree. Two sections of the Foreign Sovereign Immunities Act bear on consideration of the effect of the Treaty of Amity: sections 1604 and 1605(a)(1). Section 1604 of FSIA provides:

> Subject to existing international agreements to which the United States is a party at the time of enactment of this Act a foreign state shall be immune from the jurisdiction of the courts of the United States and of the States except as provided in sections 1605 to 1607 of this chapter.

"This exception [to FSIA] applies when international agreements 'expressly conflic[t]' with the immunity provisions of the FSIA." *Argentine Republic v. Amerada Hess Shipping Corp.*, 488 U.S. 428 (1989). The Supreme Court found no such express conflict where the international conventions "set forth substantive rules of conduct" and did "not create private rights of action for foreign corporations to recover compensation from foreign states in United States courts." *Id.* Article IV of the Treaty of Amity sets forth such substantive provisions, and hence does not pose a bar to application of FSIA. . . .[3]

---

[3] Article IV of the Treaty of Amity provides, in relevant part:

1. Each High Contracting Party shall at all times accord fair and equitable treatment to nationals and companies of the other High Contracting Party, and to their property and enterprises; shall refrain from applying unreasonable or discriminatory measures that would impair their legally acquired rights and interests; and shall assure that their lawful contractual rights are afforded effective means of enforcement, in conformity with the applicable laws.

2. Property of nationals and companies of either High Contracting Party, including interests in property, shall receive the most constant protection and security within the territories of the other High Contracting Party, in no case less than that required by international law. Such property shall not be taken except for a public purpose, nor shall it be taken without the prompt payment of just compensation. Such compensation shall be in an effectively realizable form and shall represent the full equivalent of the property taken; and adequate provision shall have been made at or prior to the time of taking for the determination and payment thereof . . . .

4. Enterprises which nationals and companies of either High Contracting Party are

In addition, pursuant to section 1605(a)(1), if the Treaty of Amity contained an explicit waiver of sovereign immunity, the foreign state would not be entitled to immunity under FSIA. However, the only express provision for waiver of sovereign immunity under the Treaty of Amity is found in Article XI, paragraph 4:

> No enterprise of either High Contracting Party, including corporations, associations, and government agencies and instrumentalities, which is publicly owned or controlled shall, if it engages in commercial, industrial, shipping or other business activities within the territories of the other High Contracting Party, claim or enjoy, either for itself or for its property, immunity therein from . . . suit.

We agree with the Ninth Circuit that this "limited waiver" "extends only to enterprises of Iran, not Iran itself" and "extends only to enterprises 'doing business' in the United States." *Berkovitz* [*v. Islamic Republic of Iran*, 735 F.2d 329 (9th Cir.), *cert. denied,* 469 U.S. 1035 (1984),] at 333. . . . In the instant case, the alleged commercial actions took place in Iran, not in the United States, and Foremost brought the action against the sovereign itself. Thus, the provisions of Article XI, paragraph 4, are not apposite and, for the purposes of the instant case, Iran did not waive its immunity in that treaty. . . .[4]

Notes and Questions on Waiver

1. *Narrowing the categories of waiver.* Each of the three types of implicit waiver identified by Congress in the legislative history of the FSIA (and cited in *Foremost*) has been litigated and narrowly interpreted.

> A. Clearly, for example, when a *foreign state files a responsive pleading*[1] *without raising the defense of sovereign immunity,* the immunity may be waived — this from the "use it or lose it" school of jurisprudence. *See, e.g., Haven v. Rzeczpospolita Polska,* 215 F.3d 727 (7th Cir. 2000). But some courts decline to make this a *per se* rule, insisting instead on additional

---

permitted to establish or acquire, within the territories of the other High Contracting Party, shall be permitted freely to conduct their activities therein, upon terms no less favorable than other enterprises of whatever nationality engaged in similar activities. Such nationals and companies shall enjoy the right to continued control and management of such enterprises; to engage attorneys, agents, accountants and other technical experts, executive personnel, interpreters and other specialized employees of their choice; and to do all other things necessary or incidental to the effective conduct of their affairs.

Treaty of Amity, Economic Relations, and Consular Rights Between the United States of American and Iran, 8 U.S.T. 899, 903–04, art. IV (1957).

[4] We do not decide here in what contexts, if any, the Treaty of Amity might constitute a waiver of immunity. We conclude only that the treaty has not effected a waiver in the instant case.

[1] Rule 7 of the Federal Rules of Civil Procedure establishes that only certain filings may be considered responsive pleadings, including a complaint, an answer, a reply to a counterclaim, an answer to a cross-claim, a third-party complaint, and a third-party answer. "No other pleading shall be allowed."

evidence that the foreign sovereign actually intended to waive the defense. In *Drexel Burnham Lambert Group, Inc. v. Committee of Receivers for Galadari,* 12 F.3d 317 (2d Cir. 1993), for example, the court ruled that the foreign defendant's failure to raise sovereign immunity immediately was not "unmistakeable" and "unambiguous." Does this additional requirement in effect convert an implicit form of waiver into an explicit form of waiver?

B. When a *foreign state agrees that the law of another country governs a contract,* the courts will routinely find a waiver of sovereign immunity. For example, the consulate of El Salvador was held to have waived sovereign immunity by signing a lease with a clause providing that "This lease shall be governed by the laws of the state where the Premises are located [i.e., California]." *Berdakin v. Consulado de la Republica de El Salvador,* 912 F. Supp. 458 (C.D. Cal. 1995). *Accord Eckert Intern., Inc. v. Government of Sovereign Democratic Republic of Fiji,* 32 F.3d 77 (4th Cir. 1994) (contract with choice of law provision requiring agreement to be construed according to Virginia law held an implicit waiver of foreign sovereign immunity.) But if the contract in which the choice-of-law clause appears is unrelated to the underlying cause of action, an implicit waiver is considerably harder to establish. *Gates v. Victor Fine Foods,* 54 F.3d 1457 (9th Cir.), *cert. denied,* 516 U.S. 869 (1995).

What exactly is the rationale for finding a waiver in choice-of-law clauses? Suppose the choice-of-law clause specified the application of some third country's law. Would that also ground a finding that sovereign immunity had been implicitly waived in the courts of the United States? What principle would support such a rule?

C. When a *foreign state agrees to arbitration in another country,* U.S. courts may find a waiver on the theory that the submission to arbitration implies a willingness to submit to the enforcement of any resulting award. In its original form, the FSIA allowed courts to infer waiver in these circumstances, based on a passage in the legislative history. But the courts generally declined to infer an implicit waiver of immunity to suit in U.S. courts from a contractual clause providing for arbitration in a country other than the United States. *See, e.g., Seetransport Wiking Trader v. Navimpex Centrala,* 989 F.2d 572, 577 (2d Cir. 1993). In *Amerada Hess v. Argentina, supra,* 488 U.S. at 442–43, the Supreme Court expressed similar doubts:

> [W]e [do not] see how a foreign state can waive its immunity under § 1605(a)(1) by signing an international agreement that contains no mention of a waiver of immunity to suit in United States courts or even the availability of a cause of action in the United States.

In 1988, Congress amended the statute to create an explicit exception to immunity in cases where a foreign state or sovereign entity has agreed to arbitrate a dispute and the arbitration agreement is or may be governed by a treaty signed by the United States calling for the recognition and enforcement of arbitral awards, such as the Convention on the Recognition and Enforcement of Foreign Arbitral Awards. 28 U.S.C. § 1605(a)(6).[2] *See,*

---

[2] Section 1605(a)(6): A foreign state shall not be immune from the jurisdiction of courts of the United States or of the States in any case —

e.g., U.S. Titan, Inc. v. Guangzhou Zhen Hua Shipping Co., Ltd., 241 F.3d 135 (2d Cir. 2001). The courts have declined to recognize the immunity defense and enforced not only arbitral judgments that have actually been awarded but the underlying obligation to arbitrate as well. *See, e.g., Cargill Int'l S.A. v. M/T Pavel Dybenko*, 991 F.2d 1012, 1016 (2d Cir. 1993).

2. *Implicit waivers.* Plaintiffs who attempt to find an implicit waiver in conduct other than that listed in the legislative history are fighting uphill. For example, an implicit waiver is unlikely to be found in a sovereign defendant's extensive business dealings in the United States (although the commercial activity exception might be triggered), or its submission to the tax authority of the United States, or its hiring of U.S. citizens. *See, e.g., Mendenhall v. Saudi Aramco*, 991 F. Supp. 856 (S.D. Tex. 1998). Similarly, courts are unlikely to infer a waiver from provisions of foreign sovereign entity's corporate charter stating that it could "sue and be sued" in its own domestic courts. Standing alone, that provision does not "evidence an intent on the part of the sovereign entity to waive immunity from suit in the United States." *General Elec. Capital Corp. v. Grossman*, 991 F.2d 1376, 1386 (8th Cir. 1992).

Arguments to the effect that egregious violations of international human rights law trigger a waiver have also been unsuccessful. *See, e.g., Frolova v. Union of Soviet Socialist Republics,* 761 F.2d 370, 378 (7th Cir. 1985); *Princz v. Federal Republic of Germany*, 26 F.3d 1166 (D.C. Cir.), *cert. denied,* 513 U.S. 1121 (1994). Germany's payment of reparations to a Holocaust survivor who was a U.S. citizen did not constitute an implied waiver. *Sampson v. Federal Republic of Germany*, 975 F. Supp. 1108 (N.D. Ill. 1997). What is the most convincing rationale for depriving plaintiffs of their day in court in these cases?

3. *Waivers by treaty.* As *Amerada Hess, Foremost,* and *U.S. Titan, supra,* suggest, sovereign immunity may be waived by treaty, but the courts have stated this principle more often than they have applied it. Only treaties like arbitration conventions and treaties of amity and commerce that explicitly mention sovereign immunity or that create (or imply) causes of action in U.S. courts have been interpreted as waivers. In *Greenpeace v. France*, 946 F. Supp. 773 (C.D. Cal. 1996), for example, an environmental group attempted to sue France for the seizure of certain U.S. flag vessels, claiming that the seizures

---

(6) in which the action is brought, either to enforce an agreement made by the foreign state with or for the benefit of a private party to submit to arbitration all or any differences which have arisen or which may arise between the parties with respect to a defined legal relationship, whether contractual or not, concerning a subject matter capable of settlement by arbitration under the laws of the United States, or to confirm an award made pursuant to such an agreement to arbitrate, if . . . (B) the agreement or award is or may be governed by a treaty or other international agreement in force for the United States calling for the recognition and enforcement of arbitral awards . . .

Section 1605(a)(6) is textually separate from the waiver provision of § 1605(a)(l), but the courts will occasionally address the arbitration and waiver exceptions together, especially if the foreign sovereign is not a party to an arbitration agreement. *See Davis v. Yemen*, 218 F.3d 1292 (11th Cir. 2000), *infra. Cf.* RESTATEMENT (THIRD) OF FOREIGN RELATIONS LAW § 456(2)(b) ("Under the law of the United States, . . . *an agreement to arbitrate is a waiver* of immunity from jurisdiction in (i) an action or other proceeding to compel arbitration pursuant to the agreement; and (ii) an action to enforce an arbitral award rendered pursuant to the agreement. . . .") (emphasis supplied).

violated France's treaty obligation not to interfere with the freedom of vessels sailing on the high seas. Acknowledging that France had explicitly agreed to abide by its international obligations under the United Nations Convention on the Law of the Sea, the court ruled that nothing in the treaty contemplated lawsuits in the United States or amounted to a waiver of sovereign immunity. Similarly, in *Haven v. Rzeczpospolita Polska* , 215 F.3d 727 (7th Cir. 2000), Poland was held not to have waived its sovereign immunity when it entered into a treaty with United States by which it agreed to compensate United States nationals for property it seized after World War II, given that the text of the treaty contained no mention of sovereign immunity and did not create a cause of action in United States courts. For an example of a treaty provision that might qualify as a waiver of immunity in U.S. courts, see Treaty of Friendship, Commerce and Navigation between the United States and Ireland, 1 U.S.T. 785, T.I.A.S. No. 2155, at article XV(3):

> No enterprise of either Party which is publicly owned or controlled shall, if it engages in commercial, manufacturing, processing, shipping or other business activities within the territories of the other Party, claim or enjoy, either for itself or for its property, immunity therein from taxation, suit, execution of judgment or other liability to which privately owned and controlled enterprises are subject therein.

On the basis of *Foremost*, what facts must a case present before this provision will be interpreted so as to defeat a claim of foreign sovereign immunity? What is the argument that this treaty provision is actually superfluous?

---

[c] The Tort Exception

§ 1605. General exceptions to the jurisdictional immunity of a foreign state

(a) A foreign state shall not be immune from the jurisdiction of courts of the United States or of the States in any case —

(5) not otherwise encompassed in paragraph (2) above [the commercial activity exception], in which money damages are sought against a foreign state for personal injury or death, or damage to or loss of property, occurring in the United States and caused by the tortious act or omission of that foreign state or of any official or employee of that foreign state while acting within the scope of his office or employment; except this paragraph shall not apply to

(A) any claim based upon the exercise or performance or the failure to exercise or perform a discretionary function regardless of whether the discretion be abused, or

(B) any claim arising out of malicious prosecution, abuse of process, libel, slander, misrepresentation, deceit, or interference with contract rights; . . .

LETELIER v. REPUBLIC OF CHILE
488 F. Supp. 665 (D.D.C. 1980)

[Orlando Letelier (once the Chilean Ambassador to the United States and subsequently a prominent critic of the Pinochet regime), and two companions, Michael and Ronni Moffitt, were driving to work in Washington, D.C. in September 1976, when a bomb planted under the driver's seat was detonated, killing both Letelier and Ronni Moffitt and seriously injuring Michael Moffitt. Plaintiffs allege that the bomb was built, planted, and detonated by Chilean agents, "acting in concert and purportedly at the direction and with the aid of defendants Republic of Chile, its intelligence organ, the Centro Nacional de Intelligencia (CNI) (formerly Direccion de Intelligencia Nacional, a/k/a DINA)." The Republic of Chile argued that the court lacked subject matter jurisdiction under the Foreign Sovereign Immunities Act.]

. . . [T]he Foreign Sovereign Immunities Act, . . . like all other statutory enactments regulating the subject matter jurisdiction of the federal district courts, delimits the boundaries within which the jurisdictional power of this Court can be exercised. . . . [T]he Act very broadly confers original jurisdiction upon federal district courts to hear any nonjury civil action against a foreign state, thereby encompassing the action plaintiffs now seek to prosecute against the Republic of Chile. The matter does not end there, however, for this jurisdictional grant is qualified in that it has been made subject to any proper interposition of the defense of sovereign immunity, a defense upon which the defendant places its greatest reliance.[1]

As a doctrine of international law requiring that, under the proper circumstances, a domestic court will relinquish jurisdiction over a foreign state, sovereign immunity first was recognized in American law in the early nineteenth century by Chief Justice Marshall in *The Schooner Exchange v. M'Faddon*, 11 U.S. (7 Cranch) 116 (1812), in which a foreign entity's plea of immunity, as supported by the executive branch, was found to be valid as within the general law and practice of nations. By this century, however, the judicial reliance upon general principles of international law to decide questions involving sovereign immunity began to give way to a deference to the practices and policies of the Department of State, as articulated in the suggestions of immunity presented to the courts by the department. As was most fully articulated in 1952 in a letter from Jack Tate, Legal Adviser to the State Department, to the Attorney General, the department's policy was to render a suggestion of immunity only in those restricted instances in which

---

[1] In addressing the question of the procedure for raising the defense of sovereign immunity, both the House and Senate committee reports concerning the Foreign Sovereign Immunities Act state that "sovereign immunity is an affirmative defense which must be specially pleaded." In this instance the Republic of Chile, while not having entered a formal appearance through counsel or having filed a responsive pleading through an accredited representative, has had the Department of State transmit to the Court a diplomatic note from the Ministry of Foreign Affairs and a note from the Embassy of Chile in which the issues of the Court's jurisdiction and Chile's sovereign immunity have been discussed. The extent to which the affirmative defense of sovereign immunity can be raised by way of such a procedure rather than by a formal appearance or the filing of a pleading is one that the Court need not answer definitively, for even assuming it has been pleaded properly, the Court still has subject matter jurisdiction for the reasons discussed *infra*.

the acts of a friendly foreign state were of a public or sovereign nature (*jure imperii*) rather than being simply private or commercial (*jure gestionis*).

The distinction between a state's public actions and its private or commercial activities was found to be one that often was easier to proclaim than to apply. The determination of the executive about what constituted a public, as opposed to a private or commercial act, frequently was subject to diplomatic rather than strictly legal considerations, thereby resulting in suggestions of immunity that were not in conformity with the policy articulated in the Tate letter. Moreover, even in those instances when executive suggestions were not involved, there was a lack of uniform judicial interpretation.

It is against this background that the Congress considered and enacted the Foreign Sovereign Immunities Act of 1976. As is made clear both in the Act and in its legislative history, one of its principal purposes was to reduce the foreign policy implications of sovereign immunity determinations and assure litigants that such crucial decisions are made on purely legal grounds, an aim that was to be accomplished by transferring responsibility for such a decision from the executive branch to the judiciary. In addition, the Act itself is designed to codify the restrictive principle of sovereign immunity that makes a foreign state amenable to suit for the consequences of its commercial or private, as opposed to public acts.

In considering the related questions of jurisdiction and sovereign immunity under the Act, one court has observed:

> The Act's central feature is its specification of categories of actions for which foreign states are not entitled to claim the sovereign immunity from American court jurisdiction otherwise granted to such states. These exceptions are contained not in the sections of the Act which describe the grounds on which jurisdiction may be obtained, however, but are phrased as substantive acts for which foreign states may be found liable by American courts. This effects an identity between substance and procedure in the Act which means that a court faced with a claim of immunity from jurisdiction must engage ultimately in a close examination of the underlying cause of action in order to decide whether the plaintiff may obtain jurisdiction over the defendant.

Yessenin-Volpin v. Novosti Press Agency, 443 F. Supp. 849, 851 (S.D.N.Y. 1978). In the instant action, relying on section 1605(a)(5) as their basis for combatting any assertion of sovereign immunity, plaintiffs have set forth several tortious causes of action arising under international law, the common law, the Constitution, and legislative enactments, all of which are alleged to spring from the deaths of Orlando Letelier and Ronni Moffitt. The Republic of Chile, while vigorously contending that it was in no way involved in the events that resulted in the two deaths, further asserts that, even if it were, the Court has no subject matter jurisdiction in that it is entitled to immunity under the Act, which does not cover political assassinations because of their public, governmental character.

As supportive of its conclusion that political, tortious acts of a government are to be excluded, the Republic of Chile makes reference to the reports of the House and the Senate Judiciary Committees with regard to the Act, in which it was stated: "Section 1605(a)(5) is directed primarily at the problem of traffic accidents but is cast in general terms as applying to all tort actions for money damages. . . . The purpose of section 1605(a)(5) is to permit the victim of a traffic accident or other noncommercial tort to maintain an action against a foreign state to the extent otherwise provided by law." It is clear from these passages, the Chilean government asserts, that the intent of Congress was to include only private torts like automobile accidents within the exclusion from immunity embodied in section 1605(a)(5).

Prominently absent from defendant's analysis, however, is the initial step in any endeavor at statutory interpretation: a consideration of the words of the statute. Subject to the exclusion of these discretionary acts defined in subsection (A) and the specific causes of action enumerated in subsection (B), neither of which have been invoked by the Republic of Chile, by the plain language of section 1605(a)(5), a foreign state is not entitled to immunity from an action seeking money damages "for personal injury or death . . . caused by the tortious act or omission of that foreign state" or its officials or employees. Nowhere is there an indication that the tortious acts to which the Act makes reference are to only be those formerly classified as "private," thereby engrafting onto the statute, as the Republic of Chile would have the Court do, the requirement that the character of a given tortious act be judicially analyzed to determine whether it was of the type heretofore denoted as *jure gestionis* or should be classified as *jure imperii*. Indeed, the other provisions of the Act mandate that the Court not do so, for it is made clear that the Act and the principles it sets forth in its specific provisions are henceforth to govern all claims of sovereign immunity by foreign states.

Although the unambiguous language of the Act makes inquiry almost unnecessary, further examination reveals nothing in its legislative history that contradicts or qualifies its plain meaning. The relative frequency of automobile accidents and their potentially grave financial impact may have placed that problem foremost in the minds of Congress, but the applicability of the Act was not so limited, for the committees made it quite clear that the Act "is cast in general terms as applying to all tort actions for money damages" so as to provide recompense for "the victim of a traffic accident or other noncommercial tort." Further, any notion that the Congress wished the courts to go outside the scheme promulgated by legislative action to determine the extent to which the defense of sovereign immunity could be invoked is foreclosed by the committee reports that not only state that "[t]his bill . . . sets forth the sole and exclusive standard to be used in resolving questions of sovereign immunity raised by foreign states before Federal and State courts in the United States," but also provide that the burden of proof shall be upon the foreign state to present evidence "that the plaintiffs claim relates to a public act of the foreign state[,] that is, an act not within the exceptions in section 1605–1607." Thus, it is apparent that the terms of section 1605(a)(5) set the sole standard under which any claim of sovereign immunity must be examined. . . .

Examining then the specific terms of section 1605(a)(5), despite the Chilean failure to have addressed the issue, the Court is called upon to consider whether either of the exceptions to liability for tortious acts found in section 1605(a)(5) applies in this instance. It is readily apparent, however, that the claims herein did not arise "out of malicious prosecution, abuse of process, libel, slander, misrepresentation, deceit, or interference with contract rights," 28 U.S.C. § 1605(a)(5)(B), and therefore only the exemption for claims "based upon the exercise or performance or the failure to exercise or perform a discretionary function regardless of whether the discretion be abused," § 1605(a)(5)(A), can be applicable.

As its language and the legislative history make apparent, the discretionary act exemption of subsection (A) corresponds to the discretionary act exception found in the Federal Tort Claims Act. As defined by the United States Supreme Court in interpreting the Federal Tort Claims Act, an act that is discretionary is one in which "there is room for policy judgment and decision." *Dalehite v. United States*, 346 U.S. 15, 36 (1953). Applying this definition to the instant action, the question becomes, would the alleged determination of the Chilean Republic to set into motion and assist in the precipitation of those events that culminated in the deaths of Orlando Letelier and Ronni Moffitt be of the kind in which there is "room for policy judgment and decision."

While it seems apparent that a decision calculated to result in injury or death to a particular individual or individuals, made for whatever reason, would be one most assuredly involving policy judgment and decision and thus exempt as a discretionary act under section 1605(a)(5)(A), that exception is not applicable to bar this suit. As it has been recognized, there is no discretion to commit, or to have one's officers or agents commit, an illegal act. Whatever policy options may exist for a foreign country, it has no "discretion" to perpetrate conduct designed to result in the assassination of an individual or individuals, action that is clearly contrary to the precepts of humanity as recognized in both national and international law. Accordingly there would be no "discretion" within the meaning of section 1605(a)(5)(A) to order or to aid in an assassination and were it to be demonstrated that a foreign state has undertaken any such act in this country, that foreign state could not be accorded sovereign immunity under subsection (A) for any tort claims resulting from its conduct. As a consequence, the Republic of Chile cannot claim sovereign immunity under the Foreign Sovereign Immunities Act for its alleged involvement in the deaths of Orlando Letelier and Ronni Moffitt.

Notes and Questions on *Letelier*

1. *International law exception?* Did the judge in *Letelier* create an exception to sovereign immunity for violations of international law? If so, does the case survive *Amerada Hess*? If the judge did not create such an exception, what exactly is the relevance of international law to the result?

2. *Jurisdiction versus enforcement.* Winning a case and collecting a judgment can be two radically different things, as the *Letelier* action demonstrates. *See* 28 U.S.C. §§ 1609–10, and the materials below on execution.

3. *The situs of a tort.* One of the recurring litigated issues under the tort exception is the situs requirement: which parts of the tort must occur in the United States before the exception is triggered? The following cases offer two contrasting approaches to that issue.

IN RE SEDCO, INC.
543 F. Supp. 561 (S.D. Tex. 1982)

The 1979 IXTOC I well disaster in the Bay of Campeche [in which the Mexican national petroleum company, in the course of drilling for oil, created a massive and deadly spill,] has produced a tangle of litigation. Before the Court, at this time, is a series of jurisdictional issues which must be untangled before discovery on the merits can begin. . . . Petroleos Mexicanos (Pemex), which is both a direct defendant to certain private and public plaintiffs and a third party defendant to claims asserted by Sedco, has moved to be dismissed from all claims on the basis of the grant of sovereign immunity provided by the Foreign Sovereign Immunity Act (FSIA). By asserting this motion, Pemex alleges that this Court lacks jurisdiction to hear claims based upon acts purportedly done in its capacity as a foreign sovereign. The issues raised by such a motion strike to the very heart of the international nature of the IXTOC I disaster. . . .

Petroleos Mexicanos was created in 1938 as a decentralized governmental agency charged with the exploration and development of Mexico's hydrocarbon resources. Unlike in the United States, the government of Mexico owns its country's natural resources, in particular, its hydrocarbon deposits. The Regulatory Law passed pursuant to the Mexican Constitution specifically creates a national oil company, Pemex, to implement the National Development Plan for hydrocarbon resources. Pemex is not privately owned and is governed by a council (Consejo de Administracion) composed of Presidential appointees. Decisions made by the governing council are made in furtherance of Mexican National policy concerning its Petroleum resources.

Beyond a doubt, Pemex is a "foreign state" as contemplated by § 1603(a) of the FSIA. . . .

[The court first determined that the commercial activity exception did not apply to this case, declaring that "Pemex was not engaged in commercial activity as contemplated by Congress in the FSIA when the IXTOC I well was drilled. . . . Because the nature of Pemex's act in determining the extent of Mexico's natural resources was uniquely sovereign, this Court finds that the commercial activity exception to the FSIA, § 1605(a)(2), is inapplicable to the facts presented by this case."]

Alternatively, it is urged that this Court exercise jurisdiction over Pemex under the "noncommercial tort" exception to the FSIA, § 1605(a)(5). . . . For jurisdiction to exist, the following must be shown: (1) a noncommercial act by the foreign state; (2) causing personal injury or damages to, or loss of property; and (3) that the claim is not based upon the exercise of a discretionary function, or upon libel, slander, misrepresentation, or interference with contract rights.

Section 1605(a)(5) is silent with respect to where the noncommercial tort must occur for jurisdiction to exist. Plaintiffs argue the tort may occur, in whole or in part, in the United States, and that the tort occurs in the United States if the acts or omissions directly affect this country. This argument may be correct in other circumstances; however, legislative history appears to reject this theory with respect to the FSIA. In describing the purpose of § 1605(a)(5), the House Committee Report accompanying the House Bill, which ultimately became the FSIA, states:

> [The non-commercial tort exception] denies immunity as to claims for personal injury or death, or for damage to or loss of property caused by the tortious act or omission of a foreign state or its officials or employees, acting within the scope of their authority; *the tortious act or omission must occur within the jurisdiction of the United States. . . .*

House Report, *supra* at 6619 (emphasis added). The primary purpose of this exception is to cover the problem of traffic accidents by embassy and governmental officials in this country. While the exception does extend generally to all noncommercial torts committed in this country, *see Letelier v. Republic of Chile*, 488 F. Supp. 665, 672 (D.D.C. 1980), this Court finds that the tort, in whole, must occur in the United States. The alleged acts or omissions made the basis of this lawsuit all took place in Mexico or its territorial waters in the Bay of Campeche, and § 1605(a)(5) is, therefore, inapplicable.

Notwithstanding the fact that the tort did not occur wholly within the United States, the acts complained of were discretionary in nature, done in furtherance of Pemex' legal mandate to explore for Mexico's hydrocarbon deposits. Discretionary acts by a sovereign are specifically immunized from suit under the FSIA. The language of this exemption and its legislative history demonstrate that it parallels the discretionary act exception to the Federal Tort Claims Act, 28 U.S.C. § 2680(a). The scope of this discretionary act exception has troubled courts for years. However, the facts of this case closely resemble those of *Dalehite v. United States*, 346 U.S. 15 (1953), still the leading case on the issue. In *Dalehite*, the Supreme Court found the government's actions in formulating and then directing the execution of a formal plan for a fertilizer export program could not form the basis of a suit under the Federal Tort Claims Act. Such actions were found to be discretionary under § 2860(a), even though an alleged abuse of that discretion resulted in the 1947 Texas City disaster.

Pemex, in this case, was executing a national plan formulated at the highest levels of the Mexican government by exploring for Mexico's natural resources. Any act performed by a subordinate of Pemex in furtherance of this exploration plan was still discretionary in nature and immune from suit under the FSIA. To deny immunity to a foreign state for the implementation of its domestic economic policies would be to completely abrogate the doctrine of foreign sovereign immunity by allowing an exception to swallow the grant of immunity preserved by § 1604. Therefore, Pemex' Motion to Dismiss all claims against it on the basis of foreign sovereign immunity must be granted.

OLSEN ex rel. SHELDON v. GOVERNMENT OF MEXICO
729 F.2d 641 (9th Cir. 1984)

. . . Appellants Olsen and Sanchez, United States citizens domiciled in California, are minor children claiming the wrongful death of their parents. As prisoners of the Mexican government, the parents of appellants were to be transferred to authorities for incarceration in the United States pursuant to the Prisoner Exchange Treaty between the United States and Mexico. On the night of October 27, 1979, a twin-propeller plane owned and operated by the Mexican government carrying guards, pilots, and appellants' parents departed Monterrey, Mexico for Tijuana, where the transfer was to take place. En route, the pilots, employees of the Mexican Department of Justice, learned of thick fog and diminishing visibility at their destination. They requested an instrument landing which, at Tijuana Airport, requires the airplane to enter United States airspace so it can approach the runway from the west. Following procedures established by a Letter of Agreement between aviation authorities of the United States and Mexico, Tijuana air control sought and received permission for the airplane to cross the border. In addition to providing access to United States airspace during hazardous weather conditions, the Letter also allows for coordinated navigational assistance.

Because its radar and instrument landing navigational system were inoperative, Tijuana air control asked its counterpart in San Diego to radio direction headings, altitude, and location data necessary for an instrument landing to the aircraft. Unfortunately, neither the San Diego air controllers nor the pilots were bilingual. Instead, the San Diego air controllers relayed the information via the telephone "hotline" to Tijuana air control who radioed their translation to the pilots. In this manner, the aircraft penetrated almost 12 miles into United States airspace, made a wide turn and began to descend toward Tijuana Airport. Having strayed one mile off the proper course, the pilot abandoned the approach at the border and re-entered Mexican airspace.

San Diego air control advised the pilot to proceed to other airports where visual landings would be possible. The pilot declined and decided to attempt another instrument landing. With the continued use of navigational data from San Diego air control, the airplane re-entered United States airspace. The pilots aligned the aircraft with the proper compass heading and descended on course, but failed to maintain the proper altitude. After striking a telephone pole, the airplane crashed three-quarters of a mile inside the United States, killing all on board. The crash site was two and one-half miles from the beginning of the runway.

DISCUSSION

The FSIA sets forth criteria which must be satisfied to establish both statutory subject matter jurisdiction and personal jurisdiction. The FSIA confers subject matter jurisdiction upon district courts in nonjury civil actions where the foreign state is not entitled to immunity as defined by the FSIA's substantive provisions. Personal jurisdiction is established whenever subject matter jurisdiction exists and service of process has been made in accord with section 1608 of the FSIA. Thus, both forms of jurisdiction turn on whether the foreign state is entitled to sovereign immunity. If the dispute does not come within one of the exceptions to sovereign immunity explicitly provided by sections 1605–1607, the district court lacks both subject matter jurisdiction and personal jurisdiction.

I. Subject Matter Jurisdiction

. . . Appellants allege that their wrongful death claims come within the so-called "noncommercial torts" exception, section 1605(a)(5). Mexico argues that section 1605(a)(5) does not apply and it is therefore immune from suit. First, Mexico contends that Congress, in enacting the FSIA, adopted the restrictive theory of sovereign immunity and that Mexico's conduct was of the public nature held to be immune under that theory. Second, Mexico asserts that the 1605(a)(5) exception to immunity requires all the acts or omissions constituting the tort to occur within the United States. Finally, Mexico characterizes its activities which led to the crash as discretionary functions, thus falling within the exception to jurisdiction set forth in section 1605(a)(5)(A). We consider these arguments in turn.

A. The FSIA and the Restrictive Theory of Sovereign Immunity.

It is clear that the FSIA, for the most part, codifies the restrictive principle of soverign [sic] immunity. Under this principle, the immunity of a foreign state is "restricted" to suits involving that state's public acts (*jure imperii*) and does not extend to suits based on its private or commercial acts (*jure gestionis*). Mexico argues that this public/private distinction applies not only to the FSIA generally, but specifically to section 1605(a)(5), the noncommercial torts exception to immunity. According to Mexico's interpretation, foreign states would be immune from jurisdiction for those torts which otherwise come within the bounds of section 1605(a)(5) but which are public in nature.

Section 1605(a)(5) cannot be read, however, other than in conjunction with section 1605(a)(5)(A), which exempts from the reach of section 1605(a)(5) those torts committed in a foreign state's discretionary capacity. Discretionary functions, as discussed below, include those acts or decisions made at the policy-making or planning level of government. Those torts involving acts or omissions of a fundamentally governmental nature are not actionable. Thus, despite section 1605(a)(5), a foreign state remains largely immunized from torts committed in its governmental capacity. Mexico's position, that governmental acts are automatically read out of section 1605(a)(5), would render section 1605(a)(5)(A) superfluous. Its argument is therefore untenable.

B. The Location of the Tortious Conduct.

Section 1605(a)(5) requires the injury complained of to occur in the United States.[1] The provision does not indicate that the conduct causing the tort must also take place in the United States. Ordinarily, this would end our inquiry and there would be no need to consider the location of the tortious conduct. Where, as in the instant case, the injuries occurred in the United States, and all other requirements of section 1605(a)(5) are met, the foreign state would not be immune. However, the legislative history to section 1605(a)(5) indicates that "the tortious act *or omission* must occur within the jurisdiction of the United States. . . .

A careful reading of the record in this case suggests that many potentially tortious acts and omissions occurring both in Mexico and the United States caused the crash. Pilot error, the absence of operational radar and navigational aids at Tijuana airport, defective aircraft instruments, the decision to forego a visual landing at another airport, inaccurate data from San Diego air control, and other factors may have contributed causally to the accident. Mexico, relying on *Matter of SEDCO*, 543 F. Supp. 561, 567 (S.D. Tex. 1982) *(SEDCO)*, contends that section 1605(a)(5) must be construed to require all of the tortious conduct occur in the United States before a foreign state will be denied immunity. In *SEDCO*, an exploratory off-shore well operated by Pemex, the Mexican national oil company, exploded in Mexican waters. The resulting oil slick washed up on the shores of Texas. Citizens there sued Pemex and other parties under section 1605(a)(5). Citing that section's legislative history requiring the tortious act or omission to occur within the United States, the court held that for the noncommercial tort exception to apply, "the tort, in whole, must occur in the United States." Thus, Mexico argues, because some allegedly tortious acts or omissions took place outside the United States — such as the maintenance of the aircraft and the inoperative radar at Tijuana airport — Mexico should be immune.

The instant case is distinguishable from *SEDCO* in one crucial respect. In *SEDCO,* none of the alleged acts or omissions, only the resultant injury, occurred in the United States. By requiring every aspect of the tortious conduct to occur in the United States, a rule such as in *SEDCO* would encourage foreign states to allege that some tortious conduct occurred outside the United States. The foreign state would thus be able to establish immunity and diminish the rights of injured persons seeking recovery. Such a result contradicts the purpose of the FSIA, which is to "serve the interests of justice and . . . protect the rights of both foreign states and litigants in United States courts." 28 U.S.C. § 1602. The FSIA requires us to protect the rights of plaintiffs while respecting the sovereignty of foreign states. Consequently, we hold that if plaintiffs allege at least one entire tort occurring in the United States, they may claim under section 1605(a)(5). In this case, appellants allege conduct constituting a single tort — the negligent piloting of the aircraft — which occurred in the United States. We are satisfied that appellants have alleged sufficient conduct occurring in the United States to bring this case

---

[1] Section 1605(a)(5) specifies that foreign states are not immune from jurisdiction in any case in which money damages are sought "for personal injury or death, or damage to or loss of property, occurring in the United States and caused by the tortious act or omission of that foreign state. . . ."

within the noncommercial torts exception as expressed in section 1605(a)(5) and its legislative history.

C. The Discretionary Function Exception.

Section 1605(a)(5)(A) provides an exception to noncommercial tort jurisdiction for claims based upon a state's discretionary function.[2] Mexico seeks to bring the airplane crash within this exception by contending that the conduct which led to the crash was discretionary.

The FSIA provides considerable guidance as to which acts or decisions constitute discretionary functions. Not only does the language of the FSIA discretionary function exception replicate that of the Federal Tort Claims Act (FTCA), 28 U.S.C. § 2680(a), but the legislative history of the FSIA, in explaining section 1605(a)(5)(A), directs us to the FTCA. To

> determine the scope of the discretionary function exception of the FSIA, we therefore turn to the interpretation given the similar FTCA provision.[3]

The seminal case defining the scope of the discretionary function exception within the context of the FTCA, *Dalehite v. United States*, 346 U.S. 15 (1953), held "discretion" to mean:

> more than the initiation of programs and activities. It also includes determinations made by executives or administrators in establishing plans, specifications or schedules of operations. Where there is room for policy judgment and decision there is discretion.

In so defining discretion, the Court adhered to the legislative purpose behind the exception: to allow government executives to make policy decisions in an atmosphere free of concern over possible litigation.

Over the years, the definition of discretion has been refined and qualified somewhat. This circuit employs a test which distinguishes between the "planning level" of governmental activity and those acts designed to carry out policy, the "operational level." *Thompson v. United States*, 592 F.2d 1104, 1111 (9th Cir. 1979).[4] Because decisions at the planning level establish governmental policy, they are not actionable. But where decisions occur at the operational level, the discretionary function exemption provides no protection from liability even though such decisions or acts may involve elements of discretion. In addition to examining the level at which the conduct occurred, we also consider two other factors which are particularly important when

---

[2] Section 1605(a)(5) does not apply to:

> (A) any claim based upon the exercise or performance or the failure to exercise or perform a discretionary function regardless of whether discretion be abused.

[3] The Federal Tort Claims Act does not apply to:

> (a) Any claim . . . based upon the exercise or performance or failure to exercise or perform a discretionary function or duty on the part of a federal agency or an employee of the Government, whether or not the discretion involved be abused.

[4] [Editor's note: for reasons you may wish to consider, the court no longer adheres to the distinction between the "planning level" and "operational level" for purposes of determining the scope of an official's discretion. *See Risk v. Halvorsen and Kingdom of Norway*, 936 F.2d 393 (9th Cir. 1991).]

determining the immunity of foreign states: The ability of United States courts to evaluate the act or omission of the state, and the potential impairing effect such an evaluation would have on the effective administration of the state's government.

We conclude that of those alleged acts or omissions on the part of Mexico which contributed to the accident, none was discretionary. First, while Mexico's decision to enter into the Prisoner Exchange Treaty with the United States or to transfer these particular prisoners to United States custody might well be deemed discretionary, those decisions are not implicated in the instant action. Rather, appellants allege that Mexico negligently maintained, directed, and piloted the aircraft. Such conduct represents measures taken to implement the broader policy or plan to exchange prisoners. The acts or omissions in question involved the transportation of prisoners, an act remote from the policy decision to transfer them. While the pilot and air controllers had considerable discretion in carrying out their assigned tasks, it is clear they acted on the operational level, far from the centers of policy judgment.

Second, this dispute does not raise questions of policy decisions of Mexico, only issues of historical fact and tort liability. Therefore, the trial court can readily evaluate the allegedly tortious acts as it is well suited to the task of determining facts and applying the relevant law.

Third, we see nothing which suggests that denying immunity will impair the effectiveness of Mexico's penal or aviation authorities. A trial on the merits will call for the testimony of individuals involved in the accident, primarily Mexican air traffic control personnel. There seems little doubt that the air traffic authorities and other relevant governmental entities can function without diminished efficacy while their employees testify in discovery or court proceedings.

In conclusion, the claims asserted by appellants fall within the exception to immunity for noncommercial torts as provided by section 1605(a)(5) of the FSIA. Additionally, the conduct of Mexican personnel which may have led to the crash occurred at the operational level and was not discretionary. Thus, Mexico is not immune under the FSIA and subject matter jurisdiction exists.

Notes and Questions on *SEDCO* and *Olsen*

1. *Pollution as an international tort.* In 1944, the *Trail Smelter Arbitration (United States v. Canada)*, 111 U.N. REP. INT'L ARB. AWARDS 1905 (1949), established that a state could not use its territory in such a way as to harm the territory of another. It was in many respects an international confirmation of the ancient *sic utere* doctrine, which has its counterparts in common law tort (and property) law. That being so, why exactly is the transborder pollution in *SEDCO* not within the tort exception?

2. *Non-territorial "jurisdiction."* The legislative history of the FSIA — though not its text — requires that the tortious act or omission occur "within the *jurisdiction* of the United States." Is that the same as requiring that the act

or omission occur *in U.S. territory* or *in the United States*? Is there any sense in which the environmental damage at issue in *SEDCO* is within the "jurisdiction of the United States" as that term is understood at international law?

3. Which case — *SEDCO* or *Olsen* — seems better reasoned? For what it's worth, the *SEDCO* court subsequently reconsidered and vacated its own order, 610 F. Supp. 306, 307-08 (S.D. Tex. 1984), demonstrating just how fact-intensive the characterization issue is under § 1605(a)(2) but not necessarily how best to conceive the requirements of the tort exception under § 1605(a)(5):

> This Court . . . gave perhaps too much weight to the evidence presented by Pemex that the well was drilled for exploratory purposes to aid the Mexican government's long range planning and policy-making process concerning the development of its minerals. That evidence was presented by the affidavits of two Mexican lawyers and a letter from a Mexican consul in Houston, Texas. Sedco has presented evidence in its Memorandum in Support of Motions for Rehearing and Reconsideration which conflicts with this Court's conclusion based on said evidence that the IXTOC I well was drilled for exploratory purposes. Sedco attached as Exhibit A to its Memorandum a copy of the Pemex drilling program for the well . . . which indicates the well was drilled for commercial exploitation. . . . There is a genuine factual dispute evidenced by conflicting affidavits and documents as to the characterization of the well. This Court would prefer to have the affiants appear in court in person in order to judge the credibility of those witnesses. Fairness thus dictates that the jurisdictional determination should be made after a full evidentiary hearing.

4. *Scope of the tort.* In a case like *Olsen*, should one qualifying tortious act in the United States bring all related tort claims within the exception? For example, if negligent piloting were the only qualifying act in the United States, should claims arising from other conduct that contributed to the accident also fall within the exception, regardless of where it occurred?

5. *"Discretionary" torts.* As noted by the *Letelier* and *Olsen* cases, the exception to immunity for non-commercial torts in the United States is itself subject to several exceptions: certain named torts come within a state's immunity, as do claims "based on the exercise or performance, or failure to exercise or perform, a discretionary function regardless of whether the discretion be abused." The meaning of this latter exception-to-the-exception for discretionary function torts is a recurring issue in litigation under § 1605(a)(5). After all, what can it mean to say that a state official has the "discretion" to commit a tort?

In *Risk v. Halvorsen and Kingdom of Norway*, 936 F.2d 393 (9th Cir. 1991), one of the relatively few family law cases brought under the FSIA, a father sued the kingdom of Norway and Norwegian consular officials for allegedly helping his wife remove his children to Norway in violation of a state court's custody order. Specifically, he claimed that the Norwegian government and its consular officials conspired to violate and in fact violated the custody order by suggesting to his wife that she return to Norway with the children; by providing travel documents for her and the children; by providing financial assistance; and by obstructing the father's effort to locate and contact his children.

In ruling against the father, the *Risk* court consulted a variety of laws — and law-types — to give meaning to the discretionary function exception in § 1605(a)(5). Particular emphasis was placed on the principles developed under the Federal Tort Claims Act, under which

> [f]irst we "must determine whether the government employee had any discretion to act or if there was an element of choice as to appropriate conduct." *Liu v. Republic of China*, 892 F.2d 1419, 1431 (9th Cir. 1989), *cert. dismissed*, 497 U.S. 1058 (1990) (citing *Berkovitz v. United States*, 486 U.S. 531, 535 (1988)). Second, we consider "whether the decisions were grounded in social, economic, and political policy," concentrating on "the nature of the conduct, rather than the status of the actor. . . ." *MacArthur Area Citizens Ass'n v. Peru*, 809 F.2d 918, 922 (D.C.Cir. 1987), *vacated on other grounds*, 823 F.2d 606 (1987) (quoting *United States v. Varig*, 467 U.S. 797, 813 (1984)).

> In *MacArthur*, a neighborhood association sued the Republic of Peru for occupation and use of a building in violation of a zoning ordinance. The circuit court for the District of Columbia held that the discretionary function exception to the FSIA applied because the establishment of a chancery in a particular building, and modification of that building for security purposes, is a discretionary act of public policy, both political and economic in nature. In *Joseph v. Nigeria*, 830 F.2d 1018 (9th Cir. 1987), *cert. denied*, 485 U.S. 905 (1988), we declined to apply the discretionary function exception to acts of officials of the Nigerian government which lead to a tort suit. In that case, the government officials were accused of destruction of the property in which the Nigerian Consulate was located. We held that while acquisition and operation of the property was a discretionary function, purely destructive acts are not part of the policy decision to establish the consulate and thus fall outside the scope of the discretionary function exception.

The *Risk* court concluded that the actions of the Norwegian officials were closer to *MacArthur* than to *Joseph*, declaring that each of the acts fell within the functions of consular officials according to the Vienna Convention on Consular Relations (VCCR), April 24, 1963, 21 U.S.T. 77:

> Article 5, sections (d) and (e) of that document, to which the United States and Norway are signatories, defines consular functions in part as "issuing passports and travel documents to nationals of the sending state . . ." and "helping and assisting nationals, both individuals and bodies corporate, of the sending state." Acts covered by the VCCR presumptively are "grounded in social, economic, and political policy" and thus the conduct of the Norwegian officials satisfies the second prong of the discretionary function analysis contained in *Liu*.

The court gave little weight to the argument that interference with custody orders violated the state penal code and that consular officials could have no discretion to commit a criminal act. In *Liu*, the widow of a citizen of the Republic of China ("ROC"), whose murder allegedly was ordered by the director of that country's Defense Intelligence Bureau, brought a wrongful death suit in federal court. The court there declined to apply the discretionary function exception, explaining that, "because the acts in this case violated ROC law, they were not discretionary and thus fell outside coverage of the discretionary function exception. . . . [W]e hold that the discretionary function exception is inapplicable when an employee of a foreign government violates its own internal law." In *Risk*, by contrast, there was no assertion that the Norwegian consular officials had violated any Norwegian law.

The court also declined to apply the *Letelier* court's conclusion that "action . . . clearly contrary to the precepts of humanity" is outside the scope of the discretionary function exception.

> In this case, the most that can be said is that Norwegian officials issued travel documents to a Norwegian citizen and her children, also citizens of Norway; that they provided funds for her travel; and that they protected her from contact by her former husband. Although these acts may constitute a crime under California law, it cannot be said that every conceivably illegal act is outside the scope of the discretionary function exception.

> Do you agree?

6. *Exceptions to the exception: connecting the dots.* Do the named torts in § 1605(a)(5)(B) — malicious prosecution, abuse of process, libel, slander, misrepresentation, deceit, or interference with contract rights — have anything in common that might explain why Congress would except them from the tort exception?

---

[d] The Takings Exception

§ 1605. General exceptions to the jurisdictional immunity of a foreign state

(a) A foreign state shall not be immune from the jurisdiction of courts of the United States or of the States in any case -

(3) in which rights in property taken in violation of international law are in issue and that property or any property exchanged for such property is present in the United States in connection with a commercial activity carried on in the United States by the foreign state; or that property or any property exchanged for such property is owned or operated by an agency or instrumentality of the foreign state and that agency or instrumentality is engaged in a commercial activity in the United States . . . .

SIDERMAN DE BLAKE v. THE REPUBLIC OF ARGENTINA
965 F.2d 699 (9th Cir. 1992), *cert. denied*, 507 U.S. 1017 (1993)

Susana Siderman de Blake and Jose, Lea, and Carlos Siderman (collectively, "the Sidermans") appeal the dismissal of their action against the

Republic of Argentina and the Argentine Province of Tucuman (collectively, "Argentina"). The Sidermans' complaint alleged eighteen causes of action arising out of the torture of Jose Siderman and the expropriation of the Sidermans' property by Argentine military officials. The district court dismissed the expropriation claims . . . but granted a default judgment to Jose and Lea Siderman on the torture claims. Argentina then entered its first appearance in the case and moved for relief from judgment on the ground that the Foreign Sovereign Immunities Act ("FSIA"), rendered it immune from the Sidermans' action. The district court granted the motion and vacated the default judgment. The Sidermans now appeal. We reverse and remand for further proceedings.

FACTS

The factual record . . . tells a horrifying tale of the violent and brutal excesses of an anti-Semitic military junta that ruled Argentina. On March 24, 1976, the Argentine military overthrew the government of President Maria Estela Peron and seized the reins of power for itself, installing military leaders of the central government and the provincial governments of Argentina. That night, ten masked men carrying machine guns forcibly entered the home of Jose and Lea Siderman, husband and wife, in Tucuman Province, Argentina. The men, who were acting under the direction of the military governor of Tucuman, ransacked the home and locked Lea in the bathroom. They then blindfolded and shackled 65-year old Jose, dragged him out of his home, tossed him into a waiting car, and drove off to an unknown building. For seven days the men beat and tortured Jose. Among their tools of torture was an electric cattle prod, which they used to shock Jose until he fainted. As they tortured him, the men repeatedly shouted anti-Semitic epithets, calling him a "Jew Bastard" and a "Shitty Jew." They inflicted all of these cruelties upon Jose Siderman because of his Jewish faith.

At the end of this nightmarish week, his body badly bruised and his ribs broken, Jose was taken out of the building and driven to an isolated area, where the masked men tossed him out of the car. The men told Jose that if he and his family did not leave Tucuman and Argentina immediately, they would be killed. On the day of Jose's release, he and Lea fled to Buenos Aires in fear for their lives. Their son Carlos followed shortly thereafter, and the night Carlos left Tucuman, military authorities ransacked his home. In June 1976, Jose, Lea, and Carlos left Argentina for the United States, where they joined Susana Siderman de Blake. She is the daughter of Jose and Lea and is a United States citizen.

Before the hasty flight from Tucuman to Buenos Aires, Jose was forced to raise cash by selling at a steep discount part of his interest in 127,000 acres of land. Prior to their departure for the United States, the Sidermans also made arrangements for someone to oversee their family business, Inmobiliaria del Nor-Oeste, S.A. ("INOSA"), an Argentine corporation. Susana Siderman de Blake, Carlos Siderman and Lea Siderman each owned 33% of INOSA and Jose owned the remaining one percent. Its assets comprised numerous real estate holdings including a large hotel in Tucuman, the Hotel Gran Corona.

The Sidermans granted management powers over INOSA to a certified public accountant in Argentina.

After the Sidermans left Argentina for the United States, Argentine military officers renewed their persecution of Jose. They altered real property records in Tucuman to show that he had owned not 127,000, but 127, acres of land in the province. They then initiated a criminal action against him in Argentina, claiming that since he owned only 127 acres he had sold land that did not belong to him. Argentina sought the assistance of our courts in obtaining jurisdiction over his person, requesting via a letter rogatory that the Los Angeles Superior Court serve him with documents relating to the action. The court, unaware of Argentina's motives, complied with the request. . . .

The Argentine military also pursued INOSA with vigor. In April 1977, INOSA was seized through a sham "judicial intervention," a proceeding in which property is put into receivership. The purported reasons for the intervention were that INOSA lacked a representative in Argentina and that INOSA had obtained excessive funds from a Tucuman provincial bank. Though these reasons were pretexts for persecuting the Sidermans because of their religion and profiting from their economic success, the Sidermans were unable to oppose the intervention because Argentine officials had imprisoned and killed the accountant to whom they had granted management powers over INOSA. In 1978, the Sidermans retained an attorney in Argentina and brought a derivative action in a Tucuman court in an effort to end the intervention. The court ordered that the intervention cease, and the order was upheld by the Supreme Court of Tucuman, but the order remains unenforced and the intervention has continued. Argentine military officials and INOSA's appointed receivers have extracted funds from INOSA, purchased various assets owned by INOSA at sharply discounted prices, and diverted INOSA's profits and revenues to themselves.

In 1982, Jose, Lea, and Carlos, who by then had become permanent residents of the United States, and Susana, a United States citizen since 1967, turned to federal court for relief. They filed a complaint asserting eighteen causes of action based on the torture and harassment of Jose by Argentine officials and the expropriation of their property in Argentina. Named defendants included the Republic of Argentina, the Province of Tucuman, INOSA, and numerous individual defendants who participated in the wrongdoing. In December 1982, the Sidermans properly served Argentina and Tucuman with the Summons and Complaint. The Argentine Embassy subsequently sought assistance from the U.S. State Department, which informed Argentina that it would have to appear and present any defenses it wished to assert to the district court, including the defense of sovereign immunity, or risk a default judgment. The State Department also provided a directory of lawyer referral services. Despite receiving this information, Argentina did not enter an appearance, and the Sidermans filed a motion for default judgment.

. . . [The district court dismissed the Sidermans' expropriation claims *sua sponte* but entered a default judgment on the torture claims, awarding Jose $2.6 million in damages and expenses and awarding Lea $100,000 for her loss of consortium claim.]

The damages award finally elicited a response from Argentina, which filed a motion for relief from judgment on the ground that it was immune from suit under the FSIA and that the district court therefore lacked both subject matter and personal jurisdiction. The United States filed a suggestion of interest, asking the court to consider the issue of foreign sovereign immunity but indicating no view of the merits. . . . [T]he district court vacated the default judgment and dismissed the Sidermans' action on the ground of Argentina's immunity under the FSIA. The Sidermans filed a timely notice of appeal . . . .

DISCUSSION

. . . The Sidermans argue that their claims . . . fall within the international takings exception to the FSIA's rule of immunity. That exception provides that a foreign state is not immune in an action in which rights in property taken in violation of international law are in issue and [1] that property or any property exchanged for such property is present in the United States in connection with a commercial activity carried on in the United States by the foreign state; or [2] that property or any property exchanged for such property is owned or operated by an agency or instrumentality of the foreign state and that agency or instrumentality is engaged in a commercial activity in the United States. Though few courts have had the opportunity to consider the international takings exception, it is clear that Jose, Lea, and Carlos Siderman cannot assert a claim that comes within this exception. In *Chuidian v. Philippine Nat'l Bank*, 912 F.2d 1095, 1105 (9th Cir. 1990), we held that the exception does not apply where the plaintiff is a citizen of the defendant country at the time of the expropriation, because "[e]xpropriation by a sovereign state of the property of its own nationals does not implicate settled principles of international law." However, Susana Siderman de Blake is eligible to invoke the international takings exception, and the Sidermans' allegations and evidence bring her claims within clause two of that exception.

Under that clause, the property at issue must have been taken in violation of international law. At the jurisdictional stage, we need not decide whether the taking actually violated international law; as long as a "claim is substantial and non-frivolous, it provides a sufficient basis for the exercise of our jurisdiction." *West v. Multibanco Comermex, S.A.*, 807 F.2d 820, 826 (9th Cir.), *cert. denied*, 482 U.S. 906 (1987). In *West*, we described three requisites under international law for a valid taking. First, "[v]alid expropriations must always serve a public purpose." Second, "aliens [must] not be discriminated against or singled out for regulation by the state." Finally, "[a]n otherwise valid taking is illegal without the payment of just compensation." These well-established principles track the RESTATEMENT OF FOREIGN RELATIONS LAW, which provides:

> A state is responsible under international law for injury resulting from: (1) a taking by the state of the property of a national of another state that (a) is not for a public purpose, or (b) is discriminatory, or (c) is not accompanied by provision for just compensation. . . .

RESTATEMENT (THIRD) OF THE FOREIGN RELATIONS LAW OF THE UNITED STATES § 712 (1987) [hereinafter "RESTATEMENT"]. The legislative history of the FSIA reveals a similar understanding of what constitutes a taking in violation of international law. *See* H.R.Rep. No. 1487, 94th Cong., 2d Sess. 19–20 (taking violates international law if it is done "without payment of the prompt adequate and effective compensation required by international law" or is "arbitrary or discriminatory in nature"). If a taking violates any one of the aforementioned proscriptions, it violates international law.

Susana Siderman de Blake's claim that Argentina violated the international law of expropriation is substantial and non-frivolous. The complaint alleges that Argentina officials seized INOSA for their personal profit and not for any public purpose. The complaint also alleges that Argentina seized INOSA because the Siderman family is Jewish — a discriminatory motivation based on ethnicity. *See* RESTATEMENT § 712 Comment f (noting that "taking that singles out aliens generally, or aliens of a particular nationality, or particular aliens, would violate international law"). Finally, none of the Sidermans has received any compensation for the seizure, let alone just compensation. As in *West*, we have no difficulty concluding that the Sidermans' complaint contains "substantial and non-frivolous" allegations that INOSA was taken in violation of international law.

Beyond establishing that property has been taken in violation of international law, Susana Siderman de Blake must demonstrate that the expropriated property, or property exchanged for it, is owned or operated by an agency or instrumentality of Argentina and that the agency or instrumentality is engaged in commercial activity in the United States. The Sidermans' allegations establish that INOSA itself has become an agency or instrumentality of Argentina. As defined by [Section 1603(b) of] the FSIA, an "agency or instrumentality" means any entity —

> (1) which is a separate legal person, corporate or otherwise, and (2) which is an organ of a foreign state or political subdivision thereof, . . . and (3) which is neither a citizen of a State of the United States . . . nor created under the laws of any third country.

As an Argentine corporation, INOSA satisfies the first and third elements of the above definition, and the Sidermans' basic allegation that Argentina has expropriated INOSA suffices as an allegation that INOSA is now an "organ" of Argentina or Tucuman. The Sidermans' allegations thus satisfy the "agency or instrumentality" definition. The final requirement under clause two — that the agency or instrumentality must be engaged in a commercial activity in the United States — is also met. The Sidermans' allegations concerning Argentina's solicitation and entertainment of American guests at the Hotel Gran Corona and the hotel's acceptance of American credit cards and traveler's checks are sufficient at this stage of the proceedings to show that Argentina is engaged in a commercial activity in the United States. The Sidermans' allegations bring Susana Siderman de Blake's expropriation claims within clause two of the international takings exception.

We hold that the Sidermans' complaint and declarations allege sufficient facts to bring their expropriation claims within both the commercial activity and international takings exceptions to the FSIA's grant of foreign sovereign immunity. We emphasize the preliminary nature of our holding; following further development of the factual record on remand, the district court ultimately must determine whether the FSIA exceptions do or do not apply to the expropriation claims. While the Sidermans have sustained their initial burden of alleging applicable exceptions to the FSIA, Argentina will have the opportunity on remand to challenge the evidence presented by the Sidermans and to present its own. Under the procedures our circuit has developed for considering jurisdiction under the FSIA, Argentina now bears the burden of proving by a preponderance of the evidence that none of the FSIA exceptions applies to the Sidermans' claims. To the extent that the jurisdictional facts are disputed on remand, the parties should be allowed to conduct discovery for the limited purpose of establishing jurisdictional facts before the claims can be dismissed. . . .

ZAPPIA MIDDLE EAST CONST. CO. LTD. v. EMIRATE OF ABU DHABI
215 F.3d 247 (2d Cir. 2000)

Plaintiff-appellant Zappia Middle East Construction Company Limited ("ZMEC") . . . is a construction company incorporated in the British Virgin Islands with a place of business in Canada. ZMEC is owned by Joseph Zappia. Mr. Zappia is a citizen of Italy and Canada and a resident of Rome, though at all times relevant to this action he resided in the Emirate of Abu Dhabi. Defendant-appellee Abu Dhabi Investment Authority ("ADIA") is an investment institution wholly owned by Abu Dhabi. ADIA owns a majority of the shares of defendant-appellee Abu Dhabi Commercial Bank ("ADCB").

From 1979 to 1982, ZMEC entered into a series of eight construction contracts in Abu Dhabi to build public works facilities in the Emirate. The contracts called for the Emirate to make periodic progress payments to ZMEC. In mid-1982, the Emirate delayed making payments, and in some instances refused to pay ZMEC the monies due under the contracts. The Emirate also allegedly forced ZMEC to perform work beyond that specified in the contracts. To remain solvent, ZMEC borrowed funds from Emirates Commercial Bank ("ECB") on unfavorable terms.

In January 1983, ZMEC reached the limit of its credit with ECB. On January 10, 1983, ZMEC entered into an agreement with ECB (the "1983 Agreement") pursuant to which day-to-day management of ZMEC was turned over to another construction contractor, Bovis International Limited ("Bovis"), and supervision of ZMEC was turned over to a management committee comprised of three representatives of ECB, one representative of Bovis, and Mr. Zappia or alternatively his assistant. The 1983 Agreement also prevented ZMEC from incurring any further debts or liabilities without the written consent of ECB.

ZMEC alleges that Mr. Zappia signed the 1983 Agreement under threat of imprisonment. At the January 10, 1983 meeting, ECB also forced Mr. Zappia to surrender his passport. Thereafter, Mr. Zappia's passport was withheld until the Emirate's acting Interior Minister returned it months later. Ten days after the 1983 Agreement was executed, ECB wrote to Sheikh Kalifa Bin

Zayed Al Nahyan ("Sheikh Kalifa"), the Crown Prince of Abu Dhabi and the Chairman of Abu Dhabi's executive council, petitioning him to direct the various government departments to extend the duration of ZMEC's projects so that Bovis could complete them.

In July 1985, more than two years after the execution of the 1983 Agreement, ECB and two other banks were recapitalized by the Emirate and merged into the newly formed ADCB. By then, several of the construction projects had been completed and Bovis was liquidating ZMEC's construction equipment and preparing claims for compensation on ZMEC's behalf. After the merger, Bovis completed the remaining projects and sold the rest of ZMEC's construction equipment. No proceeds from the sales of equipment were paid to the Emirate or ADIA, and none of the equipment or the proceeds of the sales are present in the United States.

In 1994, ZMEC instituted this suit seeking payments under the original construction contracts. ZMEC alleged that the defendants had taken its property in violation of international law and asserted jurisdiction based upon the expropriation exception to the FSIA. The case was referred to a magistrate judge for pretrial management and a report and recommendation on dispositive motions. The defendants promptly moved to dismiss the complaint for lack of subject matter jurisdiction. The parties subsequently conducted two years of discovery solely on the jurisdictional issue.

Based on the documentary evidence amassed by the parties, the magistrate judge concluded in a thorough report and recommendation that there was no evidence that ECB was controlled by the Emirate or the royal family. Consequently, the magistrate judge determined that no expropriation by the sovereign had taken place. Adopting the report and recommendation, the district judge also concluded that the evidence did not support ZMEC's assertions that the Emirate expropriated ZMEC's property and dismissed the complaint. ZMEC appeals the district court's finding that rights in intangible property are not "rights in property" under the FSIA, and that there was no expropriation by Abu Dhabi and ADIA. . . .

DISCUSSION

. . . It is undisputed that the defendants-appellees are either foreign sovereigns or instrumentalities of a foreign sovereign. In actions against foreign sovereigns or their instrumentalities, the FSIA provides the sole basis for obtaining subject-matter jurisdiction of United States courts. . . . Under the FSIA, a foreign sovereign and its instrumentalities are immune from suit in the United States courts unless a specific statutorily defined exception applies. Although this action involves a commercial contract dispute, the FSIA "commercial activities" exception does not apply because no commercial acts or their effects were felt in the United States. However, ZMEC contends that the FSIA expropriation exception applies.

The expropriation exception provides that a foreign sovereign is not immune from suit in any case

> in which rights in property taken in violation of international law are
> in issue and that property or any property exchanged for such property

is present in the United States in connection with a commercial activity carried on in the United States by the foreign state; or that property or any property exchanged for such property is owned or operated by an agency or instrumentality of the foreign state and that agency or instrumentality is engaged in a commercial activity in the United States.

28 U.S.C. § 1605(a)(3). Thus, in order to establish jurisdiction pursuant to the FSIA expropriation exception, a plaintiff must show that: (1) rights in property are in issue; (2) that the property was "taken"; (3) that the taking was in violation of international law; and (4) that one of the two nexus requirements is satisfied. The district court found that ZMEC failed to satisfy the first two criteria because intangible contract rights are not rights in property and there was no governmental taking. We need not determine whether intangible contract rights are property under the statute, however, because defendants-appellees' actions did not constitute a taking within the meaning of the FSIA.

The FSIA does not define the term "taken." However, the legislative history makes clear that the phrase "taken in violation of international law" refers to "the nationalization or expropriation of property without payment of the prompt, adequate, and effective compensation required by international law," including "takings which are arbitrary or discriminatory in nature." H.R. REP. No. 94-1487, at 19 (1976), *reprinted in* 1976 U.S.C.C.A.N. 6604, 6618. The term "taken" thus clearly refers to acts of a sovereign, not a private enterprise, that deprive a plaintiff of property without adequate compensation.

ZMEC argues that ECB and ADCB were alter egos of the Emirate, which surreptitiously expropriated ZMEC's property under the 1983 Agreement. However, government instrumentalities are presumed to be distinct and independent from their sovereign and normally are treated as such. *See First Nat'l City Bank v. Banco Para El Comercio Exterior de Cuba*, 462 U.S. 611, 626–27 (1983) [*Bancec.*] As the Supreme Court has explained,

> [f]reely ignoring the separate status of government instrumentalities would result in substantial uncertainty over whether an instrumentality's assets would be diverted to satisfy a claim against the sovereign, and might thereby cause third parties to hesitate before extending credit to a government instrumentality. As a result, the efforts of sovereign nations to structure their governmental activities in a manner deemed necessary to promote economic development and efficient administration would surely be frustrated.

Id. at 626. While the presumption of separateness is a strong one, it may be overcome if a corporate entity is so extensively controlled by the sovereign that the latter is effectively the agent of the former, or if recognizing the corporate entity as independent would work a fraud or injustice. *See id.* at 629–630.

ZMEC bears the burden of proving that the corporate entity should not be presumed distinct from a sovereign or sovereign entity. ZMEC challenges ECB's and ADCB's status as separate corporate entities on the following evidence: the Emirate forced ZMEC into debt by withholding required contract payments, which in turn lead ZMEC to take out a loan from ECB; ECB officials threatened to disavow ZMEC's checks, which could have led to Mr. Zappia's imprisonment; ECB seized Mr. Zappia's passport and submitted it to a government official who withheld it for months; the 1983 Agreement included a provision that prevented ZMEC from incurring additional debt which effectively acted as an "embargo"; after the 1983 Agreement was executed, ECB sought Sheikh Khalifa's approval of an extension of time in which to complete the construction of government buildings; and after entering into the 1983 Agreement, ECB rushed to complete the construction projects increasing ZMEC's debt exposure.

This evidence does not demonstrate a sufficient intermingling of the private bank with the sovereign to overcome the presumption of separateness. There is no evidence that Abu Dhabi or ADIA ignored ECB's separate status, or that the sovereign so abused the corporate form that considerations of fair dealing require that we disregard the presumption of separateness. The facts merely show that the government, acting as a commercial entity, reneged on its contractual obligations. ZMEC then turned to a private commercial bank, ECB, for a loan. When it could not meet its loan obligations, ECB levied on the only available security interest—ZMEC. After ECB merged into ADCB in 1985, ADCB merely acted pursuant to the agreement its predecessor had negotiated. The acts of a private commercial entity, even one that supports a government, cannot be attributed to a government that has not authorized the private entity to act on its behalf. The strong presumption of separateness cannot be overcome on the facts of this case.

ZMEC also asserts that the acts of Abu Dhabi and ADIA alone are sufficient to serve as a basis for jurisdiction under the FSIA expropriation exception. Specifically, ZMEC relies on Abu Dhabi's refusal to pay ZMEC under the construction contracts and ADIA chairman Sheikh Khalifa's ex post facto approval of the 1983 Agreement as a basis for subject matter jurisdiction. Tellingly, ZMEC does not cite any law in support of that proposition. Abu Dhabi's alleged refusal to pay ZMEC under the construction contracts no doubt supports a commercial breach of contract claim. However, breach of a commercial contract alone does not constitute a taking pursuant to international law. Moreover, the government did not seize control of ZMEC. ECB transferred the management of ZMEC to a management team that consisted solely of private actors and included Mr. Zappia. As for ADIA, it was not even a party to any of the contracts at issue in this action. Although Sheikh Khalifa was the chairman of ADIA, his ex post facto approval of the 1983 Agreement alone is not sufficient to establish jurisdiction over ADIA.

Accordingly, the district court did not err in dismissing the complaint for lack of jurisdiction. . . .

Notes and Questions on the Takings Exception

1. *International and domestic takings.* Should a U.S. court interpret the FSIA's takings exception in light of the domestic takings jurisprudence under the

Fifth Amendment to the U.S. Constitution (which provides that "[n]o person shall . . . be deprived of . . . property, without due process; nor shall private property be taken for public use, without just compensation")?

> Where the government authorizes a physical occupation of property (or actually takes title), the Takings Clause generally requires compensation. *See, e.g., Loretto v. Teleprompter Manhattan CATV Corp.*, 458 U.S. 419, 426 (1982). But where the government merely regulates the use of property, compensation is required only if considerations such as the purpose of the regulation or the extent to which it deprives the owner of the economic use of the property suggest that the regulation has unfairly singled out the property owner to bear a burden that should be borne by the public as a whole. *See, e.g., Penn Central Transp. Co. v. New York City*, 438 U.S. 104, 123–125 (1978). The first category of cases requires courts to apply a clear rule; the second necessarily entails complex factual assessments of the purposes and economic effects of government actions.

Yee v. City of Escondido, 503 U.S. 519 (1992). *See also Hodel v. Irving*, 481 U.S. 704 (1987); *Miller v. Schoene*, 276 U.S. 272 (1928). Can't every governmental regulation "be viewed as taking particular strands in the bundle of property rights"? JOSEPH SINGER, PROPERTY LAW: RULES, POLICIES, AND PRACTICES (2d ed. 1997), at 1222. Is a U.S. court precluded from designating as a § 1605(a)(3) taking any action that would be lawful if the U.S. government did the same thing without compensation?

2. *Breach of contract as a taking.* In *Zappia*, the court was willing to assume that the foreign sovereign's refusal to pay the contractor would support a commercial breach of contract claim, but it did not rise to level of a "taking" pursuant to international law. What exactly does a breach of contract claim lack that prevents it from being litigated under § 1605(a)(3)?

3. *Taking of intangible property.* Suppose the Siderman's Argentine property included trademark protection for the Hotel Gran Corona's commercial symbols or copyrights on its brochures. Would that intangible property also be within the FSIA's takings exception?

> For some purposes other than the FSIA, "[a]s defined in international law, property commonly includes intangible assets and 'any interest in property if such interest has a reasonably ascertainable value'." *Banco Nacional de Cuba v. Chemical Bank New York Trust Co.*, 822 F.2d 230, 238 (2d Cir. 1987). *Accord West v. Multibanco Comermex, S.A.*, 807 F.2d 820, 829–30 (9th Cir.), *cert. denied*, 482 U.S. 906 (1987); Christie, *What Constitutes a Taking of Property Under International Law?*, 38 BRIT. Y.B. INT'L L. 307, 318–19 (1964) ("contract and many other so-called intangible rights can, under certain circumstances, be expropriated"). *See also De Sanchez v. Banco Cent. de Nicaragua*, 770 F.2d 1385, 1395 (5th Cir. 1985).

> But there is not yet universal agreement that the taking of intangible property necessarily falls within § 1605(a)(3). Assess the court's analysis in *Intercontinental Dictionary Series v. De Gruyter*, 822 F. Supp. 662, 678 (C.D. Cal. 1993), *disapproved on other grounds, Sun v. Taiwan*, 201 F.3d 1105 (9th Cir.), *cert. denied*, 531 U.S. 979, 121 S. Ct. 427 (2000):

Headquartered in Irvine, California, [Intercontinental Dictionary Series] ("IDS") is a private, unincorporated affiliation of linguistic scholars, many from prestigious universities throughout the world. The projects undertaken by IDS focus on the compilation and eventual publication of massive linguistic dictionaries covering languages spoken in various geographic regions of the world. The goal of IDS is to create and publish a series of such dictionary volumes using an orthographically uniform word list accessed through a computer database. . . .

In connection with its work, IDS has completed a manuscript entitled "Intercontinental Dictionary Series, Volume I: South American Indian Languages." As part of its planned series, IDS has also compiled a yet unpublished manuscript entitled "Intercontinental Dictionary Series, Volume II: Austronesian Languages" (the "IDS volume"), which is the centerpiece of this litigation. Approximately half of the contributors to the latter Austronesian languages volume are citizens of the United States. Furthermore, plaintiff has obtained a Certificate of Registration of Copyright on this IDS volume.

The ANU, the national university of Australia, was created by the Australian National University Act of 1946. One of the statutorily enumerated functions of the ANU is to "encourage, and provide facilities for, post-graduate research and study, both generally and in relation to subjects of national importance to Australia." The [Research School of Pacific Studies] ("RSPS") is a division of the ANU and the individual ANU defendants are employed in various capacities by the ANU and/or the RSPS. . . .

On an unspecified date, the Australian government began the funding of a project in furtherance of the ANU's statutorily-defined objectives to research matters of importance to Australia and the surrounding Pacific region. The project resulted in the development of a yet unpublished work entitled the Comparative Austronesian Dictionary ("the CAD treatise"). Accompanying the CAD treatise are associated computer databases and word lists. Like the IDS volume, the CAD treatise is a linguistic dictionary that documents the Austronesian family of languages. According to defendants, at no time did any entity other than the ANU and its staff membership contribute any linguistic materials to the development of the CAD treatise. The project that culminated in the CAD treatise was funded by the Australian national government . . . .

In its complaint, IDS asserts that it owns the CAD treatise, the related computer database, and the word lists covering the Austronesian languages for the following reasons: (1) it applied for registration of an early draft manuscript; (2) it developed the concept for a series of linguistic dictionary volumes covering different regions of the world; and (3) it hired Dr. Tryon as "volume editor" to develop the Austronesian manuscript as a volume of IDS's series of linguistic dictionaries. Plaintiff further alleges that the ANU defendants are infringing its copyright by developing the Austronesian materials to final form in the CAD treatise, by making an agreement with the German defendants to publish the CAD treatise, by representing that the CAD treatise is the property of the ANU defendants, and by refusing to turn over the CAD treatise to IDS. The gravamen of plaintiff's complaint is that the ANU defendants, most notably Dr. Tryon, have pirated the research and development undertaken in collaboration with IDS for its volume on the Austronesian languages and have created the CAD treatise as an infringing "spin-off" of the IDS volume. . . .

28 U.S.C. § 1605(a)(3) . . . establishes two scenarios for the application of the [takings] exception: one where the property must be present in the United States, and the other, where an agent or instrumentality owns the property in question and conducts commercial activity in the United States.

The ANU defendants have asserted that this exception does not apply to intangible property. *De Sanchez v. Banco Central de Nicaragua,* 770 F.2d 1385 (5th Cir. 1985). Although the *De Sanchez* court found a determination of the question unnecessary, it delineates why courts have restricted the exception to tangible property and suggests that the court would have adopted such an interpretation if necessary to its holding. In light of the statutory language, which appears by its language to require a taking of property in violation of international law, the Court approves of the rationale discussed in *De Sanchez.* . . . Plaintiff offers no argument to the contrary, and agreed at oral argument that the international takings exception should be applied only to tangible property. Thus, for purposes of the present motion at least, the intangible intellectual property rights or the right to receive payment on a contract alleged by IDS are not grounds for applying the exception.

Regarding application of the "international takings" exception, plaintiff simply states that word lists, disks, and manuscripts associated with the IDS volume and the CAD treatise are tangible forms of property. As noted above, the exception for takings of tangible property can apply in two circumstances. The complaint . . . and the declarations filed by defendants substantiate that the final CAD manuscript and the related computer materials are located in Canberra, Australia; they have never been taken to the United States. Plaintiff's interest in these materials is "intangible" and not present in the United States as required by the first part of the exception to the FSIA. Alternatively, while the ANU defendants "own" these items as an agency or instrumentality of the Australian government, they are not engaging in a "commercial activity" within the United States, so as to satisfy the second possibility for application of the exception — namely, that the property is owned or operated by an agency or instrumentality of the foreign state and that agency or instrumentality is engaged in a commercial activity in the United States.

Accordingly, because the ANU defendants are not engaging in a commercial activity with substantial contacts to the United States, the Court determines that the "international takings" exception is inapplicable on the facts of the present case.

How might you attack this approach on appeal? How would you advise IDS to protect its rights?

---

[e]   The Arbitration Exception

§ 1605. General exceptions to the jurisdictional immunity of a foreign state

(a) A foreign state shall not be immune from the jurisdiction of courts of the United States or of the States in any case . . .

(6) in which the action is brought, either to enforce an agreement made by the foreign state with or for the benefit of a private party to submit to arbitration all or any differences which have arisen or which may arise between the parties with respect to a defined legal relationship, whether contractual or not, concerning a subject matter capable of settlement by arbitration under the laws of the United States, or to confirm an award made pursuant to such an agreement to arbitrate, if (A) the arbitration takes place or is intended to take place in the United States, (B) the agreement or award is or may be governed by a treaty or other international agreement in force for the United States calling for the recognition and enforcement of arbitral awards, the underlying claim, save for the agreement to arbitrate, could have been brought in a United States court under this section or section 1607, or (D) paragraph (1) of this subsection is otherwise applicable; . . .

S & DAVIS INTERNATIONAL, INC. v. REPUBLIC OF YEMEN
218 F.3d 1292 (11th Cir. 2000)

S & Davis International, Inc. ("S & Davis") filed suit in the Northern District of Alabama to enforce an arbitration award against the General Corporation for Foreign Trade and Grains ("General Corporation") of Yemen. The suit arose from a breach of contract dispute. S & Davis also named the Ministry of Supply & Trade (the "Ministry") and The Republic of Yemen as defendants, asserting that the General Corporation was controlled by the government. The Ministry filed a motion to dismiss, claiming immunity under the Foreign Sovereign Immunities Act of 1976 ("FSIA"). The district court held there was sufficient subject matter jurisdiction and personal jurisdiction to proceed. The Ministry appeals. . . . We affirm. . . .

On May 14, 1996, the General Corporation, a Yemeni corporation, executed a contract with S & Davis, an Alabama corporation, to purchase 300,000 metric tons of wheat at a price of $274.88 per ton. [According to the president of S & Davis,] the contract was prepared "according to the instructions of the Ministry of Supply & Trade," and "[a]ll aspects of the contract were reportedly being discussed with the Minister of Supply who appeared to [be] the principal in the transaction." In addition to the signatures of the two named parties, A.M. Ali Othman, the Minister of Supply & Trade of Yemen, also signed the contract, indicating approval by the Ministry as required under Yemeni law.

The contract specified U.S. wheat No. 2 or better with point of origin from the U.S., Canada, Australia, South Africa, or Argentina. The wheat was to be shipped from Portland, Oregon and delivered to Yemen, with freight charges calculated from Portland. The purchase price was to be paid with a letter of credit issued by the Bank of Yemen with confirmation by a "U.S.A. prime bank." . . . The contract was negotiated and signed in Yemen. However, the contract contained an arbitration agreement providing that any dispute was to be arbitrated by the Grain and Feed Trade Association ("GAFTA") in London, England. . . .

On September 14, the Embassy notified S & Davis that efforts to convince the Governor of the Central Bank of Yemen to open a letter of credit had failed. The General Corporation admits it was not able to obtain a letter of credit as required in the contract. After additional attempts through various political and diplomatic channels to open a letter of credit, on January 2, 1997, S & Davis declared the General Corporation had breached the contract and initiated GAFTA arbitration in London. Both parties agree that S & Davis had never purchased any wheat under the contract.

S & Davis sought damages against both the General Corporation and the Ministry of Trade, asserting that the General Corporation was not an independent organization with authority to contract. S & Davis maintains that the Ministry of Supply & Trade was a principal in the transaction, that it was the alter ego of the General Corporation, that it was in privity with the General Corporation and that through its interference it caused the breach of contract. S & Davis submitted an affidavit from a Yemeni solicitor, "by education, training and profession, . . . an expert in the laws of the Republic of Yemen," who stated, "[t]he Public Corporations established under the caption law bear no semblance to western business corporations. All the Yemeni Corporations, including the Public Corporation for Foreign Trade and Grains, are wholly owned by the Government of Yemen." . . .

The original GAFTA panel held that the General Corporation breached the contract by failing to open a letter of credit but concluded that S & Davis had not shown entitlement to any damages. . . . The appellate arbitration panel affirmed the finding of a breach of contract but awarded S & Davis approximately $17 million in damages against the General Corporation. . . . On December 18, 1998, S & Davis filed this suit in federal district court to enforce the arbitration award, in addition to a claim for breach of contract and enforcement of the arbitration award against the Republic of Yemen asserting that the General Corporation is a political subdivision of the Republic, and an alternative claim for tortious interference with contractual relations against the Ministry of Supply & Trade for the amount of the arbitration award. . . .

The Ministry claimed immunity under the FSIA, as a political subdivision of The Republic of Yemen. S & Davis asserted that subject matter jurisdiction was allowed under the FSIA and the Convention on the Recognition and

Enforcement of Foreign Arbitration Awards, 9 U.S.C. § 201 *et seq*. The district court . . . denied the Ministry's motion on all grounds. The Ministry timely filed a notice of appeal.

ANALYSIS

[After establishing its appellate jurisdiction and the standard on review, the court ruled that the General Corporation was not an entity separate and independent from the Yemeni ministry, citing *Bank of United States v. Planters' Bank of Georgia*, 9 Wheat. 904, 22 U.S. 904, 907 (1824) ("when a government becomes a partner in any trading company, it divests itself, so far as concerns the transactions of that company, of its sovereign character, and takes that of a private citizen. Instead of communicating to the company its privileges and its prerogatives, it descends to a level with those with whom it associates itself, and takes the character which belongs to its associates, and to the business which is to be transacted.")]

S & Davis claims that the Ministry is subject to jurisdiction pursuant to exceptions set forth in § 1605 of the FSIA; the waiver exception, 28 U.S.C. § 1605(a)(1), the arbitration exception under § 1605(a)(6)(B), and the commercial activity exception, 28 U.S.C. § 1605(a)(2). . . .

A waiver of immunity may be explicit or by implication. S & Davis asserts that by agreeing to arbitrate pursuant to the rules of GAFTA in London, the Ministry, through the General Corporation, impliedly waived its sovereign immunity. S & Davis points to the legislative history of § 1605(a)(1), which states, "with respect to implicit waivers, the courts have found such waivers in cases where a foreign state has agreed to arbitration in another country or where a foreign state has agreed that the law of a particular country should govern a contract." H. R. REP. NO. 1487, 94th Cong., 2d Sess. at 18 (1976), *reprinted in* 1976 U.S.C.C.A.N. 6604, 6617.

As provided for in the contract, the parties submitted their dispute to arbitration before GAFTA. S & Davis now seeks to have the arbitral award issued by GAFTA recognized and enforced in the courts of the United States, pursuant to the Convention on the Recognition and Enforcement of Arbitral Awards (the "Convention"), opened for signature June 10, 1958, Art. I.1, 21 U.S.T. 2517, reprinted in 9 U.S.C. § 201. The Convention provides that "it shall apply to the recognition and enforcement of arbitral awards made in the territory of a State other than the State where the recognition and enforcement of such awards are sought," Art. I, and that "[e]ach Contracting State shall recognize arbitral awards as binding and enforce them in accordance with the rules of procedure of the territory where the award is relied upon. . . ." *Id.* Art. III. Therefore, when a country becomes a signatory to the Convention, by the provisions of the Convention, the signatory State must have contemplated enforcement actions in other signatory states.

Most courts have determined that the implied waiver provision of § 1605(a)(1) must be construed narrowly. Interpreting § 1605(a)(1), the Supreme Court held "we [do not] see how a foreign state can waive its immunity under § 1605(a)(1) by signing an international agreement that contains no mention of a waiver of immunity to suit in United States courts or even the availability of a cause of action in the United States." *Argentine Republic* [*v. Amerada Hess Shipping Corp.*, 488 U.S. 428 (1989),] at 442–43.

In this case, although the United States and England are signatories to the Convention, The Republic of Yemen is not. The Ministry argues that a sovereign's agreement to arbitrate in a Convention State is not a waiver of immunity to suit in the U.S. unless the foreign sovereign is also a party to the Convention. A similar situation is found in *Creighton Ltd. v. Government of the State of Qatar*, 181 F.3d 118 (D.C. Cir. 1999). Creighton, a Cayman Islands' corporation with offices in Tennessee, contracted with the government of Qatar to build a hospital in Qatar. Following a dispute over its performance, Creighton obtained an arbitral award against Qatar from the International Chamber of Commerce in Paris and then sought to enforce the award in the district court for the District of Columbia. Due to the fact that Qatar was not a signatory to the Convention, the D.C. Circuit rejected a broad reading of the implicit waiver section that would allow waiver where the defendant sovereign is not a signatory to the Convention, finding that Qatar's "agreement to arbitrate in a signatory country, without more, [did not] demonstrate[] the requisite intent to waive its sovereign immunity in the United States." We agree that there was no waiver of sovereign immunity.

However, the court in *Creighton* found jurisdiction under the arbitration exception in § 1605(a)(6)(B), stating that "the New York Convention is exactly the sort of treaty Congress intended to include in the arbitration exception." As the court in *Creighton* noted, "[Section] 1605(a)(6) does not affect the contractual right of the parties to arbitration but only the tribunal that may hear a dispute concerning the enforcement of an arbitral award." The Ministry contends that because it was not a party to the contract, it is not subject to the arbitration agreement or award. While it is true that in *Creighton*, Qatar was a direct party to the contract, given our determination that there was sufficient evidence to show the General Corporation is an agency or instrumentality under the control of the Ministry, we find that the district court has subject matter jurisdiction pursuant to the arbitration exception under § 1605(a)(6)(B), where a foreign state has no immunity from a proceeding to confirm an award that "may be governed by a treaty . . . calling for the recognition and enforcement of arbitral awards." 28 U.S.C. § 1605(a)(6)(B).[1]

[The court also found that the commercial activity exception applied, declaring: "We are not persuaded by the Ministry's argument that this case is the same as *MOL, Inc. v. Peoples Republic of Bangladesh*, 736 F.2d 1326 (9th Cir. 1984), where the Bangladesh Ministry of Agriculture granted a ten-year license to MOL, an Oregon corporation, to export rhesus monkeys. The Ninth Circuit found this license "was not just a contract for trade of monkeys." Unlike *MOL*, the contract between S & Davis and the General Corporation was just a contract and the Ministry was more involved than a mere regulator, whose directives, not based upon regulatory reasons, controlled the General Corporation's actions. This was a commercial activity exception."]

---

[1] Neither party disputes the fact that the petition for enforcement was filed within the three year period after an award is made, as required by 9 U.S.C. § 207. Nor does the Ministry contest the validity of the award or argue to vacate the award under 9 U.S.C. § 10.

CARGILL INTERNATIONAL S.A. v. M/T PAVEL DYBENKO
991 F.2d 1012 (2d Cir. 1993)

Plaintiff-Appellant, Cargill B.V. ("CBV"), appeals from the grant of summary judgment . . . in favor of the defendant, Novorossiysk Shipping Company ("Novorossiysk"), denying plaintiffs' request to compel Novorossiysk to arbitrate in London. The district court found that Novorossiysk was a foreign sovereign and that CBV had failed to establish jurisdiction under the Foreign Sovereign Immunities Act, 28 U.S.C. §§ 1602–1611 ("FSIA"). For the reasons that follow, we reverse and remand.

BACKGROUND

On June 14, 1988, CBV, a Dutch corporation with its principal offices in Amsterdam, bought 7,000 metric tons of crude Argentine degummed soybean oil from [Cargill International S.A. ("CISA")], a company incorporated under the laws of the Netherlands Antilles and based in Geneva, Switzerland. Subsequently, CISA entered into a Charter Party with Novorossiysk, an entity wholly owned by the former Soviet Union, to transport the oil from Argentina and Brazil to the Netherlands aboard Novorossiysk's ship, the M/T Pavel Dybenko.

Under Clause 24 . . . of the Charter Party, any dispute arising out of the Charter Party is to be submitted to arbitration in either New York or London, "whichever place is specified in Part I of this charter pursuant to the laws relating to arbitration there in force." . . . Part I specifies London as the site for arbitration proceedings. In addition, Clause 28 of the Special Provisions appended to the Charter Party provides that the bills of lading should "incorporate particulars of Charter Party i.e. . . . . — Arbitration in London should be stated in the Bill of Lading." On July 16–18, 1988, the M/T Pavel Dybenko was loaded with 9,100 metric tons of degummed soyabean oil in San Lorenzo, Argentina, and on July 23, 1988, with 5,750 metric tons in Rio Grande, Brazil. Pursuant to the terms of the Charter Party, CISA, through its Argentine agents/shippers, had the bills of lading presented to the master of the Pavel Dybenko for his signature. Despite Clause 28 of the Charter Party, the bills of lading failed to "incorporate particulars" of the Charter Party, including the arbitration provision. CBV is the receiver and holder of bills of lading issued in connection with this cargo.

After arrival in Amsterdam, CBV subjected the cargo to chemical analysis and allegedly found it to have been contaminated with hydrocarbons during the course of the voyage. As a result, CBV claimed monetary damages in the amount of $920,000. CBV presented its claim to the West of England Shipowners Mutual Insurance Association ("West of England"). As security for the claim, West of England guaranteed by letter that it would appear and pay any judgment rendered by a Dutch court having jurisdiction in this case. From July, 1989 to April, 1990, the parties' insurance representatives entered into three agreements extending CISA and CBV's time to commence legal proceedings against the defendants. The last extension granted by defendants was to expire on May 9, 1990.

On May 7, 1990, the plaintiffs sought an additional three-month extension. They telexed their request to Novorossiysk's headquarters in Moscow. Apparently, the request arrived on a state holiday and received no response. As a result, on May 9, 1990, CISA designated its arbitrator in London under the terms of the Charter Party. Both CBV and CISA also brought this suit against the defendants in order to protect whatever rights they might have in the United States, the only forum in which the statute of limitations had not yet expired. No other fora remained open to them at the time. The complaint sought an order to compel Novorossiysk to arbitrate in London. . . . CISA has agreed to stay its claims pending the outcome of its arbitration in London.

In CBV's suit before the district court, it alleged jurisdiction based on three exceptions to the FSIA: the waiver exception, the arbitration exception, and the maritime lien exception, found respectively in 28 U.S.C. §§ 1605(a)(1), 1605(a)(6)(B), and 1605(b). The district court found none of the exceptions to be applicable. First, the court found no implicit or explicit waiver by Novorossiysk of its sovereign immunity due to its agreement in the Charter Party to arbitrate disputes in London. Second, the court noted that the bills of lading contained no arbitration clause and thus the arbitration exception did not apply. The court refused to consider CBV's argument that it was a third-party beneficiary of the arbitration clause in the Charter Party. According to the court, it required a "basis for subject matter jurisdiction" in order to reformulate the contract between CBV and Novorossiysk. Third, the court found that the plaintiffs had met none of the requirements to enforce a maritime lien.

Because a court has jurisdiction to determine its own jurisdiction, we reverse and remand to the district court for a determination of whether CBV can prove its third party beneficiary status and thus establish subject matter jurisdiction.

DISCUSSION

. . . As a sovereign entity under the FSIA, Novorossiysk is entitled to immunity unless one of the statutory exceptions applies. Once the defendant presents a *prima facie* case that it is a foreign sovereign, the plaintiff has the burden of going forward with evidence showing that, under exceptions to the FSIA, immunity should not be granted, although the ultimate burden of persuasion remains with the alleged foreign sovereign.

CBV argues that Novorossiysk . . . is not entitled to sovereign immunity under two exceptions to the FSIA. First, CBV contends that Novorossiysk has waived its immunity under 28 U.S.C. § 1605(a)(1), the waiver exception, by agreeing to arbitrate its dispute with CISA; second, CBV asserts that the arbitration exception, 28 U.S.C. § 1605(a)(6), also deprives Novorossiysk of immunity. . . .

1. The Waiver Argument

The waiver exception permits federal courts to assert jurisdiction over any foreign sovereign that waives its immunity "either explicitly or by implication." 28 U.S.C. § 1605(a)(1). The House Report which accompanied the FSIA listed three examples of implicit waivers: when (1) a foreign state has agreed to arbitrate in another country; (2) a foreign state has agreed that the law of a particular country shall govern; or (3) a foreign state has filed a responsive pleading but has failed to raise the defense of sovereign immunity.

In *Zernicek v. Petroleos Mexicanos*, 614 F. Supp. 407, 411 (S.D. Tex. 1985), *aff'd*, 826 F.2d 415 (5th Cir. 1987), *cert. denied*, 484 U.S. 1043 (1988), the court noted that courts have interpreted the waiver provision narrowly: "most courts have refused to find an implicit waiver of immunity to suit in American courts from a contract clause providing for arbitration in a country other than the United States." Moreover, it is rare for a court to find that a country's waiver of immunity extends to third parties not privy to the contract. When the case involves an implied waiver, we think that a court should be even more hesitant to extend the waiver in favor of third parties. We agree with these courts that such a waiver will not be implied absent strong evidence of the sovereign's intent. In *Maritime Ventures Int'l, Inc. v. Caribbean Trading & Fidelity, Ltd.*, 689 F. Supp. 1340, 1351 (S.D.N.Y. 1988), the court warned that a broader interpretation "would result in a vast increase in the jurisdiction of the federal courts over matters involving sensitive foreign relations." Because of these concerns, an agreement to arbitrate in a foreign country, without more, ought not to operate as a waiver of sovereign immunity in United States courts, especially in favor of a non-party to the agreement. Thus, CBV may not depend on Novorossiysk's agreement to arbitrate with CISA in London to show that the Soviet entity had impliedly waived its immunity to jurisdiction in the United States.

2. The Arbitration Exception

Section 1605(a)(6)(B) of the FSIA provides an exception to sovereign immunity in cases where a foreign state has agreed to arbitrate and the arbitration agreement is or may be governed by a treaty signed by the United States calling for the recognition and enforcement of arbitral awards.[1] CBV argues that it may enforce the arbitration clause contained in the Charter Party against Novorossiysk as a third party beneficiary to the Charter Party, and that this clause is governed by the Convention on the Recognition and Enforcement of Foreign Arbitral Awards, 21 U.S.T. 2517, T.I.A.S. No. 6997, 330 U.N.T.S. 3 (the "Convention").

The United States became a party to the Convention in 1970 and Congress soon enacted implementing legislation, codified as Chapter II of the Federal Arbitration Act, 9 U.S.C. §§ 201–208. Congress vested federal district courts with original jurisdiction over any action or proceeding "falling under the Convention," having deemed such an action "to arise under the laws and treaties of the United States." 9 U.S.C. § 203. *See also Dworkin-Cosell Interair Courier Serv., Inc. v. Avraham*, 728 F. Supp. 156, 158 (S.D.N.Y. 1989) (the Convention "vests United States' district courts with original jurisdiction . . . over actions concerning '[a]n arbitration agreement . . .' "). Furthermore, the statute states that "[a]n arbitration agreement . . . arising out of a legal

---

[1] As stated by Senator Mathias, the main sponsor of the bill to amend the FSIA to provide for this exception, "unless the arbitration agreement is enforceable, the arbitration is meaningless. . . . This amendment will reassure businesses that the international arbitration process will work. It does so by amending the FSIA to say that an agreement to arbitrate constitutes a waiver of immunity in an action to enforce that agreement or the resultant award." 131 Cong. Rec. S5369 (daily ed. May 3, 1985).

relationship, whether contractual or not, which is considered as commercial, including a transaction, contract, or agreement described in section 2 of this title, falls under the Convention." 9 U.S.C. § 202.[2]

As the 9th Circuit stated in *Ministry of Defense of the Islamic Republic of Iran v. Gould, Inc.,* 887 F.2d 1357, 1362 (9th Cir. 1989), *cert. denied,* 494 U.S. 1016 (1990), three basic requirements must be met for a district court to find jurisdiction under the Convention: "the award (1) must arise out of a legal relationship (2) which is commercial in nature and (3) which is not entirely domestic in scope." If a district court finds that these requirements are met, it must order arbitration unless it finds the agreement "null and void, inoperative or incapable of being performed." Convention, Article II(3).

As the Supreme Court observed in *Scherk v. Alberto-Culver Co.,* 417 U.S. 506, 520 n. 15 (1974),

> [t]he goal of the Convention, and the principal purpose underlying the American adoption and implementation of it, was to encourage recognition and enforcement of commercial arbitration agreements in international contracts and to unify the standards by which agreements to arbitrate are observed and arbitral awards are enforced in the signatory countries.

Thus, the Convention should be broadly interpreted to effectuate the goals of the legislation. Moreover, when the Convention is read together with the FSIA's arbitration exception, which gives jurisdiction if an arbitration agreement "is or may be governed" by a treaty, 28 U.S.C. § 1605(a)(6)(B) (emphasis added), it evinces a strong legislative intent to provide enforcement for such agreements. We agree with CBV that the Convention is exactly the sort of treaty Congress intended to include in the arbitration exception. If the alleged arbitration agreement exists, it satisfies the requirements for subject matter jurisdiction under the Convention and FSIA.

We believe the district court in this case erred in deciding that it could not assess CBV's third party beneficiary argument because it did not have jurisdiction to make this initial determination. Rather than considering the allegations to see if they gave the court subject matter jurisdiction, the court stated that "regardless of the merits," the contractual arguments could not be addressed. According to the court, it lacked subject matter jurisdiction because there was no arbitration agreement. We find, however, that the district court was required to weigh the contractual arguments before it could determine that no arbitration agreement existed. . . .

[T]he district court must look at the substance of the allegations to determine jurisdiction. In resolving the jurisdictional dispute, the district court must review the pleadings and any evidence before it, such as affidavits. . . . The district court, if necessary, may proceed to a trial on this issue. The Federal Arbitration Act, which applies to actions under the Convention where the two are not in conflict, 9 U.S.C. § 208, authorizes a summary trial to

---

[2] 9 U.S.C. § 206, a section of the legislation implementing the Convention, gives a district court the power to compel arbitration in accordance with the agreement, even if the site of arbitration is outside of the United States. Novorossiysk does not contest this power.

determine whether an agreement to arbitrate actually exists. 9 U.S.C. § 4 (1988).

CBV alleges that CISA and Novorossiysk intended to make CBV a third party beneficiary of the Charter Party and in particular of its arbitration clause. Thus, to determine whether subject matter jurisdiction existed, the district court ought to have determined whether, if the facts as alleged by CBV are true, the arbitration agreement in the Charter Party was intended to benefit CBV. [A] Charter Party is just a species of contract, subject to the same rules of interpretation as any other binding agreement. . . .

In order to enforce the agreement as a third party beneficiary, CBV must show that "the parties to that contract intended to confer a benefit on [it] when contracting; it is not enough that some benefit incidental to the performance of the contract may accrue to [it]." *McPheeters v. McGinn, Smith and Co., Inc.,* 953 F.2d 771, 773 (2d Cir. 1992). . . . We note that if CBV is found to be a third party beneficiary to the Charter Party, it may be proper for the district court to enforce the arbitration agreement against Novorossiysk. Because the parties have not adequately addressed this issue in their briefs, however, we leave the arguments to them and the district court. . . .

Notes and Questions on S & *Davis, Cargill,* and the Arbitration Exception

1. *Arbitral awards and agreements to arbitrate. Davis* and *Cargill* illustrate the two principal uses of the arbitration exception to foreign sovereign immunity: enforcing an award actually rendered by an arbitral panel and enforcing the underlying agreement to arbitrate. *See also U.S. Titan, Inc. v. Guangzhou Zhen Hua Shipping Co.,* 241 F.3d 135 (2d Cir. 2001). *Compare Seetransport Wiking Trader Schiffarhtsgesellschaft MBH & Co. v. Navimpex Centrala Navala,* 989 F.2d 572, 577–79 (2d Cir. 1993) (distinguishing between cases in which the plaintiff seeks to enforce award and cases in which no award yet exists). Notice also that the inherent jurisdiction of the court to determine its own jurisdiction under the FSIA may, as in *Cargill,* take the court into the merits of the underlying contractual claim. Cargill for example was trying to establish that it was a third-party beneficiary of a contract and to use that status to enforce the arbitration agreement.

2. *Relationship between § 1605(a)(1) and § 1605(a)(6).* The legislative history of the FSIA suggests that plaintiffs with an arbitration agreement in-hand may have two theories of recovery — one under the waiver exception and one under the arbitration exception. For the reasons suggested above (*see supra* page 442) and as *Cargill* itself demonstrates, the waiver exception as interpreted is considerably narrower than Congress may have had in mind. The arbitration exception appears broader (not least because it has no comparable requirement of intentionality), but it too is subject to limitations. Like what?

3. *The Federal Arbitration Act versus § 1605(a)(6).* Recall that the *Cargill* court cited *Ministry of Defense of the Islamic Republic of Iran v. Gould* for

the proposition that "three basic requirements must be met for a district court to find jurisdiction under the Convention: 'the award (1) must arise out of a legal relationship (2) which is commercial in nature and (3) which is not entirely domestic in scope.'" *Gould* did not base jurisdiction on the Foreign Sovereign Immunities Act however: the Federal Arbitration Act, 9 U.S.C. § 201 gives courts original jurisdiction over an action or proceeding that falls under the Convention. But the criteria for bringing a claim under the Convention would be irrelevant if the defendant state were not a party to that treaty.

Looking at the language of § 1605(a)(6), how would you articulate the difference between (i) jurisdiction under the Convention and the Federal Arbitration Act as summarized in *Gould* and (ii) jurisdiction under the arbitration exception of the FSIA?

4. *Personal jurisdiction under § 1605(a)(6).* Many courts continue to assume that foreign states are persons within the meaning of the Due Process Clause, suggesting in turn that they are entitled to the "minimum contacts" test of *International Shoe* for personal jurisdiction. *See supra* note 4 following *Amerada Hess*, at page 403. The Supreme Court has not finally resolved the issue and the FSIA itself suggests that personal jurisdiction is satisfied if the court has subject matter jurisdiction and the foreign state has been properly served: "[p]ersonal jurisdiction over a foreign state shall exist as to every claim for relief over which the district courts have [subject matter] jurisdiction under subsection (a) where service has been made under [28 U.S.C. § 1608]." 28 U.S.C. § 1330(b).

But the lower courts have not come to consensus on the issue. In *Creighton Ltd. v. Government of the State of Qatar*, 181 F.3d 118 (D.C. Cir. 1999), Creighton won an $8 million arbitral award from the International Chamber of Commerce in Paris and sought to enforce it in a U.S. court when enforcement in France failed. The court determined that the criteria for subject matter jurisdiction under § 1605(a)(6) had been satisfied, but the case was still dismissed for failure of personal jurisdiction. The underlying contract had been offered, accepted, and performed in Qatar, and *International Shoe* could not be satisfied by the defendant's hiring of Creighton Ltd. (a Cayman Islands corporation with offices in the state of Tennessee).

---

[f]   The Terrorism Exception

§ 1605. General exceptions to the jurisdictional immunity of a foreign state

(a) A foreign state shall not be immune from the jurisdiction of courts of the United States or of the States in any case —

(7) not otherwise covered by paragraph (2) [the commercial activity exception], in which money damages are sought against a foreign state for personal injury or death that was caused by an act of torture, extrajudicial

killing, aircraft sabotage, hostage taking, or the provision of material support or resources (as defined in section 2339A of title 18) for such an act if such act or provision of material support is engaged in by an official, employee, or agent of such foreign state while acting within the scope of his or her office, employment, or agency, except that the court shall decline to hear a claim under this paragraph —

(A) if the foreign state was not designated as a state sponsor of terrorism under section 6(j) of the Export Administration Act of 1979 (50 U.S.C. App. 2405(j)) or section 620A of the Foreign Assistance Act of 1961 (22 U.S.C. 2371) at the time the act occurred, unless later so designated as a result of such act or the act is related to Case Number 1:00CV03110 (EGS) in the United States District Court for the District of Columbia [the *Flatow* litigation, *infra*]; and

(B) even if the foreign state is or was so designated, if —

(i) the act occurred in the foreign state against which the claim has been brought and the claimant has not afforded the foreign state a reasonable opportunity to arbitrate the claim in accordance with accepted international rules of arbitration; or

(ii) neither the claimant nor the victim was a national of the United States (as that term is defined in section 101(a)(22) of the Immigration and Nationality Act) when the act upon which the claim is based occurred.

FLATOW v. IRAN
999 F. Supp. 1 (D.D.C. 1998)

[Alisa Flatow, a U.S. citizen, was a college student visiting Israel, when a suicide bomber drove a van loaded with explosives into the bus she was riding. Believing that her death was the result of state-sponsored terrorism, her father sued the Islamic Republic of Iran, its intelligence service, and various Iranian officials.]

Plaintiff brings this action pursuant to two recently enacted amendments to the FSIA, which grant jurisdiction over foreign states and their officials, agents and employees, and create federal causes of action related to personal injury or death resulting from state-sponsored terrorist attacks. Given these novel enactments, and this Court's special role in the development of foreign sovereign immunity jurisprudence, this Court has engaged in a systematic review of dispositive legal issues prior to making its determination that Plaintiff has established his claim and right to relief to the satisfaction of this Court [28 U.S.C. § 1608(e) and Fed. R. Civ. P. 55(a)] . . . .

As this action is brought against a foreign state, its intelligence service acting as its agent, and three of its officials, acting in their official capacity,[1]

---

[1] This Circuit has previously recognized that although the FSIA neither prohibits nor provides for its application to defendants who are natural persons, maintenance of a coherent practice regarding foreign sovereign immunity weighs heavily in favor of applying the FSIA to individuals. The FSIA has thus been construed to apply to individuals for acts performed in their official capacity on behalf of either a foreign state or its agency or instrumentality.

the Foreign Sovereign Immunities Act of 1976, ["FSIA"], as amended, controls this action. . . . This Court lacks jurisdiction over this matter unless it falls within one of the FSIA's enumerated exceptions to foreign sovereign immunity.

. . . In the Antiterrorism and Effective Death Penalty Act of 1996, Congress lifted the immunity of foreign states for a certain category of sovereign acts which are repugnant to the United States and the international community — terrorism [hereinafter "state sponsored terrorism exception"]. That Act created an exception to the immunity of those foreign states officially designated by the Department of State as terrorist states[2] if the foreign state commits a terrorist act, or provides material support and resources to an individual or entity which commits such an act, which results in the death or personal injury of a United States citizen.

Although the Antiterrorism Act created a forum competent to adjudicate claims arising from offenses of this nature, serious issues remained, in particular, the causes of action available to plaintiffs. Congressman Jim Saxton sponsored an amendment to 28 U.S.C. § 1605(a)(7) with the intent to clarify this and other issues. In Congressman Saxton's experience as Chairman of the House Task Force on Counterterrorism and Unconventional Warfare and member of the House National Security Committee, in order for the exception for immunity to have the desired deterrent effect, the potential civil liability for foreign states which commit and sponsor acts of terrorism would have to be substantial. Therefore, the amendment to 28 U.S.C. § 1605(a)(7) expressly provided, *inter alia*, that punitive damages were available in actions brought under the state sponsored terrorism exception to immunity. The amendment, Civil Liability for Acts of State Sponsored Terrorism, was enacted on September 30, 1996 as part of the 1997 Omnibus Consolidated Appropriations Act, and . . . is commonly referred to as the "Flatow Amendment."

Although the events complained of herein occurred more than a year prior to the enactment of the Antiterrorism and Effective Death Penalty Act of 1996, § 1605(a)(7) provides a basis for subject matter jurisdiction. Congress has expressly directed the retroactive application of § 1605(a)(7) in order to further a comprehensive counterterrorism initiative by the legislative branch of government. . . . Furthermore, the state sponsored terrorism exception to foreign sovereign immunity is a remedial statute. It creates no new responsibilities or obligations; it only creates a forum for the enforcement of preexisting universally recognized rights under federal common law and international law. . . .

SUBJECT MATTER JURISDICTION

In order to establish subject matter jurisdiction pursuant to § 1605(a)(7), a claim must contain the following statutory elements:

(1) that personal injury or death resulted from an act of torture, extrajudicial killing, aircraft sabotage, or hostage taking; and

---

[2] In addition to the Islamic Republic of Iran, the foreign states currently designated as sponsors of terrorism . . . are: Cuba, Syria, Iraq, Libya, Sudan and North Korea. [*See* 31 C.F.R. § 596.201.]

(2) the act was either perpetrated by the foreign state directly or by a non-state actor which receives material support or resources from the foreign state defendant; and

(3) the act or the provision of material support or resources is engaged in by an agent, official or employee of the foreign state while acting within the scope of his or her office, agency or employment; and

(4) that the foreign state be designated as a state sponsor of terrorism either at the time the incident complained of occurred or was later so designated as a result of such act; and

(5) if the incident complained of occurred with[in] the foreign state defendant's territory, plaintiff has offered the defendants a reasonable opportunity to arbitrate the matter; and

(6) either the plaintiff or the victim was a United States national at the time of the incident; and

(7) similar conduct by United States agents, officials, or employees within the United States would be actionable.

While elements (4)–(6) are pure questions of fact, elements (1)–(3) and (7) are mixed questions of law and fact, and, in the absence of settled precedent, require interpretation.

1. A SUICIDE BOMBING IS AN ACT OF EXTRAJUDICIAL KILLING.

Plaintiff describes the cause of his daughter's death as an "extrajudicial killing" within the meaning of § 1605(a)(7). The state-sponsored terrorism exception to immunity expressly adopts the definition of extrajudicial killing set forth in the Torture Victim Protection Act of 1991. That Act defines an "extrajudicial killing" as

a deliberate killing not authorized by a previous judgment pronounced by a regularly constituted court affording all judicial guarantees which are recognized as indispensable by civilized peoples. Such term, however, does not include any such killing that, under international law, is lawfully carried out under the authority of a foreign nation.

"Deliberate" is defined as:

. . . . carried on coolly and steadily, especially according to a preconceived design; given to weighing facts and arguments with a view to a choice or decision; careful in considering the consequences of a step;
. . . .

Other courts have found that summary executions, for example, would be considered "extrajudicial killings" within the meaning of 28 U.S.C.A. § 1350 note. See Lafontant v. Aristide, 844 F. Supp. 128 (E.D.N.Y. 1994) (dicta). In actions brought under the Alien Tort Statute and the Torture Victim Protection Act, courts have suggested, in the context of command responsibility, that a course of indiscriminate brutality, known to result in deaths, rises to the level of "extrajudicial killings." See also In re Yamashita, 327 U.S. 1 (1946) (". . . a deliberate plan and purpose to massacre and exterminate . . . unarmed noncombatant civilians . . . without cause or trial . . . and without military necessity.")

The state sponsored terrorism exception to immunity was enacted as part of a comprehensive legislative initiative to squelch international terrorism — the Antiterrorism and Effective Death Penalty Act of 1996. Previous treatments of international terrorism by Congress therefore appropriately inform the interpretation of "deliberated killing". One statute *in pari materia* defines terrorism as ". . . meaning premeditated, politically motivated violence perpetrated against noncombatant targets by subnational groups or clandestine agents." 22 U.S.C. § 2656f(d)(2). As the state sponsored terrorism exception expressly incorporates a definition from the United States criminal code chapter on international terrorism, another definition from that chapter is also apropos:

> (1) the term "international terrorism" means activities that —
>
> A. involve violent acts or acts dangerous to human life that are a violation of the criminal laws of the United States or of any State, or that would be a criminal violation if committed within the jurisdiction of the United States or of any State;
>
> B. appear to be intended —
>
> i) to intimidate or coerce a civilian population;
>
> ii) to influence the policy of a government by intimidation or coercion;
>
> iii) to affect the conduct of a government by assassination or kidnapping; and
>
> C. occur primarily outside the territorial jurisdiction of the United States, or transcend national boundaries in terms of the means by which they are accomplished, the persons they appear intended to intimidate or coerce, or the locale in which their perpetrators operate or seek asylum; . . .

18 U.S.C. § 2331. Attempts to reach a fixed, universally accepted definition of international terrorism have been frustrated both by changes in terrorist methodology and the lack of any precise definition of the term "terrorism." Therefore, the United States characterizes rather than enumerates acts for the purposes of designating foreign state sponsors of terrorism and defining criminal terrorist offenses under federal law. Each of the acts listed in § 1605(a)(7) fully conform with the foregoing definitions and provisions.

This Court concludes that a suicide bombing conforms with each of the foregoing provisions and definitions, and therefore is an act of "extrajudicial killing" within the meaning of § 1605(a)(7).

2. THE ROUTINE PROVISION OF FINANCIAL ASSISTANCE TO A TERRORIST GROUP IN SUPPORT OF ITS TERRORIST ACTIVITIES CONSTITUTES THE PROVISION OF MATERIAL SUPPORT OR RESOURCES WITHIN THE MEANING OF § 1605(a)(7).

The state-sponsored terrorism provision adopts the definition of "providing material support or resources" set forth in the federal criminal code. Section 1605(a)(7) incorporates 18 U.S.C. § 2339A by reference, which provides that:

> . . . "material support or resources" means currency or other financial securities, financial services, lodging, training, safehouses, false

documentation or identification, communications equipment, facilities, weapons, lethal substances, explosives, personnel, transportation, and other physical assets, but does not include humanitarian assistance to persons not directly involved in such violations.

This Court concludes that the routine provision of financial assistance to a terrorist group in support of its terrorist activities constitutes "providing material support or resources" for a terrorist act within the meaning of § 1605(a)(7). Furthermore, as nothing in 18 U.S.C. § 2339A or § 1605(a)(7) indicates otherwise, this Court also concludes that a plaintiff need not establish that the material support or resources provided by a foreign state for a terrorist act contributed directly to the act from which his claim arises in order to satisfy § 1605(a)(7)'s statutory requirements for subject matter jurisdiction. Sponsorship of a terrorist group which causes the personal injury or death of a United States national alone is sufficient to invoke jurisdiction.

3. THE PROVISION OF MATERIAL SUPPORT AND RESOURCES TO A TERRORIST GROUP IS AN ACT WITHIN THE SCOPE OF A FOREIGN STATE'S AGENTS' AND HIGH OFFICIALS' AGENCY AND OFFICES.

The law of *respondeat superior* demonstrates that if a foreign state's agent, official, or employee provides material support and resources to a terrorist organization, such provision will be considered an act within the scope of his or her agency, office, or employment. In the District of Columbia, whether an employer is liable for the torts of its employee depends on whether the tort was at least in part "actuated" by an intent to advance the employer's business, and the tort must be foreseeable given the employee's duties. The acts of an employee under these circumstances, whether lawful or not, and whether expressly prohibited by the employer or not, can be imputed to the employer.

In order for an agent, official, or employee's unlawful conduct to be imputed to a government, however, the government must share a degree of responsibility for the wrongful conduct. The government must have engaged in the wrongful conduct, either deliberately or permissively, as a matter of policy or custom. This Court concludes that if a foreign state's heads of state, intelligence service, and minister of intelligence routinely provide material support or resources to a terrorist group, whose activities are consistent with the foreign state's customs or policies, then that agent and those officials have acted squarely within the scope of their agency and offices within the meaning of § 1605(a)(7). . . .

4. UNITED STATES OFFICIALS WOULD BE LIABLE FOR PROVIDING MATERIAL SUPPORT OR RESOURCES TO A TERRORIST GROUP WITHIN THE UNITED STATES.

The Flatow Amendment clarifies that the liability of foreign states and their officials must be comparable to that of the United States and its agents, officials, and employees officials [sic]. This Court concludes that if officials of the United States, while acting in their official capacities, provide material support and resources to a terrorist group which executed a suicide bombing within the United States, those officials would not be immune from civil suits for wrongful death and personal injury.

[The court then discussed personal jurisdiction, the act of state doctrine (*infra*), *forum non conveniens* (*supra*), and damages and concluded:] This Court possess subject matter jurisdiction over this action and personal jurisdiction over, Defendants. Plaintiff has established to this Court's satisfaction, pursuant to 28 U.S.C. § 1608(e), and by clear and convincing evidence, that Defendants, the Islamic Republic of Iran, the Iranian Ministry of Information and Security, Ayatollah Ali Hoseini Khamenei, former President Ali Akbar Hashemi-Rafsanjani, and former Minister Ali Fallahian-Khuzestani, are jointly and severally liable for all damages awarded by this Court to Plaintiff Stephen M. Flatow, in his own right, as Administrator of the Estate of Alisa Michelle Flatow, and on behalf of decedent's heirs-at-law, for their provision of material support and resources to a terrorist group which caused the extrajudicial killing of Alisa Michelle Flatow. [The court then entered judgment in favor of the Plaintiff in an amount exceeding $247,000,000. On the issue of enforcing this judgment, see *Flatow v. Iran*, *infra* at page 500.]

Notes and Questions on *Flatow* and the Prospect of Litigating Terrorism

1. *Proliferation of cases under § 1605(a)(7).* A number of cases have been brought against foreign states under § 1605(a)(7), including: actions against Libya for the bombing of Pan Am Flight 103 over Lockerbie, Scotland, *Rein v. Socialist People's Libyan Arab Jamahiriya*, 995 F. Supp. 325 (E.D.N.Y. 1998); actions against Cuba for the destruction of a private plane, flown by Brothers to the Rescue, by the Cuban Air Force over the Straits of Florida in February 1996, *Alejandre v. The Republic of Cuba*, 996 F. Supp. 1239 (S.D. Fla. 1997); an action against Iran for the kidnapping, imprisonment, and torture of U.S. hostages in Lebanon between 1985 and 1991, *Jenco v. Islamic Republic of Iran*, 154 F. Supp.2d 27 (D.D.C. 2001) (awarding over $314 million to a variety of plaintiffs); *Cicippio v. Islamic Republic of Iran*, 18 F. Supp. 2d 62 (D.D.C. 1998) (awarding $65 million to several plaintiffs); an action against Iran for its support of Hamas, which had detonated a bomb on a bus, killing two U.S. nationals, *Eisenfeld v. Islamic Republic of Iran*, 2000 U.S. Dist. LEXIS 9545 (D.D.C. 2000). One can anticipate similar actions arising out of the September 11th attacks, if evidence emerges linking any state on the "terrorist list" to these attacks.

2. *Constitutionality of the terrorism exception.* If you were mounting a constitutional challenge to Section 1605(a)(7), what would it look like? In *Daliberti v. Republic of Iraq*, 97 F. Supp. 2d 38 (D.D.C. 2000), the court addressed three attacks on the constitutionality of the state-sponsored terrorism exception:

> (1) the requirement that a state be designated by the Secretary of State as a state sponsor of terrorism as a precondition for the filing of a lawsuit constitutes an impermissible legislative delegation of power to the Executive Branch to determine the courts' jurisdiction; (2) the statutory exception to foreign sovereign immunity set out in

28 U.S.C. § 1605(a)(7) violates Iraq's due process right to equal protection by discriminating against those sovereigns designated as state sponsors of terrorism; and (3) the FSIA as a whole, or at least the state sponsored terrorism exception, violates due process by abrogating the minimum contacts requirement that is always necessary for the exercise of personal jurisdiction.

How would you rule on these arguments if you were the judge in the case?

3. *Letelier and § 1605(a)(7).* Assuming that § 1605(a)(7) had existed at the time of Orlando Letelier's assassination, what facts would you need to change in order to bring the original *Letelier* action, *supra*, under that provision?

4. *The problem of relativism.* How, if at all, does the statute get around the problem that "one person's terrorist is another person's freedom fighter?"

---

[4]   The Problem of Executing Judgments

§ 1609. Immunity from attachment and execution of property of a foreign state

Subject to existing international agreements to which the United States is a party at the time of enactment of this Act [enacted Oct. 21, 1976] the property in the United States of a foreign state shall be immune from attachment arrest and execution except as provided in sections 1610 and 1611 of this chapter.

1610. Exceptions to the immunity from attachment or execution

(a) The property in the United States of a foreign state, as defined in section 1603(a) of this chapter, used for a commercial activity in the United States, shall not be immune from attachment in aid of execution, or from execution, upon a judgment entered by a court of the United States or of a State after the effective date of this Act, if —

(1) the foreign state has waived its immunity from attachment in aid of execution or from execution either explicitly or by implication, notwithstanding any withdrawal of the waiver the foreign state may purport to effect except in accordance with the terms of the waiver, or

(2) the property is or was used for the commercial activity upon which the claim is based, or

(3) the execution relates to a judgment establishing rights in property which has been taken in violation of international law or which has been exchanged for property taken in violation of international law, or

(4) the execution relates to a judgment establishing rights in property —

(A) which is acquired by succession or gift, or

(B) which is immovable and situated in the United States: Provided, That such property is not used for purposes of maintaining a diplomatic or consular mission or the residence of the Chief of such mission, or

(5) the property consists of any contractual obligation or any proceeds from such a contractual obligation to indemnify or hold harmless the foreign state or its employees under a policy of automobile or other liability or casualty insurance covering the claim which merged into the judgment, or

(6) the judgment is based on an order confirming an arbitral award rendered against the foreign state, provided that attachment in aid of execution, or execution, would not be inconsistent with any provision in the arbitral agreement, or

(7) the judgment relates to a claim for which the foreign state is not immune under section 1605(a)(7), regardless of whether the property is or was involved with the act upon which the claim is based.

(b) In addition to subsection (a), any property in the United States of an agency or instrumentality of a foreign state engaged in commercial activity in the United States shall not be immune from attachment in aid of execution, or from execution, upon a judgment entered by a court of the United States or of a State after the effective date of this Act, if —

(1) the agency or instrumentality has waived its immunity from attachment in aid of execution or from execution either explicitly or implicitly, notwithstanding any withdrawal of the waiver the agency or instrumentality may purport to effect except in accordance with the terms of the waiver, or

(2) the judgment relates to a claim for which the agency or instrumentality is not immune by virtue of section 1605(a)(2), (3), (5), or (7), or 1605(b) of this chapter, regardless of whether the property is or was involved in the act upon which the claim is based. . . .

(d) The property of a foreign state, as defined in section 1603(a) of this chapter, used for a commercial activity in the United States, shall not be immune from attachment prior to the entry of judgment in any action brought in a court of the United States or of a State, or prior to the elapse of the period of time provided in subsection of this section, if — (1) the foreign state has explicitly waived its immunity from attachment prior to judgment, notwithstanding any withdrawal of the waiver the foreign state may purport to effect except in accordance with the terms of the waiver, and (2) the purpose of the attachment is to secure satisfaction of a judgment that has been or may ultimately be entered against the foreign state, and not to obtain jurisdiction. . . .

LETELIER v. CHILE
748 F.2d 790 (2d Cir. 1984), *cert. denied*, 471 U.S. 1125 (1985)

The critical question posed on this appeal is whether the assets of a foreign state's wholly owned airline are subject to execution to satisfy a default judgment obtained against the foreign state. The district court, believing that Congress under the FSIA, would not have established a right to jurisdiction over the foreign state without also providing a remedy, ordered execution. We reverse although we recognize that our decision may preclude the plaintiffs from collecting on their judgment. How one wishes to decide a case comes lightly to mind, on a wing; but often how one must decide it comes arduously, weighed down by somber thought. To rule otherwise here would only illustrate once again that hard cases make bad law.

Orlando Letelier, the former Chilean Ambassador to the United States, his aide, Michael Moffitt, and Moffitt's wife, Ronni, were riding to work in Washington, D.C. in September, 1976 when an explosive device planted under the driver's seat in their car was detonated, killing both Letelier and Ronni Moffitt and seriously injuring Michael Moffitt. That assassination gives rise to the present appeal. Investigation by agencies of the United States government into these murders revealed the identity of nine assassins and their alleged connection to the government of Chile. Of the nine only Michael Vernon Townley, an American citizen working for Chilean intelligence, was convicted of a criminal offense. Three of those indicted were members of the Cuban Nationalist Movement who, although found guilty in the trial court, had their convictions reversed on appeal. Of the other five individuals indicted, none were brought to trial: three were Chilean nationals that Chile refused to extradite, and two remain at large.

In August 1978, the personal representatives of Letelier and Moffitt instituted a civil tort action in the United States District Court for the District of Columbia against the indicted individuals and the Republic of Chile. . . . All defendants defaulted, although Chile sent two Diplomatic Notes to the United States Department of State asserting its sovereign immunity and that the allegations against it were false. The State Department forwarded these Notes to the clerk of the district court. In August 1978, the trial court granted default judgments against the individual defendants. During 1979 and 1980, the district court heard plaintiffs' motion for a default judgment against Chile, and finally resolved that motion. In the former case, the court ruled that it had subject matter jurisdiction pursuant to the exception to immunity found in § 1605(a)(5) of the Act. In the latter case, the trial court relying on Townley's testimony at the criminal trial, where he had pled guilty and testified for the prosecution, granted a default judgment against the Republic of Chile and awarded plaintiffs over five million dollars including interest, compensatory and punitive damages, counsel fees, and out of pocket expenses. The Republic of Chile did not take an appeal from either of these judgments.

The resulting judgment against the Republic of Chile was entered in the United States District Court for the District of Columbia. Plaintiffs subsequently filed the judgment in the United States District Court for the Southern District of New York, for the purpose of executing on the property interests that The Republic of Chile has in the Chilean national airline, Linea Aerea Nacional-Chile or LAN, which is located in New York, and for the appointment of Michael Moffitt as a receiver of those interests to satisfy the judgment against Chile. . . . The application for execution against LAN's assets came before District Court Judge Morris E. Lasker. LAN moved to dismiss claiming that it should not be held to answer for Chilean debts and that its assets were immune from execution. Relying upon a recent decision of the United States Supreme Court, *First National City Bank v. Banco Para El Comercio Exterior de Cuba (Bancec)*, 462 U.S. 611 (1983), which based a decision to disregard separate corporation identities on "international equitable principles," Judge Lasker first held in an opinion and order that, were the facts as asserted, LAN's role in the assassination was commercial activity under the Act. He further held that to adhere to LAN's separate corporate identity would, as in *Bancec*, violate equitable principles.

Having concluded that LAN's assets were subject to execution to satisfy a judgment against Chile, the district court concluded that the language of § 1610(a)(2) did not limit execution only to commercial assets used for commercial purposes, as LAN claimed, but also permitted execution to satisfy tort judgments "so long as the assets on which the judgment creditor seeks to execute were also used commercially in the activity giving rise to the claim." The rationale for this reading of the statute was that a statute should not be interpreted to create a right without a remedy. The court reasoned that if jurisdictional immunity is lifted, the presumption is that there will be a right to execute.

Plaintiffs later sought discovery against The Republic of Chile by serving it with interrogatories and requests to produce documents and admit facts. Chile refused to comply and again filed Diplomatic Notes asserting its refusal to recognize either the validity of the default judgment or the district court's jurisdiction in the supplementary proceedings for enforcement. Judge Lasker . . . granted plaintiffs' motions for . . . sanctions against LAN consisting of adverse findings of fact that provided a basis to disregard LAN's juridical separateness, and appointed Moffitt as a receiver of LAN's assets in the United States. From the[se] rulings . . . LAN has appealed and raised a number of issues.

DISCUSSION

The principal issue is whether LAN's assets may be executed upon to satisfy the judgment obtained in the District of Columbia against Chile. This discussion necessarily focuses on the FSIA, which is the exclusive source of subject matter jurisdiction over all suits involving foreign states or their instrumentalities. According to § 1604, foreign states are immune from suit in our courts unless the conduct complained of comes within the exceptions set forth in §§ 1605 to 1607 of the Act. Similarly, under § 1609, foreign states are immune from execution upon judgments obtained against them, unless an exception set forth in §§ 1610 or 1611 of the FSIA applies.

The judgment creditors claim that § 1610(a)(2) allows them to execute upon LAN's assets in this case. Section 1610(a)(2) provides:

> The property in the United States of a foreign state . . . used for a commercial activity in the United States, shall not be immune from attachment in aid of execution, or from execution . . . if . . . the property is or was used for the commercial activity upon which the claim is based.

We consider first whether LAN's separate juridical existence may be ignored, thereby making its assets "the property in the United States of a foreign state."

I. Separate Juridical Existence

In *Bancec*, the Supreme Court determined whether a claim of a foreign agency plaintiff was subject to a set-off for the debts of its parent government. *Bancec* deserves close scrutiny because it provides a conceptual framework for resolving plaintiffs' assertion that LAN's assets should be treated as assets of Chile and because the district court relied on it to reach that conclusion.

In *Bancec*, the Cuban bank of the same name brought suit against Citibank to collect on a letter of credit issued in its favor in 1960. Citibank counter-claimed arguing that it was entitled to set-off amounts as compensation due it for the Cuban government's expropriation of Citibank's assets in Cuba. We ruled that as Bancec was not the alter ego of the Cuban government, it could not be held to account for Cuban debts. The Supreme Court reversed. Relying on the Act's legislative history, the Court noted that it was not intended to affect the substantive law of liability of a foreign state or the attribution of liability among its entities and proceeded to resolve the appeal on "equitable principles." The *Bancec* Court recognized that "government instrumentalities established as juridical entities distinct and independent from their sovereign should normally be treated as such." FSIA's legislative history provided support for that conclusion:

> Section 1610(b) will not permit execution against the property of one agency or instrumentality to satisfy a judgment against another, unrelated agency or instrumentality. There are compelling reasons for this. If U.S. law did not respect the separate juridical identities of different agencies or instrumentalities, it might encourage foreign jurisdictions to disregard the juridical divisions between different U.S. corporations or between a U.S. corporation and its independent subsidiary. However, a court might find that property held by one agency is really the property of another.

The Supreme Court concluded in *Bancec* that the presumption of separate-ness had been overcome. It reasoned that the real beneficiary of any recovery would be the Cuban government, and that Cuba should not be permitted to obtain relief in American courts without answering for its seizure of Citibank's assets. The Court commented that "Cuba cannot escape liability for acts in violation of international law simply by retransferring the assets to separate juridical entities."

Thus, *Bancec* rests primarily on two propositions. First, courts may use set-off as a unique, equitable remedy to prevent a foreign government from eluding liability for its own acts when it affirmatively seeks recovery in an American judicial proceeding. The broader message is that foreign states can-not avoid their obligations by engaging in abuses of corporate form. The *Bancec* Court held that a foreign state instrumentality is answerable just as its sovereign parent would be if the foreign state has abused the corporate form, or where recognizing the instrumentality's separate status works a fraud or an injustice.

The district court analyzed the present case in light of *Bancec* and ruled that Chile's alleged use of LAN to transport Townley and explosives to the United States were "significant steps in the conspiracy" that if proven "would constitute a gross abuse of the corporate form." Accordingly, it held, "If Chile ignored LAN's separate existence in accomplishing the wrong, it may not invoke that separate existence in order to deny the injured a remedy."

The district judge "found" the following facts based "on the record" and "established" by evidentiary sanctions imposed pursuant to Rule 37(b)(A): From January 1975 through January 1979, LAN's assets and facilities were under the direct control of Chile, which had the power to use them; Chile could have decreed LAN's dissolution and taken over property interests held in LAN's name; Chile, through its agencies, officers, and employees, intentionally used facilities and personnel of LAN to plan and carry out its conspiracy to assassinate Orlando Letelier by (a) transporting Michael Vernon Townley between Chile and the United States, (b) transporting explosives on several occasions, assisting with currency transactions involved in paying off the co-conspirators in the assassination, (d) providing a meeting place for the co-conspirators, (e) arranging for Townley to exit the United States under an alias after the assassination. By using LAN in these endeavors, the district court found, Chile ignored LAN's separate existence and abused the corporate form.

In our view this is not the sort of "abuse" that overcomes the presumption of separateness established by *Bancec*. Joint participation in a tort is not the "classic" abuse of corporate form to which the Supreme Court referred. In *Bancec*, the Court relied by analogy on the domestic law of private corporations that ignores separate juridical status "where a corporate entity is so extensively controlled by its owner that a relationship of principal and agent is created," where "the corporate form . . . is interposed to defeat legislative policies," or where recognition of corporate form "would work fraud or injustice." The facts that the district court "found" here do not add up to anything that resembles the abuses in the decisions cited in *Bancec*. None of these facts shows that Chile ignored LAN's separate status. Instead, they simply demonstrate that Michael Townley was able to enlist the cooperation of certain LAN pilots and officials with whom he had a pre-existing social relationship in pursuing his sinister goal. There was no finding that LAN's separate status was established to shield its owners from liability for their torts or that Chile ignored ordinary corporate formalities.[1]

Plaintiffs had the burden of proving that LAN was not entitled to separate recognition. A creditor seeking execution against an apparently separate entity must prove "the property to be attached is subject to execution." The evidence submitted by the judgment creditors does not reveal abuse of corporate form of the nature or degree that *Bancec* found sufficient to overcome the presumption of separate existence. As both *Bancec* and the FSIA

---

[1] Further, an "injustice" might be inflicted on third parties were LAN's separate status so easily ignored. Here, plaintiffs are attempting to obtain an affirmative recovery against a foreign agency; no equitable set-off is involved. Under these circumstances, abuse of corporate form must be clearly demonstrated to justify holding the "subsidiary" liable for the debts of its sovereign "parent," particularly, where, as here, LAN apparently has non-party private bank creditors. Concern for these non-party creditors is stronger in this case as the net result will be an out-of-pocket loss to LAN. To adopt a rule facilitating an easy piercing of the corporate veil threatens the interests of such unsuspecting third parties.

legislative history caution against too easily overcoming the presumption of separateness, we decline to extend the *Bancec* holding to do so in this case.

II. Commercial Activity

Even assuming the district court was correct in disregarding LAN's corporate form and finding that LAN's assets were Chile's property in the United States, § 1610(a)(2) also requires that the property be "used for the commercial activity upon which the claim is based." In permitting execution against LAN's assets, the court below essentially concluded that LAN's activities aided Townley in the assassination and constituted the "commercial activities" that § 1610(a)(2) requires. We cannot agree, because a consistent application of the Act, analysis of the background of its enactment, its language and legislative history, and the case law construing it compel the opposite conclusion.

We first note that the district court for the District of Columbia found that Chile lost its immunity from jurisdiction pursuant to § 1605(a)(5), the "tortious activity" exception to jurisdictional immunity. Section 1605(a)(5) specifically states that it applies to situations "not otherwise encompassed in paragraph (2)." Section 1605(a)(2) is the commercial activity exception. The jurisdictional immunity under (2) and the tort exception under (5) are mutually exclusive. If the district court in the District of Columbia lifted jurisdictional immunity based on its finding that the activities complained of were tortious, not commercial, it is inconsistent for this court to lift execution immunity based on a finding that the activities were commercial.

Our disagreement with the finding that LAN's activities were commercial rests on more than the resulting lack of symmetry in application of the FSIA. If LAN, as the trial court found, acted in complicity with the Chilean secret police in the assassination, its activities had nothing to do with its place in commerce. The nature of its course of conduct could not have been as a merchant in the marketplace. Its activities would have been those of the foreign state: governmental, not private or commercial. . . .

Congress specifically designed the execution immunity rules to "conform" to the jurisdictional immunity provisions of § 1605. Congress intended the "essential nature" of given behavior to determine its status for purposes of the commercial activities exception, and gave the courts a "great deal of latitude" to decide this issue. The legislative history makes clear that courts should not deem activity "commercial" as a whole simply because certain aspects of it are commercial. The example given is that the AID programs remain governmental even though they involve behavior traditionally performed by private persons. . . .

A private person cannot lawfully engage in murder any more than he can in kidnapping or criminal assault. Carriage of passengers and packages is an activity in which a private person could engage. But it is not for those activities that LAN's assets are being executed against. Rather, plaintiffs assert that LAN itself participated in the assassination and essentially accuse LAN of being a co-conspirator or joint tortfeasor.[2] In other words, LAN is accused of

---

[2] In fact, the court below relied on LAN's "status" as such to make its finding of apparent abuse of corporate form.

engaging in state-sponsored terrorism the purpose of which, irrelevant under the FSIA, was to assassinate an opponent of the Chilean government. Politically motivated assassinations are not traditionally the function of private individuals. They can scarcely be considered commercial activity. Viewed in this light, LAN's participation, if any, in the assassination is not commercial activity that falls within the § 1610(a) (2) exception and its assets therefore are not stripped of immunity.

III. Right Without a Remedy

The district court's principal concern with finding LAN immune from execution on its assets was that "having determined to grant jurisdiction in both commercial and tort claims, it appears out of joint to conclude that Congress intended the surprising result of allowing only commercial creditors to execute on their judgments." Hence, it concluded that Congress would not create a right without a remedy. Few would take issue with the district judge's comment as an abstract principle of statutory interpretation. Nevertheless, when drafting the FSIA, Congress took into account the international community's view of sovereign immunity. That makes a world of difference in the Act's interpretation. The Act's history and the contemporaneous passage of similar European legislation strongly support the conclusion that under the circumstances at issue in this case, Congress did, in fact, create a right without a remedy. Congress wanted the execution provisions of the FSIA to "remedy, in part, the [pre-FSIA] predicament of a plaintiff who has obtained a judgment against a foreign state." It is to that pre-FSIA plaintiff's predicament that we now turn.

To put the execution immunity provisions of the 1976 Act in proper perspective, it is helpful to examine them in light of the European Convention on State Immunity and Additional Protocol adopted in 1972 and the United Kingdom's enactment of The State Immunity Act of 1978. Although these two codifications contain vastly different approaches to execution of judgments, they are relevant to this discussion in that neither Act ensures that a party may execute on a judgment against a foreign state by attaching property, even if it may validly assert jurisdiction over that foreign state.

The European Convention, because of its members' conflicting views, decided not to provide machinery for the enforcement of judgments by execution. The Convention relied instead on the obligation of an individual State to honor judgments taken against it. . . .

The State Immunity Act, like the FSIA, grants general immunity from execution over a foreign state's property except that, unlike the FSIA, which permits execution only on property upon which the claim is based, courts in England may execute on property in use or intended to be used for commercial purposes. Hence, The State Immunity Act restricts immunity from execution more than the FSIA and subjects *any* property of the foreign state used for commercial purposes to execution.

The FSIA distinguishes between execution against property of an agency or instrumentality of a foreign state, which may be executed against regardless of whether the property was used for the activity on which the claim is based under § 1610(b)(2), and the property of the foreign state itself, which may be executed against only when the property was used for the commercial activity on which the claim is based under § 1610(a) (2). In so distinguishing, Congress sharply restricted immunity from execution against agencies and instrumentalities, but was more cautious when lifting immunity from execution against property owned by the State itself. Congress passed the FSIA on the background of the views of sovereignty expressed in the 1945 charter of the United Nations and the 1972 enactment of the European Convention, which left the availability of execution totally up to the debtor state, and its own understanding as the legislative history demonstrates, that prior to 1976 property of foreign states was absolutely immune from execution. It is plain then that Congress planned to and did lift execution immunity "in part." Yet, since it was not Congress' purpose to lift execution immunity wholly and completely, a right without a remedy does exist in the circumstances here. Our task must be to read the Act as it is expressed, and apply it according to its expressions. . . .

We hold therefore that the Foreign Sovereign Immunities Act does not allow execution against the assets of LAN, the Chilean National Airlines.[3] The court below improperly ignored defendant LAN's separate juridical status from the Republic of Chile. Ordinarily, we would remand for further evidentiary hearings on the separateness issue, but we are further persuaded, even were LAN and Chile found to be alter egos, that Congress did not provide for execution against a foreign state's property under the circumstances of this case. Congress provided for execution against property used in commercial activity upon which the claim is based. An act of political terrorism is not the kind of commercial activity that Congress contemplated.

Accordingly, we reverse the orders appealed from and dismiss the supplementary proceedings.

Notes and Questions on *Letelier*

1. *The aftermath of Letelier*. The concluding footnote in *Letelier* has an air of prescience to it. In April 1988, the government of the United States formally espoused the *Letelier* claim, invoking a 1914 treaty with Chile for the settlement of disputes, and requesting the appointment of an international commission to investigate the deaths of Letelier and Moffitt. Chile concurred in the appointment of a five-member commission and expressed its willingness to make an *ex gratia* payment to the United States for the benefit of the families (and without admitting guilt), in an amount to be determined by the commission. In January 1992, the commission awarded a total of $2.6 million.

2. *Comparing §§ 1610(a) and (b)*. Section 1610 of the FSIA distinguishes between executing a judgment against defendant *states* (§ 1610(a)) and

---

[3] Although tenuous, other remedies may still be possible. Chile itself may decide as an act of international good-will to honor the judgment of the United States District Court for the District of Columbia. Alternatively, the United States may be persuaded to bring this claim before some international tribunal as it did in *Z & F Assets Realization Corp. v. Hull,* 311 U.S. 470 (1941), or there may be a forum in South America or elsewhere equivalent to the European Court of Human Rights that will provide a judicial remedy.

executing a judgment against a state *instrumentality* (§ 1610(b)). What is the textual difference between these two types of execution? Why couldn't the *Letelier* plaintiffs prevail under either of these provisions?

3. If § 1605(a)(7) had been available to the *Letelier* plaintiffs in their original action, how might § 1610(a)(7) have compelled a different result at the enforcement stage? *Compare Alejandre v. Telefonica Larga Distancia de Puerto Rico, Inc.*, 183 F.3d 1277 (11th Cir. 1999), in which the families of Americans whose plane had been shot down by the Cuban Air Force over international waters established jurisdiction under § 1605(a)(7) and obtained a multi-million dollar judgment against the Cuban government. They then successfully moved to execute the judgment by garnishing certain debts owed by Telefonica to a Cuban telecommunications company. But citing *Letelier* and *Bancec, supra*, the court of appeals vacated the garnishment order, ruling that the Cuban telecommunications company—as an instrumentality of the Cuban government—had a separate juridical status from the government and therefore the payments to it could not be garnished to satisfy a judgment against the Cuban government. The following case offers another variation on this theme.

FLATOW v. IRAN
67 F. Supp. 2d 535 (D. Md. 1999), *aff'd*, 225 F.3d 653 (4th Cir. 2000)

Plaintiffs daughter, Alisa Flatow, was killed on April 9, 1995 in the Gaza Strip when a terrorist bomb exploded. On April 24, 1996, Congress enacted amendments to the FSIA as part of the Antiterrorism and Effective Death Penalty Act, which granted subject matter jurisdiction over a claim brought against a foreign state:

> for personal injury or death that caused by an act or torture, extrajudicial killing, aircraft sabotage, hostage taking, or the provision of material support or resources . . . for such an act if such act or provision of material support is engaged in by an official, employee or agent of such foreign state while acting within the scope of his or her office, employment, or agency. . . .

Relying on these amendments, Plaintiff filed a Complaint for wrongful death and other related causes of action against the Iranian Government, the Iranian Ministry of Information and Security, Ayatollah Ali Hoseini Khamenei, then-President Ali Akbar Hashemi-Rafsanjani, and then-Intelligence Minister Ali Fallahian Khuzestani. On March 3, 1998, Plaintiff obtained a default judgment against the Defendants, and United States District Judge Royce C. Lamberth entered judgment in favor of the Plaintiff in an amount exceeding $247,000,000. Plaintiff then began to initiate enforcement proceedings throughout the country against assets that he claims are owned by the Iranian Government. The instant proceeding includes property located at (1) 8100 Jeb Stuart Road, Rockville, Montgomery County, Md., (2) 7917 Montrose Road, Rockville, Montgomery County, Md., and (3) 12010 Seven Locks Road,

Potomac, Montgomery County, Md. Plaintiff served writs of execution upon these properties on November 9, 1998.

The Movant, the Alavi Foundation ("Foundation"), which was not named as a party to the underlying litigation, is the owner of record of these properties. The Foundation now moves [under state law] . . . to release the property in question from the levy, to quash the writs of execution issued on the property, and to enjoin the Plaintiff from issuing future writs against the Foundation's property. Under Maryland law, as a general rule, a judgment creditor may not levy against a third-party's property in order to satisfy a money judgment against a judgment debtor.

In order to levy against a third-party's property, the judgment creditor must prove that the property of a third-party can be seized because: (1) the third-party is an agent, alter ego, or instrumentality of the judgment debtor; (2) the third-party is a garnishee of the judgment debtor; or (3) there was a conveyance of property between the judgment debtor and the third-party which was motivated by the intent to defrauding creditors. Plaintiff, the judgment creditor in this case, cannot meet any of these narrowly defined bases for levying a third-party's property.

Plaintiff maintains that the property of the Foundation may be levied because the Foundation "and its assets are property in the United States of [the Iranian Government] and the [FSIA] authorizes the execution against certain assets of foreign state sponsors of terrorism, including those at issue in this proceeding, in order to satisfy judgments for which they are not immune from suit under § 1605(a)(7)." However, the Alavi Foundation is a nonprofit foundation, which was duly organized under the Not-For-Profit Corporation Law of New York State. As such, it is a citizen of the State of New York. Section 1603(b) of the FSIA, the law that governs the underlying case, provides that an " 'agency or instrumentality of a foreign state' means any entity . . . which is neither a citizen of a State of the United states as defined in section 1332(c). . . of this title. . . ." Therefore, pursuant to the FSIA, the Foundation by definition cannot be an agent, alter ego, or instrumentality of the Iranian Government.

Even if the Foundation was not a citizen of the State of New York, pursuant to the FSIA, a separately incorporated entity is entitled to a presumption of independence from a foreign sovereign. In order to overcome this presumption of independence, Plaintiff must show either that the Foundation is "so extensively controlled by" the Iranian Government "that a relationship of principal and agent is created" or that regarding the Foundation as a separate instrumentality would "work fraud or injustice" against him.

The case law in this area generally holds that a principal-agent relationship has been created for the purposes of the FSIA when the foreign sovereign exercises day-to-day control over its activities. *See McKesson Corp. v. Islamic Republic of Iran*, 52 F.3d 346, 35 1–52 (D.C. Cir. 1995); *see also Hester Int'l Corp. v. Federal Republic of Nigeria*, 879 F.2d 170, 178–80 (5th Cir. 1989) (holding that an entity in which Nigeria held 100% of its stock was not an agent because there was no showing of day-to-day control); *Baglab Ltd. v. Johnson Matthey Bankers Ltd.*, 665 F. Supp. 289, 297 (S.D.N.Y. 1987) (holding that the plaintiff failed to overcome the presumption of separateness because it failed to prove that the Bank of England exercised "general control over the day-to-day activities" of an entity so that the entity could be deemed an agent).

Plaintiff concedes that this is the general rule, but argues that the Court should apply a more lenient rule in the instant case. Plaintiff argues that the "courts have developed that standard under the rubric of a different provision of the FSIA — the commercial activities exception to foreign sovereign immunity— the history and purpose of which are not comparable to § 1605(a)(7)." Plaintiff contends that the purpose of the commercial activities exception is to facilitate "legitimate commercial intercourse by and among the community of nations," and to allow foreign governments the same type of access to the advantages of the corporate form that a private person would have. According to Plaintiff, § 1605(a)(7) was "designed to prevent foreign state sponsors of terrorism from enjoying surreptitious participation in the American marketplace and legal system, the benefits of which could eventually be turned against American interests." Plaintiff argues that cases arising under this exception should be treated differently than those cases which arise out of commercial disputes. Plaintiff states that:

> Rather than perpetuate a safe harbor for outlaws, which would be the result of a "day-to-day control" test, American courts should permit enforcement of § 1605(a)(7) judgments against non-parties to the underlying litigation when there is evidence that a judgment debtor owns covert property interests in the United States which have been sheltered in an outwardly independent third party.

The Court is not persuaded that Plaintiff's more lenient standard, which would find that an entity is an instrumentality if there is proof that the foreign sovereign has any interest in that entity, is applicable. "Congress is presumed to enact legislation with knowledge of the law, that is with the knowledge of the interpretation that courts have given the statute." *United States v. Langley*, 62 F.3d 602, 605 (4th Cir. 1995). There is nothing in the language of the provision itself, or the legislative history that indicates that Congress intended Section 1605(a)(7) to be interpreted differently than the other provisions of the statute. "Absent a clear manifestation of contrary intent, a newly-enacted or revised statute is presumed to be harmonious with existing law and its judicial construction." *Langley*, 62 F.3d at 605. Therefore, the Court finds that the day-to-day control rule is applicable to Section 1605(a)(7) as well.

Plaintiff has the burden of proving that the Foundation is not entitled to separate recognition. *See De Letelier v. Republic of Chile*, 748 F.2d at 795 ("A creditor seeking execution against an apparently separate entity must prove 'the property to be attached is subject to execution."). Most of the evidence that Plaintiff produced in this case to establish that the Iranian Government exercises control over the Foundation was presented in *Gabay v. Mostazafan Foundation of Iran*, 968 F. Supp. 895 (S.D.N.Y. 1997), *aff'd*, 152 F.3d 918 (2d Cir. 1998), *cert. denied*, 525 U.S. 1040 (1998). This Court finds, as the *Gabay* court found, that this evidence does not establish that the Iranian Government exercised such control.

Plaintiff claims that the Foundation was originally established as the Pahlavi Foundation of New York in 1973 by Shah Mohammed Reza Pahlavi as a branch of the Pahiavi Foundation, an Iranian nonprofit charitable organization founded in 1958. Plaintiff further claims that the fact that the Iranian Government controlled, and continues to control the Foundation is demonstrated by the changes in the name of the Foundation, which, in Plaintiff's view, coincided with political changes in Iran. Plaintiff notes that in March of 1979, following the Islamic Revolution in which Ayatollah Khomeini assumed power over the country, the Mostazafan Foundation of Iran was created. Plaintiff asserts that the Mostazafan Foundation of Iran then took control of the Pahlavi Foundation of Iran. Plaintiff claims that the fact that the Iranian Government confiscated the Pahlavi Foundation of New York, as well, is demonstrated by the fact that there was a turnover of the Foundation's Board of Directors, and a change of the name from Pahlavi Foundation of New York to Mostazafan Foundation of New York. Plaintiff states that the evidence "strongly suggest[s] that [the Foundation] is a *de facto* instrumentality of the Islamic Republic of Iran." Moreover, Plaintiff asserts that the Foundation has been used by the Iranian Government as part of its "ongoing fraudulent scheme to disguise its participation in the United States legal system and avoid its obligations under United States laws, in flagrant abuse of the corporate form."

The Alavi Foundation has shown that there were legitimate reasons for the changes in composition of the Board in 1979. Former Secretary of State William Rogers stated, in both his resignation letter and in deposition testimony in the *Gabay* case, that he had agreed to serve as a Board member "only until the Pahlavi Foundation began to produce income and the Foundation's subsequent achievement of that goal constituted his reason for retiring from the Board." Further, Dr. Houshang Ahmadi testified in the Gabay case that he became a Board member at the invitation of the president of the Foundation at the time, Manoucher Shafie ("Shafie"), and that his decision to become a member was not influenced by a third party. Therefore, the Court cannot find that the Iranian Government exercised control of the change in the composition of the Foundation's Board.

Movant has also provided a legitimate reason for the changes in the name of the Foundation. Shafie testified in *Gabay* that the name change from Pahlavi to Mostazafan was his idea because the name Pahlavi had become controversial, and the name Mostazafan, which means "helping needy people" fit the Foundation's purpose. Moreover, the name changes were subject to regulatory and judicial approval under New York law. Therefore, the fact that the name changes coincided with changes in the name of the foundation in Iran is not proof of day-to-day control of the Foundation by the Iranian Government.

Plaintiff has also produced certain issues of a newsletter entitled the Bonyad Local Publication, which he claims demonstrates that the Foundation was controlled by the Mostazafan Foundation of Iran, and thus the Iranian Government. Although the newspapers do demonstrate some similarities between the activities of the Alavi Foundation and the activities alleged to be the goals of the Iranian Government for the Foundation, the existence of these similarities "does not show a causal connection between the listing of the goals in the newsletters and the actual activities" of the Foundation. *Gabay,* 968 F. Supp. at 900. Moreover, in *Hester Int'l Corp.*, the court also was provided with documents, which were not authored by the Nigerian Government itself, which proclaimed that the entity involved was the representative of Nigeria. In that case, the court found that the entity, a corporation that was created and owned by the Nigerian Government, could not be considered a mere alter ego or agent of the government in spite of these documents. The Court similarly finds that the newsletters in the present case are not proof of day-to-day control.

Plaintiff has also produced documents from the Internal Revenue Service ("IRS"), which he claims indicates that the Iranian Government exercises control over the Foundation. The record shows that after ten years of debate over the subject, the IRS changed its position about whether a loan the Foundation received from a bank affiliated with the Iranian Government was deductible. The IRS had maintained that the loan was not deductible because the parties to it were not dealing at "arms-length." The Foundation asserted, as it does here, that it was independent of the Iranian Government, and thus the loan should be deductible. In 1997, the IRS gave the Foundation a substantial refund. Therefore, the documents produced by Plaintiff do not establish that the Foundation was subject to day-to-day control by the Iranian Government.

In addition to the evidence that was provided in *Gabay*, Plaintiff has also provided sworn statements from Dr. Patrick L. Clawson ("Clawson"), the Director for Research at the Washington Institute for Near East Policy, and Kenneth R. Timmerman ("Timmerman"), a journalist, to support his theory that the Foundation is controlled by the Iranian Government. Plaintiff states that if the Court held an evidentiary hearing in this matter, he is prepared to present these witnesses and at least a dozen others that would testify about a connection between the Foundation and the Iranian Government.

However, after reviewing the statements of Dr. Clawson and Mr. Timmerman, the Court does not believe that an evidentiary hearing is necessary. The Timmerman report is replete with allegations connecting the Foundation with terrorism. However, it is based upon the newsletters, anonymous interviews, and confidential informants, and generally lacks the reliability and "equivalent circumstantial guarantee of trustworthiness" to meet any of the hearsay exceptions. Dr. Clawson has expressed an opinion that the Foundation's activities "seem consistent with Iranian behavior." He has stated that he "can't prove that's the same pattern, but I just simply say it's consistent." As such, his opinion is based on speculation. "An expert's opinion should be excluded when it is based on assumptions which are speculative and are not based in the record." *Tyger Constr. Co., Inc. v. Pensacola Constr. Co.*, 29 F.3d 137, 142 (4th Cir. 1994). The Court believes, and Plaintiff has not submitted any affidavits for the other witnesses to the contrary, that any testimony at the evidentiary hearing would be of the same ilk. Thus, Plaintiff is not entitled to an evidentiary hearing.

Finally, Plaintiff maintains that during a November 2, 1998 meeting, he and his counsel met with Under Secretary of State Stuart E. Eizenstat

("Secretary Eizenstat") and with representatives of the Departments of State, Treasury, and Justice. As a result of this meeting, the Plaintiff maintains that he received more than three thousand pages of documents related to the assets of the Iranian Government. Plaintiff notes that within these pages were numerous references to the Foundation and its assets. Plaintiff also asserts that members of the Secretary Eizenstat's staff "expressly stated that the Alavi Foundation is an agency or instrumentality of the Islamic Republic of Iran controlled through the Mostazafan Foundation of Iran. . . ." Plaintiff, however, has not provided an affidavit or any other documentary evidence to support the argument that the United States Government itself has taken the official stance that the Foundation is an instrumentality of the Iranian Government. The evidence in the record supports the position that the United States Government and the State of New York have always considered the Foundation to be a separate and distinct entity from the Iranian Government. Moreover, the IRS has determined the Foundation to be a charitable organization within the meaning of the Internal Revenue Code.

The evidence in the record supports a finding that the Iranian Government does not exercise day-to-day control over the Foundation. Movant maintains, and Plaintiff has not demonstrated to the contrary, that the Foundation has been in compliance with all federal and state registration and reporting requirements since its organization, including the required annual filings with the New York's Secretary of State. Further, Movant contends, and Plaintiff concedes, it scrupulously adheres to all corporate formalities. Movant has submitted proof by affidavit that the Directors are elected by the Foundation itself, and they have regular meetings. Further, the Foundation files its own tax returns, and is in good standing with the Attorney General of New York. Plaintiff has not provided any proof that the Foundation is undercapitalized. Instead, Movant has submitted proof by affidavit that it is funded through the rental income that it receives from the interest it has in its building located in New York City. Moreover, the Foundation has its own bank accounts, and there is no proof of any commingling of funds between the Foundation and the Iranian Government, or any of its agents or instrumentalities. Movant has submitted proof by affidavit that it hires its own employees and that none of these employees are agents, officers, or employees of the Iranian Government as well. There is no evidence in the record that the Foundation shares any office space with any agent or instrumentality of the Iranian Government. Finally, Movant has submitted proof by affidavit that the Foundation has rejected requests for funding from entities affiliated with the Iranian Government. In light of these facts, the Iranian Government cannot be seen as exercising day-today control over the Foundation's activities.

Furthermore, in order to be liable as an agent, alter ego, or instrumentality, the entity generally must have some connection with the underlying dispute. *See Hercaire Int'l Inc. v. Argentina*, 821 F.2d 559, 563 (11th Cir. 1987) ("Having had no connection whatsoever with the underlying transaction which gives rises to Argentina's liability it would be manifestly unfair to subject [the entity's] assets to such attachment."). Although Plaintiff again argues that this rule should not be applied to Section 1605(a)(7), for the reasons previously explained, the Court is not persuaded. Plaintiff has not established that the Foundation has any connection with the underlying case. Nor has the Plaintiff established that regarding the Foundation as a separate instrumentality would "work fraud or injustice" against him. Therefore, the Foundation cannot be held liable for the judgment against the Iranian Government.

As Plaintiff cannot establish that the Foundation was an agent, alter ego, or instrumentality of the Iranian Government, has not proceeded by writ of garnishment, and has not argued that there was a conveyance between the Foundation and the Iranian Government that was made with the intent to defraud a judgment creditor, Plaintiff was not entitled to a levy on these properties. Therefore, the Court will release the properties from the levy, and quash the writs of execution against them. Further, pursuant to [state law], as a levy is a cloud on a property's title, the Foundation is entitled to an injunction against Plaintiff to prevent any future writs on the properties of the Foundation. Accordingly, the Court will grant the Movant's motions.

Notes and Questions on *Flatow*

1. *Jurisdiction versus enforcement.* Why might Congress rationally separate the issue of jurisdiction over a foreign state from the issue of enforcing a judgment against it? Which provisions of the FSIA indicate that obtaining subject matter or personal jurisdiction is considerably easier than enforcing a judgment in hand?

2. *Federal Rule of Civil Procedure 69(a).* Notice the extent to which the *Flatow* court relies on state and federal law. Why doesn't the FSIA pre-empt recourse to state law for all purposes? *See* Rule 69(a), F.R.C.P.:

> (a) In General. Process to enforce a judgment for the payment of money shall be a writ of execution, unless the court directs otherwise. The procedure on execution, in proceedings supplementary to and in aid of a judgment, and in proceedings on and in aid of execution shall be in accordance with the practice and procedure of the state in which the district court is held, existing at the time the remedy is sought, except that any statute of the United States governs to the extent that it is applicable. In aid of the judgment or execution, the judgment creditor or a successor in interest when that interest appears of record, may obtain discovery from any person, including the judgment debtor, in the manner provided in these rules or in the manner provided by the practice of the state in which the district court is held.

Which enforcement and execution issues under the FSIA should be controlled by state law?

3. *Legislating a result in Flatow.* As noted in the case, Congress amended the FSIA in 1998 to allow judgment creditors under § 1605(a)(7) to attach a foreign government's property in the United States if it had been blocked or frozen by the executive branch. The U.S. State Department, invoking the International Emergency Economic Powers Act in 1979, had seized small diplomatic properties in Washington, D.C. belonging to Iran, and Mr. Flatow attempted to satisfy his judgment in part by attaching these diplomatic

properties. The 1998 amendments also directed the Secretaries of Treasury and State to "fully, promptly, and effectively assist any judgment creditor or any court that has issued any such judgment in identifying, locating, and executing against the property of that foreign state or any agency or instrumentality of such state." As adopted, the amendment allowed the President to waive the requirements of this section in the "interest of national security." That waiver authority was exercised immediately and defended in the following terms:

> If the U.S. permitted attachment of diplomatic properties, then other countries could retaliate, placing our embassies and citizens overseas at grave risk. Our ability to use foreign properties as leverage in foreign policy disputes would also be undermined. . . . The Administration stands ready to work with the Flatow family, which won a U.S. court judgment against Iran, in identifying Iranian commercial assets that may be available for attachment.

What should the policy of the United States be with respect to the satisfaction of judgments against foreign states? And which branch of the government should decide this?

4. *Denouement: combining judicial and legislative strategies.* Flatow's $247 million default judgment remained unsatisfied until Congress passed the Victims of Trafficking and Violence Protection Act in October 2000, 22 U.S.C. § 7101 *et seq.*, which allows specified victims of terrorist acts to collect compensatory damages from the U.S. treasury and compelled the government to seek reimbursement from the defendant state. The Act allows the attachment of foreign property that is regulated under other statutes, including the Foreign Assistance Act of 1961, the International Emergency Economic Powers Act, and the Trading with the Enemy Act. The Treasury Department paid Flatow $26 million in January 2001. In exchange, Flatow relinquished his right to execute against or attach certain property associated with his claim. Other judgment creditors under § 1605(a)(7) have followed the Flatow's lead.

Iran passed a law allowing Iranian victims of "U.S. interference" since the Iranian coup in 1953 to sue the U.S. government in Iranian courts.

How would you respond to the argument that the legislation compensates the few at the expense of the government's ability to freeze (and unfreeze) the assets of foreign sovereigns? Or the government's ability to protect U.S. assets abroad?

B. THE ACT OF STATE DOCTRINE

Under the act of state doctrine, the courts of the United States will not judge the validity of a foreign government's official acts within its own territory. Based on both constitutional and international considerations — though compelled by neither — this doctrine of non-justiciability may be considered the foreign affairs equivalent of the political question doctrine, assuring that the courts do not infringe on the prerogatives of the political branches in matters of international relations. In the words of one court facing a politically nasty case:

> The act of state doctrine is similar to the political question doctrine in domestic law. It requires that the courts defer to the legislative and executive branches when those branches are better equipped to resolve a politically sensitive question.

International Ass'n of Machinists and Aerospace Workers v. Organization of Petroleum Exporting Countries, 649 F.2d 1354, 1358–9 (9th Cir. 1981). At the most abstract level, it is understandable that domestic courts would need some sort of safety valve for cases that touch too sharply on diplomatic or political nerves.

But the doctrine is something of a house divided against itself. The function of courts is to resolve disputes, and they should only rarely decline to resolve issues that are otherwise properly before them. For that reason, the act of state doctrine has become encrusted with multiple exceptions and limitations, each of which offers opportunities for advocacy and each of which suggests that the courts both need and avoid a doctrine that rules certain issues out-of-bounds.

The act of state doctrine arises frequently in transnational litigation, even when no foreign government is a party. After all, even private parties can argue that a finding on the merits potentially implicates some sovereign act of a foreign government, and the act of state doctrine will offer a powerful rationale for presuming the validity of that act. As you read the following cases — in which the courts struggle with the tension between applying the law and avoiding politics — consider what defines an official act in the first place. How do courts articulate the rationale for the act of state doctrine? What is the effect of applying the doctrine? And what limitations and exceptions constrain its application?

---

[1]   Introduction

RESTATEMENT (THIRD) FOREIGN RELATIONS LAW OF THE UNITED STATES
Part IV—Jurisdiction and Judgments
Chapter 4—Jurisdiction and the Law of Other States
Subchapter B—The Act of State Doctrine

§ 443. Act of State Doctrine: Law of the United States.

(1) In the absence of a treaty or other unambiguous agreement regarding controlling legal principles, courts in the United States will generally refrain from examining the validity of a taking by a foreign state of property within its own territory, or from sitting in judgment on other acts of a governmental character done by a foreign state within its own territory and applicable there.

(2) The doctrine set forth in Subsection (1) is subject to modification by act of Congress. *See* § 444.

§ 444. Act of State Doctrine: Statutory Limitation.

In the absence of a Presidential determination to the contrary, the act of state doctrine will not be applied in a case involving a claim of title or other right to property, when the claim is based on the assertion that a foreign state confiscated the property in violation of international law.

One standard version of the history of the act of state doctrine appears in *Kalamazoo Spice Extraction Co. v. Provisional Military Government of Ethiopia*, 729 F.2d 422 (6th Cir. 1984):

> [T]he roots of the doctrine can be traced to *Underhill v. Hernandez*, 168 U.S. 250 (1897), where the Supreme Court held:
>
>> Every sovereign state is bound to respect the independence of every other sovereign state, and the courts of one country will not sit in judgment on the acts of the government of another done within its own territory. Redress of grievances by reason of such acts must be obtained through means open to be availed of by sovereign powers as between themselves.
>
> Thus, the Supreme Court's decision in *Underhill* was a recognition that generally the courts of one nation will not sit in judgment on the acts of another nation when those acts occur within the latter's borders.
>
> The modern restatement of the doctrine is contained in *Banco Nacional de Cuba v. Sabbatino*, 376 U.S. 398 (1964). In *Sabbatino*, the Court stated:
>
>> The Judicial Branch will not examine the validity of a taking of property within its own territory by a foreign government, extant and recognized by this country at the time of the suit, in the absence of a treaty or other unambiguous agreement regarding controlling legal principles, even if the complaint alleges that the taking violates customary international law. 376 U.S. at 428.
>
> Justice Harlan, writing for the majority in *Sabbatino*, noted that the act of state doctrine has "constitutional underpinnings." These constitutional underpinnings, according to Justice Harlan, arise out of a recognition of the separation of powers doctrine and the fact that the executive branch is usually best equipped to deal with matters of foreign policy since this area often requires "political acts." Moreover, action by the judiciary while the executive branch is simultaneously acting upon the same matter could potentially be embarrassing or detrimental to those executive efforts.
>
> However, after *Sabbatino*, the Court began to limit the breadth of the act of state doctrine and ruled that United States courts could be the

proper forum for the adjudication of expropriation claims in certain circumstances. In *First National City Bank v. Banco Nacional de Cuba*, 406 U.S. 759 (1972) (*Citibank*), the Court ruled that expropriation claims may be heard as set-offs in some circumstances. A plurality of the Court in *Citibank* recognized the 'Bernstein exception' as a basis for a court to exercise jurisdiction over the acts of a foreign sovereign committed within that sovereign's borders. The Bernstein exception consists of a letter from the United States Department of State advising a court that foreign relations considerations do not necessitate an application of the act of state doctrine.[1]

A further narrowing of the act of state doctrine was the result in *Alfred Dunhill of London, Inc. v. Cuba*, 425 U.S. 682 (1976). The court held in *Dunhill* that immunity from the United States judiciary through the act of state doctrine was granted to foreign sovereigns for acts within their borders. However, in order for there to be act of state immunity, the act in question must be public and not commercial in nature. Justice White, writing for four of the justices, analogized the act of state doctrine with sovereign immunity and reasoned that the act of state doctrine, like sovereign immunity, should not immunize foreign sovereigns when they have acted in a commercial capacity.[2]

[2] The Doctrine Articulated

BANCO NACIONAL de CUBA v. SABBATINO
376 U.S. 398 (1964)

[After the Cuban revolution, the United States reduced the import quota on sugar from Cuba, and the government of Fidel Castro responded by nationalizing property in Cuba owned by U.S. nationals. Among the properties nationalized was a sugar estate owned by CAV, which had previously agreed to deliver a shipment of sugar to a New York commodities broker named Farr Whitlock. Following additional negotiations with the Castro government — which now claimed title to the sugar by virtue of the expropriation — Farr Whitlock completed the sale, but gave the proceeds to Sabbatino, a receiver

---

[1] The "Bernstein exception" derives its name from *Bernstein v. N.Y. Nederlandsche-Amerikaansche Stoomvaart-Maat-schaapij*, 173 F.2d 71 (2d Cir. 1949), *modified by*, 210 F.2d 375 (2d Cir. 1954) (*per curiam*) where the State Department advised the Second Circuit that foreign relations considerations did not require the application of the act of state doctrine. Justice Rehnquist's opinion in *Citibank* which found the Bernstein exception dispositive was joined only by Chief Justice Burger and Justice White. Justices Douglas and Powell concurred in two separate opinions. Consequently, it appears that the Bernstein exception may have doubtful utility since a majority of the Court did not approve its use.

[2] The decision in *Dunhill* that commercial acts of a sovereign would not be entitled to immunity under the act of state doctrine is known as the "commercial act exception". However, that exception, like the Bernstein exception, was recognized by only a plurality of the Court. Only Chief Justice Burger and Justices Powell and Rehnquist joined in Justice White's opinion creating the exception. Thus, this exception also seems to be of doubtful precedential value.

for CAV. Banco Nacional, acting as agent for the Cuban government, demanded payment from Farr Whitlock and Sabbatino, who declined. Banco Nacional then filed this suit. Sabbatino claimed title on the ground that Cuba's seizure of the estate had violated international law in that it had been uncompensated, discriminatory, and retaliatory. That argument prevailed in the lower courts, which concluded in effect that thieves could take no title, applying international legal standards to determine that the expropriation was unlawful. The case then came before the Supreme Court of the United States.]

IV.

The classic American statement of the act of state doctrine . . . is found in *Underhill v. Hernandez*, 168 U.S. 250, where Chief Justice Fuller said for a unanimous Court:

> Every sovereign state is bound to respect the independence of every other sovereign state, and the courts of one country will not sit in judgment on the acts of the government of another, done within its own territory. Redress of grievances by reason of such acts must be obtained through the means open to be availed of by sovereign powers as between themselves.

Following this precept the Court in that case refused to inquire into acts of Hernandez, a revolutionary Venezuelan military commander whose government had been later recognized by the United States, which were made the basis of a damage action in this country by Underhill, an American citizen, who claimed that he had had unlawfully assaulted, coerced, and detained in Venezuela by Hernandez.

None of this Court's subsequent cases in which the act of state doctrine was directly or peripherally involved manifest any retreat from *Underhill*. . . . On the contrary in two of these cases, *Oetjen* [*v. Central Leather Co.*, 246 U.S. 297] and *Ricaud* [*v. American Metal Co.*, 246 U.S. 304], the doctrine as announced in *Underhill* was reaffirmed in unequivocal terms.

Oetjen involved a seizure of hides from a Mexican citizen as a military levy by General Villa, acting for the forces of General Carranza, whose government was recognized by this country subsequent to the trial but prior to decision by this Court. The hides were sold to a Texas corporation which shipped them to the United States and assigned them to defendant. As assignee of the original owner, plaintiff replevied the hides, claiming that they had been seized in violation of the Hague Conventions. In affirming a judgment for defendant, the Court . . . described the designation of the sovereign as a political question to be determined by the legislative and executive departments rather than the judicial department, invoked the established rule that such recognition operates retroactively to validate past acts, and found the basic tenet of *Underhill* to be applicable to the case before it.

> The principle that the conduct of one independent government cannot be successfully questioned in the courts of another is as applicable to a case involving the title to property brought within the custody of a court, such as we have here, as it was held to be to the cases cited, in which claims

for damages were based upon acts done in a foreign country, for it rests at last upon the highest considerations of international comity and expediency. To permit the validity of the acts of one sovereign state to be reexamined and perhaps condemned by the courts of another would very certainly "imperil the amicable relations between governments and vex the peace of nations."

In *Ricaud*, the facts were similar — another general of the Carranza forces seized lead bullion as a military levy — except that the property taken belonged to an American citizen. The Court found *Underhill, American Banana [Co. v. United Fruit Co.*, 213 U.S. 347], and *Oetjen* controlling. Commenting on the nature of the principle established by those cases, the opinion stated that the rule

> does not deprive the courts of jurisdiction once acquired over a case. It requires only that when it is made to appear that the foreign government has acted in a given way on the subject-matter of the litigation, the details of such action or the merit of the result cannot be questioned but must be accepted by our courts as a rule for their decision. To accept a ruling authority and to decide accordingly is not a surrender or abandonment of jurisdiction but is an exercise of it. It results that the title to the property in this case must be determined by the result of the action taken by the military authorities of Mexico
> . . . .

In deciding the present case the Court of Appeals relied in part upon an exception to the unqualified teachings of *Underhill, Oetjen*, and *Ricaud* which that court had earlier indicated. In *Bernstein v. Van Heyghen Freres Societe Anonyme*, 2 Cir., 163 F.2d 246, suit was brought to recover from an assignee property allegedly taken, in effect, by the Nazi Government because plaintiff was Jewish. Recognizing the odious nature of this act of state, the court, through Judge Learned Hand, nonetheless refused to consider it invalid on that ground. Rather, it looked to see if the Executive had acted in any manner that would indicate that United States Courts should refuse to give effect to such a foreign decree. Finding no such evidence, the court sustained dismissal of the complaint. In a later case involving similar facts the same court again assumed examination of the German acts improper, *Bernstein v. N.V. Nederlandsche-Amerikaansche Stoomvaart-Maatschappij*, 2 Cir., 173 F.2d 71, but, quite evidently following the implications of Judge Hand's opinion in the earlier case, amended its mandate to permit evidence of alleged invalidity, subsequent to receipt by plaintiff's attorney of a letter from the Acting Legal Adviser to the State Department written for the purpose of relieving the court from any constraint upon the exercise of its jurisdiction to pass on that question.[1]

---

[1] The letter stated:

1. This government has consistently opposed the forcible acts of dispossession of a discriminatory and confiscatory nature practiced by the Germans on the countries or peoples subject to their controls.

3. The policy of the Executive, with respect to claims asserted in the United States for the restitution of identifiable property (or compensation in lieu thereof) lost through force, coercion, or duress as a result of Nazi persecution in Germany, is to relieve

This Court has never had occasion to pass upon the so-called *Bernstein* exception, nor need it do so now. For whatever ambiguity may be thought to exist in the two letters from State Department officials on which the Court of Appeals relied, is now removed by the position which the Executive has taken in this Court on the act of state claim; . . . these letters were intended to reflect no more than the Department's then wish not to make any statement bearing on this litigation. . . .

The outcome of this case, therefore, turns upon whether any of the contentions urged by respondents against the application of the act of state doctrine in the premises is acceptable: (1) that the doctrine does not apply to acts of state which violate international law, as is claimed to be the case here; (2) that the doctrine is inapplicable unless the Executive specifically interposes it in a particular case; and (3) that, in any event, the doctrine may not be invoked by a foreign government plaintiff in our courts.

V.

Preliminarily, we discuss the foundations on which we deem the act of state doctrine to rest, and more particularly the question of whether state or federal law governs its application in a federal diversity case.

We do not believe that this doctrine is compelled either by the inherent nature of sovereign authority, as some of the earlier decisions seem to imply, or by some principle of international law. If a transaction takes place in one jurisdiction and the forum is in another, the forum does not by dismissing an action or by applying its own law purport to divest the first jurisdiction of its territorial sovereignty; it merely declines to adjudicate or makes applicable its own law to parties or property before it. The refusal of one country to enforce the penal laws of another is a typical example of an instance when a court will not entertain a cause of action arising in another jurisdiction. While historic notions of sovereign authority do bear upon the wisdom or employing the act of state doctrine, they do not dictate its existence.

That international law does not require application of the doctrine is evidenced by the practice of nations. Most of the countries rendering decisions on the subject fail to follow the rule rigidly. No international arbitral or judicial decision discovered suggests that international law prescribes recognition of sovereign acts of foreign governments, and apparently no claim has ever been raised before an international tribunal that failure to apply the act of state doctrine constitutes a breach of international obligation. If international law does not prescribe use of the doctrine, neither does it forbid application of the rule even if it is claimed that the act of state in question violated international law. The traditional view of international law is that it establishes substantive principles for determining whether one country has wronged another. Because of its peculiar nation-to-nation character, the usual method for an individual to seek relief is to exhaust local remedies and then repair to the executive authorities of his own state to persuade them to

---

American courts from any restraint upon the exercise of their jurisdiction to pass upon the validity of the acts of Nazi officials.

State Department Press Release, April 27, 1949, 20 Dept. State Bull. 592.

champion his claim in diplomacy or before an international tribunal. Although it is, of course, true that United States courts apply international law as a part of our own in appropriate circumstances, *Ware v. Hylton*, 3 Dall. 199; *The Nereide*, 9 Cranch 388; *The Paquete Habana*, 175 U.S. 677, the public law of nations can hardly dictate to a country which is in theory wronged how to treat that wrong within its domestic borders. . . .

Despite the broad statement in *Oetjen* that "The conduct of the foreign relations of our government is committed by the Constitution to the executive and legislative * * * departments," it cannot of course be thought that "every case or controversy which touches foreign relations lies beyond judicial cognizance." *Baker v. Carr*, 369 U.S. 186, 211. The text of the Constitution does not require the act of state doctrine; it does not irrevocably remove from the judiciary the capacity to review the validity of foreign acts of state.

The act of state doctrine does, however, have "constitutional" underpinnings. It arises out of the basic relationships between branches of government in a system of separation of powers. It concerns the competency of dissimilar institutions to make and implement particular kinds of decisions in the area of international relations. The doctrine as formulated in past decisions expresses the strong sense of the Judicial Branch that its engagement in the task of passing on the validity of foreign acts of state may hinder rather than further this country's pursuit of goals both for itself and for the community of nations as a whole in the international sphere. Many commentators disagree with this view; they have striven by means of distinguishing and limiting past decisions and by advancing various considerations of policy to stimulate a narrowing of the apparent scope of the rule. Whatever considerations are thought to predominate, it is plain that the problems involved are uniquely federal in nature. If federal authority, in this instance this Court, orders the field of judicial competence in this area for the federal courts, and the state courts are left free to formulate their own rules, the purposes behind the doctrine could be as effectively undermined as if there had been no federal pronouncement on the subject.

We could perhaps in this diversity action avoid the question of deciding whether federal or state law is applicable to this aspect of the litigation. New York has enunciated the act of state doctrine in terms that echo those of federal decisions[, and . . .] our conclusions might well be the same whether we dealt with this problem as one of state law or federal law. However, we are constrained to make it clear that an issue concerned with a basic choice regarding the competence and function of the Judiciary and the National Executive in ordering our relationships with other members of the international community must be treated exclusively as an aspect of federal law. . . .

VI.

If the act of state doctrine is a principle of decision binding on federal and state courts alike but compelled by neither international law nor the Constitution, its continuing vitality depends on its capacity to reflect the proper distribution of functions between the judicial and political branches of the Government on matters bearing upon foreign affairs. It should be apparent that the greater the degree of codification or consensus concerning a particular area of international law, the more appropriate it is for the judiciary to render decisions regarding it, since the courts can then focus on the application of an agreed principle to circumstances of fact rather than on the sensitive task of establishing a principle not inconsistent with the national interest or with international justice. It is also evident that some aspects of international law touch much more sharply on national nerves than do others; the less important the implications of an issue are for our foreign relations, the weaker the justification for exclusivity in the political branches. The balance of relevant considerations may also be shifted if the government which perpetrated the challenged act of state is no longer in existence, as in the *Bernstein* case, for the political interest of this country may, as a result, be measurably altered. Therefore, rather than laying down or reaffirming an inflexible and all-encompassing rule in this case, we decide only that the Judicial Branch will not examine the validity of a taking of property within its own territory by a foreign sovereign government, extant and recognized by this country at the time of suit, in the absence of a treaty or other unambiguous agreement regarding controlling legal principles, even if the complaint alleges that the taking violates customary international law.

There are few, if any, issues in international law today on which opinion seems to be so divided as the limitations on a state's power to expropriate the property of aliens. There is, of course, authority, in international judicial and arbitral decisions, in the expressions of national governments, and among commentators for the view that a taking is improper under international law if it is not for a public purpose, is discriminatory, or is without provision for prompt, adequate, and effective compensation. However, Communist countries, although they have in fact provided a degree of compensation after diplomatic efforts, commonly recognize no obligation on the part of the taking country. Certain representatives of the newly independent and underdeveloped countries have questioned whether rules of state responsibility toward aliens can bind nations that have not consented to them and it is argued that the traditionally articulated standards governing expropriation of property reflect 'imperialist' interests and are inappropriate to the circumstances of emergent states.

The disagreement as to relevant international law standards reflects an even more basic divergence between the national interests of capital importing and capital exporting nations and between the social ideologies of those countries that favor state control of a considerable portion of the means of production and those that adhere to a free enterprise system. It is difficult to imagine the courts of this country embarking on adjudication in an area which touches more sensitively the practical and ideological goals of the various members of the community of nations.[2]

When we consider the prospect of the courts characterizing foreign expropriations, however justifiably, as invalid under international law and ineffective to pass title, the wisdom of the precedents is confirmed. While each of the

---

[2] There are, of course, areas of international law in which consensus as to standards is greater and which do not represent a battleground for conflicting ideologies. This decision in no way intimates that the courts of this country are broadly foreclosed from considering questions of international law.

leading cases in this Court may be argued to be distinguishable in its facts from this one[,] . . . the plain implication of all these opinions . . . is that the act of state doctrine is applicable even if international law has been violated.

The possible adverse consequences of a conclusion to the contrary of that implicit in these cases in highlighted by contrasting the practices of the political branch with the limitations of the judicial process in matters of this kind. Following an expropriation of any significance, the Executive engages in diplomacy aimed to assure that United States citizens who are harmed are compensated fairly. Representing all claimants of this country, it will often be able, either by bilateral or multilateral talks, by submission to the United Nations, or by the employment of economic and political sanctions, to achieve some degree of general redress. Judicial determinations of invalidity of title can, on the other hand, have only an occasional impact, since they depend on the fortuitous circumstance of the property in question being brought into this country. Such decisions would, if the acts involved were declared invalid, often be likely to give offense to the expropriating country; since the concept of territorial sovereignty is so deep seated, any state may resent the refusal of the courts of another sovereign to accord validity to acts within its territorial borders. Piecemeal dispositions of this sort involving the probability of affront to another state could seriously interfere with negotiations being carried on by the Executive Branch and might prevent or render less favorable the terms of an agreement that could otherwise be reached. Relations with third countries which have engaged in similar expropriations would not be immune from effect.

The dangers of such adjudication are present regardless of whether the State Department has, as it did in this case, asserted that the relevant act violated international law. If the Executive Branch has undertaken negotiations with an expropriating country, but has refrained from claims of violation of the law of nations, a determination to that effect by a court might be regarded as a serious insult, while a finding of compliance with international law would greatly strengthen the bargaining hand of the other state with consequent detriment to American interests.

Even if the State Department has proclaimed the impropriety of the expropriation, the stamp of approval of its view by a judicial tribunal, however, impartial, might increase any affront and the judicial decision might occur at a time, almost always well after the taking, when such an impact would be contrary to our national interest. Considerably more serious and far-reaching consequences would flow from a judicial finding that international law standards had been met if that determination flew in the face of a State Department proclamation to the contrary. When articulating principles of international law in its relations with other states, the Executive Branch speaks not only as an interpreter of generally accepted and traditional rules, as would the courts, but also as an advocate of standards it believes desirable for the community of nations and protective of national concerns. In short, whatever way the matter is cut, the possibility of conflict between the Judicial and Executive Branches could hardly be avoided.

Respondents contend that, even if there is not agreement regarding general standards for determining the validity of expropriations, the alleged combination of retaliation, discrimination, and inadequate compensation makes it patently clear that this particular expropriation was in violation of international law. If this view is accurate, it would still be unwise for the courts so to determine. Such a decision now would require the drawing of more difficult lines in subsequent cases and these would involve the possibility of conflict with the Executive view. Even if the courts avoided this course, either by presuming the validity of an act of state whenever the international law standard was thought unclear or by following the State Department declaration in such a situation, the very expression of judicial uncertainty might provide embarrassment to the Executive Branch.

Another serious consequence of the exception pressed by respondents would be to render uncertain titles in foreign commerce, with the possible consequence of altering the flow of international trade. If the attitude of the United States courts were unclear, one buying expropriated goods would not know if he could safely import them into this country. Even were takings known to be invalid, one would have difficulty determining after goods had changed hands several times whether the particular articles in question were the product of an ineffective state act.[3]

By discouraging import to this country by traders certain or apprehensive of nonrecognition of ownership, judicial findings of invalidity of title might limit competition among sellers; if the excluded goods constituted a significant portion of the market, prices for United States purchasers might rise with a consequent economic burden on United States consumers. Balancing the undesirability of such a result against the likelihood of furthering other national concerns is plainly a function best left in the hands of the political branches.

Against the force of such considerations, we find respondents' countervailing arguments quite unpersuasive. Their basic contention is that United States courts could make a significant contribution to the growth of international law, a contribution whose importance, it is said, would be magnified by the relative paucity of decisional law by international bodies. But given the fluidity of present world conditions, the effectiveness of such a patchwork approach toward the formulation of an acceptable body of law concerning state responsibility for expropriations is, to say the least, highly conjectural. Moreover, it rests upon the sanguine presupposition that the decisions of the courts of the world's major capital exporting country and principal exponent of the free enterprise system would be accepted as disinterested expressions of sound legal principle by those adhering to widely different ideologies. . . .

It is suggested that if the act of state doctrine is applicable to violations of international law, it should only be so when the Executive Branch expressly stipulates that it does not wish the courts to pass on the question of validity. We should be slow to reject the representations of the Government that such a reversal of the *Bernstein* principle would work serious inroads on the

---

[3] Were respondents' position adopted, the courts might be engaged in the difficult tasks of ascertaining the origin of fungible goods, of considering the effect of improvements made in a third country on expropriated raw materials, and of determining the title to commodities subsequently grown on expropriated land or produced with expropriated machinery.

maximum effectiveness of United States diplomacy. Often the State Department will wish to refrain from taking an official position, particularly at a moment that would be dictated by the development of private litigation but might be inopportune diplomatically. Adverse domestic consequences might flow from an official stand which could be assuaged, if at all, only by revealing matters best kept secret. Of course, a relevant consideration for the State Department would be the position contemplated in the court to hear the case. It is highly questionable whether the examination of validity by the judiciary should depend on an educated guess by the Executive as to probable result and, at any rate, should a prediction be wrong, the Executive might be embarrassed in its dealings with other countries. We do not now pass on the *Bernstein* exception, but even if it were deemed valid, its suggested extension is unwarranted.

However offensive to the public policy of this country and its constituent States an expropriation of this kind may be, we conclude that both the national interest and progress toward the goal of establishing the rule of law among nations are best served by maintaining intact the act of state doctrine in this realm of its application.

VII.

Finally, we must determine whether Cuba's status as a plaintiff in this case dictates a result at variance with the conclusions reached above. If the Court were to distinguish between suits brought by sovereign states and those of assignees, the rule would have little effect unless a careful examination were made in each case to determine if the private party suing had taken property in good faith. Such an inquiry would be exceptionally difficult, since the relevant transaction would almost invariably have occurred outside our borders. If such an investigation were deemed irrelevant, a state could always assign its claim. . . .

Respondents offer another theory for treating the case differently because of Cuba's participation. It is claimed that the forum should simply apply its own law to all the relevant transactions. An analogy is drawn to the area of sovereign immunity, in which, if a foreign country seeks redress in our courts, counterclaims are permissible. But immunity relates to the prerogative right not to have sovereign property subject to suit; fairness has been thought to require that when the sovereign seeks recovery, it be subject to legitimate counterclaims against it. The act of state doctrine, however, although it shares with the immunity doctrine a respect for sovereign states, concerns the limits for determining the validity of an otherwise applicable rule of law. It is plain that if a recognized government sued on a contract with a United States citizen, concededly legitimate by the locus of its making, performance, and most significant contacts, the forum would not apply its own substantive law of contracts. Since the act of state doctrine reflects the desirability of presuming the relevant transaction valid, the same result follows; the forum may not apply its local law regarding foreign expropriations.

Since the act of state doctrine proscribes a challenge to the validity of the Cuban expropriation decree in this case, any counterclaim based on asserted invalidity must fail. Whether a theory of conversion or breach of contract is the proper cause of action under New York law, the presumed validity of the expropriation is unaffected. Although we discern no remaining litigable issues of fact in this case, the District Court may hear and decide them if they develop. . . .

JUSTICE WHITE, dissenting. I am dismayed that the Court has, with one broad stroke, declared the ascertainment and application of international law beyond the competence of the courts of the United States in a large and important category of cases. I am also disappointed in the Court's declaration that the acts of a sovereign state with regard to the property of aliens within its borders are beyond the reach of international law in the courts of this country. However clearly established that law may be, a sovereign may violate it with impunity, except insofar as the political branches of the government may provide a remedy. This backward-looking doctrine, never before declared in this Court, is carried a disconcerting step further: not only are the courts powerless to question acts of state proscribed by international law but they are likewise powerless to refuse to adjudicate the claim founded upon a foreign law; they must render judgment and thereby validate the lawless act. Since the Court expressly extends its ruling to all acts of state expropriating property, however clearly inconsistent with the international community, all discriminatory expropriations of the property of aliens, as for example the taking of properties of persons belonging to certain races, religions or nationalities, are entitled to automatic validation in the courts of the United States. No other civilized country has found such a rigid rule necessary for the survival of the executive branch of its government; the executive of no other government seems to require such insulation from international law adjudications in its courts; and no other judiciary is apparently so incompetent to ascertain and apply international law.

The Court does not refer to any country which has applied the act of state doctrine in a case where a substantial international law issue is sought to be raised by an alien whose property has been expropriated. This country and this Court stand alone among the civilized nations of the world in ruling that such an issue is not cognizable in a court of law. The Court notes that the courts of both New York and Great Britain have articulated the act of state doctrine in broad language similar to that used by this Court in *Underhill*, and from this it infers that these courts recognize no international law exception to the act of state doctrine. The cases relied on by the Court involved no international law issue. For in these cases the party objecting to the validity of the foreign act was a citizen of the foreign state. It is significant that courts of both New York and Great Britain, in apparently the first cases in which an international law issue was squarely posed, ruled that the act of state doctrine was no bar to examination of the validity of the foreign act. *Anglo-Iranian Oil Co. v. Jaffrate*, (1953) Int'l L.Rep. 316 (Aden Sup. Ct.): "[T]he Iranian Laws of 1951 were invalid by international law, for, by them, the property of the company was expropriated without any compensation." *Sulyok v. Penzintezeti Kozpont Budapest*, 279 App.Div. 528, 111 N.Y.S.2d 75, *aff'd,* 304 N.Y. 704, 107 N.E.2d 604 (foreign expropriation of intangible property denied effect as contrary to New York public policy).

I do not believe that the act of state doctrine, as judicially fashioned in this Court, and the reasons underlying it, require American courts to decide cases in disregard of international law and of the rights of litigants to a full determination on the merits.

Notes and Questions on *Sabbatino*

1. *Sabbatino's narrow and contingent holding.* Notice how narrowly the court articulates its holding in *Sabbatino*:

> . . . [R]ather than laying down or reaffirming an inflexible and all-encompassing rule in this case, we decide only that the Judicial Branch will not examine the validity of a taking of property within its own territory by a foreign sovereign government, extant and recognized by this country at the time of suit, in the absence of a treaty or other unambiguous agreement regarding controlling legal principles, even if the complaint alleges that the taking violates customary international law.

What limitations on the act of state doctrine can you deduce from this one passage?

2. *International law in U.S. courts.* How would you reconcile the act of state doctrine as applied in *Sabbatino* with the axiom in *Paquete Habana* that "international law is part of our law, and must be ascertained and administered by the courts of justice . . . as often as questions of right depending upon it are duly presented for their determination"?

3. *Act of state doctrine as a choice-of-law rule.* The courts have frequently concluded that the act of state doctrine is not jurisdictional, unlike foreign sovereign immunity, but is better conceived as a choice of law rule. In *Sharon v. Time, Inc.*, 599 F. Supp. 538, 546 (S.D.N.Y. 1984), for example, the court found that "[t]he act-of-state doctrine is, in its origins and essence, a federal rule mandating a choice of law by which to judge the validity of the official actions of sovereign states. In *Ricaud v. American Metal Co. Ltd.*, 246 U.S. 304 (1918), the Court applied the act of state doctrine in the context of a claim for the return of property seized by General Carranza in the Mexican Revolution. The language in *Ricaud* illuminates the nature of the act of state doctrine as a rule for the choice of governing law:

> [The rule] does not deprive the courts of jurisdiction once acquired over a case. It requires only that, when it is made to appear that the foreign government has acted in a given way on the subject-matter of the litigation, the details of such action or the merit of the result cannot be questioned but must be accepted by our courts as a rule for their decision.

Id. at 309. The doctrine's application did not result in the loss of jurisdiction, but in a rule of law by which the decision was to be made."

From this perspective, *Sabbatino* was not a finding against U.S. jurisdiction. To the contrary, jurisdiction was evidently proper, with the court deciding the dispute by presuming the validity of Cuba's action.

4. *Definition of "public act."* What body of law — that of the situs, the United States, or international law — should control the issue of whether something is a "public act of the sovereign" or not? Is a foreign administrative official's interpretation of foreign law an act of state, or must the act be more tangible — like detaining a person, expropriating property, or promulgating regulations — to come within the doctrine? Consider the argument that extending act-of-state deference to interpretations of foreign law by foreign officials would violate Rule 44.1 of the Federal Rules of Civil procedure, which directs that U.S. courts conduct *de novo* review of foreign law. *See Riggs Nat. Corp. v. Commissioner of Internal Revenue*, 163 F.3d 1363 (D.C. Cir. 1999).

5. *Deference to the executive branch.* How much weight — and on what rationale — should the courts give to Executive Branch suggestions on the application of the act of state doctrine? Is it sensible that a doctrine with *"constitutional* underpinnings" should be manipulable by a letter to the court from the executive branch?

6. *Statutory override.* In an attempt to override the result in *Sabbatino*, Congress adopted the Hickenlooper Amendment, described in full detail below but captured in § 444 of RESTATEMENT (THIRD):

> In the absence of a Presidential determination to the contrary, the act of state doctrine will not be applied in a case involving a claim of title or other right to property, when the claim is based on the assertion that a foreign state confiscated the property in violation of international law.

Is it sensible that a doctrine with *"constitutional* underpinnings" should be manipulable by an act of Congress?

7. *Sabbatino and Erie.* What does *Sabbatino* imply, if anything, about the obligation of state courts to apply the act of state doctrine (and international law generally)? If a state had its own act of state doctrine, would a federal court in that state be obliged to apply it under the *Erie* doctrine? The *Sabbatino* court addressed the issue in the following terms, though it seems not to have averted an academic debate about the common law-making powers of the federal courts when addressing issues of customary international law.[1]

> It seems fair to assume that the Court did not have rules like the act of state doctrine in mind when it decided *Erie R. Co. v. Tompkins*. Soon thereafter, Professor Philip C. Jessup, now a judge of the International Court of Justice, recognized the potential dangers were Erie extended to legal problems affecting international relations. [In *The Doctrine of Erie Railroad v. Tompkins Applied to International Law*, 33 AM. J. INT'L L. 740 (1939),] [h]e cautioned that rules of international law should not be left to divergent and perhaps parochial state interpretations. His basic rationale is equally applicable to the act of state doctrine.

---

[1] For the leading exposition of the revisionist position that *Sabbatino* and other decisions undermine the legitimacy of customary international law as federal common law, see Curtis Bradley & Jack Goldsmith, *Customary International Law as Federal Common Law: A Critique of the Modern Position*, 110 HARV. L. REV. 815 (1997). For one conclusive rebuttal, see Harold Hongju Koh, *Is International Law Really State Law?*, 111 HARV. L. REV. 1824 (1998).

The Court in the pre-*Erie* act of state cases, although not burdened by the problem of the source of applicable law, used language sufficiently strong and broadsweeping to suggest that state courts were not left free to develop their own doctrines (as they would have been had this Court merely been interpreting common law under *Swift v. Tyson*). The Court of Appeals in the first *Bernstein* case, *supra*, a diversity suit, plainly considered the decisions of this Court, despite the intervention of *Erie*, to be controlling in regard to the act of state question, at the same time indicating that New York law governed other aspects of the case. We are not without other precedent for a determination that federal law governs; there are enclaves of federal judge-made law which bind the States. A national body of federal-court-built law has been held to have been contemplated by § 301 of the Labor Management Relations Act, *Textile Workers Union of America v. Lincoln Mills*, 353 U.S. 448. Principles formulated by federal judicial law have been thought by this Court to be necessary to protect uniquely federal interests, *D'Oench, Duhme & Co. v. Federal Deposit Ins. Corp.*, 315 U.S. 447; *Clearfield Trust Co. v. United States*, 318 U.S. 363. Of course the federal interest guarded in all these cases is one the ultimate statement of which is derived from a federal statute. Perhaps more directly in point are the bodies of law applied between States over boundaries and in regard to the apportionment of interstate waters.

In *Hinderlider v. La Plata River Co.*, 304 U.S. 92, 110, in an opinion handed down the same day as *Erie* and by the same author, Mr. Justice Brandeis, the Court declared, "For whether the water of an interstate stream must be apportioned between the two States is a question of 'federal common law' upon which neither the statutes nor the decisions of either State can be conclusive." Although the suit was between two private litigants and the relevant States could not be made parties, the Court considered itself free to determine the effect of an interstate compact regulating water apportionment. The decision implies that no State can undermine the federal interest in equitably apportioned interstate waters even if it deals with private parties. This would not mean that, absent a compact, the apportionment scheme could not be changed judicially or by Congress, but only that apportionment is a matter of federal law. *Cf. State of Arizona v. State of California*, 373 U.S. 546, 597–598. The problems surrounding the act of state doctrine are, albeit for different reasons, as intrinsically federal as are those involved in water apportionment or boundary disputes. The considerations supporting exclusion of state authority here are much like those which led the Court in *United States v. California*, 332 U.S. 19, to hold that the Federal Government possessed paramount rights in submerged lands though within the three-mile limit of coastal States. We conclude that the scope of the act of state doctrine must be determined according to federal law [adding in a footnote that "Various constitutional and statutory provisions indirectly support this determination, see U.S.Const., Art, I, § 8, cls. 3, 10; Art. II, §§ 2, 3; Art. III, § 2; 28 U.S.C. §§ 1251(a)(2), (b)(1), (b)(3), 1332(a)(2), 1333, 1350, 1351, by reflecting a concern for uniformity in this country's dealings with foreign nations and indicating a desire to give matters of international significance to the jurisdiction of federal institutions."]

---

[3] Judicial Hostility Towards a Judicially-Created Doctrine

W.S. KIRKPATRICK & CO., INC. v. ENVIRONMENTAL TECTONICS CORP., INT'L, 493 U.S. 400 (1990)

JUSTICE SCALIA delivered the opinion of the Court. In this case we must decide whether the act of state doctrine bars a court in the United States from entertaining a cause of action that does not rest upon the asserted invalidity of an official act of a foreign sovereign, but that does require imputing to foreign officials an unlawful motivation (the obtaining of bribes) in the performance of such an official act.

I

The facts as alleged in respondent's complaint are as follows: In 1981, Harry Carpenter, who was then Chairman of the Board and Chief Executive Officer of petitioner W. S. Kirkpatrick & Co., Inc. (Kirkpatrick), learned that the Republic of Nigeria was interested in contracting for the construction and equipment of an aeromedical center at Kaduna Air Force Base in Nigeria. He made arrangements with Benson "Tunde" Akindele, a Nigerian citizen, whereby Akindele would endeavor to secure the contract for Kirkpatrick. It was agreed that, in the event the contract was awarded to Kirkpatrick, Kirkpatrick would pay to two Panamanian entities controlled by Akindele a "commission" equal to 20% of the contract price, which would in turn be given as a bribe to officials of the Nigerian Government. In accordance with this plan, the contract was awarded to petitioner W. S. Kirkpatrick & Co., International (Kirkpatrick International), a wholly owned subsidiary of Kirkpatrick; Kirkpatrick paid the promised "commission" to the appointed Panamanian entities; and those funds were disbursed as bribes. All parties agree that Nigerian law prohibits both the payment and the receipt of bribes in connection with the award of a government contract.

Respondent Environmental Tectonics Corporation, International, an unsuccessful bidder for the Kaduna contract, learned of the 20% "commission" and brought the matter to the attention of the Nigerian Air Force and the United States Embassy in Lagos. Following an investigation by the Federal Bureau of Investigation, the United States Attorney for the District of New Jersey brought charges against both Kirkpatrick and Carpenter for violations of the Foreign Corrupt Practices Act of 1977, and both pleaded guilty.

Respondent then brought this civil action in the United States District Court for the District of New Jersey against Carpenter, Akindele, petitioners, and others, seeking damages under the Racketeer Influenced and Corrupt Organizations Act, the Robinson-Patman Act, and the New Jersey Anti-Racketeering Act. The defendants moved to dismiss the complaint under Rule 12(b)(6) of the Federal Rules of Civil Procedure on the ground that the action was barred by the act of state doctrine.

The District Court, having requested and received a letter expressing the views of the legal adviser to the United States Department of State as to the applicability of the act of state doctrine, treated the motion as one for summary judgment under Rule 56 of the Federal Rules of Civil Procedure and granted the motion. The District Court concluded that the act of state doctrine applies "if the inquiry presented for judicial determination includes the motivation of a sovereign act which would result in embarrassment to the sovereign or constitute interference in the conduct of foreign policy of the United States" (citing *Clayco Petroleum Corp. v. Occidental Petroleum Corp.*, 712 F.2d 404, 407 (CA9 1983)). Applying that principle to the facts at hand, the court held that respondent's suit had to be dismissed because in order to prevail, respondent would have to show that "the defendants or certain of them intended to wrongfully influence the decision to award the Nigerian Contract by payment of a bribe, that the Government of Nigeria, its officials or other representatives knew of the offered consideration for awarding the Nigerian Contract to Kirkpatrick, that the bribe was actually received or anticipated and that 'but for' the payment or anticipation of the payment of the bribe, ETC would have been awarded the Nigerian Contract."

The Court of Appeals for the Third Circuit reversed. Although agreeing with the District Court that "the award of a military procurement contract can be, in certain circumstances, a sufficiently formal expression of a government's public interests to trigger application" of the act of state doctrine, it found application of the doctrine unwarranted on the facts of this case. The Court of Appeals found particularly persuasive the letter to the District Court from the legal adviser to the Department of State, which had stated that in the opinion of the Department, judicial inquiry into the purpose behind the act of a foreign sovereign would not produce the "unique embarrassment, and the particular interference with the conduct of foreign affairs, that may result from the judicial determination that a foreign sovereign's acts are invalid." The Court of Appeals acknowledged that "the Department's legal conclusions as to the reach of the act of state doctrine are not controlling on the courts," but concluded that "the Department's factual assessment of whether fulfillment of its responsibilities will be prejudiced by the course of civil litigation is entitled to substantial respect." In light of the Department's view that the interests of the Executive Branch would not be harmed by prosecution of the action, the Court of Appeals held that Kirkpatrick had not met its burden of showing that the case should not go forward; accordingly, it reversed the judgment of the District Court and remanded the case for trial. We granted certiorari.

II

This Court's description of the jurisprudential foundation for the act of state doctrine has undergone some evolution over the years. We once viewed the doctrine as an expression of international law, resting upon "the highest considerations of international comity and expediency," *Oetjen v. Central Leather Co.*, 246 U.S. 297, 303–304 (1918). We have more recently described it, however, as a consequence of domestic separation of powers, reflecting "the strong sense of the Judicial Branch that its engagement in the task of passing on the validity of foreign acts of state may hinder" the conduct of foreign affairs, *Banco Nacional de Cuba v. Sabbatino*, 376 U.S. 398, 423 (1964). Some Justices have suggested possible exceptions to application of the doctrine, where one or both of the foregoing policies would seemingly not be served: an exception, for example, for acts of state that consist of commercial transactions, since neither modern international comity nor the current position of our Executive Branch accorded sovereign immunity to such acts, *see Alfred Dunhill of London, Inc. v. Republic of Cuba*, 425 U.S. 682, 695–706 (1976) (opinion of White, J.); or an exception for cases in which the Executive Branch has represented that it has no objection to denying validity to the foreign sovereign act, since then the courts would be impeding no foreign policy goals, *see First National City Bank v. Banco Nacional de Cuba*, 406 U.S. 759, 768–770 (1972) (opinion of Rehnquist, J.). The parties have argued at length about the applicability of these possible exceptions, and, more generally, about whether the purpose of the act of state doctrine would be furthered by its application in this case. We find it unnecessary, however, to pursue those inquiries, since the factual predicate for application of the act of state doctrine does not exist. Nothing in the present suit requires the Court to declare invalid, and thus ineffective as "a rule of decision for the courts of this country," *Ricaud v. American Metal Co.*, 246 U.S. 304, 310 (1918), the official act of a foreign sovereign.

In every case in which we have held the act of state doctrine applicable, the relief sought or the defense interposed would have required a court in the United States to declare invalid the official act of a foreign sovereign performed within its own territory. In *Underhill v. Hernandez*, 168 U.S. 250, 254 (1897), holding the defendant's detention of the plaintiff to be tortious would have required denying legal effect to "acts of a military commander representing the authority of the revolutionary party as government, which afterwards succeeded and was recognized by the United States." In *Oetjen v. Central Leather Co., supra*, and in *Ricaud v. American Metal Co., supra*, denying title to the party who claimed through purchase from Mexico would have required declaring that government's prior seizure of the property, within its own territory, legally ineffective. In *Sabbatino*, upholding the defendant's claim to the funds would have required a holding that Cuba's expropriation of goods located in Havana was null and void. In the present case, by contrast, neither the claim nor any asserted defense requires a determination that Nigeria's contract with Kirkpatrick International was, or was not, effective.

Petitioners point out, however, that the facts necessary to establish respondent's claim will also establish that the contract was unlawful. Specifically, they note that in order to prevail, respondent must prove that petitioner Kirkpatrick made, and Nigerian officials received, payments that violate Nigerian law, which would, they assert, support a finding that the contract is invalid under Nigerian law. Assuming that to be true, it still does not suffice.

The act of state doctrine is not some vague doctrine of abstention but a "principle of decision binding on federal and state courts alike." *Sabbatino, supra,* at 427. As we said in *Ricaud,* "the act within its own boundaries of one sovereign State . . . becomes . . . a rule of decision for the courts of this country." Act of state issues only arise when a court must decide — that is, when the outcome of the case turns upon — the effect of official action by a foreign sovereign. When that question is not in the case, neither is the act of state doctrine. That is the situation here. Regardless of what the court's factual findings may suggest as to the legality of the Nigerian contract, its legality is simply not a question to be decided in the present suit, and there is thus no occasion to apply the rule of decision that the act of state doctrine requires. *Cf. Sharon v. Time, Inc.,* 599 F.Supp. 538, 546 (S.D.N.Y. 1984) ("The issue in this litigation is not whether [the alleged] acts are valid, but whether they occurred").

In support of their position that the act of state doctrine bars any factual findings that may cast doubt upon the validity of foreign sovereign acts, petitioners cite Justice Holmes' opinion for the Court in *American Banana Co. v. United Fruit Co.,* 213 U.S. 347 (1909). That was a suit under the United States antitrust laws, alleging that Costa Rica's seizure of the plaintiff's property had been induced by an unlawful conspiracy. In the course of a lengthy opinion, Justice Holmes observed, citing *Underhill,* that "a seizure by a state is not a thing that can be complained of elsewhere in the courts." The statement is concededly puzzling. *Underhill* does indeed stand for the proposition that a seizure by a state cannot be complained of elsewhere — in the sense of being sought to be declared ineffective elsewhere. The plaintiff in *American Banana,* however, like the plaintiff here, was not trying to undo or disregard the governmental action, but only to obtain damages from private parties who had procured it. Arguably, then, the statement did imply that suit would not lie if a foreign state's actions would be, though not invalidated, impugned.

Whatever Justice Holmes may have had in mind, his statement lends inadequate support to petitioners' position here, for two reasons. First, it was a brief aside, entirely unnecessary to the decision. *American Banana* was squarely decided on the ground (later substantially overruled, *see Continental Ore Co. v. Union Carbide & Carbon Corp.,* 370 U.S. 690, 704–705 (1962)) that the antitrust laws had no extraterritorial application, so that "what the defendant did in Panama or Costa Rica is not within the scope of the statute." 213 U.S., at 357. Second, whatever support the dictum might provide for petitioners' position is more than overcome by our later holding in *United States v. Sisal Sales Corp.,* 274 U.S. 268 (1927). There we held that, *American Banana* notwithstanding, the defendant's actions in obtaining Mexico's enactment of "discriminating legislation" could form part of the basis for suit under the United States antitrust laws. 274 U.S., at 276. Simply put, *American Banana* was not an act of state case; and whatever it said by way of dictum that might be relevant to the present case has not survived *Sisal Sales.*

Petitioners insist, however, that the policies underlying our act of state cases — international comity, respect for the sovereignty of foreign nations on their own territory, and the avoidance of embarrassment to the Executive

Branch in its conduct of foreign relations — are implicated in the present case because, as the District Court found, a determination that Nigerian officials demanded and accepted a bribe "would impugn or question the nobility of a foreign nation's motivations," and would "result in embarrassment to the sovereign or constitute interference in the conduct of foreign policy of the United States." The United States, as *amicus curiae*, favors the same approach to the act of state doctrine, though disagreeing with petitioners as to the outcome it produces in the present case. We should not, the United States urges, "attach dispositive significance to the fact that this suit involves only the 'motivation' for, rather than the 'validity' of, a foreign sovereign act," and should eschew "any rigid formula for the resolution of act of state cases generally." In some future case, perhaps, "litigation . . . based on alleged corruption in the award of contracts or other commercially oriented activities of foreign governments could sufficiently touch on 'national nerves' that the act of state doctrine or related principles of abstention would appropriately be found to bar the suit," and we should therefore resolve this case on the narrowest possible ground, *viz.*, that the letter from the legal adviser to the District Court gives sufficient indication that, "in the setting of this case," the act of state doctrine poses no bar to adjudication.[1]

These urgings are deceptively similar to what we said in *Sabbatino*, where we observed that sometimes, even though the validity of the act of a foreign sovereign within its own territory is called into question, the policies underlying the act of state doctrine may not justify its application. We suggested that a sort of balancing approach could be applied — the balance shifting against application of the doctrine, for example, if the government that committed the "challenged act of state" is no longer in existence. But what is appropriate in order to avoid unquestioning judicial acceptance of the acts of foreign sovereigns is not similarly appropriate for the quite opposite purpose of expanding judicial incapacities where such acts are not directly (or even indirectly) involved. It is one thing to suggest, as we have, that the policies underlying the act of state doctrine should be considered in deciding whether, despite the doctrine's technical availability, it should nonetheless not be invoked; it is something quite different to suggest that those underlying policies are a doctrine unto themselves, justifying expansion of the act of state doctrine (or, as the United States puts it, unspecified "related principles of abstention") into new and uncharted fields. The short of the matter is this: Courts in the United States have the power, and ordinarily the obligation, to decide cases and controversies properly presented to them. The act of state doctrine does not establish an exception for cases and controversies that may embarrass foreign governments, but merely requires that, in the process of deciding, the acts of foreign sovereigns taken within their own jurisdictions shall be deemed valid. That doctrine has no application to the present case because the validity of no foreign sovereign act is at issue.

---

[1] Even if we agreed with the Government's fundamental approach, we would question its characterization of the legal adviser's letter as reflecting the absence of any policy objection to the adjudication. The letter, which is reprinted as an appendix to the opinion of the Court of Appeals, *see* 847 F.2d 1052, 1067–1069 (CA3 1988), did not purport to say whether the State Department would like the suit to proceed, but rather responded (correctly, as we hold today) to the question whether the act of state doctrine was applicable.

The judgment of the Court of Appeals for the Third Circuit is affirmed.

Notes and Questions on *Kirkpatrick*

1. *Reconciling Kirkpatrick and Sabbatino.* Both *Kirkpatrick* and *Sabbatino* place limits on the act of state doctrine, though they are not identical limits. How would you articulate the differences between them?

2. *Understanding Kirkpatrick.* How would you defend the twin propositions that (i) *Kirkpatrick* is not only right but obviously right; and (ii) *Kirkpatrick* is not only wrong but obviously wrong?

3. *Distinguishing foreign sovereign immunity from the act of state doctrine.* Based on what you've read so far, how would you articulate the differences between the foreign sovereign immunity doctrine and the act of state doctrine? Think specifically about the sources of controlling law in both cases, the parties entitled to invoke the doctrines, the apparent exceptions to the doctrines, and the effects of applying the doctrines.

---

[4] The Doctrine Applied (or Not)

THE REPUBLIC OF THE PHILIPPINES v. FERDINAND E. MARCOS
862 F.2d 1355 (9th Cir. 1988) (*en banc*)

The Republic of the Philippines (the Republic) brought a civil suit against its former president, Ferdinand Marcos, and his wife Imelda (the Marcoses), asserting claims under the Racketeer Influenced and Corrupt Organizations Act (RICO), 18 U.S.C. §§ 1961 *et seq.*, and other applicable law. The district court . . . entered a preliminary injunction enjoining the Marcoses from disposing of any of their assets save for the payment of attorney fees and normal living expenses. The Marcoses appealed. A panel of this court reversed, 2-1. We took the case *en banc* and now affirm the district court. . . .

The Republic alleges that the Marcoses engaged in mail fraud, wire fraud, and the transportation of stolen property in the foreign or interstate commerce of the United States. The acts alleged are crimes under 18 U.S.C. §§ 1341, 1343, and 2315. The Republic alleges that the acts were repeated, forming a pattern of predicate acts under RICO, 18 U.S.C. § 1961, and thereby giving rise to civil liability under RICO. . . .

The gravamen of the Republic's entire case is the allegation that the Marcoses stole public money:

> During his twenty years as President of the Philippines, *Mr. Marcos used his position of power and authority to convert and cause to be converted, to his use* and that of his friends, family, and associates,

money, funds, and property belonging to the Philippines and its people.
Complaint, para. 12 (emphasis added). . . .

Act of State and Political Question

Before determining whether issuance of an injunction was appropriate we consider two defenses which, if accepted, would block trial of the case: the Marcoses maintain, first, that their acts are insulated because they were acts of state not reviewable by our courts; and second, that any adjudication of these acts would involve the investigation of political questions beyond our courts' competence.

Acts of State. The classification of certain acts as "acts of state" with the consequence that their validity will be treated as beyond judicial review is a pragmatic device, not required by the nature of sovereign authority and inconsistently applied in international law. *Banco Nacional de Cuba v. Sabbatino*, 376 U.S. 398, 421–22 (1964). The purpose of the device is to keep the judiciary from embroiling the courts and the country in the affairs of the foreign nation whose acts are challenged. Minimally viewed, the classification keeps a court from making pronouncements on matters over which it has no power; maximally interpreted, the classification prevents the embarrassment of a court offending a foreign government that is "extant at the time of suit." *Id.* at 428.

The "continuing vitality" of the doctrine depends on "its capacity to reflect the proper distribution of functions between the judicial and political branches of the Government on matters bearing upon foreign relations." *Id.* at 427–28. Consequently, there are "constitutional underpinnings" to the classification. *Id.* at 423. A court that passes on the validity of an "act of state" intrudes into the domain of the political branches. . . .

As a practical tool for keeping the judicial branch out of the conduct of foreign affairs, the classification of "act of state" is not a promise to the ruler of any foreign country that his conduct, if challenged by his own country after his fall, may not become the subject of scrutiny in our courts. No estoppel exists insulating a deposed dictator from accounting. No guarantee has been granted that immunity may be acquired by an ex-chief magistrate invoking the magic words "act of state" to cover his or her past performance.

The classification might, it may be supposed, be used to prevent judicial challenge in our courts to many deeds of a dictator in power, at least when it is apparent that sustaining such challenge would bring our country into a hostile confrontation with the dictator. Once deposed, the dictator will find it difficult to deploy the defense successfully. The "balance of considerations" is shifted. *Sabbatino*, 376 U.S. at 428. *A fortiori*, when a ruler's former domain has turned against him and seeks the recovery of what it claims he has stolen, the classification has little or no applicability. The act of state doctrine is supple, flexible, *ad hoc*. The doctrine is meant to facilitate the foreign relations of the United States, not to furnish the equivalent of sovereign immunity to a deposed leader.

In the instant case the Marcoses offered no evidence whatsoever to support the classification of their acts as acts of state. The burden of proving acts of state rested upon them. *Alfred Dunhill of London, Inc. v. Republic of Cuba,*

425 U.S. 682, 695 (1976). They did not even undertake the proof. The United States, invited by the court to address this matter as an amicus, assures us that the Executive does not at present see the applicability of this defense. The act of state doctrine, the Executive declares, has "no bearing" on this case as it stands. As the doctrine is a pragmatic one, we cannot exclude the possibility that, at some later point in the development of this litigation, the Marcoses might produce evidence that would warrant its application. On the present record, the defense does not apply.

Political Questions. Bribetaking, theft, embezzlement, extortion, fraud, and conspiracy to do these things are all acts susceptible of concrete proofs that need not involve political questions. The court, it is true, may have to determine questions of Philippine law in determining whether a given act was legal or illegal. But questions of foreign law are not beyond the capacity of our courts. *See Zschernig v. Miller*, 389 U.S. 429, 461 (1968) (Harlan, J. concurring); Fed.R.Civ.P. 44.1 (allowing consideration of foreign law materials). The court will be examining the acts of the president of a country whose immediate political heritage is from our own. Although sometimes criticized as a ruler and at times invested with extraordinary powers, Ferdinand Marcos does not appear to have had the authority of an absolute autocrat. He was not the state, but the head of the state, bound by the laws that applied to him. Our courts have had no difficulty in distinguishing the legal acts of a deposed ruler from his acts for personal profit that lack a basis in law. As in the case of the deposed Venezuelan ruler, Marcos Perez Jimenez, the latter acts are as adjudicable and redressable as would be a dictator's act of rape. *Jimenez v. Aristeguieta*, 311 F.2d 547 (5th Cir. 1962). . . .

In Summation. Jurisdiction to hear the Republic's claims and to enter the preliminary injunction exists. A serious question of liability has been presented and the Republic has a fair chance of success on the merits of its case. The Marcoses have not presented any preclusive defense. The scope of the injunction is justified. It was imperative for the district court to preserve the status quo lest the defendants prevent resolution of the case by putting their property beyond the reach of the court. Hardship to the Republic would have been great and irreparable if the district court had not taken its prudent, amply justified action to keep the Marcoses' assets from disappearing.

SCHROEDER, Circuit Judge, with whom CANBY, Circuit Judge, joins concurring in part and dissenting in part. . . .

The majority of our three-judge panel concluded that the act of state doctrine bars consideration of the plaintiffs' claims. I agree with the majority of this *en banc* court that such a holding is not appropriate on this record. I do not agree with the majority, however, that this injunction can be affirmed without any regard to the act of state doctrine.

The panel majority's use of the act of state doctrine as a threshold bar in the circumstances of this case is not consistent with the development of that doctrine under Supreme Court authority. *See, e.g., Alfred Dunhill of London, Inc. v. Cuba*, 425 U.S. 682 (1976); *Banco Nacional de Cuba v. Sabbatino*, 376 U.S. 398 (1964). We have expressly stated that the act of state doctrine is not jurisdictional. *See International Association of Machinists and Aerospace Workers v. OPEC*, 649 F.2d 1354, 1359 (9th Cir. 1981), *cert. denied*, 454 U.S.

1163 (1982); *Timberlane Lumber Co. v. Bank of America*, 549 F.2d 597, 602 (9th Cir. 1976), *cert. denied*, 472 U.S. 1032 (1985). Rather, the doctrine involves the judiciary's prudential decision to refrain from adjudicating the legality of a foreign sovereign's public acts that were committed within its own territory. The Supreme Court, in addressing the act of state doctrine, has stated:

> Every sovereign state is bound to respect the independence of every other sovereign state, and the courts of one country will not sit in judgment on the acts of the government of another, done within its own territory. Redress of grievances by reason of such acts must be obtained through the means open to be availed of by sovereign powers as between themselves.

Sabbatino, 376 U.S. at 416 (quoting *Underhill v. Hernandez*, 168 U.S. 250, 252, (1897)).

The act of state doctrine "expresses the strong sense of the Judicial Branch that its engagement in the task of passing on the validity of foreign acts of state may hinder rather than further this country's pursuit of goals both for itself and for the community of nations as a whole in the international sphere." *Sabbatino*, 376 U.S. at 423. The Court further elaborated that the doctrine involves separation of powers:

> [The doctrine's] continuing vitality depends on its capacity to reflect the proper distribution of functions between the judicial and political branches of the Government on matters bearing upon foreign affairs. . . . Some aspects of international law touch much more sharply on national nerves than do others; the less important the implications of an issue are for our foreign relations, the weaker the justification for exclusivity in the political branches. . . . We decide only that the Judicial Branch will not examine the validity of a taking of property within its own territory by a foreign sovereign government, extant and recognized by this country at the time of suit.

However, these considerations are less compelling in the situation before us, where the foreign government has itself invoked our jurisdiction, and the challenged actions involve a government no longer in power. In *Sabbatino*, the Supreme Court observed that, "the balance of relevant considerations may also be shifted if the government which perpetrated the challenged act of state is no longer in existence . . . for the political interest of this country may, as a result, be measurably altered." 376 U.S. at 428. "Moreover, the act of state doctrine reflects respect for foreign states, so that when a state comes into our courts and asks that our courts scrutinize its actions, the justification for application of the doctrine may well be significantly weaker." *Republic of the Philippines v. Marcos*, 806 F.2d 344, 359 (2d Cir. 1986).

Further, the Supreme Court has noted that for the doctrine to apply the acts in question must have involved public acts of the sovereign. The Court stated that in each of its act of state decisions, the facts were sufficient to demonstrate that

> the conduct in question was the public act of those with authority to exercise sovereign powers and was entitled to respect in our courts.

> Here, no statute, decree, order, or resolution of the Cuban Government itself was offered in evidence indicating that Cuba had repudiated its obligations in general or any class thereof or that it had as a sovereign matter determined to confiscate the amounts due three foreign importers.

Alfred Dunhill, 425 U.S. at 694–95.

Accordingly, the courts have insisted that the act of state doctrine precludes review of public acts of the sovereign. *See, e.g., Marcos,* 806 F.2d at 358 ("that the acts must be public acts of the sovereign has been repeatedly affirmed"); *Filártiga v. Pena-Irala,* 630 F.2d 876, 889 (2d Cir. 1980) ("we doubt whether action by a state official in violation of the Constitution and laws of the Republic of Paraguay, and wholly unratified by that nation's government, could properly be characterized as an act of state"); *Arango v. Guzman Travel Advisors Corp.,* 621 F.2d 1371, 1380 (5th Cir. 1980) ("the act of state doctrine only precludes judicial inquiry into the legality, validity, and propriety of the acts and motivations of foreign sovereigns acting in their governmental roles within their own boundaries"); *Jimenez v. Aristeguieta,* 311 F.2d 547, 557 (5th Cir. 1962) ("judicial authorities cannot review the acts done by a sovereign in his own territory to determine illegality"); *Sharon v. Time, Inc.,* 599 F. Supp. 538, 544 (S.D.N.Y. 1984) ("the doctrine is limited to laws, decrees, decisions, seizures, and other officially authorized 'public acts' "); *see also Restatement (Second) of Foreign Relations Law* § 41 (1965) (doctrine involves refraining "from examining the validity of an act of a foreign state by which that state has exercised its jurisdiction to give effect to its public interest").

As the dissenting opinion of Judge Nelson quite rightly pointed out [in the decision of the three-judge panel], the act of state doctrine cannot bar the plaintiffs' action at this stage in the proceedings due to the distinction between the official acts and the private conduct of a former head of state. As Judge Nelson stated:

> Marcos and his agents no doubt exercised broad power, especially after the imposition of martial law in 1972. But the appropriate inquiry is not to invoke the talismanic label "dictator." The district court should determine which of the challenged acts were official and which were not. Only by doing so can the court determine the extent to which the act of state doctrine may apply.

At this point, no determinations have been made regarding the capacity in which the Marcoses were acting when the alleged unlawful conduct occurred. Accordingly, the original panel majority erred in finding that, at this stage of the litigation, the act of state doctrine bars adjudication of the bulk of the Philippine government's pendent claims.

The majority decision here, however, goes much further. It declares that the injunction can be affirmed without regard to the act of state doctrine. In my view, we should instead instruct the district court to consider to what extent, if any, the doctrine applies in the circumstances of this case, and on the basis of the record which has developed more fully during the pendency of this interlocutory appeal. Until such consideration can be given, an injunction of this breadth is not appropriate.

This *en banc* court requested the *amicus* views of the Department of State on the act of state issues. Its brief concludes that the application of the act of state doctrine at this stage is speculative and the injunction premature. The majority's reliance upon the position of the United States as support for its holding is wholly misplaced. The government urges that an injunction should not have been entered on the basis of this record. The government *amicus curiae* brief states in appropriate context as follows:

> The record before the district court, which did not include any detailed specification of the factual basis for the bulk of the nonfederal claims, did not make it possible even to analyze the extent to which those claims are properly before the court. . . .

> Even assuming jurisdiction, it is not clear at this stage that the district court should, as a prudential matter, undertake to adjudicate the bulk of the nonfederal claims. The court's capacity to do so fairly and expeditiously and without offending the sensibility of other nations cannot be resolved on this record. Adjudication in this district court may turn out to be barred by considerations of international comity and *forum non conveniens*.

> The act of state doctrine seems to us to have little or no bearing on this case at this stage of its development. The doctrine provides, in general, that the validity of specific acts of a foreign sovereign is not subject to challenge in our courts; the circumstances of a particular case may, however, make that general principle inapplicable. On the present record, it is not clear that any act of state — an act of a sovereign within its territorial jurisdiction on matters pertaining to its governmental sovereignty — is involved in this case. Nor is it clear that the case would require an adjudication of the validity of such an act, without which the case could not fairly proceed. Under these circumstances, the bearing, if any, of the act of state doctrine on this case should be determined only after further development of the case on the merits.

The United States' views are wholly in accord with those expressed in this dissent and are in conflict with the majority. . . .

BRAKA v. BANCOMER, S.N.C.
762 F.2d 222 (2d Cir. 1985)

This appeal represents [an] opportunity . . . to consider the effect of foreign financial decrees on the investments of United States entities. Because we agree with the district court that plaintiffs' recovery is barred by the act of state doctrine, we affirm the judgment of the United States District Court for the Southern District of New York, dismissing plaintiffs' complaint.

In our previous excursion into the intricacies of the act of state doctrine, *Allied Bank International v. Banco Credito Agricola de Cartago*, 757 F.2d 516 (2d Cir. 1985), we held that because the situs of the debt was in the United

States, the act of state doctrine did not operate to prevent the creditors from recovering for their losses. In the case before us, however, the doctrine does bar relief because the situs of defendant's obligations was in Mexico.

Plaintiffs are a number of United States citizens who purchased peso-and dollar-denominated certificates of deposit (CDs) from defendant Bancomer, S.A. (Bancomer). When plaintiffs' purchases were made in 1981, Bancomer was a privately run Mexican bank. Plaintiffs arranged for their purchases by telephone with Bancomer's Mexico City office. The purchases were effected either through application of plaintiffs' funds that were on deposit in Mexico or through plaintiffs' delivery of checks drawn on their New York banks payable to Bancomer's New York agency. If the latter method was used, the agency, which was not authorized to accept deposits, transmitted the funds by interbank transfer to the Mexican office. The CDs indicated that Mexico was the place of deposit and the place of payment of principal and interest, although as a convenience such payments were sometimes transmitted to plaintiffs' New York banks. The total value of the CDs was $2,100,000. . . .

. . . [S]hortly before the first certificate was to reach maturity, the Mexican Ministry of Treasury and Public Credit issued a decree requiring that all domestic obligations be performed by delivery of an equivalent amount in pesos at the prevailing exchange rate. This decree banned the use of foreign currency as legal tender. [One month later] two more decrees were issued. The first nationalized Mexico's banks, including Bancomer. The second mandated a system of exchange controls that was carried out by the subsequent issuance of rules called "General Rules for Exchange Controls." As a result of these and later decrees, plaintiffs received Mexican pesos at the officially prescribed exchange rates, approximately 70–80 pesos per dollar, when they tendered their certificates on the maturity dates. Plaintiffs allege that because they did not receive the then actual market exchange rate of 135–150 pesos per dollar, they lost over $900,000.

Plaintiffs filed suit in federal district court in New York claiming damages for breach of contract and for violation of the federal securities laws. Bancomer moved to dismiss the complaint, arguing that the court lacked jurisdiction under the Foreign Sovereign Immunities Act (FSIA), that, even if jurisdiction did exist, the act of state doctrine precluded examination of Mexico's acts, and the CDs are not "securities" and so are not subject to the securities laws. The district court considered only the first two defenses[, r]uling that . . . the FSIA did not render Bancomer immune from suit but that the act of state doctrine did bar judicial review of plaintiffs' claims.

First, the court held that Bancomer's issuance of CDs was a commercial rather than a sovereign act, and that it therefore fell within the commercial activity exception to FSIA. . . . However, the court went on to hold that the absence of immunity did not render plaintiffs' claims justiciable. Because the situs of plaintiffs' CDs was in Mexico, the court determined that act of state principles prevented judicial examination of the complaint. In addition, the court rejected plaintiffs' claims that they were harmed by a commercial activity of the Mexican government. Noting that Mexico had acted within its governmental function of setting monetary policy, the court held that Mexico's issuance of exchange controls was not a commercial activity. Therefore, the court rejected plaintiffs' claims as barred by the act of state doctrine.[1] The court dismissed plaintiffs' action pursuant to Fed. R. Civ. P. 12(b)(6) for failure to state a claim, or in the alternative, pursuant to Fed. R. Civ. P. 56, for failure to demonstrate the existence of a genuine issue of material fact.

Because we affirm the district court's dismissal of plaintiffs' complaint on act of state grounds, we need not on this appeal address appellee's claim that the court erred in failing to find Bancomer immune from suit under the FSIA. Our recent, thorough exposition of the act of state doctrine in *Allied* makes a similar discussion unnecessary here. We need recall only that the doctrine bars judicial review of "the validity of a taking of property within its own territory by a foreign sovereign government." *Banco Nacional de Cuba v. Sabbatino*, 376 U.S. 398, 428 (1964). In addition, we note that the policy concerns underlying the doctrine require that the political branches be preeminent in the realm of foreign relations. Accordingly, the Supreme Court has directed that each case be analyzed individually to determine the need for a separation of powers: "the less important the implications of an issue are for our foreign relations, the weaker the justification for exclusivity in the political branches." *Id.* at 428. Our examination of the facts in the instant case convinces us that the district court was correct in ruling that the relevant considerations mitigate against judicial intervention.

Situs of Obligation

In reviewing the district court's conclusion on the applicability of the act of state doctrine, we must first determine the situs of the property that was taken by the Mexican exchange controls. As we noted in *Allied*, "the concept of the situs of a debt for act of state purposes differs from the ordinary concept." The test we adopted in *Allied* was whether the purported taking was "able to come to complete fruition within the dominion of the [Mexican] government." Here, unlike *Allied*, it is clear that Mexico's actions meet this test.

The property at issue was Bancomer's obligation to pay the contractually mandated return on plaintiffs' investment. Plaintiffs argue that the situs of this obligation was New York. They allege that because they made some purchases by giving checks to Bancomer's New York agency and received some interest payments in New York, they could demand that Bancomer fulfill its obligation by paying them in New York.

The CDs named Mexico City as the place of deposit and of payment of interest and principal. Although some of the CDs were dollar-denominated, Bancomer never agreed to pay them in any location other than Mexico. The fact that plaintiffs' deposits were occasionally accepted and transmitted to Mexico by Bancomer's New York agency does not alter the situs of Bancomer's obligation. It is clear that the accomplishment of interbank transfers, which

---

[1] The district court also held that the Hickenlooper Amendment did not apply because currency regulations do not create "takings" within the meaning of the Amendment. In response to plaintiffs' argument that the validity of Mexico's action was not at issue because plaintiffs' dispute was only with Bancomer, the court noted that any judgment for plaintiffs would contravene Mexico's decree. Therefore, the court rejected plaintiffs' attempt to remove this question from the realm of act of state analysis.

was the extent of the New York agency's participation, does not change the contractually mandated situs of plaintiffs' property. The CDs were located in Mexico and were therefore subject to the effects of the exchange control regulations. The Mexican government "had the parties and the *res* before it and acted in such a manner as to change the relationship between the parties touching the *res*." *Tabacalera* [*Severiano Jorge, SA v. Standard Cigar Co.*], 392 F.2d [706,] 715 [(5th Cir.), *cert. denied*, 393 U.S. 924 (1968)]. To intervene to contradict the result of the exchange controls would be an impermissible intrusion into the governmental activities of a foreign sovereign.

Plaintiffs' attempt to equate their case with *Garcia* [*v. Chase Manhattan Bank*, 735 F.2d 645 (2d Cir. 1984),] is unavailing. In *Garcia* we held that the act of state doctrine did not bar recovery because the parties expressly provided for repayment at any Chase branch, anywhere in the world. Here, by contrast, no such wide-ranging agreement exists. Thus, we hold that the situs of defendant's obligation existed wholly within the boundaries of the foreign sovereign, and that the act of state doctrine therefore bars recovery.

Commercial Activity Exception

Plaintiffs assert that even if their claim is barred by the act of state doctrine, a commercial activity exception will permit them to prevail. They rely on *Alfred Dunhill of London, Inc. v. Republic of Cuba*, 425 U.S. 682, 696–706 (1976) (plurality opinion) [excerpted below, p. 548]. Plaintiffs insist that we have adopted this so-called exception, citing *Texas Trading & Milling Corp. v. Federal Republic of Nigeria*, 647 F.2d 300, 316 n.38 (2d Cir. 1981), *cert. denied*, 454 U.S. 1148 (1982), and *Hunt v. Mobil Oil Corp.*, 550 F.2d 68, 72–73 (2d Cir.), *cert. denied*, 434 U.S. 984 (1977). We do not read the dicta in those cases as an adoption of the suggested exception. Even if we decided that the act of state doctrine is not applicable to commercial transactions of foreign governments, the result here would be the same. The activity that implicates act of state concerns here was the issuance by the Mexican government of exchange controls which prevented Bancomer from performing its contractual obligations. This action, taken by the Mexican government for the purpose of saving its national economy from the brink of monetary disaster, surely represents the "exercise [of] powers peculiar to sovereigns." *Dunhill*, 425 U.S. at 704 (plurality opinion). Those sovereign powers, unlike acts that could be taken by a private citizen, trigger no commercial exception.

Plaintiffs protest that they seek no intervention into Mexico's sovereign acts; they merely request that we order Bancomer to perform its commercial contractual commitments. However, Bancomer has already paid plaintiffs all that it may under Mexican law. Were we to issue the order they seek, we would find ourselves directing a state-owned entity to violate its own national law with respect to an obligation wholly controlled by Mexican law. This would clearly be an impermissible "inquiry into the legality, validity, and propriety of the acts and motivation of foreign sovereigns acting in their governmental roles within their own boundaries." *Arango v. Guzman Travel Advisors Corp.*, 621 F.2d 1371, 1380 (5th Cir. 1980). Therefore, the action at issue is sovereign rather than commercial. We leave for another day consideration of the possible existence in this Circuit of a commercial exception to the act of state doctrine under *Dunhill*.

The act of state doctrine bars consideration of plaintiffs' complaint because the situs of defendant's obligations was in Mexico and the acts in question were taken by the Mexican government in its capacity as a sovereign. We affirm the judgment of the district court.

Notes and Questions on *Marcos* and *Braka*

1. *Contextual factors and the act of state doctrine.* Judging from the analysis in *Kirkpatrick, Marcos,* and *Braka*, what must an act be before it triggers the act of state doctrine? Are there characteristics of a case — other than the type of act in question — that might affect or determine the applicability of the act of state doctrine? For example, how should the court approach the act-of-state issue in civil cases with criminal overtones in the United States (*e.g.,* RICO and securities regulation cases)?

2. *Contractual "manipulation" of the act of state doctrine.* Doesn't the *Braka* court's fixation on the "contractually-mandated" place of repayment subvert the public values behind the act of state doctrine by subjecting it to the manipulation of private agreements?

3. *Multiple places of performance.* Would the result in *Braka* change if the debt were repayable in both Mexico and the United States?

4. *Braka and Weltover.* Is it conceivable that a foreign state could lose its sovereign immunity through the commercial activity exception (*e.g.*, *Weltover*, *supra*,) but receive the benefit of the act of state doctrine for the same activity? How could such a result be defended?

5. *The act of state doctrine and the Alien Tort Claims Act.* How do you respond to the argument that the act of state doctrine should effectively bar every human rights lawsuit under the Alien Tort Claims Act? That act requires the plaintiff to demonstrate that the defendant has committed a tort "in violation of the law of nations or a treaty of the United States." But because non-states can commit such violations in only extraordinary circumstances, virtually every defendant will be a state official whose actions must be presumed valid under the act of state doctrine. In the process of establishing jurisdiction by proving "a violation of the law of nations or a treaty of the United States," the plaintiff would also establish a compelling reason for not exercising jurisdiction. On this theory, shouldn't the act of state doctrine have compelled the opposite result in *Filártiga, supra*?

In *Filártiga* itself, the Second Circuit expressed skepticism that the act of state doctrine would pose an inevitable or fatal obstacle to human rights litigation under the Alien Tort Claims Act:

> [W]e doubt whether action by a state official in violation of the Constitution and laws of the Republic of Paraguay, and wholly unratified by that nation's government, could properly be characterized as

an act of state. Paraguay's renunciation of torture as a legitimate instrument of state policy, however, does not strip the tort of its character as an international law violation, if it in fact occurred under color of government authority.

630 F.2d at 889–90. *Accord Kadic v. Karadzic*, 70 F.3d 232, 250 (2d Cir. 1995), *cert. denied*, 518 U.S. 1005 (1996):

> It would be a rare case in which the act of state doctrine precluded suit under section 1350. *Banco Nacional [i.e., Sabbatino]* was careful to recognize the doctrine in the absence of . . . unambiguous agreement regarding controlling legal principles . . . and applied the doctrine only in a context — expropriation of an alien's property — in which world opinion was sharply divided. . . . [W]e doubt that the acts of even a state official, taken in violation of a nation's fundamental law and wholly unratified by that nation's government, could properly be characterized as an act of state.

See also Kadic v. Karadzic, 176 F.R.D. 329, 353 (C.D. Cal. 1997) ("In the context of *jus cogens* violations of international law, which are, by definition, internationally denounced, the high degree of international consensus severely undermines defendants' argument that [their] alleged activities should be treated as official acts of state.")

This approach builds on the Supreme Court's ratification requirement in *Dunhill*, 425 U.S. at 682, *infra*, and attaches a legal consequence to the political decision of governments to disclaim or deny human rights abuses. Claiming act of state "immunity" for such acts would create the dilemma of adopting, say, torture as state policy or as an expression of public authority ratified (at least metaphorically) by the state itself. In other words, the act of state doctrine, which cannot protect unofficial or unacknowledged acts of government officials, should be foreclosed when an act isn't "owned." As a result, the act of state doctrine cannot pose a *per se* barrier to human rights cases under § 1350.

---

[5] Litigating the Limitations on the Doctrine

[a] The Situs Requirement: Territoriality

REPUBLIC OF IRAQ v. FIRST NATIONAL CITY BANK
353 F.2d 47 (2d Cir. 1965)

King Faisal II of Iraq was killed on July 14, 1958, in the midst of a revolution in that country which led to the establishment of a republic, recognized by the United States in August. On July 19, 1958, the new government issued Ordinance No. 23 which decreed that "all property [of the dynasty] . . .

whether moveable or immoveable . . . should be confiscated."[1] At the time of his death, King Faisal had a balance of $55,925 and 4,008 shares of Canada General Fund, Ltd., a Canadian investment trust, in deposit and custody accounts with Irving Trust Company in New York. In October 1958, the Surrogate's Court for New York County issued to the defendant letters of administration with respect to King Faisal's New York assets. During that month the Consul General of the Republic of Iraq notified Irving Trust that the Republic claimed all assets of King Faisal by virtue of Ordinance No. 23. Notwithstanding the notice, Irving Trust subsequently transferred to the administrator the balance in the account and certificates for the shares, which were later sold.

In March 1962, the Republic brought this action against the administrator in the District Court for the Southern District of New York to recover the bank balance and the proceeds of the shares. From a judgment dismissing the complaint, the Republic appeals. We affirm. . . .

The principal questions raised in this appeal are the proper definition of the act of state doctrine and its application to foreign confiscation decrees purporting to affect property within the United States. Although difficulty is sometimes encountered in drawing the line between an "act of state" and more conventional foreign decrees or statutes claimed to be entitled to respect by the forum, the Ordinance involved in this case is nowhere near the boundary. A confiscation decree, which is precisely what Ordinance No. 23 purported to be, is the very archetype of an act of state. *See* ALI, Restatement of Foreign Relations Law of the United States § 41c (Proposed Official Draft, 1962) [hereinafter cited as Restatement].

The Supreme Court has declared that a question concerning the effect of an act of state "must be treated exclusively as an aspect of federal law." *Banco Nacional de Cuba v. Sabbatino*, 376 U.S. 398, 423–427 (1964). We deem that ruling to be applicable here even though, as we conclude below, this is not a case in which the courts of the forum are bound to respect the act of the foreign state. Like the traditional application of the act of state doctrine to preclude judgment with respect to another government's acts concerning property within its own territory at the time, the exercise of discretion whether or not to respect a foreign act of state affecting property in the United States is closely tied to our foreign affairs, with consequent need for nationwide uniformity. It is fundamental to our constitutional scheme that in dealing with other nations the country must speak with a united voice. It would be baffling if a foreign act of state intended to affect property in the United States were ignored on one side of the Hudson but respected on the other; any such diversity between states would needlessly complicate the handling of the foreign relations of the United States. The required uniformity can be secured only by recognizing the expansive reach of the principle, announced by Mr. Justice

---

[1] The ordinance included the following preamble:

> It is well known that the Iraqi Exdynasty has exerted its influence in Iraq to gain illegal wealth since its inception, as from 23rd August 1921. Consequently, in accordance with the aims of the National Movement that have been achieved by the Iraqi Army supported by the people of Iraq with their consent on 14th July, 1958, for the realization of social justice and putting an end to the illegal exploitation, we issue the following ordinance . . . .

Harlan in *Sabbatino*, that all questions relating to an act of state are questions of federal law, to be determined ultimately, if need be, by the Supreme Court of the United States.

Under the traditional application of the act of state doctrine, the principle of judicial refusal of examination applies only to a taking by a foreign sovereign of property within its own territory; when property confiscated is within the United States at the time of the attempted confiscation, our courts will give effect to acts of state "only if they are consistent with the policy and law of the United States." Restatement § 46.

In this case, neither the bank account nor the shares in the Canadian investment trust can realistically be considered as being within Iraq simply because King Faisal resided and was physically present there at the time of his death; in the absence of any showing that Irving Trust had an office in Iraq or would be in any way answerable to its courts, we need not consider whether the conclusion would differ if it did. So far as appears on this record, only a court in the United States could compel the bank to pay the balance in the account or to deliver the certificates it held in custody. The property here at issue thus was within the United States. Although the nationality of King Faisal provided a jurisdictional basis for the Republic of Iraq to prescribe a rule relating to his property outside Iraq, this simply gives the confiscation decree a claim to consideration by the forum which, in the absence of such jurisdiction, it would not possess — not a basis for insisting on the absolute respect which, subject to the qualifications of *Sabbatino*, the decree would enjoy as to property within Iraq at the time.

Extra-territorial enforcement of the Iraqi ordinance as to property within the United States at the date of its promulgation turns on whether the decree is consistent with our policy and laws.[2] We perceive no basis for thinking it to be. Confiscation of the assets of a corporation has been said to be "contrary to our public policy and shocking to our sense of justice," *Vladikavkazsky Ry. Co. v. New York Trust Co.*, 263 N.Y. 369, 378 (1934) [citations omitted]. Confiscation of the assets of an individual is no less so, even if he wears a crown. Our Constitution sets itself against confiscations such as that decreed by Ordinance No. 23 not only by the general guarantees of due process in the Fifth and Fourteenth Amendments but by the specific prohibitions of bills of attainder in Article I. It is true that since these provisions are addressed to action by the United States or a state, they might not prevent a court of the United States from giving effect to a confiscatory act of a foreign state with respect to property in the United States. But at least they show that, from its earliest days under the Constitution, this nation has had scant liking for legislative proscription of members of a defeated faction, although — or perhaps because — many states, in their dealings with property of the loyalists immediately after the Revolution, had practiced exactly that. Foreigners

---

[2] It might be argued that, with respect to the shares in the Canadian investment trust, a United States court ought to consider whether a Canadian court would regard the confiscation decree as consistent with the policy of Canada. But, apart from factors tending against such an argument, appellant has not contended that the shares should be treated differently than the bank account, it has presented no evidence as to the attitude of Canada toward foreign confiscations, and although we could take judicial notice of Canadian decisions, we are not obliged to do so under these circumstances.

entrusting their property to custodians in this country are entitled to expect this historic policy to be followed save when the weightiest reasons call for a departure. In saying this we are not guilty of disrespect to the recitals in the preamble of Ordinance No. 23; subject to the narrow exception discussed below, the policy of the United States is that there is no such thing as a "good" confiscation by legislative or executive decree.

The only cases cited to us that might seem to suggest a deviation from this view are *United States v. Belmont*, 301 U.S. 324 (1937), and *United States v. Pink*, 315 U.S. 203 (1942). Language in the latter opinion did indeed lead "some commentators to protest that the Court had laid down the revolutionary doctrine that recognition requires the recognizing state to give extraterritorial effect to all acts of state of the recognized government." The facts of the cases, however, required no such overturn of established principles. By the Litvinov agreement our Government had procured, as an incident to recognition, an assignment of the Soviet Union's claims to American assets of nationalized Russian companies, for the benefit of United States nationals whose property in the Soviet Union had been confiscated. Such action of the Chief Executive, taken under his power to conduct the foreign relations of the United States, was considered to make the Soviet confiscation decrees consistent with the law and policy of the United States from that time forward, and, as we now know from *Sabbatino*, federal law controls. In this case, by contrast, nothing remotely resembling the Litvinov agreement is present; on the contrary, the Department of State has disclaimed any interest of the executive department in the outcome of the litigation.[3]

Appellant insists that, however this may be, a New York court would give effect to Ordinance No. 23 because of the New York Decedent Estate Law, McKinney's Consol. Laws, c. 13, § 47, which provides:

> Except where special provision is otherwise made by law, the validity and effect of a testamentary disposition of any other property [i.e., other than real estate] situated within the state, and the ownership and disposition of such property, where it is not disposed of by will, are regulated by the laws of the state or country, of which the decedent was a resident, at the time of his death.

As already indicated, we read *Sabbatino* to mean that New York could not, by application of its choice of law rules, give a foreign act of state an effect, whether less or greater, differing from that dictated by federal law. But appellant's position would be baseless in any event. Not only does § 47 refer to the law existing at the time of decedent's death, but no state has been

---

[3] The Deputy Legal Adviser to the Department of State said in a letter dated January 15, 1965, to defendant's counsel:

> While the recognition of and maintenance of diplomatic relations with a foreign government are political matters within the province of the executive department of the Federal Government, questions regarding the administration of estates and the determination of rights and interests in property in the United States ordinarily are matters for determination by the courts of competent jurisdiction. Accordingly, the Department considers that the legal effect of Ordinance No. 23 as it may pertain to title to property in the United States of King Faisal II is a question for determination by the competent United States court.

stronger in its opposition to foreign confiscation decrees than New York. Indeed, it was this opposition that required the Supreme Court's intervention in the *Pink* case. We are thus confident that the courts of New York would not strain to read the general language of the Decedent Estate Law to include what on its face is a confiscation decree. . . .

Notes and Questions on *Braka* and *Iraq*

1. *The act of state doctrine in a borderless world.* Should the territorial limits at work in the act of state doctrine apply in the new era of international law, when non-territorial interests of states are routinely recognized?

2. *Where does a government act?* Virtually every foreign government's act occurs within its territory, at least at the decisional stage. Does either *Braka* or *Iraq* offer a manageable formula for determining when the foreign government's act is sufficiently extraterritorial to lose the protection of the act of state doctrine?

3. *The act of state doctrine and intangible property.* For act of state purposes, what is the situs of intangibles like insurance policies or copyrights or causes of action? What sources of law (or policy) might you consult to answer that question? *See* RESTATEMENT (THIRD) OF FOREIGN RELATIONS LAW, § 443, Reporters' Note 4 (1987):

> [I]t might be preferable to approach the question of the applicability of the act of state doctrine to intangible assets not by searching for an imaginary situs for property that has no real situs, but by determining how the act of the foreign state in the particular circumstances fits within the reasons for the act of state doctrine and for the territorial limitation.

4. *Location of a debt.* Where is a debt for purposes of the extraterritoriality exception to the act of state doctrine? In *F.&H.R. Farman-Farmaian Consulting Engineers v. Harza Engineering Co.*, 882 F.2d 281 (7th Cir. 1989), *cert. denied*, 497 U.S. 1038 (1990), the plaintiff was a former shareholder and director of an Iranian consulting firm that had been expropriated and liquidated during the Iranian Revolution. He brought suit on behalf of himself and other former shareholders to recover a debt owed to the Iranian company by Harza Engineering Company, a Delaware corporation with its principal place of business in Chicago, Illinois. The plaintiffs alleged that the extraterritoriality exception would apply, but the court rejected the argument:

> The exception to the act of state doctrine on which the plaintiffs rely requires that the act of confiscation not have been complete within the confiscating state. Equivalently, if a foreign state has made a confiscatory "taking," an act offensive to American proprieties, American courts will not lend their assistance to making the confiscation effective. So if the consulting firm had assets in Chicago, and the Iranian board of liquidators brought suit here to obtain control of those assets in conformity with the Iranian decree seizing the firm, the suit

would fail. *See, e.g., Bandes v. Harlow & Jones, Inc.*, 852 F.2d 661, 666–67 (2d Cir. 1988); *United Bank Ltd. v. Cosmic International, Inc.*, 542 F.2d 868 (2d Cir. 1976). But it is the exception that fails if the confiscation was complete within the foreign state in the sense that all of the firm's assets and operations were there, and the victim is trying to get an American court to undo the confiscation. That is this case. The consulting firm was an Iranian company all of whose assets and operations were in Iran; the revolutionary regime seized the firm and its assets; one of those assets was the firm's claim against Harza for payment for the services that the firm had rendered Harza in Iran. . . . The two Second Circuit decisions that we have cited, *Bandes* and *United Bank*, look the other way, but are distinguishable because in each a shipment of goods to or from the U.S. was contemplated. In this case, all the services under the contract were to be performed in the foreign country.

Granted, to describe the Consulting Firm's claim for payment of Harza's debt to it as an asset located in Iran, as we have done, may be thought to beg the question. A debt (like a word, a number, an idea) has no space-time location; it is not a physical object, and efforts to treat it as such, like efforts in conflicts of law jurisprudence, now largely abandoned, to find the site of a contract, seem bound to fail. This acknowledgment does not much help the plaintiffs, though, since they argue that the debt was "in" Chicago — a clearly untenable proposition. Harza's liability was the consulting firm's asset, and it is strange to describe the consulting firm as having an "American" asset by virtue merely of having a claim against an American company for services performed on that company's behalf in Iran.

The metaphysics and semantics of the issue to one side, the plaintiffs' submission that the debt is located in Chicago would if accepted greatly reduce the accepted scope of the act of state doctrine — a pertinent although not necessarily a controlling consideration. A dispute between an Iranian corporation doing business entirely in Iran, and the government of Iran, could pop up in an American court merely because the corporation was owed some money by an American firm.

Are you convinced?

---

[b] The "Unambiguous Agreement"/Clear Law Exception

KALAMAZOO SPICE EXTRACTION CO. v. PROVISIONAL MILITARY GOVERNMENT OF SOCIALIST ETHIOPIA
729 F.2d 422 (6th Cir. 1984)

This is an appeal from a district court judgment, which dismissed appellant's counterclaim. The district court held that the act of state doctrine as interpreted by the Supreme Court in *Sabbatino*, precluded judicial inquiry into the validity of an expropriation by the Ethiopian government of shares in an Ethiopian business entity held by an American corporation. Appellant, Kalamazoo Spice Extraction Company (Kal-Spice) is an American corporation which, in a joint venture with Ethiopian citizens, established the Ethiopian Spice Extraction Company (ESESCO) in 1966, an Ethiopian based corporation. Kal-Spice owned approximately 80% of the shares of ESESCO. Kal-Spice also contributed capital, built a production facility, and trained ESESCO's staff, which consisted of Ethiopian citizens. Production began in 1970 after several years of preparation, construction, and training.

The Provisional Military Government of Socialist Ethiopia (PMGSE) came to power in 1974. As part of its program to assure that Ethiopian industries would "be operated according to the philosophy of Ethiopian socialism", the PMGSE announced the seizure of "control of supervision and a majority shareholding" of a number of corporations, including ESESCO, in February 1975. As a result of the expropriation, Kal-Spice's ownership interest in ESESCO was reduced from 80% to approximately 39%. In December 1975, the PMGSE established a Compensation Commission. The Commission's purpose was to compensate those claimants whose property had been expropriated. Kal-Spice claimed it was entitled to compensation of $11,000,000. In October 1981, the PMGSE offered Kal-Spice the equivalent of $450,000 in Ethiopian currency. Kal-Spice, however, has rejected the PMGSE's offer. The PMGSE contends that Kal-Spice should have accepted the offer because: 1) Kal-Spice retains an interest in ESESCO of approximately 40% and 2) Kal-Spice carried expropriation insurance based on a total investment in ESESCO of less than $1,000,000.

A few months before the PMGSE's expropriation program, Kal-Spice placed an order with ESESCO for the purchase of spices to be delivered to Kal-Spice in Michigan between November 1, 1974, and November 5, 1975. ESESCO shipped spices worth more than 1.9 million dollars to Kal-Spice. These shipments occurred in several installments, some before the February 3, 1975, seizure of ESESCO and some after that date. The post-expropriation shipments were drawn from inventories seized on the expropriation date. According to Kal-Spice, it continued to make payments for these shipments for a while after the expropriation until it realized that the PMGSE did not intend to compensate it for the expropriated property. ESESCO, now controlled by the PMGSE, filed a breach of contract action against Kal-Spice, demanding payment for goods received by Kal-Spice. Kal-Spice counterclaimed against ESESCO as the alter ego of the PMGSE, seeking, *inter alia*, damages for the expropriation of ESESCO.

Once the suit reached the United States District Court of the Western District of Michigan, the court decided that the act of state doctrine precluded adjudication of the claims against the PMGSE based on the expropriation of Kal-Spice's interests. The district court further held that the Treaty of Amity between the United States and Ethiopia was "so inherently general, doubtful, and susceptible of multiple interpretation" that it could not be applied by a United States court to satisfy the "treaty exception" to the act of state doctrine. We disagree, and reverse and remand for the reasons set forth below. . . .

The act of state doctrine is an exception to the general rule that a court of the United States, where appropriate jurisdictional standards are met, will decide cases before it by choosing the rules appropriate for decision from among various sources of law, including international law. . . . Kal-Spice, as well as the United States Departments of State, Treasury, Justice, and the American Bar Association, as *amici curiae*, request that this Court recognize a "treaty exception" to the act of state doctrine. According to appellant and *amici*, the following language in *Sabbatino* provides the basis for a treaty exception:

> The Judicial Branch will not examine the validity of a taking of property within its own territory by a foreign sovereign government, extant and recognized by this country at the time of suit, *in the absence of a treaty or other unambiguous agreement regarding controlling legal principles*, even if the complaint alleges that the taking violates customary international law (emphasis added).

This language and the existence of a treaty between the United States and Ethiopia asserts appellant and *amici*, requires a "treaty" exception to the rule that a United States court will not exercise jurisdiction over a foreign sovereign for an act done by that sovereign within its borders. The treaty in existence between the United States and Ethiopia is the 1953 Treaty of Amity and Economic Relations (Treaty of Amity). Article VIII, paragraph two of that treaty provides:

> Property of nationals and companies of either High Contracting Party, including interests in property, shall receive the most constant protection and security within the territories of the other High contracting party. *Such property shall not be taken except for a public purpose, nor shall it be taken without prompt payment of just and effective compensation* (emphasis added).

Kal-Spice unsuccessfully argued before the district court that this treaty provision was the type referred to by the Supreme Court in *Sabbatino*, which would allow a United States court to exercise jurisdiction over a claim of expropriation of property by a foreign sovereign. Specifically, Kal-Spice alleged that the "prompt payment of just and effective compensation" provision of the Treaty of Amity set forth controlling legal principles which [were] referred to by the Supreme Court in *Sabbatino*.

The district court, however, did not agree with Kal-Spice's assertion. Instead, the district court agreed with the PMGSE's position that this provision of the treaty calling for the "prompt payment of just and effective compensation" was ambiguous. It found that this provision was "so inherently general, doubtful and susceptible to multiple interpretation that in the absence of an established body of law to clarify their meaning a court cannot reasonably be asked to apply them to a particular set of facts." The failure of the treaty to provide a controlling legal standard provided a possibility of conflict with the Executive Branch. It is this potential conflict, concluded the district court, that underlies the act of state doctrine.

We do not agree with the district court's decision that the provision of the treaty requiring payment of prompt, just, and effective compensation fails to provide a controlling legal standard. To the contrary, we find that this is a controlling legal standard in the area of international law. As the appellant and *amici* correctly point out, the term "prompt, just, and effective compensation" and similar terms are found in many treaties where the United States and other nations are parties. The 1953 United States-Ethiopia Treaty of Amity and Economic Relations is one of a series of treaties, also known as the FCN Treaties, between the United States and foreign nations negotiated after World War II. As the legislative history of these treaties indicates, they were adopted to protect American citizens and their interests abroad. Almost all of these treaties contain sections which provide for "prompt, adequate, and effective compensation", "just compensation", or similar language regarding compensation for expropriated property.

The United States District Court for the District of Columbia used a treaty to find a "treaty exception" in *American International Group, Inc. v. Islamic Republic of Iran*, 493 F. Supp. 522 (D.D.C. 1980). There, several American insurance companies held investments in insurance companies doing business in Iran. After the Iranian revolution of 1979 the Iranian government nationalized the insurance industry, and did not compensate the American companies for their investments which had been expropriated. The American insurance companies subsequently brought suit seeking damages for the property that had been expropriated without compensation.

The district court examined the 1957 Treaty of Amity between the United States and Iran, and concluded that the insurance companies were entitled to compensation. Specifically, the court examined Article IV, paragraph two, which stated:

> Property of nationals and companies of either High Contracting Party, including interests in property, shall receive the most constant protection and security within the territories of the other High Contracting Party, in no case less than that required by international law. *Such property shall not be taken except for a public purpose, nor shall it be taken without the prompt payment of just compensation.* Such compensation shall be in an effectively realizable form and shall represent the full equivalent of the property taken; and adequate provision shall have been made at or prior to the time of taking for the determination and payment thereof (emphasis added).

After examining the treaty the district court determined, *inter alia*, that the act of state doctrine did not preclude it from jurisdiction because the treaty was relevant, unambiguous, and set forth agreed-upon principles of international law, i.e., a standard for compensation for the expropriated property.[1] Accordingly, the district court granted plaintiffs' motion for a partial summary judgment on the issue of liability as a result of the expropriation of their property without compensation by the Iranian government.

---

[1] The district court also held that the act of state doctrine was inapplicable because the court was not deciding the validity of Iran's expropriation of the plaintiffs' interest, but rather it was adjudicating the failure of Iran to provide compensation for the expropriated property in violation of international law. It was also decided that the act of state doctrine did not apply because of the commercial act exception of *Alfred Dunhill of London, Inc. v. Republic of Cuba, supra. American International Group*, 439 F. Supp. at 525. We decline, however, to reverse the district court on these additional grounds. Our decision to reverse the district court is based only upon the existence of a treaty between the United States and Ethiopia which may provide a basis for Kal-Spice to receive compensation.

There is a striking similarity between the treaty in the present case and the one involved in *American International*. Both treaties contain similar provisions for compensation when property is expropriated by one of the nations that is a party to the treaty. Consequently, *American International* provides authoritative guidance to us on the use of the treaty exception, and illustrates the error of the district court's decision that the treaty in this case was too ambiguous to allow a court to exercise jurisdiction.

Banco Nacional de Cuba v. Chase Manhattan Bank, 658 F.2d 875 (2d Cir. 1981), provides an example of the utility of the "prompt, just, and effective compensation" standard that is employed in many treaties. In *Chase Manhattan Bank*, the Second Circuit was faced with the task of determining the value of Cuban branches of Chase Manhattan which had been expropriated by the Cuban revolutionary government.[2] After examining several theories regarding the appropriate standard for the compensation of expropriated property, the court concluded Chase Manhattan Bank was entitled to the net asset value of the branches that were expropriated by the Cuban government.

We do not suggest, however, by our citation of *Chase Manhattan Bank*, that the district court in the present case is bound to use the same method employed in *Chase Manhattan Bank* for determining compensation, if any, to which Kal-Spice will be entitled. There are sufficient factual differences in the present case and *Chase Manhattan Bank*, e.g., nature of the property expropriated, status of the expropriated property, the facts surrounding the expropriation, etc., which may call for a different compensation standard. The citation to *Chase Manhattan Bank* is only for the purpose of illustrating the point that the standard of compensation provided for in the Treaty of Amity between Ethiopia and the United States can provide a basis for determining the extent of compensation to which Kal-Spice may be entitled.

Moreover, the Supreme Court's decision in *Sabbatino*, in addition to the *American International* and *Chase Manhattan Bank* decisions requires a reversal of the district court decision that the 1953 Treaty of Amity was too ambiguous to be susceptible to judicial interpretation. As the Supreme Court stated in *Sabbatino*:

> It should be apparent that the greater the degree of codification or consensus concerning a particular area of international law, the more appropriate it is for the judiciary to render decisions regarding it, since the courts can then focus on the application of an agreed principle to circumstances of fact rather than on the sensitive task of establishing a principle not inconsistent with the national interest or with international justice.

Numerous treaties employ the standard of compensation used in the 1953 Treaty of Amity between Ethiopia and the United States. Undoubtedly, the

---

[2] The Second Circuit relied upon *First National City Bank v. Banco Nacional de Cuba*, 406 U.S. 759 (1972) (*Citibank*) for its holding that the act of state doctrine was inapplicable. Noting that Citibank was a plurality opinion, the Second Circuit held that the act of state doctrine does not apply where: 1) the executive branch provides a Bernstein letter advising the courts that it believes the act of state doctrine need not be applied; 2) there is no showing that an adjudication of the claim will interfere with foreign relations; and 3) the claim against the foreign sovereign is asserted by way of counterclaim and does not exceed the value of the sovereign's claim. 658 F.2d at 884.

widespread use of this compensation standard is evidence that it is an agreed upon principle in international law. Nor will adjudication in this matter interfere with any efforts by the Executive branch to resolve this matter. In fact, the Executive branch has also intervened in this matter through the Departments of State, Treasury, and Justice who have filed a joint *amicus* brief urging that the 1953 Treaty of Amity makes the act of state doctrine inapplicable. Obviously, the Executive branch feels that an adjudication in this matter is appropriate. Thus, the Supreme Court's concern in *Sabbatino* for judicial interference with foreign policy activity by the Executive branch is not a consideration in this case.

Additionally, there is a great national interest to be served in this case, *i.e.,* the recognition and execution of treaties that we enter into with foreign nations. Article VI of the Constitution provides that treaties made under the authority of the United States shall be the supreme law of the land. Accordingly, the Supreme Court has recognized that treaties, in certain circumstances, have the "force and effect of a legislative enactment." *See, e.g., Whitney v. Robertson*, 124 U.S. 190 (1888). The failure of this court to recognize a properly executed treaty would indeed be an egregious error because of the position that treaties occupy in our body of laws. . . .

Our decision that the 1953 Treaty of Amity makes the act of state doctrine inapplicable only begins this controversy. The district court must determine what rights, if any, the treaty confers upon Kal-Spice. We recognize that further proceedings will be an arduous task for all parties involved. However, proper briefing of this issue before the court should lead to the resolution of this dispute. Accordingly, the decision of the district court dismissing appellant's counterclaim is reversed and remanded for further proceedings not inconsistent with this opinion.

Notes and Questions on *Kalamazoo Spice*

1. *Meaning of "unambiguous agreement."* The *Sabbatino* court and the RE-STATEMENT (THIRD) would apply the act of state doctrine "in the absence of a treaty or other unambiguous agreement regarding controlling legal principles." Should either *jus cogens* or general customary international law qualify as an "unambiguous agreement"? Could an "unambiguous agreement" include a contract between private parties or between a private party and a state? *Cf.* RESTATEMENT (THIRD) OF FOREIGN RELATIONS LAW, § 443, comment c (1987):

> When a state has expressly subjected certain kinds of obligations to adjudication in the courts of another state, or to international arbitration . . ., it may be said to have acknowledged that its acts with respect to those obligations . . . are subject to international scrutiny; in such cases the justification for applying the act of state doctrine is significantly weaker.

2. *A per se factor?* Should the existence of a treaty foreclose the application of the act of state doctrine altogether, or should it instead be one factor of many in determining whether the doctrine applies?

3. *Limits on the treaty "exception."* Treaties that are ambiguous about the standard to apply in a case or about the class of persons within the ambit of the treaty will not overcome the act of state doctrine. *See, e.g., Dayton v. Czechoslovak Socialist Republic*, 834 F.2d 203 (D.C. Cir. 1987).

---

[c] The Commercial Activity Exception

[1] The Supreme Court Speaks (But What Does It Say?)

ALFRED DUNHILL OF LONDON, INC. v. REPUBLIC OF CUBA
425 U.S. 682 (1976)

MR. JUSTICE WHITE delivered the opinion of the Court.[1]

The issue in this case is whether the failure of respondents to return to petitioner Alfred Dunhill of London, Inc. (Dunhill), funds mistakenly paid by Dunhill for cigars that had been sold to Dunhill by certain expropriated Cuban cigar businesses was an "act of state" by Cuba, precluding an affirmative judgment against respondents.

I

. . . In 1960, the Cuban Government confiscated the business and assets of the five leading manufacturers of Havana cigars. These companies, three corporations and two partnerships, were organized under Cuban law. Virtually all of their owners were Cuban nationals. None were American. These companies sold large quantities of cigars to customers in other countries, including the United States, where the three principal importers were Dunhill, Saks & Co. (Saks), and Faber, Coe & Gregg, Inc. (Faber). The Cuban Government named "interventors" to take possession of and operate the business of the seized Cuban concerns. Interventors continued to ship cigars to foreign purchasers, including the United States importers.

This litigation began when the former owners of the Cuban companies, most of whom had fled to the United States, brought various actions against the three American importers for trademark infringement and for the purchase price of any cigars that had been shipped to importers from the seized Cuban plants and that bore United States trademarks claimed by the former owners to be their property. . . . [T]he Cuban interventors and the Republic of Cuba were allowed to intervene in these actions, which were consolidated for trial. Both the former owners and the interventors had asserted their right to some $700,000 due from the three importers for postintervention shipments: Faber, $582,588.86; Dunhill, $92,949.70; and Saks, $24,250. It also developed that as of the date of intervention, the three importers owed sums totaling $477,200 for cigars shipped prior to intervention: Faber, $322,000; Dunhill, $148,600;

---

[1] Part III of this opinion is joined only by THE CHIEF JUSTICE, MR. JUSTICE POWELL, and MR. JUSTICE REHNQUIST.

and Saks, $6,600. These latter sums the importers had paid to interventors subsequent to intervention on the assumption that interventors were entitled to collect the accounts receivable of the intervened businesses. The former owners claimed title to and demanded payment of these accounts.

Based on the "act of state" doctrine . . . the District Court held . . . that it was required to give full legal effect to the 1960 confiscation of the five cigar companies insofar as it purported to take the property of Cuban nationals located within Cuba. Interventors were accordingly entitled to collect from the importers all amounts due and unpaid with respect to shipments made after the date of intervention. The contrary conclusion was reached as to the accounts owing at the time of intervention: Because the United States courts will not give effect to foreign government confiscations without compensation of property located in the United States and because under *Republic of Iraq v. First Nat. City Bank*, 353 F.2d 47 (CA2 1965), the situs of the accounts receivable was with the importer-debtors, the 1960 seizures did not reach the preintervention accounts, and the former owners, rather than the interventors, were entitled to collect them from the importers — even though the latter had already paid them to interventors in the mistaken belief that they were fully discharging trade debts in the ordinary course of their business.

This conclusion brought to the fore the importers' claim that their payment of the preintervention accounts had been made in error and that they were entitled to recover these payments from interventors by way of setoff and counterclaim. Although their position that the 1960 confiscation entitled them to the sums due for preintervention sales had been rejected and the District Court had ruled that they "had no right to receive or retain such payment," interventors claimed those payments on the additional ground that the obligation, if any, to repay was a quasi-contractual debt having a situs in Cuba and that their refusal to honor the obligation was an act of state not subject to question in our courts. The District Court rejected this position for two reasons. First, the repayment obligated was more properly deemed situated in the United States and hence remained unaffected by any purported confiscatory act of the Cuban Government. Second, in the District Court's view, nothing had occurred which qualified for recognition as an act of state:

> [T]here was no formal repudiation of these obligations by Cuban Government decree of general application or otherwise. . . . Here, all that occurred was a statement by counsel for the interventors, during trial, that the Cuban Government and the interventors denied liability and had refused to make repayment. This statement was made after the interventors had invoked the jurisdiction of this Court in order to pursue their claims against the importers for post-intervention shipments. It is hard to conceive how, if such a statement can be elevated to the status of an act of state, any refusal by any state to honor any obligation at any time could be considered anything else.

The importers were accordingly held entitled to set off their mistaken payments to interventors for preintervention shipments against the amounts due from them for their post-intervention purchases. Faber and Saks, because they owed more than interventors were obligated to return to them, were satisfied completely by the right to setoff. But Dunhill — and at last we arrive at the issue in this case — was entitled to more from interventors — $148,000 — than it owed for postintervention shipments — $93,000 — and to be made whole, asked for and was granted judgment against interventors for the full amount of its claim, from which would be deducted the smaller judgment entered against it.

The Court of Appeals agreed that the former owners were entitled to recover from the importers the full amount of preintervention accounts receivable. It also held that the mistaken payments by importers to interventors gave rise to a quasi-contractual obligation to repay these sums. But, contrary to the District Court, the Court of Appeals was of the view that the obligation to repay had a situs in Cuba and had been repudiated in the course of litigation by conduct that was sufficiently official to be deemed an act of state: "[I]n the absence of evidence that the interventors were not acting within the scope of their authority as agents of the Cuban government, their repudiation was an act of state even though not embodied in a formal decree." Although the repudiation of the interventors' obligation was considered an act of state, the Court of Appeals went on to hold that *First Nat. City Bank v. Banco Nacional de Cuba,* 406 U.S. 759 (1972), entitled importers to recover the sums due them from interventors by way of setoff against the amounts due from them for postintervention shipments. The act of state doctrine was said to bar the affirmative judgment awarded Dunhill to the extent that its claim exceeded its debt. The judgment of the District Court was reversed in this respect, and it is this action which was the subject of the petition for certiorari filed by Dunhill. In granting the petition, we requested the parties to address certain questions, the first being whether the statement by counsel for the Republic of Cuba that Dunhill's unjust-enrichment claim would not be honored constituted an act of state. . . . We have now concluded that nothing in the record reveals an act of state with respect to interventors' obligation to return monies mistakenly paid to them. Accordingly we reverse the judgment of the Court of Appeals.

II

The District Court and the Court of Appeals . . . observed that interventors had "ignored" demands for the return of the monies [paid by mistake on preintervention accounts receivable] and had "fail[ed] to honor the importers' demand (which was confirmed by the Cuban government's counsel at trial)." This conduct was considered to be "the Cuban government's repudiation of its obligation to return the funds" and to constitute an act of state not subject to question in our courts. We cannot agree. . . .

In *The "Gul Djemal,"* 264 U.S. 90 (1924), a supplier libeled and caused the arrest of the *Gul Djemal,* a steamship owned and operated for commercial purposes by the Turkish Government, in an effort to recover for supplies and services sold to and performed for the ship. The ship's master, "a duly commissioned officer of the Turkish Navy," appeared in court and asserted sovereign immunity, claiming that such an assertion defeated the court's jurisdiction. A direct appeal was taken to this Court, where it was held that the master's assertion of sovereign immunity was insufficient because his mere representation of his government as master of a commercial ship furnished no basis for assuming he was entitled to represent the sovereign in other capacities. Here there is no more reason to suppose that the interventors possess governmental, as opposed to commercial, authority than there was to suppose that the master of the *Gul Djemal* possessed such authority. The master of the *Gul Djemal* claimed the authority to assert sovereign immunity while the interventors claim that they had the authority to commit an act of state, but the difference is unimportant. In both cases, a party claimed to have had the authority to exercise sovereign power. In both, the only authority shown is commercial authority.

We thus disagree with the Court of Appeals that the mere refusal of the interventors to repay funds followed by a failure to prove that interventors "were not acting within the scope of their authority as agents of the Cuban government" satisfied respondents' burden of establishing their act of state defense. Nor do we consider *Underhill v. Hernandez,* heavily relied upon by the Court of Appeals, to require a contrary conclusion.[2] In that case . . . it was apparently concluded that the facts were sufficient to demonstrate that the conduct in question was the public act of those with authority to exercise sovereign powers and was entitled to respect in our courts. We draw no such conclusion from the facts of the case before us now. As the District Court found, the only evidence of an act of state other than the act of nonpayment by interventors was "a statement by counsel for the interventors, during trial, that the Cuban Government and the interventors denied liability and had refused to make repayment." *Menendez v. Faber, Coe & Gregg, Inc.,* 345 F. Supp., at 545. But this merely restated respondents' original legal position and adds little, if anything, to the proof of an act of state. No statute, decree, order, or resolution of the Cuban Government itself was offered in evidence indicating that Cuba had repudiated its obligations in general or any class thereof or that it had as a sovereign matter determined to confiscate the amounts due three foreign importers.

III [*See* footnote 1, *supra.*]

If we assume with the Court of Appeals that the Cuban Government itself had purported to exercise sovereign power to confiscate the mistaken payments belonging to three foreign creditors and to repudiate interventors' adjudicated obligation to return those funds, we are nevertheless persuaded by the arguments of petitioner and by those of the United States that the concept of an act of state should not be extended to include the repudiation of a purely commercial obligation owed by a foreign sovereign or by one of its commercial instrumentalities. Our cases have not yet gone so far, and we decline to expand their reach to the extent necessary to affirm the Court of Appeals.

Distinguishing between the public and governmental acts of sovereign states on the one hand and their private and commercial acts on the other

---

[2] There the commander of a successful revolution, in control of the city of Bolivar, refused a passport to Underhill. Upon suit by Underhill for his detention, this Court refused to inquire into the propriety of the detention because "[t]he acts complained of were the acts of a military commander representing the authority of the revolutionary party as government, which afterwards succeeded and was recognized by the United States."

is not a novel approach. As the Court stated through Mr. Chief Justice Marshall long ago in *Bank of the United States v. Planters' Bank of Georgia,* 9 Wheat. 904, 907 (1824):

> It is, we think, a sound principle, that when a government becomes a partner in any trading company, it divests itself, so far as concerns the transactions of that company, of its sovereign character, and takes that of a private citizen. Instead of communicating to the company its privileges and its prerogatives, it descends to a level with those with whom it associates itself, and takes the character which belongs to its associates, and to the business which is to be transacted.

In this same tradition, *South Carolina v. United States,* 199 U.S. 437 (1905), drew a line for purposes of tax immunity between the historically recognized governmental functions of a State and businesses engaged in by a State of the kind which theretofore had been pursued by private enterprise. Similarly, in *Ohio v. Helvering,* 292 U.S. 360, 369 (1934), the Court said: "If a state chooses to go into the business of buying and selling commodities, its right to do so may be conceded so far as the Federal Constitution is concerned; but the exercise of the right is not the performance of a governmental function. . . . When a state enters the market place seeking customers it divests itself of its quasi sovereignty pro tanto, and takes on the character of a trader. . . ." It is thus a familiar concept that "there is a constitutional line between the State as government and the State as trader. . . ." *New York v. United States,* 326 U.S. 572, 579 (1946).

It is the position of the United States, stated in an *amicus* brief filed by the Solicitor General, that such a line should be drawn in defining the outer limits of the act of state concept and that repudiations by a foreign sovereign of its commercial debts should not be considered to be acts of state beyond legal question in our courts. Attached to the brief of the United States and to this opinion as Appendix 1 is the letter of November 26, 1975, in which the Department of State, speaking through its Legal Adviser agrees with the brief filed by the Solicitor General and, more specifically, declares that "we do not believe that the *Dunhill* case raises an act of state question because the case involves an act which is commercial,[3] and not public, in nature."[4]

---

[3] The dissent, assuming that the Republic of Cuba purported to exercise sovereign powers in refusing to return Dunhill's money, asserts that there is no distinction between the refusal to honor its obligation to return Dunhill's money and the original expropriation of the cigar businesses; and that the case therefore does not involve a purely commercial act. The dissent is wrong. Cuba's debt to Dunhill arose out of the conduct by Cuba's agents of a commercial business for profit. The same may not be said of conventional expropriations of foreign assets located *ab initio* inside a country's territorial borders. Dunhill was continuing to buy cigars from the interventors after intervention and Dunhill knew when the payments were made that the interventors would receive them. The debt would never have arisen if Cuba's agents had not gone into the cigar business and sold to Dunhill. This case is therefore no different from any case in which a buyer overpays for goods sold by a commercial business operated by a foreign government — a commonplace event in international commerce.

[4] The letter also takes the position that sovereign immunity, as such, does not prevent entry of an affirmative judgment on a counterclaim arising out of the same "transaction or occurrence that is the subject matter of the claim of the foreign state," and inferentially that the act of state doctrine is likewise unavailable as a method of avoiding such an affirmative judgment. In light of our conclusion that repudiation by a sovereign of a commercial debt is not an act of state, we

The major underpinning of the act of state doctrine is the policy of foreclosing court adjudications involving the legality of acts of foreign states on their own soil that might embarrass the Executive Branch of our Government in the conduct of our foreign relations. But based on the presently expressed views of those who conduct our relations with foreign countries, we are in no sense compelled to recognize as an act of state the purely commercial conduct of foreign governments in order to avoid embarrassing conflicts with the Executive Branch. On the contrary, for the reasons to which we now turn, we fear that embarrassment and conflict would more likely ensue if we were to require that the repudiation of a foreign government's debts arising from its operation of a purely commercial business be recognized as an act of state and immunized from question in our courts.

Although it had other views in years gone by, in 1952, as evidenced by . . . the Tate Letter, the United States abandoned the absolute theory of sovereign immunity and embraced the restrictive view under which immunity in our courts should be granted only with respect to causes of action arising out of a foreign state's public or governmental actions and not with respect to those arising out of its commercial or proprietary actions. This has been the official policy of our Government since that time as the [government] confirms:

> Moreover, since 1952, the Department of State has adhered to the position that the commercial and private activities of foreign states do not give rise to sovereign immunity. Implicit in this position is a determination that adjudications of commercial liability against foreign states do not impede the conduct of foreign relations, and that such adjudications are consistent with international law on sovereign immunity.

Repudiation of a commercial debt cannot, consistent with this restrictive approach to sovereign immunity, be treated as an act of state; for if it were, foreign governments, by merely repudiating the debt before or after its adjudication, would enjoy an immunity which our Government would not extend them under prevailing sovereign immunity principles in this country. This would undermine the policy supporting the restrictive view of immunity, which is to assure those engaging in commercial transactions with foreign sovereignties that their rights will be determined in the courts whenever possible.

Although at one time this Court ordered sovereign immunity extended to a commercial vessel of a foreign country absent a suggestion of immunity from the Executive Branch, and although the policy of the United States with respect to its own merchant ships was then otherwise, *Berizzi Bros. Co. v. S.S. Pesaro*, 271 U.S. 562 (1926), the authority of that case has been severely diminished by later cases such as *Ex parte Peru*, 318 U.S. 578 (1943), and *Mexico v. Hoffman*, 324 U.S. 30 (1945). In the latter case, the Court unanimously denied immunity to a commercial ship owned but not possessed by

---

do not reach the State Department's alternative position. The letter also takes the position that the overruling of *Sabbatino*, so that acts of state would hereafter be subject to adjudication in American courts under international law, would not result in embarrassment to the conduct of United States foreign policy. We need not resolve this issue either.

the Mexican Government. The decision rested on the fact that the Mexican Government was not in possession, but the Court declared:

> Every judicial action exercising or relinquishing jurisdiction over the vessel of a foreign government has its effect upon our relations with that government. Hence it is a guiding principle in determining whether a court should exercise or surrender its jurisdiction in such cases, that the courts should not so act as to embarrass the executive arm in its conduct of foreign affairs. "In such cases the judicial department of this government follows the action of the political branch, and will not embarrass the latter by assuming an antagonistic jurisdiction."

> It is therefore not for the courts to deny an immunity which our government has seen fit to allow, or to allow an immunity on new grounds which the government has not seen fit to recognize. The judicial seizure of the property of a friendly state may be regarded as such an affront to its dignity and may so affect our relations with it, that it is an accepted rule of substantive law governing the exercise of the jurisdiction of the courts that they accept and follow the executive determination that the vessel shall be treated as immune. But recognition by the courts of an immunity upon principles which the political department of government has not sanctioned may be equally embarrassing to it in securing the protection of our national interests and their recognition by other nations.

In a footnote, the Court expressly questioned the *Berizzi Bros.* holding, and two concurring Justices asserted that the Court had effectively overruled that case.

Since that time, as we have said, the United States has adopted and adhered to the policy declining to extend sovereign immunity to the commercial dealings of foreign governments. It has based that policy in part on the fact that this approach has been accepted by a large and increasing number of foreign states in the international community; in part on the fact that the United States had already adopted a policy of consenting to be sued in foreign courts in connection with suits against its merchant vessels; and in part because the enormous increase in the extent to which foreign sovereigns had become involved in international trade made essential "a practice which will enable persons doing business with them to have their rights determined in the courts."

In the last 20 years, lower courts have concluded . . . that *Berizzi Bros.* no longer correctly states the law; and they have declined to extend sovereign immunity to foreign sovereigns in cases arising out of purely commercial transactions. Indeed, it is fair to say that the "restrictive theory" of sovereign immunity appears to be generally accepted as the prevailing law in this country.

Participation by foreign sovereigns in the international commercial market has increased substantially in recent years. The potential injury to private businessmen — and ultimately to international trade itself — from a system in which some of the participants in the international market are not subject to the rule of law has therefore increased correspondingly. As noted above, courts of other countries have also recently adopted the restrictive theory of sovereign immunity. Of equal importance is the fact that subjecting foreign governments to the rule of law in their commercial dealings presents a much smaller risk of affronting their sovereignty than would an attempt to pass on the legality of their governmental acts. In their commercial capacities, foreign governments do not exercise powers peculiar to sovereigns. Instead, they exercise only those powers that can also be exercised by private citizens. Subjecting them in connection with such acts to the same rules of law that apply to private citizen is unlikely to touch very sharply on "national nerves." Moreover, as this Court has noted:

> [T]he greater the degree of codification or consensus concerning a particular area of international law, the more appropriate it is for the judiciary to render decisions regarding it, since the courts can then focus on the application of an agreed principle to circumstances of fact rather than on the sensitive task of establishing a principle not inconsistent with the national interest or with international justice.

There may be little codification or consensus as to the rules of international law concerning exercises of governmental powers, including military powers and expropriations, within a sovereign state's borders affecting the property or persons of aliens. However, more discernible rules of international law have emerged with regard to the commercial dealings of private parties in the international market. The restrictive approach to sovereign immunity suggests that these established rules should be applied to the commercial transactions of sovereign states.

Of course, sovereign immunity has not been pleaded in this case; but it is beyond cavil that part of the foreign relations law recognized by the United States is that the commercial obligations of a foreign government may be adjudicated in those courts otherwise having jurisdiction to enter such judgments. Nothing in our national policy calls on us to recognize as an act of state a repudiation by Cuba of an obligation adjudicated in our courts and arising out of the operation of a commercial business by one of its instrumentalities. For all the reasons which led the Executive Branch to adopt the restrictive theory of sovereign immunity, we hold that the mere assertion of sovereignty as a defense to a claim arising out of purely commercial acts by a foreign sovereign is no more effective if given the label "Act of State" than if it is given the label "sovereign immunity."[5] In describing the act of state

---

[5] The dissent states that the doctrines of sovereign immunity and act of state are distinct — the former conferring on a sovereign "exemption from suit by virtue of its status" and the latter "merely [telling] a court what law to apply to a case." It may be true that the one doctrine has been described in jurisdictional terms and the other in choice-of-law terms; and it may be that the doctrines point to different results in certain cases. It cannot be gainsaid, however, that the proper application of each involves a balancing of the injury to our foreign policy, the conduct of which is committed primarily to the Executive Branch, through judicial affronts to sovereign powers, against the injury to the private party, who is denied justice through judicial deference to a raw assertion of sovereignty, and a consequent injury to international trade. The State Department has concluded that in the commercial area the need for merchants "to have their rights determined in courts" outweighs any injury to foreign policy. This conclusion was reached in the context of the jurisdictional problem of sovereign immunity. We reach the same one in the choice-of-law context of the act of state doctrine.

doctrine in the past we have said that it "precludes the courts of this country from inquiring into the validity of the public acts a recognized foreign sovereign power committed within its own territory" and that it applies to "acts done within their own States, in the exercise of governmental authority." We decline to extend the act of state doctrine to acts committed by foreign sovereigns in the course of their purely commercial operations. Because the act relied on by respondents in this case was an act arising out of the conduct by Cuba's agents in the operation of cigar businesses for profit, the act was not an act of state.

[Appendices to the opinion of the court, and concurring and dissenting opinions omitted.]

Notes and Questions on *Dunhill*

1. *Rationale for a commercial activity exception.* What are the best arguments for and against the recognition of a commercial activity exception to the act of state doctrine? Could it be that there is more likely to be "unambiguous agreement" about controlling legal principles in a commercial context, or that sensitive diplomatic issues are less likely to arise? Should the Foreign Sovereign Immunities Act, with its distinction between acts *jure imperii* and acts *jure gestionis*, simply apply by analogy to act-of-state cases? Why do you suppose disagreement on these points fractured the Supreme Court in *Dunhill*?

2. *Effect of Kirkpatrick on the commercial activity exception.* The Supreme Court arguably had the perfect opportunity in *Kirkpatrick*, *supra*, to clarify the meaning of *Dunhill*, especially the plurality's suggestion that domestic courts need not apply the act of state doctrine to a foreign government's commercial acts. What does the ultimate decision in *Kirkpatrick* say, if anything, about the existence and contours of the commercial activity exception?

3. *Meaning of "commercial" in different settings.* In principle, can an act be commercial for purposes of the Foreign Sovereign Immunities Act — and therefore not be entitled to immunity — and yet be sufficiently public to qualify for act-of-state treatment — and therefore be held non-justiciable? Rereading the last footnote in *Dunhill*, what could be the practical effect of such a ruling?

4. *FSIA "commercial activity" exception compared.* Does the Foreign Sovereign Immunities Act offer useful guidance in determining whether an act is "commercial" for purposes of the act of state doctrine? Note specifically that courts are not to consider the purpose of an act in determining whether it is commercial for purposes of the FSIA. But how might purpose arguments be relevant in the act-of-state context?

5. *Problem.* Suppose that the government of Japan, in settlement of a long-standing trade dispute with the United States, capped the aggregate export of automobiles to the U.S., and then gave specific export quotas to every automobile manufacturer in Japan. If dealers in the United States then sued

the Japanese manufacturers for anticompetitive conduct and violations of U.S. antitrust law, should the act of state doctrine apply or not?

––––––––

[2] *Dunhill*'s Ambiguity in the Lower Courts

Only a plurality of the Supreme Court in *Dunhill* endorsed a commercial activity exception to the act of state doctrine, concluding that domestic courts need not presume the validity of a foreign government's commercial acts. Of course, even if a majority had endorsed the exception in principle, defining the line between commercial acts and governmental acts would be no simple task, and certainly no simpler than determining the line between *jure gestionis* and *jure imperii* for purposes of the Foreign Sovereign Immunities Act, *supra*. Perhaps because that analytical task is so difficult and because the Supreme Court's authorization in *Dunhill* is so equivocal, the lower courts have approached the commercial activity exception with hesitation and uncertainty. Consider for example the analysis of the court in *Braka v. Bancomer, supra*:

> Plaintiffs assert that even if their claim is barred by the act of state doctrine, a commercial activity exception will permit them to prevail. They rely on *Alfred Dunhill of London, Inc. v. Republic of Cuba*, 425 U.S. 682, 696–706 (1976) (plurality opinion). Plaintiffs insist that we have adopted this so-called exception, citing *Texas Trading & Milling Corp. v. Federal Republic of Nigeria*, 647 F.2d 300, 316 n.38 (2d Cir. 1981), *cert. denied*, 454 U.S. 1148 (1982), and *Hunt v. Mobil Oil Corp.*, 550 F.2d 68, 72–73 (2d Cir.), *cert. denied*, 434 U.S. 984 (1977). We do not read the dicta in those cases as an adoption of the suggested exception. Even if we decided that the act of state doctrine is not applicable to commercial transactions of foreign governments, the result here would be the same. The activity that implicates act of state concerns here was the issuance by the Mexican government of exchange controls which prevented Bancomer from performing its contractual obligations. This action, taken by the Mexican government for the purpose of saving its national economy from the brink of monetary disaster, surely represents the "exercise [of] powers peculiar to sovereigns."*Dunhill*, 425 U.S. at 704 (plurality opinion). Those sovereign powers, unlike acts that could be taken by a private citizen, trigger no commercial exception.
>
> Plaintiffs protest that they seek no intervention into Mexico's sovereign acts; they merely request that we order Bancomer to perform its commercial contractual commitments. However, Bancomer has already paid plaintiffs all that it may under Mexican law. Were we to issue the order they seek, we would find ourselves directing a state-owned entity to violate its own national law with respect to an obligation wholly controlled by Mexican law. This would clearly be an impermissible "inquiry into the legality, validity, and propriety of the acts and motivation of foreign sovereigns acting in their governmental roles within their own boundaries." *Arango v. Guzman Travel Advisors*

Corp., 621 F.2d 1371, 1380 (5th Cir. 1980). Therefore, the action at issue is sovereign rather than commercial. We leave for another day consideration of the possible existence in this Circuit of a commercial exception to the act of state doctrine under *Dunhill*.

Other courts have expressed similar hesitation. In *Honduras Aircraft Registry Ltd. v. Honduras*, 129 F.3d 543 (11th Cir. 1997), *cert. denied*, 524 U.S. 952 (1988), for example, the lower court had dismissed an act-of-state argument on the apparent ground that the case "involve[d] a perceived commercial exception to the doctrine as under the FSIA." But the court of appeals ruled that *"there is no commercial exception to the act of state doctrine* as there is under the FSIA. The factors to be considered, as recited in *Kirkpatrick*, may sometimes overlap with the FSIA commercial exception, but a commercial exception alone is not enough. The district court may have been correct in holding the doctrine was no bar to this case, but whatever the result may be it must be reached only after consideration of the pertinent factors."

As the following cases suggest, not all of the lower courts are reluctant to endorse a commercial activity exception in principle, although their somewhat conclusory opinions can hide the underlying difficulty of characterizing any particular act as "commercial" or not. (They may even endorse and apply the exception without saying so.)

ARANGO v. GUZMAN TRAVEL ADVISORS CORP.
621 F.2d 1371 (5th Cir. 1980)

Plaintiffs-appellants, Ramiro Arango and his family, attack the district court's dismissal of their tort and breach of contract claims against appellee, Compania Dominicana de Aviacion ("Dominicana"), the national airline of the Dominican Republic. Dominicana, one of four defendants against whom suit had originally been filed in a Florida state court, had removed the claims to federal district court . . . .

The Arangos' claims arose from the events of an abortive package vacation tour from Miami, Florida to the Dominican Republic. The Arangos' jaunt terminated abruptly and prematurely when Dominican immigration officials denied them entry into that country upon their arrival at the airport in Santo Domingo, apparently because of their inclusion on an official list of "undesirable aliens." The officials then compelled the Arangos' immediate, "involuntary re-routing" back to the United States via Dominicana, the air carrier on which they had arrived. Because of the unavailability of immediate return flights directly to Miami, the requirement that the Arangos leave the country resulted in their being shunted first to San Juan, Puerto Rico, and the next day to Port-au-Prince, Haiti, where they apparently were left to arrange and pay for their own return to Miami, which they finally were able to accomplish four days later.

Based on the non-performance of the vacation contract and the sundry injuries and inconveniences suffered in their "involuntary re-routing", the

Arangos brought suit in state court against four defendants, all alleged to have collaborated in the marketing and formation of the package tour so as to create a joint venture for purposes of the action arising therefrom: Guzman Travel Advisors Corp., a Florida corporation and the actual purveyor of the package tour; Trailways Travel & Tourism International Corp., also a Florida corporation and the tour organizer; Sheraton Hotels & Inns, World Corp., a foreign corporation whose local hotel was to provide food and lodging; and the appellee here, Dominicana, which was to provide air transportation and "tourist cards" necessary for entering the Dominican Republic and which had been responsible for the Arangos' carriage during their "re-routing" to the United States. Wholly owned by the Dominican government, Dominicana exercised its prerogative under the relevant provisions of the Foreign Sovereign Immunities Act of 1976 ("FSIA") as a "foreign state," to remove the action to federal district court. . . . Once in federal court, Dominicana moved to dismiss the action under Fed.R.Civ.P. 12(b)(1), (6), arguing first, that as a foreign sovereign, it was immune from the jurisdiction of the court under the pertinent provisions of the FSIA; and second, that the Arangos' complaint stated no claim upon which relief could be granted because all alleged injuries derived from the official acts of Dominican immigration authorities, which acts are insulated from judicial scrutiny in United States courts by the "act of state" doctrine. Without specifying upon which ground it relied, the district court granted the motion and dismissed the suit against Dominicana. [The court's discussion of the FSIA is omitted.]

The second theory proffered to the district court as grounds for dismissal was the act of state doctrine. "The act of state doctrine in its traditional formulation precludes the courts of this country from inquiring into the validity [or legality] of the public acts a recognized foreign sovereign power [has] committed within its own territory." *Banco Nacional de Cuba v. Sabbatino*, 376 U.S. 398, 401 (1964). Relegating grievances from acts of this sort to executive channels of international diplomacy, the rule is an embodiment of the deference to be accorded the sovereignty of other nations; it averts potential diplomatic embarrassment from the courts of one sovereign sitting in judgment over the public acts of another. *Alfred Dunhill of London, Inc. v. Republic of Cuba*, 425 U.S. 682, 697 (1975).

Unlike foreign sovereign immunity, the act of state doctrine affects the viability of the Arangos' claims against all the defendants. It does not simply relieve the foreign government of liability for its acts, but operates as an issue preclusion device, foreclosing judicial inquiry into the validity or propriety of such acts in litigation between any set of parties. Consequently, the Arangos' battery and false imprisonment claims would be foreclosed under this doctrine, as well as under the FSIA, since they would, by definition, require an adjudication of the propriety and legality of the acts of the Dominican immigration authorities and, more specifically, of Dominicana employees while effectively deployed as agents of that government under the orders of these authorities in the performance of their official governmental duties in denying the Arangos' entry into the Dominican Republic and effecting their removal.

Dominicana urges that, beyond this, since the Arangos' expulsion by Dominican authorities was the precipitating factor for all plaintiffs' claims, all should be foreclosed by the act of state doctrine. This contention accords that doctrine too great a breadth. The act of state doctrine only precludes judicial inquiry into the legality, validity, and propriety of the acts and motivations of foreign sovereigns acting in their governmental roles within their own boundaries;[1] it does not preclude judicial resolution of all commercial consequences stemming from the occurrence of such public acts. The Arangos' contract and negligence claims require only a determination of the respective rights and duties of the parties in the wake of the sovereign acts of the Dominican immigration authorities. The claims raise the questions of who bears the risk of loss following such an incident and whether there existed a duty on the part of any defendant to protect the Arangos from, or to warn of, the possibility of its occurrence. They do not necessitate a consideration or evaluation of the legitimacy of those "acts of state," themselves. Consequently, the act of state doctrine, like the FSIA, should not have required dismissal with respect to the Arangos' contract and negligence claims. . . .

VIRTUAL DEFENSE AND DEVELOPMENT INT'L, INC. v. THE REPUBLIC OF MOLDOVA
133 F. Supp. 2d 1 (D.D.C. 1999)

. . . Following the dissolution of the Union of Soviet Socialist Republics, Moldova emerged as a sovereign nation facing severe economic turmoil. In an effort to bolster its weakening economy, Moldova arranged to sell to Iran several MiG-29 planes, which were capable of firing nuclear weapons. The United States of America strongly opposed this sale on grounds of international security and, in early 1997, requested that Moldova cancel the scheduled transfer to Iran. Moldova agreed to comply.

Subsequently, in May and June of 1997, Boris Birshtein, the Economic and Commercial Advisor to the Moldovan President, contacted an international consultant in New York, regarding economic opportunities in Moldova. Among the opportunities discussed was the sale of the MiG-29 planes. On August 5, 1997, [the consultant] contacted Virtual to relay the message that Moldova was interested in having Virtual negotiate the sale of the MiG-29 planes to an entity approved by the United States. In September 1997, Virtual's President traveled to Moldova to work out the details of such an agreement. Subsequently, on September 17, 1997, the Prime Minister of Moldova sent a letter to Virtual stating that "[o]n behalf of the Republic of Moldova the Company [Virtual] is provided with authorization to initiate and sustain discussions with governments and/or private business entities concerning the realization of these aircrafts. This authorization is provided taking into account that this deal will be carried out with partners from [the] United States of America or other states with the authorization of the USA Government."

---

[1] Dominicana's sale of airline tickets and tourist cards to the Arangos and its activities and omissions in connection therewith, which took place wholly in the United States, are not "acts of state" insulated under the doctrine. Cf. *Alfred Dunhill of London, Inc. v. Republic of Cuba*, 425 U.S. 682, 695–706 (plurality of four Justices ruling that act of state doctrine does not apply to purely commercial acts of a sovereign).

Virtual alleges that a contract existed between it and Moldova whereby Virtual would receive a commission of fifteen percent upon successfully negotiating the sale of the MiG-29 planes. In its complaint, Virtual alleges that it negotiated a sale of the MiGs from Moldova to the United States for $60 million for which Virtual is entitled to its fifteen percent commission. In actuality, the MiGs were sold to the United States for $40 million in cash and $100 million in the form of economic aid. Contrary to Virtual's assertion that it negotiated this sale, Moldova alleges that "the negotiations between the United States and Moldova were nearly complete by the time Virtual was provided authorization to explore whether other possible purchasers for the MiGs existed."

Following the sale, Virtual demanded payment of its commission in the amount of $9 million and was denied the fees. Consequently, Virtual filed a complaint in this court seeking damages for breach of contract and *quantum meruit*. . . .

[The court first ruled that the case fell within the commercial activity exception to the Foreign Sovereign Immunities Act, 28 U.S.C. § 1605(a)(2), citing the legislative history of the act:

> [T]he fact that goods or services to be procured through a contract are to be used for public purpose is irrelevant; it is the essentially commercial nature of an activity or transaction that is critical. Thus a contract by a foreign government to buy provisions or equipment for its armed forces or to construct a government building constitutes a commercial activity.

H. Rep. No. 94-1487, 94th Cong., 2d Sess., reprinted in 1976 U.S. CODE CONG. & AD. NEWS 6604, 6615. In this case, "Moldova acted as a private participant in the market when it engaged in discussions with Virtual regarding the sale of the MiGs and when it eventually sold the MiGs to the United States. The mere fact that the goods sold by Moldova were MiG-29 planes does not change the nature of Moldova's actions. The court also found that the statutorily required nexus to the United State was satisfied.]

. . . Having determined that it has jurisdiction over this case, the court must next consider the appropriateness of exercising its jurisdiction over a foreign state in light of the "act of state" doctrine. Unlike the FSIA, the act of state doctrine is not jurisdictional, but prudential. "The act of state doctrine is similar to the political question doctrine in domestic law. It requires that the courts defer to the legislative and executive branches when those branches are better equipped to resolve a politically sensitive question." *International Ass'n of Machinists and Aerospace Workers v. Organization of Petroleum Exporting Countries,* 649 F.2d 1354, 1358–9 (9th Cir. 1981) [hereinafter *IAM*]. In addition, the act of state doctrine aims to keep the courts "from deciding a case when the outcome turns upon the legality or illegality (whether as a matter of United States, foreign, or international law) of official action by a foreign sovereign performed within its own territory." *Riggs Nat'l Corp. & Subsidiaries v. Commissioner of Internal Revenue Serv.,* 163 F.3d 1363, 1367 (D.C. Cir. 1999) (citing *W.S. Kirkpatrick & Co., Inc. v. Environmental Tectonics Corp.,* 493 U.S. 400, 406 (1990)). The burden of proving that the court should apply the act of state doctrine and abstain from hearing the case is on the party asserting the applicability of the doctrine. Consequently, the burden in this case is on Moldova to demonstrate that the act of state doctrine should be applied.

Essentially, if a state is acting in the public interest then it is asserting its sovereignty and the act of state doctrine may apply. This may be so even if a court has jurisdiction over the foreign sovereign pursuant to the commercial activity exception to the FSIA. Consequently, under the act of state doctrine, a United States court would be discouraged from hearing even cases premised on commercial activities if hearing such cases would require the court to pass judgment on an underlying sovereign act. As the Ninth Circuit has noted,

> [t]he act of state doctrine is not diluted by the commercial activity exception which limits the doctrine of sovereign immunity. While purely commercial activity may not rise to the level of an act of state, certain seemingly commercial activity will trigger act of state considerations. . . . While the FSIA ignores the underlying purpose of a state's action, the act of state doctrine does not.

IAM, 649 F.2d at 1360.

The Supreme Court has suggested a "balancing approach" when deciding if the act of state doctrine applies. It is necessary to balance the judiciary's interest in hearing a case involving a commercial activity with the desire to avoid matters of foreign affairs controlled by the executive or legislative branches. *See Banco Nacional de Cuba v. Sabbatino*, 376 U.S. 398, 428 (1964) ("Some aspects of international law touch more sharply on national nerves than do others; the less important the implications of an issue are for our foreign relations, the weaker the justification for exclusivity in the political branches."). In balancing these interests, a court should be mindful that the decision to deny judicial relief to a party should not be made lightly. Viewing the facts of this case in light of this standard, the court concludes that the defendant has not met its burden of showing that the act of state doctrine should be applied.

To meet its burden and show that the act of state doctrine should apply to the sale of the MiG-29 planes and the alleged agreement to pay Virtual a commission fee, Moldova must show that it was acting in the public interest of its country and that a judicial inquiry into this action would either (1) cause harm to the interests of another branch of the United States government, or (2) question the legality of Moldova's sovereign actions.

This case is distinguishable from other instances in which courts chose to apply the act of state doctrine. In *IAM*, the court was asked to question the validity of OPEC's alleged price fixing practices. Despite the commercial aspect of the action the court chose not to hear the case noting that "OPEC's 'price fixing' activity has a significant sovereign component. . . . [T]he act of state doctrine remains available when such caution is appropriate, regardless of any commercial component of the activity involved." The *IAM* court reasoned that use of the act of state doctrine was appropriate because the record "contain[ed] extensive documentation of the involvement of our executive and legislative branches with the oil question. . . . It is clear that OPEC and its activities are carefully considered in the formulation of American foreign policy." Additionally, "[t]he United States and other nations have supported the principle of supreme state sovereignty over natural resources."

Here, the court is not asked to question the validity of a sovereign action, such as price fixing, but is merely asked to adjudicate a contract claim. In *Alfred Dunhill of London v. Republic of Cuba*, the court "declined to extend the act of state doctrine to acts committed by foreign sovereigns in the course of their purely commercial operations. Because the act relied on by respondents in this case was an act arising out of the conduct by Cuba's agents in the operation of cigar businesses for profit, the act was not an act of state." The actions that took place between Virtual and Moldova in this case are more similar to the activities at issue in *Dunhill* than they are to the sovereign actions of the OPEC countries at issue in *IAM*. Furthermore, Moldova has offered little evidence to demonstrate that the executive or legislative branches of the United States government have considerable involvement or interest in the issues presented by this case. In absence of evidence to the contrary, the court finds that this case involves a contract question that does not tread upon Moldova's sovereignty or hamper the objectives of another branch of the United States government. Accordingly, the court concludes that application of the act of state doctrine is not appropriate in this case. . . .

WORLD WIDE MINERALS LTD. v. REPUBLIC OF KAZAKHSTAN
116 F. Supp. 2d 98 (D.D.C. 2000)

After gaining independence from the Soviet Union in 1991, Kazakhstan began to seek foreign investment. Among the areas of interest to foreign companies were the northern and southern uranium mines of Kazakhstan. In June of 1996, World Wide Minerals Ltd., a Canadian corporation, submitted a proposal for the management of the northern mines complex in Kazakhstan. World Wide was simultaneously negotiating with the Kazakhstan Joint Stock Company of Atomic Power, Engineering, and Industry (KATEP) for the right to export and sell uranium from Kazakhstan. On July 2, 1996, World Wide and KATEP agreed on the points of negotiation. They called for good faith negotiations on the issue of marketing the uranium. No final agreement to market the uranium was ever reached.

On October 7, 1996, Kazakhstan and World Wide entered into the Management Agreement. Under this agreement, World Wide took over the state controlled holding company for the northern mines complex. World Wide committed to paying the debt of the holding company, some 5 million dollars. This agreement indicated that an export license would be required for World Wide to sell the uranium. World Wide was entitled to terminate the agreement if the license was not received by December 16, 1996. . . . World Wide never received the export license, but did not suspend activities until April 1997.

On March 25, 1997, World Wide, through its wholly owned subsidiary World Wide Resource Finance Inc., entered into the Pledge Agreement with the State

Committee of Kazakhstan. This agreement secured the loans of the Management Agreement. Under Article 19 of the Pledge Agreement, the parties indicated that any disputes would be addressed first by negotiations, and then by arbitration under UNCITRAL. Paragraph 19.5 provided that the parties would not be restricted in their right to settle disputes in court. That paragraph also provides that Kazakhstan waives immunity "for the purposes of the United States Foreign Sovereign Immunities Act of 1976 in any action or proceedings to which such Act applies."

On January 15, 1997, World Wide contracted with Nuclear Fuel Resources Inc., (NFR) of Colorado to market uranium from the northern mines. NFR and World Wide then entered into an agreement to provide uranium to Consumer's Energy, a Michigan corporation, on March 27, 1997. When the export license was not issued, World Wide could not perform its duties under the contract. As a result of the failure to obtain the export license, World Wide suspended operations at the Northern Mines. Kazakhstan informed World Wide that it would not be able to grant an export license because of an earlier agreement with Nukem Inc., a U.S. company, for exclusive marketing of the uranium. This agreement had been kept confidential. In July of 1997, Nukem took over the failed contract with Consumer's Energy. On August 1, 1997, Kazakhstan terminated the northern mines management agreement. Plaintiffs filed suit, alleging breach of contract, conspiracy, violations of the RICO statute and, in the proposed second amended complaint violations of the Sherman Act. . . .

[The court first ruled that Kazakhstan had waived the defense of foreign sovereign immunity. *See* 28 U.S.C. § 1605(a)(1).]

The act of state doctrine bars consideration of claims when the resolution of a case turns on the legality or illegality of official action taken by a foreign sovereign in its own territory. . . . Kazakhstan has raised the act of state doctrine as a defense. The defendants claim that in order to give relief this court must find invalid the denial of the export license and other governmental enactments. Kazakhstan has demonstrated that granting World Wide relief would require a judgment on the acts of a sovereign state. World Wide repeatedly indicates that its damages were caused by the inability to obtain an export license for uranium and the nationalization of property. The regulations regarding the issuance of export licenses were specifically enacted by Kazakhstan in the interests of international and national security. If liability were attributed to Kazakhstan for the alleged damages suffered by World Wide, Kazakhstan would be faced with a judgment that designated its denial of the export license as invalid. The same is true of a judgment concerning the alleged nationalization of property.

World Wide claims that it only seeks investigation into the conspiracy against it. World Wide maintains that the facts here are similar to those in *Kirkpatrick*, and therefore the ruling in that case should guide the decision. In *Kirkpatrick*, the Supreme Court considered the application of the act of state doctrine to a claim for damages under the Racketeer Influenced and Corrupt Organizations Act. The plaintiff claimed that the defendant, a private corporation, had bribed Nigerian officials in order to obtain a contract. The Court held that the act of state doctrine did not apply because the validity of the contract was not at issue.

In contrast, the validity of the contract is at issue in this case. Unlike the facts in *Kirkpatrick*, the defendant here is a foreign sovereign, not a private company. To investigate the conspiracy, we must examine the contracts with Nukem, since these led to the denial of World Wide's export license. These contracts were based on the internal laws and decrees of the Republic of Kazakhstan. Kazakhstan would be faced with an investigation directly concerning its governmental acts. Investigation of the claims against Kazakhstan would be in direct conflict with the ruling in *Kirkpatrick*.

By way of comparison, the act of state doctrine would not bar claims against Nukem because the situation would be analogous to *Kirkpatrick*. If the court allowed such damages its findings might suggest that the contract was invalid, but Kazakhstan's governmental decrees would not be directly implicated. Here however, the claim for damages is against Kazakhstan, thus involving the legality of the governmental actions. As such, this court cannot consider any of the claims against Kazakhstan or its instrumentalities due to the act of state doctrine. . . .

Notes and Questions on the Commercial Activity Exception

1. *The test for commerciality.* In *Arango*, what is the test for distinguishing justiciable from non-justiciable issues under the act of state doctrine? What, if anything, does the distinction between a government's act and its commercial consequences say about the court's attitude towards the act of state doctrine?

2. *Reconciling the principal cases.* Can *World Wide Minerals* and *Virtual Defense* be distinguished or reconciled? Should the identity of the defendant matter (as it did in *World Wide Minerals*)? Which case seems more consistent with *Kirkpatrick*?

3. *The commercial activity exception and the separation of powers.* Maybe asking if there is a commercial activity exception to the act of state doctrine is the wrong question, seeking some absolute resolution to what is ultimately a separation-of-powers issue, where absolutes are unavailable and undesirable. After all, there may be areas of constitutional law where stability and accommodation are better served by relative uncertainties and *ad hoc* judgments than by determinate rules. Besides, it's possible that the body of case law under the act of state doctrine offers advocates sufficiently clear *strategic goals* in their adversarial characterizations of any particular governmental act, even if *rules* are hard to come by.

For example, at a minimum, we know — in contrast to the Foreign Sovereign Immunities Act — that there is no statutory directive allowing domestic courts to adjudicate the validity of a foreign government's commercial act. We also know from *Dunhill* that only a plurality of the Supreme Court is willing to endorse such a *per se* exception. And yet, as the cases in this section suggest, the courts are willing to make commerciality one factor among many in determining whether the doctrine should apply or not. And, as suggested in *Arango*, *Virtual Defense*, and *World Wide Minerals*, the further down the chain of proximate cause the plaintiff's commercial claim is from a governmental act (*e.g.,* a regulation or a decision not to issue a license), the less likely it is that the courts will defer on act-of-state grounds. Query whether the commercial consequences of non-commercial acts *per se* should always be justiciable, or whether the separation-of-powers rationale for the act of state doctrine counsels against words like "always" and "*per se.*"

---

[d] Congressional "Overrides:" The Second Hickenlooper Amendment and its Modern Progeny

Like all creatures of the common law, the act of state doctrine bends to the will of Congress, and there have been periodic efforts to legislate the doctrine out of existence. But just as the political question doctrine serves too useful a function to be abandoned altogether in domestic litigation, so too with the act of state doctrine and the safety-valve it offers in some transnational cases. As a consequence, legislation comprehensively banning act-of-state abstention is unlikely to see the light of day. But in specific *classes* of cases, Congress has felt that the rights of plaintiffs to their day in court should prevail over the political or diplomatic disruption that might flow from adjudication. Advocates must be aware of the lurking Congressional authority to modify the act of state doctrine.

The most famous example of a Congressional override of the doctrine is the Second Hickenlooper Amendment, adopted in the mid-1960s in response to the Supreme Court's decision in *Sabbatino*, and ultimately codified as part of the Foreign Assistance Act of 1965:

> Notwithstanding any other provision of law, no court in the United States shall decline on the ground of the federal act of state doctrine to make a determination on the merits giving effect to the principles of international law in a case in which a claim of title or other right to property is asserted by any party including a foreign state (or a party claiming through such state) based upon (or traced through) a confiscation or other taking after January 1, 1959, by an act of that state in violation of the principles of international law, including the principles of compensation and the other standards set out in this subsection: *Provided*, that this subparagraph shall not be applicable
>
> (1) in any case in which an act of a foreign state is not contrary to international law or with respect to a claim of title or other right to property acquired pursuant to an irrevocable letter of credit of not more than 180 days duration issued in good faith prior to the time of the confiscation or other taking, or
>
> (2) in any case with respect to which the President determines that application of the act of state doctrine is required in that particular case by the foreign policy interests of the United States and a suggestion to this effect is filed on his behalf in that case with the court.

The courts have generally construed the Second Hickenlooper Amendment to assure that its remedial purpose is served. But *Sabbatino* remains good law, even if its fullest implications are controversial, and the Hickenlooper Amendment — like all statutory enactments — requires (and rewards) careful parsing. Consider for example whether the amendment might apply to claims of title to specific property before the court, but not to claims for compensation for the taking of property that is not before the court. Could a breach of contract claim come within the amendment?

The explicit reach of the Second Hickenlooper Amendment is one recurring issue, periodically reappearing long after the *Sabbatino* decision that provoked it, but there is no doubt that the amendment was intended to constrict the applicability of the act of state doctrine in explicitly defined cases. Counsel must frequently determine whether Congress has *implicitly* overridden the act of state doctrine in other settings. As the materials after *West* and *Faysound* suggest, the central question is whether certain provisions of a statute — a cause of action for example or a grant of subject matter jurisdiction — might be so incompatible with act-of-state deference as to override it, even in the absence of a Hickenlooper-like reference to the doctrine itself.

WEST v. MULTIBANCO COMERMEX, S.A.
807 F.2d 820 (9th Cir. 1987)

[Plaintiffs were individual U.S. investors who had purchased peso-and dollar-denominated certificates of deposit from defendant banks. In an effort to maintain the exchange value of the peso, the Mexican government adopted regulations *inter alia* "eliminating all bank deposits in foreign currency and specifying that repayment of those deposits were to be made in pesos at a rate of exchange to be determined by Banco de Mexico, Mexico's central bank." In addition the government nationalized the private banking system in Mexico and banned the transfer of dollars abroad. When the certificates later matured, plaintiffs suffered significant financial losses and sued for repayment at face value. Defendants raised multiple defenses including the act of state doctrine, to which the plaintiffs interposed the second Hickenlooper Amendment. Defendants argued that that statute does not apply to certificates of deposit.]

. . . West claims that the 'conversion' of his dollar-denominated certificate of deposit to pesos at a rate of exchange specified by the government — a rate less than the market rate of exchange — was a taking of his property in violation of international law. This is an expropriation claim. Before reaching the merits of that claim, we must . . . consider the applicability of the act of state doctrine and determine whether it is permissible for us to examine the challenged actions of the Mexican government. . . .

Congress has adopted a specific statutory provision requiring federal courts to examine the merits of controversies involving expropriation claims. The so-called Second Hickenlooper Amendment, overrides the judicially developed doctrine of act of state. Hickenlooper was passed in response to the Supreme Court's decision in *Sabbatino,* which barred adjudication of an expropriation claim on act of state grounds. The amendment states in part:

> No court in the United States shall decline on the ground of the federal act of state doctrine to make a determination on the merits giving effect to the principles of international law in a case in which a claim of title or other rights to property is asserted by any party . . . based upon (or traced through) a confiscation or other taking . . . by an act of that state in violation of the principles of international law, including the principles of compensation . . . .

When Hickenlooper governs, courts are barred from invoking the judicially created doctrine under which we refrain from consideration of cases involving acts of foreign governments or foreign officials.[1]

Defendants argue that Hickenlooper is inapplicable because rights arising out of ownership of certificates of deposit are contractual, and hence not 'tangible property' which can be taken by expropriation within the meaning of the amendment. Although this proposition finds support in case law, it is based largely upon an overly formalistic attachment to private law categories and is contrary to the motivating policies of the Hickenlooper Amendment.

Defendants' construction would unnecessarily restrict the scope of Hickenlooper. As the District of Columbia Circuit has noted, the "broad, unqualified language of the carefully drafted amendment" should not be undermined by the importation of external constraints on interpretation. *Ramirez de Arellano v. Weinberger*, 745 F.2d 1500, 1542 n.180 (D.C. Cir. 1984) (en banc), *vacated and remanded because of subsequent legislation*, 471 U.S. 1113 (1985). The legislative history to Hickenlooper supports the rejection of a constricted interpretation and makes it clear that the protection afforded U.S. investments was to be broad in scope:

> The sponsors of the amendment referred to it as the "Rule of Law" amendment; they viewed it as authorizing courts to apply established law [in] suits challenging expropriations. Congressional intent to overturn *Sabbatino* was never limited to a single narrow class of cases. The purposes of the amendment include the promotion and protection of United States investment in foreign countries (which characteristically has always principally been land, minerals, and large fixed immovables), and securing the right of a property holder to a court hearing on the merits.

Id.

Moreover, the tangible/intangible characterization of property interests, urged by the defendants, is a distinction without a difference. This distinction is not generally recognized in international, federal, or state law. *Oakland v. Oakland Raiders (Raiders I)*, 32 Cal. 3d 60, 646 P.2d 835 (1982) (at least

---

[1] Congress's ability to override the act of state doctrine is directly related to the underpinnings of that doctrine. In *Sabbatino*, the Supreme Court explained that the act of state doctrine was grounded largely upon "the competence and function of the Judiciary . . . in ordering our relationships with other members of the international community." In addition to concerns of institutional competence, the Court indicated that the "absence of a treaty or other unambiguous agreement regarding controlling legal principles" gave it pause. In the context of expropriation claims, Congress has determined both that the courts are competent to resolve such claims (unless the President specifically directs otherwise in a particular case) and that the relevant content of international law is clear.

for "eminent domain purposes, neither the federal nor the state Constitution distinguishes between property which is real or personal, tangible or intangible").

Although the certificates of deposit may be characterized as intangible property or contracts, they are "property interests" that are protected under international law from expropriation. For example, in its adjudication of disputes involving claims for compensation for alleged takings of property — bank deposits in Czechoslovakia — the Foreign Claims Settlement Commission observed that while "the relationship between a depositor and bank arises only out of contract[,] . . . a contract right is property." Panel Opinion No. 1, (revised), Fourteenth Semiannual Report to the Congress for the Period Ending June 30, 1961, 124, 125 (Foreign Cl. Settlement Comm'n) (footnote omitted). The Commission ruled that the "right to payment of [a] deposit is regarded as property" and provides a basis for an expropriation claim. Here, we have citizens who purchased certificates of deposit. Such contracts are properly understood as investments and are therefore the type of "property" that Hickenlooper sought to protect. *Cf. Kaiser Aetna v. United States*, 444 U.S. 164, 175 (1979) (some of the factors to be considered in determining whether government action effected a "taking" of property are "the economic impact of the regulation, its interference with reasonable investment backed expectations, and the character of the governmental action").

In sum, the rights arising from a certificate of deposit are "rights to property" capable of being expropriated by foreign states under international law within the meaning of Hickenlooper. We reject the construction suggested by the defendants and hold that the "tangibleness" of property is not the dispositive factor.[2] Accordingly, the amendment is applicable and we are free to adjudicate the plaintiffs' claims on the merits.

[The court then ruled that the actions of the Mexican government did not constitute a taking in violation of international law. The court concluded: "The courts of this country should not operate as an international deposit insurance company, hauling foreign sovereigns before us whenever disgruntled investors so desire. West and his fellow plaintiffs chose to purchase both dollar and peso certificates of deposit because of the extraordinary rates of return. The actions of the government of Mexico and the losses they occasioned were within the purview of the risks associated with those potentially extraordinary returns. The judgment of the District Court is affirmed."]

---

[2] We do not intend to suggest by our discussion in the text that every contract claim is encompassed by the protections of Hickenlooper.

FAYSOUND LTD. v. WALTER FULLER AIRCRAFT SALES, INC.
748 F. Supp. 1365 (W.D. Ark. 1990), *appeal dismissed*, 940 F.2d 339 (8th Cir. 1991), *cert. denied*, 502 U.S. 1096 (1992)

[Faysound Limited ("Faysound"), a Hong Kong corporation, purchased a Falcon aircraft from the manufacturer at a cost of over nine million dollars. The plane was then leased to a Philippine corporation, United Coconut Chemicals ("UNICHEM") for a period of five years. Shortly before the lease was to expire, Ferdinand Marcos, the President of the Philippines, was deposed. The new government established the Philippine Commission on Good Government ("PCGG"), with significant powers to recover the "ill-gotten wealth" of the Marcos family and its cronies. The PCGG instituted an action against one Eduardo Cojuango, Jr., a wealthy associate of former President Marcos, who held substantial interests in UNICHEM. The PCGG issued a writ of sequestration against the airplane, but never served or notified Faysound. The sequestration order ultimately expired under Philippine law, and the PCGG sought judicial approval to sell the plane. When it appeared that the Philippine court would not approve the sale, the PCGG withdrew its request for judicial approval and sold the airplane to defendant Walter Fuller Aircraft Sales, Inc., in a transaction considered by both a Philippine court and a U.S. court to be the result of corruption and bribery. The plane was then flown by Fuller to Little Rock, Arkansas, for reconditioning. Faysound then sought to recover the plane from Fuller, who alleged that the act of state doctrine barred recovery.]

Defendant seeks to defend a clear expropriation of plaintiff's property on the ground of the "act of state" doctrine. This doctrine was articulated in *Banco Nacional de Cuba v. Sabbatino,* where the Castro government in Cuba expropriated a shipment of sugar sold under a futures contract while the sugar was being loaded on a ship in Cuba. The Supreme Court held:

> The Judicial Branch will not examine the validity of a taking of property within its own territory by a foreign sovereign government, extant and recognized by this country at the time of suit, in the absence of a treaty or other unambiguous agreement regarding controlling legal principles, even if the complaint alleges that the taking violates customary international law.

This case comes clearly within the exception noted. Both the United States and the Philippines are signatories to the Geneva Convention, which covers property rights in aircraft along with other aviation subjects. While the *Sabbatino* Court was not anxious to enter the conflict of ideologies involved in the Cuba expropriation, it acknowledged that most principles of international law are not so difficult:

> There are, of course, areas of international law in which consensus as to standards is greater and which do not represent a battleground for conflicting ideologies. This decision in no way intimates that the courts of this country are broadly foreclosed from considering questions of international law.

The Geneva Convention represents an area of broad international consensus. The Treaty in Article I provides as follows:

(1) The Contracting States undertake to recognize:

(a) rights of property in aircraft;

(b) rights to acquire aircraft by purchase coupled with possession of the aircraft;

(c) rights to possession of aircraft under leases of six months or more;

(d) mortgages, hypotheques and similar rights in aircraft which are contractually created as security for payment of an indebtedness;

> *Provided* that such rights

(i) have been constituted in accordance with the law of the Contracting State in which the aircraft was registered as to nationality at the time of their constitution, and

(ii) are regularly recorded in a public record of the Contracting State in which the aircraft is registered as to nationality.

(2) Nothing in this Convention shall prevent the recognition of any rights in aircraft under the law of any Contracting State; but Contracting States shall not admit or recognize any right as taking priority over the rights mentioned in paragraph (1) of the Article.

The case at bar is clearly within the exception noted in *Sabbatino*. The expropriation in that case was not proscribed by a treaty couched in clear and unambiguous terms. Congress almost immediately enacted legislation to overrule the decision. The Second Hickenlooper Amendment, was "enacted to make sure that the United States not become a 'thieves market' for the product of foreign expropriation." 110 CONG. REC. 19,557, 88th Cong. 2d Sess. (1964):

> The amendment is designed to discourage uncompensated expropriation of foreign investment by preserving the right of the original owners to attack any taking in violation of international law if the property involved comes before a U.S. court. Because the United States is the largest market for the products of many U.S. owned companies in foreign countries, the knowledge that this market will be denied to stolen property should discourage seizure of that investment.

On remand of the *Sabbatino* case from the Supreme Court of the United States, the District Court and the Court of Appeals for the Second Circuit held that the Hickenlooper Amendment compelled a different result and had in effect vitiated the *Sabbatino* decision. *Banco Nacional de Cuba v. Farr,* 243 F. Supp. 957 and 272 F. Supp. 836 (S.D.N.Y. 1965), *aff'd* 383 F.2d 166 (2d Cir. 1967), *cert. denied*, 390 U.S. 956 (1968). . . .

Fuller argues that the Hickenlooper Amendment applies only if the property of a United States citizen is involved and only when the expropriated property or its proceeds were in the United States when the expropriation occurred. For its claim that the Amendment does not apply to aliens, Fuller Aircraft cites the First Hickenlooper Amendment, rather than the Second Hickenlooper Amendment. Unlike the Second Hickenlooper Amendment, the First

Hickenlooper Amendment by its terms refers only to United States citizens. The Second Hickenlooper Amendment contains no such limitation. Indeed, the Reporters for the Restatement of the Foreign Relations Law of the United States disagree with Fuller Aircraft's contention. "The Amendment, if otherwise applicable, would apparently apply to a claim by an alien as well as by a national of the United States. . . ." RESTATEMENT (THIRD) OF THE FOREIGN RELATIONS LAW OF THE UNITED STATES, § 444, Reporter's Note 6.

Fuller Aircraft is similarly misguided in arguing that the Second Hickenlooper Amendment does not apply because the Falcon was not in the United States when the expropriation occurred. Comment e to § 444 of the RESTATEMENT OF THE FOREIGN RELATIONS LAW OF THE UNITED STATES provides:

> e. Claim to specific property. The exception to the Act of State Doctrine embodied in the Second Hickenlooper Amendment has been held to be limited to actions asserting title to property before the court. Thus, if the plaintiff claims ownership of a vessel that has been taken by a foreign state and the vessel is at a port in the United States, the plaintiff may rely on the Amendment in asserting title before a court in the United States . . . .

> In order for the Hickenlooper Amendment to apply, the plaintiff must allege and prove that the property that is the subject of the claim is in the United States or was there at the time the action was commenced.

As noted above, the *Sabbatino* case makes a clear exception where the expropriation is covered by a treaty. The act of state doctrine "was never intended to apply when an applicable bilateral treaty governs the legal merits of the controversy." *Ramirez de Arellano v. Weinberger*, 745 F.2d 1500, 1540 (D.C. Cir. 1984). The provisions of the Treaty set out are clear and unambiguous. They provide governing legal standards for the Court's determination of the issues:

> Additionally, there is a great national interest to be served in this case, *i.e.*, the recognition and execution of treaties that we enter into with foreign nations. Article VI of the Constitution provides that treaties made under the authority of the United States shall be the supreme law of the land. Accordingly, the Supreme Court has recognized that treaties, in certain circumstances, have the "force and effect of a legislative enactment." See, e.g., *Whitney v. Robertson,* 124 U.S. 190 (1888). The failure of this Court to recognize a properly executed treaty would indeed be an egregious error because of the position that treaties occupy in our body of laws.

Kalamazoo Spice Extraction Co. v. Provisional Military Gov't of Socialist Ethiopia, 729 F.2d 422, 428 (6th Cir. 1984). . . .

Another serious question in this case is whether the acts of the PCGG were true "acts of state." Fuller must prove that PCGG exercised sovereign power in its sequestration and sale of the Falcon. We hold it did not exercise such power. The only evidence offered to show that PCGG had authority to sell the plane in the exercise of Philippine sovereignty is an affidavit from Rosalio DeLeon, a PCGG Commissioner. DeLeon's motives and actions are highly suspect. He is the brother-in-law of Ben Cuevo, one of the Philippine "middle men" appointed as exclusive agent by Fuller.

Plaintiff has submitted the deposition testimony of Art Condes, one of the main players in the attempt to sell the Falcon, that DeLeon was to receive a bribe of $150,000. Plaintiff has also submitted an affidavit from a former Solicitor General and Supreme Court Justice, specifically controverting DeLeon's affidavit with regard to the PCGG's authority under a Writ of Sequestration:

> Assuming, however, that the Falcon aircraft had been validly seques-tered . . . there can be hardly any doubt that the sequestration of the aircraft may be deemed to have been "automatically lifted" as of August 2, 1987. . . . But even if it is assumed that the sequestration of June 19, 1986, on the Falcon aircraft continues to be effective, PCGG had no authority to sell the aircraft. The power to sell property pertains to the owner (Article 428 and 429, Civil Code). And the Supreme Court has ruled that sequestration does not vest in the PCGG the right of ownership.

Assuming that the above conduct raises factual issues that are not appropri-ate for disposition by summary judgment, there are other factors that as a matter of law preclude Fuller reliance on the "act of state" doctrine. To establish that sale of the plane was an act of state, Fuller relies on three executive orders of President Aquino which are summarized as follows. Executive Order No. 1 creates the PCGG for the purpose of recovering all ill-gotten wealth. It charges the PCGG with the task of assisting Aquino in (1) recovering all ill-gotten wealth accumulated by Marcos and his close asso-ciates; (2) investigating cases of graft and corruption assigned to it by the President; (3) sequestering or placing or causing to be placed under its control or possession any building or office wherein any ill-gotten wealth or properties may be found; and (4) provisionally taking over in the public interest or to prevent its disposal or dissipation, business enterprises and properties of Marcos and his close associates.

Executive Order No. 2 addresses the funds, money, assets, and properties illegally acquired or misappropriated by Marcos and his associates. This order (1) authorizes the freezing of all assets and properties in the Philippines in which Marcos or his associates have an interest or participation; (2) prohibits any person from transferring, conveying, or otherwise depleting or concealing such assets; (3) requires all persons in the Philippines holding such assets to make such disclosure; and (4) authorizes the PCGG to request and appeal to foreign governments wherein any such assets or properties may be found to freeze them pending adjudication of ownership in the Philippine Court.

Executive Order No. 14 gives [a special Philippine] Court original jurisdic-tion over cases involving the ill-gotten wealth of Marcos and his associates. No provision of these executive orders authorizes the expropriation and sale of property belonging without question to a Hong Kong national.

The writ of sequestration that PCGG issued against Eduardo Cojuangco, Jr. surely cannot be the "act of state" on which Fuller relies. Cojuangco did not own the plane. A company in which he owned stock leased the plane. The lease had almost expired. The owner of the plane is not a party to the sequestration order. In any event sequestration by the PCGG vests no title in the latter, as the Philippine Supreme Court has aptly pointed out. It is a method of conserving the property pendente lite.

> The act of sequestration, freezing or provisional takeover of property does not import or bring about a divestment of title over said property; does not make the PCGG the owner thereof. In relation to the property sequestered, frozen or provisionally taken over, the PCGG is a conservator, not an owner. Therefore, it cannot perform strict acts of ownership. *Baseco v. PCGG*, 150 S. Ct. Rep. Ann. 81, 236 (Philippine S. Ct. 1987).

As a matter of fact, Fuller in his original brief identified the PCGG as a receiver. A court-supervised trustee does not exercise sovereign power under the "act of state" doctrine. The PCGG as a receiver must act under the authority of a court. By President Aquino's Executive Order No. 14, that court was the [special Philippine] Court. That Court denied PCGG the authority to sell this plane and scathingly denounced its action in regard to the seizure and attempted sale of the plane. The order was never reversed or vacated by the Supreme Court.

To qualify as an act of state, it is necessary to prove that the act "occurred as a result of a considered policy determination by a government to give effect to its political and public interest — matters that would have significant impact on American foreign relations." *Mannington Mills, Inc. v. Congoleum Corp.*, 595 F.2d 1287, 1295 (3rd Cir. 1979). The Court in *Mannington Mills* refused to grant "act of state" status to a foreign sovereign's grant of a patent. Similarly, a foreign judicial judgment in a case involving private litigants does not rise to the status of an act of state. *Timberlane Lumber Co. v. Bank of America*, 549 F.2d 597, 607–08 (9th Cir. 1976). Nor does a party's initiation of foreign judicial proceedings amount to an act of state. *Dominicus Americana Bohio v. Gulf & Western*, 473 F. Supp. 680, 689 (S.D.N.Y. 1979). And as the Supreme Court stressed in *Alfred Dunhill of London, supra,* a foreign naval officer's operation of the foreign sovereign's ship on behalf of the sovereign does not give rise to an act of state. . . .

CONCLUSION

The PCGG expropriated an expensive airplane without any legal basis whatsoever. Although the plane was leased to a company in which an associate of Ferdinand Marcos was a stockholder, the Marcos associate owned no interest whatsoever in the plane, and the lease was near the end of its term. The plane was nevertheless seized and sold in a transaction having the strong odor of corruption. The sale was made in the face of an adverse ruling by the Philippine court having supervision over it — a ruling never reversed by the Philippine Supreme Court. The seizure and sale violated the specific terms of the Treaty known as the Geneva Convention covering property rights in aircraft. It violated principles of international law, the Second Hickenlooper Amendment, as well as principles of Philippine law enunciated by the Philippine court having jurisdiction over this matter.

Notes and Questions on *West* and *Faysound*

1. *Explicit overrides: sufficient but necessary?* The Second Hickenlooper Amendment overrides the act of state doctrine by name: "no court . . . shall decline on the ground of the federal act of state doctrine to make a determination on the merits giving effect to the principles of international law. . . ." Similarly, under paragraph 1 of section 301(a) of the Cuban Liberty and Democratic Solidarity (Libertad) Act of 1996, (the Helms-Burton Act), 22 U.S.C.§ 6082, Congress provided a civil action for trafficking in certain property confiscated by the Cuban Government on or after January 1, 1959, and explicitly overrode the act of state doctrine:

> (6) No court of the United States shall decline, based upon the act of state doctrine, to make a determination on the merits in an action brought under paragraph (1).

See also The Federal Arbitration Act, 9 U.S.C. § 15:

> Enforcement of arbitral agreements, confirmation of arbitral awards, and execution upon judgments based on orders confirming such awards shall not be refused on the basis of the Act of State doctrine.

Must a statute be this explicit before it will be held to override the act of state doctrine? Consider *Daliberti v. Republic of Iraq*, 97 F. Supp. 2d 38, 55 (D.D.C. 2000), in which the court based subject matter jurisdiction on the terrorist exception to foreign sovereign immunity, 28 U.S.C. 1605(a)(7), and rejected the state defendant's act of state claim on the following grounds:

> While the act of state doctrine seeks to prevent courts from interfering in the foreign affairs powers of the President and the Congress, it does not prohibit Congress and the Executive from using the threat of legal action in the courts as an instrument of foreign policy. The designation of Iraq as a terrorist state was made by the Secretary of State on behalf of the Executive Branch under an express grant of authority by Congress. For this Court to grant defendant's motion to dismiss on act of state grounds would constitute more of a judicial interference in the announced foreign policy of the political branches of government than to allow the suit to proceed under the explicit authorization of Congress.

Are you persuaded that a statutory grant of jurisdiction or a statutory right of action implicitly overrides the act of state doctrine? Should claims under every broadly-worded federal statute (e.g. antitrust, securities regulation, RICO) be exempt from the act of state doctrine?

2. *Effect of the statute.* Does the Hickenlooper Amendment promote international law or its opposite?

3. *Interpreting the Second Hickenlooper Amendment.* In *Hunt v. Coastal States Gas Producing Co.*, 583 S.W.2d 322 (Tex. 1979), the Supreme Court of Texas identified three elements to a claim under the Second Hickenlooper Amendment:

> 1. Expropriated property must come within the territorial jurisdiction of the United States.

2. The act of the expropriating nation must be in violation of international law.

3. The asserted claim must be a claim of title or other right to property.

What large classes of claims would these restrictions effectively keep out of U.S. courts? Consider the following observations about the Second Hickenlooper Amendment from the Court of Appeals for the District of Columbia Circuit:

> We reject the . . . suggestion that the word "property" in the statute must invariably be limited to expropriated personal property located in the United States. . . . It may be that a primary purpose of the statute was to prevent invocation of the act of state doctrine when property expropriated in a foreign country subsequently makes its way into the United States, but this was not the sole situation in which the amendment was to be activated. . . . [T]he broad, unqualified language of the carefully drafted amendment belies the narrow reading . . . . The sponsors of the amendment referred to it as the "Rule of Law" amendment; they viewed it as authorizing courts to apply established law [in] suits challenging expropriations. Congressional intent to overturn *Sabbatino* was never limited to a single narrow class of cases. The purposes of the amendment include the promotion and protection of United States investment in foreign countries (which characteristically has always principally been land, minerals, and large fixed immovables), and securing the right of a property holder to a court hearing on the merits. . . . Gutting the amendment by the addition of external language . . . would be inconsistent with these purposes and we decline to adopt it.

Ramirez de Arellano v. Weinberger, 745 F.2d 1500, 1541 n.180 (D.C.Cir. 1984), *vacated on other grounds*, 471 U.S. 1113 (1985). Which of these two approaches seems more persuasive?

4. *Problem.* The analysis in *Faysound* is partly driven by the existence of a treaty and so might be considered another example of the *Sabbatino* court's willingness to subordinate the act of state doctrine to "a treaty or other otherwise unambiguous agreement regarding controlling legal principles." *See Kalamazoo Spice Extraction Co., supra.* But *Faysound* is also clearly an example of the courts' interpretation of the Hickenlooper Amendment. Suppose the plane had been sold and the proceeds came into the United States instead of the plane itself? Same result?

5. *Incorporating international law standards into statutes.* Should every Congressional directive to apply international law be interpreted as an implicit override of the act of state doctrine? Consider for example the federal law governing the conservation of marine sanctuaries, 16 U.S.C. § 1435:

> This chapter and the regulations issued under . . . this title shall be applied in accordance with generally recognized principles of international law, and in accordance with treaties, conventions, and other agreements to which the United States is a party.

Are such provisions superfluous in light of the principle that statutes "ought never to be construed to violate the law of nations if any other possible construction remains," *Murray v. The Schooner Charming Betsy*, 6 U.S. (2 Cranch) 64, 118 (1804) or do such explicit directives assist a court with an act-of-state issue before it?

---

[e] The Power of Executive Suggestion: The *"Bernstein Exception"*

In 1937, a German Jew named Arnold Bernstein was forced by the Nazis to surrender the ownership of his shipping company to a Nazi agent, who subsequently transferred some of the company's vessels to Belgian and Dutch companies. After the war, Bernstein sued the Belgian company to recover damages for the forced transfer of the ship and other assets. The company invoked the act of state doctrine, claiming that its title was valid under the laws of Germany at the time and that the courts of the United States should not judge its validity. Despite Bernstein's claim that the Nazi government was no longer in existence, the Second Circuit Court of Appeals applied the act of state doctrine, declaring that the executive branch had shown no "positive intent" to override the doctrine. *Bernstein v. van Heyghen Frères Société Anonyme*, 163 F.2d 246 (2d Cir. 1947), *cert. denied*, 322 U.S. 772 (1947); *Bernstein v. N.Y. Nederlandsche-Amerikaansche Stoomvaart-Maatschaapij*, 173 F.2d 72 (2d Cir. 1949).

Bernstein then requested the Department of State to respond to the Second Circuit's decision, which it did in no uncertain terms:

> This Government has consistently opposed the forcible acts of dispossession of a discriminatory and confiscatory nature practices by the Germans on the countries or peoples subject to their controls. . . . The Policy of the Executive, with respect to claims asserted in the United States for the restitution of identifiable property (or compensation in lieu thereof) lost through force, coercion, or duress as a result of Nazi persecution in Germany, is to relieve American courts from any restraint upon the exercise of their jurisdiction to pass upon the acts of Nazi officials.

The Second Circuit then modified its earlier decision, removed the act-of-state barrier, and the defendants settled. *Bernstein v. N.Y. Nederlandsche-Amerikaansche Stoomvaart-Maatschaapij*, 210 F.2d 375 (2d Cir. 1954) (*per curiam*). For the last half-century, the executive branch's authority to override the act-of-state doctrine has been known as the "*Bernstein* exception," but its status as law remains controverted, and the *Sabbatino* decision explicitly avoided the issue. 376 U.S., at 420 ("This Court has never had occasion to pass upon the so-called *Bernstein* exception, nor need it do so now.")

The cause of the continuing controversy isn't obscure. On one hand, there is the "one-voice orthodoxy" under which the executive enjoys far-ranging power in foreign affairs, assertedly unconstrained by the structural limitations at work in domestic matters. The orthodoxy is captured in the famous observation of John Marshall as a member of the House of Representatives that "The President is the sole organ of the nation in its external relations, and its sole representative with foreign nations." And there is precedent for exclusive executive dominance in such matters, especially in the area of war powers. *See, e.g., United States v. Curtiss-Wright Corp.*, 299 U.S. 304 (1936). On the other hand, the courts have never embraced the full implications of executive supremacy where their own prerogatives and jurisdiction are involved. To the contrary, our "cultural commitment to judicial oversight"[1] places a heavy burden of justification on those who would carve out any *per se* category of judicial incompetence. Against this backdrop, the act of state doctrine — and particularly the validity of the *Bernstein* exception — should be seen as a clinic in the continuing political and legal debate about the powers of the presidency.

The tension is illustrated by the Supreme Court's disjointed holding in *First National City Bank ("FNCB") v. Banco Nacional de Cuba*, 406 U.S. 759 (1972). In *FNCB*, the State Department had submitted a letter to the court suggesting that the act of state doctrine need not apply to the specific issue in the case:

> The Department of State believes that the act of state doctrine should not be applied to bar consideration of a defendant's counterclaim or set-off against the Government of Cuba in this or like cases.

Justice Rehnquist, joined by Chief Justice Burger and Justice White, ruled that the *Bernstein* exception applied and was dispositive:

> where the Executive Branch, charged as it is with primary responsibility for the conduct of foreign affairs, expressly represents to the Court that application of the act of state doctrine would not advance the interests of American foreign policy, that doctrine should not be applied by the courts.

Justices Douglas concurred in the result but disagreed with the analysis, declaring among other things that the plurality's reasoning converted the court into "a mere errand boy for the Executive which may choose to pick some people's chestnuts out of the fire but not others." Justice Powell also concurred in the result, holding the case justiciable, but offered yet another rationale for the result. He was not prepared to give the executive branch dispositive power over the courts' exercise of jurisdiction, but he thought *Sabbatino* should be narrowed so as not to cover FNCB's counterclaims, concluding that the courts should adjudicate foreign expropriations "[u]nless it appears that an exercise of jurisdiction would interfere with delicate foreign relations conducted by the political branches." In his view, no such conflict had been shown.

The four dissenting justices rejected all three of the rationales advanced by the fractured majority and concluded that *Sabbatino* compelled the application of the act of state doctrine. With respect to the *Bernstein* exception itself, the dissenters explained that the "Executive Branch, however extensive its powers in the area of foreign affairs, cannot by simple stipulation change a political question into a cognizable claim."

---

[1] Abram Chayes, *The Role of the Judge in Public Law Litigation*, 89 HARV. L. REV. 1281, 1307 (1976).

When the smoke cleared, the *Bernstein* exception had been adopted by three justices but explicitly rejected by six. Since *FNCB*, the lower courts have viewed executive suggestions as one relevant factor in the application or rejection of the act of state doctrine, but not a dispositive one.

In the human rights litigation against the deposed president of the Philippines, Ferdinand Marcos, for example, the U.S. government appeared *amicus curiae* and declined the court's invitation to address the act of state issue definitively, preferring to base its argument on a narrow interpretation of the Alien Tort Claims Act. But the government also assured the court that

> the entertainment of these suits would not embarrass the relations between the United States and the Government of the Philippines. Indeed, the Government of the Philippines has filed a brief *amicus curiae* arguing that these suits should be permitted to proceed in the district courts.

The government disavowed the usual inference from this information, opting not to offer decisive guidance on the applicability of the act of state doctrine. But the government's assurance was consistent with its previously-expressed views about the general propriety of litigating international human rights claims in domestic courts. In its submissions in the *Filártiga* litigation, for example, the United States declared that, when an individual has suffered a denial of his right to be free from torture,

> there is little danger that judicial enforcement will impair our foreign policy efforts. To the contrary, a refusal to recognize a private cause of action in these circumstances might seriously damage the credibility of our nation's commitment to the protection of human rights.

The government has filed similar submissions in other human rights cases, *see, e.g., Kadic v. Karadzic*, 70 F.3d 232, 239–40 (2d Cir. 1995), *cert denied*, 518 U.S. 1005 (1996) ("The Executive Branch has emphatically restated in this litigation its position that private persons may be found liable under the Alien Tort Act for acts of genocide, war crimes, and other violations of international humanitarian law.") This approach seems entirely consistent with a prior administration's views outside the context of human rights litigation:

> In general, [the State] Department's experience provides little support for a presumption that adjudication of acts of foreign states in accordance with relevant principles of international law would embarrass the conduct of foreign policy.

Letter of Monroe Leigh, Legal Advisor to the Department of State, attached as Appendix I to the opinion of the Court in *Alfred Dunhill of London, Inc. v. Republic of Cuba*, 425 U.S. 682, 706 (1976), at 710. Evidently, there are times when abstention is more embarrassing than adjudication.

Acknowledging that the courts will give respectful consideration to executive submissions without making them dispositive, should courts distinguish between types of executive suggestion, giving more (or less) weight to "green-light" assurances that a case can go forward than to "red light" efforts to derail a case? And suppose the executive branch remains pointedly silent in a case. How should its silence be interpreted?

C. THE POLITICAL QUESTION DOCTRINE

The act of state doctrine is sometimes described as the foreign affairs equivalent of the political question doctrine. Both are prudential doctrines under which a court will decline to exercise jurisdiction it admittedly has, because the issues presented are non-justiciable, and both explicitly reflect the constitutional separation of powers. But it is a mistake to assume on the basis of these similarities that the political question doctrine has no independent role to play in international civil cases. To the contrary, there may be cases in which the act of state doctrine cannot apply, because the legitimacy of no foreign government's act is challenged, and yet the political question doctrine may nonetheless preclude the court from adjudicating the case. *See, e.g., Made in the USA Foundation v. United States*, 242 F.3d 1306 (11th Cir. 2001) (the issue of whether NAFTA was a "treaty" requiring Senate ratification pursuant to the Treaty Clause held to be a nonjusticiable political question.)

The political question doctrine — when it is deployed in international cases — generally rests on the suspicion that international law qualifies as a branch of "politics" and not "law." In essence, the political question doctrine limits the exercise of federal jurisdiction and forecloses judicial inquiry into the propriety (or wisdom) of political decisions based on executive discretion. *Iwanowa v. Ford Motor Co.*, 67 F. Supp.2d 424, 483–84 (D.N.J. 1999). The Supreme Court has warned the lower courts not to intrude in such matters, reasoning that:

> [t]he very nature of executive decisions as to foreign policy is political, not judicial. Such decisions are wholly confided by our Constitution to the political departments of the government, Executive and Legislative. They are delicate, complex, and involve large elements of prophecy. They are and should be undertaken only by those directly responsible to the people whose welfare they advance or imperil. They are decisions of a kind for which the Judiciary has neither aptitude, facilities nor responsibility and which has long been held to belong in the domain of the political power not subject to judicial intrusion or inquiry.

Chicago & Southern Air Lines v. Waterman S.S. Corp., 333 U.S. 103, 111 (1948).

The fountainhead of the political question doctrine is *Baker v. Carr*, 369 U.S. 186, 217 (1962), in which the Court offered some guidance for the identification of non-justiciable issues:

> Prominent on the surface of any case held to involve a political question is found [1] a textually demonstrable constitutional commitment of the issue to a coordinate political department; or [2] a lack of judicially discoverable and manageable standards for resolving it; or [3] the impossibility of deciding without an initial policy determination of a kind clearly for nonjudicial discretion; or [4] the impossibility of a court's undertaking independent resolution without expressing lack of the respect due coordinate branches of government; or [5] an

unusual need for unquestioning adherence to a political decision already made; or [6] the potentiality of embarrassment from multifarious pronouncements by various departments on one question.

As shown in *767 Third Avenue Associates*, *infra*, these standards are likely to apply when a case implicates the explicit and exclusive constitutional powers of the executive branch, especially the recognition of foreign governments. But, as the *Baker* court itself recognized, "it is error to suppose that every case or controversy which touches foreign relations lies beyond judicial cognizance." 369 U.S. at 211. Indeed, most of the decisions in this book would have been unresolvable if diplomatic or political repercussions were enough to derail them under the political question doctrine.

Perhaps because the political question doctrine cannot be given its fullest literal scope — at least not without damaging the independence of the judiciary or ignoring its obligation to resolve disputes that come before it — the courts have shown a certain reluctance to invoke it. In *Committee of United States Citizens Living in Nicaragua v. Reagan*, 859 F.2d 929 (D.C. Cir. 1989), for example, plaintiffs challenged the U.S. government's funding of the *contras* in Nicaragua in violation of the decision by the International Court of Justice declaring such action to be in breach of international law. The lower court dismissed the case, declaring it non-justiciable and invoking the political question doctrine. But the court of appeals rejected that conclusion "particularly to the extent that appellants seek to vindicate personal rights rather than to conform America's foreign policy to international norms." *Id.* at 932. The political question doctrine, with its "shifting contours and uncertain underpinnings" and its "susceptibility to indiscriminate and overbroad application," could not displace whatever legal standards applied:

> Such basic norms of international law as the proscription against murder and slavery may well . . . restrain our government in the same way that the Constitution restrains it. If Congress adopted a foreign policy that resulted in the enslavement of our citizens or other individuals, that policy might well be subject to challenge in domestic courts under international law. . . .

Id. at 941. As a consequence, advocates can avoid the political question doctrine if they can prove that there is law for the court to apply or — in the words of *Baker v. Carr* — that there are "judicially manageable standards" and no textual commitment of the issue "to a coordinate branch of government." Which of these tests did the following case flunk?

———

767 THIRD AVENUE ASSOCIATES v. CONSULATE GENERAL OF SOCIALIST FEDERAL REPUBLIC OF YUGOSLAVIA
218 F.3d 152 (2d Cir. 2000)

On its face, this case concerns nothing more than a garden-variety landlord-tenant dispute. Plaintiffs (the landlords) are seeking to recover unpaid rent for offices leased to the former Socialist Federal Republic of Yugoslavia (SFRY) for use as consular offices in New York. Unfortunately for the landlords, the SFRY has ceased to exist. Beginning in 1991, the SFRY faced political upheaval and military conflict that eventually led to its disintegration. As a result, the SFRY has been replaced by five successor states: Slovenia, Croatia, Bosnia-Herzegovina, Macedonia, and the Federal Republic of Yugoslavia which is composed of Serbia and Montenegro (FRY) (successors or successor states). A by-product of this conflict has been a number of civil suits in this country involving the SFRY, its agencies and state-owned companies, and the successor states, regarding their assets and liabilities in the United States.

The landlords are suing the former SFRY and the five successor states. The landlords appeal from a judgment of the United States District Court for the Southern District of New York, Constance B. Motley, J., holding that the issues of whether any or all of defendant states succeed to the liabilities of the SFRY, and, if so, in what proportion, raise political questions that a federal court is not competent to decide. Instead of simply dismissing, however, the court issued an indefinite stay of the action. For the reasons set forth below, we affirm the district court's decision as to justiciability, vacate the stay order, and remand to the district court with instructions to enter a judgment for defendants and dismiss the complaint.

I. Background

. . . Much has been written about the sad events in the Balkans in the last decade leading to the breakup of the former SFRY and the emergence of the successor states. For the purposes of this appeal, we see no need to add to the volumes of print on the subject except to cite those facts pertinent to the appeal. Slovenia and Croatia formally declared independence in June 1991. Macedonia issued a declaration of independence in September 1991 and adopted a constitution in November 1991. Bosnia-Herzegovina declared its independence in March 1992. The United States recognized Slovenia, Croatia, and Bosnia-Herzegovina in April 1992. In the following month, the three republics were admitted to the United Nations.[1] On April 27, 1992, the republics of Serbia and Montenegro declared themselves, under the name of FRY, the continuation and sole successors of the former SFRY. Neither the United States nor the European Community recognized the FRY.[2] The Arbitration Commission, an arm of the International Conference on Former Yugoslavia which coordinated peacemaking efforts during the conflict, issued a number of opinions relevant to the succession of the successor states from the SFRY. Among its recommendations, the Commission noted that aspects of succession involving "state property, archives and debts" are issues that must be resolved "by negotiation and agreement" among the successor states.

On May 24, 1992, the United States formally acknowledged that the SFRY had ceased to exist. In addition, SFRY's assets in this country have been

[1] Macedonia was not admitted to the United Nations until April 1993. Recognition of Macedonia by most EU states did not come until December 1993, and the United States recognized Macedonia in February 1994.

[2] *See also* Security Council Resolution 777, September 19, 1992, recommending that the FRY cannot automatically continue the membership of the former SFRY and must apply for membership.

blocked by executive orders. . . . The wars between the FRY and the other successor states, most notably Bosnia-Herzegovina, raged from the end of 1991 until 1995. In late 1995, following intense negotiations mediated primarily by the United States, the FRY and the successor states signed the Dayton Accords marking the end of the armed conflict in Bosnia. Simultaneously, a Peace Implementation Council was established in order to arrive at a comprehensive resolution of succession issues among the successor states. The United States and the successors claim that negotiations on these subjects have been sporadic but are still continuing. . . .

As a result of the disintegration of the SFRY in 1991 and in opposition to Serbia's conduct, the United States Department of Treasury ordered the SFRY to close its consular offices and terminate all operations by May 31, 1992. The State Department also ordered all SFRY personnel to leave the United States by June 7, 1992. The landlords now allege that the SFRY breached the lease [and its] extensions by failing to pay the rent owed under the leases. The landlords claim that the total rent owed is $2,262,224 plus interest. . . .

[In a separate proceeding, the landlords alleged that the United States' forced closure of SFRY's consular offices "constituted a regulatory taking of its property, consisting of the benefits of its leases, for which it was entitled to just compensation under the Fifth Amendment." The trial court granted the United States' motion for summary judgment, holding that the plaintiffs "had no compensable investment-backed expectation 'to be free from government interference with [their] contract rights.'" The Court of Appeals for the Federal Circuit affirmed.]

In February 1996, the landlords filed the present action for the entire amount of rent owed under the 1991 lease extensions, naming as defendants the SFRY and the five successor states (FRY, Slovenia, Croatia, Macedonia, and Bosnia-Herzegovina). . . . As the district court noted, the five successor states all filed "essentially similar, but somewhat divergent, dispositive motions." The common thread in all of the motions was the argument that their liability could not be determined without first answering nonjusticiable political questions.

In addition, the United States submitted a statement of interest on behalf of the State Department asserting that

> [i]t is the fundamental position of the United States . . . that the . . . SFRY, has ceased to exist and that no state represents its continuation. . . . [E]ach of the states that is before your Honor today that has emerged on its territory . . . is a successor. Each has interests in the assets and liabilities of the former SFRY, but those interests have not yet been determined by the executive.

The United States explained that the policy of the executive branch has been that allocation of these interests should be determined through international negotiations. . . .

In an extensive and thorough opinion, the district court concluded that this case posed a question that is "'beyond the competence and proper institutional role of the federal courts.'" . . . The district court's decision that this case is nonjusticiable rested primarily on the lack of judicially recognizable standards. However, the court also relied on other prongs of the political question doctrine. The judge stated that allocating liability among the successor states could trespass on the executive branch's authority in foreign policy, and thereby raise separation of powers concerns. Additionally, the judge recognized the need for uniform judicial pronouncements on this subject. Mindful that other district courts in this circuit have concluded that this type of case presents nonjusticiable political questions, a contrary finding could create the " 'potentiality of embarrassment from multifarious pronouncements by various departments on one question.' "

The court then considered the landlords' two proposed methods of allocating the alleged SFRY liabilities among the various defendants: (1) impose the same allocation of SFRY assets and liabilities used by the International Monetary Fund (IMF); or (2) apply a rule of joint and several liability. The district court rejected both suggestions. First, the judge noted that IMF allocation was inappropriate as it related only to state debt to the IMF, and the United States has "expressly reject[ed] use of the IMF percentages outside the IMF context." Next, the court rejected joint and several liability on the ground that "it would not avoid any political questions, but simply would decide them implicitly and in a chaotic fashion." The court pointed out that imposing joint and several liability would not only potentially lead to inequitable distribution of the debt, but would likely conflict with future political settlement of the debt allocation. . . . This appeal followed.

II. Discussion

. . . [T]he primary question raised by this appeal [is] whether the landlords' claims and the relief they seek "are of the type which admit of judicial resolution." *Powell v. McCormack*, 395 U.S. 486, 517 (1969). The landlords ask this court to determine (1) that the successors are liable for debt incurred by the SFRY; and (2) the proper allocation of that debt among the successors. The landlords argue that this determination does not require the resolution of political questions because there is no textual commitment of these issues to other branches of the government, the Executive has recognized the successors, application of New York State principles of joint-and-several liability provide a judicially manageable standard for fashioning relief, and "even applying international law" leads "automatically" to the same result.

We agree with the district court that virtually all of the *Baker v. Carr* factors, apply to this case. In *Baker*, the Court specifically addressed application of the political question doctrine to questions involving foreign relations. The Court noted that "[n]ot only does resolution of such issues frequently turn on standards that defy judicial application, or involve the exercise of a discretion demonstrably committed to the executive or legislature; but many such questions uniquely demand single-voiced statement of the Government's views."

Because the "nonjusticiability of political questions is primarily a function of the constitutional separation of powers . . . the dominant consideration in any political question inquiry is whether there is a textually demonstrable constitutional commitment of the issue to a coordinate political department."

Lamont v. Woods, 948 F.2d 825, 831 (2d Cir. 1991). In *Oetjen v. Central Leather Co.*, 246 U.S. 297, 302 (1918), the Supreme Court held that "[t]he conduct of the foreign relations of our Government is committed by the Constitution to the Executive and Legislative — 'the political' — Departments of the Government, and the propriety of what may be done in the exercise of this political power is not subject to judicial inquiry or decision."

In *Can v. United States,* 14 F.3d 160 (2d Cir. 1994), this court considered a claim by a group of citizens of the Republic of South Vietnam who sought to obtain title to assets of the former Republic of South Vietnam in the United States. We held that "[t]he recognition of any rights of succession to a foreign sovereign's power or property is in the first instance constitutionally committed to the executive branch. . . ." We conclude that these precedents squarely apply here.

In its *amicus* brief to us, the government argues that "liability, if any exists, cannot attach to the Successor Defendants in the absence of a political determination, which has not yet been made. . . ." It further represents to us that "[t]he policy of the United States has been to encourage successors to agree among themselves regarding [debt] allocation," and that "the United States continues to support the international process as the means to pursue resolution." Thus, the executive branch has apparently made the initial policy determination that resolution of issues such as debt allocation among the successors to the SFRY must be resolved in an international forum. This position is understandable in light of the still volatile atmosphere in the Balkans. A determination by this court of the allocation of debt among the successors might hinder or prejudice the future resolution of this issue through negotiations or another determination by the Executive. Such an outcome would directly "interfere with executive foreign policy prerogatives," *Can*, 14 F.3d at 163.

The landlords argue that *Can* is distinguishable. They point out that in *Can* the United States had not recognized any government as the legitimate representative of the Republic of Vietnam, the state there involved, but in this case the President has actually recognized Slovenia, Macedonia, Bosnia, and Croatia as successors to the SFRY. The distinction is not dispositive. The plaintiffs in *Can* did not ask the court to recognize their sovereignty; they simply asked for recognition of their rights in certain property of the Republic of Vietnam. We stressed in *Can* that such a determination might "prejudice other claimants" and could conflict with a future determination by the President. The same concerns arise here where the landlords ask us to find that at least some of the successors have rights and obligations with respect to SFRY's property and the extent of those rights and obligations. This is precisely the type of determination that is reserved to the Executive in the first instance, and which has yet to be made.

The district court relied primarily on the second *Baker* factor ("a lack of judicially discoverable and manageable standards for resolving [the question]") in support of its conclusion that this case does not lend itself to judicial resolution. As the Supreme Court noted in *Nixon v. United States*, 506 U.S. 224, 228–29 (1993):

the concept of a textual commitment to a coordinate political department is not completely separate from the concept of a lack of judicially discoverable and manageable standards for resolving it; the lack of judicially manageable standards may strengthen the conclusion that there is a textually demonstrable commitment to a coordinate branch.

Applying this thinking to state succession, we concluded in *Can* that we "have no standards for judging a claim of succession to a former sovereign, even where that succession is only to property rather than to government power." We reasoned that questions of title were "inextricably intertwined with the question of state succession and sovereignty," which are reserved to determination by the executive branch. Moreover, with respect to the landlords' claim that joint and several liability principles provide a judicially manageable standard for fashioning relief, the district court rejected that view and we agree. Such state law principles have no basis in international law, which is the body of law we must turn to in this case. *See First Nat'l City Bank v. Banco Para El Comercio Exterior de Cuba*, 462 U.S. 611, 622 n. 11 (1983) (international, not state, law governs the allocation of liabilities among foreign states). Indeed, the landlords do not point to any case where a court applied such a rule to determine the liabilities of successor states based on the liabilities of a defunct predecessor state.

Finally, international law does not support the landlords' claim that the successor states are automatically liable to the landlords. The RESTATEMENT (THIRD) OF FOREIGN RELATIONS LAW § 209(2) provides that: "Subject to agreement between predecessor and successor states, responsibility for the public debt[3] of the predecessor, and rights and obligations under its contracts, remain with the predecessor state. . . ." Clearly, no agreement between the SFRY and the successors regarding assumption of SFRY's liabilities has been formulated yet. None of the exceptions listed in the Restatement to this general rule applies. Accordingly, there is no rule of law that automatically subrogates successor states to their predecessor's debt. . . . It may be, as the landlords claim, that principles of equity and international comity suggest some equitable assumption of a predecessor state debt. However, the federal courts do not have the authority or the means to determine the equitable distribution of the public debt of a foreign state among several successor states. . . .

We have considered all of the landlords' arguments properly before us and none justifies a reversal on the issue of justiciability. . . . [The court then ruled that nothing in the Foreign Sovereign Immunities Act superceded the political question doctrine and required the court to resolve an issue that the court considered non-justiciable.]

We affirm the district court's decision as to justiciability. . . .

---

[3] Public debt is defined as debt owed by "one state to another or to an international organization, as well as to . . . private foreign individuals or corporations. . . ." RESTATEMENT (THIRD) OF FOREIGN RELATIONS LAW § 209, cmt. b.

Notes and Questions on the Political Question Doctrine

1. *Treaty interpretation as a political question.* Suppose that the successor governments in *767 Third Avenue Associates* resolved the debt and asset allocation issues by treaty or another type of agreement. Would the interpretation of that treaty also be considered a political question? *See* RESTATEMENT (THIRD) OF FOREIGN RELATIONS LAW § 209, note 6 ("apportionment [of successor liability] is sometimes so complex and controversial as to defy judicial creativity, but in several instances international agreements made such apportionments and courts have interpreted and enforced them"). Although the executive branch clearly has a profound role to play in the interpretation of international treaties, *Sumitomo Shoji America, Inc. v. Avagliano*, 457 U.S. 176 (1982), the courts have never ruled that the interpretation of treaties — which the Supremacy Clause of the Constitution declares to be "the Supreme *Law* of the Land" along with federal statutes — is a political question.

2. *Distinguishing the political question doctrine from the act of state doctrine.* In a domestic court, what kind of international issues — other than those arising out of recognition and succession disputes — are likely to be considered non-justiciable under *Baker v. Carr*, and yet *not* trigger the act of state doctrine? Consider for example *Kwan v. United States,* 84 F. Supp 2d 613 (E.D. Pa. 2000) ("it is well established that the judiciary cannot order the government of the United States to comply with the terms of an agreement with another sovereign"); *Iwanowa v. Ford Motor Co.,* 67 F. Supp. 2d 424 (D.N.J. 1999) (issue of war reparations affects relations with international community and is therefore a political question); *Goldwater v. Carter*, 444 U.S. 996 (1979) (authority of the President to abrogate a treaty presents a nonjusticiable political question).

D. DIPLOMATIC AND CONSULAR IMMUNITY

As a matter of international and domestic law, a foreign state's diplomatic agents, once accredited and accepted, are immune from "arrest, detention, criminal process, and, in general, civil process in the receiving state." RESTATEMENT (THIRD) OF THE FOREIGN RELATIONS LAW OF THE UNITED STATES, § 464. But considerable confusion can rest inside the phrase "in general." Unlike criminal proceedings, as to which a diplomatic agent's immunity is absolute unless waived by the sending state, civil proceedings are subject to a somewhat qualified regime. The agent does not enjoy immunity for example from civil actions that arise out of professional or commercial activity that is outside her official functions, which means in turn that the courts are obliged to determine what the scope of those functions is. Is a diplomat immune from civil proceedings for abusing a domestic employee in his official residence? If a consul signs a lease for the consulate and then breaches it, will she be liable for damages? If a diplomat assaults a protester at the embassy gates, will he be immune from civil process? What if a consular official issues a visa to enable one parent to violate a local custody order —

will that fall within an official function? Courts that confront these issues operate within a regime of domestic statutes, treaties, and an ancient custom, shaped by every nation's need for diplomatic communications (and the desire to assure reciprocal treatment for their own diplomats abroad).

To understand how the domestic courts approach these issues, first read through the Diplomatic Relations Act (excerpted below, with a complete version of the act in the Documents Supplement). Then consider the two dominant treaties in the field — the Vienna Convention on Diplomatic Relations and the Vienna Convention on Consular Relations (also excerpted below, with complete versions in the Documents Supplement). Finally, as you consider the two district court cases interpreting this body of law, *Berdakin* and *Mukaddam*, imagine how you might frame the arguments on appeal.

28 U.S.C. § 1351. Consuls, vice consuls, and members of a diplomatic mission as defendant

The district courts shall have original jurisdiction, exclusive of the courts of the States, of all civil actions and proceedings against —

(1) consuls or vice consuls of foreign states; or

(2) members of a mission or members of their families (as such terms are defined in section 2 of the Diplomatic Relations Act).

UNITED STATES DIPLOMATIC RELATIONS ACT
22 U.S.C. 254

§ 254a. Definitions

As used in this Act —

(1) the term "members of a mission" means—

(A) the head of a mission and those members of a mission who are members of the diplomatic staff or who, pursuant to law, are granted equivalent privileges and immunities,

(B) members of the administrative and technical staff of a mission, and

(c) members of the service staff of a mission,

as such terms are defined in Article 1 of the Vienna Convention;

(2) the term "family" means—

(A) the members of the family of a member of a mission described in paragraph (1)(A) who form part of his or her household if they are not nationals of the United States, and

(B) the members of the family of a member of a mission described in paragraph (1)(B) who form part of his or her household if they are not nationals or permanent residents of the United States, within the meaning of Article 37 of the Vienna Convention;

(3) the term "mission" includes missions within the meaning of the Vienna Convention and any missions representing foreign governments, individually or collectively, which are extended the same privileges and immunities, pursuant to law, as are enjoyed by missions under the Vienna Convention; and

(4) the term "Vienna Convention" means the Vienna Convention on Diplomatic Relations of April 18, 1961 (T.I.A.S. numbered 7502; 23 U.S.T. 3227), entered into force with respect to the United States on December 13, 1972.

§ 254b. Privileges and immunities of mission of nonparty to Vienna Convention

With respect to a nonparty to the Vienna Convention, the mission, the members of the mission, their families, and diplomatic couriers shall enjoy the privileges and immunities specified in the Vienna Convention.

§ 254c. Extension of more favorable or less favorable treatment than provided under Vienna Convention; authority of President

The President may, on the basis of reciprocity and under such terms and conditions as he may determine, specify privileges and immunities for the mission, the members of the mission, their families, and the diplomatic couriers which result in more favorable treatment or less favorable treatment than is provided under the Vienna Convention.

§ 254d. Dismissal on motion of action against individual entitled to immunity

Any action or proceeding brought against an individual who is entitled to immunity with respect to such action or proceeding under the Vienna Convention on Diplomatic Relations, under section 254b or 254c of this title, or under any other laws extending diplomatic privileges and immunities, shall be dismissed. Such immunity may be established upon motion or suggestion by or on behalf of the individual, or as otherwise permitted by law or applicable rules of procedure.

VIENNA CONVENTION ON DIPLOMATIC RELATIONS
DONE AT VIENNA, ON 18 APRIL 1961
500 U.N.T.S. 95, 23 U.S.T. 3227

The States Parties to the present Convention, . . . [b]elieving that an international convention on diplomatic intercourse, privileges and immunities would contribute to the development of friendly relations among nations, irrespective of their differing constitutional and social systems, . . . [h]ave agreed as follows:

ARTICLE 3

1. The functions of a diplomatic mission consist *inter alia* in:

(a) representing the sending State in the receiving State;

(b) protecting in the receiving State the interests of the sending State and of its nationals, within the limits permitted by international law;

(c) negotiating with the Government of the receiving State;

(d) ascertaining by all lawful means conditions and developments in the receiving State, and reporting thereon to the Government of the sending State;

(e) promoting friendly relations between the sending State and the receiving State, and developing their economic, cultural and scientific relations. . . .

ARTICLE 4

1. The sending State must make certain that the *agrément* of the receiving State has been given for the person it proposes to accredit as head of the mission to that State.

2. The receiving State is not obliged to give reasons to the sending State for a refusal of *agrément*.

ARTICLE 9

1. The receiving State may at any time and without having to explain its decision, notify the sending State that the head of the mission or any member of the diplomatic staff of the mission is *persona non grata* or that any other member of the staff of the mission is not acceptable. In any such case, the sending State shall, as appropriate, either recall the person concerned or terminate his functions with the mission. A person may be declared *non grata* or not acceptable before arriving in the territory of the receiving State. . . .

ARTICLE 22

1. The premises of the mission shall be inviolable. The agents of the receiving State may not enter them, except with the consent of the head of the mission.

2. The receiving State is under a special duty to take all appropriate steps to protect the premises of the mission against any intrusion or damage and to prevent any disturbance of the peace of the mission or impairment of its dignity.

3. The premises of the mission, their furnishings and other property thereon and the means of transport of the mission shall be immune from search, requisition, attachment or execution.

ARTICLE 24

The archives and documents of the mission shall be inviolable at any time and wherever they may be.

ARTICLE 29

The person of a diplomatic agent shall be inviolable. He shall not be liable to any form of arrest or detention. The receiving State shall treat him with due respect and shall take all appropriate steps to prevent any attack on his person, freedom or dignity.

ARTICLE 30

1. The private residence of a diplomatic agent shall enjoy the same inviolability and protection as the premises of the mission.

2. His papers, correspondence and, except as provided in paragraph 3 of Article 31, his property, shall likewise enjoy inviolability.

ARTICLE 31

1. A diplomatic agent shall enjoy immunity from the criminal jurisdiction of the receiving State. He shall also enjoy immunity from its civil and administrative jurisdiction, except in the case of:

(a) a real action relating to private immovable property situated in the territory of the receiving State, unless he holds it on behalf of the sending State for the purposes of the mission;

(b) an action relating to succession in which the diplomatic agent is involved as executor, administrator, heir or legatee as a private person and not on behalf of the sending State;

(c) an action relating to any professional or commercial activity exercised by the diplomatic agent in the receiving State outside his official functions.

2. A diplomatic agent is not obliged to give evidence as a witness.

3. No measures of execution may be taken in respect of a diplomatic agent except in the cases coming under sub-paragraphs (a), (b) and (c) of paragraph 1 of this Article, and provided that the measures concerned can be taken without infringing the inviolability of his person or of his residence. . . .

ARTICLE 32

1. The immunity from jurisdiction of diplomatic agents and of persons enjoying immunity under Article 37 may be waived by the sending State.

2. Waiver must always be express.

3. The initiation of proceedings by a diplomatic agent or by a person enjoying immunity from jurisdiction under Article 37 shall preclude him from invoking immunity from jurisdiction in respect of any counter-claim directly connected with the principal claim.

4. Waiver of immunity from jurisdiction in respect of civil or administrative proceedings shall not be held to imply waiver of immunity in respect of the execution of the judgment, for which a separate waiver shall be necessary.

ARTICLE 41

1. Without prejudice to their privileges and immunities, it is the duty of all persons enjoying such privileges and immunities to respect the laws and regulations of the receiving State. They also have a duty not to interfere in the internal affairs of that State.

2. All official business with the receiving State entrusted to the mission by the sending State shall be conducted with or through the Ministry for Foreign Affairs of the receiving State or such other ministry as may be agreed.

3. The premises of the mission must not be used in any manner incompatible with the functions of the mission as laid down in the present Convention or by other rules of general international law or by any special agreements in force between the sending and the receiving State.

ARTICLE 42

A diplomatic agent shall not in the receiving State practice for personal profit any professional or commercial activity.

VIENNA CONVENTION ON CONSULAR RELATIONS (selected provisions)
DONE AT VIENNA, ON 24 APRIL 1963
596 U.N.T.S. 262, 21 U.S.T. 78

The States Parties to the present Convention, . . . [b]elieving that an international convention on consular relations, privileges and immunities would also contribute to the development of friendly relations among nations, irrespective of their differing constitutional and social systems, . . . have agreed as follows:
. . .

ARTICLE 5
Consular Functions

Consular functions consist in:

(a) protecting in the receiving State the interests of the sending State and of its nationals, both individuals and bodies corporate, within the limits permitted by international law;

(b) furthering the development of commercial, economic, cultural and scientific relations between the sending State and the receiving State and otherwise promoting friendly relations between them in accordance with the provisions of the present Convention;

(c) ascertaining by all lawful means conditions and developments in the commercial, economic, cultural and scientific life of the receiving State, reporting thereon to the Government of the sending State and giving information to persons interested;

(d) issuing passports and travel documents to nationals of the sending State, and visas or appropriate documents to persons wishing to travel to the sending State;

(e) helping and assisting nationals, both individuals and bodies corporate, of the sending State;

(f) acting as notary and civil registrar and in capacities of a similar kind, and performing certain functions of an administrative nature, provided that there is nothing contrary thereto in the laws and regulations of the receiving State;

(g) safeguarding the interests of nationals, both individuals and bodies corporate, of the sending State in cases of succession *mortis causa* in the territory of the receiving State, in accordance with the laws and regulations of the receiving State;

(h) safeguarding, within the limits imposed by the laws and regulations of the receiving State, the interests of minors and other persons lacking full capacity who are nationals of the sending State, particularly where any guardianship or trusteeship is required with respect to such persons;

(i) subject to the practices and procedures obtaining in the receiving State, representing or arranging appropriate representation for nationals of the sending State before the tribunals and other authorities of the receiving State, for the purpose of obtaining, in accordance with the laws and regulations of the receiving State, provisional measures for the preservation of the rights and interests of these nationals, where, because of absence or any other reason, such nationals are unable at the proper time to assume the defence of their rights and interests;

(j) transmitting judicial and extrajudicial documents or executing letters rogatory or commissions to take evidence for the courts of the sending State in accordance with international agreements in force or, in the absence of such international agreements, in any other manner compatible with the laws and regulations of the receiving State;

(k) exercising rights of supervision and inspection provided for in the laws and regulations of the sending State in respect of vessels having the nationality of the sending State, and of aircraft registered in that State, and in respect of their crews;

(l) extending assistance to vessels and aircraft mentioned in sub-paragraph (k) of this Article and to their crews, taking statements regarding the voyage of a vessel, examining and stamping the ship's papers, and, without prejudice to the powers of the authorities of the receiving State, conducting investigations into any incidents which occurred during the voyage, and settling disputes of any kind between the master, the officers and the seamen in so far as this may be authorized by the laws and regulations of the sending State;

(m) performing any other functions entrusted to a consular post by the sending State which are not prohibited by the laws and regulations of the receiving State or to which no objection is taken by the receiving State or which are referred to in the international agreements in force between the sending State and the receiving State.

ARTICLE 10
Appointment and Admission of Heads of Consular Posts

1. Heads of consular posts are appointed by the sending State and are admitted to the exercise of their functions by the receiving State. . . .

ARTICLE 23
Persons Declared "Non Grata"

1. The receiving State may at any time notify the sending State that a consular officer is *persona non grata* or that any other member of the consular staff is not acceptable. In that event, the sending State shall, as the case may be, either recall the person concerned or terminate his functions with the consular post. . . .

ARTICLE 31
Inviolability of the Consular Premises

. . . 2. The authorities of the receiving State shall not enter that part of the consular premises which is used exclusively for the purpose of the work of the consular post except with the consent of the head of the consular post or of his designee or of the head of the diplomatic mission of the sending State. The consent of the head of the consular post may, however, be assumed in case of fire or other disaster requiring prompt protective action.

3. Subject to the provisions of paragraph 2 of this Article, the receiving State is under a special duty to take all appropriate steps to protect the consular premises against any intrusion or damage and to prevent any disturbance of the peace of the consular post or impairment of its dignity. . . .

ARTICLE 33
Inviolability of the Consular Archives and Documents

The consular archives and documents shall be inviolable at all times and wherever they may be.

ARTICLE 36
Communication and Contact with Nationals of the Sending State

1. With a view to facilitating the exercise of consular functions relating to nationals of the sending State:

(a) consular officers shall be free to communicate with nationals of the sending State and to have access to them. Nationals of the sending State shall have the same freedom with respect to communication with and access to consular officers of the sending State;

(b) if he so requests, the competent authorities of the receiving State shall, without delay, inform the consular post of the sending State if, within its consular district, a national of that State is arrested or committed to prison or to custody pending trial or is detained in any other manner. Any communication addressed to the consular post by the person arrested, in prison, custody or detention shall also be forwarded by the said authorities without delay. The said authorities shall inform the person concerned without delay of his rights under this sub-paragraph;

(c) consular officers shall have the right to visit a national of the sending State who is in prison, custody or detention, to converse and correspond with him and to arrange for his legal representation. They shall also have the right to visit any national of the sending State who is in prison, custody or detention in their district in pursuance of a judgment. Nevertheless, consular officers shall refrain from taking action on behalf of a national who is in prison, custody or detention if he expressly opposes such action.

2. The rights referred to in paragraph 1 of this Article shall be exercised in conformity with the laws and regulations of the receiving State, subject to the proviso, however, that the said laws and regulations must enable full effect to be given to the purposes for which the rights accorded under this Article are intended.

ARTICLE 41
Personal Inviolability of Consular Officers

1. Consular officers shall not be liable to arrest or detention pending trial, except in the case of a grave crime and pursuant to a decision by the competent judicial authority.

2. Except in the case specified in paragraph 1 of this Article, consular officers shall not be committed to prison or liable to any other form of restriction on their personal freedom save in execution of a judicial decision of final effect.

3. If criminal proceedings are instituted against a consular officer, he must appear before the competent authorities. Nevertheless, the proceedings shall be conducted with the respect due to him by reason of his official position and, except in the case specified in paragraph 1 of this Article, in a manner which will hamper the exercise of consular functions as little as possible. When, in the circumstances mentioned in paragraph 1 of this Article, it has become necessary to detain a consular officer, the proceedings against him shall be instituted with the minimum of delay.

ARTICLE 43
Immunity from Jurisdiction

1. Consular officers and consular employees shall not be amenable to the jurisdiction of the judicial or administrative authorities of the receiving State in respect of acts performed in the exercise of consular functions.

2. The provisions of paragraph 1 of this Article shall not, however, apply in respect of a civil action either:

(a) arising out of a contract concluded by a consular officer or a consular employee in which he did not contract expressly or impliedly as an agent of the sending State; or

(b) by a third party for damage arising from an accident in the receiving State caused by a vehicle, vessel or aircraft.

ARTICLE 45
Waiver of Privileges and Immunities

1. The sending State may waive, with regard to a member of the consular post, any of the privileges and immunities provided for in Articles 41 [and] 43. . .

2. The waiver shall in all cases be express, except as provided in paragraph 3 of this Article, and shall be communicated to the receiving State in writing.

3. The initiation of proceedings by a consular officer or a consular employee in a matter where he might enjoy immunity from jurisdiction under Article 43 shall preclude him from invoking immunity from jurisdiction in respect of any counter-claim directly connected with the principal claim.

4. The waiver of immunity from jurisdiction for the purposes of civil or administrative proceedings shall not be deemed to imply the waiver of immunity from the measures of execution resulting from the judicial decision; in respect of such measures, a separate waiver shall be necessary.

ARTICLE 55
Respect for the Laws and Regulations of the Receiving State

1. Without prejudice to their privileges and immunities, it is the duty of all persons enjoying such privileges and immunities to respect the laws and regulations of the receiving State. They also have a duty not to interfere in the internal affairs of that State.

2. The consular premises shall not be used in any manner incompatible with the exercise of consular functions.

3. The provisions of paragraph 2 of this Article shall not exclude the possibility of offices of other institutions or agencies being installed in part of the building in which the consular premises are situated, provided that the premises assigned to them are separate from those used by the consular post. In that event, the said offices shall not, for the purposes of the present Convention, be considered to form part of the consular premises.

ARTICLE 57
Special Provisions Concerning Private Gainful Occupation

1. Career consular officers shall not carry on for personal profit any professional or commercial activity in the receiving State.

2. Privileges and immunities provided in this Chapter shall not be accorded:

(a) to consular employees or to members of the service staff who carry on any private gainful occupation in the receiving State;

(b) to members of the family of a person referred to in sub-paragraph (a) of this paragraph or to members of his private staff;

(c) to members of the family of a member of a consular post who themselves carry on any private gainful occupation in the receiving State.

MUKADDAM v. PERMANENT MISSION OF SAUDI ARABIA
TO THE UNITED NATIONS
111 F. Supp. 2d 457 (S.D.N.Y. 2000)

Plaintiff Rajaa Al Mukaddam ("Mukaddam") was employed by the defendant Permanent Mission of Saudi Arabia to the United Nations (the "Mission") for over 14 years. Plaintiff contends that she was wrongfully terminated by the defendant in April 1998 following a pattern of harassment and gender discrimination that began in 1996 and asserts claims of wrongful termination and retaliation under Title VII of the Civil Rights Act of 1964 and the New York State Human Rights Law. The defendant contends that its status as the Permanent Mission of Saudi Arabia entitles it to immunity from suit in the United States and renders the statutes under which plaintiff sues inapplicable. It therefore moves to dismiss plaintiff's claims on the grounds that this Court lacks subject matter and personal jurisdiction and that plaintiff's complaint fails to state a claim upon which relief can be granted. . . .

Mindful of the diplomatic and sovereign immunity concerns raised by this case, the Court invited the United States Department of State and the Office of Legal Affairs of the United Nations to express any views they might have on the Mission's motion to dismiss. The Department of State submitted a Statement of Interest in which it set forth the United States' view on the parameters of immunity to suit of Saudi Arabia under the Foreign Sovereign Immunities Act ("FSIA") and the Vienna Convention on Diplomatic Relations and Optional Protocol on Disputes (the "Vienna Convention"). . . . The United States does not interpret Article 7 of the Vienna Convention as providing immunity from claims by employees of diplomatic missions, but rather as limiting receiving states from imposing restrictions, other than those set forth in the articles enumerated in Article 7, on the acceptance of mission personnel. The United States acts consistently with this view and defends cases in foreign courts involving conditions of employment or discharge at its diplomatic and consular missions in other countries, generally considering them to be commercial in nature.

The United Nations submitted a letter setting forth its position that any measure, such as legal process, that might impede the maintenance of Permanent Missions to the United Nations or their ability to discharge their official functions would contravene the Charter of the United Nations and the Agreement between the United Nations and the United States of America regarding the Headquarters of the United Nations. In addition, the United Nations interprets the Vienna Convention's grant of authority to "freely appoint" mission staff as extending to the freedom to decide whether to continue or terminate such appointments and finds that subjecting such decisions to the jurisdiction of the receiving state would violate the sending state's sovereign immunity. The United Nations concluded that this case does not arise out of commercial activities of Saudi Arabia and that the exercise of jurisdiction in this case would contravene all three of the aforementioned international agreements. . . .

[T]he issue before the Court on this motion to dismiss is not whether . . . plaintiff will ultimately prevail but whether the claimant is entitled to offer evidence to support [her] claims. . . .

[The court first addressed the impact of the FSIA and concluded "[having] found that plaintiff was neither a civil servant nor a diplomatic officer, and that her employment was commercial activity, this Court holds that the Mission's employment of plaintiff constitutes commercial activity within the meaning of the FSIA. Since this activity took place in the United States, and plaintiff's discriminatory discharge and retaliation claims are based upon this activity, the Court holds that plaintiff's allegations, if proved, would establish that her employment comes within the commercial activity exception to the FSIA. . . . The FSIA was enacted in 1976, four years after the United States became a party to the Vienna Convention. In consequence, the FSIA is subject to the Vienna Convention as a pre-existing international agreement, and the Court must consider its application in deciding whether jurisdiction exists to adjudicate this matter."]

The Vienna Convention was opened for signature in 1961 and signed by the President of the United States in 1972. By its terms, diplomats and their household family members enjoy absolute immunity from criminal prosecution and, with three limited exceptions, immunity from civil suit.[1] In addition, the convention declares the premises of a mission inviolable.

The defendant asserts that Article 7 of the Vienna Convention applies to this action and provides it with absolute immunity from any legal challenge with respect to the hiring and firing of Mission staff. Article 7 provides, in relevant part, that "[s]ubject to the provisions of Articles 5, 8, 9, and 11, the sending State may freely appoint the members of the staff of [its] mission." The term "members of the staff of the mission" is defined to include "members of the diplomatic staff, of the administrative and technical staff and of the service staff of the mission."

The Mission's interpretation of Article 7 is overly broad and ignores the context of the language upon which it relies. The provisions to which Article 7 is subject address issues such as the accreditation of the head of a mission and the appointment of diplomatic staff, notice to the receiving state of the same, the receiving state's rights to declare an individual "persona non grata," and the need for a mission to stay within reasonable size. Read in context, Article 7 simply provides that the sending state may appoint its own staff without approval of the receiving state unless one of the restrictions enumerated in Articles 5, 8, 9, or 11 applies. For example, Article 8 provides that a sending state may not appoint a citizen of the receiving state as a diplomatic staff member without the consent of the receiving state. This reading does not approach the Mission's interpretation of Article 7 as providing an "absolute grant of immunity" from "any legal challenge to the hiring and firing of Mission staff."

The broad grant of immunity that the defendant seeks to invoke is simply not found in the Vienna Convention on Diplomatic Relations. The Vienna

---

[1] *See* Vienna Convention, Art. 31(1) (a diplomatic agent enjoys immunity from civil suit except in cases of (a) a real action relating to private, immovable property situated in the receiving state, unless the property is held on behalf of the sending state for purposes of the mission, (b) an action relating to succession not on behalf of the sending state, or (c) an action relating to any professional or commercial activity outside of a diplomat's official functions); 37(1) (extending immunity to members of the household family of a diplomatic agent).

Convention provides immunity to diplomatic agents and their families, but not to foreign states or their Missions, except in particular circumstances. And just as the FSIA does not affect "either diplomatic or consular immunity," neither does diplomatic or consular immunity affect foreign sovereign immunity under the FSIA. If jurisdiction over a foreign sovereign, or an agency or instrumentality of that sovereign, is properly asserted under the provisions of the FSIA, as the Court has found that it is here, the Vienna Convention does not immunize that sovereign or its instrumentality from suit. In consequence, the Vienna Convention does not prevent the Court from exercising jurisdiction in this case.

[The court then ruled that the mission is an employer under Title VII of the Civil Rights Act of 1964 and the New York State Human Rights Law. The defendant's motion to dismiss was denied in all relevant respects.]

BERDAKIN v. CONSULADO DE LA REPUBLICA DE EL SALVADOR
912 F. Supp. 458 (C.D. Cal. 1995)

Plaintiff Daniel Berdakin leased office space at 2412 W. Seventh Street in Los Angeles to defendant Consulado de la Republica de El Salvador ("the Consulate"). He alleges that the Consulate breached the lease, and is suing for damages. The Consulate and defendant Consul General, Gerardo Sol Mixco ("the Consul"), have entered special appearances for the limited purpose of contesting personal and subject matter jurisdiction. Accordingly, defendants have moved to vacate the summons and dismiss the complaint for lack of jurisdiction. . . .

On March 15, 1992, plaintiff Daniel Berdakin entered into a lease with the Consulate for office space at 2412 W. Seventh Street, Los Angeles, for a term of 72 months. The Consul executed the lease on behalf of the Consulate. In or about July 1995, defendants vacated the premises and ceased payment of rent. Berdakin filed a complaint for rent and other damages in Los Angeles Superior Court on July 25, 1995, and purported to serve the summons and complaint upon Vice-Consul Victor Ollua at the Consulate's new premises on August 14, 1995. . . . Defendants removed the action to this Court . . . as an action against a foreign sovereign state as defined by [the Foreign Sovereign Immunities Act (FSIA),] 28 U.S.C. § 1603. The Consulate and the Consul now move to vacate the summons and dismiss the complaint on the grounds that this Court lacks both personal and subject matter jurisdiction.

DISCUSSION

. . .

A. The Consulate's Immunity under the FSIA

It should be noted as a preliminary matter that the FSIA applies only to states and their instrumentalities, and not to the Consul himself, and concomitantly, that the Vienna Convention's consular immunity doctrine applies only to the Consul himself, and not to the Consulate. The Consulate qualifies as a "foreign state" under the FSIA, rather than merely an agency or instrumentality of a foreign state. [The court ruled that the Consulate, though presumptively immune from jurisdiction under the FSIA, had waived immunity by entering into a lease controlled by California law and had engaged in a commercial activity in the United States, both of which were sufficient to overcome its immunity. In a separate ruling however, the court determined that the consulate had not been served in accordance with the service provisions of the FSIA, 28 U.S.C.§ 1608(a).] . . .

B. The Consul's Immunity under the Vienna Convention [on Consular Relations]

The Court will now address the issue of the Consul's immunity under Article 43 of the Vienna Convention. Since the FSIA does not apply to the Consul himself, the Court has jurisdiction over plaintiff's claim against the Consul under 28 U.S.C. § 1351, but the Court cannot possess jurisdiction over the Consul if he is protected by consular immunity. Article 43 provides that the Consul "shall not be amenable to [suit in the United States] in respect of acts performed in the exercise of consular functions." Article 5 lists 12 such functions, and contains a catch-all clause, 5(m), which defines "consular functions" in relevant part as "any other functions entrusted to a consular post by the sending State which are not prohibited by the laws and regulations of the receiving state or to which no objection is taken by the receiving state." The Consul contends that he acted "in the exercise of consular functions" in entering into the lease and in terminating it and thus is immune under Article 5(m). He argues that he acted within the scope of his official duties in signing the lease on behalf of the Consulate, and that he was entrusted with the function of securing office space for the operation of the Consulate.

The Court has been unable to locate much authority construing "consular functions." Nevertheless, several recent cases shed some light on the matter. In *Gerritsen v. de la Madrid Hurtado*, 819 F.2d 1511, 1515–16 (9th Cir. 1987) (*Gerritsen I*), the Ninth Circuit held that it was not a consular function to beat and threaten physical violence against a leafletter to prevent him from distributing his wares in front of the consulate. Such conduct constituted interference with the internal affairs of the receiving State in violation of Article 55(1) and of international law, and thus was outside the scope of Article 5(a) because that provision grants immunity only "within the limits permitted by international law." Nor was it immune under the catch-all provision, since the crimes alleged were "prohibited by the laws and regulations of the receiving State."

On remand, the District Court held that consular immunity applied to the allegations remaining after the Court of Appeals' decision. After analyzing the cases and international practice, the Court articulated a two-pronged test to determine whether consular immunity applies to conduct alleged to have been "in the exercise of" a consular function. First, the Court should consider "whether there is a logical connection between the act and the purported function," and second, it should decide "whether the act is a reasonable means to the fulfillment of the function." *Gerritsen v. Escobar y Cordova*, 721 F. Supp. 253, 259 (C.D. Cal. 1988). The Court then identified some relevant criteria for these determinations: "(1) the subjective intent of the consular official, based on objective evidence, in performing a particular act; (2) whether the act furthered some function of the consulate; (3) whether the act is of a personal character; (4) the seriousness of the act; and (5) the absence or presence of a malicious motive in the performance of a particular act." The consular functions alleged to have been furthered were the maintenance of "the peace and dignity of the consular offices" and "the protection of [the] consular premises," which the Court held to be legitimate consular functions under Article 5(m)'s catch-all provision. The Court then found that the alleged acts were in fact "attempts to protect the consulate," and thus held that consular immunity applied.

In a related case, the Ninth Circuit held that consular officials were entitled to immunity with respect to verbal threats and warnings made in order to "maintain the peace and dignity" of the consulate and to protect its premises. *Gerritsen v. Consulado General De Mexico*, 989 F.2d 340, 346 (9th Cir.), *cert. denied*, 510 U.S. 828 (1993) (*Gerritsen II*). Unlike the physical violence dealt with in *Gerritsen I*, the conduct in *Gerritsen II* was not "*per se* illegal in this country" and it was undertaken in furtherance of legitimate consular objectives.

The Ninth Circuit came to a different conclusion in *Joseph v. Office of Consulate General of Nigeria*, 830 F.2d 1018 (9th Cir. 1987). In *Joseph*, the consulate leased a house for use as a residence by its employees. Plaintiff sued in tort, alleging that Olalandu, a consular employee who had lived in the house, had left it in a severely damaged condition. The Court stated that "[t]he 'exercise' of a consular function necessarily implies an attempt by an employee to perform his or her consular duties successfully," and held that "no public interest or function of the Consulate or Nigeria was furthered by the allegedly tortious acts performed by Olalandu." *See also State v. Doering-Sachs*, 652 So.2d 420 (Fla. Ct. App.), 659 So.2d 1088 (Fla. 1995) (no connection between defendant's criminal activity — resisting arrest and threatening with a firearm — and the consular function he was performing).

In *Risk v. Halvorsen*, 936 F.2d 393, 397–98 (9th Cir. 1991), *cert. denied*, 502 U.S. 1035 (1992), the Ninth Circuit held that issuing passports and helping the sending state's nationals were consular functions under Article 5(d) and (e). This was so even though the conduct at issue (helping plaintiff's ex-wife leave the country with her and plaintiff's children, in violation of a custody decree) might have been criminal under California law, because (d) and (e) do not limit immunity to conduct permitted by international law (unlike (a)) or the receiving state's laws and regulations (unlike (m)).

Like the instant case, *Koeppel & Koeppel v. Federal Republic of Nigeria*, 704 F. Supp. 521 (S.D.N.Y. 1989), involved a claim of breach of a lease. The Court held that sheltering a Nigerian national overnight in the consulate (in violation of the lease) was a consular function because, unlike the vandalism in *Joseph* or the beatings in *Gerritsen I*, it had "a clear public purpose" and was intended to protect the interests of a national under Article 5(a). The plaintiff in *Koeppel & Koeppel* contended that defendant could not be immune because its conduct breached the lease and thereby violated the law of the receiving state, but the Court disagreed. "Plaintiff's argument suggests that no immunity should be afforded if the consular official's conduct involves breach of the law. If this were the rule, however, there would be no immunity. Every lawsuit asserted against a consular official accuses him or her of some violation of legal rights. Some unfairness to the wronged party is inherent in the notion of immunity." If all illegality negated immunity, immunity would only offer protection where no protection was needed.

In *Ford v. Clement*, 834 F. Supp. 72 (S.D.N.Y. 1993), *aff'd without opinion*, 29 F.3d 621 (2d Cir. 1994), *cert. denied*, 513 U.S. 974 (1994), a former Vice-Consul claimed consular employees harassed her in order to force her out of her job. The Court held that "the management and supervision of the Vice Consul and other consular staff" were consular functions since "they are fundamental to the efficient execution of all of the other consulate functions enumerated by the Vienna Convention." "Moreover, they are necessarily entrusted to the Consul General and indeed lie at the core of any efforts by the Consul General to perform its designated functions."

Miles Management Corp. v. Republic of South Africa, 1994 WL 714584 (N.D. Ill.), involved facts very similar to those of the instant case. The consul signed leases on behalf of the consulate for apartments and parking spaces, and the consulate abandoned the premises before the end of the lease. The Court held the Consul immune under section (m). "Entering into a lease was a function entrusted to a consular post by the sending State and this act is in no way prohibited by the laws and regulations of the receiving State." The Court was untroubled by the fact that "breaching the lease agreement is prohibited by law," stating that "what is important here is that in entering into the contract (or lease) consul acted in the exercise of consular functions."

The Court has considered these cases and concludes that the Consul is entitled to immunity from this suit. As was true in *Ford* and *Miles Management*, here the suit against the Consul arises out of his performance of a function inherent in his position. The Consul clearly was entrusted with the function of entering into a lease in order to secure office space for the operation of the Consulate; if it were otherwise, the Consul could not carry out any of the functions of his office, since without a lease such as the one entered into by the Consul, there could be no Consulate at all.

The Court therefore concludes that obtaining space in which to operate the Consulate is a legitimate consular function, and that entering into a lease to procure such space is a reasonable means of fulfilling that function. The possibility that the Consul's actions in vacating the premises constitute a breach of the lease does not affect the Court's conclusion that the Consul's acts which plaintiff complains of were performed in the exercise of consular functions. Some illegal acts, such as beating a protester, cannot be performed in the exercise of consular functions because they are categorically unlawful acts that cannot constitute legitimate consular functions. But other illegal acts may be performed in the exercise of consular functions, because it is not the illegality itself that takes an act outside the ambit of consular functions. Rather, as the term "consular functions" suggests, it is the fact that an act is not a legitimate consular function — whether or not the act is illegal — that renders its performance outside the exercise of consular functions.

In this case, the function (obtaining office space for the operation of the Consulate) obviously has been entrusted to the Consul and obviously is not "prohibited by the laws and regulations" of this country. This case thus falls squarely within the language of Article 5(m), and it is irrelevant that the manner in which the Consul performed this function is alleged to have violated the law. Article 5(m) requires that the function be legal, but Article 43 does not require that the conduct in the exercise of that function also be legal. If that were the law, consular immunity would only immunize legal conduct, and the doctrine would thus be a nullity. As Judge Leval explained in *Koeppel & Koeppel*, if no illegal act could be performed in the exercise of consular functions, there would be no such thing as consular immunity. If an act were legal, there could be no liability, and if it were illegal, there could be no immunity.

The Consul is therefore not "amenable to the jurisdiction" of this Court under Article 43(1).[1] The Court grants defendants' motion to vacate the summons and dismiss the complaint as to the Consul for lack of personal jurisdiction.

CONCLUSION

The Court hereby grants defendants' motion to vacate the summons and dismiss the complaint as to the Consulate for lack of personal jurisdiction, and hereby grants said motion as to the Consul for lack of subject matter jurisdiction. In light of the Court's holding that it possesses subject matter jurisdiction under the FSIA over plaintiff's claim against the Consulate, plaintiff may seek to refile his complaint as to the Consulate and serve the Consulate in accordance with the requirements of the FSIA.

Notes and Questions on *Berdakin*, *Mukaddam*, and Diplomatic or Consular Immunity

1. *Arguments on appeal.* Drawing on the text and purposes of the relevant treaties and statutes, how would you frame the arguments on appeal in *Berdakin* and *Mukaddam*?

2. *State Department certification.* The status of a particular person as a diplomat or consul — and therefore entitled to immunity in the first place — is generally a function assigned to the State Department, whose certifications are determinative. *Abdulaziz v. Metropolitan Dade County*, 741 F.2d 1328, 1331 (11th Cir. 1984). In this respect, the practice under the Diplomatic Relations Act recalls the approach to foreign sovereign immunity before the passage of the FSIA. Why would the State Department support the transfer of its authority to the courts in sovereign immunity cases but not in diplomatic immunity cases?

---

[1] Article 43 provides that no immunity attaches to a consular employee in an action "(a) arising out of a contract concluded by a consular officer or a consular employee in which he did not contract explicitly or impliedly as an agent of the sending State; or (b) by a third party for damage arising from an accident in the receiving State caused by a vehicle, vessel or aircraft." These exclusions are manifestly inapplicable.

3. *Waiver.* The immunity of diplomatic and consular agents may be waived by the sending state, but that waiver must be explicit in most cases. *Cf. Libra Bank Ltd. v. Banco Nacional de Costa Rica*, 676 F.2d 47, 49 (2d Cir. 1982) (requiring an explicit waiver prevents "inadvertent, implied or constructive waiver in cases where the intent of the foreign state is equivocal or ambiguous"). Implicit waivers are limited by the relevant treaties, excerpted above and in the Documents Supplement. *See* Vienna Convention on Diplomatic Relations, art. 32(3); Vienna Convention on Consular Relations, art. 45(3).

4. *Lease disputes.* It is now generally recognized that an embassy's breach of a lease will expose it to damages. *International Road Federation v. Embassy of the Democratic Republic of the Congo*, 131 F. Supp. 2d 248 (D.D.C. 2001).

5. *Abuse of domestic employees.* Do the cases summarized in *Berdakin* suggest how the courts will (or should) address allegations that a diplomat abused his domestic employee? *See Tabon v. Mufti*, 73 F.3d 535 (4th Cir. 1996); *Park v. Shin*, __ F. Supp. 2d __, 2001 U.S. Dist. LEXIS 11580 (N.D. Cal. 2001).

E. HEAD-OF-STATE IMMUNITY

LAFONTANT v. ARISTIDE
844 F. Supp. 128 (E.D.N.Y 1994)

The question posed by this case is whether the recognized head of a state who has violated the civil rights of a person by having him killed can avoid civil prosecution in this country by virtue of his status. The answer is yes. Defendant seeks dismissal as a matter of law. For purposes of this opinion only it must be assumed that plaintiffs allegations are true. . . .

According to the complaint, on January 7, 1991, Dr. Roger Lafontant, along with others, attempted a coup d'etat to prevent Haitian president-elect, Jean-Bertrand Aristide, from taking office. The next day, the coup was thwarted. Lafontant had been a central figure in Haitian politics for many years; he had held the position of Secretary of the Interior, Secretary of Defense, and other positions in former Haitian governments. He was arrested and jailed for his participation in the failed coup and sentenced to life imprisonment on July 29, 1991. President Aristide then, it is alleged, instructed Captain Stagne Doura, a member of the Armed Forces of Haiti, to execute Lafontant. These orders were carried-out by Private First Class Sincere Leus who shot and killed Lafontant in a Haitian prison at midnight, September 29, 1991. President Aristide's conduct, it is alleged, under color of law of the Republic of Haiti, constituted a criminal act and tort that was not officially sanctioned or in furtherance of the defendant's official function as President.

Two days after this killing, President Aristide was exiled from Haiti following a successful military coup. He has since been living in the United States. The United States government has consistently recognized Jean-Bertrand Aristide as the current lawful head-of-state of the Republic of Haiti. When President Bush received the credentials of President Aristide's designated ambassador . . . he publicly stated that "the United States continues to recognize President Aristide as the duly elected President of Haiti." In a speech by Secretary of State James Baker on October 2, 1991 before the Organization of American States he declared, "we [the United States government] will not recognize this outlaw regime." . . .

In reply to defendant's suggestion of immunity, plaintiff [a resident of New York and the widow of Lafontant] submitted what purports to be a letter signed by President Aristide on September 30, 1991, relinquishing his title as President of the Republic of Haiti. She also relies on the fact that on October 6, 1991, the parliament of Haiti applied Article 149 of the Constitution of Haiti which governs succession in the event of a presidential vacancy. On October 8, 1991, a judge of the Supreme Court of Haiti, Joseph Nerette, was sworn in as temporary President of Haiti. Mr. Nerette chose Jean Jacques Honorat as Prime Minister on October 11, 1991. On October 16, the new government was approved by the parliament. This government functioned in Haiti until June 19, 1992, when President Nerette stepped aside. An agreement was signed between the defendant and Lieutenant General Raoul Cedras allowing President Aristide to return to Haiti by October 30, 1993 (the Governor's Island Agreement). President Aristide did not return to Haiti by that date and has remained continuously outside Haiti since the coup d'etat.

Defendant questions the assertion that the agreement "permits" President Aristide to return to Haiti. He claims that the agreement provides for the nomination of a Prime Minister, commander-in-chief of the Armed Forces, and the granting of an amnesty, all to be undertaken "by the President of the Republic." It is his contention that the "President of the Republic" refers to President Aristide. Plaintiff has also submitted a copy of an arrest warrant dated November 6, 1991, issued for President Aristide's arrest by a criminal court in Haiti. This warrant charges President Aristide with the assassination of plaintiff's husband, Dr. Lafontant.

The Justice Department submitted a suggestion of immunity letter. It states in pertinent part:

> The United States has an interest and concern in this action against President Aristide insofar as the action involves the question of immunity from the Court's jurisdiction of the head-of-state of a friendly foreign state. The United States' interest arises from a determination by the Executive Branch of the Government of the United States, in the implementation of its foreign policy and in the conduct of its international relations, that permitting this action to proceed against President Aristide would be incompatible with the United States' foreign policy interests. . . .

A. Common Law Head-of-State Immunity

A head-of-state recognized by the United States government is absolutely immune from personal jurisdiction in United States courts unless that immunity has been waived by statute or by the foreign government recognized by the United States. A visiting head-of-state is generally immune from the jurisdiction of a foreign state's courts. *See, e.g., Saltany v. Reagan*, 702 F.Supp. 319 (D.D.C. 1988), *aff'd in part, rev'd in part on other grounds*, 886 F.2d 438 (D.C. Cir. 1989), *cert. denied*, 495 U.S. 932 (1990) (granting head-of-state immunity to Prime Minister of England in suit alleging violations of international law); *Kilroy v. Windsor*, Civ. No. C-78-291 (N.D.Ohio 1978) (Prince Charles, The Prince of Wales, granted immunity from suit alleging human rights violations in Northern Ireland), excerpted in 1978 DIG. U.S. PRAC. INT'L L. 641–43; *Psinakis v. Marcos*, Civ. No. C-75-1725 (N.D.Cal. 1975), excerpted in 1975 DIG. U.S. PRAC. INT'L L. 344–45 (immunity granted to then-President Marcos following suggestion of immunity by the Executive Branch); *Kendall v. Saudi Arabia*, 65 Adm. 885 (S.D.N.Y. 1965), reported in 1977 *Dig. U.S. Prac. Int'l L.* 1017, 1053-34.

Head-of-state immunity, like foreign sovereign immunity, is premised on the concept that a state and its ruler are one for purposes of immunity. As early as 1812, the Supreme Court embraced the notion, grounded in customary international law, that a head-of-state is absolutely "exempted" from the jurisdiction of the receiving state's courts. *Schooner Exchange v. M'Faddon*, 11 U.S. (7 Cranch) 116 (1812). This absolute form of immunity is based on the notion that all states are equal and that no one state may exercise judicial authority over another. The foreign head-of-state, as representative of his nation, enjoys extraterritorial status when traveling abroad because he would not intend "to subject himself to a jurisdiction incompatible with his dignity, and the dignity of his nation." *Id.* at 137.

Head-of-state immunity is also supported by the doctrine of comity — that is to say, each state protects the immunity concept so that its own head-of-state will be protected when he or she is abroad. Comity has been described as:

> neither a matter of absolute obligation . . . nor of mere courtesy and good will . . . [b]ut it is the recognition which one nation allows within its territory to the legislative, executive or judicial acts of another nation, having due regard both to international duty and convenience, and to the rights of its own citizens or of other persons who are under the protection of its laws.

Hilton v. Guyot, 159 U.S. 113, 163–64 (1895). This concept of doing to others as you would have them do to you is the principal rationale for a number of important doctrines of international law. *See, e.g., Mitsubishi Motors Corp. v. Soler Chrysler-Plymouth, Inc.,* 473 U.S. 614 (1985) (rationale for enforcing arbitration agreements in international contracts rests on comity); *The Bremen v. Zapata Off-Shore Co.,* 407 U.S. 1 (1972) (rationale for enforcing forum selection clauses in international contracts rests on comity); *First Nat'l City Bank v. Banco National de Cuba,* 406 U.S. 759, 762 (1972) (Act of State rule based on comity). Like the related doctrine of diplomatic immunity, head-of-state immunity is required to safeguard mutual respect among nations. Heads of state must be able to freely perform their duties at home and abroad without the threat of civil and criminal liability in a foreign legal system. *See* Note, *Resolving the Confusion Over Head of State Immunity: The Defined Rights of Kings*, 86 COLUM. L. REV. 169 (1986).

The immunity extends only to the person the United States government acknowledges as the official head-of-state. Recognition of a government and its officers is the exclusive function of the Executive Branch. Whether the recognized head-of-state has *de facto* control of the government is irrelevant;

the courts must defer to the Executive determination. Presidential decisions to recognize a government are binding on the courts, and the courts must give them legal effect. *United States v. Pink,* 315 U.S. 203, 230 (1942) (Executive Branch's determination that recognition of Soviet Union required settlement of claims is binding on the courts).

Since determination of who qualifies as a head-of-state is made by the Executive Branch, it is not a factual issue to be determined by the courts. No judicial hearing or factual determination aside from receipt of the State Department's communication is warranted. In *United States v. Noriega,* 746 F. Supp. 1506 (S.D. Fla. 1990), General Noriega, prosecuted criminally in this country, challenged jurisdiction, arguing that he was entitled to head-of-state immunity. Noriega had never been officially recognized by the United States as the head-of-state of Panama. Instead, the United States had recognized President Eric Arturo Delvalle, even though General Noriega held *de facto* power in Panama and was dealt with as if he were head-of-state by United States officials. General Noriega argued that because he was the *de facto* ruler of Panama, he was entitled to head-of-state immunity. This argument was rejected because the grant of immunity is a privilege which the United States may withhold from any claimant. The fact that Noriega controlled Panama did not entitle him to head-of-state immunity absent explicit recognition from the United States. The court noted that if Noriega's argument that he was entitled to head-of-state immunity were accepted, "illegitimate dictators [would be granted] the benefit of their unscrupulous and possibly brutal seizures of power."

In *Saltany v. Reagan,* 702 F. Supp. 319 (D.D.C. 1988), residents of Libya brought suit against Prime Minister Margaret Thatcher of the United Kingdom, for alleged violations of international law. Pursuant to 28 U.S.C. § 517, the State Department submitted an immunity letter, suggesting that the court grant Prime Minister Thatcher immunity as the head of government of a friendly foreign state. The court accepted the State Department's suggestion as conclusive, and granted immunity. . . .

The government of a foreign state which is recognized by the Executive Branch may waive its head-of-state immunity. In *In re Grand Jury Proceedings,* 817 F.2d 1108 (4th Cir. 1987), *cert. denied,* 484 U.S. 890 (1987), Ferdinand and Imelda Marcos, the former leaders of the Philippines, were found civilly liable for failing to comply with federal grand jury subpoenas. The court held that the doctrine of head-of-state immunity is not an individual right but an "attribute of state sovereignty," a privilege that can be revoked by the foreign state. Corazon Aquino was recognized by the United States as the then head-of-state of the Philippines. The Aquino government waived Mr. and Mrs. Marcos' residual head-of-state or diplomatic immunity in a note to the United States government. The court honored President Aquino's waiver, holding that application of head-of-state immunity to the Marcoses would "clearly offend the present Philippine government, and would therefore undermine the international comity that the head-of-state immunity doctrine is designed to promote."

Similarly, the court held that the foreign government waived immunity in *Paul v. Avril,* 812 F. Supp. 207 (S.D.Fla. 1993). Prosper Avril, the ex-Lieutenant-General of the Armed Forces of Haiti and former military ruler of Haiti was sued for alleged violations of international law. Defendant moved to dismiss, claiming head-of-state immunity. The government of Haiti waived any immunity enjoyed by Mr. Avril. Mr. Avril argued that by following Haiti's suggestion of waiver the court would "encourage countries to disavow those former leaders who do not curry favor with the new government." The court held that the Haitian government then recognized by the United States could waive head-of-state immunity of the former head of military government, and that waiver extends to whatever "residual" head-of-state immunity defendant possessed. . . .

B. Application of Common Law Immunity to Facts

President Aristide is the head-of-state of the Republic of Haiti who is recognized by the U.S. government. He enjoys head-of-state immunity unless there has been a waiver of immunity. Plaintiff contends that the Republic of Haiti has waived President Aristide's immunity. She argues that the failure of the military rulers of Haiti to comply with the terms of the Governor's Island Agreement constitutes an implied waiver of President Aristide's right to legally govern Haiti and claim head-of-state immunity.

This argument is invalid for several reasons. First, the terms of the Governor's Island agreement do not explicitly or implicitly condition President Aristide's status as President of Haiti on his return to Haiti. Second, even if the agreement did provide for the forfeiture of President Aristide's status, recognition of a head-of-state by courts of the United States is an issue for resolution by the Executive Branch of the United States government. A court may not make an independent inquiry into the facts underlying our government's decision.

The warrant for President Aristide's arrest issued by a Haitian court and a personal note allegedly signed by President Aristide that purports to declare his renunciation of the Presidential office are without effect on the issue of immunity. Assuming without deciding that these documents are valid, they cannot affect the court's treatment of the suggestion of immunity. The court must rely on the Executive's determination of who is a lawful head-of-state. Here there has been no explicit waiver of President Aristide's immunity recognized as a waiver by the United States. Unlike *In re Mr. and Mrs. Doe*, 860 F.2d 40 (2d Cir. 1988), where the recognized Philippines government specifically waived the Marcoses' head-of-state immunity, the unrecognized *de facto* rulers of Haiti have no power to and have not undertaken any action accepted by our government as an implicit waiver of immunity. While not decisive, we note that the recognized Ambassador of Haiti to the United States has submitted a letter stating affirmatively that President Aristide is the head-of-state of the Republic of Haiti, and that the embassy does not waive any of the sovereign, head-of-state, or diplomatic immunities that he may enjoy.

The United States government does not recognize the *de facto* military rulers of Haiti. It has repeatedly condemned their regime. The United Nations has also severely criticized their illegal seizure of power. *See* THE SITUATION OF DEMOCRACY AND HUMAN RIGHTS IN HAITI: REPORT OF THE SECRETARY GENERAL, U.N. GAOR, 47th Sess., Agenda Item 22, U.N. Doc. A/47/975 (July 12, 1993). Because the United States does not recognize the *de facto* government, that government does not have the power to waive President Aristide's immunity.

Granting President Aristide head-of-state immunity will further the goals of comity. The State Department, in its suggestion of immunity letter, states that "permitting this action to proceed against President Aristide would be incompatible with the United States' foreign policy interests." The United States foreign policy goal of encouraging democratic elections is strengthened by recognizing President Aristide as the democratically elected head of Haiti. Numerous Executive Orders supporting President Aristide establish that the Republic of Haiti is a "friendly foreign state." Even, however, if the goal of the United States were less lofty, it would make no difference. In this matter the courts are bound by executive decision. . . .

[The court then ruled that no statute had modified the ancient common law rule of head-of-state immunity. In particular, nothing in the Foreign Sovereign Immunities Act, 28 U.S.C. § 1330, 1602 *et seq.*, or the Torture Victim Protection Act, 28 U.S.C. § 1350 note, altered the traditional standards.]

Notes and Questions on *Lafontant* and Head-of-State Immunity (including *Former* Heads-of-State)

1. *Articulating the doctrine's rationale and limitations.* The *quid pro quo* for the absolute form of immunity extended in *Lafontant* is that only recognized heads of state can qualify for it. Family members and close advisors may qualify for some other kind of immunity in the right circumstances, but head-of-state immunity is strictly limited. *See In re Estate of Ferdinand E. Marcos Human Rights Litigation,* 978 F.2d 493 (9th Cir. 1992), *cert. denied,* 508 U.S. 972 (1993). Why is it sensible, given the functional rationale behind the doctrine, to draw such formal distinctions?

2. *Former Head-of-State immunity.* In what circumstances should a *former* head-of-state receive immunity in U.S. courts comparable to that extended in *Lafontant*? *Compare Nixon v. Fitzgerald,* 457 U.S. 731 (1982) (establishing a former U.S. president's "absolute immunity from damages liability predicated on his official acts"). From one perspective, the prospect of a sitting head-of-state's future liability in U.S. courts might compromise current foreign relations and thereby justify a former-head-of-state immunity. And the power of reciprocity shouldn't be discounted: one rationale for a broad-based immunity for former heads-of state grows out of the prospect that former U.S. presidents could otherwise face suit in foreign lands for official actions taken while in office. The contingency is obviously remote, but should ex-President Clinton be vulnerable — even in principle — to suit in the courts of Yugoslavia for the civilian deaths caused by NATO's bombing of Belgrade? *See Herbage v. Meese,* 747 F. Supp. 60 (D.D.C. 1990) *aff'd,* 946 F.2d 1564 (D.C. Cir. 1991).

In the U.S. litigation against Ferdinand Marcos, the former president of The Philippines, the defendant argued in favor of a common law immunity for former heads of state, citing a New York state court decision, *Hatch v. Baez,*

14 Hun. 596 (N.Y. Sup. Ct. 1876), which had suggested that former head-of-state immunity should be recognized in order to protect the ongoing diplomatic relations of the United States. But the demise of absolute immunity among nations in the intervening century, *see, e.g.,* The Foreign Sovereign Immunities Act of 1976, 28 U.S.C. § 1604, 1605, combined with the refusal of New York courts to follow *Hatch* in actions against the deposed Shah of Iran, robbed *Hatch* of whatever precedential value it may once have had. *See, e.g., Islamic Republic of Iran v. Mohammed Reza Pahlavi,* 62 N.Y.2d 474 (1984), *cert. denied,* 469 U.S. 1108 (1985). Given the reluctance of domestic courts to embrace new forms of immunity without either legislative authorization or guidance from the executive branch, *Hatch* has become too slender a reed to support *Lafontant*-like immunity for former heads-of-state.

Marcos' argument for immunity by virtue of his position as a former head-of-state was ultimately rejected on multiple grounds: neither the United States government nor the post-Marcos government in the Philippines had requested immunity, the clear implication being that a domestic court's decision on the immunity of former heads of state is affected by, if not determined by, such submissions. *Estate of Domingo v. Republic of the Philippines,* 694 F. Supp. 782, 786 (D. Wash. 1988), *appeal dismissed, Estate of Domingo, by Mast,* 895 F.2d 1416 (9th Cir. 1990). The courts are especially unlikely to extend immunity for acts that were illegal or *ultra vires.* In *Mr. and Mrs. Doe v. United States,* 860 F.2d 40 (2d Cir. 1988), the court ruled that head-of-state immunity for former President Marcos and his wife had been waived by the Philippines. In dicta, however, the court stated "we believe there is respectable authority for denying head-of-state immunity to a former head-of-state for private or criminal acts in violation of American law." *Id.* at 45. *See also Republic of the Philippines v. Marcos,* 806 F.2d 344 (2d Cir. 1986) (former head of state not immune from suit on the basis of his private acts); *In re Grand Jury Proceedings,* 817 F.2d 1108 (4th Cir. 1987).

Cases against former heads of state are obviously rare, and so courts have not had the opportunity to define precisely how much weight should be given to executive suggestions of immunity, as distinct from the submissions of the foreign government or the court's independent determination that the acts were *ultra vires* or illegal. Is former head-of-state immunity an issue — like foreign sovereign immunity — in which the executive branch might be expected to support a statutory transfer of power to the courts? *Cf.* The Foreign Sovereign Immunities Act, 28 U.S.C. § 1602 ("The Congress finds that the determination *by United States courts* of the claims of foreign states to immunity from the jurisdiction of such courts would serve the interests of justice and would protect the rights of both foreign states and litigants in United States courts. . . . Claims of foreign states to immunity should henceforth be decided by courts of the United States and of the States. . . .") (emphasis supplied).

Chapter 7
TRANSNATIONAL *RES JUDICATA*

Domestic courts increasingly confront legal disputes which already bear the fingerprints of some foreign court or arbitral tribunal. Defendants who lost in a prior proceeding may wish to relitigate their liability in another foreign forum or block the enforcement of the judgment against assets located there. Plaintiffs who lost in the first proceeding may simply want another bite at the apple. In either case, the enforcement court will face a difficult question: how much weight — if any — does that prior foreign decision deserve? Should the doctrines of *res judicata*, which preclude the relitigation of cases and issues in domestic courts, also apply in these international settings, and if so, on what rationale? A generous approach to the recognition or enforcement of foreign judgments might serve efficiency and fairness, on the theory that "one trial of an issue is enough."[1] But there are also reasons of principle and pragmatics for resisting any automatic deference to foreign judgments, no matter how inefficient relitigation may seem.

In August 2000, for example, a French judge found the internet company, Yahoo!, Inc., in violation of French law because Yahoo hosted websites that contained anti-Semitic and Nazi revisionist literature and that held auctions of Nazi paraphernalia. "Exhibition with intent to sell" the Nazi paraphernalia was — according to the court — a wrong committed on French territory every time a French user accessed one of the websites and was an "offense against the collective memory of a country profoundly wounded by the atrocities committed by and in the name of the Nazi criminal enterprise."[2] If French citizens had been able to obtain a civil judgment against Yahoo on this basis, and then attempted to enforce that judgment in the United States, would a U.S. court enforce the judgment?[3] If not, on what grounds could it disregard a final and formal judgment of another sovereign nation?

In the United States, the presumption has historically been that the judgments of a nation's courts, like that nation's laws, are strictly territorial. "No law has any effect, of its own force, beyond the limits of the sovereignty from which its authority is derived." *Hilton v. Guyot*, 159 U.S. 113, 163 (1895). A state might be obliged by treaty to give a foreign judgment effect within its territory, or it may have reasons of its own to recognize and enforce it. But it has that choice: sovereignty, for all of its abstract quality, has certain concrete manifestations, and the discretion to ignore foreign judgments is apparently one of them.

But a policy of automatically ignoring foreign judgments has costs of its own: it's wasteful and potentially inequitable to reconsider an issue that has

---

[1] *Baldwin v. Iowa State Traveling Men's Association*, 283 U.S. 522, 525 (1931).

[2] Carl S. Kaplan, *French Nazi Memorabilia Case Presents Jurisdiction Dilemma*, N.Y. Times, Aug. 11, 2000, *available at* www.nytimes.com/2001/08/11/technology/11CYBERLAW.html.

[3] *Yahoo! Inc. v. La Ligue Contre le Racisme et L'Antisemitisme*, 145 F. Supp. 2d 1168 (N.D. Cal. 2001) and 169 F. Supp. 2d. 1181 (N.D. Cal. 2001).

already been resolved once, even under foreign procedures or standards. States may also be interested in maximizing the extraterritorial effects of their own judgments, and the *quid pro quo* is a reciprocal respect for foreign judgments. States could of course avoid the either-or extremes of automatic enforcement and automatic rejection of foreign judgments, but then the formula and the institutional process for picking winners and losers becomes paramount. Should judges be in the business of deciding which countries' judgments deserve respect and which ones do not? If not, whose job is it? And which criteria are the most appropriate?

As shown in this chapter, the doctrinal structure of *res judicata* in transnational cases reflects these competing principles and offers advocates certain strategic targets in their effort to enforce — or resist — foreign judgments in domestic courts.

A. FOREIGN JUDGMENTS IN U.S COURTS

Domestic civil procedure courses typically focus on types of *res judicata*, that is, the variety of doctrines which preclude the relitigation of a case or an issue. Typically, for example, first-year law students in the United States study the doctrines of *merger* — which melds the plaintiff's cause of action into a final judgment and thereby prevents her from relitigating the same claim — and *bar* — which allows a successful defendant to block a second action on the same claim. These two doctrines are sometimes classified as examples of *claim preclusion*, working in cases that involve a common cause of action and common parties (or those in privity with them). They stand in contrast to *issue preclusion*, which "extends the *res judicata* effect of a judgment to encompass the same issues arising in a *different action . . . and even to different parties* where the issue has been determined in prior litigation with adequate opportunity to be heard for the party to be precluded."[4]

In most courses, students also study the impact of the Full Faith and Credit Clause of the Constitution,[5] under which "Full Faith and Credit shall be given in each State to the Public Acts, Records, and Judicial Proceedings of every

---

[4] Scoles, Hay, Borchers, Symeonides, CONFLICT OF LAWS 1141 (3d ed. 2000) (emphasis supplied). The standards governing these two types of preclusion vary somewhat, but there tend to be common elements. *Claim preclusion* "gives dispositive effect to a prior judgment if a particular issue, although not litigated, could have been raised in the earlier proceeding" and requires: "(1) a final judgment on the merits in a prior suit involving; (2) the same parties or their privies; and (3) a subsequent suit based on the same cause of action." *Churchill v. Star Enter.*, 183 F.3d 184, 194 (3d Cir. 1999). Issue preclusion by contrast "prevents parties from litigating again the same issues when a court of competent jurisdiction has already adjudicated the issue on its merits," *Witkowski v. Welch*, 173 F.3d 192, 198 (3d Cir. 1999) and requires that "(1) the issue decided in the prior adjudication must be identical with the one presented in the later action; (2) there must have been a final judgment on the merits; (3) the party against whom collateral estoppel is asserted must have been a party or in privity with the party to the prior adjudication; and (4) the party against whom collateral estoppel is asserted must have had a full and fair opportunity to litigate the issue in question in the prior adjudication." *Schroeder v. Acceleration Life Ins. Co. of Pennsylvania*, 972 F.2d 41, 45 (3d Cir. 1992).

[5] U.S. CONST. Art. IV, § 1.

other State." Taken in conjunction with its implementing legislation,[6] the Full Faith and Credit Clause establishes a mandatory regime under which each state must recognize every final judgment rendered by every other state, subject only to strict exceptions.[7] These provisions were intended to forge one nation out of different states, each with its own court system and its own local politics.

Intuitively, one might have expected similarly federal standards to govern the *res judicata* effects of foreign judgments, on the theory that relations with a foreign government can be compromised by the decision to discount (or disregard) the judgments of its courts and that that prospect implicates uniquely national concerns. In principle, an international treaty or a federal statute could define the weight to be given to foreign judgments, and federal standards in those forms actually do govern the enforceability of foreign *arbitral awards*. But no treaty or statute of general application exists with respect to *foreign judgments* in U.S. courts, and the result is that *state law — not federal law — generally provides the standards for recognition and enforcement of judgments.* This means, for example, that the preclusion effects of a Belgian judgment sued upon in the state courts of Massachusetts would be governed by Massachusetts law.[8] If the same judgment were sued upon in California, that state's law would determine the *res judicata* effects. The problem is that any system defined by the law of the fifty states is potentially no system at all, and the prospect for chaos (or at least for intense forum-shopping) cannot be dismissed. From this perspective, the contrast between the *res judicata* regime governing sister-state judgments and the approach to foreign judgments is fundamental and clearly marked.

On the other hand, uniform laws have been proposed and in some cases widely adopted, which bring a measure of harmony out of the potential chaos. The Uniform Foreign Money-Judgments Recognition Act, for example, establishes a uniform presumption of enforceability subject to a uniform set of defenses, as shown below. The Uniform Child Custody Jurisdiction Act, amended as the Uniform Child Custody Jurisdiction and Enforcement Act, promotes the uniform recognition of judgments that take the form of foreign custody decrees, and the Uniform Enforcement of Foreign Judgments Act has been

---

[6] The implementing legislation, 28 U.S.C. § 1738, provides that judicial proceedings "shall have the same full faith and credit in every court within the United States . . . as they have by law or usage in the courts of such State . . . from which they are taken."

[7] For example, a judgment issued by a court without personal or subject matter jurisdiction is not entitled to full faith and credit in the courts of a sister state. If the defendant received inadequate notice of the proceeding or was deprived of an opportunity to be heard, the resulting judgment need not be enforced or recognized. A judgment obtained through fraud will be similarly treated. RESTATEMENT (SECOND) CONFLICTS OF LAWS §§ 104, 105. Public policy is not a recognized exception to the requirements of the Full Faith and Credit Clause. *Id.*, § 117. *Fauntleroy v. Lum,* 210 U.S. 230 (1908).

[8] A federal court in Massachusetts would have to follow the state rule, assuming that its jurisdiction were grounded in the diversity or alienage clauses of the Constitution. "Diversity" and "alienage" refer to the judicial power of the federal courts under Article III, § 2 of the Constitution, over "all Cases . . . between Citizens of different States . . . and between a State, or the Citizens thereof, and foreign States, Citizens, or Subjects." *See also* 28 U.S.C. § 1332 (establishing *inter alia* the federal courts' subject matter jurisdiction in certain civil actions "between citizens of different States" and "between citizens of a State and citizens or subjects of a foreign state.")

interpreted to create a registration procedure for foreign country judgments. In short, though the relevant law governing the recognition and enforcement of foreign judgments continues to be state law, and though there is some variation among the states themselves, there is a remarkable convergence in the substantive standards that the courts apply.

---

[1]   Foreign Judgments in the Absence of Statutes or Treaties: The Permissive Regime of *Hilton v. Guyot*

HILTON v. GUYOT
159 U.S. 113 (1895)

JUSTICE GRAY delivered the opinion of the Court.

[Gustave Guyot, a French citizen, sued Henry Hilton, a U.S. citizen, and others, in France, on a contract claim. Hilton appeared in the French court, defended the case on the merits, and lost. That judgment was affirmed by a French appellate court but not before Hilton and his co-defendant had successfully removed their assets from France. The defendants failed to pay the French judgment, and Guyot attempted to enforce the judgment against them in the United States. A federal court in New York enforced the foreign judgment, and Hilton sought review in the Supreme Court.]

International law, in its widest and most comprehensive sense — including not only questions of right between nations, governed by what has been appropriately called the 'law of nations,' but also questions arising under what is usually called 'private international law,' or the 'conflict of laws,' and concerning the rights of persons within the territory and dominion of one nation, by reason of acts, private or public, done within the dominions of another nation — is part of our law, and must be ascertained and administered by the courts of justice as often as such questions are presented in litigation between man and man, duly submitted to their determination. The most certain guide, no doubt, for the decision of such questions is a treaty or a statute of this country. But when, as is the case here, there is no written law upon the subject, the duty still rests upon the judicial tribunals of ascertaining and declaring what the law is, whenever it becomes necessary to do so, in order to determine the rights of parties to suits regularly brought before them. In doing this, the courts must obtain such aid as they can from judicial decisions, from the works of jurists and commentators, and from the acts and usages of civilized nations.

No law has any effect, of its own force, beyond the limits of the sovereignty from which its authority is derived. The extent to which the law of one nation, as put in force within its territory, whether by executive order, by legislative act, or by judicial decree, shall be allowed to operate within the dominion of another nation, depends upon what our greatest jurists have been content to call "the comity of nations." Although the phrase has been often criticized, no satisfactory substitute has been suggested.

"Comity," in the legal sense, is neither a matter of absolute obligation, on the one hand, nor of mere courtesy and good will, upon the other. But it is the recognition which one nation allows within its territory to the legislative, executive, or judicial acts of another nation, having due regard both to international duty and convenience, and to the rights of its own citizens, or of other persons who are under the protection of its laws.

Mr. Justice Story, in his COMMENTARIES ON THE CONFLICT OF LAWS, treating of the question in what department of the government of any state, in the absence of any clear declaration of the sovereign will, resides the authority to determine how far the laws of a foreign state shall have effect, and observing that this differs in different states, according to the organization of the departments of the government of each, says: "In England and America the courts of justice have hitherto exercised the same authority in the most ample manner, and the legislatures have in no instance (it is believed) in either country interfered to provide any positive regulations. The common law of both countries has been expanded to meet the exigencies of the times as they have arisen . . . ." §§ 23, 24. . . .

Mr. Wheaton, [a prominent nineteenth-century publicist in international law,] says: . . .

> No sovereign is bound, unless by special compact, to execute within his dominions a judgment rendered by the tribunals of another State; and if execution be sought by suit upon the judgment, or otherwise, the tribunal in which the suit is brought, or from which execution is sought, is, on principle, at liberty to examine into the merits of such judgment, and to give effect to it or not, as may be found just and equitable. The general comity, utility and convenience of nations have, however, established a usage among most civilized States, by which the final judgments of foreign courts of competent jurisdiction are reciprocally carried into execution, under certain regulations and restrictions, which differ in different countries.

[H. Wheaton, International Law § 147 (8th ed. 1866)]. Chancellor Kent [a British jurist, frequently cited by the Supreme Court as an authority on the common law] says: "The effect to be given to foreign judgments is altogether a matter of comity, in cases where it is not regulated by treaty." 2 Kent Com. (6th ed.) 120.

In order to appreciate the weight of the various authorities cited at the bar, it is important to distinguish different kinds of judgments. Every foreign judgment, of whatever nature, in order to be entitled to any effect, must have been rendered by a court having jurisdiction of the cause, and upon regular proceedings and due notice. In alluding to different kinds of judgments, therefore, such jurisdiction, proceedings and notice will be assumed. It will also be assumed that they are untainted by fraud . . . .

A judgment *in rem*, [for example] adjudicating the title to a ship or other movable property within the custody of the court, is treated as valid everywhere. . . . A judgment affecting the status of persons, such as a decree confirming or dissolving a marriage, is [similarly] recognized as valid in every country, unless contrary to the policy of its own law. . . . Other foreign judgments which have been held conclusive of the matter adjudged were judgments discharging obligations contracted in the foreign country between citizens or residents thereof. . . .

The extraterritorial effect of judgments *in personam*, at law or in equity, may differ, according to the parties to the cause. A judgment of that kind between two citizens or residents of the country, and thereby subject to the jurisdiction, in which it is rendered, may be held conclusive as between them everywhere. So, if a foreigner invokes the jurisdiction by bringing an action against a citizen, both may be held bound by a judgment in favor of either. And if a citizen sues a foreigner, and judgment is rendered in favor of the latter, both may be held equally bound.

The effect to which a judgment, purely executory, rendered in favor of a citizen or resident of the country, in a suit there brought by him against a foreigner, may be entitled in an action thereon against the latter in his own country — as is the case now before us — presents a more difficult question, upon which there has been some diversity of opinion. . . .

[Justice Gray then examined English cases in detail, on the ground that] they directly bear upon the question what was the English law, being then our own law, before the Declaration of Independence. They demonstrate that by that law, as generally understood, . . . a judgment recovered in a foreign country for a sum of money, when sued upon in England, was only *prima facie* evidence of the demand, and subject to be examined and impeached. . . .

The law upon this subject, as understood in the United States, at the time of their separation from the mother country, was that . . . all the courts of the several Colonies and States were deemed foreign to each other, and consequently judgments rendered by any one of them were considered as foreign judgments, and their merits reexaminable in another Colony, not only as to the jurisdiction of the court which pronounced them, but also as to the merits of the controversy, to the extent to which they were understood to be reexaminable in England. . . . It was because of that condition of the law, as between the American Colonies and States, that the United States, at the very beginning of their existence as a nation, ordained that full faith and credit should be given to the judgments of one of the States of the Union in the courts of another of those States. . . .

The decisions of this court have clearly recognized that judgments of a foreign state are *prima facie* evidence only, and that, but for those constitutional and legislative provisions, judgments of a State of the Union, when sued upon in another State, would have no greater effect. . . . In the courts of the several States, it was long recognized and assumed, as undoubted and indisputable, that by our law, as by the law of England, foreign judgments for debts were not conclusive, but only *prima facie* evidence of the matter adjudged. . . .

Mr. Justice Story, in his Commentaries on the Conflict of Laws, . . . after reviewing many English authorities, said, . . .

> It is, indeed, very difficult to perceive what could be done, if a different doctrine were maintainable to the full extent of opening all the evidence and merits of the cause anew on a suit upon the foreign

judgment. Some of the witnesses may be since dead; some of the vouchers may be lost or destroyed. The merits of the cause, as formerly before the court upon the whole evidence, may have been decidedly in favor of the judgment; upon a partial possession of the original evidence, they may now appear otherwise. . . .

Indeed, the rule that the judgment is to be *prima facie* evidence for the plaintiff would be a mere delusion, if the defendant might still question it by opening all or any of the original merits on his side; for under such circumstances it would be equivalent to granting a new trial. It is easy to understand that the defendant may be at liberty to impeach the original justice of the judgment by showing that the court had no jurisdiction, or that he never had any notice of the suit; or that it was procured by fraud; or that upon its face it is founded in mistake; or that it is irregular and bad by the local law. . . To such an extent the doctrine is intelligible and practicable. Beyond this, the right to impugn the judgment is in legal effect the right to retry the merits of the original cause at large, and to put the defendant upon proving those merits. . . .

After stating the effect of the Constitution of the United States, and referring to the opinions of some foreign jurists, and to the law of France, which allows the merits of foreign judgments to be examined, Mr. Justice Story concluded his treatment of the subject as follows:

It is difficult to ascertain what the prevailing rule is in regard to foreign judgments in some of the other nations of continental Europe; whether they are deemed conclusive evidence, or only *prima facie* evidence. Holland seems at all times, upon the general principle of reciprocity, to have given great weight to foreign judgments, and in many cases, if not in all cases, to have given to them a weight equal to that given to domestic judgments, wherever the like rule of reciprocity with regard to Dutch judgments has been adopted by the foreign country whose judgment is brought under review. This is certainly a very reasonable rule, and may perhaps hereafter work itself firmly into the structure of international jurisprudence. . . .

In view of all the authorities upon the subject, and of the trend of judicial opinion in this country and in England, following the lead of Kent and Story, we are satisfied that, where there has been opportunity for a full and fair trial abroad before a court of competent jurisdiction, conducting the trial upon regular proceedings, after due citation or voluntary appearance of the defendant, and under a system of jurisprudence likely to secure an impartial administration of justice between the citizens of its own country and those of other countries, and there is nothing to show either prejudice in the court, or in the system of laws under which it was sitting, or fraud in procuring the judgment, or any other special reason why the comity of this nation should not allow it full effect, the merits of the case should not, in an action brought in this country upon the judgment, be tried afresh, as on a new trial or an appeal, upon the mere assertion of the party that the judgment was erroneous in law or in fact. . . .

It is next objected that in those courts one of the plaintiffs was permitted to testify not under oath, and was not subjected to cross-examination by the opposite party, and that the defendants were, therefore, deprived of safeguards which are by our law considered essential to secure honesty and to detect fraud in a witness; and also that documents and papers were admitted in evidence, with which the defendants had no connection, and which would not be admissible under our own system of jurisprudence. But it having been shown by the plaintiffs, and hardly denied by the defendants, that the practice followed and the method of examining witnesses were according to the laws of France, we are not prepared to hold that the fact that the procedure in these respects differed from that of our own courts is, of itself, a sufficient ground for impeaching the foreign judgment. . . .

It must, however, always be kept in mind that it is the paramount duty of the court, before which any suit is brought, to see to it that the parties have had a fair and impartial trial, before a final decision is rendered against either party. When an action is brought in a court of this country, by a citizen of a foreign country against one of our own citizens, to recover a sum of money adjudged by a court of that country to be due from the defendant to the plaintiff, and the foreign judgment appears to have been rendered by a competent court, having jurisdiction of the cause and of the parties, and upon due allegations and proofs, and opportunity to defend against them, and its proceedings are according to the course of a civilized jurisprudence, and are stated in a clear and formal record, the judgment is *prima facie* evidence, at least, of the truth of the matter adjudged; and it should be held conclusive upon the merits tried in the foreign court, unless some special ground is shown for impeaching the judgment, as by showing that it was affected by fraud or prejudice, or that, by the principles of international law, and by the comity of our own country, it should not be given full credit and effect. . . .

But whether those decisions can be followed in regard to foreign judgments, consistently with our own decisions as to impeaching domestic judgments for fraud, it is unnecessary in this case to determine, because *there is a distinct and independent ground upon which we are satisfied that the comity of our nation does not require us to give conclusive effect to the judgments of the courts of France*; *and that ground is, the want of reciprocity*, on the part of France, as to the effect to be given to the judgments of this and other foreign countries. . . .

[After an exhaustive analysis of recognition practices in countries around the world, Justice Gray concluded:] [T]here is hardly a civilized nation . . . which, by its general law, allows conclusive effect to an executory foreign judgment for the recovery of money. . . . The prediction of Mr. Justice Story . . . has thus been fulfilled, and the rule of reciprocity has worked itself firmly into the structure of international jurisprudence. The reasonable, if not the necessary, conclusion appears to us to be that judgments rendered in France, or in any other foreign country, by the laws of which our own judgments are reviewable upon the merits, are not entitled to full credit and conclusive effect when sued upon in this country, but are *prima facie* evidence only of the justice of the plaintiffs' claim.

In holding such a judgment, for want of reciprocity, not to be conclusive evidence of the merits of the claim, we do not proceed upon any theory of retaliation upon one person by reason of injustice done to another; but upon the broad ground that international law is founded upon mutuality and reciprocity, and that by the principles of international law recognized in most civilized nations, and by the comity of our own country, which it is our judicial duty to know and to declare, the judgment is not entitled to be considered conclusive.

By our law, at the time of the adoption of the Constitution, a foreign judgment was considered as *prima facie* evidence, and not conclusive. There is no statute of the United States, and no treaty of the United States with France, or with any other nation, which has changed that law, or has made any provision upon the subject. It is not to be supposed that, if any statute or treaty had been or should be made, it would recognize as conclusive the judgments of any country, which did not give like effect to our own judgments. In the absence of statute or treaty, it appears to us equally unwarrantable to assume that the comity of the United States requires anything more.

If we should hold this judgment to be conclusive, we should allow it an effect to which, supposing the defendants' offers to be sustained by actual proof, it would, in the absence of a special treaty, be entitled in hardly any other country in Christendom, except the country in which it was rendered. If the judgment had been rendered in this country, or in any other outside of the jurisdiction of France, the French courts would not have executed or enforced it, except after examining into its merits. The very judgment now sued on would be held inconclusive in almost any other country than France. In England, and in the Colonies subject to the law of England, the fraud alleged in its procurement would be a sufficient ground for disregarding it. In the courts of nearly every other nation, it would be subject to reexamination, either merely because it was a foreign judgment, or because judgments of that nation would be reexaminable in the courts of France.

CHIEF JUSTICE FULLER, with whom JUSTICES HARLAN, BREWER, and JACKSON, dissenting.

Plaintiffs brought their action on a judgment recovered by them against the defendants in the courts of France, which courts had jurisdiction over person and subject-matter, and in respect of which judgment no fraud was alleged, except in particulars contested in and considered by the French courts. The question is whether under these circumstances, and in the absence of a treaty or act of Congress, the judgment is reexaminable upon the merits. This question I regard as one to be determined by the ordinary and settled rule in respect of allowing a party, who has had an opportunity to prove his case in a competent court, to retry it on the merits, and it seems to me that the doctrine of *res judicata* applicable to domestic judgments should be applied to foreign judgments as well, and rests on the same general ground of public policy that there should be an end of litigation.

This application of the doctrine is in accordance with our own jurisprudence, and it is not necessary that we should hold it to be required by some rule of international law. The fundamental principle concerning judgments is that disputes are finally determined by them, and I am unable to perceive why a judgment *in personam* which is not open to question on the ground of want of jurisdiction, either intrinsically or over the parties, or of fraud, or on any other recognized ground of impeachment, should not be held *inter partes*, though recovered abroad, conclusive on the merits. . . .

In any aspect, it is difficult to see why rights acquired under foreign judgments do not belong to the category of private rights acquired under foreign laws. Now the rule is universal in this country that private rights acquired under the laws of foreign states will be respected and enforced in our courts unless contrary to the policy or prejudicial to the interests of the state where this is sought to be done; and although the source of this rule may have been the comity characterizing the intercourse between nations, it prevails to-day by its own strength, and the right to the application of the law to which the particular transaction is subject is a juridical right.

It is held by the majority of the court . . . that although no special ground exists for impeaching the original justice of a judgment, such as want of jurisdiction or fraud, the right to retry the merits of the original cause at large, defendant being put upon proving those merits, should be accorded in every suit on judgments recovered in countries where our own judgments are not given full effect, on that ground merely.

I cannot yield my assent to the proposition that because by legislation and judicial decision in France that effect is not there given to judgments recovered in this country which, according to our jurisprudence, we think should be given to judgments wherever recovered, (subject, of course, to the recognized exceptions,) therefore we should pursue the same line of conduct as respects the judgments of French tribunals. The application of the doctrine of *res judicata* does not rest in discretion; and it is for the government, and not for its courts, to adopt the principle of retorsion, if deemed under any circumstances desirable or necessary.

Notes and Questions on *Hilton v. Guyot*

1. *Holding versus dicta: the decline of reciprocity as a precondition for recognition or enforcement.* In *Hilton*, the Supreme Court ruled that the Full Faith and Credit Clause does not apply to the judgments of foreign countries and that the French judgment would not be recognized or enforced in the United States in the absence of reciprocity, that is, proof that a French court would enforce a U.S. judgment in similar circumstances.[1] But the Court also indicated in *dicta* that it could give the French judgment a *presumptive validity* in certain circumstances:

> [1] where there has been opportunity for a full and fair trial abroad [2] before a court of competent jurisdiction, [3] conducting the trial upon regular proceedings, [4] after due citation or voluntary appearance of the defendant, and [5] under a system of jurisprudence likely to secure an impartial administration of justice between the citizens

---

[1] In the Court's words, "the judgment rendered in a foreign country is allowed the same effect only as the courts of that country allow to the judgments of the country in which the judgment in question is sought to be executed."

of its own country and those of other countries, and [6] there is nothing to show either prejudice in the court, or [7] in the system of laws under which it was sitting, or [8] fraud in procuring the judgment, or [9] any other special reason why the comity of this nation should not allow it full effect, the merits of the case should not, in an action brought in this country upon the judgment, be tried afresh. . . .

Id. at 202–3.

Over time, these *dicta* have had more staying power than the reciprocity requirement at the heart of *Hilton*'s 5-4 holding. Though reciprocity has not entirely disappeared as a factor in the recognition and enforcement of foreign judgments, the idea that "courts are required to do, not as justice and reason require, but as they are done by," *MacDonald v. Grand Trunk Railway Co.*, 71 N.H. 448, 456 (1902), has had more critics than adherents. A handful of states by statute require reciprocity as a precondition for recognition and enforcement, but reciprocity as endorsed by the *Hilton* court "is no longer an element of the federal law of enforcement of foreign judgments." *McCord v. Jet Spray International Corp.*, 874 F. Supp. 436 (D. Mass. 1994) (quoting *Tahan v. Hodgson*, 662 F.2d 862, 867 & n. 21 (D.C.Cir. 1981)) (emphasis supplied).

The continuing vitality of *Hilton* rests instead on its specification of the defenses to recognition and enforcement and its endorsement of comity as the essence of U.S. courts' approach to foreign judgments, at least in the absence of a controlling statute or treaty. According to the Court,

> [t]he extent to which the law of one nation, as put in force within its territory . . . by judicial decree, shall be allowed to operate within the dominion of another nation, depends upon what our greatest jurists have been content to call "the comity of nations." Although the phrase has been often criticized, no satisfactory substitute has been suggested. "Comity," in the legal sense, is neither a matter of absolute obligation, on the one hand, nor of mere courtesy and good will, upon the other. But it is the recognition which one nation allows within its territory to the . . . judicial acts of another nation, having due regard both to international duty and convenience, and to the rights of our own citizens or of other persons who are under the protection of its laws.

Hilton, 159 U.S., at 163–64. In effect, as shown in the cases below, *Hilton*-based comity means that a foreign judgment will be enforced *unless* one of the defenses specified there is applicable.

2. *State law versus federal law.* The result in *Hilton v. Guyot* was not compelled by the Constitution or federal legislation. But because the court's jurisdiction was grounded in the diversity of the parties, it was empowered under then-prevailing doctrine to articulate a federal general common law governing the recognition of foreign judgments. *Cf. Swift v. Tyson*, 41 U.S. 1 (1842). The relationship between federal and state courts in diversity cases was fundamentally reconfigured forty-three years later in *Erie Railroad Co. v. Tompkins*, 304 U.S. 64 (1938), which held that "[t]here is no federal general common law" and which obliged a federal court with diversity jurisdiction to apply the

substantive law of the state in which it sat. Of course, if there were a federal rule on the subject — in the form of a statute or a treaty — and that rule were otherwise constitutional, it would prevail by reason of the Supremacy Clause. But there is no such pre-emptive federal rule governing the recognition of foreign judgments — at least not yet — and the federal courts sitting in diversity continue to apply the recognition standards of the states in which they operate. *See, e.g., Southwest Livestock and Trucking Co., Inc. v. Ramon*, 169 F.3d 317 (5th Cir. 1999), *infra. See also* RESTATEMENT (SECOND) CONFLICTS OF LAWS § 98, cmt. c. As shown in the next section, the potential chaos of fifty different systems for the recognition of foreign judgments has been contained somewhat by the wide adoption of the Uniform Foreign Money-Judgments Act and the American Law Institute's adoption of the RESTATE-MENT (THIRD) OF FOREIGN RELATIONS LAW and the RESTATEMENT (SECOND) OF CONFLICTS.

3. *Comity defined.* The *Hilton* court's definition of comity continues to echo in the decided cases. "Comity is a recognition which one nation extends within its own territory to the legislative, executive, or judicial acts of another. It is not a rule of law, but one of practice, convenience, and expediency. Although more than mere courtesy and accommodation, comity does not achieve the force of an imperative or obligation. Rather, it is a nation's expression of understanding which demonstrates due regard both to international duty and convenience and to the rights of persons protected by its own laws. Comity should be withheld only when its acceptance would be contrary or prejudicial to the interest of the nation called upon to give it effect. . . ." *Somportex, Ltd. v. Philadelphia Chewing Gum Co.*, 453 F.2d 435 (3d Cir. 1971), *cert. denied*, 405 U.S. 1017 (1972).

Academics have expressed considerably more skepticism about the concept of comity than the courts have. *See, e.g.*, Michael D. Ramsey, *Escaping "International Comity,"* 83 IOWA L. REV. 893 (1999); Joseph H. Sommer, *Against Cyberlaw*, 15 BERK. TECH. L.J. 1145 (2000) (assessing effect of globalization on comity); Harold Maier, *Extraterritorial Jurisdiction at a Crossroads: An Intersection Between Public and Private International Law*, 76 AM. J. INT'L L. 280, 281 (1982) (comity is "an amorphous never-never land whose borders are marked by fuzzy lines of politics, courtesy and good faith"); Joel R. Paul, *Comity in International Law*, 32 HARV. INT'L L. J. 1, 3–4 and notes 4–14 (1991) (comity defined variously as "the basis of international law, a rule of international law, a synonym for private international law, a rule of choice of law, courtesy, politeness, convenience or goodwill between sovereigns, a moral necessity, expediency, reciprocity or 'consideration of high international politics concerned with maintaining amicable and workable relationships between nations' ").

4. *Recognition versus enforcement.* The law has traditionally distinguished between the *enforcement* and the *recognition* of a foreign judgment, though few courts or commentaries preserve the distinction in its pure form. Arthur T. von Mehren & Donald T. Trautman, *Recognition of Foreign Adjudications: A Survey and a Suggested Approach*, 81 HARV. L. REV. 1601, 1608 (1968). "Enforcement" is typically sought by the judgment-creditor seeking the relief awarded by the court that issued the judgment in question and forcing the

judgment-debtor to satisfy it. When a foreign judgment is "enforced," the court's compulsory and remedial powers — *e.g.,* attachment, execution, sequestration, and the like — are recruited to satisfy the foreign judgment. "Recognition" by contrast might be sought by either party seeking to preclude the relitigation of a particular issue or claim — *e.g.,* issues of fact or the defendant's underlying liability. From this perspective, recognition of a judgment is a precondition for its enforcement.

5. *Error as a ground for non-recognition.* The *Hilton* court said that it would be unwilling to ignore a foreign judgment just because it was "erroneous in law or in fact." The failure of reciprocity or fraud might derail the preclusive effects of a foreign judgment, but an error in the judgment would not suffice. Under both the Full Faith and Credit Clause and *Hilton*, the policy against relitigating adjudicated disputes is sufficiently strong as to bar a second action, even where further investigation of the law or the facts indicates that the controversy was erroneously decided. How would you explain the rationale for this rule to a non-lawyer?

6. *Different procedures as a ground for non-recognition.* Recall that Hilton attempted to block the enforcement of the French judgment on the ground that

> one of the plaintiffs [in the French trial] was permitted to testify not under oath, and was not subjected to cross-examination by the opposite party, and that the defendants were, therefore, deprived of safeguards which are by our law considered essential to secure honesty and to detect fraud in a witness; and also that documents and papers were admitted in evidence, with which the defendants had no connection, and which would not be admissible under our own system of jurisprudence.

Mere differences in procedure are routinely insufficient, standing alone, to deny comity to a foreign judgment. In Judge Cardozo's famous observation, "we are not so provincial as to say that every solution of a problem is wrong because we deal with it otherwise at home." *Loucks v. Standard Oil Co.,* 224 N.Y. 99, 110–11, 120 N.E. 198, 201 (1918). A measure of deference to the judgments of foreign courts — even if they use different judicial procedures — facilitates and stabilizes relationships at the international plane (and not coincidentally encourages the recognition and enforcement of U.S. judgments in foreign courts). But it's equally true that a judgment that results from either particular or systemic violations of due process is not entitled to comity. *Compare S.C. Chimexim S.A. v. Velco Enterprises Ltd.,* 36 F. Supp. 2d 206 (S.D.N.Y. 1999) (Romanian judgment enforced) *Bank Melli Iran v. Pahlavi,* 58 F.3d 1406 (9th Cir. 1995) (Iranian judgment not enforced), *infra.* How would you go about determining whether a particular foreign judicial practice was a "mere" difference in procedure or a violation of due process? On which side of the line is the right of cross-examination? The doctor-patient privilege? The choice of law?

As you think through this problem, it may be helpful to distinguish between the concept of constitutional due process and the *Hilton*-based concept of international due process that is "simple and basic enough to describe the judicial processes of civilized nations, and which is fundamentally fair." *Society of Lloyd's v. Ashenden*, 233 F.3d 473 (7th Cir. 2000).

7. *Problem: assigning the burden of proof.* Who should bear the burden of proof when a foreign judgment is at issue? Should the party relying on the judgment be required to demonstrate that none of the *Hilton* exceptions to comity apply? Or should the party resisting enforcement be obliged to demonstrate that comity should be denied?

One leading commentary argues that "[t]here is much sense in making the party who claims the unusual occurrence plead it affirmatively so that the usual assumptions may be indulged in as a matter of course wherever there is no such claim." 5 Charles A. Wright & Arthur R. Miller, FEDERAL PRACTICE AND PROCEDURE § 1271, at 445 (1990) (citation omitted). And several courts assume that the *Hilton* conditions are affirmative defenses, placing the burden of non-recognition on those who resist it. *See* cases cited in *Bank Melli Iran v. Pahlavi*, 58 F.3d 1406 (9th Cir. 1995). But another well-respected commentator takes a contrasting view, arguing that the burden of proof in "establishing the conclusive effect of a foreign judgment is on the party asserting conclusiveness." 11 Jack B. Weinstein et al., NEW YORK CIVIL PRACTICE ¶ 5302.01 (1998), and the Second Circuit has ruled that

> [A] plaintiff seeking enforcement of a foreign country judgment granting or denying recovery of a sum of money must establish *prima facie*: (1) a final judgment, conclusive and enforceable where rendered; (2) subject matter jurisdiction; (3) jurisdiction over the parties or the *res*; and (4) regular proceedings conducted under a system that provides impartial tribunals and procedures compatible with due process.

Ackermann v. Levine, 788 F.2d 830, 842 n. 12 (2d Cir. 1986). Under this approach, a plaintiff attempting to recover on a foreign judgment would first establish a *prima facie* case, and then defendant could raise defenses like fraud or public policy.

As shown below, the contemporary law of transnational *res judicata* distinguishes between mandatory and discretionary grounds for declining to extend comity to a foreign judgment. How might that distinction be useful in assigning the burden of proof?

---

[2] Approximate Harmony: Uniform Acts and Restatements

The *Hilton dicta*, which lay out the grounds *other than reciprocity* for denying comity to a foreign judgment, have been enumerated and recombined in various ways over the last century, although the broad outlines of the comity doctrine remain stable. The Eighth Circuit Court of Appeals, for example, has interpreted *Hilton* to mean that a foreign judgment will be given preclusive effect if five factors are present. *Shen v. Leo A. Daly Co.*, 222 F.3d 472, 476 (8th Cir. 2000) ("Previously litigated claims should not be retried if the reviewing court finds that the [1] foreign court provided a full and fair trial of the issues in a court of competent jurisdiction, [2] the foreign forum ensured the impartial administration of justice, [3] the foreign forum ensured that the trial was conducted without prejudice or fraud, [4] the foreign court had proper jurisdiction over the parties, and [5] the foreign judgment does not violate public policy.") Comparing that summary of *Hilton* — a common law decision of the Supreme Court — with both the Uniform Foreign Money-Judgments Act (UFMJRA) and the RESTATEMENT (THIRD) OF FOREIGN RELATIONS LAW will suggest an important substantive convergence among these three very different legal authorities.

THE UNIFORM FOREIGN MONEY-JUDGMENTS RECOGNITION ACT — 1962 (selected provisions)
13 U.L.A. 149

§ 1. Definitions.

As used in this Act:

(1) "foreign state" means any governmental unit other than the United States, or any state, district, commonwealth, territory, insular possession thereof, or the Panama Canal Zone, the Trust Territory of the Pacific Islands, or the Ryukyu Islands;

(2) "foreign judgment" means any judgment of a foreign state granting or denying recovery of a sum of money, other than a judgment for taxes, a fine or other penalty, or a judgment for support in matrimonial or family matters.

§ 2. Applicability.

This Act applies to any foreign judgment that is final and conclusive and enforceable where rendered even though an appeal therefrom is pending or it is subject to appeal.

§ 3. Recognition and Enforcement.

Except as provided in section 4, a foreign judgment meeting the requirements of section 2 is conclusive between the parties to the extent that it grants or denies recovery of a sum of money. The foreign judgment is enforceable in the same manner as the judgment of a sister state which is entitled to full faith and credit.

§ 4. Grounds for Non-recognition.

(a) A foreign judgment is not conclusive if

(1) the judgment was rendered under a system which does not provide impartial tribunals or procedures compatible with the requirements of due process of law;

(2) the foreign court did not have personal jurisdiction over the defendant; or

(3) the foreign court did not have jurisdiction over the subject matter.

(b) A foreign judgment need not be recognized if

(1) the defendant in the proceedings in the foreign court did not receive notice of the proceedings in sufficient time to enable him to defend;

(2) the judgment was obtained by fraud;

(3) the [cause of action] [claim for relief] on which the judgment is based is repugnant to the public policy of this state;

(4) the judgment conflicts with another final and conclusive judgment;

(5) the proceeding in the foreign court was contrary to an agreement between the parties under which the dispute in question was to be settled otherwise than by proceedings in that court; or

(6) in the case of jurisdiction based only on personal service, the foreign court was a seriously inconvenient forum for the trial of the action.

§ 5. Personal Jurisdiction.

(a) The foreign judgment shall not be refused recognition for lack of personal jurisdiction if

(1) the defendant was served personally in the foreign state;

(2) the defendant voluntarily appeared in the proceedings, other than for the purpose of protecting property seized or threatened with seizure in the proceedings or of contesting the jurisdiction of the court over him;

(3) the defendant prior to the commencement of the proceedings had agreed to submit to the jurisdiction of the foreign court with respect to the subject matter involved;

(4) the defendant was domiciled in the foreign state when the proceedings were instituted, or, being a body corporate had its principal place of business, was incorporated, or had otherwise acquired corporate status, in the foreign state;

(5) the defendant had a business office in the foreign state and the proceedings in the foreign court involved a [cause of action] [claim for relief] arising out of business done by the defendant through that office in the foreign state; or

(6) the defendant operated a motor vehicle or airplane in the foreign state and the proceedings involved a [cause of action] [claim for relief] arising out of such operation.

(b) The courts of this state may recognize other bases of jurisdiction.

Notes and Questions on the UFMJRA

1. *Convergence.* A majority of jurisdictions in the United States has enacted the UFMJRA.[1] In the remaining states, either the principles and standards

---

[1] (As of 1 May 2001): Alaska, California, Colorado, Connecticut, Delaware, District of Columbia, Florida, Georgia, Hawaii, Idaho, Illinois, Iowa, Maine, Maryland, Massachusetts, Michigan, Minnesota, Missouri, Montana, New Jersey, New Mexico, New York, North Carolina, Ohio, Oklahoma, Oregon, Pennsylvania, Texas, Virgin Islands, Virginia, and Washington.

of the Act have been followed (even when the Act itself is not cited by name), or the courts consult Sections 481–486 of the Restatement (Third) of Foreign Relations Law, which were drafted with the UFMJRA as a model. The substantive overlap between the UFMJRA and the Restatement (Third) is quite considerable, including both the presumption of enforceability (§ 481) and the two-tiered specification of defenses (§ 482):

§ 481. Recognition and Enforcement of Foreign Judgments.

(1) Except as provided in § 482, a final judgment of a court of a foreign state granting or denying a sum of money, establishing or confirming the status of a person, or determining interests in property, is conclusive between the parties, and is entitled to recognition in courts in the United States.

§ 482. Grounds for Nonrecognition of Foreign Judgments.

(1) A court in the United States may not recognize a judgment of the court of a foreign state if:

(a) the judgment was rendered under a judicial system that does not provide impartial tribunals or procedures compatible with due process of law; or

(b) the court that rendered the judgment did not have jurisdiction over the defendant in accordance with the law of the rendering state and with the rules set forth in § 421 [see Note and Question #5, infra.]

(2) A court in the United States need not recognize a judgment of the court of a foreign state if:

(a) the court that rendered the judgment did not have jurisdiction of the subject matter of the action;

(b) the defendant did not receive notice of the proceedings in sufficient time to enable him to defend;

(c) the judgment was obtained by fraud;

(d) the cause of action on which the judgment was based, or the judgment itself, is repugnant to the public policy of the United States or of the State where recognition is sought;

(e) the judgment conflicts with another final judgment that is entitled to recognition; or

(f) the proceeding in the foreign court was contrary to an agreement between the parties to submit the controversy on which the judgment is based to another forum.

The consequence of the substantial overlap between the UFMJRA and the Restatement (Third) is that — with the notable and well-rehearsed exceptions noted below — even states which have not formally adopted the uniform act tend to adhere to comparable standards.

2. *Exclusions*. Subject only to limited fairness and public policy protections, the UFMJRA assures that foreign judgments for a sum of money will be conclusive and enforceable between the parties — that they will in fact be "enforceable in the same manner as the judgment of a sister state which is entitled to full faith and credit." But notice the implicit and explicit exclusions:

A. *The Revenue Rule.* Section 1(2) excludes money judgments "for taxes, a fine or other penalty. . . ." *Compare* § 483 of the RESTATEMENT (THIRD) FOREIGN RELATIONS LAW:

§ 483. Recognition and Enforcement of Tax and Penal Judgments

Courts in the United States are not required to recognize or to enforce judgments for the collection of taxes, fines, or penalties rendered by the courts of other states.

The exclusion stems from an ancient *per se* refusal to enforce the tax and criminal laws of foreign states. *See, e.g., Her Majesty v. Gilbertson*, 597 F.2d 1161 (9th Cir. 1979) (U.S. court declines to enforce Canadian certificate of tax assessment on U.S. citizens); *Overseas Inns SA v. U.S.*, 911 F.2d 1146, 1149 (5th Cir. 1990) ("Comity does not reach so far as to allow one country to adversely affect another's tax revenues.").

1. Does the revenue rule continue to make sense? *See United States v. Trapilo*, 130 F.3d 547, 550 n.4 (2d Cir. 1997) ("[i]n an age when virtually all states impose and collect taxes and when instantaneous transfer of assets can be easily arranged, the rationale for not recognizing or enforcing tax judgments is largely obsolete" (quoting RESTATEMENT (THIRD) OF THE FOREIGN RELATIONS LAW OF THE UNITED STATES § 483, Reporters Note 2 at 613 (1987)). Other courts have decided to narrow the application of the revenue rule. *See, e.g., The European Community v. RJR Nabisco, Inc.*, 150 F.Supp. 2d 456, 476 (E.D.N.Y. 2001) ("The policy concerns that give rise to and justify the revenue rule do not warrant elevating the doctrine to a categorical limitation upon the powers conferred upon the federal courts by the Constitution.").

2. Isn't the revenue rule in effect a reverse act of state doctrine?[2] That doctrine reflects the truism that foreign sensitivities (and their separation of powers implications) generally cut *in favor* of presuming the validity of a foreign government's official acts within its own territory. To that extent, those acts are "recognized" in U.S. courts. It was for precisely that reason that the *Sabbatino* decision — presuming the validity of an expropriation by the Castro government in Cuba — was so controversial. Why wouldn't at least that amount of deference attach to the tax assessment of a country like Canada in *Gilbertson*, *supra*?

B. *Family law judgments.* Section 1(2) also excludes from the presumption of enforceability "a judgment for support in matrimonial or family matters." The rationale for the rule is that foreign courts should not become enmeshed in on-going family relationships centered in other states. But the increased mobility of families, and the importance of enforcing support obligations generally, have convinced some states to adopt the 1956 United Nations Convention on the Recovery of Maintenance Abroad and to propose the development of a new Hague convention on the enforcement of maintenance obligations.

C. *Distinguishing judgments by the type of relief awarded.* A "money judgment" within the meaning of the UFMJRA is obviously in contrast to

---

[2] *See* Chapter 6[B], *supra.*

a decree or judgment of equity in which the court orders some other type of relief, such as an injunction or specific performance. Should the preclusive effects of a foreign judgment vary depending on the type of relief granted? In *Baker v. General Motors Corp.*, 522 U.S. 222 (1998), a purely domestic case arising under the Full Faith and Credit Clause, the Supreme Court said in *dicta*, "[t]here is no reason why the preclusive effects of an adjudication on parties and those 'in privity' with them . . . should differ depending solely upon the type of relief sought in a civil action." After *Baker*, what is the prognosis for any notion of *res judicata* that rests on the ancient distinction between relief at law and relief at equity? What are the best arguments for not taking *Baker* out of its domestic constitutional setting and expanding it to an international comity setting?

3. *Definition of final judgment.* When is a foreign judgment sufficiently "final" to qualify for recognition or enforcement, and which jurisdiction's law determines finality? Under Section 2 of the Act, "any foreign judgment that is final and conclusive and enforceable *where rendered*" is entitled to the presumption of enforceability, even if an appeal is pending. The enforcing court may wish to stay its decision until the appeals process abroad is completed, but nothing in the act requires that delay. By contrast, any judgment that is subject to modification on a continuing basis will not qualify as final for purposes of the UFMJRA.

4. *Grounds for non-recognition.* Section 4 of the UFMJRA is divided into two parts, distinguishing between the seemingly mandatory grounds upon which a foreign judgment "is not conclusive" and the seemingly discretionary grounds upon which a foreign judgment "need not be recognized." Section 482 of the Restatement (Third) follows a similar structure, though you'll notice that the language is slightly different. You will also notice that the two provisions are substantively similar and, in many places, identical. Understanding that the drafters of the Restatement (Third) based their work in part on the UFMJRA, the differences between the two take on greater significance. What changes did they make, and what practical difference might the different terminology make? Consider for example the Restatement drafters' decision to move the failure of subject matter jurisdiction from the mandatory category to the discretionary category, *compare* UFMJRA, § 4(a)(3) *with* Restatement (Third) § 482(2)(a), and their decision to drop the *forum non conveniens* defense in personal service cases, UFMJRA § 4(b)(6).

5. *Personal jurisdiction.* Under *Hilton*, the UFMJRA, and the Restatement (Third), personal jurisdiction is a non-negotiable precondition for the recognition or enforcement of a foreign judgment. But what's the right test for determining whether personal jurisdiction was satisfied? Will U.S. courts sitting at the enforcement stage insist that foreign courts abide by the minimum contacts analysis of *International Shoe* and its progeny? Will state courts give their long-arm statutes an extraterritorial application by declining comity to foreign judgments that are based on some other jurisdictional nexus?

Section 5 of the UFMJRA offers a non-exclusive list of affiliations that will satisfy the personal jurisdiction requirement, including *inter alia* personal service; voluntary general appearance; prior consent to jurisdiction; and domicile or various corporate affiliations. Compare the language of Section 5 with the Restatement (Third) provisions on personal jurisdiction:

§ 421. Jurisdiction to Adjudicate

(1) A state may exercise jurisdiction through its courts to adjudicate with respect to a person or thing if the relationship of the state to the person or thing is such as to make the exercise of jurisdiction reasonable.

(2) In general, a state's exercise of jurisdiction to adjudicate with respect to a person or thing is reasonable if, at the time jurisdiction is asserted:

(a) the person or thing is present in the territory of the state, other than transitorily;

(b) the person, if a natural person, is domiciled in the state;

(c) the person, if a natural person, is resident in the state;

(d) the person, if a natural person, is a national of the state;

(e) the person, if a corporation or comparable juridical person, is organized pursuant to the law of the state;

(f) a ship, aircraft or other vehicle to which the adjudication relates is registered under the laws of the state;

(g) the person, whether natural or juridical, has consented to the exercise of jurisdiction;

(h) the person, whether natural or juridical, regularly carries on business in the state;

(i) the person, whether natural or juridical, had carried on activity in the state, but only in respect of such activity;

(j) the person, whether natural or juridical, had carried on outside the state an activity having a substantial, direct, and foreseeable effect within the state, but only in respect of such activity; or

(k) the thing that is the subject of adjudication is owned, possessed, or used in the state, but only in respect of a claim reasonably connected with that thing.

(3) A defense of lack of jurisdiction is generally waived by any appearance by or on behalf of a person or thing (whether as plaintiff, defendant, or third party), if the appearance is for a purpose that does not include a challenge to the exercise of jurisdiction.

6. *State-to-state variations.* Despite the considerable unifying force of the UFMJRA and the Restatement (Third), there continue to be some substantive differences among the states in their approach to foreign judgments. A handful of jurisdictions for example have inserted a reciprocity requirement in their versions of the UFMJRA. Nor is there a single agreed formula for allocating the burden of proof in foreign judgment cases, with some jurisdictions requiring the party invoking the judgment to demonstrate that it is free of all potential defenses and others insisting that the party impugning the foreign judgment must demonstrate that one of the defenses applies.

7. *Other uniform acts.* The Uniform Foreign Money-Judgments Recognition Act is not the only uniform act with implications for judgments from other

countries. For example: (a) the Uniform Child Custody Jurisdiction Act, amended as the Uniform Child Custody Jurisdiction and Enforcement Act, allows for the recognition of foreign custody decrees; (b) the Uniform Enforcement of Foreign Judgments Act, which creates a registration procedure for judgments rendered by sister states, has been interpreted to apply to foreign country judgments, *see, e.g., Tjontveit v. Den Norske Bank ASA*, 997 F. Supp. 799 (S.D. Tex. 1998); and (c) the Uniform Foreign-Money Claims Act addresses issues that can arise when an award is specified in foreign currency, *see, e.g., Manches & Co. v. Gilbey*, 419 Mass. 414, 646 N.E.2d 86 (1995).

---

[3]   Litigating the Standards for Recognition and Enforcement

[a]   Notice and Jurisdiction

By far the most common grounds for not extending comity to a foreign judgment are the failure of personal or subject matter jurisdiction in the foreign court and the inadequacy of notice to the defendant that the fireworks had started. In one famous case,

> *Buchanan v. Rucker*, 9 East 192, 103 Eng. Rep. 546 (K.B. 1808), an English court had to decide whether to enforce a foreign judgment from the island of Tobago. Service of process had been obtained by nailing the summons to the courthouse door in Tobago. The defendant had no notice of the summons and, indeed, had never set foot on Tobago. Refusing to enforce the judgment, Lord Ellenborough illustrated the jurisdictional and notice limitation on the comity doctrine, asking "can the island of Tobago pass a law to bind the rights of the whole world? Would the world submit to such an assumed jurisdiction?"

Cunard Steamship Co., Ltd. v. Salen Reefer Services AB, 773 F.2d 452, 457 (2d Cir. 1985). Given the constitutional dimension of jurisdiction and notice questions in the United States, the issues of jurisdiction and notice may be viewed as specialized applications of the more general due process defense to foreign judgments.

The procedures employed by the foreign tribunal need not be identical to those employed in American courts, but the procedures must be "compatible with the requirements of due process of law." *See, e.g., Ingersoll Milling Machine Co. v. Granger*, 833 F.2d 680, 687 (7th Cir. 1987). So for example, in *Koster v. Automark Indus., Inc.*, 640 F.2d 77 (7th Cir. 1982), a Dutch default judgment was denied enforcement in federal district court on the ground that the defendant's business contacts with the Netherlands were insufficient to satisfy constitutional due process standards. The lack of notice in a timely way similarly flunks the due process test. *Choi v. Kim*, 50 F.3d 244 (3d Cir. 1994). And the failure to comply with the Hague Service Convention may also bar the recognition or enforcement of a foreign judgment. *Arco Electronics Control, Ltd. v. Core Intern.*, 794 F. Supp. 1144 (S.D. Fla. 1992). As you read the following case, consider this question: does the foreign court have to satisfy

International Shoe and its progeny, or should international comity soften those standards?

———

S.C. CHIMEXIM S.A. v. VELCO ENTERPRISES LTD.
36 F. Supp. 2d 206 (S.D.N.Y. 1999)

In this diversity case, plaintiff S.C. Chimexim S.A. ("Chimexim") seeks to enforce a $201,087 judgment rendered in its favor by a tribunal in Bucharest, Romania (the "Bucharest Judgment") against defendant Velco Enterprises, Ltd ("Velco"). Velco moves to dismiss the amended complaint pursuant to Federal Rules of Civil Procedure 12(b)(1), 12(b)(2), and 12(b)(6). . . .

Chimexim is a Romanian corporation with principal offices located in Bucharest, Romania. Velco is a Connecticut corporation with its principal place of business in New York. In addition, at relevant times to this suit, Velco had a "Representative Office" in Romania, which was authorized by the Ministry of Foreign Trade Organization Department to do business in Romania. The Authorization states that Velco's principal place of business is New York and that the scope of activity of the Representative Office is "to support the trading activity of Velco[] in Romania concerning the import and export of chemical products." The Representative Office was staffed by an office manager, two secretaries, and a messenger, and it was open approximately forty hours a week.[1]

Chimexim and Velco are in the business of purchasing, selling, and distributing industrial chemicals, plastics, and related raw materials. Chimexim and Velco bought and sold various products from and to one another. This case arises from a transaction involving Chimexim's sale of polyvinylchloride ("PVC") to Velco. Chimexim apparently performed its end of the bargain but was not paid in full by Velco. Thus, in 1991, Chimexim and Velco entered into an "Agreement" that purported "to settle" Velco's outstanding invoices in the amount of $307,000. The Agreement provided that: (1) Velco would pay $75,000 to Chimexim the week of October 21, 1991; (2) the $232,000 balance would be discharged by Velco to Chimexim based on "developments [of] bilateral business between the two companies" — each company agreeing to sell each other's products at competitive prices, and Velco promising to reserve a 3% commission to Chimexim on its purchases and sales; and (3) when Velco reached a settlement with one of its Brazilian clients, concerning non-delivery of PVC that affected Velco's agreement with Chimexim, Chimexim and Velco would "discuss a fair basis [for] their respective final settlement."

Velco paid Chimexim $75,000 as set forth in the Agreement. Chimexim contends that Velco failed to adhere to the remaining terms of the Agreement. Velco contends that the Agreement precluded Chimexim from pursuing claims against it in Romania. . . .

---

[1] Velco contends that the Representative Office's function "was to facilitate Velco's transaction of business with Romanian companies . . . . [and was not] authorized to transact business on behalf of Velco." Chimexim alleges, on the other hand, that the Representative Office initiated negotiations with it for the transaction at issue.

On January 25, 1996, Chimexim's attorney in Bucharest apparently served a "Notification" on Velco demanding payment of $201,087 under the Agreement. The Notification stated that if Velco did not pay said amount to Chimexim by February 16, 1996, the "debtor will be prosecuted, according to the Romanian legislation, with all consequences arising from this regarding compensation [] and expenses." Velco neither admits nor denies receiving the Notice, but it is undisputed that Velco did not remit payment.

On June 19, 1996, Chimexim brought suit against Velco in Romania before the Bucharest Tribunal, Commercial Section (the "Tribunal"), to recover the unpaid balance on the PVC transaction. Chimexim's application to the Tribunal stated the relevant facts discussed above, including information about the PVC transaction and the parties' Agreement to settle. The application also stated that Velco owed a balance of $201,087 on the $307,000 initially due to Chimexim under the Agreement. Attached to the application were twenty-five documents submitted in support of the claim, including a copy of the Agreement.

Chimexim served Velco at its Representative Office with a summons by posting the summons in the case on the Office's door. Velco denies that it was properly served, and maintains that its Representative Office never received the summons. Velco failed to appear before the Tribunal. Accordingly, on July 10, 1996, the Tribunal entered judgment against Velco in the amount of $201,087. In its judgment, the Tribunal concluded that Velco owed Chimexim $201,087 and that the "procedure was legally carried out." The judgment also stated that Velco was "legally summoned at the office of its representative in Romania." In addition. the judgment noted that the Tribunal analyzed "the proofs that have been produced for the cause, [and] considers the action of [Chimexim] as founded and is going to accept it as such to oblige [Velco] to pay the amount of $201,087 . . . according to the agreement concluded between the parties."

Velco appealed the judgment to Bucharest's Court of Appeal. In its appeal, Velco asserted four grounds for reversal: (1) the "introductory application" (or initial pleading) was insufficiently "stamped" (noting that the application did not make reference to the applicable law or invoke the proper grounds and was not filed with the sufficient number of stamps); (2) insufficient service of process (noting that the proof of service carried neither "the seal of Velco . . . nor the signature of any employee of the Representative Office, although the above-mentioned headquarters were permanently manned"); (3) lack of personal jurisdiction because only the Representative Office was allegedly served and it "cannot validly represent Velco . . . in court"; and (4) the Tribunal "mistakenly settled the case, without actually investigating the merits of the dispute and by breaching [certain provisions of Romania's] Civil Code" (arguing *inter alia* that the Agreement barred the suit). . . .

. . . [T]he three-judge panel of the Court of Appeal rejected Velco's appeal and affirmed the Tribunal. The Court of Appeal stated that it considered the following in rendering its decision: (1) Chimexim's claim that Velco owed it $201,087, and the documents submitted by Chimexim to support its claim; and (2) each of Velco's four grounds of appeal. The Court of Appeal concluded that "the criticism against the award is unfounded and the appeal groundless."

In so concluding, the Court of Appeal stated that it: (1) rejected Velco's argument concerning the insufficiency of the stamping on the summons; (2) determined that service was proper; (3) agreed that the court had personal jurisdiction over the Representative Office "as long as the representative has legal personality and represents the interests of the parent company on the Romanian Territory"; and (4) rejected Velco's argument that the Tribunal did not investigate the merits of the claim.

On October 2, 1998, Velco appealed to the Supreme Judicial Court of Romania. A hearing on that appeal was scheduled for February 4, 1999. Neither party has informed the Court as to the disposition, if any, of that appeal. Neither the Court of Appeal nor the Supreme Judicial Court stayed the execution of judgment. . . .

On January 1, 1998, Chimexim filed suit against Velco in this Court, seeking to enforce its Bucharest Judgment. . . . The parties conducted discovery, limited to the question of jurisdiction. These motions followed.

DISCUSSION

A. Applicable Law

1. Comity

The recognition of foreign judgments "is governed by principles of comity." *Pariente v. Scott Meredith Literary Agency, Inc.*, 771 F. Supp. 609, 615 (S.D.N.Y. 1991) The seminal case in the area of enforcing foreign judgments, *Hilton v. Guyot*, explained the doctrine of comity as follows:

> No law has any effect . . . beyond the limits of the sovereignty from which its authority is derived. The extent to which the law of one nation, as put in force within its territory, . . . by judicial decree, shall be allowed to operate within the dominion of another nation, depends upon what our greatest jurists have been content to call the "comity of nations". . . . "Comity" . . . is the recognition which one nation allows within its territory to the . . . judicial acts of another nation, having due regard both to international duty and convenience, and to the rights of its own citizens, or of persons who are under the protection of its laws.

159 U.S. at 163–64. The Supreme Court in *Hilton* held that if the foreign forum provides a full and fair trial before a court of competent jurisdiction, "under a system of jurisprudence likely to secure an impartial administration of justice . . . and there is nothing to show either prejudice . . . or fraud in procuring the judgment," the judgment should be enforced and not "tried afresh." *Id.* at 202–03.

The practice of extending " 'comity whenever the foreign court ha[s] proper jurisdiction and enforcement does not prejudice the rights of United States citizens or violate domestic public policy,' has consistently been followed in this Circuit." *Pariente*, 771 F. Supp. at 615. . . .

2. New York Law — Article 53

New York law governs actions brought in New York to enforce foreign judgments. In New York, "courts 'generally will accord recognition to the judgments rendered in a foreign country under the doctrine of comity absent a showing of fraud in the procurement of the foreign judgment or unless recognition of the foreign judgment would offend a strong policy of New York.'" *Allstate Ins. Co. v. Administratia Asigurarilor de Stat*, 962 F. Supp. 420, 425 (S.D.N.Y. 1997) Indeed, New York has a "long-standing" tradition of "permitting the enforcement of [foreign] country money judgments." *Fairchild, Arabatzis & Smith, Inc. v. Prometco Co.*, 470 F. Supp. 610, 615 (S.D.N.Y. 1979). David Siegel, PRACTICE COMMENTARIES, MCKINNEY'S CONS.LAWS OF NEW YORK, Book 7B, CPLR C5304:1, at 548 (McKinney's 1997) (describing New York as "generous" in the recognition of the judgments of foreign nations) (hereinafter "Siegel Commentaries").

New York has codified the principles of comity by statute as the "Uniform Foreign Money-Judgments Recognition Act," N.Y. C.P.L.R. ("CPLR") Article 53. Article 53 provides that "a foreign country judgment . . . is conclusive between the parties to the extent that it grants or denies recovery of a sum of money." CPLR § 5303. The article applies to "any foreign country judgment which is final, conclusive and enforceable where rendered even though an appeal therefrom is pending or it is subject to appeal." CPLR § 5302.

A foreign country judgment is "not conclusive" if: (1) "the judgment was rendered under a system which does not provide impartial tribunals or procedures compatible with the requirements of due process of law"; or (2) "the foreign court did not have personal jurisdiction over the defendant." CPLR § 5304(a). These bases of non-recognition preclude courts from recognizing the foreign judgment as a matter of law. SIEGEL COMMENTARIES at 543–49; 11 Jack B. Weinstein et al., NEW YORK CIVIL PRACTICE ¶ 5304.01 (1998) (hereinafter "WEINSTEIN CPLR").

A foreign country judgment "need not be recognized," however, if: (1) the foreign court did not have subject matter jurisdiction; (2) the defendant in the proceedings in the foreign court did not receive notice of the proceedings in sufficient time to enable a defense; (3) the judgment was obtained by fraud; (4) the cause of action violates public policy; (5) the judgment conflicts with another final and conclusive judgment; (6) the proceeding in the foreign country was contrary to an agreement between the parties under which the dispute in question was to be settled otherwise than by proceedings in that court; or (7) the foreign court was a seriously inconvenient forum for the trial of the action. CPLR § 5304(b). These bases of non-recognition are discretionary.

A foreign country judgment "shall not be refused recognition for lack of personal jurisdiction" if, *inter alia*: (1) defendant was served in person in the foreign state; (2) defendant voluntarily appeared in the proceedings, other than for the purpose of protecting property seized; (3) defendant had its principal place of business, was incorporated, or had otherwise acquired corporate status in the foreign state; or (4) defendant had a business office in the foreign state and the proceedings in the foreign court involved a cause of action arising out of business done by defendant in the foreign state. CPLR § 5305.

If any of the above bases for personal jurisdiction apply, "recognition [of the foreign judgment] may not be refused for lack of personal jurisdiction, although recognition may be refused on one of the discretionary grounds listed in [§ 5304(b)]." SIEGEL COMMENTARIES at 549. . . .

[The court ruled that "plaintiff has the burden of proving that no mandatory basis for non-recognition pursuant to CPLR § 5304(a) exists and that defendant has the burden of proving that a discretionary basis for non-recognition pursuant to CPLR § 5304(b) applies.]

Velco's Motion to Dismiss

Velco moves to dismiss this case pursuant to Federal Rules of Civil Procedure 12(b)(1) and 12(b)(2). Rules 12(b)(1) and 12(b)(2), however, are the "means for challenging the jurisdiction of the court before whom a matter is pending." *Canadian Imperial Bank of Commerce v. Saxony Carpet Co.,* 899 F. Supp. 1248, 1251 (S.D.N.Y. 1995), *aff'd,* 104 F.3d 352 (2d Cir. 1996). Velco seeks to invoke these rules to challenge the jurisdiction of the Romanian court, not this Court. Thus, Velco's reliance on Rules 12(b)(1) and 12(b)(2) is erroneous and its motion to dismiss on these bases is denied.

Velco's motion to dismiss for failure to state a claim upon which relief can be granted is similarly denied. . . . Chimexim's allegations concerning the Bucharest Judgment clearly suffice to state a claim — the amended complaint states that Chimexim holds a final, conclusive, and enforceable foreign judgment against Velco for monetary damages. . . .

Chimexim's Cross-Motion for Summary Judgment

Chimexim's's cross-motion for summary judgment raises three issues: (1) whether Chimexim has met its burden of showing that the Bucharest Judgment is final and executory under Romanian law; (2) if so, whether Chimexim has met its burden of showing that no mandatory basis for non-recognition exists; and (3) if so, whether Velco has met its burden of establishing that one of the discretionary exceptions for not recognizing a foreign judgment exists. These issues involve questions of both law and fact.

1. Finality

Velco contends that the Bucharest Judgment is not final, conclusive, and enforceable because it is on appeal to Romania's Superior Court. I reject the argument because the undisputed evidence in the record demonstrates the contrary. Three Romanian lawyers declare that the Bucharest Judgment is final and executory under Romanian law, notwithstanding Velco's latest appeal. Moreover, Velco does not contest the fact that neither the Court of Appeal nor the Superior Court stayed execution of the Bucharest Judgement. Finally, Article 53 specifically states that it applies to judgments "even though an appeal therefrom is pending or is subject to appeal." CPLR § 5302. Hence, there is no genuine issue of material fact as to presumptive validity of the Bucharest Judgment.

2. Chimexim's Contentions Concerning Recognition

Chimexim contends that this Court should enforce the Bucharest Judgment because: it was rendered under a system which provides impartial tribunals and procedures compatible with the requirements of due process of law, and because the Romanian courts had personal jurisdiction over Velco. Velco disagrees. I discuss these issues in turn.

a. Impartial Tribunal and Due Process

The materials submitted to the Court as well as the Court's own research demonstrate that the Romanian judicial system comports with the requirements of due process. Velco's sweeping allegation that the Bucharest Judgment is unenforceable because the "Romanian judicial system is incompatible with due process" is rejected, as a matter of law. Because I conclude that the Romanian judicial system comports with the requirements of due process, I also conclude that there is no genuine issue of material fact in this respect for trial.

The record establishes the following: First, the Romanian government and its judicial system have undergone extensive reform since the fall of the Communist regime in 1989 and the adoption of the Romanian Constitution in 1991. As one of Velco's own submissions observes:

> Six years after the fall of Ceausescu, Romania is a greatly changed society with many of the institutional features of democracy, a nascent capitalist economy, and an identifiable path toward gradual integration with Europe.

(Excerpt from Thomas Carothers, *Assessing Democracy Assistance: The Case of Romania* 15 (Carnegie Endowment for International Peace 1996) (hereinafter "CARNEGIE ASSESSMENT")). Likewise, as another of Velco's submissions states:

> The Romanian Constitution contains basic due process guarantees, but the procedures necessary to implement these guarantees are not strictly followed. The Constitution provides free access to justice, procedural due process, and guarantees the right to the assistance of an attorney. . . . All persons are considered equal before the court and entitled to their day in court. There is some evidence that these guarantees are not always accorded. Under the Constitution, all parties to a judicial proceeding are provided with a right of appeal.

See also Robert B. Yegge, 37:3 *Judges' J.* 41 (1998) (detailing . . . judicial reform efforts in Romania since 1991 and observing that "[t]here has been significant social and political change in Romania" since it democratized, and that U.S. assistance with judicial reform has succeeded).

Second, the Romanian judicial system now has the earmarks of an independent system that is capable of duly administering justice. There is a Constitution that sets forth certain due process guarantees, including procedural due process. There is a Judiciary Law that establishes the judiciary as an independent branch of government. There is judicial tenure for at least some judges. There are three levels of appellate review, and in the instant case Velco has taken advantage of that right to appellate review.

Third, as expert testimony submitted by Chimexim demonstrates, due process in fact is provided under Romanian law. Constantine I. Manzini, a Romanian lawyer who is also admitted to practice law in New York, declares that "Romania provides impartial tribunals as well as procedures compatible with the requirements of due process of law." In the context of this particular case, Victor Anagnoste, a Romanian lawyer who is president of the Romanian Bar Association, declares that "[d]ue process and procedures compatible with the requirements of due process were accorded to defendant." Velco failed to submit any expert opinion suggesting that Romanian tribunals are not impartial or that Romanian civil courts do not provide litigants with due process.

Finally, the United States entered into a trade relations treaty with Romania in 1992, which provided that:

> [n]ationals and companies of either [the United States or Romania] shall be accorded national treatment with respect to access to all courts and administrative bodies in the territory of the other [country], as plaintiffs, defendants or otherwise. They shall not claim or enjoy immunity from suit or execution of judgment, proceedings for the recognition and enforcement of arbitral awards, or other liability in the territory [of either country] with respect to commercial transactions.

The language of the trade agreement demonstrates that the United States was willing to recognize Romania's judicial system.

On the basis of this record, which includes the unrebutted affidavits of Chimexim's expert witnesses, I can only conclude that Chimexim has met its burden of demonstrating that the Romanian judicial system comports with the requirements of due process.

As noted, the record does demonstrate that the Romanian judicial system is far from perfect. As Velco points out, "corruption remains a concern" in Romania and there "is some evidence that [due process] guarantees are not always accorded."[2] No judicial system operates flawlessly, however, and unfortunately injustices occur from time to time even in our own system. Velco's general (and conclusory) assertions are not sufficient to create a genuine issue of fact that Romania's judicial system as a whole is devoid of impartiality or due process.[3]

b. Personal Jurisdiction

---

[2] *See also* CARNEGIE ASSESSMENT at 53 ("Since 1989, the rule of law in Romania has improved significantly. Serious shortcomings do remain, however, including: illegal behavior, particularly corruption by government officials; a common attitude at the higher levels of the power structure that the government and the state are above the law; and only weak institutional reform processes concerning both the law-making and law-enforcing processes. The judicial system has undergone partial reforms, including the creation of a Superior Council of Magistrates, the restoration of the pre-communist-era appeals courts, and the establishment of judicial tenure for at least some judges. Yet major problems remain.").

[3] Velco also states that there are "no cases involving . . . recognition of judgments issuing from former Soviet-bloc nations, much less Romania." Likewise, however, there are no cases involving non-recognition of Romanian judgments on the basis that its courts deny litigants due process. Although a judge in this district denied summary judgment enforcing a Bucharest judgment, the court did so on the ground that issues of fact existed. *See Allstate Ins. Co. v. Administratia Asigurarilor de Stat*, 962 F. Supp. 420, 426 (S.D.N.Y. 1997) (holding that "this Court cannot determine with any certainty . . . . that the Bucharest Court possessed jurisdiction") . . . . Moreover, the *Allstate* judgment was allegedly entered in 1983, "long before the Romanian government was democratized." *Id.*

Chimexim also contends that the Bucharest Judgment is entitled to recognition because the Bucharest courts had personal jurisdiction over Velco. I agree. Pursuant to CPLR § 5305(a), at least three separate bases existed for the Tribunal to exercise jurisdiction over Velco in Romania.

1) Voluntary Appearance

First, Velco voluntarily appeared in the proceedings, other than for the purpose of protecting property seized or protesting jurisdiction. Velco contends that its appeal from the Bucharest Judgment does not constitute a voluntary appearance. Velco is mistaken.

One of Velco's arguments on appeal concerned the merits of the underlying dispute. Velco argued that the Tribunal "mistakenly settled the case, without actually investigating the merits of the dispute and by breaching [certain provisions of Romania's] Civil Code." Because it appeared in the Romanian proceedings in part to attack the Bucharest Judgment on the merits, Velco cannot now complain that the Romanian courts did not have personal jurisdiction over it. "If the judgment debtor did any more than [it] had to do . . . to preserve [a] jurisdictional objection in the foreign court, [it] would thereby have submitted voluntarily to its jurisdiction and forfeited the right to claim an exception." SIEGEL COMMENTARIES at 556.

On this basis alone, Chimexim has met its burden of proving that the Romanian courts had personal jurisdiction over Velco. After all "[i]f any one of [the bases for personal jurisdiction listed in CPLR § 5305(a) is] present, recognition may not be refused for lack of personal jurisdiction." SIEGEL COMMENTARIES at 549.

2) Corporate Status & Cause of Action Arising from Foreign Office

Even were I to conclude that Velco did not voluntarily appear, I would still find that personal jurisdiction was proper because: (1) Velco's Representative Office had acquired a corporate status in Romania (CPLR § 5304(a)(4)); and (2) Velco had a business office in Romania and the underlying dispute "involved a cause of action arising out of business done by [Velco] through that office" in Romania. CPLR § 5304(a)(5).

It is undisputed that Velco's Representative Office was authorized to do business in Romania by Romania's Ministry of Foreign Trade Organization Department. Thus, Velco acquired a "corporate status" in Romania, even though its principal place of business was New York and it was incorporated in Connecticut. Velco's Representative Office was registered in Romania and was authorized to "to support the trading activity of Velco[] in Romania concerning the import and export of chemical products."

In addition, Chimexim's claim against Velco arose out of business done by Velco through its foreign office. The purchase orders for the PVC transaction state that they were "conveyed through Velco Bucharest." Velco itself admits in its reply memorandum that the PVC purchase orders were "transmitted, in the first instance through the representative office. . . ." Velco urges the Court to consider its Representative Office — which was open approximately forty hours a week, and staffed by four full-time individuals — to have functioned "as no more than a messenger." The undisputed facts demonstrate the contrary, and no reasonable factfinder could conclude otherwise on this record.

Accordingly, the Romanian courts had at least three valid bases for exercising personal jurisdiction over Velco. In short, Chimexim has met its burden of proving that no mandatory basis exists for not recognizing the Bucharest Judgment.

3. Velco's Contentions Concerning Non-Recognition

Velco contends that this Court should exercise its discretion to deny enforcement of the Bucharest judgment because: (a) the Romanian courts did not have subject matter jurisdiction; (b) the Bucharest Judgment is contrary to the parties' 1991 Agreement; and/or (c) Velco did not receive notice in sufficient time to enable it to defend. Each of these contentions is rejected. The Romanian courts had subject matter jurisdiction over the underlying case, and Velco offers no valid argument or evidence to the contrary. Likewise, the Bucharest Judgment does not conflict with the parties' 1991 Agreement. The Agreement nowhere states that Chimexim was precluded from bringing suit against Velco. Moreover, the issue as to whether the Agreement barred suit was specifically raised by Velco on appeal and rejected. Finally, I do not accept Velco's contention that it did not receive notice in sufficient time to enable it to defend. Even accepting Velco's contention that its Representative Office did not receive the summons, the evidence presented demonstrates that Velco mounted a vigorous defense against the Tribunal's decision on appeal, and that the Court of Appeal duly considered its arguments. The Court of Appeal, however, was unpersuaded and determined that the evidence presented warranted an affirmance of the Tribunal's decision. I will not second-guess that determination.

CONCLUSION

For the reasons set forth above, Velco's motion to dismiss is denied and Chimexim's cross-motion for summary judgment is granted. The Bucharest Judgment will be granted comity.

Notes and Questions on the Jurisdictional Prerequisite

1. *International disagreement on the legitimate grounds of personal jurisdiction.* There continues to be considerable international disagreement between civil law and common law jurisdictions over the legitimacy of two bases of personal jurisdiction: the defendant's brief presence in the rendering state ("tag" jurisdiction) and the mere presence of his or her assets in the rendering state. Attorneys trained in the civil law tradition have expressed a measure of outrage that a person stopping over in New York (or most other states) can be served with process there, and attorneys trained in the common law tradition are sometimes stunned to discover that an alien with assets in a civil law jurisdiction (a bank account, an umbrella) may be sued for a debt there. The consequence is that the principle that foreign judgments will only

be recognized if the rendering court has jurisdiction — clear as it is in the abstract — has its difficulties in application across legal cultures.

2. *Estoppel on issues of fairness.* Should a party, like Velco, which litigates a case in a foreign court be estopped from challenging its fairness and impartiality at the enforcement stage in the United States? After all, under the doctrine of claim preclusion as generally understood, a final judgment by a court of competent jurisdiction on the merits of an action precludes parties from litigating issues that *were or could have been* raised in that action.

But the fairness criterion is so fundamental that the courts have been reluctant to subject it to arguments from estoppel or waiver. For example, in *Bridgeway Corp. v. Citibank,* 45 F. Supp. 2d 276 (S.D.N.Y. 1999), *aff'd,* 201 F.3d 154 (2d Cir. 2000), Bridgeway, a Liberian company had deposited funds in U.S. dollars in an account at Citibank Liberia. In 1991, with the chaos of civil war in Liberia, Citibank — headquartered in the United States — decided to close down its Liberian operation. Bridgeway insisted on the repayment of its funds in U.S. dollars, but Citibank refused and remitted funds instead to an intermediary in Liberian dollars. Bridgeway sued in Liberia, seeking repayment of the deposit in U.S. dollars, and lost at the trial level on the ground that the local banking laws gave Citibank discretion to repay deposits in either U.S. or Liberian currency. On Bridgeway's appeal, the Supreme Court of Liberia reversed and ruled in favor of Bridgeway, which then sought enforcement of the judgment in the United States.

If you represented Bridgeway in the enforcement action, you would probably argue that Citibank had voluntarily litigated the case on the merits in Liberia, without challenging either the fairness of the proceedings or the failure of the Liberian judiciary generally to meet due process standards. After all, you might point out, the Liberian judicial system was modeled on systems in the United States. But the U.S. court in *Bridgeway* went the other way: because of the civil war and the suspension of the Liberian constitution in particular, the court concluded that Liberian judges effectively served at the pleasure of the warring factions. The political and social pressure to which the judges were subjected meant that the system itself was not fair and impartial.

3. *The effect of treaties.* The treaty in *Chimexim* provided that:

> [N]ationals and companies of either [the United States or Romania] shall be accorded national treatment with respect to access to all courts and administrative bodies in the territory of the other [country], as plaintiffs, defendants or otherwise. They shall not claim or enjoy immunity from suit or execution of judgment, proceedings for the recognition and enforcement of arbitral awards, or other liability in the territory [of either country] with respect to commercial transactions.

The *Chimexim* court concluded that this language "demonstrates that the United States was willing to recognize Romania's judicial system." Is that clearly right or is there a narrower explanation of the treaty-parties' intent? Consider for example the 1951 Friendship, Commerce and Navigation Treaty between the United States and Greece, 5 U.S.T. 1829:

> Nationals and companies of either Party shall be accorded national treatment and most-favored-nation treatment with respect to access

to the courts of justice . . . in all degrees of jurisdiction, both in pursuit and in defense of their rights. [National treatment is defined as that treatment which is] "accorded within the territories of a Party upon terms no less favorable than the treatment accorded therein, in like situations, to nationals, companies, products, vessels or other objects, as the case may be, of such Party.

See Vagenas v. Continental Gin Co., 988 F.2d 104, 106 (11th Cir.), *cert. denied*, 510 U.S. 947 (1993) (elevating a Greek judgment to the status of sister state judgment under the Greek-U.S. treaty).

4. *Effect of a pending appeal.* Notice that the existence of an appeal as in *Chimexim* does not prevent a judgment from being sufficiently final to justify the extension of comity to a foreign judgment. *See* UFMJRA, § 2, *supra.*

---

[b] Due Process Abroad

BANK MELLI IRAN v. PAHLAVI
58 F.3d 1406 (9th Cir.), *cert. denied*, 516 U.S. 989 (1995)

Bank Melli Iran and Bank Mellat ("the Banks") filed this action for the purpose of enforcing certain judgments, which they had obtained against Shams Pahlavi in the tribunals of Iran. She is a resident of California and is the sister of the former Shah of Iran. The district court determined that at the times that the judgments were obtained, Pahlavi could not have obtained due process of law in the courts of Iran. It, therefore, granted summary judgment in her favor. The Banks appeal and we affirm. . . .

In January of 1979, the Shah of Iran fled the country in the midst of the series of events that ultimately resulted in the creation of the Islamic Republic of Iran. Prior to that time, Pahlavi, the Shah's older sister, had signed a number of promissory notes. The Banks, which were the holders of those notes and which are at the very least closely associated with the government, brought collection actions against Pahlavi in the courts of Iran. They served her by publication and in 1982 and 1986 obtained default judgments in the total amount of $32,000,000. They now seek to enforce those judgments pursuant to the Algerian Accords[1] and pursuant to the California Uniform Foreign Money-Judgments Recognition Act, Cal. Civ. Proc. Code §§ 1713–1713.8 ("Foreign Money-Judgments Act" or the "Act").

---

[1] See our discussion of the background and implementation of the Accords in *Islamic Rep. of Iran v. Boeing Co.*, 771 F.2d 1279, 1282–84 (9th Cir. 1985), *cert. dismissed*, 479 U.S. 957 (1986) ["In January 1981, the United States and Iran reached an agreement on the release of the American hostages held in Iran. The settlement was contained in five separate agreements (the Accords), the first two of which established a framework for settling claims between the two nations, and claims in which a national of one party sued the other party. On February 24, 1981, President Reagan issued Exec. Order No. 12294, 3 C.F.R. 139 (1982) (Executive Order), which ratified President Carter's previous executive orders and his execution of the Accords. *Id.* at 140. The Treasury Department subsequently promulgated regulations in conjunction with the Executive Order to implement the Accords. See 31 C.F.R. pt. 535 (1984)."]

Pahlavi filed a motion to dismiss pursuant to Federal Rule of Civil Procedure 12(b)(6) to which she attached a number of documents containing extrinsic evidence to support her assertion that the judgments were rendered without due process of law. . . . [T]he district court . . . converted it to a motion for summary judgment. . . [and] granted summary judgment for Pahlavi. It is from that judgment that the Banks have now appealed. . . .

DISCUSSION

[The court first acknowledged the issue of which party bears the burden of proving that one of the defenses to enforcement applies, but concluded that it need not resolve the issue, "because, as we will show, whether Pahlavi had to put in sufficient evidence to sustain a defense or whether she had only to point to weaknesses in the Banks' case, she carried her burden. As the district court pointed out, Pahlavi's position was so persuasive that the Banks were going to have to point to something that refuted it. That was neither improper nor unfair."]

. . . It has long been the law of the United States that a foreign judgment cannot be enforced if it was obtained in a manner that did not accord with the basics of due process [citing *Hilton v. Guyot* and § 482(1)(a) of the Restatement (Third) of Foreign Relations Law, *supra*]. We are aware of no deviation from that principle. In fact, as we have already shown, it was expressly incorporated into the Foreign Money-Judgments Act. Cal. Civ. Proc. Code § 1713.4. It can hardly be gainsaid that enforcement will not be permitted under California law if due process was lacking when the foreign judgment was obtained. Faced with that ineluctable proposition, the Banks argue that the Algerian Accords have somehow elided the due process requirement from the law of the United States as far as Pahlavi is concerned. With that we cannot agree.

The Algerian Accords do provide that Iran [and its instrumentalities] can bring actions to recover any of its assets from the family of the former Shah. . . . They also provide that in litigation against the Shah's family "the claims of Iran should not be considered legally barred either by sovereign immunity principles or by the act of state doctrine and that Iranian decrees and judgments relating to such assets should be enforced by such courts in accordance with United States law." It is upon this language that the Banks rest their claim that the United States courts cannot consider whether the judgments were obtained in accordance with due process. That is a foundation that crumbles under the weight the Banks seek to place upon it.

It is true that "[t]he clear import of treaty language controls unless 'application of the words of the treaty according to their obvious meaning effects a result inconsistent with the intent or expectations of its signatories.' " *Sumitomo Shoji Amer., Inc. v. Avagliano*, 457 U.S. 176, 180 (1982) (citation omitted). Where the Banks' argument goes awry is in the suggestion that the language in question removes due process considerations from the purview of the United States courts. In the first place, it is notable that the Accords eliminate certain defenses — sovereign immunity and the act of state doctrine — but otherwise provide that enforcement of judgments shall be "in accordance with United States law." That law, of course, includes the due process requirement which we have already delineated.

Secondly, when Warren Christopher, then the former Deputy Secretary of State and one of the chief architects of the Algerian Accords, addressed the concerned members of the Committee on Foreign Affairs of the House of Representatives in 1981, he assured them that "Iran's claims to the property of the Shah and his family will have to be adjudicated in U.S. courts in full accordance with due process of law." It would be most surprising if what he really meant was that due process would be applicable if the initial action were brought in the courts of the United States, a rather obvious point, but that those same courts would be expected to enforce any judgment obtained in Iran, regardless of due process considerations. Absent strong evidence to the contrary — evidence not present in this record — the only reasonable inference is that the United States intended that enforcement "in accordance with United States law" include the due process requirements that are usually demanded by our courts when they review foreign judgments.

Finally, a construction of the Algerian Accords that permitted the taking of assets from a resident of this country by means of a judgment obtained without due process of law would raise grave questions about the enforceability of that part of the Accords. That question would be lurking in the case were we to accept the position that the Banks argue for. We see no reason to stretch the language of the Accords and thereby create those questions because we have no reason to think that the Accords were intended to change the law of this country in that backhanded a fashion. Thus, we hold that attempts to enforce judgments under the Algerian Accords are not exempt from due process defenses. . . .

Having so held, we are left with the question of whether the district court properly granted Pahlavi summary judgment on the due process issue. That is, did she show that she could not get due process in Iran? On this record, the answer is yes, as a precis of the evidence will show.

Pahlavi attached various reports to her motion to dismiss. Those included consular information sheets which gave travel warnings from 1981 through 1993 and noted that anti-American sentiment could make it dangerous to travel in Iran. In particular, the State Department noted that "U.S./Iranian dual nationals have often had their U.S. passports confiscated upon arrival and have been denied permission to depart the country documented as U.S. citizens." While those advisories apply to American nationals, there is no reason to believe that the Shah's sister would have fared any better. Further, a 1991 report on terrorism was attached. That report stated that even then Iran was a continuing state sponsor of terrorism. The report recounted the assassination of a former Iranian prime minister and his aide in Paris, France. Again, one would anticipate that the Shah's sister would encounter great danger should she try to enter Iran.

In addition, other materials from the Department of State were obtained, pursuant to the request of the district court. One of those documents is the portion of the Country Report on Human Rights Practices for 1982 regarding Iran. *See* REPORT BY DEPARTMENT OF STATE TO COMMITTEE ON FOREIGN RELATIONS U.S. SENATE AND COMMITTEE ON FOREIGN RELATIONS U.S. HOUSE

OF REPRESENTATIVES, 98th Cong.2d Sess. 1141 (Joint Comm. Print 1983). That report indicates that trials are rarely held in public, that they are highly politicized, and that the regime does not believe in the independence of the judiciary. *See also* COUNTRY REPORT FOR 1986 at 1159 (report detailing denials of fair public trial and discussing the purchase of verdicts in civil trials); COUNTRY REPORT FOR 1983 at 1259 (same); COUNTRY REPORT FOR 1984 at 1238 (same); COUNTRY REPORT FOR 1985 at 1237 (same). In addition, a 1990 declaration from Laurence Pope, a State Department official, was submitted. Pope declared that under the post-Shah regime "judges are subject to continuing scrutiny and threat of sanction and cannot be expected to be completely impartial toward U.S. citizens," and that "U.S. claimants can have little reasonable expectation of justice." The declaration also pointed out the fact that attorneys in Iran "have been officially discouraged from representing politically undesirable interests," and, "[w]itnesses to events living in Iran . . . are likely to be subject to the same risks as lawyers." Those observations concentrated on the effect upon American citizens, but it can hardly be doubted that they would apply equally to Pahlavi. Further, the COUNTRY REPORT FOR 1986 suggested that people like Pahlavi (those with close ties to the Shah's regime) could not return to Iran without reprisals. That report also indicated that the revolutionary courts could take over cases that were formerly within civil court jurisdiction and could overturn the decisions of civil courts. Also, restraints on arbitrary actions of the revolutionary courts had been greatly weakened.

Pahlavi did not put in a declaration which specifically stated that she would be treated badly by the regime. Her failure to present that more specific evidence does weaken her position somewhat. Nevertheless, a common sense reading of the evidence indicates that if it were the only evidence placed before the trier of fact, a verdict would be directed in her favor on the ground that she could not possibly have obtained a fair hearing before the courts of Iran had she attempted to fight the Banks' claims against her.

That conclusion is further buttressed by decisions which recognize that in the early to mid-1980s Americans could not get a fair trial in Iran. *See McDonnell Douglas Corp. v. Islamic Rep. of Iran*, 758 F.2d 341, 346 (8th Cir.) ("We thus take judicial notice that litigation of the dispute in the courts of Iran would, at the present time, be so gravely difficult and inconvenient that McDonnell Douglas would for all practical purposes be deprived of its day in court."), *cert. denied*, 474 U.S. 948 (1985); *Rockwell Int'l. Sys., Inc. v. Citibank, N.A.*, 719 F.2d 583, 587–88 (2d Cir. 1983) ("Neither [party] argues that the post-revolutionary Iranian judicial system is capable of affording an adequate remedy; courts that have passed on this contention have consistently rejected it."); *Harris Corp. v. National Iranian Radio and Television*, 691 F.2d 1344, 1357 (11th Cir. 1982) ("It is clear that the Islamic regime now governing Iran has shown a deep hostility toward the United States and its citizens, thus making effective access to the Iranian courts unlikely."). There is no reason to think that Pahlavi would have had better access to justice. After all, much of the hostility to United States citizens stemmed from this country's connection to the Shah's regime, and it is hardly necessary to say that Pahlavi's connection was, if anything, closer.

Of course, had the Banks put in any evidence of substance, summary judgment might have been averted. But the Banks' response to Pahlavi's evidence was information and belief declarations from their counsel. Those were entitled to no weight because the declarant did not have personal knowledge. . . . In addition, even if the material had been in proper form, the matters addressed by the declaration and the exhibits did not directly come to grips with the question placed at issue: whether Pahlavi could receive a fair trial in Iran. Instead, the information submitted merely indicated that service was made by publication, that Pahlavi should have received notice, and that Iranian experts had considered the claims against Pahlavi. Portions of the written law of Iran were also included. . . .

In short, the Banks failed to show that there was a material issue of fact on the question of whether Pahlavi could receive a trial in Iran that would be characterized by a "system of jurisprudence likely to secure an impartial administration of justice." *Hilton*, 159 U.S. at 202. Thus, summary judgment was properly granted in her favor.

CONCLUSION

Nations are not inexorably bound to enforce judgments obtained in each other's courts. However, our courts will enforce foreign judgments that arise out of proceedings which comport with basic principles of due process. Neither the Foreign Money-Judgments Act nor the Algerian Accords nor any case interpreting them deviates from that principle. The evidence in this case indicated that Pahlavi could not expect fair treatment from the courts of Iran, could not personally appear before those courts, could not obtain proper legal representation in Iran, and could not even obtain local witnesses on her behalf. Those are not mere niceties of American jurisprudence. They are ingredients of "civilized jurisprudence." *Hilton*, 159 U.S. at 205. They are ingredients of basic due process. [The district court's grant of summary judgment is affirmed.]

Notes and Questions on *Bank Melli Iran*

1. *Proving the due process argument.* To what sources should advocates turn in order to give content to their assertion that a particular foreign legal system comports with the requirements of due process (or not)? Compare the sources in *Bank Melli Iran* with those in *Chimexim*. Notice anything useful?

2. *Politics and the due process argument.* At the time of the decision in *Bank Melli Iran*, Iran was an enemy of the United States. Is due process just a fancy legal name for international politics, suggesting that states friendly to the United States are more likely to have courts that comport with due process than are the enemies of the United States? On the other hand, on what principle should the courts of the United States be completely insensitive to the effects of their judgments in the world outside the courtroom?

3. *Due process and extraterritoriality*. Does the result in *Bank Melli Iran* reflect an inappropriate exportation of US constitutional standards? Or is the source of law governing that issue outside (or beyond) the Constitution?

4. *Due process and fraud*. Litigants in the United States attempting to resist the enforcement or recognition of a foreign judgment will occasionally argue that that judgment was obtained through fraud. Some older cases, including *Hilton*, distinguish confusingly between "extrinsic" fraud — fraud committed on the foreign court and relating to matters other than those that were litigated — and "intrinsic" fraud — fraud relating to issues which were committed in the presence of the court or litigated in the prior proceeding, including *e.g.* perjurious testimony. *Hilton*, 159 U.S. at 207; *Fairchild, Arabatzis & Smith, Inc. v. Prometco (Produce & Metals) Co.*, 470 F. Supp. 610, 615 (S.D.N.Y. 1979). *See* 11 C. WRIGHT & A. MILLER, FEDERAL PRACTICE AND PROCEDURE, § 2861 (1973). Modern authorities tend to reject the distinction, and fraud that effectively deprives a party of her day in court in violation of the due process standard will bar recognition or enforcement of the resulting judgment, whether it is "extrinsic" or "intrinsic." *See, e.g., Bandai America, Inc. v. Bally Midway Mfg. Co.*, 775 F.2d 70, 73 (3d Cir. 1985), *cert. denied*, 475 U.S. (1986). As a consequence, despite the analytical differences between the tort-based, "private" conception of fraud and the constitutional, "public" conception of due process, the two standards have tended to converge in practice.

---

[c] Public Policy

The most common grounds for challenging foreign judgments in U.S. courts are jurisdiction and notice as in *Chimexim, supra*. But it well-established that comity will not be extended to foreign proceedings if doing so would be contrary to the policies, or prejudicial to the interests, of the United States. *See, e.g., Allied Bank Int'l v. Banco Credito Agricola de Cartago*, 757 F.2d 516, 522 (2d Cir. 1985). "No nation is under an unremitting obligation to enforce foreign interests which are fundamentally prejudicial to those of the domestic forum. Thus, from the earliest times, authorities have recognized that the obligation of comity expires when the strong public policies of the forum are vitiated by the foreign act." *Laker Airways Ltd. v. Sabena, Belgian World Airlines*, 731 F.2d 909, 937 (D.C.Cir. 1984). Though often used to challenge jurisdiction to prescribe or the international choice-of-law as in *Laker Airways* or *Hartford Insurance*, Chapter 4(B)(2), *supra*, public policy can also constrain the recognition and enforcement of foreign judgments. As you consider the two cases that follow, try to identify the sources of the public policy at issue. What does it say about the public policy defense that it works in one case and not in the other?

SOUTHWEST LIVESTOCK AND TRUCKING COMPANY, INC. v. RAMON
169 F.3d 317 (5th Cir. 1999)

Defendant-Appellant, Reginaldo Ramon, appeals the district court's grant of summary judgment in favor of Plaintiffs-Appellees, Southwest Livestock & Trucking Co., Inc., Darrel Hargrove and Mary Jane Hargrove. Ramon contends that the district court erred by not recognizing a Mexican judgment, that if recognized would preclude summary judgment against him. We vacate the district court's summary judgment and remand.

I

Darrel and Mary Jane Hargrove (the "Hargroves") are citizens of the United States and officers of Southwest Livestock & Trucking Co., Inc. ("Southwest Livestock"), a Texas corporation involved in the buying and selling of livestock. In 1990, Southwest Livestock entered into a loan arrangement with Reginaldo Ramon ("Ramon"), a citizen of the Republic of Mexico. Southwest Livestock borrowed $400,000 from Ramon. To accomplish the loan, Southwest Livestock executed a *"pagare"* — a Mexican promissory note — payable to Ramon with interest within thirty days. Each month, Southwest Livestock executed a new *pagare* to cover the outstanding principal and paid the accrued interest. Over a period of four years, Southwest Livestock made payments towards the principal, but also borrowed additional money from Ramon. In October of 1994, Southwest Livestock defaulted on the loan. With the exception of the last *pagare* executed by Southwest Livestock, none of the *pagares* contained a stated interest rate. Ramon, however, charged Southwest Livestock interest at a rate of approximately fifty-two percent. The last *pagare* stated an interest rate of forty-eight percent, and under its terms, interest continues to accrue until Southwest Livestock pays the outstanding balance in full.

After Southwest Livestock defaulted, Ramon filed a lawsuit in Mexico to collect on the last *pagare*. The Mexican court granted judgment in favor of Ramon, and ordered Southwest Livestock to satisfy its debt and to pay interest at forty-eight percent. Southwest Livestock appealed, claiming that Ramon had failed to effect proper service of process, and therefore, the Mexican court lacked personal jurisdiction. The Mexican appellate court rejected this argument and affirmed the judgment in favor of Ramon.

After Ramon filed suit in Mexico, but prior to the entry of the Mexican judgment, Southwest Livestock brought suit in United States District Court, alleging that the loan arrangement violated Texas usury laws. Southwest Livestock then filed a motion for partial summary judgment, claiming that the undisputed facts established that Ramon charged, received, and collected usurious interest in violation of Texas law. Ramon also filed a motion for summary judgment. By then, the Mexican court had entered its judgment, and Ramon sought recognition of that judgment. He claimed that, under principles of collateral estoppel and *res judicata*, the Mexican judgment barred Southwest Livestock's suit. The district court judge referred both motions to a magistrate judge.

The magistrate judge . . . first addressed whether the Texas Uniform Foreign Country Money-Judgment Recognition Act (the "Texas Recognition Act") required the district court to recognize the Mexican judgment. As the magistrate judge observed, a judgment "that is not refused recognition . . . is conclusive between the parties to the extent that it grants or denies recovery of a sum of money." The magistrate judge concluded that, contrary to Southwest Livestock's position, the Mexican court properly acquired personal jurisdiction over Southwest Livestock, and therefore, lack of jurisdiction could not constitute a basis for nonrecognition. Nonetheless, according to the magistrate judge, "the district court would be well within its discretion in not recognizing the Mexican judgment on the grounds that it violates the public policy of the state of Texas." Thus, the magistrate judge decided that the Mexican judgment did not bar Southwest Livestock's suit. The magistrate judge then addressed whether the district court should apply Texas or Mexican law to its resolution of Southwest Livestock's usury claim. The magistrate judge concluded that, under Texas choice-of-law rules, the district court should apply Texas law. Under Texas law, Ramon undisputably charged usurious interest.

The district court adopted the magistrate judge's recommendation, granting Southwest Livestock's motion for summary judgment as to liability under Texas usury law, and denying Ramon's motion for summary judgment. The district court agreed that the Mexican judgment violated Texas public policy, and that Texas law applied. The district court then heard evidence on the question of damages and granted $5,766,356.93 to Southwest Livestock. The district court also ordered that amount to "increase by $1,677.00 for every day after November 17, 1997, until the date this Judgment is signed," and awarded Southwest Livestock post-judgment interest and attorneys' fees. Ramon appealed. . . .

II

We must determine first whether the district court properly refused to recognize the Mexican judgment. Our jurisdiction is based on diversity of citizenship. Hence, we must apply Texas law regarding the recognition of foreign country money-judgments. *See Erie R.R. Co. v. Tompkins*, 304 U.S. 64 (1938) (holding that in a diversity action, a federal court must apply the law of the forum state); *Success Motivation Institute of Japan, Ltd. v. Success Motivation Institute Inc.*, 966 F.2d 1007, 1009–10 (5th Cir. 1992) ("*Erie* applies even though some courts have found that these suits necessarily involve relations between the U.S. and foreign governments, and even though some commentators have argued that the enforceability of these judgments in the courts of the United States should be governed by reference to a general rule of federal law.").

Under the Texas Recognition Act, a court must recognize a foreign country judgment assessing money damages unless the judgment debtor establishes one of ten specific grounds for nonrecognition. *See* Tex. Civ. Prac. & Rem. Code Ann. § 36.005 (West 1998).[1] Southwest Livestock contends that it established

---

[1] Tex. Civ. Prac. & Rem. Code Ann. § 36.005 (West 1998) provides:

(a) A foreign country judgment is not conclusive if:

a ground for nonrecognition. It notes that the Texas Constitution places a six percent interest rate limit on contracts that do not contain a stated interest rate. It also points to a Texas statute that states that usury is against Texas public policy. *See* Vernon's Tex. Civ. Stat., art. 5069-1C.001 ("All contracts for usury are contrary to public policy"). Thus, according to Southwest Livestock, the Mexican judgment violates Texas public policy, and the district court properly withheld recognition of the judgment.

. . . In reviewing the district court's decision, we note that the level of contravention of Texas law has "to be high before recognition [can] be denied on public policy grounds." *Hunt v. BP Exploration Co. (Libya) Ltd.*, 492 F.Supp. 885, 900 (N.D.Tex. 1980). The narrowness of the public policy exception reflects a compromise between two axioms — *res judicata* and fairness to litigants — that underlie our law of recognition of foreign country judgments.

To decide whether the district court erred in refusing to recognize the Mexican judgment on public policy grounds, we consider the plain language of the Texas Recognition Act. Section 36.005(b)(3) of the Texas Recognition Act permits the district court not to recognize a foreign country judgment if "the cause of action on which the judgment is based is repugnant to the public policy" of Texas. This subsection of the Texas Recognition Act does not refer to the judgment itself, but specifically to the "cause of action on which the judgment is based." Thus, the fact that a judgment offends Texas public policy does not, in and of itself, permit the district court to refuse recognition of that judgment. *See Norkan Lodge Co. Ltd. v. Gillum*, 587 F. Supp. 1457, 1461 (N.D. Tex. 1984) (noting that a "judgment may only be attacked in the event that 'the cause of action [on] which the judgment is based is repugnant to the public policy of this state,' not the judgment itself").

In this case, the Mexican judgment was based on an action for collection of a promissory note. This cause of action is not repugnant to Texas public policy. *See, e.g., Akin v. Dahl*, 661 S.W.2d 914 (Tex. 1983) (enforcing a suit for the collection of a promissory note). Under the Texas Recognition Act, it

---

(1) the judgment was rendered under a system that does not provide an impartial tribunal or procedures compatible with the requirements of due process of law;

(2) the foreign country court did not have personal jurisdiction over the defendant; or

(3) the foreign country court did not have jurisdiction over the subject matter.

(b) A foreign country judgment need not be recognized if:

(1) the defendant in the proceedings in the foreign country court did not receive notice of the proceedings in sufficient time to defend;

(2) the judgment was obtained by fraud;

(3) the cause of action on which the judgment is based is repugnant to the public policy of this state;

(4) the judgment conflicts with another final and conclusive judgment;

(5) the proceeding in the foreign country court was contrary to an agreement between the parties under which the dispute in question was to be settled otherwise than by proceedings in that court;

(6) in the case of jurisdiction based only on personal service, the foreign country court was a seriously inconvenient forum for the trial of the action; or

(7) it is established that the foreign country in which the judgment was rendered does not recognize judgments rendered in this state that, but for the fact that they are rendered in this state, conform to the definition of "foreign country judgment."

is irrelevant that the Mexican judgment itself contravened Texas's public policy against usury. Thus, the plain language of the Texas Recognition Act suggests that the district court erred in refusing to recognize the Mexican judgment.

Southwest Livestock, however, argues that we should not interpret the Texas Recognition Act according to its plain language. Southwest Livestock contends that Texas courts will not enforce rights existing under laws of other jurisdictions when to do so would violate Texas public policy. It believes that the reasoning of the Texas Supreme Court in *DeSantis v. Wackenhut Corp.*, 793 S.W.2d 670 (Tex. 1990), requires us to affirm the district court's decision not to recognize the Mexican judgment. In *DeSantis*, the Court refused to apply Florida law to enforce a noncompetition agreement, even though the agreement contained an express choice of Florida law provision, and Florida had a substantial interest in the transaction. The Court concluded that "the law governing enforcement of noncompetition agreements is fundamental policy in Texas, and that to apply the law of another state to determine the enforceability of such an agreement in the circumstances of a case like this would be contrary to that policy." *Id.* at 681. Southwest Livestock argues similarly that the law governing usury constitutes a fundamental policy in Texas, and that to recognize the Mexican judgment would transgress that policy.

We find that, contrary to Southwest Livestock's argument, *DeSantis* does not support the district court's grant of summary judgment.

First, in *DeSantis* the Court refused to enforce an agreement violative of Texas public policy; it did not refuse to recognize a foreign judgment. Recognition and enforcement of a judgment involve separate and distinct inquiries. *See Guinness v. Ward,* 955 F.2d 875, 889 (4th Cir. 1992) (noting the difference between recognizing and enforcing a foreign judgment); *see also Restatement (Third) of Foreign Relations Law* § 481 cmt. b (1986) (distinguishing between the recognition and enforcement of judgments).

Second, unlike in *DeSantis*, where the plaintiff sought to use foreign law offensively to enforce the noncompetition agreement, in this case, Ramon seeks recognition of the Mexican judgment as an affirmative defense to Southwest Livestock's usury claim. Different considerations apply when a party seeks recognition of a foreign judgment for defensive purposes. As Justice Brandeis once stated:

> [T]he company is in a position different from that of a plaintiff who seeks to enforce a cause of action conferred by the laws of another state. The right which it claims should be given effect is set up by way of defense to an asserted liability; and to a defense different considerations apply. A state may, on occasion, decline to enforce a foreign cause of action. In so doing, it merely denies a remedy leaving unimpaired the plaintiff's substantive right, so that he is free to enforce it elsewhere. But to refuse to give effect to a substantive defense under the applicable law of another state, as under the circumstances here presented, subjects the defendant to irremediable liability. This may not be done.

Bradford Elec. Light Co. v. Clapper, 286 U.S. 145, 160 (1932); *cf. Resource Sav. Assoc. v. Neary*, 782 S.W.2d 897, 900 (Tex. App. — Dallas 1989, *writ denied*) (noting that because a party sought recognition of a foreign judgment for defensive purposes different considerations applied, but refusing to recognize the foreign judgment nonetheless).

Third, *DeSantis* involved a noncompetition agreement, and as we have explained elsewhere, "noncompetition agreements implicate an arguably stronger Texas public policy than usurious contracts" [citation omitted].

We find our decision in *Woods-Tucker Leasing Corp. v. Hutcheson-Ingram Development Co.*, 642 F.2d 744 (5th Cir. 1981), more helpful than *DeSantis*. In *Woods-Tucker*, we considered "whether a bankruptcy court sitting in Texas should honor a party contractual choice of Mississippi law in determining whether to apply the Texas or Mississippi usury statute to a transaction . . . between a Texas partnership and a Mississippi-headquartered corporate subsidiary of a Georgia corporation." In deciding to honor the parties' choice of Mississippi law, we noted that applying Mississippi law did not offend any Texas fundamental public policy:

> To be sure, it is the underlying policy of each state's usury laws to protect necessitous borrowers within its borders. Yet, as we have noted, we have found no Texas cases that have invalidated a party choice of law on grounds that the application of a foreign usury statute would violate public policy.

We also relied on the Supreme Court's decision in *Seeman v. Philadelphia Warehouse Co.*, 274 U.S. 403 (1927). In *Seeman*, the Supreme Court emphasized its policy of "upholding contractual obligations assumed in good faith." It stated that, although parties may not willfully evade otherwise applicable usury laws by "entering into [a] contract . . . [that] has no normal relation to the transaction," if the rate of interest "allowed by the laws of the place of performance is higher than that permitted at the place of the contract," the parties may contract for a higher rate of interest without incurring the penalties of usury. *Woods-Tucker*, and its reliance on *Seeman*, indicates that, although Texas has a strong public policy against usury, this policy is not inviolable.

We are especially reluctant to conclude that recognizing the Mexican judgment offends Texas public policy under the circumstances of this case. The purpose behind Texas usury laws is to protect unsophisticated borrowers from unscrupulous lenders. *See Woods-Tucker*, 642 F.2d at 753 n. 13 ("[I]t is the underlying policy of each state's usury laws to protect necessitous borrowers within its borders"). . . . This case, however, does not involve the victimizing of a naive consumer. Southwest Livestock is managed by sophisticated and knowledgeable people with experience in business. Additionally, the evidence in the record does not suggest that Ramon misled or deceived Southwest Livestock. Southwest Livestock and Ramon negotiated the loan in good faith and at arms length. In short, both parties fully appreciated the nature of the loan transaction and their respective contractual obligations.

Accordingly, in light of the plain language of the Texas Recognition Act, and after consideration of our decision in *Woods-Tucker* and the purpose behind

Texas public policy against usury, we hold that Texas's public policy does not justify withholding recognition of the Mexican judgment. The district court erred in deciding otherwise.

YAHOO!, INC. v. LA LIGUE CONTRE LE RACISME ET L'ANTISEMITISME
169 F. Supp. 2d 1181 (N.D. Cal. 2001)

Defendants La Ligue Contre Le Racisme Et l'Antisemitisme ("LICRA") and L'Union Des Etudiants Juifs De France, citizens of France, are non-profit organizations dedicated to eliminating anti-Semitism. Plaintiff Yahoo!, Inc. ("Yahoo!") is a corporation organized under the laws of Delaware with its principal place of business in Santa Clara, California. Yahoo! is an Internet service provider that operates various Internet websites and services that any computer user can access at the Uniform Resource Locator ("URL") www.yahoo.com. Yahoo! services ending in the suffix, ".com," without an associated country code as a prefix or extension (collectively, "Yahoo!'s U.S. Services") use the English language and target users who are residents of, utilize servers based in and operate under the laws of the United States. Yahoo! subsidiary corporations operate regional Yahoo! sites and services in twenty other nations, including, for example, Yahoo! France, Yahoo! India, and Yahoo! Spain. Each of these regional web sites contains the host nation's unique two-letter code as either a prefix or a suffix in its URL (e.g., Yahoo! France is found at www.yahoo.fr and Yahoo! Korea at www.yahoo.kr). Yahoo!'s regional sites use the local region's primary language, target the local citizenry, and operate under local laws.

Yahoo! provides a variety of means by which people from all over the world can communicate and interact with one another over the Internet. Examples include an Internet search engine, e-mail, an automated auction site, personal web page hostings, shopping services, chat rooms, and a listing of clubs that individuals can create or join. Any computer user with Internet access is able to post materials on many of these Yahoo! sites, which in turn are instantly accessible by anyone who logs on to Yahoo!'s Internet sites. As relevant here, Yahoo!'s auction site allows anyone to post an item for sale and solicit bids from any computer user from around the globe. Yahoo! records when a posting is made and after the requisite time period lapses, sends an e-mail notification to the highest bidder and seller with their respective contact information. Yahoo! is never a party to a transaction, and the buyer and seller are responsible for arranging privately for payment and shipment of goods. Yahoo! monitors the transaction through limited regulation by prohibiting particular items from being sold (such as stolen goods, body parts, prescription and illegal drugs, weapons, and goods violating U.S. copyright laws or the Iranian and Cuban embargos) and by providing a rating system through which buyers and sellers have their transactional behavior evaluated for the benefit of future consumers. Yahoo! informs auction sellers that they must comply with Yahoo!'s policies and may not offer items to buyers in jurisdictions in which the sale of such item violates the jurisdiction's applicable laws. Yahoo! does not actively regulate the content of each posting, and individuals are able to post, and have in fact posted, highly offensive matter, including Nazi-related propaganda and Third Reich memorabilia, on Yahoo!'s auction sites.

On or about April 5, 2000, LICRA sent a "cease and desist" letter to Yahoo!'s Santa Clara headquarters informing Yahoo! that the sale of Nazi and Third Reich related goods through its auction services violates French law. LICRA threatened to take legal action unless Yahoo! took steps to prevent such sales within eight days. Defendants subsequently utilized the United States Marshal's Office to serve Yahoo! with process in California and filed a civil complaint against Yahoo! in the Tribunal de Grande Instance de Paris (the "French Court"). The French Court found that approximately 1,000 Nazi and Third Reich related objects, including Adolf Hitler's *Mein Kampf, The Protocol of the Elders of Zion* (an infamous anti-Semitic report produced by the Czarist secret police in the early 1900's), and purported "evidence" that the gas chambers of the Holocaust did not exist were being offered for sale on Yahoo.com's auction site. Because any French citizen is able to access these materials on Yahoo.com directly or through a link on Yahoo.fr, the French Court concluded that the Yahoo.com auction site violates Section R645-1 of the French Criminal Code, which prohibits exhibition of Nazi propaganda and artifacts for sale.

On May 20, 2000, the French Court entered an order requiring Yahoo! to (1) eliminate French citizens' access to any material on the Yahoo.com auction site that offers for sale any Nazi objects, relics, insignia, emblems, and flags; (2) eliminate French citizens' access to web pages on Yahoo.com displaying text, extracts, or quotations from *Mein Kampf* and *Protocol of the Elders of Zion*; (3) post a warning to French citizens on Yahoo.fr that any search through Yahoo.com may lead to sites containing material prohibited by Section R645-1 of the French Criminal Code, and that such viewing of the prohibited material may result in legal action against the Internet user; (4) remove from all browser directories accessible in the French Republic index headings entitled "negationists" and from all hypertext links the equation of "negationists" under the heading "Holocaust." The order subjects Yahoo! to a penalty of 100,000 Euros for each day that it fails to comply with the order. The order concludes:

> We order the Company YAHOO! Inc. to take all necessary measures to dissuade and render impossible any access via Yahoo.com to the Nazi artifact auction service and to any other site or service that may be construed as constituting an apology for Nazism or a contesting of Nazi crimes.

High Court of Paris, May 22, 2000, Interim Court Order No. 00/05308, 00/05309. The French Court set a return date in July 2000 for Yahoo! to demonstrate its compliance with the order.

Yahoo! asked the French Court to reconsider the terms of the order, claiming that although it easily could post the required warning on Yahoo.fr, compliance with the order's requirements with respect to Yahoo.com was technologically impossible. The French Court sought expert opinion on the matter and on November 20, 2000, "reaffirmed" its order of May 22. The French Court ordered Yahoo! to comply with the May 22 order within three (3) months or face a penalty of 100,000 Francs (approximately U.S. $13,300) for each day of non-compliance. The French Court also provided that penalties assessed against Yahoo! Inc. may not be collected from Yahoo! France. Defendants again utilized the United States Marshal's Office to serve Yahoo! in California with the French Order. Yahoo! subsequently posted the required warning and prohibited postings in violation of Section R645-1 of the French Criminal Code from appearing on Yahoo.fr. Yahoo! also amended the auction policy of Yahoo.com to prohibit individuals from auctioning:

> Any item that promotes, glorifies, or is directly associated with groups or individuals known principally for hateful or violent positions or acts, such as Nazis or the Ku Klux Klan. Official government-issue stamps and coins are not prohibited under this policy. Expressive media, such as books and films, may be subject to more permissive standards as determined by Yahoo! in its sole discretion.

Yahoo Auction Guidelines (visited Oct. 23, 2001). Notwithstanding these actions, the Yahoo.com auction site still offers certain items for sale (such as stamps, coins, and a copy of Mein Kampf) which appear to violate the French Order. While Yahoo! has removed the *Protocol of the Elders of Zion* from its auction site, it has not prevented access to numerous other sites which reasonably "may be construed as constituting an apology for Nazism or a contesting of Nazi crimes."

Yahoo! claims that because it lacks the technology to block French citizens from accessing the Yahoo.com auction site to view materials which violate the French Order or from accessing other Nazi-based content of websites on Yahoo.com, it cannot comply with the French order without banning Nazi-related material from Yahoo.com altogether. Yahoo! contends that such a ban would infringe impermissibly upon its rights under the First Amendment to the United States Constitution. Accordingly, Yahoo! filed a complaint in this Court seeking a declaratory judgment that the French Court's orders are neither cognizable nor enforceable under the laws of the United States. . . .

OVERVIEW

As this Court and others have observed, the instant case presents novel and important issues arising from the global reach of the Internet. Indeed, the specific facts of this case implicate issues of policy, politics, and culture that are beyond the purview of one nation's judiciary. Thus, it is critical that the Court define at the outset what is and is not at stake in the present proceeding.

This case is not about the moral acceptability of promoting the symbols or propaganda of Nazism. Most would agree that such acts are profoundly offensive. By any reasonable standard of morality, the Nazis were responsible for one of the worst displays of inhumanity in recorded history. This Court is acutely mindful of the emotional pain reminders of the Nazi era cause to Holocaust survivors and deeply respectful of the motivations of the French Republic in enacting the underlying statutes and of the defendant organizations in seeking relief under those statutes. Vigilance is the key to preventing atrocities such as the Holocaust from occurring again. Nor is this case about the right of France or any other nation to determine its own law and social policies. A basic function of a sovereign state is to determine by law what forms of speech and conduct are acceptable within its borders. In this instance, as a nation whose citizens suffered the effects of Nazism in ways that are incomprehensible to most Americans, France clearly has the right to enact and enforce laws such as those relied upon by the French Court here.

What is at issue here is whether it is consistent with the Constitution and laws of the United States for another nation to regulate speech by a United States resident within the United States on the basis that such speech can be accessed by Internet users in that nation. In a world in which ideas and information transcend borders and the Internet in particular renders the physical distance between speaker and audience virtually meaningless, the implications of this question go far beyond the facts of this case. The modern world is home to widely varied cultures with radically divergent value systems. There is little doubt that Internet users in the United States routinely engage in speech that violates, for example, China's laws against religious expression, the laws of various nations against advocacy of gender equality or homosexuality, or even the United Kingdom's restrictions on freedom of the press. If the government or another party in one of these sovereign nations were to seek enforcement of such laws against Yahoo! or another U.S.-based Internet service provider, what principles should guide the court's analysis?

The Court has stated that it must and will decide this case in accordance with the Constitution and laws of the United States. It recognizes that in so doing, it necessarily adopts certain value judgments embedded in those enactments, including the fundamental judgment expressed in the First Amendment that it is preferable to permit the non-violent expression of offensive viewpoints rather than to impose viewpoint-based governmental regulation upon speech. The government and people of France have made a different judgment based upon their own experience. In undertaking its inquiry as to the proper application of the laws of the United States, the Court intends no disrespect for that judgment or for the experience that has informed it. . . .

LEGAL ISSUES

. . . The French order prohibits the sale or display of items based on their association with a particular political organization and bans the display of websites based on the authors' viewpoint with respect to the Holocaust and anti-Semitism. A United States court constitutionally could not make such an order. The First Amendment does not permit the government to engage in viewpoint-based regulation of speech absent a compelling governmental interest, such as averting a clear and present danger of imminent violence. In addition, the French Court's mandate that Yahoo! "take all necessary measures to dissuade and render impossible any access via Yahoo.com to the Nazi artifact auction service and to any other site or service that may be construed as constituting an apology for Nazism or a contesting of Nazi crimes" is far too general and imprecise to survive the strict scrutiny required by the First Amendment. The phrase, "and any other site or service that may be construed as an apology for Nazism or a contesting of Nazi crimes" fails to provide Yahoo! with a sufficiently definite warning as to what is proscribed.

Phrases such as "all necessary measures" and "render impossible" instruct Yahoo! to undertake efforts that will impermissibly chill and perhaps even censor protected speech. "The loss of First Amendment freedoms, for even minimal periods of time, unquestionably constitutes irreparable injury." *Elrod v. Burns*, 427 U.S. 347, 373 (1976) *citing New York Times Co. v. United States*, 403 U.S. 713 (1971).

Rather than argue directly that the French order somehow could be enforced in the United States in a manner consistent with the First Amendment, Defendants argue instead that at present, there is no real or immediate threat to Yahoo!'s First Amendment rights because the French order cannot be enforced at all until after the cumbersome process of petitioning the French court to fix a penalty has been completed. They analogize this case to *Int'l Soc. for Krishna Consciousness of California, Inc. v. City of Los Angeles,* 611 F. Supp. 315, 319–20 (C.D.Cal. 1984), in which the City of Los Angeles sought a declaratory judgment that a resolution limiting speech activities adopted by its Board of Airport Examiners was constitutional. The district court concluded that the action was unripe because the resolution could not take effect without ratification by the City Council, which had not yet occurred. The cases, however, are distinguishable. While Defendants present evidence that further procedural steps in France are required before an actual penalty can be fixed, there is no dispute that the French order is valid under French law and that the French Court may fix a penalty retroactive to the date of the order. The essence of the holding in the *Krishna Consciousness* case is that the subject resolution had no legal effect at all. . . .

Defendants next argue that this Court should abstain from deciding the instant case because Yahoo! simply is unhappy with the outcome of the French litigation and is trying to obtain a more favorable result here. Indeed, abstention is an appropriate remedy for international forum-shopping. In *Supermicro Computer, Inc. v. Digitechnic, S.A.*, 145 F. Supp.2d 1147 (N.D. Cal. 2001), a California manufacturer was sued by a corporate customer in France for selling a defective product. The California company sought a declaratory judgment in the United States that its products were not defective, that the French customer's misuse of the product caused the product to fail, and that if the California company was at fault, only limited legal remedies were available. The court concluded that the purpose of the action for declaratory relief was to avoid an unfavorable result in the French courts. It noted that the action was not filed until a year after the French proceedings began, that the French proceedings were still ongoing, and that the French defendants had no intent to sue in the United States. It concluded that the declaratory relief action clearly was "litigation involving the same parties and the same disputed transaction."

In the present case, the French court has determined that Yahoo!'s auction site and website hostings on Yahoo.com violate French law. Nothing in Yahoo!'s suit for declaratory relief in this Court appears to be an attempt to relitigate or disturb the French court's application of French law or its orders with respect to Yahoo!'s conduct in France. Rather, the purpose of the present action is to determine whether a United States court may enforce the French order without running afoul of the First Amendment. The actions involve distinct legal issues, and as this Court concluded in its jurisdictional order, a United States court is best situated to determine the application of the United States Constitution to the facts presented. No basis for abstention has been established.

Comity

No legal judgment has any effect, of its own force, beyond the limits of the sovereignty from which its authority is derived. However, the United States Constitution and implementing legislation require that full faith and credit be given to judgments of sister states, territories, and possessions of the United States. The extent to which the United States, or any state, honors the judicial decrees of foreign nations is a matter of choice, governed by "the comity of nations." *Hilton v. Guyot*, 159 U.S. 113, 163 (1895). Comity "is neither a matter of absolute obligation, on the one hand, nor of mere courtesy and good will, upon the other." *Hilton*, 159 U.S. at 163–64. United States courts generally recognize foreign judgments and decrees unless enforcement would be prejudicial or contrary to the country's interests. *Somportex Ltd. v. Philadelphia Chewing Gum Corp.*, 453 F.2d 435, 440 (3d Cir. 1971), *cert. denied*, 405 U.S. 1017 (1972); *Laker Airways v. Sabena Belgian World Airlines*, 731 F.2d 909, 931 (D.C.Cir. 1984) ("[T]he court is not required to give effect to foreign judicial proceedings grounded on policies which do violence to its own fundamental interests."); *Tahan v. Hodgson*, 662 F.2d 862, 864 (D.C.Cir. 1981) ("[R]equirements for enforcement of a foreign judgment expressed in *Hilton* are that . . . the original claim not violate American public policy . . . that it not be repugnant to fundamental notions of what is decent and just in the State where enforcement is sought.").

As discussed previously, the French order's content and viewpoint-based regulation of the web pages and auction site on Yahoo.com, while entitled to great deference as an articulation of French law, clearly would be inconsistent with the First Amendment if mandated by a court in the United States. What makes this case uniquely challenging is that the Internet in effect allows one to speak in more than one place at the same time. Although France has the sovereign right to regulate what speech is permissible in France, this Court may not enforce a foreign order that violates the protections of the United States Constitution by chilling protected speech that occurs simultaneously within our borders. . . .

The reason for limiting comity in this area is sound. "The protection to free speech and the press embodied in [the First] amendment would be seriously jeopardized by the entry of foreign judgments granted pursuant to standards deemed appropriate in [another country] but considered antithetical to the protections afforded the press by the U.S. Constitution." [*Bachchan v. India Abroad Publications, Inc.*, 585 N.Y.S.2d 661 (N.Y. Sup. Ct. 1992)] at 665. Absent a body of law that establishes international standards with respect to speech on the Internet and an appropriate treaty or legislation addressing enforcement of such standards to speech originating within the United States, the principle of comity is outweighed by the Court's obligation to uphold the First Amendment. . . .

If a hypothetical party were physically present in France, engaging in expression that was illegal in France but legal in the United States, it is unlikely that a United States court would or could question the applicability of French law to that party's conduct. However, an entirely different case would be presented if the French court ordered the party not to engage in the same expression in the United States on the basis that French citizens (along with anyone else in the world with the means to do so) later could read, hear, or see it. While the advent of the Internet effectively has removed the physical and temporal elements of this hypothetical, the legal analysis is the same.

In light of the Court's conclusion that enforcement of the French order by a United States court would be inconsistent with the First Amendment, the factual question of whether Yahoo! possesses the technology to comply with the order is immaterial. Even assuming for purposes of the present motion that Yahoo! does possess such technology, compliance still would involve an impermissible restriction on speech.

CONCLUSION

Yahoo! seeks a declaration from this Court that the First Amendment precludes enforcement within the United States of a French order intended to regulate the content of its speech over the Internet. Yahoo! has shown that the French order is valid under the laws of France, that it may be enforced with retroactive penalties, and that the ongoing possibility of its enforcement in the United States chills Yahoo!'s First Amendment rights. Yahoo! also has shown that an actual controversy exists and that the threat to its constitutional rights is real and immediate. Defendants have failed to show the existence of a genuine issue of material fact or to identify any such issue the existence of which could be shown through further discovery. Accordingly, the motion for summary judgment will be granted. . . .

Notes and Questions on the Public Policy Doctrine

1. *Proving the exception.* At some level of abstraction, every difference in substantive law reflects a difference in public policy, but the courts have said repeatedly that "mere" differences in the applicable legal standard are not enough to trigger the public policy exception. Consider for example the following formulation of the public policy defense from *McCord v. Jet Spray*, 874 F. Supp. 436 (D. Mass. 1994):

> The public policy exception operates only in those unusual cases where the foreign judgment is "repugnant to fundamental notions of what is decent and just in the State where enforcement is sought." [citations omitted]. Under the "classic formulation" of the public policy exception, a judgment is contrary to the public policy of the enforcing state where that judgment " 'tends clearly' to undermine the public interest, the public confidence in the administration of the law, or security for

individual rights of personal liberty or of private property" . . . (quoting *Somportex v. Philadelphia Chewing Gum*, 453 F.2d 435, 443 (3d Cir. 1971), *cert. denied*, 405 U.S. 1017 (1972)).

Advocates have a broad array of possible sources to try to prove the forum's commitment to a particular public policy, but what types of evidence persuaded the courts in *Southwest Livestock* and *Yahoo!*? Note that the *Yahoo!* court is not alone in concluding that First Amendment concerns make some foreign judgments contrary to public policy in U.S. courts. *See, e.g., Bachchan v. India Abroad Publications, Inc.*, 154 Misc.2d 228, 585 N.Y.S.2d 661 (N.Y. Sup. Ct. 1992) (declining to enforce a British libel judgment because of its chilling effect on First Amendment rights); *Telnikoff v. Matusevitch*, 347 Md. 561, 702 A.2d 230 (1997) (same). But just because "constitutional policies" are *sufficient* to trigger the exception doesn't imply that they're *necessary* before the exception can apply. What are the advantages and disadvantages of a rule requiring that a public policy be of constitutional origin or dimension before it can block the recognition or enforcement of a foreign judgment?

2. *Agreements versus judgments.* On what grounds (and to what end) does the *Southwest Livestock* court distinguish between declining to enforce an agreement and declining to enforce a judgment? What gives that distinction such weight in the decision? Is there any reason to think that agreements will be either more or less contrary to public policy than a formal judgment from another sovereign state?

3. *Interstate judgments distinguished from international judgments.* In *Thomas v. General Motors Corp.*, 522 U.S. 222 (1998), the Supreme Court disapproved any broad-gauged public policy defense to the recognition or enforcement of a judgment from a sister state of the Union:

> A court may be guided by the forum State's "public policy" in determining the *law* applicable to a controversy. *See Nevada v. Hall*, 440 U.S. 410, 421–424 (1979). But our decisions support no roving "public policy exception" to the full faith and credit due *judgments*. . . . In assuming the existence of a ubiquitous "public policy exception" permitting one State to resist recognition of another State's judgment, the District Court in [this case] misread our precedent. "The full faith and credit clause is one of the provisions incorporated into the Constitution by its framers for the purpose of transforming an aggregation of independent, sovereign States into a nation." *Sherrer v. Sherrer*, 334 U.S. 343, 355 (1948). We are "aware of [no] considerations of local policy or law which could rightly be deemed to impair the force and effect which the full faith and credit clause and the Act of Congress require to be given to [a money] judgment outside the state of its rendition." *Magnolia Petroleum Co. v. Hunt*, 320 U.S. 430, 438 (1943).

Id. at 233–34 (emphasis in original). Does or should *Thomas* constrain the public policy exception in international cases?

4. *Offensive versus defensive uses of judgments.* Should the preclusion effects of a foreign judgment vary according to whether it is sued upon as a ground for recovery or interposed as a defense? Justice Brandeis, in distinguishing between the offensive and the defensive use of a judgment drew the distinction in these terms (also quoted in *Southwest Livestock, supra*):

[T]he [defendant] company is in a position different from that of a plaintiff who seeks to enforce a cause of action conferred by the laws of another state. The right which it claims should be given effect is set up by way of defense to an asserted liability; and to a defense different considerations apply. A state may, on occasion, decline to enforce a foreign cause of action. In so doing, it merely denies a remedy leaving unimpaired the plaintiff's substantive right, so that he is free to enforce it elsewhere. But to refuse to give effect to a substantive defense under the applicable law of another state, as under the circumstances here presented, subjects the defendant to irremediable liability. This may not be done.

Bradford Elec. Light Co. v. Clapper, 286 U.S. 145, 160 (1932). Should the contours of the public policy exception vary depending on whether a plaintiff or a defendant is invoking it?

B. INNOCENTS ABROAD: U.S. JUDGMENTS IN FOREIGN COURTS AND THE DEVELOPMENT OF THE HAGUE JUDGMENTS CONVENTION

At a minimum, globalization has meant that litigants in U.S. courts must be conscious early in a case that the value of a U.S. judgment may depend upon its recognition or enforcement abroad. Liability may be established in a federal district court in Chicago, for example, but there can be no recovery without the assistance of a court in the country where the defendant's assets are. And defendants who prevail in a U.S. court will wish to erect that judgment as a summary defense to any effort by the plaintiffs to relitigate the same issue in a different forum. But the relatively accommodating regime of *Hilton v. Guyot* and the Uniform Foreign Money Judgments Recognition Act, *supra*, is not characteristic of other nations' approach to U.S. judgments, and the assumption has long been that U.S. litigants do not compete on a level playing field: "U.S. courts are quite liberal in their approach to the recognition and enforcement of judgments rendered in foreign jurisdictions, whereas the reverse is not true."[1]

It is impossible here to canvass transnational *res judicata* practices around the world. (Indeed, the very multiplicity of approaches may prove to be the most significant problem facing a litigant eager to enforce a U.S. judgment abroad.) But it is possible to define and illustrate the *types* of obstacles that U.S. judgments encounter abroad and to understand the virtue and the vice of a treaty-based solution to the recurring problems of interjurisdictional recognition:

1. *Extraterritorial application of U.S. law*. Foreign courts may resist the recognition or enforcement of a U.S. judgment that is perceived to rest on an illegitimate extraterritorial application of U.S. law. For example, "[t]he

---

[1] Matthew H. Adler, *If We Build It, Will They Come? — The Need for a Multilateral Convention on the Recognition and Enforcement of Civil Monetary Judgments*, 26 LAW & POL'Y INT'L BUS. 79, 94 (1994).

United Kingdom has provided, by legislation, that U.S. antitrust judgments are not enforceable in British courts, and both Australia and Canada have given their Attorneys General authority to declare such judgments unenforceable or to reduce the [antitrust damage awards] that will be enforced."[2] Even in the absence of such blocking legislation in the foreign forum, the policy framework may differ so fundamentally that a U.S. judgment grounded in the offensive law will not be enforced, though "mere differences" in substantive law tend not to trigger the same hostility.

2. *Aggressive interpretations of personal jurisdiction.* Foreign courts will decline to enforce a U.S. judgment that rests on objectionable exercises of personal jurisdiction, such as "tag" or transient jurisdiction based on the defendant's temporary presence in the forum, *see, e.g., Burnham v. Superior Court*, 495 U.S. 604 (1990), minimal or incidental effects within the state of extraterritorial conduct outside of it, *see, e.g., United States v. Aluminum Co. of America (Alcoa)*, 148 F.2d 416 (2d Cir. 1945), or most controversially, on the activities within the forum of an alleged "co-conspirator," *see, e.g., United Phosphorus Ltd. v. Angus Chem. Co.*, 43 F. Supp. 2d 904 (N.D. Ill. 1999).

3. *Per se categories of unenforceable judgments.* Traditionally at least, the courts of one nation would not recognize or enforce foreign judgments grounded in the "public law" of another, including judgments for the collection of taxes, fines, and penalties, and U.S. judgments that could be characterized as such were typically unenforceable abroad. Similarly, foreign courts tended not to recognize or enforce awards that were provisional, modifiable, or otherwise non-final (like many family law judgments) or which granted a form of relief that violated local public policy or was generally unavailable in the foreign legal system.

4. *Improper service and other procedural failings.* Foreign courts have occasionally declined to enforce a U.S. judgment if the defendant was not served in a way that the enforcing court considers proper. Class actions, summary judgments, and default judgments, though proper under the Federal Rules of Civil Procedure and equivalent state rules, have also occasionally encountered difficulty when enforcement is sought in foreign courts, typically on the ground that the defendant did not receive a full trial on the issue of his or her individual liability.

5. *Excessive damage awards.* The American jury is neither mirrored nor conspicuously respected in foreign court systems around the world. In part, that reflects the tendency of the American system to rely on private litigation and juries to constrain the conduct of defendants through the award of compensatory and punitive damages, in contrast to other legal cultures which rely predominantly on administrative law and institutions to control hazardous behaviors.

In 1992, in an effort to overcome these obstacles and improve the reception of U.S. judgments abroad, the United States proposed that the Hague Conference on Private International Law — which had developed conventions

---

[2] William S. Dodge, *Antitrust and the Draft Hague Judgments Convention*, 32 LAW & POL'Y INT'L BUS. 363 (2001).

on international judicial assistance, *supra*, Chapter 5 — develop the first global treaty addressing both the bases for personal jurisdiction and the recognition and enforcement of foreign judgments.[1] But international law-making of this sort, "[l]ike reform of judicial administration in the United States, . . . is 'no sport for the short-winded.' "[2] After nearly a decade of negotiations, the proposed Hague Judgments Convention, reproduced in the Documents Supplement, continues to be highly controversial, and its eventual promulgation by the Hague Conference — let alone its adoption by the United States and other governments — remains highly problematic.

Beth Van Schaack, *In Defense of Civil Redress:*
The Domestic Enforcement of Human Rights Norms in the
Context of the Proposed Hague Judgments Convention
42 HARV. INT'L L. J. 141, 171–78 (2001) [*]

The proposed Hague Convention on Jurisdiction and the Enforcement of Civil Judgments ("the Hague Convention"), if it enters into force, will create the foundation for an extensive enforcement regime that will enable plaintiffs litigating in Contracting States to seek enforcement of their civil judgments in any Contracting State in which the defendant holds assets. . . .

A. Background to the Hague Convention Project

There is no global convention in force governing the recognition and enforcement of foreign judgments. In the 1960s, the Hague Conference on Private International Law drafted a convention governing recognition and enforcement of foreign judgments, but it did not directly govern the exercise

---

[1] Although no universal treaty exists to resolve conflicts in the rules governing the recognition and enforcement of foreign court judgments, regional treaties in Europe and the Americas have settled interjurisdictional practices there, typically on the basis of reciprocity. The recognition of judgments among members of the European Communities for example has been regulated since 1975 by the Brussels Convention on Jurisdiction and the Enforcement of Judgments in Civil and Commercial Matters, Sept. 27, 1968, 1972 O.J. (L 299) 32, *reprinted in* 8 I.L.M. 229 (1969), usefully conceived as the Full Faith and Credit Clause of the European common market. Bartlett, *Full Faith and Credit Comes to the Common Market*, 24 INT'L & COMP. L. Q. 44 (1975). The Lugano Convention, Sept. 16, 1988, 1988 O.J. (L 319) 9, *reprinted in* 28 I.L.M. 620 (1989), extended the effects of the Brussels Convention to members of the European Free Trade Association, not all of whom were members of the European Union. The Brussels Convention is reproduced in the Documents Supplement. A similar treaty has been adopted by the Organization of American States, the Inter-American Convention on Extraterritorial Validity of Foreign Judgments and Arbitral Awards, 1439 U.N.T.S. 8, *reprinted in* 18 I.L.M. 1224, which is also reproduced in the Documents Supplement. The United States is not a party to either of these regional treaties, and no treaty to which the United States is a party — with the exception of certain tax treaties and certain friendship, commerce and navigation treaties as interpreted — requires the recognition of foreign judgments.

[2] Stephen B. Burbank, *Jurisdictional Equilibration, the Proposed Hague Convention and Progress in National Law*, 49 AM. J. COMP. L. 203 (2001) (*quoting* ARTHUR T. VANDERBILT, ed., MINIMUM STANDARDS OF JUDICIAL ADMINISTRATION xix (1949)).

[*] ©2001 Harvard Int'l L. Journal. [Editor's note: some footnotes omitted or edited and renumbered.]

of jurisdiction.[1] There are very few signatories, and events within the European Community eventually superseded this effort.

The Brussels Convention, as the Convention on Jurisdiction and the Enforcement of Judgments in Civil Matters[2] is commonly known, was adopted by delegations from the six original members of the European Economic Community.[3] Unlike the Convention on the Recognition and Enforcement of Foreign Judgments in Civil and Commercial Matters ("the Recognition Convention"), the Brussels Convention is a double convention with respect to domiciliaries of Contracting States in that it governs both the exercise of jurisdiction and the enforcement of judgments.[4]

In keeping with continental notions of personal jurisdiction based on an objective relationship between the defendant and the forum, the Brussels Convention adopts the general rule that the defendant may be sued in the jurisdiction in which he or she is domiciled or habitually resident, regardless of the defendant's nationality.[5] Beyond this general rule, the Brussels Convention adopts a series of claim-specific rules. For example, tort claims

---

[1] *See* Convention on the Recognition and Enforcement of Foreign Judgments in Civil and Commercial Matters, Feb. 1, 1971, 1144 U.N.T.S. 249 [hereinafter Recognition Convention]. The United States is not a party to this or any other bilateral or multilateral enforcement treaty. An optional Supplementary Protocol to the 1971 Convention dealt with jurisdiction and obliged member states to eschew recourse to certain bases of jurisdiction. *See* Convention on the Recognition and Enforcement of Foreign Judgments in Civil and Commercial Matters, Feb. 1, 1971, Supplementary Protocol, 1144 U.N.T.S. 249, 271–72. However, the Supplementary Protocol's implementation was prohibitively cumbersome, as it required the execution of separate bilateral agreements between and among the states desiring to avail themselves of its provisions.

[2] The negotiation process began in 1959, and the Brussels Convention was eventually promulgated in 1968. Convention on Jurisdiction and the Enforcement of Judgments in Civil and Commercial Matters, Sept. 27, 1968, 1978 O.J. (L 304) 78, *reprinted in* 8 I.L.M. 229 (1969) [hereinafter Brussels Convention]. The companion Lugano Convention extends the provisions of the Brussels Convention to the six member states of the European Free Trade Association (Austria, Finland, Iceland, Norway, Sweden, and Switzerland) and is open to new members; however, new parties must negotiate accession treaties with all other members. European Communities-European Free Trade Association, Convention on Jurisdiction and Enforcement of Judgments in Civil and Commercial Matters, Sept. 16, 1988, 1988 O.J. (L 319) 9, *reprinted in* 28 I.L.M. 620 (1989). Other European states, including Spain and Portugal, later acceded to the Brussels Convention.

[3] The six original members of the European Economic Community were France, Germany, Italy, Belgium, the Netherlands, and Luxembourg.

[4] *See* Arthur T. von Mehren, *Enforcing Judgments Abroad: Reflections on the Design of Recognition Conventions*, 24 BROOK. J. INT'L L. 17, 17–18 (1998). A double convention governs both jurisdiction to adjudicate and recognition of foreign judgments. *Id.* There are two variations of double conventions. In a pure double convention, all jurisdictional bases that a state is not obliged by the convention to offer are prohibited. *Id.* at 19. In contrast, in a mixed convention, there are three groups of jurisdictional bases: first, required bases which the state must allow if the litigation falls within the scope of the convention; second, permitted bases that the state may allow, but judgments rendered on such a basis are not entitled to automatic enforcement under the convention; and third, prohibited bases that a state may not allow in litigation that is within the scope of the convention. *Id.*

[5] According to Article 2, "[s]ubject to the provisions of this Convention, persons domiciled in a Contracting State shall, whatever their nationality, be sued in the courts of that State." Brussels Convention, *supra*, art. 2. Article 52 leaves the definition of "domicile" to the state's local law. With respect to legal persons, "domicile" is the seat of the corporation as defined by the private international law of the forum state according to Article 53.

may be brought in the jurisdiction in which the harmful event occurred.[6] Thus, the plaintiff suing a natural person in tort may exercise personal jurisdiction according to two provisions of the Brussels Convention: the general rule of domicile or the claim-specific rule of locus of harm.

The Brussels Convention has the effect of dividing jurisdiction into two lists: a required (white) list and a prohibited (black) list with respect to domiciliaries of Contracting States.[7] All Contracting Parties must make available the bases of jurisdiction enumerated on the required list to all parties who are litigating matters within the scope of the Brussels Convention. Defendants who are domiciliaries of Contracting States may not be sued except under bases enumerated under the Brussels Convention, even if those bases exist under national law. Therefore, Contracting States may not allow plaintiffs who are litigating matters within the scope of the Brussels Convention against domiciliaries of another Contracting State to utilize these prohibited bases of jurisdiction, even though they are otherwise permitted under national law. Article 3 of the Brussels Convention sets forth an exemplary, not exhaustive, list of prohibited bases, and identifies provisions in the national legal systems of Contracting States that constitute prohibited bases.[8] For example, Article 3(2) specifically prohibits the exercise of transient jurisdiction as it is practiced in Ireland and the United Kingdom.[9]

The Brussels Convention is the first multilateral convention to regulate both jurisdiction and enforcement. Under this system, the enforcing court need not scrutinize the court of origin's jurisdictional basis, since the Brussels Convention itself ensures that jurisdiction was proper before the court of origin. Any judgment rendered by a Contracting State according to the Brussels Convention's jurisdictional rules is to be automatically enforced by the courts of other Contracting States with no reference to the merits of the case.[10]

The Brussels Convention does not regulate the exercise of jurisdiction over domiciliaries of non-Contracting States. Rather, Article 4(1) of the Brussels Convention preserves for Contracting States the use of exorbitant grounds of

---

[6] According to this provision, a person domiciled in a Contracting State may be sued "in matters relating to tort, delict or quasi-delict, in the courts for the place where the harmful event occurred." *Id.*, art. 5(3). The European Court of Justice has defined "tort" by what it is not. *See* Case 189/87, *Kalfelis v. Schroder*, 1988 E.C.R. 5565, 5585 ("[T]he concept of 'matters relating to tort, delict and quasi-delict' covers all actions which seek to establish the liability of a defendant and which are not related to a 'contract' within the meaning of Article 5(1).").

[7] Thus, the Brussels Convention is a pure double convention with respect to domiciliaries of Contracting States.

[8] "Exorbitant jurisdiction can be defined as those assertions of jurisdiction that are not generally recognized by accepted principles of international law." John Fitzpatrick, *The Lugano Convention and Western European Integration: A Comparative Analysis of Jurisdiction and Judgments in Europe and the United States*, 8 CONN. J. INT'L L. 695, 703 n.34 (1993).

[9] *See* Brussels Convention, *supra*, art. 3(2). Similarly, the Brussels Convention forbids the exercise of jurisdiction based solely on the nationality of the plaintiff as allowed under French law, CODE CIVIL [C.CIV.] art. 14, and on the basis of the defendant's ownership of property within the forum as allowed under German law, ZIVILPROZESSORDNUNG [ZPO] [civil procedure statute] § 23.

[10] *See* Brussels Convention, *supra*, art. 26 ("A judgment given in a Contracting State shall be recognized in other Contracting States without any special procedure being required."); *id.* art. 29 ("Under no circumstances may a foreign judgment be reviewed as to its substance.").

jurisdiction against domiciliaries of non-Contracting States. At the same time, such judgments must be recognized and enforced by other Contracting States pursuant to Article 26. In other words, non-domiciliary defendants may be sued under any jurisdictional basis and may have any resultant judgment automatically enforced against them, but they do not benefit from the Brussels Convention's jurisdictional regime or defenses to enforcement as provided in Article 27. Thus, the Brussels Convention does not concern itself with non-domiciliary defendants until the time of enforcement. This aspect of the Brussels Convention has been the subject of indignant criticism.[11]

The Convention purports to provide a remedy for this asymmetry at Article 59, which invites non-Contracting States to ratify bilateral conventions on the recognition and enforcement of judgments with Contracting States. In these bilateral agreements, Contracting States pledge not to enforce judgments rendered on the basis of a jurisdictional rule on the Brussels Convention's prohibited list. This remedy has proven illusory. For example, the United States attempted to negotiate a bilateral enforcement treaty with the United Kingdom, after the latter acceded to the Brussels Convention, in order to prevent judgments rendered pursuant to Article 4 against U.S. parties initiated in member states from being recognized and enforced in the United Kingdom. The treaty negotiations failed in part due to the influence of British insurance companies, who were fearful of U.S. jury verdicts, punitive damage awards (particularly in products liability cases), and antitrust remedies.

As a result of the widespread implementation of the Brussels Convention regime, judgments against domiciliaries of Contracting States are freely enforced throughout Europe. In contrast, it is more difficult for litigants outside the Brussels Convention ambit to enforce judgments abroad.[12] For example, U.S. judgments may be difficult to enforce overseas, in part due to the prevalence (or perception of the prevalence) of large jury awards containing punitive or multiple damages. In contrast, foreign judgments are generally liberally enforced in the United States. Although there is no uniform enforcement regime in place within the United States due to congressional inaction, judgments issuing from foreign tribunals are freely recognized and enforced either on principles of common law or pursuant to the Uniform Foreign Money Judgments Recognition Act, which has been adopted by approximately half of the states.

The operation of the Brussels Convention has been quite successful in Europe. The system is predictable and reliable, and the enforcement of foreign judgments occurs by operation of law without a de novo review of the judgment and thus at only minimal judicial cost. Over time, many states lobbied for the creation of a more inclusive and worldwide enforcement regime to replace the current patchwork approach, and the Hague Convention project was born.

---

[11] *See, e.g.*, Fitzpatrick, *supra*, at 703 n.36, 724 (describing the system as "blatantly discriminatory" with a "significant negative impact on foreign parties doing business in the EC," and noting that the Convention has the effect of reinforcing "judgments based on exorbitant assertions of jurisdiction by guaranteeing their recognition and enforcement throughout Western Europe").

[12] *See* Linda J. Silberman & Andreas F. Lowenfeld, *A Different Challenge for the ALI: Herein of Foreign Country Judgments, an International Treaty, and an American Statute*, 75 IND. L.J. 635, 638–39 (2000).

B. The Launching of the Hague Convention

The United States initiated the current Hague Convention project in May 1992 with a proposal to the Hague Conference on Private International Law.[13] One commentator has noted the unequal negotiating positions of the United States vis-a-vis the members of the Brussels Convention, notwithstanding U.S. economic and diplomatic strength. On the one hand, the United States stands to gain significantly from the proposed Hague Convention. First, parties resident in the United States would gain protection from assertions of jurisdiction based on Europe's exorbitant bases of jurisdiction. Second, parties litigating in the United States would gain greater predictability in enforcement, because they would have access to a more uniform enforcement regime.

In contrast, parties litigating in Europe already benefit from a successful enforcement regime among themselves. Given the already liberal enforcement record for foreign judgments within the United States, the new Hague Convention can only offer a marginal increase in assurance that foreign judgments will be enforced here. Thus, the main bargaining chip for the United States is the relinquishment of forms of U.S. jurisdiction deemed exorbitant from a continental perspective. These are principally transient (or tag) jurisdiction and general doing-business jurisdiction,[14] both of which have received constitutional blessing from U.S. courts and are particularly important for civil human rights litigation.[15]

---

[13] *See* Ronald A. Brand, *Tort Jurisdiction in a Multilateral Convention: The Lessons of the Due Process Clause and the Brussels Convention*, 24 BROOK. J. INT'L L. 125, 126 n.1 (1998). The formal negotiations began in June 1997. *Id.* In November 1998, the drafting committee produced a preliminary consolidated text that was on the table for negotiations in June 1999. *See* SPECIAL COMM'N ON INT'L JURISDICTION AND THE EFFECTS OF FOREIGN JUDGMENTS IN CIV. AND COM. MATTERS, HAGUE CONF. ON PRIVATE INT'L LAW, PROPOSAL BY THE DRAFTING COMMITTEE (Working Document No. 144E, Nov. 20, 1998) [hereinafter Working Document No. 144E]. Because a number of key provisions remained bracketed after the June 1999 proceedings, another negotiation session was added in October 1999 in preparation for the final diplomatic conference that was originally to be held in October 2000. The October 1999 session produced a substantial draft text, but a number of issues remained outstanding for the final Diplomatic Session, including the reach of exclusive jurisdiction, the treatment of default judgments, e-commerce, intellectual property, reporting requirements, relations with other conventions, and the content of a human rights exception. On February 22, 2000, the U.S. delegation wrote to the Secretary General of the Hague Conference on Private International Law and argued that there was not enough common ground in the preliminary text to warrant the convening of a full Diplomatic Conference in October 2000.

[14] *See* Eric B. Fastiff, *The Proposed Hague Convention on the Recognition and Enforcement of Civil and Commercial Judgments: A Solution to Butch Reynolds's Jurisdiction and Enforcement Problems,* 28 CORNELL INT'L L.J. 469, 485 (1995) (noting that relinquishing tag jurisdiction "is the carrot which is enticing the Europeans (and the Japanese and Canadians) to join the negotiations").

[15] Despite initial support from the United States, observers increasingly question whether the United States will sign and ratify the Hague Convention once it is opened for signature. [According to] Jeffrey Kovar, Assistant Legal Advisor for Private International Law, U.S. Department of State, . . . "[a]s a general matter . . . the U.S. delegation believes the October 1999 draft is not an effective vehicle for achieving a convention to which the United States can become a party." Kovar went on to note that "[t]he October 1999 draft presents a deal on jurisdiction that is heavily weighted against U.S. jurisdictional practices. The Bar would reject it in this country." . . .

Working Document 144E, an early consolidated draft text prepared by the drafting committee for the June 1999 negotiations,[16] was loosely based on the Brussels Convention model and envisioned a pure double convention in which some bases of jurisdiction were required and all bases not required were prohibited. Working Document 144E, like the Brussels Convention, included a basic rule governing the exercise of general jurisdiction. Under this rule, a natural person could be sued where the person was habitually resident or domiciled, and legal persons could be sued in their place of incorporation or central management, or in their place of principal activity if the other locations could not be determined.

Working Document 144E also recognized claim-specific bases for jurisdiction over contract and tort claims. Echoing the general rule of the Brussels Convention, Article 10 provided that,

> [t]he plaintiff may commence an action based on a claim in tort or delict in the courts of the Contracting State — (a) in which the act or omission of the defendant that caused the injury occurred, or (b) in which the injury arose, provided that the defendant could reasonably foresee that the activity giving rise to the claim could result in such injury in that State . . . .

Finally, Working Document 144E provided for jurisdiction over a defendant legal entity in the state in which a branch, agency, or other establishment of the defendant was situated or had acted on behalf of the defendant as long as the suit arose out of that activity.

Article 20 of Working Document 144E outlined eight prohibited bases of jurisdiction. Most importantly for litigation seeking to enforce human rights norms, this prohibited list included jurisdiction premised on "(e) the carrying on of commercial or other activities by the defendant within the territory of the State; [and] (f) the service of a writ upon the defendant within the territory of the State."[17] The original Hague Convention draft was a pure double convention in that the prohibited list was exemplary, rather than exhaustive, and every basis of jurisdiction not required was prohibited.

Like the Brussels Convention, the enforcement provisions of Working Document 144E were quite liberal. As a general rule, it provided that "[a] decision rendered in a Contracting State shall be recognised in another Contracting State if it is final in the State of origin." At the same time, a court was to decline recognition and enforcement if "the decision was rendered by a court not having jurisdiction under this Convention." The enforcing court was not to undertake a review on the merits of the decision rendered by the court of origin. From the start of the negotiations, the United States advocated that the Hague Convention be a mixed, rather than a pure double, convention. A mixed convention envisions three categories of jurisdictional bases: a mandatory list, a prohibited list, and a permissive ("gray") list. The permissive

---

[16] This text holds no official status. It was promulgated by the drafting committee to focus the negotiations.

[17] Article 20 also prohibited the exercise of general jurisdiction within a particular forum based on the presence of property in that forum, the nationality of either the plaintiff or defendant, the domicile of the plaintiff, a unilateral specification of the forum by the plaintiff, and an assertion of specific jurisdiction premised on transient jurisdiction or commercial activity.

list would comprise bases of jurisdiction existing in national law that were neither mandatory nor prohibited. Litigants would be allowed to utilize such bases against residents of Contracting States, but the enforcement of the resultant judgment by the courts of other Contracting States would be discretionary.

The United States argued that a mixed convention was necessary to avoid preempting idiosyncratic jurisdictional rules and freezing permitted bases of jurisdiction despite developments in business methods, technology, and communications. In a proposal submitted to the Special Commission on International Jurisdiction and the Effects of Foreign Judgments in Civil and Commercial Matters ("the Special Commission") during the June 1999 proceedings, the United States reproduced Article 20 with its list of prohibited bases of jurisdiction, but included at Article 21 a residual provision to the effect that "[t]his Convention does not affect the status under the law of each Contracting Party of rules of jurisdiction or competence neither required nor prohibited by this Convention." This proposal ensured that the list of prohibited bases of jurisdiction was exhaustive, so that states could utilize any basis of jurisdiction not expressly prohibited; the enforcement of judgments on bases of jurisdiction not contained in the mandatory list, however, would not be guaranteed. This position was ultimately adopted by the drafters.

STATEMENT OF JEFFREY D. KOVAR,
Assistant Legal Adviser for Private International Law
U.S. Department of State, before the Subcommittee on
Courts and Intellectual Property, Committee on the Judiciary,
U.S. House of Representatives
(June 29, 2000)

The Department is leading U.S. efforts at the Hague Conference on Private International Law to negotiate a Convention on Jurisdiction and the Recognition and Enforcement of Foreign Civil Judgments. The Hague project — which was undertaken at the initiative of the United States — would create harmonized rules of jurisdiction in international civil cases as well as common rules for enforcing abroad the resulting judgments. A successful convention would level the international playing field for American litigants and fill a major gap in the legal infrastructure of the global marketplace.

Although international commerce, trade, and communications are accelerating at a breathtaking pace, and the growth of the Internet promises to make boundaries less and less relevant for commerce, the judicial settlement of transnational disputes remains largely confined to national territories. There is no effective regime for coordinating and enforcing the work of national courts in resolving transnational legal disputes. If this widening gap between the global marketplace and the isolated national court systems is not addressed, it could well slow progress and inhibit growth in trade.

The Hague Convention negotiations, if successfully concluded, hold out the promise of addressing this important need. In this testimony, we will provide some history and background to the Hague negotiations, including how the Convention would work, describe some of the major obstacles facing our delegation, explain how we are addressing the critical issues of electronic commerce and intellectual property, and give some sense of what we think the road ahead looks like.

BACKGROUND

The recognition and enforcement of judgments from one jurisdiction to another has long been understood as a fundamental requirement for fully integrated markets. Thus, the framers of the U.S. Constitution included the Full Faith and Credit Clause to ensure that judgments from one state would be enforceable in every other. In the same way, as part of their movement toward a unified market several European countries concluded a convention in 1968 to provide recognition and enforcement of each other's judgments. This convention, called the Brussels Convention, became a required ticket of admission to the Common Market and then the European Union. . . .

For many countries, the enforcement of foreign judgments is not a matter of general law but is addressed through treaties. The United States is not a party to any convention or bilateral agreement on the recognition and enforcement of foreign judgments. We made an effort to conclude a treaty with the United Kingdom in the 1970s, but it was ultimately blocked by the U.K. insurance industry, which was nervous about the enforcement of U.S. tort judgments against them in U.K. courts. By contrast with the practice of most countries, however, the United States has led the way in enforcing foreign country judgments on the basis of comity. The Supreme Court embraced this approach over 100 years ago in the case of *Hilton v. Guyot*, 159 U.S. 113 (1895). Judgments from countries with reliable legal systems are now predictably enforceable in federal and state courts in the United States under the common law or under the Uniform Foreign Money Judgments Act. Although the Supreme Court in *Hilton* suggested that it was appropriate also to require a showing of reciprocity in the country where the judgment was rendered, this requirement is no longer a part of most state law.

Thus, while U.S. courts are perceived as the most open in the world to the recognition and enforcement of foreign civil judgments in the absence of a treaty obligation to do so, the ability of U.S. judgment holders to enforce their judgments abroad is much more problematic. Even in those countries that will, in principle, enforce foreign judgments in the absence of a treaty, the reach of U.S. long-arm jurisdiction, what they perceive to be "excessive" jury awards, and punitive damages are sometimes considered reasons not to enforce U.S. judgments. U.S. litigants deserve the same opportunity to have their judgments enforced abroad as that enjoyed by foreign litigants in the United States.

THE NEGOTIATIONS

The successful negotiation at the Hague Conference of a convention on jurisdiction and the recognition and enforcement of foreign civil judgments would be a huge step toward an international regime for enforcing foreign court judgments. The negotiations, which have been underway since 1996, involve more than 45 countries from around the world, including virtually all major U.S. trading partners. The Hague Conference is well known here for producing the Conventions on Service of Process and the Taking of Evidence Abroad, Abolishing the Requirement of Legalization, and International Child Abduction to which we are a party. Moreover, the Hague Intercountry Adoption Convention is currently being considered by the House and Senate for advice and consent to ratification and implementing legislation, and has solid support from the adoption community. The Hague Conference has traditionally been a professional and non-political forum of experts in the area of conflict of laws.

If successful, the Hague Jurisdiction and Judgments Convention would establish a regime governing jurisdiction to sue defendants from party states in tort and contract, and would improve predictability in the enforcement of the resulting judgments. This requirement that the Convention create uniform rules of jurisdiction comes as a surprise to many Americans. It reflects both the approach of the Brussels Convention and a deep-seated feeling among many other delegations that they do not wish to enforce U.S. judgments unless we make our jurisdiction practices consistent with their view of what constitutes appropriate international rules. Since litigants from most developed countries have no substantial difficulties enforcing judgments in the United States, their governments believe they have substantial negotiating leverage over us. This would perhaps not be the case if our states included reciprocity requirements in their law.

Agreeing on a rigid set of jurisdictional rules poses special difficulties for the United States. Because the Due Process Clause puts limits on the extension of jurisdiction over defendants without a substantial link to the forum, the United States is unable to accept certain grounds of jurisdiction as they are applied in Europe under the Brussels and Lugano Conventions. For example, we cannot, consistent with the Constitution, accept tort jurisdiction based solely on the place of the injury, or contract jurisdiction based solely on place of performance stated in the contract.

At the same time, civil law attorneys (and their clients) are profoundly uncomfortable with jurisdiction based on doing business or minimum contacts, which they find vague and unpredictable. They feel strongly that certain aspects of U.S. jurisdictional practice must be restricted under the Convention. Although this divide has been partially bridged by agreement to permit some grounds of jurisdiction under national law to continue outside the Convention, critical choices and hard negotiations remain. If the Convention is to regulate jurisdiction in international litigation it must bridge vast differences in approach toward general and specialized jurisdiction among the various countries involved. It must also provide strong and clear benefits to outweigh the inevitable concerns about giving up some current litigation options in international cases.

Apart from jurisdiction, agreement must also be reached on how to handle a huge array of issues raised by this sweeping and ambitious project. Some of the issues include: concurrent filings in the courts of more than one state; *forum non conveniens*; provisional and protective measures; punitive, non-compensatory and "excessive" damages; a lack of fairness or impartiality in the judgment court; and scope of application to government litigation.

The fifth negotiating session in October 1999 produced a preliminary draft text, and the original schedule called for a final negotiating session this coming fall. However, after extensive consultations with industry and consumer groups, the private bar, and with government litigators, the Department of State concluded that this text is not close to being ratifiable in the United States and cannot be an effective vehicle for final negotiations. Acutely aware of the need for more time, in May [2000] we successfully requested the Hague Conference to extend the negotiations for another year or more, and to split the final session into two parts. We also secured a commitment from other delegations to make a renewed effort to seek real compromises on these difficult issues by meeting informally before the next session in June 2001 to try to achieve new drafts. Frankly, if other delegations do not begin to show more flexibility on many key provisions, we will be unable to achieve a convention that could attract sufficient support in the United States.

ELECTRONIC COMMERCE AND INTELLECTUAL PROPERTY ISSUES

When the Hague Convention negotiations were first proposed by the United States in 1992, and when they began four years later, no one predicted the immensely difficult issues that would suddenly arise from the explosion of electronic commerce. . . . Recognizing that revising rules of jurisdiction applicable to the Internet raised issues that had not yet been explored, the Hague Conference held a roundtable workshop in Geneva in September 1999, then called a special experts meeting in Ottawa last February devoted only to electronic commerce issues raised by the draft Convention. Because the issues relate to commercial electronic transactions, the Department of State specifically sought the assistance of the Department of Commerce with this phase of the discussions. The Ottawa session provided an opportunity for interested business and consumer groups to engage delegations and begin to educate them about the special litigation problems that arise from commerce on the Internet. . . .

Similarly, the special litigation issues raised by international patent, trademark, and copyright litigation, including through the Internet, call for experts to consider carefully the potential effects of the current draft on international litigation involving intellectual property (IP) rights. Under the Brussels Convention, and reflected in the current draft of the Convention, jurisdiction over certain types of claims involving registered intellectual property rights is limited to the country of registration. This requirement has led to major clashes of interpretation among Brussels Convention parties, and those concerns have in turn been raised over the Hague draft. Recognizing these difficulties, the Hague Conference has asked the World Intellectual Property Organization (WIPO) to convene a meeting of experts to address the problems of jurisdiction in international litigation involving IP rights. The Department of Commerce, especially the Patent and Trademark Office, is providing assistance with this aspect of the discussions.

There is no consensus on the electronic commerce and intellectual property issues in the United States or elsewhere, and the Department believes we must take an extremely careful and deliberate approach in the Hague negotiations. We do not have firm views on the proper outcome of these provisions, and are seeking to consult as widely as possible and ensure that all the various interests are heard. We hope very much that effective solutions will emerge that will enable the Convention to move forward to a successful conclusion.

THE ROAD AHEAD

A carefully conceived and properly balanced Hague Convention would represent a tremendous opportunity for many American litigants, and we are trying vigorously to reach the right balance of provisions to enable us to achieve a convention to which the United States could become a party. However, given the strong litigation orientation of our society and the differences between our established jurisdiction practices and those of many of the other participating countries at the Hague, the Convention negotiations present special challenges. When you add the enormous uncertainties raised by the growth of trade and commerce on the Internet, and the complex choices for intellectual property litigation, the obstacles can seem overwhelming. Nevertheless, the promise is great, and we hope that we can ultimately succeed. . . .

Notes and Questions

1. *A moving target.* Progress on the proposed Hague convention on judgments has been glacial. In June 2001, delegates to the Hague Conference discussed the preliminary draft convention drawn up in October 1999 and confronted a range of disagreements in specialized areas of law — notably e-commerce and intellectual property. The delegates drew up a new version of an interim text, also reproduced in the Document Supplement, with multiple provisions in brackets, indicating in some cases a profound disagreement about basic approaches, let alone the details of the treaty. The delegates directed the policy-making body of the Hague Conference to "examine whether conditions are met for a successful conclusion of these negotiations, including sufficient agreement on the way to approach critical areas where consensus is still lacking, a result-oriented method of negotiations, and a schedule for any future negotiations." That process can be expected to take several years, and the draft Hague convention on judgments continues to be a moving target as a consequence.

2. *Civil and commercial matters within the scope of the proposed convention.* Under Article 1, the draft convention applies to "civil and commercial matters" and specifically excludes "revenue, customs, [and] administrative matters," perpetuating the reluctance to enforce the public law of another state. Some admittedly "civil and commercial" matters — like domestic relations, insolvency, and the status and legal capacity of natural persons — are expressly excluded from the draft convention, Article 1(2). Even with the clarity of these exclusion clauses, however, there is no consensus about the meaning of "civil and commercial matters," even though that phrase recurs in other Hague

conventions. *See, e.g.*, RESTATEMENT (THIRD) OF THE FOREIGN RELATIONS LAW OF THE UNITED STATES § 471, cmt. f (noting that the United Kingdom interprets "civil and commercial matters" under the Hague Service Convention as meaning any non-criminal proceeding and Germany interprets the phrase to more broadly exclude any "public law" judgment). Is the protection of intellectual property like copyrights and patents an "administrative" matter or a "civil or commercial matter"? What about private actions under U.S. securities laws? What about human rights cases under the Alien Tort Claims Act, *supra*?

3. *Rules versus principles*. The draft convention follows the approach of Brussels and Lugano Conventions in adopting definite rules governing jurisdiction — implemented through the sanction of non-recognition — as distinct from the more impressionistic jurisdictional inquiry under the Due Process Clause of the U.S. Constitution, with its inquiry into "minimum contacts" and notions of "fair play and substantial justice." Which approach — rules or principles — seems preferable?

4. *Lists of "black," "white," and "gray" and Supreme Court precedent*. The draft convention prohibits the exercise of jurisdiction by a state party on the basis of certain contacts standing alone ("the black list"), requires the recognition of judgments based on other contacts ("the white list"), and allows but does not require recognition of judgments based on yet other contacts ("the gray list"). Looking over these provisions, and recalling that no treaty can compel what the Constitution forbids, which Supreme Court precedents on personal jurisdiction seem most vulnerable to being overridden if the convention were adopted by the United States without reservations?

5. *The proposed convention and Filártiga*. Article 10(1) of the interim text, addressing jurisdiction over torts, provides:

> A plaintiff may bring an action in tort [or delict] in the courts of the State — a) in which the act or omission that caused injury occurred, or b) in which the injury arose, unless the defendant establishes that the person claimed to be responsible could not reasonably foresee that the act or omission could result in an injury of the same nature in that State.

How would this provision affect the enforceability of judgments under the Alien Tort Claims Act, like *Filártiga*, *supra*?

C. PARALLEL PROCEEDINGS

Transnational *res judicata* by its nature deals with one jurisdiction's response to the final judgments from another. But increasingly, parties attempt to litigate identical or related issues in more than one country simultaneously. The wrong may occur in several places at once, as in multiterritorial infringements of copyrights, or the defendant and its assets may be located in two or more jurisdictions. Duplicative litigation has its obvious costs, not the least of which is the risk of contradictory judgments, but there are circumstances in which parallel litigation is unavoidable. Broadly speaking, U.S. courts that confront these situations have three alternatives: (i) do nothing and allow both proceedings to continue simultaneously, (ii) stay or dismiss the local proceeding, or (iii) attempt to derail the foreign proceeding. The following materials explore the logic — and the limits — of each alternative.

---

[1] Alternative #1: Simultaneous Proceedings

The general rule is that "parallel proceedings on the same *in personam* claim should ordinarily be allowed to proceed simultaneously, at least until a judgment is reached in one which can be pled as *res judicata* in the other." *Laker Airways, Ltd. v. Sabena Belgian World Airlines,* 731 F.2d 909, 926 (D.C. Cir. 1984). In part, the predisposition to allow simultaneous litigation follows from the federal courts' "virtually unflagging obligation" to exercise the jurisdiction conferred upon them, *Colorado River Water Conserv. Dist. v. United States,* 424 U.S. 800, 817 (1976). *See also Quackenbush v. Allstate Ins. Co.,* 517 U.S. 706, 723 (1996) ("federal courts have the power to dismiss or remand cases based on abstention principles only where the relief being sought is equitable or otherwise discretionary.") There is some empirical evidence that U.S. courts routinely permit the parallel proceedings to continue in both courts, but there are considerable disadvantages to this approach. "Simultaneous adjudications regarding identical facts and highly similar legal issues creates the risk of inconsistent judgments," *EFCO Corp. v. Aluma Systems USA,* 983 F. Supp. 816, 824 (S.D. Iowa 1997), and can create an unseemly race to judgment, as both courts attempt to issue a decision that will be entitled to *res judicata* in the other.

ABDULLAH SAYID RAJAB AL-RIFAI & SONS W.L.L. v. McDONNELL DOUGLAS FOREIGN SALES CORP.
988 F. Supp. 1285 (E.D. Mo. 1997)

. . . On July 28, 1997, plaintiff filed its one-count complaint seeking money due for commissions earned under a representation agreement with defendant. . . . [D]efendant filed a motion to dismiss or, in the alternative, to stay the case based on the existence of a pending case in Kuwait which defendant contends addresses the identical issues raised in the present case. . . .

Plaintiff Abdullah Sayid Rajab Al-Rifai & Sons W.L.L. ("ASRR") is a trading and contracting company organized under Kuwaiti law, with its principal place of business in Kuwait. Defendant McDonnell Douglas Foreign Sales Corporation ("MDFSC") is a wholly owned subsidiary of McDonnell Douglas Corporation ("MDC") organized under the laws of the Virgin Islands which transacts substantial business in Missouri. Beginning in 1974 [and renewed by agreement in 1985], plaintiff, through its now deceased principal, Colonel Abdullah Sayid Rajab Al-Rifai ("Colonel Al-Rifai"), entered into a series of representation agreements with MDC and two of its wholly-owned subsidiaries, McDonnell Douglas International Sales Corporation ("MDISCO") and defendant MDFSC. . . . In exchange for its services, plaintiff was to receive prescribed commissions under the representation agreements.

[Claiming that the 1985 representation agreement had been wrongfully terminated,] Plaintiff instituted a suit against MDISCO on December 3, 1994, before the Court of First Instance in the Commercial Circuit of the State of Kuwait ("the Kuwaiti Action"). In the Kuwaiti Action, plaintiff seeks statutory damages for non-renewal of the representation agreements and payment of all commissions then due. . . . The Court of First Instance reserved judgment on plaintiff's claims for commissions arising out of the aircraft sale and referred the matter to the Experts Department of the Kuwaiti Ministry of Justice ("the Experts Department") for an accounting of the commissions due to plaintiff. *Id.* In late October of 1997, the Experts Department found for plaintiff in the amount of $637,588 for commissions relating to the aircraft sale. Subsequent to the Experts Department's recommendation, the matter was referred back to the Court of First Instance for a final determination. . . . In the present case [filed in federal district court in July 1997], plaintiff alleges that defendant has not fully paid plaintiff's commissions under the 1985 agreement for the sale of . . . F-18 aircraft to Kuwait. . . .

DISCUSSION

Based on deference to the pending Kuwaiti action, defendant seeks to have the instant action dismissed or, in the alternative, stayed pending the outcome of the Kuwaiti proceedings.

A. Motion to Dismiss

In determining whether to dismiss the instant action in favor of the Kuwaiti action the Court is mindful of the "virtually unflagging obligation of the federal courts to exercise the jurisdiction given them." [*Colorado River Water Conserv. Dist. v. United States*, 424 U.S. 800, 817 (1976).] Federal courts "have a strict duty to exercise the jurisdiction that is conferred upon them by Congress." *Quackenbush v. Allstate Ins. Co.*, 517 U.S. 706(1996). Defendant urges the Court to dismiss the present action because it presents the same claims and issues as the Kuwaiti action which has been pending since December of 1994. . . . [D]efendant argues that the Court has the inherent power to control its own docket, ensuring judicial efficiency and fairness. Moreover, defendant asserts that the Court has the inherent power to dismiss this action based on the pendency of a related foreign proceeding. *See* [*inter alia*] *Evergreen Marine Corp. v. Welgrow Int'l, Inc.*, 954 F. Supp. 101, 103 (S.D.N.Y. 1997); *Dragon Capital Partners v. Merrill Lynch Capital Services, Inc.*, 949 F. Supp. 1123, 1127 (S.D.N.Y. 1997). Based upon these cases from the Southern District of New York, defendant urges the Court to exercise "international abstention." In this line of cases, the New York courts have analyzed several relevant factors to determine whether an action should be dismissed or stayed including: "the similarity of parties and issues involved in the foreign litigation; the promotion of judicial efficiency; adequacy of relief available in the alternative forum; issues of fairness to and convenience of the parties, counsel and witnesses; the possibility of prejudice to any of the parties; and the temporal sequence of the filing of the actions." *Evergreen Marine Corp. v. Welgrow Int'l,*

Inc., 954 F. Supp. 101, 103 (S.D.N.Y. 1997). Defendant contends that each of these factors weighs in favor of dismissing the action. . . .

In support of its motion to dismiss, defendant analogizes the present situation to that presented in *Colorado River Water Conservation Dist. v. United States,* 424 U.S. 800 (1976), where parallel proceedings to those in the federal district court were pending before a state forum. Factors relevant to the determination of whether to dismiss the federal action include: "the inconvenience of the federal forum; the desirability of avoiding piecemeal litigation; and the order in which jurisdiction was obtained by the concurrent forums" with no one factor being necessarily determinative. Neither the Supreme Court nor the Eighth Circuit Court of Appeals has squarely addressed the issue of whether a district court may dismiss a case based on the pendency of an action in a foreign country.

Plaintiff argues that the Supreme Court's recent decision in *Quackenbush v. Allstate Ins. Co.,* 517 U.S. 706 (1996) precludes the dismissal of the instant case. In *Quackenbush,*[1] the Court held that "federal courts have the power to dismiss or remand cases based on abstention principles only where the relief being sought is equitable or otherwise discretionary." The *Quackenbush* Court reviewed the various abstention doctrines,[2] but made no mention of any type of international abstention.[3]

Defendant contends that the Supreme Court's holding in *Quackenbush* is inapplicable because it does not address the issues of deference to pending foreign actions. Defendant argues that *Quackenbush* is aimed solely at *Burford* abstention and its accompanying principles of federalism and state sovereignty and does not impact the validity of the New York cases which instead address foreign actions and accompanying principles of comity. At least two Southern District of New York cases facing the issue of deference to foreign proceedings have been decided subsequent to *Quackenbush.* Neither decision addresses the *Quackenbush* decision and both decisions continue to espouse the district court's inherent power to dismiss an action based on the pendency of a related proceeding in a foreign jurisdiction. The *Evergreen* court

---

[1] *Quackenbush* discussed *Burford* abstention. *See Burford v. Sun Oil Co.,* 319 U.S. 315 (1943) (abstention proper where federal review would be disruptive of state efforts to establish a consistent policy relating to a matter of substantial public interest).

[2] In *Quackenbush,* the Court reviewed the recognized abstention doctrines. *See, e.g., Younger v. Harris,* 401 U.S. 37 (1971) (abstention proper where there would be potential interference with a pending state criminal proceeding); *Railroad Comm'n of Tex. v. Pullman Co.,* 312 U.S. 496 (1941) (abstention proper where a federal constitutional question may be avoided if state court is given an opportunity to rule on a question of ambiguous state law); *Louisiana Power & Light Co. v. Thibodaux,* 360 U.S. 25 (1959) (abstention proper where federal litigation would be hindered by an unresolved question of state law); *Colorado River Water Conservation Dist. v. United States,* 424 U.S. 800 (1976) (abstention proper in limited circumstances where case is duplicative of a pending state proceeding). The facts presented here do not fall into any of the above-mentioned categories of abstention.

[3] The issue is not one of international comity which is defined as "the recognition which one nation allows within its territory to the legislative, executive, or judicial acts of another nation, having due regard both to international duty and convenience and to the rights of its own citizens or of other persons who are under the protection of its laws." *Dragon Capital Partners v. Merrill Lynch Capital Serv., Inc.,* 949 F. Supp. 1123, 1126 n. 8 (S.D.N.Y. 1997), quoting Black's Law Dictionary 267 (6th ed. 1990). "Comity refers to deference to another sovereign's definite law or judicial decision" and not to pending proceedings.

states, "the considerations involved in deferring to state court proceedings are different from those involved in deferring to foreign proceedings, where concerns of international comity arise and issues of federalism and federal supremacy are not in play." *Evergreen*, 954 F. Supp. at 104 n. 1.

Despite the contention that *Quackenbush* only prohibits dismissal of actions at law under *Burford* abstention and is therefore inapplicable to the present issue, other courts have read *Quackenbush* more broadly. The Eighth Circuit has stated "[i]n *Quackenbush*, the Court 'decided that federal courts have the power to dismiss or remand cases based on abstention principles only where the relief being sought is equitable or otherwise discretionary.'" *Warmus v. Melahn*, 110 F.3d 566, 567 (8th Cir. 1997). . . . The Eighth Circuit has recognized that in actions at law, the court does not have power to dismiss an action based on abstention principles. . . .

The Court finds that an outright dismissal of the instant action at law is improper in light of *Quackenbush*. Because plaintiff's claim is for money due, this is a legal action that does not involve equitable or discretionary relief. Accordingly, the Court will not dismiss the instant action.

B. Motion to Stay

Although the Court will not dismiss this action, the *Quackenbush* decision does not preclude the Court from issuing a stay. The *Quackenbush* Court emphasized the difference between an outright dismissal and a stay. "[A]n order merely staying the action does not constitute abnegation of judicial duty. On the contrary, it is a wise and productive discharge of it. There is only postponement of decision for its best fruition." Federal courts do have the power, based on abstention principles, to stay actions for damages. [The court assessed multiple factors to determine the propriety of a stay: the similarity of the two actions, the degree of progress already made in the foreign action, the adequacy and appropriateness of the foreign forum, and judicial efficiency and deference to foreign proceedings. It concluded:] [D]ue to the dissimilarity of the parties, the convenience of the present forum and the likelihood of dismissal of at least a portion of the foreign action, the Court finds that a stay pending the outcome of the litigation in Kuwait is also inappropriate.

Notes and Questions on the Predisposition to Allow Simultaneous Proceedings

1. *The Quackenbush analogy. Burford* abstention is a way for one sovereign (the federal government) to respect the prerogatives of another (a state government). Isn't the analogy to international proceedings fairly direct? And doesn't that imply that the failure to abstain as in *Al-Rifai* violates the principles adopted by the Supreme court in *Burford* and *Quackenbush*?

2. *Negative effects.* What are the principal disadvantages of proceeding as the court has directed in *Al-Rifai*?

3. Are you convinced by the court's effort to clarify that the issues before it

are not to be resolved by reference to comity? What is the court trying to accomplish and avoid by portraying its analysis this way?

---

[2]   Alternative #2: *Lis alibi pendens* — Abstention, Stays, and Dismissals

TURNER ENTERTAINMENT CO. v. DEGETO FILM GmbH
25 F.3d 1512 (11th Cir. 1994)

[Turner Entertainment had a licensing agreement with a German television cooperative, ARD, under which ARD was allowed to broadcast certain works owned by Turner. The agreement gave ARD a right to telecast the programs "by all means and methods now or hereafter known including but not limited to . . . [direct broadcast satellites] and/or communication satellite for purposes of so-called home television reception," so long as the works were broadcast in German and so long as the broadcast were limited to the territory specified in the agreement. In 1993, nine years after the agreement had been concluded, ARD announced its intention to broadcast certain licensed works over the newly-developed ASTRA satellites, a technology which enabled ARD to meet its legal obligation to telecast to the entire German public, now also including the former German Democratic Republic. But because the ASTRA satellites had a broadcast "footprint" five times larger than the licensed territory, Turner attempted to block the broadcasts, and ARD filed a declaratory judgment action in Germany, seeking judicial confirmation of its interpretation of the agreement — allowing the ASTRA broadcasts. Turner filed suit in the United States one week later.

The U.S. district court granted an injunction prohibiting ARD from the ASTRA broadcasts and denied ARD's motion to dismiss or stay the U.S. litigation in light of the parallel proceedings in Germany. The German court subsequently ruled that the parties had not contemplated the new technology and that ARD therefore had no absolute right to broadcast via ASTRA. But it also determined that ARD was "compelled as a practical matter to broadcast outside the licensed territory in order to fulfill its legal obligation to bring its telecasts to the German public." Applying the doctrine of good faith, the German court ruled that ARD should be allowed to broadcast via the ASTRA satellite but for an increased fee to be determined at a later stage in the proceeding.]

A. Whether to Dismiss or Stay the Domestic Litigation: International Abstention

ARD appeals the district court's denial of its Motion to Dismiss or Stay the American Litigation in deference to the parallel German proceedings.[1] In the

---

[1] All of the parties to the American litigation are parties in the German litigation. Although some of the parties in the German litigation are absent from this action, the central issue is the same in both cases: whether the Agreement permits ARD to broadcast Turner-licensed works via the ASTRA satellite.

period since the district court denied the appellants' Motion to Dismiss or Stay the American Litigation, the German court has rendered a decision on the merits of the dispute, although it has not determined the fee to be paid by ARD to Turner. The existence of the German judgment adds new considerations to the decision whether to continue the American litigation. The issue is whether a federal court, which properly has jurisdiction over an action, should exercise its jurisdiction where parallel proceedings are ongoing in a foreign nation and a judgment has been reached on the merits in the litigation abroad.

Federal courts have a "virtually unflagging obligation" to exercise the jurisdiction conferred upon them. *Colorado River Water Conserv. Dist. v. United States*, 424 U.S. 800, 817 (1976). Nevertheless, in some private international disputes the prudent and just action for a federal court is to abstain from the exercise of jurisdiction. Therefore, federal courts have begun to fashion principles that guide courts' actions in cases of concurrent jurisdiction in a federal court and the court of a foreign nation. This circuit has never considered the question of "international abstention." In other federal courts, at least two distinct but very similar approaches to international abstention have developed. Both have lifted criteria for analysis from case law concerning concurrent jurisdiction between federal and state courts.

One approach has taken the criteria enunciated in *Colorado River* and applied them to the international context. These cases have at times injected the special concerns of "international comity" into the abstention analysis. Another line of international abstention cases, developed in the Southern District of New York, applies a similar set of principles, with a clearer emphasis on the concerns of international comity implicated by the exercise of jurisdiction. These two sets of principles overlap to a large extent, and we find both lines of cases helpful to our analysis. Taking the two approaches together, courts have sought to fashion principles that will promote three readily identifiable goals in the area of concurrent international jurisdiction: (1) a proper level of respect for the acts of our fellow sovereign nations — a rather vague concept referred to in American jurisprudence as international comity; (2) fairness to litigants; and (3) efficient use of scarce judicial resources.[2]

1. International Comity

The ramifications of international comity, in the abstention context, are suggested in the leading Supreme Court case, *Hilton v. Guyot,* 159 U.S. 113 (1895):

> "Comity," in the legal sense, is neither a matter of absolute obligation, on the one hand, nor of mere courtesy and good will, upon the other. But it is the recognition which one nation allows within its territory to the legislative, executive, or judicial acts of another nation, having due regard both to international duty and convenience, and to the rights of its own citizens, or of other persons who are under the protection of its laws. . . .

---

[2] Some courts have added to the consideration of these criteria a general rule that federal courts should assume jurisdiction in parallel proceedings until a judgment is reached in one court.

. . . In the context of international abstention case law, the meaning of international comity[3] is derived from [*Hilton*.][4] General comity concerns include: (1) whether the judgment was rendered via fraud; (2) whether the judgment was rendered by a competent court utilizing proceedings consistent with civilized jurisprudence; and (3) whether the foreign judgment is prejudicial, in the sense of violating American public policy because it is repugnant to fundamental principles of what is decent and just.

Turner does not argue that the decision was rendered by fraud, or that the German court is not a competent court which follows civilized procedures. Germany's legal system clearly follows procedures that ensure that litigants will receive treatment that satisfies American notions of due process. Turner's sole argument is that the German court's decision is contrary to federal or Georgia public policy because it abrogates Turner's freedom of contract. [The court concluded that the German court had reasonably interpreted the licensing agreement and that its decision had not violated federal or state policy governing the freedom and the sanctity of contracts.] . . .

Also relevant to considerations of international comity are the relative strengths of the American and German interests. In the instant case, the contract was written in English, with an American as one party to the contract, and includes a choice of law and forum selection provision designating this federal court and the applicable law (although the choice of law and forum is concurrent with Germany's). However, the central question in the case — whether the Agreement does or should permit ARD to broadcast via ASTRA — requires a thorough knowledge of European broadcasting technology and markets, and requires reference to European law. Most of the witnesses and experts in the litigation would be European. Furthermore, although an American entity is a party to the contract, there also are German parties, and the choice-of-law and forum provisions also designate the German court and law. More importantly, the Agreement calls for performance of the contract, for the most part, in Germany, and the German interest and connection to the case is much more significant than the American.

Although Turner attempts to present the case as a garden variety contract action, there are complicated issues surrounding the case that require extensive knowledge of the European television market. Given exclusive jurisdiction over the matter, the federal forum would without doubt be capable of rendering a just result. However, the German court would seem to be the most sensible venue to determine a just result in this case. There appears to be no clear federal interest in trying this case. Certainly much is at stake in this litigation for both parties. However, the public interest in the litigation is more conspicuous in Germany, because the German parties include the German state broadcasters, and the salient issues in the case are of great moment to

---

[3] . . . Although international comity is a rather nebulous set of principles that may be applicable whenever a court's decision will have ramifications beyond its territorial jurisdiction and into that of another nation, our use of the term is informed and guided by the international abstention case law.

[4] We note that the criteria set out below have been developed for the purpose of considering actions brought to enforce foreign judgments. Although this appeal does not contain an enforcement action, the same criteria are readily applicable in the present context because a judgment has been rendered in the parallel proceeding.

the state of television in Germany and the rest of Europe. There is no comparable federal interest in maintaining jurisdiction over the litigation.

While courts regularly permit parallel proceedings in an American court and a foreign court, once a judgment on the merits is reached in one of the cases, as in the German forum in this case, failure to defer to the judgment would have serious implications for the concerns of international comity. For example, the prospect of "dueling courts," conflicting judgments, and attempts to enforce conflicting judgments raise major concerns of international comity.

In sum, international comity concerns favor deference to the German proceedings in the instant case.

2. Fairness

With respect to the goal of fairness, relevant considerations include: (1) the order in which the suits were filed; (2) the more convenient forum; and (3) the possibility of prejudice to parties resulting from abstention.

The instant lawsuits were filed almost simultaneously. The record reflects that the German action was filed one week prior to the American litigation, and the record does not show that the American suit was a reaction to the German suit. We note that none of the cases regarding concurrent international jurisdiction give priority solely on the basis of first-filing in a case where the suits were filed so closely together. Whatever weight is to be accorded this one-week priority, of course, points toward the German forum. The other factors point even more strongly in that direction.

With respect to convenience of the forum, the weightier German interest, discussed above, indicates that the German court provides a more convenient forum for the litigation, as does the fact that most of the witnesses and experts in the litigation would be European, and the fact that the Agreement calls for performance of the contract, for the most part, in Germany. The significantly greater German interest in the litigation, discussed above, also supports the more general notion that concerns of fairness favor the German forum.

Before accepting or relinquishing jurisdiction, a federal court must be satisfied that its decision will not result in prejudice to the party opposing the stay. Ensuring the ability of the parties to fully and fairly litigate their claims in some tribunal surely is a paramount goal of international abstention principles. *See Hilton v. Guyot,* [*supra* at] 205 ("It must, however, always be kept in mind that it is the paramount duty of the court before which any suit is brought to see to it that the parties have had a fair and impartial trial, before a final decision is rendered against either party.") In the instant case, we see nothing that has occurred in the German proceedings to indicate that staying the litigation will foreclose any chance for Turner to obtain a fair and just result. For example, nothing has occurred in the German proceedings to date to dispel the expectation that Turner will have ample opportunity to fairly present to the German trial court at the next stage of the proceedings its evidence regarding the value of the ASTRA broadcasts in the areas outside the licensed territory defined in Paragraph 4 of the Agreement. In sum, we conclude that fairness in this case indicates deference to the German proceedings.

3. Judicial Resources

Finally, courts have considered the efficient use of scarce judicial resources. Criteria relevant to efficiency include (1) the inconvenience of the federal forum; (2) the desirability of avoiding piecemeal litigation; (3) whether the actions have parties and issues in common; and (4) whether the alternative forum is likely to render a prompt disposition. We have already discussed the convenience of the federal forum. The desire to avoid piecemeal litigation is also relevant to the convenience of the forum. If both proceedings continued, the courts' calendars would have to be synchronized and the litigation would have to move back and forth across the Atlantic. We have already noted that the actions involve substantially the same parties and issues. Finally, the German court would seem as likely as the American forum to render a prompt disposition. Although the appeal of the German decision will not be heard until [next year,] the German litigation has moved much farther along than the American action. There has been no discovery in the American litigation, while a trial on the merits has already occurred in Germany. Overall, we readily conclude that concerns regarding judicial efficiency militate strongly in favor of staying or dismissing the instant action in favor of the German litigation. . . .

In summary, we conclude that the relevant concerns of international comity, fairness, and efficiency point overwhelmingly, at this stage of the litigation, to deference to the German forum which has already rendered a judgment on the merits. We also conclude that at this stage of the litigation, the appropriate resolution is a stay rather than a dismissal of the American action. The German court has yet to rule on appeal or to determine the manner or amount of the fee that the appellants shall pay to Turner. After the German litigation is complete, Turner may seek a hearing to determine whether the final results have altered any issues addressed herein. If not, the action should be dismissed. Either party also may add an action for enforcement of the foreign judgment at an appropriate time. . . . [F]or the same reasons that we have decided to stay the instant suit, we conclude that the preliminary injunction entered by the district court must be vacated.

Notes and Questions on Domestic Divestiture and *Turner Entertainment*

1. *Applying the abstention doctrine.* To appreciate just how fact-dependent the decision to abstain is, try altering the facts in *Turner Entertainment* one at a time, and determine whether that change (a) would and (b) should change the result:

(i) Suppose — all other things remaining the same — that there hadn't been an intervening judgment in Germany and the U.S. court was deciding the case while a decision on the merits was pending in that country.

(ii) Suppose that Turner Entertainment Company were owned by a Japanese media conglomerate and that the real party-in-interest was not a U.S. citizen.

(iii) Suppose that the parallel proceedings involved different parties, with Turner Entertainment and ARD in the U.S. litigation, and Turner Entertainment and ARD's public broadcasting subsidiary — over which no U.S. court would have personal jurisdiction — in the German litigation.

(iv) Suppose that the action had first been filed in the United States instead of in Germany.

(v) Suppose the contract had a choice-of-law or choice-of-forum provisions that unambiguously selected the United States.

(vi) In some respects, the German judgment "split the baby," allowing ARD to complete the broadcast but requiring additional payment to Turner. Suppose that court had interpreted the contract exactly as ARD had argued.

2. *Articulating the abstention standards.* To date, the *Turner Entertainment* approach has been approved in a variety of cases and rejected in none. But the considerations governing stays have been articulated in various ways and in various combinations. *See, e.g., Goldhammer v. Dunkin' Donuts, Inc.*, 59 F. Supp. 2d 248 (D. Mass. 1999):

> The federal trial courts have developed a roster of relevant factors in determining whether to grant a stay because of parallel litigation in a foreign forum: (1) similarity of parties and issues involved in the foreign litigation; (2) the promotion of judicial efficiency; (3) adequacy of relief available in the alternative forum; (4) issues of fairness to and convenience of the parties, counsel, and witnesses; (5) the possibility of prejudice to any of the parties; and (6) the temporal sequence of the filing of the actions. . . . The overarching concerns for a federal court facing concurrent international jurisdiction are demonstrating a proper level of respect for the acts of other sovereign nations, ensuring fairness to litigants, and efficiently using scarce judicial resources.

Given the similarity between these factors and the criteria for a *forum non conveniens* dismissal (Chapter 3, *supra)*, it is standard for litigants to combine motions to dismiss, with motions in the alternative to stay, the local proceedings.

3. *Extending Quackenbush to international proceedings. Quackenbush v. Allstate Ins. Co.*, 517 U.S. 706 (1996), was decided two years after *Turner Entertainment.* As noted in *Al-Rifai, supra*, the Supreme Court there declared that "federal courts have the power to dismiss or remand cases based on abstention principles only where the relief being sought is equitable or otherwise discretionary." Otherwise, "federal courts have a strict duty to exercise the jurisdiction that is conferred upon them by Congress." *Id.*, at 716, 723. On the surface, *Quackenbush* might be interpreted to preclude the exercise of discretion in *Turner Entertainment.* But the courts have been unwilling to assume that *Quackenbush* can be extended from its domestic setting to an international setting. "Read in the proper context . . . the Supreme Court's admonition [in *Quackenbush*] that courts generally must exercise their nondiscretionary authority in cases over which Congress has granted them jurisdiction can apply only to those abstention doctrines

addressing the unique concerns of federalism." *Posner v. Essex Insur. Co.*, 178 F.3d 1209, 1223 (11th Cir. 1999). Does that distinction make sense?

---

[3]   Alternative #3: The Antisuit Injunction

KIRBY ENGINEERING v. NORFOLK SOUTHERN RAILWAY COMPANY
71 F. Supp.2d 1363 (N.D. Ga. 1999)

This is an action. . . to recover damages for equipment damaged during shipping. It is before the Court on Defendant's Motion to Enjoin Plaintiffs From Pursuing a Parallel Cause of Action in Australia. At issue is the standard by which the Court should issue an antisuit injunction against prosecution of a parallel foreign *in personam* action. For the reasons set forth below, the Court will deny the motion.

[Plaintiff Kirby Engineering, an Australian firm, contracted with International Cargo Control, Inc. (ICC) to ship eight containers of equipment from Australia to a General Motors plant in Huntsville, Alabama. ICC contracted with Hamburg Sud, an ocean carrier, to transport the equipment from Australia to Savannah, Georgia, and that voyage was completed without incident by Hamburg Sud's subsidiary, Columbus Line, Inc. Columbus Line in turn had subcontracted with the defendant, Norfolk Southern Railway, to carry the equipment from Savannah to Huntsville. There was no direct contractual relationship between Kirby and Norfolk Southern. On October 9, 1997, the train carrying Kirby's equipment derailed in Alabama before reaching its destination, causing more than $2 million in damage. Kirby sued ICC and Hamburg Sud in Australia and initiated this action in the United States against Norfolk Southern. Norfolk Southern challenged the jurisdiction of the Australian court and moved to stay that action pending the disposition of the U.S. case, but the motion to stay was denied.]

It is undisputed that federal courts possess the discretionary power to enjoin parties subject to their jurisdiction from pursuing parallel *in personam* litigation before foreign tribunals. Nevertheless, parallel *in personam* proceedings should ordinarily be allowed to proceed simultaneously, at least until judgment is reached in one which can be pled as *res judicata* in the other. When to invoke the power to enjoin a foreign proceeding is the rub. That the injunction operates only against the parties, and not directly on the foreign court, does not obviate the need for due regard to principles of international comity, as such an order effectively invades the jurisdiction of a sovereign government.

The Eleventh Circuit has not yet addressed this issue. Other Circuits have adopted one of two approaches. Some circuits follow a so-called restrictive approach in granting antisuit injunctions. The restrictive approach places a premium on preserving international comity. Under this approach, courts should enjoin parties from prosecuting parallel foreign *in personam* actions only for one of two reasons: when necessary to protect the forum court's jurisdiction over the matter at issue, or to protect important public policies. Other circuits issue antisuit injunctions more freely. For convenience, the Court will refer to this view as the liberal approach. The liberal approach places less importance on international comity in deciding international jurisdictional disputes. Instead, the liberal approach focuses on whether duplicative litigation is "vexatious." In these circuits, a duplication of the parties and issues, alone, generally suffices to justify issuing an antisuit injunction.

Each of the two approaches considers the effect an antisuit injunction will have on comity. Accordingly, it is important to define this somewhat elusive concept. The Supreme Court has defined comity as "the recognition which one nation allows within its territory to the legislative, executive or judicial acts of another nation, having due regard both to international duty and convenience, and to the rights of its own citizens or of other persons who are under the protection of its laws." *Hilton v. Guyot,* 159 U.S. 113, 164 (1895). Although comity is not required by international law, "comity attempts to ensure the development of a working international dispute resolution system by advocating respect or deference for a foreign jurisdiction's laws." The difficulty in applying such an amorphous concept arises from the fact that, legally, comity is neither an absolute obligation nor a matter of mere courtesy and good will. Put another way, comity is a continual give-and-take of jurisdictional respect.

Of the two approaches to antisuit injunctions, the liberal approach sets a lower bar for enjoining parties from prosecuting foreign parallel *in personam* actions. The Fifth, Seventh, and Ninth Circuits have adopted or incline toward this approach. *See, e.g., Kaepa v. Achilles,* 76 F.3d 624 (5th Cir. 1996); *Philips Medical Sys. Int'l B.V. v. Bruetman,* 8 F.3d 600, 605 (7th Cir. 1993); *Seattle Totems Hockey Club, Inc. v. National Hockey League,* 652 F.2d 852 (9th Cir. 1981)[, *cert. denied,* 457 U.S. 1105 (1982)]. Generally, courts in these circuits grant antisuit injunctions if a duplication of parties and issues exists between a suit in the forum court and a foreign suit. While not excluding considerations of international comity, this standard focuses on the "potentially vexatious nature" of concurrent foreign litigation. *Kaepa,* 76 F.3d at 627.

Among the circuits following this approach, *Seattle Totems* is a leading case. There, the Ninth Circuit affirmed an antisuit injunction granted against the defendant, the National Hockey League (NHL), in an antitrust action. The NHL had sought to file a suit involving the same breach of contract claim in Canadian courts as the case in district court. The NHL admitted that under Fed. R. Civ. P. 13(a), their contract claim would constitute a compulsory counterclaim in the U.S. antitrust suit. Canadian law, however, did not require the defendant to assert a compulsory counterclaim. The Ninth Circuit affirmed the district court's injunction and invocation of Rule 13(a) to govern the pending litigation rather than Canadian law. In reaching its holding, the Ninth Circuit adopted factors set forth by the Fifth Circuit in [*In re Unterweser Reederei, Gmbh,* 428 F.2d 888, 896 (5th Cir. 1970), *rev'd on other grounds sub. nom., M/S Bremen v. Zapata Off-Shore Company,* 407 U.S. 1 (1972)]. The court stated that "foreign litigation may be enjoined when it would (1) frustrate a policy of the forum issuing the injunction; (2) be vexatious or oppressive; (3) threaten the issuing courts [sic] *in rem* or *quasi in rem* jurisdiction, or (4) where the proceedings prejudice other equitable consider-ations." In reaching its decision, the Ninth Circuit considered factors from *forum non conveniens* doctrine such as convenience to the parties and wit-nesses, the efficient administration of justice, and the potential prejudice to one party. . . .

The restrictive approach places a premium on international comity. Adopted by the D.C., the Second, and the Sixth Circuits, the restrictive approach per-mits such injunctions against parallel *in personam* foreign actions only for two reasons. *See, e.g., Laker Airways v. Sabena*, 731 F.2d 909 (D.C. Cir. 1984); *China Trade & Dev. Corp.*, 837 F.2d 33, 36 (2d Cir. 1987); *Gau Shan Co. v. Bankers Trust,* 956 F.2d 1349 (6th Cir. 1992). These circuits require the party seeking the injunction to show that prosecution of the foreign suit presents a threat to the forum court's jurisdiction or imperils important public policies of the forum court.

The leading case adopting the restrictive approach is *Laker Airways*. In that case, the district court enjoined American and other non-British defendants from seeking relief in English courts as an attempt to evade United States antitrust laws. Upholding the injunction, the D.C. Circuit found that the antitrust laws clearly applied to the conduct underlying the claims. The court found that "a preliminary injunction [was] imperative to preserve the court's jurisdiction." Thus, although the D.C. Circuit affirmed the lower court, it adopted a higher standard than the Fifth, Seventh and Ninth Circuits for issuing foreign antisuit injunctions. Because the foreign action directly infringed on the jurisdiction of the United States courts, the injunction was appropriate.

Adopting the reasoning from *Laker Airways*, the Second Circuit reversed an antisuit injunction in *China Trade*. This admiralty action involved a contract between China Trade, an importer, and a Korean shipper for the shipping of soybeans from the U.S. to China. The Korean vessel ran aground and ruined China Trade's soybean cargo. China Trade sued in U.S. district court for its losses, and the parties began discovery. Before trial, the Korean shipper filed suit in South Korea seeking the equivalent of a declaratory injunction to avoid liability. China Trade moved in district court for an injunction against the Korean action. Finding identical parties and issues in both actions, and considering factors of vexatiousness and expense, the district court permanently enjoined the shipper from prosecution of the Korean action. The Second Circuit reversed. Addressing jurisdictional concerns, the court found that the Korean court had attempted neither to enjoin nor usurp the district court's jurisdiction over the matter. Regarding policy concerns, the court found no evidence that the Korean shipper sought to evade any impor-tant public policy of the United States courts. The court held that an injunction is not appropriate merely to prevent a party from seeking slight advantages in substantive or procedural law in a foreign court. Moreover, the possibility that a U.S. judgment might be unenforceable in the Korean court was only speculation. Thus, the Second Circuit held that enjoining the foreign suit was unjustified.

As these cases show, courts adopting the restrictive approach issue antisuit injunctions sparingly. As with the liberal approach, courts in restrictive circuits generally make a threshold finding that the foreign action involves identical parties and issues. Whereas other circuits require little more than identical parties and issues, the courts following the restrictive approach recognize only two grounds warranting a foreign antisuit injunction even with identical parties and issues: (1) to protect the forum's jurisdiction over the matter at issue, or (2) to prevent evasion of the forum's important public polices. In these circuits, a duplication of the parties and issues, alone, is not sufficient to enjoin a foreign suit.

[The court then distinguished the *Bremen* case, *supra*, on the ground that *Bremen* "turned on a forum selection clause and the weight the clause warranted. Here, there is no contractual forum selection clause agreed to by Kirby and Norfolk Southern because no direct contract exists between the two parties. Although Kirby spends much of its brief describing the forum selection clause ICC entered with Columbus Line [which specified that actions under the contract would be brought in Australia], that contract has no bearing on the jurisdiction of the dispute between Kirby and Norfolk Southern."]

Having duly considered the arguments and authority raised by both sides, the Court adopts the restrictive approach. The alternative too freely allows courts to invade the jurisdiction of sovereign governments. Moreover, the underlying justification for the liberal approach reflects an antiquated view of commerce. As noted above, the factors adopted by the Fifth and Ninth Circuits can be traced at least to the middle of this century. Today's world is one of economic interdependence. "[E]conomic interdependence requires cooperation and comity between nations." [*Gau Shan*, 956 F.2d at 1354.] When American companies accept business from foreign firms, they also accept the possibility of concurrent jurisdiction with foreign courts over disputes arising from that relationship. We cannot capitalize on world markets "exclusively on our terms, governed by our laws, and resolved in our courts." *Bremen*, 407 U.S. at 9. Following the reasoning of *Bremen*, parties can agree in advance on where their disputes should be resolved. Where, as here, the parties have not selected a forum, concurrent jurisdiction should be expected. Comity dictates deference and mutual respect for concurrent foreign jurisdiction. Thus, a duplication of parties and interests, alone, should not justify the issuance of a foreign antisuit injunction.

Courts generally should allow parallel proceedings on the same *in personam* claim to proceed simultaneously until a judgment is reached in one jurisdiction. Such a judgment can then be pled as *res judicata* in the other jurisdiction. Consequently, courts should rarely enjoin litigants from proceeding in courts of foreign countries. As a prerequisite to obtaining a foreign antisuit injunction, a threshold finding of identical parties and issues must be made. Such a threshold showing is not present here. The Australian action involves parties not before this court and, apparently, not subject to this court's jurisdiction. These circumstances are quite different from cases such as *Seattle Totems* and *Kaepa* where a defendant in United States district court runs to a foreign tribunal to file "mirror-image claims." Because the parties and issues before the Australian court do not mirror the instant action, that case is not properly labeled a "parallel" action. The same result obtains if the actions are viewed as parallel. Neither of the two grounds which warrant an injunction are present. The Australian proceedings neither threaten this Court's jurisdiction nor impede or evade important public policies of this Court.

Here, . . . many factors favor litigation of this case in the United States. Most of the witnesses reside here. Nothing in the record, however, indicates that this Court's jurisdiction is threatened. There is no evidence that the Australian court would enter an antisuit injunction. The fact that Norfolk Southern's ability to present live witnesses will be restricted in Australia does not pose a threat to the jurisdiction of this court; it is only a threat to Norfolk Southern's interest in defending itself from this lawsuit. An injunction, however, is not appropriate "merely to prevent a party from seeking 'slight advantages in the substantive or procedural law to be applied in a foreign court.' " [*Gau Shan*, 956 F.2d at 1356.] Thus, no jurisdictional concerns justify enjoining the foreign proceeding.

An antisuit injunction may also be appropriate when a party seeks to evade some important public policy of the forum court through litigation in a foreign proceeding. Antisuit injunctions based on an attempted evasion of the forum's public policies are warranted "only when the strongest equitable factors favor its use." *Laker Airways*, 731 F.2d at 931. Here, equity does not warrant an injunction. There is no evidence from which to infer that Kirby filed its suit in Australia in an attempt to evade the public policies of this forum. The record establishes that Kirby was bound by forum-selection clauses in the applicable contracts to litigate against ICC and Hamburg Sud in Australia. Indeed, in a recent judgment issued by the Supreme Court of New South Wales, Australia, the court recognized that Kirby can only seek relief against ICC and Hamburg Sud in that forum. Additionally, no procedural injustice will result from concurrent jurisdiction. Norfolk Southern argues that its defenses to the claims in Australia will require numerous witnesses, physical evidence, charts, computer models, and photographs. Norfolk Southern alleges that its ability to present its defense will be hamstrung with the "perfunctory manner" by which it contends the Australian court operates. While these procedural hindrances raise valid concerns, Norfolk Southern's opposing parties will face the same obstacles. Moreover, allowing Kirby to further litigate in Australia will not pose an unreasonable expense on Norfolk Southern. As Norfolk Southern recognizes, Australian procedural rules permit very little live testimony. Thus, while the vast majority of witnesses necessary for Norfolk Southern's defense may reside in the United States, their depositions — already necessary for this case — can be used in the Australian proceedings. Any other procedural disadvantages Norfolk Southern might face are neither unreasonable nor unexpected in light of its decision to transport international cargo without bargaining for a United States forum. The right to a fair trial is an important public policy in this Court. Norfolk Southern has not shown that it will forfeit that right absent an antisuit injunction.

Norfolk Southern also argues that an injunction should issue because simultaneous litigation of the Australian action is duplicative. Norfolk Southern also contends that because virtually all of their witnesses are in the United States, the trial should only occur here. While these arguments may support the transfer of a case on grounds of *forum non conveniens*, they do not warrant the issuance of an antisuit injunction. "Considerations that are appropriate in deciding whether to decline jurisdiction are not as persuasive when deciding whether to deprive another court of jurisdiction." *Kaepa*, 76 F.3d at 631 (dissent). Indeed, if the Court were to hold that duplication of parties and convenience to litigants were a sufficient basis to issue a foreign antisuit injunction, parallel proceedings would never be permitted.

Moreover, resolution of this case will not resolve the Australian action in whole. The core of that case — Kirby's suit against ICC and Hamburg Sud — still must be tried. Enjoining Kirby from simultaneously prosecuting the Australian action would unnecessarily delay those proceedings. Respect for international comity, and due regard for the sovereignty of the Australian judicial system, dissuades this Court from unnecessarily enjoining an action in the Australian courts. Insisting on a parochial concept that all disputes should be resolved in our courts will neither encourage the expansion of American commerce nor endear us to our neighbors. Accordingly, the motion should be denied. . . .

Notes and Questions on Antisuit Injunctions

1. *Keeping Kirby in perspective. Kirby* should not be overinterpreted. After all, the courts continue to be split on both the propriety of antisuit injunctions and the criteria for issuing them. *See, e.g., General Elec. Co. v. Deutz AG*, 129 F. Supp.2d 776 (W.D. Pa. 2000). The *Kirby* court deliberately chose — and defended — only the "restrictive" approach to antisuit injunctions, placing international comity at the heart of its analysis. But consider again the factors that the "permissive" courts use in considering such relief. Recall for example the Ninth Circuit's analysis in *Seattle Totems Hockey Club, Inc., supra*, 652 F.2d at 855 (citing Fifth Circuit precedent):

> A federal district court with jurisdiction over the parties has the power to enjoin them from proceeding with an action in the courts of a foreign country, although the power should be used sparingly. . . . [F]oreign litigation may be enjoined when it would (1) frustrate a policy of the forum issuing the injunction; (2) be vexatious or oppressive; (3) threaten the issuing court's *in rem* or *quasi in rem* jurisdiction; or (4) where the proceedings prejudice other equitable considerations. . . . [A]llowing simultaneous prosecution of the same action in a foreign forum thousands of miles away would result in "inequitable hardship" and "tend to frustrate and delay the speedy and efficient determination of the cause."

What are the best arguments for this approach to antisuit injunctions? If the Supreme Court determined that a cert-worthy conflict existed among the federal circuit courts of appeal, which route would you expect it to take, and on what rationale?

2. *Antisuit injunctions correlated to the type of jurisdiction.* Why does the *Kirby* court emphasize the difference between *in personam* actions on one hand and *in rem* or *quasi-in-rem* actions on the other? What possible difference can that make? As noted by the *Kirby* court, 71 F.Supp. 2d at 1370:

Courts have a duty to protect their legitimately conferred jurisdiction in order to provide justice to the parties subject to that jurisdiction. Consequently, when a litigant's action in a foreign tribunal threatens to undermine the jurisdiction of the court, the court may consider the effectiveness and propriety of enjoining the litigant's participation in the foreign proceeding. Such threats, however, are rare. Two circumstances present this threat. First, concurrent proceedings pose an inherent threat to *in rem* or *quasi in rem* jurisdiction. Where jurisdiction arises solely from the presence of property within the forum, that jurisdiction is threatened if a foreign court orders the transference of the property to another location. No such concern is present in the instant case. Secondly, with *in personam* cases, "if a foreign court is not merely proceeding in parallel but is attempting to carve out exclusive jurisdiction over the action, an injunction may also be necessary to protect the enjoining court's jurisdiction." *Gau Shan*, 956 F.2d at 1356. As in *Laker Airways*, where the foreign parallel action was interdictory and not parallel, an antisuit injunction is proper. A foreign parallel action is interdictory when it was instituted in the foreign court solely to terminate the United States claim. Such a direct interference with the jurisdiction of a United States court warrants the "defensive issuance of an antisuit injunction." *Gau Shan*, 956 F.2d at 1356.

3. *The concept of the "adjudicating forum" under the CJMA.* The Conflict of Jurisdiction Model Act, reprinted in full in the Document Supplement, attempts to limit parallel proceedings and therefore creates more doctrinal space for antisuit injunctions than the *Kirby* case would allow. "It is an important public policy of this State to encourage the early determination of the adjudicating forum for transnational civil disputes, to discourage vexatious litigation and to enforce only those foreign judgments which were not obtained in connection with vexatious litigation, parallel proceedings or litigation in inconvenient forums." CJMA, § 1. The Act has only been adopted in one state since 1989, but it does reflect the aversion of its drafters (the American Bar Association Section on International Law and Practice) to parallel proceedings.

In essence, the CJMA prohibits recognition of a foreign judgment in parallel proceedings unless a local court has first designated the foreign court a proper "adjudicating forum." The factors for selecting the proper forum are laid out in Section 3:

A determination of the adjudicating forum shall be made in consideration of the following factors:

a. the interests of justice among the parties and of worldwide justice;

b. the public policies of the countries having jurisdiction of the dispute, including the interest of the affected courts in having proceedings take place in their respective forums;

c. the place of occurrence, and of any effects, of the transaction or occurrence, and of any effects, of the transaction or occurrence out of which the dispute arose;

d. the nationality of the parties;

e. substantive law likely to be applicable and the relative familiarity of the affected courts with that law;

f. the availability of a remedy and the forum most likely to render the most complete relief;

g. the impact of the litigation on the judicial systems of the courts involved, and the likelihood of prompt adjudication in the court selected;

h. location of witnesses and availability of compulsory process;

i. location of documents and other evidence and ease or difficulty associated with obtaining, reviewing or transporting such evidence;

j. place of first filing and connection of such place to the dispute;

k. the ability of the designated forum to obtain jurisdiction over the person and property that are the subject of the proceeding;

l. whether designation of an adjudicating forum is a superior method to parallel proceedings in adjudicating the dispute;

m. the nature and extent of litigation that has proceeded over the dispute and whether a designation of an adjudicating forum will unduly delay or prejudice the adjudication of the rights of the original parties; and

n. a realigned plaintiff's choice of forum should rarely be disturbed.

How do these standards differ from those articulated in *Hilton v. Guyot* or the Uniform Enforcement of Foreign Money-Judgments Act, *supra*? If you were a member of a state legislature and the question arose whether to adopt the CJMA, how would you vote and how would you explain your vote? Why do you suppose that only one state — Connecticut — has adopted the act?

D. THE ENFORCEMENT OF FOREIGN ARBITRAL AWARDS IN DOMESTIC COURTS

[1] The System Established

Arbitration is often portrayed as an alternative to litigation, especially in international business transactions, where market players seek the efficient and cheap resolution of disputes. "As a speedy and informal alternative to litigation, arbitration resolves disputes without confinement to many of the procedural and evidentiary structures that protect the integrity of formal trials." *Forsythe Int'l SA v. Gibbs Oil Co.*, 915 F.2d 1017, 1022 (5th Cir. 1990). But the realities of contemporary legal practice do not always support a pristine distinction between litigation and arbitration, and transnational lawyers must be prepared to resort to domestic courts when one party declines either to submit to arbitration as specified in a contract or to honor an arbitral award that has been issued. The courts of the United States may also become enmeshed in the arbitration process when parties disagree about whether their arbitration contract covers the substantive dispute between them or if questions arise about the arbitral tribunal's procedure, composition, location, and the scope of its mandate.

The legal regime governing these enforcement questions is quite distinct from that governing the judgments of foreign courts as in *Hilton v. Guyot*, where comity and the absence of international treaty or federal statutory standards have created a discretionary and decentralized world. By contrast, the enforcement of arbitral awards is controlled by a widely-adopted treaty, the Convention on the Recognition and Enforcement of Foreign Arbitral Awards, 330 U.N.T.S. 3, 21 U.S.T. 2517, T.I.A.S. 6997 (1958) (the New York Convention), and a federal statute, the Federal Arbitration Act, 9 U.S.C. 1-14, 201–208 (FAA).[1] It may seem anomalous, especially after studying the act of state doctrine, that the more informal, less state-centered "judgment" — the arbitration — is entitled to more uniform and more certain treatment than the formal judgment of a foreign court. But the complexity and uncertainty of the old arbitral enforcement procedures led to the drafting of the New York Convention and its adoption by more than 120 countries.[2] Specifically, prior to the convention, the winners of an arbitral award were obliged to seek and receive two judicial recognitions of the award: one in the country where the award was made and another in the country where enforcement was sought. The commercial community, frustrated with this "double exequatur" procedure, developed a treaty that streamlined the process, accelerating the enforcement of both the underlying agreement to arbitrate and any resulting award.

As shown in the following excerpt, the Convention applies "to the recognition and enforcement of arbitral awards made in the territory of a State *other than* the State where the recognition and enforcement of such awards are sought," Article I(1), thus introducing a strong territorial element to its application and apparently excluding purely domestic arbitrations.[3] For all qualifying awards, the Convention and its implementing statute establish a strong presumption of enforceability: when a party brings an action to confirm an arbitration award falling under the Convention, a court "shall confirm the award unless it finds one of the grounds for refusal or deferral of recognition or enforcement of the award specified in the said Convention." 9 U.S.C. § 207. Those defenses are laid out in Article V of the Convention, which provides that a court may refuse to enforce or recognize an arbitration award "only" upon proof of the conditions specified there. But refusing defensively to enforce or recognize an award in one jurisdiction is one thing: vacating it offensively for all purposes is quite another, and neither the New York Convention nor its implementing

---

[1] Chapter 1 of the FAA, codified at 9 U.S.C. § 1 *et seq.*, contains general provisions relating to arbitration and is sometimes referred to as the "domestic FAA," although it applies to arbitration agreements that arise out of a transaction in domestic and foreign commerce. Chapter 2 of the FAA, 9 U.S.C. §§ 201–208, which is the principal focus of this section, implements the New York Convention and is sometimes referred to as the "Convention Act." Chapter 3 of the FAA, 9 U.S.C. §§ 301–07, implements the Inter-American Convention on International Commercial Arbitration, Jan. 30, 1975, 14 I.L.M. 336 (the "Panama Convention"). Chapter 3 of the FAA is sometimes referred to as the Panama Convention Act.

[2] The New York Convention is also significant as a model for regional arbitration agreements (*e.g.*, the European Convention on International Commercial Arbitration (Geneva 1961)) and numerous bilateral investment treaties. *See generally* Albert Jan van Den Berg, THE NEW YORK ARBITRATION CONVENTION OF 1958 (1951); W. Laurence Craig, William W. Park, & Jan Paulsson, INTERNATIONAL CHAMBER OF COMMERCE ARBITRATION (3d ed. 2000).

[3] *But see* Notes and Questions #4, *infra*.

legislation authorizes a U.S. court to take that more invasive step. *See, e.g., Lander Co. Inc. v. MMO Invs., Inc.*, 107 F.3d 476, 478 (7th Cir. 1997), *cert. denied*, 522 U.S. 811 (1997) ("the New York Convention contains no provision for seeking to vacate an award"). Article V(1)(e) suggests instead that a party may request a competent authority in the country in which, or under the law of which, the award was made, to set aside or suspend the award.

UNITED NATIONS CONVENTION ON THE RECOGNITION AND ENFORCEMENT OF FOREIGN ARBITRAL AWARDS (NEW YORK CONVENTION) (selections)
21 U.S.T. 2517, T.I.A.S. No. 6997, 330 U.N.T.S. 38.

Article I

1. This Convention shall apply to the recognition and enforcement of arbitral awards made in the territory of a State other than the State where the recognition and enforcement of such awards are sought, and arising out of differences between persons, whether physical or legal. It shall also apply to arbitral awards not considered as domestic awards in the State where their recognition and enforcement are sought. . . .

Article II

1. Each Contracting State shall recognize an agreement in writing under which the parties undertake to submit to arbitration all or any differences which have arisen or which may arise between them in respect of a defined legal relationship, whether contractual or not, concerning a subject matter capable of settlement by arbitration.

2. The term "agreement in writing" shall include an arbitral clause in a contract or an arbitration agreement, signed by the parties or contained in an exchange of letters or telegrams.

3. The court of a Contracting State, when seized of an action in a matter in respect of which the parties have made an agreement within the meaning of this article, at the request of one of the parties, refer the parties to arbitration, unless it finds that the said agreement is null and void, inoperative or incapable of being performed.

Article III

Each Contracting State shall recognize arbitral awards as binding and enforce them in accordance with the rules of procedure of the territory where the award is relied upon, under the conditions laid down in the following articles. There shall not be imposed substantially more onerous conditions or higher fees or charges on the recognition or enforcement of arbitral awards to which this Convention applies than are imposed on the recognition or enforcement of domestic arbitral awards. . . .

Article V

1. Recognition and enforcement of the award may be refused, at the request of the party against whom it is invoked, only if that party furnishes to the competent authority where the recognition and enforcement is sought, proof that:

(a) The parties to the agreement referred to in article II were, under the law applicable to them, under some incapacity, or the said agreement is not valid under the law to which the parties have subjected it or, failing any indication thereon, under the law of the country where the award was made; or

(b) The party against whom the award is invoked was not given proper notice of the appointment of the arbitrator or of the arbitration proceedings or was otherwise unable to present his case; or

(c) The award deals with a difference not contemplated by or not falling within the terms of the submission to arbitration, or it contains decisions on matters beyond the scope of the submission to arbitration, provided that, if the decisions on matters submitted to arbitration can be separated from those not so submitted, that part of the award which contains decisions on matters submitted to arbitration may be recognized and enforced; or

(d) The composition of the arbitral authority or the arbitral procedure was not in accordance with the agreement of the parties, or, failing such agreement, was not in accordance with the law of the country where the arbitration took place; or

(e) The award has not yet become binding on the parties, or has been set aside or suspended by a competent authority of the country in which, or under the law of which, that award was made.

2. Recognition and enforcement of an arbitral award may also be refused if the competent authority in the country where recognition and enforcement is sought finds that:

(a) The subject matter of the difference is not capable of settlement by arbitration under the law of that country; or

(b) The recognition or enforcement of the award would be contrary to the public policy of that country.

Article VI

If an application for the setting aside or suspension of the award has been made to a competent authority referred to in article V(1)(e), the authority before which the award is sought to be relied upon may, if it considers it proper, adjourn the decision on the enforcement of the award and may also, on the application of the party claiming enforcement of the award, order the other party to give suitable security.

Chapter 2 of the Federal Arbitration Act, reproduced in the Document Supplement, attempts to make domestic enforcement standards largely congruent with the New York Convention.[4] Under the implementing statute, foreign arbitral awards are presumed to be conclusive, and may only be denied recognition or enforcement if the court finds that one of the defenses laid out in the Convention applies:

> Within three years after an arbitral award falling under the Convention is made, any party to the arbitration may apply to any court having jurisdiction under this chapter for an order confirming the award as against any other party to the arbitration. The court shall confirm the award unless it finds one of the grounds for refusal or deferral of recognition or enforcement of the award specified in the said Convention.

9 U.S.C. § 207. The doctrine that emerges from the combined effect of the New York Convention and the Federal Arbitration Act, as amended by the Convention Act,[5] has been summarized in the Restatement (Third) of U.S. Foreign Relations Law in the following terms:

§ 487. Recognition and Enforcement of Foreign Arbitral Agreements and Awards

Under the Convention on the Recognition and Enforcement of Foreign Arbitral Awards, and subject only to the defenses set forth in § 488,

(1) a court in a state party to the Convention must recognize and enforce an arbitral award, rendered in a state party to the Convention pursuant to a valid written agreement to arbitrate, at least if the legal relationship that gave rise to the controversy was commercial in character;

(2) a court in a state party to the Convention must, at the request of any party to an action, stay or dismiss the action pending arbitration if an agreement to arbitrate falling under the Convention is in effect and covers the controversy on which the action is based.

§ 488. Grounds for Nonrecognition of Foreign Arbitral Awards

Under the Convention on the Recognition and Enforcement of Foreign Arbitral Awards,

(1) a court in a state party to the Convention may deny recognition or enforcement to a foreign arbitral award if

(a) the agreement to arbitrate was not valid under the applicable law;

(b) the party against which the award was rendered did not receive proper notice of the proceedings or was otherwise not afforded an opportunity to present its case;

(c) the award deals with matters outside the terms of the agreement to arbitrate;

---

[4] For an analysis of the discrepancies between the Convention Act and the New York Convention, see Susan Karamanian, *The Road to the Tribunal and Beyond: International Commercial Arbitration and United States Courts*, 34 G. WASH. INT'L L. REV. 17 (2001).

[5] *See* note 1, *supra*.

(d) the constitution of the arbitral tribunal or the arbitral procedure was contrary to the agreement of the parties or to the law of the state where the arbitration took place; or

(e) the award has not yet become binding on the parties, or has been suspended or set aside by a competent court in the state where it was made.

(2) A court of a state party to the Convention may also deny recognition or enforcement to a foreign arbitral award that meets the requirements of § 487 if, under the law of that state,

(a) the subject matter of the controversy is not capable of settlement by arbitration; or

(b) recognition or enforcement of the award would be contrary to public policy.

Notes and Questions

1. *The New York Convention versus the draft Hague Judgments Convention.* Focusing specifically on the defenses to enforcement, what substantive similarities and differences are there between the regime governing arbitral awards and that governing foreign judgments, *supra*? Why do you suppose that a global treaty regime governing arbitrations has worked relatively successfully for decades and a global treaty regime governing judgments continues to be elusive and controversial?

2. *Dependency on national law.* Although the New York Convention offers an international framework for the enforcement of arbitral awards, it is

> [n]ational law [that] gives arbitration its legally binding character. Courts become actors in arbitration when business managers ask that arbitration agreements and awards be enforced against recalcitrant parties, that assets be attached, that the scope of the arbitration clause be determined, or that poorly drafted (sometimes pathological) arbitration clauses be made workable. The authority of an arbitrator, therefore, derives not only from the consent of the parties, but also from the several legal systems that support the arbitral process: the law that enforces the agreement to arbitrate, the forum called on to recognize and enforce the award, and the law of the place of the proceedings.

William W. Park, *The Internationalization of Law and Legal Practice: National Law and Commercial Justice: Safeguarding Procedural Integrity in International Arbitration*, 66 TUL. L. REV. 647, 655–56 (1989) (citations omitted). It is possible in short to overstate both the distinction between litigation and arbitration and the distinction between international and domestic law.

3. *Defenses under the Convention.* The New York Convention establishes a presumption in favor of the recognition and enforcement of foreign arbitral awards, subject to limited defenses: the agreement is invalid (Article V(1)(a));

notice is inadequate or a party was otherwise unable to present a case (Article V(1)(b)); the award exceeds the scope of the submission to arbitration (Article V(1)(c)); the composition of the arbitral body violated the parties' agreement or local law (Article V(1)(d)); the award is not yet binding or has been suspended by a competent authority (Article V(1)(e)); the subject matter is not capable of settlement by arbitration in the country where recognition is sought (Article V(2)(a)); or the enforcement of the award would be contrary to the public policy of the state where enforcement is sought (Article V(2)(b)). Reviewing the text of Article V, what is the difference between the defenses in paragraph 1 of Article V and those in paragraph 2? Is the list of defenses in Section 488 of the Restatement (Third) identical to those in Article V of the Convention? What significance, if any, would you attach to the differences?

4. *International and "non-domestic" awards.* As noted above, under the first sentence of Article I(1), the New York Convention adopts a territorial approach to arbitral awards, applying "to the recognition and enforcement of arbitral awards made in the territory of a State other than the State where the recognition and enforcement of such awards are sought." But the second sentence of Article I(1) adds confusingly that "[i]t shall also apply to arbitral awards not considered as domestic awards in the State where recognition and enforcement are sought." Why is the second sentence necessary? Are there awards which are "non-domestic" for purposes of the second sentence of Article I(1) but which do not satisfy the territorial criterion under the first sentence for convention treatment?

Section 202 of the implementing legislation illustrates how an award can be non-domestic and yet not satisfy the territoriality requirement:

> An arbitration agreement or arbitral award arising out of a legal relationship, whether contractual or not, which is considered as commercial, . . . falls under the Convention. An arbitration agreement or award that arises out of such a relationship which is entirely between United States citizens shall be deemed not to fall under the Convention *unless that relationship involves property located abroad, envisages performance or enforcement abroad, or has some other reasonable relation with one or more foreign states.*

9 U.S.C. § 202 (emphasis supplied). That an award can fall within the convention by virtue only of its "reasonable relation with one or more foreign states" suggests that the margins of the treaty regime are potentially indefinite. *See, e.g., Industrial Risk Insurers v. M.A.N. Guttehoffnungshutte GmbH*, 141 F.3d 1434 (11th Cir. 1998), *cert. denied*, 525 U.S. 1068 (1999) (arbitral award made in United States, under U.S. law, falls within the New York Convention if party to arbitration is domiciled or has its principal place of business outside of United States); *Lander Co. Inc. v. MMP Invs., Inc.*, 107 F.3d 476 (7th Cir.), *cert. denied*, 522 U.S. 811 (1997) (New York Convention applies to arbitration award made in United States as between two domestic corporations when the contract contemplated distribution abroad). Does the domestic legislation overinterpret Article I of the Convention? Is an expansive application necessarily a bad thing?

5. *Manifest disregard.* In principle, an arbitral award will be set aside if it was made in "manifest disregard" of the applicable law — a "judicially crafted

exception to the general rule that arbitrators' 'erroneous interpretation or applications of law are not reversible.' " *Bowen v. Amoco Pipeline Co.*, 254 F.3d 925, 932 (10th Cir. 2001) (quoting *ARW Exploration Corp. v. Aguirre*, 45 F.3d 1455, 1463 (10th Cir. 1995)). The "manifest disregard" standard introduces a potential wildcard into the enforcement process, and for that reason courts describe the doctrine as "severely limited," *Government of India v. Cargill Inc.*, 867 F.2d 130, 133 (2d Cir. 1989), and applicable only in extraordinary circumstances, as for example if the arbitrators "understood and correctly stated the law but proceeded to ignore it." *Kanuth v. Prescott, Ball, & Turben, Inc.*, 949 F.2d 1175, 1179 (D.C. Cir. 1991). *See also Dirussa v. Dean Witter Reynolds Inc.*, 121 F.3d 818, 821 (2d Cir. 1997), *cert. denied*, 522 U.S. 1049 (1998):

> we have cautioned that manifest disregard "clearly means more than error or misunderstanding with respect to the law." The error must have been obvious and capable of being readily and instantly perceived by the average person qualified to serve as an arbitrator. Moreover, the term "disregard" implies that the arbitrator appreciates the existence of a clearly governing legal principle but decides to ignore or pay no attention to it. Thus, to modify or vacate an award on this ground, a court must find both that (1) the "arbitrators knew of a governing legal principle yet refused to apply it or ignored it altogether," and (2) the "law ignored by the arbitrators . . . [was] 'well defined, explicit, and clearly applicable' " to the case.

Id. (citing *Folkways Music Publishers, Inc. v. Weiss*, 989 F.2d 108, 112 (2d Cir. 1993)). One commentator has suggested that actually satisfying this strict standard "will never happen in our lifetimes," no matter how many courts reaffirm their hypothetical power to review awards on that basis. Alan Scott Rau, *The New York Convention in American Courts*, 7 AM. REV. INT'L ARB. 213, 238 (1997). Notice however that *DiRussa, Kanuth*, and *Bowen* — though useful in giving content to the manifest disregard standard generally — are domestic cases with no connection to the New York Convention. Is there a textual basis in the Convention (or the implementing legislation or the Restatement) for suggesting that the manifest disregard standard should be easier or harder to satisfy in international arbitration cases?

6. *The convention and its implementing statute in state courts.* Under the Supremacy Clause of the Constitution, the New York Convention "controls any case in any American court falling within its sphere of application. . . . [A]ny dispute involving international commercial arbitration which meets the Convention's jurisdictional requirements, whether brought in state or federal court, must be resolved with reference to that instrument." *Filanto, S.p.A. v. Chilewich Int'l Corp.*, 789 F. Supp. 1229, 1236 (S.D.N.Y. 1992). But even arbitration cases that are filed in state courts may not stay there long, because, in implementing the convention, Congress adopted a broad removal provision "so that parties seeking to guarantee enforcement of arbitral contracts and awards could elect to escape the uncertainty of the laws of the fifty states for the comparative uniformity of federal law." *Caringal v. Karteria Shipping Ltd.*, 108 F. Supp.2d 651, 654 (E.D. La. 2000). And in those cases that do remain in state court, the Convention and its implementing statute

have been held to pre-empt inconsistent state law. *See, e.g., F.A. Richards & Assocs. v. General Marine Catering Co.*, 688 So.2d 199 (La. App. 1997).

---

[2] Enforcing the Agreement to Arbitrate

MITSUBISHI MOTORS CORP. v. SOLER CHRYSLER-PLYMOUTH, INC.
473 U.S. 614 (1985)

JUSTICE BLACKMUN delivered the opinion of the Court. The principal question presented by these cases is the arbitrability, pursuant to the Federal Arbitration Act, 9 U. S. C. § 1 et seq., and the Convention on the Recognition and Enforcement of Foreign Arbitral Awards (Convention), T.I.A.S. No. 6997, of claims arising under the Sherman Act, 15 U. S. C. § 1 *et seq.*, and encompassed within a valid arbitration clause in an agreement embodying an international commercial transaction.

I

Petitioner-cross-respondent Mitsubishi Motors Corporation (Mitsubishi) is a Japanese corporation which manufactures automobiles and has its principal place of business in Tokyo, Japan. Mitsubishi is the product of a joint venture between, on the one hand, Chrysler International, S.A. (CISA), a Swiss corporation registered in Geneva and wholly owned by Chrysler Corporation, and, on the other, Mitsubishi Heavy Industries, Inc., a Japanese corporation. The aim of the joint venture was the distribution through Chrysler dealers outside the continental United States of vehicles manufactured by Mitsubishi and bearing Chrysler and Mitsubishi trademarks. Respondent-cross-petitioner Soler Chrysler-Plymouth, Inc. (Soler), is a Puerto Rico corporation with its principal place of business in . . . Puerto Rico.

On October 31, 1979, Soler entered into a Distributor Agreement with CISA which provided for the sale by Soler of Mitsubishi-manufactured vehicles within a designated area, including metropolitan San Juan. On the same date, CISA, Soler, and Mitsubishi entered into a Sales Procedure Agreement (Sales Agreement) which, referring to the Distributor Agreement, provided for the direct sale of Mitsubishi products to Soler and governed the terms and conditions of such sales. Paragraph VI of the Sales Agreement, labeled "Arbitration of Certain Matters," provides:

> All disputes, controversies or differences which may arise between [Mitsubishi] and [Soler] out of or in relation to Articles I-B through V of this Agreement or for the breach thereof, shall be finally settled by arbitration in Japan in accordance with the rules and regulations of the Japan Commercial Arbitration Association.

Initially, Soler did a brisk business in Mitsubishi-manufactured vehicles. As a result of its strong performance, its minimum sales volume, specified by Mitsubishi and CISA, and agreed to by Soler, for the 1981 model year was substantially increased. In early 1981, however, the new-car market slackened. Soler ran into serious difficulties in meeting the expected sales volume, and by the spring of 1981, it felt itself compelled to request that Mitsubishi delay or cancel shipment of several orders. About the same time, Soler attempted to arrange for the transshipment of a quantity of its vehicles for sale in the continental United States and Latin America. Mitsubishi and CISA, however, refused permission for any such diversion, citing a variety of reasons,[1] and no vehicles were transshipped. Attempts to work out these difficulties failed. Mitsubishi eventually withheld shipment of 966 vehicles, apparently representing orders placed for May, June, and July 1981 production, responsibility for which Soler disclaimed in February 1982.

The following month, Mitsubishi brought an action against Soler in the United States District Court for the District of Puerto Rico under the Federal Arbitration Act and the Convention.[2] Mitsubishi sought an order, pursuant to 9 U.S.C. §§ 4 and 201,[3] to compel arbitration in accord with para. VI of the Sales Agreement. Shortly after filing the complaint, Mitsubishi filed a request for arbitration before the Japan Commercial Arbitration Association.

---

[1] The reasons advanced included concerns that such diversion would interfere with the Japanese trade policy of voluntarily limiting imports to the United State; that the Soler-ordered vehicles would be unsuitable for use in certain proposed destinations because of their manufacture, with use in Puerto Rico in mind, without heaters and defoggers; that the vehicles would be unsuitable for use in Latin America because of the unavailability there of the unleaded, high-octane fuel they required; that adequate warranty service could not be ensured; and that diversion to the mainland would violate contractual obligations between CISA and Mitsubishi.

[2] The complaint alleged that Soler had failed to pay for 966 ordered vehicles; that it had failed to pay contractual "distress unit penalties," intended to reimburse Mitsubishi for storage costs and interest charges incurred because of Soler's failure to take shipment of ordered vehicles; that Soler's failure to fulfill warranty obligations threatened Mitsubishi's reputation and goodwill; that Soler had failed to obtain required financing; and that the Distributor and Sales Agreements had expired by their terms or, alternatively, that Soler had surrendered its rights under the Sales Agreement.

[3] Section 4 provides in pertinent part:

> A party aggrieved by the alleged failure, neglect, or refusal of another to arbitrate under a written agreement for arbitration may petition any United States district court which, save for such agreement, would have jurisdiction under title 28, in a civil action or in admiralty of the subject matter of a suit arising out of the controversy between the parties, for an order directing that such arbitration proceed in the manner provided for in such agreement. . . . The court shall hear the parties, and upon being satisfied that the making of the agreement for arbitration or the failure to comply therewith is not in issue, the court shall make an order directing the parties to proceed to arbitration in accordance with the terms of the agreement.

Section 201 provides: "The Convention on the Recognition and Enforcement of Foreign Arbitral Awards of June 10, 1958, shall be enforced in United States courts in accordance with this chapter." Article II of the Convention, in turn, provides:

> 1. Each Contracting State shall recognize an agreement in writing under which the parties undertake to submit to arbitration all or any differences which have arisen or which may arise between them in respect of a defined legal relationship, whether contractual or not, concerning a subject matter capable of settlement by arbitration.
>
> . . .
>
> 3. The court of a Contracting State, when seized of an action in a matter in respect of which the parties have made an agreement within the meaning of this article, shall, at the request of one of the parties, refer the parties to arbitration, unless it finds that the said agreement is null and void, inoperative or incapable of being performed. . . .

Soler denied the allegations and counterclaimed against both Mitsubishi and CISA. It alleged numerous breaches by Mitsubishi of the Sales Agreement, raised a pair of defamation claims, and asserted causes of action under the Sherman Act; the federal Automobile Dealers' Day in Court Act; the Puerto Rico competition statute; and the Puerto Rico Dealers' Contracts Act. In the counterclaim premised on the Sherman Act, Soler alleged that Mitsubishi and CISA had conspired to divide markets in restraint of trade. To effectuate the plan, according to Soler, Mitsubishi had refused to permit Soler to resell to buyers in North, Central, or South America vehicles it had obligated itself to purchase from Mitsubishi; had refused to ship ordered vehicles or the parts, such as heaters and defoggers, that would be necessary to permit Soler to make its vehicles suitable for resale outside Puerto Rico; and had coercively attempted to replace Soler and its other Puerto Rico distributors with a wholly owned subsidiary which would serve as the exclusive Mitsubishi distributor in Puerto Rico.

After a hearing, the District Court ordered Mitsubishi and Soler to arbitrate each of the issues raised in the complaint and in all the counterclaims save two and a portion of a third. With regard to the federal antitrust issues, it recognized that the Courts of Appeals, following *American Safety Equip. Corp. v. J.P. Maguire & Co.*, 391 F.2d 821 (CA 2 1968), uniformly had held that the rights conferred by the antitrust laws were "of a character inappropriate for enforcement by arbitration," . . . quoting *Wilko v. Swan*, 201 F.2d 439, 444 (CA2 1953), *rev'd*, 346 U.S. 427 (1953). The District Court held, however, that the international character of the Mitsubishi-Soler undertaking required enforcement of the agreement to arbitrate even as to the antitrust claims. It relied on *Scherk v. Alberto-Culver Co.*, 417 U.S. 506, 515–520 (1974), in which this Court ordered arbitration, pursuant to a provision embodied in an international agreement, of a claim arising under the Securities Exchange Act of 1934 notwithstanding its assumption, arguendo, that *Wilko, supra,* which held nonarbitrable claims arising under the Securities Act of 1933, also would bar arbitration of a 1934 Act claim arising in a domestic context.

The United States Court of Appeals for the First Circuit affirmed in part and reversed in part. . . . It . . . rejected Soler's suggestion that it could not have intended to arbitrate statutory claims not mentioned in the arbitration agreement. Assessing arbitrability "on an allegation-by-allegation basis," the court then read the arbitration clause to encompass virtually all the claims arising under the various statutes, including all those arising under the Sherman Act. . . . [A]fter endorsing the doctrine of *American Safety*, precluding arbitration of antitrust claims, the Court of Appeals concluded that neither this Court's decision in *Scherk* nor the Convention required abandonment of that doctrine in the face of an international transaction. Accordingly, it reversed the judgment of the District Court insofar as it had ordered submission of "Soler's antitrust claims" to arbitration. Affirming the remainder of the judgment, the court directed the District Court to consider in the first instance how the parallel judicial and arbitral proceedings should go forward.

We granted certiorari primarily to consider whether an American court should enforce an agreement to resolve antitrust claims by arbitration when that agreement arises from an international transaction.

II

At the outset, we address the contention raised in Soler's cross-petition that the arbitration clause at issue may not be read to encompass the statutory counterclaims stated in its answer to the complaint. In making this argument, Soler . . . argues that as a matter of law a court may not construe an arbitration agreement to encompass claims arising out of statutes designed to protect a class to which the party resisting arbitration belongs "unless [that party] has expressly agreed" to arbitrate those claims, by which Soler presumably means that the arbitration clause must specifically mention the statute giving rise to the claims that a party to the clause seeks to arbitrate. Soler reasons that, because it falls within the class for whose benefit the federal and local antitrust laws and dealers' Acts were passed, but the arbitration clause at issue does not mention these statutes or statutes in general, the clause cannot be read to contemplate arbitration of these statutory claims.

We do not agree, for we find no warrant in the Arbitration Act for implying in every contract within its ken a presumption against arbitration of statutory claims. The Act's centerpiece provision makes a written agreement to arbitrate "in any maritime transaction or a contract evidencing a transaction involving commerce . . . valid, irrevocable, and enforceable, save upon such grounds as exist at law or in equity for the revocation of any contract." 9 U. S. C. § 2. The "liberal federal policy favoring arbitration agreements," *Moses H. Cone Memorial Hospital v. Mercury Construction Corp.*, 460 U.S. 1, 24 (1983), manifested by this provision and the Act as a whole, is at bottom a policy guaranteeing the enforcement of private contractual arrangements: the Act simply "creates a body of federal substantive law establishing and regulating the duty to honor an agreement to arbitrate."[4] As this Court recently observed, "[the] preeminent concern of Congress in passing the Act was to enforce private agreements into which parties had entered," a concern which "requires that we rigorously enforce agreements to arbitrate." *Dean Witter Reynolds Inc. v. Byrd,* 470 U.S. 213, 221 (1985).

Accordingly, the first task of a court asked to compel arbitration of a dispute is to determine whether the parties agreed to arbitrate that dispute. The court is to make this determination by applying the "federal substantive law of arbitrability, applicable to any arbitration agreement within the coverage of the Act." *Moses H. Cone Memorial Hospital,* 460 U.S., at 24. And that body of law counsels

> that questions of arbitrability must be addressed with a healthy regard for the federal policy favoring arbitration. . . . The Arbitration Act establishes that, as a matter of federal law, any doubts concerning the scope of arbitrable issues should be resolved in favor of arbitration, whether the problem at hand is the construction of the contract language itself or an allegation of waiver, delay, or a like defense to arbitrability." *Moses H. Cone Memorial Hospital,* 460 U.S., at 24–25.

---

[4] The Court previously has explained that the Act was designed to overcome an anachronistic judicial hostility to agreements to arbitrate, which American courts had borrowed from English common law.

Thus, as with any other contract, the parties' intentions control, but those intentions are generously construed as to issues of arbitrability. There is no reason to depart from these guidelines where a party bound by an arbitration agreement raises claims founded on statutory rights. Some time ago this Court expressed "hope for [the Act's] usefulness both in controversies based on statutes or on standards otherwise created," *Wilko v. Swan*, 346 U.S. 427, 432 (1953), and we are well past the time when judicial suspicion of the desirability of arbitration and of the competence of arbitral tribunals inhibited the development of arbitration as an alternative means of dispute resolution. . . . Of course, courts should remain attuned to well-supported claims that the agreement to arbitrate resulted from the sort of fraud or overwhelming economic power that would provide grounds "for the revocation of any contract." 9 U. S. C. § 2; *The Bremen v. Zapata Off-Shore Co.*, 407 U.S. 1, 15 (1972). But, absent such compelling considerations, the Act itself provides no basis for disfavoring agreements to arbitrate statutory claims by skewing the otherwise hospitable inquiry into arbitrability.

That is not to say that all controversies implicating statutory rights are suitable for arbitration. There is no reason to distort the process of contract interpretation, however, in order to ferret out the inappropriate. Just as it is the congressional policy manifested in the Federal Arbitration Act that requires courts liberally to construe the scope of arbitration agreements covered by that Act, it is the congressional intention expressed in some other statute on which the courts must rely to identify any category of claims as to which agreements to arbitrate will be held unenforceable. For that reason, Soler's concern for statutorily protected classes provides no reason to color the lens through which the arbitration clause is read. By agreeing to arbitrate a statutory claim, a party does not forgo the substantive rights afforded by the statute; it only submits to their resolution in an arbitral, rather than a judicial, forum. It trades the procedures and opportunity for review of the courtroom for the simplicity, informality, and expedition of arbitration. We must assume that if Congress intended the substantive protection afforded by a given statute to include protection against waiver of the right to a judicial forum, that intention will be deducible from text or legislative history. Having made the bargain to arbitrate, the party should be held to it unless Congress itself has evinced an intention to preclude a waiver of judicial remedies for the statutory rights at issue. Nothing, in the meantime, prevents a party from excluding statutory claims from the scope of an agreement to arbitrate. . . .

III

We now turn to consider whether Soler's antitrust claims are nonarbitrable even though it has agreed to arbitrate them. In holding that they are not, the Court of Appeals followed the decision of the Second Circuit in *American Safety Equipment Corp. v. J. P. Maguire & Co.*, 391 F.2d 821 (1968). Notwithstanding the absence of any explicit support for such an exception in either the Sherman Act or the Federal Arbitration Act, the Second Circuit there reasoned that "the pervasive public interest in enforcement of the antitrust laws, and the nature of the claims that arise in such cases, combine to make . . . antitrust claims . . . inappropriate for arbitration." We find it unnecessary to assess the legitimacy of the *American Safety* doctrine as applied to agreements to arbitrate arising from domestic transactions. As in *Scherk v. Alberto-Culver Co.*, 417 U.S. 506 (1974), we conclude that concerns of international comity, respect for the capacities of foreign and transnational tribunals, and sensitivity to the need of the international commercial system for predictability in the resolution of disputes require that we enforce the parties' agreement, even assuming that a contrary result would be forthcoming in a domestic context.

Even before *Scherk*, this Court had recognized the utility of forum-selection clauses in international transactions. In *The Bremen, supra,* an American oil company, seeking to evade a contractual choice of an English forum and, by implication, English law, filed a suit in admiralty in a United States District Court against the German corporation which had contracted to tow its rig to a location in the Adriatic Sea. Notwithstanding the possibility that the English court would enforce provisions in the towage contract exculpating the German party which an American court would refuse to enforce, this Court gave effect to the choice-of-forum clause. It observed:

> The expansion of American business and industry will hardly be encouraged if, notwithstanding solemn contracts, we insist on a parochial concept that all disputes must be resolved under our laws and in our courts. . . . We cannot have trade and commerce in world markets and international waters exclusively on our terms, governed by our laws, and resolved in our courts. 407 U.S., at 9.

Recognizing that "agreeing in advance on a forum acceptable to both parties is an indispensable element in international trade, commerce, and contracting," the decision in *The Bremen* clearly eschewed a provincial solicitude for the jurisdiction of domestic forums.

Identical considerations governed the Court's decision in *Scherk*, which categorized "[an] agreement to arbitrate before a specified tribunal [as], in effect, a specialized kind of forum-selection clause that posits not only the situs of suit but also the procedure to be used in resolving the dispute." In *Scherk*, the American company Alberto-Culver purchased several interrelated business enterprises, organized under the laws of Germany and Liechtenstein, as well as the rights held by those enterprises in certain trademarks, from a German citizen who at the time of trial resided in Switzerland. Although the contract of sale contained a clause providing for arbitration before the International Chamber of Commerce in Paris of "any controversy or claim [arising] out of this agreement or the breach thereof," Alberto-Culver subsequently brought suit against Scherk in a Federal District Court in Illinois, alleging that Scherk had violated § 10(b) of the Securities Exchange Act of 1934 by fraudulently misrepresenting the status of the trademarks as unencumbered. The District Court denied a motion to stay the proceedings before it and enjoined the parties from going forward before the arbitral tribunal in Paris. The Court of Appeals for the Seventh Circuit affirmed, relying on this Court's holding in *Wilko v. Swan*, 346 U.S. 427 (1953), that agreements to arbitrate disputes arising under the Securities Act of 1933 are nonarbitrable. This Court reversed, enforcing the arbitration agreement even while assuming for purposes of the decision that the controversy would be nonarbitrable under the holding of *Wilko* had it arisen out of a domestic transaction. Again, the Court emphasized:

> A contractual provision specifying in advance the forum in which disputes shall be litigated and the law to be applied is . . . an almost indispensable precondition to achievement of the orderliness and predictability essential to any international business transaction. . . . A parochial refusal by the courts of one country to enforce an international arbitration agreement would not only frustrate these purposes, but would invite unseemly and mutually destructive jockeying by the parties to secure tactical litigation advantages. . . . [It would] damage the fabric of international commerce and trade, and imperil the willingness and ability of businessmen to enter into international commercial agreements.

Accordingly, the Court held Alberto-Culver to its bargain, sending it to the international arbitral tribunal before which it had agreed to seek its remedies.

The Bremen and *Scherk* establish a strong presumption in favor of enforcement of freely negotiated contractual choice-of-forum provisions. Here, as in *Scherk*, that presumption is reinforced by the emphatic federal policy in favor of arbitral dispute resolution. And at least since this Nation's accession in 1970 to the Convention, and the implementation of the Convention in the same year by amendment of the Federal Arbitration Act, [footnote omitted] that federal policy applies with special force in the field of international commerce. Thus, we must weigh the concerns of *American Safety* against a strong belief in the efficacy of arbitral procedures for the resolution of international commercial disputes and an equal commitment to the enforcement of freely negotiated choice-of-forum clauses.

At the outset, we confess to some skepticism of certain aspects of the *American Safety* doctrine. As distilled by the First Circuit, the doctrine comprises four ingredients. First, private parties play a pivotal role in aiding governmental enforcement of the antitrust laws by means of the private action for treble damages. Second, "the strong possibility that contracts which generate antitrust disputes may be contracts of adhesion militates against automatic forum determination by contract." Third, antitrust issues, prone to complication, require sophisticated legal and economic analysis, and thus are "ill-adapted to strengths of the arbitral process, *i.e.*, expedition, minimal requirements of written rationale, simplicity, resort to basic concepts of common sense and simple equity." Finally, just as "issues of war and peace are too important to be vested in the generals, . . . decisions as to antitrust regulation of business are too important to be lodged in arbitrators chosen from the business community — particularly those from a foreign community that has had no experience with or exposure to our law and values."

[The Court rejected the second, third, and fourth concerns, noting *inter alia* the neutrality and expertise, in matters of law and fact, available in arbitral proceedings.]

We are left, then, with the core of the *American Safety* doctrine — the fundamental importance to American democratic capitalism of the regime of the antitrust laws. Without doubt, the private cause of action plays a central role in enforcing this regime. As the Court of Appeals pointed out:

> A claim under the antitrust laws is not merely a private matter. The
> Sherman Act is designed to promote the national interest in a competi-
> tive economy; thus, the plaintiff asserting his rights under the Act has
> been likened to a private attorney-general who protects the public's
> interest.

The treble-damages provision wielded by the private litigant is a chief tool
in the antitrust enforcement scheme, posing a crucial deterrent to potential
violators.

The importance of the private damages remedy, however, does not compel
the conclusion that it may not be sought outside an American court. Notwithstanding its important incidental policing function, the treble-damages cause
of action conferred on private parties by § 4 of the Clayton Act, and pursued
by Soler here . . . seeks primarily to enable an injured competitor to gain
compensation for that injury.

> Section 4 . . . is in essence a remedial provision. It provides treble damages
> to "[any] person who shall be injured in his business or property by reason
> of anything forbidden in the antitrust laws . . . ." Of course, treble damages
> also play an important role in penalizing wrongdoers and deterring wrong-
> doing, as we also have frequently observed. . . . It nevertheless is true that
> the treble-damages provision, which makes awards available only to injured
> parties, and measures the awards by a multiple of the injury actually
> proved, is designed primarily as a remedy.

Brunswick Corp. v. Pueblo Bowl-O-Mat, Inc., 429 U.S. 477, 485–486
(1977). . . . [A]t least where the international cast of a transaction would
otherwise add an element of uncertainty to dispute resolution, the prospective
litigant may provide in advance for a mutually agreeable procedure whereby
he would seek his antitrust recovery as well as settle other controversies.

There is no reason to assume at the outset of the dispute that international
arbitration will not provide an adequate mechanism. To be sure, the international arbitral tribunal owes no prior allegiance to the legal norms of particular states; hence, it has no direct obligation to vindicate their statutory
dictates. The tribunal, however, is bound to effectuate the intentions of the
parties. Where the parties have agreed that the arbitral body is to decide a
defined set of claims which includes, as in these cases, those arising from the
application of American antitrust law, the tribunal therefore should be bound
to decide that dispute in accord with the national law giving rise to the claim.[5]

---

[5] In addition to the clause providing for arbitration before the Japan Commercial Arbitration
Association, the Sales Agreement includes a choice-of-law clause which reads: "This Agreement
is made in, and will be governed by and construed in all respects according to the laws of the
Swiss Confederation as if entirely performed therein." The United States raises the possibility
that the arbitral panel will read this provision not simply to govern interpretation of the contract
terms, but wholly to displace American law even where it otherwise would apply. The International Chamber of Commerce opines that it is "[conceivable], although we believe it unlikely, [that]
the arbitrators could consider Soler's affirmative claim of anticompetitive conduct by CISA and
Mitsubishi to fall within the purview of this choice-of-law provision, with the result that it would
be decided under Swiss law rather than the U.S. Sherman Act." At oral argument, however,
counsel for Mitsubishi conceded that American law applied to the antitrust claims and represented
that the claims had been submitted to the arbitration panel in Japan on that basis. Tr. of Oral.
Arg. 18. The record confirms that before the decision of the Court of Appeals the arbitral panel
had taken these claims under submission.

And so long as the prospective litigant effectively may vindicate its statutory cause of action in the arbitral forum, the statute will continue to serve both its remedial and deterrent function.

Having permitted the arbitration to go forward, the national courts of the United States will have the opportunity at the award-enforcement stage to ensure that the legitimate interest in the enforcement of the antitrust laws has been addressed. The Convention reserves to each signatory country the right to refuse enforcement of an award where the "recognition or enforcement of the award would be contrary to the public policy of that country." Art. V(2)(b). While the efficacy of the arbitral process requires that substantive review at the award-enforcement stage remain minimal, it would not require intrusive inquiry to ascertain that the tribunal took cognizance of the antitrust claims and actually decided them.[6]

As international trade has expanded in recent decades, so too has the use of international arbitration to resolve disputes arising in the course of that trade. The controversies that international arbitral institutions are called upon to resolve have increased in diversity as well as in complexity. Yet the potential of these tribunals for efficient disposition of legal disagreements arising from commercial relations has not yet been tested. If they are to take a central place in the international legal order, national courts will need to "shake off the old judicial hostility to arbitration," *Kulukundis Shipping Co. v. Amtorg Trading Corp.*, 126 F.2d 978, 985 (CA2 1942), and also their customary and understandable unwillingness to cede jurisdiction of a claim arising under domestic law to a foreign or transnational tribunal. To this extent, at least, it will be necessary for national courts to subordinate domestic notions of arbitrability to the international policy favoring commercial arbitration.[7]

We therefore have no occasion to speculate on this matter at this stage in the proceedings, when Mitsubishi seeks to enforce the agreement to arbitrate, not to enforce an award. Nor need we consider now the effect of an arbitral tribunal's failure to take cognizance of the statutory cause of action on the claimant's capacity to reinitiate suit in federal court. We merely note that in the event the choice-of-forum and choice-of-law clauses operated in tandem as a prospective waiver of a party's right to pursue statutory remedies for antitrust violations, we would have little hesitation in condemning the agreement as against public policy.

[6] *See* n.[5], *supra*. We note, for example, that the rules of the Japan Commercial Arbitration Association provide for the taking of a "summary record" of each hearing, Rule 28.1; for the stenographic recording of the proceedings where the tribunal so orders or a party requests one, Rule 28.2; and for a statement of reasons for the award unless the parties agree otherwise, Rule 36.1(4). Needless to say, we intimate no views on the merits of Soler's antitrust claims.

[7] We do not quarrel with the Court of Appeals' conclusion that Art. II(1) of the Convention, which requires the recognition of agreements to arbitrate that involve "subject matter capable of settlement by arbitration," contemplates exceptions to arbitrability grounded in domestic law [citing authorities]. And it appears that before acceding to the Convention the Senate was advised by a State Department memorandum that the Convention provided for such exceptions. *See* S. Exec. Doc. E, 90th Cong., 2d Sess., 19 (1968).

In acceding to the Convention the Senate restricted its applicability to commercial matters, in accord with Art. I(3). Yet in implementing the Convention by amendment to the Federal Arbitration Act, Congress did not specify any matters it intended to exclude from its scope. In *Scherk*, this Court recited Art. II(1), including the language relied upon by the Court of Appeals, but paid heed to the Convention delegates' "frequently [voiced] concern that courts of signatory countries in which an agreement to arbitrate is sought to be enforced should not be permitted to decline enforcement of such agreements on the basis of parochial views of their desirability

Accordingly, we "require this representative of the American business community to honor its bargain," *Alberto-Culver Co. v. Scherk*, 484 F.2d 611, 620 (CA7 1973) (Stevens, J., dissenting), by holding this agreement to arbitrate "[enforceable] . . . in accord with the explicit provisions of the Arbitration Act." *Scherk*, 417 U.S., at 520. The judgment of the Court of Appeals is affirmed in part and reversed in part, and the cases are remanded for further proceedings consistent with this opinion.

JUSTICE POWELL took no part in the decision of these cases.

JUSTICE STEVENS, with whom JUSTICE BRENNAN joins, and with whom JUSTICE MARSHALL joins except as to Part II, dissenting.

. . . This Court agrees with the Court of Appeals' interpretation of the scope of the arbitration clause, but disagrees with its conclusion that the clause is unenforceable insofar as it purports to cover an antitrust claim against a Japanese company. This Court's holding rests almost exclusively on the federal policy favoring arbitration of commercial disputes and vague notions of international comity arising from the fact that the automobiles involved here were manufactured in Japan. Because I am convinced that the Court of Appeals' construction of the arbitration clause is erroneous, and because I strongly disagree with this Court's interpretation of the relevant federal statutes, I respectfully dissent. In my opinion, (1) a fair construction of the language in the arbitration clause in the parties' contract does not encompass a claim that auto manufacturers entered into a conspiracy in violation of the antitrust laws; (2) an arbitration clause should not normally be construed to cover a statutory remedy that it does not expressly identify; (3) Congress did not intend § 2 of the Federal Arbitration Act to apply to antitrust claims; and (4) Congress did not intend the Convention on the Recognition and Enforcement of Foreign Arbitral Awards to apply to disputes that are not covered by the Federal Arbitration Act. . . .

The Court's [precedents] . . . explain why it makes good sense to draw a distinction between statutory claims and contract claims. In view of the Court's repeated recognition of the distinction between federal statutory rights and contractual rights, together with the undisputed historical fact that arbitration has functioned almost entirely in either the area of labor disputes or in "ordinary disputes between merchants as to questions of fact," it is reasonable to assume that most lawyers and executives would not expect the language in the standard arbitration clause to cover federal statutory claims. Thus, in my opinion, both a fair respect for the importance of the interests that Congress has identified as worthy of federal statutory protection, and a fair appraisal of the most likely understanding of the parties who sign

---

or in a manner that would diminish the mutually binding nature of the agreements." 417 U.S., at 520, n.15. There, moreover, the Court dealt, arguendo, with an exception to arbitrability grounded in express congressional language; here, in contrast, we face a judicially implied exception. The utility of the Convention in promoting the process of international commercial arbitration depends upon the willingness of national courts to let go of matters they normally would think of as their own. Doubtless, Congress may specify categories of claims it wishes to reserve for decision by our own courts without contravening this Nation's obligations under the Convention. But we decline to subvert the spirit of the United States' accession to the Convention by recognizing subject-matter exceptions where Congress has not expressly directed the courts to do so.

agreements containing standard arbitration clauses, support a presumption that such clauses do not apply to federal statutory claims. . . .

The Court has repeatedly held that a decision by Congress to create a special statutory remedy renders a private agreement to arbitrate a federal statutory claim unenforceable. Thus, . . . the express statutory remedy provided in the Ku Klux Klan Act of 1871, the express statutory remedy in the Securities Act of 1933, the express statutory remedy in the Fair Labor Standards Act, and the express statutory remedy in Title VII of the Civil Rights Act of 1964, each provided the Court with convincing evidence that Congress did not intend the protections afforded by the statute to be administered by a private arbitrator. The reasons that motivated those decisions apply with special force to the federal policy that is protected by the antitrust laws. . . .

The Sherman and Clayton Acts reflect Congress' appraisal of the value of economic freedom; they guarantee the vitality of the entrepreneurial spirit. Questions arising under these Acts are among the most important in public law. . . .

The Court assumes for the purposes of its decision that the antitrust issues would not be arbitrable if this were a purely domestic dispute, but holds that the international character of the controversy makes it arbitrable. The holding rests on vague concerns for the international implications of its decision. . . .

International Obligations of the United States

Before relying on its own notions of what international comity requires, it is surprising that the Court does not determine the specific commitments that the United States has made to enforce private agreements to arbitrate disputes arising under public law. As the Court acknowledges, the only treaty relevant here is the Convention on the Recognition and Enforcement of Foreign Arbitral Awards. . . . As the Court acknowledged in *Scherk v. Alberto-Culver Co.*, the principal purpose of the Convention "was to encourage the recognition and enforcement of commercial arbitration agreements in international contracts and to unify the standards by which agreements to arbitrate are observed and arbitral awards are enforced in the signatory countries." However, the United States, as *amicus curiae*, advises the Court that the Convention "clearly contemplates" that signatory nations will enforce domestic laws prohibiting the arbitration of certain subject matters. This interpretation of the Convention was adopted by the Court of Appeals, and the Court declines to reject it. The construction is beyond doubt.

Article II(3) of the Convention provides that the court of a Contracting State, "when seized of an action in a matter in respect of which the parties have made an agreement within the meaning of this article, shall, at the request of one of the parties, refer the parties to arbitration." This obligation does not arise, however, (i) if the agreement "is null and void, inoperative or incapable of being performed," Art. II(3), or (ii) if the dispute does not concern "a subject matter capable of settlement by arbitration," Art. II(1). The former qualification principally applies to matters of fraud, mistake, and duress in the inducement, or problems of procedural fairness and feasibility. The latter clause plainly suggests the possibility that some subject matters are not capable of arbitration under the domestic laws of the signatory nations, and that agreements to arbitrate such disputes need not be enforced.

This construction is confirmed by the provisions of the Convention which provide for the enforcement of international arbitration awards. Article III provides that each "Contracting State shall recognize arbitral awards as binding and enforce them." However, if an arbitration award is "contrary to the public policy of [a] country" called upon to enforce it, or if it concerns a subject matter which is "not capable of settlement by arbitration under the law of that country," the Convention does not require that it be enforced. Arts. V(2)(a) and (b). Thus, reading Articles II and V together, the Convention provides that agreements to arbitrate disputes which are nonarbitrable under domestic law need not be honored, nor awards rendered under them enforced. . . .

International Comity

It is clear then that the international obligations of the United States permit us to honor Congress' commitment to the exclusive resolution of antitrust disputes in the federal courts. The Court today refuses to do so, offering only vague concerns for comity among nations. The courts of other nations, on the other hand, have applied the exception provided in the Convention, and refused to enforce agreements to arbitrate specific subject matters of concern to them.

It may be that the subject-matter exception to the Convention ought to be reserved — as a matter of domestic law — for matters of the greatest public interest which involve concerns that are shared by other nations. The Sherman Act's commitment to free competitive markets is among our most important civil policies. This commitment, shared by other nations which are signatory to the Convention, is hardly the sort of parochial concern that we should decline to enforce in the interest of international comity. Indeed, the branch of Government entrusted with the conduct of political relations with foreign governments has informed us that the "United States' determination that federal antitrust claims are nonarbitrable under the Convention . . . is not likely to result in either surprise or recrimination on the part of other signatories to the Convention." . . .

The Court's repeated incantation of the high ideals of "international arbitration" creates the impression that this case involves the fate of an institution designed to implement a formula for world peace. But just as it is improper to subordinate the public interest in enforcement of antitrust policy to the private interest in resolving commercial disputes, so is it equally unwise to allow a vision of world unity to distort the importance of the selection of the proper forum for resolving this dispute. Like any other mechanism for resolving controversies, international arbitration will only succeed if it is realistically limited to tasks it is capable of performing well — the prompt and inexpensive resolution of essentially contractual disputes between commercial partners. As for matters involving the political passions and the fundamental interests of nations, even the multilateral convention adopted under the auspices of the United Nations recognizes that private international arbitration is incapable of achieving satisfactory results.

In my opinion, the elected representatives of the American people would not have us dispatch an American citizen to a foreign land in search of an uncertain remedy for the violation of a public right that is protected by the Sherman Act. This is especially so when there has been no genuine bargaining over the terms of the submission, and the arbitration remedy provided has not even the most elementary guarantees of fair process. Consideration of a fully developed record by a jury, instructed in the law by a federal judge, and subject to appellate review, is a surer guide to the competitive character of a commercial practice than the practically unreviewable judgment of a private arbitrator.

Notes and Questions on *Mitsubishi*

1. *Determining whether a "subject matter" is "capable of settlement by arbitration" within the meaning of the New York Convention.* The New York Convention explicitly recognizes that some subject matters can be excluded from resolution through arbitration, allowing a party for example to declare that it will only apply the convention to commercial relationships, Article I(3), and imposing the obligation to recognize an arbitration agreement only with respect to "a subject matter capable of settlement by arbitration, Article II(1). The *Mitsubishi* court noted that the implementing legislation by contrast does not explicitly exclude any matters from its scope — other than non-commercial and non-legal relationships, neither of which was at issue in *Mitsubishi* — and on that basis recognized a powerful presumption in favor of arbitrating even statutory claims: "questions of arbitrability must be addressed with a healthy regard for the federal policy favoring arbitration. . . . [A]ny doubts concerning the scope of arbitrable issues should be resolved in favor of arbitration." In some circumstances, one federal regulatory policy (*e.g.,* antitrust standards) must evidently give way to another, namely the federal policy favoring arbitration in international business disputes.

A. Why should there be such a tilt towards arbitration when arbitration generally requires the parties to waive prerogatives to discovery, jury trials and other procedural rights in the U.S. judicial system?

B. Does the *Mitsubishi* policy mean in effect that private parties may opt out of statutory regulation through an artful choice of foreign arbitration under foreign law? Or is there a more moderate interpretation of *Mitsubishi*?

In approaching this question, consider the reality that, every so often, oral arguments (and footnotes) really do matter. The parties in *Mitsubishi* had selected the laws of the Swiss Confederation to govern their contract substantively, and a literal interpretation of their choice — combined with the decision to allow such private choices to trump public laws — might preclude the application of U.S. antitrust law. But according to footnote 5 [orginally footnote 19] of the court's opinion, "[a]t oral argument, . . . counsel for Mitsubishi conceded that *American law applied to the antitrust claims and represented that the claims had been submitted to the arbitration panel in Japan on that basis"* (emphasis supplied). The court continued:

> We therefore have no occasion to speculate on this matter at this stage in the proceedings, when Mitsubishi seeks to enforce the agreement to arbitrate, not to enforce an award. Nor need we consider now the effect of an arbitral tribunal's failure to take cognizance of the statutory cause of action on the claimant's capacity to reinitiate suit in federal court. We merely note that in the event the choice-of-forum and choice-of-law clauses operated in tandem as a prospective waiver of a party's right to pursue statutory remedies for antitrust violations, we would have little hesitation in condemning the agreement as against public policy.

The famous "footnote 19" has been the subject of intense scrutiny. *Simula, Inc. v. Autoliv, Inc.,* 175 F.3d 716 (9th Cir. 1999), for example, like *Mitsubishi,* raised the prospect of arbitrating U.S. antitrust claims in a foreign arbitral tribunal. The plaintiffs argued that arbitration in Switzerland, as required by the agreement, would deprive them of certain antitrust remedies because the tribunal was not obliged to apply U.S. law. The court ruled that footnote 19 was not binding: "we do not believe *dictum* in a footnote regarding antitrust law outweighs the extended discussion and holding in *Scherk* on the validity of clauses specifying the forum and applicable law." *Id.* at 723 (quoting *Richards v. Lloyd's of London,* 135 F.3d 1289, 1295 (9th Cir.) *(en banc), cert. denied,* 525 U.S. 943 (1998). Can the *Simula* approach be reconciled with the *Mitsubishi* court's requirement that the "prospective litigant [be able] effectively [to] vindicate its statutory cause of action in the arbitral forum"?

C. *Relationship between arbitrability and the enforcement of a subsequent award: the "second look" doctrine.* According to the *Mitsubishi* court, "[h]aving permitted the arbitration to go forward, the national courts of the United States will have the opportunity at the award-enforcement stage to ensure that the legitimate interest in the enforcement of the antitrust laws has been addressed." The court was willing to consider the statutory claims arbitrable in part because a U.S. court could take a "second look" at the case when it came back for enforcement. Why might the Supreme Court rule as it did despite the inefficiency of leaving the applicable rule unclear and allowing the arbitrator to apply the "wrong" law? Of what value is the "second look" doctrine in those common circumstances in which the prevailing party in the arbitration seeks enforcement in countries *other than* the United States? And what should the "second look" be under *Mitsubishi*: a searching *de novo* look at the arbitrators' analysis and disposition of U.S. law or a deferential look to assure that U.S. law was considered and applied?

D. *U.S. regulatory policy in foreign arbitrations.* How confident are you that an arbitral proceeding will be able to understand U.S. law and thereby protect the U.S. statutory rights of the parties? On what assumptions do you make your assessment? How should the Japanese arbitrators resolve the case if there turn out to be irreconcilable differences in the statutory rights of the parties under Japanese, Swiss, and U.S. law?

2. *When is there an agreement to arbitrate in the first place?* It isn't always obvious under the New York Convention when the parties have agreed to arbitrate their differences, and litigation continues to swirl around this jurisdictional requirement. The starting point is Article II(1), which requires each contracting state to recognize "an agreement in writing," and Article II(2), which defines "agreement in writing" to include "an arbitral clause in a contract or an arbitration agreement, signed by the parties or contained in an exchange of letters or telegrams." In *Sphere Drake Ins. PLC v. Marine Towing, Inc.*, 16 F.3d 666 (5th Cir.), *cert. denied*, 513 U.S. 871 (1994), for example, the court ruled that the phrase "signed by the parties or contained in an exchange of letters or telegrams" modified only the words "arbitration agreement", suggesting that an arbitration clause in an unsigned "contract" could fall within the Convention: "Because what is at issue here is an arbitral clause in a contract, the qualifications applicable to arbitration agreements do not apply. A signature is therefore not required." 16 F.3d, at 669. By contrast, in *Kahn Lucas Lancaster, Inc. v. Lark Int'l Ltd.*, 186 F.3d 210 (2d Cir. 1999), the court ruled that both "an arbitral clause in a contract" *and* "an arbitration agreement" must be signed or contained in an exchange of letters or telegrams. An arbitration clause in a series of purchase orders did not create an agreement under the Convention because only one of the parties had signed them. The result in *Kahn Lucas* is consistent with the negotiating history of the Convention and the authoritative non-English language versions of the treaty.

3. *International versus domestic arbitrations.* Consider how critical *Mitsubishi's* international setting is to its holding. Would the result be the same for example if the parties and the transaction were entirely domestic? Recall that *American Safety Equipment Corp. v. J.P. Maguire*, cited prominently in *Mitsubishi*, had held that federal antitrust claims are nonarbitrable in a domestic context. But

> concerns of international comity, respect for the capacities of foreign and transnational tribunals, and sensitivity to the need of the international commercial system for predictability in the resolution of disputes require that we enforce the parties' agreement, even assuming a contrary result would be forthcoming in a domestic context.

Mitsubishi, 473 U.S., at 629. Are you convinced? If so, how do you respond to the argument that *Mitsubishi* promotes a kind of lawlessness in international commercial settings that circumvents the will of Congress? *See* Hannah L. Buxbaum, *The Private Attorney General in a Global Age: Public Interests in Private International Antitrust Litigation*, 26 YALE J. INT'L L. 219, 244 (2001).

4. *The "very limited inquiry" on a motion to compel arbitration.* Courts have articulated a "very limited," two-step inquiry to determine whether they should compel arbitration on a party's motion. *See, e.g., Ledee v. Ceramiche Ragno*, 684 F.2d 184 (1st Cir. 1982). The first step requires the court to address four separate questions: (1) Is there an agreement in writing to submit the dispute to arbitration? (2) Does the agreement call for arbitration in the territory of a Convention signatory? (3) Does the arbitration agreement arise out of a defined legal relationship, whether contractual or not? (4) Is one of

the parties to the agreement a non-U.S. citizen, or does the relationship bear some reasonable relation to one or more foreign states? If these four criteria are met, the court will undertake the second step of the analysis and determine, in the words of Article II(3) of the New York Convention, whether the agreement to arbitrate is "null and void, inoperative or incapable of being performed." Given the convention's goal of encouraging arbitrations, this exclusionary language is narrowly construed. *DeMercurio v. Sphere Drake Ins., PLC*, 202 F.3d 71 (1st Cir. 2000).

> *Problem.* Suppose that a party resisted arbitration on the ground that the arbitration clause appeared in an adhesion contract. Should the court compel arbitration and require the arbitral tribunal to address the validity of the underlying contract, or should the court resolve the validity of the contract first? Does the Convention or the implementing statute or *Mitsubishi* offer a definitive answer? *Compare*, in the setting of a *domestic* arbitration, *Prima Paint v. Flood & Conklin Mfg. Co.*, 388 U.S. 395 (1967) (claim of fraud in the inducement of a contract was for the arbitrators under a clause calling for the arbitration of any controversy or claim arising out of or relating to the contract or a breach of the contract) *with Sphere Drake Ins. Ltd. v. All American Ins. Co.*, 256 F.3d 587 (7th Cir. 2001) (attempting to limit *Prima Paint* and allowing the court to determine the agreement's validity).

5. *Arbitrations outside of the New York Convention.* What difference might it make at the enforcement stage if the parties' agreement called for arbitration in a country that is not a party to the New York Convention? Are there any circumstances in which this might be a rational bargaining position for one of the parties?

6. *Bitter with the sweet.* What is your reaction to the following observation from Justice Steven's dissent: "When Mitsubishi enters the American market and plans to engage in business in that market over a period of years, it must recognize its obligation to comply with American law and to be subject to the remedial provisions of American statutes." Is this an argument-type you've seen before in this course in other contexts?

---

[3] Enforcing the Award (or Not)

EUROPCAR ITALIA, S.p.A. v. MAIELLANO TOURS, INC.
156 F.3d 310 (2d Cir. 1998)

Defendant-appellant Maiellano Tours, Inc. ("Maiellano") appeals from [a] judgment . . . granting plaintiff-appellee Europcar Italia S.p.A.'s ("Europcar") motion for summary judgment on its action for the enforcement of a foreign arbitration award under the Convention on the Recognition and Enforcement of Foreign Arbitral Awards of 1958, as implemented by 9 U.S.C. § 201 *et seq.* (the "Convention"). In October 1988, the parties entered into an agreement (the "1988 agreement") whereby Europcar, an Italian car rental business, agreed to provide rental car services in Italy to customers sent to it by

Maiellano, an American travel agency. The 1988 agreement contained an arbitration clause providing that the agreement would be governed by Italian law and that

> [a]ny dispute arising from or in connection with this agreement, included [sic] those related to its validity, performance or termination will be submitted to and finally resolved by a sole arbitrator appointed by the legal counsels selected by the parties. The sole arbitrator shall decide under the rules known in the Italian legal system as *"arbitrato irrituale in equita"* (informal proceedings).

A dispute arose in 1991 as to which party was entitled to certain value-added-tax refunds that had been remitted by the Italian tax authority to Maiellano. Unable to agree on a sole arbitrator as required by the 1988 agreement, the parties entered into a supplemental arbitration agreement, which provided in relevant part:

> [t]he agreement between Maiellano Tours, Inc. and Europcar Italia S.p.A. is regulated by Italian law. In the event that any dispute shall arise with respect to the application of this agreement, including its validity, execution or resolution, it shall be settled by a final arbitration by an Arbitration Panel of three arbitrators, as amicable adjusters, appointed as follows: each part [sic] will appoint an arbitrator, and the third arbitrator, who will act as President of the Panel will be mutually appointed by the two arbitrators so appointed. . . . The Panel will decide the controversy pursuant to the rules set forth in the Italian legal system for the *"Arbitrato Irrituale in Equita (procedimento informale)"* (Informal arbitration on equitable grounds).

Thus, as in the 1988 agreement, the procedure to be used was *"arbitrato irrituale"* and the arbitration panel's decision was to be a "final arbitration." Following written submissions and hearings, the selected panel issued an award in favor of Europcar in June of 1992.

In July 1992, Europcar commenced an action in the Italian courts to confirm the arbitration award and to obtain an order of payment. Maiellano countered by commencing a collateral action to have the award set aside on the ground of fraud, alleging that the arbitrator's decision was based on a February 20, 1979, agreement (the "1979 agreement") that contained a forged Maiellano signature. The Tribunal of Rome consolidated the actions and by a decision dated March 30, 1996, ruled in favor of Europcar and rejected all of Maiellano's claims. The tribunal found that Maiellano had not raised the issue of forgery to the arbitrators and that the arbitrators' decision was based principally on the parties' ten-year business relationship rather than on any particular written agreement. Maiellano appealed the Tribunal of Rome's confirmation of the arbitral award to the Roman Court of Appeals.

On August 4, 1994, while the above litigation was underway in the Italian courts, but before the outcome of the proceedings in the Tribunal of Rome, Europcar filed an action in the Eastern District of New York seeking recognition and enforcement of the arbitral award pursuant to the Convention and 9 U.S.C. § 207. Maiellano opposed enforcement, arguing, *inter alia,* that the district court lacked subject matter jurisdiction because *arbitrato irrituale* is not covered by the Convention and, in the alternative, that the district court should defer its decision pending the outcome of the trial of the Tribunal of Rome in accordance with *Spier v. Calzaturificio Tecnica S.p.A.*, 663 F. Supp. 871 (S.D.N.Y. 1987). Europcar moved for summary judgment in October of 1994, and the district court . . . entered judgment for Europcar in the amount of $1,102,283 with interest and costs. This appeal followed.

DISCUSSION

The Convention provides for the enforcement of arbitration agreements and the confirmation of foreign arbitral awards. District courts have been given original jurisdiction over actions or proceedings falling under the Convention, 9 U.S.C. § 203, and any party to a foreign arbitration may seek confirmation in a district court of an arbitral award within three years after the award is made, 9 U.S.C. § 207. "The court shall confirm the award unless it finds one of the grounds for refusal or deferral of recognition or enforcement of the award specified in the . . . Convention." The grounds for refusing to enforce an award are limited to the specific defenses enumerated in Article V of the Convention, which provides in relevant part:

> 1. Recognition and enforcement of the award may be refused . . . only if [the] party [requesting refusal] furnishes . . . proof that: . . . . (e) The award has not yet become binding on the parties, or has been set aside or suspended by a competent authority of the country in which, or under the law of which, that award was made.
>
> 2. Recognition and enforcement of an arbitral award may also be refused if the competent authority in the country where recognition and enforcement is sought finds that: . . . (b) The recognition or enforcement of the award would be contrary to the public policy of [the] country [in which enforcement is sought].

The party opposing enforcement has the burden of proving the existence of one of these enumerated defenses. On appeal, Maiellano argues, *inter alia*, that (1) the district court did not have jurisdiction under the Convention to confirm an award granted under *arbitrato irrituale*; (2) the award should not have been enforced because the parties did not intend to be bound by the arbitration award; (3) the district court should have refused to enforce the award because it was based on a forged contract and, therefore, is contrary to United States public policy; and, in any event, (4) the district court should have suspended its decision to await the outcome of the pending Italian litigation.

A. Enforceability of *arbitrato irrituale* Award

Maiellano contends that awards granted under the Italian rules known as *arbitrato irrituale* do not give rise to a binding arbitral award of the sort entitled to enforcement under the Convention because *arbitrato irrituale* is an informal, extralegal process that lacks procedural safeguards. Moreover, confirmation of the award here would give it greater legal status than it would be accorded in Italy because under Italian law, such arbitral awards are considered to be contractual agreements that are not automatically enforceable, but rather are subject to *de novo* review by an Italian court. Therefore,

Maiellano contends, it would be inappropriate to confirm such awards through the summary proceeding and deferential enforcement envisioned by the Convention. Maiellano supports these arguments with a decision by Germany's highest court . . . that held that awards rendered under *arbitrato irrituale* were not enforceable under the Convention, as well as opinions of academicians, including one of the draftsmen of the Convention, that state that the Convention was not meant to apply to *arbitrato irrituale.* . . .

Europcar, on the other hand, points to four decisions of the Italian Supreme Court, the Corte de Cassazione, that have expressly held that *arbitrato irrituale* does fall under the Convention. The Corte di Cassazione recognized that such awards would be treated differently under the Convention than under Italian law. Nevertheless, it held that in order to be enforceable under the Convention, awards must only be binding on the parties, not necessarily judicially binding in the originating country, and that although awards under *arbitrato irrituale* are merely contractual, and therefore are not immediately enforceable in Italy, they are nevertheless binding on the parties. The Corte di Cassazione concluded that in light of the differences in arbitration among the signatory countries, the Convention should be read broadly to cover both formal and informal arbitration. Whether or not the Convention applies to *arbitrato irrituale* is, as far as we can tell, a matter of first impression for any United States federal court. Indeed, apart from the above-cited cases in Germany and Italy, the matter apparently has yet to be ruled on by the Permanent Court of International Justice at the Hague [sic] or the courts of any other signatory countries. The only other federal court to be presented with the issue declined to resolve the matter and instead adjourned the proceedings to await the outcome of parallel proceedings in Italy. The district court below found the Italian cases persuasive and held that awards under *arbitrato irrituale* are enforceable under the Convention.

. . . . [T]he issue of whether or not *arbitrato irrituale* is enforceable under the Convention presents a close question and there are compelling arguments on both sides. Because resolution of this issue is not necessary to the disposition of this case, however, we leave decision on the matter for another day.

B. Parties' Intent to be Bound

Maiellano next argues that the parties did not intend to be legally bound by the arbitral award, but only to have it serve as a "contractual advisory". The district court properly rejected this argument. As the district court noted, both arbitration agreements stated unambiguously that the arbitration was to finally resolve the dispute and the arbitrators found that the parties intended to be bound by their award. Absent extraordinary circumstances, a confirming court is not to reconsider the arbitrator's findings. Moreover, as discussed above, awards under *arbitrato irrituale* are contractually binding on the parties even if they are not automatically enforceable. Accordingly, the district court did not err in determining that the arbitration award at issue was binding upon the parties under the Convention.

C. Alleged Forgery of Agreement

Maiellano also argues that the award was based on the allegedly forged 1979 agreement and therefore enforcement would be contrary to United States public policy. The Convention provides that a federal court "shall confirm the award unless it finds one of the grounds for refusal or deferral of recognition or enforcement of the award specified in the said Convention." 9 U.S.C. § 207. Article V(2)(B) of the Convention allows a court to refuse enforcement where to do so would violate the public policy of the enforcing state. However, this public policy exception is to be construed very narrowly and should be applied "only where enforcement would violate our 'most basic notions of morality and justice.'" *Waterside Ocean Navigation Co. v. International Navigation Ltd.*, 737 F.2d 150, 152 (2d Cir. 1984). No such public policy concerns are implicated in this case.

Maiellano has apparently confused the issue of a fraudulently obtained arbitration agreement or award, which might violate public policy and therefore preclude enforcement, with the issue of whether the underlying contract that is the subject of the arbitrated dispute was forged or fraudulently induced — a matter to be determined exclusively by the arbitrators. *See Prima Paint Corp. v. Flood & Conklin Mfg. Co.*, 388 U.S. 395, 403–04 (1967). Indeed, the supplemental arbitration agreement at issue here, whose validity Maiellano does not dispute, incorporates this rule of law by expressly providing that "any dispute [arising] with respect to the application of [the 1988] agreement, including its validity, execution or resolution, . . . shall be settled by a final arbitration by an Arbitration Panel." Thus, if Maiellano failed to raise the issue of the forged 1979 agreement to the arbitrators, the issue is forfeited. And if Maiellano did raise the issue to the arbitrators, it cannot seek to relitigate the matter here. It is also significant that the Italian Tribunal, in confirming the arbitration award, determined that the arbitrators had based their decision primarily on the ten-year business relationship that had existed between the parties, and that the allegedly forged 1979 agreement had only a minor influence on their decision. Furthermore, even if the arbitrators erroneously determined that the 1979 agreement was valid, an arbitration award cannot be avoided solely on the ground that the arbitrator may have made an error of law or fact. Thus, we agree with the district court that enforcement of the arbitration award would not violate public policy.

D. District Court's Decision not to Adjourn Proceedings

A court has discretion to adjourn enforcement proceedings where an application has been made in the originating country to have the arbitral award set aside or suspended. Article VI of the Convention provides

> If an application for the setting aside or suspension of the award has been made to a competent authority [of the country in which, or under the law of which, that award was made], the authority before which the award is sought to be relied upon may, if it considers it proper, adjourn the decision on the enforcement of the award and may also, on the application of the party claiming enforcement of the award, order the other party to give suitable security.

Maiellano urges that proceedings in the district court should have been adjourned or suspended until his appeal in Italy was decided. The district court denied Maiellano's application to adjourn the enforcement proceedings, finding that the confirmed award was immediately enforceable under Italian law notwithstanding the pending appeal and that the defendant had not sought a stay of enforcement in the Italian courts, and concluding that adjournment would thwart arbitration's twin goals of "settling disputes efficiently and avoiding long and expensive litigation." *See Folkways Music Publishers, Inc. v. Weiss*, 989 F.2d 108, 111 (2d Cir. 1993). . . .

The issue of whether or not to adjourn under Article VI of the Convention is a relatively undeveloped area of the law. Few courts of appeals have spoken on the issue, and district courts have resolved it in divergent ways. Guidance as to when it is appropriate to stay enforcement of an award under the Convention is virtually non-existent. It is plain to us, however, that a district court faced with a decision whether to adjourn arbitral enforcement proceedings to await the outcome of foreign proceedings must take into account the inherent tension between competing concerns. On the one hand, the adjournment of enforcement proceedings impedes the goals of arbitration — the expeditious resolution of disputes and the avoidance of protracted and expensive litigation. Under the law of many countries, an arbitration award is final, binding, and enforceable even if subject to further appeal in court. A stay of confirmation should not be lightly granted lest it encourage abusive tactics by the party that lost in arbitration.

On the other hand, certain considerations favor granting a stay. One of the grounds for refusing to enforce an award under Article V(1)(e) is if the award "has been set aside or suspended by a competent authority of the country in which . . . the award was made." Thus, where a parallel proceeding is ongoing in the originating country and there is a possibility that the award will be set aside, a district court may be acting improvidently by enforcing the award prior to the completion of the foreign proceedings. Moreover, where, as here, it is the plaintiff who first sought to enforce his award in the originating country, the argument for enforcement by the plaintiff in the district court loses force because the possibility of conflicting results and the consequent offense to international comity can be laid at the plaintiff's door.

The limited scope of review allowed under the Convention also favors deference to proceedings in the originating country that involve less deferential standards of review on the premise that, under these circumstances, a foreign court well-versed in its own law is better suited to determine the validity of the award. *Cf. Ottley v. Schwartzberg*, 819 F.2d 373, 377 (2d Cir. 1987) ("[C]onfirmation of an arbitration award is a summary proceeding that merely makes what is already a final arbitration award a judgment of the court.").

In the instant case, it is plain that the district court's decision not to adjourn was based on the general objectives underlying the arbitration of disputes. However, it does not appear to us that the district court adequately considered the competing concerns just outlined. We think that a proper balancing of these concerns should lead a district court to consider several factors, including

(1) the general objectives of arbitration — the expeditious resolution of disputes and the avoidance of protracted and expensive litigation;

(2) the status of the foreign proceedings and the estimated time for those proceedings to be resolved;

(3) whether the award sought to be enforced will receive greater scrutiny in the foreign proceedings under a less deferential standard of review;

(4) the characteristics of the foreign proceedings including (i) whether they were brought to enforce an award (which would tend to weigh in favor of a stay) or to set the award aside (which would tend to weigh in favor of enforcement); (ii) whether they were initiated before the underlying enforcement proceeding so as to raise concerns of international comity; (iii) whether they were initiated by the party now seeking to enforce the award in federal court; and (iv) whether they were initiated under circumstances indicating an intent to hinder or delay resolution of the dispute;

(5) a balance of the possible hardships to each of the parties, keeping in mind that if enforcement is postponed under Article VI of the Convention, the party seeking enforcement may receive "suitable security" and that, under Article V of the Convention, an award should not be enforced if it is set aside or suspended in the originating country. . .; and

(6) any other circumstances that could tend to shift the balance in favor of or against adjournment. For example, in the instant case the controversy surrounding the enforceability of *arbitrato irrituale* may tend to favor adjournment because an Italian judgment confirming the award could itself be recognized and enforced in the district court.

While this is not an exhaustive list, we think it adequately represents the various concerns that come into play when a district court is asked to adjourn enforcement proceedings to await the outcome of parallel foreign proceedings. Because the primary goal of the Convention is to facilitate the recognition and enforcement of arbitral awards, the first and second factors on the list should weigh more heavily in the district court's determination. In the instant case, however, we think the district court should reconsider its decision not to adjourn enforcement of the arbitral award in light of the foregoing considerations. Of course, by so doing, we do not intend in any way to influence the district court's decision. . . .

BAKER MARINE (NIG.) LTD. v. CHEVRON (NIG.) LTD.
191 F.3d 194 (2d Cir. 1999)

. . . Baker Marine, Danos, and Chevron are corporations involved in Nigeria's oil industry. In September 1992, Baker Marine and Danos entered a contract to bid to provide barge services for Chevron. Baker Marine agreed it would provide local support, while Danos agreed it would provide management and technical equipment. The bid by Baker Marine and Danos was successful, and in October 1992, the two companies jointly entered a contract with Chevron to provide barge services.

The contract with Chevron included provisions for the arbitration of disputes which the contract between Baker Marine and Danos incorporated by reference. These provisions stated that "[a]ny dispute, controversy or claim arising out of this Contract, or the breach, termination or validity thereof, shall be finally and conclusively settled by arbitration in accordance with the Arbitration Rules of the United Nations Commission on International Trade Law (UNCITRAL)." Two different clauses further specified that the arbitration "procedure (insofar as not governed by said UNCITRAL rules . . .) shall be governed by the substantive laws of the Federal Republic of Nigeria" and that the contracts "shall be interpreted in accordance with the laws of the Federal Republic of Nigeria." The contracts also provided that "judgment upon the award of the arbitrators may be entered in[] any court having jurisdiction thereof," and that the contract and awards under it "shall be governed by the 1958 United Nations Convention on Recognition and Enforcement of Foreign Arbitration Awards ['Convention' or 'New York Convention']." The United States and Nigeria are parties to the Convention.

Baker Marine charged Chevron and Danos with violating the contracts. Pursuant to those contracts, the parties submitted to arbitration before panels of arbitrators in Lagos, Nigeria. By written decisions of early 1996, one panel of arbitrators awarded Baker Marine $2.23 million in damages against Danos[, and] a second panel awarded Baker Marine $750,000 in damages against Chevron. Baker Marine promptly sought enforcement of both awards in the Nigerian Federal High Court. Danos and Chevron appealed to the same court to vacate the awards on various grounds. By written opinions of November 1996 and May 1997, the Nigerian court set aside the two arbitration awards. In the Chevron action, the court concluded that the arbitrators had improperly awarded punitive damages, gone beyond the scope of the submissions, incorrectly admitted parole evidence, and made inconsistent awards, among other things. The court found that the Danos award was unsupported by the evidence.

In August 1997, Baker Marine brought these actions in the Northern District of New York seeking confirmation of the awards under the United States law implementing the Convention, chapter 2 of the Federal Arbitration Act ("FAA"), 9 U.S.C. §§ 201–09. The district court denied Baker Marine's petitions to enforce the arbitral awards, concluding that under the Convention and principles of comity, "it would not be proper to enforce a foreign arbitral award under the Convention when such an award has been set aside by the Nigerian courts." Baker Marine appeals.

. . . Baker Marine argues that the district court's ruling failed to give effect to Article VII of the Convention, which provides that the Convention shall not "deprive any interested party of any right he may have to avail himself of an arbitral award in the manner and to the extent allowed by the law or the treaties of the count[r]y where such award is sought to be relied upon." Art. VII(1). Baker Marine contends that the awards were set aside by the Nigerian courts for reasons that would not be recognized under U.S. law as valid grounds for vacating an arbitration award, and that under Article VII, it may invoke this country's national arbitration law, notwithstanding the action of the Nigerian court.

We reject Baker Marine's argument. It is sufficient answer that the parties contracted in Nigeria that their disputes would be arbitrated under the laws of Nigeria. The governing agreements make no reference whatever to United States law. Nothing suggests that the parties intended United States domestic arbitral law to govern their disputes.[1] The "primary purpose" of the FAA is "ensuring that private agreements to arbitrate are enforced according to their terms." *Volt Information Sciences, Inc. v. Board of Trustees*, 489 U.S. 468, 479 (1989). . . . Furthermore Baker Marine has made no contention that the Nigerian courts acted contrary to Nigerian law. . . .

Baker Marine makes a further argument premised on the language of Article V(1)(e) of the Convention. Article V(1)(e) provides that when a party seeks confirmation of an award, "[r]ecognition and enforcement of the award may be refused" if the award has been set aside by a competent authority of the country in which the award was made. Baker Marine argues that this use of the permissive "may," rather than a mandatory term, implies that the court might have enforced the awards, notwithstanding the Nigerian judgments vacating them. It is sufficient answer that Baker Marine has shown no adequate reason for refusing to recognize the judgments of the Nigerian court.[2] . . .

The judgments of the district court declining to enforce the arbitration awards are affirmed. The applications for sanctions are denied.

Notes and Questions on *Europcar* and *Baker Marine*

1. *Assessing the foreign effect of a local award.* The *Europcar* court explicitly dodged the question of whether the Convention applied to the informal Italian procedure of *arbitrato irrituale*. In the future, there will likely be scattered cases in which that specific question will recur. But the case (and that inconclusive part of it) is included here, because it raises issues that are fundamental in the litigation of cases under the New York Convention: specifically, what are the relative powers of the local court where the award is issued

---

[1] Furthermore, as a practical matter, mechanical application of domestic arbitral law to foreign awards under the Convention would seriously undermine finality and regularly produce conflicting judgments. If a party whose arbitration award has been vacated at the site of the award can automatically obtain enforcement of the awards under the domestic laws of other nations, a losing party will have every reason to pursue its adversary "with enforcement actions from country to country until a court is found, if any, which grants the enforcement." Albert Jan van den Berg, THE NEW YORK ARBITRATION CONVENTION OF 1958: TOWARDS A UNIFORM JUDICIAL INTERPRETATION 355 (1981).

[2] This case is unlike *In re Chromalloy Aeroservices*, 939 F. Supp. 907 (D.D.C. 1996), on which Baker Marine relies. In that case, the government of Egypt had entered a contract with an American company agreeing that disputes would be submitted to arbitration and that the decision of the arbitrator could not "be made subject to any appeal or other recourse."*Id.* at 912. After the arbitrator entered an award in favor of the American company, the American company applied to the United States courts for confirmation of the award, and the Egyptian government appealed to its own courts, which set aside the award. The district court concluded that Egypt was seeking "to repudiate its solemn promise to abide by the results of the arbitration," and that recognizing the Egyptian judgment would be contrary to the United States policy favoring arbitration. Unlike the petitioner in *Chromalloy*, Baker Marine is not a United States citizen, and it did not initially seek confirmation of the award in the United States. Furthermore, Chevron and Danos did not violate any promise in appealing the arbitration award within Nigeria. Recognition of the Nigerian judgment in this case does not conflict with United States public policy.

and the foreign court where the award is sought to be enforced? The Convention establishes a presumption in favor of enforcing the award, limits the defenses available in the enforcement court, and requires the party opposing enforcement to establish one of these defenses. In addition, the enforcement court can only decide whether to give the award effect, leaving the local court in the country where the award was made with the exclusive authority to annul or vacate the award altogether. But which country's law should control the effect of an award under the Convention? Drawing on the *Europcar* court's inconclusive discussion of the issue, how would you articulate the competing arguments in principle, and how would you decide the issue in *Europcar* if the issue *had* to be resolved? Is there any provision of the Convention that offers definitive guidance on the choice-of-law issue?

2. *Standard of review.* What does the language of discretion in Articles V and VI of the New York Convention suggest about the proper standard of review in enforcement cases? Should a reviewing court for example be bound by the arbitrators' findings of fact? Should arbitral awards be analogized to foreign judgments in this regard (or even to an appellate court's review of a trial court's findings of fact), or not?

3. *The public policy defense.* Article V(2)(b) of the New York Convention provides that enforcement may be resisted if "[t]he recognition or enforcement of the award would be contrary to the public policy" of that country. In order to prevent this defense from swallowing the presumption of enforceability altogether, the courts have interpreted the exception narrowly, allowing the defense, in the words of the *Europcar* court, "only where enforcement would violate our 'most basic notions of morality and justice.'" Why doesn't the prospect of a U.S. court facilitating fraud by enforcing the award in *Europcar* violate basic notions of morality and justice? What would? *Compare Southwest Livestock and Trucking Co. v. Ramon*, 169 F.3d 317 (5th Cir. 1999), *supra*, addressing the public policy exception to the enforcement of foreign court judgments.

4. *Adjournment.* The court of appeals in *Europcar* vacated the judgment below and remanded the case to the district court, directing it to reconsider its decision not to adjourn the enforcement proceedings pending the outcome of the Italian appeal. But it also laid out certain factors to guide the court's resolution of the issue. The court was evidently trying to balance two attractive but irreconcilable objectives: resisting adjournments for fear of frustrating the federal policy in favor of arbitration (and potentially rewarding dilatory tactics by the loser in the arbitration) versus granting adjournments to assure that the underlying award is final and proper in all respects (and potentially to assure consistency with any parallel proceedings that may be underway in the nation where the award was issued). Which way does each of the *Europcar* factors cut?

And what is the proper showing required to justify adjournment? Is it analogous to the issuance of an injunction or perhaps the even higher standard governing the stay of an injunction pending appeal in U.S. courts? Notice that there is no hint in the *Europcar* list of factors suggesting that the party seeking adjournment under Article VI must satisfy so demanding a standard. Article VI after all requires only that an "*application* for the setting aside or suspension of the award" be made to the competent authority. ALBERT JAN VAN DEN BERG, THE NEW YORK ARBITRATION CONVENTION OF 1958 (1981), at 351. The fact that adjournment under Article VI is a temporary and discretionary form of relief may also justify the lesser showing that an application for suspension has been filed in the country of origin, as distinct from the showing that the award has actually been suspended there, which might justify the more extreme sanction of non-enforcement under Article V. Does the courts' experience with parallel proceedings in litigation, *supra*, offer any guidance in the arbitral setting?

5. *Effect of foreign nullification on U.S. enforcement. Baker Marine* indicates that the state where the award is rendered retains a measure of control over its extraterritorial effect. *See also Spier v. Calzaturificio Tecnica, S.p.A.,* 71 F. Supp. 2d 279 (S.D.N.Y. 1999). But in what circumstances should the enforcement court decline to give effect to the judgment of a local court *nullifying* the award?

Consider the case of *In re Chromalloy Aeroservices,* 939 F. Supp. 907 (D.D.C. 1996), distinguished in a footnote in *Baker Marine.* In *Chromalloy,* an arbitral panel in Egypt, applying Egyptian law, ordered the Egyptian government to pay Chromalloy more than $17 million for the breach of a military procurement contract. One month after Chromalloy sought to enforce that award in a U.S. court, the Egyptian government filed an appeal with the Egyptian Court of Appeal, seeking nullification of the award — an appeal it ultimately won. The U.S. court declined to give any effect to the Egyptian court judgment and enforced the underlying award anyway, despite its nullification by the court in Egypt. The decision to enforce the award drew in part on the strong presumption in favor of international arbitration adopted in *Mitsubishi* and *Scherk, supra*: "A decision by this Court to recognize the decision of the Egyptian court would violate this clear U.S. public policy," and nothing in the act of state doctrine, *supra*, Chapter 6, or international comity required an overriding deference to the Egyptian court's judgment.

Is it a violation of the New York Convention for a U.S. court to give a foreign award *more* weight than it has in the courts of the nation where it was rendered? Is the *Baker Marine* court's effort to distinguish *Chromalloy* convincing? Should the result have been the same in *Baker Marine* if — as in *Mitusbishi* — arbitration under local rules had been chosen in one nation to resolve disputes under the contract but the contract itself was to be governed by the law of a different nation? On the enforceability of annulled arbitral awards, *see generally Hilmarton v. OTV,* 1993 REV. ARB 315 and 322, and 1994 REV. ARB. 327, in which a French court recognized an award that had been annulled by a Swiss cantonal court. Eric Schwartz, *A Comment on Chromalloy: Hilmarton a l'Americaine,* 14 J. INT. ARB. 125 (1997).

Chapter 8
PROFESSIONAL RESPONSIBILITY IN TRANSNATIONAL CASES

During a recent visit to the International Criminal Tribunal for the former Yugoslavia, I met one of the staff lawyers who explained that in discussing preparation of the witnesses for cross-examination during trial, several lawyers from different countries expressed opposing views on the ethics questions involved. An Australian lawyer felt that from his perspective, it would be unethical to prepare a witness; a Canadian lawyer said it would be illegal; and an American lawyer's view was that not to prepare a witness would be malpractice.

— Mary C. Daly, *The Dichotomy Between Standards and Rules: A New Way of Understanding the Differences in Perceptions of Lawyer Codes of Conduct by U.S. and Foreign Lawyers*, 32 VAND. J. TRANSNAT'L L. 1117 (1999)

A. INTRODUCTION

In the United States, the law of professional responsibility — *i.e.*, the law governing lawyers — is decentralized and various, with each state authorized to regulate the profession in its own way. The result is a nationwide patchwork of standards governing such issues as the obligations of loyalty and independence, the unauthorized practice of law, the definition of misconduct and malpractice, conflicts of interest, confidentiality, the obligations of partnership and other forms of association, advertising, and billing practices. These are matters that go to the heart of a lawyer's work, but unfortunately, except on television, ethical problems tend not to announce themselves when they arrive in the office.

The potential consequences of violating the rules of professional conduct, whether intentionally or not, can be marked and range from the forfeiture of fees or disqualification from a particular representation, to malpractice liability, suspension from the practice of law, fines, disbarment, and even criminal sanctions. Ideally, when the potential penalties sting like that, the rules should be clear, uniform, routinely respected, and enforced. Within the United States, there have been efforts to harmonize domestic standards of professional responsibility through the American Law Institute's Restatement (Third) of the Law Governing Lawyers and the American Bar Association's Model Rules of Professional Conduct and Model Code of Professional Responsibility. But it takes legislative or judicial action in each state for the provisions in these instruments to become effective, and state-to-state variance — even an irreconcilable diversity among states on some issues — remains a reality. At the federal level, aside from Rule 11 of the Federal Rules of Civil Procedure, which offers a narrow definition of sanctionable conduct in federal litigation, there is no national standard governing an attorney's professional responsibility in civil litigation: each federal district court is empowered to adopt its own rules of conduct.[1]

Patchy as the traditional domestic law of professional responsibility is, ethical issues become exponentially more complicated as the practice of law crosses international borders or takes virtual and electronic form. Legal cultures vary, sometimes profoundly, in their conception of the attorney's role and the propriety of certain professional conduct. For example,

(1) *the unauthorized practice of law*. The role of a lawyer varies from country to country, and non-lawyers in one jurisdiction may routinely handle matters that must be handled in another jurisdiction by lawyers admitted to practice there. Some lawyerly functions in U.S. litigation, like pre-trial depositions, are either unknown or are functions of the court in other legal systems. In a transnational case with contacts in both places, which definition of the lawyer's function should control and on what rationale? And in those common circumstances when a lawyer must advise a client on the law of a foreign jurisdiction, what steps must be taken to assure that he or she is not committing the unauthorized practice of law there (or negligence locally)? If a lawyer must retain local counsel abroad, what are his or her obligations of due diligence in assuring that foreign attorney's professionalism?

(2) *conflicts of interest*. Lawyers engaged in a transnational practice with multiple clients (especially when the clients assume complex corporate forms) may find themselves disqualified from a representation or sanctioned for simultaneously representing clients with adverse interests. The standards defining and governing such conflicts — and the extent to which they may be waived by the clients' consent — vary from jurisdiction to jurisdiction, and the transnational litigator must be prepared to identify the existence of the conflict under applicable standards and take lawful and appropriate steps to resolve them;

(3) *the "zealous representation" of a client's interest*. Lawyers in the United States are obliged to represent the interests of their clients zealously, consistent with the tenets and assumptions of the adversarial system. The common law system generally empowers attorneys and judges in the evolution of the law, and the incremental process by which the law emerges is the direct result of articulating and protecting a client's interest. In civil law countries, or countries where the inquisitorial system is in operation, the lawyers' role is more confined, and the attorney's obligation as an officer of the court may trump her obligation as an advocate for her client. It is possible as a result that conduct considered obligatory in one jurisdiction is considered unethical (or distinctly counter-productive) in another;

(4) *definition of malpractice*. As suggested by Professor Daly's experience at the Yugoslavian War Crimes Tribunal, *supra*, definitions of malpractice are not universal. In a purely domestic case within the United States, the Model Code and the Model Rules might serve as the standard for defining malpractice liability, despite the fact that the framers of those instruments

---

[1] 28 U.S.C. § 2071.

expressly disclaimed that intention.[2] But by what standard would a lawyer determine her professional obligation of full and competent representation in a case that crossed borders with a system where malpractice was defined more abstractly, or which prohibited action required by U.S. rules, or which required action prohibited by U.S. rules?

(5) *fees.* As an attorney's clients become less local, fee expectations become a matter of potential controversy. The American rule, under which each party generally bears its own attorneys fees, does not apply abroad; indeed, in many other nations, attorneys fees are routinely awarded to the party that prevails in a litigation, a risk that can deter the filing of litigation in the first place. Similarly, contingent fee arrangements, common in the United States, are perceived as patently unethical — generating litigation and promoting overzealous advocacy — in many other countries, where lawyers receive a set fee for defined services regardless of the result in a particular case. Minimum fee schedules of that sort are thought to assure the lawyer's independence and her equal treatment of all cases, but similar approaches in the United States have been held to violate American antitrust laws;

(6) *limits on advertising.* In *Bates v. State Bar of Arizona*, 433 U.S. 350 (1977), the Supreme Court ended a long-standing ban on lawyer advertising in the United States. Today, "[a]lmost the only restraints on advertisements that can . . . safely be imposed by state bar authorities are those on false or misleading publications, characteristically phrased in terms that seem to be borrowed from rules governing purchases and sales of securities."[3] In foreign countries, the commercial speech of lawyers may also be protected in principle but is subject to greater (if more indefinite) restrictions;[4]

(7) *client confidentiality and the attorney-client privilege.* The attorney-client relationship creates expectations of trust — that the client and lawyer will discuss matters that no one else is to know, that the client's secrets will be protected, and that communications within the attorney-client privilege and the attorney's work-product will not be disclosed to third parties. But these expectations are bound by culture and geography: the law defining the relationship between a lawyer and her clients determines which expectations are reasonable and which are not. In those foreign jurisdictions where the lawyer's obligation to the court (or to public order) can outweigh the lawyer's obligation to his or her client, the U.S. version of a privilege

---

[2] Thomas Morgan, *American Perspectives on the Duty of Loyalty*, RIGHTS, LIABILITY, AND ETHICS IN INTERNATIONAL LEGAL PRACTICE 2 (Mary Daly and Roger Goebel, eds., 1995).

[3] Detlev F. Vagts, *Professional Responsibility in Transborder Practice: Conflict and Resolution*, 13 GEO. J. LEGAL ETHICS 677, 681 (2000).

[4] An American firm attempted to celebrate the opening of its Berlin office by hosting a reception to which non-clients were invited but were stopped by German authorities on the ground that the reception amounted to inappropriate promotion. *See also* the judgment of the European Court of Human Rights in *Casado Coca v. Spain, Series A, No. 285*, 18 Eur. H.R. Rep. 1, 4 (1994):

Members of the Bar must show regard for truth, rigour and exactness without detracting from other members' advertisements by imitating them or inviting confusion with them, without lapsing into self-praise and comparison with or denigration of their colleagues and without citing their own professional success, their clientele or the financial terms on which they provide services.

for attorney-client communications and for attorney work product will seem extravagant and improper. Information that is protected in one jurisdiction may be subject to mandatory disclosure in another. If the attorney-client relationship is centered in a jurisdiction which restricts these privileges and the litigation occurs in a jurisdiction with a more expansive set of protections, which law should apply? Or suppose one office of a multi-jurisdictional law firm is obliged locally to disclose a client's intention to commit a crime: may the firm — must the firm — disclose relevant information from intra-firm communications with an office in another jurisdiction which is locally forbidden from disclosing that information?;

(8) *limits on multi-disciplinary practice (M.P.)*. The transnational practice of law is increasingly multi-disciplinary, as lawyers attempt to go into partnership with other types of professionals who are not lawyers, such as accountants, to offer an integrated form of business planning advice. But, as a generalization, the accountant is professionally obligated to make client information public, and the attorney is professionally obligated to keep client information confidential. Can a single organization be structured to include both professions? The M.P. lawyer may also be an employee of a large corporation, raising the prospect of a conflict of interest: the employer could require the lawyer to act in the best interest of the corporation's shareholders by maximizing profits while the lawyer's duty of loyalty to the client and zealous representation would require a very different, potentially less profitable course of action. Nations have responded with disparate regulations on the legality of such associations. What constraints does this diversity place on lawyers in a restrictive jurisdiction who wish to create, perform extraterritorial work with, or refer a local client to a multi-disciplinary firm that is lawful in its home jurisdiction?;

(9) *the rights and obligations of partnership*. With the globalization of practice, attorneys must be conscious of the differing standards governing the obligations of partners to one another and to the public at large. What fiduciary obligations does one member of the firm owe to the others? How will the firm's profits be distributed? What happens to firm assets and liabilities if the firm is dissolved? And, if each partner in a global firm can only practice in a jurisdiction where he or she is admitted, must the definition of "practice" become more refined? Should we distinguish for example between a "practice" that provides transnational *business* advice (*e.g.,* U.S. lawyers advising a European company on legal questions arising in a worldwide global market) and a "practice" that provides transnational *litigation* advice, which inevitably raises more localized concerns?

As suggested by these examples and by the cases that follow, the ethical and disciplinary issues that arise in a transnational setting are frequently handled as a choice-of-law problem, with courts and regulators choosing among competing jurisdictions' rules for a dispositive standard. But how helpful is this? As shown in Chapter 4, *supra,* choice-of-law techniques in the domestic setting tend to fall into three categories: the territorial or "vested rights" approach of the First Restatement of Conflicts, the rebuttable presumptions or "most significant relationship" test of the Second Restatement of Conflicts, and the policy-oriented approach of "interest analysis." But each of these three approaches is indeterminate in its own way, and each introduces a potential wildcard into litigation. As a consequence, clarifying that choice-of-law doctrines apply to transnational questions of professional responsibility doesn't necessarily make the difficulties go away. To the contrary, it may simply raise another round of difficulty. If geographical concerns are relevant, for example, which place qualifies as the attorney's "home" jurisdiction: where the lawyer is admitted to practice, where he or she is employed, where the work is performed or centered, or where the client is? Should any additional disciplinary authority reside in a jurisdiction if some foreign attorney purports to be an expert in that jurisdiction's law? And if the issues are to be resolved by reference not to these geographical facts but to the underlying policies behind the rules in conflict or by reference to the most significant relationship test, how much advance guidance can these amorphous standards give to lawyers making concrete, day-to-day decisions about their professional conduct?

The history of choice-of-law doctrine suggests that the difficulty might be minimized by unifying the underlying principles of substantive law: choice-of-law problems in a contracts case for example tend to disappear when the doctrines of contract law are the same in all relevant jurisdictions or where some treaty, like the Convention on Contracts for the International Sale of Goods, has harmonized the law internationally. It may seem utopian to imagine supra-national rules of professional responsibility, when there is nation-to-nation disagreement about the role of lawyers and when the profession itself moves uneasily between one self-image as a traditional service profession and another as a contemporary for-profit business. It may also be easier to articulate standards for cross-border lawyering than to develop cross-border disciplinary institutions for enforcing them. But it is now possible to see the earliest hints of an emerging international consensus on what a lawyer's professional ethics entail, regardless of location. The Council of the Bars and Law Societies of the European Union ("CCBE"), for example, which represents the legal profession in the various nations that make up the European Union, has adopted a code of conduct for lawyers in the region and urged member-states to adopt the code as "enforceable rules."[5] The United Nations Congress on the Prevention of Crime and the Treatment of Offenders has promulgated Guidelines on the Role of Prosecutors and Basic Principles on the Role of Lawyers, which lay out a lawyer's baseline duties and privileges. And the International Criminal Tribunal for the Former Yugoslavia has promulgated a Code of Professional Conduct for Defence Counsel appearing before the tribunal. (A copy of each of these instruments is in the Documents Supplement). Especially as the World Trade Organization works towards liberalizing trade in services, including legal services,[6] these and future "public" international instruments may help to minimize the "private"

---

[5] CCBE Code, Rule 1.3.2. *See generally* Robert J. Goebel, *Lawyering in the European Community: Progress Towards Community-Wide Rights of Practice*, 15 FORD. INT'L L.J. 556 (1992). The CCBE Code includes both choice-of-law provisions and substantive provisions governing lawyers' professional obligations.

[6] SYDNEY M. CONE, INTERNATIONAL TRADE IN LEGAL SERVICES: REGULATION OF LAWYERS AND FIRMS IN GLOBAL PRACTICE (1996).

international law problem of choosing an applicable law of professional responsibility in transnational cases.

B. THE UNAUTHORIZED PRACTICE OF LAW

American Bar Association, Model Rules of Professional Conduct, Rule 5.5 (a), (b), Unauthorized Practice of Law:

A lawyer shall not . . . [p]ractice law in a jurisdiction where doing so violates the regulation of the legal profession in that jurisdiction. . . [nor] assist a person who is not a member of the bar in the performance of activity that constitutes the unauthorized practice of law.

RESTATEMENT (THIRD) OF THE LAW GOVERNING LAWYERS, § 3, Jurisdictional Scope of the Practice of Law by a Lawyer:

A lawyer currently admitted to practice in a jurisdiction may provide legal services to a client:

(1) at any place within the admitting jurisdiction;

(2) before a tribunal or administrative agency of another jurisdiction or the federal government in compliance with requirements for temporary or regular admission to practice before that tribunal or agency; and

(3) at a place within a jurisdiction in which the lawyer is not admitted to the extent that the lawyer's activities arise out of or are otherwise reasonably related to the lawyer's practice under subsection (1) or (2).

Comment e:

The rules governing interstate practice by nonlocal lawyers were formed at a time when lawyers conducted very little practice of that nature. Thus, the limitation on legal services threatened by such rules imposed little actual inconvenience. However, as interstate and international commerce, transportation, and communications have expanded, clients have increasingly required a truly interstate and international range of practice by their lawyers. . . . Applied literally, the old restrictions on practice of law in a state by a lawyer admitted elsewhere could seriously inconvenience clients who have need of such services within the state. Retaining locally admitted counsel would often cause serious delay and expense and could require the client to deal with unfamiliar counsel. Modern communications, including ready electronic connection to much of the law of every state, makes concern about a competent analysis of a distant state's law unfounded. Accordingly, there is much to be said for a rule permitting a lawyer to practice in any state, except for litigation matters or for the purpose of establishing a permanent in-state branch office. Results approaching that rule may arguably be required under the federal interstate commerce clause and the privileges and immunities clause. The approach of . . . Section [3] is more guarded. However, its primary focus is appropriately on the needs of clients.

BIRBROWER, MONTALBANO, CONDON & FRANK, P.C. v.
SUPERIOR COURT OF SANTA CLARA COUNTY
17 Cal. 4th 119, *cert. denied*, 525 U.S. 920 (1998)

[The California state] Business and Professions Code section 6125 states: "No person shall practice law in California unless the person is an active member of the State Bar." We must decide whether an out-of-state law firm, not licensed to practice law in this state, violated section 6125 when it performed legal services in California for a California-based client under a fee agreement stipulating that California law would govern all matters in the representation. . . .

I. Background

. . . Birbrower is a professional law corporation incorporated in New York, with its principal place of business in New York. During 1992 and 1993, Birbrower attorneys, defendants Kevin F. Hobbs and Thomas A. Condon (Hobbs and Condon), performed substantial work in California relating to the law firm's representation of [ESQ Business Services, Inc. (ESQ), a California corporation]. Neither Hobbs nor Condon has ever been licensed to practice law in California. None of Birbrower's attorneys were licensed to practice law in California during Birbrower's ESQ representation. . . . In July 1992, the parties negotiated and executed the fee agreement in New York, providing that Birbrower would perform legal services for ESQ, including "All matters pertaining to the investigation of and prosecution of all claims and causes of action against Tandem Computers Incorporated [Tandem]." The "claims and causes of action" against Tandem, a Delaware corporation with its principal place of business in Santa Clara County, California, related to a software development and marketing contract between Tandem and ESQ. . . . The Tandem Agreement stated that "The internal laws of the State of California (irrespective of its choice of law principles) shall govern the validity of this Agreement, the construction of its terms, and the interpretation and enforcement of the rights and duties of the parties hereto." Birbrower asserts, and ESQ disputes, that ESQ knew Birbrower was not licensed to practice law in California.

While representing ESQ, Hobbs and Condon traveled to California on several occasions. In August 1992, they met in California with ESQ and its accountants. During these meetings, Hobbs and Condon discussed various matters related to ESQ's dispute with Tandem and strategy for resolving the dispute. They made recommendations and gave advice. During this California trip, Hobbs and Condon also met with Tandem representatives on four or five occasions during a two-day period. At the meetings, Hobbs and Condon spoke on ESQ's behalf. Hobbs demanded that Tandem pay ESQ $15 million. Condon told Tandem he believed that damages would exceed $15 million if the parties litigated the dispute. Around March or April 1993, Hobbs, Condon, and another Birbrower attorney visited California to interview potential arbitrators and to meet again with ESQ and its accountants. Birbrower had previously filed a demand for arbitration against Tandem with the San Francisco offices of the American Arbitration Association (AAA).

In August 1993, Hobbs returned to California to assist ESQ in settling the Tandem matter. While in California, Hobbs met with ESQ and its accountants to discuss a proposed settlement agreement Tandem authored. Hobbs also met with Tandem representatives to discuss possible changes in the proposed agreement. Hobbs gave ESQ legal advice during this trip, including his opinion that ESQ should not settle with Tandem on the terms proposed.

ESQ eventually settled the Tandem dispute, and the matter never went to arbitration. But before the settlement, ESQ and Birbrower modified the contingency fee agreement. The modification changed the fee arrangement from contingency to fixed fee, providing that ESQ would pay Birbrower over $1 million. The original contingency fee arrangement had called for Birbrower to receive "one-third (1/3) of all sums received for the benefit of the Clients . . . whether obtained through settlement, motion practice, hearing, arbitration, or trial by way of judgment, award, settlement, or otherwise . . . ."

In January 1994, ESQ sued Birbrower for legal malpractice and related claims in Santa Clara County Superior Court. Birbrower . . . filed a counterclaim, which included a claim for attorney fees for the work it performed in both California and New York. . . . ESQ argued that by practicing law without a license in California and by failing to associate legal counsel [locally] while doing so, Birbrower violated section 6125, rendering the fee agreement unenforceable. Based on these undisputed facts, the Santa Clara Superior Court granted ESQ's motion for summary adjudication[, concluding that] (1) Birbrower was "not admitted to the practice of law in California"; (2) Birbrower "did not associate California counsel"; (3) Birbrower "provided legal services in this state"; and (4) "The law is clear that no one may recover compensation for services as an attorney in this state unless he or she was a member of the state bar at the time those services were performed." . . . The Court of Appeal . . . affirmed[,] . . . concluding] that Birbrower's violation barred the firm from recovering its legal fees under the written fee agreement, including fees generated in New York by the attorneys when they were physically present in New York, because the agreement included payment for California or "local" services for a California client in California. . . . We granted review to determine whether Birbrower's actions and services performed while representing ESQ in California constituted the unauthorized practice of law under section 6125 and, if so, whether a section 6125 violation rendered the fee agreement wholly unenforceable.

II. Discussion

A. The Unauthorized Practice of Law

[Under section 6125 of the State Bar Act], the general rule has been that, although persons may represent themselves and their own interests regardless of State Bar membership, no one but an active member of the State Bar may practice law for another person in California. The prohibition against unauthorized law practice is within the state's police power and is designed to ensure that those performing legal services do so competently. A violation of section 6125 is a misdemeanor. Moreover, "No one may recover compensation for services as an attorney at law in this state unless [the person] was at the time the services were performed a member of The State Bar." *Hardy v. San Fernando Valley C. of C.*, 99 Cal. App. 2d 572, 576 (1950).

Although the Act did not define the term "practice law," case law explained it as " 'the doing and performing services in a court of justice in any matter depending therein throughout its various stages and in conformity with the adopted rules of procedure.' " *People v. Merchants Protective Corp.*, 189 Cal. 531, 535 (1922). *Merchants* included in its definition legal advice and legal instrument and contract preparation, whether or not these subjects were rendered in the course of litigation. [*People v. Ring*, 26 Cal.App. 2d. Supp. 768 (1937)] later determined that the Legislature "accepted both the definition already judicially supplied for the term and the declaration of the Supreme Court [in *Merchants*] that it had a sufficiently definite meaning to need no further definition. The definition . . . must be regarded as definitely establishing, for the jurisprudence of this state, the meaning of the term 'practice law.' "

In addition to not defining the term "practice law," the Act also did not define the meaning of "in California." In today's legal practice, questions often arise concerning whether the phrase refers to the nature of the legal services, or restricts the Act's application to those out-of-state attorneys who are physically present in the state. Section 6125 has generated numerous opinions on the meaning of "practice law" but none on the meaning of "in California." In our view, the practice of law "in California" entails sufficient contact with the California client to render the nature of the legal service a clear legal representation. In addition to a quantitative analysis, we must consider the nature of the unlicensed lawyer's activities in the state. Mere fortuitous or attenuated contacts will not sustain a finding that the unlicensed lawyer practiced law "in California." The primary inquiry is whether the unlicensed lawyer engaged in sufficient activities in the state, or created a continuing relationship with the California client that included legal duties and obligations.

Our definition does not necessarily depend on or require the unlicensed lawyer's physical presence in the state. Physical presence here is one factor we may consider in deciding whether the unlicensed lawyer has violated section 6125, but it is by no means exclusive. For example, one may practice law in the state in violation of section 6125 although not physically present here by advising a California client on California law in connection with a California legal dispute by telephone, fax, computer, or other modern technological means. Conversely, although we decline to provide a comprehensive list of what activities constitute sufficient contact with the state, we do reject the notion that a person automatically practices law "in California" whenever that person practices California law anywhere, or "virtually" enters the state by telephone, fax, e-mail, or satellite. *See, e.g., Baron v. City of Los Angeles*, 2 Cal.3d 535, 543, 86 Cal. Rpt. 673, 469 P.2d 353, (1970) ("practice law" does not encompass all professional activities.) . . . We must decide each case on its individual facts.

This interpretation acknowledges the tension that exists between interjurisdictional practice and the need to have a state-regulated bar. As stated in the American Bar Association Model Code of Professional Responsibility, Ethical Consideration EC 3-9,

Regulation of the practice of law is accomplished principally by the respective states. Authority to engage in the practice of law conferred in any jurisdiction is not per se a grant of the right to practice elsewhere, and it is improper for a lawyer to engage in practice where he is not permitted by law or by court order to do so. However, the demands of business and the mobility of our society pose distinct problems in the regulation of the practice of law by the states. In furtherance of the public interest, the legal profession should discourage regulation that unreasonably imposes territorial limitations upon the right of a lawyer to handle the legal affairs of his client or upon the opportunity of a client to obtain the services of a lawyer of his choice in all matters including the presentation of a contested matter in a tribunal before which the lawyer is not permanently admitted to practice.

Baron implicitly agrees with this canon. . . .

Exceptions to section 6125 do exist, but are generally limited to allowing out-of-state attorneys to make brief appearances before a state court or tribunal. They are narrowly drawn and strictly interpreted. For example, an out-of-state attorney not licensed to practice in California may be permitted, by consent of a trial judge, to appear in California in a particular pending action. . . . The Act also does not regulate practice before United States courts. Thus, an out-of-state attorney engaged to render services in bankruptcy proceedings [is] entitled to collect his fee. *But see* U.S. Dist. Ct. Local Rules, Northern Dist. Cal., rule 11-1(b); Eastern Dist. Cal., rule 83-180; Central Dist. Cal., rule 2.2.1; Southern Dist. Cal., rule 83.3 c.1.a. [. . . conditioning admission to their respective bars (with certain exceptions for some federal government employees) on active membership in good standing in California State Bar].) Finally, California Rules of Court permits the State Bar to issue registration certificates to foreign legal consultants who may advise on the law of the foreign jurisdiction where they are admitted. These consultants may not, however, appear as attorneys before a California court or judicial officer or otherwise prepare pleadings and instruments in California or give advice on the law of California or any other state or jurisdiction except those where they are admitted. The Legislature has recognized an exception to section 6125 in international disputes resolved in California under the state's rules for arbitration and conciliation of international commercial disputes. This exception states that in a commercial conciliation in California involving international commercial disputes, "The parties may appear in person or be represented or assisted by any person of their choice. A person assisting or representing a party need not be a member of the legal profession or licensed to practice law in California." Likewise, the Act does not apply to the preparation of or participation in labor negotiations and arbitrations arising under collective bargaining agreements in industries subject to federal law.

B. The Present Case

The undisputed facts here show that neither *Baron*'s definition nor our "sufficient contact" definition of "practice law in California" would excuse Birbrower's extensive practice in this state. Nor would any of the limited statutory exceptions to section 6125 apply to Birbrower's California practice.

As the Court of Appeal observed, Birbrower engaged in unauthorized law practice in California on more than a limited basis, and no firm attorney engaged in that practice was an active member of the California State Bar. . . . Birbrower attorneys traveled to California to discuss with ESQ and others various matters pertaining to the dispute between ESQ and Tandem. Hobbs and Condon discussed strategy for resolving the dispute and advised ESQ on this strategy. Furthermore, during California meetings with Tandem representatives in August 1992, Hobbs demanded Tandem pay $15 million, and Condon told Tandem he believed damages in the matter would exceed that amount if the parties proceeded to litigation. Also in California, Hobbs met with ESQ for the stated purpose of helping to reach a settlement agreement and to discuss the agreement that was eventually proposed. Birbrower attorneys also traveled to California to initiate arbitration proceedings before the matter was settled. As the Court of Appeal concluded, ". . . the Birbrower firm's in-state activities clearly constituted the [unauthorized] practice of law" in California.

Birbrower contends, however, that section 6125 is not meant to apply to any out-of-state attorneys. Instead, it argues that the statute is intended solely to prevent nonattorneys from practicing law. This contention is without merit because it contravenes the plain language of the statute. Section 6125 clearly states that no person shall practice law in California unless that person is a member of the State Bar. The statute does not differentiate between attorneys or nonattorneys, nor does it excuse a person who is a member of another state bar. . . .

Birbrower next argues that we do not further the statute's intent and purpose — to protect California citizens from incompetent attorneys — by enforcing it against out-of-state attorneys. Birbrower argues that because out-of-state attorneys have been licensed to practice in other jurisdictions, they have already demonstrated sufficient competence to protect California clients. But Birbrower's argument overlooks the obvious fact that other states' laws may differ substantially from California law. Competence in one jurisdiction does not necessarily guarantee competence in another. By applying section 6125 to out-of-state attorneys who engage in the extensive practice of law in California without becoming licensed in our state, we serve the statute's goal of assuring the competence of all attorneys practicing law in this state.

California is not alone in regulating who practices law in its jurisdiction. Many states have substantially similar statutes that serve to protect their citizens from unlicensed attorneys who engage in unauthorized legal practice. Like section 6125, these other state statutes protect local citizens "against the dangers of legal representation and advice given by persons not trained, examined and licensed for such work, whether they be laymen or lawyers from other jurisdictions." *Spivak v. Sachs*, 16 N.Y.2d 163 (1965). Whether an attorney is duly admitted in another state and is, in fact, competent to practice in California is irrelevant in the face of section 6125's language and purpose. . . . [A] decision to except out-of-state attorneys licensed in their own jurisdictions from section 6125 is more appropriately left to the California Legislature.

Assuming that section 6125 does apply to out-of-state attorneys not licensed here, Birbrower alternatively asks us to create an exception to section 6125 for work incidental to private arbitration or other alternative dispute resolution proceedings. Birbrower points to fundamental differences between private arbitration and legal proceedings, including procedural differences relating to discovery, rules of evidence, compulsory process, cross-examination of witnesses, and other areas. As Birbrower observes, in light of these differences, at least one court has decided that an out-of-state attorney could recover fees for services rendered in an arbitration proceeding. *See Williamson v. John D. Quinn Const. Corp.*, 537 F. Supp. 613, 616 (S.D.N.Y. 1982). In *Williamson*, a New Jersey law firm was employed by a client's New York law firm to defend a construction contract arbitration in New York. It sought to recover fees solely related to the arbitration proceedings, even though the attorney who did the work was not licensed in New York, nor was the firm authorized to practice in the state. In allowing the New Jersey firm to recover its arbitration fees, the federal district court concluded that an arbitration tribunal is not a court of record, and its fact-finding process is not similar to a court's process. The court relied on a local state bar report concluding that representing a client in an arbitration was not the unauthorized practice of law. But as *amicus curiae,* the State Bar of California observes, "While in *Williamson* the federal district court did allow the New Jersey attorneys to recover their fees, that decision clearly is distinguishable on its facts. . . . [¶] In the instant case, it is undisputed that none of the time that the New York attorneys spent in California was" spent in arbitration; *Williamson* thus carries limited weight. Birbrower also relies on California's rules for arbitration and conciliation of international commercial disputes for support. As noted, these rules specify that, in an international commercial conciliation or arbitration proceeding, the person representing a party to the conciliation or arbitration is not required to be a licensed member of the State Bar.

We decline Birbrower's invitation to craft an arbitration exception to section 6125's prohibition of the unlicensed practice of law in this state. Any exception for arbitration is best left to the Legislature, which has the authority to determine qualifications for admission to the State Bar and to decide what constitutes the practice of law. Even though the Legislature has spoken with respect to international arbitration and conciliation, it has not enacted a similar rule for private arbitration proceedings. Of course, private arbitration and other alternative dispute resolution practices are important aspects of our justice system. Section 6125, however, articulates a strong public policy favoring the practice of law in California by licensed State Bar members. In the face of the Legislature's silence, we will not create an arbitration exception under the facts presented. . . .

In its reply brief to the State Bar's *amicus curiae* brief, Birbrower raises for the first time the additional argument that the Federal Arbitration Act (FAA) preempted the rules governing the AAA proposed arbitration and section 6125. The FAA regulates arbitration that deals with maritime transactions and contracts involving the transportation of goods through interstate or foreign commerce. Although we need not address the question . . . and note that the parties' settlement agreement rendered the arbitration unnecessary, we reject the argument for its lack of merit. First, the parties incorporated a California choice-of-law provision in the Tandem Agreement, indicating they intended to apply California law in any necessary arbitration, and they have not shown that California law in any way conflicts with the FAA. Moreover, in interpreting the California Arbitration Act stay provisions, the high court observed that the FAA does not contain an express preemptive provision, nor does it "reflect a congressional intent to occupy the entire field of arbitration." *Volt Info. Sciences v. Leland Stanford Jr. Univ.*, 489 U.S. 468, 477 (1989).

Finally, Birbrower urges us to adopt an exception to section 6125 based on the unique circumstances of this case. Birbrower notes that "Multi-state relationships are a common part of today's society and are to be dealt with in commonsense fashion." In many situations, strict adherence to rules prohibiting the unauthorized practice of law by out-of-state attorneys would be " 'grossly impractical and inefficient.' " Although, we recognize the need to acknowledge and, in certain cases, to accommodate the multi-state nature of law practice, the facts here show that Birbrower's extensive activities within California amounted to considerably more than any of our state's recognized exceptions to section 6125 would allow. Accordingly, we reject Birbrower's suggestion that we except the firm from section 6125's rule under the circumstances

C. Compensation for Legal Services

Because Birbrower violated section 6125 when it engaged in the unlawful practice of law in California, the Court of Appeal found its fee agreement with ESQ unenforceable in its entirety. Without crediting Birbrower for some services performed in New York, for which fees were generated under the fee agreement, the court reasoned that the agreement was void and unenforceable because it included payment for services rendered to a California client in the state by an unlicensed out-of-state lawyer. . . . We agree with the Court of Appeal to the extent it barred Birbrower from recovering fees generated under the fee agreement for the unauthorized legal services it performed in California. We disagree with the same court to the extent it implicitly barred Birbrower from recovering fees generated under the fee agreement for the limited legal services the firm performed in New York. . . .

Some jurisdictions have adopted a[n] exception to the general rule of nonrecovery for in-state services, if an out-of-state attorney "makes a full disclosure to his client of his lack of local license and does not conceal or misrepresent the true facts." For example, in *Freeling v. Tucker*, 49 Idaho 475 (1930), the court allowed an Oklahoma attorney to recover for services rendered in an Idaho probate court. Even though an Idaho statute prohibited the unlicensed practice of law, the court excused the Oklahoma attorney's unlicensed representation because he had not falsely represented himself nor deceptively held himself out to the client as qualified to practice in the jurisdiction. In this case, Birbrower alleges that ESQ at all times knew that the firm was not licensed to practice law in California. Even assuming that is true, however, we reject the full disclosure exception for the same reasons we reject the argument that section 6125 is not meant to apply to non-attorneys. Recognizing these exceptions would contravene not only the plain language of section 6125 but the underlying policy of assuring the competence of those practicing law in California. . . .

Because Birbrower practiced substantial law in this state in violation of section 6125, it cannot receive compensation under the fee agreement for any of the services it performed in California. Enforcing the fee agreement in its entirety would include payment for the unauthorized practice of law in California and would allow Birbrower to enforce an illegal contract.

Birbrower asserts that even if we agree with the Court of Appeal and find that none of the above exceptions allowing fees for unauthorized California services apply to the firm, it should be permitted to recover fees for those limited services it performed exclusively in New York under the agreement. In short, Birbrower seeks to recover under its contract for those services it performed for ESQ in New York that did not involve the practice of law in California, including fee contract negotiations and some corporate case research. Birbrower thus alternatively seeks reversal of the Court of Appeal's judgment to the extent it implicitly precluded the firm from seeking fees generated in New York under the fee agreement.

We agree with Birbrower that it may be able to recover fees under the fee agreement for the limited legal services it performed for ESQ in New York to the extent they did not constitute practicing law in California, even though those services were performed for a California client. Because section 6125 applies to the practice of law in California, it does not, in general, regulate law practice in other states. Thus, although the general rule against compensation to out-of-state attorneys precludes Birbrower's recovery under the fee agreement for its actions in California, the severability doctrine may allow it to receive its New York fees generated under the fee agreement, if we conclude the illegal portions of the agreement pertaining to the practice of law in California may be severed from those parts regarding services Birbrower performed in New York. . . .

The fee agreement between Birbrower and ESQ became illegal when Birbrower performed legal services in violation of section 6125. It is true that courts will not ordinarily aid in enforcing an agreement that is either illegal or against public policy. Illegal contracts, however, will be enforced under certain circumstances, such as when only a part of the consideration given for the contract involves illegality. In other words, notwithstanding an illegal consideration, courts may sever the illegal portion of the contract from the rest of the agreement. If the court is unable to distinguish between the lawful and unlawful parts of the agreement, "the illegality taints the entire contract, and the entire transaction is illegal and unenforceable." . . .

In this case, the parties entered into a contingency fee agreement followed by a fixed fee agreement. ESQ was to pay money to Birbrower in exchange for Birbrower's legal services. The object of their agreement may not have been entirely illegal, assuming ESQ was to pay Birbrower compensation based in part on work Birbrower performed in New York that did not amount to the practice of law in California. The illegality arises, instead, out of the amount to be paid to Birbrower, which, if paid fully, would include payment for services rendered in California in violation of section 6125. Therefore, we conclude the Court of Appeal erred in determining that the fee agreement between the parties was entirely unenforceable because Birbrower violated section 6125's prohibition against the unauthorized practice of law in California. Birbrower's statutory violation may require exclusion of the portion of the fee attributable to the substantial illegal services, but that violation does not necessarily entirely preclude its recovery under the fee agreement for the limited services it performed outside California. . . .

III. Disposition

We . . . affirm the Court of Appeal judgment to the extent it concluded that Birbrower's representation of ESQ in California violated section 6125, and that Birbrower is not entitled to recover fees under the fee agreement for its local services. We reverse the judgment to the extent the court did not allow Birbrower to argue in favor of a severance of the illegal portion of the consideration (for the California fees) from the rest of the fee agreement, and remand for further proceedings consistent with this decision.

EL GEMAYEL v. SEAMAN
72 N.Y.2d 701 (1988)

The question presented for our review is whether services rendered by plaintiff to defendant in connection with a Lebanese legal matter constituted the unlawful practice of law in New York such that the contract for such services is illegal and therefore unenforceable. We agree with the courts below that plaintiff's conduct did not constitute the unlawful practice of law in New York within the meaning of Judiciary Law § 478 and that, therefore, the contract is not void on this ground.

The undisturbed factual determinations of the trial court demonstrate that plaintiff, an attorney admitted to practice in Lebanon but not in any jurisdiction in the United States, resides in Washington, D.C., and maintains an office at Georgetown University where he serves as a Middle Eastern law consultant. In April 1982, defendant's granddaughter Jeneane Aoude was abducted by her natural father from her home in Newton, Massachusetts, in violation of a Massachusetts decree awarding custody to Jeneane's mother, and defendant's daughter, Mary Aoude. Jeneane was subsequently located in Lebanon. Referred by the pastor of Mary's church, defendant and Mary Aoude, then residing together in Phoenix, New York, sought plaintiff's advice on whether Lebanese courts would honor the Massachusetts custody decree. Plaintiff, in a letter addressed to Mary in Massachusetts, rendered his legal opinion that Lebanese courts would honor that Massachusetts decree. He billed Mary $2,000 for this service and was paid in full.

Defendant and Mary Aoude remained in regular contact with plaintiff after he rendered this opinion and, as the trial court found, he subsequently agreed to assist them in getting the child back, while defendant agreed to pay his fee and expenses. The bulk of plaintiff's services were performed in Lebanon, where he confirmed the child's exact location, instituted four separate court actions against Mary's ex-husband, and ultimately assisted Mary in spiriting the child out of Lebanon and back to the United States. Plaintiff's activities in the United States included the commencement of investigations through his Beirut office, accompanying Mary and her Massachusetts attorney to a Massachusetts court to obtain a copy of the judgment awarding Mary custody which would be recognized in Lebanon, authenticating documents so that they might be used in Lebanon, helping Mary complete a power of attorney form, and assisting her in applying for a Lebanese visa. Plaintiff's only contacts with New York during this time, however, were his frequent phone calls to Mary and defendant in Phoenix, New York, to report on and discuss the progress of the case. Additionally, after Mary returned from Lebanon with Jeneane, plaintiff made a single visit to Phoenix to return luggage Mary had left in Lebanon. While in Phoenix, he also discussed his bill with defendant. Plaintiff subsequently mailed a bill for his services to defendant in New York.

When defendant failed to pay the bill, plaintiff commenced this action, asserting causes of action in contract and *quantum meruit*. Defendant asserted . . . that inasmuch as plaintiff had engaged in the unlawful practice of law, any contract for his services was unenforceable. . . .

Judiciary Law § 478 provides:

> It shall be unlawful for any natural person to practice or appear as an attorney-at-law or as an attorney and counselor-at-law for a person other than himself in a court of record in this state, or to furnish attorneys or counsel or an attorney and counsel to render legal services, or to hold himself out to the public as being entitled to practice law as aforesaid, or in any other manner * * * without having first been duly and regularly licensed and admitted to practice law in the courts of record of this state, and without having taken the constitutional oath.

Its purpose is to protect the public in this State from "the dangers of legal representation and advice given by persons not trained, examined and licensed for such work, whether they be laymen or lawyers from other jurisdictions." As a matter of public policy, a contract to provide services in violation of the statute is unenforceable in our State courts. Moreover, violation of Judiciary Law § 478 is a misdemeanor, and its provisions also may be enforced in civil actions by the Attorney-General or a bar association formed in accordance with the laws of this State.

It is settled that the "law" contemplated by Judiciary Law § 478 includes foreign as well as New York law (*Matter of New York County Lawyers Assn. [Roel]*, 3 NY2d 224). In *Roel*, we held that . . . the predecessor of Judiciary Law § 478, prohibited the activities of a Mexican attorney who admittedly practiced foreign law in his New York office by advising members of the public on Mexican law. The practice of Lebanese law likewise falls within the purview of the statute. The issue, however, is whether plaintiff's activities in New York appropriately can be considered the "practice" of Lebanese law.

The "practice" of law reserved to duly licensed New York attorneys includes the rendering of legal advice as well as appearing in court and holding oneself out to be a lawyer. Additionally, such advice or services must be rendered to particular clients . . . and services rendered to a single client can constitute the practice of law.

Spivak [*v. Sachs*, 211 N.E. 2d 329, 16 N.Y.2d 163 (1965)] held that a California attorney engaged in the unlawful practice of law by assisting an acquaintance in New York with her divorce. In so doing, the California attorney became substantially involved in the client's New York affairs — spending 14 days in New York attending meetings, reviewing drafts of a separation agreement, discussing the client's financial and custody problems, recommending a change in New York counsel and, based on his knowledge of New York and California law, rendering his opinion as to the proper jurisdiction for the divorce action and related marital and custody issues. While holding that these activities plainly constituted the "practice" of law, we also recognized that the statute . . . should not be construed to prohibit "customary and innocuous practices." We noted that: "recognizing the numerous multi-State transactions and relationships of modern times, we cannot penalize every instance in which an attorney from another State comes into our State for conferences or negotiations relating to a New York client and a transaction somehow tied to New York".

Here, unlike *Spivak*, plaintiff's contacts with New York were, as [the lower court] found, incidental and innocuous. Although plaintiff engaged in substantial litigation in Lebanon, where he was licensed, and even arguably provided legal services while in Washington, D.C., and Massachusetts, his contact with New York consisted entirely of phone calls to defendant and her daughter Mary in New York in which they discussed the progress of the legal proceedings in Lebanon. There was but a single visit to Phoenix, New York, after the successful completion of his legal services. We conclude that, in the circumstances of this case, phone calls to New York by plaintiff, an attorney licensed in a foreign jurisdiction, to advise his client of the progress of legal proceedings in that foreign jurisdiction, did not, without more, constitute the "practice" of law in this State in violation of Judiciary Law § 478. To adopt a *per se* rule such as advanced by defendant would impair the ability of New York residents to obtain legal advice in foreign jurisdictions on matters relating to those jurisdictions since the foreign attorneys would be unable to recover for their services unless they were licensed both in New York as well as in the foreign jurisdiction.

We do not have occasion to decide, however, whether a contract for legal services, rendered in a foreign jurisdiction to a New York client and which constitute the illegal practice of law in that foreign jurisdiction, is enforceable in this State. Although it is undisputed that plaintiff is not a licensed attorney in either Washington, D.C., or Massachusetts, defendant has failed to allege or prove that plaintiff's conduct in either place was unlawful under the law of that jurisdiction. . . .

Notes and Questions on *Birbrower* and *El Gemayel*

1. *Analysis and implications.* Are *Birbrower* and *El Gemayel* irreconcilable as a matter of law, or can they be distinguished on the facts? At a minimum, the two cases suggest that problems of interpretation lurk beneath the surface of the simple territorialism expressed in the state prohibitions on the unauthorized practice of law: it is one thing for these rules to allow only lawyers

admitted by a state to practice within that state, but it is quite another to determine what is meant by "practicing law" and when it is carried on "in-state."

A. *What qualifies as "practicing law"?* There is no doubt that appearing before the local courts qualifies as practicing law, and, according to *Birbrower*, giving advice regarding local arbitration (even if it never occurred) also qualifies as practicing law. The result in the case may reflect notions of professionalism, consumer protection, or sheer economic self-interest, but is its conclusion that the New York lawyers were "practicing law" in California clearly erroneous? Did the *El Gemayel* court adopt a narrower definition of "practice"? Suppose the New York lawyers in *Birbrower* had limited themselves to advising only on an international transaction involving a California client and a foreign business. Same result? Should the unauthorized practice statutes distinguish litigation advice from all other forms of representation, especially on international business transactions or federal law (like tax and immigration issues)? On what principle might that distinction rest?

B. *What qualifies as practicing "in-state"?* Has the *Birbrower* court announced a *per se* territorial rule, or are multiple facts combined to compel the result in the case? What factors that might account for the result in *Birbrower* are absent from *El Gemayel*? Is there any part of the *El Gemayel* opinion suggesting that the court would disagree with the statement in *Birbrower* that "one may practice law in the state in violation of [the prohibition on the unauthorized practice of law] although not physically present here by advising a California client on California law in connection with a California legal dispute by telephone, fax, computer, or other modern technological means"?

2. *Safe harbors and risk factors.* A strictly literal application of Model Rule 5.5, or Section 3 of the Restatement, or the state laws of the sort at issue in *Birbrower* and *El Gemayel* might make the contemporary practice of law impossible, since neither clients nor their problems are confined by state or national boundaries. But there are relatively easy cases, *i.e.,* permissible forms of transboundary legal advice that should not violate the prohibition on the unauthorized practice of law:

[A] lawyer conducting activities in the lawyer's home state may advise a client about the law of another state, a proceeding in another state, or a transaction there, including conducting research in the law of the other state, advising the client about the application of that law, and drafting legal documents intended to have legal effect there. There is no *per se* bar against such a lawyer giving a formal opinion based in whole or in part on the law of another jurisdiction, but a lawyer should do so only if the lawyer has adequate familiarity with the relevant law. It is also clearly permissible for a lawyer from a home-state office to direct communications to persons and organizations in other states (in which the lawyer is not separately admitted), by letter, telephone, telecopier, or other forms of electronic communication. On the other hand, as with litigation, it would be impermissible for a lawyer to set up an office for the general practice of nonlitigation law in a jurisdiction in which the lawyer is not admitted . . . .

RESTATEMENT (THIRD) OF THE LAW GOVERNING LAWYERS § 3, cmt e.

In the following cases, assume that Lawyer is admitted to practice in the United States, specifically State A, but not in Country B. Which hypotheticals raise the greatest risk of committing the unauthorized practice of law in Country B or elsewhere? In each case, what additional facts would be useful (or essential)?

A. *Offering an opinion about foreign law to a local client*. Lawyer offers an opinion about the applicability and meaning of Country B's laws on intellectual property to a corporate client, headquartered in State A but with operations worldwide, including in Country B.

B. *Negotiating or concluding a transaction in a foreign country on behalf of a local client*. Lawyer travels to Country B to negotiate a contract on behalf of a State A client. The transaction is virtually identical to other deals negotiated by Lawyer in other countries, and the client has retained Lawyer specifically because of her expertise in applicable U.S. antitrust, banking, and environmental law.

C. *Offering legal advice to a foreign client in a foreign jurisdiction*. Relying exclusively on web-based and telephone communications, Lawyer advises a client resident in or headquartered in Country B about (i) arbitration practice under the rules of the United Nations Commission on International Trade Law, (ii) the antitrust law of the United States, (iii) a property transaction in Country B, and (iv) the wills and estates law of a third country.

D. *Opening a branch office*. Lawyer, a partner in Hypothetical Law Firm in State A, opens a branch office of the firm in Country B and hires only associates who are admitted in Country B. She takes up residence in Country B and supervises the operations of the branch office, but she is not admitted to practice law in Country B.

E. *Virtual advice and referral*. On its website, Hypothetical Law Firm A hyperlinks to the websites of foreign law libraries and databases as well as foreign firms, in exchange for reciprocal treatment on their websites.

3. *Pro hac vice admissions*. Is admission *pro hac vice* a practical solution to the issue in *Birbrower*?

Apparently all states provide . . . a procedure for temporary admission of an unaddicted lawyer, usually termed admission *pro hac vice*. . . . Although the decision is sometimes described as discretionary, a court will grant admission *pro hac vice* if the lawyer applying for admission is in good standing in the bar of another jurisdiction and has complied with applicable requirements (sometimes requiring the association of local counsel), and if no reason is shown why the lawyer cannot be relied upon to provide competent representation to the lawyer's client in conformance with the local lawyer code. . . . Some jurisdictions impose limitations, such as a maximum number of such admissions in a specified period. Admission *pro hac vice* normally permits the lawyer to engage within the jurisdiction in all customary and appropriate activities in conducting the litigation, including appropriate office practice. Activities in contemplation of such admission are also authorized, such as investigating facts or consulting with the client within the jurisdiction prior to drafting a complaint and filing the action.

RESTATEMENT (THIRD) OF THE LAW GOVERNING LAWYERS, § 3, comment e. But the *pro hac vice* option is at best a partial solution to the *Birbrower* problem. Few jurisdictions extend the privilege of *pro hac vice* admission from litigation counseling to arbitration or mediation counseling, let alone to transnational counseling for local clients. Even litigators cannot generally take advantage of *pro hac vice* admissions until a case is actually filed, meaning that pre-trial work may qualify as the unauthorized practice of law. Some states also limit the frequency with which a lawyer or a firm may appear *pro hac vice*.

4. *Associating with local counsel.* Suppose a lawyer attempted to minimize the risk of committing the unauthorized practice of law by suggesting that the client retain an attorney admitted in the foreign jurisdiction. *See, e.g., Fought & Co. v. Steel Eng'g & Erection, Inc.*, 951 P.2d 487 (Hawaii 1998) (Oregon lawyer who, acting on behalf of an Oregon-based client, had hired and directed local counsel in in-state litigation, had not committed the unauthorized practice of law and therefore was not precluded from recovering court-awarded fees). Aside from logistical and cost considerations, what are the attorney's professional obligations in recommending a foreign attorney?

Under Model Rule 5.1(c), one lawyer is responsible for another lawyer's violation of the Rules of Professional Conduct if:

(1) the lawyer orders or, with knowledge of the specific conduct, ratifies the conduct involved; or

(2) the lawyer is a partner in the law firm in which the other lawyer practices or the non-lawyer is employed, or has supervisory authority over the other lawyer or non-lawyer, and knows of such conduct, or in the exercise of reasonable management or supervisory authority should have known of the conduct so that reasonable remedial action could be or could have been taken at a time when its consequences could be or could have been avoided or mitigated.

Suppose Local Lawyer urges Client to retain foreign counsel and Client agrees. Foreign Lawyer issues an opinion to the client. Local Lawyer may have avoided committing the unauthorized practice of law, but is she free from imputed liability under Model Rule 1.5 if she does no more than making it clear that the opinion was obtained for and at the request of the client and that she is acting merely to transmit the opinion to the client? *See* Ronald A. Brand, *Professional Responsibility in a Transnational Transactions Practice*, 17 J. L. & COMM. 301, 331 (1998); *Wildermann v. Wachtell*, 267 N.Y.S. 840, 842 (Sup. Ct. N.Y. County 1933), *aff'd mem.*, 271 N.Y.S. 954 (App. Div. 1st Dep't 1934) ("A lawyer should not be held to a stricter rule in foreign matters than the exercise of due care in recommending a foreign attorney.").

5. *Choice of law.* In interstate cases *within* the United States, Rule 8.5 of the Model Rules of Professional Conduct offers a choice-of-law algorithm for clarifying which jurisdiction has disciplinary authority:

(a) Disciplinary Authority. A lawyer admitted to practice in this jurisdiction is subject to the disciplinary authority of this jurisdiction, regardless of where the lawyer's conduct occurs. A lawyer may be subject to the disciplinary authority of both this jurisdiction and another jurisdiction where the lawyer is admitted for the same conduct.

(b) Choice of Law. In any exercise of the disciplinary authority of this jurisdiction, the rules of professional conduct to be applied shall be as follows:

(1) for conduct in connection with a proceeding in a court before which a lawyer has been admitted to practice (either generally or for purposes of that proceeding), the rules to be applied shall be the rules of the jurisdiction in which the court sits, unless the rules of the court provide otherwise; and

(2) for any other conduct,

(i) if the lawyer is licensed to practice only in this jurisdiction, the rules to be applied shall be the rules of this jurisdiction, and

(ii) if the lawyer is licensed to practice in this and another jurisdiction, the rules to be applied shall be the rules of the admitting jurisdiction in which the lawyer principally practices; provided, however, that if particular conduct clearly has its predominant effect in another jurisdiction in which the lawyer is licensed to practice, the rules of that jurisdiction shall be applied to that conduct.

The commentary that follows the Rule limits its relevance in disciplinary issues that cross international borders: "[t]he choice of law provision is not intended to apply to transnational practice. Choice of law in this context should be the subject of agreements between jurisdictions or of appropriate international law." Is there any part of Rule 8.5(b) that raises special difficulties in an international or web-based environment? Is there any reason that ethical conflicts in a transnational setting could not be resolved under the principles announced in other restatements, like the Restatement (Second) of Conflicts or the Restatement (Third) of Foreign Relations Law (*supra*, chapter 4)?

6. *Client consent.* In *Birbrower*, why wouldn't the client's informed consent allow the representation, so long as the legal advice did not involve representation in litigation in the courts of California? Assuming completely informed consent about a lawyer's admission status, shouldn't clients have the freedom to choose the counsel they want?

7. *The legislative aftermath of Birbrower.* In response to the *Birbrower* decision, the California legislature amended the law governing the unauthorized practice of law by permitting an out-of-state lawyer to conduct in-state arbitration, so long as he or she is associated with local counsel who was designated as counsel of record and so long as the out-of-state lawyer agreed to be subject to local jurisdiction for disciplinary purposes. *See* Cal. Code Civ. Pro. § 1282.4 (1999). But problems arguably remain:

The corrective legislation, as implemented by the California State Bar and the California Supreme Court, does not extend to persons not admitted as lawyers in United States jurisdictions. Moreover, § 1282.4 has no application at all to arbitrations falling within the definitions of an "international" and "commercial" arbitration set forth in [other provisions of California law].

Thus, neither lawyers from other United States jurisdictions nor foreign lawyers are protected from the rule in *Birbrower* in international arbitrations with situs in California, and the option of associating local counsel does not offer a solution if dictum in *Birbrower* is to be credited. There is a hint in *Birbrower* that international arbitrations might be handled differently, but little reliance can be placed on the court's discussion; the provision in question clearly applies only to international *conciliations*. Indeed, the existence of an express exception for international conciliations but not for international arbitrations supports the contrary argument that persons not admitted to the California bar may not act as advocates in international arbitrations in California.

Richard A. Eastman, *International Decision: Birbrower, Montalbano, Condon & Frank v. Superior Court*, 94 Am. J. Int'l L. 400, 404 (2000) (citations omitted). For that reason, *Birbrower* has been criticized as inconsistent with "the on-going liberalization of representation in international arbitration." *Id.*

THE SPECIAL PROBLEM OF TRANSNATIONAL AFFILIATIONS AND FOREIGN LEGAL CONSULTANTS

American Bar Association, Model Rules of Professional Conduct, Rule 5.4(b)-(d):

(b) A lawyer shall not form a partnership with a nonlawyer if any of the activities of the partnership consist of the practice of law.

(c) A lawyer shall not permit a person who recommends, employs, or pays the lawyer to render legal services for another to direct or regulate the lawyer's professional judgment in rendering such legal services.

(d) A lawyer shall not practice with or in any form of a professional corporation or association authorized to practice law for a profit, if:

> (1) a nonlawyer owns any interest therein, except that a fiduciary representative of the estate of a lawyer may hold the stock or interest of the lawyer for a reasonable time during administration;

> (2) a nonlawyer is a corporate director or officer thereof; or

> (3) a nonlawyer has the right to direct or control the professional judgment of a lawyer.

RESTATEMENT (THIRD) OF THE LAW GOVERNING LAWYERS, § 2, Admission to Practice Law:

> In order to become a lawyer and qualify to practice law in a jurisdiction of admission, a prospective lawyer must comply with requirements of the jurisdiction relating to such matters as education, other demonstration of competence such as success in a bar examination, and character.

Comment g:

> *Foreign legal consultants.* A substantial number of American jurisdictions . . . provide arrangements for admission to practice of law-trained

persons admitted to practice in non-United States jurisdictions. The arrangements arose from both international and American bar concern to provide an appropriate response to the requirements of transborder law practice and commerce. In some states, the admission is limited to advising clients on the applicability of the law of the lawyer's home jurisdiction. In each state, the lawyer is admitted subject to the lawyer code of the admitting state. Similarly, other nations are increasingly providing methods by which American and other countries' lawyers may gain admission to practice.

IN THE MATTER OF ALBERT F. DALENA
157 N.J. 242 (1999)

This attorney disciplinary case concerns an allegation that respondent was involved in the unauthorized practice of law by associating with Carlo Maccallini, a foreign attorney who has not complied with the Foreign Legal Consultant Rule. Respondent was admitted to practice law in New Jersey in 1959. He practices law in Madison, New Jersey, under the firm name Dalena, Dalena and DeStefano. He has no prior disciplinary history. Our statement of the facts is taken from respondent's stipulated facts.

Dalena & Maccallini is a partnership organized under the laws of the Republic of Italy and does not maintain a bona fide office for the practice of law in New Jersey. Maryann T. Sagert, a resident of Illinois, contacted the American Consulate in Rome seeking an attorney fluent in English and Italian. She was referred to Maccallini in Italy whom she retained to settle the estate of her late father who was a resident of Italy. Respondent prepared and executed a retainer agreement with Sagert in New Jersey using the letterhead for Dalena & Maccallini, which is respondent's law office address.

A dispute arose between the Dalena & Maccallini firm and Sagert concerning the reasonableness of a $4,646.50 fee charged for services rendered in connection with the estate matter. That bill prompted Sagert to file a fee arbitration request against Carlo Maccallini with the Morris County . . . Fee Arbitration Committee. . . . While the fee arbitration was pending, Sagert also filed a grievance against Maccallini with the District . . . Ethics Committee (DEC). . . . Sagert alleged in the complaint that Maccallini accomplished nothing while representing her in Italy. The DEC inquired of respondent whether Maccallini had complied with [the Foreign Legal Consultant Rule] and whether Maccallini was associated with respondent in his law firm. Respondent provided the following information:

> Mr. Maccallini requested my assistance in contacting Maryann Sagert and an agreement was entered with Dalena & Maccallini which was used as an intermediary and convenience by Carlo Maccallini in Rome. I practice each day as the Senior Partner of the firm above listed on this letterhead (Dalena, Dalena & DeStefano). Carlo Maccallini did not maintain an office for practice as a Foreign Legal Consultant here in New Jersey, but he used Dalena & Maccallini as a convenience for

his clients for whom he was doing work in Italy. Dalena & Maccallini has no listed telephone number in any telephone book, or any law library, legal periodical, Martindale Hubbel or other publication. Carlo Maccallini has not held himself out as a Foreign Legal Consultant, but he has held himself out as an attorney licensed in the Republic of Italy to see clients here in the United States.

Respondent forwarded with the above written explanation a copy of a newspaper advertisement taken out by Maccallini, which typically appeared in American newspapers. Respondent explained that such advertisements

indicate that Carlo Maccallini is available for appointments for problems in Italy and is not associated with the firm Dalena, Dalena & DeStefano. There is no mention of Dalena & Maccallini. The practice of Mr. Maccallini in coming to the United States goes back about 14 years. Customarily, Mr. Maccallini comes to the United States to see clients for cases that he has in Italy. He does so twice a year and generally for three or four day periods. The total time spent in the United States seeing clients generally extends not more than 7 days over a yearly period.

Based on the recommendation of the DEC investigator, the DEC dismissed the grievance for lack of jurisdiction over Maccallini. Sagert filed a notice of appeal with the [Disciplinary Review Board (DRB)], stating that, when she retained Dalena & Maccallini, she believed "that Mr. Maccallini was a part of the firm in New Jersey." According to Sagert, respondent assured her that she "would have the 'United States law' to protect her if the job wasn't being done in Italy."

. . . [T]he DRB reversed the DEC's dismissal of Sagert's grievance and remanded the matter to the Office of Attorney Ethics (OAE) for further investigation. [T]he DRB Counsel [subsequently] advised the OAE that the DRB was concerned about the propriety of the business relationship between respondent and Maccallini. . . . Counsel for the OAE requested respondent to provide specific information concerning the legal and financial structure of Dalena & Maccallini. [R]espondent informed the OAE that

there are no written agreements concerning the association of Dalena & Maccallini. That relationship is an ad-hoc relationship. Dalena & Maccallini does not do business in the State of New Jersey. The office acts as a convenience for Carlo Maccallini in doing business in Italy and meeting with American clients here.

To further explain the financial arrangement between respondent and Maccallini, respondent supplied copies of bills given to Sagert. Respondent revised his [earlier] response to the statement that Dalena & Maccallini is a law firm that has been in existence for approximately fourteen years and is located in Rome, Italy. He asserted that the listing of a New Jersey office on Dalena & Maccallini's letterhead meant that it is

merely a satellite office of the firm practicing in Italy. The office here in New Jersey has what is best described as an "ad-hoc" relationship with the Rome office. The New Jersey office does not constitute a "bona fide" office as described under our Court Rules. It serves only the Italian law firm as a communication center for correspondence and documents and convenience to American clients and others who have matters pending in Italy.

Respondent further explained that the Italian law firm of Dalena & Maccallini has clients throughout the United States and that the firm has no New Jersey practice presently or at any time. Respondent added that

> although Dalena & Maccallini is not a law firm which has a New Jersey practice, it clearly constitutes a "partnership" for purposes of the practice of law within the Republic of Italy. I have not, either by means of expressed statements or by implication, misled to [sic] the public the nature of the partnership of Dalena & Maccallini. It has always been made clear to our clients that the firm does not have a New Jersey practice. . . . By way of further explanation, Carlo Maccallini does advertise and meet with clients on matters solely concerning the Republic of Italy. He does not practice New Jersey law, and any fees earned by Dalena & Maccallini have to do with foreign matters.

Respondent stated that he and Maccallini had considered certification under [the Foreign Legal Consultant Rule] but had concluded that certification was inappropriate because Maccallini is not "domiciled or has a permanent presence in the State of New Jersey," he "does not intend to maintain a bona fide office in the State of New Jersey," and he has not used, and does not intend to use, the title of "foreign legal consultant." Respondent admits that Maccallini occasionally meets with clients in the law offices of Dalena, Dalena & DeStefano, regarding matters of Italian law. Although there is no New Jersey Lawyers' Diary listing or telephone number for Dalena & Maccallini, there is a small plaque at the rear of the Dalena, Dalena & DeStefano office that reads "Dalena & Maccallini."

The OAE requested that respondent provide copies of retainer agreements between Dalena & Maccallini and New Jersey residents, identical or similar to the agreement with Sagert. Respondent certified that he has no such agreements in his possession because all retainer agreements with Dalena & Maccallini are kept in the firm's Rome office. He also certified that there are no pending matters in which Dalena & Maccallini represents New Jersey clients pursuant to fee agreements similar to the agreement between Dalena & Maccallini and Sagert.

The OAE argued before the DRB that respondent committed the following unethical violations:

> 1. That he assisted Maccallini in engaging in the unauthorized practice of law, . . . because Maccallini was not a certified Foreign Legal Consultant; and

> 2. That he implied that he was engaged in the practice of law in New Jersey in partnership with Maccallini, . . . based on respondent signing the fee agreement with Sagert in New Jersey on the Dalena & Maccallini letterhead that contained his New Jersey address.

Based on its *de novo* review of the record, the DRB found that respondent engaged in the unauthorized practice of law with Maccallini . . . and that respondent also violated [the law] in that he used a firm name and letterhead that were misleading. The DRB explained the violations rather succinctly:

> Although not cited by the OAE, [the relevant] rule states that an attorney shall not use a firm name, letterhead or other designation that [contains]

false or misleading communications. Again, one could look at respondent's letterhead and retainer agreement and find it misleading, not as to whether it is a partnership or it has a New Jersey practice, but as to whether it is a New Jersey partnership.

Accordingly, the Board found a violation . . . . In addition, by not specifically identifying Maccallini as a foreign legal consultant, . . . both in the letterhead and in the sign "Dalena & Maccallini," respondent assisted Maccallini in creating the impression that Maccallini was permitted to practice in New Jersey within the partnership.

The DRB concluded that respondent's unethical conduct warrants the imposition of a reprimand as the appropriate sanction. Our independent examination of the record convinces us that some of the legal conclusions reached by the DRB are clearly and convincingly established by the record. The DRB properly rejected respondent's assertion that a foreign attorney has the discretion whether to apply for certification pursuant to [the Foreign Legal Consultant Rule] when a certification is required. That rule prescribes the requirements for a certification and the practice of law in New Jersey by foreign legal consultants. In relevant part, it provides:

> (a) Certification of Foreign Legal Consultants. A person who is admitted to practice in a foreign country as an attorney . . . and who complies with the provisions of this rule may be certified by the Supreme Court as a foreign legal consultant and, in that capacity, may render legal services within this state to the extent permitted by this rule.

> (b) Eligibility. In its discretion the Supreme Court may certify as a foreign legal consultant an applicant who:

>> (1) for a period of not less than 5 to 7 years immediately preceding the date of the application has been admitted to practice and has been in good standing as an attorney or counselor at law or the equivalent in a foreign country and has engaged either (A) in the practice of law in such country or (B) in a profession or occupation which requires as a prerequisite admission to practice and good standing as an attorney or counselor at law or the equivalent in such country;

>> (2) possess the good moral character customarily required for admission to the practice of law in this State; and

>> (3) intends to maintain, within this State, a bona fide office for practice as a foreign legal consultant. * * *

> (e) Scope of Practice. A person licensed as a foreign legal consultant under this rule may render and be compensated for the performance of legal services within the State, but specifically shall not: * * *

>> (5) render professional legal advice on the laws of this State or the United States of America . . . or any foreign country other than a country to the bar of which the foreign legal consultant is admitted as an attorney . . . .

>> (7) use any title other than "foreign legal consultant"; provided that such persons's authorized title and firm name in the foreign country

in which such person is admitted to practice as an attorney or counselor of law or the equivalent may be used, provided that the title, firm name, and the name of such foreign country are stated together with the title "foreign legal consultant" and further provided that such does not create the impression that the foreign legal consultant holds a plenary license to practice law in this State.

The rule requires certification by the Supreme Court, among other things, before a foreign legal consultant can practice law in New Jersey. The meaning of the word "may" in the rule could not be simpler or clearer: the Court may or may not grant the certification, in its discretion. It does not mean, as respondent contends, that the foreign attorney may or may not apply for certification, at his or her discretion, and still practice law in New Jersey. The word "may" is clearly intended to vest discretionary authority with the Court and not the applicant. A foreign attorney must first apply for certification as a foreign legal consultant if he or she wishes to render legal advice in New Jersey; the Supreme Court then may or may not grant certification. After being certified, the foreign legal consultant is not authorized to render legal advice on New Jersey law, but only on the law of the foreign country in which the attorney is admitted.

Although it is clear that a foreign attorney must be certified . . . as a foreign legal consultant before he or she is authorized to give legal advice in New Jersey, the Court has never decided what conduct by a New Jersey attorney while assisting an uncertified, or even a certified, foreign legal consultant violates our Rules of Professional Conduct. The novelty of issues raised in this case is important because at the close of this century, unlike at its beginning, lawyers frequently are called on to participate in or give advice concerning transactions or events in other countries. For that reason, we must rethink what is meant by the practice of law in New Jersey by a foreign legal consultant and the ethical issues arising from the association of a New Jersey attorney with foreign legal consultants.

The New Jersey State Bar Association has filed an *amicus curiae* brief. It consulted with members of the International Law Section, the Unlawful Practice Committee, and the Professional Responsibility Committee, and concluded that [the Foreign Legal Consultant Rule] has fostered a whole host of unanswered (or unanswerable) questions. We agree with the State Bar that the following are among the most significant issues that need clarification:

1. When does a foreign attorney need to be certified under [the Foreign Legal Consultant Rule]?

2. In general, what restrictions should be imposed on a New Jersey attorney's relationships with foreign counsel — those who are certified and those who are not?

3. How may an attorney advertise or otherwise make known any relationship with foreign counsel?

4. May a New Jersey attorney, by public advertisement or otherwise, promote the use of foreign counsel in matters involving the practice of law in that counsel's jurisdiction? . . .

5. May New Jersey attorneys allow a foreign attorney to use their office to meet with clients as a convenience once a year? Twice a year? Once a month?

6. May New Jersey attorneys use their offices to fax information from a foreign attorney's client to that foreign attorney in the foreign attorneys own country?

7. May New Jersey attorneys advise their clients that the foreign attorney will be available for certain dates for consultation on matters pending in the foreign attorney's country?

8. May New Jersey attorneys be reimbursed for any overhead, *i.e.*, faxing and mailing, done as an accommodation to the foreign attorney?

9. Do the answers to these questions depend on whether or not the foreign attorney is certified as a foreign legal consultant?

10. What actions are permissible if the foreign attorney is certified that are not permissible if the foreign attorney is not certified?

Because the issues presented are of first impression and because we agree that major clarifications of [the Foreign Legal Consultant Rule] are required, we have decided not to address whether respondent committed unethical conduct. The Court will instead refer the matter to a committee to study the problems and make recommendations to the Court. Even if we were satisfied that there is clear and convincing evidence that respondent engaged in the unauthorized practice of law with an uncertified foreign legal consultant, and that respondent's letterhead is misleading, because the Court has never interpreted [the Foreign Legal Consultant Rule], and because of the numerous important questions concerning its meaning, this would not be an appropriate case to impose a public reprimand. We therefore, dismiss the complaint and refer this matter to a committee to study the issues raised.

AMERICAN BAR ASSOCIATION
STANDING COMMITTEE ON ETHICS AND PROFESSIONAL RESPONSIBILITY
Formal Opinion 01-423 (2001)

Forming Partnerships With Foreign Lawyers

As business has become more international in scope, American business officials wish to be represented by law firms capable of advising them concerning the laws of foreign countries. To meet these expectations, more U.S. law firms have sought to gain international legal expertise. Some of these firms have formed partnerships and similar affiliations with lawyers from other countries.[1]

---

[1] Law firms generally conduct their international services in one of several modes: (1) the global firm endeavors to maintain an office in each major jurisdiction and some minor jurisdictions, providing in-depth, local law coverage; (2) the international firm seeks a presence in most major

Growing numbers of foreign-based law firms have acquired expertise in the law and practices of jurisdictions foreign to them by hiring locally-licensed lawyers to help advise their clients. Some of these foreign-based law firms either have hired U.S. lawyers or merged with U.S. law firms in order to provide legal advice in matters dependent upon U.S. law.

The Committee is asked whether the practice of U.S. lawyers forming partnerships with foreign lawyers[2] violates the Model Rules of Professional Conduct proscriptions against forming law partnerships or similar associations with nonlawyers, and against sharing legal fees with nonlawyers, and against engaging in or assisting another in the unauthorized practice of law. After considering the purposes for these proscriptions, the Committee concludes that the Model Rules do not prohibit U.S. lawyers from forming partnerships with foreign lawyers[3] for the purpose of practicing law. The foreign lawyers must, however, be members of a recognized legal profession in the foreign jurisdiction and the arrangement must be in compliance with the law of the foreign and U.S. jurisdictions where the firm practices.

Forming Partnerships With Foreign Lawyers Does Not Violate Any Model Rule

No provision of the Model Rules specifically addresses whether a foreign lawyer may be admitted to partnership in a U.S. firm. There are, however, prohibitions in Rule 5.4 [*supra*] against nonlawyers sharing in legal fees or being partners or holding any other interest or office in an organization that practices law. Therefore, if a member of the legal profession of a foreign country were considered a "nonlawyer" under Rule 5.4, he would be prohibited from being a partner in a U.S. law firm.

The prohibitions in Rule 5.4 are directed mainly against entrepreneurial relationships with non-lawyers and primarily are for the purpose of protecting a lawyer's independence in exercising professional judgment on the client's behalf free from control by nonlawyers. This Committee consistently has interpreted Rule 5.4 with this purpose in mind, and on occasion has rejected

---

jurisdictions and a few minor ones in which clients need their presence, but with little emphasis on local law capabilities; (3) the international network calls for exclusive or nonexclusive cross-referrals and local law capabilities among firms in each major jurisdiction and many minor ones, with firms in each jurisdiction qualified to provide local law expertise. Each pays a membership fee based on size and agrees to provide any other member firm free advice on a matter. . . .

[2] The term "foreign lawyer" is used here to denote a person who has not been licensed generally to practice law by any state, territory, or commonwealth of the United States, but who is authorized to practice in a recognized legal profession by a jurisdiction elsewhere. Foreign legal consultants are considered foreign lawyers for this purpose, even though they may have qualified under the laws of a state to counsel clients in that jurisdiction on the laws of a non-U.S. jurisdiction. *See, e.g.*, New York Rules of the Courts of Appeals, Rules for the Licensing of Legal Consultants, N.Y.R.Ct. § 521.1 *et seq.* (McKinney 2000).

[3] The analysis in this opinion also applies to holding membership in limited liability companies, to owning shares in professional associations, and to owning an interest in any other type of entity that practices law.

a literal application of its provisions that did not accord with the purpose for the Rule.[4]

Rule 5.4 accomplishes this purpose by requiring that lawyers, to the exclusion of nonlawyers, own and control law practices, which thus helps assure that clients are accorded the protections of the professional standards lawyers must maintain. The Committee believes that foreign lawyers who are members of a recognized legal profession are qualified to accord these same protections to clients of U.S. law firms in which they become partners. Therefore those foreign lawyers should be considered lawyers rather than nonlawyers for purposes of Rule 5.4.

This concept finds support in Rule 7.5(b) because that rule recognizes that there may be associations in law practice with lawyers not admitted in the jurisdiction, and requires only that the firm indicate "the jurisdictional limitations on those not licensed to practice in the jurisdiction where the office is located."[5] When the Model Rules were adopted, some U.S. law firms had foreign lawyers as partners; hence, any intent to render the practice a rules violation needed to be clearly stated. Yet nothing in this or any other Model Rule, or in the legislative history of the Model Rules, suggests that the term "jurisdiction" as used in Rule 7.5(b) excludes jurisdictions outside the United States.

The American Bar Association has, moreover, recognized the desirability of assuring the availability of foreign lawyers to assist clients in the United States with issues involving foreign law and has furthered the reciprocal opportunities for U.S. lawyers to practice abroad by adopting a "Model Rule for the Licensing of Legal Consultants." This rule specifies that licensed foreign legal consultants may be partners in law firms, thus according some recognition to the arrangement.[6]

---

[4] *See, e.g.*, ABA Formal Op. 93-374, FORMAL AND INFORMAL ETHICS OPINIONS 1983-1998 at 182–184 (analyzing the four paragraphs of Rule 5.4 in light of its purpose to protect professional independence and concluding that the rule is not violated by a lawyer's sharing court-awarded fees with a *pro bono* organization that sponsors the litigation; the conclusion was based partly on the absence in such fee-sharing of any threat to the lawyer's independent professional judgment); ABA Formal Op. 88-356, *id.* at 35 (paying service fee to a temporary lawyer agency based on a percentage of lawyer's wages did not constitute illegal fee-splitting under Rule 5.4(a) or a violation of Rule 5.4(c)).

[5] Rule 7.5(b). In the former Model Code of Professional Responsibility, the similar provision, DR 2-102(D), was phrased prohibitively rather than permissively and provided that a law partnership

> shall not be formed or continued between or among lawyers licensed in different jurisdictions unless all enumerations of the members and associates of the firm on its letterhead and in other permissible listings make clear the jurisdictional limitations on those members and associates of the firm not licensed to practice in all listed jurisdictions; however, the same firm may be used in each jurisdiction.

We believe the DR is the same in substance as Model Rule 7.5(b), which sets the parameters for properly listing nonadmitted lawyers in such a way as to comply with the Rule 7.1 proscription against making "a false or misleading communication about the lawyer or the lawyer's services."

[6] Once licensed, and with specified limitations on the scope of the legal consultant's practice, the consultant is subject to the licensing jurisdiction's rules of professional conduct and to discipline there and is subject to the attorney-client, work-product, and similar professional privileges. §§ 5, 6, *id.* at 31–33. Not surprisingly, restrictions on the scope of practice, § 4, *id.* at 31, resemble those that lawfully could be imposed on a legal professional licensed in one

Rule 5.5[7] provides a basis for disciplining lawyers when they violate or assist in a violation of a jurisdiction's law practice admissions standards and unauthorized practice of law regulations.[8] These standards and regulations are for the purpose of protecting clients and the jurisdiction's legal system from the adverse effects of incompetence or unethical conduct.[9] The rule is not violated by a foreign lawyer who, although a partner or associate in a law firm that has an office to practice law in the jurisdiction, nevertheless does not himself "practice law" in the jurisdiction as the term is defined here.

For these reasons, the Committee is of the opinion that U.S. lawyers may in general form partnerships with foreign lawyers provided the foreign lawyers satisfy the requirements described in the next part.

The Foreign Lawyer Must Be a Member of a Recognized Legal Profession

In order to quality as a foreign lawyer for purposes of Rule 5.4, a person must be a member of a recognized legal profession in a foreign jurisdiction. The term "profession" itself generally connotes the attributes of education and formal training, licensure to practice, standards, and a system of sanctions for violations of the standards. There nevertheless is no arbitrary definition of "lawyer" or "legal profession" that must be applied to determine whether a person in a foreign jurisdiction is a lawyer. The determination essentially is factual, requiring consideration of the jurisdiction's legal structure as well as the nature of the services customarily performed by the persons in question.

European community member country wishing to practice in another. . . .The ABA Model Foreign Consultant Rule is nearly identical to the New York Rule on licensing foreign legal consultants. *supra* note [2].

[7] Rule 5.5 states:

A lawyer shall not:

(a) practice law in a jurisdiction where doing so violates the regulation of the legal profession in that jurisdiction; or

(b) assist a person who is not a member of the bar in the performance of activity that constitutes the unauthorized practice of law.

[8] . . ."Practicing law" is a regulatory concept dependent upon the law of each jurisdiction. Appropriate authorization to practice in a jurisdiction usually is gained through bar examination and general admission; admission as a lawyer either on motion or through a shorter bar examination; *pro hac vice* admission for occasional appearances in courts, arbitrations, or administrative hearings; authorization for in-house counsel to represent her employer; special licensure as a foreign legal consultant; or (as allowed by statute, rule or custom) temporary appearances in a jurisdiction in futherance of matters having a relationship to another jurisdiction in which the lawyer is authorized to handle the legal matter. *See* 1 RESTATEMENT (THIRD) OF THE LAW GOVERNING LAWYERS, Topic 2, Title B § 3(3), *Jurisdictional Scope of the Practice of Law by a Lawyer* 24 (2000) (hereinafter "RESTATEMENT"), defining the jurisdictional scope of the practice of law by a lawyer as including provision of legal services to a client "at a place within a jurisdiction in which the lawyer is not admitted to the extent that the lawyer's activities arise out of or are otherwise reasonably related to the lawyer's practice in another jurisdiction where authorized."

[9] *See, e.g.*, RESTATEMENT, Topic 2, Title A, *Admission to Practice Law, Introductory Note, supra* note [8], at 16: "[i]n general, a jurisdiction's requirements for admission and for renewal of a license to practice law are best designed when directed primarily toward protecting the legal system against incompetent practitioners or those whose professional acts would predictably cause harm to clients, the legal system or the public."

Generally speaking, a person who is specially trained to provide advice on the law of the foreign jurisdiction and to represent clients in its legal system, and is licensed by the jurisdiction to do so, will qualify as a foreign lawyer. Before accepting a foreign lawyer as a partner, the responsible lawyers of a U.S. law firm must take reasonable steps to ensure that the foreign lawyer is a member of a recognized legal profession authorized to engage in the practice of law in the foreign jurisdiction and that the arrangement complies with the law of the jurisdictions where the firm practices.[10] For example, foreign lawyers admitted to practice in Sweden, Japan, Great Britain and other European Union countries would satisfy these requirements and have been found by bar association ethics committees to qualify for partnership in U.S. law firms.[11]

If, however, professionals in a foreign jurisdiction are not members of a recognized legal profession in that jurisdiction, the professionals should, in our opinion, be considered nonlawyers rather than lawyers for purposes of Model Rule 5.4. Hence, they would not be eligible for partnership in a U.S. law firm. For example, qualification as foreign lawyer for purposes of Rule 5.4 ordinarily should be accorded members of the profession of *avocat* (courtroom lawyer) or *conseil juridique* (transactional or business lawyer), but might not be accorded members of the profession of *notario* or notary, a substantially different functionary in most civil law jurisdictions.[12] In some countries,

---

[10] State and local bar ethics committees have imposed similar obligations on lawyers in firms that admit foreign lawyers to partnership. *See, e.g.,* Association of the Bar of the City of New York Committee on Prof. and Judicial Ethics Formal Op. 81-72 (commenting on letterhead designations of foreign lawyers and noting that whether New York lawyers may form a partnership relationship with a foreign law firm requires a factual inquiry "whether the training of and ethical standards applicable to the foreign lawyer are comparable to those for an American lawyer" such that the foreign lawyer is a "lawyer" within the meaning of DR 3-103(A) of the New York Code of Professional Responsibility); Utah State Bar Ethics Advisory Op. 96-14 (January 24, 1997) (Utah lawyer may form a partnership or associate with legal practitioners from a foreign country who are authorized by the laws of the foreign country to engage in the functional equivalent of U.S. legal practice.)

[11] *See* New York State Bar Ass. Committee on Prof. Ethics Op. 658 (1994) (under DR's 2-102(C), 2-102(D), 3-103(A), it is permissible for Swedish law firm to form partnership with New York firm, subject to compliance with law; New York State Bar Ass. Committee on Prof. Ethics Op. 646 (1993) (approving partnership with Japanese lawyer practicing in New York); New York State Bar Ass. Committee for Prof. Ethics and Conduct Op. 542 (1982) (approving partnership with British solicitor to practice in New York). Philadelphia Bar Ass. Prof. Guidance Committee Guidance Op. No. 92-19, 1992 WL 405939 (December 1992) (Pennsylvania lawyers may form partnerships with lawyers admitted to practice outside U.S.); Iowa Supreme Court Bd. of Prof. Ethics and Conduct Op. 97-25 (March 3, 1998) (Iowa lawyer may practice law in a partnership that includes English solicitors practicing in England and Wales). *Compare with* Virginia Legal Ethics Op. 1743 (April 13, 2000) (improper for a Virginia lawyer to form partnership with a foreign legal consultant not admitted to practice in the U.S.; lawyer licensed in another country considered "non-lawyer" for purposes of Virginia's Unauthorized Practice of Law Rules, Va. S. Ct. R., pt. 6 § 1). . . .

[12] In Belgium, "[t]ransfer of real estate and authentication of signatures, wills, etc. is the monopoly of notaries, who remain organized separately from the lawyers. Whereas lawyers have the possibility to advise in matters falling within the competence of notaries, they have no authority to perform the official functions of a notary. Quite often, the notary and lawyer will therefore work together although it is not yet permitted that lawyers and notaries combine their offices in the firm." Roel Nieuwdorp, *Belgium* in Law Without Frontiers, A Comparative Survey of the Rules of Professional Ethics Applicable to Cross-Border Practice of Law 30 (Edwin Godfrey ed. 1995), a publication containing essays on the ethical and regulatory rules applicable in most European Union countries.

moreover, there may be no recognized legal profession. In that case, admitting the foreign professional also would not be ethically permissible under Rule 5.4.[13]

The law and ethical standards applicable to the legal profession in foreign countries will differ from some of the law and ethical standards that apply to U.S. lawyers. For example, the scope of client confidentiality may differ, just as Rule 1.6 and the attorney-client privilege differ among United States jurisdictions.[14] This difference would not disqualify a foreign lawyer from partnership in a U.S. law firm. However, when necessary to enable a client to make informed decisions about representation in a foreign jurisdiction where the attorney-client privilege is materially more limited than in the United States, a lawyer working on the matter in a U.S. office has an obligation under Rules 1.4 and 1.6 to explain the risks of diminished protection to the client. Moreover, responsible lawyers in U.S. law firms must, in accordance with Rule 5.1,[15] make reasonable efforts to ensure that client information respecting matters in their U.S. offices is protected in accordance with Rule 1.6, that conflicts with the interests of clients with U.S. matters are managed as Rule

---

[13] The Model Rules would not, however, bar a contractual relationship with a separate organization in which the foreign professionals were partners that could, with appropriate disclosures, also be partly owned by U.S. lawyers as a law-related entity. *See* Rule 5.7. Lawyers also may use nonlawyers as "paraprofessionals" to assist them in the performance of legal services as long as the nonlawyers are supervised appropriately. *See* Rule 5.5 cmt. [1] (not assisting unauthorized practice for a lawyer to employ "the services of paraprofessionals and [delegates] functions to them, as long as the lawyer supervises the delegated work and retains responsibility for their work" as provided in Rule 5.3).

[14] Wholly apart from admission of foreign lawyers to partnership, protecting client confidences is a major concern in any transnational legal representation. In most civil law countries, the attorney-client privilege applies differently, and may not apply at all in some circumstances where it would be applicable in the United States, e.g., to communications with in-house, corporate counsel. *See generally* Daiske Yoshida, *The Applicability of the Attorney-Client Privilege to Communications with Foreign Legal Professionals*, 66 FORDHAM L. REV. 209, 227 (1997); Joseph Pratt, *The Parameters of the Attorney-Client Privilege for In-House Counsel at the International Level: Protecting the Company's Confidential Information*, 20 N.W.J. INT'L LAW & BUS. 145, 159 (1999).

[15] Rule 5.1 states:

(a) partner in a law firm shall make reasonable efforts to ensure that the firm has in effect measures giving reasonable assurance that all lawyers in the firm conform to the Rules of Professional Conduct.

(b) lawyer having direct supervisory authority over another lawyer shall make reasonable efforts to ensure that the other lawyer conforms to the Rules of Professional Conduct.

(c) lawyer shall be responsible for another lawyer's violation of the Rules of Professional Conduct if:

(1) the lawyer orders or, with knowledge of the specific conduct, ratifies the conduct involved; or

(2) the lawyer is a partner in the law firm in which the other lawyer practices, or has direct supervisory authority over the other lawyer, and knows of the conduct at a time when its consequences can be avoided or mitigated but fails to take reasonable remedial action.

1.7 and related rules require, and that all the lawyers in the firm comply with other applicable rules of professional conduct.[16]

Finally, when foreign lawyers are partners in or otherwise are associated with U.S. law firms, the U.S. lawyers in the firm are prohibited by Rule 5.5(b) from assisting their foreign partners and associates in what would be deemed the unauthorized practice of law in any U.S. jurisdiction. Calling upon a foreign lawyer to provide advice on the law of a foreign jurisdiction to a client who is located in a U.S. jurisdiction, however, ordinarily should not violate Rule 5.5 even though the foreign lawyer neither is admitted to practice generally nor licensed as a foreign legal consultant as long as the foreign lawyer is not regularly in the jurisdiction and the matter has a relationship to the jurisdiction in which the foreign lawyer is admitted or otherwise permitted to practice.[17]

Summary

In the Committee's opinion, it is ethically permissible under the Model Rules for U.S. lawyers to form partnerships or other entities in which foreign lawyers are partners or owners, as long as the foreign lawyers are members of a recognized legal profession in the foreign jurisdiction, and the arrangement complies with laws of the U.S. and foreign jurisdictions in which the firm practices. Persons who are not members of a recognized legal profession, including those from jurisdictions with no recognized legal profession, do not qualify as lawyers for purposes of Rule 5.4. Responsible lawyers in a U.S. law firm must make reasonable efforts to ensure that foreign lawyers admitted to partnership or ownership in the firm satisfy these requirements; that the arrangement is in compliance with the law of jurisdictions where the firm practices; that matters in their U.S. offices that involve representation in a foreign jurisdiction are managed in accordance with applicable Model Rules; and that lawyers in the firm comply with other applicable ethics rules.

Notes and Questions on *Dalena* and Opinion 01-423

1. *Devising an appropriate rule.* If you were preparing a legislative framework for foreign legal consultants in the United States, how would you answer each

---

[16] We apply the term "rules of professional conduct" to mean the Model Rules, if in effect in a jurisdiction, but if not, other denominated ethical and disciplinary standards in effect in U.S. and foreign jurisdictions, the rules in which apply to the conduct in question. We do not, however, address here the difficult choice-of-law issues that arise when determining which jurisdictions' ethical and disciplinary standards apply to lawyers engaged in a multinational legal matter. *See* Model Rule 8.5(b).

[17] *See, e.g.,* Virginia Unauthorized Practice of Law Committee Op. No. 195 (April 13, 2000); RESTATEMENT, *supra* note [8], at 24, Topic 2, Title B § 3, *Jurisdictional Scope of the Practice of Law by a Lawyer* 24 (incidental work in a jurisdiction where a lawyer is not admitted to practice that is related to a legal matter on which the lawyer works from an office in a jurisdiction where the lawyer is admitted does not involve unauthorized practice of law). From an ethical standpoint, a foreign lawyer should be afforded the same treatment although the law in each jurisdiction determines what conduct constitutes unauthorized practice of law.

of the ten questions raised by the *Dalena* court? Should a minimalist approach to regulation — perhaps a simple reciprocity — be the preferred approach in order to accommodate foreign sensibilities? What competing concerns might cut the other way? Does the ABA Opinion answer the *Dalena* questions (or provide an approach for answering them)? *See also* Opinion No. 278 of the Legal Ethics Committee of the District of Columbia Bar (1998), *Partnership with Foreign Lawyer*: "A lawyer who is licensed to practice in the District of Columbia may join in a partnership or in other forms of professional association with a foreign lawyer who is not licensed to practice in any jurisdiction in the United States so long as the partnership or association will not compromise the D.C. lawyer's ability to uphold ethical standards. . . ." Is there some reason that bar associations might wish to avoid too much clarity in such matters?

2. *Distinguishing foreign legal consultants from partners.* How do the privileges and obligations of foreign lawyers as "foreign legal consultants" — as defined by the New Jersey rule in *Dalena* — differ from the privileges and obligations of foreign lawyers as "partners" — as defined in the ABA Opinion?

3. *Aiding and abetting.* Over a quarter-century ago, in *Bluestein v. State Bar*, 529 P.2d 599 (Cal. 1974), Bluestein was suspended from the practice of law for aiding and abetting the unlicensed practice of law in California. He had shared an office with one Lynas, who held himself out as an expert in the law of Spain but who was not admitted to practice law in California. Bluestein described Lynas as an associate, listed him on the letterhead as "Of Counsel", and introduced him to clients seeking advice on Spanish law. " 'Whether a person gives advice as to [local] law, federal law, the law of a sister state, or the law of a foreign country, he is giving legal advice. . . . To hold otherwise would be to state that a member of the [State] bar only practices law when he deals with local law, a manifestly anomalous statement.' " 529 P.2d at 606 (citing *In re Roel*, 3 N.Y.2d 224 (Ct. App. 1957)). In light of *Birbrower*, *El Gemayel*, *Dalena*, and ABA Opinion 01-423, how might you advise Mr. Bluestein if he came to you today and asked for detailed advice about structuring a formal relationship with Mr. Lynas?

4. *Transnational affiliations with non-lawyers: multidisciplinary practice (MDP).* A bedrock principle of American legal practice has been that lawyers are categorically prohibited from sharing fees with a non-lawyer and from entering into a partnership with a non-lawyer "if any of the activities of the partnership consist of the practice of law." *See, e.g.,* American Bar Association, Model Rule 5.4(a) and (b). The justification for these twin prohibitions has traditionally been that the lawyer's independent judgment and loyalty to her client are unacceptably jeopardized by any economic relationship with non-lawyers, who are not subject to the same rules of professional responsibility. But, with the globalization of business, the transnational practice of law has come under some market pressure to become multi-disciplinary, as clients seek advice from a single source that combines expertise in law, public relations, accounting, and even engineering. Today, some of the largest transnational "law firms" in the world are (or grew out of) the largest accounting firms. These integrated cross-disciplinary entities are lawful in

some states[1] and in some foreign countries, including Germany, France, Spain, Canada, and Australia.[2] But many bar organizations — including the American Bar Association — have reacted with skepticism and caution. Consider the following position statement adopted by the Council of the Bars and Law Societies of the European Community (CCBE):

POSITION ON INTEGRATED FORMS OF CO-OPERATION BETWEEN LAWYERS AND PERSONS OUTSIDE THE LEGAL PROFESSION (ATHENS 1999)

One-sided loyalty to the interests of clients, which is one of the lawyer's principal duties, can be jeopardised when a lawyer is closely tied to persons or institutions which require him to respect other loyalties — in particular where those other loyalties are, viewed on their own merits, legitimate or even salutary. . . . [The] duty [of confidentiality] also is a source of major difficulties when lawyers combine their services in integrated co-operation with other professionals, if those other professionals have different rights and duties as concerns confidentiality. This can readily be envisaged when the co-operation involves professionals having a duty to positively denounce (to public authorities) illegal activities of their clients — which is the case . . . with accountants in some jurisdictions.

The duty to maintain their independence, to avoid conflicts of interests and to respect client confidentiality are particularly endangered when lawyers exercise their profession in an organisation which, factually or legally, allows non-lawyers a relevant degree of control over the affairs of the organisation. Interests conflicting with the stated duties of lawyers, arising from the concerns of the non-lawyers involved, may then directly influence the organisation's aims or policies. As already indicated, the interests involved may, viewed by themselves, be legitimate and salutary, rendering their potential influence particularly insidious. . . .

The negative aspects inherent to inter-professional co-operation as indicated above, must be balanced against the legitimate interest in the free pursuit of economic activity . . . In this respect it has been advanced that there is a relevant demand on the part of users of professional services, for the forms of service made possible by integrated professional organisations, and that this demand may not justifiably be denied. CCBE observes, however, that there is no actual evidence of the existence of any public consensus as to the desirability or the legitimacy of the forms of integrated co-operation examined here; whilst it is a matter of overriding public interest, that the negative aspects considered above be effectively dealt with. . . .

CCBE respects that in a number of jurisdictions forms of integrated co-operation between lawyers and non-lawyers are permitted, and are effectively carried on. In some of the relevant jurisdictions the local regulatory

---

[1] *See* American Bar Association, Center for Professional Responsibility, *Status of Multidisciplinary Practice Studies by State (and Some Local Bars)* (November 21, 2001), www.abanet.org/cpr/mdp-state_action.html (*accessed on* 29 December 2001).

[2] Aubrey M. Connatser, *Multidisciplinary Partnerships in the United States and the United Kingdom and Their Effect on International Business Litigation*, 36 TEX. INT'L L.J. 365 (2001).

situation obviates some of the problems discussed above, as for example where rules on confidentiality are applicable to other professionals on the same footing as they apply to lawyers. Where integrated co-operation is permitted, there is also often a body of rules intended to provide for the problems discussed, such as rules on internal partitioning of the relevant organization (colloquially referred to as the use of "Chinese Walls"). CCBE does not accept that, given circumstances and/or specific professional rules such as these, the likelihood of the actual occurrence of breaches of lawyer independence, of client confidentiality or of the respect for the avoidance of conflicts of interests, will be appreciably lessened. The complexities alone that are necessarily attendant upon an organization as under consideration here, and upon the application of rules of the type indicated, make it unlikely that the relevant problems can truly be adequately met. . . .

CCBE consequently advises that there are overriding reasons for not permitting forms of integrated co-operation between lawyers and non-lawyers with relevantly different professional duties and correspondingly different rules of conduct. In those countries where such forms of co-operation are permitted, lawyer independence, client confidentiality and disciplinary supervision of conflicts-of-interests rules must be safeguarded.

Would MDPs be objectionable even if the non-lawyers in the organization were subject to precisely the same professional strictures as the lawyer? Consider Rule 5.4(b) of the District of Columbia Rules of Professional Conduct:

(b) A lawyer may practice law in a partnership or other form of organization in which a financial interest is held or managerial authority is exercised by an individual non-lawyer who performs professional services which assist the organization in providing legal services to clients, but only if:

(1) The partnership or organization has as its sole purpose providing legal services to clients;

(2) All persons having such managerial authority or holding a financial interest undertake to abide by these Rules of Professional Conduct;

(3) The lawyers who have a financial interest or managerial authority in the partnership or organization undertake to be responsible for the nonlawyer participants to the same extent as if nonlawyer participants were lawyers . . .;

(4) The foregoing conditions are set forth in writing.

As a matter of policy, how confident are you that the restrictions of the D.C. rule will avoid the dangers that gave rise to the original prohibition on fee-splitting and affiliations with non-lawyers? As a matter of law, would a lawyer who is subject to the CCBE Code violate it by referring a European client with a trans-Atlantic merger issue to an MDP established under the D.C. rules? Would a lawyer who is admitted both in the District of Columbia and in a member-state of the European Union be allowed to enter into an MDP or not?

C. CONFLICTS OF INTEREST

American Bar Association, Model Rules of Professional Conduct, Rule 1.7, Conflict of Interest: General Rule:

(a) A lawyer shall not represent a client if the representation of that client will be directly adverse to another client, unless:

(1) the lawyer reasonably believes the representation will not adversely affect the relationship with the other client; and

(2) each client consents after consultation.

(b) A lawyer shall not represent a client if the representation of that client may be materially limited by the lawyer's responsibilities to another client or to a third person, or by the lawyer's own interests, unless:

(1) the lawyer reasonably believes the representation will not be adversely affected; and

(2) the client consents after consultation. When representation of multiple clients in a single matter is undertaken, the consultation shall include explanation of the implications of the common representation and the advantages and risks involved.

The Council of the Bars and Law Societies of the European Union (CCBE), Code of Conduct, Rule 3.2: Conflict of Interest:

3.2.1 A lawyer may not advise, represent or act on behalf of two or more clients in the same matter if there is a conflict, or a significant risk of a conflict, between the interests of those clients.

3.2.2 A lawyer must cease to act for both clients when a conflict of interests arises between those clients and also whenever there is a risk of a breach of confidence or where his independence may be impaired.

3.2.3 A lawyer must also refrain from acting for a new client if there is a risk of a breach of confidence entrusted to the lawyer by a former client or if the knowledge which the lawyer possesses of the affairs of the former client would give an undue advantage to the new client.

3.2.4 Where lawyers are practising in association, paragraphs 3.2.1 to 3.2.3 above shall apply to the association and all its members.

Japan Federation of Bar Associations, Code of Ethics for Practicing Attorneys:

Article 25. *Notification of Special Relation*. If an attorney has a special relation with the opposite party in a matter and it may be prejudicial to the fiduciary relationship between him or her and his or her client, he or she shall notify the client of such circumstances.

Article 26. *Matters Which May Not Be Handled*. An attorney shall not handle the following matters, except the third and fourth matters with client consent:

(1) A matter in which the opposite party has consulted the attorney, and the degree and method of the consultation are based on a fiduciary relationship;

(2) A matter in which a client's interest conflicts with that of a client in another matter the attorney is handling;

(3) A matter in which the opposite party is at the same time represented by the attorney in another matter;

(4) A matter in which the attorney was asked by the opposite party to take another matter the attorney is handling;

(5) A matter which the attorney handled in the past as a public servant, a person who engaged in public affairs under laws and rules, or an arbitrator.

Article 27. *A Matter Which May Not Be Handled Due to a Relation with Another Attorney or His or Her Client.* An attorney shall not participate in a matter which may keep him or her from maintaining fairness due to his or her relation with another attorney in the same office or with such attorney's clients.

Article 28. *Learning of Conflict after Taking a Matter.* If an attorney learns, after taking a matter, that the circumstances come under Article 27, he or she shall notify the client, without delay, of such circumstances and take a proper step to resolve the conflict of interest.

Article 32. *Possibility of Conflict of Interests.* If an attorney has more than two clients who are parties to the same matter and there is a possibility of conflict of interests between them, the attorney shall notify each of such clients of the circumstances.

IMAGE TECHNICAL SERVICES, INC. v. EASTMAN KODAK COMPANY
820 F. Supp. 1212 (N.D. Cal. 1993)

[Independent service organizations ("ISOs"), which service copiers and other office machinery, brought an antitrust action against the equipment manufacturer, Eastman Kodak Company ("Kodak"), alleging that Kodak refused to sell certain products to the ISOs and refused to sell parts to the equipment owners unless they agreed not to use the ISOs' services. Here] Kodak brings a motion to disqualify plaintiffs' counsel, the Coudert Brothers Law Firm ("Coudert"). Upon consideration of the briefs and arguments of the parties, and good cause appearing therefrom, Kodak's motion to disqualify the Coudert firm is granted.

FACTS AND BACKGROUND

The Coudert firm has provided legal services to Eastman Chemical, one of Kodak's three major operating divisions, for the last six years. These services have covered a vast array of legal matters, including competition law questions, joint ventures, contract issues, tax issues, and questions concerning environmental law. Coudert preformed this work out of the Washington, D.C., New York, Paris, Brussels, Hong Kong, and Singapore offices. For purposes of this motion, it is undisputed that the work performed by Coudert for Eastman Chemicals did not involve issues directly relevant to this litigation.[1]

. . . For purposes of the present motion, it is sufficient to note that in 1991, Kodak appealed to the United States Supreme Court a judgment of the Ninth Circuit reversing and remanding the [district court's] order . . . dismissing plaintiffs' federal antitrust claims. Coudert was asked by . . . counsel for the ISOs to participate in the briefing before the Supreme Court. The ISOs' primary contact with the Coudert firm was Douglas Rosenthal. A conflicts check performed by Coudert disclosed that the firm had an ongoing relationship with Eastman Chemical and Kodak Pathe. The work for Eastman Chemical was performed primarily by Coudert's Hong Kong office. Mr. Rosenthal asked Owen Nee, the managing partner of Coudert's Hong Kong Office, to disclose the conflict to the Eastman Chemical representatives, and obtain their consent to Coudert's representation of the ISOs.

Mr. Nee planned to discuss the conflict during a separately arranged meeting on other business with Barry Falin, Director of Business Development for the Filter Products Organization of Eastman Chemicals, and Michael Chung, Manager of the Filter Products Organization. In preparation for that meeting, Mr. Nee discussed with Mr. Rosenthal what information was to be given to the Eastman Chemical business representatives. Mr. Rosenthal telefaxed Mr. Nee on July 13, 1991, as follows:

> I have seen your fax of today and have spoken both to Ken Katz and Steve Hudspeth. I am authorized by both of them to affirm we trust your judgment about what to say, in passing, about our involvement in the Kodak Supreme Court case, when you meet with officials of Kodak Chemical dealing with China this Monday.
>
> As a small modification to your proposed statement, might I suggest the following:
>
> Our San Francisco office is going to participate in a brief contrary to the interests of the Kodak Corporation in the Supreme Court Appeal; and after review of the matter we have determined that the China representation is sufficiently distant that the actions of the San Francisco office do not constitute a conflict of interest.[2]

After the meeting took place on July 23, 1991, Mr. Nee wrote Mr. Rosenthal and Mr. Hudspeth informing them that he "explained the matter in the form [they] sent to [him] by [their] telefax on July 12, 1991." Neither the documents submitted in opposition to Kodak's motion, nor the declaration of Mr. Nee, reflect that Coudert advised Falin and Chung of the nature of the conflict, the potential exposure to Kodak, or even that Kodak was a party to the

---

[1] Coudert also represented a separately incorporated independent French subsidiary of Kodak, Kodak Pathe. For purposes of this opinion, the court deems Coudert's representation of Pathe irrelevant. *See* State Bar of California Standing Committee on Professional Responsibility and Conduct, Formal Opinion No. 1989-113 (Parent and subsidiary corporations are separate entities, therefore, representation of a wholly owned subsidiary, let alone a separately incorporated subsidiary, does not create a conflict of interest).

[2] Coudert's San Francisco office participated in two *amicus* briefs to the Supreme Court. Coudert's Washington, D.C. office "participated" in the brief for respondents on the merits before the Supreme Court.

Supreme Court action. Mr. Nee's telefax goes on to state that Messrs. Falin and Chung approved of Coudert's representation of the ISOs. Neither Messrs. Falin and Chung recall any such conversations. Mr. Chung testified specifically that even if he had been so informed, he did not recall Mr. Nee disclosing that Coudert would represent the ISOs at the district court level, or explaining the potential exposure Kodak faced in this action.

On September 20, 1991, Kodak was served with Respondent's Brief in the U.S. Supreme Court appeal. The brief identified Coudert as co-counsel for the ISOs. There is some dispute about when Coudert disclosed to Kodak that it would participate in the district court trial on remand. However, the parties agree that on July 30, 1992, Gordon Spivack of Coudert's New York office informed [the] Senior Vice President and General Counsel of Eastman Kodak, that Coudert would participate in the preparation and trial of the ISO case in this court. . . .

DISCUSSION

A. Applicable Rules of Conduct

Rule 110-3 of the Local Rules of Court for the Northern District of California provides that the conduct of counsel before this court is governed by "the standards of professional conduct required of members of the State Bar of California and contained in the State Bar Act, the Rules of Professional Conduct of the State Bar of California, and decisions of any court applicable thereto."[3] Under California law, the decision whether or not to disqualify counsel is a matter addressed to the discretion of the trial judge.

At the time Coudert began its representation of the ISOs, the 1989 version of Rule 3-310 of the California Rules of Professional Conduct were [sic] in effect. That version states in relevant part:

> (A) If a member has or had a relationship with another party interested in the representation . . . the member shall not accept or continue such representation without all affected clients' informed written consent.

> (B) A member shall not concurrently represent clients whose interests conflict, except with their informed written consent.

Under California authority, an attorney's conduct is to be evaluated by the Rules of Professional Responsibility in effect at the time of that conduct, even where subsequent amendments to those Rules are in force at the time of decision. As this court must apply California Rules of Professional

---

[3] Coudert argues that the California Rules of Professional Conduct do not apply to this case because the Coudert lawyers who represented the ISOs before the U.S. Supreme Court were acting outside of California, and were not members of the California Bar Association. This argument is without merit. First, as stated above, the standards of professional conduct before this court are those applicable under the California Rules of Professional Responsibility. Second, by Coudert's own admission, the disclosure made to the Hong Kong Eastman Chemical officials was that the San Francisco office would participate in briefs before the Supreme Court. Aside from the fact that such a disclosure is insufficient to meet Coudert's duties to its clients (*see* Sect. C below), the disclosure about the San Francisco attorneys directly raises the duty of attorneys who are members of the California bar.

Responsibility, including California case law, this court will apply the rules in effect at the time Coudert states that it obtained consent.[4]

B. Written Consent

At the time Coudert was invited to participate in the brief before the Supreme Court in 1991, Coudert was actively representing Eastman Chemicals in a variety of international matters. Therefore, Coudert's representation of the ISOs conflicted with the interests of its existing client, Kodak. In 1991, Rule 3-310(B) provided that "[a] member shall not concurrently represent clients whose interests conflict, except with their informed written consent . . . ." Coudert admits that it failed to obtain written consent from Kodak before representing the ISOs.

C. Informed Consent

Since Coudert failed to obtain written consent as required under former California Rule 3-310(B), Coudert failed to obtain consent. Even if written consent was not required, the court finds that Coudert failed to obtain "informed consent" under *Unified Sewerage Agency, Etc. v. Jelco Inc.,* 646 F.2d 1339 (9th Cir. 1981). Plaintiffs argue that under *Jelco* this court is bound by a federal standard for disqualification motions.[5] The court does not apply the federal standard for the reasons stated in this opinion but finds that the consent obtained here would be insufficient to meet Coudert's burden under the federal standard. Plaintiffs offer the declaration of Mr. Nee, in which he states that during a July 1992 meeting with Barry Falin and Michael Chung, businessmen who were managers at Eastman Chemical in Hong Kong, he disclosed to Eastman Chemical the representation of the ISOs. Coudert's own characterization of the disclosures fails to meet the requirements announced in *Jelco*. *Jelco*, as in this case, involved an issue of representation adverse to a present client. In reviewing the obligations of counsel as to present clients, the Ninth Circuit stressed that "representation adverse to a present client must be measured not so much against the similarities in litigation, as against the duty of undivided loyalty which an attorney owes to each of his clients."

The *Jelco* court held that to avoid disqualification under Disciplinary Rule DR5-105(B) of the Code of Professional Responsibility of the State of Oregon,[6]

---

[4] Plaintiffs argue that federal standards should determine what version of the rules apply. As Kodak correctly points out, the resolution of this issue does not materially alter the outcome of this motion. The California Rules of Professional Responsibility are disciplinary rules, and merely inform the law controlling motions to disqualify. The "rules are not intended to supersede existing law relating to . . . motions for disqualification of counsel due to conflict of interest . . . ." Discussion to Rule 1-100. Under California law, there is a clear prohibition of attorneys representing two or more clients in the same matter without informed written consent. It is immaterial that the new version may have created a lesser standard as plaintiffs suggest.

[5] At the district court level, pursuant to that court's local rules, the Code of Professional Responsibility of the State of Oregon was applied. While the Ninth Circuit in *Jelco* relied upon cases applying American Bar Association Model Rules of Professional Conduct (similar to those found in the Oregon rules) in reviewing the standard for disqualification, the Ninth Circuit expressly declined to express an opinion as to which law applied.

[6] Disciplinary Rule DR5-105(B) provides that: "A lawyer shall not continue multiple employment if the exercise of his independent professional judgment on behalf of a client will be or is likely to be adversely affected by his representation of another client, except to the extent permitted under DR5-105(C)." Code of Professional Responsibility of the State of Oregon (1980).

an attorney must satisfy DR5-105(C)'s two conditions: "First, each client must consent to the multiple representation after full disclosure of the risks. Second, it must be 'obvious' that the attorney can adequately represent the interests of each client." As to the consent prong of this analysis, the court cited *In re Boivin,* 271 Ore. 419, 533 P.2d 171 (1975), as the leading Oregon case on the meaning of "consent" in Canon 5 of the disciplinary rules of the State Bar of Oregon. In *Boivin,* the court stated that consent must be informed consent, made after full disclosure of all material facts:

> To satisfy the requirement of full disclosure by a lawyer before undertaking to represent two conflicting interests, it is not sufficient that both parties be informed of the fact that the lawyer is undertaking to represent both of them, but he must explain to them the nature of the conflict of interest in such detail so that they can understand the reasons why it may be desirable for each to have independent counsel, with undivided loyalty to the interests of each of them.

Plaintiffs argue that the consent obtained from Mr. Falin was informed and, moreover, that Kodak's decision to continue to employ Coudert, even after the current motion was filed, is indicative of Kodak's consent. The court disagrees. As stated above, there is a dispute about Mr. Falin's consent. Moreover, such consent is not informed consent. By Coudert's own admission, Messrs. Falin and Chung were told only that the San Francisco office of Coudert was going to participate in a brief before the Supreme Court adverse to Kodak's interests. Coudert did not explain how the representation would be adverse to Kodak's interest, nor did Coudert inform Kodak of the fact that Coudert's New York and San Francisco offices were actually going to appear on the brief before the Supreme Court. In fact, the July 13, 1991 telefax and Mr. Nee's declaration do not state that Mr. Nee told Messrs. Falin and Chung that Kodak was a party to the action before the Supreme Court, the nature of the underlying action, or the potential exposure to Kodak, should the ISOs prevail.[7]

In *Jelco,* the court found that counsel had twice alerted Jelco's counsel to the potential conflict and asked whether Jelco wished to continue counsel's retainer. On two separate occasions after full disclosure of the conflicts, and discussions with its own attorneys, Jelco consented to the representation. In contrast, the disclosure made by Coudert in this matter cannot be construed as "informed."

The form, content, and nature of the disclosure to Messrs. Falin and Chung was deficient under the standards for informed consent. Under both the California and ABA Rules of Professional Conduct, Coudert owes its client, Kodak, the highest level of undivided loyalty. Coudert's duties to disclose any representation adverse to the interests of Kodak cannot be fulfilled by mentioning "in passing" participation in a brief contrary to the interests of the client without stating the details of why the interests are contrary. The exposure Kodak faces in this action is substantial. Coudert's failure to fully disclose that exposure, as well as the extent of its participation in this action,

---

[7] *See Florida Ins. Guar. Ass'n, Inc. v. Carey Canada,* 749 F. Supp. 255 (S.D. Fla. 1990), in which that court, in granting a motion to disqualify counsel, found "most gravely, [the fact that] the . . . 'consultation' did not disclose the magnitude of the adverse interests at issue. . . ." *Id.* at 259.

falls short of the "undivided loyalty" it owes to its client. The details are essential to informed consent so that the client can weigh and measure the nature of the contrary interests and give informed consent based upon knowledge of material facts.

D. Waiver

"Where the party opposing the motion can demonstrate *prima facie* evidence of unreasonable delay in bringing the motion causing prejudice to the present client, disqualification should not be ordered." *Western Continental Co. v. Natural Gas Corp.*, 212 Cal. App. 3d 752, 763, 261 Cal. Rptr. 100 (1989). Plaintiffs argue that Kodak waived its right to object to its representation of the ISOs by failing to object in a timely fashion. Coudert's name appeared on Respondent's Brief before the Supreme Court, which was served on September 20, 1991. Accordingly, plaintiffs' argument that Kodak had notice of the adverse representation well before the instant motion is without merit. In order to successfully claim laches as a defense to this motion, plaintiffs must establish (a) Kodak long ago had notice of the adverse representation, (b) Kodak intentionally delayed moving for Coudert's disqualification, (c) plaintiffs are severely burdened by the delay, and (d) the extreme and intentional delay allowed Kodak to obtain a tactical advantage.

In this day of multinational corporations and law firms, it is possible that a corporation would not be aware of the law firms representing its overseas divisions. Moreover, while Coudert is charged with the responsibility of performing conflict checks upon taking on a new client, Kodak as the client is under no such obligation. Absent some showing that Kodak was aware of Coudert's dual representation prior to September 1992, the court will make no finding of waiver based on the appearance of the Coudert firm on a brief before the Supreme Court.

Plaintiffs have not shown that Kodak has gained any tactical advantage from the alleged delay in bringing this motion after September 1992. Even assuming that Coudert did disclose the conflicting representation, Coudert's disclosure indicated only that Coudert would participate in a brief before the Supreme Court. Coudert did not indicate that it would participate in this action at the district court level until July 1992, after the case had been remanded back to this court. Since the matter was remanded, the action has been stayed. The court finds that in light of the procedural history of this case, and Coudert's involvement, the delay was not extreme, prejudicial, intentional, a severe burden; nor did the delay allow Kodak any tactical advantage.

E. Policy Considerations

Plaintiffs argue that an order disqualifying Coudert would violate policy. This argument ignores the long-standing rule in both California and Ninth Circuit cases prohibiting attorneys from accepting employment adverse to a current client without the client's informed consent. In light of this court's ruling that Coudert failed to secure Kodak's informed consent to the adverse representation, the policy issues triggered by this motion tip decidedly toward Kodak. The court and the legal profession have a strong interest in insuring that counsel fulfill the highest duty of loyalty to clients. While plaintiffs' argument that multinational clients (such as Kodak) will often consult international law firms (such as Coudert) on discreet legal issues is well taken, plaintiffs have cited to no California or Ninth Circuit authority creating an exception to the rules about representation adverse to an existing client because of these factors.

Whether a matter is international, multinational, or domestic, the standard of conduct for explanation of material facts underlying a potential conflict of interest is the same. The duty to the client of undivided loyalty and necessity of informed client consent to adverse representation applies internationally no matter how difficult the communication hurdles. Law is a profession of service premised upon representation of the client with the highest duty of loyalty and the deepest regard for the trust of the client. Therefore, policy requires the disqualification of Coudert.

Notes and Questions on *Kodak*

1. *Conflicts of interest generally.* Reflecting concerns with an attorney's duty of loyalty and the protection of client confidentiality, Section 201 of the Restatement (Third) of the Law Governing Lawyers states a general prohibition on the representation of clients with adverse interests, recognizing four categories of conflicts:

> Unless all affected clients and other necessary persons consent to the representation under the limitations and conditions provided in § 202,[1] a lawyer may not represent a client if the representation would involve a conflict of interest. A conflict of interest exists if there is a substantial risk that the lawyer's representation of the client would be materially and adversely affected [i] by the lawyer's own interest, or by the lawyer's duties [ii] to another current client, [iii] to a former client, or [iv] to a third person.

The breadth of this definition — and the rigidity of the prohibition on representations where undivided loyalty is, or is perceived to be, impossible — is counter-balanced somewhat by a liberal standard of client consent. That is, with limited exceptions, clients may waive their objection to their attorney's conflicts, so long as they are fully informed of the extent and the nature of the conflict.

---

[1] § 202. Client Consent to a Conflict of Interest

(1) A lawyer may represent a client notwithstanding a conflict of interest prohibited by § 201 if each affected client or former client gives informed consent to the lawyer's representation. Informed consent requires that the client or former client have reasonably adequate information about the material risks of such representation to that client or former client.

(2) Notwithstanding the informed consent of each affected client or former client, a lawyer may not represent a client if:

(a) the representation is prohibited by law;

(b) one client will assert a claim against the other in the same litigation; or

(c) in the circumstances, it is not reasonably likely that the lawyer will be able to provide adequate representation to one or more of the clients.

The commentary to this section illustrates the special "circumstances" in subsection (2)(c) by reference only to representations in certain criminal cases and in certain class actions.

A. But why in *Kodak* was there a conflict in the first place if, as the court notes, "the work performed by Coudert for Eastman Chemicals did not involve issues directly relevant to this litigation"?

B. Assuming that there *were* a conflict requiring consent, recall that the California lawyers in *Kodak* requested and received what they considered a valid consent under California rules. The ethical violation apparently lay in the defective information conveyed to the client by the lawyers in Hong Kong. On what principle would they be subject to California's ethical standards and its courts?

2. *Varying standards of client consent in a transnational setting.* Under Model Rule 1.7, *supra*, the ban on the simultaneous representation of clients with adverse interests can be overcome only if, in addition to the lawyer's reasonable belief that the representation of one client "will not adversely affect the relationship with the other client," each client "consents to the representation after consultation." *See, e.g., Equal Employment Opportunity Commission v. Orson H. Gygi Co., Inc.,* 749 F.2d 620, 622 (10th Cir. 1984). Some states modify Model Rule 1.7 to clarify that a lawyer may not represent adverse interests in the same matter, *even with client consent*. Compare that with CCBE Code Rule 3.2 on conflicts of interest, *supra*, which has *no* provision dealing with consent,[2] and the Japan Federation of Bar Associations, *supra*, which identifies only a narrow class of conflicts that *aren't* consentable. Does this suggest that the *Kodak* court's statement — "whether a matter is international, multinational or domestic, the standard of conduct for explanation of material facts underlying a potential conflict of interest is the same" — may be misleading at best? Would the result have been the same under the Japanese Code of Ethics, *supra*, if the lawyers in question had all been members of the Japanese bar?

3. *Imputation of conflicts, ethical screens, and the international merger of law firms.* The *Kodak* case illustrates the principle that "a conflict of interest held by one attorney in a law firm normally extends to the entire firm, no matter how large. In such a circumstance, if the conflict requires the disqualification of that attorney, the entire firm must be disqualified, including all attorneys in all offices of the firm." *Value Property Trust v. Zim Co.,* 195 B.R. 740 (C.D. Cal. 1996); *Westinghouse Electric Corp. v. Kerr-McGee Corp.,* 580 F.2d 1311,

---

[2] Professor Daly warns against any over-interpretation of the CCBE text and its silence with respect to client consent, concluding that the conflicts of interest addressed in foreign codes of professional conduct

   mostly resemble the sorts of direct adversity in relationships that even clients in the United States cannot generally waive. The absence of a waiver provision in the CCBE Code reflects a sustained confidence in a lawyer's ability to identify a conflict and a willingness to decline a representation through an exercise of self-discipline. Analyzing conflict of interest norms from this comparative perspective can lead to significant insights into the underlying philosophical assumptions about the nature of the attorney-client relationship. The United States has essentially adopted an autonomy model. It defines conflicts broadly, imposes on a lawyer the duty to inform the client fully of the conflict, and leaves the decision on consent or waiver to the client. Outside the United States, the model is one of paternalism. It leaves the evaluation of a conflict to the lawyer and makes no provision for informing the client or obtaining consent.

Mary C. Daly, *The Ethical Implications of the Globalization of the Legal Profession: A Challenge to the Teaching of Professional Responsibility in the Twenty-First Century,* 21 FORD. INT'L L.J. 1239, 1289–90 (1998).

1318 (7th Cir.), *cert. denied*, 439 U.S. 955 (1978). In *Zim*, a firm with four hundred attorneys, practicing in sixteen offices in seven foreign countries and the United States, was disqualified from a representation because of a conflict of interest held by one attorney, who was not a partner at the firm but who was "of counsel" at the firm's office in Washington, D.C. Lawyers in small firms or partnerships, the legal departments of corporations, legal services organizations, and other forms of association are similarly treated. Thomas D. Morgan, *Conflicts of Interest and the New Forms of Professional Associations*, 29 S. TEX. L. REV. 215 (1998).

A. *Gotcha.* This rule of imputation, though intended to protect client confidentiality and assure a lawyer's loyalty, may also trigger a tactical game, in which one side seeks not to promote professional ethics but to disadvantage its adversary by disqualifying its lawyers, sometimes in the middle of a case. Does *Kodak* illustrate that principle too?

B. *Screens.* Some jurisdictions have recognized a limited exception to the general rule of imputation, permitting a law firm to construct an "ethical screen" around the disqualified attorney in certain circumstances:

> Such an ethical wall must be as imposing and impregnable as the Great Wall of China (and thus it has been called a "Chinese wall"). Traditionally, an ethical wall has been permitted only for former government attorneys entering private practice. . . . Certain courts . . . have also permitted such a wall when an attorney moves from one law firm to another. . . . The typical elements of an ethical wall are: physical, geographic, and departmental separation of attorneys, prohibitions against and sanctions for discussing confidential matters; established rules and procedures preventing access to confidential information and files; procedures preventing a disqualified attorney from sharing in the profits from the representation; and continuing education in professional responsibility.

Zim, 195 B.R. at 756 (citations omitted). The Restatement acknowledges that "[imputation creates burdens both for clients and lawyers" and observes that

> Some clients who wish to be represented by a trusted or highly recommended lawyer or law firm must forgo the engagement. A single personally prohibited lawyer can conflict out literally hundreds of lawyers in a firm. Prospective imputed prohibition inhibits mobility of lawyers from one firm or employer to another. The burden of prohibition should end when material risks to confidentiality and loyalty resulting from shared income and access to information have been avoided by appropriate measures. . . .

RESTATEMENT (THIRD) OF THE LAW GOVERNING LAWYERS, § 124, comment b. If you were assisting Coudert Brothers in the construction of an ethical screen when it undertook the potentially inconsistent representations, what specific procedures and standards would you advise the firm to adopt? How would you account for the fact that ethical screens are disapproved in some nations where Coudert operates? *See In re A Firm of Solicitors*, 2 W.L.R. 809 (1992) (expressing British skepticism about "Chinese walls") and *Prince Jefri Bolkiah v. KPMG*, 2. W.L.R 215 (H.L.) (1998) (ethical screens in multidisciplinary practice).

C. *International mergers.* As international law firms grow or develop transnational networks, and their representations become more complex, potential conflicts of interest abound. Sometimes the conflicts result from client activity like mergers with, or acquisitions of, other companies, *see, e.g., Gould v. Mitsui Mining and Smelting Co.,* 738 F. Supp. 1121 (N.D. Ohio 1990), but the increasingly common international merger of law firms can raise even more intractable conflicts, as each firm brings its own diverse clientele to the merger table. *See, e.g.,* Krysten Crawford, *Clifford Chance's World of Challenges: Compensation, Client Conflicts Have Put Ambitious Mega-Merger Between New York, London Firms to the Test,* 24 LEGAL TIMES 22 (November 19, 2001). In the latter circumstances, a lawyer's continuing obligation of loyalty generally prevents the resulting firm from dropping the less-profitable clients just to make the conflict disappear. Indeed, unless the problem is resolved prior to the merger by following proper procedures for withdrawal (including the protection of client confidentiality) or by obtaining the clients' consent, the new firm may be required to withdraw from representing both clients, or it may in especially serious circumstances face sanctions.

D. CLIENT CONFIDENTIALITY AND THE ATTORNEY-CLIENT PRIVILEGE

American Bar Association, Model Rules of Professional Conduct, Rule 1.6, Confidentiality of Information:

(a) A lawyer shall not reveal information relating to representation of a client unless the client consents after consultation, except for disclosures that are impliedly authorized in order to carry out the representation, and except as stated in paragraph (b).

(b) A lawyer may reveal such information to the extent the lawyer reasonably believes necessary:

(1) to prevent the client from committing a criminal act that the lawyer believes is likely to result in imminent death or substantial bodily harm; or

(2) to establish a claim or defense on behalf of the lawyer in a controversy between the lawyer and the client, to establish a defense to a criminal charge or civil claim against the lawyer based upon conduct in which the client was involved, or to respond to allegations in any proceeding concerning the lawyer's representation of the client.

Comment 5:

The principle of confidentiality is given effect in two related bodies of law, the attorney-client privilege (which includes the work product doctrine) in the law of evidence and the rule of confidentiality established in professional ethics. The attorney-client privilege applies in judicial and other proceedings in which a lawyer may be called as a witness or otherwise required to produce evidence concerning a client.

The rule of client-lawyer confidentiality applies in situations other than those where evidence is sought from the lawyer through compulsion of law. The confidentiality rule applies not merely to matters communicated in confidence by the client but also to all information relating to the representation, whatever its source. A lawyer may not disclose such information except as authorized or required by the Rules of Professional Conduct or other law.

The Council of the Bars and Law Societies of the European Union (CCBE), Code of Conduct, Rule 2.3: Confidentiality:

2.3.1 It is of the essence of a lawyer's function that he should be told by his client things which the client would not tell to others, and that he should be the recipient of other information on a basis of confidence. Without the certainty of confidentiality there cannot be trust. Confidentiality is therefore a primary and fundamental right and duty of the lawyer.

The lawyer's obligation of confidentiality serves the interest of the administration of justice as well as the interest of the client. It is therefore entitled to special protection by the state.

2.3.2 A lawyer shall respect the confidentiality of all information that becomes known to him in the course of his professional activity.

2.3.3 The obligation of confidentiality is not limited in time.

2.3.4 A lawyer shall require his associates and staff and anyone engaged by him in the course of providing professional services to observe the same obligation of confidentiality.

Japan Federation of Bar Associations, Code of Ethics for Practicing Attorneys, Article 20, Maintenance of Confidentiality:

An attorney shall not disclose or utilize, without any good reason, confidential information of a client which is obtained in the course of his or her practice. The same prohibition applies to confidential information of a client of another attorney practicing in the same office, which may be obtained in the course of his or her practice.

RENFIELD CORP. v. REMY MARTIN & CO.
98 F.R.D. 442 (D. Del. 1982)

This is an antitrust action brought by plaintiffs Renfield Corporation and Renfield Importers ("Renfield") against E. Remy Martin & Co., S.A. ("Remy S.A."), Remy Martin Amerique, Inc. ("Remy Amerique"), and other defendants. Renfield has moved under Fed.R.Civ.P. 37(a)(2) for an order compelling production of certain documents withheld by the Remy defendants on the ground of attorney-client privilege. In the alternative, Renfield seeks an *in camera* inspection of these documents by the Court to determine on a document-by-document basis whether they are protected by the attorney-client privilege. . . .

The communications at issue are 119 documents that reflect communications between officials of both Remy defendants and employees of Remy S.A.

identified as its French "in-house counsel." Renfield challenges Remy's assertion of the attorney-client privilege on the basis that the privilege does not apply to communications with French "in-house counsel." I shall consider separately the documents located in the offices of Remy S.A. in France and those located in the New York offices of Remy Amerique.

A. Documents Located in the Offices of Remy S.A. in France.

The parties are not in disagreement that the Hague Evidence Convention governs discovery of any of the documents located in France; they are in disagreement, however, as to the meaning of the relevant provisions of that Convention. Two provisions are pertinent. Article 21(e) provides that:

> A person requested to give evidence may invoke the privileges and duties to refuse to give the evidence contained in Article 11.

Article 11, in turn, provides that:

> The person concerned may refuse to give evidence insofar as he has a privilege or duty to refuse to give the evidence — (a) under the law of the State of execution; or (b) under the law of the State of origin. . . .

Defendants read these provisions to assure that a witness will have the benefit not only of privileges recognized by the forum State, but also privileges recognized by the State where the letters are executed.[1]

Renfield reads them to permit a witness to assert only a privilege of the State of origin or State of execution which is otherwise applicable under conflict of laws principles. While there is room for argument, I find Renfield's reading of the language employed less plausible than that of defendants'. Moreover, I believe defendant's interpretation is more compatible with the limited "legislative history" of the Convention currently available to me. Both the United States and France in their answers to Question 10 of the "Questionnaire on the Taking of Evidence Abroad"[2] made in preparation for the Hague Convention evinced their intent that the treaty be a privilege-creating, rather than privilege-limiting, law.[3] Thus, I conclude that if a privilege is recognized by either French or United States law, the defendants may invoke it.

For the purpose of this motion, I assume that French law would not grant a privilege to refuse to disclose these documents. Therefore, I must consider

---

[1] Article 11 goes on to indicate that a signatory of the Convention may elect to afford the witness the benefit of the privileges of other jurisdictions, such as the privilege recognized by the witness's domicile.

[2] Question 10 reads:

What privileges are available to witnesses appearing under a letter rogatory—
   a. only those of the law of the requested State?
   b. only those of the law of the requesting State?
   c. each privilege decreed either by the law of the requested State or by that of the requesting State?
   d. only those decreed by both legislations cumulatively?

[3] Under Renfield's reading, the only effect of this provision of Article 11 is to limit the privileges otherwise available to the witness, *i.e.,* to restrict otherwise applicable privileges to those recognized by the State of execution and the State of origin, excluding, for example, otherwise applicable privileges recognized by the law of the witness's domicile, absent a special undertaking from the State of origin.

whether United States law provides such a privilege. I conclude that it does. Preliminarily, it is clear that the communications were intended and reasonably expected to be confidential.[4] Thus, the only issue of any substance is whether the privilege is available where the attorney is a French "in-house counsel." Plaintiffs have urged that because French "in-house counsel" are not members of a bar, the privilege is unavailable. In order to decide this, it is necessary to have some understanding of the structure of the French legal profession.

The organization of the French legal profession is unlike that in the United States.[5] In France, there are several categories within the practicing legal profession and each category performs a different function that, in the United States, would all be performed by an American lawyer. For example, the "*avocat*" provides legal advice to clients and appears in court but may not be employed by any person or organization. The "*conseil juridique*" is allowed to provide legal advice but may not appear in court and may only be employed by, or associated with, other "*conseils juridiques.*" Thus, an individual who is employed by a corporation is not permitted by law to be on the list of "*avocats*" or "*conseils juridiques.*" Nevertheless, these individuals are not prohibited from giving legal advice.

Because there is no clear French equivalent to the American "bar," in this context membership in a "bar" cannot be the relevant criterion for whether the attorney-client privilege is available. Rather, the requirement is a functional one of whether the individual is competent to render legal advice and is permitted by law to do so. French "in-house counsel" certainly meet this test; like their American counterparts, they have legal training and are employed to give legal advice to corporate officials on matters of legal significance to the corporation.[6]

B. Documents in the New York Office of Remy Amerique.

The Hague Evidence Convention is not applicable to documents located in the United States. Therefore, I must apply choice-of-law principles to determine whether United States or French privilege law applies. There is no dispute that the choice-of-law standard is that the applicable law is that of

---

[4] The communicators did not expect the recipients to share the information other than perhaps with outside counsel. Renfield erroneously equates the issue of whether the communications were reasonably expected to be confidential with the issue of whether they are protected by an attorney-client privilege under the law which would be applicable under conventional conflict of law principles. To equate those issues in this context would be to defeat what I believe to be the intent of the Hague Evidence Convention — that a witness shall not be limited to the attorney-client privilege law of the jurisdiction whose laws would be applicable under such conflicts rules.

[5] [Editor's note: The details of the court's description of the French legal profession are no longer accurate, though its key conclusions that the profession in France is not structured like the profession in the United States and that a variety of French professionals "are not prohibited from giving legal advice" remain true. *See* Robert J. Goebel, *Lawyers in the European Community: Progress Towards Community-Wide Rights of Practice*, 15 FORDHAM INT'L L.J. 556, 563 (1992).]

[6] In a related argument, Renfield asserts that, as a matter of law, the communications cannot be treated as ones seeking legal advice where the lawyers are French and, therefore, presumptively unqualified to render advice on United States law. I disagree. While the fact that a lawyer is not a member of the bar of a United States jurisdiction may be relevant in determining whether a communication is for the purpose of securing legal advice, it is not necessarily determinative of that issue.

the state with the most significant relationship with the communications. RESTATEMENT (SECOND) OF CONFLICT LAWS § 139(1) (1971). In this case, the United States has the most significant relationship with the communications. The officials located in the New York office of Remy Amerique are the ones who have sought the legal advice and the United States has the same interest in protecting the freedom of these individuals to obtain legal advice as it does for any other American residents. For the same reasons stated above in connection with the Remy S.A. documents, the United States privilege law does recognize the Remy Amerique communications as privileged. It follows, therefore, that the attorney-client privilege is also appropriately applied to communications of Remy Amerique officials with French "in-house counsel." . . . While the fact of foreign lawyers being consulted on United States law might, in some factual context, raise an issue of whether the communications were for the purpose of seeking legal, as contrasted with business advice, the background of the attorneys involved in these communications is such that their nationality raises no question in my mind about the defendants' representation.

Notes and Questions on *Renfield* and Client Confidentiality

1. *Transnational perspectives on the attorney-client privilege.* In *Upjohn Co. v. United States*, 449 U.S. 383, 389 (1981), the Supreme Court declared that

> [t]he attorney-client privilege is the oldest of the privileges for confidential communications known to the common law. Its purpose is to encourage full and frank communication between attorneys and their clients and thereby promote broader public interests in the observance of law and administration of justice. The privilege recognizes that sound legal advice or advocacy serves public ends and that such advice or advocacy depends upon the lawyer's being fully informed by the client.

As *Renfield* suggests, the virtues of the privilege are so self-evident in the United States that a client's communications with in-house corporate lawyers are covered by the privilege, and even a lawyer admitted to practice in a foreign nation is a "lawyer for the purposes of the privilege. . . ." RESTATEMENT (THIRD) OF THE LAW GOVERNING LAWYERS, § 72, cmt e.

But the rules can be quite different in foreign jurisdictions, and even some U.S. courts have reached decisions that are not entirely consistent with *Renfield. See, e.g., Honeywell v. Minolta*, 1990 U.S. Dist. Lexis 5954 (N.J. 1990). In *AM&S Europe Ltd. vs. Commission of the European Communities*, Case 155/79, [1982] E.C.R. 1575, [1982] 2 C.M.L.R. 264, the European Court of Justice (ECJ) recognized that an attorney-client privilege exists in various forms throughout Europe, but it also articulated limitations on the privilege that differentiate it from the privilege as applied in U.S. courts. Specifically, the ECJ upheld a fine against a company for withholding documents which included communications to and from an in-house lawyer on the ground that the privilege is intended to foster — and is therefore limited to — communications emanating from an "independent" lawyer. The implication of *AM&S Europe*, contrary to *Renfield*'s implications, is that a European client's communications with in-house counsel or with U.S. lawyers not admitted in Europe would not be protected by the privilege.

There are additional differences. In the United States, an attorney's work product — the material gathered in anticipation of litigation or in preparation for trial — receives limited protection under U.S. law, which generally terminates with the litigation, Fed. R. Civ. P. 26(b)(3), and the privilege to refuse disclosure of a client's confidential communications can be waived by the client. In some foreign jurisdictions, work product is variously defined and subject to disparate levels of protection, and the client's waiver is not necessarily binding on the attorney, who may have independent professional reasons to assert the privilege.

A. *Generally*. As you read through the confidentiality provisions of the Model Rules, the CCBE Code, and the Japan Bar Federation Code of Ethics, *supra*, how would you articulate the differences among them? Which provides the greatest scope of protection for client communications?

B. *Testing the principle*. How should a court in the United States resolve the following hypothetical cases and according to what rationale?

1. A communication is not protected in Country A, where it took place, but is sought as evidence in a civil proceeding in the United States, where it would have been protected had it occurred in its entirety there.

2. The reverse of Case 1: a communication is protected in Country A, where it took place, but is sought as evidence in a civil proceeding in the United States, where it would not have been protected had it occurred there.

3. Numerous attorney-client communications occur by telephone, fax, and e-mail, but the attorney and the client are in two different jurisdictions, one of which would protect the communications (had it occurred entirely within its territory) and the other of which would not.

4. An attorney whose state of licensure requires lawyers to disclose client fraud on the court is retained by a client in a foreign jurisdiction, where lawyers have no right, let alone an obligation, to breach the client's confidence.

2. Lex fori and evidentiary privileges. It is axiomatic that the law of the forum, *lex fori*, governs procedural matters, and, though the line between substance and procedure is notoriously difficult to draw, issues of discovery and evidence have routinely been treated as matters of procedure. "It seems obvious that foreign law cannot be permitted to obstruct the investigation and discovery of facts in a case, under rules established as conducive to the proper and orderly administration of justice in a court of the United States. Even if a foreign government were itself a party, it must conform to the law of the forum and make discovery upon order of the court." *Societe Internationale v. Rogers*, 357 U.S. 197, 213 (1958). But confidentiality privileges are not merely logistical arrangements for the administration of justice in a courtroom, like the format of a brief. They serve fundamental interests and values that lie outside the litigation by encouraging certain professional and personal relationships or the protection of privacy. Should attorney confidentiality rules — despite their evidentiary impact — be subject only to the *lex fori*, to the exclusion of the law of the place where the client relationship is centered or where the evidence is located?

As noted in *Renfield,* Article 11 of the Hague Evidence Convention provides for the recognition of foreign privileges in the processing of letters rogatory:

> In the execution of a Letter of Request the person concerned may refuse to give evidence in so far as he has a privilege or duty to refuse to give the evidence (a) under the law of the State of execution; or (b) under the law of the State of origin, and the privilege or duty has been specified in the Letter, or, at the instance of the requested authority, has been otherwise confirmed to that authority by the requesting authority. . . .

When discovery is sought in a country that is *not* a party to the Hague Evidence Convention and a privilege is asserted which is unavailable in U.S. law, U.S. courts have undertaken a tailored inquiry into the scope of the asserted privilege and its conformity to U.S. standards, but nothing guarantees that the privilege will receive extraterritorial recognition in the United States. *United States v. First National City Bank*, 396 F.2d 897 (2d Cir. 1968); *Minpeco, S.A. v. Conticommunity Services, Inc.*, 116 F.R.D. 517 (S.D.N.Y. 1987); *Bristol-Meyers Squibb Co. v. Rhone-Poulenc Rover, Inc.*, 188 F.R.D. 189, 200 (S.D.N.Y. 1999) (confidentiality protections for French patent agent under French law held not comparable to U.S. law of privileges). Should attorney-client privileges be subject to the same analysis as bank secrecy and other commercial confidentiality laws?

3. *Federal Rule of Evidence 501.* Federal Rule of Evidence 501, though not drafted to address the unique difficulties of international civil litigation in U.S. courts, provides: "Except as otherwise required by the Constitution of the United States or provided by Act of Congress or in rules prescribed by the Supreme Court pursuant to statutory authority, the privilege of a witness, person, government, State, or political subdivision thereof shall be governed by the principles of the common law as they may be interpreted by the courts of the United States in the light of reason and experience." How would you convince a court that FRE 501 is sufficiently broad to allow (or require) the recognition of confidentiality privileges arising out of a foreign attorney-client privilege, even if they are not identical to the privileges generally recognized in the United States?

4. *E-mail and confidentiality.* Do attorneys and clients have a reasonable expectation of privacy in unencrypted e-mail sent over the internet?

E.   TOWARDS AN INTERNATIONAL CONCEPTION OF THE PROFESSION

The history of the legal profession worldwide suggests that localism and exclusionary regulation are common; indeed, Professor Richard Abel has "chronicle[d] a continuous succession of protectionist strategies: lawyers against non-lawyers; lawyers admitted to one court against those admitted to others; lawyers performing one function against those performing others (*e.g.* barristers and solicitors; *avocats, avoues,* and *conseils juridiques*); and lawyers from one geographic jurisdiction against those from others."[1] In these circumstances, we may be skeptical that professional protectionism will erode, "given national differences of law, language, history, and culture."[2]

But even an understandable skepticism should not obscure the convergence over the last decade towards an international conception of lawyers' professional obligations. In part, the trend is driven by the liberalization of trade in services under the auspices of the General Agreement on Tariffs and Trade/World Trade Organization, and on a regional basis by the European Union and the North American Free Trade Agreement. In the effort to assure that member states do not discriminate against foreign goods and services solely on the basis of their origin, states have had to define what is essential and non-territorial about the profession. But the GATT/WTO, the EU, and NAFTA do not draw on a clean slate: in recent years, there have been numerous international initiatives to define common ground among lawyers, assuring a balance between their rights and their duties.[3]

The United Nations for example has adopted "Basic Principles on the Role of Lawyers" (reproduced in the Document Supplement), which were "formulated to assist Member States in their task of promoting and ensuring the proper role of lawyers" and which

> should be respected and taken into account by Governments within the framework of their national legislation and practice and should be brought to the attention of lawyers as well as other persons, such as judges, prosecutors, members of the executive and the legislature, and the public in general. These principles shall also apply, as appropriate, to persons who exercise the functions of lawyers without having the formal status of lawyers.

The Basic Principles are admittedly non-binding, but as shown repeatedly in the history of international law (and as suggested in Chapter 1, *supra*), soft law is not irrelevant and can illuminate the next step in the development of authoritative standards.

It is therefore potentially significant that the Basic Principles on the Role of Lawyers address such topics as access to lawyers and legal services, special safeguards in criminal justice matters, qualifications and training, duties and responsibilities, guarantees for the functioning of lawyers, freedom of expression and association, professional associations, and disciplinary proceedings. Of necessity, the principles are articulated at a fairly high level of abstraction. For example, Principle 12 provides that "[l]awyers shall at all times maintain the honour and dignity of their profession as essential agents of the administration of justice." Principle 15 provides that "[l]awyers shall always loyally

---

[1] Richard L. Abel, *Symposium: The Future of the Legal Profession: Transnational Law Practice,* 44 CASE W. L. REV. 737 (1994).

[2] *Id.*

[3] *Cf. In re Application of Collins-Bazant,* 561 N.W.2d 209 (Neb. 1997) and 578 N.W.2d 38 (Neb. 1998) (NAFTA does not automatically allow Canadian to take Nebraska bar exam).

respect the interests of their clients." And Principle 13 — addressing the duties of lawyers to their clients — includes:

(a) Advising clients as to their legal rights and obligations, and as to the working of the legal system in so far as it is relevant to the legal rights and obligations of the clients;

(b) assisting clients in every appropriate way, and taking legal action to protect their interests;

(c) assisting clients before courts, tribunals or administrative authorities, where appropriate.

As the cases in this chapter show, difficult questions of interpretation inevitably swirl around these generalizations, and the hard law emerges from between these soft lines.

That process is more advanced now in international criminal litigation than in international civil litigation. The International Criminal Tribunal for the Former Yugoslavia has adopted a Code of Professional Conduct for Defence Counsel appearing before it (also to be found in the Documents Supplement). In its specificity and in the prospects for actual enforcement, the Tribunal's code of conduct compares favorably with national codes like those in the United States, Japan, and the CCBE states. Consider for example Article 9 of the ICTY Code, addressing conflicts of interest:

(1) Counsel owes a duty of loyalty to his or her Client. Counsel must at all times act in the best interests of the Client and must put those interests before their own interests or those of any other person.

(2) In the course of representing a Client, Counsel must exercise all care to ensure that no conflict of interest arises.

(3) Without limiting the generality of sub-articles (1) and (2), Counsel must not represent a Client with respect to a matter if:

(a) such representation will be or is likely to be adversely affected by representation of another Client;

(b) representation of another Client will be or is likely to be adversely affected by such representation;

(c) the Counsel's professional judgement on behalf of the Client will be, or may reasonably be expected to be, adversely affected by:

(i) the Counsel's responsibilities to, or interests in, a third party; or

(ii) the Counsel's own financial, business, property or personal interests; or

(iii) the matter is the same or substantially related to another matter in which Counsel had formerly represented another client ("the former client"), and the interests of the Client are materially adverse to the interests of the former client, unless the former client consents after consultation.

(4) Counsel must not accept compensation for representing a Client from a source other than that Client or, if assigned by the Tribunal, from a source other than the Tribunal, unless:

(a) that Client consents after consultation; and

(b) there is no interference thereby with the Counsel's independence of professional judgement nor with the Client-Counsel relationship.

(5) Where a conflict of interest does arise, Counsel must -

(a) promptly and fully inform each potentially affected Client of the nature and extent of the conflict; and

(b) either:

(i) take all steps necessary to remove the conflict; or

(ii) obtain the full and informed consent of all potentially affected Clients to continue the representation, so long as Counsel is able to fulfill all other obligations under this Code.

Similarly detailed provisions address confidentiality, attorney misconduct, dealing with unrepresented persons, candor toward the tribunal, and diligence, *inter alia*. The Tribunal acknowledges that these provisions draw on national codes from around the world. The process of harmonization, begun over forty years ago by the private International Bar Association's International Code of Ethics for the Legal Profession and developed by the CCBE and the Union Internationale des Advocats, continues.

The evolution of an international conception of a lawyer's professional obligations reflects a now-characteristic law-making process, with several common characteristics. First, "public" organizations like the United Nations and "private" organizations like the ABA and the CCBE develop a range of norms, frequently responding to or incorporating one another's work. Second, the emergence of norms occurs over time, frequently beginning in soft law declarations of principles which gradually harden in specific institutional settings into enforceable principles. Third, the norms are enforced in a variety of settings, including the domestic courts of nations around the world, confirming that these courts are not hermetically sealed off from the international legal order but make essential contributions to its constant refinement.

TABLE OF CASES

[Principal cases appear in capitals; References are to pages.]

[Principal cases appear in capitals; References are to pages.]

[Principal cases appear in capitals; References are to pages.]

C

[Principal cases appear in capitals; References are to pages.]

[Principal cases appear in capitals; References are to pages.]

[Principal cases appear in capitals; References are to pages.]

[Principal cases appear in capitals; References are to pages.]

I

[Principal cases appear in capitals; References are to pages.]

[Principal cases appear in capitals; References are to pages.]

[Principal cases appear in capitals; References are to pages.]

[Principal cases appear in capitals; References are to pages.]

[Principal cases appear in capitals; References are to pages.]

[Principal cases appear in capitals; References are to pages.]

[Principal cases appear in capitals; References are to pages.]

[Principal cases appear in capitals; References are to pages.]

[Principal cases appear in capitals; References are to pages.]

X

Y

Z

INDEX

[References are to page numbers.]

[References are to page numbers.]